PSYCHOLOGY

PSYCHOLOGY
THE SCIENCE
OF BEHAVIOR

NEIL R. CARLSON

UNIVERSITY OF MASSACHUSETTS

ALLYN AND BACON, INC.

BOSTON, LONDON, SYDNEY, TORONTO

Series Editor: Bill Barke

Library of Congress Cataloging in Publication Data

Carlson, Neil R., 1942–
    Psychology : the science of behavior.

    Bibliography: p. A13
    Includes index.
    1. Psychology.   2. Psychology, Physiological.
3. Neuropsychology.   I. Title.
BF121.C35   1984   150   83-15510
ISBN 0-205-08038-3
ISBN 0-205-79836-1 (International)
Printed in the United States of America.
10 9 8 7 6 5 4 3 2   89 88 87 86 85 84

The author would like to thank Leslie Evans for the artwork prepared for the part openings and chapter numbers and to acknowledge the contributions of the following authors, publishers, and photographers who granted permission to reproduce their materials.

Chapter 1

FIGURE 1.1 p. 5—The Granger Collection. FIGURE 1.2 p. 7—The Granger Collection (photo and title page). FIGURE 1.3 p. 7—Historical Pictures Service, Chicago. FIGURE 1.4 p. 8—Historical Pictures Service, Chicago. FIGURE 1.5 p. 8—Culver Pictures (photo) and The Granger Collection (title page). FIGURE 1.6 p. 9—The Granger Collection. FIGURE 1.7 p. 10—The Granger Collection. FIGURE 1.8 p. 11—The Granger Collection. FIGURE 1.9 p. 12—The Bettmann Archive. FIGURE 1.10 p. 13—The Granger Collection. FIGURE 1.11 p. 13—Culver Pictures. FIGURE 1.13 p. 15—The Bettmann Archive. FIGURE 1.14 p. 16—The Granger Collection. FIGURE 1.15 p. 17—The Bettmann Archive. FIGURE 1.16 p. 18—The Bettmann Archive. FIGURE 1.17 p. 19—The Bettmann Archive. FIGURE 1.18 p. 20—The Granger Collection. FIGURE 1.19 p. 21—Historical Pictures Service, Chicago. FIGURE 1.20 p. 22—Culver Pictures.

Chapter 2

FIGURE 2.1 p. 30—The Granger Collection. FIGURE 2.2 p. 32—The Bettmann Archive. FIGURE 2.4 p. 36—Arthur Tress. FIGURE 2.5 p. 37—Cary Wolinsky/Stock, Boston. FIGURE 2.15 p. 49—The Bettmann Archive.

Chapter 4

FIGURE 4.1 p. 118—Mark Antman/The Image Works. FIGURE 4.7 p. 123—F. Roche/Animals Animals. FIGURE 4.10 p. 127—Official United States Navy Photograph. FIGURE 4.12 p. 131—Leonard Freed/Magnum Photos. FIGURE 4.13 p. 133—Susan Lapides. FIGURE 4.15 p. 136—Nina Leen/*Life Magazine*, Time Inc. FIGURE 4.16 p. 137—Wide World Photos. FIGURE 4.23 p. 147—Wide World Photos. FIGURE 4.24 p. 148—Will Rapport/Courtesy of B.F. Skinner. FIGURE 4.25 p. 150—Peter Menzel/Stock, Boston.

Chapter 5

FIGURE 5.1 p. 163—Frank Siteman. FIGURE 5.2 p. 164—John D. Cunningham. FIGURE 5.3 p. 165—Frank Siteman. FIGURE 5.7 p. 171—Frank Siteman. FIGURE 5.8 p. 172—Paul Conklin. FIGURE 5.14 p. 180—Frank Siteman. FIGURE 5.27 p. 195—John D. Cunningham.

(continued after Subject Index)

To my family:
Alice and Fritz
Kerstin and Paul
Mary

CONTENTS

PART E · SOCIAL BEHAVIOR

CHAPTER 14 · EMOTION 520

CHAPTER 15 · SOCIAL PSYCHOLOGY 562

CHAPTER 16 · PERSONALITY 610

PREFACE

Writing an introductory psychology text is a long and often lonely task. Many times I asked myself why I had begun such a time-consuming project. Fortunately, an answer was always available. I wrote my first book, *Physiology of Behavior,* because I was not satisfied with the texts that were then available, and having a sabbatical leave, decided to see whether I would be able to write a book that my students could learn from. I found that I enjoyed writing more than I had expected, and once the book was finished I was receptive to my editor's suggestion that I consider writing an introductory psychology text. I enjoy teaching the course, and the prospect of writing a book that covered such a broad field was just the challenge I wanted.

My own students are diverse in their ability and interests. The best are as good as the best students anywhere; they are eager to learn and easy to teach. But there are others who learn slowly or who are not very interested in what college has to offer them academically. Lecturing to such a group has taught me as much as them. The material must be presented in a straightforward fashion. All steps must be explained; one cannot assume that students will figure out the intervening logical conclusions by themselves. But the unfolding story must be interesting to the better students, and must challenge their intellect, as well. There must be a point to the humorous anecdotes that provide gratifying laughter, and they must be an integral part of the discourse, not tacked on. As I began writing this book I tried out my new outlines on my classes by incorporating them into my lectures. Their responses helped me realize what made sense and what did not. Sometimes I found myself in the midst of a detailed explanation looking at a roomful of blank faces and realized that the topic

was unimportant and boring to me, too, so I deleted it from the manuscript. At other times their questions inspired new explanations and examples that I quickly incorporated into the text. Therefore, I must share authorship with hundreds of students who unwittingly assisted me in my task.

When I took my first psychology course as an undergraduate I was surprised to learn that psychological investigation was actually a scientific enterprise. I had thought that psychologists knew about all the real, often hidden reasons for our behavior, and that I would now learn all their secrets. I had never really considered where this knowledge came from. I learned quickly that psychologists knew much less about the important questions than I thought they did, but their pursuit of knowledge was more interesting than I had suspected it could be.

It is the fascination and excitement of the pursuit of knowledge that I try to convey in my lectures, and which I have tried to convey in this text. The scientific method is an outstandingly successful intellectual achievement. It permits the practitioner to enjoy a mixture of speculation, logical deductions, and empirical data collection. Those of us who enjoy gadgets can spend time with computers and other hardware. Those of us who enjoy watching social interactions can design experiments that present interesting situations and observe our subjects' behavior. And then we can teach our students about what we discover, and how we discover it.

I have tried to explain how psychologists go about discovering the causes of behavior, and, of course, I have summarized the important things we have learned. I have tried to integrate findings across different subdisciplines and show the student that all of what we do is related, even though different psychologists concern themselves with different phenomena, or with different levels of analysis of these phenomena. Because we are living organisms, I have tried to show the pervasive importance of the biological approaches to behavior, including the functional, ecological approach and the physiological approach. Although there is a chapter devoted to the biology of behavior I have included relevant biological research in most chapters of the book. I spent my most recent sabbatical leave in a neurology department at a medical center, and I have discussed what I learned about the effects of damage to the human brain in the context of perception, memory, consciousness, language, emotion, and other topics.

The strengths of this book are, I think, the organization and selection of topics, the artwork, the use of everyday examples to illustrate and explain behavioral phenomena, detailed coverage of the most important principles of psychology, and a personal writing style. I have been selective in the topics I have included. I believe that a student is not well served by reading an encyclopedic collection of briefly summarized phenomena. Psychology is getting to be a mature science. If a phenomenon is worth mentioning it is worth explaining well enough so that a student can understand what is known about its causes and appreciate its relation to other phenomena.

Each chapter in the text is preceded by a list of learning objectives. These objectives provide a quick summary of the topics that are covered and provide a focus for student self-testing. The questions in the study guide are designed to help the students master these objectives, and the questions in the test bank are designed to test their mastery.

I have provided summaries where they will do the most good: just after a sizable chunk of material has been covered. Each chapter contains a number of these interim summaries, usually after each major heading. These provide students with a place to relax a bit and review what they have just read. Taken together, they provide a much longer summary than a student could or would tolerate at the end of a chapter, and will, I believe, serve them better. The concluding remarks at the end of the chapter are just that: remarks that bring the chapter to an end, perhaps summarizing some of the important issues and providing some context and closure.

To give students an appreciation for the discovery process that takes place in the laboratory or field, I have included discussions of both real experiments and "thought experiments." I invite them to try to reason out the best approach to a problem or to find the defect in a seemingly logical experiment. (You will find these discussions marked with a vertical bracket running alongside the text.) These guided discoveries are functional teaching tools, not embellishments. I have not included any "boxes." I find them to be distracting, and so do many of my students. They often interrupt one's reading of the main text. Why not, I always think, include the material as part of the text? If it is worth saying it is worth integrating with the continuing discussion. Digressions and anecdotes are interesting, and we all use them in lectures, but we insert them where they are appropriate. I have, indeed, included them in the text. In addition, I have included descriptive and inferential statistics in the chapter on methods, not in an appendix. I suspect that few statistical appendices are assigned or read.

There is more to a book like this one than the words. Often, graphs, drawings, diagrams, or photographs illustrate or elaborate points in ways that words cannot. I am pleased with the assistance that the editorial and production staff at Allyn and Bacon gave me in preparing the visual material. I think this material is informative as well as aesthetically pleasing. Consequently, each chapter ends not only with a review of newly introduced terms, but with a list of the figures that illustrate them, as well.

A complete teaching package accompanies this text, including a study guide, an instructor's manual, test items (both in printed form and on floppy disks for microcomputers), and films. The entire teaching package is closely integrated. The learning objectives presented at the opening of each chapter serve as the organizing principle for the ancillary material, resulting in what I believe is the most integrated and closely focused teaching package available for the basic introductory psychology course.

ACKNOWLEDGMENTS

As the writer I get to think of the book as "mine," but it belongs to many other people. I acknowledge their contributions and thank them. Bill Barke, the psychology editor at Allyn and Bacon, found reviewers to read successive approximations of the final version of the text, gathered a group of people to create the ancillary material, convinced the management to put their best people to work on the production of the book, and provided me with those necessary social reinforcers to keep my enthusiasm high during such a long project. Allen Workman, the developmental editor, gave me lessons on clear writing, especially on tying related topics together and providing smooth transitions. I also thank Wendy Ritger, who coordinated the preparation of the ancillary material, and Lauren Whittaker, who helped with the photo research and procurement of illustrations.

Many colleagues assisted me by reading drafts of chapters of the book and evaluating them and suggesting changes. The following people reviewed early versions.

Paul Bell
Colorado State University

John Best
Indiana University

Nancy Breland
Trenton State College

Rachel Clifton
University of Massachusetts

Sally Diveley
Trenton State University

John Donahoe
University of Massachusetts

Henry Ellis
University of New Mexico

Scott Fraser
University of Southern California

William Froming
University of Florida

Arnold Glass
Rutgers College

Donald Hoffeld
Louisiana State University

Kent Johnson
Morningside Learning Center

Lawrence Kameya
Case Western Reserve University

James Kilkowski
University of California

John Lamberth
Temple University

Donald Meichenbaum
University of Waterloo

Melinda Novak
University of Massachusetts

Edgar O'Neal
Tulane University

John Santelli
Fairleigh Dickinson University

Paul Tacon
York University

Michael Terman
Northeastern University

Joann Veroff
University of Michigan

Jean Volckmann
Pasadena City College

John Wright
Washington State University

The most recent, almost-ready drafts were read by

Robert Arkin
University of Missouri

William Beatty
North Dakota State University

Michael Best
Southern Methodist University

Douglas Bloomquist
Framingham State College

Anthony Caggiula
University of Pittsburgh

Charles Crowell
University of Notre Dame

David Dodd
University of Utah

Leslie Fisher
Cleveland State University

Carl Gustavson
North Dakota State University

John Hall
Pennsylvania State University

William Johnson
University of Mississippi

Marguerite Kermis
Canisius College

Marjorie Lewis
Illinois State University

Gerald Mendelsohn
University of California, Berkeley

Steven Mewaldt
Marshall University

Yvonne Hardaway Osborne
Louisiana State University

Merle Prim
Western Washington University

Michael Scheier
Carnegie-Mellon University

Robert Stern
Pennsylvania State University

William Timberlake
Indiana University

Paul Wellman
Texas A&M University

Then, when the book was "finished," I wrote a description of what I had done, and the people listed above read and commented on this description of the finished product. I used their comments to do some final editing and rewriting. I am very grateful to these readers for their comments, which helped shape the final form of the manuscript.

The writing was still not complete. My copy-editor, Anne Hawthorne, dug into it and proved that I still had far to go. Her tough-minded, no-nonsense (sometimes I found myself saying "brutal") editing tightened and improved my prose.

I want to thank the people who prepared the ancillary material for doing such a fine job, and for tolerating my last-minute changes, which forced them to revise their own work. Eric Carlson (Mount Holyoke College), Rosalind Burns (University of Massachusetts), and Madeleine McKivigan (Greater New Haven State Technical College) wrote the study guide; George Rebec (Indiana University) wrote the instructor's manual; and Bill Williams (Eastern Washington University) wrote the bank of test questions.

Finally, I thank my family for tolerating my spending so much time working on the book and for putting up with my grouchiness when work seemed to be going slowly. My wife Mary helped me by reading my manuscripts, finding and consulting references for me, typing an early version of the manuscript onto floppy diskettes and typing and editing the study guide. She provided support and solace, too, but I'll thank her personally for that.

TO THE READER

You purchased this book because it was assigned to you, and this semester you will be spending a considerable amount of time reading it. I hope that you will enjoy it; learning about psychology can be fun. If it were not I would never have finished writing this book, and I would long ago have tired of lecturing about it to my students.

There are some things you should know about the book before you start reading. As you will see, each chapter begins with a list of learning objectives that specify the concepts that you are to learn. If, after reading each chapter, you can answer these objectives, then you have mastered the material. If you find yourself hesitating, then you have only to refer back to those pages listed after each learning objective. The text you will need to review is signaled by a small diamond-shaped symbol: ◆. I suggest that you skim through the objectives before reading each chapter; you will see where the discussion will lead you. (The learning objectives also serve as a point of departure for the study guide that accompanies this text.)

In addition to the concepts introduced by the learning objectives, key terms are also specially marked in text. Each one appears in boldface italic where the definition or description is given. A list of these terms appears at the end of each chapter, with the appropriate page of text listed.

The book contains tables, graphs, diagrams, drawings, and photographs. They are there to illustrate a point, and in some cases, to make a point that cannot be made with words alone. I am always annoyed when illustrations accompany text without a clear indication of when I should stop reading and consult them. If I look at the illustration too soon I will not understand it. If I look at it too late I will have struggled with text that I could have understood more clearly had I only looked at the illustration first. Therefore, I have added explicit references so that you will be spared this kind of annoyance. These are in boldface, like this: (See **Figure 5.10.**) If you wait until you see a figure or table reference before looking away from the text you will be consulting the illustration at the most appropriate time. Sometimes it is best to look at a figure more than once; in such cases I provide more than one reference to it.

Each chapter will take some time to read carefully. Rather than provide a long summary at the end of each chapter I have provided interim summaries—reviews of the information that has just been presented. When you reach these in your reading, take the opportunity to relax and think about what you have read. You might even want to take a five-minute break after reading the interim summary, then read it once again to remind yourself of what you just read, and go on to the next section. If you read the material this way you will learn it with much less effort than you would otherwise have to expend.

I have included as part of the text several demonstrations and experiments that you may want to try, and some "thought experiments" that will help illustrate important principles. (They are marked in text by a vertical bracket.) I urge you to try them. I use them in my lectures, and my students have found them worthwhile. Most of them are fun, help break up the chore of reading a long chapter, and are not hard to remember when it comes to examination time.

I have not met you, but I feel as if I have been talking to you during the several years I have been writing and rewriting this book. Writing is an unsocial activity in the sense that it is done alone. It is even an antisocial activity when the writer must say, "No, I'm too busy writing to talk with you now." So as I wrote this book I consoled myself by imagining that you were listening to me. You will get to meet me, or at least do so vicariously, through my words, as you read this book. If you then want to make the conversation two-way, please write to me at the Department of Psychology, Tobin Hall, University of Massachusetts, Amherst, 01003. I hope to hear from you.

PSYCHOLOGY

PART · A
THE SCIENCE
OF BEHAVIOR

For countless years people have grappled with the most basic of intellectual problems: understanding the way that we humans gain knowledge about ourselves, our behavior, and our environment. From the earliest times of recorded history this issue has been argued by philosophers. One important result of their thoughts and arguments was the birth of science. Philosophers developed a system of observation and reasoning that they used to explain the causes of natural phenomena and the special relation of the human species to the universe. The spirit of their inquiry and their attempt to classify and catalog the knowledge that they gained are the foundations upon which the modern scientific method was built.

For over 2000 years, dating from the time of Ancient Greece, philosophers relied upon logic and speculation to answer questions about the nature of the universe and the human mind. To them, experimentation and documentation of physical phenomena to verify their conclusions was, quite literally, inconceivable. The animating spirit of the world was divine; thus, truth had to be deduced. It was not until the fourteenth century that the spirit of the Renaissance challenged this approach to the study of natural phenomena. Now, logical reasoning began to be supported and supplemented by direct observation, using the scientific instruments that had just been invented. The initial focus of investigations led to the development of such scientific disciplines as physics and biology. But it was not until the late nineteenth century that scientists and philosophers were prepared to deal with the human mind and human behavior as physical phenomena. As you will see in Chapter 1, scientists eventually realized that the study of human behavior need not be different in practice from that of the physical and biological sciences. Objective investigation could effectively be applied to the human mind. Psychology, as a science, was born.

Chapter 2 follows up on the historical perspective of Chapter 1 with a description of the scientific method, as it applies to psychologists' attempts to understand human behavior. You will learn how psychologists perform experiments and carry out objective observations of behavior. As you will see, an understanding of the scientific method will help you deal with a wide variety of intellectual issues.

THE NATURE
OF PSYCHOLOGY

LEARNING ◆ OBJECTIVES

PSYCHOLOGY IS both a scientific discipline and a profession. Psychologists are probably the most diverse group of people in our society to share the same title. According to the 1980 census, there are 119,000 people in the United States who are employed as psychologists. They engage in research, teaching, counseling, and psychotherapy; they advise industry and governmental agencies about personnel matters, the design of products, advertising and marketing, and legislation; they devise and administer tests of personality, achievement, and ability. Psychologists study phenomena as diverse as physiological processes within the nervous system, genetics, environmental events, mental abilities, and social interactions. And yet, psychology is a new discipline; the first person to call himself a psychologist died in 1920.

In this book we shall study the science of psychology. The primary emphasis is on the discovery of the causes of human behavior. I shall describe the applications of these discoveries to the treatment of mental disorders and the improvement of society, but the focus will be on the way in which psychologists discover facts. In this chapter I shall examine the history of psychology: its origins in philosophy and biology, and its evolution as an independent science. Then I shall describe what present-day psychologists do.

HISTORY OF PSYCHOLOGY

Although philosophers and other thinkers have been concerned with psychological issues for a long time, the science of psychology is comparatively young; it started in Germany in the late nineteenth century. Why did it start there, at that time? As we shall see, the time and place were ripe for the establishment of an academic discipline devoted to the study of the human mind. The German university system was well established, and professors were highly respected members of society. The aca-

demic tradition in Germany emphasized a scientific approach to a large number of subjects, such as history, phonetics, archaeology, aesthetics, and literature. Thus, in contrast to the more traditional philosophical approach to the study of the human mind by the French and British, German scholars were more open to the possibility that the human mind could be studied scientifically. Experimental physiology, one of the most important roots of experimental psychology, was well established there. A more mundane and practical reason that favored Germany as the birthplace of psychology was the fact that universities were well financed; there was money to support researchers who wanted to expand scientific investigation into new fields.

But first we must trace the roots of psychology back through philosophy and the natural sciences, which provided the methods with which to study human behavior. These roots took many centuries to develop. Let us examine them, and see how the stage was set for the emergence of the science of psychology in the late nineteenth century.

PHILOSOPHICAL ROOTS OF PSYCHOLOGY

Each of us is conscious of our existence. Furthermore, we are aware of this consciousness. Although we often find ourselves doing things that we had not planned to do (or had planned *not* to do), by and large we feel that we are in control. That is, our behavior is controlled by our consciousness. We consider alternatives, make plans, and then act. We get our muscles moving; we engage in behavior.

Consciousness is a private experience, and yet it has a history. At present, even though we can experience only our own consciousness directly, we attribute consciousness to our fellow human beings, and, at least to some extent, other animals as well. To the degree that our behaviors are similar we tend to assume that our mental states, too, resemble each other. Much earlier in the history of our species, people were very generous in attributing a life-giving *animus*, or spirit, to anything that seemed to move or grow independently. Because they knew that the movements of their bodies were controlled by their minds or spirits, they then inferred that the sun, moon, wind, tides, and other moving objects were similarly animated. This primitive philosophy is called *animism* (from the Latin *animare:* to quicken, enliven, endow with breath or soul). Even gravity was explained in animistic terms: rocks fell to the ground because the spirits within them wanted to be reunited with Mother Earth.

Obviously, our interest in animism is a historical one. No educated person in our society believes that rocks fall because they "want to." Rather, we believe that they fall owing to the existence of natural forces inherent in physical matter, even if we do not understand what these forces are. But it is instructive to note the different interpretations placed upon the same events. Surely we are just as prone to subjective interpretations of natural phenomena, albeit more sophisticated ones, as our ancestors were. In fact, when we try to explain why people do what they do, we tend to attribute at least some of their behavior to the action of a motivating spirit; namely, a will. On a philosophical level this explanation of behavior may suit our needs. However, on a scientific level, we need to record our experience in more concrete terms so that the judgments we make are as free as possible from subjective interpretation.

The best means we have to ensure objectivity is the scientific method. Psychology as a science must be based on the assumption that behavior is strictly subject to physical laws just like any other natural phenomenon. The rules of scientific research impose discipline on humans whose natural inclinations might lead them to incorrect conclusions. It was natural for our ancestors to believe that rocks had spirits, just as it is natural for people to believe that behavior can be affected by an intangible will. The idea that feelings, emotions, imagination, and other private experiences can be conceived of as products of physical laws of nature did not come easily; it evolved through many centuries.

We begin in Ancient Greece, where thinkers broke from the common reliance upon mythology as an explanation for humanity's relation to the universe. This change in approach occurred with the Greek philosophers of the late sixth and fifth centuries B.C. They perceived humans as thinking creatures, capable of using the rational faculties of the mind to explain the phenomena of the perceptual world. We can trace the beginning of the scientific method back to these philosophers, and to their reliance upon observation as the source of knowledge.

FIGURE 1.1 Aristotle (384–322 B.C.) used the evidence of physical phenomena as the basis for conclusions he would draw about the human condition and the natural world. His explanations were given in terms of observable physical qualities (wet/dry, hot/cold); he sought to explain phenomena in terms of their natural causes.

Aristotle was probably the most mature and comprehensive thinker of Ancient Greece. (See **Figure 1.1**.) By carefully and systematically observing what he could of nature, and by reasoning from these observations, he created a system of knowledge that had a profound impact on biology as well as philosophy. His purpose in obtaining this knowledge was to help answer philosophical questions; however, it served an even greater purpose.

For many centuries, Aristotle's writings about natural phenomena were used as the authority on subjects relating to the physical universe. His interpretations were accepted by subsequent generations, with little attempt being made to verify them. Intellectual activity was instead focused upon problems of a religious nature. Philosophy, as it developed in Europe through the Middle Ages, was primarily Christian philosophy. Philosophers were concerned with the discovery of revealed truth, not the advancement of science. This relegation of science to minor status is more easily understood when you realize that the primary concept of the mind and body was a dualistic one.

Dualism, the division of the world into two independent elements, mind and matter, was the basis of philosophical thought well into the seventeenth century. The mind—more appropriately, the soul—was believed to be a nonphysical entity, in contrast to the physical body. Because scholarly activity was the domain of Christian philosophers and theologians, the study of these scholars was limited to the relation of humans to God. They sought to discover religious truths; observation of natural phenomena was useful only in what it revealed about the nature of God and only when it did not contradict established beliefs.

Scholarly activity moved into a more specialized setting with the founding of universities in the thirteenth century. These universities, established by the Church, became centers of *Scholasticism,* a philosophical–theological movement that sought to reconcile the truth of God's revelation with the truths discovered by human reason and observation—even those that seemed to be contradictory. This synthesis did not survive continued scrutiny. By the fourteenth century scholars abandoned the effort to reconcile faith and reason. They concluded that the existence of God and the immortality of

the soul were not to be proved; instead, knowledge of these came only through intuition and mystical experience. For the first time, theology and philosophy became separate disciplines, fundamentally unrelated. Now, scholars of what was called natural philosophy turned their efforts toward study of the tangible objects of the world and began to collect a large body of scientific data.

Outside the universities, with the flowering of the Italian Renaissance, people were taking more of an interest in the secular world. This intensification of the secular spirit in Western European thought, literature, and art reflected a very basic change in attitude that came to be identified as *humanism.* Its primary characteristic was the focusing of interest upon human nature and the human condition. Renewed interest in the physical world, combined with a general optimism and confidence in the wisdom and self-sufficiency of humankind helped to promote the cause of science. Because universities were still under the control of the Church, special societies and academies were established to further scientific inquiry.

René Descartes, a French philosopher and mathematician, emerged from this climate. (See **Figure 1.2**.) He advocated a sober, impersonal investigation of natural phenomena using sensory experience and human reasoning. This stance challenged the established authority of the Church. He assumed that the world was a purely mechanical entity that, having once been set in motion by God, ran its course without divine interference. Thus, to understand the world, one had only to understand how it was constructed.

To Descartes, animals were mechanical devices; their behavior was controlled by environmental stimuli. His view of the human body was much the same: it was a machine. What set humans apart from the rest of the world was the fact that they possessed a mind. This was a uniquely human attribute and was not subject to the physical laws of the universe.

Descartes was a proponent of dualism, believing in two distinct entities: mind and matter. However, his thinking differed significantly from that of his predecessors. He was the first to propose a link between the human mind and its purely physical housing. This link is absolutely vital to the evolution of a psychological science.

DISCOURS
DE LA METHODE
Pour bien conduire ſa raiſon, & chercher
la verité dans les ſciences.

FIGURE 1.2   René Descartes (1596–1650) in his
Discourse on Method was the first to write about
scientific theory and methodology. As the inventor of
analytic geometry he contributed an important tool to
physical science.

Descartes reasoned that mind and body could
interact. The mind controlled the movements of
the body; the body, through its sense organs, supplied the mind with information about what was
happening in the environment. This philosophical
approach, reasonably enough, was called *interac-
tionism.* Descartes hypothesized that this interaction between mind and body took place in the
pineal body, a small organ situated on top of the
brain stem, buried beneath the large cerebral hemispheres. (See **Figure 1.3.**) When the mind decided
to perform an action, it tilted the pineal body in
a particular direction, causing fluid to flow into
the proper set of nerves. This caused the appro-

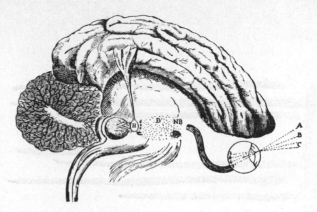

FIGURE 1.3   The pineal body (H), as conceived
of by Descartes, was the structure through which the
mind could control the body.

priate muscles to inflate and move. Let us see how
Descartes came up with this mechanical concept of
the body's movements.

Western Europe in the seventeenth century was
the scene of great advance in the sciences. It was
not just the practical application of science that
impressed Europeans, it was the beauty, imagination, and fun of it as well. Craftsmen constructed
elaborate mechanical toys and devices. As a young
man Descartes was greatly impressed by the moving statues in the Royal Gardens. A person wandering through the gardens, stepping on a hidden
plate, would activate hydraulically operated mechanisms that would cause statues to move and dance.
These devices served Descartes as models in theorizing about how the body worked. He conceived
of the muscles as balloons. They became inflated
when a fluid passed through the nerves that connected them to the brain and spinal cord, just as
water flowed through pipes to activate the statues.
This inflation was the basis of the muscular contraction that causes us to move.

This story illustrates one of the first times that
a technological device was used as a model for explaining how the nervous system works. In science
a *model* is a relatively simple system that works
on known principles and that does at least some of
the things that a more complex system does. For
example, when it was understood that elements of
the nervous system communicate by means of electrical impulses, people invented models of the brain

that were based upon telephone switchboards and, more recently, computers. Abstract models, which are completely mathematical in their properties, have also been developed.

Although Descartes's model of the human body was mechanical, it was controlled by the nonmechanical (in fact, nonphysical) mind. Humans were born with a special capability that made them more than simply the sum of their parts; their knowledge was more than a physical phenomenon.

Descartes did recognize that some movements were automatic and involuntary. For example, the application of a hot object to the hand would cause an almost immediate withdrawal of the arm away from the source of stimulation. Reactions like this did not require participation of the mind. Descartes called them *reflexes* (from the word "reflection"). Energy coming from the outside stimulus would be reflected through the nervous system to the muscles, which would contract. The term is still in use today, and is used in exactly the same sense; of course, we explain the operation of a reflex differently. (See **Figure 1.4.**)

With the work of the English philosopher John Locke the mechanization of the whole world was complete. (See **Figure 1.5.**) Locke did not exempt the mind from the mechanical laws of the material universe. Descartes's rationalism (pursuit of truth through reason) was supplanted by *empiricism*—pursuit of truth through observation and experi-

FIGURE 1.5   John Locke (1632–1704) in his *Essay Concerning Human Understanding* proposed the theory that the human mind, void of all knowledge at birth, learns knowledge through perception and reason.

FIGURE 1.4   Descartes's diagram of a withdrawal reflex from his *Traité de l'Homme*.

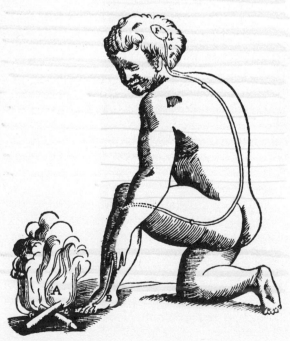

ence. Locke rejected the notion that ideas were innately present in an infant's mind. Instead, all knowledge must come through experience. It is empirically derived. (In Greek, *empeirā* means "experience.") His model of the mind was a tablet of soft clay, smooth at birth, ready to accept the writings of experience upon it.

George Berkeley, Irish philosopher and mathematician, expanded upon Locke's ideas. (See **Figure 1.6.**) He agreed with Locke that all knowledge was empirically derived and that the mind of an infant was like a smooth, clean slate of clay, but he disagreed about how experience wrote upon it.

Locke believed that our knowledge of complex experiences was nothing more than linkages of simple, primary sensations: simple ideas combined to form complex ones. In contrast, Berkeley believed that our knowledge of events in the world did not come simply from direct experience, but instead was the result of inferences based upon the accumulations of past experiences. In other words, we must learn how to perceive. For example, our per-

FIGURE 1.6   George Berkeley (1685–1753) further refined the ideas of John Locke by suggesting that human perception, and hence knowledge, was much more complex than the simple act of perceiving would seem to indicate. Humans had to learn to perceive.

ception of depth involves several elementary sensations, such as observing the relative movements of objects as we move our head and the convergence of our eyes (crossing or uncrossing of the eyes for near or distant objects). Although our knowledge of depth seems to be immediate and direct, it is actually a secondary, complex response constructed from a number of simple elements. Perceptions even involve integration of the activity of different sense organs, as when we see, hear, feel, and smell the same object.

As you can see, the philosophers Locke and Berkeley were grappling with the structure of the human mind and the way people acquire knowledge. They were dealing with the concept of learning. (In fact, modern psychologists are still concerned with the issues that Berkeley raised.) As philosophers, they were trying to fit the unquantifiable variable—reason—into the equation.

It was with the work of the English philosopher James Mill that the pendulum took its full swing from animism (physical matter possessed of spirits) to full-blown materialism (mind as matter). (See **Figure 1.7.**) Mill worked on the assumption that humans and animals were fundamentally the same. Both humans and animals were thoroughly physical in their makeup and were completely subject to the physical laws of the universe. Essentially, he agreed with Descartes's approach to understanding the human body, but rejected the concept of an immaterial mind. Mind, to Mill, was as passive as the body. It responded to the environment in precisely the same way. The mind, no less than the body, was a machine.

Mill's philosophy obviously precluded the concept of freedom of will. People were *not* able to choose what they did. Instead, their behavior was determined by physical events: environmental events that affected their sense organs and internal, physiological events that occurred within their bodies. Mind had no creative functions; the association of ideas occurred automatically and required no effort of will.

A staunch advocate for applying the methods of scientific investigation to the study of humans was Auguste Comte, a French mathematician and philosopher. (See **Figure 1.8.**) With absolute confidence in the value of factual data, he began to compile a systematic survey of all knowledge. He

FIGURE 1.7 James Mill (1773–1836) believed that the working of the human mind was a purely physical phenomenon, as subject to the laws of nature as any other natural phenomenon. He disavowed any creative function to the mind.

limited the scope of his project to facts that were indisputably true, those that could be observed objectively. He believed that the search for absolute truths was better abandoned for the more sensible discovery of physical laws, dealing with scientific—i.e., positive—facts. As applied to the study of humans, this meant behavior that could be observed: *social* events can be studied; private events cannot. Thus, speculation about what was going on in a person's mind was better abandoned for study of what a person actually did and said. This philosophical approach to knowledge is called *positivism.*

◆   Interim summary: We can see that by the mid-nineteenth century philosophy had embraced three concepts that would lead to the objective investigation of the human mind: the principles of materialism, empiricism, and positivism. Materialism maintained that all natural phenomena could be explained in terms of physical entities: the inter-

FIGURE 1.8   Auguste Comte (1798–1857) is credited with establishing sociology as a separate discipline. He placed great faith in statistics and amassed a vast amount of data on social, and hence behavioral, phenomena.

action of matter and energy. Empiricism emphasized that all knowledge is acquired by means of sensory experience; no knowledge is innate. Positivism insisted on the strict adherence to the testimony of direct observation of physical events, which for psychology means behavior. By directing attention to tangible, sensory components of human activity, these concepts laid the foundation for a scientific approach in psychology. At this point the divisions between science and philosophy were still blurred. It is in the development of the natural sciences, especially biology and physiology, that we find the ingredients needed to unite with the critical, analytical components of philosophy to form the separate scientific discipline of psychology: experimentation and verification.

BIOLOGICAL ROOTS OF PSYCHOLOGY

René Descartes and his model of muscular physiology provides a good beginning for a discussion of the biological roots of psychology. Descartes's concept was based on an actual working model whose movements seemed similar to those of human beings. Recognition of that similarity served as proof of his theory; he did not have the means available to offer a more scientific proof. But development of technology soon made experimentation and manipulation possible. Truth need not only be reasoned; it could be demonstrated and verified. Thus, Descartes's hydraulic model of muscular movement was shown to be incorrect by Luigi Galvani (1737–1798), an Italian physiologist who discovered that muscles could be made to contract by applying an electrical current directly to them, or to the nerve that was attached to them.

With the work of the German physiologist Johannes Müller we note a very definite transition from the somewhat isolated instances of research into human physiology to the progressively more direct exploration of the human body. Müller was a forceful advocate of applying experimental procedures to the study of physiology. (See **Figure 1.9.**) According to him, biologists should do more than observe and classify; they should remove or isolate various organs, test their responses to chemicals, and manipulate other conditions in order to see how the organism worked. His most important contribution to what would become the science of psychology was his *doctrine of specific nerve energies.* He noted that the basic message within all nerves was the same—an electrical impulse. What, then, accounts for the brain's ability to distinguish different kinds of sensory information? That is, why do we see what our eyes detect, hear what our ears detect, and so on? After all, the optic nerves and the auditory nerves both send the same kind of message to the brain.

The answer is that the messages are sent over different channels. Because the optic nerves are attached to the eyes, the brain interprets impulses received from these nerves as visual sensations. You have probably already noticed that rubbing your eyes causes sensations of flashes of light. When you rub your eyes, the pressure against them stimulates visual receptors located inside. The brain then interprets these messages as sensations of light.

Müller's doctrine had important implications. If the brain recognizes the nature of a particular sensory input by means of the particular nerve that

FIGURE 1.9   Johannes Müller (1801–1858) provided the basis for subsequent studies on the specialized functions of various parts of the nervous system. He said that it is not the message sent by

excitation of sensory receptors that causes us to experience different sensations; it is the channel that picks up and transmits the message and that portion of the brain that receives it.

brings the message, then perhaps the brain is similarly specialized, with different parts having different functions. If the nerves that send the messages are anatomically distinct, then those regions of the brain that receive these messages must also be anatomically distinct. Müller's ideas have endured, forming the basis for investigations of the functions of the nervous system. The work is important, too, because of its implications. For centuries, thinking or consciousness had been identified as the distinguishing feature of the human mind and had been

localized as a function of the brain. Now the components of the nervous system were being identified and their means of operation were being explored.

Pierre Flourens, a French physiologist, provided experimental evidence for the implications of Müller's doctrine of specific nerve energies. (See Figure 1.10.) He removed various parts of the nervous system of animals and found that the resulting effects depended upon the parts that were removed. He observed what the animal could no longer do

FIGURE 1.10 Pierre Flourens (1794–1867) used experimental ablation to begin mapping out the functions of various portions of the brain.

FIGURE 1.11 Paul Broca (1824–1880) identified the physical basis of speech production as being located in a certain part of the human brain. A postmortem examination of a patient who had suffered speech loss revealed damage to the left cerebral hemisphere.

and concluded that the missing capacity must have been the function of the part he had removed. For example, if an animal could not move its leg after part of its brain was removed, then that region must normally control leg movements. This method (called *experimental ablation*, from *ablātus*, "carried away") was soon adopted by neurologists, and is still used by scientists today. Using this method, Flourens claimed to have discovered the regions of the brain that controlled heart rate and breathing, purposeful movements, and visual and auditory reflexes.

The person to apply the logic of Flourens's method to humans was Paul Broca. (See **Figure 1.11**.) In 1861 Broca, a French surgeon, performed an autopsy on the brain of a man who had had a stroke several years before; the stroke had caused him to lose the ability to speak. Broca discovered that part of the cerebral cortex on the left side of the man's brain was damaged. He suggested that this region of the brain is a center for speech.

Although subsequent research has found that speech is not controlled by a single "center" in the brain, the comparison of postmortem anatomical findings with a patient's behavioral and intellectual deficits has become an important means of studying the function of the brain. Psychologists can

operate on the brains of laboratory animals, but they obviously cannot operate on the brains of humans. Instead, they must study the effects of brain damage that occurs from natural causes.

In 1870 the German physiologists Gustav Fritsch and Eduard Hitzig introduced the use of electrical stimulation to the mapping of the functions of the brain. The results of this method complemented those produced by the experimental destruction of nerve tissue in animals, and provided some answers that the method of experimental ablation could not. For example, Fritsch and Hitzig discovered that applying a small electrical shock to different parts of the cerebral cortex caused movements of different parts of the body. In fact, the body appeared to be "mapped" on the surface of the brain. (See **Figure 1.12**.)

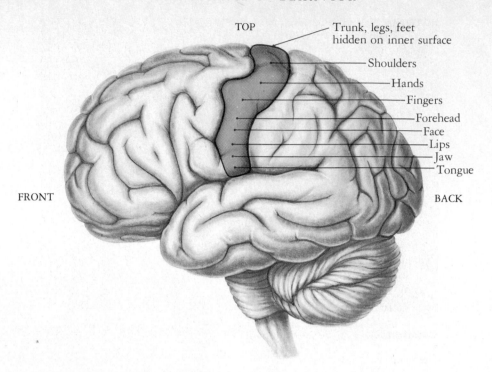

TOP

Trunk, legs, feet
hidden on inner surface

Shoulders

Hands

Fingers

Forehead

Face

Lips

Jaw

Tongue

FRONT

BACK

FIGURE 1.12   Cortical motor map. Stimulation
of various parts of motor cortex cause contraction of
muscles in various parts of the body.

The work of the German physicist and physiologist Hermann von Helmholtz did much to demonstrate that mental phenomena could be explained by physiological means. (See **Figure 1.13.**) This extremely productive scientist made contributions to both physics and physiology. He devised a mathematical formulation of the law of conservation of energy. He invented the ophthalmoscope (a device used to examine the retina of the eye). He devised a theory of color vision and color blindness that was proved to be largely correct in the middle of the twentieth century. He studied audition, music, eye movements, the formation of ice, geometry, and allergies.

Helmholtz actively disassociated himself from natural philosophy. Müller, under whom Helmholtz had conducted his first research, believed that human organs were endowed with a vital nonmaterial force that coordinated physiological behavior, a force that was not subject to experimental investigation. Helmholtz would allow no such restrictions nor would he come to his research with some conclusions already made. He advocated a purely scientific approach with conclusions based on objective investigation and precise measurement.

Until Helmholtz's time it was believed that the transmission of impulses through nerves was as fast as the speed of electricity in wires, which is virtually instantaneous, considering the small distances that have to be traveled within the human body. However, Helmholtz successfully measured the speed of the nerve impulse and found that it was only about 90 feet per second, which is considerably slower. This suggested to later researchers that the nerve impulse is more complex than a simple electrical current passing through a wire, which is indeed true.

Helmholtz also attempted to measure the speed of a person's reaction to a physical stimulus, but abandoned this because there was too much variability from person to person. However, this variability interested scientists who followed him; they tried to explain the reason for individual differences

FIGURE 1.13   Hermann von Helmholtz (1821–1894), through his laboratory research, demonstrated the ability and the willingness to analyze philosophical assumptions on which much of science was then based.

in behavior. The fact that the velocity of nerve impulses and a person's reactions to stimuli could be measured suggested to later researchers that mental events themselves could be the subject of scientific investigation. It seemed possible that if the proper techniques could be developed, one could investigate what went on within the human brain. Thus, Helmholtz's research was very important in setting the stage for the science of psychology.

Interim summary: To summarize our history thus far we return to Auguste Comte. His "law of three stages," which traced human intellectual development, offers us an interesting analogy. Humans had moved from a theological stage (the world and human destiny explained in terms of gods and spirits), through a transitional stage (explanations given in the philosophical terms of essences, final causes, and other abstractions), to the modern positive stage (explanations given in the scientific terms of natural laws and empirical data). We can relate the development in the approach to the study of the human mind to Comte's three stages: from animism, through theology and philosophy, into biology and physiology. This leads us to Wilhelm Wundt and his laboratory.

MAJOR TRENDS IN THE DEVELOPMENT OF PSYCHOLOGY

◆ Psychology began in Germany in the late nineteenth century with Wilhelm Wundt. (See **Figure 1.14.**) Wundt was the first person to call himself a psychologist. He shared the conviction of other German scientists that all aspects of nature, including the human mind, could be studied scientifically. His book *Principles of Physiological Psychology* was the first textbook of psychology.

The fact that Germany was the birthplace of psychology had as much to do with social, political, and economic influences as with the abilities of its scientists and scholars. Germany, since the time of the Holy Roman Empire in the fourteenth century, was much more decentralized than the

FIGURE 1.14 Wilhelm Wundt (1832–1920) founded the first psychological laboratory in Leipzig in 1879. As a scientist he regarded description as the problem of science and observation as its method. As a psychologist he was interested in the introspective analysis of the contents of human consciousness.

other European nations. In Britain and France, the strong centralized power of the Church, monarchies, and nobility found its way into the universities. On the other hand, Germany was divided into small independent principalities, linked together by a growing system of trade. (In fact, this interest in commerce led to important developments in mathematics and practical science.)

Unlike the monarchies of Europe, Germany's social structure was less stratified, more fluid and individualistic. There was freedom to exploit one's inventions for private gain unhindered by state suppression. Human activity was focused less on finding the glory of God and more toward a more

disciplined commitment to cooperation in working for the common good. Growth in commerce and industry placed commercial value on science, and natural philosophy (what would become natural science) passed from the hands of gentleman scholars and amateurs to a group of professionals and the German universities. It was in this climate that Müller, Helmholtz, and Wundt conducted their research.

Structuralism

◈ Wundt's experimental method was called *structuralism*. Its subject matter was the *structure* of the mind, built from the elements of consciousness such as ideas and sensations. Its raw material was supplied by trained observers who described their own experiences. The observers were taught to engage in *introspection* (literally, "looking within"). They observed stimuli and described their experiences. Wundt and his associates made inferences about the nature of mental processes by seeing how changes in the stimuli caused changes in the verbal reports of their trained observers.

Wundt was particularly interested in the problem that had intrigued George Berkeley: how did basic sensory information give rise to complex perceptions? His trained observers attempted to ignore complex perceptions and report only the elementary ones. For example, the sensation of seeing a patch of red is an immediate and elementary one whereas the perception of an apple is a complex one.

Wundt was a very ambitious and prolific scientist who wrote many books and trained many other scientists in his laboratory. However, his method did not survive the test of time; structuralism died out in the early twentieth century. The major problem with his approach was the difficulty encountered by observers in reporting the raw data of sensation, data unmodified by experience. In addition, the emphasis of psychological investigation shifted from the study of the human mind to the study of human behavior. And now that cognitive psychologists have resumed the study of the human mind we have newer and better methods for studying it than were available to Wundt. However, although structuralism has been supplanted, Wundt's contribution must be acknowledged. He established psychology as an experimental science, independent of philosophy. He trained a great number of psychologists, many of whom established their own laboratories and continued the evolution of the new discipline.

Functionalism

◆ The next major trend in psychology was *functionalism*. This approach, which began in the United States, was in large part a protest against the structuralism of Wundt. While structuralists were interested in what they saw as the components of consciousness (ideas, sensations), the functionalists focused on the operations of conscious activity (perceiving, learning). Functionalism grew from the new perspective on nature that was being supplied by Charles Darwin and his followers. Functionalism stressed the biological significance (function) of natural processes, including behaviors. The em-

FIGURE 1.15   Charles Darwin (1809–1882) was the first scientist to provide adequate evidence for the theory of evolution and to explain how the process of natural selection produces adaptation. Psychologists adapted this concept of functional evolution in their study of human behavior.

phasis was on overt, observable behavior, and not on private mental events.

Charles Darwin proposed the theory of evolution in his book *On the Origin of Species by Means of Natural Selection*. (See **Figure 1.15**.) As you know, his work, more than that of any other person, revolutionized biology. The concept of *natural selection* showed how the consequences of an animal's characteristics affected its ability to survive. Instead of simply identifying, describing, and naming species, biologists attempted to understand the adaptive significance of the ways in which species differed.

Darwin's theory suggested that behaviors, like other biological characteristics, could best be explained by understanding their role in the adaptation of an organism to its environment. Behavior had a biological context. Darwin assembled evidence that suggested that behaviors, like body parts, could be inherited. In his book *The Expression of the Emotions in Man and Animals* he suggested that the facial gestures that animals make in expressing emotions had descended from movements that previously had other functions. New areas of exploration were opened for psychologists by the suggestion that a continuity existed among the various species of animals, and that behaviors, like parts of the body, had evolutionary histories.

The most important psychologist to embrace functionalism was William James. (See **Figure 1.16**.) Although James was a champion of experimental psychology, he himself did not appear to enjoy doing research, but spent most of his time reading, thinking, teaching, and writing during his tenure as professor of philosophy (later, professor of psychology) at Harvard University. His course entitled "The Relations between Physiology and Psychology" was the first course in experimental psychology to be offered in the United States.

James was a brilliant writer and thinker. Although he did not produce any significant experimental research, his teaching and writing influenced those who followed him. His theory of emotion is one of the most famous and durable of any psychological theory. It is still quoted in textbooks today. (Yes, you will read about it later.) Psychologists still find it worthwhile to read James's writings; he supplied ideas for experiments that still sound fresh and new today.

FIGURE 1.16   William James (1842–1910) established a functional point of view in psychology. He treated thinking and knowledge as instruments in the struggle to live, assimilating mental science to biological disciplines.

Unlike structuralism, functionalism was not supplanted; instead, its major tenets were absorbed by its successor, behaviorism. One of the last of the functionalists, James Angell, described its fundamental principles. (1) Functional psychology is the study of mental *operations* and not mental *structures*. (For example, the mind remembers; it does not contain a memory.) It is not enough to compile a catalog of what the mind does; one must try to understand what the mind accomplishes. (2) Mental processes are not studied as isolated and independent events, but as part of the biological activity of the organism. These processes are part of the organism's adaptation to the environment, and are a product of its evolutionary history. The fact that we are conscious implies that consciousness has adaptive value for our species. (3) Functional psychology studies the relation between environment and the response of the organism. There is no meaningful distinction between mind and body; they are part of the same entity.

Freud's Psychodynamic Theory

While psychology was developing as a fledgling science, an important figure was formulating a theory of human behavior that would greatly affect psychology and psychiatry and radically influence intellectuals of all kinds. Sigmund Freud began his

FIGURE 1.17   Sigmund Freud (1856–1939) was the first to employ psychoanalytic methods in his treatment of patients. In doing so, he successfully treated illnesses that seemed to have no apparent organic explanation. Freud believed such illnesses were manifestations of an unconscious mental life; to treat the patient one had to bring to the consciousness of the sufferer the facts and circumstances of earlier, repressed experiences and feelings.

career as a neurologist, so his work was firmly rooted in biology. He soon became interested in behavioral and emotional problems, and began formulating his psychodynamic theory of personality, which was to evolve over his long career. Although his approach to theory was speculative rather than scientific, he remained convinced that the biological basis of his theory would be established some day. (See **Figure 1.17**.)

Freud and his theory are discussed in detail in Chapter 16. His theory of the mind (and personality) included structures, but his structuralism was quite different from Wundt's. He devised his concepts of ego, superego, id, and other mental structures through talking with his patients, not through laboratory experiments. His hypothetical mental operations included many that were unconscious, and hence not available to introspection. Also unlike Wundt, Freud emphasized function; his mental structures served biological drives and instincts, and reflected our animal nature.

Freud's influence upon clinical practice and

therapy represented a high point in emphasizing internal mental events, which stood in sharp contrast to the opposite approach of the behaviorists.

Behaviorism

◆ The next major trend in psychology, *behaviorism,* directly followed from functionalism. It went several steps further in its rejection of the special nature of mental events. Drawing from Comte's positivism, it denied that mental events were properly the subject matter of psychology. Psychology was the study of behavior, and mental events were not behavior. They could not be observed, so they were outside the realm of scientific inquiry.

◆ Edward Thorndike was an American psychologist who studied the behavior of animals. (See **Figure 1.18.**) His studies of the learning behavior of cats led him to formulate the *law of effect.* He placed cats in a cage that was equipped with a latch. The cats, who were hungry, had to operate

FIGURE 1.18   Edward Thorndike (1874–1949) established animal psychology as a natural science. As a functionalist he was interested in learning theory; he used the learned behavior demonstrated by his laboratory animals to support his theories.

the latch in order to leave the cage and eat the food that was placed in a dish outside. Thorndike observed that the cats' restless activity eventually resulted in their operating the latch. On subsequent trials the cats' behavior became more and more efficient, until they operated the latch as soon as they were placed into the cage. He called the process "learning by trial and accidental success."

Thorndike noted that some events, usually those that one would expect to be pleasant, seemed to "stamp in" a response that had just occurred. Other, apparently noxious events, seemed to "stamp out" the response, or make it less likely to occur. (Nowadays, we call these processes "reinforcement" and "punishment.") Thorndike's law of effect was defined as follows:

> Any act which in a given situation produces satisfaction becomes associated with that situation, so that when the situation recurs the act is more likely than before to recur also. Conversely, any act which in a given situation produces discomfort becomes disassociated from that situation, so that when the situation recurs the act is less likely than before to recur. (Thorndike, 1905, p. 203)

The law of effect is certainly in the functionalist tradition. It observes that the consequences of a behavior act back upon the organism to affect the likelihood that the response that just occurred will occur again. The cat accidentally presses the latch and the consequences of this act (being able to leave the cage and eat) make pressing the latch become more likely the next time the cat is put into the cage. This is very similar to the principle of natural selection; organisms that successfully adapt to their environment are more likely to survive and breed, thus producing more organisms like themselves.

Although Thorndike insisted that the subject matter of psychology was behavior, his explanations had somewhat mentalistic terms. For example, in his law of effect he spoke of "satisfaction," which is certainly not a phenomenon that can be directly observed. Later behaviorists threw out terms like "satisfaction" and "discomfort" and replaced them with more objective terms, reflecting the behavior of the organism rather than any feelings it might have.

◆ Another major figure in the development of the behavioristic trend was not a psychologist at all,

FIGURE 1.19   Ivan Pavlov (1849–1936) supplied psychology wih the discovery of the conditioned reflex. His story is one of those happy occurrences in which research reveals a significant, though unsought, result.

but a Russian physiologist. Ivan Pavlov studied the physiology of digestion. (See **Figure 1.19.**) In the course of studying the stimuli that produce salivation, he discovered that hungry dogs would salivate at the sight of the attendant who brought in their dish of food. Pavlov found that a dog could be trained to salivate at completely arbitrary stimuli, such as the sound of a bell, if the stimulus was quickly followed by the delivery of a bit of food into the animal's mouth.

Pavlov's discovery had profound significance for psychology. His principles showed that through experience, an animal could learn to make a response to a stimulus that had never caused this response before. This could explain how organisms learn cause-and-effect relations in the environment. Thorndike's law of effect suggested an explanation for the adaptability of an individual's behavior to its particular environment. Two important behavioral principles had been discovered.

Behaviorism as a formal discipline within psychology began with the publication of a book by

John B. Watson, *Psychology from the Standpoint of a Behaviorist*. Watson was a professor of psychology at Johns Hopkins University. (See **Figure 1.20**.) He was a popular teacher and writer, and was a very successful advocate of behaviorism. Even after being fired from his position at Johns Hopkins and embarking on a highly successful career in advertising, he continued to lecture and write magazine articles about psychology.

According to Watson, psychology was a natural science that studied only observable events: the behavior of organisms. He believed that the elements of consciousness studied by the structuralists were too subjective to lend themselves to scientific investigation. He wanted to restrict psychology to the objective study of stimuli and the behaviors they produced. Even thinking was reduced to a form of behavior—talking to one's self.

FIGURE 1.20   John B. Watson (1878–1958) sought to make psychology a purely objective experimental branch of natural science by restricting it to the study of relations between environmental events (stimuli) and behavior (responses).

Now what can we observe? We can observe *behavior—what the organism does or says*. And let us point out at once: that saying is doing—that is, *behaving*. Speaking overtly or to ourselves (thinking) is just as objective a type of behavior as baseball. (Watson, 1930, p. 6)

Behaviorism is still very much alive today in psychology. Its advocates include B. F. Skinner, whose name is undoubtedly familiar to you. Behaviorism has given birth to the technology of teaching machines (which have since been replaced by computers), the use of behavior modification in instruction of the mentally retarded, and the use of behavior therapy for treatment of mental disorders. Research on the nature of the basic principles that were discovered by Thorndike and Pavlov still continues.

Psychologists, including modern behaviorists, have moved away from the strict behaviorism of Watson; mental processes such as imagery and attention are again considered to be proper subject matter for scientific investigation. But Watson's emphasis on objectivity in psychological research remains in what some call "methodological behaviorism." Even those modern psychologists who most vehemently protest against the perceived narrowness of behaviorism use the same principles of objectivity to guide their research. As research scientists they must uphold the principles of objectivity that evolved from positivism to functionalism to behaviorism. A person who studies private mental events knows that these events can only be studied indirectly, by means of behavior—verbal reports. Psychologists realize that these reports are not pure reflections of these mental events; like other behaviors these responses can be affected by a variety of factors. But as much as possible, they strive to maintain an objective stance to ensure that their research findings will be valid and capable of being verified.

Oh yes, I mentioned that Watson was fired from his professorship at Johns Hopkins. He got in trouble for pursuing a pioneering research project. Long before Masters and Johnson studied the physiology of the human sexual response, Watson measured and recorded various physiological reactions of a man and a woman who were engaged in intercourse. Clearly, it was research done before its time, but the fact that most bothered the university administration was that the subjects in this investigation were Watson and his young research assistant. (They later married.)

Reaction Against Behaviorism: The Cognitive Revolution

◆ The emphasis on behaviorism restricted the subject matter of psychology to observable behaviors. For many years such concepts as consciousness were considered to be outside the domain of psychology. As one psychologist put it: ". . . psychology, having first bargained away its soul and then gone out of its mind, seems now . . . to have lost all consciousness" (Burt, 1962, p. 229). During the past two decades many psychologists have protested against the restrictions of behaviorism and have turned to the study of consciousness, feelings, dreams, and other private events. However, they have not gone back to the introspective methods that were employed by structuralists like Wundt. They still use objective research methods, just as behaviorists do.

Let me give an example of the kinds of private events that have been studied objectively. A number of psychologists have studied *imagery*. If you close your eyes and imagine what the open pages of this book look like, you are producing an image of what you have previously seen. This image exists only within your brain, and it can be experienced by you and no one else. I have no way of knowing whether your images are like mine any more than I know whether the color red looks the same to you as it does to me. The *experience* of imagery cannot be shared.

But behaviors that are based upon images can, indeed, be measured. For example, Kosslyn (1973) asked a group of people to memorize several drawings. Then he asked them to imagine one of them, focusing their attention on a particular feature of the image. Next, he asked them a question about a detail of the image that was either "near" the point they were focusing on, or "far" from it. For example, if they were picturing a boat, he might ask them to imagine that they were looking at its stern (back). Then he might ask them whether the boat had a rudder at the stern, or whether a rope was fastened to its bow. Since the bow is at the

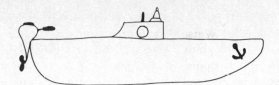

FIGURE 1.21   A drawing used in the imagery study by Kosslyn. (From Kosslyn, S.M. *Perception and Psychophysics*, 1973, *14*, 90–94.)

opposite end of the boat, it should be located at the "opposite end" of the image. (See **Figure 1.21**.)

Kosslyn found that people could very quickly answer a question about features of the boat that were near the place they were focusing on, but they took longer to answer a question about a part that was farther away. It was as if they had to scan their mental images to get from one place to the other.

Because we cannot observe what is happening within a person's head, the concept of imagery remains hypothetical. However, this hypothetical concept very nicely explains and organizes some concrete results—namely, the amount of time that it takes for a subject to give an answer. Although the explanation for the results of this experiment is phrased in terms of private events (images), the behavioral data (how long it takes to answer the questions) are empirical and objective.

Interim summary: We can see that psychology has come a long way in a relatively short time. The first laboratory of experimental psychology was established in 1879, not too much over a century ago. Nineteenth-century philosophers set the stage for psychology through the doctrine of positivism; the biologists provided the means through the establishment of the science of experimental physiology. Wilhelm Wundt established psychology as a discipline that was independent of philosophy. Even though his structuralism did not last, the interest in psychology did not abate. It took on added breadth and scope with the emergence of functionalism, which grew out of Darwin's theory of evolution with its stress on the adaptive value of biological phenomena. Functionalism gave rise to the objectivity of behaviorism which, despite the reaction of many modern psychologists, still dominates the way we do research.

WHO ARE WE?

Psychologists come in many varieties. Some of us are scientists; some of us are clinical practitioners, helping people with mental disorders or problems of adjustment to daily life; some of us work for marketing and advertising firms; some of us design instruments. As I have already told you, this book will emphasize the science of psychology, and will discuss the ways in which we try to discover the causes of human behavior. But first let me describe the variety of problems that we study.

EXPLAINING BEHAVIOR

The goal of research in psychology is to understand human behavior: to explain why people do what they do. Different kinds of psychologists are interested in different kinds of behaviors, and different levels of explanation. Therefore, before I describe the various types of psychologists, I must discuss the meaning of the term "explanation."

How do psychologists "explain" behavior? In general, we discover its causes—those events that are responsible for its occurrence. If we can describe the events that caused the behavior to occur, we have "explained" it. Different psychologists look for different types of *causal events.* Some look inside the organism for physiological causes such as the activity of nerve cells or the secretions of glands. Others "look inside" the organism in a metaphorical sense, explaining behaviors in terms of hypothetical mental states like anger, fear, or a need to achieve. Still others look only for environmental events that cause behaviors to occur.

Research psychologists differ from each other in two principal ways: they study different types of *phenomena* and they look for different *causal events.* That is, they explain different types of behaviors, and they explain them in terms of different causes. Two different kinds of psychologists might both be interested in the same psychological phenomenon (for example, memory) but attempt to explain it in terms of different causal events. These dis-

tinctions will become clear to you as I describe the different types of psychologists.

TYPES OF PSYCHOLOGISTS

Physiological psychologists study almost all behavioral phenomena that can be observed in nonhuman animals. They study such topics as learning, memory, sensory processes, emotional behavior, motivation, sexual behavior, and sleep. They look for causal events in the organism's physiology, especially the nervous system and its interaction with glands that secrete hormones. The reason that almost all physiological psychologists study animals is that physiological experiments cannot ethically be performed with humans.

Psychophysiologists generally study human subjects. They measure people's physiological reactions, such as heart rate, blood pressure, electrical resistance of the skin, muscle tension, and electrical activity of the brain. These measurements provide an indication of a person's degree of arousal or relaxation. Most psychophysiologists investigate phenomena like stress and emotions. A practical application of their techniques is the lie detector test.

Comparative psychologists, like physiological psychologists, mostly study the behavior of animals other than humans. They also study similar behavioral phenomena. However, comparative psychologists explain behavior in terms of adaptation to the environment; thus, they are the direct descendents of the functionalist tradition in psychology. They are more likely than most other psychologists to study inherited behavioral patterns: *species-typical behaviors* such as courting and mating, predation, defensive behaviors, and parental behaviors.

In the past the term *experimental psychologist* described a very large group of scientists in the mainstream of the behavioristic tradition. Today this term is usually applied to those psychologists who are interested in the general principles of learning, perception, motivation, and memory. Some experimental psychologists investigate the behavior of animals, but most of them study human behavior. The causal events that they study are almost exclusively environmental in nature.

Cognitive psychologists almost exclusively study

humans, although investigators have begun to study animal cognition. They study complex processes like perception, memory, attention, and concept formation. To them, causal events are functions of the human brain responding to environmental events, but most of them do not study physiological mechanisms. Their explanations are phrased in terms of the characteristics of inferred processes or structures of the mind, such as imagery, attentional processes, and language mechanisms.

Experimental neuropsychologists are closely allied with both cognitive psychologists and physiological psychologists. They are generally interested in the same phenomena that are studied by cognitive psychologists, but attempt to discover the particular brain mechanisms that are responsible for cognitive processes. One of their principal research techniques is the ablation method, which I described earlier; they study the behavior of people whose brains have been damaged by natural causes.

Developmental psychologists study physical, cognitive, emotional, and social development, especially of children. Some of them study phenomena of adolescence or adulthood, in particular the effects of aging. The causal events they study are as comprehensive as all of psychology: physiological processes, cognitive processes, and social influences.

Social psychologists study the effects of people upon people. The phenomena they study include perception (of one's self as well as others), cause-and-effect relations in human interactions, attitudes and opinions, interpersonal relationships, and emotional behaviors, such as aggression and sexual behavior.

Personality psychologists study individual differences in temperament and patterns of behavior. They look for causal events in a person's past history, both genetic and environmental. Some personality psychologists are closely allied with social psychologists; others work on problems related to adjustment to society, and hence study problems of interest to clinical psychologists.

Psychometricians devise ways to measure human personality and ability. Psychometricians develop psychological tests, some of which you have taken during your academic career. These tests are used by school systems, counselors, clinical psy-

chologists, and employers. In general, most psychometricians are interested in the practical issues of measurement, and most of them do not seek causes in a person's hereditary or environmental history. However, their tests are often used by other psychologists to investigate the causes of behavior.

Most *clinical psychologists* are practitioners who attempt to help people solve their problems, whatever the causes. Others are scientists who do research. They study *psychopathology* (mental disorders) and problems of adjustment. They look for a wide variety of causal events, including genetics, physiology, and environmental phenomena such as parental upbringing, interactions with siblings, and other social stimuli.

Besides clinical psychology, the applied areas of psychology include *counseling, educational psychology, school psychology, industrial and organizational psychology,* and *engineering psychology.* Counselors help people with minor problems of everyday life and assist them with vocational and academic guidance. Educational psychologists often conduct basic research, but most attempt to apply the principles discovered by experimental, cognitive, social, and developmental psychologists to the task of education. School psychologists are counselors within elementary and secondary school systems. Industrial and organizational psychologists are usually employed in industry, where they advise management about the application of psychological principles to running a business. In addition, many industrial and organizational psychologists are scientists who do basic research in academic institutions. Engineering psychologists assist in the design of products so that they can most quickly, accurately, and comfortably be used by humans.

WHERE DO PSYCHOLOGISTS WORK?

◈ Most psychologists who are scientists work in colleges and universities where they teach and conduct research, although some are employed by private or governmental research institutions. Most applied psychologists work in private practices, school systems, industry, or government; some are hired by colleges and universities to teach students who want to become applied psychologists themselves. A survey taken by the American Psychological As-

TABLE 1.1   Employment of academic and applied psychologists

GROUP	EMPLOYMENT (PERCENT OF TOTAL NUMBER[a])		TOTAL NUMBER[b]
	Colleges and universities	Private practice, school systems, government, and industry	
Academic Psychologists			
Cognitive	89.3%	10.6%	216
Comparative	66.4	33.6	77
Developmental	84.8	14.9	854
Educational	78	21.2	1187
Experimental	75	24.6	1490
Personality	81.1	18.9	347
Physiological	75.6	24.2	356
Social	79.6	20	1052
Applied Psychologists			
Clinical	23.3%	75.6%	9757
Counseling	43.5	56	2377
Engineering	4.3	95.1	188
Industrial/organizational	39.3	65	1200
Psychometrics	47.3	52.8	152
School	35.9	63.9	975

[a]Percentages may not total 100% because some respondents did not indicate their place of employment; they may total over 100% because some respondents work for more than one organization.

[b]The total number includes only people employed in psychology-related jobs full time.

Note. From Stapp, J.; Fulcher, R.; Nelson, S.D.; Pallak, M.S.; and Wicherski, M. "The Employment of Recent Doctorate Recipients in Psychology: 1975 through 1978." *American Psychologist,* 1981, *36,* 1211–1254.

sociation in 1978 and published in 1982 will illustrate the places of employment of various types of psychologists (Stapp, Fulcher, Nelson, Pallak, and Wicherski, 1981).

The data are presented in Table 1.1, which contains the numbers of psychologists with doctoral degrees who are hired by various kinds of organizations. The data are only approximate figures for psychologists as a group, since questionnaires were mailed only to members of the American Psychological Association (APA). This group is the largest organization of psychologists in the United States and Canada, but not all psychologists belong to it. For example, approximately 70 percent of the members of my own department at the University

of Massachusetts belong to the APA. Clinical psychologists who engage in private practice are probably the most likely to be members; the APA serves clinical psychologists in a professional capacity similar to that provided for physicians by the American Medical Association. Many research psychologists do not regard membership as important to their careers. Nevertheless, the figures still indicate the general trends. (See **Table 1.1.**)

CONCLUDING REMARKS

Although psychology is a young science, it has a long history, traced back through its roots in philosophy and biology. Today, psychologists are a diverse group, studying the complete range of human behaviors, and looking for a wide variety of causal events. In the next chapter I shall describe the basic research techniques of psychology: the rules we must obey if we are to make conclusions about cause-and-effect relations in human behavior. In succeeding chapters I shall tell you about some of the things that psychologists have discovered through their research.

GUIDE TO TERMS INTRODUCED IN THIS CHAPTER

SUGGESTIONS FOR FURTHER READING

If you are interested in reading more about the history of science in general, you might want to consult *The Origins of Modern Science: 1300–1800* by H. Butterfield (New York: Macmillan, 1959) and *Science and the Modern World,* by A.N. Whitehead (New York: Macmillan, 1925).

There are several books that describe the history of psychology, including its philosophical and biological roots, and you might prefer to read one of them, and expand your reading from there if you want to learn more. An excellent introduction, which includes excerpts from the original writings of several historical figures, is *A History of Modern Psychology* (3rd ed.) by D. Schultz (New York: Academic Press, 1981). The classic text, rather heavygoing for the casual reader, is *A History of Experimental Psychology,* by E.G. Boring (New York: Appleton, 1950). Also recommended is S. Lachman's *History and Methods of Physiological Psychology* (Detroit: Hamilton, 1963). For a biographical approach, see R.I. Watson's *The Great Psychologists: From Aristotle to Freud* (Philadelphia: Lippincott, 1963).

In a more general historical vein we have C.H. Haskin's *Rise of Universities* (Ithaca: Cornell University Press, 1957). This neat little book is a must for those of you wondering how universities were founded. There are separate chapters on the medieval professor and the medieval student. For a look at how some of the great Renaissance artists and thinkers rejected the medieval exploration of the world and returned to the Greek and Roman ideas that placed the human, and not God, in the center of the universe, see *The Humanism of Italy* (New York: Macmillan, 1920) by H.O. Taylor.

THE WAYS AND
MEANS OF
PSYCHOLOGY

LEARNING ◆ OBJECTIVES

PSYCHOLOGISTS ATTEMPT to explain behavior—to understand its causes. As scientists, we believe that behaviors can be studied objectively, like any other natural phenomena. Like other scientists, psychologists must follow the procedures and principles of the scientific method. That is what this chapter is about.

The *scientific method* permits a person to discover the causes of a natural phenomenon, including an organism's behavior. There are other approaches to the understanding of natural phenomena, but the scientific method has become the predominant method of investigation for a very practical reason: *it works better than any other method we have discovered*. The generalizations obtained by following the scientific method are the ones that are most likely to survive the test of time. (See **Figure 2.1.**)

In this chapter you will learn how the scientific method is used in psychology. What you learn will

FIGURE 2.1   René Descartes outlined his principles of scientific inquiry in 1637.

The first . . . never to accept anything as true that I did not know to be evidently so. . . .

The second, to divide each of the difficulties . . . into as many parts as might be possible and necessary in order best to solve it.

The third to conduct my thoughts in an orderly way, beginning with the simplest objects and the easiest to know, in order to climb gradually, as by degrees, as far as the knowledge of the most complex. . . .

And the last, everywhere to make such complete enumerations and such general reviews that I would be sure to have omitted nothing.

(From Descartes, R. *Discourse on Method.* translated by F. E. Sutcliffe. Baltimore: Penguin Books, 1968, 41.)

help you understand the experiments that will be described in the remaining chapters of the book. But understanding the scientific method is even more important than that; what you learn here can be applied to everyday life. Knowing how a psychologist can be fooled by the results of an experiment unless he or she uses the proper procedures can help us all avoid being fooled by more casual observations.

◆ A sound experiment, which follows the necessary procedures, is not necessarily an important one. Not all properly designed experiments are *worthwhile;* some studies are trivial, and some conditions are so contrived as to have no relevance to what goes on in a more natural environment. All that is promised by use of the scientific method is that the particular question being asked of nature will be answered unambiguously. If a scientist asks a trivial question, nature will return a trivial answer.

It is important to note that no area of psychological investigation is inherently more "scientific" than any other. For example, the physiological analysis of hunger is not inherently more scientific than an investigation of the social factors affecting a person's willingness to help someone. A scientist is a person who follows the scientific method while investigating natural phenomena. A scientist does not necessarily need a laboratory, or any special apparatus. Depending on the question being asked, he or she might need no more than a pad of paper and a pencil, and some natural phenomenon (like another person's behavior) to observe.

THE SCIENTIFIC METHOD

What can a scientist hope to accomplish, and what rules must be followed? As we shall see, a scientist attempts to discover *relations* among events, and to phrase these relations in language that is precise enough to be understood by others but general enough to apply to a wide variety of phenomena. As we have already seen in Chapter 1, this language takes the form of "explanations," which are general statements about events that cause phenomena to occur. But what is the nature of the general statement? The answer should become clear as we see how psychologists use the scientific method.

◆ The scientific method consists of four major steps,

listed below. The list is meant as an overview. Some new terms are introduced here without definition, but they will be described in detail later.

1. *Identify the problem and formulate hypothetical cause-and-effect relations among variables.* This step involves classification of variables (behaviors and environmental and physiological events) into the proper categories and description of the relations in general terms. An example might be the following hypothesis: "Humiliation increases a person's susceptibility to propaganda." This statement describes a relation between two events—humiliation, and susceptibility to propaganda—and states that an increase in one causes an increase in the other.

2. *Design and execute the experiment.* This step involves the manipulation of *independent variables* and observation of *dependent variables.* For example, if we wanted to test the hypothesis that I just suggested, we would have to humiliate people and see whether that experience altered their susceptibility to propaganda. But how would we humiliate them, and how would we measure their susceptibility to propaganda? The variables must be *operationally defined,* and the independent variable must be *controlled* so that definitive conclusions may be made.

3. *Determine the truth of the hypothesis by examining the data from the experiment.* Do the results support the hypothesis, or do they suggest that the facts are otherwise? This step often involves special procedures to determine whether an observed relation is *statistically significant.*

4. *Communicate the results.* Once a psychologist has learned something about the causes of behavior from an experiment or observational study, he or she must inform other psychologists (and perhaps others, as well) about the new information. In most cases, this communication will be accomplished by writing an article that includes a description of the procedure and results and a discussion of their significance. The article will be sent to one of the many journals that publish results of psychological experiments. Thus, other psychologists will be able to incorporate these findings into their own thinking and hypothesizing.

Now that I have presented an overview of the scientific method, let me describe its components and the rules that govern it.

HYPOTHESES

◆ A *hypothesis* is the starting point of any experiment. It is an idea, phrased as a general statement, that the scientist wishes to test in an experiment. In the original Greek, *hypothesis* means "suggestion," and the word still conveys the same meaning. When a scientist forms a hypothesis, he or she is simply suggesting that a relation exists among various phenomena (like the one that might exist between humiliation and a person's susceptibility to propaganda). Thus, a hypothesis is a *tentative statement about a relation between two or more events.*

Hypotheses do not spring out of the air; they occur to a scientist as a result of his or her own research or scholarship. Experiments breed experiments. That is, worthwhile research does not merely answer questions; it suggests new questions to be asked—new hypotheses to be tested. Productive and creative scientists formulate new hypotheses by thinking about the implications of experiments that they themselves perform, or those that they learn about.

THEORIES

◆ A *theory* is an elaborate form of hypothesis. In fact, a theory can be seen as a way of organizing a system of related hypotheses to explain some larger aspect of nature. Furthermore, good theories fuel the creation of further hypotheses. (More accurately, a good scientist, contemplating a good theory, thinks of good hypotheses.) For example, Einstein's theory of relativity states that time, matter, and energy are interdependent. Changes in any one can produce changes in the others. The hypotheses that were suggested by this theory revolutionized science; the field of nuclear physics largely rests on experiments that were suggested by Einstein's theory.

Within psychology, the most influential people

FIGURE 2.2   Freud founded the Psychological Wednesday Circle, which eventually became the International Psycho-Analytical Association; the influence of his theory of personality spread throughout the western world. He is shown here as a guest of Clark University in 1908, seated with G.S. Hall and C. Jung to his left, with A.A. Brill, E. Jones, and S. Frenczi standing behind.

have been those who suggested a new way of looking at nature—a way that organized previously unrelated facts and hypotheses into a cohesive theoretical framework. Sigmund Freud's theory of personality certainly changed the way scientists looked at human behavior. It even affected novelists, playwrights, historians, and political scientists. In fact, even though much of Freud's theory has not been scientifically verified, it is so comprehensive, and provides an "explanation" for so much of human behavior, that it continues to exert considerable influence today. (See **Figure 2.2.**)

Much research in psychology is based on frameworks that are larger in scope than hypotheses, but smaller in scope than full-fledged theories. A psychologist might publish an article that seems to pull together the results of many previous experiments on a particular topic. For example, the "frustration-aggression hypothesis," which you will learn about in a later chapter, suggests that organisms have a tendency to become aggressive when they do not achieve a goal that they have become accustomed to achieving in a particular situation. This hypothesis is less comprehensive than Freud's theory of personality, but it makes a prediction that might fit a wide variety of situations. Indeed, many experiments were performed to test this hypothesis under different conditions. While the ideas that most psychologists construct fall short of constituting a theory, they serve a similar function by getting researchers to think about old problems in new ways, and in showing how findings that did not appear to be related to each other can be explained by a single concept. There is even a scientific journal (*Psychological Reviews*) that is devoted to articles that the authors hope will have theoretical significance.

VARIABLES

◆ The hypothesis that I proposed earlier—"Humiliation increases a person's susceptibility to propaganda"—describes a relation between humiliation and susceptibility to propaganda. Scientists refer to these two components as *variables*: things that can vary. Variables are quantities, characteristics, or phenomena that a scientist either measures or *manipulates* when he or she performs an experiment. *Manipulate* literally means "to handle," from

manus, "hand." Psychologists use the word to refer to setting the value of a variable for experimental purposes. The results of this manipulation determine whether the hypothesis is true or false.

To test the "humiliation" hypothesis in an experiment, we would set the value of people's humiliation at a high level and then measure their susceptibility to propaganda. The first variable—the one that the experimenter manipulates—is called the ***independent variable.*** The second one, which the experimenter measures, is the ***dependent variable.*** An easy way to keep them straight is to remember this: a hypothesis always describes how a dependent variable *depends* on the value of an independent variable. For example, susceptibility to propaganda (dependent variable) depends upon the level of a person's humiliation (independent variable). (See **Figure 2.3.**)

As we saw, hypotheses are expressed in general terms. This means that the variables that hypotheses deal with are also general rather than specific. That is, we want to understand the behavior of people in general, not just one particular person in one particular situation. Thus, variables are *categories* into which various behaviors are classified. For example, if one person hits, kicks, or throws something at someone else, we could label all of these behaviors as "interpersonal aggression." Presumably, they might have very similar causes. Therefore, a psychologist must know enough about a particular type of behavior to be able to classify it correctly.

◆ Although one of the first steps in psychological investigation involves naming and classifying behaviors, we must be careful to avoid committing the ***nominal fallacy.*** The nominal fallacy refers to the erroneous belief that one has explained an event simply by naming it. (*Nomen* means "name.") Clas-

FIGURE 2.3 Independent and dependent variables.

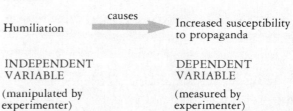

Humiliation	causes →	Increased susceptibility to propaganda
INDEPENDENT VARIABLE		DEPENDENT VARIABLE
(manipulated by experimenter)		(measured by experimenter)

sifying a behavior does not explain it; it only prepares the way toward discovering events that cause
it. For example, suppose that we see someone frown
and shout at other people without provocation,
criticize their work when it is really acceptable,
and generally act unpleasantly toward everyone
around him. Someone says, "Boy, he's really angry
today!" Does this statement "explain" his behavior?

It does not; it only *describes* it. Instead of saying
he is angry, it might be better to say he is *engaging
in angry or hostile behaviors*. That statement does not
pretend to explain why he is acting the way he is.
To say "he is angry" suggests the presence of an
internal state that is responsible for producing his
behavior; that is, his anger causes his behavior. But
all that we have observed is his behavior, not his
internal state. Even if he is experiencing feelings
of anger, these feelings still do not explain his
behavior. What we really need to know is what
events made him act the way he did. Perhaps he
has a painful toothache. Perhaps he just learned
that he missed out on an important promotion that
he expected to earn. Perhaps he had a terrible fight
with his wife. Perhaps he just read a book that
advised him to be more assertive. Events like these
are causes of both the behavior and the feelings,
and unless these are discovered we cannot say that
we have "explained" his behavior.

Of course, a large number of events precede any
behavior. Many of these events are completely unrelated to the observed behavior. When I get off
the train it is because the conductor announces my
stop, and not because one person coughs, another
turns the pages of her newspaper, another crosses
his legs, another looks at her watch, and so on.
The task of a psychologist is to determine which
of the many events that occur before a particular
behavior caused that behavior to happen.

OPERATIONAL DEFINITION

Hypotheses are phrased in general terms, but experiments (step 2 of the scientific method) require
that something *particular* be done. In our "humiliation" experiment, an experimenter does not simply
"humiliate" the subjects; he or she must arrange a
particular situation that is expected to cause hu-

miliation. Similarly, the experimenter does not
simply "measure susceptibility to propaganda"; he
or she tests the subjects' opinion on a particular
topic, has them watch a film that promotes a point
of view on the topic, and then tests their opinion
again. Generalities must be translated into specific
operations.

This translation of generalities into specific
operations is called an *operational definition*. For
the purposes of the experiment, general terms are
defined as a set of particular operations that are
performed to assign their value (independent variable) or to measure them (dependent variable).
This task can be one of the stickiest ones a psychologist encounters. Although we do our thinking and general hypothesizing in general terms like
"humiliation" or "susceptibility to propaganda,"
we must translate these concepts into specific operations when we perform an experiment.

Here is an example of an operational definition:

"Humiliation" is the state that occurs when a person
spends fifteen minutes working on an insoluble task
and is subsequently informed by the experimenter—
in a contemptuous manner—that his or her performance is so poor that he or she (a student) should
probably consider quitting school, since even most
below-average students can do much better.

The operational definition of "susceptibility to
propaganda" would include a description of the
opinion test that was used and the propaganda film
that was shown to the subjects.

The importance of providing an operational
definition of experimental variables should be obvious. If an experiment is to be understood and
evaluated by other people (step 4 of the scientific
method), the investigator must provide others with
an adequate description of the procedures that he
or she used. Communicating the results is as important a part of the scientific method as obtaining
them.

There are a variety of ways to translate a general
concept into a set of operations. The experimenter
may or may not succeed in manipulating the desired independent variable, or in measuring the
desired dependent variable. For example, another
investigator might use a different set of operations
to produce humiliation. Suppose that the results
of his or her experiment were different from ours?

Which set of results should people accept? Which operational definition of humiliation is correct?

Validity of an Operational Definition

The question of the "correctness" of an operational definition of a variable brings us to the issue of *validity*. Everyone knows the meaning of the word *valid:* well-grounded, fit, appropriate. Thus, the validity of an operational definition refers to how appropriate it is—how accurately it represents the variable whose value it sets or measures. Obviously, validity is very important; if an operational definition is not valid, an experiment that uses it cannot provide meaningful results.

How can the validity of an operational definition be determined? Unfortunately, there is no simple answer to this question. Various techniques have been used but none of them is foolproof. To begin with, an investigator will examine the *face validity* of the operations. This is just a fancy way of saying that he or she will think about them and decide whether they make sense: on the *face* of it, do the operations appear to manipulate or measure the variable in question? My earlier definition of humiliation—having someone fail at a task that the experimenter says is a simple one—makes sense (at least to me), so it has some face validity. When a psychologist tries to decide how to test a particular hypothesis, he or she uses common sense to arrive at operations that have face validity.

Given enough time, the validity of an operational definition will emerge (or so we hope). Investigators will compare the results of their experiments with those of others, and see whether they are compatible. If a new set of operations produces results that are very different from previous ones, then at first we may question the validity of the new approach. However, the new and different results sometimes point out the inadequacy of the operations that *everyone else* has been using. It sometimes happens that a psychologist will devise a procedure for producing or measuring a state that is so clever, and so simple to do, that it will be adopted by everyone who is studying the issue. If the procedure is not valid, then neither are the results that were obtained by all those who have used it. If someone devises a new *and valid* set of operations, his or her results will differ from

the rest, and the general tendency will be for others to reject the new approach, and stick with the familiar one.

Fortunately, truth eventually seems to win out. Most scientists who are clever enough to devise a better operational definition are also usually stubborn enough to persist until they have convinced others to question the validity of the old procedures. To do this they will perform a set of experiments that demonstrate how well their procedure works, and try to show that it reconciles results that previously appeared to be contradictory. They will be demonstrating that their method of defining the term has greater *construct validity* than the old method.

I have just defined *construct validity* by means of an example, and I am sure that now you would like a more concise definition. Unfortunately, this is not easy to do. *Construct,* as a noun (pronounced *CON strukt*), is defined as "something assembled from simple elements, especially a concept." The elements, in the case of construct validity, are the pieces of evidence, obtained from a number of studies, that show that the operational definition works—that the results of experiments that use it make sense. Validity is *constructed,* piece by piece.

Reliability of an Operational Definition

Having carefully designed an experiment, the psychologist must then decide how best to conduct it. This brings us to the second part of step 2 of the scientific method. The psychologist must decide what subjects will be used, what instructions will be given, and what equipment and material will be used. He or she must ensure that the data that are collected will be accurate; otherwise, all effort will be in vain.

If the procedure that is described by an operational definition gives consistent results under consistent conditions, the procedure is said to be *reliable.* Note, however, that it may or may not be *valid.* For example, suppose that I operationally define susceptibility to propaganda as the length of a person's thumb; the longer the person's thumb, the more susceptible he or she is to propaganda. Even though this measurement can be made accurately and reliably, it is still nonsensical, having nothing to do with susceptibility to propaganda.

(Of course, most examples of reliable but invalid operational definitions are much more subtle than this.) It is usually much easier to achieve reliability than validity; reliability is mostly a result of care and diligence on the part of the experimenter.

Let us look at an example. Suppose that you want to measure people's reading speed. You select a passage of prose and see how much of it each person can read in five minutes. This operational definition of reading speed certainly has face validity, so long as you choose a passage that is reasonably easy for a normal adult to understand. But suppose that you test people in a building that is located under the flight path of an airport. At times, the noise of planes flying overhead creates a terrible din. At other times, all is quiet. If a person is tested when planes are roaring overhead, the distracting noise might very well disrupt his or her reading, and produce a low score. The on-again,

off-again noise would affect the accuracy of the measurement. It would lower its reliability.

An alert, careful experimenter can control most of the extraneous factors that could affect the reliability of his or her measurements. Conditions throughout the experiment should always be as consistent as possible. For example, the same instructions should be given to each person who participates in the experiment, all mechanical devices should be in good repair, and all assistants hired by the experimenter should be well trained in performing their tasks. Noise and other sources of distraction should be kept to a minimum. (See **Figure 2.4.**)

Often experimenters attempt to measure variables that cannot be specified as precisely as reading speed. For example, suppose that a psychologist wants to count the number of friendly interactions that a child makes with other children in a group.

FIGURE 2.4   The apparatus in a well-equipped sleep laboratory is elaborate, but research there is not necessarily more "scientific" than research that uses nothing more complicated than a paper and pencil. The methods, not the equipment, define the scientific nature of research.

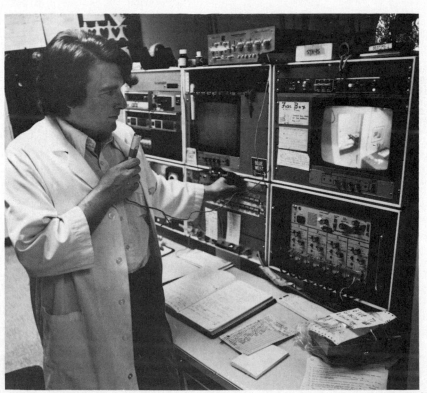

This measurement would require someone to watch that child and count the number of times a friendly interaction occurs. But it is difficult to be absolutely specific about what constitutes a "friendly interaction" and what does not. What if the child looks at another child and they appear to exchange a look? One person might say that the look conveyed interest in what the other child was doing, so it should be scored as a friendly interaction. Another person denies that anything passed between them, and says that a friendly interaction should not be scored.

The solution in this case is, first of all, to try to specify as precisely as possible the criteria for scoring a friendly interaction. Then two or more people should watch the child's behavior and score it independently. That is, they should not be aware of the other person's ratings. If their ratings agree, we can say that the scoring system has high *interrater reliability.* If they disagree, interrater reliability is low, and there is no point in continuing the experiment. Instead, the rating system should be refined and the raters should be trained to apply it consistently. Any investigator who performs an experiment that requires some degree of subjective judgment in the measurement of dependent variables must be sure that interrater reliability is sufficiently high. (See **Figure 2.5.**)

RELATIONS AMONG VARIABLES

A hypothesis, you will recall, makes a tentative statement about the existence of a relation among two or more variables. An experiment is the procedure for testing the hypothesis to determine whether these variables *are* related. A scientist performs an experiment by altering the value of the independent variable (such as degree of humiliation), and then observing whether this change affects the dependent variable (in this case, susceptibility to propaganda). If an effect is seen, we can con-

FIGURE 2.5   To be sure that observations of behavior are reliable, two or more observers independently rate the behavior. If their ratings agree, the measurement is said to have high interrater reliability.

clude that there is a cause-and-effect relation between the variables.

Causal Relations

◆ The goal of scientific investigation is to discover the events that cause other events to occur. When the value of an independent variable is manipulated and corresponding changes are observed in the value of the dependent variable, we conclude that the variables are **causally related.** That is, changes in X *cause* changes in Y. (Be careful to read *cau sal,* not *cas u al;* the two words have very different meanings.) Causation is probably one of the earliest concepts that a human learns. A baby discovers that some of its actions have reliable consequences. For example, thrashing around in the crib results in jiggling a mobile overhead, and crying (usually) results in parental attention.

Noncausal Relations

Noncausal relations are much more difficult to describe, probably because we have so little practice in distinguishing them from causal ones. I am sure that you could think of many causal relations; for example, the speed of a car is related to the position of the accelerator pedal, and the rate at which an ice cube melts is related to the room temperature. However, it takes some practice to think of examples of noncausal relations.

Here is a hypothetical example of noncausal relation. The number of tractors sold in a particular town is likely to be related to (but not caused by) the number of bottles of French wine that are sold there per capita. The relation is probably inverse; that is, high values of one variable are associated with low values of the other. Towns that sell many tractors probably sell relatively few bottles of French wine and vice versa. The values of both variables probably depend upon the amount of urbanization in a given location: large industrialized cities will sell more French wine and fewer tractors per capita, whereas towns in agricultural regions will sell more tractors and less French wine. Farmers, not city-dwellers, buy tractors, and city people tend to drink more French wine.

However, to determine for certain whether the relation is causal or noncausal, we would have to do an experiment; we would have to manipulate one of the variables and look for changes in the

other. I rather doubt that anyone would bother to sell French wine at bargain prices in agricultural areas to see whether increased wine sales would affect sales of tractors.

Why should we be concerned with the distinction between causal and noncausal relations? After all, a psychologist would appear to have no reason to be interested in noncausal relations. Psychologists, like other scientists, should be concerned with cause and effect. However, there are two reasons why noncausal relations are important to psychologists: (1) They can be something to guard against; a psychologist must be sure he or she has not mistaken a noncausal relation for a causal one. (2) They can be used for practical purposes—for making predictions. I will describe the problems first, and then, in a later section on psychological testing, I will discuss the potential usefulness of noncausal relations.

Interim summary: The scientific method is a method of inquiry that allows us to determine the causes of natural phenomena. Experiments test the truth of a hypothesis, which is a tentative statement about a causal relation between an independent variable and a dependent variable. To perform an experiment, a scientist alters the value of the independent variable and looks for changes in the dependent variable. Because a hypothesis is stated in general terms, the scientist must specify the particular operations that he or she will perform to manipulate the independent variable and measure the dependent variable. That is, an operational definition must be provided.

As we saw, it often takes some ingenuity to devise a valid operational definition for a variable. But this definition is of the utmost importance. A good operational definition is not only a necessary part of the procedure by which a hypothesis is tested, it can also eliminate confusion by giving concrete form to the hypothesis, making its meaning absolutely clear to other psychologists.

CONTROL OF INDEPENDENT VARIABLES

There is yet another problem that must be solved in designing an experiment: making sure that the procedure alters the independent variable, and *only* the independent variable. In most experiments we are interested in the effects of a small number of independent variables (usually, just one) on a dependent variable. For example, if we want to determine whether noise has an effect on people's reading speed, we must choose our source of noise carefully. If we use the sound from a television set to supply the noise and find that it slows people's reading speed, we cannot conclude that the effect was caused purely by "noise." We might have selected a very interesting program (as unlikely as that may seem), thus distracting the subjects' attention from the material that they were reading. If we want to do this experiment properly, we should use noise that is neutral, and not a source of interest by itself: noise like the *sssh* sound that

is heard when an FM radio is tuned between stations.

In the example I just described, the experimenter intended to test the effects of an independent variable (noise) on a dependent variable (reading speed). By using a television to provide the noise, the experimenter was inadvertently testing the effect of other variables besides noise on reading speed. The experimenter had introduced extra, unwanted independent variables.

Confounding of Variables

◆ One of the meanings of the word *confound* is "to fail to distinguish." This is precisely the meaning that applies here. If an experimenter accidentally manipulates more than one independent variable,

FIGURE 2.6   A schematic representation of the flawed "predator" experiment, page 40.

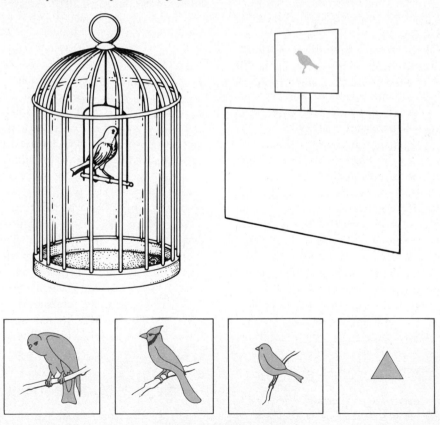

Stimuli arranged in order
of similarity to predator

it is impossible to distinguish the effects of any one of them on the dependent variable. There are many ways in which *confounding of variables* can occur. The best way to understand the problems that can arise is to examine some of the mistakes that an experimenter can make.

When I was a graduate student, I accompanied several fellow students to hear a talk that was presented by a visitor to the Zoology Department. He described research he had conducted in a remote area of South America. He was interested in determining whether a particular species of bird could recognize a large bird that normally preys upon it. He had constructed a set of cardboard models that bore varying degrees of resemblance to the predator: from a perfect representation to two models of a noncarnivorous bird to a neutral stimulus (a triangle, I think). The experimenter somehow restrained each of the birds that were being tested and suddenly presented the bird with each of the test stimuli, in decreasing order of similarity to the predator—that is, from predator to harmless birds to triangle. He observed a relation between the amount of alarm that the birds showed and the similarity that the model bore to the predator. The most predator-like model produced the greatest response. (See **Figure 2.6** on page 39.)

As one of us pointed out—to the embarrassment of the speaker and his hosts—the study contained a fatal flaw that made it impossible to conclude whether a relation existed between the independent variable (similarity of the model to the predator) and the dependent variable (amount of alarm). Can you figure it out? Read the previous paragraph, consult Figure 2.6, and think about the problem for a while before you read on.

* * *

Here is the answer. To test the birds' responses to the models, the investigator had to present them at different times. Is it reasonable to suppose that the presentation of one stimulus has an effect on the response produced by the next stimulus? Of course it is. It is very likely that even if the birds were shown the *same* model again and again, they would exhibit less and less of a response. We very commonly observe a phenomenon called *habituation* when a stimulus is presented repeatedly. The last presentation produces a much smaller response than the first. Consequently, we do not know whether the decreases in signs of alarm were caused by stimuli that looked less and less like the predator or whether the decreases were simply due to habituation. The investigator's trip to South America was a waste of time, at least insofar as this experiment was concerned. (See **Figure 2.7**.)

Could the zoologist have carried out his experiment in a way that would have permitted a relation to be inferred? Yes, he could have; perhaps the solution has occurred to you already. (If it has not, think about it for a while.) The experimenter should have presented the stimuli in different orders to different birds. Some birds would see the predator first, others would see the triangle first, and so on. Then he could have calculated the average amount of alarm that the birds showed to each of the stimuli with the assurance that the results would not be contaminated by habituation. This procedure is called *counterbalancing*. To

FIGURE 2.7   Habituation may have taken place in the "predator" experiment.

counterbalance means to "weigh evenly," and this would have been accomplished by making sure that each of the models was presented equally often (to different birds, of course) as the first, second, third, or fourth stimulus. Now, the effects of habituation are spread equally among all the stimuli. (See **Figure 2.8.**)

Let us look at another example of an extra, unwanted independent variable intruding into an experiment. Suppose that we want to determine whether the viewing of violence on television might increase a child's level of aggression. We would select two television shows, one violent and the other nonviolent. We would show the violent program to one group of children, and the nonviolent one to another group, and then observe the behavior of both groups. We might place the children in a room full of toys and count the number of destructive acts they commit (such as knocking down towers of blocks, banging toy trucks into the

furniture and walls, or fighting with other children). We would train our observers well and make sure that the interrater reliability of the measurement was high.

The design of this experiment is simple and straightforward, but to be able to infer a causal relation between violence in the program and the children's subsequent behavior we must be sure that the treatment of both groups is identical in every way except for the amount of violence they see. But how can we select, from the programs available on television, two that are identical except for the amount of violence they contain? Obviously we cannot. And the differences could be very important. Suppose that the children who watched the violent program found it to be very interesting but the children who watched the nonviolent one found it to be extremely dull and boring. We might expect a group of angry and hostile children to emerge from watching the nonviolent

FIGURE 2.8   The order of presentation of the models in the "predator" experiment should have been counterbalanced.

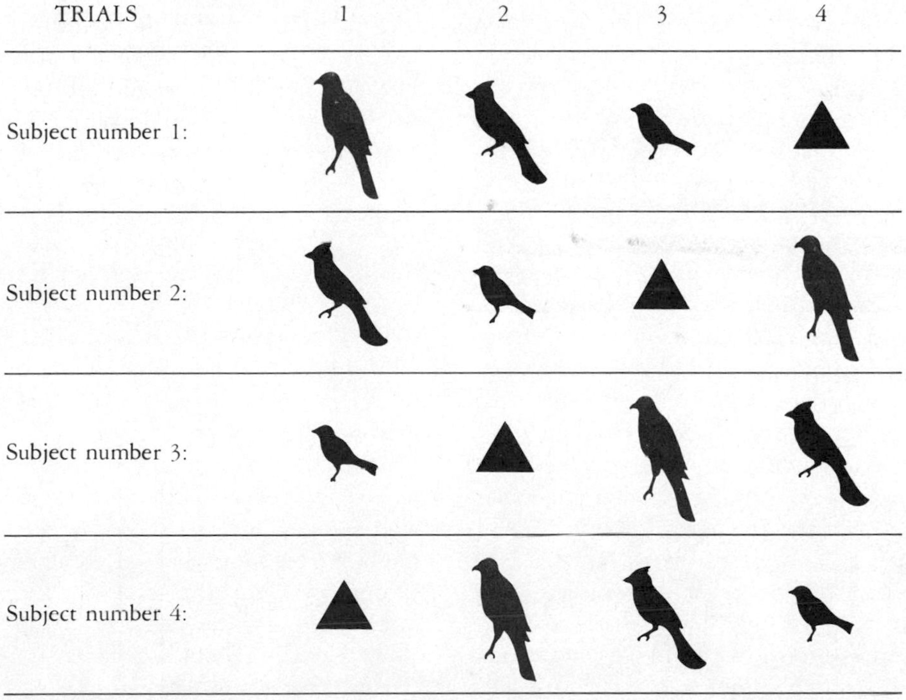

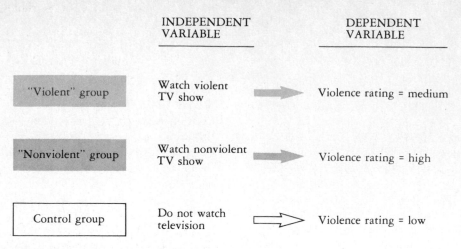

FIGURE 2.9   Possible outcomes of an experiment testing the effects of watching a violent television program. This design includes a control group.

program, having been forced to undergo such a tedious experience.

Our study might then indicate that violent television programs *reduced* the frequency of violent play in children, and we might therefore favor the hypothesis that viewing a violent program serves as a *cathartic* experience—one that purges a child's pent-up hostilities. Of course, we would have really proved nothing of the kind. The higher level of violence in the group of children who watched the nonviolent program was caused by their having been forced to watch a program that bored them.

What solutions are there to this problem? First, it would be worthwhile to add another group of children, who would not watch a television program. This group is called a **control group**. A control group is a "no treatment" group; it is used to contrast the effects of manipulating an independent variable with no treatment at all. If we had used such a group, perhaps we would have seen that the children who watched the nonviolent program were more violent and aggressive than the children who did not watch television at all, and we would realize that something was wrong. Watching a nonviolent program was not the neutral experience we had thought it would be. (See **Figure 2.9**.)

Ideally, we would also want to consider producing our own television shows. That way, we could keep them as similar as possible, having them differ principally in the amount of violence they portrayed. This task would obviously be a chal-

lenge; the programs would have to be equally lively, interesting, and plausible, but only one would contain violence.

Confounding of Subject Variables

My examples so far have dealt with the confounding of independent variables, which are manipulated by the experimenter. But there is another source of confounding: variables that are inherent in the subjects whose behavior is being observed. Here is an example of a study with confounded subject variables. Suppose that a professor wanted to determine which of two teaching methods worked better. She taught two courses in introductory psychology, one that met at 8 A.M. and another that met at 4 P.M. She used one teaching method for the morning class and another for the afternoon class. At the end of the semester she found that the final-examination scores were higher for her morning class. Therefore, she concluded that she would henceforth use that particular teaching method for all of her classes.

What is the problem? The two groups of subjects for the experiment are not equivalent. People who sign up for a class that meets at 8 A.M. are likely to be somewhat different from those who sign up for a 4 P.M. class. Also, learning efficiency might vary at different times of the day. It is possible that the school schedules some kinds of activities (like long laboratory courses or athletic practice) late in the afternoon, which means that

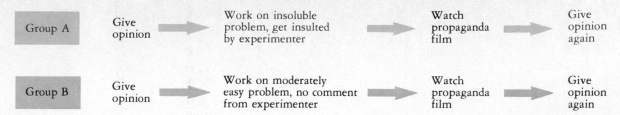

FIGURE 2.10   Design of the "humiliation" experiment with an operational definition of the independent variable, humiliation.

some students will not be able to enroll in the 4 P.M. class. For a variety of reasons, the students in the two classes would probably not be equivalent. Therefore, we could not conclude that differences in their final-exam scores were solely a result of the different teaching methods.

Subjects must be carefully assigned to the various groups that participate in an experiment. The usual way to assign them is by *random selection.* One way to accomplish this would be to assemble the names of the available subjects and then toss a coin for each one to determine their assignment to one of the two groups. (More typically, the assignment is made by computer, or by consulting a list of random numbers.) We can expect people to have different abilities, personality traits, and other characteristics that might affect the outcome of the experiment. But if they are randomly assigned to the experimental conditions, we can expect that the composition of the groups will be approximately the same.

A second way to assign subjects to groups is *matching.* Equivalent groups of subjects are assembled by measuring various subject variables, such as age, socioeconomic status, and intelligence. Subjects are then assigned to groups so that the average age, socioeconomic status, and intelligence of the groups are equal. This method is used much less often than random selection in assembling groups of people for experiments. However, it is an absolute necessity for observational studies, which will be discussed later.

A psychologist must remain alert to the problem of confounded subject variables after he or she has designed the experiment and randomly assigned subjects to the various groups. Some problems will not emerge until the investigation is actually performed. Let us go back to an earlier question: Does humiliation increase a person's susceptibility to propaganda?

As you will recall, for this experiment we would ask people's opinions about a particular issue. Then we would give one group of them an impossible task, and subject them to scorn and ridicule for performing so poorly. Another group would be given an easier task, and their performance would not be commented upon. Next, all of the subjects would be shown a propaganda film designed to change their opinion, and then their opinion would be tested again. Susceptibility to propaganda, the independent variable, would be indicated by the degree to which their opinions changed. (See **Figure 2.10**.)

The design of this experiment is sound. Assuming that the subjects were really humiliated, that our test is a valid measure of opinions on an issue, and that the propaganda film is related to that issue, we should be able to make conclusions about the effects of humiliation on susceptibility to this type of propaganda. However, the experiment, as performed under real conditions, might not work out the way we want it to. Suppose that some of our humiliated subjects become disgusted and walk away. If this happens, we will now be comparing the behavior of two groups of subjects of somewhat different character—a group of people who are willing to submit to ridicule and a group of randomly selected people, some of whom *would have* left, had they been subjected to the humiliating treatment. We would have inadvertently added another variable to our original hypothesis: people who will tolerate a degrading experience might be more susceptible to propaganda, compared with most other people. (See **Figure 2.11**.)

The moral of this example? An experimenter must continue to attend to the possibility of con-

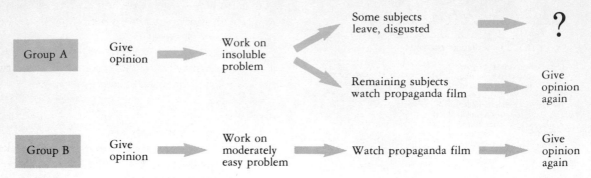

CONFOUNDED VARIABLES

FIGURE 2.11   A possible problem with the "humiliation" experiment: loss of subjects from the "humiliated" group.

founded variables even after the experiment has been designed. The solution in this case? There probably is none. Because we cannot force subjects to continue to participate, there is a strong possibility that some subjects will leave. Any experimenter who presents subjects with an unpleasant experience confronts this danger. Some psychological variables are, by their very nature, difficult to investigate.

The Problem of Subjects' Expectancies

◆ When subjects take part in an experiment, they are not simply passive participants whose behavior is controlled solely by the independent variables selected by the experimenter. The subjects know they are being observed by a psychologist, and this knowledge is certain to affect their behavior in some way. In fact, some subjects may try to outwit the psychologist by acting in a way opposite to that which they think is expected. However, most subjects will try to cooperate because they do not want to ruin the experiment for the investigator. In fact, they may even try to figure out what question is being asked so that they can act accordingly. Because the study is being run by a psychologist, some subjects are unlikely to take what he or she says at face value and will look for devious motives behind an apparently simple task. Actually, most experiments are not devious at all; they are what they appear to be.

"Devious" studies do not always succeed in fooling the subjects. For example, suppose that you were a participant in an experiment that was represented to be a learning study. On the table in front of you is an assortment of knives and pistols. The experimenter says, "Oh, ignore them. Someone else left them here. They have nothing to do with this study." Would you believe him? Probably not, and you would undoubtedly try to figure out what the presence of these weapons is supposed to do to your behavior. You might suspect (in this case correctly) that the psychologist is trying to determine whether the presence of weapons will increase your hostility. Having decided this, you might (a) try to act naturally, so you will not hurt the experiment, (b) act aggressively, to help the experimenter get the results he wants, or (c) act nonaggressively, to prove that you are immune to the effects of objects that are associated with violence. The results of this study might not show the effects of the presence of weapons on aggression, but rather on the numbers of people who select strategies (a), (b), or (c).

An experimenter must always remember that his or her subjects do not merely react to the independent variable in a simple-minded way. If a psychologist wants to assess the effects of weapons on aggression, he or she had better have a plausible reason for their presence.

SINGLE-BLIND STUDIES   Suppose that we want to study the effects of a stimulant drug, such as am-

F.T.C. Disputes Validity Of Research on Listerine

By BOYCE RENSBERGER

"Tests made over a 12-year period proved that people who gargled with Listerine full strength twice a day, every day, had fewer colds and milder colds than those who did not."

That statement and others like it have been used for years by the makers of nonprescription drugs in an attempt to persuade consumers that scientific evidence supports their advertising claims. Rarely, however, are the details of the cited research ever made public, even through scientific journals, so that the adequacy of the research methods can be evaluated.

Now, however, with the recent ruling by the Federal Trade Commission that Listerine's future advertising must deny past claims that it can prevent and cure the common cold, the F.T.C. has released documents describing the research in detail.

After asking a number of eminent scientists to evaluate the research, the commission decided that the experiments were designed in such a way that they permitted biased results in favor of Listerine.

• • •

According to the F.T.C.'s documents, the 12-year tests that Warner-Lambert relied on were conducted during the winters of 1930 to 1942 on two groups of people—those who gargled with Listerine and those who did not.

Normally, drug testing observes standard rules intended to reduce any chance of subtle bias, such as selecting experimental and control groups to be evenly matched and keeping the subjects ignorant of what results are hoped for.

Instead of an independent scientist and a disinterested experimental group, Warner-Lambert conducted the Listerine research on its own employees in the factory. Employees were allowed to choose which group they would be in. Naturally, the F.T.C.'s experts said, those who believed in gargling joined that group, while those who did not remained nongarglers.

• • •

The garglers in the 12-year test, already believing in the usefulness of gargling, undoubtedly reported fewer cold symptoms than those who did not gargle.

Experts who testified at the F.T.C. hearings said that a properly designed study would have assigned people to the two groups randomly and given the control group a placebo, or similar-appearing dummy medication so that neither group would know which was getting the real thing. The placebo effect would thus be the same for both groups.

Article to be continued in Figure 2.13.

FIGURE 2.12   The company that markets Listerine, a mouthwash, formerly claimed that daily use of their product warded off colds, but the research on which this claim was based was flawed. A single-blind procedure was not used; selection of the subjects for the experimental and control groups was not random.

phetamine, on a person's ability to perform a task that requires fine manual dexterity. We would administer the drug to one group of subjects and leave another group untreated. (Of course, the experiment would have to be supervised by a physician, who would prescribe the drug.) We would determine how many times the subjects in each group could thread a needle in a ten-minute period (our operational definition of manual dexterity). We would then see whether differences in the number of needle-threadings were causally related to the effects of the drug.

But there is a problem. For us to conclude that a causal relation exists, the treatment of the two groups must be identical except for the single variable that is being manipulated. In this case, the *mere administration* of a drug might have effects on behavior, independent of any pharmacological effects. If subjects know that they have just taken an amphetamine pill, their behavior is very likely to be affected by this knowledge, as well as by the drug circulating in their bloodstream.

The answer, of course, is to give pills to members of both groups. One group would receive amphetamines, the other would receive an inert pill— a *placebo.* (The word comes from the Latin *placere,* "to please." A physician sometimes gives a placebo to hypochondriacal patients, to placate them.) Subjects would not be told which pill they received. With this improved experimental procedure, if we observe differences in the needle-threading ability of the two groups, we can infer that they were produced by the pharmacological effects of amphetamine. The procedure is called a ***single-blind*** study; the subjects do not know what kind of pill they are taking. (See **Figure 2.12**.

DOUBLE-BLIND STUDIES   Let us look at another example, in which it is important to keep the experimenter, as well as the subjects, in the dark. Suppose that we believe that if patients with mental disorders take a particular drug, they will be easier to talk with. We give the drug to some patients, and administer a placebo to others. We talk with all patients afterward, and rate the quality of the conversation. But "quality of conversation" is a difficult dependent variable to measure, and the rating is therefore likely to be affected by ***subjective*** factors; that is, factors that are a matter of personal judgment. The fact that we know which patients received the drug means that we will very likely rate more highly the quality of conversation with the drugged patients. I am not saying that we would intentionally cheat, but even honest people tend to perceive results in a way that favors their own preconceptions.

What do we do about such a problem? In this case the answer is simple. Just as the patients should not know whether they are receiving a drug or a placebo, neither should the experimenter. Someone *else* should administer the pill, or give the experimenter a set of identical-looking pills in a set of coded containers, so that both experimenter and patient would be unaware of the nature of the contents. Now the ratings cannot be affected by experimenter bias. We call this method the *double-blind* procedure.

The double-blind procedure does not apply only to experiments that use drugs as the independent variable. Suppose that the last experiment I described attempted to evaluate the effects of a particular kind of psychotherapy on the ability of a therapist to communicate with a patient. If the same person did both the psychotherapy and the rating, that person might tend to see the results in a light that was most favorable to his or her own expectations. In this case, it would be best to have one person perform the psychotherapy and another person evaluate the quality of conversation with the patients. The evaluator would not know whether a particular patient had just received psychotherapy or was a member of the control group, which remained untreated. (See **Figure 2.13**.)

FIGURE 2.13   The Listerine saga continues. A second experiment was conducted, ostensibly using the double-blind procedure, but the design was flawed. Among other things, the physician who rated the boys' health could smell the mouthwash on their breath. Even if the results had been favorable to the company, they would not have been justified in using them to support their claims.

Research on Listerine

By BOYCE RENSBERGER

Continued from Figure 2.12.

For 25 years, Warner-Lambert accepted the 12-year test as a truly scientific experiment documenting the cold-fighting properties of Listerine. But, as the company's officials testified, doubts did creep up and it was decided to make a new test in 1967.

The company hired a pediatrician and sent him to St. Barnabas Catholic School in the Bronx. About 1,500 students were divided, this time randomly, into garglers and nongarglers and instructed to report to the pediatrician any morning they thought they had a cold.

Gargled in School

The doctor, Benjamin W. Nitzberg, went to the school at 10 A.M. every day during the November-to-April test periods. To insure that the garglers participated in the test, they were made to gargle in school at 9 o'clock every morning, using bottles labeled "Warner-Lambert Research Institute."

A proper experimental design, experts told the F.T.C., would keep the examining physician ignorant of which group any person belongs to. If the doctor knows which group a person is in and believes the drug to be effective and is in the pay of a manufacturer who would like favorable results, there is a good chance that at least borderline situations would be called in favor of the biases.

Students who wished to report to Dr. Nitzberg had to do so within an hour or so of gargling with Listerine. Thus, Dr. Nitzberg could hardly avoid smelling Listerine on the breath of those who gargled.

The F.T.C. also found that students were not kept ignorant of the expected outcome of the tests. In fact, the purpose of the experiment was so well known that parents of nongarglers complained to school officials because they thought their children were being denied protection against colds.

Colored Water Used

Near the end of the four-year study, the Warner-Lambert researchers did recognize the lack of a placebo and thereafter had former nongarglers gargle with water colored to resemble Listerine.

However, F.T.C. investigators found that, since the placebo lacked Listerine's strong flavor and odor, by now well known to the entire school (which Dr. Nitzberg said smelled like a Listerine factory during the tests), few students were in doubt as to what they were gargling with.

Investigators and medical experts also found fault with the conditions under which Dr. Nitzberg examined the children. During much of the study, he had to look for 14 symptoms and rate the severity of each on a six-point scale. The average time Dr. Nitzberg allotted to this for each child was between one and a half and two minutes.

The results of the study showed that Listerine users had slightly more colds than those who did not use it, and their colds lasted slightly longer on the average.

When those results became evident, Warner-Lambert dropped references to the 12-year test in its advertising and ended the St. Barnabas tests.

OBSERVATIONAL STUDIES

There are some variables, especially subject variables, that a psychologist cannot manipulate. For example, a person's sex, income, social class, and personality are determined by factors not under the psychologist's control. Nevertheless, these variables are often of interest. Because they cannot be altered by the psychologist, they cannot be investigated in an experiment—the only means by which a causal relation can be proved. A different approach is used; an *observational study* is performed.

The basic principle of an observational study is very simple—measure two variables, as they are found to exist, in each member of a group of people, and determine whether the variables are related. Studies like this are often encountered in investigations of the effects of personality variables. For example, we might ask whether shyness (a personality variable) is related to daydreaming. We would decide how to assess a person's shyness and the amount of daydreaming that he or she engages in each day, and then take the measure of these two variables for a group of people. If shy people tended to daydream more (or less) than people who were not shy, we would conclude that the variables were related.

Of course, we could not conclude that the variables were *causally* related. Suppose that we found that shy people spent more time daydreaming. Shyness might have caused the daydreaming, or excessive daydreaming might have caused the shyness, or perhaps some other variable that we did not measure caused both shyness and an increase in daydreaming. Observational studies do not permit us to make definite conclusions about cause and effect. (See **Figure 2.14**.)

A good illustration of this principle is provided by an interesting observational study. This study attempted to determine whether membership in the Boy Scouts would affect a person's subsequent participation in community affairs (Chapin, 1947). The investigator compared a group of men who had once been Boy Scouts with a group who had not. He found that the men who had been Boy Scouts tended to join more community-affairs groups as adults.

The investigator wanted to conclude that the experience of being a Boy Scout increased a person's

FIGURE 2.14   Correlations do not necessarily indicate cause-and-effect relations: daydreaming could cause shyness or shyness could cause daydreaming.

Daydreaming keeps a person from making many contacts with other people; experiences in fantasies are more successful and gratifying than those in real life.

He does not know how to respond in the company of other people.

Person has poor social skills; finds contacts with other people uncomfortable.

He turns to daydreaming because he receives no gratification from social contacts.

tendency to join community organizations. However, this conclusion is not warranted. All we can say is that people who join Boy Scouts tend to join community organizations later in life. It could be that people who, for one reason or another, are "joiners" tend to join the Boy Scouts when they are young and community organizations when they are older. To determine cause and effect we would have to make some boys join the Boy Scouts and prevent others from doing so, and see how many organizations members of each group would voluntarily join later in life. Here, then, is a question that we shall never answer.

◆   When a psychologist attempts to study the effects of a variable that he or she cannot alter (like sex, age, socioeconomic status, or personality characteristics), he or she will generally try to *match* the subjects on all the relevant variables except the one being studied. That is, if a psychologist wants to study the effects of shyness on daydreaming, he or she might gather two groups of subjects, shy and "nonshy." The people would be selected in such a way that the effects of other variables would be minimized. The average age, intelligence, income, etc., of the two groups would be the same. The psychologist would have to think of as many variables as possible that might affect daydreaming, and see that the people in each group (shy and nonshy) scored similarly on these other variables.

If, after following this matching procedure, the investigator found that shyness was still related to daydreaming, we could be somewhat more confident that the relation was causal. (However, the matching procedure still does not help us decide which is cause and which is effect. Shyness could cause daydreaming, or daydreaming could cause shyness.) The weakness in the matching procedure is that a psychologist might not know all the variables that should be held constant. If the two groups are not matched on an important variable, then the results will be misleading.

Interim summary: Psychologists are interested in explaining the causes of behavior—that is, discovering causal relations. To do so they form hypotheses, manipulate independent variables, and measure dependent variables. If this procedure is to work, they must be certain that other variables are controlled. If an extra independent variable is inadvertently manipulated, and if this extra variable has an effect on (is causally related to) the dependent variable, then the experimenter will mistake a noncausal relation for a causal one. The experimenter will conclude that the dependent variable is causally related to the independent variable, when it is actually related to the extra (confounded) variable. One of the worst embarrassments that an investigator can suffer is to have a colleague point out in a journal article that he or she failed to control for confounding variables, and hence drew incorrect conclusions.

GENERALITY

◆ When we carry out an experiment, we are usually not especially interested in the particular subjects whose behavior we observe. Instead, we probably assume that our subjects are representative of the larger population. In fact, a group of subjects is usually referred to as a **sample** of the larger population. (The words *sample* and *example* have the same root.) If we study the behavior of a group of five-year-old children, we probably want to make conclusions about five-year-olds in general. That is, we want to be able to **generalize** our specific results to the population as a whole—to conclude that the results of our study tell us something about human nature in general, and not simply about our particular subjects.

Many psychologists recruit their subjects from introductory courses in psychology. Thus, the results of experiments that use these students as subjects can be generalized only to other groups of students who are recruited in the same way. In the strictest sense, the results cannot be generalized to students in other courses, or to adults in general, or even to all students enrolled in Introductory Psychology—after all, students who volunteer to serve as subjects might be very different from those who do not. If this is the case, it would hardly seem worthwhile to do the experiments. Even if we used truly random samples of all age groups of adults in our area, we could not generalize the results to people who live in other geographical regions.

But we are not so strict, of course. Most of us assume that a relation among variables that is ob-

FIGURE 2.15   Harry Truman, the winner of the 1948 U.S. presidential election, appears to enjoy the premature headline proclaiming Dewey's victory. The *Chicago Daily News* based their news story on the opinion polls instead of waiting for the verdict from the voting polls. Modern polling techniques are much more accurate; in fact, some people claim that some voters on the west coast of the U.S. did not bother to vote in the 1980 presidential election because the winner had already been announced on radio and television.

served in one group of humans will also be seen in other groups, so long as the relation is a relatively strong one and the sample of subjects is not an especially unusual one. (For example, we might expect that data obtained from prison inmates will have less generality than data obtained from college students.) Generalization from a particular sample of subjects to a larger population is one of those cases in which scientific practice usually does not rigorously follow scientific law.

The practice of generalizing occurs in observational studies just as much as it does in experiments. In one famous case, its limitations were demonstrated with a vengeance. During the United States presidential campaign of 1948, poll-takers predicted, from a sampling of the populace, that Dewey would easily defeat Truman. Of course, they were wrong—embarrassingly so. The subjects that were sampled had been drawn from telephone directories. In 1948, a smaller percentage of the population had telephones than today, and those who did not have telephones tended to be poorer than those who did. A much higher proportion of this second group (people without telephones) voted for Truman; hence, the samples drawn by poll-takers were not representative of the population to which they wanted to generalize—registered U.S. voters. (See **Figure 2.15**.)

CASE STUDIES

Not all investigations make use of groups of subjects. *Case studies* investigate the behavior of individuals, and for some phenomena this method is very effective. Suppose that we are investigating a potential food additive. We feed a small amount to a rat, who immediately has a convulsion and dies. We would have very strong evidence that the compound is poisonous. Perhaps we would try it on one more rat to be sure that the first one was not about to die anyway. If the second rat dies, we would probably not bother to do further testing. The response is so closely tied to the administration of the compound that we are willing to conclude that one event caused the other.

Psychologists often take advantage of "experimental manipulations" that occur because of events outside their control. For example, David Margolin and I studied a woman who had received a serious skull fracture in an automobile accident. The damage to her brain made it impossible for her to read, although her vision was almost normal. We gave her lists of words like these: "rose, violet, carrot, petunia, daffodil" and asked her to choose the one that did not belong with the others. She would point to the word "carrot" even though she could not read it, and had no idea why she chose the one she did. Her performance proves that people can have some idea of the meaning of words that does not depend upon their "saying the words to themselves."

Obviously, we cannot fracture the skulls of a group of people to study phenomena like this experimentally. Instead, we carefully study patients whose brains have been damaged by accident or disease and then form hypotheses that can be tested with groups of normal people.

Case studies are also performed by clinical psychologists, who observe the behavior of their clients, and listen to what they have to say about their lives. Often, the psychologist tries to correlate events that occurred in the client's past (perhaps in childhood) with his or her present behavior and personality. Studies like these are called *retrospective* ("backward-looking"), and their validity depends heavily on the client's memory for past events. Because recollections are often faulty, one must be very cautious about accepting the conclusions of retrospective studies whose results cannot be independently verified.

ETHICS

Unlike some other scientists, psychologists always study living subjects. This means that a psychologist must obey ethical rules as well as scientific ones. Even psychologists who use animal subjects must be sure that they are adequately fed and comfortably housed, and must not inflict unnecessary pain. Rules for care and treatment of animals have been established by such societies as the American Psychological Association.

Much more care is needed in the treatment of human subjects, not only because they are members of our own species, about whom we care the most, but also because it is possible to hurt people in very subtle ways. For example, let us consider (for the last time) the hypothetical experiment on humiliation and susceptibility to propaganda. For the experiment to be scientifically valid, it is necessary actually to humiliate someone. But does a psychologist have the right to do so, even in the interest of science? Suppose that some of the subjects feel *very* humiliated, and suffer a real loss of self-esteem? (After all, if the experiment is to work, they *should*.)

In the United States, federal regulations state that all departments of psychology that engage in federally funded research must have a committee that reviews the ethics of all experiments that use humans as subjects. The committee must review the experiments before they can be performed, to ensure that subjects will be treated properly. In addition, the American Psychological Association has its own ethical guidelines for human research. Review committees are in everyone's interest; both the experimenters and their subjects can be sure that the experimental procedures are unlikely to produce harm.

DESCRIPTIONS OF OBSERVATIONS

In most of the examples I have cited so far, the behavior of a number of subjects was observed. I implied that the data obtained from them would be used to represent a particular value of a variable. This means, of course, that a single number will be used to represent the results of several observations. There is nothing novel about such a procedure. I am sure that all of you know how to calculate the average of a set of numbers; you are familiar with this common *measure of central tendency*. You might be less familiar with measures of variability, which tell us how groups of numbers differ from each other, or with measures of relations, which tell us how closely related two sets of numbers are.

These measures, which describe the results of experiments, are called *descriptive statistics.* They are used for two reasons. First, the investigator calculates them and uses their values to determine whether the hypothesis is true (step 3 of the scientific method). Second, the investigator uses these values to communicate the results of the experiment accurately and succinctly to others (step 4 of the scientific method).

MEASURES OF CENTRAL TENDENCY

The Mean

◆ When we say that the average weight of an adult male in North America is 173 pounds or that the average density of population in the United States is 63.9 people per square mile, we are using a *measure of central tendency,* a statistic that represents a number of observations. The most common measure of central tendency is the average, which psychologists and statisticians usually refer to as the *mean.* As everyone learns in elementary school, the mean is calculated by adding the individual values of the sample and dividing by the number of observations. The mean is the most commonly used measure of central tendency in reports of psychological experiments.

The Median

When we want to choose a measure for descriptive purposes that is most representative of a sample of numbers, we should use the *median,* and not the mean. It is because of this fact that we usually read the term "median family income" rather than "mean family income" in newspapers or magazine articles.

Let us see why the median is a more representative measure than the mean. The median is defined as *the midpoint of a set of values arranged in numerical order.* The median of the set of values listed in Table 2.1 is 5, since that number is at the midpoint. The mean, however, is 8, since $2 + 3 + 5 + 14 + 16 = 40$; $40/5 = 8$. (See **Table 2.1.**)

How can we assess the accuracy with which a measure of central tendency represents a sample of several numbers? We will calculate the difference between each score and the measure of central tendency and add these differences up. We will then divide this total figure by the number of scores, and thus obtain the *average deviation* of each score from the measure of central tendency. The measure of central tendency that deviates the least, on the average, from the individual scores in the sample can then be regarded as the most representative. (See **Table 2.2.**)

We find that the average difference between each score and the mean is 5.6; the average difference between each score and the median is 5.0. Therefore, the median can be said to represent the sample better than the mean does. To take an example that makes more intuitive sense than a set of five numbers, consider a small town that contains 100 families. Ninety-nine of the families, all of whom work in the local textile mill, make between $10,000 and $15,000 per year. However, the income of one family is $2 million per year. This family consists of a novelist and her husband who moved to the area because of its mild climate. The mean income for the 99 families who work in the mill is $12,500 per year. The mean income for the town as a whole, considering the novelist as well as the mill workers, is $32,375 per year. However, the median income is $12,500 per year. Clearly, this figure represents the typical family income of this town better than $32,375.

Why, then, would we ever bother to use the mean rather than the median? There are three reasons: (1) The mean is easier to calculate when the sample is large; it is easier to add up a large set of numbers than it is to arrange them in numerical order. (2) Most samples are not like my example of ninety-nine low values and one very high one; in most cases the mean and median are not very different. (3) For reasons that I shall explain later, the mean has mathematical properties that make it more useful than the median.

TABLE 2.1   Mean of a sample of five scores

	2
	3
	5 ←*median*
	14
	16
Total:	40
Mean:	40/5 = 8

TABLE 2.2 Calculation of average deviation

Scores	Difference between score and median (5)	Difference between score and mean (8)
2	3	6
3	2	5
5	0	3
14	9	6
16	11	8
	Total: 25	Total: 28
	Average deviation: 25/5 = 5.0	Average deviation: 28/5 = 5.6

MEASURES OF VARIABILITY

◆ Many experiments produce two sets of numbers—scores of subjects in the experimental group and scores of members of the control group. If the mean scores of these two groups differ, then the experimenter concludes that the independent variable had an effect. As we shall see in a later section, the psychologist must decide whether the difference between the two groups is larger than what would probably occur by chance. To make this decision, he or she calculates a measure of variability, against which the difference in the means can be compared.

The Range

◆ Two samples can have the same measure of central tendency and still be very different. For example, the mean and median of both sets of numbers listed in Table 2.3 are the same, but the samples are clearly different. The scores in Sample B are more disparate. (See **Table 2.3.**)

One way of stating the difference between the two samples is to say that the numbers in Sample A range from 8 to 12 while the numbers in Sample B range from 0 to 20. To put it another way the range of Sample A is 4 (12 − 8 = 4) and the range of Sample B is 20 (20 − 0 = 20).

The *range* is especially easy to calculate for small samples: simply subtract the lowest score from the highest score. However, this measure of variability is not used very often to describe the results of

psychological experiments because another measure of variability, the variance, has more useful mathematical properties.

Variance and Standard Deviation

In an earlier example I calculated the average deviation from the mean and median for a set of five numbers. The average deviation is, of course, a measure of the degree to which scores differ from each other. However, this measure is almost never used, except for demonstrations like the one I presented. What is used is the *variance,* which is the *average of the squared deviation of each score from the mean.* To calculate this measure you square each deviation score (multiply it by itself). Then you

TABLE 2.3 Two samples with the same means but different ranges

Sample A	Sample B
8	0
9	5
10 ←*median*	10 ←*median*
11	15
12	20
Total: 50	Total: 50
Mean: 50/5 = 10	Mean: 50/5 = 10
Range: 12 − 8 = 4	Range: 20 − 0 = 20

TABLE 2.4 Calculation of variance and standard deviation

Scores	Difference between score and mean (deviation score)	Squared difference between score and mean (squared deviation score)
2	6	36
3	5	25
5	3	9
14	6	36
16	8	64
Total: 40		Total: 170
Mean: 40/5 = 8		Variance: 170/5 = 34
		Standard deviation: $\sqrt{34}$ = 5.83

calculate the mean of these values. (See **Table 2.4.**)

The number most often used to report the amount of variability is the ***standard deviation,*** which is simply the square root of the variance. The square root of 34 is 5.83, so the standard deviation of our sample is 5.83. (See **Table 2.4.**) If you look back at the earlier example (Table 2.2), where I used the same set of numbers to calculate how closely the mean and median represent the scores, you will find that the average deviation of the scores from the mean is 5.6. That is close to the standard deviation of 5.83. For most samples of numbers, these two measures will be close in value. It is only because of special mathematical properties of the *standard* deviation that we use it instead of the *average* deviation. These properties concern the assessment of statistical significance, which I will discuss later.

MEASUREMENT OF RELATIONS

◆ In many studies—especially observational studies—the investigator wants to measure the degree to which two variables are related. For example, suppose that a psychologist has developed a new aptitude test and wants to sell the test to college admissions committees to use for screening applicants. Before they would consider buying the test, he would have to show that a person's score on the test was related to his or her success in college.

The psychologist would give the test to a number of freshmen entering college, and would later obtain their average grades. The psychologist would then measure the relation between test scores and grades. But how does one measure a relation?

Let us suppose that we gave the test to ten students entering college, and later obtained their average grades. We would have two scores for each person, as shown in Table 2.5. (See **Table 2.5.**)

TABLE 2.5 Test scores and average grades of ten students

Student	Test score	Average grade[a]
A.C.	15	2.8
B.F.	12	3.2
G.G.	19	3.5
L.H.	8	2.2
R.J.	14	3.0
S.K.	11	2.6
P.R.	13	2.8
A.S.	7	1.5
J.S.	9	1.9
P.V.	18	3.8

[a] 0 = F, 4 = A

We can examine the relation between these variables by plotting the scores on a graph. For example, A.C. received a test score of 15 and earned an average of 2.8 (B minus). We could represent this student's score as a point on the graph shown in Figure 2.16. The horizontal axis represents the test score and the vertical axis represents the average grade. A point is placed on the graph that corresponds to the score of student A.C. on both of these measures. (See **Figure 2.16.**)

We can construct a graph that contains the scores of all ten students, and then look at the distribution of scores to determine whether they are related. Examination of this graph, called a *scatter plot,* shows that the points are not randomly distributed; instead, they tend to be located along a diagonal line that runs from the lower left to the upper right. (See **Figure 2.17.**)

The data shown in Figure 2.17 illustrate that a rather good relation exists between a student's test score and average grade. High scores are associated with good grades, low scores with poor grades. However, the psychologist who developed the test would want a more convenient way to communicate the strength of the relation, and would probably calculate the *correlation coefficient.* The

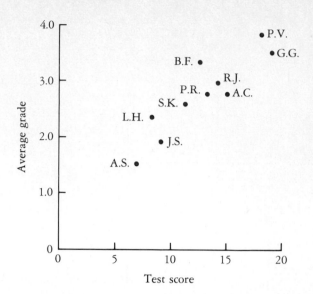

FIGURE 2.17   A scatter plot of the test scores and average grades of ten students.

correlation between the scores in my example is + .9. (I will not bother you with the details of how this measure is calculated.) A correlation this high is indeed an excellent one, and a psychologist would be delighted to have developed a test whose scores correlated with college grades this well. The value of a correlation can vary from 0 (no relation) to 1.0 (perfect relation). A perfect relation means that if we know the value of a person's score on one measure, then we can determine precisely what his or her score will be on the other. Thus, a correlation of + .9 is very close to perfect; the hypothetical aptitude test of our example is indeed a very good indicator of how well a student will do in college.

◆   I should note that correlations may be negative as well as positive. A *negative correlation* indicates that high values on one measure are associated with low values on the other, and vice versa. An example of a negative correlation would be the relation between an adult's age and the number of remaining teeth. The older a person is, the more likely it becomes that some teeth will be lost. Another example would be the correlation between the average score of a professional golfer and the amount of money he or she wins in a year. Since low golf scores indicate more skill, players with the lowest scores will tend to win the most money,

FIGURE 2.16   An example of the graphing of one data point: the test score and average grade of student A.C.

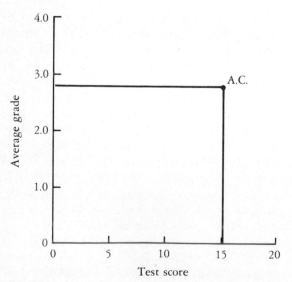

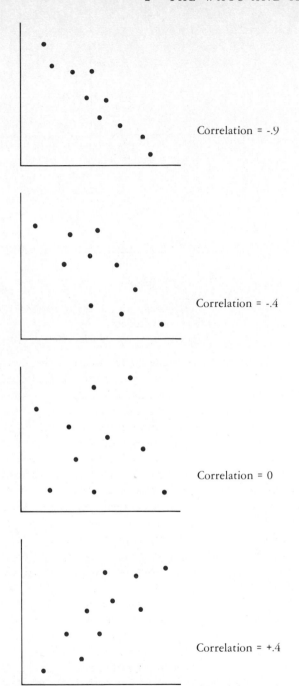

FIGURE 2.18 A variety of scatter plots, indicating several different correlations.

be considered an almost-perfect relation, but in this case high scores on one measure predict low scores on the other. Scatter plots for high and low correlations, both positive and negative, are shown in Figure 2.18. (See **Figure 2.18.**)

The correlation coefficient has an interesting property—it allows us to determine how much of the variability in one measure can be accounted for by using the value of the other measure. Because this concept will come up again in later chapters when I discuss psychological tests of ability and temperament, it is worthwhile describing it here. Consider our hypothetical aptitude test. If its correlation with the students' average grades was 0, then our best guess for any student's average grade would be the mean of all the students' grades. The variability around the mean is, of course, the variance. But if the correlation between the test and the average grade were .9, then knowing a student's test score would be very useful. We would use the students' test scores and the value of the correlation coefficient to calculate a predicted average grade for each student. If we then calculated the variability between the predicted grades and the ones that the students actually earned, the result would be much lower than the variability around the mean. The better the correlation, the more the variability is reduced. In the ideal case (correlation of 1.0) there is no variation between predicted and actual grades. To put it another way, the test would be able to *account for* all the variability of the students' grades.

The percentage of the variability that can be accounted for is equal to the square of the correlation coefficient. Thus, a correlation of $+.9$ means that 81% ($.9^2 = .81$) of the variability in the average grades of a group of students can be predicted by knowing their scores on our hypothetical test. (Note that a correlation of $-.9$ works just as well, since $-.9^2 = .81$.) To put it another way, only 19% (100% $-$ 81%) of the variability of the grades would be determined by factors *other than* those measured by the test.

Unfortunately, real aptitude tests do not predict grades this well. A test-maker would probably be pleased with a correlation of $+.6$, which would mean that the test measures factors that account for only 36% of the variability in a student's score, leaving 64% to factors not being measured.

and those with the highest scores will win the least.

In terms of predicting the value of one measure by using the other, a negative correlation is just as good as a positive one. A correlation of $-.9$ can

ASSESSING THE SIGNIFICANCE OF RELATIONS

Scientific investigations, whether they consist of experiments or observational studies, are concerned with relations. Sometimes the relation is calculated directly, by computing a correlation coefficient. Other times (for example, in an experiment) two or more values of the independent variable are selected and the dependent variable is measured. The results, usually expressed as means and standard deviations, indicate whether the independent variable had an effect—that is, whether the mean values of the dependent measure were different. Next I shall discuss the procedure that helps us decide whether a difference observed between group means is likely to reflect a real effect of the independent variable, or whether the results are due to chance.

STATISTICAL SIGNIFICANCE

When we perform an experiment, we select a sample of subjects from a larger population—the one to which we want to generalize. In so doing, we hope that the results will be similar to those we might have obtained had we observed all members of the population. We assign the subjects to groups in an unbiased manner (usually by random selection), alter only the relevant independent variables, and measure the dependent variable with a valid method. In other words, we put into practice the procedures I have outlined in this chapter. After we have completed the experiment, we must decide whether our results indicate that there is a relation between independent and dependent variables; that is, we must decide whether the results are *statistically significant.*

The concept of statistical significance is not an easy one to grasp, so I want to make sure you understand the purpose of this discussion. Suppose that we want to determine whether the presence of other people affects the speed at which a person can solve simple arithmetic problems. We would test members of the experimental group with other people watching them; members of the control group would work alone. We would then calculate the mean number of problems that were solved by each group. If the means were different, we would conclude that the presence of an audience does affect the rate at which a person can solve arithmetic problems.

TABLE 2.6   Heights (in inches) of selected sample of students

Name ends in consonant		Name ends in vowel
65	61	67
67	68	68
71	70	62
72	65	63
73	73	62
65	60	64
74	70	60
74	72	63
67	63	61
69	67	69
68	73	63
75	66	65
72	71	69
71	72	71
65	64	69
66	69	65
70	73	70
72	75	63
72	72	63
71	66	64
62	71	65
62	68	63
80	70	66
	75	62
		72
		65
		66
		65
		65

Total: 3257

Mean: 3257/47 = 69.3

Total: 1890

Mean: 1890/29 = 65.2

Difference between means: 69.3 − 65.2 = 4.1

But how different is different? Suppose that we tested two groups of people, *both* of whom performed alone. Would the mean scores be precisely the same? Of course not. *By chance,* one mean would be a little higher. Now back to our experiment. Suppose we found that the mean score for the group that worked in the presence of an audience was lower than the mean score for the group that performed alone. Could we conclude that the presence of an audience disrupted our subjects' performance, or was the difference between the mean scores merely due to chance? This is the kind of question that every psychologist must ask after an experiment is over.

ASSESSMENT OF DIFFERENCES BETWEEN SAMPLES

The obvious way to determine whether the group means differ significantly is to look at the size of the difference. If it is large, then we can be fairly confident that the independent variable had a significant effect. If it is small, then the difference is probably due to chance. What we need are guidelines to help us determine when a difference is large enough to be statistically significant.

The following example will explain how these guidelines are constructed. I distributed cards to students in one of my classes to collect some data that I could analyze to explain some statistical concepts. I will use the data for that purpose here.

There were 76 students in the class. Their average height was 67.2 inches. I performed an observational study to test the following hypothesis: People whose first names end with a vowel will, on the average, be shorter than people whose first names end with a consonant. (I will tell you later why I expected this hypothesis to be confirmed.)

I divided the subjects into two groups: those whose first names ended with a vowel and those whose first names ended with a consonant. Table 2.6 contains a listing of these two groups. Indeed, the means for the two groups differed by 4.1 inches. (See **Table 2.6**.)

A difference of 4.1 inches seems large, but how can we be sure that it is not due to chance? What we really need to know is how large a difference would there be if the means had been calculated from two groups that were randomly selected, and

TABLE 2.7 Heights (in inches) of a random division of the class into two groups

Group A		Group B	
65	71	63	62
72	63	62	63
72	74	70	65
69	72	70	75
61	71	65	71
69	65	64	80
66	71	75	71
70	67	63	68
66	72	70	71
65	66	75	73
66	72	67	62
65	73	65	72
64	63	68	65
72	69	63	72
63	62	69	66
65	60	67	73
62	70	68	65
67	68	60	73
	69		61
	64		74
Total: 2561		Total: 2588	
Mean: 67.4		Mean: 68.1	

Difference: -0.7

not chosen on the basis of a variable that is related to height. For comparison, I divided the class into two random groups. To do this I shuffled the cards with the students' names on them, and then dealt them out into two piles. Then I calculated the mean height of the people whose names were in each of the piles. This time, the difference between the means was 0.7 inches. (See **Table 2.7**.)

I divided the class into two random groups five more times, calculating the means, and the difference between the means, each time. The differences ranged from 0.2 inches to 0.7 inches. (See **Table 2.8**.) It began to look like a mean difference of 4.1 inches was bigger than what one would expect by chance.

TABLE 2.8   Mean heights (in inches) of five random divisions of the class into two groups

Group A	Group B	Difference
67.6	67.9	−0.3
68.1	67.4	0.7
67.8	67.6	0.2
67.9	67.5	0.4
68.0	67.4	0.6

Next I divided the class into two random groups 1000 times. (I used my home computer to do the chore.) *Not once* in 1000 times was the difference between the means of the two randomly chosen groups greater than 3.0 inches. Therefore, I can conclude that if the class is divided randomly into two groups, the chance that the means of their heights will differ by 4.1 inches is much less than one time in a thousand, or 0.1% of the time. Thus, I can safely say that when I divided the students into two groups based upon the last letters of their first names, I was dividing them on a basis that

was related to their height. The division was *not* equivalent to random selection. A person's height *is* related to the last letter of his or her first name.

Figure 2.19 presents a *frequency distribution* of the differences between the means of the 1000 random divisions of the class. The height of a point represents the number of times (frequency) the difference between the means fell into a particular range. For example, the difference between the means fell between −0.2 inches and +0.2 inches 170 times. (See **Figure 2.19**.)

Suppose that the difference between the means in our observational study had been smaller than 4.1 inches. Suppose it had been 2.3 inches. Would we conclude that the difference represented a real relation, or would we decide that the difference was due to chance? Figure 2.19 would help us decide.

We can see that only 15 out of 1000 times (1.5%) will the difference between the means of the two groups be as large or larger than 2.3 inches: 11 + 4 = 15. (See **Figure 2.19**.) This means the following: If we obtained a difference of 2.3 inches between the means of the groups and concluded that the populations represented (people whose first names end in vowels and people whose first names

FIGURE 2.19   A frequency distribution that illustrates the number of occurrences of various ranges of mean differences in heights. The group of 76

people was divided randomly into two samples 1000 times.

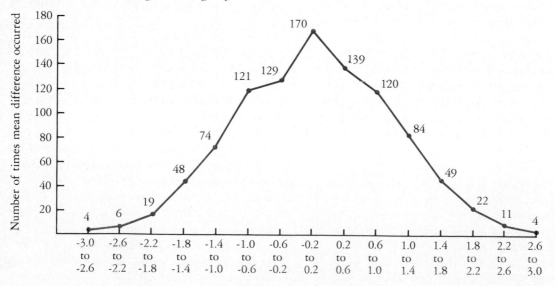

end in consonants) tend to have different heights, *the likelihood of our being wrong is 1.5%*. The calculations show that we will obtain a difference of at least 2.3 inches purely by chance only 1.5% of the time. Since 1.5% is a small likelihood, we would probably conclude that the relation was statistically significant.

The method I used to determine the significance of my original findings from the group of 76 students (a difference of 4.1 inches) uses the same principles that a psychologist uses to determine whether the results observed in a given experiment represent a real difference or are just due to chance. In my example we considered two possibilities: (1) the difference in the means was due to chance and (2) the difference in the means occurred because the last letter of a person's first name is related to his or her height. We found that a difference of 4.1 inches would be expected less than one time in a thousand. Therefore, we rejected alternative (1) and concluded that alternative (2) was correct. My original hypothesis was right.

◆   Ordinarily, psychologists who conduct experiments or observational studies like this one would not use their computers to divide their subjects' scores randomly 1000 times. Instead, they would calculate the mean and standard deviation for each group and consult a table that statisticians have prepared for them. The table (which is based upon the special mathematical properties of the mean and standard deviation that I have alluded to several times) will tell them how likely it is that their results could have been obtained by chance—in my case, that the last letter of a person's first name is not related to his or her height. If the likelihood is low enough, they will conclude that the results that they obtained are statistically significant. Most psychologists consider a 5% probability to be statistically significant but are much more comfortable with 1%.

Interim summary: If a psychologist tests a hypothesis by comparing the scores of two groups of subjects, he or she must have some way of determining whether the observed difference in the mean scores is larger than one would expect by chance. My example was an observational study; I certainly did not *manipulate* my students' names—they already had them when they came to my class. How-

ever, the procedure I followed is based upon the same logic that a psychologist would follow in assessing the significance of the results of an experiment.

A psychologist performs an experiment by observing the performance of two or more groups of subjects who have been exposed to different conditions, representing different values of the independent variable. Next, the psychologist calculates the group means and standard deviations of the dependent variable. He or she uses a formula and consults a special table that statisticians have devised so that others can estimate the likelihood of getting such results when the independent variable actually has *no effect* on the dependent variable. If the probability of obtaining these results by chance is sufficiently low, the psychologist will reject the possibility that the independent variable had no effect, and decide in favor of the alternative—that it really *did* have an effect, and that a causal relation exists.

I must emphasize that statistical tests help us to decide whether results are representative of the larger population, but not whether they are *trivial*. For example, suppose that a school system decided to perform an experiment to try a new teaching method. They found that the test scores of students who were taught by the new method were "significantly" better than those of students who were taught by the old method. However, the difference was very small: the students who learned from the new method did only slightly better. (A small difference can be statistically significant if the variability within the group is small enough, or if the groups of subjects are very large.) Since it would be very expensive to change all classes over to the new method, the school system would probably decide to continue with the present one. Tests of significance tell us whether differences are large enough so that they are probably not due to chance; they do not tell us whether the differences are large enough to be *important*.

I should now tell you why I originally hypothesized that the last letter of a person's first name is related to his or her height. Females are more likely than males to have first names that end in a vowel (Paula, Angela, Anna, etc.). Because females tend to be shorter than males, I expected that a group of students whose first names ended in vowels would be shorter, on the average, than those whose names ended in consonants. Indeed, the data proved me correct.

PSYCHOLOGICAL TESTS

◆ As you undoubtedly know, psychologists devise and administer all kinds of tests: aptitude tests, intelligence tests, personality tests, and tests to diagnose various mental disorders. These tests are used for many reasons, such as deciding which children need special training or instruction, helping a person decide what kind of career to pursue, selecting among a number of job applicants, or evaluating the effectiveness of a particular kind of psychotherapy. Tests are also used in basic research. For example, if we wanted to see whether shy people daydream more than people who are not shy, we would probably use a personality test that was designed to measure a person's degree of *introversion.*

Psychological tests can be viewed as operational definitions of people's behavioral characteristics: verbal fluency, introversion, mathematical ability, anxiety, abstract reasoning ability, or authoritarianism, to mention a few. Like any other operational definition, a psychological test can have high or low validity. A valid test accurately measures what it purports to measure. Tests can be evaluated on face validity or, in the case of complex personality characteristics (like authoritarianism or introversion), construct validity. That is, if the results of research consistently show the tests to be useful, their validity will be accepted by psychologists.

◆ A third type of validation is possible with some kinds of psychological tests: *predictive validity.* In the section on measurement of relations, I described a hypothetical test that was designed to predict a student's average grade in college. Such a test would be useful for admissions committees in deciding which applicants should be accepted. The test's predictive validity is determined by administering it to a number of entering freshmen, and then correlating their scores with the average grades that they earn in college. The higher the correlation, the greater the predictive validity.

Note that predictive validity says nothing about causal relations; it merely says how useful a score is in predicting the value of another variable. When an admissions committee administers a test for college entrance they do not care precisely what the test measures, only how well the scores correlate with scholastic performance. Thus, psychological tests can make practical use of noncausal relations.

CONCLUDING REMARKS

The scientific method consists of a logical system of inquiry with sensible rules that must be followed if a person wants to draw accurate conclusions about the causes of natural phenomena. These rules were originally devised by philosophers who attempted to determine how we can understand reality. Because we are all, by our natures, intuitive psychologists, trying to understand why other people do what they do, it is especially important to realize how easily we can be fooled about the actual causes of behavior. Thus, everyone, not just the professional psychologist, is well served by knowing the basics of the scientific method.

GUIDE TO TERMS INTRODUCED IN THIS CHAPTER

average deviation　p. 51　Table 2.2
case study　p. 49
causal relation　p. 38
confounding of variables　p. 40　Figure 2.6
construct validity　p. 35
control group　p. 42　Figure 2.9
correlation coefficient　p. 54　Figure 2.18
counterbalancing　p. 40　Figure 2.8
dependent variable　p. 33　Figure 2.3
descriptive statistics　p. 50
double-blind procedure　p. 46　Figure 2.13
face validity　p. 35
frequency distribution　p. 58　Figure 2.19
generalization　p. 48
hypothesis　p. 32
independent variable　p. 33　Figure 2.3
interrater reliability　p. 37　Figure 2.5
manipulation　p. 33

SUGGESTIONS FOR FURTHER READING

There are several standard textbooks that discuss the scientific method in psychological research. Some good ones are *Experimental Methodology* (2nd ed.) by L.B. Christensen (Boston: Allyn and Bacon, 1980), which covers ethical and practical issues as well as theoretical ones; and *Methods Toward a Science of Behavior and Experience* by W. Ray and R. Ravizza (Belmont, California: Wadsworth Publishing, 1981), which contains a variety of examples of psychological research.

The Game of Science (4th ed.) by G. McCain and E. M. Segal (Belmont, California: Brooks/Cole, 1981) and *Pitfalls in Human Research* by T.X. Barber (New York: Pergamon Press, 1976) are rather entertaining accounts of the whys and wherefores of the scientific method. Most of us enjoy reading about the mistakes of others, perhaps thinking that we could have done things better. Barber's book allows us to indulge in this activity; it discusses specific instances of studies that were flawed.

PART • B

FOUNDATIONS

OF BEHAVIOR

The three chapters in this section deal with fundamental processes that are used by many psychologists to explain behavior. Chapter 3 describes the basic functions of the human nervous system—the physiological processes that are necessary for perception, memory, decision making, emotion, planning, and the execution of behavior—and briefly reviews how psychologists and other scientists study these functions. After describing the basic functions of nerve cells, it explains how drugs that alter a person's behavior affect the functioning of these cells. This chapter provides a foundation for what you will learn in later chapters.

Chapters 4 and 5 explore the basic learning processes: classical conditioning, instrumental conditioning, and the mechanisms of motivation and reinforcement. A basic understanding of these processes can help us understand the causes of complex behaviors that will be described in later chapters. These chapters provide explicit examples of how the scientific method, described in Chapter 2, is used to investigate the nature and causes of behavior.

BIOLOGY
OF BEHAVIOR

LEARNING ◆ OBJECTIVES

THERE ARE many ways to study human behavior; one important approach is the study of the biology of behavior. Human behavior is organized and controlled by the nervous system. We learn about the world through the activity of our sense organs, and we interact with it through the contractions of our muscles. Between sense organs and muscles lies the nervous system, where perceiving, learning, decision making, and all our mental processes take place. In this chapter I shall describe the general structure of the human nervous system, review the methods used to study its functions, and summarize what has been learned from this study. I shall also describe the effects of drugs that alter behavior and discuss the physiological basis of these effects.

INVESTIGATIONS OF THE BIOLOGY OF BEHAVIOR

◆ The efforts of scientists in many different fields contribute to our understanding of the biology of behavior. *Neuroanatomists* study the structure of the nervous system; *cell biologists* explore the functions of its cells; *neurophysiologists* investigate how nerve cells transmit information; *neurochemists* study the chemistry of the nervous system; and *psychopharmacologists* use drugs to uncover its functions. All these scientists provide the basic tools that others use to study the biology of behavior. However, the research performed by *neurologists, physiological psychologists,* and *neuropsychologists* has the most relevance to psychology.

◆ Neurologists are physicians (M.D.s) who specialize in the treatment of diseases of the nervous system. These physicians were the first to study the role that the nervous system plays in human behavior. They observed that damage to various portions of the human brain produced different kinds of disorders, which suggested that different parts of the brain have different functions. Today neurologists use this information in making their diagnoses. For example, if a patient loses sensation to pain in the right leg, loses sensation to touch in the left leg, and has difficulty making accurate, rapid movements of either arm and hand, a neurologist can be almost certain that a particular region of the left side of the lower part of the brain has been damaged.

The studies that began with the efforts of neurologists in the last century and the early part of this century have been continued and extended by neuropsychologists. Neurologists are primarily interested in the diagnosis and treatment of disease and injury. They study the patient's deficits to determine what parts of the nervous system are damaged and to assess the proper course of treatment and probability of recovery. In contrast, neuropsychologists try to learn how the nervous system organizes and controls human behavior. Neuropsychologists, too, study patients who have sustained damage to some portion of the nervous system. They use their assessment skills to determine which sensory, motor, or cognitive abilities have been disrupted by the injury, and then draw inferences about the psychological functions that are performed by various parts of the nervous system.

Basically, neuropsychologists use the following logic: if damage to a particular part of the nervous system (structure A) impairs a person's ability to perform a particular function (function B), we can infer that structure A plays a role in the execution of function B. For example, if a person can no longer see after the back part of the brain is destroyed, we can be fairly certain that the back part of the brain plays a role in vision. Much of what we know about the functions of various parts of the brain was obtained by using this inferential strategy. As you learned in Chapter 1, it is called the *ablation method.*

◆ Physiological psychologists use a wider range of research techniques (which will be described in greater detail in the next section). These scientists perform most of their investigations with laboratory animals. Unlike neuropsychologists, who assess the behavior of patients whose nervous systems have been damaged by injury or disease, physiological psychologists can operate on their animals and produce damage to any structure of the brain. They can also insert wires to stimulate the brain with electricity or to record the electrical activity that the brain produces. They can inject drugs or remove pieces of tissue for chemical analysis. Although the animals they study lack many abilities that humans possess (such as speech), physiological psychologists can use them to conduct investigations that cannot be performed with humans.

RESEARCH METHODS OF PHYSIOLOGICAL PSYCHOLOGY

◆ The most common research method used by physiological psychologists is the one that is also used by neuropsychologists: correlation of a behavioral deficit with the location of damage to the nervous system. But instead of waiting until a patient accidentally suffers damage to a particular part of the brain, the physiological psychologist operates on a laboratory animal in order to produce that damage. This technique is called *lesion production.* A le-

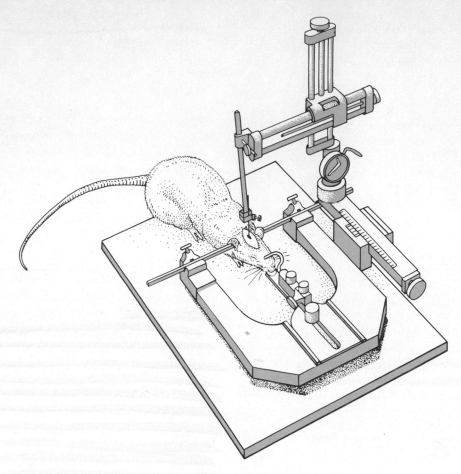

FIGURE 3.1   A stereotaxic apparatus, used to
insert a wire or metal tube into a specific portion of
an animal's brain.

a lesion

sion is an injury; this technique permits the investigator to direct and control the injury to a particular part of the brain. He or she then studies the results.

An animal is anesthetized and prepared for surgery, a hole is drilled in the skull, and part of the brain is destroyed. If the region that is under investigation is located in the depths of the brain, a special device is used: a **stereotaxic apparatus**. *Stereotaxic* means "solid arrangement"; it refers to the ability to manipulate an object in three-dimensional space. A stereotaxic apparatus permits a physiological psychologist to insert a fine wire into a precise location in the brain. Electrical current is then passed through the wire, and a small portion of the brain around the tip of the wire is destroyed. After the animal recovers from the oper-

ation (within a few days), its behavior can be assessed. (See **Figure 3.1**.)

A stereotaxic apparatus can also be used to insert wires for recording the electrical activity of nerve cells in particular regions of the brain. The wire is inserted and attached to an electrical connector glued to the animal's skull, and the scalp is sewed together. The connector is later attached to a wire leading to electronic devices that record the electrical activity of the brain while the animal is performing various behaviors. (See **Figure 3.2**.) As we shall see later, nerve cells transmit information from place to place by means of electrical charges; the wire in the brain detects these charges.

A wire placed in an animal's brain can be used to lead electrical current into the brain as well as out of it. The electrical connector on the animal's

FIGURE 3.2 A permanently attached set of wires (electrodes) in an animal's brain, with a connecting socket cemented to the skull.

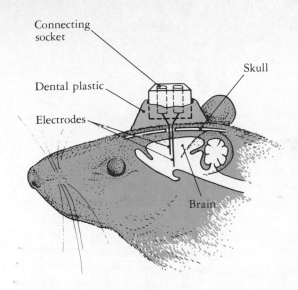

skull is attached to an electrical stimulator, and current is sent to a portion of the animal's brain. The experimenter then assesses the effects of this artificial stimulation on the animal's behavior. One example of an experiment that uses this technique is shown in **Figure 3.3.** A rat is pressing a lever attached to an electrical switch that turns on a stimulator. The stimulator sends a brief pulse of electricity through a wire placed in the rat's brain. If the tip of the wire is located in certain parts of the brain, the animal will press the lever again and again. This fact suggests that these parts of the brain play a role in reward mechanisms. (Chapter 5 discusses this phenomenon in more detail.)

Different drugs affect different types of nerve cells of the brain in different ways, and many of the hormones that are produced by the glands of the body affect behavior by stimulating nerve cells.

Physiological psychologists often use these chemicals in their investigations to determine how their behavioral effects are produced.

Although physiological psychologists regularly use many other techniques, lesion production,

FIGURE 3.3 When the rat presses the switch it receives a brief pulse of electricity to its brain, through wires like those shown in Figure 3.2

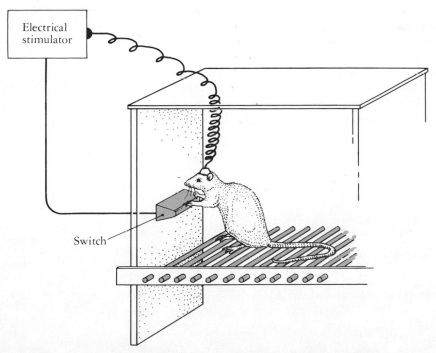

electrical recording, electrical stimulation, and the administration of drugs and hormones are the ones most frequently used and illustrate the rationale for the basic research methods of physiological psychology.

ASSESSING DAMAGE TO THE HUMAN BRAIN

Physiological psychologists know the location of the lesions in the brains of their laboratory animals because they placed them there. In addition, they can confirm the precise location of the lesions by performing an autopsy after behavioral testing is completed. Neuropsychologists have a more difficult task. Their subjects are human beings, whose brains can be examined only when they die, and then only if a patient's family gives permission for an autopsy. Sometimes brain damage is caused by surgical removal of a tumor or diseased region of the brain; in such cases the neurosurgeon can provide the neuropsychologist with drawings of the parts that were removed. However, most human brain lesions are produced by natural causes, such as a stroke. Most strokes are produced when a blood clot obstructs an artery in the brain and blocks the supply of oxygen and nutrients to a particular region, causing that region to die. No surgery takes place, so a neurosurgeon's report is not available.

Until recently, it was not possible to determine the location of brain lesions until the patient died and an autopsy was performed. Now, however, a diagnostic machine is available that has revolutionized the practice of neurology and has aided neuropsychological research: the *CAT scanner.*

CAT stands for *computerized axial tomography. Axis,* "wheel," refers to the circular movement of the X-ray tube and detector around the person's head; *tomos,* "cut," describes the fact that the picture looks like a slice. A CAT scanner sends a narrow beam of X rays through a person's head. A detector measures the amount of radiation that gets through to the other side. The beam is moved around the patient's head and a computer calculates the amount of radiation that passes through. The result is a two-dimensional image of a "slice" of the person's head, parallel to the top of the skull. (See **Figure 3.4.**) Figure 3.5 shows a picture produced by a CAT scanner (left) and a photograph

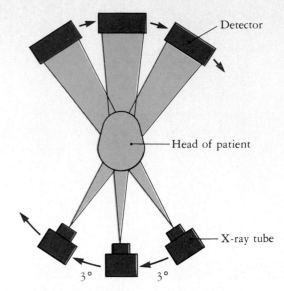

FIGURE 3.4 A schematic representation of a CAT scanner. (Redrawn from Carlson, N.R. *Physiology of Behavior,* 2nd ed. Boston: Allyn and Bacon, 1981.)

of the corresponding slice through a human brain. (See **Figure 3.5.**)

The development of the CAT scanner has made it possible to determine whether a person's neurological symptoms are caused by localized brain injury, such as those produced by a stroke or brain tumor. Many patients have been spared unnecessary brain surgery because the CAT scanner revealed that a brain tumor was *not* present. Others have received timely surgery because the CAT scanner revealed the presence of a tumor that had not been suspected. One case I learned about involved a ten-year-old boy who complained of headaches. The family physician suspected that the headaches were psychological in origin but decided to refer the boy to a neurologist for a CAT scan, mainly because the procedure is relatively harmless (the exposure to radiation is low) and it is always good medical practice to rule out more serious organic problems. To everyone's surprise, the scan of the boy's brain revealed the presence of a large lesion that looked like a tumor. Neurosurgery was performed immediately, and a tumor was found and removed. If a CAT scan had not been done, the growing tumor would have eventually pro-

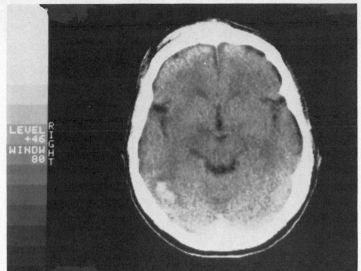

FRONT

BACK

FIGURE 3.5   An image from a CAT scan (left) and a photograph of an actual slice of a brain (right), cut in approximately the same plane. (CAT scan courtesy of Dr. J.McA. Jones, Good Samaritan Hospital, Portland, Oregon. Photograph from DeArmond, S.J., Fusco, M.M., and Dewey, M.M. *Structure of the Human Brain: A Photographic Atlas*, 2nd ed. New York: Oxford University Press, 1976.)

duced unmistakable neurological symptoms, but the early detection and surgery will certainly work in favor of the boy's chances for recovery.

The CAT scan has become an indispensable tool for neuropsychological research. Now the investigator can determine the approximate location of a brain lesion while the patient is still alive. Knowing the results of behavioral testing and the location of the brain damage, the researcher can make inferences about the normal function of the missing brain tissue. Figure 3.6 shows a complete set of CAT scans, from a person who has difficulties perceiving and drawing pictures of three-dimensional objects. You will have no trouble spotting the lesion. (See **Figure 3.6**.)

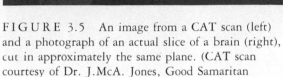

STRUCTURE AND FUNCTION OF THE NERVOUS SYSTEM

The anatomy of the brain is very complex. Although we now know a great deal about the various brain regions and the pathways of the nerve fibers that connect them, we have only an elementary knowledge about what specific functions each of these regions and connecting pathways perform. In a sense, neuroanatomists have provided a challenge to other neuroscientists: here is a map of the brain—now you fill in the functions. This challenge will continue to occupy our efforts for many years to come.

THE CENTRAL NERVOUS SYSTEM

The brain and spinal cord are the most protected organs of the body. The brain is encased in the skull, which consists of a very tough set of bones; the spinal cord runs through the middle of a column of hollow bones, the vertebrae. (See **Figure 3.7**.) Both the brain and the spinal cord (which together are referred to as the *central nervous system*) are surrounded by the *meninges*. (*Meninges* is the plural of *meninx*, "membrane." You have probably heard of *meningitis*, which is an inflammation of the meninges.) Three different sets of membranes encase the brain. The outer one is a thick, tough, unstretchable wrapping, rather like soft parchment. The inner one is thin and delicate and adheres directly to the brain. The middle one is spongy and is filled with a fluid.

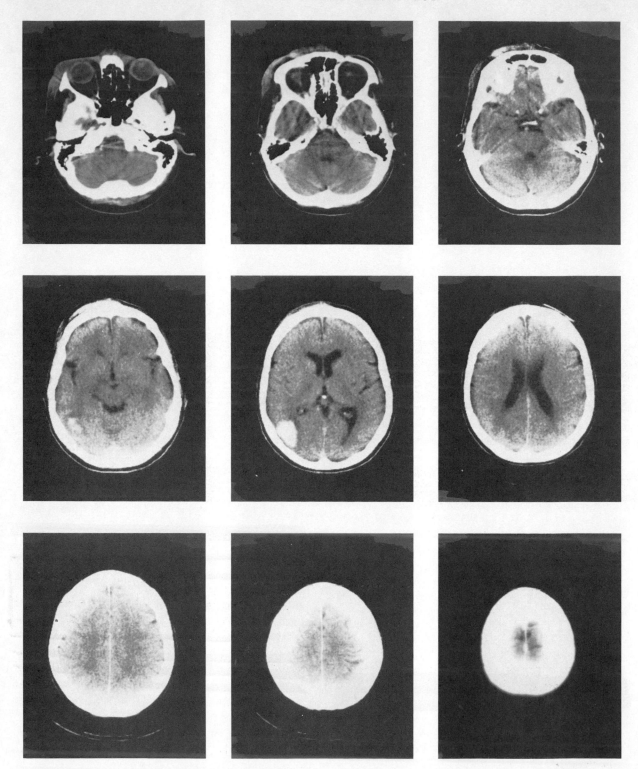

FIGURE 3.6   A complete set of CAT scans from a patient with a lesion in the right occipital-parietal area. Note that left and right are reversed. (Courtesy of Dr. J.McA. Jones, Good Samaritan Hospital, Portland, Oregon.)

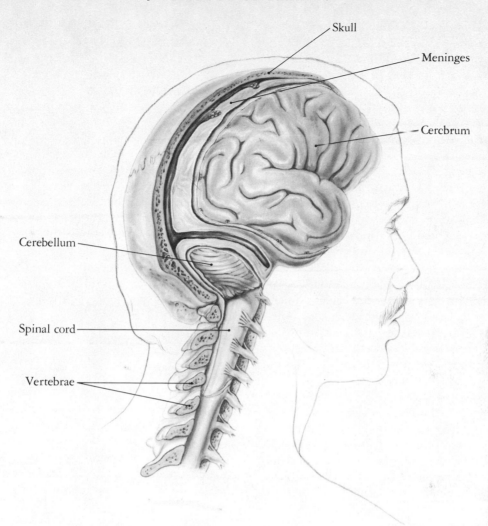

Skull

Meninges

Cerebrum

Cerebellum

Spinal cord

Vertebrae

FIGURE 3.7   The central nervous system: brain and spinal cord. (Adapted from Carlson, N.R. *Physiology of Behavior,* 2nd ed. Boston: Allyn and Bacon, 1981.)

The average human brain weighs approximately 1200–1500 grams (approximately 3 pounds). It is extremely soft and fragile. Because of its great delicacy, and because we often move our heads around, the brain is provided with a cushioning device: *cerebrospinal fluid,* or *CSF.* CSF is similar to blood plasma, the clear liquid that remains when the red and white cells are removed from blood. This fluid is produced continuously by specialized blood vessels located in hollow chambers of the brain called *ventricles.*

CSF flows out of the ventricles into the space between the outer (tough) and inner (delicate) meninges, providing a liquid cushion around the entire brain. As a result, the brain floats instead of resting directly on the base of the skull. Because an object weighs less when it is submerged in liquid, the effective weight of the brain is reduced from well over a kilogram to less than 80 grams (2.8 ounces). Without the cushioning effect of CSF our brain would be brusied and injured by any rapid movement of our head.

THE PERIPHERAL NERVOUS SYSTEM

◆ The business of the brain is to control the movements of the muscles—to produce appropriate behaviors in appropriate situations. Of course, we use

our brains for thinking as well as for moving, but if we could not perceive the world or move our muscles, we would have nothing to think about. Thus a brain is useful only if it can receive sensory information and exert control on the muscles. These processes require the peripheral nervous system.

The *peripheral nervous system* consists of the nerves that connect the central nervous system with sense organs, muscles, and glands. The sense organs detect changes in the environment and send signals through the nerves to the central nervous system. The brain makes appropriate responses by sending signals over the nerves to the muscles (causing behavior) and the glands (producing adjustments in internal physiological processes).

Nerves are bundles of many thousands of individual nerve fibers, all wrapped in a protective set of meninges, just like the brain. Under a microscope, nerves look something like telephone cables. (See **Figure 3.8.**) Like the individual wires in a telephone cable, nerve fibers transmit messages through the nerve, from brain to muscle or gland, or from sense organ to brain.

Some nerves are attached to the spinal cord. These serve all of the body below the neck, conveying sensory information from the skin and carrying messages to muscles and glands. For example, if you stub your toe, the pain you feel comes from sense receptors at the ends of nerve fibers in your toe. These fibers run through nerves attached to the lower part of the spinal cord. The information is sent up to the brain through bundles of nerve fibers that run the length of the spinal cord. Other nerves are attached directly to the base of the brain; these serve muscles and sense receptors in the neck and head. For example, when you taste your food the sensory information gets to your brain through nerves that travel from your tongue to the base of your brain.

Each nerve fiber has its own function; it conveys information about what is happening at a particular part of the body, or it carries messages from the brain to a particular muscle or gland. (Do you remember Müller's doctrine of specific nerve energies from Chapter 1?) Figures 3.9 and 3.10 show the location of some of the major *spinal nerves* (attached to the spinal cord) and the *cranial nerves* (attached directly to the brain). The pictures in Figure 3.10 illustrate the kinds of sensory information and muscle control conveyed by the various cranial nerves. (See **Figures 3.9 and 3.10.**)

SENSORY INPUT TO THE BRAIN

Cerebral Cortex

We perceive information about the world when messages about events that occur there are sent from sense receptors to the central nervous system, through nerve fibers in spinal or cranial nerves. Sensory information goes to a variety of locations within the brain, but the most important of these (so far as conscious perception is concerned) is the *cerebral cortex.* The word *cortex* means "bark." The cerebral cortex consists of a thin layer of tissue approximately three millimeters thick and containing billions of nerve cells. It is here that perceptions take place, memories are stored and retrieved, and plans are formulated and executed.

The cerebral cortex covers the surface of the *cerebral hemispheres,* the two large masses that form the greatest bulk of the human brain. Figure 3.11 shows two views of the human brain and illustrates the extent of the cerebral cortex. The gray shading is appropriate, since the cerebral cortex is often referred to as the brain's *gray matter.* The drawing on the left shows how the brain looks from the side, with the front of the brain at the left. (See **Figure 3.11, left.**) The drawing on the right shows the brain sliced through the middle, from front to back, with the left half cut away. You see the inner surface of the right side of the brain. (See **Figure 3.11, right.**)

FIGURE 3.8   A nerve consists of a sheath of tissue that encases a bundle of individual nerve fibers (axons).

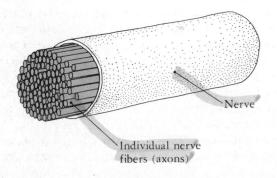

Nerve

Individual nerve fibers (axons)

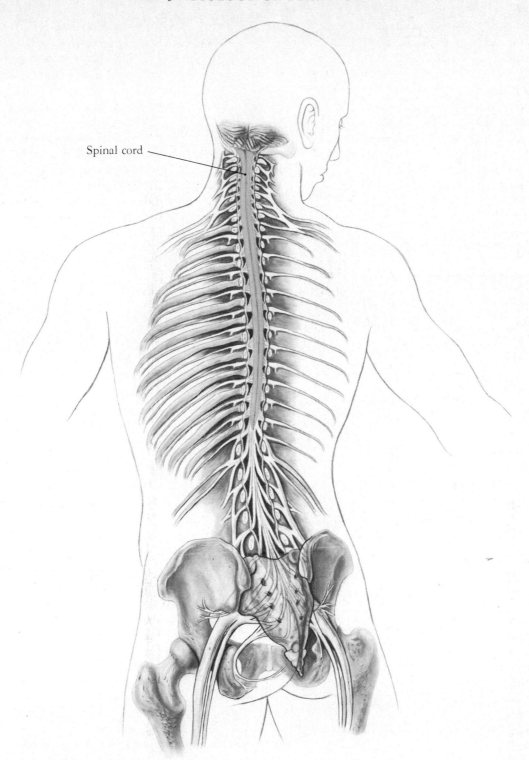

Spinal cord

FIGURE 3.9   The spinal cord and spinal nerves.
(Adapted from Carlson, N.R. *Physiology of Behavior*,
2nd ed. Boston: Allyn and Bacon, 1981.)

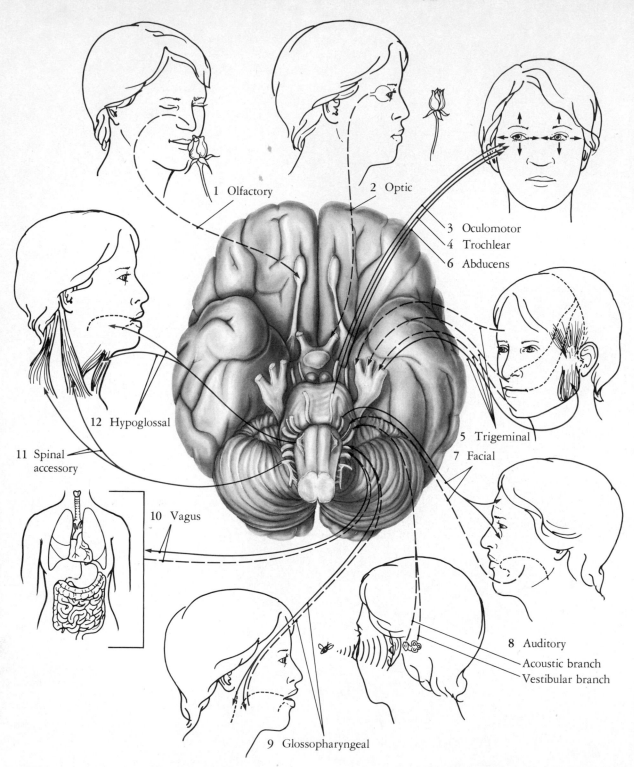

1 Olfactory

2 Optic

3 Oculomotor
4 Trochlear
6 Abducens

5 Trigeminal

7 Facial

12 Hypoglossal

11 Spinal
accessory

10 Vagus

8 Auditory
Acoustic branch
Vestibular branch

9 Glossopharyngeal

FIGURE 3.10   The cranial nerves and their
functions. Solid lines indicate motor functions; dashed
lines indicate sensory functions. (Redrawn from
Carlson, N.R. *Physiology of Behavior*. 2nd ed. Boston:
Allyn and Bacon, 1981.)

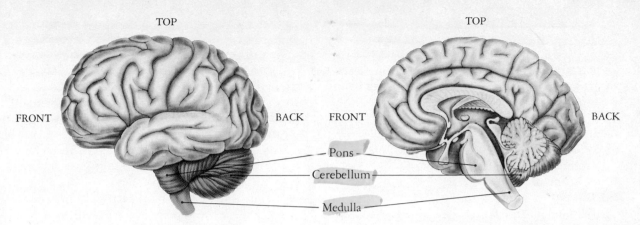

FIGURE 3.11   Side views of the human brain: intact (left) and sliced through the middle from front to back (right). The cerebral hemispheres are shown in gray.

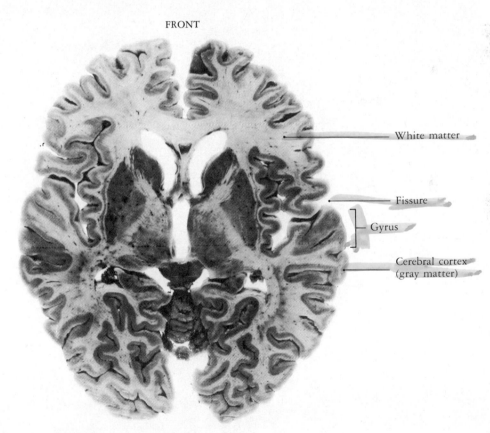

FIGURE 3.12   A photograph of a slice of a human brain. Note the fissures and gyri, and the layer of cerebral cortex that follows these convolutions. (Adapted from DeArmond, S.J., Fusco, M.M. and Dewey, M.M. *Structure of the Human Brain: A Photographic Atlas*, 2nd ed. New York: Oxford University Press, 1976.)

notes

The human cerebral cortex is very wrinkled; it is full of bulges (*gyri*) separated by grooves. These grooves (called *sulci* if they are small and *fissures* if they are large and deep) increase the amount of area the cortex occupies. If the surface of the brain were smooth (as it is in most other animals), the total area of the cerebral cortex would be much smaller. **Figure 3.12** on the preceding page shows a slice through the cerebral hemispheres; note how the cerebral cortex follows the grooves.

Thalamus

All sensory information (except for olfaction, the sense of smell) is sent to the *thalamus* before it reaches the cerebral cortex. The thalamus is a part of the *subcortical area* of the cerebral hemispheres. If you stripped away the cerebral cortex, you would find a layer of nerve fibers that connect the cortex with the rest of the brain. These fibers are referred to as *white matter,* because of the shiny white appearance of the substance that coats and insulates them. If you then stripped away the white matter you would reach the heart of the cerebral hemispheres—the subcortical area. The thalamus is part of this region.

Almost all parts of the brain come in pairs: a left portion and a right portion, one in each hemisphere. Thus the thalamus has two parts, one in each side of the brain. Each part looks rather like a football, with the long axis oriented from front to back. (See **Figure 3.13**.) Nerve fibers from the various sensory systems enter the thalamus from below, and other sets of fibers exit from the top and travel to specific regions of the cerebral cortex.

FIGURE 3.13   The thalamus.

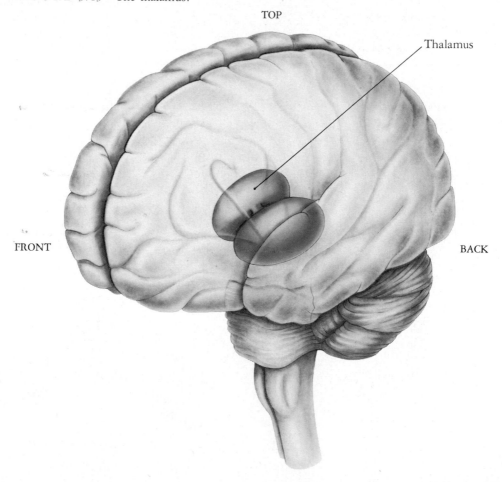

TOP

Thalamus

FRONT

BACK

The thalamus has been referred to as the "relay station" of the brain because it passes information from the sensory systems along to the cerebral cortex.

Sensory Areas of the Cerebral Cortex

◆ We become aware of events in our environment by means of five major *sensory modalities:* vision, audition, olfaction, gustation (taste), and the somatosenses (touch, pain, temperature). A sixth, the vestibular system (pertaining to balance), does not provide us with conscious sensations of environmental events; we use the information from this system for orientation and control of posture, becoming aware of its activity only when it makes us feel dizzy or nauseated. (*Modality* literally means "measure," or "method"; in this case it refers to a particular kind of stimulus that we can perceive.)

The three *primary sensory areas* of the cerebral cortex receive sensory information that is relayed from the thalamus. (See **Figure 3.14**.) The *primary visual cortex,* which receives visual information, is located at the back of the brain, mostly hidden from view on the inner surfaces of the cere-

bral hemispheres. The *primary auditory cortex* is also mostly hidden from view on the surface of a deep groove called the *lateral fissure.* The *primary somatosensory cortex,* located just behind the *central fissure,* receives information from the body senses: touch, pain, and temperature. (*Soma* means "body.")

Interim summary: An example will summarize what I have written so far. Suppose you see a rose, and then pick it and smell it. You see it because light reflected from it stimulates sensory receptors in the retinas of your eyes. The stimulation is transmitted through nerve fibers contained in the *optic nerves,* one of the pairs of cranial nerves. These fibers travel to the thalamus, where information is passed to a new set of fibers that travel to primary visual cortex at the back of your brain.

When you pick the rose you feel the stem and perhaps get pricked by a thorn. The pressure of the stem on your skin and the small injury caused by the thorn stimulate touch and pain receptors within your skin. The sensory information is transmitted to the spinal cord by means of a spinal

FIGURE 3.14   Primary sensory and motor areas of the human brain. (Adapted from Carlson, N.R.

Physiology of Behavior, 2nd ed. Boston: Allyn and Bacon, 1981.)

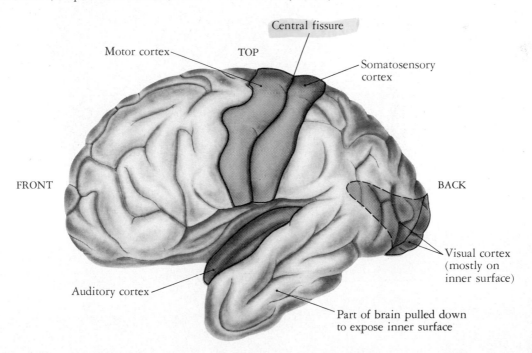

nerve. It is then sent up through the spinal cord to the thalamus, and then relayed to primary somatosensory cortex, just behind the central fissure.

When you sniff the odor of the rose, the aromatic molecules stimulate olfactory receptors embedded in the ceiling of your nasal cavity. The information is then transmitted to the brain through the **olfactory nerves,** one of the pairs of cranial nerves. Olfactory information (smell) does not get relayed through the thalamus. Instead, it is transmitted to various subcortical structures and directly to the cerebral cortex.

Of course, when you experience the sight, feel, and odor of a rose you perceive it as a single object; these separate sensory experiences are united. This unity is provided by connections between the regions of the cerebral cortex that analyze the individual sensory components.

MOTOR OUTPUT FROM THE BRAIN

As I mentioned earlier, the brain is the organ that controls behavior; that is, it moves the muscles. Muscular movement is referred to as **motor activity.** (The word *motor* is used in its original sense, referring to movement, not mechanical engines.) Many different motor systems control our behavior. The movement of the eyes, the hands and fingers, the arms and legs, the trunk, and the muscles used for speech all appear to have separate control

FIGURE 3.15   The basal ganglia. (Adapted from Carlson, N.R. *Physiology of Behavior,* 2nd ed. Boston: Allyn and Bacon, 1981.)

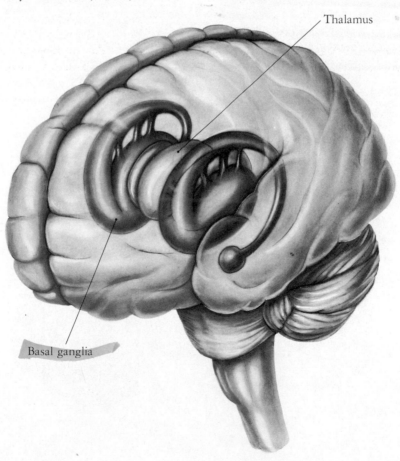

Thalamus

Basal ganglia

mechanisms (which interact and cooperate with each other, of course).

◆ Control of hand and finger movements is most highly developed in primates and in a few other mammals, such as the raccoon. The principal area that controls these movements is the *primary motor cortex,* that part of the cerebral cortex located just in front of the central fissure (and immediately adjacent to the primary somatosensory cortex; look back at **Figure 3.14.**) Commands to move the hands and fingers are initiated elsewhere in the cerebral cortex. These commands produce activity in nerve cells within the primary motor cortex and are transmitted through nerve fibers that travel down through the subcortical areas to the spinal cord. There, information is transmitted out through spinal nerves to the muscles that perform the movements.

The control of other types of movements, such as postural adjustments and larger movements of the arms and legs, involves a set of subcortical structures called the *basal ganglia.* These structures are located deep within the brain, beneath the cortex and underlying white matter, and just in front of the thalamus. (See **Figure 3.15.**) Like the thalamus, they are two-sided structures, one portion in each cerebral hemisphere.

Postural movements and movements of the arms and legs are initiated by activity in various regions of the brain that stimulate nerve cells in the basal ganglia. The pathway from these structures down to the spinal cord is very complicated, involving at least a dozen separate regions of the brain (including several parts of the thalamus) along with their interconnections. Eventually nerve cells in the spinal cord are stimulated and messages are sent through spinal nerves to the appropriate muscles.

One structure deserves special mention with respect to motor activity: the *cerebellum* ("little brain"). The cerebellum is well named; Figure 3.16 shows you that the cerebellum indeed looks like a miniature brain, nestled beneath the overhanging back part of the cerebral hemispheres. (See **Figure 3.16.**) The cerebellum receives information from the various motor systems of the brain and provides an important degree of coordination among them. It smooths out movements, especially those that involve rapid changes in direction. It monitors in-

FIGURE 3.16 The cerebellum.

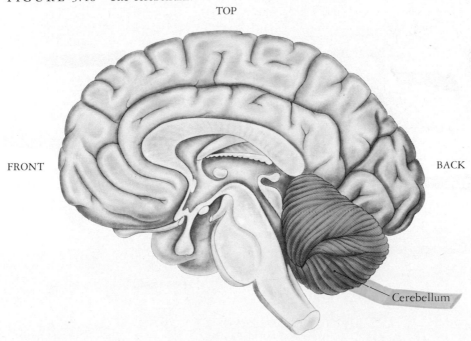

TOP

FRONT

BACK

Cerebellum

formation from the vestibular system (concerned with balance) and keeps us from falling down when we stand or walk. It also plays a large role in the control of eye movements.

Many neurological disorders can affect the motor systems of the brain. One of them, *Parkinson's disease,* is caused by the death of a particular set of nerve cells, which control the general activity of the basal ganglia. People with Parkinson's disease have difficulty initiating movements, and when they walk they do so with an awkward, shuffling gait. Their arms and hands shake, especially when they are at rest. If you hold their arm and try to bend their elbow or wrist, you will find it difficult to do so; all of their arm muscles are contracted, producing a degree of rigidity. When these people talk, their voice lacks force, so the listener has to strain to hear them.

The symptoms of Parkinson's disease tell us something about the role played by the basal gan-

glia and allow us to make inferences about the way the brain carries out its tasks. Obviously, the basal ganglia are involved in walking and maintenance of normal posture, control of the arms and hands, and control of at least some of the muscles that support speech. Fortunately there is a drug that greatly alleviates the symptoms of Parkinson's disease; later in this chapter I will describe how this drug works.

ASSOCIATION AREAS OF THE CORTEX

Primary sensory and motor cortex are only a small fraction of the total area of the cerebral cortex. The rest of the cerebral cortex accomplishes what is done between sensation and action: perception, concept formation, memory, planning, and all the rest. These processes take place in the *association areas* of the cerebral cortex. (The term comes from early theories of brain function that assumed that

FIGURE 3.17   The four lobes of the cerebral cortex. (Adapted from Carlson, N.R. *Physiology of Behavior,* 2nd ed. Boston: Allyn and Bacon, 1981.)

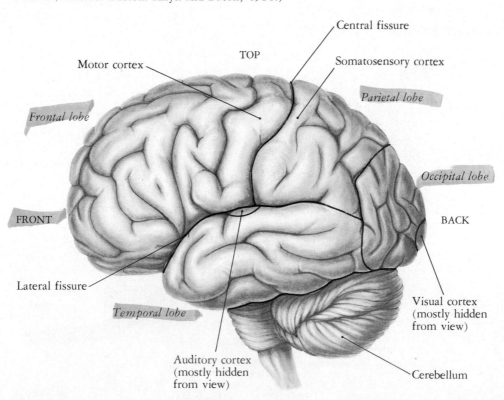

elements of perception and movement were linked together—associated—here.) To understand these processes better, we must examine the anatomy and functions of other subdivisions of the cerebral cortex.

The central fissure provides an important dividing line between the frontal area of the brain and the posterior regions. You may have noted that all the primary sensory areas lie behind the central fissure, and the primary motor area lies in front of it. The remaining areas of these two regions of the cortex perform similar functions. The frontal cortex is involved with movement-related activities, such as planning and initiation of behavior. The posterior cortex is important for sensation and perception, concept formation, and storage of most memories.

A more specific division of the cerebral cortex will help us to identify its parts. The cerebral cortex is divided into four areas, or *lobes,* named for the bones of the skull that cover them: the *frontal lobe, parietal lobe, temporal lobe,* and *occipital lobe.* (See **Figure 3.17.**) The frontal lobe includes

everything in front of the central fissure except the tip of the temporal lobe, which projects forward beneath the central fissure. The parietal lobe lies behind the central fissure, above the lateral fissure. The temporal lobe lies beneath the lateral fissure. The occipital lobe lies at the very back of the brain, behind the parietal and temporal lobes. Thus, the motor cortex is in the frontal lobe, the somatosensory cortex is in the parietal lobe, the auditory cortex is in the temporal lobe, and the visual cortex is in the occipital lobe.

Sensory Association Areas

Each primary sensory area of the cortex sends information to adjacent areas of *sensory association cortex.* (See **Figure 3.18.**) For example, the primary visual cortex, mostly hidden in the inner surfaces of the cerebral hemispheres, sends information to the *visual association cortex.* Similarly, the primary auditory cortex sends information to the *auditory association cortex,* and the primary somatosensory cortex sends information the *somatosensory association cortex.*

FIGURE 3.18 The primary sensory areas of the cortex communicate with association areas.

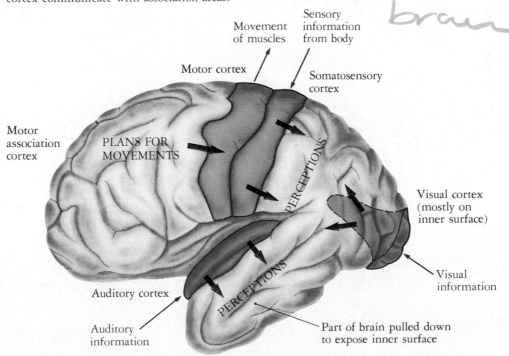

Visual, somatosensory, and auditory association cortex perform perceptual analyses of the information they receive from the relevant primary sensory cortex and probably also play a role in storing memories related to them. These areas can be conceived of as secondary sensory regions.

◆ Secondary sensory regions of cortex are primarily *unimodal* in nature—that is, they receive information from only one sensory modality. Other areas of the association cortex, residing at the junctions of the posterior lobes of the brain, are *polymodal*—they receive information from more than one sensory modality. These tertiary areas of sensory cortex include the border between the parietal and occipital cortex, the temporal and occipital cortex, and the region where all three posterior lobes converge. (See **Figure 3.17.**)

The polymodal association cortex performs higher-order analyses of sensory information and represents abstract information in ways that are independent of the individual sensory modalities. For example, you can think of a tree as a visual image of a particular tree, you can imagine how the bark of various trees feels, you can imagine the sound of wind rustling some leaves, or you can think about the wood products that can be made from lumber. You can also think about the sound of the word *tree,* an abstract line drawing that might represent it, or the visual appearance of the letters TREE. The various thoughts and associations can be started by the sight of an actual tree, by the sound of the word, or by the printed words you have just read.

I will say more about the functions of the sensory association cortex when I describe the disorders that are caused by damage to the various lobes of the brain.

Motor Association Areas

◆ Just as regions of the posterior association cortex are related to sensory images and memories, the frontal association cortex is involved in the planning and execution of movements. Some regions have rather specific functions, such as the *frontal eye fields,* which control voluntary eye movements, and *Broca's speech area,* which is necessary for the production of proper speech. (See **Figure 3.19.**) The rest of the frontal cortex receives information

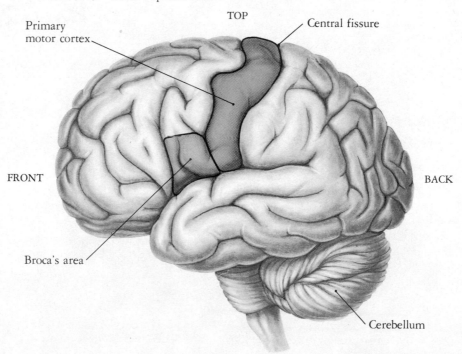

FIGURE 3.19   Broca's speech area.

Primary motor cortex

TOP

Central fissure

FRONT

BACK

Broca's area

Cerebellum

from the sensory association areas in the posterior part of the brain and integrates this information into plans of action.

Interim summary: In an earlier example I outlined the neural events that accompanied your perception of a rose. Now we can consider the neural events that cause your muscles to move so that you can pick it and smell it. Your perception of a rose causes you to remember how beautiful one looks in a vase on your desk. Retrieval of this memory (probably located in visual association areas in your occipital and temporal lobes) causes messages to be sent to the motor association cortex in your frontal lobes. There, plans are made to pick the rose. Impulses are sent to your primary motor cortex, and from there to the motor systems in your basal ganglia that control your walking up to the rose bush.

As you walk, your balance is maintained by mechanisms that involve your basal ganglia and cerebellum. Next, activity of your motor association cortex excites nerve cells in the arm and hand regions of your primary motor cortex, moving the muscles of your arm and hand so that you pick the rose and bring it up to your nose. The accuracy of this reaching and grasping movement is controlled by your cerebellum. Finally, your motor association cortex stimulates circuits that control respiration, so that you sniff air that contains the scent of the flower.

IMPORTANT SUBCORTICAL STRUCTURES

So far I have described four important regions of the brain: the cerebral cortex, thalamus, basal gan-

FIGURE 3.20 The hypothalamus and the pituitary gland. (Adapted from Carlson, N.R.

Physiology of Behavior, 2nd ed. Boston: Allyn and Bacon, 1981.)

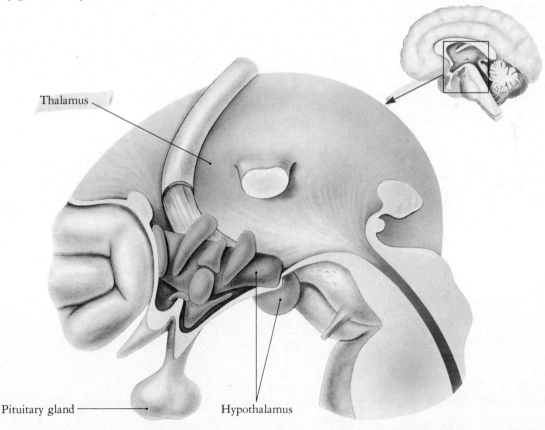

Thalamus

Pituitary gland

Hypothalamus

glia, and cerebellum. Three other brain structures, located subcortically, are important enough to warrant attention here.

Hypothalamus

Hypo- means "less than" or "beneath," and as its name suggests, the **hypothalamus** is located below the thalamus, at the base of the brain. (See **Figure** 3.20 on the preceding page.) The hypothalamus is a small region, consisting of less than one cubic centimeter of tissue. Its relative importance far exceeds its size.

The hypothalamus participates in two major functions: **homeostasis** and control of **species-typical behaviors.** *Homeostasis* (from the root words *homoio,* "similar," and *stasis,* "standstill") refers to

TABLE 3.1   The major endocrine glands, the hormones they secrete, and their principal functions

Gland	Hormone	Function
Adrenal gland		
Cortex	Aldosterone	Excretion of sodium and potassium
	Androgens	Growth of pubic and underarm hair; sex drive (women)
	Cortisol	Metabolism, response to stress
Medulla	Epinephrine, norepinephrine	Metabolism, response to stress
Hypothalamus[a]	Releasing hormones	Control of anterior pituitary hormone secretion
Kidneys	Renin	Control of aldosterone secretion; blood pressure
Ovaries	Estradiol	Maturation of female reproductive system; secondary sex characteristics
	Progesterone	Maintenancy of lining of uterus; promotion of pregnancy
Pancreas	Insulin, glucagon	Regulation of metabolism
Pituitary		
Anterior	Adrenocorticotrophic hormone	Control of adrenal cortex
	Gonadotrophic hormones	Control of testes and ovaries
	Growth hormone	Growth; control of metabolism
	Prolactin	Milk production
	Thyroid-stimulating hormone	Control of thyroid gland
Posterior	Antidiuretic hormone[b]	Excretion of water
	Oxytocin[b]	Release of milk
Testes	Testosterone	Maturation of male reproductive system; sperm production; secondary sex characteristics; sex drive (men)
Thyroid	Thyroxine	Energy metabolism; growth and development

[a]The hypothalamus, although it is part of the brain, secretes hormones; thus it can be considered to be an endocrine gland.

[b]These hormones are produced by the hypothalamus but are transported to and released from the posterior pituitary gland.

the maintenance of a proper balance of physiological variables such as temperature, concentration of fluids, and amount of nutrients stored. Species-typical behaviors are the behaviors exhibited by most members of a species that are important to survival, such as eating, drinking, fighting, sexual behavior, and care of offspring.

The hypothalamus receives information from the sensory modalities, especially from somatosensory receptors inside the body; thus, it is informed about changes in the organism's physiological status. It also contains specialized sensors that monitor various characteristics of the blood that flows through the brain, such as temperature, nutrient content, and amount of dissolved salts. In turn, the hypothalamus controls the *pituitary gland,* which is located on the end of a stalk attached directly to the base of the hypothalamus. (See **Figure 3.20.**)

The pituitary gland has been called the "master gland" because it controls the activity of the rest

of the *endocrine glands,* which secrete hormones. Thus, by controlling the pituitary gland the hypothalamus exerts control over the entire endocrine system. Some of these hormones have important effects on behavior and will be discussed later (in Chapters 7 and 14). **Table 3.1** lists of some of the endocrine glands and the functions they regulate.

The hypothalamus also controls much of the activity of the *autonomic nervous system.* This division of the peripheral nervous system consists of nerves that control motor functions other than those performed by the skeletal muscles, such as sweating, crying, salivation, secretion of digestive juices, changes in the size of blood vessels (which causes changes in blood pressure), and secretion of some hormones. The autonomic nervous system has two branches, the **sympathetic** and the **parasympathetic.** The sympathetic branch directs activities that involve the expenditure of energy, whereas the parasympathetic branch controls quiet activities. Psy-

TABLE 3.2 Major functions of the autonomic nervous system

ORGAN	EFFECT OF ACTIVITY OF AUTONOMIC NERVE FIBERS	
	Sympathetic	Parasympathetic
Adrenal medulla	Secretion of epinephrine and norepinephrine	
Bladder	Inhibition of contraction	Contraction
Blood vessels		
Abdomen	Construction	
Muscles	Dilation	Constriction
Skin	Constriction or dilation	Dilation
Heart	Faster rate of contraction	Slower rate of contraction
Intestines	Decreased activity	Increased activity
Lacrimal glands	Secretion of tears	
Liver	Release of glucose	
Lungs	Dilation of bronchi	Constriction of bronchi
Penis	Ejaculation	Erection
Pupil of eye	Dilation	Constriction
Salivary glands	Secretion of thick, viscous saliva	Secretion of thin, enzyme-rich saliva
Sweat glands	Secretion of sweat	
Vagina	Orgasm	Secretion of lubricating fluid

chophysiologists monitor many of the responses of the autonomic nervous system, and in so doing can measure its activity and its relation to psychological phenomena like emotions. (See **Table 3.2.**)

The homeostatic functions of the hypothalamus can involve either nonbehavioral physiological changes or overt behaviors. Nonbehavioral changes include regulation of temperature by sweating or increasing metabolic rate. Overt behaviors include putting on or taking off a coat, turning the thermostat up or down, and adding another log to the fire.

Damage to an animal's hypothalamus disrupts a variety of homeostatic activities. These might include impaired regulation of body temperature, changes in food intake, sterility, or stunting of growth. Obviously, the hypothalamus is a very important structure.

The hypothalamus exerts a great deal of control over *species-typical behaviors*. Physiological psychologists often refer to them as the *four Fs:* feeding, fighting, fleeing, and mating. However, this classification omits other species-typical behaviors that are controlled by the hypothalamus: drinking, nest-building, care of offspring, and various behaviors that conserve body heat.

Pons

◆ The *pons* is a large bulge in the brain stem, below the point at which it attaches to the cerebral hemispheres. *Pons* means "bridge"; it received its name from the prominent bundles of nerve fibers that pass through it. (See **Figure 3.21.**) The pons contains circuits of nerve cells with functions related to sleeping and alertness, attention, and movement. These play an especially important role in the organization of species-typical behaviors.

Our degree of arousal (alertness) varies greatly

FIGURE 3.21   The pons, showing the reticular formation and periaqueductal gray matter.

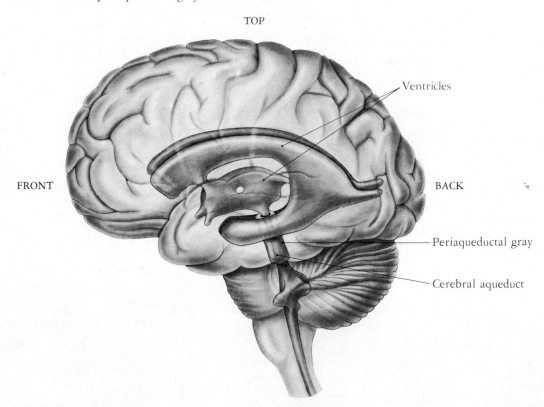

TOP

FRONT

BACK

Ventricles

Periaqueductal gray

Cerebral aqueduct

during the day. At times we are attentive, while at other times we are very relaxed and out of touch with what is going on in the environment. Control of arousal is an important function of the *reticular formation,* a tangle of nerve cells and fibers located in the depths of the pons. (*Reticulum* means "net," and refers to this tangle.) When an electrical current is passed through a wire that has been inserted into parts of the reticular formation, an animal becomes alert and attentive. The reticular formation sends nerve fibers to the thalamus and to the cerebral cortex. When it is stimulated, it sends messages through these fibers that activate nerve cells in the cortex, making them more responsive to sensory information. Presumably, the artificial electrical stimulation mimics the effects of natural stimuli (like sudden, loud noises) that also cause arousal.

The pons also contains circuits of nerve cells that control the complex movements that constitute species-typical behaviors. Although the hypothalamus plays a major role in determining *when* an animal fights, feeds, flees, or performs other species-typical behaviors, this structure does not control the patterns of muscular movements that produce these behaviors. Instead, parts of the pons appear to be the most important brain regions for programming these movements. Damage to the pons disrupts or abolishes species-typical behaviors, and, conversely, direct electrical stimulation will produce them.

Control of species-typical behavior patterns is shared by portions of the reticular formation and another part of the pons, the *periaqueductal gray matter.* When people refer to "gray matter" they usually mean the cerebral cortex. However, there are other regions of gray matter, located subcortically. One of the most important of these areas is the periaqueductal gray matter. (See **Figure 3.21.**) The pons contains a tube called the *cerebral aqueduct,* which interconnects two of the brain's ventricles. (An aqueduct is a channel that carries a supply of water—in this case it carries cerebrospinal fluid.) Thus, the mass of neurons surrounding this aqueduct are periaqueductal (*peri* means "surrounding").

Besides being involved in species-typical behaviors, the periaqueductal gray matter controls an animal's tolerance to pain. Since this function is related to the role of opiates, it will be discussed later.

Medulla

◆ The *medulla* ("marrow") is the lowest part of the brain, located just above the spinal cord. (See **Figure 3.22.**) The medulla is vital for life; a very small lesion located in a critical region of this structure will cause immediate death.

The medulla controls the so-called *vital functions:* heart rate, blood pressure, and respiration. The control mechanisms for these functions are contained in the reticular formation of the medulla (an extension of the reticular formation of the pons). The medulla also plays an important role in other physiological activities, such as vomiting, coughing, and sneezing. The medulla receives sensory information directly from receptors within the body and exerts its effects through nerve fibers that travel out through the cranial and spinal nerves. In addition, the medulla receives information from the hypothalamus, which exerts some of its control over the autonomic nervous system by influencing the activity of this structure.

In addition to these functions, the medulla participates in the control of sleep. This interesting behavior will be described in Chapter 10.

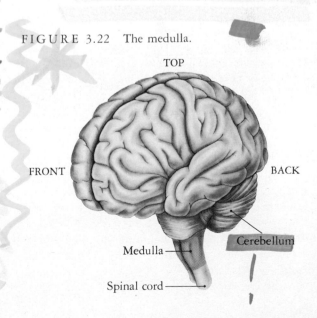

FIGURE 3.22   The medulla.

TOP

FRONT

BACK

Cerebellum

Medulla

Spinal cord

Interim summary: We return to our example of the rose one last time. In addition to the sensory and motor activity you consciously initiate in your desire to hold and to smell the flower, there are many functions being controlled by your brain that you are not aware of. The day is hot and sunny, so your hypothalamus, which contains temperature receptors and also receives information from temperature receptors in your skin, causes you to sweat, and hence keeps your body from overheating. Messages received from your optic nerves activate neurons within your pons that constrict your pupils and also make you squint against the bright light. As you bend to pick the rose, the lowering of your head causes a sudden rise in blood pressure there, which is detected by receptors in your blood vessels. Information from them is sent through a cranial nerve to your medulla, which sends a message to your heart, slowing it, and to blood vessels, relaxing muscles in their walls so that the blood pressure in your head will not get dangerously high. As you stand and raise your head again after picking the rose, the process is reversed, so that your brain continues to receive its share of the flow of blood.

As you can see, this seemingly simple act involves very complex neural activity.

COMPLEX FUNCTIONS OF THE CEREBRAL CORTEX

◆ As we saw earlier, the central fissure divides the brain in two regions, a front part (frontal lobe) and a back part (parietal, occipital, and temporal lobes). The regions in front of the central fissure are concerned with motor functions, the regions behind it with sensory functions. This section describes the types of deficits that are produced by damage to particular areas of the human cerebral cortex, and the inferences that have been made about their functions. As we saw earlier, much of what we know about the functions of the human brain came from observations of the behavior of people whose brains were damaged; the missing functions are presumably what the damaged parts previously did. Now I shall describe some of these observations, and the conclusions derived from them.

LATERALIZATION OF FUNCTION

Although the two cerebral hemispheres cooperate with each other, they do not perform idential functions. Some functions are *lateralized*—located primarily in one side of the brain. In general, the left hemisphere plays a role in verbal functions and in the *analysis* of information—the extraction of the elements that make up the whole of an experience. This ability makes the left hemisphere particularly good at recognizing serially ordered events—that is, events whose elements occur one at a time. In contrast, the right hemisphere is specialized for *synthesis;* it is particularly good at putting isolated elements together to perceive things as a whole.

In almost all people the left hemisphere is specialized for speech, but in some, especially those who are left-handed or ambidextrous (equally agile with their left or right hand), the *right* hemisphere performs this role. Thus, my descriptions of the functions of the left and right hemispheres should be reversed for these people.

OCCIPITAL LOBE

◆ The primary business of the occipital lobe is seeing. (See **Figure 3.23.**)

Damage to the primary visual cortex produces blindness, and a small lesion in the primary visual cortex produces a "hole" in the field of vision. However, a person with such a lesion can move his or her eyes around and eventually see everything in the environment. In contrast, damage to the visual association cortex (which includes parts of the parietal and temporal lobes as well as the occipital lobe) does not damage the primary sensory function; no blindness results. However, such damage will impair the ability to recognize objects by sight. This deficit is called *visual agnosia* (*a-*, "without"; *gnōsis*, "knowledge").

As I mentioned earlier, the left hemisphere is specialized for perception of fine details. Damage to the visual association cortex of the left hemisphere produces deficits in the ability to recognize details of a visual scene: angles, curves, and line segments. It also produces severe deficits in the ability to read. On the other hand, damage to the visual association cortex of the right hemisphere

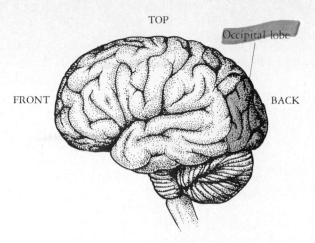

FIGURE 3.23 The occipital lobe.

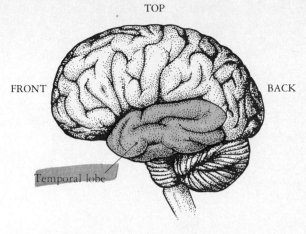

FIGURE 3.24 The temporal lobe.

produces deficits in visual recognition of familiar objects; the person might be able to walk around without bumping into things and to point to objects that an experimenter holds up, but be unable to name the objects or identify their functions.

TEMPORAL LOBE

The principal sensory function of the temporal lobe is hearing, but this lobe is also involved in vision, memory, and variables related to personality and social behavior. (See **Figure 3.24.**)

Auditory and Speech Functions

Damage to the temporal lobe results in a variety of symptoms, depending on which region is destroyed and which lobe (left or right) is affected. The primary auditory cortex is located on the inner surface of the temporal lobe. The auditory association cortex is located on the sides of the temporal lobes, back toward the occipital lobes. One of the most important language areas of the brain is a region of the auditory association cortex on the left side of the brain called *Wernicke's area*. (See **Figure 3.25.**) This region, named after its discoverer, is necessary for the identification of spoken words.

Damage to Wernicke's area results in *Wernicke's aphasia*. This term is not really accurate, since *asphasia* means "without speech," and most people with Wernicke's aphasia can utter words.

However, it is difficult for them to comprehend speech, although they almost always understand the meaning of nonspeech sounds. For example, they recognize the ringing of a telephone and will move out of the way when they hear the honking of a horn.

In a few very rare cases, patients can lose the ability to understand speech but can produce meaningful speech by themselves. I once met a patient with temporal lobe damage who had excellent hearing and could recognize sounds such as the jingling of keys or the snapping of fingers. However, he could not understand one word that was spoken to him. His own speech was excellent, and he could read and answer questions that were put to him in writing. This syndrome is called *pure word-deafness.*

Much more commonly, people with Wernicke's aphasia are unable to read or to produce meaningful speech. Here is a sample of the speech of a person with Wernicke's aphasia:

EXAMINER: What kind of work did you do before you came into the hospital?

PATIENT: Never, now mista oyge I wanna tell you this happened when happened when he rent. His— his kell come down here and is—he got ren something. It happened. In thesse ropiers were with him for hi—is friend—like was. And it just happened so I don't know, he did not bring around anything. And he did not pay it. And he roden all o these

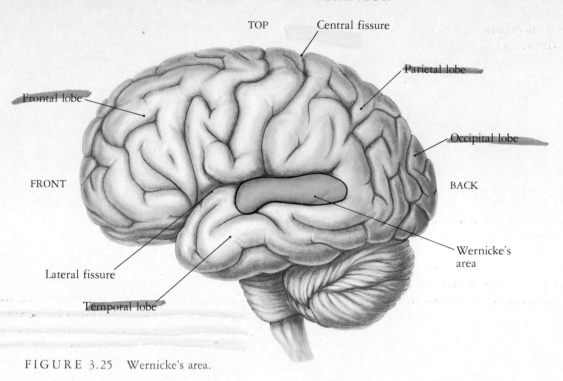

FIGURE 3.25   Wernicke's area.

arranjen from the pedis on from iss pescid. In these floors now and so. He hadn't had em round here.

(Kertesz, 1981, p. 73)

Damage to the auditory association cortex in the right hemisphere does not seriously affect speech perception or production, but it does affect the ability to recognize patterns of tones and rhythms. This deficit is called *amusia,* because of the inability to comprehend music. Damage to the right auditory association cortex can also impair the ability to judge the location of sounds in the environment. As we shall see, the right hemisphere is very important in perception of space. The contribution of the right temporal lobe to this function is to participate in perceiving the placement of sounds.

Memory

Bilateral damage to the temporal lobes (that is, damage to both sides) usually results in severe loss of memory. In some cases, the patient has a relatively good memory for events that occurred before the injury but becomes almost totally incapable of learning anything new. This important syndrome is discussed in much more detail in Chapter 11.

Damage that is restricted to one temporal lobe usually produces only mild memory deficits. Damage in the left temporal lobe produces deficits in memory for verbal information, while right temporal lobe damage produces deficits in memory for pictures and other nonverbal information.

Social Behavior

Damage to various portions of the temporal lobes can affect social behavior and emotional reactions. For example, a person with damage to a temporal lobe (especially the right) very often becomes a compulsive talker who harangues any available listener, even if the listener shows no sign of interest in what is being said. This fact suggests that the right temporal lobe normally plays a role in evaluating the appropriateness of thoughts and speech. People with abnormally functioning temporal lobes are often very egocentric, suspicious, and preoccupied with religious issues.

Sexual behavior also appears to be at least partly under the control of the temporal lobes. A particular kind of epilepsy is caused by abnormal activity of neurons in the temporal lobe. Patients who have this form of epilepsy occasionally show unusual sexual behavior, including fetishism (attachment to unusual sexual objects) and sexual attraction to young children. If a portion of the defective temporal lobe is removed, the abnormal sexual behavior usually disappears. In other cases of temporal lobe epilepsy, the reverse is seen; people show a *lack* of interest in sexual activity. Surgery usually causes an increase in sexual interest.

PARIETAL LOBE

◆ The principal sensory function of the parietal lobe is somatosensory perception, but this part of the brain does much more than mediate our awareness of what is happening in the body and on its surface. The functions of the parietal lobe overlap with those of the occipital and temporal lobes. Thus, the back and lower parts of the parietal lobe are concerned with visually and acoustically related functions. In addition, the parietal lobe is very important in our perception of space and our awareness of the location of our own bodies in space. (See **Figure 3.26.**)

◆ Damage to the left parietal lobe (and its junction with the temporal and occipital lobes) can result in a variety of disorders, including loss of the ability to read (*alexia*) or write (*agraphia*).

Damage restricted to the parietal lobe usually impairs a person's ability to draw. When the left hemisphere is damaged, the primary deficit seems to be in construction; the person has trouble making his or her hand go where it should. In contrast,

FIGURE 3.26   The parietal lobe.

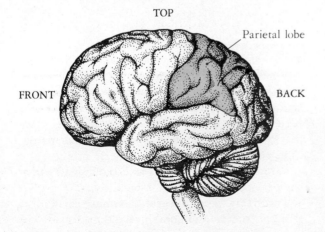

TOP

Parietal lobe

FRONT   BACK

the primary deficit produced by damage to the right parietal lobe is perceptual; the person can analyze the picture into its constituent parts but has trouble integrating these parts into a consistent whole.

Figure 3.27 shows two drawings of a bicycle by patients who both had suffered damage to one parietal lobe. The drawing on the left, by a person with left parietal damage, is in relatively good proportion, but the details are very sketchy. It is clumsily drawn, as if it were drawn by a young child. (See **Figure 3.27, left.**) In contrast, the drawing by the patient with right parietal damage is smoothly executed and shows good detail, but the parts are not all placed appropriately. (See **Figure 3.27, right.**) There is another peculiarity that is shown in the right-hand drawing. Look at the drawing again to see whether you notice it.

The patient with right parietal lobe damage showed another common symptom: *sensory neglect.* He did not attempt to draw the spokes in the left part of the wheels. People with damage to the right parietal lobe tend not to notice objects that are located toward their left, and neglect the left side of objects that they are attending to. For example, a person who is given a pancake for breakfast may eat only the right half. The spokes are missing from the drawing of the bicycle because the patient was not even aware of the existence of the left sides of the wheels. Figure 3.28 shows this phenomenon even more graphically; this picture of a clock was drawn by a person who had sustained damage to the right parietal lobe. (See **Figure 3.28.**)

Sometimes people with damage to the right parietal lobe even fail to be aware of the left side of their own body. For example, a person might dress only one half of the body, putting a shirt or coat on only the right arm. If someone calls their attention to their left arm, they will see it and recognize it, but might say that it belongs to someone else. A man might shave only the right side of his face.

Severe bilateral parietal lobe damage leads to *apraxia*—loss of the ability to produce particular movements on command. For example, a person might be unable to draw a picture, demonstrate how to make conventional gestures (such as saluting, waving a hand, blowing a kiss), or use a common tool. Most neurologists and neuropsychologists believe the left parietal lobe plays an

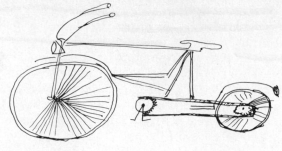

FIGURE 3.27   Drawings of a bicycle by patients with damage to the left hemisphere (left) and the right hemisphere (right). (From Lezak, M.D.

Neuropsychological Assessment. New York: Oxford University Press, 1976.)

important role in our ability to keep track of the location of the moving parts of our body, whereas the right parietal lobe helps us keep track of the space around us. Obviously, damage to both regions would be expected to produce severe difficulty in moving parts of our body through space.

People with parietal lobe damage usually have difficulty at performing arithmetic calculations. This deficit, called *acalculia,* is probably related to other spatially related functions of the parietal lobe. Try to multiply 55 by 12 without using pencil and paper. Close your eyes and work on the problem for a while. Try to analyze how you did it.

* * *

Most people report that they try to imagine the numbers arranged one above the other as they would

FIGURE 3.28   Drawing of a clock by a patient with damage to the right parietal lobe. (From Kaplan, E. and Velis, D.C. *The Neuropsychology of 10 after 11,* paper presented at the International Neuropsycholotical Society Annual Meeting, 1983.)

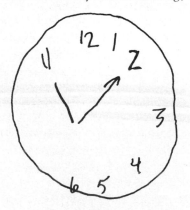

be if paper and pencil were being used. In other words, they "write" the problem out mentally. Apparently, damage to the parietal lobes makes it impossible for people to keep the numbers straight.

Another problem that is commonly encountered in people who have sustained parietal lobe damage is difficulty in answering questions such as "What do you call the son of your mother's sister?" Think about the question, and how you go about answering it. Do you automatically name the relationship, or do you have to "picture" something in your head? What do you think this has to do with spatially related functions?

* * *

Perhaps you pictured part of a "genealogical tree," with your mother above you, her sister to the side, and her son below her. He, of course, would be your cousin. We cannot be sure that everyone follows this strategy, but we do know that parietal lobe damage impairs the kind of reasoning that is necessary for answering questions about the names of family relationships.

FRONTAL LOBE

The principal function of the frontal lobe is motor; primary motor cortex is located in the back of the frontal lobe, just ahead of the central fissure. (See **Figure 3.29.**) However, the frontal lobe does much more. Its functions seem to be related to planning, changing strategies, self-awareness, attention to emotionally related stimuli, and spontaneity of behavior.

For many years, neurologists and anatomists thought the frontal lobes were the "seat of the

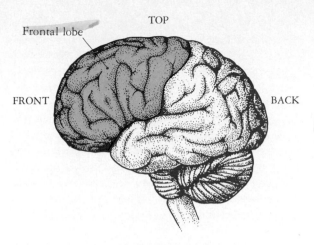

FIGURE 3.29   The frontal lobe.

human intellect." After all, they are by far the largest lobes of the cerebral cortex, and they are proportionately larger in humans than in any other species. Since we regard ourselves as the most intelligent species of animal, the conclusion seems inescapable that the frontal lobes are responsible for our intellectual capacities.

This conclusion is wrong. Damage to the frontal lobes—even very extensive damage—does not make a person stupid. The effects of frontal lobe damage are severe, but they cannot be characterized as intellectual deterioration. Many studies have shown that if a person with frontal lobe damage can be properly motivated, the person will often perform just as well on standard intelligence tasks as before the brain damage occurred. Thus, the ability to think and reason is not dependent on frontal cortex.

The general deficits produced by destruction of the front part of the frontal lobes are the following: (1) *slowing* of thoughts and behavior, (2) *perseveration* (that is, continuing with a strategy that used to work even though it no longer does), (3) *loss of self-awareness* and changes in emotional reactions, and (4) *deficiencies in planning*. Damage to the back portions of the frontal lobes leads to problems in the control of eye movement, and destruction of a particular region there causes a form of aphasia.

Except for language functions (which will be discussed shortly), the frontal lobes show less of a right-left difference in function than any other cortical region. A person with extensive frontal lobe damage shows a great deal of behavioral inertia; he or she may sit still, staring vacantly into the distance. Various reflexes that are otherwise seen only in infants are easily triggered. These include sucking on an object placed near the mouth, and tightly grasping an object placed against the palm. Presumably the frontal lobes in normal adults suppress these responses, which are produced by various subcortical regions of the brain.

Loss of spontaneity also accompanies frontal lobe damage. When a person is asked to say or write as many words as possible he or she will have great difficulty coming up with more than a few, even though there is no problem in understanding words or identifying objects by name. In addition to this loss of spontaneity, patients have difficulty changing strategies. If they are given a task to solve, they may solve it readily but will fail to abandon this strategy and learn a new one if the problem is changed (perseveration). For example, suppose an experimenter asks a person with frontal lobe damage to sort a deck of cards into two stacks. The person is told "correct" whenever he or she puts a red card on the right stack or a black card on the left stack. The person soon learns what to do. But now suppose the experimenter changes the rules of the game without warning, and says "correct" when the patient puts jacks, queens, kings, and aces on the right and number cards on the left. A person without brain damage will soon realize that the rules have changed, and will learn the new sorting strategy. However, the person with frontal lobe damage will show perseveration, continuing to use the old sorting strategy, even though he or she clearly realizes that it is no longer valid.

People with damaged frontal lobes often have rather bland personalities. They react with indifference to events that would normally be expected to affect them emotionally. For example, they may show no signs of distress at the death of a close relative, even though they obviously understand what has happened. They have little insight into their own problems and are uncritical of their performance on various tasks. They are even indifferent to pain, although they report feeling the pain just as much as they did before the damage occurred.

In terms of daily living, the most important consequence of damage to the frontal lobes is probably lack of foresight and difficulty in planning. A person with frontal lobe damage might perform fairly well on a test of intelligence but be unable to hold a job. Presumably, planning is related to the general motor functions of the region in front of the central fissure. Just as we can use the occipital, temporal, and parietal regions of the brain to imagine something we have perceived, we can use the frontal region to imagine something we might do. Perhaps we test various possible actions by imagining ourselves doing them and guessing what the consequences of these actions might be. When people's frontal lobes are damaged their behavior often becomes more impulsive because their ability to plan their actions is lost.

Broca's speech area, located just below and ahead of primary motor cortex, is essential for the production of speech. Damage to this region results in a form of aphasia (**Broca's aphasia**) characterized by slow, labored, difficult speech that lacks grammatical structure. Here is a good example of the speech of a patient with Broca's aphasia who is talking about a dental appointment:

> Ah . . . Monday . . . ah Dad and Paul [patient's name] . . . and Dad . . . hospital. Two . . . ah doctors . . . , and ah . . . thirty minutes . . . and yes . . . ah . . . hospital. And, er Wednesday . . . nine o'clock. And er Thursday, ten o'clock . . . doctors. Two doctors . . . and ah . . . teeth. Yeah, . . . , fine. (Goodglass, 1976, p. 278)

People with Broca's aphasia have difficulty finding words and fail almost entirely to find the "little words," such as articles (*a, the*) and prepositions (*of, to, in,* and so on). They also fail to add grammatical inflections (like the *-s* to "he walks" or the *-ed* to "they played"). However, there is usually relatively little loss in the ability to *understand* speech. It remains to be seen just what role Broca's area plays in the translation of thoughts into speech.

Interim summary: From this brief tour around the brain you have learned about the general structure and some of the functions of the human brain. The central fissure divides the cerebral cortex into two major regions. The frontal lobes are concerned with motor functions, including planning and formulation of strategies as well as precise movements of the arms and legs. The three lobes behind the central fissure are generally concerned with sensa-

tion: somatosenses in the parietal lobe, vision in the occipital lobe, and audition in the temporal lobe. The other functions of these lobes are related to these sensory processes; for example, the parietal lobes are concerned with perception of space as well as knowledge about the body.

The right and left hemispheres are somewhat specialized. The left hemisphere is mostly concerned with details of perception and with events that occur one after the other, such as the series of sounds that make up speech. The right hemisphere is mostly concerned with the general form and shape of things, including the assessment of social situations.

Many subcortical structures have specialized functions. The *basal ganglia* are concerned with movement; the *thalamus* relays sensory information to the appropriate regions of sensory cortex; the *hypothalamus* controls many of the body's glands and regulates eating, drinking, body temperature, and other processes that are vital to normal physiological functioning; the *reticular formation* of the *pons* controls attention and arousal, and it and the *periaqueductal gray matter* control the execution of species-typical behaviors such as fighting; and the *medulla* controls vital functions such as heart rate and breathing. Finally, the *cerebellum* (not a part of the cerebral hemispheres) plays an important role in the control of movements, especially rapid, skilled ones.

With this basic understanding of the structure of the nervous system and its general functions, we can turn to the structure and functions of the elements that make it up—the nerve cells.

NEURONS

STRUCTURE

Neurons, or nerve cells, are the elements of the nervous system that bring sensory information to the brain, store memories, reach decisions, and control the activity of the muscles. A neuron is shown in Figure 3.30. There are four principal parts.

1. The **soma,** or cell body, is the largest part of the neuron, and contains the mechanisms that control the metabolism and maintenance of the cell.

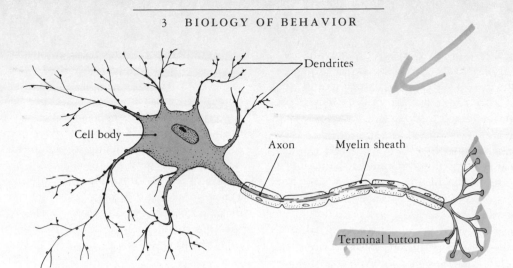

FIGURE 3.30 A schematic drawing of a neuron.
(Redrawn from Carlson, N.R. *Physiology of Behavior*,
2nd ed. Boston: Allyn and Bacon, 1981.)

The soma also receives messages from other neurons. (See **Figure 3.30.**)

2. The ***dendrites,*** or treelike growths attached to the soma, function principally to receive messages from other neurons. They transmit the information that they receive down their "trunks" to the soma. (See **Figure 3.30.**)

3. The ***axon*** carries messages away from the soma toward the cells with which the neuron communicates. An axon is usually much longer than the illustration shows —as much as tens of thousands of times longer than the diameter of its soma. (See **Figure 3.30.**) The message carried by the axon involves an electrical current, but it does not travel

FIGURE 3.31 Various shapes of neurons.
(Redrawn from Carlson, N.R. *Physiology of Behavior*,
2nd ed. Boston: Allyn and Bacon, 1981.)

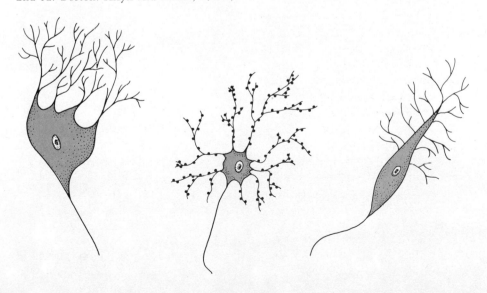

down the axon the way electricity travels through a wire. For one thing, electricity travels through a wire at the rate of 186,000 miles per second (the speed of light), or almost 200 million meters per second. As Helmholtz discovered, the axon transmits information at a much slower rate—less than 200 meters per second.

A useful analogy in understanding the nature of the message carried by the axon is that of a fuse used for explosives. When one end of such a fuse is lit, the flame travels to the opposite end, where the explosive is located. Similarly, when an axon is "triggered" at one end, it sends an electrical message called the *action potential* down to the other end. (Of course, there is no explosion at the end.) Unlike an explosive fuse, the axon is reusable; messages can be sent down it repeatedly.

4. The ***terminal buttons*** are located at the ends of the "twigs" that branch off the axons. (See Figure 3.30.) Terminal buttons secrete a chemical called a ***transmitter substance*** whenever an action potential is sent to them down the axon. The transmitter substance affects the activity of the other cells with which the neuron communicates. Thus, the message from one neuron to another (or from neuron to muscle or gland) is actually conveyed by a chemical. Most drugs that affect the nervous system, and hence alter a person's behavior, do so by affecting these chemical transmissions of messages from cell to cell.

Not all neurons look like the one shown in Figure 3.30. Figure 3.31 illustrates other shapes. (See **Figure 3.31.**)

FIGURE 3.32   Synapses between several neurons. (Redrawn from Carlson, N.R. *Physiology of Behavior*, 2nd ed. Boston: Allyn and Bacon, 1981.)

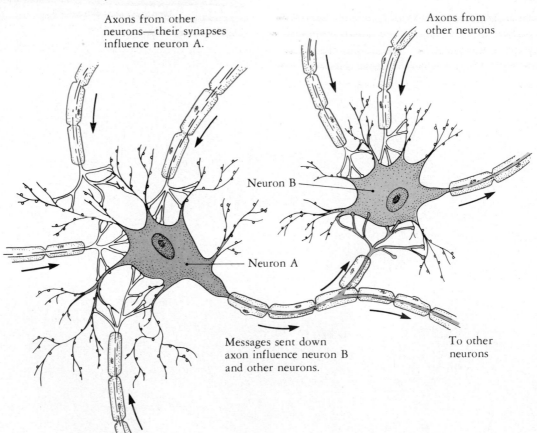

Axons from other neurons—their synapses influence neuron A.

Axons from other neurons

Neuron B

Neuron A

Messages sent down axon influence neuron B and other neurons.

To other neurons

Many axons, especially long ones, are insulated with a substance called myelin. The white matter on the outer part of the spinal cord gets its color from the *myelinated* (that is, myelin-covered) axons that travel through it. Myelin, part protein and part fat, is produced by special cells that individually wrap themselves around segments of the axon, leaving small bare patches of the axon between. (Look back at **Figure 3.30.**) The principal function of myelin is to insulate axons from each other and thus prevent the scrambling of messages. Its importance is demonstrated by the effects of multiple sclerosis, in which a loss of myelin produces severe disturbances in sensory functions and motor control.

FUNCTIONS

Neurons communicate by means of *synapses,* conjunctions of terminal buttons of one neuron with the somatic or dendritic membrane of another. (See **Figure 3.32.**) Many terminal buttons form synapses with a single neuron, and this neuron in turn forms synapses with many others. The drawing is considerably simplified; an individual neuron can have tens of thousands of synapses on it.

Figure 3.33 illustrates the relation between a *motor neuron* and a muscle. A motor neuron is one that forms synapses with a muscle. When its axon fires, all the muscle fibers with which it forms synapses will contract with a brief twitch. (See **Figure 3.33.**) A muscle consists of thousands of individual muscle fibers. It is controlled by a large number of motor neurons, each of which forms synapses with different groups of muscle fibers. The strength of a muscular contraction, then, depends on the number of motor neurons whose axons are firing at a given time.

SYNAPSES

Effects of Synaptic Transmission

There are basically two types of synapses: *excitatory synapses* and *inhibitory synapses.* Excitatory synapses do just what their name implies. When they are activated by an action potential they release a transmitter substance that excites the neurons upon which they synapse. The effect of this

FIGURE 3.33   Synapses between terminal buttons of the axons of a motor neuron and a muscle.

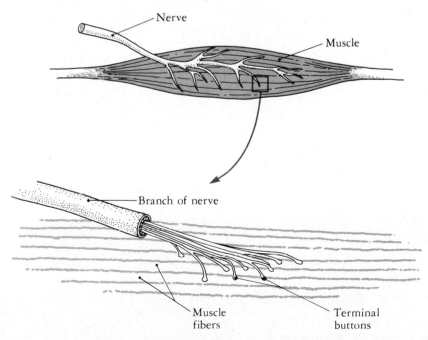

excitation is to make it more likely that the syn-apsed-upon neurons (*postsynaptic neurons*) will "fire," that is, send an action potential down their axons. (The neuron that synapses with—sends messages to—the postsynaptic neuron is called the *presynaptic neuron.*)

Inhibitory synapses do just the opposite. When they are activated, they lower the probability that the axon of the postsynaptic neuron will fire. Thus, the rate at which a particular axon fires is deter-mined by the activity of the synaptic inputs to the dendrites and soma of the cell. If the excitatory synapses are more active, it will fire at a high rate. If the inhibitory synapses are more active, it will fire at a low rate, or perhaps not at all. (See **Figure 3.34.**)

♦ The contest between excitatory and inhibitory synapses, called *neural integration,* is the basis for decision making. *Integration* simply means "ad-dition"; the effects of the excitatory and inhibitory synapses add together, and the result determines the activity of the axon of the postsynaptic neuron.

FIGURE 3.34   Synapses that excite (E) or inhibit (I) the postsynaptic neuron.

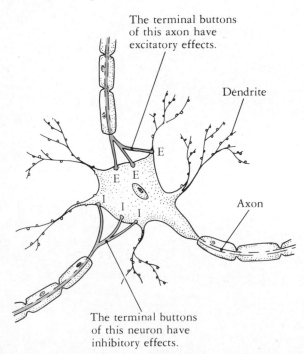

The terminal buttons of this axon have excitatory effects.

Dendrite

Axon

The terminal buttons of this neuron have inhibitory effects.

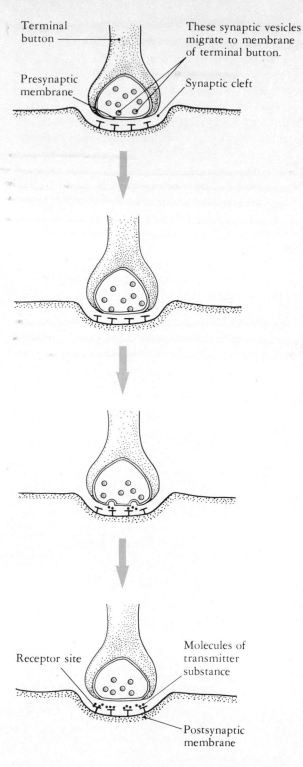

Terminal button

These synaptic vesicles migrate to membrane of terminal button.

Presynaptic membrane

Synaptic cleft

Receptor site

Molecules of transmitter substance

Postsynaptic membrane

FIGURE 3.35   The release of a transmitter substance from a terminal button.

If excitation dominates, the axon will fire rapidly. If inhibition dominates, it will be silent. In turn, the activity of the terminal buttons of this neuron play a role in determining the rate of firing of the axons of *other* neurons. The importance of neural integration will be demonstrated later, in the discussion of reflexes.

Mechanisms of Synaptic Transmission

Terminal buttons excite or inhibit their postsynaptic cells by releasing transmitter substances. These chemicals are stored within small round containers called *synaptic vesicles*. (*Vesicle* means "small sac.") **Figure 3.35** shows the sequence by which the vesicles release transmitter substances.

When an axon fires, the action potential travels to all its terminal buttons. The arrival of an action potential at a terminal button causes some of the synaptic vesicles located closest to the *presynaptic membrane* to attach and adhere to it, and then to break open, spilling their contents into the space

between the terminal button and the membrane of the postsynaptic cell—the *synaptic cleft*. (See **Figure 3.35**.) The transmitter substance causes reactions in the postsynaptic neuron that either excite or inhibit it. These reactions are triggered by special submicroscopic structures in the postsynaptic membrane called *receptor sites*.

A molecule of transmitter substance acts upon a receptor site like a key upon a lock. When the presynaptic membrane releases a transmitter substance, molecules find their way to the receptor sites and activate them. In turn, the receptor sites produce excitatory or inhibitory effects on the postsynaptic neuron. (See **Figure 3.36**.) Many drugs produce their effects by stimulating or blocking these postsynaptic receptor sites.

The excitation or inhibition produced by a synapse is brief; the effects soon pass away. The two mechanisms that terminate these effects are chemical deactivation and re-uptake. In the first case, the transmitter substance is actually destroyed. The

FIGURE 3.36 The activation of receptor sites by a transmitter substance released from the terminal button.

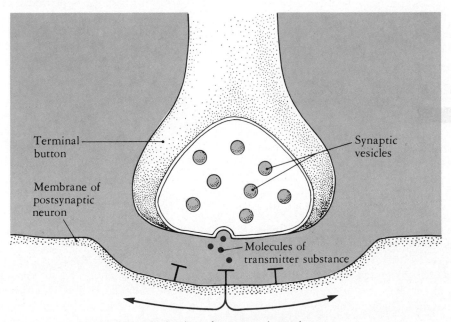

Activation of receptor site excites or inhibits postsynaptic neuron.

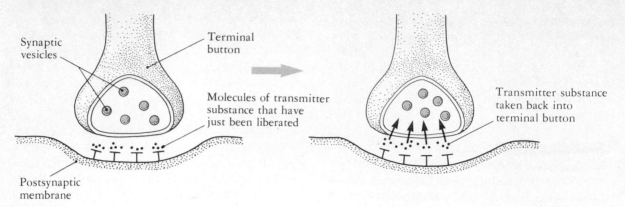

FIGURE 3.37   A schematic representation of re-uptake.

more common process is *re-uptake*. Most transmitter substances are recycled by the terminal buttons. The chemical is released by the terminal button and quickly taken up again, so that it has only a brief time to stimulate the postsynaptic receptor sites. (See **Figure 3.37**.) The transmitter substance is then reused; newly formed synaptic vesicles, manufactured in the terminal button, are filled with the recycled chemical. The rate at which the terminal button takes back the transmitter substance obviously determines how prolonged the effects of the chemical on the postsynaptic neuron will be. As we shall see, some drugs affect the nervous system by altering the rate of re-uptake.

REFLEXES

The interconnections of the billions of neurons in our central nervous system provide us with the capacities for perception, decision making, memory, and action. Although it is impossible to draw a "neural wiring-diagram" for such complex functions, we can do so for some of the simpler reflexes that are triggered by certain kinds of sensory stimuli. For example, when your finger is pricked by a pin, your hand withdraws. When your eye is touched, you close your eyes and draw your head back. When a baby's cheek is touched, it turns its mouth toward the object, and if the object is of the appropriate size and texture, the baby begins

to suck. All these activities occur quickly, without requiring thought. Their usefulness is obvious.

A simple *withdrawal reflex,* which is produced by a noxious stimulus (such as a pinprick) requires three types of neurons. *Sensory neurons* detect the noxious stimulus and convey this information to the spinal cord. *Interneurons* receive the sensory information and in turn convey it to the *motor neurons* that cause the appropriate muscle to contract. (See **Figure 3.38**.) The sequence is simple and straightforward. A noxious stimulus applied to the skin produces a burst of action potentials in the sensory neurons. Their axons fire, liberating an excitatory transmitter substance that stimulates the interneurons. Then the interneurons fire, exciting motor neurons, which in turn cause the muscle fibers with which they synapse to contract. (See **Figure 3.38**.)

The next figure adds a bit of complexity to the circuit. Suppose you have removed a hot casserole from the oven. As you start over to the table to put it down, the heat begins to penetrate the rather thin potholders you are using. This noxious stimulus excites the motor neurons that control the muscles that open your hands. And yet you manage to get the dish to the table without dropping it. How is this accomplished?

As we saw earlier, the activity of a neuron depends on the relative activity of the excitatory and inhibitory synapses on it. The hot object causes the stimulation of a number of excitatory synapses on the motor neurons that control the muscles that

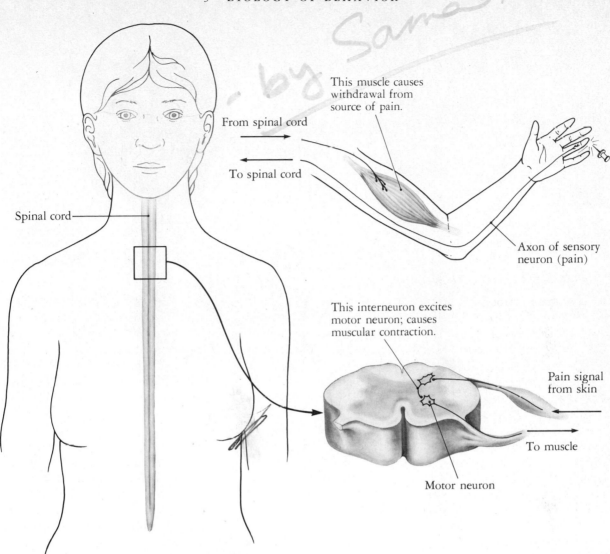

by Samag

This muscle causes
withdrawal from
source of pain.

From spinal cord

To spinal cord

Spinal cord

Axon of sensory
neuron (pain)

This interneuron excites
motor neuron; causes
muscular contraction.

Pain signal
from skin

To muscle

Motor neuron

FIGURE 3.38   A schematic representation of the
elements of a withdrawal reflex.

open your hands, but this excitation is counter-
acted by inhibition from another source—your brain.
Figure 3.39 shows an axon from a neuron in the
brain that forms synapses with an interneuron, which
in turn forms synapses with a motor neuron that
causes the hands to open. (See **Figure 3.39.**) The
effect of the interneuron is inhibitory; when this
neuron is stimulated its terminal buttons inhibit
firing of the motor neurons and thus prevent your
hands from opening. This inhibition provides a

practical example of neural integration; it reverses
the effect of the excitation arising from the withdrawal reflex.

PHARMACOLOGY
OF NEURONS

Although the action potential, the message that is
sent from one end of an axon to the other, consists

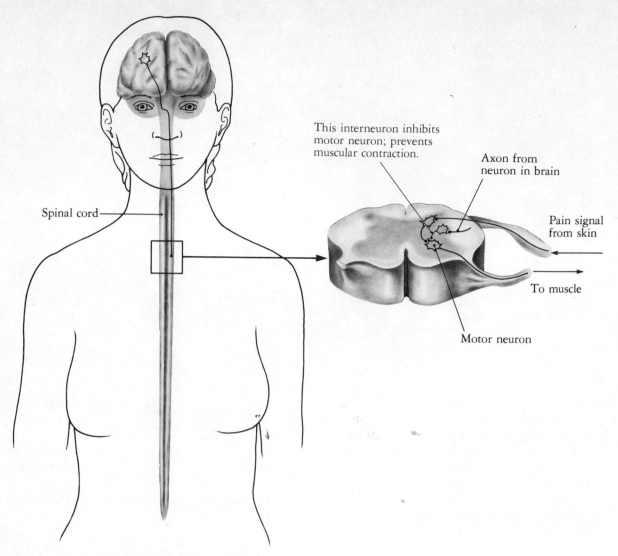

This interneuron inhibits
motor neuron; prevents
muscular contraction.

Axon from
neuron in brain

Pain signal
from skin

Spinal cord

To muscle

Motor neuron

FIGURE 3.39   A schematic representation of a
withdrawal reflex being inhibited by the brain.

of an electrical charge, most of the important events that take place within the nervous system are chemical in nature. Communication between neurons, between sensory receptor and neuron, and between neuron and muscle takes place chemically; a terminal button secretes a chemical that has an excitatory or inhibitory effect on another cell. There are many different kinds of neurotransmitter substances in the brain, and various drugs affect their production or release, mimic their effects on the receptor sites, block these effects, or interfere with mechanisms that deactivate the neurotransmitters once they are released. By altering the normal activity of a particular transmitter substance, a drug affects perceptions, thoughts, and behaviors that it controls. In this section we will study the ways that drugs can affect the nervous system, and hence behavior.

STIMULATION OR
INHIBITION OF AXONS

Some drugs affect the conduction of action potentials by the axon. A few drugs excite the axon, but

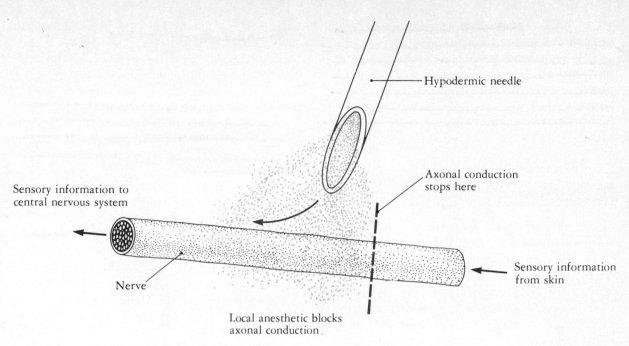

Hypodermic needle

Axonal conduction
stops here

Sensory information to
central nervous system

Sensory information
from skin

Nerve

Local anesthetic blocks
axonal conduction

FIGURE 3.40   The effects of a local anesthetic
such as Novocain.

these chemicals are relatively rare. More important
are the *local anesthetics,* which block conduction
of action potentials down axons. These drugs permit painless surgery, such as the removal of a tooth
or the stitching up of a wound. By blocking axonal
conduction, they prevent pain messages from
reaching the central nervous system. (See **Figure
3.40.**) Typical local anesthetics include Novocain
and cocaine. (Other effects of cocaine will be described later.)

There are also drugs that decrease the excitabil-
ity of the axon but do not prevent the occurrence
of action potentials. They make it necessary for
more excitatory synapses to be active before the
axon will fire. Such drugs are used to treat *epilepsy,* a disorder produced by abnormal, continuous firing of cerebral neurons. Epilepsy is caused
by overexcitability of neurons, and the drug thus
restores things to normal.

STIMULATION OR INHIBITION OF THE RELEASE OF TRANSMITTER SUBSTANCES

Some drugs cause terminal buttons to release their
neurotransmitter, and thus mimic the effect of fir-

ing of the axons to which the terminals are attached. There are many different kinds of transmitter substances, and the effects of a particular
drug are more or less specific to one transmitter
substance. Therefore, not all neurons are affected
by a drug that facilitates or inhibits release of a
particular transmitter substance. An example of such

FIGURE 3.41   The effects of botulinum toxin,
which prevents the release of a transmitter substance
from terminal buttons.

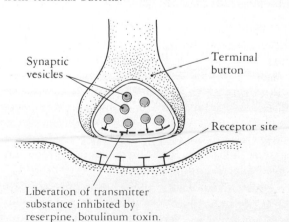

Synaptic
vesicles

Terminal
button

Receptor site

Liberation of transmitter
substance inhibited by
reserpine, botulinum toxin.

a drug is the venom of the black widow spider, which causes the release of *acetylcholine*, an important transmitter substance. In contrast, botulinum toxin, a poison that is sometimes present in improperly canned food, completely blocks the release of acetylcholine. An extremely small amount—less than one millionth of a gram—can kill a person. (See **Figure 3.41**.)

FACILITATION OF THE SYNTHESIS OF TRANSMITTER SUBSTANCES

◆ Transmitter substances are synthesized by neurons from raw ingredients present in the fluid that bathes them. The synthesis of some transmitter substances can be facilitated by administering the appropriate raw ingredient. I mentioned earlier that Parkinson's disease, a serious motor disorder, is caused by the death of neurons that regulate the activity of the basal ganglia. These neurons secrete a transmitter substance called *dopamine*, which is synthesized from L-DOPA, an amino acid. L-DOPA greatly alleviates the symptoms of Parkinson's disease by providing the patient's neurons with much more raw material than is normally present. The few surviving dopamine-secreting neurons produce more dopamine than they usually do, and hence are able to release more of the transmitter substance. The increased release of dopamine partially compensates for the loss of dopamine-secreting neurons; the activity of the basal ganglia is brought closer to normal.

STIMULATION OR INHIBITION OF RECEPTOR SITES

Transmitter substances produce their effects by stimulating postsynaptic receptor sites, which in turn excite or inhibit the postsynaptic neurons.
◆ Some drugs mimic the effects of particular transmitter substances by directly stimulating particular kinds of receptor sites. For example, isoproterenol stimulates receptor sites on neurons that open the air passages to the lungs, and hence is used to treat asthma. This drug and others like it are often inhaled directly into the lungs.

Some drugs block receptor sites, making them inaccessible to the transmitter substance and thus inhibiting synaptic transmission. (If we use a lock-and-key analogy to describe these effects of a transmitter substance on a receptor site, then a drug that blocks receptor sites can be said to clog up the lock so that the key will no longer fit into it.) For example, curare is a poison that was discovered by South American Indians, who use it on the darts of their blowguns. This drug blocks the receptor sites on muscles, which are normally stimulated by acetylcholine. Thus, the drug prevents synaptic transmission in muscles and causes paralysis. The victim is unable to breathe, and consequently suffocates. (See **Figure 3.42**.)

Some medically useful chemicals work by blocking receptor sites. For example, chlorpromazine alleviates the symptoms of schizophrenia, apparently by blocking receptor sites in the brain that are normally stimulated by dopamine. (Drugs like chlorpromazine are discussed in more detail in Chapter 18.)

A drug that blocks receptor sites can have a *stimulating* effect on the nervous system. For example, a poison called strychnine blocks receptor sites that respond to an inhibitory transmitter substance. By blocking the effects of an inhibitory transmitter substance, strychnine removes some of the inhibition that normally counterbalances excitation; the result is excessive neural activity, sometimes leading to convulsions and death. (See **Figure 3.43**.)

FIGURE 3.42   The effects of curare, which blocks receptor sites and thus prevents the transmitter substance from activating them.

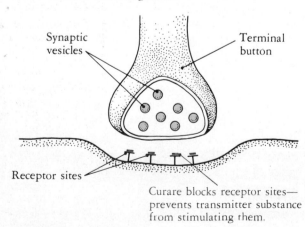

Synaptic vesicles

Terminal button

Receptor sites

Curare blocks receptor sites—prevents transmitter substance from stimulating them.

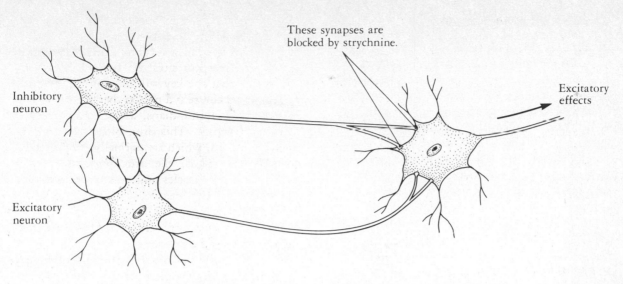

These synapses are
blocked by strychnine.

Inhibitory
neuron

Excitatory
effects

Excitatory
neuron

FIGURE 3.43   By blocking receptor sites at
inhibitory synapses, strychnine can have an excitatory
effect on the nervous system.

INHIBITION OF RE-UPTAKE

Most transmitter substances are taken back into the
terminal buttons soon after they are released. Re-
uptake thus keeps the effects of synaptic transmission brief. Some drugs inhibit the process of
re-uptake, so the transmitter substance remains in
the synaptic cleft for a longer time and continues
to stimulate the postsynaptic receptor sites. Therefore, inhibition of the process of re-uptake *increases*
the effect of the transmitter substance. The excitatory effects of cocaine and amphetamine are produced by the inhibition of the re-uptake of certain
transmitter substances. (See **Figure 3.44.**)

FIGURE 3.44   Cocaine and amphetamine prevent
re-uptake of certain transmitter substances, thus
prolonging their effect on the postsynaptic neuron.

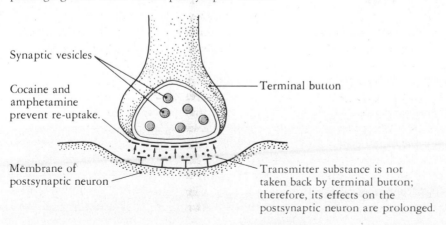

Synaptic vesicles

Cocaine and
amphetamine
prevent re-uptake.

Terminal button

Membrane of
postsynaptic neuron

Transmitter substance is not
taken back by terminal button;
therefore, its effects on the
postsynaptic neuron are prolonged.

POPULAR DRUGS

A number of drugs are taken not for any therapeutic use, but rather for the pleasurable effects they give the user. We might call them "recreational drugs," although people who become addicted to them, and have to organize their lives around procuring them, can hardly be said to be having fun. The majority of people who use drugs are not physiologically addicted to them, although many might become unhappy and distressed if they learned that their supply of their favorite drugs was to be terminated.

This section explains only the pharmacological effects of these drugs as they affect the nervous system, not why a person becomes an addict. As we shall see, detoxification is not much of a medical problem; under medical supervision, an addict can safely be withdrawn from a drug without inordinate suffering. However, addiction is more than a simple physiological response; many former addicts become hooked on the drug again.

I shall describe (1) drugs that generally depress the central nervous system (alcohol, barbiturates, tranquilizers, and volatile solvents), (2) opiates such as heroin and morphine, (3) hallucinogenic and consciousness-altering drugs (LSD and marijuana), and (4) stimulants (cocaine and amphetamine). Tobacco and caffeine, other much-used drugs, also affect the central nervous system, but they are less potent, pharmacologically, than the other drugs.

DRUGS THAT DEPRESS THE CENTRAL NERVOUS SYSTEM

Alcohol

Although we know that alcohol depresses neurons, especially those in the cerebral cortex, we do not really know how it does so. Alcohol is a potent drug; it produces intoxication in most people with a blood alcohol content of approximately 0.12 percent—about five 1.5-ounce shots of 80-proof (40 percent) alcohol. However, there are large individual differences. Some people appear to be only mildly intoxicated with blood alcohol levels of up to 0.30 percent.

Use of alcohol unquestionably can produce addiction. A person who abruptly stops drinking after severe and prolonged intoxication will suffer profound withdrawal symptoms: fevers, restlessness, nausea, and the hallucinations of *delerium tremens.* These effects can be very severe; sometimes they even cause death. Other depressants, such as tranquilizers, can be administered to ease withdrawal from alcohol. Unlike a heroin addict, who can safely take an amount of the drug that would kill someone who does not use it, the *tolerance* of chronic alcoholics is not higher than that of nonaddicts; that is, they cannot safely tolerate larger doses of alcohol than nonaddicts can.

When used in moderate doses, alcohol is often regarded as a stimulant. Most of this effect probably results from depression of brain mechanisms (especially those of the frontal lobe) that normally inhibit behavior. When released from this inhibition, many people do and say things they normally would not. (How many people recall with regret what they did or said at a party the previous evening?)

Prolonged and heavy use of alcohol can have disastrous effects. Chronic alcoholics usually lack a well-balanced diet because they consume many hundreds of calories from alcohol each day and consequently eat less food. Furthermore, alcohol interferes with absorption of B vitamins from the intestinal tract. These two effects of alcohol consumption increase the likelihood of suffering a vitamin deficiency. The result of a prolonged vitamin B deficiency is brain damage; in particular, many chronic alcoholics suffer from *Korsakoff's syndrome,* a severe deficit in the ability to learn anything new. For example, institutionalized patients suffering from Korsakoff's syndrome cannot find their way around the grounds without assistance, and may report to questioners that they arrived at the institution only a few days before, even though they may have been there for many years.

Barbiturates, Tranquilizers, and Aromatic Solvents

Other drugs also depress the central nervous system. Barbiturates and aromatic solvents (such as volatile constituents of substances like airplane glue and paint thinner) are most similar in effect to alcohol. Tranquilizers vary in their specific mode of action, but their general effects are to depress the activity of neurons. They are generally safer than the other depressants—few people die from tranquilizer overdose.

The effects of depressant drugs are additive; a nonlethal dose of alcohol and a nonlethal dose of barbiturates, taken together, can kill. Chronic barbiturate addicts suffer withdrawal symptoms when they cease taking the drug, and the reaction can be severe. Chronic use of barbiturates is less likely to produce long-term damage than chronic use of alcohol, since no calories are supplied by the drug, and the addict is more likely to obtain a well-balanced diet.

OPIATES

◈ **Opium,** derived from a sticky resin produced by the opium poppy, has been eaten and smoked for centuries. One of the naturally occurring ingredients of opium, **morphine,** is sometimes used as a painkiller but has largely been supplanted by synthetic opiates. **Heroin,** a compound produced from morphine, is the most commonly abused opiate.

Recently, the effects of opiates have become better understood. **Opiate receptors,** similar to the postsynaptic receptor sites that respond to transmitter substances, have been discovered on neurons in the brain. These receptors exist because the brain produces it own opiates, called **endorphins,** or "inner morphine." During times of stress, or during sexual activity, fighting, or other behaviors that are important to species survival, specialized neurons release endorphins into the fluid that bathes the cells of the brain. The endorphins then stimulate the opiate receptors and produce **analgesia,** or lessening of pain. (This primary effect of opiates explains why many heroin addicts nod off and do not awaken when they burn their fingers or chest with cigarettes.) The analgesic effect appears to be mediated principally by neurons in the periaqueductal gray matter, which contain many opiate receptors.

When injected into a vein, heroin and other opiates produce a "rush" that the user finds intensely pleasurable. So, too, do the endorphins, a fact that has led neuroscientists to speculate that these naturally produced chemicals are important in the regulation of mood.

Chronic use of opiates produces physiological tolerance and addiction; that is, progressively more of the drug must be injected to produce the rush, and withdrawal symptoms occur when a chronic user stops taking it. The chief symptoms of withdrawal are nausea, abdominal pains (cramps), and restlessness. Today the symptoms of opiate withdrawal in North America are likely to be much less severe than they were twenty-five or thirty years ago because street heroin is usually no stronger than 2 percent. An addict with a typical eight-to-ten-bag-per-day habit simply does not take enough of the drug to cause dangerously severe withdrawal symptoms. Thus, addicts are "protected" from more severe symptoms by high price and low quality.

Authoritative sources (such as Hoffman, 1975) state that the symptoms of opiate withdrawal are often no worse than those of a severe cold. (In fact, addicts who are undergoing medically supervised withdrawal may exaggerate their symptoms in order to obtain a larger dose of the drug being used to ease their symptoms.) When the cost of their habit becomes too high, many addicts voluntarily go "cold turkey" for several days so they can obtain a high from smaller, and cheaper, doses. Several days of abdominal cramps, retching, and nausea cannot be called pleasant, but withdrawal from opiates is less traumatic than the popular media imply.

Chronic use of opiates is unlikely to produce long-term damage that can be attributed *directly* to the drug. For example, addicted dentists and physicians usually continue to practice. However, most addicts do not observe aseptic techniques when they inject the drug into a vein. As a result, heroin addicts have a high incidence of hepatitis (a liver disease), endocarditis (inflammation of the membrane that lines the interior of the heart), and other infectious diseases. Furthermore, most manufacturers and distributors of heroin take little care in its production and dilution. Quinine, milk sugar, and talc are commonly used to cut the drug, and many deaths attributed to overdose probably occurred because of a reaction to impure adulterants.

In addition to drugs that block postsynaptic receptor sites, and hence inhibit synaptic transmission, there are drugs that block opiate receptors. These drugs, called **opiate antagonists,** have saved many lives in the emergency room, where they are used to treat drug overdoses. However, they are not of much use in controlling heroin addiction. The most effective of these drugs (naloxone) must be injected, and none of the opiate antagonists is effective for more than a few minutes. Furthermore, they are expensive and produce varying degrees of unpleasant side effects. The best hope in preventing addiction is to determine the factors that predispose an individual to drug use and then develop ways to help people avoid their use.

HALLUCINOGENIC AND CONSCIOUSNESS-ALTERING DRUGS

LSD (lysergic acid diethylamide), peyote (or its derivative, mescaline), and various other drugs produce vivid visual hallucinations that some people find very enjoyable. These drugs appear to exert their effects by inhibiting the activity of neurons that secrete a transmitter substance, *serotonin*. Research with animals suggests that these neurons may play a role in preventing dreaming except when it is appropriate (that is, during sleep); thus perhaps the LSD trip bears a resemblance to what goes on during dreams. (Sleep and dreaming are discussed in Chapter 10.)

So far as we know, the lethal dose of the commonly used hallucinogens is very high; it is estimated that a lethal amount of LSD would be hundreds of thousands of times greater than a pharmacologically effective dose. In fact there appears to be no undisputed case of death that can be attributed directly to the *pharmacological* effects of LSD, although there have been reports of people who have jumped from buildings or entered a busy street, convinced of their invincibility while under the influence of hallucinogens. Nor is there good evidence for tolerance or pharmacological addiction; a user of LSD or marijuana does not have to increase the dose to obtain the same effect, and no withdrawal symptoms are seen.

The pharmacological effects of marijuana, the most popular consciousness-altering drug, are not known. Although studies have shown that a high dose of THC (tetrahydrocannabinol), the active ingredient in marijuana, alters the activity of neurons in various parts of the brain, no one knows why, or whether these particular alterations are the ones that cause the consciousness-altering effects. So far as we know, marijuana does not exert its effects by interacting with any one transmitter substance.

There is no evidence for long-term damage from the hallucinogens; reports of chromosomal damage have not been convincingly shown. LSD does appear to affect the reproductive process, since pregnancy is rare among women who are heavy and continuous users. Marijuana mimics some of the effects of estrogen (a female hormone) and suppresses the effects of testosterone (a male hormone), but these effects are probably not clinically significant (men who habitually smoke marijuana have become fathers).

Although the effects of hallucinogens have been likened to mental disorders, most experts disagree. People who are under the influence of a hallucinogen do not resemble people with mental disorders. A psychiatrist is unlikely to mistake a person under the influence of LSD or another hallucinogen for a person with schizophrenia. The drugs that can mimic mental disorders are the stimulants: amphetamine and cocaine.

STIMULANT DRUGS

Many drugs stimulate the nervous system; the ones most frequently used recreationally are amphetamine and cocaine. These drugs have remarkably similar effects: they facilitate the release and retard the re-uptake of two transmitter substances, dopamine and *norepinephrine*. In addition, cocaine is a potent local anesthetic, blocking axonal conduction. It is still the drug of choice in anesthesia of the eye and its associated membranes during surgery.

Amphetamine is swallowed or injected. The immediate effects are euphoria and a perceived abundance of energy. Users of this drug are generally friendly and gregarious, at least in the early stages of a binge. When injected, amphetamine produces a rush (distinct from that of heroin) that results in a prolonged high. As the high wears off, the user typically repeats the injection. After several days, a high becomes more difficult to sustain and the side effects of the drug (muscular pain, severe teeth-grinding, tremors, feelings of paranoia) intensify. The user stops taking the drug and "crashes," sleeping for up to a few days. Upon awakening, the user feels depressed and anxious and often begins to take the drug again to eliminate these symptoms and to regain the pleasurable high.

Cocaine, a much more expensive drug (regarded by users as the "king of drugs"), is usually sniffed into the mucous membranes of the nasal passages. Use of cocaine is generally limited by its high cost. Around the turn of the century, cocaine was commonly injected rather than sniffed by its users. (Sigmund Freud was a user for a while, and praised the delights of this drug until some users began to die from its effects.) The effects of cocaine injections are the same as those of amphetamine injections.

Long-term, heavy use of amphetamine has serious effects, attested to by the slogan "Speed kills." Chronic, heavy users suffer psychotic reactions (symptoms of mental disorders) that usually cannot be distinguished from true schizophrenia. (Chapter 17 discusses the physiology of schizophrenia, including its relation to amphetamine psychosis.) Beside the psychotic side effects, heavy use of amphetamines has been reported to produce permanent deficits in memory, and the life-style of amphetamine addicts results in malnutrition and other disorders caused by injection of unsterile substances.

Interim summary: The basic element of the nervous system is the neuron, with its soma, dendrites, axon, and terminal buttons. One neuron communicates with another (or with muscle or gland cells) by means of synapses, junctions of terminal buttons of the presynaptic neuron with the membrane of the postsynaptic cell. Communication is chemical in nature; when an action potential travels down an axon, it causes a transmitter substance to be released from the synaptic vesicles that are located in the terminal buttons. Molecules of the transmitter substance stimulate the receptor sites on the postsynaptic neuron, which either excite or inhibit the firing of the postsynaptic cell. The combined effects of excitatory and inhibitory synapses on a particular neuron determine its rate of firing.

Drugs can facilitate or interfere with synaptic activity. Facilitators include drugs that directly stimulate the receptor sites, thus mimicking the effects of the transmitter substance itself (such as asthma medication); drugs that cause the release of a transmitter substance (such as the venom of the black widow spider); the raw material out of which transmitter substances are produced (such as

L-DOPA, used to treat Parkinson's disease); and drugs that inhibit re-uptake of a neurotransmitter (such as amphetamine and cocaine). Drugs that interfere with synaptic activity include those that block receptor sites (such as curare, which paralyzes the muscles); and those that inhibit the release of a transmitter substance (such as botulinum toxin).

Many chemicals found in nature have pleasurable effects, and many more have been synthesized in the laboratory. Alcohol, barbiturates, tranquilizers, and volatile solvents depress the activity of the central nervous system, whereas amphetamine and cocaine stimulate it. The opiates mimic substances the brain itself produces, causing analgesia and an intensely enjoyable "rush." Probably, the brain's own opiates (the endorphins) are involved in mood as well as reduction of pain while engaging in important behaviors such as fighting and mating. Although the physiological causes of the effects of marijuana are not known, LSD, mescaline, and related drugs inhibit the activity of synapses that use serotonin, a transmitter substance. It is possible that the hallucinogenic effects of these drugs are related to dreaming.

CONCLUDING REMARKS

This chapter has explained the basic structure of the brain; the workings of its elements, the neurons; and how behaviorally active drugs exert their effects. Later chapters will build on the foundation provided here by discussing what psychologists have learned about human behavior and its physiological basis.

GUIDE TO TERMS INTRODUCED IN THIS CHAPTER

acalculia p. 94
acetylcholine p. 106
action potential p. 98
agraphia p. 93
alexia p. 93
amusia p. 92

SUGGESTIONS FOR
FURTHER READING

Several excellent books will tell you more about the effects of brain damage on human brain functions. *The Shattered Mind* (New York: Vintage Press, 1975) by Howard Gardner describes the effects of strokes on intellectual and verbal abilities. The book is full of detailed descriptions of cases studied by Dr. Gardner. If you are interested in this topic you will enjoy this book.

The Integrated Mind (New York: Plenum Press, 1978) by Michael S. Gazzaniga and Joseph E. LeDoux, which sounds like the counterpart to Gardner's book, describes studies of people whose brains have been surgically disconnected into two relatively independent right and left cerebral hemispheres. These studies permit interesting inferences about differences in the functions of the two sides of the brain. The book is somewhat more formal than Gardner's, but it is clearly written.

Many people have been concerned about problems that might arise from our discoveries about human brain functions. For example, is it possible to control people's thoughts and behaviors by artificially stimulating their brains with electrical current? Are there potential abuses of psychosurgery, such as prefrontal lobotomies? Eliot Valenstein confronts these issues in a book appropriately called *Brain Control* (New York: Wiley-Interscience, 1973). He points out the significant problems encountered in evaluating the effects of these procedures and also documents past mistakes.

If you are interested in learning more about the effects of drugs that are often abused you may want to read the third edition of *A Primer of Drug Action* by Robert M. Julien (San Francisco: W. H. Freeman, 1981). The discussions of chemistry are quite complex for readers without a background in this subject, but the rest of the book contains much helpful information about the effects of popular drugs and their use and abuse in society.

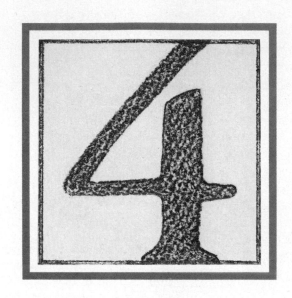

LEARNING:

BASIC PRINCIPLES

LEARNING ◆ OBJECTIVES

1. Describe what psychologists mean by "learning," and how it relates to environmental events, the nervous system, and behavior. pp. 116–117
2. Describe the process of habituation, both short-term and long-term, including its evolutionary significance for organisms. 117–118
3. Illustrate the difference between classical conditioning and habituation with an original example. 118–119
4. Describe delayed conditioning, trace conditioning, simultaneous conditioning, and backward conditioning, including their procedures and relative effectiveness. 120–121
5. Diagram the process of classical conditioning. Include all technical terms and abbreviations. 121–122
6. Differentiate between defensive and consummatory reflexes. 122
7. Describe two aspects of the biological significance of classical conditioning. 122–123
8. Describe the process of latent inhibition, including the role habituation plays in this learning process. 123–124
9. Give an original example of classical conditioning from your own life. Diagram the example and label all the parts with technical terms and abbreviations. 124–125
10. Describe the process of extinction and spontaneous recovery in classical conditioning, including similarities to and differences from habituation. 125
11. Compare phobias with fetishes. Include a diagram of the classical conditioning of each. 125–126
12. Describe the process of reinforcement in instrumental conditioning and the importance of its immediacy. Differentiate between reinforcement and reward. 127
13. Compare positive reinforcement, negative reinforcement, punishment, and response cost. 128
14. Describe the research by Logan on the importance of immediacy of reinforcement. 130
15. Explain how preference can be measured. 130
16. Describe the Premack principle and its use in making a preference hierarchy. 131
17. Describe the importance of the fact that reinforcement contingencies must restrict the preferred behavior. 131–132
18. Compare primary and secondary (conditioned) reinforcers and describe their origins. 132
19. Describe the biological significance of conditioned reinforcement. 133
20. Compare classical conditioning with instrumental conditioning. 133
21. Give everyday examples of social reinforcement. 133
22. Describe reinforcement as the recognition of progress toward doing something correctly. 134
23. Define the method of successive approximations (shaping). 135–137
24. Describe how an operant chamber is used to shape the behavior of a small rodent or bird. 135–136

WE ARE what we are because of history, both our ancestors' history and the history of our own lives. The evolution of our species was shaped by the process of natural selection: mutations introduced variability, and those changes that produced favorable consequences were maintained. Our be-haviors are similarly selected: behaviors that produce favorable consequences are repeated, while behaviors that produce unfavorable consequences tend not to recur. In other words, we learn from experience.

◆   Learning refers to relatively longlasting changes

in an individual's behavior that are produced by environmental events. The word *behavior* in this definition is absolutely essential, because the only evidence of learning is a change in behavior. The process is an adaptive one; the changes in behavior are the result of interactions with the environment. As conditions change, new behaviors are learned and old ones are eliminated.

Undoubtedly, learning takes place within the nervous system; experiences alter the structure and chemistry of the brain, and these changes affect the individual's subsequent behavior. If we had some way of directly monitoring the status of the neurons that participate in the learning process, we could determine that learning has occurred. But there is no way to study changes that remain private. If a person "thinks about" what he or she has learned but makes no response that others can see or hear, we cannot possibly know that learning has taken place. Thus we must look at overt behaviors.

Many psychologists make a distinction between learning and performance. For them, learning is defined as the changes within the nervous system that have been brought about by experience. Performance is the behavioral change (or new behavior) that is produced by the internal change. Performance occurs only when the situation is appropriate. For example, a person may have learned a new dance, but unless the right music is playing and a suitable partner is available the performance of what the person learned will not take place. Performance can also depend upon internal states; a rat that has been taught by a psychologist to run through a maze for a piece of food will do so only if it is hungry.

This chapter considers the general laws of learning, as they apply to humans and animals. The next chapter will discuss the motivational factors that affect performance and the nature of reinforcement and punishment—two processes that greatly affect learning.

Most of my examples in this chapter are of humans in real-life situations, but some are of animals, either in their natural habitats or in the laboratory, because the principles of learning were discovered through laboratory research. When I describe general principles that apply equally to humans and to other animals, I use the term *organism* as the most inclusive one available.

HABITUATION

There are many events that cause us to react automatically. For example, a sudden, unexpected noise causes an *orienting response*—we become alert and turn our head toward the source of the noise. However, if the noise occurs again and again, we gradually cease to respond to it—we eventually ignore it. *Habituation,* learning *not* to respond to an event that occurs repeatedly, is the simplest form of learning. Even animals with very primitive nervous systems are capable of habituation. For example, if we tap the shell of a land snail with the point of a pencil, it will withdraw its body into its shell. After half a minute or so it will extend its body out of its shell and continue with whatever it was doing. If we tap it again it will again withdraw, but this time it will stay inside its shell a shorter time. Another tap will cause it to withdraw again, but for even less time. Eventually it will stop responding to the tap. The withdrawal response will have habituated.

From an evolutionary perspective, habituation makes sense. If a once-novel stimulus occurs again and again without any important result, the stimulus has no significance to the organism. (A *stimulus* is any physical event that can be detected by an organism's sense receptors.) Obviously it is a waste of time and energy to keep responding to a stimulus that has no importance. Consider what would happen to a land snail in a rainstorm if its withdrawal response never habituated. And consider how distracting it would be to have your attention diverted every time a common household noise occurred.

The simplest form of habituation is temporary, or *short-term habituation*. Suppose we tap a snail's shell until the withdrawal response habituates. If we tap its back again the next day we will find that it withdraws into its shell again and continues to do so for several more taps. It takes just as long for habituation to occur as it did the day before. And if we repeat our experiment every day afterward, the same thing will happen; the snail does not "remember" what happened previously.

Animals with more complex nervous systems are capable of *long-term habituation*. A hunting dog may be frightened the first few times it hears the sound of a shotgun, but it soon learns not to re-

FIGURE 4.1   Although a subway rider is assaulted by intense auditory stimuli and is jostled by movements of the car, responses to these stimuli soon habituate.

spond to it. This habituation carries across from day to day, or even from one hunting season to the next.

Certainly, habituation is the least interesting form of learning, but it is a useful one: it permits us to get more important things done, relatively free from distraction by petty events. It also affects more complex (and interesting) forms of learning, as we shall see. (See **Figure 4.1**.)

CLASSICAL CONDITIONING

In contrast to habituation, which occurs when nothing important happens, *classical conditioning* occurs when an organism encounters an unimpor-

tant, unexpected stimulus followed by an important one that is capable of causing an automatic reaction. The pairing of unexpected stimulus with important stimulus causes the reaction to become conditioned to the unexpected stimulus.

Many of your behaviors have been shaped by this learning process. For example, suppose that you are seated in a small room and someone attaches a large rubber balloon to an electric pump, gradually inflating it to a diameter of two feet, its maximum size. The rubber looks very thin and taut. The pump continues to rumble on, putting more air into the straining membrane, which is now about eighteen inches from your face. What are you likely to do? It is a pretty safe bet that you are grimacing and squinting through partly closed eyelids, your

FIGURE 4.2   Classical conditioning: the child watches the balloon grow large until it bursts, which causes a defensive startle reaction.

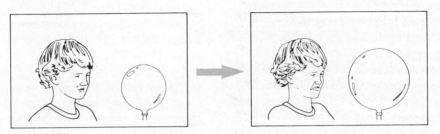

FIGURE 4.3   After the child's first experience with a bursting balloon, the mere sight of an inflating balloon elicits a defensive reaction.

head is hunched down, and you might even be holding your hands over your ears. Why?

You know that the balloon is ready to burst, and when it does it will make a very loud noise. You undoubtedly learned about balloons early in childhood; in fact you probably cannot remember your first encounter with one. But let us analyze how a person learns to flinch defensively at the sight of a thinly stretched balloon. Suppose we inflate a balloon in front of a young boy who has never seen one before. The child will turn his eyes toward the enlarging balloon, but he will not flinch. When the balloon finally explodes, the noise and the blast of air will cause a defensive startle reaction—the subject will squint, grimace, move his head forward, raise his shoulders, and suddenly move his arms toward his body. A bursting balloon is an undeniably important stimulus, one that causes a defensive reaction. Figure 4.2 illustrates what we have done so far.

We will probably not have to repeat the experience many times until our subject reacts the way you do—by flinching defensively before the bal-loon actually bursts. Perhaps one experience will be enough. A previously neutral stimulus (over-inflated balloon), followed by an important stimulus (the explosion that occurs when the balloon bursts), can now trigger the response. The defensive flinching response has been *classically conditioned* to the sight of an overinflated balloon. (See Figure 4.3.)

THE WORK OF IVAN PAVLOV

Ivan Pavlov, a Russian physiologist, carried out the pioneering studies in classical conditioning. (He performed such an impressive and authoritative series of experiments over his long career that this form of learning is called "classical" out of respect for his work.) Pavlov's interest in the digestive process led him to study the neural control of saliva-tion and secretion of digestive juices. One of the surgical procedures he developed to study the func-tions of the digestive system of dogs, his experi-mental animals, consisted of diverting the duct of a salivary gland from the inside of the mouth to the outside of the cheek. Pavlov then inserted a small tube in the duct and collected drops of saliva as they were secreted by the salivary gland.

During his studies Pavlov noticed that after a dog had participated in an experiment for a while, it would begin to salivate as soon as he or one of his assistants entered the room. He expected salivation to occur when the dogs received their food during the course of the experiment; he was surprised that it began earlier than that. At first, Pavlov regarded this anticipatory secretion of saliva as an annoying complication. However, he soon realized that the phenomenon had important implications. He knew that both dogs and humans begin to salivate at the beginning of a meal, even before food enters their mouth. The sight of the food itself is sufficient to stimulate salivation. Previously, scientists believed that this salivation was nothing more than an automatic, reflexive response. But obviously Pavlov's dogs had *learned* to salivate when they saw him or one of his assistants. Therefore, it seemed possible that the salivation that normally occurs at the beginning of a meal is also learned.

Pavlov devised a new apparatus to investigate this phenomenon, which he called "psychic secretion." He struck a tuning fork to make a sound, and half a second later gave the dog some food.

He found that salivation very quickly became conditioned to the tone. (See **Figure** 4.4.) In later studies he used an electric bell as a noise source, and varied the time intervals between the presentation of the sound and the food. Conditioning occurred only when the food followed the sound within a short time. If the bell *followed* the food, the animal never learned to salivate to it. Thus, the sequence and timing of events are important factors in classical conditioning.

Figure 4.5 shows the relative effectiveness of four pairings of stimuli. The most effective pairing, called *delayed conditioning,* is shown at the top of Figure 4.5. The previously neutral stimulus (sound of the bell) occurs first and is still present when, after a short delay, the food is put into the dog's mouth. (See **Figure** 4.5.) *Trace conditioning* is somewhat less effective than delayed conditioning. A bell rings, and the food is delivered after an interval of time. Trace conditioning is probably less effective than delayed conditioning because the stimuli are not present at the same time; a *memory* of the bell is paired with the food, and the memory is less effective than the sound itself. (The term *trace* refers to the neural event in the brain that encodes the memory of the stimulus. See **Figure** 4.5.)

Simultaneous conditioning, in which the neu-

FIGURE 4.4　Pavlov's original procedure for classical conditioning. The experimenter strikes the tuning fork and then presents the food. Saliva is collected in the tube.

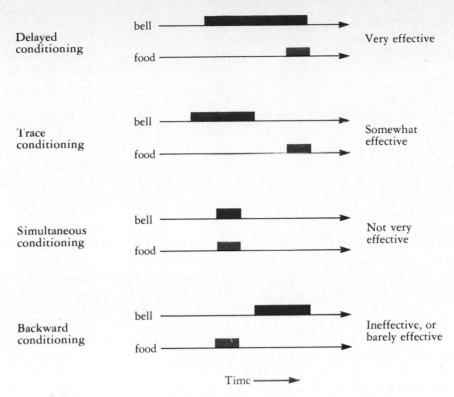

FIGURE 4.5   A comparison of the effectiveness of four kinds of stimulus presentation in classical conditioning.

tral stimulus and the eliciting stimulus are presented simultaneously, is not very effective. Perhaps the simultaneous presentation causes the elicited response to "swamp" the neutral stimulus so that it is less likely to be noticed. (See **Figure** 4.5.) The final form of conditioning, *backward conditioning* (the reverse of trace conditioning), is extremely ineffective; there is disagreement about whether this procedure works at all. (See **Figure** 4.5.) It seems that classical conditioning, then, which entails pairing a neutral stimulus with an eliciting stimulus, requires that the neutral stimulus be presented first.

It is important to understand that classical conditioning is adaptive learning. It is a modification of an already existing stimulus-response relation; a response that is automatically produced by a stimulus becomes linked to a new one. (Remember that Pavlov was originally studying reflex reactions when he made his discovery.) The process is illustrated in Figure 4.6.

◆   The eliciting stimulus upon which the learning depends is referred to as the *unconditional stimulus,* or *US.* The response it elicits, which occurs naturally prior to learning, is called the *unconditional response,* or *UR.* Conditioning occurs when a neutral, noneliciting stimulus, called the *conditional stimulus,* or *CS,* is paired with the unconditonal stimulus (and thus with the unconditional response). Once learning occurs, the conditional stimulus produces the response by itself—now called the *conditional response,* or *CR.* (See **Figure 4.6.**)

If you think about them, the terms make sense. The unconditional stimulus automatically produces the unconditional response; no conditions have to be met. Once the conditions of pairing have been met, the conditional stimulus elicits what is now called the conditional response. The basic form of the response in both instances is the same; what differs is the stimulus that elicits it. (Because of a translation error, many people use the terms *un-*

CONDITIONING PROCEDURE

Neutral stimulus (bell) + Eliciting stimulus (food) ⟶ Elicited response (salivation)
Unconditional stimulus (US)   Unconditional response (UR)

AFTER CONDITIONING

Previously neutral stimulus (bell) ⟶ Response (salivation)
Conditional stimulus (CS)   Conditional response (CR)

FIGURE 4.6   The process of classical conditioning.

conditioned and conditioned, but the terms conditional and unconditional are more appropriate.)

THE ELICITED RESPONSE

Two kinds of naturally occurring responses can be classically conditioned to neutral stimuli: defensive and consummatory reflexes. (No, I did not misspell that word, as you shall see.) A *defensive reflex* is one made in response to an *aversive stimulus*—one that the organism tends to avoid. The response either protects part of the body or moves part of the body away from the source of the aversive stimulation. You have already encountered an example of a defensive reflex: the bursting of a balloon elicits flinching, which causes the eyelids to close and thus protects the eyes from objects that might be blown into them. Similarly, reflexive ducking is a response to a suddenly looming object that is rapidly approaching someone's face. The stimulus elicits the movement, which serves to avoid a collision.

This is probably a good place to make sure that everyone understands my use of the term "elicit." Many people confuse *elicit*, which means "to evoke, to bring out," with *illicit*, which means "not allowed, not sanctioned by law." We can sometimes *elicit* an *illicit* response, but that is another matter altogether.

A *consummatory reflex* is somewhat less straightforward than a defensive reflex. In general, consummatory reflexes are components of behaviors that are directed toward some object (or toward another organism), and have relevance to an organism's survival and the propagation of its spe-

cies. The word is *consummatory*, not *consumatory*. The behavior *consummates*, or "finishes," a sequence. Sometimes that sequence involves consuming something, but often it does not. Consider a consummatory behavior such as the attack of a male wolf on a rival that intrudes upon his territory. A number of reflexes accompany the attack. The wolf's pupils dilate, his eyes widen, his heart rate and blood pressure increase, and the fur on the back of his neck stands up. (See **Figure 4.7.**) Or consider the consummatory act of eating. The behavior is accompanied by reflexes such as salivation, secretion of digestive juices, and release of insulin into the bloodstream. All these reflexes can be classically conditioned—even the release of insulin into the bloodstream.

You might ask *why* classical conditioning takes place. What is its utility? In general, it permits an organism to prepare for events that will soon occur. For example, it is useful to have learned to to duck your head when you hear the buzz of a wasp near your ear. Similarly, your digestive system can do its job more easily if you have learned to salivate before food enters your mouth, and if your stomach secretes digestive juices before you swallow your food.

Classical conditioning has a second function, which is even more important than the first: once defensive or consummatory responses have become classically conditioned to new stimuli, those previously neutral stimuli can shape the behavior of the organism. Because a neutral stimulus becomes desirable when it is associated with a desirable stimulus, or undesirable when it is associated with an undesirable one, our behavior can be modified

[handwritten margin note: organisms tend to avoid aversive stimuli]

[handwritten margin note: defensive reflex]

FIGURE 4.7 The wolf's ears flatten, his lips pull back and expose his teeth, and the fur on his back stands up when another male invades his territory. These reflexes, which signal an impending attack, can be classically conditioned to neutral stimuli.

by these stimuli, with their newly acquired significance to us. Because of this phenomenon, classical conditioning plays an important role in emotions; it has a significant effect on what frightens, angers, or attracts us. (You will learn more about such conditioned reinforcers and conditioned punishers later in this chapter.)

THE ROLE OF THE NEUTRAL STIMULUS

Habituation and Latent Inhibition

◆ A "neutral" stimulus is neutral only with respect to the response that is triggered by the unconditional (eliciting) stimulus. Thus a balloon getting larger is at first neutral with respect to the defensive response caused by an explosion; initially, the neutral stimulus does not produce the defensive

reaction. And, indeed, it never will if the filling of the balloon goes "unnoticed," even when it is regularly followed by the bursting of the balloon. The conditional stimulus must not be neutral with respect to an orienting response.

What determines whether a stimulus will be "noticed"? You already know part of the answer. You will recall that a stimulus that is repeatedly presented *by itself* may produce an orienting response at first, but eventually the response habituates. Once the orienting response has habituated, if the stimulus is now followed by an unconditional stimulus that elicits a defensive or consummatory reflex, the reflex will *not* become conditioned to the neutral stimulus. (See **Figure 4.8.**) A stimulus to which the organism has become completely habituated will not serve as a stimulus for classical conditioning. The organism just does not pay attention to it. (Sometimes conditioning will occur

LATENT INHIBITION

Habituation to neutral stimulus ⎰ Sound of bell ——————▶ Orienting response
                                    repeat until
                                 ⎱ Sound of bell ——————▶ *No* response

then

Attempt at classical conditioning ⎰ Sound of bell + Food ——————▶ Salivation
                                     repeat several times

Test to see whether classical
conditioning occurred ⎰ Sound of bell ——————▶ *No* salivation

FIGURE 4.8   The process of latent inhibition.

even after habituation to the neutral stimulus, but the process takes much longer.)

If you think about it, this effect of habituation on classical conditioning makes sense. A stimulus that occurs regularly, without any special consequences, is not important. It would be a waste of the organism's time and energy to respond to it. If nothing important follows its occurrence, the stimulus ceases to produce an orienting response; it becomes part of the background. If an important stimulus (one that elicits a defensive or consummatory reflex) occurs, any stimulus that has already been occurring regularly is not likely to be related to it. The stimuli that help predict the occurrence of the unconditional stimulus are almost always novel ones, and it is to these that the organism will learn to respond.

The failure of an elicited response to become conditioned to a stimulus that no longer produces an orienting response is called *latent inhibition.* (*Latent* means "hidden" or "concealed.") The term suggests that previous exposure to a neutral stimulus inhibits its potential to become part of a classically conditioned reflex. Whether the process involves actual neural inhibition is not known.

CLASSICAL CONDITIONING IN EVERYDAY LIFE

In the laboratory, a response may be conditioned to an arbitrary stimulus: salivation may be conditioned to the sound of a bell. The only reason the

sound of the bell precedes the food is that the experimenter has arranged the sequence of these events. However, in everyday life, most conditional responses are made to conditional stimuli that are causally related to the unconditional stimuli that originally elicited the responses. For example, the sight of lightning and the sound of thunder are causally related. In fact they are different sensory aspects of a single event: the lightning heats the air and produces a sudden explosion of sound. It is only because sound travels more slowly than light that the two stimuli occur at different times. Someone who is frightened by the sound of thunder is likely to show signs of distress to a sudden flash of light from the sky even before hearing the thunder.

You can probably think of examples of classically conditioned responses of your own. For instance, if your employer (or parent or spouse or teacher) addresses you in a particular tone of voice (conditional stimulus), you may get a queasy feeling in your stomach (conditional response) because that tone of voice was followed by unpleasant scenes in the past (unconditional stimuli). People, tones of voice, objects, and places can all serve as conditional stimuli for unpleasant conditional responses, such as the queasy feeling. In fact this conditioning can result in development of a phobia, a phenomenon discussed in the next section.

Pleasant reactions can also be classically conditioned. A person may feel a warm wave of remembrance (conditional response) upon hearing a song (conditional stimulus) that was associated with a happy romance (during which there were many unconditional stimuli). Even the pleasure received from the sight of a loved one is partly a result of classical conditioning; the presence of that person has been associated with enjoyable events. Similarly, money has meaning for us because it has been associated with desirable commodities. Conditioned reinforcers such as these are discussed later in this chapter.

EXTINCTION

The pairing of a neutral stimulus with an eliciting stimulus leads to classical conditioning; the previously neutral stimulus becomes a conditional stimulus that produces the conditional response. However, classical conditioning is not necessarily permanent. Although the response will occur when the conditional stimulus is presented by itself, the unconditional stimulus must occur occasionally, or the conditional stimulus will lose its ability to elicit the response.

For example, suppose we train a dog to salivate (conditional response) to the sound of a bell (conditional stimulus) by following the sound with an injection of food (unconditional stimulus) into the dog's mouth. Soon the sound of the bell will elicit salivation even when no food is injected. Now suppose that we permanently disconnect the device that injects the food into the dog's mouth but continue to ring the bell every few minutes. For a while, the dog salivates whenever the bell is rung, but eventually it secretes less and less saliva; finally, the dog stops responding. *Extinction* has taken place. The response has been *extinguished*. (Note that responses, not organisms, are extinguished. Students sometimes write, in exams or papers, that "the animal was extinguished." Obviously, an extinguished animal is a dead one.)

Figure 4.9 presents data obtained from one of Pavlov's dogs during extinction. The dog had previously been trained to salivate in response to a noise. Pavlov then presented the noise (CS) every three minutes without the food (US) and counted drops of saliva (CR). By the ninth presentation of the noise alone, the response was completely extinguished. (See **Figure** 4.9.)

The procedure that produces the extinction of a conditional response is exactly the same as the one

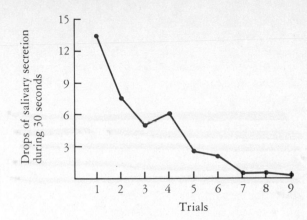

FIGURE 4.9 Extinction of a classically conditioned salivation response. (From Hall, J. F. *An Invitation to Learning and Memory.* Boston: Allyn and Bacon, 1982. Based on data from Pavlov, 1927.)

that produces habituation of an orienting response. In other words, extinction of a conditional response can be described as habituation caused by the repeated presentation of the conditional stimulus by itself.

Extinction is usually not permanent. Given a rest period after a series of presentations of the conditional stimulus alone, the organism will once again emit the conditional response when the conditional stimulus is presented. This phenomenon is appropriately called *spontaneous recovery*. However, unless the unconditional stimulus is also presented, the response will extinguish even more quickly than it did the first time.

CLASSICAL CONDITIONING AND ABNORMAL REACTIONS TO STIMULI

Many people are troubled by behaviors that they wish they could stop doing or by thoughts and fears that trouble them. One way or another, most of these undesirable responses are learned. Just the existence of two extreme forms of such responses—phobias and fetishes—provides ample evidence that classical conditioning does indeed have an effect on emotions and behaviors.

Phobias are unreasonable fears of specific objects or situations, such as spiders, automobiles, or enclosed spaces. Presumably, at some time early in life, the person was exposed to the now-fearsome object in conjunction with a stimulus that elicited pain or fear. For example, being stuck in a hot, overcrowded elevator for a few hours with fellow passengers who are sweating, screaming, and vomiting might be expected to lead to a distrust of elevators afterward and even to produce a full-fledged phobia.

Fetishes are abnormal sexual attachments to objects, such as articles of clothing. It is probable that they occur because of the prior association of some stimulus that most people find neutral with sexual stimuli, which most people do *not* find neutral. One possible scenario might involve a teenage boy masturbating while looking at a sexually arousing picture of a woman wearing high-heeled shoes. The pleasurable stimuli associated with his arousal and orgasm could be conditioned to the shoes worn by the woman, and the boy would subsequently become a shoe fetishist. However, fetishism cannot be that simple; there must be other factors operating, too. Some people are undoubtedly more susceptible than others to developing fetishes. Nevertheless, there is good laboratory evidence that both fear and sexual arousal can be conditioned to neutral stimuli. Let us consider fear (phobia) first.

Campbell, Sanderson, and Laverty (1964) performed an experiment that few people would be inclined to volunteer for. The experiment was an attempt to condition a fear reaction to a neutral stimulus by presenting it just once in conjunction with an aversive one. They turned on a tone, which was to serve as the conditional stimulus, then injected a drug that produces temporary paralysis. The drug does not affect consciousness; the subject remains aware of everything that happens. The subjects tried desperately to breathe, but their muscles did not respond. (Needless to say, they were given artificial respiration.) Obviously, this was an intensely terrifying experience.

When the conditional stimulus (tone) was presented later to the subjects, their autonomic nervous system produced responses that are usually associated with fear. Moreover, these responses did not extinguish, even after the conditional stimulus was presented many times. This experiment provides support for the suggestion that a phobia can be learned through classical conditioning.

In a rather unusual study of fetishes, Rachman and Hodgson (1968) conditioned a sexual response to an object popular among fetishists, women's knee-length boots. Their subjects, young single males, were shown first a color slide of the boots, then a slide of an attractive, naked woman. Sexual arousal was measured by a device called a *plethysmograph*, which measures changes in an object's size. In this case it was attached to the subjects' penises, to make an accurate record of their erections.

The experiment worked. The pairing of the boots as a conditional stimulus and pictures of naked women as unconditional stimuli did result in classical conditioning: the subjects' penises enlarged somewhat in response to the picture of the boots. The subjects even responded to color slides of shoes. Repeated presentation of the conditional stimulus alone (without the naked women) led to extinction. Fortunately, the experiment did not turn the subjects into shoe and boot fetishists.

In fact, the same principles of classical conditioning used in these experiments to induce phobias and fetishes can also be used to abolish them in people who want to be rid of them. Chapter 18 discusses these procedures.

Interim summary: I have so far discussed two forms of learning that help shape behavior: habituation and classical conditioning. Habituation in effect screens out stimuli that experience has shown to be unimportant. This allows organisms to respond to more important stimuli, such as those related to survival and propagation. Thus, habituation plays an important role in the second form of learning, classical conditioning.

The process of classical conditioning takes place when a neutral conditional stimulus occurs just before an unconditional stimulus that elicits a defensive or consummatory behavior. The response that an organism makes to the unconditional stimulus is already a natural part of its behavior; what the organism learns is to make it in response to new stimuli. The neutral stimulus is linked to the unconditional stimulus (either naturally, because the two are causally related, or artificially, in an experiment). The organism learns to respond directly to the once-neutral stimulus. The range of behaviors that can be classically conditioned is limited to those that are automatically elicited by unconditional stimuli. However, through classical conditioning, stimuli that were previously neutral with respect to an organism's behavior can be made to be important, and this importance can have profound effects on a limitless variety of behaviors.

INSTRUMENTAL CONDITIONING

Just as habituation and classical conditioning play a part in shaping behavior, so too does instrumental conditioning. The principle behind it will be familiar to you: when an organism is rewarded for a particular action, its tendency will be to repeat that action, and conversely, when an organism is punished for a particular action, its tendency will be to avoid repeating that action. You may recognize this principle as Thorndike's law of effect. (See **Figure 4.10**.)

◆ The essence of instrumental conditioning is the occurrence of a rewarding or punishing stimulus immediately after an organism performs a particular behavior; the presentation of the stimulus is *contingent* upon the organism's behavior. (A *contingency* is another name for a causal relation; in this case it refers to the fact that the stimulus occurs only when the behavior does.) The effect of the stimulus is to increase or decrease the probability that the organism will perform that behavior again. In a general sense, instrumental conditioning is a description of the ways that the consequences of an organism's actions cause its behavior to adapt to its environment.

REINFORCEMENT AND PUNISHMENT

Because it has fewer connotations, most psychologists prefer to use the term *reinforcement* rather than *reward*. A stimulus that increases the probability of a response that it follows is called a **reinforcing stimulus,** or simply a **reinforcer.** In common usage the term *reward* implies that an organism has done something "good," and deserves a special treat. The neutrality of the process of reinforcement becomes clear when we think of it as the natural consequence of a behavior. Sometimes we deliberately set up a contingency between response and reinforcer (for example, when we train a pet to do a trick). But many reinforcement contingencies are unintentional. Suppose that a large, friendly dog jumps up on a small child with a candy bar who is playing in a park. The child takes fright, drops the candy bar, and runs away. The dog sees something fall at its feet, sniffs it, discovers that it smells tasty, and eats it. Suppose further that the dog now tends to jump up on small children playing in the park. We would conclude that the first child inadvertently reinforced the dog's behavior by dropping the candy bar. However, we would not want to say that she intended to *reward* it.

The behaving organism, and not the agent that delivers the stimulus, determines whether or not a particular stimulus is reinforcing. Suppose that a mother decides to punish her child's whining. Every time the child whines, she says sternly, "Stop

FIGURE 4.10 Instrumental conditioning: the trainer is teaching the dolphin to rescue divers. He does so by rewarding the appropriate behaviors.

whining!" and delivers a lecture on the subject. Unfortunately, the child continues to whine several times a day, and in fact seems to do it even more frequently. Without intending to do so, the mother has actually reinforced whining. Although the rebuke was meant to be aversive to the child, the attention she gave was apparently reinforcing enough to increase the child's frequency of whining.

The term *instrumental conditioning* reflects the fact that the behavior of the organism is *instrumental* in determining whether the reinforcing or punishing stimulus occurs. It involves a stimulus change that is contingent upon a response. The stimulus can be either an *appetitive stimulus* (one that an organism tends to approach) or an aversive one (one that an organism tends to avoid). Please note the use of the term *stimulus change* rather than simply *stimulus;* a behavior may be reinforced or punished by the *removal* of a stimulus, not only by its administration.

Suppose you have to walk barefoot across a large asphalt parking lot on a very hot, sunny day. As you walk, your feet get hotter and hotter. The pain becomes intense, and you look around for some relief. You see a puddle of water in a patch of shade provided by a large truck. You step into the puddle and find it to be delightfully cool on your feet. This stimulus change—removal of an aversive stimulus—is certainly reinforcing.

The type of reinforcement I just described is called *negative reinforcement.* (The other form of reinforcement, the occurrence of a preferred stimulus, is sometimes called *postive reinforcement,* but most psychologists simply call it *reinforcement,* as I do in this book.) Many people confuse negative reinforcement with punishment, but the terms refer to entirely different phenomena. *Punishment* refers to the suppressing effect of an aversive stimulus that occurs right after a particular behavior. *Negative reinforcement* is a particular kind of reinforcement; it refers to the reinforcing effect of the removal of an aversive stimulus immediately after a particular behavior. These contingencies are clearly different: punishment causes a behavior to decrease, whereas negative reinforcement causes a behavior to increase.

Just as the termination of an aversive stimulus is reinforcing, the termination of an appetitive stimulus is punishing. Suppose you meet a person

to whom you find yourself attracted. You engage the person in conversation and enjoy the friendly attention that you receive. You talk for a while and are pleased to find that the other person also seems to be attracted to you. Then you make a disparaging remark about a well-known politician, and your new friend's smile disappears. You quickly change the subject and never bring it up again. The behavior (disparaging remark) is followed by removal of an appetitive stimulus (a warm, friendly smile). The removal of the smile punishes the behavior.

This type of punishment is called *response cost;* a particular response (behavior) costs the organism the presence of a reinforcing stimulus. Just as negative reinforcement involves the removal of an aversive stimulus, punishment, in the form of response cost, involves the removal of an appetitive stimulus. Thus, there are four types of instrumental conditioning—two kinds of reinforcement and two kinds of punishment—caused by the administra-

FIGURE 4.11   Reinforcement and punishment produced by the onset or removal of an appetitive or aversive stimulus.

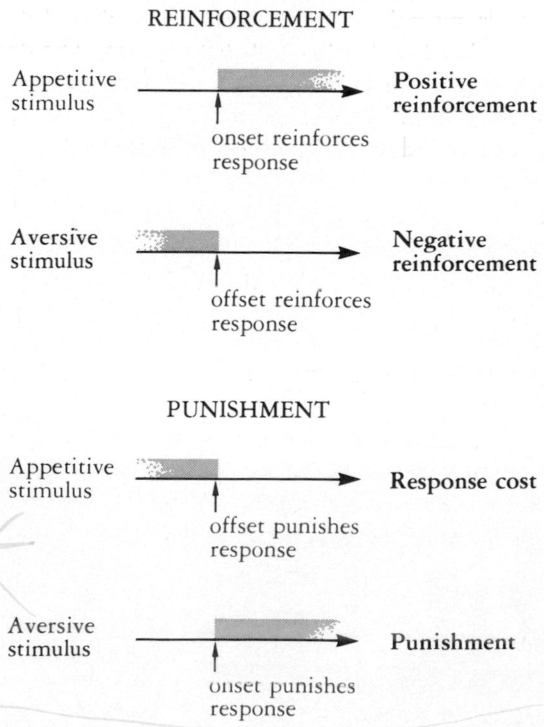

REINFORCEMENT

Appetitive stimulus — onset reinforces response → **Positive reinforcement**

Aversive stimulus — offset reinforces response → **Negative reinforcement**

PUNISHMENT

Appetitive stimulus — offset punishes response → **Response cost**

Aversive stimulus — onset punishes response → **Punishment**

[handwritten margin notes: "negative reinforcement removal of an aversive stimuli"]

[handwritten note at bottom: "omission (in lecture)"]

tion or termination of appetitive or aversive stimuli. (See **Figure 4.11**.)

The following examples describe stimuli that could serve as reinforcers or punishers. See if you can identify the response that is reinforced or suppressed, the reinforcing or punishing stimulus, and the type of instrumental conditioning: reinforcement, negative reinforcement, punishment, or response cost.

1. A woman staying in a rented house cannot get to sleep because of the very unpleasant screeching noise made by the furnace. She goes to the basement, tries to discover the source of the noise, and finally kicks the side of the oil burner. The noise ceases. The next time the furnace makes the noise, she immediately goes to the basement and kicks the side of the oil burner.

2. A man decides to press his trousers while watching an important football game. During a time-out he brings the iron and ironing board into the living room and plugs in the iron. Immediately the tube goes blank; he has blown a fuse. By the time he gets the superintendent of the apartment building to unlock the room that contains the fuse box, he has missed two touchdowns. He never again tries to iron his clothes while watching television.

3. A woman returns home from work and discovers that her dog has soiled the carpet. The dog runs to greet her, and she says, "Naughty boy!" and slaps him. When she comes home the next day she calls her dog, but he stays where he is, hiding under the sofa.

4. A little boy goes for a walk down the street and sees a strange dog. He says, "Hi, doggy!" The dog runs over to him, wagging its tail exuberantly, jumps on him, and knocks him down. The dog attempts to lick his face, but he squirms away and runs home. The next time he sees the dog, he turns away from it.

5. A man visits the lunch counter of a new restaurant and is served by an attractive, friendly waitress. He visits the restaurant for lunch several times during the next week.

* * *

Example 1 illustrates negative reinforcement. The unpleasant noise (aversive stimulus) is terminated when the woman kicks the side of the oil burner (response). Example 2 illustrates response cost. The football game (appetitive stimulus) disappears from the screen of the television set when the man plugs the iron into the wall socket (response); thus, the act of plugging the iron into the wall is punished.

Example 3 illustrates punishment, but not of the response that the woman intends. She slaps the dog, delivering an aversive stimulus, but the response she punishes is the one that the dog has just made: running up to her when she enters the door. Since the dog soiled the rug some time ago, this response is not punished. Example 4 is a straightforward illustration of punishment. The response of saying "Hi, doggy!" is punished by the fall to the ground. Example 5 is an obvious illustration of reinforcement. Entering the restaurant and sitting at the lunch counter is reinforced by a friendly interaction with a pleasant and attractive woman.

Some Complications

Rarely does an instance of instrumental conditioning belong to only one of the four classes described in the previous section. If we examine each situation more closely, we will find that reinforcement or punishment is provided by more than one stimulus. Kicking the oil burner was reinforced by the termination of an irritating noise, so this example is clearly an instance of negative reinforcement. But it is more than that. The aversive stimulus is terminated by the kick, but the kick also made it possible for the woman to go to sleep, and her realization of this fact served as a reinforcer. The second example, the loss of part of the football game, was an instance of response cost, but it was also straightforward punishment; the man realized that he would have to go to some trouble to turn the electricity on again. In almost every case, careful analysis will reveal that a particular instance of instrumental conditioning involves more than one reinforcing or punishing stimulus.

Immediacy of Reinforcement and Punishment

Reinforcement or punishment occurs only when a stimulus *immediately* follows the behavior, within a second or two. (The ability of many organisms—particularly humans—to tolerate a long delay between their work and the reward they receive for it appears to contradict this statement. However, it can be explained by a phenomenon called conditioned reinforcement, which will be discussed later in this chapter.)

An experiment by Logan (1965) illustrates nicely the importance of the immediacy of reinforcement. Logan trained hungry rats to run through a simple maze in which a single passage led to two corridors. At the end of one corridor they would find a small piece of food. At the end of the other corridor they would receive much more food, but it would be delivered only after a delay. Although the most intelligent strategy would be to enter the second corridor and wait for the larger amount of food, the rats chose to take the small amount of food that was delivered right away. Immediacy of reinforcement took precedence over quantity.

There is an exception to the rule that reinforcers (or punishers) must immediately follow a behavior. In most of our dealings with things in the physical world, events that are causally related occur close to each other in time. It makes good sense for organisms to be affected only by events that follow their behavior after a brief interval. Those events that occur later are probably not causally related to the behavior. However, some important stimuli produce effects that are delayed for several hours. For example, if we eat food that contains something toxic (such as poisonous mushrooms), we will not get sick immediately. And yet, organisms are able to learn not to eat things that make them sick (assuming that they survive the experience). The interval between eating a novel food and getting sick can be very long but can still lead to instrumental conditioning. The next chapter discusses this phenomenon in more detail.

REINFORCEMENT AND BEHAVIORAL PREFERENCE

You will recall from the section on classical conditioning that unconditional stimuli are those that elicit defensive or consummatory responses. Similarly, stimuli that serve as reinforcers or punishers also elicit responses: usually, reinforcers elicit consummatory responses whereas punishers elicit defensive responses. If a stimulus does not elicit a behavior, it probably will not serve as a punisher or reinforcer. (Some stimuli can elicit a covert response rather than an overt one, and may still serve

as a punisher or reinforcer. For example, imagine a croupier placing a stack of chips before a cool and sophisticated gambler who has just won at roulette. The gambler might not show any overt signs of pleasure, but we would be foolish to conclude that winning had no effect simply because we could not see a response.)

The Premack Principle — imp

Some stimuli—food to a hungry animal, water to a thirsty one, warmth to a cold one—are obviously reinforcing. Other stimuli, not related to survival, are not so easy to predict. Premack (1965) has suggested that an animal's own preference can be used to determine whether a stimulus will serve as a reinforcer or punisher. An animal can be put into an apparatus that is divided into two compartments. The stimulus to be tested can be made available in one of the compartments but not in the other. Or two different stimuli can be presented, one on one side, a second on the other side. The relative amount of time that the animal spends in the two compartments reveals its preference. As you would expect, a hungry animal will stay where the food is, and a thirsty animal will stay where the water is. Similarly, if an animal stays in a compartment containing a window that permits it to look out, then we know that the opportunity to look outside is a reinforcer, and that we can alter the animal's behavior by unshuttering a window for a brief time whenever it performs a particular response.

Sometimes an organism surprises us with its choice. Countless numbers of children have participated in learning experiments that required them to work a knob on a device resembling a pinball machine in order to receive an M&M candy (Premack, 1965). In other words, a response was reinforced with the delivery of M&Ms. (M&Ms, sugar-coated chocolate candies, are widely used because they are of a small, uniform size and can easily be dispensed, one at a time, by an automatic dispensing machine.) Premack found that some children, if given the choice, would play with the knob rather than eat an M&M: it was more fun to play the "game" than to eat an M&M. Premack turned the contingency around; he offered these children an M&M, and if they ate it they got a chance to play with the knob for a while. The

FIGURE 4.12   On a hot day, playing in cool water is a highly preferred behavior.

children quickly learned to eat M&Ms so that they could get a chance to play. Again, it is clear that the *subject*, and not the *experimenter*, determines which stimuli will serve as reinforcers.

The first part of the ***Premack principle*** states that an organism has different preferences for performing different behaviors. (See **Figure 4.12**.) A large list of behaviors can be assembled, ranked in order of preference from low to high. (Such a list is called a ***preference hierarchy***.) Some behaviors are very high on the list, some are neutral, and some are so low on the list that they will be avoided. (Screaming in response to the pain caused by having one's foot pounded by a sledge hammer would be a behavior that is low on most people's list.) The second part of the Premack principle states

that an organism will perform a behavior that is low in the hierarchy in order to gain the opportunity to perform a preferred behavior. Thus, if a child prefers playing with the knob to eating M&Ms, he or she can be trained to eat M&Ms if this behavior is reinforced by the opportunity to play with the knob. If a rat prefers eating food to running through a maze, it can be trained to run through the maze by reinforcing this behavior with the opportunity to eat food.

A case reported by Tyson (1980) illustrates this principle. The sole pleasure of a severely retarded man appeared to be making other residents' beds in the ward of the institution in which he lived. This resident also resisted bathing, so that whenever he became so dirty and smelly that the attendants and fellow residents could not stand it, he was forcibly stripped, put into a bathtub, and washed. The ordeal was unpleasant both for the resident and for the attendants who had to wash him. Tyson decided to make use of the Premack principle. After obtaining permission from the ethics review board of the institution, he made bedmaking contingent on bathing; that is, the resident was permitted to make beds only after he bathed. The contingency worked; within a few days he was bathing regularly.

Stimuli, then, are reinforcing when they permit a particular behavior to occur, and each organism has its own set of preferences for engaging in a particular behavior. A hungry animal prefers eating to most other behaviors; for this animal, food is reinforcing because it permits eating. Obviously, it is futile to label stimuli as reinforcers or punishers without taking the organism's preference into account. Who could have predicted that the opportunity to make beds would serve as a reinforcer?

Restriction of the Preferred Behavior Through Reinforcement Contingencies

Suppose you are seated in front of a television, watching your favorite program. You have a large bowlful of popcorn in your lap, and you munch on it as you watch. Someone approaches you and offers to give you a piece of popcorn every time you press a button. This contingency (one piece of popcorn for each button press) is unlikely to affect your behavior. You can already eat a handful of popcorn whenever you want, so it is unlikely that the promise of popcorn for button pressing will alter what you are doing. Now suppose you are watching television without a bowl of popcorn in your lap because you had no popcorn in the house. The offer will probably seem more worthwhile, and you might start pressing the button. The point is this: if the opportunity to engage in a particular behavior is not limited, then it is difficult to use the opportunity to engage in that behavior as a reinforcer. Timberlake and Allison (1974) have emphasized that it is not enough to know an organism's relative preference for engaging in each of two behaviors to predict which behavior can be used to reinforce the other. The reinforcement contingency must also *restrict* the organism's opportunity to engage in the behavior that is being used as the reinforcer.

Again suppose you are watching television and munching on a bowlful of popcorn. This time someone much stronger than you takes the bowl away from you, announces that you cannot eat any more of it, and then offers you the opportunity to obtain popcorn by pressing the button. Now the contingency is more likely to be successful.

Of course, it is also likely that you would resent being manipulated so obviously and would refuse to press the button. Your refusal does not mean that the principle of reinforcement does not work in this case—it only means that meekly eating popcorn that is doled out by someone who took it from you is very low on your list of preferred behaviors. Thus, a reinforcement contingency is effective only when the organism is currently unable to perform the preferred behavior as often as it would like to. The contingency then permits the organism to engage in the preferred behavior more often by performing the less preferred one. This principle clearly operates in the case of the man who was induced to bathe in order to make beds. Before the contingency was put into effect he got to make beds as often as he liked. The contingency (no bedmaking until after taking a bath) restricted his opportunity to make beds. Thus, an opportunity to make beds was able to reinforce bathing.

Behaviors can move up or down an organism's list of preferences; their position is not fixed. The simplest way to cause a behavior to move up the list is to deprive the organism of the opportunity to engage in it. If you have not eaten for two days, eating is very high on your list. If you have been cooped up in a room all day, going for a walk in the fresh air becomes a preferred activity. These factors are related to motivation, which will be discussed in the next chapter.

CONDITIONED REINFORCEMENT AND PUNISHMENT

Some reinforcers and punishers have obvious biological significance; they are important to an individual's survival or to the survival of its species. For example, food, warmth, and sexual contact are reinforcing, and stimuli that cause pain are punishing. These stimuli are called *primary reinforcers* and *primary punishers.* Other classes of reinforcers and punishers are not so obvious, as we just saw. This section explains how neutral stimuli can become reinforcing or punishing to an organism through the process of classical conditioning.

For humans, stimuli like money, admission tickets, the smell of delicious food, or parking tickets can serve as reinforcers or punishers, but only if the person has learned something about them. These stimuli are called *conditioned reinforcers* and *conditioned punishers.* (Sometimes they are called *secondary reinforcers* or *secondary punishers.*) Conditioned reinforcers and punishers derive their reinforcing or punishing properties from association with primary reinforcers or punishers. The distinction between them cannot always be made with certainty. For example, given the fact that food is considered to be a primary reinforcer, then a caterpillar would have to be said to be a primary reinforcer for a member of one of several South American tribes. However, few North Americans would consider a caterpillar to be food. Experience in the two cultures has determined which items are considered to be food. Mother's milk is undoubtedly a primary reinforcer, and a caterpillar is a conditioned (learned) reinforcer.

A stimulus becomes a conditioned reinforcer or punisher by means of classical conditioning. That is, if a neutral stimulus occurs regularly just before an appetitive or aversive stimulus, then the neutral stimulus itself becomes an appetitive or aversive stimulus. If *this* stimulus occurs immediately after a behavior, it serves to reinforce or punish that behavior. For example, money is regularly associated with appetitive stimuli (those things that money will buy), so it becomes a conditioned reinforcer. In contrast, the sight of a flashing light on top of

FIGURE 4.13   Social reinforcers are especially potent for humans. As her smile attests, this person's behavior is being reinforced by the social interaction, not punished by a dunk in the water.

a police car serves as a conditioned punisher to a person who is driving too fast, because such a sight precedes an unpleasant set of stimuli—a lecture by a police officer and a speeding ticket. The ticket itself is also a conditioned punisher because it signals the loss of an appetitive stimulus: money.

The phenomena of conditioned reinforcement and punishment are extremely important. They permit an organism's behavior to be affected by stimuli that are not biologically important themselves but which are regularly associated with the onset or termination of biologically important stimuli. Indeed, stimuli can even become conditioned reinforcers or punishers by being associated with *other* conditioned reinforcers or punishers. (The speeding ticket is just such an example.) If only primary reinforcers and punishers were able to control an organism's behavior, that behavior would not be very flexible. The organism would never learn to perform behaviors that had only long-range benefits; its behavior would be controlled on a moment-to-moment basis. Conditioned reinforcers and punishers (such as money, grades, smiles, and frowns) make it possible for behavior to be altered by a wide variety of contingencies. (See Figure 4.13.)

Interim summary: Classical conditioning and instrumental conditioning complement each other.

As you have seen, these forms of learning are not mutually exclusive. The pairings of neutral stimuli with appetitive and aversive stimuli (classical conditioning) determine which stimuli become conditioned (secondary) reinforcers and punishers. The contingencies between an organism's behavior and these stimuli (instrumental conditioning) adapt its behavior to its environment.

The major difference between these two types of conditioning is the nature of the contingencies: classical conditioning involves a contingency between stimuli (CS and US) whereas instrumental conditioning involves a contingency between an organism's behavior and appetitive or aversive stimuli.

SOCIAL REINFORCEMENT AND PUNISHMENT

For humans (and probably for many other animals) there is a class of conditioned reinforcers known as *social reinforcers,* as well as a complementary class known as *social punishers.* These stimuli consist of behaviors of other people, especially those that indicate approval or rejection. A smile, a nod, or a frown can serve as potent reinforcers or punishers. Sometimes the control of social reinforcers is very subtle, as the following example will show. Carl Rogers is an esteemed psychotherapist who has pioneered "client-centered therapy." He and his followers attempt to provide a consistent, supportive environment in which their clients can talk about their problems and eventually be helped. Rogers used to refer to his form of therapy as nondirective, on the grounds that he said nothing to guide his patients but let them find their own way to mental and emotional health.

Charles Truax (1966) suspected that client-centered therapy was not purely nondirective so he obtained permission from Rogers (and his clients) to record some therapy sessions and classified the statements made by the client into several categories. One of the categories included statements of improving mental health, such as "I'm feeling better lately" or "I don't feel as depressed as I used to." After each of the patient's statements, Truax noted Rogers's reaction to see whether he gave a positive response. Typical positive responses were "Oh, really? Tell me more" or "Uh-huh. That's nice" or just a friendly "Mm." Truax found that of the eight categories of client responses, only those that indicated progress were regularly followed by a positive response from Rogers. Not surprisingly, during their therapy the clients made more and more statements indicating progress.

This experiment attests to the effectiveness of social reinforcement and its occurrence in unexpected places. Rogers is an effective and conscientious psychotherapist, but he had not intended to single out and reinforce clients' realistic expressions of progress in therapy. (Obviously, he does not uncritically reinforce exaggerated or unrealistic positive statements.) When Rogers realized that he was reinforcing positive statements he stopped referring to his therapy as nondirective, since it obviously was not.

CONDITIONING OF COMPLEX BEHAVIORS

◆ Most of our behaviors, especially long sequences of behaviors, are products of conditioned reinforcers. Consider the behavior of a young child who is learning to print letters. She sits at her school desk, producing long rows of letters. What maintains her behavior? Why is she devoting her time to a task that appears to involve so much effort? The answer is that her behavior produces stimuli that are reinforcing. In other words, the effects of her behavior serve to reinforce that very behavior. In previous class sessions, the teacher has demonstrated how to print the letters and has praised the girl for printing them herself. The act of printing has been reinforced, and thus the printed letters that this act produces come to serve as conditioned reinforcers. The child prints a letter, sees that it looks approximately the way it should, and her behavior is reinforced by the sight of the letter. *Doing something correctly,* or making progress toward that goal, can provide very effective reinforcement.

This fact is often overlooked by people who take a limited view of the process of reinforcement, thinking that it has to resemble the delivery of a small piece of food to a rat after it presses a lever. Some people even say that because reinforcers are rarely delivered to humans immediately after they perform a behavior, instrumental conditioning must not play a significant role in human learning. Perhaps we psychologists who teach introductory psychology must take some of the blame for this misunderstanding. We often illustrate an explanation of instrumental conditioning with examples taken from the laboratory, so when students think of instrumental conditioning they often think only of rats pressing levers or running through mazes.

It is true that most of the phenomena of instrumental conditioning have been discovered in experiments with animals, but the process of reinforcement in real life is indeed similar to what is observed in the laboratory. Psychologists sometimes unintentionally emphasize *procedures* rather than processes; they say that a reinforcer is *delivered* because in the controlled circumstances of experiments psychologists do deliver reinforcers to their subjects. However, the overwhelming majority of reinforcers are not delivered by another agent; they are *obtained* by the organism that is doing the behaving. The reinforcement occurs as a natural consequence of the behavior. Only in the laboratory, in social situations, or in the classroom does a person *deliver* a reinforcer to another person. Most reinforcers are self-administered.

A good synonym for the conditioned reinforcement that shapes and maintains our behavior is *satisfaction.* Usually we work hard at some task because it "give us satisfaction." An artist who produces a fine painting gains satisfaction from the image that emerges as she works on it, and receives even stronger satisfaction from looking at the finished product. This satisfaction derives from a lifetime of experience. The artist knows what looks good; she recognizes a painting that will be valued as a piece of art by critics and peers. When she produces one herself she delivers her own conditioned reinforcer.

Shaping

Laboratory experiments have shown the importance of conditioned reinforcers in the instrumental conditioning of sequences of behavior. You already know that reinforcement increases the probability that a particular response will occur again. But suppose you want to train an animal to perform a completely new response—one that you have never seen it make. How can you do so, since a behavior must occur before it can be reinforced? The answer lies in the procedure of *shaping*, reinforcing a succession of responses that are increasingly similar to the one you want the animal to perform. The

reinforcer is a previously neutral stimulus that has been associated with a primary reinforcer.

Psychologists who study instrumental conditioning often use hungry rats as subjects and require them to press a small lever attached to a wall in order to obtain food. They generally use an apparatus called an *operant chamber*. (See **Figure 4.14.**) (The term comes from *operant conditioning,* which many psychologists use synonymously with instrumental conditioning, although some make a distinction that need not concern us here.) The device is also referred to as a *Skinner box,* after B.F. Skinner of Harvard University, who invented it and pioneered the modern study of instrumental conditioning. (Skinner himself dislikes the term Skinner box. See **Figure 4.15.**)

The lever on the wall of the chamber is attached to an electrical switch wired to electronic control equipment or a computer. A mechanical dispenser can automatically drop molded pellets of food, about the size of a very small pea, into a dish in the chamber. Thus, the delivery of a food pellet can be made contingent upon the rat's pressing the lever. The operant chamber shown in Figure 4.14

FIGURE 4.14   An operant chamber.

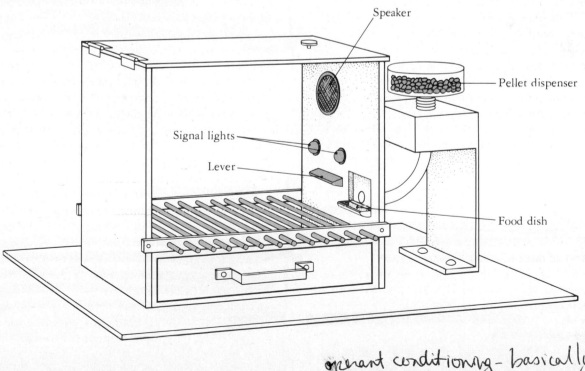

Speaker

Pellet dispenser

Signal lights

Lever

Food dish

operant conditioning - basically
instrumental conditioning

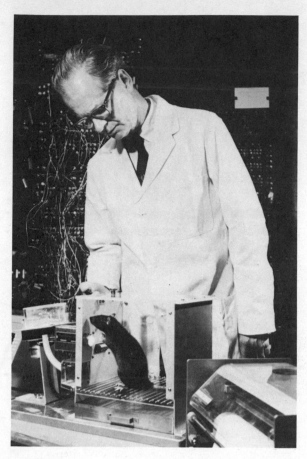

FIGURE 4.15   B. F. Skinner, the inventor of the operant chamber, in his laboratory.

contains two lights and a loudspeaker mounted on the wall near the lever, so that both visual and auditory stimuli can be presented. (See **Figure 4.14.**)

If we put a hungry rat into the apparatus, the animal will explore the chamber and may even depress the lever, perhaps while attempting to climb the wall. But we would probably have to wait a long time for the pressing of the lever to be reinforced by the delivery of the food. Reinforcement must be *immediate,* and unless the rat finds the food right after pressing the lever, some other behavior, not lever pressing, will be reinforced. The delivery of the food pellet after an accidental lever press will probably reinforce the rat's approach to the dish, so the animal will tend to remain in its vicinity, and the animal's rate of lever pressing may therefore *decrease.*

To deliver immediate reinforcement we establish an auditory stimulus as a conditioned reinforcer. An auditory stimulus is best for our purpose because the rat will perceive it wherever the animal is in the cage. A buzzer or other noise-making device is not necessary, because pellet dispensers make a noise of their own when they deliver a piece of food. To begin with, we operate the pellet dispenser and let the rat find the pellet. After it eats the food, we deliver a few more pellets while the rat is in the vicinity of the food dish, until the noise of the pellet dispenser becomes a conditioned reinforcer. Then we wait until the rat leaves the food dish and turns in the direction of the lever. As soon as the animal turns, we operate the dispenser. The rat hears the noise and returns to the dish to eat the piece of food. Since the noise, now a conditioned reinforcer, was presented immediately after the turning movement, the turning movement is reinforced. The rat soon turns away from the food dish, so we activate the dispenser again.

Once the behavior of turning away from the food dish is firmly established we reinforce a behavior even closer to lever pressing. We wait until the rat turns even farther away from the dish, approaching very near to the lever, before we activate the dispenser. (It is still the *noise,* not the food, that reinforces the behavior. The food simply serves to maintain the noise as a conditioned reinforcer.) Soon the rat is rapidly shuttling between lever and food dish. Now we wait until it touches the lever with any part of its body (it will usually bump the lever with its nose). Then we require it to put its front feet on the lever, and finally we activate the dispenser only when the rat actually presses the lever down, operating the switch. Now we can connect the switch to the dispenser and let the device operate automatically.

The formal name for shaping is the **method of successive approximations.** A reinforcer (almost always a conditioned reinforcer) is delivered immediately after responses that at first only approximately resemble the response that is to be conditioned (the **target behavior**). Successive responses must resemble the target behavior even more closely to be reinforced, until the goal is reached. (See **Figure 4.16.**)

The method of successive approximations can be

FIGURE 4.16 The Suzuki method teaches children to play violin by means of a technique that resembles shaping. The sounds a child produces successively approximate violin playing. The expression on the smallest child's face suggests that his behavior is not meeting the current criterion.

used to train an animal to perform just about any response that it is physically capable of doing. The tricks of performing dolphins and trained seals are developed by reinforcing a succession of responses that are increasingly similar to the desired one. The trainers usually reinforce the animals' behavior by producing a noise (such as the sound of a whistle) that has been paired with the delivery of food.

Shaping is a formal training procedure, but something like it also occurs in the real world. A teacher praises poorly formed letters produced by a child who is just beginning to print, but as time goes on, only more accurately drawn letters bring approval. The method of successive approximations can also be self-administered. Consider the acquisition of skills through trial and error. To begin with, you must be able to recognize the target behavior—that is, the behavior of a person with the appropriate skill. Your first attempts produce behaviors that vaguely resemble those of a skilled performer, and you are satisfied by the results of these attempts. In other words, the stimuli that are produced by your behavior serve as conditioned reinforcers for that behavior. As your skill develops, crude approximations to the final behavior become less reinforcing; you are satisfied only when your behavior improves so that it more closely resembles the target behavior. Your own criterion changes as you become more skilled. This process is perfectly analogous to the use of changing criteria in training an animal to perform a complex behavior.

Chaining of Response Sequences

◆ By now it is clear that the consequences of a behavior can be reinforcing; that is, the stimuli that

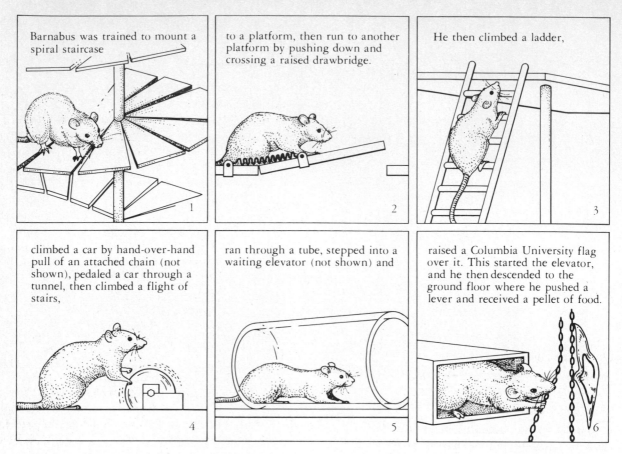

Barnabus was trained to mount a spiral staircase	to a platform, then run to another platform by pushing down and crossing a raised drawbridge.	He then climbed a ladder,
1	2	3
climbed a car by hand-over-hand pull of an attached chain (not shown), pedaled a car through a tunnel, then climbed a flight of stairs,	ran through a tube, stepped into a waiting elevator (not shown) and	raised a Columbia University flag over it. This started the elevator, and he then descended to the ground floor where he pushed a lever and received a pellet of food.
4	5	6

FIGURE 4.17   Barnabus the rat was taught a long sequence of behaviors. (From Ferster, C. B., and Perrot, M. C. *Behavior Principles.* New York: Appleton-Century-Crofts, 1968.)

the behavior produces can serve as conditioned reinforcers. This phenomenon is very important for maintaining long sequences of responses. Pierrel and Sherman (1963) performed a demonstration illustrating the power of the shaping method. (See **Figure 4.17.**) They trained a rat named Barnabus to climb a spiral stairway, lower a drawbridge and cross over to a platform, climb a ladder, pull a chain to fetch a toy car, climb into it and pedal it through a tunnel to another stairway, climb the stairs, run through a tube, get into an elevator, raise a small flag of Columbia University (which causes the elevator to descend), ride the elevator to the ground, and press a lever. After all this, the rat received a food pellet.

How can an animal be trained to perform such a long sequence of behaviors? First of all, the components of the sequence are shaped *backward* from

the order in which they are to be performed; the rat first learns to press the lever, then to operate the elevator, then to run through the tube, and so on. But because the entire sequence is so long, it is difficult to see how the early behaviors can be effectively reinforced. The trainer cannot simply deliver a food pellet, because the animal would then run directly to the food dish, omitting the rest of the responses in the chain. Instead, each behavior is reinforced by the *opportunity to perform the next behavior in the sequence.*

Suppose we want to train a rat to press four levers, each mounted on one wall of an operant chamber. We designate the levers as A, B, C, and D, and they are to be pressed in that sequence. We first train the rat to press lever D, the last in the sequence. Now, how can we train it to press lever C? We cannot deliver a piece of food when

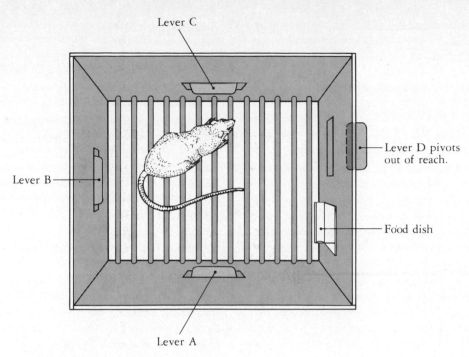

Lever C

Lever D pivots
out of reach.

Lever B

Food dish

Lever A

FIGURE 4.18   An apparatus that could be used
to train a rat to press four levers in sequence.

it approaches and presses lever C, because then it
will not bother to press lever D. Instead, we use
the *opportunity to press lever D* as a conditioned reinforcer. We block access to lever D by sliding it
back on a pivot so that it is outside the wall of the
cage, where the animal cannot reach it. (See **Figure
4.18.**) The rat will investigate the wall that contains the missing lever, but finally it will turn
away. As soon as it does, we operate the mechanism that pivots the lever back into the chamber.
(This mechanism makes a noise, of course.) The
rat turns to look at the source of the noise and sees
the lever back in position. The rat presses it and
receives a pellet of food. After each food pellet is
delivered, lever D is removed and the sound of the
mechanism that pivots it back into the chamber is
used to reinforce successive approximations to
pressing lever C. Pressing lever C permits the rat
to press lever D, which permits it to eat a pellet
of food. Next, lever C is removed and the rat is
trained to press lever B, and so on. Every response
in the chain is reinforced by a conditioned reinforcer, namely, the opportunity to perform the next
response.

You should realize that none of these responses
is being reinforced by the delivery of food. Like
the other responses, responding to lever D is reinforced by a conditioned reinforcer—in this case,
the sound of the pellet dispenser. However, the
primary reinforcer—food—is essential to the process;
it establishes the conditioned reinforcers that shape
the behavior. Ultimately, the consequence of the
rat's sequence of behaviors is to receive a pellet of
food.

EXTINCTION

We have seen how responses may be reinforced by
their consequences. When a response produces a
reinforcing stimulus, that response becomes more
frequent. But sometimes the environment changes,
so that the contingency between response and reinforcement no longer exists. If this happens, there
is no reason to continue to respond. In fact, if a
reinforcer no longer follows the response, the organism will eventually stop responding. This phenomenon, referred to as extinction, was described
earlier in the discussion of classical conditioning.

Extinction takes place only when the organism makes the response that was formerly reinforced. Suppose a rat is trained in an operant chamber to press a lever for food pellets. If the animal is taken out of the chamber for a few days, its behavior will not extinguish—it will continue to respond when it is placed into the operant chamber again. For extinction to take place the animal must press the lever and *not* receive food for doing so.

When an animal's behavior is no longer reinforced its rate of responding will usually increase at first. The increase is soon followed by a slow-down, and finally a long pause in responding. Periodically, at irregular intervals, the animal will respond again, usually in bursts. Finally, responding will cease. The behavior has been extinguished.

Suppose we train a rat to press a lever for food reinforcement and allow the animal to respond, one hour each day, for several days. Then one day we turn off the food dispenser so that the response will become extinguished. Within an hour, the animal ceases to respond. We take the animal out of the operant chamber and put it back in its cage. The next day we again put the rat in the operant chamber. We find that it quickly runs to the lever and begins responding once more. This phenomenon is called spontaneous recovery: after an interval without any opportunity to respond, the animal's rate of responding recovers spontaneously. Unless the animal's behavior is reinforced again, it does not respond very long; the response soon extinguishes. (You will recall that extinguished conditional responses—CRs—also show spontaneous recovery.)

Extinction makes good sense in a natural environment. If a response no longer "works" there is no point in persisting in making it; doing so expends energy unnecessarily and keeps the organism from discovering a response that will work. Similarly, spontaneous recovery makes good sense. Perhaps conditions have changed again, and the response will produce the reinforcer once more. It is certainly worth a try.

You can probably think of several examples of extinction of human behavior. Some instances are acts of nature. An angler catches a lot of fish in one place and hence comes back to try it again. Even if no more fish are ever caught there, he or she will probably still try the spot a few more times, spending less time there on each subsequent visit. Other instances of extinction are deliberately produced. Sometimes social reinforcers are withheld in order to extinguish another person's behavior. If you find someone's conversation boring, you will probably stop smiling, nodding, and showing the signs of interest that serve as social reinforcers.

Sometimes parents find it necessary to extinguish a child's behavior, such as crying at bedtime.

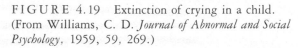

FIGURE 4.19   Extinction of crying in a child. (From Williams, C. D. *Journal of Abnormal and Social Psychology,* 1959, *59,* 269.)

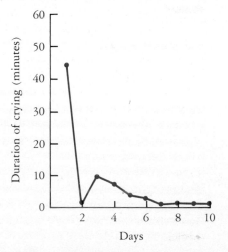
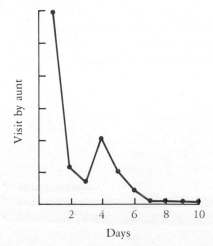

When a baby cries, a parent's usual response is to go to it and pick it up to find out what it needs or just to comfort it. The attention serves as a reinforcer. In a few cases the crying gets out of hand—the infant cries as soon as it is put down. The baby comes to rule the household, demanding constant attention, and soon the parents become exhausted. Most parents report feeling hostility toward their baby when it just will not let them put it to bed, and also feeling guilty about their hostility. When it is clear that the baby has acquired the habit of crying whenever it is put to bed, it is time to begin the process of extinction.

The first thing to do, of course, is to make sure the baby is healthy, dry, and comfortable. Then the parents have to resolve to sit still and listen to the piteous wails of a baby protesting its abandonment. The ordeal will have to be repeated a few times, but eventually the baby's crying will be extinguished. And the household will be much happier. When the behavior is extinguished, the parents' own anxiety is diminished, and they can enjoy their roles as parents more.

Figure 4.19 presents data from the extinction of a baby's bedtime crying. Note the spontaneous recovery that occurred when an aunt watched the infant while the parents went out; she "could not stand to hear the poor thing crying." (See **Figure 4.19**.)

Extinction of a previously reinforced response does more than reduce the probability of that response; it also increases the probability of other responses, especially aggressive ones. For example, a pigeon subjected to the frustration of extinction will learn to peck a plastic disk that opens a door so that another pigeon can be attacked (Azrin, 1964). The phenomenon of extinction appears to cause a variety of behaviors. Chapter 14 discusses this topic further.

INTERMITTENT REINFORCEMENT

So far we have considered situations in which a reinforcing stimulus is presented after each response (or, in the case of extinction, not at all). But reinforcing every response may soon lead to *satiation;* the animal may finally get as much as it wants of the reinforcer and thus stop working for it. Also, the behavior of an animal that receives a reinforcer for each response will extinguish fairly quickly if reinforcement is discontinued. However, if reinforcers are received after some, but not all, responses, then the behavior will be very resistant to extinction.

Intermittent reinforcement is the rule in real life. Usually, not every response that we make is reinforced. Sometimes a kind word is ignored, sometimes it is appreciated. Not every fishing trip is rewarded with a catch, but some are, and that fact is enough to keep a person trying. In this section I shall describe various patterns of intermittent reinforcement.

Intermittent Reinforcement and Resistance to Extinction

Imagine that you have been locked up in a room that is empty except for a refrigerator stocked with food. After exploring your cell, you decide to have a bite to eat. You get some food out of the refrigerator and begin eating. As you are eating, you realize that you have nothing to drink and find that there are no beverages in the refrigerator. You notice a recess in the wall, containing a small cup set under a metal spout. A pushbutton is located on the wall beneath the recess. You press the button, and the spigot dispenses a small amount of water into the cup. You drink the water, replace the cup, and press the button again. You repeat the process until you get as much water as you want.

Suppose that you spend several days in the room, obtaining food from the refrigerator and water from the dispenser mounted in the wall. Then one day the dispenser suddenly stops working. You press the button several times, but nothing happens. What would you do next? You would probably pound on the wall, hit the button several times, and start pacing around the room. (You would be displaying the aggressive responses that are produced by the frustration of extinction.) Every now and then you would come back to try the dispenser, but you would not work long at pressing the button. You would probably become quite upset and agitated, but the total number of times that you would press the button would be small. Your response would rather rapidly be extinguished.

Suppose, however, that your original experience with the water dispenser had been different. The first time you pressed it, water was delivered, but you had to press it twice before it would work again. As time went on, the operation of the dispenser became more and more erratic; sometimes it took only one or two presses to make it work, and at other times it required a hundred presses or more.

Now suppose that, unknown to you, the dispenser is permanently turned off. The next time you become thirsty, you approach and begin pressing the button. Nothing happens. You keep pressing and pressing—many more times than you did in the first example. You begin to get desperate, and perhaps you begin to bang and kick the wall, but you keep working away at the button. Finally you leave, perhaps pacing around the room, but you return now and then to the button, pressing it many times before you leave.

Your behavior follows the rule that a response that has been reinforced intermittently is resistant to extinction—*it is harder to extinguish a response that has been reinforced intermittently.* The more responses you have had to make for each reinforcement, the longer you will respond during extinction. And I am sure the reason is obvious to you. In the first example, it was immediately apparent when extinction began—the dispenser went from one squirt of water per press to no water at all. You would probably have said to yourself, "Oh no! This thing is broken!" In the second case, you were accustomed to making many responses per reinforcement, and it would take many more responses before you decided that the dispenser was not working any more. I doubt whether an animal other than a human would decide that the dispenser was broken, but the behavior of rats, pigeons, monkeys, and humans would be the same under these conditions—even to pacing around and the banging on the wall.

Here is the most likely explanation for the effects of partial intermittent reinforcement on extinction. Continuous reinforcement (that is, reinforcement after every response) is very different from extinction; the very first nonreinforced response signals the fact that conditions have changed. However, intermittent reinforcement and extinction are much more similar. A nonreinforced response is not a novel event to an organism that has been reinforced intermittently; in the past, many responses were not reinforced. Thus, the onset of extinction does not present a distinctive signal. Only after many responses have gone unreinforced can the organism detect that the reinforcement contingencies have changed. Because an organism that has been trained with intermittent reinforcement is accustomed to making nonreinforced responses, it takes longer for the behavior to be extinguished.

Schedules of Reinforcement

B.F. Skinner, who pioneered the field of instrumental conditioning, invented procedures for administering intermittent reinforcement. These procedures are called *schedules of reinforcement.* There are two types of schedules, *response-dependent schedules* and *response-and-time-dependent schedules.*

RESPONSE-DEPENDENT SCHEDULES OF REINFORCEMENT   If an animal receives a reinforcer for each response, the ratio of responses to reinforcers is one to one. We call this a *continuous reinforcement schedule* (or *CRF*). A reinforcer following every second response—two responses per reinforcer—would be called a *fixed-ratio schedule* (*FR*) of two, or *FR-2.* One reinforcer for three responses would be called FR-3, and so on. Fixed-ratio schedules of up to several hundred responses per reinforcer can be used to keep an animal responding, but it is necessary to start at an easy schedule, and then gradually increase the work required. If the schedule is increased too fast, the response may extinguish.

An animal that is working on a long fixed-ratio schedule (say, FR-75) will usually pause for a while after obtaining a reinforcer, then start in again at a steady rate until the next reinforcer is delivered. The more responses that are required per reinforcement, the longer the pause before the animal gets back to work. This phenomenon is called, appropriately enough, a *postreinforcement pause.* It is as if the animal rests for a while before working again.

People rarely encounter fixed-ratio schedules in real life. A possible example might be the harvesting of crops when a person is paid for each

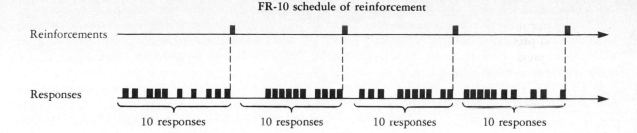

FR-10 schedule of reinforcement

Reinforcements

Responses

10 responses   10 responses   10 responses   10 responses

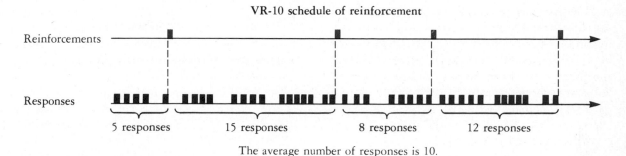

VR-10 schedule of reinforcement

Reinforcements

Responses

5 responses   15 responses   8 responses   12 responses

The average number of responses is 10.

FIGURE 4.20   Fixed-ratio (FR) and variable-ratio (VR) schedules of reinforcement.

container filled—such as a basket of apples or a box of tomatoes. Of course, payment is not made each time a container is filled, but is deferred until the end of the day or the end of the week. However, the immediate reinforcer is the satisfaction provided by filling the container. (Remember, satisfaction is another word for the conditioned reinforcement that accompanies progress.)

Variable-ratio schedules (**VR**) are slightly more complicated but are much more common in life outside the laboratory. When working on a VR-10 schedule of reinforcement, an animal receives, *on the average,* one reinforcer for every ten responses, although a particular reinforcer might be obtained after as few as two or as many as twenty responses. The point is that the *mean* number of responses per reinforcer on a VR-10 schedule is 10. **Figure 4.20** illustrates FR and VR schedules of reinforcement.

The behavior of an animal on a variable-ratio schedule of reinforcement is different from that of one on a fixed-ratio schedule. On a variable-ratio schedule, responding is generally steady and is not marked by pauses after each reinforcement, unless

the ratio is very high. The animal gets right back to work again after a rather brief pause. What accounts for this difference in postreinforcement pausing? The answer is that postreinforcement pauses do indeed follow reinforcement, but they are controlled by the work that is to come, not the work that was just completed. That is, the pause anticipates the number of responses that will have to be made before the next reinforcer is received. It should really be called a "preresponding pause."

Before I describe an experiment that showed that the pause is indeed controlled by the number of responses that lie ahead for the animal and not the number of responses just made, I would like you to think about this problem. How would you test this possibility? You will recall from Chapter 2 that the only way to determine whether a dependent variable is affected by a particular independent variable is to vary one and see whether the other is affected. To see whether this variable affects the duration of the pause, you would have to vary the number of responses that the animal must make after receiving a reinforcer. You could not use a fixed-ratio schedule, because all reinforcers require the same number of responses. For example, on an FR-10 schedule of reinforcement you do not know whether a pause is as long as it is because the previous reinforcement required ten responses or because the next one will require ten responses. How would you set up the experiment?

* * *

To determine which possibility is correct you must vary the required number of responses by training the animal on a schedule that uses two types of trials, for example, an FR-5 and FR-25. The trials alternate, so that the animal has to press the lever five times for a food pellet, then twenty-five, then five, and so on. If the duration of pausing is controlled by the work that was just performed, there should be long pauses after the animal makes twenty-five responses. If the pause is controlled by the work to come, the animal should make the long pause after the FR-5, in anticipation of the FR-25 that is to follow. (See **Figure** 4.21.)

Figure 4.21 shows that an animal trained on such a schedule will make a long pause after the FR-5 and a short pause after the FR-25. Because higher ratios of responses to reinforcements normally produce longer pauses, we must conclude that it is the work yet to come, and not the work just completed, that determines the duration of the postreinforcement pause. Because an animal cannot predict how many responses will be required on the next trial in a variable-ratio schedule of reinforcement, pauses tend to be shorter than they are on a fixed-ratio schedule.

In real life we often encounter variable-ratio

FIGURE 4.21   Use of two VR schedules of reinforcement show that a postreinforcement pause is actually a preresponding pause.

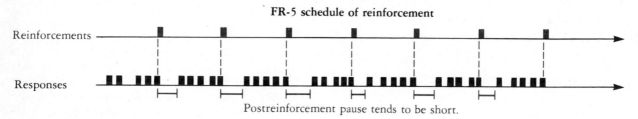

FR-5 schedule of reinforcement

Postreinforcement pause tends to be short.

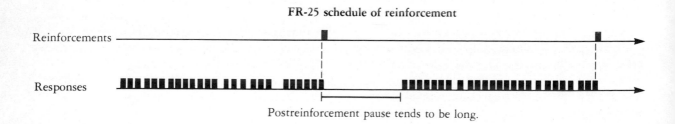

FR-25 schedule of reinforcement

Postreinforcement pause tends to be long.

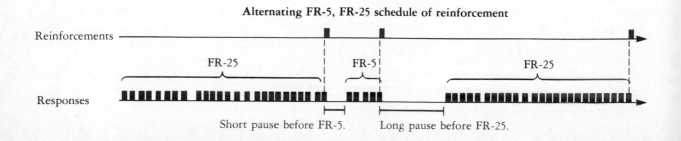

Alternating FR-5, FR-25 schedule of reinforcement

Short pause before FR-5.   Long pause before FR-25.

schedules of reinforcement. Any skilled activity that requires a discrete attempt (response) that can be scored as successful or unsuccessful will be reinforced according to a variable-ratio schedule. The average number of responses per reinforcer is determined by the person's skill. If you go bowling and get a strike 25 percent of the time, you are being reinforced on a VR-4 schedule—an average of one strike (reinforcer) for every four attempts made (responses). A traveling salesman who manages to make a sale to 10 percent of the people he visits is reinforced on a VR-10 schedule.

There is even an apparatus that automatically dispenses reinforcers on a VR schedule—a slot machine. Some percentage of the pulls of the handle will be reinforced with a payoff. The owner of the machine sets the probability of a payoff and thus determines the value of the ratio of responses to reinforcers, keeping it high enough to produce a good profit, but low enough to maintain a steady rate of responding from the customer. Variable-ratio schedules are very effective at producing a high rate of responding—the next response could bring the payoff. Furthermore (to the delight of the person who owns the machine), responding that has been reinforced on a VR schedule is very resistant to extinction.

RESPONSE-AND-TIME-DEPENDENT SCHEDULES OF REINFORCEMENT In response-and-time-dependent schedules, reinforcement is not contingent on the number of responses produced, but on the amount of time that has elapsed since the last reinforcer was delivered. After receiving a reinforcer, an organism will not get a chance to receive another one until a predetermined interval of time has elapsed. When that time is up, the next response that is made will be reinforced.

◆ Let us first examine a *fixed-interval schedule* of reinforcement (**FI**). Suppose that a rat is pressing a lever for food pellets that are being delivered on an FI-30-second schedule of reinforcement. The rat receives a food pellet (from the previous response), and a timer is started. The animal eats the food and starts pressing the bar agin, but nothing happens. Finally the timer gets to 30 seconds. The next time the rat presses the lever the food dispenser delivers another pellet of food. The timer is reset to zero and begins measuring another 30-second interval. You should note that no matter how rapidly the rat presses the lever, the minimum time between deliveries of food pellets is 30 seconds. It is the first response that occurs *after* the elapsed time that gets the pellet. (See **Figure 4.22**.)

The behavior of an animal that is being reinforced on a fixed-interval schedule is similar to that of most students working on a term paper—a long pause during which nothing is done, then a frantic burst of activity as the deadline approaches. Although there is no deadline for the rat and no food pellet for the student their patterns of responding are similar. The rat working on an FI-30-second schedule learns that a response made soon after receiving a food pellet is never reinforced and stops responding then. Time passes, and the rat approaches the lever. The animal starts pressing— slowly at first, then steadily faster. As you might expect, an animal will pause longer after each reinforcement on a FI-2-minute schedule than it will on an FI-30-second schedule.

FIGURE 4.22   Fixed-interval-30-second schedule of reinforcement.

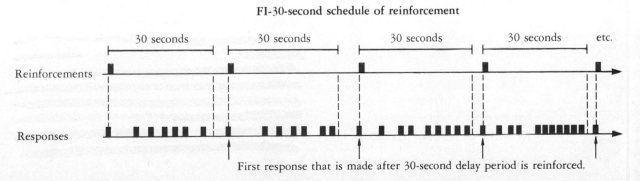

FI-30-second schedule of reinforcement

First response that is made after 30-second delay period is reinforced.

If a rat whose lever pressing is being reinforced on an FI-30-second schedule could look at a clock, it would wait exactly 30 seconds before making a response. If we give it something like a clock, it will indeed wait until the interval has elapsed. If a buzzer sounds as soon as the interval is over, the rat will soon learn to wait for that sound before it responds. We call this schedule a *cued* FI schedule; the buzzer serves as a cue that the interval is over.

A *variable-interval schedule* (VI) bears the same similarity to a fixed-interval schedule that a variable-ratio schedule does to a fixed-ratio schedule. After each reinforcement a timer is started, and responses are ignored until the timer gets to the end of the interval. Once the time is up, the next response will be reinforced. When an organism works for reinforcers that are delivered on a VI-1-minute schedule, the opportunity for reinforcement occurs, *on the average,* every 60 seconds. Sometimes it will receive a reinforcer for a response made a few seconds after the last reinforcer. At other times, two or three minutes must elapse.

When an organism's behavior is reinforced by a variable-interval schedule, it responds at a steady, even pace. The next opportunity for reinforcement may be very near, or it may be far away, so there is no point in working *too* hard. Psychologists use variable-interval schedules of reinforcement more than any other. The organism's rate of responding is very stable and is sensitive to changes in motivation (such as hunger) and to other variables that affect its physiological state. For example, researchers in the pharmaceutical industry often administer a drug to rats who are responding on a variable-interval schedule in order to determine whether the drug affects their rate of responding. Sedatives will slow the response rate; stimulants will raise it.

My favorite example of a variable-interval schedule in real life is fishing. One form of fishing consists of casting a lure into the water and retrieving it in such a way as to simulate a minnow. If no fish is present, none will be caught. Even if one is present it may not bite. Every now and then, a hungry, eager-to-bite fish will come by. If a lure is moving through the water at the same time, the angler may get a fish. After a fish is caught another may come by soon, or not for a long time. The only way to find out is to cast the lure. Because

intermittent reinforcement produces resistance to extinction, catching a fish now and then is enough to keep the angler's behavior going through long periods during which no fish are caught. You never know—that next cast might hook the big one.

SUPERSTITIOUS BEHAVIOR

Whenever a reinforcing stimulus is presented to an organism, the probability increases that the organism will repeat the behavior that it just performed. Normally, the behavior is instrumental in obtaining the reinforcer; there is a cause-and-effect relation between response and reinforcement. We learn to press the button on a drinking fountain because the response makes the water flow. A duck learns to swim up to people on the shore of a lake in the park because swimming up to people often results in their throwing food. But the response does not have to *cause* reinforcement for the relation to be learned; even an irrelevant response can be affected by a reinforcing stimulus.

Consider the following example, based on an experiment by Skinner (1948). We place a hungry pigeon inside a small enclosure and automatically give it a bit of food every fifteen seconds. After several pieces of food have been delivered, we look in on the bird, and find it spinning around frantically, counterclockwise. We remove the bird and place another one inside the chamber. We find that after receiving several pieces of food the pigeon is standing in the middle of the floor, bobbing its head up and down like a mechanical toy. A third animal persists in flapping its wings.

As you might have guessed from the title of this section, the birds have acquired *superstitious behaviors.* (Note that the term *superstitious behavior* is not synonymous with the term *superstition.* A fear of black cats or Friday the thirteenth is not a superstitious behavior; it is a superstition, or piece of folklore that we learn from others.)

What causes the development of superstitious behaviors? Here is Skinner's analysis. When a reinforcer is intermittently given to an animal regardless of what the animal does, it will seldom just wait quietly for more to be delivered. Instead, the animal will tend to continue doing what it was doing when the reinforcement occurred. Perhaps the first pigeon was turning around when the food dispenser was first operated. The pigeon heard the noise, turned toward its source, and saw the food. It ate, waited in the vicinity of the food dispenser, and finally turned to go. Just then, another bit of food was delivered, so the bird went back to eat it. The next time, the pigeon turned away a little sooner and made a couple of revolutions before some food was dispensed again. From then on the pigeon went into a spin after each reinforcement. From the bird's point of view, the response was what brought the food. Similarly, head bobbing and wing flapping were accidentally reinforced in the other pigeons because these behaviors happened to occur immediately before food was delivered to them.

It appears that we humans are not immune from acquiring superstitious behaviors. If you watch a baseball game, you will probably see some super-stitious behaviors. Most baseball pitchers perform a little ritual before throwing the ball. Typical behaviors include scuffing the ground with a shoe, rubbing the ball, pulling at one's hat, hunching one's shoulders, rubbing one's chest, and turning the ball in the glove. Each pitcher has a different routine. The same holds true for bowling, or golf, or just about any other endeavor that requires per-formance of a skilled behavior. Whether they are relevant or irrelevant, those behaviors that preceded successful pitches, strikes, or golf strokes will tend to be repeated. (See **Figure 4.23**.)

We can only speculate about the many taboos and rituals that are a part of all human culture, and try to imagine which of these developed from behaviors that were inadvertently reinforced some-time long ago.

FIGURE 4.23   Baseball pitchers often engage in peculiar behaviors before throwing the ball; presumably, these are superstitious behaviors, previously reinforced by successful pitches.

Interim summary: You now have a more complete picture of how classical conditioning and instrumental conditioning work to adapt an organism's behavior to an ever-changing environment. The learning process is not geared to an accumulation of facts; rather it involves recognition of those stimuli that have importance for an organism, which may change with time and circumstance. Intermittent reinforcement and spontaneous recovery tend to keep responses alive, habituation and extinction tend to eliminate them.

Whereas classical and instrumental conditioning appear simple when compared to complex behaviors such as reading and writing, they do in fact have very subtle manifestations and involve behaviors far more complex than the reflex reactions that Pavlov started with—superstitious behaviors for instance. For humans, instrumental conditioning involves a large number of conditioned reinforcers, including progress, satisfaction, and a variety of social reinforcers. The reinforcers themselves will vary in their influence as changes in the preference hierarchy of behaviors occur.

BEHAVIORS ELICITED BY THE REINFORCER

As we have seen, a stimulus must elicit a behavior if that stimulus is to serve as a reinforcer. Food does not reinforce an organism's behavior unless it elicits eating (or, in the case of an animal like a squirrel, storing it away). Behaviors also occur *in anticipation* of reinforcing stimuli. Autoshaping and interim behavior are examples of such anticipation.

Autoshaping

A number of years ago, Breland and Breland (1961) reported that instrumental conditioning sometimes produced unexpected results. The Brelands made commercial use of instrumental conditioning to train animals to perform for various clients. For example, they trained a pig to pick up a large wooden coin, carry it in its mouth to a piggy bank, and deposit it. This sequence was reinforced by a small piece of food. (The client was a bank that wanted to display the animal's behavior as an advertising stunt in a window.) The pig readily learned the task and performed well at first. However, after

several weeks the pig began dropping the coin, rooting it with its nose, and tossing it into the air. In other words, it began treating the coin as it would treat a piece of food, in a sense anticipating the food that had regularly followed performance of the task during the training period. The Brelands reported similar "misbehavior" from a variety of species. Instead of doing what the trainers taught them to do, the animals began to exhibit behaviors that were appropriate to their particular species. The Brelands called this phenomenon *instinctive drift*—the intrusion of species-typical consummatory responses into a sequence of instrumentally conditioned behaviors.

Brown and Jenkins (1968) discovered a phenomenon that seems to be identical to instinctive drift. This phenomenon suggests that classical and instrumental conditioning are even more closely related than was previously thought. They placed hungry pigeons in an operant chamber that contained a small, round, translucent plastic disk, located on one wall above a small drawer containing food. This arrangement is typically used by psy-

FIGURE 4.24   A pigeon pecking on a response disk. Note the food drawer, below.

chologists who wish to study instrumental conditioning in pigeons. The pigeon pecks at the plastic disk, operating a miniature switch behind it, which signals the electronic control device that a response has occurred. Pecking can be reinforced by opening the drawer for a few seconds and allowing the pigeon to eat a few pieces of grain. (See **Figure** 4.24.)

Brown and Jenkins turned on a light behind the plastic disk for a few seconds and then opened the drawer to present food to the pigeons. The food was presented *noncontingently*—the pigeons did not have to make any response for the drawer to open. The investigators were surprised to discover that the pigeons soon began pecking at the disk.

Brown and Jenkins called this phenomenon *autoshaping* because the pigeons appeared to "shape themselves" to make the response. The phenomenon is a very strong one. Williams and Williams (1969) discovered that once responding was produced by means of autoshaping, pigeons would continue to peck the disk even if pecking now caused a delay in the delivery of food (response cost). Thus, pecking that is produced by the autoshaping procedure is resistant to punishment.

Why does a pigeon bother to peck the disk when the food drawer opens automatically? The answer seems to be that the pecking is elicited by the reinforcer (food) and can be seen as part of the consummatory response (eating). As you know, a pigeon eats by pecking at its food. Intermittent reinforcement causes the probability of the appropriate consummatory responses to increase, and the light makes the disk become a salient stimulus. Thus, the pigeon pecks at it.

An experiment by Moore (1973) supported this analysis. He used the autoshaping procedure to establish pecking in hungry pigeons, who received food, and in thirsty pigeons, who received water. However, the pecking responses differed for the two groups. Hungry pigeons made short, forceful pecks, with their beak open (as they do when they eat a piece of grain). Thirsty pigeons made a sidewise movement with their head and pulsated their throat (as they do when they drink). It was as if the hungry pigeons "ate" the disk and the thirsty ones "drank" it. The relation between the reinforcer and the response strongly suggests that the response is elicited by the reinforcer.

The phenomenon of autoshaping appears to consist of a mixture of classical and instrumental conditioning. In fact, Donahoe, Crowley, Millard, and Stickney (1982) have suggested that classical and instrumental conditioning may be controlled by common mechanisms; they may be different sides of the same coin. Most psychologists have focused on the fact that the experimental procedures are very different for classical and instrumental conditioning, but this does not mean that these phenomena are biologically different.

Interim Behavior

As we have seen, if organisms receive intermittent, free (noncontingent) reinforcers, they will develop superstitious behaviors. However, if training continues for a large number of sessions, these idiosyncratic responses will eventually drop out and be replaced with rather stereotyped behaviors. Staddon and Simmelhag (1971) repeated Skinner's procedure and obtained the same results; their pigeons acquired a variety of superstitious behaviors, presumably through accidental reinforcement of whatever the animals were doing at the time the food was delivered. However, as the investigators continued the training sessions they found that the behavior of their animals became more and more similar; they began pecking against the wall of the chamber near the food dispenser. Wing flapping, head bobbing, turning, and other peculiar behaviors disappeared.

Staddon and Simmelhag called the stereotyped pecking responses *interim behaviors*. These responses, which resemble the ones elicited by food, eventually occur *in anticipation* of delivery of the reinforcer. Subsequent research has shown that when appetitive stimuli are delivered noncontingently, different species exhibit different interim behaviors. Even different breeds of pigeons exhibit somewhat different behaviors. This fact suggests that their particular form of behavior is largely controlled by genetic factors. Undoubtedly, interim behaviors are similar to the behaviors seen during autoshaping. They also resemble the instinctive drift observed by the Brelands.

In the case of autoshaping, turning on the light behind the plastic disk just before opening the food drawer makes the disk a very obvious stimulus. Therefore, the animals quickly begin directing their responses to the disk. In the case of superstitious behaviors, placing the animals in plain chambers, with no special features except the food drawer, allows more chance for idiosyncratic responses to develop, at least at first. Eventually, even these animals settle upon the species-typical behavior of pecking at the wall near the food dispenser.

IMITATION

We learn from experience; our behavior is reinforced or punished by its consequences. But we can also learn by a less direct method—observing the behavior of others. Video-game machines usually have instructions printed on them, and often flash instructions on the screen. But it is much easier to learn how to play the game by first watching someone who has had experience with it. Likewise, one of the best ways to improve your tennis game (beside taking lessons) is to watch experts play. (See **Figure 4.25**.)

Humans are not the only animals who learn by imitation. A pigeon that watches another bird per-

FIGURE 4.25   Humans learn many behaviors through imitation.

forming a complex operant task will learn the task much more quickly than one that has not had this opportunity. Why do organisms learn to imitate the behavior of others? Is this tendency innate?

There are clear examples from nature that imitation does seem to be an innate tendency. Many species of birds must learn to sing their characteristic song; if they are raised apart from other birds they will never sing, or they will sing a peculiar song that bears little resemblance to that of normally raised birds. However, if they hear the normal song played over a loudspeaker, they will sing properly when they become adults. They learn the song, but clearly there were no external reinforcement contingencies; nothing in the environment reinforced their singing the song. (This phenomenon is an excellent example of the distinction between learning and performance. A baby bird hears the proper song but does not sing it until adulthood. The changes that take place in its brain do not manifest themselves in behavior for many months.)

But even though some instances of learning by observation may not require reinforcement, there is strong evidence that imitating the behavior of other organisms may be reinforcing. Baer, Peterson, and Sherman (1967) studied three severely retarded children who had never been seen to imitate the behavior of other people. When the experimenters tried to induce them to do what they themselves did, like clap their hands, the children were unresponsive. Next, experimenters tried to induce and reinforce imitative behavior in the children. An experimenter would look at a child, say "Do this," and perform a behavior. If the child made a similar response, he was immediately praised and given a piece of food. At first the children were physically guided to make the response; if the behavior to be imitated was clapping, the experimenter would clap his hands, hold the child's hands and clap them together, then praise the child and give him some food.

The procedure worked. The children learned to imitate the experimenters' behaviors. But even more important, the children had not simply learned to mimic a specific set of responses; they had acquired the *general tendency to imitate*. When the experimenters performed new behaviors and said "Do this," the children would imitate them.

Obviously, training retarded children is much more effective when they pay attention to their teachers and imitate their behaviors when requested to do so. The procedure I just described has proved to be extremely useful for teaching children behaviors that will help them lead useful lives. But the theoretical significance of this demonstration is also important. The experiment indicates that imitation, as a general tendency, is subject to reinforcement (and presumably also to punishment). An organism can learn more than a particular response to a particular stimulus; it can learn a strategy that can be applied to a variety of situations.

An interesting issue that remains controversial in psychology is the acquisition of language by children. Why do children learn to imitate the verbal behavior of older children and adults? Is the tendency innate, like the learning of songs by some species of birds, or is it subject to the contingencies of reinforcement and punishment? Chapter 12 discusses this topic in detail.

DISCRIMINATION

◆ Most of my descriptions of instrumental conditioning so far have involved responses and reinforcing or punishing stimuli. But in instrumental conditioning *discriminative stimuli* also play an essential role. Suppose you owned a dog, and wanted to teach it to bark whenever you said, "Speak!" First, you would probably get a few pieces of food that the dog liked. Then you would attract its attention, and say, "Speak!" while waving a piece of food in front of it. The dog would begin to show signs of excitement at the sight of the food and

FIGURE 4.26 The response patterns of a rat that is pressing a lever on a discrimination schedule (light on: VI 30 seconds; light off: extinction).

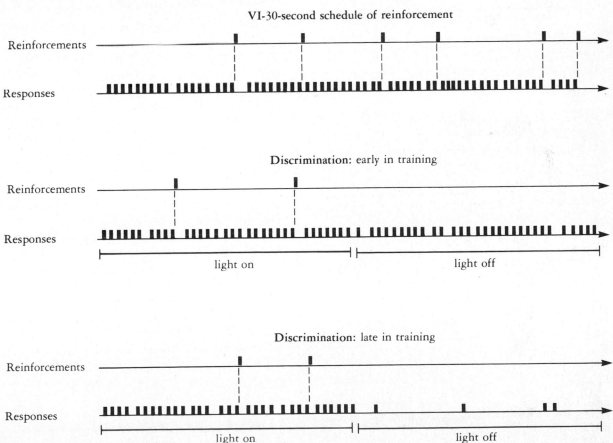

VI-30-second schedule of reinforcement

Reinforcements

Responses

Discrimination: early in training

Reinforcements

Responses

light on   light off

Discrimination: late in training

Reinforcements

Responses

light on   light off

would finally let out a bark. Immediately, you would feed it. After letting it finish eating you would bring out another piece of food and again say, "Speak!" This time the dog would probably bark a little sooner. After several trials, the dog would bark whenever you said "Speak!" even if no food was visible.

You would not reinforce barking whenever it occurred, but only when you had first presented the stimulus "Speak!" At all other times barking would be under an extinction schedule. The dog would learn to *discriminate* between the two conditions, and to respond appropriately. The word "Speak" serves as the discriminative stimulus.

Every instance of instrumental conditioning involves discriminative stimuli, even if they are not explicitly delivered like "Speak!" If you have been reinforced for telling funny jokes, you will do so only when there are other people present; you will not tell jokes in an empty room. The presence of other people serves as the discriminative stimulus for telling jokes. Similarly, a rat that has been trained to press a lever for food pellets will not make pressing movements with its paws unless there is a lever to push. And an angler will not cast his or her lure into a swimming pool. We all learn that there are some conditions under which responding is worthwhile, and some conditions under which it is useless.

In the laboratory, we might place a hungry rat in an operant chamber and train it to press a lever. When we get it to respond to a VI-30-second schedule of reinforcement we turn on a light located just above the lever and continue to reinforce responding on the same schedule. After a minute, we turn off the light and start an extinction schedule; no responses are reinforced. A minute later we turn the light back on and start the VI-30-second schedule again. We alternate periods of a VI-30-second schedule with periods of extinction, the light being illuminated only when the animal is able to obtain food. The light serves as a discriminative stimulus, because it permits the rat to discriminate between the two conditions. The rat soon learns to stop responding when the light goes off but to start responding again when it goes on. (See **Figure 4.26.**)

Discrimination tasks permit us to assess an animal's perceptual abilities. Suppose we wanted to determine whether an animal has color vision. First, we would put a window of frosted glass in the wall of an operant chamber, just above the lever. (If the species could not press a lever, we would provide a different kind of task for it to perform.) We would then shine lights of different colors on the back of the translucent screen, say, red when food was available and green when an extinction schedule was in effect. If the animal learns to discriminate, responding faster when the red light is on, then it must have color vision. (See **Figure 4.27.**)

The task I have just described is called *successive discrimination;* the stimuli are present in *succession,* one after the other. There is never more than one discriminative stimulus present at one

FIGURE 4.27   The response patterns of an animal that has been trained on a discrimination schedule (red: reinforced; green: nonreinforced). *Top:* The animal has color vision. *Bottom:* The animal does not have color vision.

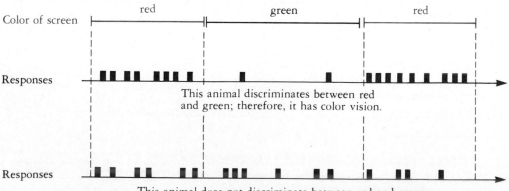

This animal discriminates between red and green; therefore, it has color vision.

This animal does not discriminate between red and green; therefore, there is no evidence it has color vision.

Lamp is off   Lamp is on

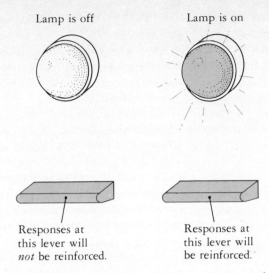

Responses at this lever will *not* be reinforced.

Responses at this lever will be reinforced.

FIGURE 4.28   Simultaneous discrimination task.

time. On the other hand, **simultaneous discrimination** presents two or more stimuli at the same time, and the animal chooses a particular response from the available alternatives. For example, an operant chamber might contain two levers, each with a light mounted above it. At any given time, only one of the levers is "working"; the responses to the other will not be reinforced. Furthermore, only one of the lights is on at any one time—the one above the lever that is working. The animal learns very soon to respond only to the lever with a light on over it. (See **Figure 4.28.**)

Discrimination tasks are common in real life. For example, we usually talk about different things with different people. We learn that some friends do not care for sports, so we do not talk about this topic with them, because we will receive few reinforcers (such as nods or smiles). Instead, we discuss topics that have interested them in the past. A person with good social skills is one who is particularly adept at observing signs of interest in someone he or she has just met, and who selects topics of conversation, and even conversational styles, that elicit signs of interest.

GENERALIZATION

No two stimuli are precisely alike. If you say "Speak!" many times, the sounds you produce will be very similar, but careful analysis of recordings would show that each time the word is pronounced somewhat differently. However, once your dog is trained it responds by barking every time you say the word, ignoring these slight differences. In other words, your dog does not discriminate between the slightly different sounds. Instead, it shows *generalization.*

The word *general* comes from the Latin *generalis,* "belonging to a kind or species." The definition fits precisely. Once an organism has learned to respond to a particular discriminative stimulus, it is said to be *generalizing* when it responds in the same manner to stimuli that are similar to the original one.

Let me give a more typical example of generalization. Honig, Boneau, Burstein, and Pennypacker (1963) trained a pigeon to peck at a translucent plastic disk. When it contained a vertical line (projected onto the back of the disk) pecking was reinforced on a VI-60-second schedule. When the disk did not contain a line, responses were not reinforced (extinction schedule). After several sessions the pigeons learned the discrimination task (to peck when a line was present, not to peck when it was absent). Then they were tested for generalization: lines with different orientations

FIGURE 4.29   A generalization gradient for a pigeon originally trained to peck at a disk containing a vertical line (90°). (From Honig, W. K., Boneau, C. A., Burstein, K. R., and Pennypacker, H. C. *Journal of Comparative and Physiological Psychology,* 1963, 56, 111–116.)

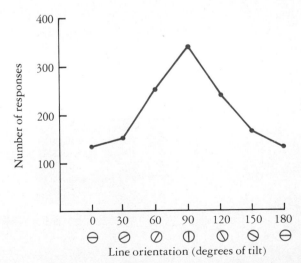

were projected onto the disk and the animals' responses were counted.

Figure 4.29 shows the results. The circles below the horizontal axis illustrate the orientation of the line. Note that the birds made the most responses to the vertical lines and responded less and less to lines tilted progressively farther away from the vertical. They responded according to the similarity between the original training stimulus and the test stimulus. (See **Figure 4.29.**)

Generalization is not restricted to laboratory demonstrations; it includes some of the most complex behaviors that we can perform. For example, in *concept formation,* a person learns a strategy (that is, a complex pattern of behavior) that solves a particular problem (that is, provides a reinforcer—probably a conditioned reinforcer such as satisfaction). When that person encounters a situation that shares some elements with the original one, he or she is likely to *generalize* the strategy to the new situation. Of course, merely identifying the process of concept formation as a form of generalization does little to explain it. We still have to find out how people are able to learn the complex behaviors required to solve the problem, and how they detect the common elements in similar situations. But perceiving the process in these terms helps outline a strategy for research on this phenomenon.

The learning of concepts is not restricted to humans. Herrnstein and Loveland (1964) trained pigeons to respond to the concept of a human being.

First they trained the birds to peck at a translucent plastic disk. Then they assembled a set of more than a thousand 35-millimeter color slides. Some of the slides contained photographs of humans, depicted in a wide variety of scenes and poses. Other slides did not contain human figures. Herrnstein and Loveland selected a group of slides, with and without human figures, from the larger set and projected them to the translucent disk, where the birds could see them. (See **Figure 4.30.**) Then they started discrimination training. When a human figure was projected, pecking was reinforced on a VI-60-second schedule of reinforcement. When the projected image was that of a scene that did not contain a human, pecking was not reinforced; a disk with no human figure was the discriminative stimulus that signaled extinction.

The birds quickly learned to respond to the concept of "human being." Their performance on the original set of slides generalized to slides they had not seen before. The birds became as good as the experimenters at detecting whether a human figure was present in the image. In fact they even responded to a scene that supposedly did not contain a human. When the experimenters looked at the slide more carefully, they discovered a person hidden away in the corner whom they had missed when they first sorted the slides.

Herrnstein and Loveland concluded that although they had demonstrated that pigeons were capable of learning the concept of a human being, the fact that they performed so rapidly and so well

FIGURE 4.30   Two of the slides used in the Herrnstein and Loveland Study. (Courtesy of R. J. Herrnstein, Harvard University.)

suggested that they *already* possessed the concept. The birds had probably learned this concept by observing humans before being brought into the laboratory; when they made mistakes while learning the discrimination task they often responded to stimuli that are normally associated with humans, such as automobiles, boats, and houses.

DISCRIMINATION AND GENERALIZATION IN CLASSICAL CONDITIONING

◆ Both discrimination and generalization involve detection of distinctions and similarities between different stimuli. These phenomena operate in both instrumental conditioning and classical conditioning. For example, if the first bursting balloon that you experience is blue, you will nevertheless flinch at the sight of a red balloon that is about to explode; your response will generalize to other conditional stimuli. Similarly, the process of conditioned reinforcement makes a *class* of stimuli serve as reinforcers. For example, social reinforcers are probably established through contact with a few people (such as members of your immediate family) very early in life. Your behavior is then reinforced by smiles and nods from other people whom you had not met earlier. The reinforcing effect of these gestures generalizes to similar gestures made by different people.

Discrimination in classical conditioning involves making conditional responses to some stimuli but not to others. For example, if one elevator in the building where you work sometimes makes frightening lurches when it stops at a floor, you may feel uneasy while riding it but not in the others, which always travel smoothly. Your response (feeling of uneasiness) discriminates between stimuli (the elevators). Discriminations can even be made on the basis of complex stimuli: compare how you might feel if you are approached by an unsavory character who asks for the time under these two conditions—a busy sidewalk full of other pedestrians and a deserted street at night.

AVERSIVE CONTROL: ESCAPE AND AVOIDANCE RESPONSES

◆ Through negative reinforcement, organisms learn an *escape response.* Negative reinforcement is the termination of an aversive stimulus that is contingent upon a specific behavior; thus, the organism escapes from the aversive stimulus by performing the appropriate response. (In this context the organism does not necessarily have to run away in order to "escape" the aversive stimulus.) Under some conditions, the organism can do more than escape the aversive stimulus—it can learn to produce a response that will *prevent* the occurrence of the aversive stimulus. The organism will learn an *avoidance response.*

Let me give an example. Suppose you meet a man at a party who backs you against the wall and subjects you to the most tedious and tiresome conversation that you have ever experienced. This obnoxiously and aggressively boring person clearly delivers aversive stimuli. You experience a great sense of relief when you finally manage to break away from him. A few days later you attend another party. You are having a good time until you see your tormenter from the earlier party heading your way. The gleam in his eyes foretells another long harangue. You suddenly remember that you have business elsewhere, make your excuses to your host, and leave. You do not want to repeat your earlier experience.

The behavior that brings about the termination of an aversive stimulus is called an escape response. The behavior that prevents another aversive stimulus from occurring is called an avoidance response. Clearly, leaving the second party before the bore could get to you is an avoidance response. Psychologists disagree about what produces and maintains avoidance responses, but most would probably support the following explanation. The sight of your tormenter at the second party serves as a conditioned aversive stimulus, because the sight of him was paired with the boring conversation. Once you go out the door you can no longer see him, so leaving the party (the avoidance response) is reinforced by the termination of a conditioned aversive stimulus.

Avoidance and Species-Typical Defense Reactions

◆ Although appetitive stimuli can reinforce a wide variety of responses, aversive stimuli can negatively reinforce only a much smaller range of responses. For example, it is virtually impossible to teach pigeons to peck at a plastic disk in order to turn off an aversive stimulus such as electric shock, yet appetitive stimuli such as food or water can easily reinforce the same response. The reason for this discrepancy is that aversive stimuli usually elicit *species-typical defense reactions* that prevent the organism from emitting the response that the experimenter is attempting to reinforce (Bolles, 1970). When a pigeon receives an electric shock it begins flapping its wings; it *never* delivers a peck to the disk.

Thus, although the principles of reinforcement and punishment appear to apply to any organism with a sufficiently complex nervous system (including all vertebrates that have been tested and some invertebrates, such as the octopus), the fact is that reinforcers (both positive and negative) sometimes elicit behaviors that are incompatible with the response that is to be reinforced. The natural history of the species must be taken into account whenever we attempt to explain its behavior in terms of its conditioning history.

Maintenance of Fears by Negative Reinforcement

You will recall that phobias can be viewed as conditioned aversive stimuli because they are acquired through classical conditioning. Phobias can last throughout a person's life. A person who was hurt or frightened by a dog during childhood may fear dogs permanently even though he or she is never attacked by one again. Why do these phobias not extinguish? There appear to be two reasons. First, the avoidance behavior is negatively reinforced. The sight of a dog is a conditioned aversive stimulus, and turning away from it terminates the aversive stimulus, which negatively reinforces the avoidance behavior. Second, the person never stays near a dog long enough for extinction to occur. (Remember that extinction, in classical conditioning, requires that the conditional stimulus be presented again and again without the unconditional stimulus.)

In the case of the boring person whom you met at the party, an external stimulus—the sight of the person—elicited the avoidance response. Sometimes avoidance responses are elicited by internal stimuli. The most common internal stimulus for avoidance responding is an estimate of elapsed time.

Suppose you are driving a car on a long trip when suddenly a leak develops in the radiator. You are not aware of the leak until the temperature gauge tells you that the engine has overheated. You pull over to the side of the road and find that the radiator is dry. Getting it filled again is a long, unpleasant task: you have to flag down another motorist, get a ride to a gas station, borrow a can of water, get a ride back to your car, put the water into the radiator, and drive back to the gas station to fill it up completely. Obviously, running out of water produces a number of aversive stimuli. You do not have enough time to get the radiator repaired, so you realize that you will have to stop and refill the radiator periodically to keep the engine from overheating again. The internal stimulus that elicits this avoidance response is your estimate of the time that has elapsed since you last filled the radiator.

Interim summary: Our earlier discussions focused on the adaptive nature of learning, an organism responding to its environment. But the same contingencies can produce different responses in different species; the effects of heredity and environment interact. Species-typical behaviors are seen in instinctive drift, autoshaping, interim behaviors, and species-typical defense reactions.

Generalization is a necessary component of all forms of learning, because no two stimuli, and no two responses, are precisely the same; thus, generalization embodies the ability to apply what is learned from one experience to similar ones. Discrimination involves detecting essential differences between stimuli and situations, and responding only when appropriate. When these abilities are added to the capacity to learn from the experience of others through imitation, we begin to see how the simple principles discussed here apply to subtle and complex forms of human behavior.

CONCLUDING REMARKS

I described three basic types of learning in this chapter: habituation, classical conditioning, and instrumental conditioning. Habituation is important because it permits an organism to stop responding to a stimulus that has no importance for it. Classical conditioning is important because a conditional stimulus serves as a useful indication (often a warning) that the unconditional stimulus will probably follow. Even more significantly, classical conditioning establishes previously neutral stimuli as conditioned appetitive or aversive stimuli, so that they can serve as reinforcers or punishers. Instrumental conditioning is important because it is the means of modifying an organism's behavior by contingencies in the environment. Human behavior is reinforced so effectively by conditioned reinforcers and punishers that we tend to overlook the importance of instrumental conditioning for ourselves, but careful analysis usually reveals the relevant contingencies.

The information presented in this chapter has direct bearing on topics discussed in later chapters. For example, social reinforcers are obviously relevant to the social behavior of humans, and a person's motivation is determined largely by the types of stimuli that serve as conditioned reinforcers and punishers. Emotional responses are largely controlled by classical conditioning. In fact, the use of principles of instrumental conditioning has become so widespread in clinical and educational psychology that a new field of therapy, called *behavior therapy,* has emerged.

The next chapter examines the nature of reinforcement, punishment, and the variables that affect motivation—all important features of learning.

GUIDE TO TERMS INTRODUCED IN THIS CHAPTER

SUGGESTIONS FOR FURTHER READING

I can recommend two useful books for those who want to learn more about the basic principles of learning: *Elementary Principles of Behavior* by D.L. Whaley and R.W. Malott (New York: Appleton-Century-Crofts, 1971), and the second edition of *Human Operant Behavior* by E.P. Reese (Dubuque, Ia.: W.C. Brown, 1978). Both books are well written and entertaining and contain many specific examples of human learning. Reese's book also contains examples of using operant techniques (instrumental conditioning) to change one's own behavior, such as studying or dieting more effectively.

An excellent primary source of information regarding classical conditioning is contained in Pavlov's own lectures, *Conditioned Reflexes*, translated by G.V. Anrep (London: Oxford University Press, 1927).

LEARNING:

MECHANISMS

OF MOTIVATION

LEARNING ◆ OBJECTIVES

WHEN WE investigate the causes of human behavior we immediately encounter inconsistency. If behavior is determined by people's interactions with the environment, then why does a person not always act the same way in what appears to be the same situation?

There are many reasons for inconsistent behavior. At one time a person fixes a meal or goes to a restaurant; at another time he or she does not. The inconsistency can be explained by the presence or absence of hunger. A person who usually picks up hitchhikers does not do so if he learns that a convict has just escaped from a nearby penitentiary. A person who likes to play tennis will probably turn down a game if she is suffering from a severe headache.

All of these reasons for inconsistent behavior are aspects of *motivation* (derived from a Latin word meaning "to move"). Of course, once the reasons are known, the behaviors are no longer considered "inconsistent." In common usage motivation refers to a driving force that moves us to a particular action; for example, behaviors that are likely to help us attain success, recognition, and financial well-being, as well as more prosaic ones that provide the next meal or drink of water. However, it is more accurate to think of motivation not as a force, but as the behavioral effects of appetitive and aversive stimuli, and of discriminative stimuli that in the past have been associated with them. For example, if you learn that a store is holding a half-price sale on some clothes that you particularly want (appetitive stimuli), you are likely to try to rearrange your schedule so that you can attend the sale before the clothes are sold. On the other hand, if you see dark clouds and hear thunder and remember that you parked your convertible with its top down, you are likely to stop what you are doing and get to it quickly so that you can prevent rain from ruining the upholstery (an aversive stimulus). In these two examples, discriminative stimuli (the ad for the sale and the dark clouds and thunder) motivate your behavior in anticipation of reinforcement or avoidance of punishment.

Motivation also encompasses the effects of events that alter the degree to which stimuli are able to reinforce or punish your behavior. For example, going without eating for several hours puts eating

FIGURE 5.1   These pastries displayed in the window serve as discriminative stimuli to motivate passersby to enter and make a purchase.

near the top of your preference hierarchy and increases the ability of stimuli that have been associated with food to reinforce your behavior.

Motivation, then, includes two types of phenomena. First, discriminative stimuli, previously associated with reinforcement or punishment, elicit a class of behaviors that bring an organism in contact with a reinforcer or that avoid contact with a punisher. For example, if something reminds you of an interesting person you met recently, you may try to meet that person again by consulting a telephone directory and making a telephone call. Many such discriminative stimuli will present themselves during the course of a single day. The second phenomenon may not be so obvious in its workings. It involves events such as deprivation of contact with a particular reinforcer, increasing an organism's preference for a particular behavior. This category includes reinforcers more subtle than food or water; after spending much time performing routine tasks we become motivated to perform behaviors such as going for a walk or talking with some friends. (See **Figure 5.1.**)

In Chapter 4 we dealt with the learning process; we saw how an organism acquires a repertoire of behaviors through experience with its environment. This chapter explores this process further, examining the environmental and biological factors that affect motivation. First, we shall examine the nature of reinforcement, which serves as the basis for motivation. We shall see that reinforcing stimuli have many effects besides the strengthening of a particular response. Next, we shall examine motivation based on physiological need—hunger. Hunger, which has been intensely studied by psychologists and physiologists, serves as a model for the other biological drives. This chapter deals with the basics; later chapters will deal with more complex aspects of motivation, including its sexual, emotional, and social components.

REINFORCEMENT

As we saw in the previous chapter, an organism's behavior can be reinforced by the opportunity to engage in a preferred behavior. That is, an organism will perform a behavior low in its preference hierarchy if doing so enables it to perform one high in its preference hierarchy. For example, a person will work (engage in a nonpreferred behavior) in order to receive money (which permits engaging in a variety of preferred behaviors). Whether or not a stimulus serves as a reinforcer depends upon whether the behavior associated with it is a preferred one or a nonpreferred one. And the hierarchy is not fixed; eating starts going up the hierarchy several hours after a meal. Therefore, to understand motivation we must know more about what causes behaviors to move up or down the preference hierarchy.

THE DRIVE-REDUCTION HYPOTHESIS

The earliest attempt to explain the nature of reinforcement held that physiological needs—needs caused by deprivation of the necessities of life—are unpleasant, and that conversely, satisfaction of these needs is pleasant, and thus reinforcing. For example, a need for nutrients causes an unpleasant state called hunger. This aversive condition is reduced when the organism eats some food. You will recall that the reduction or elimination of an aversive stimulus can serve as a negative reinforcer. Thus, the **need-reduction hypothesis** suggested that, to a hungry organism, the presence of food serves as a negative reinforcer by terminating an aversive physiological need.

The concept of need reduction was soon expanded, because not all motivation could be explained by the presence of physiological needs like the ones for food and water. For example, behaviors can be reinforced by giving an organism the opportunity to explore a novel environment or to engage in sexual activity, even though there is no physiological *need* for exploration or sexual contact as there is for food or water. (See **Figure 5.2**.) However, organisms seem to be "driven" to explore or engage in sexual behavior. Therefore, the **drive-reduction hypothesis** replaced the need-reduction hypothesis. *Drives* were conceived of as un-

FIGURE 5.2   Rats appear to enjoy running in a wheel. This behavior is difficult to explain in terms of need reduction.

pleasant physiological conditions that motivated an organism to perform behaviors that had previously reduced them.

The modification presented a serious problem. Theoretically, at least, physiological need can be measured, so it is possible to determine when it is present. If physiological measurements show that a person is dehydrated, we know that he or she is thirsty and thus is likely to perform behaviors that were previously reinforced by the opportunity to drink. However, we have no way of measuring other drives, those not based on physiological need, to determine whether or not they are present. Suppose you obtain great pleasure from watching a set of color slides taken by a friend while on vacation. According to the drive-reduction hypothesis, your "exploratory drive" or "curiosity drive" is high, and looking at vacation slides reduces it, providing reinforcement. But there is no way to measure this drive and thus confirm that it actually exists.

The most important logical problem with the drive-reduction hypothesis is that a great many events can serve as reinforcers. (See **Figure 5.3**.) If these events are reinforcing because they reduce a drive, then we are forced to postulate a large num-

ber of drives, none of which can be measured. For example, you will remember the resident of an institution for the retarded whose bathing was reinforced by the opportunity to make the other residents' beds. Is it reasonable to suppose that there is some sort of drive—say, a neatness drive—that is reduced by making beds?

Besides the logical problem with the drive-reduction hypothesis of reinforcement, there is an empirical one. Even reinforcers such as food and water, which are certainly associated with physiological needs, do not appear to reduce drive. Rather, they appear to *increase* it.

At first it might seem absurd to suggest that reinforcement is the result of events that increase drive—after all, we eat to make hunger go away, don't we? However, the answer seems to be no, we do not. It is certainly true that eating makes hunger go away, but we need not assume that this is why we eat. In fact, the *immediate* effect of eating is to increase drive; smelling, tasting, and swallowing food makes us become more hungry, not less. Only later, after swallowing many mouthfuls of food, do we experience satiety.

In what has become a classic experiment, Shef-

FIGURE 5.3 The drive-reduction hypothesis states that behaviors are motivated by drives. But what drive is this woman reducing as she rows her shell?

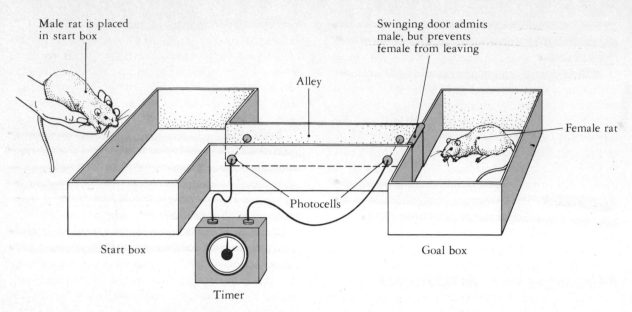

FIGURE 5.4   The procedure of the experiment by Sheffield, Wulff, and Backer (1951).

field, Wulff, and Backer (1951) permitted male rats to run down a runway to a goal box containing a sexually receptive female rat. (See **Figure 5.4.**) The males were allowed to engage in preliminary sexual activity, but as soon as they mounted the female the experimenter removed them from the goal box. The males were not permitted to ejaculate; thus, the behavior of running toward the goal box was followed by increases in drive. Instead of finding this treatment aversive, the males ran toward the females faster and faster; their approach was reinforced by sexual behavior that was never completed. The drive-reduction hypothesis clearly cannot explain this effect.

INCREASING DRIVES THROUGH REINFORCEMENT: ELECTRICAL STIMULATION OF THE BRAIN

◆ In 1954, James Olds and Peter Milner discovered quite by accident that electrical stimulation of parts of the brain can reinforce an animal's behavior. The investigators were trying to determine whether electrical stimulation of the reticular formation (in the back part of the brain) would help rats learn to run through a maze faster. They had heard that electrical stimulation of some parts of the brain could be aversive—that animals would work to avoid

having the current turned on. They decided to make sure that this was not the case for their rats, because aversive stimulation might interfere with the animals' performance in the maze.

Olds and Milner operated on a group of rats, inserting a small wire in their brains. Because this surgical procedure had only recently been developed and was not very accurate, one of the wires wound up about half a brain-length away from its target. This mistake was a lucky one for the investigators, because they discovered a phenomenon they would not have seen had the wire been located where they originally intended it to be. Here is Olds's report of what happened:

> I applied a brief train of 60-cycle sine-wave electrical current whenever the animal entered one corner of the enclosure. The animal did not stay away from that corner, but rather came back quickly after a brief sortie which followed the first stimulation and came back even more quickly after a briefer sortie which followed the second stimulation. By the time the third electrical stimulus had been applied the animal seemed indubitably to be "coming back for more." (Olds, 1973, p. 81)

Realizing that they had witnessed something important, Olds and Milner put more wires in rats' brains, and allowed them to press a switch that controlled the current to the brain. The rats quickly learned to press the switch at a rate of over 700 times per hour. Subsequent studies obtained response rates of several thousand presses per hour. (See **Figure 5.5.**)

Why does electrical stimulation of the brain reinforce an animal's behavior? Does the stimulation reduce drive? The answer appears to be quite the opposite. Electrical stimulation of the brain elicits a variety of consummatory behaviors. For example, electrical stimulation of the hypothalamus can elicit eating, drinking, mating, fighting, escape, and object carrying.

The electrical stimulation does more than simply force an animal to perform a particular behavior. For example, stimulation that causes an animal to eat does not merely produce automatic chewing and swallowing movements. Instead, when the current is turned on, the animal will seek out food and will even work for its delivery. A rat satiated by a large meal will still press a lever for the delivery of food if its lateral hypothalamus is electrically stimulated. Thus, the stimulation seems to make the animal hungry. If hunger can be conceived of as a drive, then stimulation appears to increase the level of that drive.

The drive-reduction hypothesis of reinforcement states that drives like hunger are unpleasant. Ac-

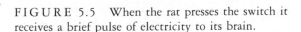

cordingly, electrical brain stimulation that makes an animal hungry should be aversive. Yet the facts are just the opposite; this stimulation is *reinforcing*—animals will work to receive stimulation that makes them hungry. The same is true for stimulation that elicits the other behaviors—drinking, mating, attack, and so on.

An ingenious experiment by Mendelson (1966) used electrical stimulation to test the drive-reduction hypothesis. He attempted to train several groups of rats to run through a maze to a goal box containing food. All rats had just eaten, so they were satiated, but they could be made hungry by electrical stimulation of the hypothalamus.

The first group consisted of rats that were made hungry the entire time they were in the maze; stimulation began as soon as they were placed in the start box and continued until they found the food and ate it. (See **Figure 5.6, left.**) These animals learned the task. The rats in the second group were not made hungry until they reached the goal box, where the current was turned on, making them eat. (See **Figure 5.6, middle.**) These animals also learned the task. With a third group of rats Mendelson attempted to reinforce behavior through drive reduction. He made the rats hungry as soon as they entered the maze but turned the current

FIGURE 5.5 When the rat presses the switch it receives a brief pulse of electricity to its brain.

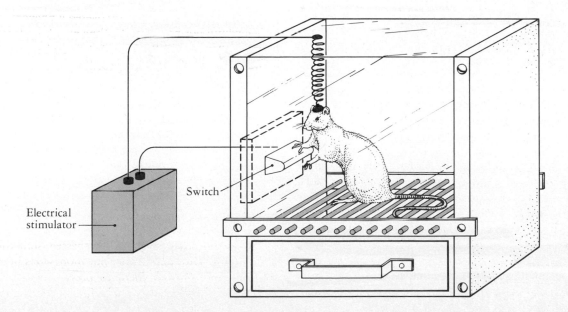

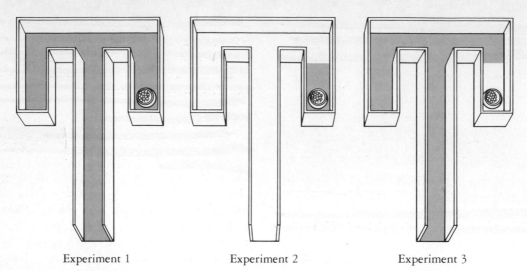

Experiment 1   Experiment 2   Experiment 3

FIGURE 5.6   The procedure of the experiment by Mendelson (1966). The electrical stimulation was turned on when the rat was in the shaded portion of the maze.

off when they entered the goal box. (See **Figure 5.6, right.**) These rats did *not* learn to run through the maze; reduction of drive did not reinforce their approach to the goal box.

Two interesting conclusions can be made about the role of drive and its reduction in reinforcement. First, consider the behavior of the rats in the second group. They were not hungry when placed in the start box, and continued not to be hungry until they got to the goal box. If they were not hungry at the start, then what motivated them to learn to run to the goal box? It appears that drive is not always necessary for performance.

This condition of Mendelson's experiment reminds me of a practice among some wealthy residents of the Roman empire. After gorging themselves on a lavish banquet, they would empty their stomachs by eating some seeds of the *nux vomica,* which cause vomiting. The diners would rest a bit and then start in on a new banquet. Right after the first meal they were satiated, like Mendelson's rats were when they entered the maze. Like the rats running toward the goal box, they got rid of this satiety. Vomiting or electrical stimulation reinstated hunger, and eating commenced once more. Thus, the act of eating itself, and not the satiety it produces, appears to be the pleasurable event.

The second conclusion from Mendelson's experiment is that drive reduction does not appear to be an effective reinforcer. The rats in the third group did not learn to run toward the goal box, where the stimulation (and hence their hunger) was turned off. If we examine our own behavior, we will find that most events that we find reinforcing are also exciting, or drive-increasing. The reason a rollercoaster ride is fun is certainly not because it *reduces* drive. The same is true for skiing, surfing, or viewing a horror film. Likewise, an interesting, reinforcing conversation is one that is exciting, not one that puts you to sleep. The experiences we really want to repeat (that we find reinforcing) are ones that increase, rather than decrease, our level of arousal. *thus- drive reduction disproved*

OPTIMAL LEVELS OF AROUSAL

The drive-reduction hypothesis states that all reinforcement is *negative* reinforcement, and thus motivation consists of a drive toward termination of aversive stimuli. However, as we just saw, activities like eating or sexual behavior appear to increase drive rather than reduce it. Yet there are times when a person wants nothing more than some peace and quiet. And, of course, negative reinforcement is accomplished by the removal of aversive stimuli. In an attempt to find a common explanation for both positive and negative reinforcement some psychologists have proposed the *optimal level hypothesis* of reinforcement and punishment: when the arousal level is too high, less stimulation is reinforcing; when it is too low, more stimulation is desired.

The hypothesis that organisms seek an optimal level of arousal is certainly plausible. Any kind of activity—even the most interesting and exciting one—eventually produces satiety; something that was once reinforcing becomes bothersome. (Even the most avid video-game player eventually moves on to something else.) Presumably, participation in an exciting behavior gradually raises an organism's arousal above its optimal level. However, the logical problem that plagues the drive-reduction hypothesis also applies to the optimal-level hypothesis. Just as we cannot measure an organism's drive or arousal, we cannot say what its optimal level should be. If we observe an animal approaching a stimulus, we might be tempted to say that its level of arousal was too low, so the animal was seeking to raise it. Conversely, if we saw it moving away from a stimulus, we might conclude that its level of arousal was too high. But because the inference was made from *observing* the animal's behavior we cannot turn around and use it to *explain* the behavior.

ACTIVATING EFFECTS OF REINFORCEMENT

◆ Before an experiment by Sheffield and Campbell (1954), it was generally believed that increases in drive automatically led to increases in an animal's behavior. For example, when a wild rat used up all the locally available food it would become hungry. The drive of hunger would make it become more and more active, and this increased activity would eventually lead the animal to find some food. Similarly, researchers noticed that caged rats that were fed only once a day would become very active just before feeding time; a person who entered the animal colony at this time could not fail to notice the animals' restless activity.

The hypothesis that drives have activating effects on behavior made good evolutionary sense. It explained how new responses are added to an animal's repertoire of behaviors. In the case of the wild rat, the general increase in activity would eventually cause the animal to make a response that permits it to perform the consummatory behavior of eating. Eating would reinforce the behaviors that preceded.

To test the hypothesis Sheffield and Campbell placed individual rats in cages designed to record their locomotor activity without disturbing them. Each cage was mounted on springs so that it would tilt slightly and cause electrical contacts to close whenever the rat moved around. The cages were enclosed in lightproof and soundproof chambers to eliminate extraneous sights and sounds. The rats were given one meal each day, which they ate within an hour or so. Therefore, by mealtime the next day the rats were very hungry. However, there was only a *very slight* increase in activity as the animals got hungrier. Increased drive by itself did *not* produce a corresponding increase in activity. The experimenters then added a new variable, presenting some stimuli just before the rats were fed: the ventilating fan was turned off and a light was turned on. Within a few days the stimulus change caused a dramatic increase in the rats' activity. These results tell us that increasing hunger is translated into behavior only in the presence of stimuli that have been associated with eating.

As for the dramatic increase in the activity of the hungry rats just before feeding time, the answer is simple: the rats have learned that the entry of a person into the room is associated with being fed. The animals' caretaker is a stimulus that occurs just before food is placed into their cages, and to a rat one person is probably much like another.

◆ Thus it appears that drive increases an animal's level of activity only in an environment containing stimuli that have been associated with reinforcement in the past. Rats apparently do not search a small cage for food unless there are stimuli there that predict its delivery. It makes sense for a hungry animal not to engage in aimless behavior in a confined space when there are no prospects for food but instead conserve its energy until conditions become more favorable.

ADJUNCTIVE BEHAVIORS: ELICITING EFFECTS OF REINFORCEMENT

◆ When a strongly motivated organism receives reinforcers on an intermittent schedule, it engages in *adjunctive behavior,* behavior that is viewed as an *adjunct*, or side effect, of that reinforcement (Falk, 1972; Staddon, 1976). As we saw in Chapter 4, it is also referred to as *interim behavior*.

Suppose lever pressing of a hungry rat is being reinforced by a schedule of reinforcement that permits it to receive one pellet of food every two minutes (FI-2-minute). All lever presses made before the two minutes have elapsed will go unreinforced; therefore, the animal eventually learns to pause for a rather long time after each food pellet is received. But what does the animal do during this time? Instead of sitting patiently, waiting until nearly two minutes have elapsed, the animal becomes very active, engaging in various consummatory behaviors, depending on what is available in the apparatus. A dish of water will elicit drinking; a block of wood, gnawing; another animal, attack. It is as if the continuous but brief and infrequent opportunity to engage in a much-preferred consummatory behavior causes so much activation that the animal expresses it in whatever other consummatory behavior can possibly be performed.

Adjunctive behavior is a very powerful phenomenon; hungry rats that drink water during an intermittent schedule of reinforcement with food will consume a measure approximately equal to one-third of their body weight in a few hours. This drinking has been called **schedule-induced polydipsia**. (Dipsas was a mythical serpent whose bite caused great thirst; thus, *dipso-* refers to drinking.) Other researchers have elicited similar examples of adjunctive behaviors: hungry pigeons will peck at various items in the environment—even other pigeons—if food is delivered intermittently (Flory, 1969; Miller and Gollub, 1974); rats that are not thirsty will drink water if the opportunity to run in activity wheels is provided on an intermittent schedule (Wayner, Singer, Cimino, Stein, and Dworkin, 1975); and people will smoke and eat more than they otherwise would if they are allowed to work on problem-solving tasks only intermittently (Wallace and Singer, 1976).

The last finding suggests that at least one cause of smoking and overeating is a person's environment; if someone is often in a situation in which reinforcing stimuli occur intermittently, he or she is likely to engage in adjunctive behavior, including eating or smoking (and, undoubtedly, gum chewing, nail biting, and aggression toward oth-

ers). Such a situation might involve doing monotonous work that provides little intrinsic gratification. Such work is reinforced on a very "lean" schedule—a paycheck every week. Interesting work—that is, work that provides reinforcers besides a weekly paycheck—is less likely to produce adjunctive behaviors.

Interim summary: When most people use the word *motivation* they think of an inner force that drives an organism's behavior toward a particular goal. However, it is better described as a tendency to perform a class of behaviors that bring an organism in contact with an appetitive stimulus or take it away from an aversive one. Formerly, psychologists believed all reinforcement to be negative; that is, aversive drives were produced by deprivation and reduced by performing the appropriate consummatory behavior. However, the fact that a large variety of stimuli could serve as reinforcers led to an unacceptable number of hypothetical drives. Since the only evidence for these drives was the behavior that they were meant to explain, logically their presence could not be experimentally verified.

Beginning with the discovery of reinforcing brain stimulation by Olds and Milner investigators could produce reinforcers at will, without having to deprive their subjects of appetitive stimuli. The observation that reinforcement and drive induction appeared to be synonymous led to the hypothesis that reinforcement involved increases, not decreases, in drive. A modified version of this hypothesis, which suggested that organisms strive to attain optimal levels of arousal, provided a way to explain reinforcement and punishment as two sides of the same coin, but it introduced another problem: the optimal level could be determined only by observing the organism's behavior, and therefore could not be used as an *explanation* of that behavior.

Besides making a particular behavior become more likely, the process of reinforcement, especially intermittent reinforcement, can cause an animal to emit behaviors that are not directly reinforced. These behaviors include a large number of responses that have been referred to as *instinctive*, such as drinking, gnawing, and fighting. The nature of the response depends upon the organism's species (that is, it depends on the nature of the behavioral patterns organized in its brain) and on the stimuli that are available to permit the behavior to occur.

PERSEVERANCE

Some people work hard even though the rewards for their work seem to occur very seldom. We refer to these people as "well motivated." Others give up easily or perhaps never try. Understanding the process of reinforcement helps us explain why some people persevere while others do not.

Effects of Intermittent Reinforcement

◆ We saw in Chapter 4 that when an organism's behavior is no longer reinforced, the behavior eventually ceases, or extinguishes. If the behavior was previously reinforced every time it occurred, ex-

FIGURE 5.7   Intermittent reinforcement leads to perseverance. Playing the slot machine (reinforced on a variable-ratio schedule) can be addictive.

tinction is very rapid. However, if it was previously reinforced only intermittently, the behavior persists for a long time. Intermittent reinforcement leads to perseverance, even when reinforcers are no longer received. (See **Figure 5.7**.)

Many human behaviors are reinforced on intermittent schedules that require the performance of long sequences of behaviors over long intervals of time. It seems likely that a person's previous experience with various schedules of reinforcement affects how long and how hard the person will work between occasions of reinforcement. If all attempts at a particular endeavor are reinforced (or if none are) the person is unlikely to pursue a long and difficult project that includes that endeavor as a source of reinforcement. If we knew more about a person's previous history with various schedules of reinforcement we would probably know more about his or her ability to persevere when the going got difficult (that is, when reinforcements became scanty).

The Role of Conditioned Reinforcement

◆ Another phenomenon that affects the ability to persevere is conditioned reinforcement. When stimuli are associated with reinforcers, they eventually acquire reinforcing properties of their own. For example, the sound of the food dispenser reinforces the behavior of a rat that is being trained to press a lever.

If a person has regularly been exposed to particular stimuli in association with reinforcers, that person's behavior can be reinforced by those stimuli. In addition, if that person has learned how to recognize self-produced stimuli as conditioned reinforcers, the performance of the behaviors that produce them will be "self-reinforcing." For example, the little schoolgirl in Chapter 4 who tirelessly practiced writing a letter of the alphabet did so because she had learned to recognize that letter and had previously been praised by her teacher (and perhaps her parents, as well) for producing letters that looked the way they should. Thus, the production of a properly formed letter provided a conditioned reinforcer, which kept her working. As you learned earlier, the usual name for this process is satisfaction. (See **Figure 5.8**.)

At least one real-life setting has provided good evidence that this explanation is a plausible one.

FIGURE 5.8   Doing something correctly produces
a self-generated reinforcer we call "satisfaction."

Bolstad and Johnson (1972) attempted to train a group of rowdy, unruly children to behave more cooperatively in the schoolroom. Some children were given points that they could exchange for prizes (such as pencils, erasers, and notepads) whenever they refrained from engaging in disruptive behaviors. Others were also given a chance to earn prizes, but had to rate their own behavior; they were awarded points only if their ratings matched those of the experimenters (and met the criterion). The purpose of this training in assessment skills was to teach them how to recognize their own "good" behavior so that its recognition might serve as its own reward.

The children who were evaluated by the experimenters alone did begin to behave better than they had before (and better than control subjects whose good behavior had not been reinforced). However, the behavior of the children who had learned to rate their own behavior improved even more. Most significantly, when points were no longer awarded (extinction schedule) the children who had learned to rate their own behavior continued to be better behaved, whereas the externally evaluated children began to misbehave again. Presumably, the children who rated their own behavior were better at discriminating the stimuli that had to be present for reinforcement to occur, and thus became more aware of conditioned reinforcers.

This experiment suggests that a long-term behavior change requires more than reinforcement of desirable behaviors; it should also involve the development of self-generated stimuli that can continue to reinforce those behaviors. Motivation is not merely a matter of wanting to do well and to work hard. It also involves the ability to be reinforced by the immediate products of the work that is being done.

FAILURE TO PERSIST: "LEARNED HELPLESSNESS" — *imp*

A large body of evidence suggests that organisms can learn that they are powerless to affect their own destinies. Maier and Seligman (1976) report a series of experiments demonstrating that animals can learn that their own behavior *has no effect* on an environmental event. This result is exactly the opposite of what has been assumed to be the basis of learning. All the examples of learning and conditioning cited so far have been instances in which one event predicts the occurrence of another. *Learned helplessness* involves learning that an aversive event *cannot* be avoided or escaped.

Overmeier and Seligman (1967) conducted the basic experiment. They placed a dog in a cloth sling, with its legs protruding through four holes in the cloth. They then administered a series of inescapable, unpredictable shocks through metal plates taped to the bottoms of the dog's hind feet. (See **Figure 5.9**.) Next, they placed the dog in a large box equipped with a floor composed of metal rods. A stimulus was presented (for example, the light was dimmed), and shortly afterward, electric current was passed through the floor, giving the dog a shock. If the animal jumped over a small barrier after the warning stimulus was presented, the dog could avoid the shock (See **Figure 5.10**.) Normal dogs learned to jump over the barrier and avoid the shock, but dogs who had previously received inescapable shocks in the sling failed to learn. They just squatted in the corner and took the shock, as if they had learned that it made no difference what they did. They had learned to be helpless.

The phenomenon of learned helplessness is obviously relevant to motivation; if an organism learns that its behavior is irrelevant, it will not be motivated to attempt behaviors that might help it to avoid or escape from aversive stimuli. Similarly, perhaps some people give up in difficult situations because they have learned in the past that their efforts are fruitless. Perhaps even infants can learn helplessness. Studies have shown that babies soon learned to "give up" and be passive and apathetic when they were raised in environments that did not respond to anything that they did (for example, in some institutions that resembled warehouses more than nurseries).

FIGURE 5.9   Learned helplessness: the method used to administer inescapable shocks in the study by Overmeier and Seligman (1967).

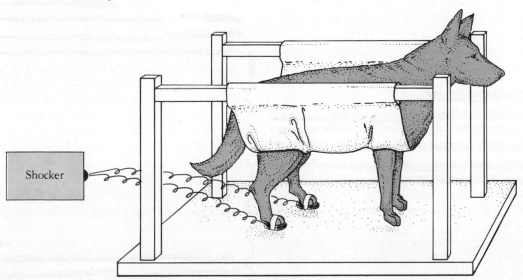

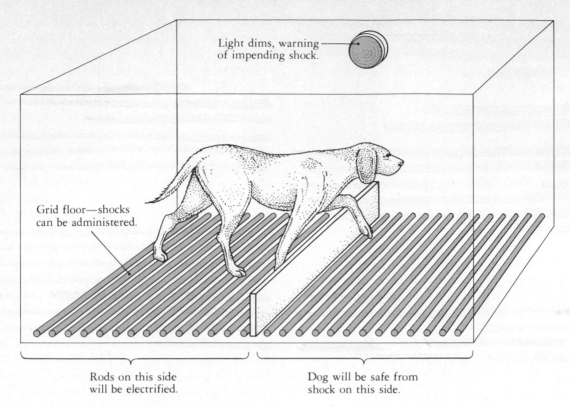

Light dims, warning of impending shock.

Grid floor—shocks can be administered.

Rods on this side will be electrified.

Dog will be safe from shock on this side.

FIGURE 5.10   Learned helplessness: the apparatus used to train an avoidance response in the experiment by Overmeier and Seligman (1967).

The causes of learned helplessness remain a controversial issue among psychologists who study learning and conditioning. The standard explanation for this phenomenon is that the organism learns that its behavior is *not* related to the aversive stimulus. The rest of this section describes two other possible explanations.

Competing Responses

Evidence obtained by Anderson, Crowell, Cunningham, and Lupo (1979) suggests that instead of learning that their own behavior is ineffectual, organisms may acquire behaviors that later compete with what would be the appropriate response. The investigators strapped rats to a platform and applied shocks to their feet. One group of rats received inescapable foot shock; the shock was delivered no matter what the rats did. Another group also received electrical shock to their feet, but for these rats the shock could be escaped if they re-

mained perfectly still: the shock was turned on, and if the rats remained still for two seconds, it was turned off again. These rats quickly learned to remain still. They did not learn that their behavior was irrelevant; they learned that moving prolonged the shock, and that remaining still ended it. Control rats received no training during this phase of the experiment. (See the left half of **Figure 5.11**.)

Next, the experimenters placed the rats in an apparatus similar to that used by Seligman in his experiments with dogs. They were placed in a *shuttle box,* a box divided into two chambers by a small hurdle. The rats could avoid shock by running from one chamber to the other. Those rats with a history of inescapable foot shock eventually learned to jump over the hurdle, but their performance was worse than that of control subjects; thus, they demonstrated a degree of learned helplessness. However, the performance of the rats that had learned to hold still was *even worse.* Clearly, this group failed to

Control group: no initial training.

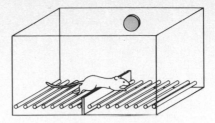

Rat readily learns to avoid shock
by jumping into second chamber.

Inescapable-shock group

Shock is inescapable;
rat learns helplessness.

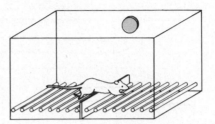

Rat learns to avoid shock, but not
as readily as control subjects.

Escapable-shock group

Rat can escape shock
by remaining still;
rat learns response.

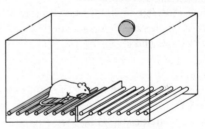

Rat's previously learned escape
response interferes with learning
new avoidance response; this
group performs the worst.

FIGURE 5.11   Learned helplessness: the
procedure used by Anderson, Crowell, Cunningham,
and Lupo (1979).

learn the avoidance response because the behavior
they had previously learned—holding still—interfered with the new behavior to be learned—running to the other chamber. These rats had not
learned to be helpless; they had learned a competing response that made it difficult for them to learn
a new one. (See the right half of **Figure 5.11**.)

It is quite possible that *both* groups of rats performed worse than control rats on the avoidance

task because they had both learned incompatible
responses. When rats (and many other animals)
receive a painful shock they make a species-typical
response called *freezing.* They tense their muscles
and become immobilized. It is possible that the
rats who were given inescapable shock also learned
to freeze because the posture made the shock feel
somewhat less painful. The slight reduction in the
aversive effects of shock would have reinforced

	First day	Second day	Results
Group A	Rats are given shock from which they can escape.	1. Rats are given one "priming" shock. 2. Sensitivity to pain is tested.	No appreciable change in rats' sensitivity to pain.
Group B	Rats are given shock from which they *cannot* escape.	1. Rats are given one "priming" shock. 2. Sensitivity to pain is tested.	*Rats in group B are less sensitive to pain.*

FIGURE 5.12   The procedure used in the experiment by Maier and Jackson (1979).

freezing, which later competed with the avoidance behavior.

Seligman's explanation of learned helplessness is that organisms learn that nothing they do has an effect on what happens to them. The results of the experiment by Anderson and his colleagues suggest that at least part of the reason for learned helplessness is interference caused by competing behaviors that were learned while the animals were given inescapable shocks.

Analgesic Effects of Inescapable Pain

When pain and stress cause the release of endorphins in the brain, these chemicals produce a variety of effects, including *analgesia*—reduction of pain. It appears that inescapable pain, one of the conditions created in experiments on learned helplessness, can cause a decrease in an animal's sensitivity to pain. Perhaps this analgesia is at least partially responsible for the animal's difficulty in learning later that the painful stimuli can be avoided.

Maier and Jackson (1979) subjected rats to either escapable or inescapable elecrical shock. The next day they gave the rats a single "priming" shock and then tested their sensitivity to pain. The rats that had previously received the inescapable shock were less sensitive to pain than control animals. In contrast, the rats that had previously received escapable shocks were *not* less sensitive to pain. (See **Figure 5.12**.)

It appears that previous exposure to unavoidable pain activates brain mechanisms that produce analgesia when the painful situation recurs. Studies have shown that these mechanisms appear to include the secretion of endogenous opiates within the brain. This analgesia could certainly cause the learning of a subsequent avoidance response to be retarded. The pain is simply less intense, so the organism is less likely to learn the avoidance response.

DRUGS AND REINFORCEMENT

Humans find the ingestion of a variety of chemicals reinforcing; the sap of the opium poppy, the juice of the coca leaf, the resin of the hemp plant, and any number of synthetically produced compounds. The behavior of people who take these drugs is strongly motivated toward acquiring them. We cannot explain the reinforcing effects of all of these substances, but we are making some progress in understanding why some people enjoy taking stimulants, such as amphetamine and cocaine, and the opiates, such as morphine or heroin. What is even more important is that investigations of the physiological effects of reinforcing drugs may help us to understand the nature of the reinforcement process, and hence motivation.

Stimulants

Amphetamine, cocaine, and various other drugs act as stimulants, but even more important, their physiological effects are very reinforcing. People, rats, monkeys, dogs, and many other animals will work hard in order to receive these drugs. Why?

As you learned in Chapter 3, stimulants like amphetamine and cocaine appear to produce their reinforcing effect by slowing the re-uptake of the transmitter substance dopamine. Because dopamine is taken back into the terminal button more slowly it is in contact with the postsynaptic neuron for a longer time, and thus exerts a more profound effect. Perhaps the motivating effects of reinforcing stimuli are produced by increased activity of neurons that secrete dopamine. Besides being reinforcing in their own right, drugs like amphetamine and cocaine enhance the effects of a variety of other reinforcers, including electrical stimulation of the brain (Stein and Ray, 1960).

Many experiments have investigated the role of dopamine, and the results have suggested that it is an essential transmitter substance in brain mechanisms of reinforcement and motivation. In one study, pimozide, a drug that *blocks* the effects of dopamine, was shown to reduce the reinforcing effects of food, water, and electrical stimulation of the brain (Rolls, Rolls, Kelly, Shaw, Wood, and Dale, 1974). When rats receive this drug they no longer perform a response that was previously performed for one of these reinforcers. If a similar drug is injected directly into a part of the brain that contains dopamine-secreting terminal buttons, it diminishes the reinforcing effects of electrical stimulation of the brain (Clavier and Routtenberg, 1980). Because stimulation of the dopamine synapses enhances reinforcement and inhibition reduces it, it seems reasonable to conclude that they play an important role in reinforcement.

Opiates

You learned in Chapter 3 that opiates such as morphine and heroin affect behavior because they mimic the effects of the brain's own opiates (the endorphins) that are released in times of stress or arousal (including inescapable shock to the feet) by stimulating receptors on neurons in the brain. Study of the release of endorphins has relevance for the phenomenon of learned helplessness, since one of the effects of these substances is analgesia.

The other effect of opiates is reinforcement. When an organism is aroused (such as during fighting or sexual behavior) some cells in its brain secrete endorphins. These chemicals circulate throughout the brain and stimulate the appropriate receptors, activating neural systems that decrease pain. The stimulation also increases the organism's attention to what is happening and keeps the organism doing whatever it was doing (that is, reinforces its behavior). The survival value of this system is obvious: it is important that a fighting or mating organism continue what it is doing and not be easily inhibited by pain. A fighting organism that suddenly stops because of pain may be killed; a mating one will not reproduce.

When a person takes an opiate, the drug artificially stimulates the endorphin receptors in his or her brain and thus activates mechanisms of arousal, analgesia, and reinforcement. The analgesia is probably irrelevant in this case, but the activating and reinforcing effects are certainly not.

Interim summary: We have seen that reinforcing stimuli have at least three effects. They elicit consummatory behaviors; they reinforce the behaviors that precede them; and, if they occur intermittently and infrequently, they elicit a variety of consummatory behaviors that are not related to any physiological need. In combination these effects lead to complex and varying behaviors as the organism responds to both internal (physiological) and external (environmental) stimuli.

In order to understand what motivates an organism's behavior we must study more than the straightforward effects of instrumental and classical conditioning; we must analyze the interplay of a host of conditioned reinforcers and punishers. We must identify discriminative stimuli and examine of the role of schedules of reinforcement (related to perseverance) and extinction. Such an analysis can account for the striving of humans for social and financial goals, as well as more prosaic behaviors motivated by needs for nutrition and warmth.

One of the effects of experience is to diminish an organism's ability to cope with new situations, as the phenomenon of learned helplessness demonstrates. We do not know whether learned helplessness stems from learning that one's behavior is ineffectual, from learning incompatible responses, or from analgesia produced by stressful situations. (Perhaps all three factors operate to some extent.) However, learned helplessness remains of practical importance, since it may well be a factor in psychological disorders such as depression.

Studies of the physiological and behavioral effects of drugs and electrical stimulation of the brain have increased our understanding of neural mechanisms of reinforcement and motivation. Because the blocking of dopamine receptors diminishes the effectiveness of reinforcers and because drugs that increase the activity of dopamine serve as potent reinforcers, the studies suggest that the secretion of dopamine is an essential component of reinforcement.

In the next section we will concentrate on a single phenomenon—hunger—and see how learning and physiological needs combine to motivate behavior.

MOTIVATION PRODUCED BY NEED: HUNGER

◆ Physiological needs can be very potent motivators: starving people have killed others for food. And you can undoubtedly imagine how hard you would struggle to breathe if something obstructed your windpipe. To survive, we all need air, food, water, various vitamins and minerals, and protection from extremes in temperature. Complex organisms possess physiological mechanisms that detect deficits or imbalances associated with these needs and mechanisms that permit them to engage in behaviors—*regulatory behaviors*—that can bring conditions back to normal. This process of detection and correction is called *homeostasis* ("stable state"). Deficits or imbalances can be said to motivate an organism because they cause it to perform the appropriate regulatory behaviors.

THE PROCESS OF REGULATION

The first behaviors performed by the earliest forms of life were undoubtedly associated with regulation. Today, the simplest self-contained forms of animal life are single-celled organisms such as free-living protozoa found in the oceans. The life processes of these organisms are adjusted to their environment—to the salts in the seawater, the prevailing temperature and oxygen level, and the nutrients that are available (usually single-celled plants). Their repertoire of regulatory behaviors is very limited. At best, they can swim more rapidly if conditions become unfavorable, and perhaps reach a more suitable environment. If not, they will die.

More complex organisms like ourselves are not as dependent on a constant environment. Our species covers the globe, from the deserts to the rain forests to the arctic wastelands. We can even survive in space and walk on the moon. Even so, the individual cells of our bodies are just as fragile as the cells of less adventuresome organisms; it is the complexity of our *organs* and *behavior* that gives us our freedom.

As more complex organisms evolved and moved from the sea to land, they took some seawater with

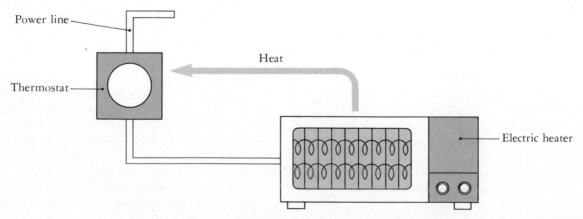

FIGURE 5.13   An electric heater and thermostat illustrate the principles of regulation.

Power line

Heat

Thermostat

Electric heater

them, enclosed in a relatively waterproof skin. Today, the cells of our bodies remain bathed in seawater and are as dependent on it as the free-living protozoa in the ocean. For our cells to survive, our internal seawater must contain the correct balance of minerals, oxygen, and nutrients and be kept at the proper temperature. Our regulatory behaviors keep the characteristics of that seawater at their optimal value.

The commonly understood meaning of the word *regulation* is "control." However, to an engineer or to a psychologist interested in motivation, regulation has a more specific meaning. A *regulatory system* consists of the following elements: a *system variable,* with its *set point;* a *detector;* and a *correctional mechanism.* Consider a small room that is kept warm by a thermostatically controlled electric heater. (See **Figure 5.13.**) The *system variable* is, of course, the room temperature—the characteristic that is being regulated. The *set point* is the temperature to which the thermostat is set—say, 68° F. The *detector* is the thermostat. If the room temperature drops below the set point, the thermostat detects this event and turns on the electric heater, the *correctional mechanism.* The heater warms the room (corrects the deviation of the system variable) until the set point is reached. The thermostat detects the warmth provided by the heater and switches the heater off. This effect of the correctional mechanism—to shut itself off—is called *negative feedback:* an event feeds back upon itself in a negative, or self-controlling way.

The processes that regulate our intake of food and water resemble this simple scheme. But investigators are finding that there are many different kinds of system variables, set points, detectors, and correctional mechanisms, and that their interactions are more complex than simple negative feedback.

The effects of hunger and the factors that control eating have stimulated many thousands of studies by psychologists and physiologists. Hunger can be reliably produced, its effects can be measured, and the behaviors it produces can be readily observed. In addition, the phenomenon is important; the effects of overeating and starvation can be seen in all parts of the world. Hunger is also familiar; we all know firsthand what it feels like. Besides being intrinsically important and interesting, hunger serves as a model for other behaviors motivated by need.

Simply put, hunger is aroused when there is a deficit in the body's supply of stored nutrients, and it is satisfied by a meal that replenishes this supply. A person who exercises vigorously uses up the stored nutrients more rapidly and consequently must eat more food. Thus, the amount of food a person normally eats is regulated by need. What, exactly, causes a person to start eating, and what brings the meal to an end? These are simple questions, but the answers are complex. There is no single physiological measure that can tell us reliably whether a person should be hungry. Hunger is determined by a variety of conditions, so instead of asking what the *cause* of hunger is, we must ask what the *causes* are.

WHAT STARTS A MEAL?

Although hunger and satiety appear to be two sides of the same coin, investigations have shown that the factors that cause a meal to begin are different from the ones that end it. Therefore, I shall consider these two sets of factors separately.

Cultural and Social Factors

Most of us in Western society eat three times a day. When the time for a meal comes, we get hungry and eat, consuming a relatively constant amount of food. The regular pattern of food intake is not determined solely by biological need; it is at least partially determined by habit. If you have ever had to miss a meal, you may have noticed that your hunger did not continue to grow indefinitely. Instead, it subsided some time after the meal would normally have been eaten, only to grow again just before the scheduled time of the next one. Hunger, then, can wax and wane according to a learned schedule.

Besides learning *when* to eat, we learn *what* to eat. Most of us would refuse to eat fresh clotted seal blood, but many Eskimos consider it a delicacy. What we accept as food depends on our culture. Our tastes are also shaped by habits acquired early in life. A child whose family eats nothing but simple "meat-and-potato" dishes will probably not become a venturesome gastronome.

Our immediate environment also affects our

FIGURE 5.14 People tend to eat more in company than alone.

hunger. We are much more likely to feel hungry, and to consume more food, in the presence of companions who are doing the same. (See **Figure 5.14**.) Even a chicken that has finished its meal will start eating again if it is placed among other chickens who are busily eating. Similarly, you may sometimes join some friends at their table just after you have eaten. You say, no, you don't want to eat . . . well, perhaps just a bite to keep them company—and you eat almost as much as they do.

Physiological Factors

Cultural and social factors assuredly influence hunger. But everyone would also agree that the "real" reason for hunger must be related to the fact that the body needs nourishment: if all other factors were eliminated, hunger would be determined by some internal physiological state. What are the internal factors that cause hunger?

THE EMPTY-STOMACH HYPOTHESIS For many years, theorists suggested that hunger resulted from an empty stomach. The walls of an empty stomach rubbed against each other, producing what we commonly identify as hunger pangs. Cannon and Washburn (1912) were the first to test this reasonable-sounding hypothesis scientifically. (Cannon also suggested that thirst was produced by a dry mouth, since a loss of body fluid resulted in a decreased flow of saliva. Some skeptics called Cannon's explanation of hunger and thirst the "spit and rumble theory.")

Cannon persuaded his assistant, Washburn, to swallow a small balloon attached to the end of a flexible rubber tube. Once the balloon was in Washburn's stomach and had been inflated, Cannon attached the rubber tube to a pressure-sensitive recording device. This permitted him to record stomach contractions, which would squeeze the balloon and hence increase the pressure in the rubber tube.

The experiment showed a relatively good correspondence between the occurrence of "hunger pangs," as reported by Washburn, and stomach contractions, as recorded by the pressure-sensitive device. However, subsequent research called into question the conclusion that these contractions are what *cause* hunger.

The best evidence against the empty-stomach hypothesis is that removal of the stomach does not abolish hunger pangs. Inglefinger (1944) interviewed patients whose stomach had been removed because of cancer or large ulcers; their esophagus had been attached directly to their small intestine. Because they had no stomach to catch and hold food, they had to eat small, frequent meals. However, despite their lack of a stomach, these people reported the same feelings of hunger and satiety that they had had before the operation.

Another objection to the empty-stomach hypothesis is that it basically ignores what regulation is all about. As the diagram in Figure 5.15 shows, an organism's intake is food, and its output is the result of metabolism—heat and work. (See **Figure 5.15**.) When the system is in balance, intake equals output. Output can vary; if we exercise more than usual or if the environment gets cooler, we begin to use more of our body's stored fuel. If our body weight is to be kept constant despite an increase in output, our food intake must increase. In fact

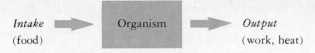

FIGURE 5.15   If weight is to be kept constant, input and output must be equal.

most of us manage to regulate our food intake very well. Because an increased expenditure of energy does not cause our stomach to empty faster Cannon's scheme cannot account for our ability to compensate for changes in the rate at which our body burns its fuel. Whatever mechanisms control our intake of food must somehow assess the amount of fat and other forms of stored nutrients that our bodies contain.

◆ THE GLUCOSTATIC HYPOTHESIS   One of the most important fuels for the body is glucose. Under normal conditions glucose is the only fuel consumed by the brain. (If a person skips several meals his or her liver will begin to manufacture **ketones** from fat; these chemicals can also be used by the brain. A shift of the brain's metabolism from glucose to a mixture of glucose and ketones probably accounts for the "high" that many people experience after fasting for a few days.)

Glucose is a simple sugar. The body can convert any foodstuff into glucose, so a person does not need to eat sugar in order to keep glucose in the blood. Normally, the body stores a portion of the nutrients received from a meal in the form of animal starch (*glycogen*). This starch is later broken

FIGURE 5.16   Metabolic pathways used when the digestive system contains food, and when it is empty.

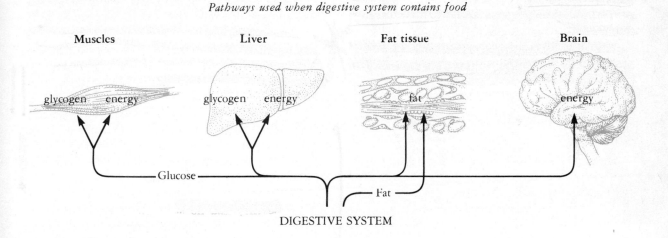

Pathways used when digestive system contains food

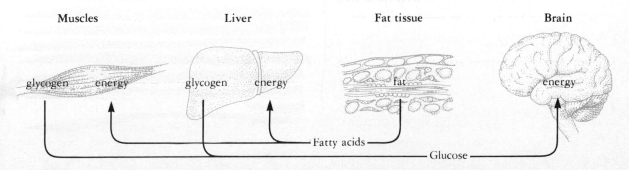

Pathways used when digestive system is empty

down into glucose to supply energy until another meal is consumed and the supply of stored fuel is replenished. While the animal starch is being broken down the brain is the only organ that uses glucose. The rest of the body lives chiefly on fatty acids, which are withdrawn from storage in fat tissue. (See **Figure 5.16.**)

Because glucose is such an important fuel, it was suggested that hunger might occur when the level of glucose in the blood became low, presumably after the most easily utilized store of fuel, animal starch, had been depleted. According to Mayer's (1955a) *glucostatic hypothesis,* a decrease in the amount of glucose in the blood stimulates glucose-sensitive neurons in the brain (*glucostats*), which act as detectors of the blood glucose level. (The term gluco*stat* is analogous to thermo*stat,* except that it refers to the measurement of glucose rather than temperature.) Mayer suggested that these detectors activate neural circuits that make a person hungry, and thus stimulate the correctional mechanism—eating. (See **Figure 5.17.**) However, medical evidence indicated that this explanation was not sufficient.

Mayer realized that glucostats could not simply measure the amount of glucose in the blood; the symptoms of *diabetes mellitus* (sugar diabetes)

proved this. People with untreated diabetes mellitus have a very high level of glucose in their blood, and consequently, in their urine. (The name can be roughly translated as "sweet urine," and indeed, the disease used to be diagnosed by taste.) According to the simplest form of the glucostatic hypothesis, these people should not be hungry— hunger is caused by a *low* blood glucose level. And yet, despite the high level of glucose in the blood, one of the symptoms of untreated diabetes is chronic hunger.

Diabetes is caused by a lack of insulin, a hormone that is normally secreted by the pancreas. For glucose to enter cells, insulin must be present in the fluid surrounding them. Thus, a lack of insulin prevents cells from using glucose even if it is present in large quantities. Without insulin, cells will starve. Once this fact is understood, it comes as no surprise that a person with untreated diabetes feels hungry; if someone's cells cannot *use* glucose, it may as well not be there. (A person's diabetes is usually treated with injections of insulin, so their cells *can* use glucose.)

Mayer's hypothesis states that glucostats respond not merely to the level of glucose in the blood, but to its *availability.* Hunger occurs whenever glucose is unavailable, whether because of a low level of glucose in the blood or because of a lack of the insulin necessary for its utilization by cells. (See **Figure 5.18.**)

For a long time, investigators assumed that the detectors that signaled hunger were located in the brain, but they had difficulty locating them. A chance observation led to a solution. In the late 1960s, Mauricio Russek noticed that an injection of glucose into the abdominal cavity of a hungry dog reduced the animal's hunger, whereas an injection of the same amount of glucose into the dog's bloodstream had little effect on the amount of food it subsequently ate. If the glucose detectors were located in the brain, the injections of glucose into the blood should have been more effective, because a substance reaches the brain much faster when it is injected directly into the bloodstream. Russek (1971) therefore reasoned that the receptors might be somewhere in the abdomen instead of in the brain.

Where in the abdomen might the detectors be?

FIGURE 5.17   Mayer's glucostatic hypothesis.

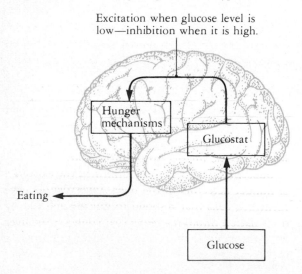

Excitation when glucose level is low—inhibition when it is high.

Hunger mechanisms

Glucostat

Eating

Glucose

DIGESTIVE SYSTEM

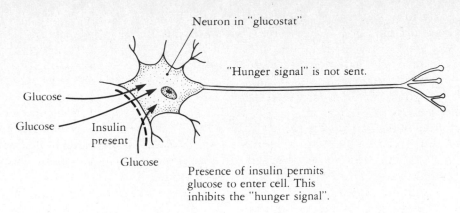

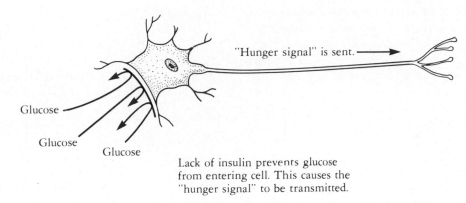

FIGURE 5.18 Because of the effects of insulin, glucostats must be sensitive to the availability of glucose.

Russek noted that all water-soluble nutrients that are absorbed from the intestines are carried by the bloodstream directly to the liver. Some of these nutrients get no farther; the liver stores them as animal starch. (See **Figure 5.19.**) The liver is the first to "know" whether nutrients are being absorbed from the intestine, and it also serves as a major storage site for animal starch. Therefore, the liver appeared to be a good candidate in Russek's search for the detectors for hunger.

Russek operated on a dog and installed a small plastic tube in the blood vessel that transports nutrients from intestine to liver. He deprived the animal of food for a while so that it would be hungry. Just before allowing the dog to eat, he injected a small amount of glucose into the blood vessel leading to the liver. The injection produced

a sudden loss of hunger; the dog ate very little. Control injections of nonnutritive solutions had no effect, and neither did injections of glucose into a vein in the neck. (See **Figure 5.20.**) The results indicate that the detectors for hunger are located in the liver; an injection of glucose into the blood vessel that serves the liver deceives these detectors just as holding a lighted candle under a thermostat will cause the furnace to be turned off.

Subsequent studies have confirmed the existence of hunger detectors in the liver. Investigators have identified cells that respond to glucose and convey information through a nerve that connects the liver with the brain. The precise nature of these detectors is not yet known, and it is debatable whether they respond specifically to the availability of glucose or to the availability of other nutrients, as

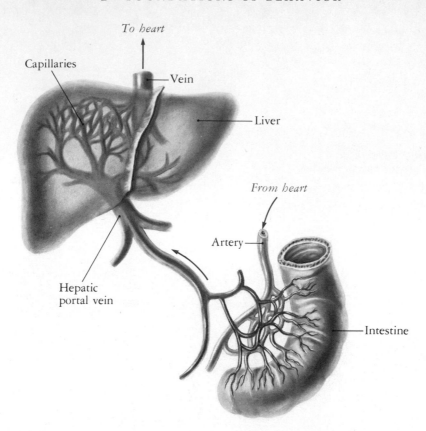

To heart

Capillaries

Vein

Liver

From heart

Artery

Hepatic
portal vein

Intestine

FIGURE 5.19   Nutrients received from the
intestine are sent directly to the liver. (Adapted from

Carlson, N.R. *Physiology of Behavior*, 2nd ed. Boston:
Allyn and Bacon, 1981.)

well. However, we can conclude that the internal stimulus for hunger is a decreased availability of nutrients (principally glucose). The detectors in the liver signal the brain and stimulate hunger.

◆ THE FAT-DETECTOR HYPOTHESIS   The sugar-detector, or glucostatic, hypothesis explains why we get hungry between meals, but it does not account for long-term regulation of body weight. Between meals we use up our easily converted supply of animal starch, so the level of glucose begins to fall. However, long-term regulation is considerably more complex. A thin person and an obese person can store away approximately the same amount of animal starch, but their bodies contain very different amounts of fat. What monitors and regulates the amount of body fat?

If a piece of fat tissue is removed from a mouse or a rat (these animals have discrete fat "organs"), the animal will start eating more and the remain-

ing fat tissue will grow until the animal regains its normal size. And if a small piece of fat tissue is transplanted from one mouse into another, the tissue will wither away. However, if the piece of fat tissue is transplanted into a mouse from which a large piece of fat tissue has just been removed, the transplanted tissue will grow and flourish (Liebelt, Bordelon, and Liebelt, 1973). These results suggest that when an animal's supply of fat tissue falls below a certain level, some signal (presumably a hormone or other chemical) is sent to the remaining tissue to cause it to grow. This implies the existence of detectors of total body fat and a set point for this variable.

Some monitoring system, then, may provide long-term regulation of total body fat, although the mechanism by which this happens is not yet understood. Perhaps if there is less fat than there should be, a chemical is secreted that encourages the fat tissue to absorb nutrients and grow. The

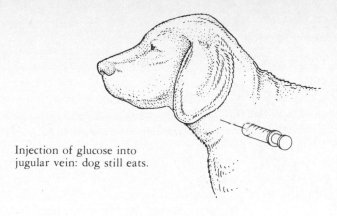

Injection of glucose into
jugular vein: dog still eats.

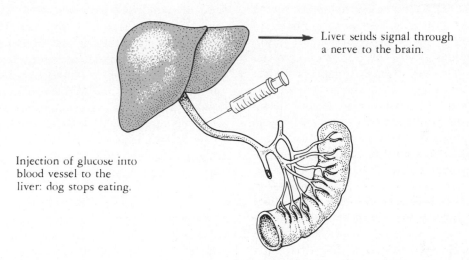

Liver sends signal through
a nerve to the brain.

Injection of glucose into
blood vessel to the
liver: dog stops eating.

FIGURE 5.20   The experiment by Russek (1971).

fat tissue then takes up some of the available nutrients, the organism gets more hungry than usual by the time of the next meal, eats more food, and body weight gradually increases.

Interim summary: From a physiological standpoint the answer to the question "What starts a meal?" seems to be "The decreased availability of nutrients in the bloodstream." This lack of available nutrient (primarily glucose) is measured by detectors in the liver, which signal the brain to stimulate hunger. Beyond this daily short-term regulation, our body also controls the long-term regulation of body weight. The exact mechanism for this is not yet clearly understood; however, it too must enter into the equation.

Cultural and social factors also play a role, especially in what we eat, but also in when we eat. The number of meals per day, their timing, and even their size are often determined by social custom. This is then reinforced by habit. Beyond this, certain environmental factors may come into play; the mere presence of food can stimulate hunger, especially when we see others partaking.

WHAT STOPS A MEAL?

It appears that receptors in the liver detect when supplies of stored energy are low by measuring glucose or some other nutrient in the blood. Through their connection with the brain, these receptors are able to stimulate hunger. But what ends hunger?

What stops a meal? 186

What brings a meal to its finish? Consider what happens when you eat. Your stomach fills with food, and the digestive process begins. However, for a good part of an hour no appreciable amount of nutrient is absorbed from the intestines into the bloodstream. Therefore, the body's supply of fuel is not replenished until a rather long time after the meal begins; the liver does not receive information about the meal until many minutes have elapsed. If you were to continue to eat until your body's need for nutrients was satisfied, your stomach would burst. Detectors somewhere other than the liver must stop the meal.

◆ The first effect of food is excitatory; the sight, smell, and taste of food makes a hungry person even hungrier. You may recall sitting down to a meal, starting to eat, and remarking, "I didn't realize how hungry I was." And in fact you *weren't* that hungry until you started eating. This effect works in other animals, too. Animal trainers customarily give their animals a piece of food before having them perform their tricks; the food piques their appetite and gets them going. This excitatory effect explains why we call premeal snacks "appetizers." As anyone handed a bowlful of potato chips knows, you can't eat just one. This phenomenon is consistent with evidence indicating that reinforcing stimuli cause an increase in drive, and not a decrease.

Sometimes, when teaching a class that meets just before lunchtime, I demonstrate the excitatory effect of eating on hunger. I pass a bowl of potato chips around, asking each person to take only one. When everyone has done so we each eat one potato chip. Then I ask them to think about how they feel: are they more or less hungry than they were before? How would they like to have some more potato chips? (I eat a few more, myself.) Does the idea of lunch seem attractive to them?

◆ Although the immediate effect of eating is to induce even more hunger, the entry of food into the stomach eventually has an inhibitory effect on eating, which suggests that the stomach contains receptors that detect the presence of food. It has been known for a long time that hunger can be abolished by injecting food into an animal's stomach by means of a flexible tube. Even though the animal does not get to taste and smell the food, it will not subsequently eat. More recently, it was shown how precisely the stomach can measure its contents. Davis and Campbell (1973) allowed rats to eat their fill and then removed some food from their stomachs. When they let the rats eat again, they ate almost exactly as much as had been taken out.

The stomach appears to contain receptors that inform the brain about the quality of its contents, as well as its quantity. Deutsch, Young, and Kalogeris (1978) injected either milk or a dilute salt solution into hungry rats' stomachs, and thirty minutes later allowed them to eat. The rats that received injections of milk ate less than the ones that received the salt solution. Since the rats could not taste what was put in their stomachs, the effect had to come from receptors there. The nature of these receptors is not known, but they must respond to some chemicals present in food.

◆ Small amounts of nonnutritive substances in the stomach do not reduce a hungry organism's intake of food. If the stomach is *very* full, its distension causes pain, which will suppress intake, but this kind of inhibition is different from true satiety. You can try an experiment of your own: Drink two large glasses of water when you are very hungry and see whether this satisfies your appetite.

◆ Interim summary: The answer to the question "What stops a meal?" seems to be "The entry of food into the stomach." We get hungry when cells in the liver detect a low level of nutrients in the blood and signal this fact to the brain. We eat, and the *immediate* effect of eating is to become even more hungry. As the stomach fills with food, detectors there signal the brain when enough has been received; satiety takes the place of hunger and the meal ends. Thus, this dual action of excitation and inhibition creates a balance. It also makes it more likely that food will be eaten in meals, rather than in little snacks throughout the day.

BRAIN MECHANISMS

You may recall from Chapter 3 that the hypothalamus, a small region situated at the base of the brain, is concerned with the *four F's*, which include *feeding*. For years researchers thought that they had identified two areas of the hypothalamus that may play a role in the control of hunger: a feeding mechanism in the *lateral hypothalamus* and a satiety mechanism in the *ventromedial hypothala-*

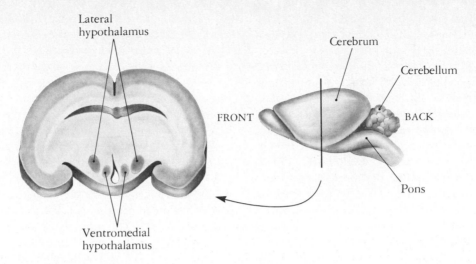

FIGURE 5.21   The ventromedial and lateral
hypothalamic areas.

mus. (See **Figure 5.21.**) However, more recent
evidence suggests that these conclusions were premature.

The Lateral Hypothalamus and Hunger

A number of years ago, Anand and Brobeck (1951)
surgically destroyed the lateral hypothalamus of a
group of rats. The animals stopped eating and
drinking and subsequently died. Later experiments
succeeded in keeping rats alive by injecting food
directly into their stomach long enough for them
to begin eating on their own again. After about
two weeks the animals did begin to eat again, but
they ate less than normal. Recovery occurred but
was not complete.

These experiments suggested that the lateral
hypothalamus was an integral part of the neural
circuits that mediate hunger. When the lateral
hypothalamus is active, we are hungry; when it is
inactive, we are not. Other experiments have shown
that stimulation of the lateral hypothalamus can
make nonhungry animals eat.

More recent studies raised the possibility that
destruction of the lateral hypothalamus affects not
hunger but the brain mechanisms needed for the
behavior of eating. The hypothalamus is a very
important integrating area; it receives sensory input and controls motor output. Normally, a hungry animal will respond to the stimuli associated
with food by eating. Perhaps lateral hypothalamic
damage somehow breaks this link. In fact, studies

have shown that damage to motor systems that are
controlled by the hypothalamus, or to sensory systems that bring information to it, will result in a
lack of eating.

The Ventromedial Hypothalamus and Satiety

Many years ago, researchers observed that tumors
of the ventromedial hypothalamus caused extreme

FIGURE 5.22   An obese rat that has overeaten
because its ventromedial hypothalamus was destroyed.
The rat weighs 1080 grams. (Photograph courtesy of
Dr. N.E. Miller, The Rockefeller University.)

overeating and subsequent obesity. Later, Hetherington and Ranson (1939) duplicated these effects in animals by destroying this region surgically. As **Figure 5.22** shows, the obesity of rats with ventromedial hypothalamic damage can only be described as gross. Researchers hypothesized that receptors in a stomach full of food sent signals to the ventromedial hypothalamus, activating it. In turn, the ventromedial hypothalamus inhibited the lateral hypothalamic "hunger mechanism." Thus, damage to the ventromedial hypothalamus would remove the inhibition and cause overeating. In support of this hypothesis, electrical stimulation of the ventromedial hypothalamus was found to *stop* eating. (See **Figure 5.23.**)

This evidence suggested that ventromedial hypothalamic damage does not actually make the animal hungry; rather, it takes the brake off the eating mechanism. In fact, although rats with ventromedial hypothalamic damage will eat a lot of food, they only eat food that tastes good to them. They will not touch food that has been made somewhat bitter by the addition of quinine, although normal hungry rats will. They are also lazy; they will go without food rather than work hard for it by pressing a lever many times for each pellet.

Other experiments have suggested that the concept of a ventromedial hypothalamic "satiety" system is too simple. For one thing, obesity appears to be caused not by damage to neural cell bodies of the ventromedial hypothalamus, but by damage to bundles of axons that pass through this region (Gold, Jones, Sawchenko, and Kapatos, 1977). For another, damage to the ventromedial hypothalamus alters the metabolism of fat tissue. Friedman and Stricker (1976) suggest that under normal conditions, fat tissue works like a sponge, absorbing excess nutrients when there is plenty of food in the digestive tract and releasing nutrients during times of fasting. Metabolic studies suggest that the fat tissue of the brain-damaged rats fails to release nutrients when they are needed. These animals *need* to eat more than normal rats do, because their fat cells are constantly absorbing nutrients from their blood and failing to release them later.

OBESITY

Overeating and the obesity it produces are problems that afflict many people, especially those in affluent societies, where food is easy to obtain. Obesity is a serious health problem; many scientists believe that being overweight is the most important causal factor in heart and blood-vessel disease. And in many societies people consider fat to be ugly. With these compelling reasons to eat moderately, why does the behavior of many people appear to flout their control mechanisms?

There is no single, all-inclusive answer, but many partial ones. Six hypothetical explanations are described below.

Habit

Habit plays an important role in the control of food intake. Early in life, when we are most active, we form our ideas about how much food constitutes a meal. Later in life we become less active, but we do not always reduce our food intake accordingly. We fill our plates according to what we think is a proper-sized meal (or perhaps the plate is filled for

FIGURE 5.23   Electrical stimulation of the medial hypothalamus causes a hungry animal to stop eating.

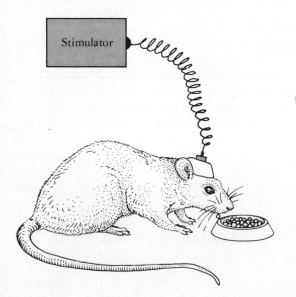

Hungry rat stops eating as soon as electrical stimulation is delivered to the ventromedial hypothalamus

Stimulator

us), and we eat everything, ignoring the satiety signals that might tell us to stop before the plate is empty.

Arousal

Eating can sometimes occur as a response to arousal or stress. Perhaps it provides a degree of comfort. If people feel anxious, lonely, and unloved, eating can make them feel much better. (Of course, the *effects* of eating—obesity—can make people feel even more anxious and unloved and perpetuate the cycle.)

A phenomenon that was discovered by researchers working with rats suggests a possible mechanism for stress-induced eating. Many psychologists have noticed that rats often begin to eat and drink after being handled. For example, if you remove a number of rats from their cages, weigh them, and then return them to their cages, you will soon hear the crunching sound of food pellets being eaten. Antelman and Szechtman (1975) reasoned that the handling, a form of mild stress, might activate mechanisms that are involved in eating. So they devised an easily administered way of producing mild stress, pinching a rat's tail gently with a pair of padded pliers, and found that it induced eating. Normal animals that were pinched twice a day got fatter than nonpinched controls. Even animals with lateral hypothalamic damage could be made to eat by this means and to recover quickly from the effects of hypothalamic surgery (Antelman, Rowland, and Fisher, 1975).

Studies have shown that eating is not the only response that is stimulated by the mild stress of tail pinch. The behavior that is observed depends upon what is available to the animal: if food is present, it eats; if water is present, it drinks; if another male rat is present, it fights; if a female rat is present, it tries to copulate. In other words, mild stress stimulates the entire range of species-typical behaviors.

Antelman and his colleagues suggested that the tail-pinch phenomenon they discovered might explain stress-induced eating. Their rats ate because of tail pinch; obese humans might eat because of unhappiness. Antelman, Szechtman, Chin, and Fisher (1976) found that drugs that block dopamine receptors eliminate stress-induced eating in rats. Perhaps these findings will help control stress-induced obesity in humans.

Metabolism

Some people appear to be destined for obesity; they become fat even though they eat less food than most thin people do. Rose and Williams (1961) studied pairs of people who were matched for weight, height, age, and activity. Some of these pairs differed by a factor of two in their intake of food. These results make it clear that some people convert their food into body tissue (principally fat) very efficiently but others do not. People with an efficient metabolism have difficulty keeping thin, while people with an inefficient metabolism can eat large meals without getting fat. In fact, some people must live on a "semistarvation" diet to maintain their weight at normal levels. In a society that produces an abundance of food and admires thinness, inefficiency in producing fat is a definite advantage.

Nonobese people respond to overeating very differently from obese people. For example, Sims and Horton (1968) fed volunteer subjects of normal weight up to 8000 calories a day, which is much more than most obese people normally consume. Their weight gain was rather modest, ranging between 15 and 25 percent. Furthermore, when the subjects were permitted to select their own diet, they quickly returned to their normal weights. Quick and relatively painless weight loss is clearly not the experience of most obese people who attempt to lose weight.

Differences in metabolism appear to have a hereditary basis. Griffiths and Payne (1976) reported that the children of obese parents ate less than the children of nonobese parents but weighed more; their metabolisms were more efficient. James and Trayhurn (1981) have suggested that metabolic efficiency is advantageous in some cultures. For example, physically active lactating women in Gambia manage to maintain their weight on only 1500 calories per day (Whitehead et al., 1978). This efficiency allows people to survive in environments in which food is scarce; however, it can be a disadvantage when food is readily available, because it promotes obesity.

Some researchers have suggested that differences in the activity of **brown fat cells** are responsible for differences in metabolism that can predispose people toward obesity. Brown fat tissue is a major source of heat production; it converts the energy of stored nutrients into heat. Thus, it is very important to organisms that live in cold climates. When rats were fed a very palatable high-fat diet their caloric intake increased by 80 percent but their weight gain was only 27 percent (Rothwell and Stock, 1977). The discrepancy is accounted for by a large increase in energy expenditure, principally through heat production in brown fat tissue. Genetically obese mice and normal ones differ primarily in the ability of their brown fat tissue to produce heat; the brown fat tissues of obese mice produces little heat (Trayhurn, Thurlby, Woodward, and James, 1979). Although people have brown fat cells, investigators still disagree about whether the differences in metabolic efficiency are caused by differences in the ability of these cells to produce heat (Blaza, 1983, Himms-Hagen, 1980).

Developmental Factors

Events that occur early in life can predispose a person toward obesity. Whatever its cause, obesity during childhood is a very strong predictor of obesity during adulthood (Stunkard and Burt, 1967). It has been suggested that juvenile obesity predisposes a person toward adult obesity through an increase in the number of fat cells. Obese people have, on the average, five times as many fat cells as nonobese people (Hirsch and Knittle, 1970). In addition, it has been shown that rats who are fed a fattening diet early in life will grow an increased number of fat cells. In contrast, if they are fattened up during adulthood, their fat cells will grow in size but not increase in number (Knittle and Hirsch, 1968). Perhaps juvenile obesity causes an increase in the number of fat cells, which makes it difficult for the person to lose weight later in life.

Another early event has been shown to predispose people toward obesity: early prenatal malnutrition. During the winter of 1944–1945 people in the Netherlands suffered a severe shortage of food. Even pregnant women received an extremely meager diet. A follow-up study of draftees in the Dutch armed forces showed that men whose mothers had been malnourished during the first two trimesters of pregnancy were twice as likely to become obese later in life (Ravelli, Stein, and Susser, 1976). Thus, it appears that inadequate nutrition of a fetus can predispose it to obesity later in life.

A later study with rats (Jones and Friedman, 1982) confirmed these results. Pregnant rats were fed only 50 percent of their normal diet during the first two weeks of gestation (corresponding approximately to the first two trimesters of a human pregnancy). Their offspring were the same size and weight as those of normally fed mothers, but when their male offspring reached puberty, they gained weight faster than controls. (Female offspring were tested, but they were not affected.) The experimental rats not only ate more than control rats did, but also converted calories of food into body mass more efficiently. The authors observed abnormalities in fat cells that may have been responsible for this effect.

This phenomenon may help explain why obesity is seen more often in people of lower socioeconomic status (Goldblatt, Moore, and Stunkard, 1965). Perhaps mothers in this group are more likely to receive inadequate nutrition during pregnancy. The fact that this form of obesity is seen only in males and only after puberty suggests that it might be triggered by male sex hormones.

Activity

Obviously, people who eat a constant number of calories each day will gain weight if they exercise less, and lose weight if they exercise more. A study reported by Mayer (1955b) suggests that activity has a strong effect on eating and body weight. Mayer and his colleagues studied a group of men in a racially homogeneous community in India. They measured food intake and body weight, and estimated the amount of energy the men expended in their jobs. People who expended moderate amounts of energy (such as clerks, mechanics, drivers, and carriers) all weighed about the same, although those who worked the hardest (carriers) ate more food than clerks, who expended the least physical energy. These people matched their food intake to their expenditure of energy. (See **Figure 5.24**.)

However, the relation between food intake and physical activity broke down in the case of people with sedentary occupations: head clerks, supervisors, and shop owners. These people expended very little energy but ate almost as much as the carriers, who worked the hardest. Their weight was correspondingly higher: the shop owners weighed approximately 45 percent more than the carriers. (See **Figure 5.24**.)

The results suggest that relative inactivity leads

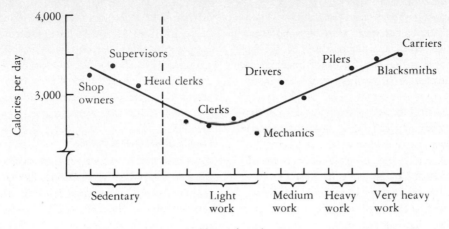

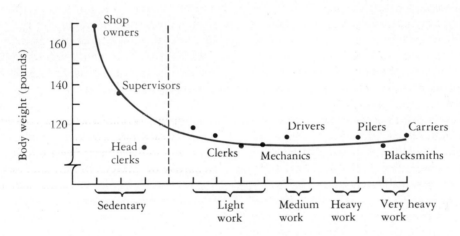

FIGURE 5.24   Food intake (calories per day) and body weight of people with various occupations in a town in India. (From Mayer, J., in *Weight Control: A Collection of Papers Presented at the Weight Control Symposium*, edited by E.S. Eppright, P. Swanson, and C.A. Iverson. Ames Ia.: Iowa State College Press, 1955.)

to obesity. Of course, we must recognize the fact that the most sedentary people also had the highest incomes, which could influence their diet; an observational study like this one does not permit us to determine causes unequivocally.

Responsiveness to Food-Related Stimuli

Schachter (1971) noted that obese rats with ventromedial hypothalamic damage were very sensitive to the external stimuli associated with eating (such as the taste of food) but tended to ignore the internal stimuli (feedback signals that normally produce satiety). Through several ingenious experiments, he demonstrated that obese people are also remarkably sensitive to external stimuli related to eating. Compared with nonobese controls, obese subjects were more affected by taste; they drank much more of a good-tasting milkshake, but less if it was made slightly bitter with quinine. Like rats with ventromedial hypothalamic damage, they were finicky.

Obese subjects were also affected more by the amount of food that was present; they tended to eat what was available, whereas nonobese controls stopped when they were full. The obese people were also more likely to be fooled into eating when falsely informed that it was time for a meal. When a clock was rigged to run fast, they accepted that it was time to eat, and ate a large meal. Nonobese subjects were also deceived, but they paid more attention to their internal satiety signals; they ate much less.

Schachter also found that obese people did not seem really to be *hungry;* they just could not control their eating. Like the obese rats with ventromedial hypothalamic damage, the obese subjects would not work hard for food. When Schachter placed a bowl of nuts in front of his subjects, virtually all the obese people (nineteen out of twenty) ate nuts that were shelled, and therefore easy to eat, but only one out of twenty ate unshelled nuts. Approximately half the nonobese people ate some nuts—with or without shells.

Subsequent research has not obtained such clear-cut results. Many studies have found that obese and nonobese subject do *not* differ in sensitivity to internal satiety signals. Rodin (1981) reports that a number of studies have found that most people, thin or fat, are rather poor at changing their intake of food when the experimenter makes changes in the caloric richness of their diet. (The changes are disguised, and cannot be recognized by taste or texture.) These results suggest that learning is very important in the control of food intake. The degree to which people respond to internal and external stimuli related to hunger seems to be an individual characteristic related only slightly to body weight (Rodin, 1981).

Interim summary: The one conclusion we can be sure about is that obesity has many causes. For any individual, genetic and/or environmental factors may interact to cause the person's weight to deviate from the norm. Thus, no single program can help all people lose weight. More research on the causes of obesity may lead to ways of determining which factors are responsible for an individual's excessive weight.

DIETARY SELECTION

Some organisms follow very simple strategies for the selection of food: they eat only one kind of food, and they recognize it innately. For example, the koala bear of Australia is a gastronomic spe-

cialist; it eats only the leaves of one species of eucalyptus tree. However, many other animals (including humans and rats) will eat almost anything that grows or moves. How do generalists like these manage to select foods that provide a balanced diet and at the same time avoid the many poisonous substances that occur in nature?

Conditioned Aversion

Rats are true generalists; they can live on almost anything that provides calories. However, they must learn through experience what is safe to eat and what is not. Therefore, they tend to approach any new food very cautiously. In terms of dietary selection they show **neophobia,** fear of novelty. They nibble a small amount of a new food, and if they do not become sick by the next day, they come back and eat the food readily. If they get sick (and survive), they will shun the food from then on. This phenomenon, the avoidance of a novel food whose ingestion is followed by sickness, is referred to as **conditioned aversion.**

The kinds of conditioning that I described in Chapter 4 occur only when the eliciting stimulus follows the neutral stimulus within a very short interval. However, when a rat eats a poisonous food it usually becomes sick many minutes later. The fact that rats who survive a taste of poisonous food later shun it appears to violate the rule that learning occurs only when the interval between the stimuli is very short. An experiment by Garcia and Koelling (1966) suggests that conditioned aversions obey a different set of time constraints. They trained and tested several groups of thirsty rats. All rats were allowed to drink some water, with which a particular novel stimulus was associated. Some rats drank water flavored with saccharine, which they had never tasted before. Others drank bright, noisy water: a special contact-sensitive circuit flashed a light and caused a clacking noise each time the rats' tongue touched the waterspout. (See **Figure 5.25.**)

The rats were further subdivided with two different aversive stimuli used at different time intervals. Half the rats from each group received an unpleasant foot shock immediately after drinking the water. (This contingency is similar to the ones that you encountered in Chapter 4.) The others received an injection of a chemical (lithium chlo-

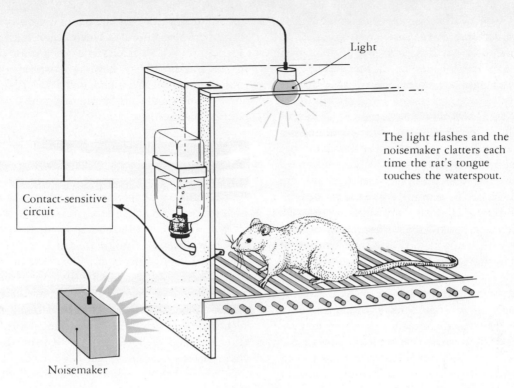

The light flashes and the noisemaker clatters each time the rat's tongue touches the waterspout.

Light

Contact-sensitive circuit

Noisemaker

FIGURE 5.25   Conditioned aversion: a rat drinks bright, noisy water in the experiment by Garcia and Koelling (1966).

ride) that made them sick a few hours later. (This contingency is similar to what would happen if a rat ate a poisonous food.) When they were tested the next day, only two of the four groups of rats showed an aversion to drinking: those that had received shock after drinking the bright, noisy water,

and those that had become sick after drinking the water flavored with saccharine. (See **Figure 5.26.**) Thus, the rats easily learned that auditory and visual stimuli had been followed by the pain of foot shock, delivered almost immediately, but not that auditory and visual stimuli had been followed sev-

FIGURE 5.26   The results of the experiment by Garcia and Koelling (1966).

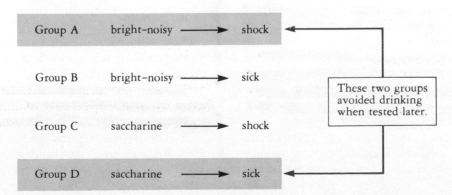

Group A   bright–noisy ———▶ shock

Group B   bright–noisy ———▶ sick

Group C   saccharine ———▶ shock

Group D   saccharine ———▶ sick

These two groups avoided drinking when tested later.

eral hours later by a feeling of sickness. They also readily learned that a novel taste was followed by a feeling of sickness later, but not that a novel taste was followed by the pain of foot shock.

This experiment provides two important facts: (1) rats can learn about associations between internal sensations (being sick) and novel tastes, and (2) the interval between the two stimuli can be very long. These facts suggest that the brain mechanisms that are responsible for a conditioned taste aversion are different from the ones that mediate an aversion caused by stimuli applied to the outside of the body (such as painful foot shock). It appears that conditioned aversions serve to protect animals from poisonous foods by enabling them to learn to avoid eating them. (In turn, most poisons that are produced by animals and plants serve to protect *them* from being eaten.) Since few naturally occurring poisons cause sickness *immediately*, it is necessary for neural mechanisms that mediate conditioned aversions to be capable of learning the association between events that are separated in time. Most other cause-and-effect relations involve events that occur closely in time; hence, the neural mechanisms that mediate an organism's ability to learn about them operates under different time constraints.

Although rats acquire conditioned aversions only to tastes, other animals can form conditioned aversions to visual stimuli. Some animals (especially birds) recognize their food by sight. Because many birds eat food that is encased in a tasteless husk (like the coating of a seed), they have no opportunity to taste the food they eat. Thus, if their conditioned aversions depended on taste, they would never be able to learn what foods to avoid. Indeed, Wilcoxon, Dragoin, and Kral (1971) found that quail (a species of seed-eating bird) can form a conditioned aversion to visual stimuli better than they can to taste.

Humans are as susceptible as other animals to conditioned aversions. Undoubtedly, many flavor aversions are acquired during childhood. Perhaps a bout of stomach flu led to an aversion for whatever meal was eaten just before. A friend of mine traveled with her parents by air many times when she was a child. At that time, the flight attendants distributed spearmint-flavored chewing gum to re-duce pain from the middle ear that occurred as the plane gained altitude. (Chewing moves the eustachian tube, which makes it easier for air pressure in the middle ear to become balanced with the cabin pressure.) My friend invariably got airsick, and even now she feels ill whenever she detects the odor of spearmint.

Selection of an Appropriate Diet

The phenomenon of conditioned aversion plays a role in the selection of an appropriate diet. Rozin and Kalat (1971) showed that when rats are fed nothing but a thiamine-deficient diet (one that lacks vitamin B$_1$), they will eat less and less of it. They will paw through the food, scatter it around the cage, and if possible, dump the container of food over. The conditioned aversion demonstrates that they learn the association between the taste and the illness produced by the vitamin deficiency. If these vitamin-deficient rats are given the opportunity to try some food that tastes different from their old, thiamine-free diet, they will begin to eat it. If the new diet contains thiamine and therefore makes them feel better when they eat it, they will continue to consume this food and will never go back to the old diet. (See **Figure 5.27.**)

In the wild, an animal may occasionally find a particular food in plentiful supply and eat that food exclusively. If the diet lacks some essential ingredient, the animal will begin to feel ill, and a conditioned aversion to that food will result. The animal will eat less of it, and hunger will drive it to seek food elsewhere. Thus, it will be likely to encounter a food that contains the missing ingredient. This mechanism is an excellent example of the marvelous economy of nature. The ability to form a conditioned aversion to whatever food was eaten before an illness permits an animal to adjust its diet to *any* kind of deficiency. The animal does not have to be able to taste the missing ingredient; it only has to be able to detect its own illness and move on to other sources of food.

The most important factor in dietary selection by humans is cultural influence; people learn to eat what other people in their culture eat. In most cases, the diet that a particular culture has is the result of a long history of experimentation. Thus, an individual who conforms to the cultural dietary

FIGURE 5.29 The dietary habits of rats are very adaptable. Unfortunately, this adaptability means their diet often includes food that was stored for our own consumption.

norms is unlikely to suffer severe vitamin or mineral deficiencies. For example, a diet that consists solely of vegetables must be carefully chosen, because most plants lack one or more of the essential amino acids. However, cultures with a tradition of vegetarianism eat mixtures of foods that provide all the essential amino acids. Presumably, their dietary norms developed through experience with the effects of eating different combinations of foods.

For very practical reasons, we know little about the role that conditioned aversions play in the dietary selection of humans. People who have eaten diets lacking essential nutrients generally have done so because poverty or isolation permitted no choice. For example, a sailor on a boat whose provisions lacked fresh fruit and meat was bound to develop scurvy; a conditioned aversion to his diet could not lead him to select foods that were unavailable. A properly controlled study would have to expose in-

fants (whose dietary habits have not yet been influenced by their culture) to diets with specific deficiencies. Obviously, the information that might be provided by such a study does not warrant the risks.

Interim summary: With a look at the phenomenon of hunger we get a better idea of the complexity of what appears to be a straightforward behavioral response (eating) to a specific physiological need for nutrition. Cultural and social factors play an important role in teaching us when to eat, what to eat, and perhaps how much to eat. Physiological factors control our ingestion of nutrients to provide sufficient resources for our normal expenditure of energy, with additional amounts being stored for possible future use. But the dividing line between external and internal factors is really not so neatly drawn. Particular eating habits, especially those learned during infancy, can override the physiological signals that would otherwise produce satiety. And experiences such as prenatal malnutrition can alter metabolism, and thus affect hunger.

CONCLUDING REMARKS

We have seen that motivation is closely related to the effects of appetitive and aversive stimuli; hence, I have discussed the nature of reinforcement and phenomena that are associated with pain. Reinforcing stimuli increase the frequency of the behaviors that precede them, produce an increase in arousal, and elicit species-typical consummatory behaviors. The adjunctive behaviors that accompany intermittent reinforcement probably account for many human behaviors. These behaviors, as well as the process of reinforcement itself, appear to involve systems of dopamine-secreting neurons.

Another aspect of motivation is tied to a person's perseverance; a "well-motivated" person is willing to work hard, even if the work is not immediately successful. We saw that two factors greatly influence an organism's output of effort: conditioned reinforcement and previous experience with various schedules of reinforcement.

Motivation also arises from physiological needs. For example, hunger occurs when detectors in the liver respond to a reduction in available nutrients. The ingestion of food immediately increases hunger (which probably relates to its reinforcing effect). However, satiety soon follows, even though the food has not yet been digested and therefore the condition that caused the hunger has not yet returned to normal. This satiety is produced by detectors located in the walls of the stomach.

We have taken a close look at how internal and external factors interact with the body's regulatory functions to produce obesity. There appear to be several causes of this condition, including habit, arousal (which is probably related to adjunctive behaviors), metabolic differences, developmental factors, differences in activity, and responsiveness to food-related stimuli.

Even though most instances of conditioning involve very brief intervals between the conditional and unconditional stimuli or between behavior and reinforcer or punisher, conditioned aversions can be acquired when sickness follows the detection of a novel taste by several hours. This phenomenon has obvious adaptive significance, helping ensure the survival of species that consume a variety of foods.

GUIDE TO TERMS INTRODUCED IN THIS CHAPTER

SUGGESTIONS FOR FURTHER READING

Few books written for the general public discuss the basic mechanisms of motivation and reinforcement, although many discuss social motivation (these will be mentioned later). There are textbooks, such as *Theory of Motivation,* 2nd ed., by R.C. Bolles (New York: Harper

& Row, 1975) and *Human Motivation* by R. Geen, R. Arkin, and W. Beatty (Boston: Allyn & Bacon, 1984).

Books on the physiology of reinforcement include *Drives and Reinforcement* by J. Olds (New York: Raven Press, 1977) and *Brain Stimulation Reward,* edited by A. Wauquier and E.T. Rolls (Amsterdam: North Holland, 1976). E.S. Valenstein's *Brain Control* (New York: Wiley, 1973), already recommended in Chapter 3, discusses studies of reinforcing brain stimulation in humans. At the risk of being perceived as immodest, I can point out Chapters 12 (hunger), 13 (thirst), and 17 (reinforcement and punishment) of my book, *Physiology of Behavior,* 2nd ed. (Boston: Allyn & Bacon, 1981).

Many books have been written about diets and dieting. I will not recommend any of them, but I can suggest that you read a book by A. Stunkard, *The Pain of Obesity* (Palo Alto, Calif.: Bull, 1976), which discusses experimental evidence about this topic.

PART • C
THE HUMAN
ORGANISM

Thus far we have studied the nature of psychology and the scientific method, some basic principles of behavior, including its biological basis, and mechanisms of learning and reinforcement. In this section we will explore development of the human organism and the nature and organization of the perceptual processes.

Human development embraces many aspects of behavior, including perception, cognition, emotion, and social interaction. (Later chapters will discuss these phenomena in adults.) Normal, healthy human development requires physical and social interaction with others: caretakers in early life and peers during childhood. The need for other people does not end with childhood; it remains with us throughout our lives.

Sexual behavior is a social behavior of the utmost importance to our species, and to ourselves as individuals. Even though actual sexual contact with another person occupies only a small portion of our life span, our view of our own sexuality has important influences on our behavior and self-concept. Chapter 7 discusses sexual development and the factors that determine sexual behavior.

Chapters 8 and 9 present what we know about human sensation and perception and methods devised to investigate these processes. As we saw in Chapter 1, these investigations grew out of the philosophers' primary question about the nature of humans: "how do we obtain knowledge?"

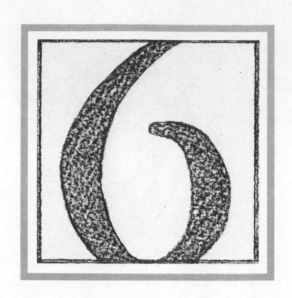

HUMAN
DEVELOPMENT

LEARNING ◆ OBJECTIVES

HUMAN LIFE is characterized by growth and change. We all begin existence as a single fertilized egg, and from that moment until the time we die we are continuously changing. Some of the changes are rapid and momentous; others are so slow that we do not notice them until we look back and see how different we are from the way we once were.

Developmental psychology is the study of these changes and of what causes them. Because developmental psychologists are concerned with physical, perceptual, cognitive, emotional, and social development, their research interests are closely related to every area of psychological inquiry, from physiological psychology to group dynamics. An examination of human development thus provides a good introduction to many of the other topics that psychologists study.

First, let us examine the basic processes that shape our physical development.

GENETIC MECHANISMS

CHROMOSOMES

Our bodies consist of many trillions of cells, all descendants of a single fertilized egg that must contain the information necessary to construct a human being. This information resides in the nucleus of the cell in twenty-three pairs of chromosomes, and in the course of our physical development, copies of these chromosomes will be included in each of these trillions of cells. This must certainly be the most efficient means of information storage found anywhere in nature; a set of human chromosomes can easily fit on the point of a pin.

The functional unit of the chromosome is the *gene;* every chromosome consists of many thousands of them, each of which contains the instructions necessary to produce a particular protein. (See **Figure 6.1.**) Through their ability to control the kinds and amounts of proteins that are manufactured, genes control the very nature of a living organism. Proteins have three basic functions: (1) they constitute much of the body's structure, including bones and cartilage; (2) they provide most of the moving force within our body, both moving our muscles and transporting substances from one place to another within cells; and (3) they serve as *enzymes.* In this last role, proteins control all of a cell's daily activities. If we are to understand how chromosomes direct the development of a human being, we must understand what enzymes do.

If the body is to live and function, its cells must constantly rearrange molecules of matter. For example, cells break down chemicals that are absorbed from the digestive system in order to extract energy, they synthesize hormones and transmitter substances, and they produce material to repair damage caused by wear or injury. To perform these and many other tasks, cells contain a rich diversity of chemicals that can be combined, split apart, and recombined in countless ways.

When we eat, we ingest complex molecules in the form of animal or plant tissue and then proceed to break these molecules down to simple ones. Next, we reverse the process, rearranging these simple molecules into complex molecules that we need. Both the splitting and the rearrangement are controlled by enzymes. Enzymes act as biological catalysts; they determine the kinds of destructive and synthetic reactions that occur without themselves becoming part of the final product. Enzymes serve much as marriage brokers or divorce judges do: they preside over the union or dissolution of various molecules, maintaining order by enforcing the instructions contained in the chromosomes.

FIGURE 6.1 Genes specify the production of proteins.

Each gene contains the instructions for manufacturing a protein.

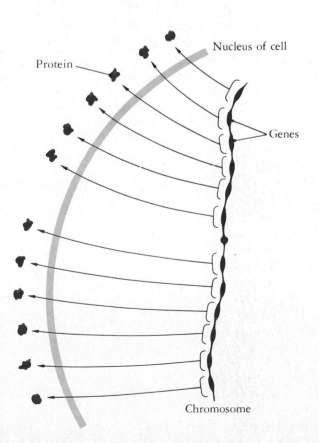

Nucleus of cell

Protein

Genes

Chromosome

DIFFERENTIATION

A fertilized human egg is nothing more than a very large cell containing the twenty-three pairs of human chromosomes. This cell divides and redivides,

FIGURE 6.2 A human egg 30 hours after fertilization; it has just divided into two cells.

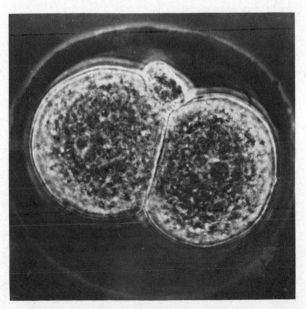

with each division doubling the previous number of cells. (See **Figure 6.2.**) Just before a cell divides it duplicates all of its parts; it produces a duplicate set of chromosomes, one set going to each of the two new cells. At first the same cell is replicated, creating a single mass of identical cells. Then, according to a special internal mechanism, the cells produced in this sequence of divisions undergo *differentiation.* Thus a single cell develops into a complex organism consisting of thousands of *different* kinds of cells.

Just as a cook keeps more recipes on file than are necessary for the preparation of a given meal, chromosomes contain more sets of instructions than any one cell will use in its lifetime. For example, a liver cell contains the instructions for producing sex hormones that it will never manufacture, and the chromosomes of a brain cell contain the information that is needed to produce saliva. Different cells use different sets of recipes in their daily activities. As a fertilized egg divides and redivides, some process, which we do not yet understand, deactivates some of the genes of the newly formed cells. Different sets of genes become deactivated in different cells at different times, and thus the cells take on different functions.

The factors that control development of a human organism are incredibly complex. For example, the most complicated organ—the brain—consists of many billions of neurons (nerve cells), all of which are connected to other neurons. In addition, many of these nerve cells are connected with sense receptors, muscles, or glands. During development, these billions of neurons must establish the proper connections, so that the eyes send their information to the visual cortex, the ears send theirs to the auditory cortex, and the nerve cells controlling movement connect with the appropriate muscles.

Experiments have shown that as the axons of developing neurons grow, they thread their way through a tangle of other growing cells, responding to physical and chemical signals along the way, much as a salmon swims upriver to the tributary in which it was spawned. During this stage of development, differentiating cells can be misguided by false signals. For example, if a woman contracts German measles during early pregnancy, there is a significant risk that toxic chemicals pro-

duced by the disease virus will adversely affect the development of her fetus. Sometimes these chemicals can misdirect the interconnections of brain cells and produce mental retardation. Thus, although development of a human organism is programmed genetically, environmental factors can affect development even before a person is born.

HEREDITY AND EVOLUTION

Long before the development of the science of genetics it was apparent that organisms tended to pass their traits on to their offspring. Physical characteristics such as the color of skin, hair, or eyes were observed to run in families. This observation had practical applications; selective breeding of livestock and pets was a highly developed art thousands of years ago. For example, the numerous breeds of dogs that exist today are the result of human intervention in the evolutionary process. Several factors affect the genetic composition of a species: genetic diversity, mutations, and natural selection.

Genetic Diversity

With the exception of genetically identical siblings (such as identical twins and triplets) and a few

FIGURE 6.3   Human chromosomes removed from the nucleus of a cell that was just ready to divide. Because the chromosomes had just duplicated in preparation for cell division, we see a total of 92 chromosomes: duplicates of each of 23 pairs.

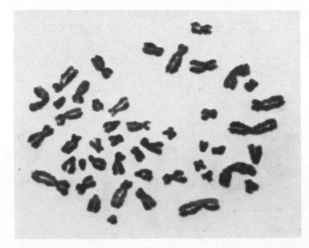

inbred strains of laboratory animals, all members of a species possess different assortments of genes. All members do have the same number of chromosomes in their cells (mosquitos: 3 pairs; frogs: 13 pairs; humans: 23 pairs; dogs: 39 pairs), and these chromosomes are similarly divided into the functional units we call genes. (See **Figure 6.3.**) However, each gene may take one of several forms, each of which contains the recipe for a different protein. The various forms that a particular gene can take are called *alleles.* (The word *allele,* like *alias,* comes from the Greek word for "other.") The major reason for individual differences in humans' physical structure is that people's chromosomes contain different collections of alleles.

Each gene directs the production of a particular protein, but several different proteins can perform the same basic task. To simplify a very complex subject, I will use an example of a simple hereditary trait. The iris of the human eye contains pigment that blocks light so that it can enter only through the pupil. Several different pigments (produced by different proteins) serve this function equally well; blue, green, and brown irises all work quite effectively.

The color of a person's eyes (the color of the iris) is a genetically determined trait; that is, the color of the pigment found in the iris depends on which iris-pigment genes have been inherited from the parents. One variety of this gene contains the in-

structions for the synthesis of brown pigment; another variety produces blue pigment. Similarly, some genes produce straight hair, while others produce curly hair. Thus, although the chromosomal blueprints for constructing a human are fairly standard (all human chromosomes contain genetic codes for eye color and hair texture), there are enough options so that each model will be somewhat different from the next.

The active unit in determining eye color is the allele. Some alleles produce the proteins that result in the development of blue-pigmented irises, and other alleles produce brown irises. But heredity is more complicated than this. Our cells contain twenty-three *pairs* of chromosomes, half of each pair from each parent. Thus, for each gene provided by the mother, there is a mate provided by the father. In many cases this pair of genes will consist of different alleles. Sometimes, as in the case of eye color, a particular allele dominates. For example, a person with a blue-eye allele on one chromosome and a brown-eye allele on the other will have brown eyes; brown iris pigment is a *dominant trait* (always expressed). In order for a person to have blue iris pigment, a *recessive trait,* the alleles on both chromosomes must be the blue type. **Figure 6.4** shows the possible combinations of alleles for brown and blue eyes.

The particular assortment of alleles that an organism possesses is called its **genotype;** the observ-

FIGURE 6.4   Dominant and recessive traits: blue eyes occur only when both alleles for eye color are of the "blue" type, but brown eyes occur when either (or both) are of the "brown" type.

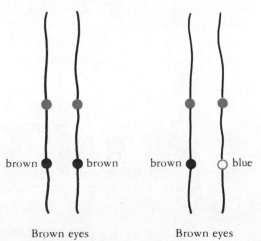

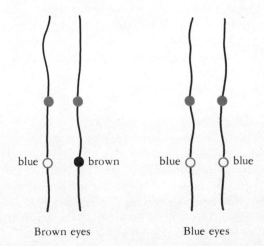

brown ● ● brown   brown ● ○ blue   blue ○ ● brown   blue ○ ○ blue

Brown eyes   Brown eyes   Brown eyes   Blue eyes

able traits that genotypes produce are called *phenotypes*. All genotypes that contain at least one brown-eye allele will produce the phenotype of brown eyes; only those with two blue-eye alleles will produce blue eyes.

Sometimes, some alleles of a particular gene will produce proteins that do not function properly. Thus, their presence on a person's chromosomes causes a genetically produced disorder. For example, some alleles of the genes for iris pigment do *not* produce a pigment. Someone with a pair of these alleles will have transparent irises, which means that he or she will be bothered by bright light. Similarly, deficits in color vision and some forms of mental retardation occur in people who inherit faulty genes.

◆   Only a few traits are determined by a single pair of genes. Most organisms, including humans, have many complex characteristics, called *polygenic traits*, which are determined by the interactions of many genes at many different locations. For example, the structure of the brain is a product of the activity of a very large number of genes. Therefore, it is reasonable to suppose that intellectual and behavioral traits are influenced by many genes.

It is obvious that genetic diversity among members of a species will produce diversity in phenotype—in appearance and behavior. Although each member of a species will carry genes for the same basic physiological mechanisms, the details of many traits will vary. If genes of individual members of a species vary, so will their bodies, their brains, and their behavioral traits. This diversity among members of a species (and between different species) came about through mutations of genes, which produced the diversity of alleles and the proteins they produce, and the process of natural selection, which determined which of these new alleles would survive.

Mutation

◆   The coding performed by chromosomes and their genes is accomplished by a set of chemical building blocks called *nucleotides*. Each gene contains a certain arrangement of nucleotides, and it is the particular order in which these nucleotides are arranged that determines which protein the gene will produce. In other words, the recipe for a protein consists of a particular sequence of nucleotides. (See

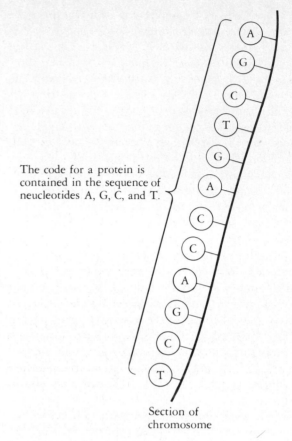

The code for a protein is contained in the sequence of neucleotides A, G, C, and T.

Section of chromosome

FIGURE 6.5   A simplified drawing of a gene; the nucleotides spell out "words" that specify how the cell should construct a particular protein.

Figure 6.5.) If something disrupts or rearranges the sequence of nucleotides (that is, causes a *mutation*), the gene will contain the recipe for a new protein. The new protein may or may not do the job that the original protein performed. If it works, all is well. If it does *not* work, and if the protein that the gene produces normally performs an important function, the mutation will prevent development or at least produce a genetic disorder.

Mutations can be caused by radiation or toxic chemicals, which can make a chromosome break apart at some point. (Since radiation is continuously present in the form of cosmic rays and the decay of isotopes in the earth itself, mutations are not recent phenomena.) When the parts of the chromosome rejoin, some of the nucleotides may be arranged in a different sequence. Unless the cell that sustains this mutation is one that produces sperm or eggs, the effect will probably not be detected. But if it occurs in a cell that gives rise to a new organism, that organism's chromosomes will contain the mutation; a new allele will be present in its genes.

Natural Selection

Occasionally a mutation produces a useful trait; the protein that the new allele produces works as well as or even better than the old one. Organisms with this allele will have a good chance of reproducing and passing the mutation on to their offspring. In very rare cases the mutations confer a *reproductive advantage;* the animals may mature more quickly; compete more successfully for food, shelter, or mates; produce a larger number of offspring; or nourish and care for their offspring more effectively than other members of their species. If such a reproductive advantage occurs, it is likely that the new allele will become more prevalent in the species. Over thousands of generations good mutations will predominate, and bad ones will be weeded out, in the process called *natural selection.* (See **Figure 6.6.**)

A great deal of genetic diversity is seen in wide-ranging species such as humans, because different sets of alleles are advantageous in different environments. For example, dark skin is advantageous in regions near the equator, which receive strong sunlight all year long, whereas light skin is advantageous in the temperate zones. Most anthropologists believe that our ancestors evolved in Africa and had dark skin. As some humans migrated to temperate zones, light skin became advantageous because it permitted sunlight (which was less intense there) to be absorbed more easily. The absorption of sunlight is important because it assists the conversion of some of the body's cholesterol into vitamin D, which is necessary for normal growth of bones. A sunscreen, in the form of darkly pigmented skin, would be a disadvantage in areas where sunlight is sparse. (Today skin color is not a significant factor in determining whether our bodies receive a sufficient amount of vitamin D, since foods rich in vitamin D are easily obtained.)

The complete set of alleles possessed by members of a particular species is called its *gene pool.* The size of the gene pool can vary for different

FIGURE 6.6 Mutations in the ancestors of present-day giraffes resulted in long necks. This trait was advantageous because the animals could eat food that others could not reach. Thus, the process of natural selection favored giraffes with long necks.

species. All members of a species with a small gene pool will resemble each other closely because the pool contains a limited number of different alleles. Genetic diversity in itself is an advantage to a species. For example, when England became industrialized, the air became filled with pollutants, and the environment became dirtier. This darkening of the environment made light-colored moths of a particular species more visible to predatory birds, and as a result they were detected and eaten at a much greater rate. Dark-colored moths of the same species, formerly in a minority, thrived in the dirtier environment because they blended in with it. After a few years, moths whose chromosomes contained alleles for darkly pigmented wings became more prevalent. If the gene pool of the species had not contained alleles for dark wings, the species might have been wiped out in some areas. Because we do not know what challenges the future will bring for our own species, it is to our advantage that the human gene pool contain as many different genetic traits as possible. No single genotype can be "best" under all conditions.

EVOLUTION OF BEHAVIOR

The connection between genes and an organism's anatomy is relatively direct; genes produce proteins that affect physical development and structure. The genetic control of behavior is much less direct. Genes cannot produce behavior, they can only shape the development of organs that affect behavior. Just as animals can be bred for their size, or the amount of milk they produce, or the thickness of their fur, they can be bred for behavioral traits. Some dogs

were bred to be gentle, and others to be fierce hunters. Although we do not know the physical basis for these differences in temperament, we assume that they stem from variations in the structural characteristics of the brain. These structural variations cause different brains to function somewhat differently and to make various behaviors more or less likely.

Several years ago, a psychologist attempted to breed rats for a particular behavioral capacity—the ability to learn to run through a maze (Tryon, 1940). He deprived the animals of food for a while to make them hungry, then placed them in the starting box of a maze. The rats wandered through the maze and eventually discovered and ate the food in the goal box. (See **Figure 6.7**.) Then they were removed from the goal box and put back into the starting box. Each time this was done, the rats found the food more quickly, until they were running directly to the goal box.

Some rats learned the maze in fewer trials than others. If the ability to learn a maze depends on characteristics of the brain that are genetically controlled, then the offspring of "bright" rats should be quicker at learning the maze than the offspring

FIGURE 6.7   A rat in Tryon's experiment learns to run to the food faster and faster each trial, making fewer errors each time.

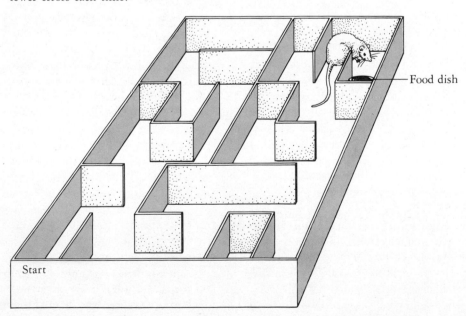

Food dish

Start

of "dull" rats. This is precisely what Tryon observed. He bred the fastest maze learners with each other and the slowest maze learners with each other. As generations passed, the offspring of the two groups of animals became increasingly different in their maze-learning abilities. **Figure 6.8** shows the effects of this selective breeding.

It is clear that maze-learning ability is affected by genetic factors. But it is also clear that a rat's ability to learn a maze is not an indication of its overall intelligence. Subsequent studies showed that

FIGURE 6.8   The effects of selective breeding of the fastest and slowest learners of a maze. (From Tryon, R.C. *Yearbook of the National Society for Studies in Education,* 1940, *39,* 111–119.)

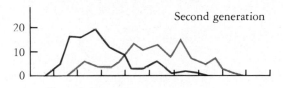

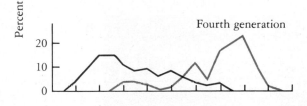

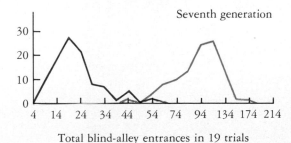

——— Offspring of maze-bright rats

——— Offspring of maze-dull rats

maze-bright rats were superior to maze-dull rats in learning a few types of tasks, but their performance was equal on many others (Searle, 1949).

Tryon's experiment is especially important because it marks the beginning of a special interdisciplinary field shared by psychology and zoology: *behavioral genetics.* Behavioral geneticists study the effects of genotypic variation on behavior; they attempt to understand how differences in inherited structure cause differences in behavior.

Interim summary: Fertilization begins a process that sees a single cell develop into a complex organism. In humans this development is directed by the genetic material contained in just twenty-three pairs of chromosomes, too small to see without a microscope. Through a process of replication and differentiation the genes contained in the original set of chromosomes will control the growth and cellular activity of the entire organism. This control is accomplished by the genes' ability to manufacture the appropriate proteins at the appropriate time.

The relation between genotype—an individual collection of alleles—and phenotype—an individual collection of physical and behavioral traits—is complex. Some alleles are dominant, some are recessive, and most traits are polygenic, controlled by the interactions of many different alleles. Human diversity itself can be traced to mutations in our ancestors' genes, which provided new alleles, and the process of natural selection, which weeded out of the gene pool most of the ones that did not work well. Each person has a different genotype, or assortment of alleles, and hence is unique. Phenotypes differ—some people are short, some tall; some have blue eyes, some brown; some have a dark complexion, some light; and so forth. Even our behaviors are influenced by our genes; although our brains, the organs that produce our behavior, are all basically similar, the details of their parts and interconnections differ.

PRODUCTION OF GAMETES

Fertilization requires the production of ova (eggs) and sperm. Approximately 500,000 ova are present in the female's body from birth, representing an enormous potential for genetic diversity among her

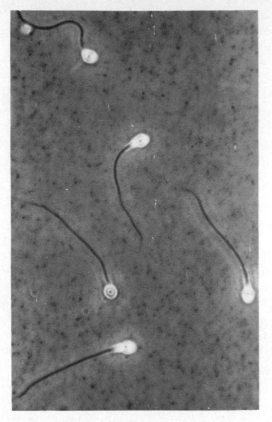

FIGURE 6.9   Human sperm.

offspring. After puberty, one of a woman's ovaries will produce a ripe ovum each month, which is discharged into the abdominal cavity. (This discharge of the ovum is called *ovulation.*) One of the fallopian tubes picks up the ovum and conveys it toward the woman's uterus. An *ovum* is the largest cell of the human body; it is approximately the size of the head of a pin. It has a yolk that contains nutrients to sustain its growth for a few days. *Sperm* are small cells that swim by lashing their long tails back and forth. (See **Figure 6.9**) They are produced daily in a man's testes and are carried in a fluid called semen. Over the course of a man's life his testes will produce billions of sperm.

Ova and sperm are collectively referred to as **gametes** (from the Greek *gamos,* "marriage"). They are produced by the division of cells in the ovaries and testes. This division is special; it results in cells that have only half the normal number of chromosomes. Instead of twenty-three *pairs* of chromosomes, sperm and ova contain twenty-three *single* chromosomes—one member of each pair.

FERTILIZATION

Once a man ejaculates semen into a woman's vagina, the sperm begin their journey into the uterus

FIGURE 6.10   Fertilization of a human ovum.

and up the fallopian tubes. *Fertilization* occurs if a sperm meets and unites with an ovum traveling downward through one of the fallopian tubes. (See **Figure 6.10.**) As we saw, sperm and ova contain twenty-three single chromosomes—one member of each pair. When an ovum is fertilized, the pairs are reconstituted in a single cell called a *zygote,* with one member of each new pair coming from one parent. Thus, each parent contributes half of a child's genetic material. (See **Figure 6.11.**)

The number of genetically different offspring that a single couple could produce is astronomical. Because each sperm or ovum contains one member of each of twenty-three pairs of chromosomes, each

parent can produce 2^{23} (8,388,608) genetically different sperm or ova. This number must then be squared because of the fact that the offspring's genotype results from the combination of both sperm and ovum. Thus, a single couple has the genetic potential to produce 70,368,774,177,664 unique offspring.

A single ejaculation of semen contains hundreds of millions of sperm and thus might appear to be a wasteful expenditure of genetic material—only one sperm unites with the ovum. But the trip through the woman's reproductive system is so arduous that only a few of the millions of sperm ever get near the ovum. Furthermore, it is thought that

FIGURE 6.11   Each parent contributes one half of his or her child's chromosomes through the sperm or ovum.

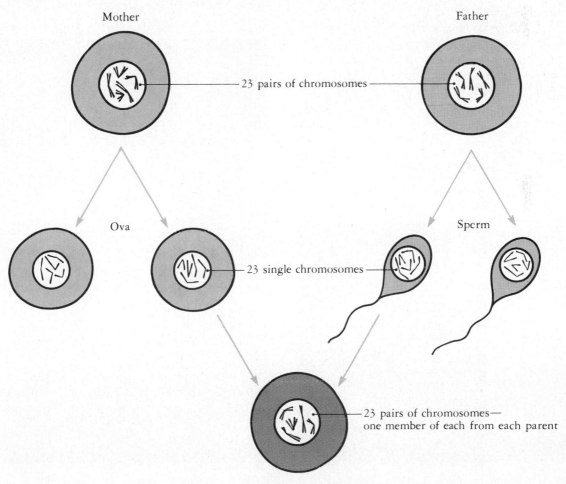

Mother

Father

23 pairs of chromosomes

Ova

Sperm

23 single chromosomes

23 pairs of chromosomes—
one member of each from each parent

Fertilized ovum—zygote

sperm release a chemical that breaks down a barrier surrounding the ovum, permitting one of them to enter and fertilize it. Thus, although only one sperm contributes its genetic material to the beginning organism, fertilization requires the presence of many sperm, all of them secreting their barrier-softening material.

DEVELOPMENT IN THE UTERUS

The fertilized ovum, sustained by its yolk, continues to travel down the fallopian tube, dividing and redividing. When the developing organism reaches the uterus it attaches itself to the wall of the uterus and begins to grow tendrils that intertwine with the rich supply of blood vessels located there. The mass of dividing cells begins to differentiate into various kinds of tissue, and at this moment when the cells begin to specialize the organism becomes an *embryo.* (See **Figure 6.12.**)

The embryo develops an *amniotic sac,* a membrane that completely encases it in a watery fluid. It also develops a *placenta,* an organ that draws nourishment from the mother and passes waste products to her to be excreted. These transfers are conveyed by blood vessels in the umbilical cord, which connects the fetus to the placenta. (See **Figure 6.13.**)

By the time the embryo becomes a *fetus* (in approximately eight weeks) it is unmistakably human in appearance. When it is four months old the mother can feel its movements. In another month it is capable of responding to the environment; it can swallow some of the amniotic fluid in which it floats, and sometimes it even develops hiccups. The sucking reflex is well developed before birth; pictures taken of fetuses by means of sonar have caught them in the act of sucking their thumbs.

As we saw earlier, drugs and toxins can have disastrous effects on fetal development. There is some evidence that even a single alcoholic "binge" during a critical stage of pregnancy can cause permanent damage to the fetus. One of the most common drug-induced abnormalities, the *fetal alcohol syndrome,* is seen in many offspring of women who

FIGURE 6.13   A human fetus (at 14 weeks) encased in its amniotic sac, with the umbilical cord and placenta.

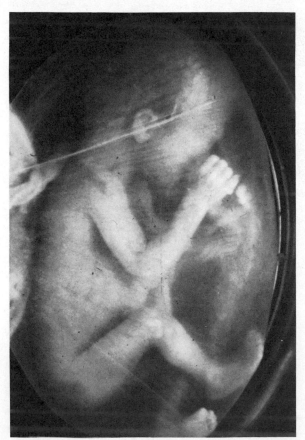

FIGURE 6.12   A human embryo 38 days after fertilization.

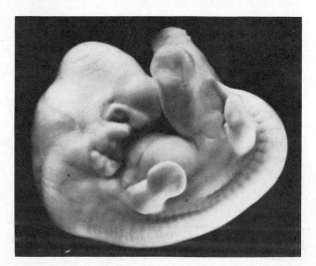

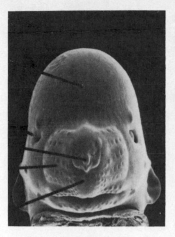
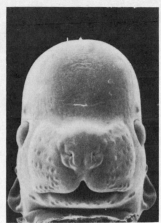

Narrow forehead

Short palpebral
fissures

Small nose

Long upper lip
with deficient
philtrum

FIGURE 6.14   A child with fetal alcohol syndrome, along with magnified views of a rat fetus whose mother received alcohol during pregnancy (left) and a normal rat fetus (right). (From Sulik, K.K., Johnston, M.C., and Webb, M.A., *Science,* 1981, *214,* 936–938.)

are chronic alcoholics. The children are much smaller than average, have characteristic facial abnormalities, and more significantly, are mentally retarded. Figure 6.14 shows the face of a child with fetal alcohol syndrome, along with the face of a normal mouse fetus and a mouse fetus whose mother received alcohol during early pregnancy. (See **Figure 6.14.**)

THE BIRTH PROCESS

By the time the fetus is born its organs have developed sufficiently that it can sustain life on its own. Labor begins as a series of rhythmic contractions of the uterus, which consists mostly of muscle tissue. The junctions of the pelvic bones that surround the mother's vagina have been softened by a hormone secreted in late pregnancy, and these bones are now capable of separating to permit passage of the fetus. The contractions push the head of the fetus against the amniotic sac, which then ruptures, discharging amniotic fluid.

As labor continues the opening at the mouth of the uterus widens until contractions finally expel the baby's head, the largest part of its body; once this is delivered to the outside world the rest follows easily. The umbilical cord is cut and tied after contractions can no longer be detected from its blood vessels, and soon afterward the placenta is expelled. The human species has just gained a new member.

EFFECTS OF THE BIRTH PROCESS ON DEVELOPMENT

Birth probably comes as a shock to the baby, and it is an exhausting (though usually rewarding) experience for the mother, but most births have no adverse effects upon mother or infant. However, a difficult delivery occasionally damages the baby and affects its subsequent development.

At birth there is an abrupt change in the baby's circulatory system. Previously the placenta has delivered nutrients and oxygen, but once the baby leaves the uterus it must obtain its own oxygen. Before birth a special blood vessel causes blood to bypass the baby's lungs. As soon as the baby is born this blood vessel clamps shut, and blood begins circulating through the lungs. The placenta gives a final contraction, squeezing out the last bit of oxygen-containing blood that the baby will receive from it.

For approximately three-quarters of a minute the baby receives no oxygen from its environment. The level of carbon dioxide in the blood increases until the respiratory centers of the medulla respond, and the baby gasps its first breath. This sudden intake of air—the first time the lungs are inflated—appears to shock and surprise the baby, because it usually begins to cry.

Thus, all newborn babies go through a period of *anoxia,* or oxygen deprivation. Most of them experience no harm at all, but those who fail to begin breathing promptly may sustain some brain damage. Slowness in beginning to breathe can result from the premature delivery of a baby with an underdeveloped brain or from an especially slow or fast delivery. During a long labor the circulation of the placenta may begin to shut down before the baby emerges; a short labor can cause the baby to be delivered before its own preparations for breathing are complete. The process of labor and delivery is not simply an expulsion of the fetus; it involves a series of interdependent changes in mother, placenta, and baby.

Anoxia can also be produced by mechanical problems during delivery. A difficult delivery can cause compression of the umbilical cord, shutting off the flow of blood. Or the umbilical cord can become wrapped around the baby's neck, pinching its blood vessels. The cord must be untangled by the person who is assisting with the delivery.

Careful studies of children who had suffered from anoxia at birth (Graham, Ernhart, Thurston, and Craft, 1962; Corah, Anthony, Painter, Stern, and Thurston, 1965) found that symptoms were most severe early in life; the babies did not respond normally to sensory stimuli and were more irritable than normal infants. By the time they were three years old, the anoxic babies were essentially normal in physical development and sensory capacities, but their cognitive development lagged behind that of normal three-year-olds. Furthermore, both the psychologists and the parents noted personality differences between the anoxic and normal children. Some of the effects of anoxia continued to diminish, and by age seven the neurological and cognitive development of most of these children was similar to that of children whose births had been normal. However, a few children had longlasting deficits: distractibility, insensitivity in social interactions, emotional instability, and poorer cognitive performance, especially in abstract verbal abilities.

Medication administered to the mother during labor and delivery can also affect a baby's subsequent development. Drugs that circulate in a mother's bloodstream can be transferred to the baby and can have a more pronounced effect on its immature nervous system and metabolism. For example, it is clear that anesthetics given to the mother during childbirth depress the baby's normal functioning. Small metal disks harmlessly pasted to the scalp can record electrical activity from the baby's brain. These recordings show a decrease in the brain's electrical activity for several days after birth if the mother received a general anesthetic during labor and delivery (Hughes, Ehemann, and Brown, 1948). In addition, the baby eats less and is less active for a few days. Sensitive measures of sensory, motor, and cognitive functioning can detect the effects of childbirth anesthetics even a month after delivery (Conway and Brackbill, 1970). Consequently, although the mothers of many normal—even brilliant and talented—individuals received a general anesthetic during childbirth, today most obstetricians tend to use local anesthetics to block axonal conduction below the spinal cord, or to combine local anesthetics around the birth canal with the techniques of natural childbirth.

GENETIC ABNORMALITIES THAT HARM DEVELOPMENT

Down's Syndrome

◆ The best-known genetic deficit that produces mental retardation is called *Down's syndrome.* This disorder was previously called *Mongolism,* because of the slight facial resemblance the afflicted children have to people of Mongolian origin. It is usually produced by a chromosomal abnormality—an extra twenty-first chromsome.

A cell produces a duplicate set of chromosomes just before it divides. At this time it is easy to see the individual chromsomes. Living cells can be obtained from a person by scraping the lining of the mouth. Once these cells are properly prepared and dyed, individual chromosomes can be photographed under a microscope and the pairs of chromsomes arranged according to size. A baby suffering from Down's syndrome will be found to have three twenty-first chromosomes instead of two. It is not known how the extra chromosome produces its harmful effects.

Children with Down's syndrome are typically

FIGURE 6.15   A child with Down's syndrome.

affectionate, loving, and cheerful. (See **Figure 6.15**.) Some of them are only moderately retarded; some score as well on tests of intelligence as people considered normal. Therefore, many such children remain with their families instead of living in an institution for mentally retarded children. However, children with Down's syndrome are more susceptible than normal ones to a variety of physical disorders and therefore have a limited life expectancy.

Phenylketonuria

Phenylketonuria (PKU) is an inherited, recessive disorder that occurs only if both alleles for a particular gene are faulty. (See **Figure 6.16**.) PKU results from the absence of an enzyme that is produced only by the normal allele. The enzyme causes one amino acid (phenylalanine) to be converted into another (tyrosine). The unconverted phenylalanine in a baby with PKU accumulates in the blood and damages the cells of the brain. Mental retardation occurs as a result of this damage.

Fortunately, PKU can be treated. A special diet containing very little phenylalanine keeps the blood level of this amino acid low and allows the nervous system to develop normally. Once it is mature enough, the nervous system builds barriers that protect it from excessive levels of phenylalanine in the blood, and the dietary restriction can be relaxed somewhat.

Early treatment is vital, because the harmful effects of early brain damage are permanent. After the first twenty-five weeks of postpartum life, it is too late to prevent mental retardation. Reliable, valid test for PKU are now available, and many countries require that all newborn infants be tested for the disorder.

Interim summary: Fertilization of an ovum by the sperm determines the genetic blueprint for an individual. The eventual expression of this blueprint involves a complex interaction between the developing organism and its environment that begins long before the child is born. We have learned some details of this interaction by studying the causes of genetically and environmentally produced defects.

Some defects are clearly of genetic origin, such as Down's syndrome. Others, such as the fetal alcohol syndrome, result from an unhealthy prenatal environment. The range of defects can vary widely. Some, like transparent irises, will have only a slight impact on a person's health and ability to survive. Others may seriously impair health or shorten a person's life. Good nutrition, abstinence from drugs (including alcohol), and good medical care will provide an optimal prenatal environment for a developing organism. In the case of some genetic

FIGURE 6.16   Phenylketonuria (PKU) is caused by a recessive gene.

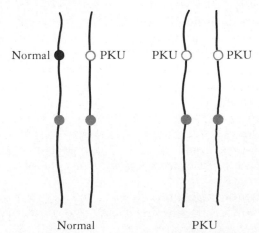

disorders, such as phenylketonuria, special post-natal treatment will minimize deleterious effects. It is clear that good care of our offspring must begin before they are born.

PHYSICAL AND PERCEPTUAL DEVELOPMENT OF THE INFANT

By general agreement, the newborn baby is called an infant (*infant* means "unable to speak") until two years of age, even though normal infants begin to speak during their second year. A newborn human infant is a helpless creature, absolutely dependent on adult care. But recent research has shown that the newborn does not passively await the ministrations of its caretaker; it very quickly develops skills that shape the behavior of the adults with whom it interacts.

MOTOR DEVELOPMENT

◆ At birth, the infant's most significant movements are reflexes—automatic movements in response to specific stimuli. The most important reflexes are the *rooting, sucking,* and *swallowing* responses. If a baby's cheek is lightly touched, it will turn its head so that the object reaches its lips (the rooting response). If the object is of the appropriate size, texture, and temperature, the baby will open its mouth and begin to suck. Obviously, these reflexes are extremely important for the baby's survival. A bottle-fed infant does not need the rooting response to eat, because the nipple is placed directly into its mouth, but babies were not bottle-fed when these reflexes evolved. As we shall see later in this chapter, these behaviors, along with smiling and crying, are important for an infant's social development.

A newborn infant can also respond to noxious stimuli by withdrawing, but these reflexes tend to be rather diffuse. An older child will pull its arm back if its hand strikes a hot or sharp object, but a baby's withdrawal reflex lacks such precision—the entire body participates in the movement. Because the baby's own organized movements are so

limited, it must depend on adult intervention to protect it from harm and to provide it with food.

Normal motor development follows a distinct pattern, although individual children progress at different rates. For example, Shirley (1933) carried out a careful, thorough study of the stages of development of the ability to walk. **Figure 6.17** shows her results.

Two general trends stand out in the development of good motor control: *cephalocaudal development* and *proximodistal development* (Appleton, Clifton, and Goldberg, 1975). *Cephalocaudal* ("head to tail") refers to the fact that an infant learns to control the movements of the upper part of its body first. In fact, a newborn baby has rather good control of its eye movements, and the presence of the rooting, sucking, and swallowing responses demonstrates control of some movements of the head, mouth, lips, tongue, and throat. *Proximodistal* ("near to far") refers to the fact that a baby can control its arms long before it can control its hands and fingers.

Development of motor skills requires two ingredients: maturation of the child's nervous system and lots of practice. Development of the brain is not complete at birth; a great deal of growth occurs during the first several months (Dekaban, 1970). In fact, some changes are still taking place in early adulthood. But motor development is not merely a matter of using differeng neuromuscular systems once they develop. Instead, physical development of the nervous system depends, to a large extent, on the baby's own movements while interacting with the environment. The infant's movements greatly affect the development of its nervous system.

A normal infant in a stimulating and nonrestrictive environment will practice its developing motor skills. This often means hard work; a young child has to put real effort into mastering new skills. Why does it bother to do so? People who have studied child development have noted how persistent a child's efforts can be, and how well they are directed at a specific goal (R. White, 1959; B. White, 1972).

A good example is the energy an infant expends in learning how to walk. By the end of its first year of life, a baby can get from place to place very

FIGURE 6.17   Milestones in a child's motor development. (After Shirley, M.M. *The First Two Years,* vol. 2. *Intellectual Development.* Minneapolis: University of Minnesota Press, 1933.)

efficiently by crawling. However, it soon begins to struggle with standing upright and taking a few steps. If the baby tries to get somewhere fast, it drops to all fours and crawls. But if it is exploring in a more leisurely fashion, it tries to walk, even though this means of locomotion is slow, tedious, and punctuated by frequent falls. For an infant, mastery of the skill of walking seems to serve as its own reward.

Studies have shown that children who have spent their infancy lying on their backs in cribs in institutional nurseries do not develop the normal motor skills of children who are raised in homes or in institutions that provide more stimulation and opportunity for movement and exploration (Dennis, 1960). Crawling and walking are among the skills that can be severely retarded.

The damage caused by early deprivation can be

reversed only by careful and painstaking programs of remedial training in the basic motor skills. These have been identified as twelve major movements (reach, point, touch, grasp, place, release, pull, push, shake, squeeze, tap, and twist). Normal infants, in a stimulating environment in which they can interact with objects and caretakers, will engage every day in 10,000 to 20,000 behaviors that exercise these twelve movements (Desjardins, 1980). Children with retarded motor development must receive specific training in behaviors that use these basic movements. Although it is very difficult to compensate for the effects of early deprivation, systematic training can bring the motor performance of these children to a point where they can function normally in society.

PERCEPTUAL DEVELOPMENT

Almost everyone who has watched a newborn baby has wondered what its perception of the world is like. What can it see? What can it hear? Until a few years ago, we could only speculate about the answers to these questions.

If we want to study how older children or adults perceive the world, we can simply ask them about their experiences. We can determine how large an object must be for them to see it, or how loud a sound must be for them to hear it. But we cannot talk to an infant and expect to get any answers. So we must use its behavior as an indicator of what it can perceive.

It has been clear for a long time that the various senses function at least to a certain extent in a newborn baby. We know that its auditory system can detect sounds, because the baby will show a startled reaction when it is presented with a sudden, loud noise. Similarly, a bright light will elicit eye closing and squinting. A cold object or a pinch will produce crying, so the sense of touch must be present. If a baby is held firmly and tilted backward, it will stiffen and flail its arms and legs, so we must conclude that it has a sense of balance.

Research indicates that even an unborn fetus has a sense of taste. When a pregnant woman accumulates too much amniotic fluid, the condition can be corrected by injecting a sugar solution into the fluid. The fetus obviously detects the sweet taste, because it usually swallows enough fluid to elim-

inate the excess (Bookmiller and Bowen, 1967). The swallowed fluid enters the bloodstream of the fetus and is then transported through the placenta to the mother, who excretes it in her urine.

Beyond these simple demonstrations, most recent investigations of the perceptual ability of newborn infants have taken advantage of cephalocaudal development—the fact that babies can move their head, eyes, and mouth rather accurately.

Perception of Patterns

Most investigations of infant perception have concentrated on vision, probably because it is such an important sense for humans. No careful observer ever doubted that a baby's eyes can respond to light; a newborn infant will close its eyes and screw up its face if the level of illumination is too high. But what about its ability to perceive objects?

A clever technique, first reported by Stirnimann (1944) and later developed by Fantz (1961), takes advantage of a young infant's rather good control over its eye movements. The baby lies on its back a few inches beneath a plywood screen, and various stimuli are placed on this ceiling. A small peephole permits the experimenter to watch the baby from above. (See **Figure 6.18.**) Typically, two different visual stimuli are placed side by side. The lighting is arranged so that the experimenter can see which stimulus the baby is looking at; the reflection is visible on the surface of the baby's eyes. The experimenter then records how much time the infant spends looking at each stimulus. If the baby spends more time looking at one stimulus, regardless of whether it is placed on the left or the right, clearly the infant can tell the stimuli apart. (On the other hand, the fact that a baby spends the same amount of time looking at both stimuli is not proof that it *cannot* tell them apart; possibly the infant finds them equally interesting.)

This technique quickly established the fact that even newborn infants show a preference for some kinds of patterns; for example, they tend to look at checkerboards more than at solid colors (Fantz, 1961). The newborn infants also appeared to spend more time looking at a picture of a human face than at other stimuli. This finding caused much excitement among researchers in child development, because it suggested that a baby could recognize a human face even without benefit of

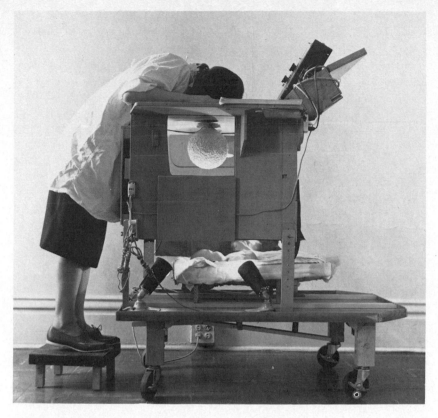

FIGURE 6.18 The apparatus used by Fantz in his experiments. (From Fantz, R.L. *Scientific American,* 1961, *204,* 66–72.)

experience. However, later experiments failed to confirm these results (Fantz and Nevis, 1967; Koopman and Ames, 1968); it appears that babies do *not* spend more time looking at a human face until they reach the age of two months (Maurer and Salapatek, 1976). Thus, there is no evidence for an unlearned ability to recognize the human face.

More recently, investigators have used modern technology to refine Fantz's technique (Haith, 1969, 1976; Salapatek, 1975). A harmless spot of infrared light, invisible to humans, is directed onto the baby's eyes. A special television camera, sensitive to infrared light, records the spot and superimposes it on an image of the display that the baby is looking at. The technique is precise enough to determine *which parts* of a stimulus the baby is scanning. For example, Salapatek (1975) reported that a one-month-old infant does not look at the

inside of a figure; instead, its gaze seems to be "trapped" by the edges. However, by the age of two months, the baby scans across the border to investigate the interior of a figure. **Figure 6.19** shows a computer-drawn reconstruction of the paths followed by the eye scans of infants of these ages. (The babies are looking at *real* faces, not the drawings shown in the figure.)

Haith (1976) has devised a theoretical model that appears to explain the scanning behavior of young infants. For reasons that will be explained in Chapter 8, the light detectors of the eye respond at a very high rate when they are presented with a pattern that contains light/dark *contrast*. Thus, if a baby is looking directly at a region of contrast, the light detectors in its eyes will be very active. Haith has shown that if an alert, awake baby sees nothing but a solid gray field, its eyes will roam about as if the infant were looking for something. If the

1-Month-old

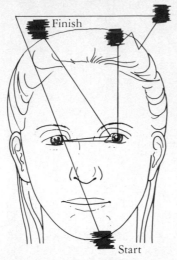

2-Month-old

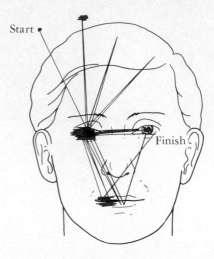

FIGURE 6.19   The scanning sequence used by children viewing actual faces. (After Salapatek, P. In *Infant Perception: From Sensation to Cognition,* vol. 1:

Basic Visual Processes, edited by L. B. Cohen and P. Salapatek. New York: Academic Press, 1975.)

baby sees a pattern with some light/dark contrast, its eyes will stop moving as soon as they encounter the pattern, and will then pass back and forth repeatedly across the region of contrast.

Clearly, then, a baby's visual system is most stimulated by change, becoming highly active when the infant moves its gaze back and forth against a region full of contrast. Haith suggested that the rule governing an infant's visual exploration is the following: maximize the activity of the visual system. This hypothetical rule accounts for the preferences that babies show for one pattern over another; they spend more time looking at the patterns with the highest local contrast.

It appears that the presence of a rich and varied visual environment is an absolute requirement for normal development of the visual system of the brain. For example, Riesen (1961) showed that when a chimpanzee is raised in the dark or in a lighted but visually sterile and homogeneous environment, the animal's visual system does not develop normally. After a few months of visual deprivation, the animal is virtually blind. Perhaps the strategy of keeping the activity of the visual system as high as possible is an innate behavioral tendency that makes the child participate in its own visual development.

Perception of Space

◆ The ability to perceive three-dimensional space comes at an early age. Gibson and Walk (1960) placed six-month-old babies on what they called a visual cliff—a platform containing a checkerboard pattern. The platform adjoined a glass shelf mounted several feet over a floor, which was also covered by the checkerboard pattern. Most babies who could crawl would not venture out onto the glass shelf. The infants acted as if they were afraid of falling. (See **Figure 6.20**.)

Even before they are capable of crawling, infants show an increase in heart rate when they are placed on top of the glass shelf (Campos, Langer, and Krowitz, 1970). Because increases in heart rate are associated with fear, it is reasonable to infer that the babies perceived that they were suspended a considerable distance above the floor and consequently became frightened. These results suggest that depth perception develops very early.

As we shall see in Chapter 8, people perceive depth by several means. One of the most important of these involves the use of *stereoscopic cues.* Stereoscopes are devices that show two slightly different pictures, one to each eye, and give the impression of a three-dimensional space. They sim-

FIGURE 6.20   A visual cliff. The child does not
cross the glass bridge. (From Gibson, E.J., and
Walk, R.R. *Scientific American,* 1960, *202,* 2–9.)

ulate the slightly different view of the real world
that each of our eyes has, since our eyes are located
in slightly different places.

To study the development of depth perception
by means of stereoscopic cues, Fox, Aslin, Shea,
and Dumais (1979) presented a special stereoscopic
image to infants. They used ***random-dot stereo-***
grams, which consist of two sets of apparently random, meaningless dots. When viewed by the naked
eye, random-dot stereograms do not contain any
detectable pattern. However, when a person looks
at them through special glasses the dots appear to
fuse and give the impression of a three-dimensional
image of an object.

Fox and his colleagues fitted infants with special
glasses and showed them random-dot stereograms
on a television screen. These stereograms could be
moved in a sequence that gave, to an adult ob-

server, the impression of movement of a real object. Once the baby appeared to be looking at the
stereogram, the investigators started the machine
so that the image moved around. An observer
watched to see whether the baby followed the image with its eyes. Their results indicate that the
ability to use stereoscopic cues develops between
the ages of three-and-a-half to six months; younger
infants showed no signs of following a moving image, and older ones tracked the image with their
eyes.

Studies with animals have shown that stereoscopic vision can occur only after neurons in the
visual cortex become connected with receptor cells
in both eyes (Hubel and Wiesel, 1970). These connections depend on visual experience; if an animal
can use only one eye at a time the connections never
occur, and the animal never acquires stereoscopic

vision. Thus, there is a critical period for the development of these connections; once it is over they cannot be established. (Hubel and Wiesel won a Nobel Prize in 1981 for this discovery.)

This critical period has important implications for human development. If an infant's eyes do not move together properly so they both are directed toward the same place in the environment, the infant never develops stereoscopic vision, even if the eye movements are later corrected by surgery on the eye muscles. Banks, Aslin, and Letson (1975) studied infants whose eye-movement deficits were later corrected surgically. Their results show that critical period ends sometime between one and three years of age; if surgery occurs later stereoscopic vision will not develop.

Interim summary: You now have a better idea of the importance of the interaction between hereditary and environmental factors in an infant's physical development, and how crucial the timing between the two can be. Genetically, an infant has the potential to develop skills that coincide with the maturation of its nervous system. But in order for this potential to be realized, the infant's environment must supply it with the opportunity to test and practice these skills. If an infant is deprived of the opportunity to practice them at crucial times, then the skills may fail to develop, which will affect his or her performance as an adult. As we shall see in the section on social development, an infant has certain innate behaviors that help ensure that it receives the proper attention and stimulation from its caregivers at the appropriate time.

COGNITIVE DEVELOPMENT

THE IMPORTANCE OF A RESPONSIVE ENVIRONMENT

As a child grows, its nervous system matures and it undergoes new experiences. Perceptual and motor skills develop in complexity and competency. The child learns to recognize particular faces and voices, begins to talk and respond to the speech of others, and learns how to solve problems. In short, the child's cognitive capacities develop.

Cognition means "to get to know." Thus, an

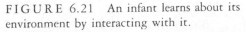

FIGURE 6.21   An infant learns about its environment by interacting with it.

infant's cognitive development is the process by which it gets to know things about itself and its world. (See **Figure 6.21.**) There is evidence that one of the first steps in cognitive development is learning that events in the environment are often contingent on the infant's own behavior. The most stimulating environment, which is most effective in promoting cognitive development, is one in which the infant's behavior has tangible effects.

In an experiment testing this hypothesis, Watson and Ramey (1972) presented three groups of infants with a mobile ten minutes per day for fourteen days. A pillow containing a pressure-sensitive switch was placed under the babies' head, and the mobile was suspended above their face. For one group, the mobile automatically rotated whenever an infant moved its head and activated the switch. For another, the mobile remained stationary. For the third group, the mobile intermittently moved on its own (*not* in response to head movement).

The babies whose head movements caused the mobile to rotate learned to move their head, and they continued to do so when tested two weeks and six weeks afterward. They had learned the contingency between head turning and mobile movement. When the babies in the second group were later given the opportunity to make the mobile move by turning their head, they readily learned to do so. However, the babies for whom the mobile had moved randomly on its own did *not* learn to control it. It was as if they had learned that nothing they could do affected the movements of the mobile. Although this phenomenon does not involve aversive stimuli, you will recognize its similarity to the studies on learned helplessness that were described in Chapter 5. (See **Figure 6.22.**)

FIGURE 6.22   The procedure and results of the experiment by Watson and Ramey (1972).

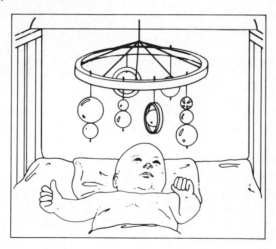

	First condition	Later condition
Group A	Head turning causes mobile to move. *Babies learn to move head.*	Head turning causes mobile to move. *Babies continue to move head.*
Group B	Mobile remains stationary.	Head turning causes mobile to move. *Babies learn to move head.*
Group C	Mobile intermittently moves on its own.	Head turning causes mobile to move. *Babies do not learn to move head.*

These results may have implications for infant-rearing practices. In some tragic cases, babies have been raised in unresponsive, unstimulating institutions (Goldfarb, 1955). In the worst institutions, nothing a child did had any effect on what happened to it. Crying did not result in handling or feeding; the babies were fed and changed on a rigid schedule. The cribs were plain and often visually isolated from each other. Movements made by the baby had no effect; there was nothing to shake or manipulate.

Many babies reared in such environments simply stop trying to affect anything in their environment. A six-month-old baby that has been institutionalized from birth is generally passive and apathetic. In contrast, a home-reared child of the same age is much more active and responsive to its environment (Lewis and Goldberg, 1969). Clearly, a responsive environment is very important for an infant's cognitive development. As we shall see later, the normal social interactions that parents engage in with their infants follow this principle; most parents play a "contingency game" with their babies that promotes early cognitive development.

THE WORK OF JEAN PIAGET

The most influential student of child development was Jean Piaget, a Swiss psychologist. (See **Figure 6.23.**) Piaget formulated the most complete and detailed description of the process of cognitive development that we now have. His conclusions were based on his observations of the behavior of children—first, his own children at home, and later other children at his Center of Genetic Epistemology in Geneva. He noticed that children of similar age tended to engage in similar behaviors and to make the same kinds of mistakes in problem solving. He concluded that these similarities were a result of a sequence of development that is followed by all normal children. Completion of each period, with its corresponding abilities, is the prerequisite for the next.

◆ According to Piaget, a child's cognitive development consists in the acquisition of *cognitive structures,* rules that are used for understanding and dealing with the world, for thinking and solving problems. The two principal types of cognitive structures are *schemas* and *concepts.* A *schema* is a

FIGURE 6.23   Jean Piaget (1896–1980) was this century's most influential student of cognitive development.

set of rules that defines a particular category of behavior—how the behavior is executed, and under what conditions. For example, the cognitive structure of an infant includes sucking schemas, reaching schemas, and looking schemas.

Piaget suggested that a child acquires knowledge of the environment by developing mental structures called *concepts*. Concepts are rules that describe properties of environmental events and their relations with other concepts. For example, concepts about the existence of various objects include what the objects do, how they relate to other objects, and what happens when they are touched or manipulated. Thus, the cognitive structure of an infant includes concepts of such things as rattles, balls, crib slats, hands, and other people.

◆ An infant acquires the rules that constitute its

schemas and concepts by interacting with its environment, a process that Piaget called *assimilation.* An infant assimilates new classes of stimuli (concepts) to its behavioral schemas; that is, the stimuli begin to elicit the behavior. For example, the *object concept* is assimilated to the *reaching schema;* the infant first learns to perceive visual stimuli with certain properties as objects, then learns to control its arm and hand movements, and finally learns to reach for an object that is within its field of vision. (In terms of instrumental conditioning, it learns the discriminative stimuli that signal that a particular behavior, such as reaching, will be reinforced, in this case by obtaining an interesting object.)

The assimilation of a concept to a behavioral schema leads to *accommodation;* that is, the behavioral schema is adjusted as the infant learns about the properties of the concept. For example, once infants have learned to reach for objects, they learn how to adjust their hand opening and closing to grasp objects of different sizes and shapes. As they learn more about various classes of objects (that is, develop more concepts) they also develop new behavioral schemas—dropping schemas, banging schemas, and so on—as they discover the properties of these objects. Assimilation of new stimuli to behavioral schemas leads to accommodation of new behaviors, which leads to the assimilation of new stimuli, and so on. Interaction with the environment teaches a child what it needs to know in order to learn new things.

PIAGET'S FOUR PERIODS OF COGNITIVE DEVELOPMENT

◆ Although development is a continuous process, the cognitive structures of children of different ages differ enough from each other to permit inferences about the rules they use to understand their environment and control their behavior. Piaget has divided cognitive development into four periods. What a child learns in one period enables that child to progress to the next.

The Sensorimotor Period

The *sensorimotor period* lasts for approximately the first two years of life. During this period cognition is closely tied to external stimulation. At first, the child appears to lose all interest in an object that disappears from its sight; the proverb "out of sight, out of mind" seems particularly appropriate. In addition, cognition consists entirely in behavior. Thinking is doing.

◆ Piaget subdivided the sensorimotor period into six stages in accordance with the rules that make up their schemas and concepts. According to Piaget, the best way to investigate an infant's object concept is to see what it does when an object disappears or is hidden. Piaget's observations include many descriptions of what his children did when he hid an interesting object.

STAGE 1 (0–2 MONTHS) At this stage, the infant does not appear to have a concept for objects. It can look at visual stimuli and will turn its head and eyes toward the source of a sound, but hiding an object elicits no particular response.

STAGE 2 (2–4 MONTHS) The infant now becomes able to follow moving objects with its eyes. If an object disappears behind a barrier the infant will continue to stare at the place where the object disappeared, but it will not search for it. If the object does not soon reappear, the infant appears to lose interest. Piaget calls this phenomenon *passive expectation;* the baby appears to expect the object to reappear but does not actively search for it.

STAGE 3 (4–6 MONTHS) The infant can now grasp and hold objects. If an object is completely hidden under a cloth the infant will not attempt to retrieve it. However, it will reach for an object that is at least partly visible. (See **Figure 6.24.**)

A stage 3 infant can also anticipate the future position of a moving object. If a moving object passes behind a screen, the infant turns its eyes toward the far side of the screen; it appears to anticipate the reappearance of the object on the other side.

STAGE 4 (6–12 MONTHS) The infant grasps objects, turns them over, investigates their properties. From looking at an object from various angles, the infant learns that it can change its visual shape and still be the same object. In addition, if an object is hidden, the infant will actively search for it; the infant's object concept contains the rule of

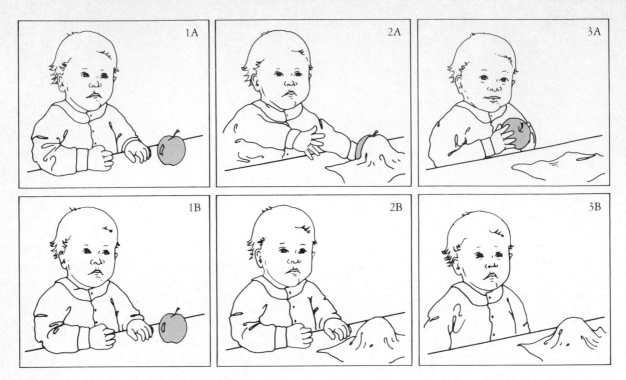

FIGURE 6.24   A stage 3 infant will reach for a partially covered object (2A), but not for a completely covered one (2B). (After Bower, T.G.R., *Perception in* *Infancy,* 2nd ed. San Francisco: W.H. Freeman, 1972.)

permanence. For a stage 4 infant a hidden object still exists. "Out of sight" is no longer "out of mind."

The behavioral schemas for dealing with hidden objects are still not fully developed. Even though the child can retrieve a hidden object, it has difficulty in shifting its strategy for searching. If the infant has been permitted to uncover an object hidden in the same place several times, the infant will persist in looking for the object in the same place even if it is hidden in a new place. Here is Piaget's description of this behavior.

> At [ten months, eighteen days] Jacqueline is seated on a mattress without anything to disturb or distract her (no coverlets, etc.). I take her parrot from her hands and hide it twice in succession under the mattress, on her left. . . . Both times Jacqueline looks for the object immediately and grabs it. Then I take it from her hands and move it very slowly before her eyes to the corresponding place on her right, under the mattress. . . . Jacqueline watches this movement but at the moment when the parrot disappears . . . she turns to her left and looks where it was before. . . . (1964, p. 51) (See **Figure 6.25.**)

STAGE 5 (12–15 MONTHS)   By early in its second year an infant will search for a hidden object in the last place it saw it hidden; it no longer persists in looking in a place where it previously succeeded in finding the object. However, the infant can keep track only of changes that it can see in the hiding place. For example, if an adult picks up an object, puts it under a cloth, drops the object while her hand is hidden, closes her hand again, and removes it from the cloth, the infant will look for the object in her hand. When it does not find the object there, the infant looks puzzled or upset and does not search for the object under the cloth. (See **Figure 6.26.**)

STAGE 6 (15–18 MONTHS)   According to Piaget, the infant begins to think during this stage. Thought

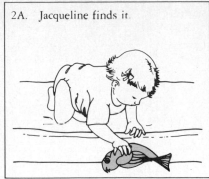

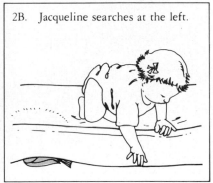

Sequence A is
repeated twice.

FIGURE 6.25   Characteristic behavior of a stage
4 infant: Piaget's interaction with his daughter,
Jacqueline.

is closely tied to motor schemas and concepts of the properties of objects, but the beginnings of symbolic representation are evident. The following quotation from Piaget illustrates how his sixteen-month-old daughter Lucienne used a motor schema to solve a problem—an early example of thinking. While playing with his daughter, Piaget hid a watch chain inside an empty match box.

I put the chain back into the box and reduce the opening to 3 mm. It is understood that Lucienne is not aware of the functioning of the opening and closing of the match box and has not seen me prepare the experiment. She only possesses two preceding schemas: turning the box over in order to empty it of its contents, and sliding her fingers into the slit to make the chain come out. It is of course this last procedure that she tries first: she puts her finger inside and gropes to reach the chain, but fails completely. A pause follows during which Lucienne manifests a very curious reaction. . . .

She looks at the slit with great attention; then, several times in succession, she opens and shuts her mouth, at first slightly, then wider and wider!

[Then] . . . Lucienne unhesitatingly puts her finger in the slit, and instead of trying as before to reach the chain, she pulls so as to enlarge the opening. She succeeds and grasps the chain. (1952, pp. 337–338)

At this stage of development, the object concept is rather mature. Permanence is complete, and the infant can infer which movements an object makes while it is out of sight. If a hand containing an object goes into a hiding place and comes out empty, the child immediately looks for the object in the appropriate hiding place.

Other cognitive structures develop by the end of the sensorimotor period. The infant begins to differentiate self from other objects in the environment, and gains an appreciation of time and space.

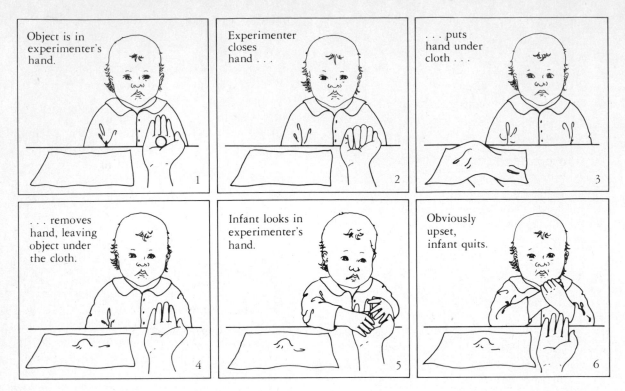

FIGURE 6.26   A stage 5 infant will not realize that the object has been left under the cloth. (After Bower, T.G.R., *Perception in Infancy*, 2nd ed. San Francisco: Freeman, 1972.)

It actively experiments with objects and discovers the consequences of these experiments. For example, the infant may learn what happens when a light switch is moved or the knob of a television is turned. By the end of this period the infant has a good start acquiring language ability. It knows the meaning of several dozen words and can produce a good number of its own.

The Preoperational Period

◆ Piaget's second period of cognitive development, the *preoperational period,* lasts from approximately age two to age seven. This period is characterized by rapid development of language ability and of the ability to represent things symbolically—the *symbolic function.* The child arranges toys in new ways to represent other objects (for example, a row of blocks can represent a train), begins to classify and categorize objects, and starts learning to count and to manipulate numbers. (See **Figure 6.27.)**

Piaget asserted that development of the sym-bolic function actually begins during the sensori-motor period, when an infant starts imitating events in its environment. For example, when Lucienne imitated the opening of the match box by opening her mouth, she was representing a concept symbolically by means of a behavioral schema that she possessed. Similarly, a child might represent a horse by making galloping movements with its feet or a bicycle by making steering movements with its hands. Symbolic representations like these are called *signifiers;* a motor act represents a concept because it resembles either the movements the object makes or the movements the child makes when interacting with the object. Even a very young infant demonstrates the beginnings of this function; a baby will often make shaking movements with its hand when it sees its rattle.

Concepts can also be represented by words, which are symbols that have no physical resemblance to the concept. (Piaget referred to such abstract symbols as *signs.*) Signifiers are personal, derived from the child's own interactions with objects. Therefore, only the child itself and perhaps members of the immediate family will understand the child's signifiers. However, signs are social conventions; they are understood by all members of society. Once a child is able to use words to talk and think about reality it has made an important step in cognitive development.

Piaget's work demonstrated quite clearly that a child's representation of the world is different from that of an adult. For example, most adults realize that a volume of water remains constant when poured into a narrower container, despite the fact that its level is now higher. However, early in the preoperational period children will fail to recognize this fact; they will say that the taller container contains more water. (See **Figure 6.28**.) The ability to realize that an object retains mass, number, or volume when it undergoes various transformations is called *conservation;* the transformed object *conserves* its original properties.

Similarly, if a child is shown two rows of five plastic disks, one spaced farther apart than the other, the child will report that the longer row has more disks. This occurs even when the rows have first been spaced equally and the child has seen the experimenter move the disks apart. Somehow the number of objects is perceived as increasing as the row gets longer. Number is not conserved. Piaget concluded that the abilities to perceive the conservation of number, mass, weight, and volume are attributes of increasing development; he found number to be conserved by age six, whereas con-

FIGURE 6.27 During the preoperational period a child creates assemblies that represent other objects.

FIGURE 6.28 Early in the preoperational period, a child does not conserve volume.

servation of volume did not occur until age eleven. (See **Figure 6.29.**)

More recent evidence suggests that a child's ability to conserve various physical attributes occurs earlier than Piaget supposed. Part of the problem might be in the child's understanding of words like *more* and *larger*. A child's concept of *more* appears to be less restrictive than that of an adult. Perhaps *more,* for a young child, refers to a general concept of larger, longer, occupying more space. If this is so

the fact that the longer row is said to have more disks does not necessarily demonstrate a failure to conserve number.

Gelman (1972) found that when the task is changed, even three-year-old children are able to demonstrate conservation of number. Instead of using the word *more,* Gelman showed children two toy platters, each containing a row of toy mice. A platter with a larger number of mice was called the "winner," while the one with a smaller number

FIGURE 6.29   Various tests of conservation. (Adapted from Lefrancois, G.R., *Of Children.* Belmont, Calif.: Wadsworth, 1973.)

1. Conservation of mass

The experimenter presents two balls of clay.

The experimenter rolls one ball into a "sausage" and asks the child whether they still contain the same amount of clay.

2. Conservation of length

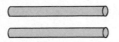   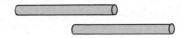

The experimenter presents two dowels.

The experimenter moves one dowel to the right and asks the child whether they are still the same length.

3. Conservation of number

The experimenter presents two rows of poker chips.

The experimenter moves one row of chips apart and asks the child whether each row still contains the same number.

of mice was called the "loser." The children were invited to play a game. They watched the experimenter hide the platters under two cans, and then move the cans around the table. Each child had to point to the can that contained the "winner," which was then uncovered. If the uncovered plate contained the original number of mice, the children were satisfied that it was still the winner, even if the experimenter tricked them and lengthened or shortened the row of mice. The children noticed that the mice had been moved, but still identified the plate as the "winner." However, if mice were removed from the plate containing the larger number, the children were disturbed and asked where the missing mice were.

Clearly, the children were able to respond to the concept of number and recognized that a larger number of mice was still a larger number of mice even if the row was lengthened or shortened. It thus seems likely that children learn to conserve number before they learn the adult meaning of the word *more*.

Another study provides further support for this conclusion. Murray (1972) found that children can be trained by their peers to conserve various physical attributes. On the basis of prior testing, several groups of three six-year-old children were formed, with two "conservers" and one "nonconserver" in each group. The groups were given the problems that they had seen on the test and were asked to solve them again and discuss them. The adult observers did not tell the children the correct solutions. During this discussion the conservers brought the nonconservers around to the correct point of view. Moreover, the training transferred to *new* problems; the reformed nonconservers acted like conservers when presented with new problems on their own.

It seems unlikely that children can learn principles of conservation in a single session with their peers. It is even less likely that the concept of conservation of one physical attribute will immediately generalize to other attributes. Instead, it seems more likely that the social interaction taught these children the more customary meaning of the words *more, larger,* and so on. If the children already realized that physical attributes remained the same even when objects were transformed in various ways but still used the words *more* and *larger* in a less discriminating way, then their rapid transformation from nonconserver to conserver is understandable.

These studies do not demonstrate that Piaget's concept of conservation was incorrect; rather, they show that an estimate of a child's cognitive ability is significantly affected by the testing method.

The Period of Concrete Operations

The *period of concrete operations* spans approximately ages seven to eleven years. It is characterized by emergence of the ability to perform logical analysis, by an increase in the ability to empathize

FIGURE 6.30 Reasoning: If A is bigger than B, and B is bigger than C, then A is bigger than C.

with the feelings and attitudes of others, and by an understanding of more complex cause-and-effect relations. The child becomes much more skilled at the use of symbolic thought. For example, during most of the period of concrete operations children can arrange a series of objects in order of size, and can compare any two objects and say which is larger. However, if they are told that A is larger than B and B is larger than C, they cannot infer that A is larger than C. During the later part of this period and the beginning of the next (the period of formal operations) children become capable of this type of reasoning even if they have never directly observed A and C together. (See **Figure 6.30**.)

Other psychologists have suggested that the increases in children's cognitive abilities are due not solely to basic changes in the structure of the cognitive processes, but also to increased memory capacity. For example, if a child cannot simultaneously remember that A is larger than B and that B is larger than C, then it is impossible to reason that A is larger than C.

◆ An important form of growth during the period of concrete operations is the transition from *egocentrism* to the ability to understand another person's point of view. In this context *egocentrism* does not mean selfish; it refers to a child's belief that others see the world precisely the way that he or she does. For example, a child who is explaining a story or sequence of events to another person is likely to omit many important details, apparently because of the belief that other people know and understand what the child does. A child often uses pronouns without considering that another person might not understand to whom or what they refer.

The Period of Formal Operations

The final stages of cognitive development, the *period of formal operations,* begins at twelve years of age, and includes the use of an essentially adult form of logic and symbolic representation; that is, in solving problems, the child learns to formulate a set of alternatives and to test these alternatives against reality. Not everyone reaches this stage of

FIGURE 6.31   During the period of formal operations children learn adult forms of logic and

problem-solving strategy. Teaching and imitation are especially important for developing these skills.

cognitive development; in fact, an investigation by Graves (1972) found that some adults do not conserve volume. This final period of cognitive development takes the child into the realm of adult abilities.

◆ Why does a child pass from one stage of cognitive development to the next? What motivates a child to change its way of reasoning and perceiving? According to Piaget the important principle is *cognitive disequilibrium* (*disequilibrium* means "lack of balance"). Disequilibrium is produced when a child encounters unexpected feedback from the environment as its developing ability to explore brings it in contact with new concepts that it cannot easily assimilate to its existing behavioral schemas. This disequilibrium requires the child to acquire new concepts and new behavioral schemas. For example, when an infant encounters another infant for the first time, it meets an object that is interesting to touch and grasp but can also itself move and do unexpected things, such as touch and grab. The infant must develop a concept for this new object and learn new ways of dealing with it.

In addition, if children who are at a particular stage of cognitive development observe an adult or older child solving a problem by the rules that belong to another stage, they are put off balance by the fact that the other person's solution is different from their own. This disparity is motivating; the child seeks to reduce it by learning the new rules. A child who is sufficiently mature will learn to imitate the older model and will begin to pass to the new stage. Thus, children can learn new concepts and behavioral schemas socially, by observing the behavior of other people. (See **Figure 6.31**.)

◆ Although Piaget's work has dominated twentieth-century child psychology, not all of his conclusions have been uncritically accepted. Perhaps the major criticism is that Piaget did not always define his terms operationally; consequently it is difficult for others to interpret the significance of his generalizations. Many of his studies lack the proper controls that were discussed in Chapter 2. Thus, much of his work is not scientific, in that there is no way to identify causal relations among variables. Nevertheless, his meticulous and detailed observations have been extremely important in the field of child development and have had a

great influence on educational practice. His theoretical framework is providing a basis for more scientific studies and will undoubtedly continue to do so for many years.

Interim summary: An important distinction between humans and other species lies in our cognitive abilities. The first step in a child's cognitive development is its learning that many events are contingent on its behavior. This understanding occurs gradually, controlled by the development of its nervous system and through increasingly complex interactions with its environment.

Jean Piaget divided a child's cognitive development into four periods, which are widely, if not universally, accepted. The periods are determined by the joint influences of the child's experiences and maturation of its nervous system. They consist of the sensorimotor period, the preoperational period, the period of concrete operations, and the period of formal operations.

An infant's earliest cognitive abilities are closely tied to the external stimuli in its immediate environment; objects exist for the infant only when they are present. Gradually the infant begins to differentiate itself from other objects in its environment, and learns that objects exist even when they are hidden. The development of object permanency leads to the ability to represent things symbolically, which is a prerequisite for the use of language. Next, the ability to perform logical analysis and to understand more complex cause-and-effect relations develops. Around the age of twelve a child develops more adultlike cognitive abilities—abilities that may allow it to solve difficult problems by means of abstract reasoning.

As you can see, behavioral development reflects physical maturation. Physical maturation and learning interact; it is important that a child grow up in a responsive and varied environment.

SOCIAL DEVELOPMENT DURING INFANCY

DEVELOPMENT OF ATTACHMENT

Normally, the first adults with whom an infant interacts are its parents. In most cases, one parent,

FIGURE 6.32   Parents and children readily form durable attachments.

usually the mother, serves as the primary caregiver. As many studies have shown, a close relationship called *attachment* is extremely important for the infant's social development. Because two people are involved, interactions must work both ways, with each of the actors fulfilling needs of the other. Formation of a strong and durable bond depends on the behavior of both people. (See **Figure 6.32**.)

A newborn infant is completely dependent upon its parent (or other caregiver) to supply it with nourishment, to keep it warm and clean, and to protect it from harm. But to most parents, this role of primary caregiver is much more than a duty; it is a source of joy and satisfaction. Most parents anticipate the birth of their child with the expectation that they will love and cherish it. And when the child is born, most of them do exactly that. As time goes on, and as parent and child interact, they become strongly attached to each other. What factors cause this attachment to occur?

Infant-parent attachment is probably at least partly innate. In studies of many species of mammals that care for their young, researchers have found that mothers are strongly motivated to perform this role. For example, the responsiveness of a mother rat occurs first around the time of birth as a result of the secretion of hormones by her endocrine glands. Even a female rat with no offspring will take care of another rat's infants if she receives injections of the proper sequence of hormones (Moltz, Lubin, Leon, and Numan, 1970). This readiness to care for young can also be induced simply by placing infant rats in the female's cage; after a few days the rat begins caring for them (Wiesner and Sheard, 1933), although the young rats have to be removed periodically to be fed by a nursing mother. Moreover, mother rodents will respond automatically to stimuli that are provided by their offspring. For example, a baby mouse makes a high-frequency sound when it is cold. (This special cry is too high for humans to hear, but researchers can detect it by using an electronic device.) In response to this cry, a mother mouse will run toward the source of the sound and search vigorously until she finds the baby mouse. One experimenter observed that female mice would rip the covering off a speaker that was presenting the recorded distress cry of an infant mouse (Noirot, 1972).

We humans are capable of performing a wider variety of behaviors, and do not have to rely on automatic, innate behaviors in order to take care of our young. Today we can read books on child care, attend classes, and talk with other people who have raised children. But how did distant ancestors who were unable to communicate through language learn to take care of their infants?

The answer comes from an analogous behavior—mating—that is an innate tendency in all species of animals that reproduce sexually. For species that have helpless offspring, caring for infants is just as important as sexual behavior. Sexual contact is pleasurable and reinforcing because of its importance in species survival. Both the female and the male provide stimuli that elicit behaviors from the opposite sex, and these behaviors tend to lead to intercourse. Although learning often plays an important role in sexual behavior, the tendency is inherited; the brain contains the necessary mechanisms. For species whose young are helpless at birth, caregiving is just as much a reproductive behavior as intercourse. Therefore, the human brain must be a product of an evolutionary process that has selected mechanisms that guarantee that a mother will normally take care of her infant, providing it with the things it needs for normal development.

However, although maternal hormones may play a role in the development of a human mother's affection for her infant, this factor cannot be the critical one, for human fathers can develop equally strong attachments with their infants. In our society today fathers are much more likely to share in caregiving with mothers, and occasionally a father assumes the role of primary caregiver. Enough fathers are now assuming this role that researchers can study the phenomenon.

Finally, the behavior of a human mother (or other caregiver) is not a stereotyped sequence of innate behaviors. It is clear that a human mother learns how to care for her infant. But her most important teacher is her child.

BEHAVIORS OF THE INFANT THAT FOSTER ATTACHMENT

◆ There is evidence that human infants are innately able to produce special behaviors that shape and control the behavior of their caregiver: rooting, sucking, cuddling, looking, smiling, and crying.

Rooting

Prechtl (1958) was the first to describe thoroughly both the rooting response of the human infant and the conditions under which it occurs. As we saw, the rooting response orients the infant's lips to the nipple so that it can suck. But even when the breast is not presented, an infant will occasionally engage in rooting behavior; it will place its face against a soft object (such as a blanket or its parent's shoulder, if it is being held there) and make side-to-side head-turning movements, as if it is trying to burrow into whatever it is pushing against. This behavior is most likely to occur when the infant is hungry. Parents recognize this fact; thus, the rooting response tells the parent that it is time to feed the infant.

Sucking

A baby must be able to suck in order to obtain milk. But not all sucking is related to nourish-

ment. Piaget (1952) noted that infants often suck on objects even when they are not hungry. Nonnutritive sucking appears to be an innate behavioral tendency in infants. It serves to inhibit a baby's distress. The behavior is not unique to humans; a young monkey often holds on to its mother's nipple with its lips even when it is not feeding. This behavior is undoubtedly important in forming the attachment between a mother monkey and her baby. In modern society a mother covers her breasts between feedings or feeds her baby with a bottle, so a baby's nonnutritive sucking must involve inanimate objects or its own thumb. In the Ganda society in Uganda, mothers were observed to give their babies access to a breast when they were fussy, just as mothers in other cultures would give them a pacifier (Ainsworth, 1967).

Cuddling

The infants of all species of primates have special reflexes that encourage front-to-front contact with the mother. For example, a baby monkey clings to its mother shortly after birth. This clinging leaves the mother free to use her hands and feet. A human infant is carried by its parent, and does not hold on by itself. However, the infant does adjust its

FIGURE 6.33   A cuddly surrogate mother. (Harry F. Harlow, University of Wisconsin Primate Laboratory.)

FIGURE 6.34   An isolated infant monkey clings to its cuddly surrogate mother if it is frightened by novel stimuli. (Harry F. Harlow, University of Wisconsin Primate Laboratory.)

posture to mold itself to the contours of a parent's body. If the parent makes a sudden movement, the baby makes a reflexive clinging movement. This movement is not strong enough to keep the baby from falling should the parent actually let go of it; probably it is a vestige of the more powerful clinging response seen in infant monkeys.

One of the earliest explanations for the phenomenon of attachment was the so-called *cupboard theory*: mother provides food when her infant is hungry, warmth when it is cold, dryness when it is wet and uncomfortable. Thus, she provides primary reinforcers. Through classical conditioning, she becomes a reinforcing stimulus—a conditioned reinforcer. As a result of this conditioning, the baby clings to her and shows other signs of attachment. However, a series of experiments by Harry Harlow, late director of the primate laboratory at the University of Wisconsin, showed unequivocally that the cupboard theory cannot account for signs of attachment behavior in monkeys; instead, clinging to a soft, cuddly form appears to be an innate reinforcer (Harlow, 1970). Harlow and his colleagues isolated baby monkeys from their moth-

ers immediately after birth and raised them alone in a cage containing two mechanical *surrogate mothers* (*surrogate* means "substitute"). One surrogate mother was made of bare wire mesh but contained a bottle that provided milk. The other surrogate was padded and covered with terrycloth but provided no nourishment (See **Figure 6.33.**)

If the cupboard theory were valid, the babies should have learned to cling to the model that provides it with milk. However, they did not; the babies preferred to cling to the cuddly surrogate, and went to the wire model only to eat. If they were frightened, they would rush to the cloth-covered model for comfort. (See **Figure 6.34.**) These results indicate that close physical contact with a cuddly object is a biological need for a baby monkey, just as hunger and thirst are. A baby monkey clings to and cuddles with its mother because the contact is innately reinforcing, not because she also provides it with food. Undoubtedly, physical contact with a soft object is also inherently reinforcing for human infants.

Looking

Vision is not a passive sensory system; it is coupled with the behavior of looking. The eyes see best what is at the center of gaze, so it is necessary to move them in order to see important visual features of the environment. Wolff (1966) showed that infants can control their eyes well enough to pursue a moving object visually within one day of delivery.

As we saw earlier, newborn infants tend to look at objects that maximize stimulation of the visual system. However, by the age of two months, infants prefer to look at faces, especially at eyes (Fantz and Nevis, 1967). This behavior undoubtedly facilitates eye-to-eye contact between parent and child.

Looking is more than an adjunct to vision; it serves as a signal to the parent. Even a very young infant seeks eye-to-eye contact with its parents. If a parent does not respond when eye contact is made, the baby usually shows signs of distress. Tronick and his colleagues (1978) observed face-to-face interactions between mothers and their infants. When the mothes approached their babies they typically smiled and began talking in a gentle, high-pitched voice. In return, they received a smile and an outreach of arms and legs from the infant. The moth-

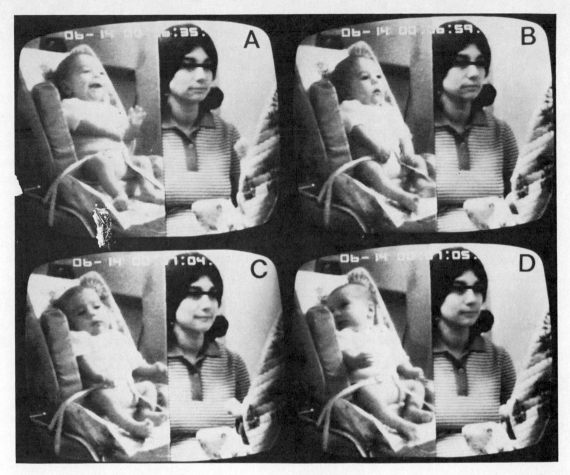

FIGURE 6.35   Reaction of an infant to its mother's expressionless face. Although each panel shows mother and infant side by side, they actually faced each other. The infant greets its mother with a smile and, getting no response, eventually turns away from her. (From Tronick, E., Als, H., Adamson, L., Wise, S., and Brazelton, T.B. *Journal of the American Academy of Child Psychiatry*, 1978, *17*, 1–13.)

ers poked and gently shook their babies, making faces at them. The babies responded with facial expressions, wiggles, and noises of their own.

To show that the interaction was really two-sided, the experimenters had each mother approach her baby while keeping her face expressionless, or mask-like. At first the infant made its usual greetings, but when the mother did not respond, it turned away. (See **Figure 6.35**.) From time to time the infant looked at her again, producing a brief smile but again turning away when she continued to stare without changing her expression. These interactions were recorded on videotape and were scored by raters who did not know the purpose of

the experiment, so the results were not biased by the experimenters' expectations.

Each mother found it very hard to resist her baby's invitation to interact; in fact, some of the mothers broke down and smiled back. Most of the mothers who managed to hold out (for three minutes) later apologized to their babies, saying something like "I am real again. It's all right. You can trust me again. Come back to me." (Tronick, Als, Adamson, Wise, and Brazelton, 1978, p. 10).

This study made it clear that the looking behavior of an infant is an invitation for the mother to respond. If she does not, the infant is disturbed and avoids further visual contact.

Smiling

For almost any human, but especially for a parent, the smile of an infant is an exceedingly effective reinforcer. (See **Figure 6.36**.) For example, the day after reading an article about imitation of facial expressions by newborn infants I had a conversation with a woman who was holding her two-month-old daughter. The baby was alert, actively looking at the people around her. For approximately five minutes she made no particular facial expression. Then I remembered the article and mentioned it to the baby's father, who was also present. He suggested I see whether his daughter would imitate my facial expression. I stuck out my tongue and immediately the baby smiled, made a noise, and stuck out its tongue. I can still feel the delight that her smile gave me.

FIGURE 6.36   If you did something that made this baby smile at you, you would probably do it again.

Like the high-frequency cry of a baby mouse, the smiling of a human infant seems to be an innate behavior. Babies can produce smiles within a few hours after birth. Although parents are often told that early smiles are not smiles at all but merely grimaces caused by the discomfort of intestinal gas, in fact infants rarely smile when they are uncomfortable. Even blind infants smile early in life (Izard, 1971). Parents of these babies must deliberately reinforce this behavior by making noises or touching them, or the smiling soon disappears. Normally, parents' facial responses reinforce and maintain the smiling of sighted infants.

Wolff (1963) studied the development of smiling in infants and observed the stimuli that elicited it. During the first month the sound of a voice, especially a high-pitched voice, can elicit smiles. Moreover, people appear to recognize this fact; when they approach a baby and talk to it they tend to raise the pitch of their voice (Tronick et al., 1978).

During the first months of life a baby often smiles spontaneously, without any obvious eliciting stimulus. Spontaneous smiling increases in frequency, peaks, and then declines. The peak occurs between eleven and fourteen weeks in infants who are raised in a family, and between sixteen and twenty weeks in those who are raised in an institution (Ambrose, 1961). Presumably, spontaneous smiling decreases earlier in family situations because there is more likely to be a primary caregiver to whom the infant becomes attached; the smile is now elicited only by certain stimuli.

By the time an infant is five weeks old, visual stimuli begin to dominate as elicitors for smiling. A face (especially a moving one) is a more reliable elicitor of a smile than a voice is; even a moving mask will cause an infant to smile. Later (at approximately three months of age), specific faces—those of people to whom the infant has become attached—will elicit smiles. The significance of these facts should be obvious. An infant's smile is a very potent reinforcer. Since it is elicited by the sound of a human voice, and later by the sight of a human face, the infant's smile reinforces the parent for approaching his or her baby. Almost every parent reports that parenting becomes a real joy once the baby starts smiling when he or she approaches; the infant is now a "person." Once the contingency is established (smiling when the parent's face is seen) the parent becomes eager to spend time with his or her infant.

At around three months an infant also begins to smile at the effects of its own activities. A par-ticularly effective elicitor of smiling is the detection of environmental events that are contingent on its own behavior. In the experiment described earlier, Watson (1973) observed that soon after two-month-old infants had learned to move their heads in order to make a mobile turn, they began to smile as soon as the mobile turned. In contrast, control subjects did *not* smile when the mobile moved independently of their head turning. Thus, it was not the movement of the mobile that made the infants smile; it was the fact that the mobile moved *in response to their own behavior*. In other words, it was the contingency that elicited a smile. (See **Figure 6.37**.)

Watson also studied the interactions between parents and babies and concluded that a considerable amount of time is spent playing the "contingency game." For example, each time an infant opens its mouth, the parent pokes the baby's abdomen; whenever it stretches its arms out, the parent touches its nose. The parent's response is contingent on some behavior produced by the infant. Infants appear to take great delight in games like these; whenever the contingent stimulus (such as touching or poking) is produced by the parent,

FIGURE 6.37 A contingency between movement of the mobile and head turning leads to increased head turning and also to smiling. (From Bower, T.G.R. *Perception in Infancy*, 2nd ed. San Francisco: Freeman, 1978 after Watson, 1973.)

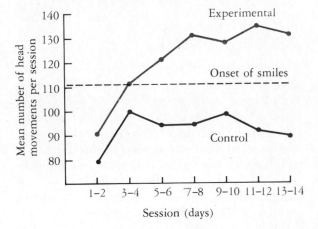

FIGURE 6.38 Babies reinforce game playing with smiles and thus encourage adults to perform behaviors that promote the babies' cognitive development.

the baby smiles, wiggles, makes cooing or gurgling sounds, and otherwise indicates its pleasure. The effect of these behaviors is, of course, to reinforce game playing by the parent.

Playing the contingency game is undoubtedly a significant part of an infant's cognitive development. Detection of contingencies appears to be innately reinforcing for infants; it produces smiling and other behaviors that reinforce the parental behavior that brought about the contingency, making it more likely that the parent will repeat the behavior. Thus, an infant reinforces behaviors of its parent that provides it with important cognitive exercise. (See **Figure 6.38.**)

Crying

Babies are equipped with a very effective aversive stimulus. For almost any adult, the sound of an infant's crying is intensely irritating. A parent who hears the sound from his or her own infant is very likely to approach it and pick it up. A young infant usually cries only when it is hungry, cold, or in pain (Wolff, 1969). In these situations, only the intervention of an adult can bring relief, so the crying obviously serves as a means of summoning aid.

The stimuli that *terminate* a baby's crying include rocking motions, soft repetitive sounds, objects that permit nonnutritive sucking (such as a pacifier), and the sight of a human face. But the most effective stimulus is being picked up and cuddled. As you learned in Chapter 4, termination of an aversive stimulus serves as a negative reinforcer. The cessation of a baby's crying when its parents pick it up reinforces the adult's behavior; consequently, the parent learns to pick up the infant when it cries.

Everyone knows that children can be "spoiled"; when things are made too easy for them, they come to believe that their every whim will be (and should be) gratified. But research has made it clear that a parent's attention does not "spoil" a very young infant.

In the first few months of life, it is very important for a parent to respond promptly when a baby cries. Bell and Ainsworth (1972) found that babies whose caregivers responded quickly to crying during the first three months of life actually cried *less* during the last four months of their first year

than did infants with unresponsive caregivers. Instead of becoming spoiled, these babies learned to cry only when they needed attention from their caregiver. The infants with responsive caregivers also learned to communicate effectively with behaviors other than crying, such as prespeech sounds and facial gestures. Just as it is important for parents to play the contingency game with their infants, it is important for babies to learn that their communicative behaviors (such as crying) can affect the behavior of other people.

THE CRITICAL PERIOD FOR ATTACHMENT

◆ For many species there is a critical period in which attachment must occur, or it will fail to develop. For example, many young birds are able to move about and feed themselves very soon after hatching. Because these birds must follow their mother around, it is important for them to become attached to her. This form of attachment is called *imprinting* (Lorenz, 1957); a baby bird learns to follow the first moving object that it encounters—normally its mother—within the first day or two of life. If it is kept isolated during this time, it will fail to become imprinted; it will never learn to follow its mother (or any other moving object, for that matter). (See **Figure 6.39.**)

Evidence suggests that there is also a critical period, though a much longer one, for the development of attachment between human parents and their infants (Ainsworth, 1973). Most infants become attached to their parents by six to nine months of age. Once attachment is formed, infants become very disturbed if they are separated from their primary caregivers, and they do not readily accept substitutes. (As we shall see later, babies do form secondary attachments to people other than their primary caregivers, but this is a different matter.)

Infants who are raised in an institution or who otherwise lack primary caregivers during the early months of life can apparently form a normal attachment if they are adopted soon after their first birthday (Gardner, Hawkes, and Burchinal, 1961). However, infants older than eighteen months do not readily form attachments with foster parents (Provence and Lipton, 1962).

Many studies have shown that infants who are

FIGURE 6.39   Konrad Lorenz was the first
moving object these young graylag geese saw after
they hatched, so they became imprinted on him.
When he goes for a swim they follow him the way
they would follow their mother.

separated from their parents during the first year
of life show a sequence of responses: protest, despair, and detachment (Bowlby, 1960). During the
stage of *protest* an infant actively and vigorously
performs the behaviors that normally call its parents, apparently in attempts to bring its parents
to it. The infant also appears to be angry when the
parents do not appear. Later, during the stage of
despair, the infant becomes inactive and withdrawn, responding little to other people in its environment. Finally, *detachment* becomes complete;
the infant again appears normal to its caretakers
and becomes more accepting and cheerful. However, if the infant is now reunited with a parent it
shows no evidence of the previous special bond
between them.

Similar research has emphasized the importance
of a parent's sustained presence during the first year
of life. For example, if a baby must spend time in
a hospital the parent should, if possible, stay with
the baby in its room. At the very least, the parent
should visit frequently and interact with the infant
as much as possible.

Some studies have shown that a particular aspect
of attachment may occur very early in life. In some
mammalian species, mothers will accept and care
for their infants only if they are able to see and
smell their offspring during the first day of life.
For example, if a lamb is removed from its mother

immediately after birth and is brought back a day
later, the mother will reject it. However, if a ewe
is in contact with her lamb for just a few minutes
after birth, she will accept it and take care of it
when it is given back to her the next day (Klopfer,
Adams, and Klopfer, 1964).

A few studies have suggested that a similar phenomenon occurs in humans; a mother experiences
bonding with her infant if the baby is placed naked
against her skin. For example, Klaus, Jerauld,
Krieger, McAlpine, Steffa, and Kennell (1972) performed an experiment with mothers who were
having their first child. The control group experienced what was then the usual hospital procedure, seeing their babies for a short time at birth
and feeding them (by bottle) five times a day. The
other mothers (the extended-contact group) received their babies for an hour soon after birth and
for five hours each afternoon on the next three days.
Thus, these mothers were in contact with their
babies for sixteen hours more than the mothers in
the control group. A month later the mothers were
interviewed during their infant's one-month
checkup. The mothers in the extended-contact group
acted more concerned about their babies, holding
and fondling them more than the mothers in the
control group. Differences in the behavior of the
two groups of mothers were still present as long
as two years later.

This study, then, suggested that mothers and babies should be together as much as possible during the first few days of life. Indeed, as a result of such studies, many hospitals have changed their procedures to ensure that a mother becomes bonded to her infant; the baby is placed against its mother's abdomen so that skin-to-skin contact occurs.

Although these studies are interesting, their conditions were not sufficiently controlled to prove that a maternal bond develops this early. The mothers in the experimental groups were aware that they were being treated differently, because they had their babies with them longer than other mothers who shared the rooms. In addition, nurses may have inadvertently communicated to the mothers that it was important to spend more time with their infants. Thus, if several months later the mothers were observed to interact with their babies slightly more, any of these variables may have accounted for this result. More recent research conducted under carefully controlled conditions has failed to confirm the results of the earlier studies. For example, Svejda, Campos, and Emde (1980) first made sure that the mothers in their study who received extended contact with their babies did not perceive themselves as "special." These investigators found that extended contact had no effect on interactions between mothers and their infants.

Certainly, increased contact between a mother and her infant soon after birth is worthwhile and rewarding. But it is probably important to make nurses, obstetricians, pediatricians, and other hospital personnel aware that there does appear to be a special bond that must form within a few hours of an infant's birth. If a premature or sick infant must be taken away from its mother immediately after birth, the mother should not be made to believe that she has missed an important aspect of motherhood—bonding. She should not be made to feel guilt and regret about a phenomenon that apparently does not exist.

THE ROLE OF ATTACHMENT IN AN INFANT'S ENVIRONMENTAL INTERACTION

◆ To develop normally, an infant must learn to explore and interact with its environment, exercising its own power of locomotion. Because the environ-

ment contains many dangers, it is advantageous for an infant to be frightened by unfamiliar stimuli and seek contact with its parent. This tendency makes it more likely that the parent will be able to prevent his or her baby from being harmed.

The presence of a baby's primary caregiver when it first becomes able to explore its environment provides considerable reassurance. Although the unfamiliar environment produces fear, the parent provides a *secure base* that the infant can leave from time to time to see what the world is like. Two studies have demonstrated the effectiveness of this reassurance (Rheingold, 1969; Rheingold and Eckerman, 1970). Ten-month-old infants were placed one at a time in a large, strange room. If the infant's mother was present, it explored and played with toys. If its mother was absent, the infant cried and showed other signs of distress. It did not explore the room. If an infant was brought by its mother into an adjoining room, it was likely to leave its mother and enter the large room by itself, explore the room, and play with toys, apparently secure in the knowledge that its mother was available nearby. Most of the infants crawled back and forth between the rooms during the observation.

Other researchers have made similar observations in studies of baby monkeys. For example, Harlow and his colleagues observed that an infant monkey who has been raised in isolation forms an attachment to a cuddly surrogate (Harlow, 1970). In unfamiliar situations the presence of this surrogate can provide reassurance; if the surrogate is present the baby monkey will explore happily. However, if the monkey is alone in the cage, or if only the wire surrogate is present, the baby will retreat in fear and huddle in a corner. (See **Figure 6.40.**)

A baby monkey will be reassured by the cuddly surrogate even if the behavior of the surrogate is the *source* of the infant's distress. Harlow and his colleagues constructed cuddly surrogates that were capable of rather nasty behaviors. One kind would periodically shake so violently that the infant would be flung off. The other contained a series of blunt brass spikes that would protrude from time to time, pushing the baby off. Both behaviors caused fear and distress in the baby monkeys, but as soon as the models stopped shaking or the brass spikes

FIGURE 6.40   If only a wire surrogate is present, an isolated infant monkey hides in the corner when frightened. (Harry F. Harlow, University of Wisconsin Primate Laboratory.)

were retracted, the babies ran to them and desperately clung to them.

This phenomenon is probably related to one that is seen in humans. Most people are shocked by the fact that battered and abused children are usually very closely attached to the parents who mistreat them. It is not unusual for a severely injured child to resist being separated from a parent who has just beaten it. The child needs consolation after the distressing experience and, as soon as the beating is over, turns to the parent (who is now usually remorseful) for comfort. The parent holds and comforts the child, thus reinforcing it for coming back. To a compassionate observer, a pathological attachment such as this is especially tragic.

INTERACTIONS WITH PEERS

◆Although the attachment between an infant and its primary caregiver is the most important social interaction in early life, a child's social development must also involve other people. A normal infant develops attachments with other adults and with older siblings, if there are any. But interaction with peers, children of a similar age, is especially important to social development.

Studies by Harlow and his colleagues have shown that social contact with peers is essential to an infant monkey's social development; in fact these interactions appear to be even more important than interactions with its mother. An infant monkey

that is raised with only a cuddly surrogate mother can still develop into a reasonably normal adult. However, an isolated monkey that does not interact with other juveniles before puberty shows severe deficits. When a previously isolated adolescent monkey is introduced to a colony of normally reared age-mates, it will retreat with terror and huddle in a corner in a desperate attempt to hide. (See **Figure 6.41.**)

Similarly, although the ability to become sexually aroused appears to be innate, normal sexual behavior—especially male sexual behavior—must be learned. A male monkey that has been isolated during childhood will fail to mate. Although he will become greatly aroused by the presence of a sexually receptive female, he appears unable to figure out how to perform intercourse. For a female monkey, interaction with peers during childhood is important for subsequent maternal behavior. Although a previously isolated female will eventually permit a gentle, experienced male to copulate with

FIGURE 6.41   An adult female monkey who was isolated during infancy hides to avoid the approach of a male. (Harry F. Harlow, University of Wisconsin Primate Laboratory.)

FIGURE 6.42 A monkey mother who was isolated during infancy ignores her infant. (Harry F. Harlow, University of Wisconsin Primate Laboratory.)

cope with fear, when to be dominant, and when not to challenge a more powerful, and aggressive, playmate. Young monkeys, like human children, engage in play, and this play appears to teach them what they need to know in order to form adult relationships. Females, for example, must learn not to fear the bold approach of a much-larger male, whose sexual overtures closely resemble aggressive gestures and postures.

Subsequent studies from Harlow's laboratory (such as Suomi and Harlow, 1972; Novak and Harlow, 1975) have shown that it is possible to eliminate the pathologically fearful behavior shown by a monkey that was raised in isolation. If there is a critical period during which monkeys learn to interact with their peers, it does not seem to be an absolute one. The important variable seems to be the abruptness with which a formerly isolated monkey is brought into social situations. If it is first placed with a younger, not-so-threatening "therapist" monkey, it can gradually learn how to interact normally with older monkeys. Thus, regardless of the specific stage of development at which socialization occurs, learning how to cope with a strange environment must be a gradual process.

◆   An experiment by Fuhrman, Rahe, and Hartup (1979) demonstrates that research with nonhuman primates can have important implications for the understanding of human development. These researchers used the "juvenile therapist" technique

her, she will not interact with her infant when it is born. She is likely to ignore it, stepping on it as if it were just another inanimate object in her environment. (See **Figure 6.42.**) If she pays attention to it she is likely to treat it brutally.

Apparently, social interaction helps young monkeys learn how to respond to each other—how to

Hartup, W.W. *Child Development*, 1979, 50, 915–922.)

FIGURE 6.43 Effects of pairing with "peer therapists" on the social interactions of isolated children. (From Fuhrman, W., Rahe, D.F., and

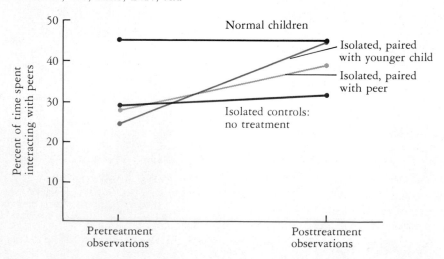

that Harlow and his associates discovered to improve peer interactions among socially withdrawn children, ages two-and-one-half to six-and-one-half years. The children appeared to be relatively isolated from their peers, spending less than a normal amount of time with them. Each child was paired with a partner for a series of ten play sessions of twenty minutes each. The partner was another child of the same age or twelve to twenty months younger. Interactions with peers were observed before, during, and after the play sessions. The play sessions were successful; they increased the amount of time that the isolated children spent with their peers. Furthermore, the children who were paired with younger "therapists" showed the greatest change. Control subjects, who did not participate in play sessions with another child, showed no change over the four-to-six-week period. (See **Figure 6.43**.)

There are tragic examples that show the importance of age-mate attachments in children, especially when normal relationships with adults have been thwarted. Freud and Dann (1951) studied six German Jewish children whose parents were murdered during World War II. The children were raised in a nursery in England after the war. They were initially very hostile toward adult caretakers and rejected their attention. They displayed an amazing degree of tenderness and solicitude toward each other, sharing toys and food without selfishness and quickly and aggressively defending each other against outsiders. They vigorously resisted being separated, even for short times. Eventually they began to direct some of their affection toward adults and finally socialized with them more normally. The intense nature of this relationship attests to the importance of attachments among peers, especially when normal parent-child attachments are unavailable.

Interim summary: Because a baby is totally dependent upon its parents, the development of attachment between parent and infant is crucial to its survival. A baby has the innate ability to shape and reinforce the behavior of its parent. To a large extent the baby is its parent's teacher. Infant and parent reinforce each other's behavior, which facilitates the development of a durable attachment between them. This relationship develops over several months; at least in humans, the time for attachment is not restricted to a few hours after birth.

Some of the behaviors that babies possess innately are rooting, sucking, cuddling, looking, smiling, and crying. These behaviors are instrumental in satisfying physiological needs and promoting parental responses. In the case of smiling, the behavior develops as the child matures; the baby first smiles spontaneously, then in response to visual stimuli (especially its caregiver), and eventually it learns to smile at its own activities, particularly those that produce reactions in its environment. Thus, smiling encourages caregivers to arrange a responsive environment (playing the "contingency game"), which in turn facilitates the baby's cognitive development.

Harlow's studies with monkeys have shown that clinging, one of the important behaviors in attachment, is an innate tendency, and does not have to be reinforced by food or warmth. Infant humans and monkeys are normally afraid of novel stimuli, but the presence of their caregiver (or cuddly surrogate) provides a secure base from which they can explore a new environment.

Development also involves the acquisition of social skills. Interaction with peers is probably the most important factor in social development. Research with monkeys has shown that deprivation of contact with peers has even more serious effects than deprivation of contact with their mother. Studies with human children suggest that peer interaction is just as important in our species.

ADULT DEVELOPMENT

Puberty (from Latin *puber*, "adult") marks the beginning of the transition from childhood to adulthood. Many physical events occur during this stage: people reach their ultimate height, develop secondary sex characteristics (including breasts, muscles, and body hair), and become capable of reproduction. These changes are discussed in the next chapter. There is also a change in social role. As a child, a person is dependent on parents, teachers, and other adults; as an adolescent, he or she is expected to assume more responsibility. Relations among peers also suddenly change; members of one's own sex become potential rivals for the attention of members of the other sex.

STAGES OF DEVELOPMENT

◈ It is much easier to outline child development than adult development; children change faster, and the changes are closely related to age. Adolescence, the last clearly defined stage of human development, occurs at about the same age in all people, and is characterized by similar kinds of changes. Adult development is much more variable, because physical changes in adults are more gradual.

Mental and emotional changes during adulthood are closely related to individual experience. Some people achieve success and satisfaction with their careers, some hate their jobs; some marry and have happy family lives, while others never adjust to the role of spouse and parent. Crises occur at different times for different people, and they do not come in the same order. No one description of adult development will fit everyone.

Thus, we can note only some general trends. Physically, we decline after early adulthood, although the decline need not be rapid; a healthy, active person can retain his or her vitality for many years. Sexual performance may decline with age, but the rate of decline is closely related to a person's activity and attitudes. Intellectual changes are also variable and are particularly difficult to assess.

PHYSICAL CHANGES

◈ Unlike the rapid physical changes that occur during prenatal development, childhood, and adolescence, the changes that occur during adulthood—except for sudden changes caused by accident or disease—are gradual. People are unlikely to notice these changes until they try to do something they have not done for several years and find it more difficult than it used to be, such as playing a sport that they have not practiced since college days.

Physical changes in adulthood occur at different rates in different individuals. People who are different from each other in early adulthood become even more different as they grow older. Therefore, it is difficult to categorize people's physical condition by age.

Most physical functions decline during adulthood. As people age, their muscles become weaker, their bones become brittle through loss of calcium, their lungs become less efficient, and the walls of their blood vessels lose some elasticity and may become coated with atherosclerotic plaques, which increase the risk of heart attack or stroke. As their bodies lose their resiliency people find it harder to recover from the stress of illness or injury. Physical stress that would be relatively minor in a young adult has much more serious consequences in an older person.

After adolescence, bones do not change in length. Thus, people's height remains constant for many years. In their fifties, people become somewhat shorter as they lose some of the material in the disks between their vertebrae. In addition to this real loss in height, many older people adopt a stooped posture (often because of arthritis), which produces an apparent additional loss in height.

Arthritis, a disease of the joints (from Greek *arthron,* "joint"), follows heart disease as the second largest cause of disability in adulthood. The pain of arthritis can seriously limit a person's flexibility and range of movements, and this enforced reduction in exercise can itself have deleterious effects on health. In addition, muscles lose strength and connective tissues such as ligaments lose their elasticity, and the skin loses fat tissue, which makes the body (and especially the limbs) look more frail. Skin loses its elasticity, resulting in wrinkles and folds. Hair eventually turns gray, and many men lose theirs. Although people's bones stop growing, their cartilage continues to grow slowly; consequently, old people have disproportionately large noses and ears.

Finally, the effects of *looking* old can be more devastating than the purely physical effects on a person's functional capacity. The sex life of a person who is regarded as sexually unattractive because of age will suffer even if he or she is physiologically capable of vigorous sexual performance. The intellectual and physical skills of an older person will go untested if he or she is regarded as "too old for the job." These age-related effects are purely social; they depend on people's attitudes toward old people.

The nervous system, like other organ systems, also declines with age. Neurons degenerate and die, and because they cannot be replaced, their loss is permanent. For example, in the brain of an older person the sulci (grooves in the cerebral cortex) become wider as the brain tissue between them degenerates. These age-related changes are apparent in CAT scans of older people. However, there is not a strong correlation between the loss of brain tissue and decline in intellectual performance. Some people may have substantial cortical degeneration but still function well intellectually. Figure 6.44 shows a CAT scan of the brain of a 101-year-old man. Although age caused loss of cortical tissue that has made the sulci more prominent, this man was physically and intellectually active at the time when the scan was taken. (See **Figure 6.44**.)

Although cortical degeneration is not closely related to intellectual ability, there are various diseases that can cause severe impairment. Pre-senile dementias refer to a class of diseases characterized by progressive loss of cortical tissue and corresponding loss of mental functions. (*Senile* means "old," *dementia* means literally "an undoing of the mind.") The most prevalent form of dementia is called **Alzheimer's disease.** People with this disorder rapidly lose the gray matter of the cerebral cortex. (See **Figure 6.45**.) The cause of the degeneration is not known, and there is no useful medical treatment. The disease progresses from disruption of memory to decline in language functions to loss of physical control and finally to premature death.

An even more significant cause of mental deterioration in old age is depression, a psychological disorder. Many people find old age an unpleasant condition: they are declining physically; they no longer have jobs or family-related activities that confirm their usefulness to other people; and many old friends have died, are infirm, or have moved away. With this strong sense of loss or deprivation, older people become depressed; they lose their appetites for food and for living in general, appear sad and confused, have trouble concentrating, and suffer losses in memory. Too often these symptoms of depression are diagnosed as dementia. Yet unlike dementia, depression is treatable with psychotherapeutic and pharmacological methods, as we shall see in Chapter 18.

One means of monitoring changes in the nervous system is the *electroencephalogram,* or *EEG.* An

EEG is a recording of the electrical activity of the brain, obtained through small metal disks pasted on the scalp. A normal EEG shows regular patterns of activity indicating that neurons in many parts of the brain are synchronized in their activity. For

FIGURE 6.44   A CAT scan of a 101-year-old person. Although there is evidence of some loss of cortical tissue, the person is active and intelligent. (CAT scan courtesy of Dr. J.McA. Jones, Good Samaritan Hospital, Portland, Oregon.)

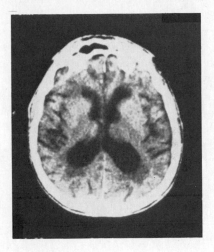

FIGURE 6.45   A CAT scan of a person with Alzheimer's disease. Note the severe widening of the sulci and enlargment of the ventricles (dark areas in the middle of the scan). (CAT scan courtesy of Dr. J.McA. Jones, Good Samaritan Hospital, Portland, Oregon.)

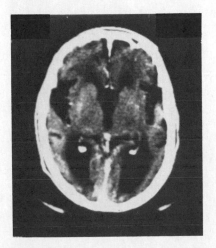

example, when a person is quietly resting, an EEG shows regular oscillations of *alpha activity* in the range of eight to twelve times per second.

Alpha activity shows a general slowing with age. In young adults the average frequency is about 10.3 cycles per second; in people in their sixties the average frequency has declined to approximately 9 cycles per second. Because a variety of brain pathologies, including dementing illnesses and diseases of the cerebral blood vessels, cause slowing of alpha activity, it seems likely that this gradual decline in the frequency of alpha activity is an indication of associated declines in physiological functioning.

Aging affects sensory functions. For example, vision grows less effective as the transparent portions of the eye become yellowed and somewhat cloudy. In addition, the lens of the eye becomes less flexible, so that it becomes more difficult for a person to focus upon objects close to the eye. As a result, most people need reading glasses later in life. People also lose the ability to hear high-pitched sounds, and at the same time high-pitched sounds begin to produce pain. (This fact undoubtedly accounts for some of the disagreements between older and younger people about what constitutes a tolerable volume at which music should be played.)

Although it is easy to measure decline in their sensory systems, older people often show very little *functional* change. Most learn to make adjustments for their sensory losses, using additional cues to help them decode sensory information. For example, people with hearing loss can learn to attend

FIGURE 6.46   Concert pianist Wanda Landowska performed publically well into her 80s. Old age does not preclude artistic and intellectual performance.

more carefully to other people's gestures and lip movements; they can also profitably use their experience to infer what was said.

All these physical changes appear to be related to lifestyle. People who are active both physically and intellectually are likely to continue to be active and productive in old age. With a flexible attitude, individuals can accommodate their interests and activities to inevitable changes in physical abilities. There is no reason why a reasonably healthy person of *any* age should stop enjoying life. (See **Figure 6.46**.)

INTELLECTUAL CHANGES

◆ One of the topics of adult development that has received the most attention is intellectual development. Psychologists have studied the effects of education and experience on intellectual abilities and have questioned whether intelligence inevitably declines with age. Most of us can conceive of a future when we can no longer run as fast as we do now or perform well in a strenuous sport, but we do not like to think of being outperformed intellectually by younger people. And in fact research indicates that people can get old without losing their intellectual skills.

Intelligence and Age: Problems of Interpretation

As we get older, our joints will get stiff, and our muscles and ligaments will become less flexible and resilient. Is the same true for our brain? Will we start to lose our memory, find it difficult to reason, and generally become a little fuzzy about everything? The graph presented in **Figure 6.47** supposedly shows how intelligence changes with age. The downward slope depicted there does not look very promising. However, the studies suggesting that intelligence declines with age have used methodologies that are open to challenge.

There are several obstacles to obtaining an accurate and unbiased estimate of the relation between age and intelligence. The first is the fact that age is usually correlated with other variables. You will recall from Chapter 1 that we can assess the effects of one variable upon another only when all other variables are held constant. Suppose that we perform a *cross-sectional study*—a slice through the various age layers of society. We obtain a sam-

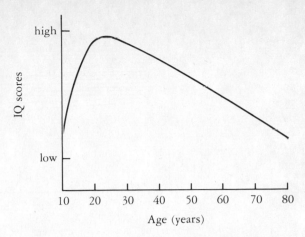

FIGURE 6.47 A traditional graph showing that IQ inevitably declines with age. (From Jones, H.E., and Kaplan, O.J., in *Mental Disorders in Later Life*, 2nd ed., edited by O.J. Kaplan. Stanford, Calif.: Stanford University Press, 1956.)

ple of healthy twenty-year-olds, thirty-year-olds, and so on, up to age eighty. We administer various intelligence tests to all our subjects and then compare the performances of the various age groups. Would we be justified in saying that the results represent the effects of age on intellectual functions? What factors other than age might account for differences in the results?

* * *

We would *not* be justified in saying that the results represent only the effects of aging, because many other variables are confounded with this one. For one thing, the people of different ages may have had very different environments; for example, the twenty-year-old people in our sample will all have received their education recently, whereas the eighty-year-old people will have been educated early in this century, when educational norms and requirements were very different: far fewer people went to college, many did not even finish high school, and those who did went to schools that were very different from high schools today. Furthermore, the health care that the older people's mothers received during pregnancy and their own health care during childhood will probably not have been as good as the care that children and pregnant women receive now.

Another factor that could contribute to a measured decline in intelligence with age is a phenomenon

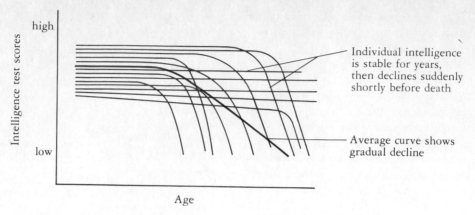

FIGURE 6.48   A possible cause of an apparent decline in intelligence with age. If individuals who show the death drop die at different times, the averaged data will indicate a smooth decline even though each individual showed a sharp drop soon before death.

called **death drop** (Jarvik and Blum, 1971; Riegel and Riegel, 1972). Shortly before dying of natural causes, people often suffer a sudden, severe decline in intellectual abilities. Because more old people than young ones die of natural causes, a sample of old people is more likely to contain members who are undergoing this decline, and hence the average performance for older people will be lower. **Figure 6.48** illustrates how an increase in the proportion of people experiencing death drop can make an average curve show a fictitious gradual decline.

Given that the cross-sectional method cannot yield accurate estimates of the effects of aging in times during which the environment is changing (and this certainly applies to our century), what method do you think would be better? How could we avoid the problems inherent in cross-sectional studies? At first glance, the ideal method would seem to be a **longitudinal study**—that is, observation of the intellectual performance of the same group of people throughout their lives. Because the various age groups consist of the same sample of people, age would not be confounded with environmental differences. But this method introduces other problems. What do you think they might be?

* * *

Some of the problems with a longitudinal study are practical in nature: such a study is expensive and depends on a long-term commitment of resources, whereas most granting agencies limit their funding commitments to three years. Because the investigator might not live as long as his or her subjects, a team of people must carry out the study, adding younger recruits from time to time. And because the person who begins such a study might not be able to participate in its completion, there is less incentive to perform a longitudinal study than a cross-sectional one, which provides immediate results.

Besides the expense, difficulty, and delay of gratification, there are methodological problems inherent in longitudinal studies. Perhaps people from poor families who received poor nutrition and health care and an inadequate education would score less well on intelligence tests. If, because of chronic poor health, these people die sooner than those with a history of good health care, the mean intelligence of long-lived groups will rise, because it contains only healthy survivors. Thus, the method may provide *inflated* estimates of the mean intellectual ability of old people, relative to younger ones.

Research has shown that indeed, group composition changes in the course of a longitudinal study. People who score poorly on intelligence tests tend not to be available for later testing. For example, in 1956 Riegel, Riegel, and Meyer (1967) tested 380 German men and women between the ages of fifty-five and seventy-five. Five years later only 202 were available for testing; the others had died, were in poor health, or were simply reluctant to be tested again. Five years after that the sample was reduced still further. An analysis showed that the original scores of people who could not be retested tended to be lower than those of people who could be retested. Thus, the people who remained were those who originally scored best on the intelligence tests. Such changes in the composition of a group make it impossible to obtain a pure measure of the effect of age on intellectual performance.

Because of the problems inherent in cross-sectional and longitudinal methods, results must be viewed with some skepticism. For example, the shape of the curve relating age to intellectual performance may not be valid. Both methods indicate a decline in performance with age, although longitudinal studies show the decline beginning later in life—not until the fifties.

Specific Abilities and Age

◈ Whatever the true shape of the curve may be, studies have shown clearly that aging affects different intellectual abilities to different degrees. Cattell (1971) divided these abilities into two major categories. In general, old people in good health do well on tests of *crystallized intelligence*—abilities that depend on knowledge and experience—until they die. Vocabulary, the ability to see similarities between objects and situations, and general information are all aspects of crystallized intelligence.

Fluid intelligence—the capacity for abstract reasoning—appears to decline with age (Baltes and Schaie, 1974; Horn, 1976). The ability to solve puzzles, to memorize a series of arbitrary items such as nonsense words or letters, to classify figures into categories, and to change problem-solving strategies easily and flexibly are aspects of fluid intelligence.

The fact that older people excel in crystallized intelligence and younger people excel in fluid intelligence is reflected in the kinds of intellectual endeavor that the two age groups seem to be best suited for. For example, most great mathematicians make their most significant contributions during their twenties or early thirties; apparently the ability to break out of the traditional ways of thinking and to conceive new strategies is crucial in such achievements. In contrast, great contributions to literature and philosophy, in which suc-

cess depends heavily on knowledge and experience, tend to be made by older people.

At least three reasons may account for older people's apparent decline in fluid intelligence. (1) The abilities that constitute fluid intelligence may be especially sensitive to the inevitable deterioration in the brain that accompanies aging. (2) People's previous experience may cause them to adhere rigidly to particular problem-solving strategies even when a more flexible approach would be more effective. In this case the decline would be due to experience rather than to a real loss of intellectual capacity. (3) People may learn so much and see so many relations among variables that they have difficulty focusing on the simple answer.

In support of the third suggestion, Kogan (1973) compared the strategies used by college students and members of a senior citizens club (average age seventy-three) to classify a number of objects and photographs. The older people were more likely to classify the items according to functional relations. For example, they might group pipes with matches. Younger people were more likely to classify objects according to physical characteristics (such as having handles) or according to a common general concept (such as kitchen utensils). Kogan attributed the difference to experience; the older subjects used a more subtle and less conventional scheme. Kogan noted that children who are rated as more creative also tend to classify according to functional relations rather than by type or physical characteristics. Thus, the behavior of the older people could be taken as evidence of a higher stage of cognitive development, and not as evidence of intellectual deterioration.

Many studies have shown that old people learn lists of words more slowly than young people do. However, some studies have shown that crystallized intelligence can sometimes facilitate new learning (Canestrari, 1966; Lair, Moon, and Kausler, 1969). Both young people and older people were given lists of words arranged in pairs. Some pairs were frequently associated ones (such as chair and table); others were unrelated. Older people learned the frequently associated pairs (but not the unrelated pairs) faster than the younger people did.

Other studies have shown that experience and accumulated crystallized intelligence can work to an older person's disadvantage. For example, when

Ruch (1934) asked people to learn false equations such as $3 \times 5 = 6$, or neutral equations such as $A \times M = B$, older people found it more difficult to learn the false equations than the neutral ones; their experience and practice interfered with the learning of equations that were contrary to fact. (It is questionable whether this tendency should be considered a liability.)

This finding suggests why people may have problems adapting to the demands of their society when they are older. Although they have had more opportunity to accumulate the experience that leads to crystallized intelligence they also run the risk of becoming obsolete; many of the skills they have learned are no longer needed. Of course, some facts do not change; 3×5 continues to equal 15, but many facts that were previously important may become less so through civilization's acquisition of more knowledge. Older strategies may also become less efficient as society and workplaces change. Researchers must carefully distinguish between obsolescence and decline in intellectual functioning, because obsolescence can be overcome (at least theoretically) through education and retraining.

Older people have difficulty responding and performing quickly. When time pressures prevail, their performance is worse than that of younger people. However, when time requirements are relaxed, the performance of old people improves much more than that of young people (Arenberg, 1973; Botwinick and Storandt, 1974).

Part of the age-related decline in speed can be attributed to deterioration in sensory functions and to difficulty in changing strategies to meet new demands. But another important reason for decreased speed is caution; older people appear to be less willing to make mistakes. In many endeavors this caution is valuable. Many societies reserve important decision-making functions for older people because they are less likely to act too hastily. A study by Leech and Witte (1971) illustrates these effects of caution on performance. The investigators found that old people who were paid for each response they made—correct or incorrect—learned lists of pairs of words faster than old people who were paid only for correct responses. The payment for incorrect responses increased their willingness to make a mistake, and this relaxation of their

normal caution paid off in an increased speed of learning.

In a review of human abilities, Horn (1976) summarized the features of aging as follows:

> In general . . . the findings suggest that if one lives long enough he will experience difficulties, relative to his skills at an earlier age, in organizational thinking, perceiving relationships, forming hypotheses, making integrations, and shifting from one learning or thinking task to another. . . . But some intellectual changes with age in adulthood reflect changes in styles of thinking which are not indicative of decreased abilities to cope but instead indicate increased capacities (p. 470)

CONCLUDING REMARKS

This chapter has followed human development from fertilized ovum to old age. Because early development is very rapid, Piaget and other psychologists have divided it into stages. Physical and intellectual capacities develop quickly during the first two decades of life and then decline, at a slower or faster rate, depending on individuals' environments, life-styles, and attitudes. As people gain education and experience, their ability to function and perform can continue to increase even though the brain has completed its development. All of us who plan to get old hope that the fruits of research will help us remain healthy and functional throughout our lives.

GUIDE TO TERMS INTRODUCED IN THIS CHAPTER

accommodation　p. 225

allele　p. 205　Figure 6.4

alpha activity　p. 248

Alzheimer's disease　p. 247　Figure 6.45

amniotic sac　p. 212　Figure 6.13

anoxia　p. 214

assimilation　p. 225

attachment　p. 234

behavioral genetics　p. 209

SUGGESTIONS FOR FURTHER READING

Many excellent books have been written about human development. The second edition of a book by T.G.R. Bower, called *Development in Infancy* (San Francisco: W.H. Freeman, 1982), contains fascinating accounts of the perceptual and cognitive abilities of young infants, as well as some studies that have caused controversy among developmental psychologists. *A Child's Eye View: Understanding the Development and Behavior of Children,* by C.K. Tomlinson (New York: St. Martin's Press, 1980) is a wonderful book that tries to explain children's behavior in light of the recent findings in the field of cognitive development.

Vitality and Aging: Implications of the Rectangular Curve by J.F. Fries and L.M. Crapo (San Francisco: W.H. Freeman, 1981) looks at the other end of the age continuum. The fact that people are living longer than ever before creates problems for individuals and society. This very readable book discusses theories of aging, factors that affect longevity, and the quality of people's later years. For a broad overview of the many factors that affect the aging process, see M. Kermis's *The Psychology of Human Aging: Theory, Research, and Practice* (Boston: Allyn and Bacon, 1984).

7

SEXUAL
DEVELOPMENT
AND BEHAVIOR

LEARNING ◆ OBJECTIVES

SEXUAL IDENTITY is an aspect of our self-image that begins to be established at a very early age. We are treated as males or females right from the time of birth. When someone announces the birth of a baby most of us immediately ask "Is it a boy or a girl?" And once we find out the baby's sex we interact with it in subtly different ways. (See **Figure 7.1.**)

We also make distinctions between sexually immature people and those who have reached puberty. In the past, our ancestors marked the transition from childhood to adulthood with various kinds of ritual ceremonies. Today there are only a few remnants of these ceremonies in Western society, mostly in the form of religious confirmations. But we continue to act differently toward adults and children. And even more significantly, our own self-image begins to change drastically when we reach puberty.

The role of sexual behavior in the survival of our species is obvious. We have been shaped by the evolutionary process so that sexual behavior has profound personal significance for us; sexual activity is part of almost everyone's life. This chapter is concerned with sexual development and sexual behavior. First we shall examine the biological differences between male and female sexual development. Then we shall consider the biological and cultural variables that produce differences in the behavior of males and females. Finally, we shall study human sexual behavior, its mechanisms, and its variations.

SEXUAL DEVELOPMENT

CHROMOSOMAL DETERMINATION OF SEX

A person's genetic sex is determined by the father's sperm at the time of fertilization. You will recall from Chapter 6 that each human parent contributes one member of each of the twenty-three pairs of the offspring's chromosomes. When the chromosomes of the sperm and ovum unite, the pairs are joined together. Twenty-two of these pairs are *autosomes* ("independent bodies"); they determine the organism's physical development independent of its sex. The last pair consists of two *sex chromosomes,* which determine whether the offspring will be a boy or a girl.

There are two types of sex chromosomes: **X** *chromosomes* and **Y** *chromosomes.* Females have two X chromosomes (XX); thus, all the ova that a woman produces will contain an X chromosome.

256

FIGURE 7.1   Differential treatment of males and females begins early in their lives.

On the other hand, males have an X and a Y chromosome (XY). When a man's sex chromosomes divide, half the sperm contain an X chromosome and the other half a Y chromosome. A Y-bearing sperm produces an XY fertilized ovum, and therefore a male. An X-bearing sperm produces an XX fertilized ovum, and therefore a female. (See **Figure 7.2.**)

But how does the presence or absence of a single Y chromosome determine whether an organism will become a male or a female? What directs the sequence of events during development of the sex organs? These questions have been answered by the study of organisms with genetic anomalies; we observe that something is missing or defective early in development and find out what the consequences are. Through these means we have learned more about sexual development than any other aspect of prenatal development. Genetic defects that produce faulty hearts, lungs, brains, or kidneys are

usually fatal; the developing organism does not survive, and therefore cannot be studied. However, genetic defects that affect the reproductive organs generally do not kill the organism, although they may prevent it from becoming a parent. Developmental anomalies in sex organs have been studied in a variety of animals, including our own species. Experimental research with other mammals and studies of these anomalies have led to a good understanding of sexual development.

DEVELOPMENT OF THE GONADS

Through the fourth week of *gestation* the development of male and female fetuses is identical. (*Gestation*, from the Latin word for "carrying," refers to the period of pregnancy.) Both sexes have a pair of identical **primordial gonads** (*primordial* means "first origin"; *gonads* are testes or ovaries). The primordial gonads are said to be **bipotential;** that is,

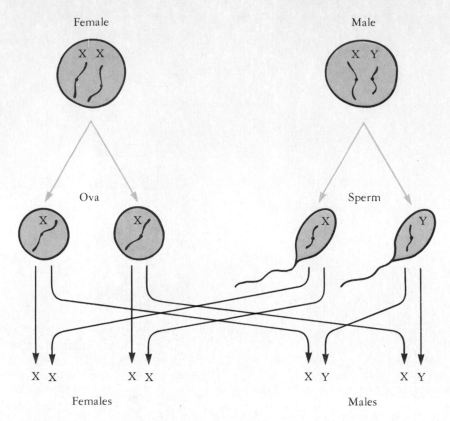

FIGURE 7.2   Determination of gender.

they can become either testes or ovaries. The determining factor appears to be a single gene on the Y chromosome. If it is present, cells produce a protein called the **H-Y antigen,** which causes the primordial gonads to become testes. If the gene is not present, H-Y antigen is not produced and the gonads develop into ovaries. (See **Figure 7.3.**)

The rest of sexual development is determined by the presence of testes or ovaries. Thus, an extremely important part of our identities—our gender—is largely determined by a protein whose production is controlled by a single gene.

DEVELOPMENT OF THE INTERNAL SEX ORGANS

Two different systems serve as *precursors* for the internal sex organs—the initial rudimentary structures from which they develop. While the gonads are developing, the precursors for *both* male and female internal sex organs are present: the *Müller-*

ian system (female) and the *Wolffian system* (male). (See **Figure 7.4, A.**)

Development of Male Internal Sex Organs

If the fertilized ovum contains an X and a Y chromosome the primordial gonads become testes. The testes begin to secrete hormones called *androgens* ("male-producing," from Greek *andros,* "man"; *gennan,* "to produce"). The most important androgen is *testosterone.* Androgens stimulate the development of the Wolffian system into *sperm ducts, seminal vesicles,* and *epididymises.* The testes also secrete another hormone (the *Müllerian inhibiting substance*), which prevents the female Müllerian system from developing. (See **Figure 7.4, C and E.**)

To see whether androgens are necessary for the development of male internal sex organs, Jost (1969) removed the testes from a male rabbit fetus while it was still in its mother's uterus. As a result of this surgery the Müllerian system, and not the

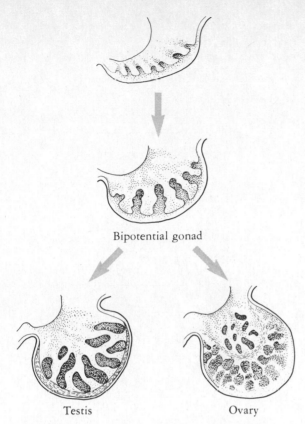

Bipotential gonad

Testis   Ovary

FIGURE 7.3 Differentiation of the gonads. The inner part of the bipotential gonads develops into testes, or the outer part develops into ovaries. (Adapted from Burns, R.K. In *Analysis of Development*, edited by B.H. Willier, P.A. Weiss, and V. Hamberger. Philadelphia: Saunders, 1955.)

Wolffian system, developed; the animal was born with fallopian tubes, a uterus, and a vagina. (However, the animal was unable to reproduce, because it did not have ovaries.) Findings such as these have given rise to the dictum "Nature's impulse is to create a female." Regardless of genetic sex, the organism will become a female if testes (and the hormones they secrete) are not present.

This experiment does not prove that androgens are responsible for the development of male sex organs; it is possible that other secretions of the testes accomplish this. However, other experiments have shown that if injections of testosterone are given to a male fetus whose testes have been removed or to a female fetus (with or without ovaries) the Wolffian system will develop—the inter-

nal sex organs will be male. Thus, the action of testosterone can contradict the tendency to produce a female. There is also a genetic anomaly that prevents the cells of an organism from responding to androgens. Fetuses with this anomaly become female even though they are genetically male. This condition, called androgen insensitivity syndrome, is discussed later.

Development of Female Internal Sex Organs

If the primordial gonads develop into ovaries, then the Müllerian system will develop into the female internal sex organs—fallopian tubes, uterus, and vagina. The Wolffian system will fail to grow. (See **Figure 7.4, B and D**.)

Although most females are born with ovaries, the presence of these organs is not necessary for prenatal development as a female. Thus, the factor that causes the development of female internal sex organs is simply the *absence of testes*. We know this because humans who fail to develop any gonads—neither testes nor ovaries—become female. (This genetic anomaly, called Turner's syndrome, is discussed later.)

It appears that female hormones are not necessary for female development, because the absence of ovaries in a fetus does not prevent the development of female sex organs. Even though the mother's ovaries produce female sex hormones and these hormones can cross the placenta and enter the circulation of the fetus, this fact does not account for female development; the blood of fetuses contains a protein that inactivates the mother's hormones (Aussel, Uriel, and Mercier-Bodard, 1973).

DEVELOPMENT OF THE EXTERNAL GENITALIA

The *external genitalia* are derived from a single set of bipotential precursors. Just as the primordial gonads can become either testes or ovaries, the *primordial phallus* can become a *glans penis* or a *clitoris,* the *genital swelling* can become a *scrotum* or *labia majora* (outer lips), and the *genital tubercle* can become a *penis shaft* or *labia minora* (inner lips). (See **Figure 7.5.**)

The process that controls development of the internal sex organs also controls development of the

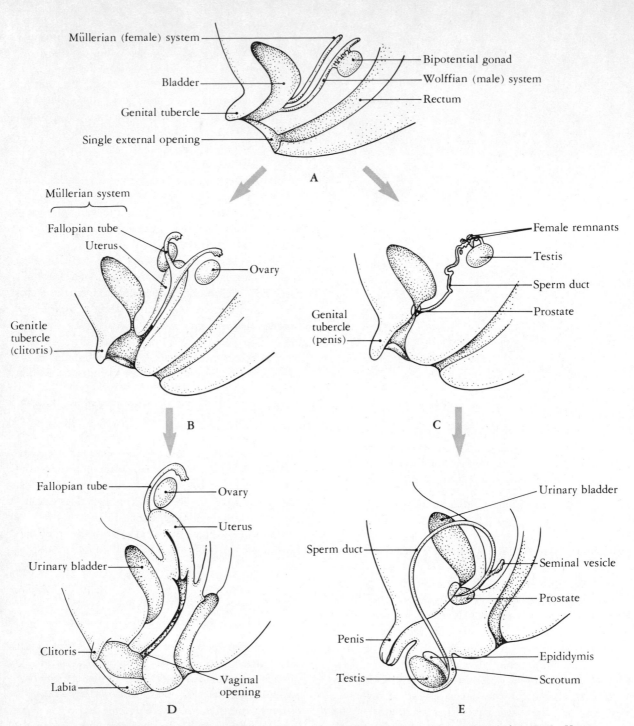

FIGURE 7.4 Differentiation and development of the internal sex organs. (Adapted from Masters, W.H., Johnson, V.E., and Kolodny, R.C. *Human Sexuality.* Boston: Little, Brown, 1982.)

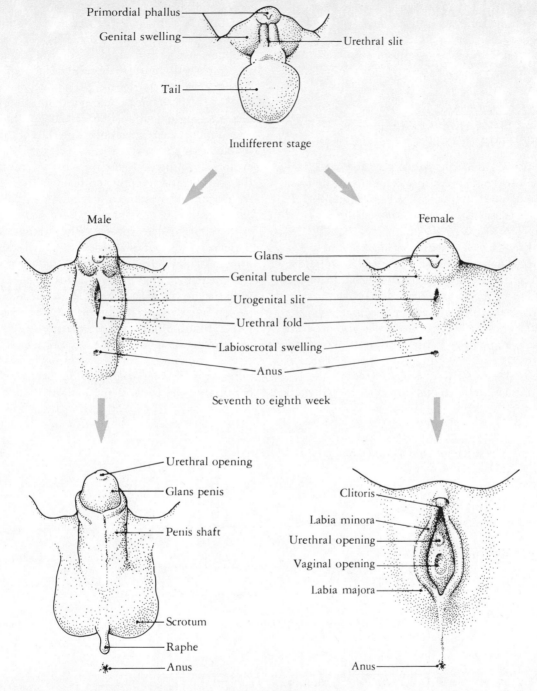

Primordial phallus
Genital swelling
Urethral slit
Tail

Indifferent stage

Male   Female

Glans
Genital tubercle
Urogenital slit
Urethral fold
Labioscrotal swelling
Anus

Seventh to eighth week

Urethral opening
Glans penis
Penis shaft

Clitoris
Labia minora
Urethral opening
Vaginal opening
Labia majora

Scrotum
Raphe
Anus   Anus

Twelfth week

FIGURE 7.5 Differentiation and development of
the external genitalia.

genitalia. If the fetus possesses testosterone-secreting testes, its genitals will be male. If the fetus has no testes, if they secrete no testosterone, or if the cells cannot respond to testosterone, its genitals will be female.

ORGANIZATIONAL AND ACTIVATIONAL EFFECTS OF SEX HORMONES

◆ We have seen that the presence or absence of androgens early in prenatal life determines which set of genitals and internal sex organs develop. Testosterone causes *androgenization* of the fetus; it becomes a male. Without androgens, the fetus becomes a female, whether or not it has ovaries. Androgenization is called an *organizational effect;* the effect irreversibly *organizes* the subsequent development of the fetus. Once the Wolffian system develops, the Müllerian system disappears, and the external genitalia become male; the potential for becoming a female is permanently lost. Thus, organizational effects occur during a critical period of development, early in prenatal life.

In contrast, *activational effects* are mostly transitory and reversible and occur after sexual differentiation is complete. For example, testosterone causes a man's beard to grow. The effect is activational, not organizational; surgical removal of the testes will cause the beard to stop growing. Activational effects depend on the *continued* presence of the hormone. If the hormone is no longer secreted, the activational effects disappear.

Hormones exert their effects on cells of the body by interacting with specialized receptors. These receptors are proteins, and they behave much like the postsynaptic receptors on neurons that respond to transmitter substances. For example, both men and women have cells in their facial skin that contain testosterone receptors. When testosterone is present in sufficient quantities, these cells cause the growth of facial hair. Normally, only a man has enough testosterone present in his blood to stimulate the growth of facial hair. However, if a woman has an androgen-secreting tumor, she, too, will grow a beard. Similarly, breast tissue contains cells that are sensitive to female sex hormones. These cells normally grow only in a woman who has passed puberty, when her ovaries begin secreting these hormones. The parts of the body that contain re-

FIGURE 7.6   Puberty is initiated when the hypothalamus stimulates the pituitary gland to secrete gonadotropic hormones.

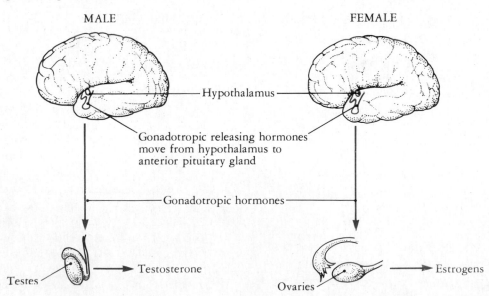

ceptors sensitive to a particular hormone are called that hormone's *target tissue.*

FURTHER SEXUAL DEVELOPMENT AT PUBERTY

◆ The internal sex organs and genitalia do not change much for several years after birth, but they begin to develop again at puberty. When boys and girls are about twelve to fourteen, their brains secrete hormones that begin the process of sexual maturation. No one knows what awakens this process and causes the hormonal secretions to begin at this time.

The *gonadotropic releasing hormones,* which begin the process, are secreted by the hypothalamus, located at the base of the brain. These hormones are carried by blood vessels to the *anterior pituitary gland,* which in turn is stimulated to secrete *gonadotropic hormones. Gonadotropic* ("gonad-changing") describes the effects of the hormones: they stimulate the gonads (testes or ovaries) to secrete sex hormones. These sex hormones act on various organs of the body and initiate the changes that accompany sexual maturation. (See **Figure 7.6.**)

The sex hormones secreted by the gonads cause growth and maturation of the external genitalia and of the gonads themselves. In addition, these hormones cause the maturation of ova and the production of sperm. All of these developments are considered *primary sex characteristics.* The sex hormones also stimulate the development of *secondary sex characteristics*—the physical changes that distinguish a male from a female. Before puberty boys and girls look much the same. If they have similar hair styles and clothing, it is difficult to determine their gender without looking at their genitals. (See **Figure 7.7.**) At puberty, females grow breasts, their pelvises widen, and they reach their final height. Males continue to grow for a longer time, so that on the average they become taller than females. Their muscles grow larger, they grow facial hair, and their voices get deeper. Both males and females grow pubic hair and axillary (underarm) hair.

In males, the sex hormone that induces these changes is the androgen testosterone. In females, the changes are produced chiefly by *estradiol* and

FIGURE 7.7   The facial features and physiques of preadolescent boys and girls are very similar.

androstenedione (AD). Estradiol is an *estrogen,* which is the principal class of female hormones. Despite the fact that androstenedione is an important sex hormone in women, it is classified as an *androgen.*

Table 7.1 lists the effects of each of these hormones. Testosterone, the primary sex hormone in males, produces the physical changes that occur at puberty: maturation of the genitals, beard growth, muscular development, and lowering of the voice. It also causes the bones to stop growing, ending the growth spurt that occurs at the beginning of puberty. (Another hormone, appropriately named *growth hormone,* causes this spurt.) In the past, many cultures have removed boys' testes (that is, castrated them) to preserve their fine soprano voice for the choir, to enhance their value as homosexual

TABLE 7.1   The principal sex hormones and their effects

Class	Principal hormones (where produced)	Effects
Androgens	Testosterone (testes)	Maturation of male genitals; production of sperm; growth of facial, pubic, and axillary hair; enlargement of larynx; inhibition of bone growth
	Androstenedione (AD) (adrenals)	In females, growth of pubic and axillary hair; less important than testosterone in males
Estrogens	Estradiol (ovaries)	Maturation of female genitals, growth of breasts, alterations in fat deposits, growth of uterine lining, inhibition of bone growth
Gestagens	Progesterone (ovaries)	Maintenance of uterine lining

Adapted from Carlson, N.R. *Physiology of Behavior*, 2nd ed. Boston: Allyn and Bacon, 1981.

prostitutes, or to make them trustworthy guards for a rich man's harem. These men usually grew very tall and had especially long arms, because testosterone was not present to halt bone growth.

In females, estradiol produces most of the changes that occur during puberty. Like testosterone, it inhibits bone growth and causes the genitals to mature. Estradiol also stimulates growth of the breasts, causes the pelvis to widen, and produces changes in the layer of fat beneath the skin and in the texture of the skin itself. This last change explains why older women, whose ovaries no longer secrete hormones, often use skin creams that contain estrogens. In fact in one unusual case, a six-year-old girl who had begun to show signs of puberty was found to have been eating her grandmother's skin cream. The cream contained enough estrogen to stimulate the changes that normally occur several years later.

Estrogens do not stimulate the growth of pubic and axillary hair in women; AD is responsible for this change. AD is produced not by the ovaries, but by the *adrenal glands,* which sit on top of the kidneys.

The activational effects of sex hormones on the internal sex organs and the external genitalia are sex-specific; that is, testosterone can cause the maturation of the penis and scrotum only in a male—only a male possesses the genetic potential for these

structures. But males and females are bipotential for many secondary sex characteristics; both males and females can grow breasts, a beard, or wider hips or develop strong muscles or a deep voice. This bipotentiality remains with us all our lives.

For example, occasionally a man must take estrogen pills to suppress a cancer whose growth depends on testosterone. His testes will stop secreting testosterone, and he will soon become *sterile* and *impotent;* that is, he will not produce sperm and will be unable to have an erection. His beard will disappear, deposits of fat will grow on his hips, his skin will become smoother and softer, and his breasts will begin to grow. However, if he was previously heterosexual he will not begin to develop homosexual tendencies. And his voice will remain low; a man's larynx enlarges at puberty, and the change is permanent.

A woman who receives testosterone pills will grow facial hair and her voice will deepen permanently. Her skin will become more coarse and wrinkled, and she will stop ovulating and menstruating. Her breasts will not change much in size, just as a man's larynx does not get smaller if he takes estrogen. The woman's sex drive will not be reduced; in fact, it may even increase, even though her bodily changes are likely to make her less attractive to men. As we shall see, some data suggest that women's sex drive is stimulated by androgens.

Interim summary: Early prenatal development of males and females is identical until the Y chromosome of males, through the activity of the H-Y antigen produced by one of its genes, causes the bipotential primordial gonads to develop as testes. Females lack a Y chromosome, and the absence of the H-Y antigen permits the primordial gonads to become ovaries. The fetal gonads secrete testosterone and Müllerian inhibiting substance, which cause the male Wolffian system to develop and the Müllerian system to regress. Lacking these hormones, the Müllerian system of the female fetus (or the prenatally castrated male fetus) develops. The bipotential external genitalia similarly develop into the male or female form, depending on the presence or absence of testosterone.

Puberty begins the final phase of sexual maturation. It is initiated by the secretion of gonadotropic releasing hormones by the hypothalamus, which cause the anterior pituitary gland to secrete the gonadotropic hormones, which, in turn, stimulate the ovaries and testes to produce estradiol and testosterone. These hormones cause the internal sex organs and external genitalia to assume their adult form and function, and promote the development of secondary sex characteristics.

EFFECTS OF SEX HORMONES ON BEHAVIOR

ORGANIZATIONAL EFFECTS OF PRENATAL ANDROGENIZATION

As we have seen, a fetus will become physically female, regardless of chromosomal sex, unless it is androgenized. Androgens also appear to affect behavior.

Organizational Effects on Sexual Behavior
Evidence of the effects of prenatal androgenization on sexual behavior comes largely from research with rats, mice, and hamsters. These animals are ideal subjects for such research, because much of the androgenization of male rodents occurs after they are born. In contrast, most other male mammals

(including humans) are androgenized long before birth. Mice, rats, and hamsters are born in a very immature form; they actually look like fetuses. (See **Figure 7.8.**) Thus, castration of a male rat soon after birth is roughly equivalent to prenatal castration of most other mammals. The rat that is castrated early will develop female-like genitals. Even if the animal receives injections of testosterone when it reaches adulthood, it will not attempt to mount and copulate with a receptive female rat. However, if it is given the appropriate female sex hormones when it reaches adulthood, it will respond to a male rat with normal female sexual behavior. Thus, nature's tendency is to produce a female whose sexual behavior is also female.

On the other hand, if we remove the ovaries of a female rat and give it an injection of testosterone immediately after birth, the animal will act like a normal male when it grows up. That is, if we give it further injections of testosterone as an adult it

FIGURE 7.8   A female mouse carrying one of her newborn offspring.

will mount and copulate with a receptive female. The injection of testosterone immediately after birth androgenizes the rat's sexual behavior. (See **Figure 7.9**.)

There are two types of behavioral androgenization: *masculinization* and *defeminization*. Masculinization is the organization of male sexual behavior—responding to a receptive female by mounting her and engaging in pelvic thrusting. Defeminization is the abolition of the tendency to engage in female sexual behavior—responding to a male by presenting the hindquarters, arching the back, and moving the tail to the side. These two types of behavioral androgenization occur at different times in different animals—either prenatally or shortly after birth (Plapinger and McEwen, 1978). The term "defeminization" is used because without the action of androgens on the developing brain the sexual behavior of a male rodent will be female.

FIGURE 7.9   Experimental androgenization of rats.

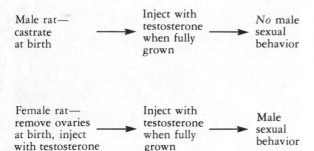

FIGURE 7.10   The experiment by Nadler (1968).

The behaviorally organizing effects of testosterone, masculinization and defeminization, appear to take place in the brain. Nadler (1968) castrated male rats and placed a very small amount of testosterone directly in the hypothalamus. The small amount of testosterone had no effect on the animals' genitals; these became female. However, the testosterone did androgenize the brain; when these rats received injections of testosterone in adulthood, they attempted to copulate with receptive females. Control subjects, who were also castrated at birth but received placebo injections in the hypothalamus or injections of testosterone in parts of the brain other than the hypothalamus, did not attempt to copulate. (See **Figure 7.10**.)

Another study lends further support to the conclusion that androgens exert an organizational effect on gender-related behavior. Beach (1970) androgenized female beagle dogs. As you know, adult male and female dogs urinate differently: the female squats, the male lifts its leg. The androgenized females acted like males, lifting a leg to urinate. Like males, they also urinated more frequently, as if to mark every tree and post in their environment.

The available evidence, which will be reviewed in a later section, suggests that prenatal androgenization of the brain does affect gender-related social behavior in humans, but not *sexual* behavior. The explanation for the species difference in the effects on sexual behavior lies in the difference between human sexual behavior and the sexual behavior of most other mammals. Most mammals display *sex-*

Male rat—castrated at birth.

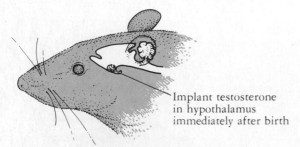

Male rat—castrated at birth.

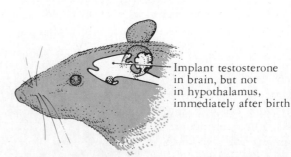

ual dimorphism in their behaviors; that is, male and female sexual behavior are distinct. (*Dimorphic* means "two forms.") The male copulates by mounting the female from behind, inserting his penis, and thrusting back and forth with his pelvis. A female stands rigidly to support the weight of the male, arches her back, and moves her tail (if any), which exposes her genitals. During copulation she remains still; only the male moves.

Human sexual behavior is not nearly so sexually dimorphic. Although the essentials of human copulation are the same as for other mammals—the penis slides in and out of the vagina—the body movements that accomplish this are not at all stereotyped. Men and women can have intercourse in a variety of positions, and the man, the woman, or both of them can produce movement of the penis within the vagina. Either sex can perform pelvic thrusts, and either sex can hold still while the other moves. Nor does the sexual behavior of male and female homosexuals differ in most important respects from that of their heterosexual counterparts. Humans receive sexual gratification by stimulation of their genitals. Both heterosexuals and homosexuals may engage in oral and manual stimulation of their partner's genitals. The difference consists in the gender of the person's partner (and, consequently, the nature of the partner's genitals).

The question that we should ask, then, is this: Does naturally occurring prenatal androgenization "masculinize" a human male, making it likely that he will respond sexually to females when he reaches puberty, and also "defeminize" him, making it unlikely that he will respond sexually to other males? Prenatal androgenization causes the development of male internal sex organs and genitalia, and that fact in itself necessarily affects sexual behavior. But evidence indicating that prenatal androgenization helps determine sexual preference in humans is weak.

Gender-related Differences in the Human Brain

Although studies have clearly established that prenatal androgenization affects brain development in a variety of animals (Goy and McEwen, 1980), information about gender-related differences in the structure of the human brain remains scanty, and none of the observed brain differences appear to be related to sexual behavior or to gender-related social behavior. For example, Wada, Clarke, and

Hamm (1975) found a small difference between males and females in the average size of two different cortical areas of the brain. Similarly, de Lacoste-Utamsing and Holloway (1982) found significant differences in the shape of the corpus callosum, the band of white matter that connects the two cerebral hemispheres.

There is evidence that male and female human brains differ in their degree of asymmetry; the functions of the right and left hemispheres tend to differ more in males than in females. For example, McGlone (1977) found that the effects of left-hemisphere lesions (produced by strokes or tumors) are more severe in men than women. Men tend to suffer more loss of verbal skills. Presumably, women's verbal abilities involve the right hemisphere to a greater extent than do men's; therefore, when women sustain damage to the left hemisphere, they can use the remaining functions in the right hemisphere more effectively.

The differences appear to account for the general tendencies of women to excel in verbal skills and of men to excel in skills related to spatial perception (Harris, 1978). Because differences in male and female social behavior are small when compared with the more rigidly stereotyped behaviors of other animals, any corresponding differences in brain structure are probably subtle. Differences in sexual preference (that is, the preference for a sexual partner of a particular gender) probably involve subcortical brain mechanisms, perhaps in the vicinity of the hypothalamus, and these areas have not yet been studied carefully in humans.

Organizational Effects on Social Behavior

People are justifiably sensitive to statements that behavioral differences in males and females are biologically determined because these alleged differences have been used to justify the exclusion of women from positions of status and power in society and ensure the persistence of a complacent population of homemakers. Most cultures, including our own, have some degree of bias against women's achievement in professions that are considered "masculine." (See **Figure 7.11**.) In general, girls are expected to be more interested in motherhood and homemaking, while boys are expected to be more independent and career-oriented. Although this cultural stereotype is changing, it continues to affect men's and women's

FIGURE 7.11   This photograph captures people's
attention because it is still unusual for women to
occupy positions of authority over men.

FIGURE 7.12   When boys and girls conform to
cultural stereotypes, is their behavior solely
determined by learning and imitation or are there also
innate dispositions to engage in different kinds of
activities?

self-image and aspirations. Young boys still tend
to play more roughly and actively and take more
of an interest in mechanical devices; young girls
still tend to play more quietly. Are these differences in behavior solely a result of socialization, or
does biology, in the form of prenatal androgenization, also play a role? (See **Figure 7.12**.)

The following evidence, though still inconclusive, suggests that prenatal androgens, through their
organizational effect on the developing brain, can

influence social behavior. However, this influence is not very strong.

EFFECTS ON FEMALE SOCIAL BEHAVIOR AND GENDER IDENTITY   Normally, a female human fetus is not exposed to significant amounts of androgens, so her body develops female characteristics. However, several years ago a number of female fetuses were inadvertently exposed to a chemical that partially androgenized them. Their mothers, who had a history of spontaneous abortions (miscarriages), were given a synthetic progesteronelike chemical to support their pregnancy. *Progesterone* (*pro,* "for"; *gestare,* "to carry") is the principal pregnancy hormone. It stimulates growth of the lining of the uterus and suppresses the activity of the muscles that ultimately contract to expel the newborn infant. If progesterone levels are too low, the muscular wall of the uterus begins to contract prematurely, and the fetus is aborted. Therefore, drugs with progesteronelike effects are sometimes used to help a woman complete a pregnancy successfully.

Unfortunately, a synthetic progesteronelike drug that was used during the 1950s had unexpected side effects: it caused partial androgenization of female fetuses (Money and Ehrhardt, 1972). Boys were unaffected, but some girl babies were born with an enlarged clitoris and partly fused labia majora. (You will remember that these genitals arise from the same primordial tissue that produces the penis and scrotum; see Figure 7.5 on page 261.) The masculinization of the genitals was corrected surgically and does not appear to have caused any problems. The internal sex organs were normal.

Money and Ehrhardt studied ten of these girls to determine whether their early exposure to an adrogenizing hormone had any effect on their subsequent behavior. They also studied a group of fifteen girls with *adrenogenital syndrome,* a disorder caused by secretion of abnormally high amounts of androgens by the adrenal glands before and after birth. The hypersecretion of androgens is corrected by medication or surgical removal of the adrenal glands, but the prenatal effects cause some masculinization.

Money and Ehrhardt compared the interests of both groups with the interests of a control group of normal girls. Normal children show a wide range in interests; some boys and girls have mostly "masculine" interests, others have mostly "feminine" interests, and still others are in between. The sample of girls in the control group showed a considerable variation in interests. In contrast, the ten androgenized girls and the fifteen girls with adrenogenital syndrome were on the "masculine" side of the continuum; for example, they referred to themselves as "tomboys," they preferred vigorous athletic sports to quiet play, and did not like to wear "feminine" clothing. They also preferred to play with boys rather than other girls. (See **Table 7.2.**)

TABLE 7.2   Sex-role related behavior in fetally androgenized girls (compared with a matched group of control subjects)

Behavioral signs	Progesteronelike drug	Adrenogenital syndrome
Known to self and mother as "tomboy"	More	More
Satisfaction with female sex role	Same	Less
Athletic interests and skills	More	More
Preference for male instead of female playmates	Prefer male	Prefer male
Childhood fights	Same	Same
Preference for slacks instead of dresses	Prefer slacks	Prefer slacks
Interests in jewelry, perfume, and hair styling	Same	Same

Adapted from Money, J., and Ehrhardt, A. *Man & Woman, Boy & Girl.* Baltimore: Johns Hopkins University Press, 1972.

There was nothing unusual about these children as individuals. All were happy to be girls and accepted their gender identity as female. Their social behavior was not abnormal; after all, many girls are bored by dolls and prefer to play very active games. And today many girls in North America prefer slacks to skirts and dresses. But the fact that *as a group* the androgenized girls differed significantly from the control group suggests that the androgens had an effect on their brains, and thus on their behavior.

◆   Prenatal androgenization does appear to increase the incidence of masculine behavior in female rhesus monkeys. Young male monkeys are much more likely than females to initiate periods of play, to engage in rough-and-tumble play, and to make playful threat gestures. Males also tend to mount other juvenile monkeys in a way that mimics adult sexual behavior, whereas females tend to present their hindquarters. Goy and Goldfoot (1973) administered androgens to pregnant rhesus monkeys and when the female babies were born, isolated them from their mothers, so that the mothers would not notice their daughters' masculinized genitals and somehow behave differently toward them. The androgenized females acted like males. Their play behavior was more aggressive, and they tended to mount other monkeys more than to present themselves.

There is no doubt that androgens can affect the brain development of various species of laboratory animals. Numerous studies have shown that some neurons develop differently if androgens are present. Presumably, prenatal androgenization causes some differences in the neural connections within the human brain. However, no research has shown that particular regions control a person's interest in "masculine" versus "feminine" activities.

What we are left with is the fact that androgens can alter the development of brain cells, and the hypotheses that prenatal androgenization can "bias" a person's social behavior toward the masculine end of the continuum. Possibly, a slight modification in the brain of an androgenized girl makes her become more active physically, and this increased activity brings her into the company of boys and into their active games.

The case of the prenatally androgenized girls does not provide conclusive evidence that andro-

gens have organizational effects on behavior. The girls' parents knew that the infants had been affected by the drug or the adrenal hormone, because their genitals were somewhat masculinzed. Possibly as a result of this knowledge they treated their daughters somewhat differently, and this treatment affected their behavior. However, it seems more likely that the parents would instead emphasize their daughters' identities as girls.

◆ EFFECTS ON A FEMALE'S SEXUAL PREFERENCES   A follow-up study of the androgenized girls found that as women, ranging in age from sixteen to twenty-seven years, they were heterosexual in sexual orientation (Money and Mathews, 1982). Most of the women were married or were dating men. Their sexual responses were also normal. Of the six women who could be questioned about their sexuality, four had engaged in intercourse or oral-genital stimulation with men. One eighteen-year-old reported having had no erotic experience, including masturbation. The other women appear to have experienced normal orgasm. Thus, we can conclude that although prenatal androgenization may have a small effect on a girl's social behavior, it does not appear to prevent a normal response to sexual stimulation or the formation of heterosexual attachments in adulthood. In other words, there is no evidence that prenatal androgenization "defeminizes" a woman's sexual preference as it does in female rodents.

Prenatal Androgenization versus Socialization

Males and females are treated differently from birth onward. Comments about newborn babies tend to be sex-typed; observers talk about the masculine appearance and behavior of male babies and the feminine appearance and behavior of female babies (Oakley, 1972). Children constantly hear comments such as "Boys will be boys" or "Girls don't do that," and adults encourage them to play with particular kinds of toys. (See **Figure 7.13.**) Television programs, advertisements, and stories (including fairy tales read to very young children) convey the information that males and females are different in interests and behavior. With such powerful and pervasive social stimuli it should not be surprising that children exhibit gender-related behaviors at a very early age. Although it is possible

FIGURE 7.13   Boys and girls are often encouraged to behave in different ways.

that sexual preference in adulthood is strongly biased by prenatal sex hormones, most gender-related behaviors are undoubtedly learned through socialization.

One famous study suggested that socialization can not only reinforce the effects of a person's prenatal hormone exposure, but even reverse them. Money and Ehrhardt (1972) reported the case of a seven-month-old baby boy born in 1963 who was brought to a physician for circumcision—removal of the fold of skin that covers the glans penis. The skin was to be cut with a cautery, a special surgical instrument that cuts with a spark of electricity. Unfortunately, the device was turned up too high, and when the physician applied it, the boy's penis burned up in a flash of smoke. Ten months later, after much consultation and soul-searching, they decided to raise their son as a girl. They renamed the child and undertook the first of several stages of plastic surgery. The mother reported later: "I started dressing her not in dresses, but, you know, in little pink slacks and frilly blouses . . . and letting her hair grow" (Money and Ehrhardt, 1972, p. 119). The child accepted the sex reassignment well, taking on characteristics that she perceived as feminine. She became neat and tidy. According

to her mother, "She likes for me to wipe her face. She doesn't like to be dirty, and yet my son is quite different. I can't wash his face for anything. . . . She seems to be daintier. Maybe it's because I encourage it. . . . One thing that really amazes me is that she is so feminine" (pp. 119–120).

The son she referred to is the identical twin brother of the child raised as a girl. As a genetically identical twin who was also normally androgenized prenatally, he has been an ideal control subject. The children have differed only in the way they are dressed and in the way other people treat them.

For a decade this study was taken as evidence that socialization can undo the effects of prenatal androgenization. However, Diamond (1982) provides evidence that the child's later social development was not as smooth as it appeared earlier. The young woman was teased by other children and called "cavewoman," apparently because of her masculine gait. She does not appear to be happy; she has diffficulty making friends and finds it difficult to accept her gender identity as a female.

Of course, the facts of this case do not necessarily prove that socialization *cannot* reverse the effects of prenatal androgenization. After all, there can be many reasons for a person's unhappiness and difficulty in making friends. But this outcome weakens the conclusion that socialization can undo the effects of prenatal androgenization.

ANDROGEN INSENSITIVITY SYNDROME: FEMALES WITH MALE GENES

◆ You will recall that hormones produce their organizational and activational effects by stimulating receptors located in the cells of target tissue. There are specific receptors for androgens, for estrogens, and for progesterone. These receptors are found in cells in many organs, including the brain, sex organs, genitals, fat tissue, muscle, and skin. The appropriate hormone produces changes in the cells by stimulating the receptors.

Because of a genetic defect, the cells of people with *androgen insensitivity syndrome* do not possess androgen receptors. These people are genetically XY males, but they develop as females. (See **Figure 7.14.**) Under the influence of the Y chromosome, their primordial gonads develop into testes, and their testes secrete androgens. But because the cells of their bodies possess no androgen receptors, the hormones fail to masculinize their internal sex organs or genitals. Their genitals are essentially female, although the vagina is often rather shallow. (Corrective surgery can lengthen the vagina, if necessary.)

In most cases, the syndrome is not recognized at birth, because physicians rarely perform careful pelvic examinations of infant girls, and these children are reared as girls. Their behavior is indistinguishable from that of normal XX females. As girls, they show similar preferences in the choice of clothing and adornments, playmates, games, and toys. They happily accept their gender as female.

All testes produce some estradiol along with a much larger amount of testosterone. In normal males, the effects of the testosterone dominate. But in people with androgen insensitivity syndrome, it is as if the testosterone does not exist. Therefore, testicular estrogen feminizes them at puberty, and they become women. As adults, they function as normal women, although they do not menstruate and cannot have children, because they lack ovaries and a functional uterus. Most of them regard their breasts, clitoris, and vagina as sexually responsive

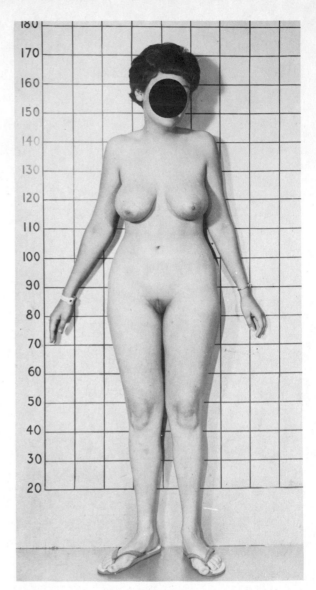

FIGURE 7.14   An XY female with androgen insensitivity syndrome. (From Money, J., and Ehrhardt, A.A., *Man & Woman, Boy & Girl.* Copyright 1972 by The Johns Hopkins University Press, Baltimore, Maryland. By permission.)

regions, and most report that they achieve orgasm in sexual intercourse with men.

TURNER'S SYNDROME: THE LACK OF FETAL HORMONES

◆ People with a chromosomal abnormality known as the XO condition, or *Turner's syndrome,* have only one sex chromosome rather than two. With only one X chromosome, neither testes nor ovaries develop from the primordial gonads, which remain as undifferentiated streaks of tissue in the adult. Therefore, the fetus produces no gonadal sex hormones. Following the rule that nature's tendency is to create a female, the person develops feminine internal sex organs and genitals.

Turner's syndrome is typically not recognized at birth, because the baby looks like a normal girl. However, when the time for puberty comes, the girl shows no signs of maturation except for the growth of pubic and axillary hair. (These, you will recall, are stimulated by the androgen AD.) With proper medical diagnosis and administration of estrogen, the girl will reach sexual maturity.

The lack of prenatal fetal sex hormones has very little effect on the subsequent behavior of girls with Turner's syndrome. Ehrhardt, Greenberg, and Money (1970) compared the behavior of fifteen of these girls with matched controls and found no difference on most measures. In fact, on three measures (athletic interests, fighting, and interest

TABLE 7.3 Sex-role-related behavior in girls with Turner's syndrome

Behavioral signs	Comparison with matched control subjects
Known to self and mother as "tomboy"	Same
Satisfaction with female sex role	Same
Athletic interests and skills	Less
Preference for male instead of female playmates	Same
Childhood fights	Less
Preference for slacks instead of dresses	Same
Interest in jewelry, perfume, and hair styling	More

Adapted from Money, J., and Ehrhardt, A. *Man & Woman, Boy & Girl*. Baltimore: Johns Hopkins University Press, 1972.

in personal adornment), the girls with Turner's syndrome were more "feminine" than the controls. (See **Table 7.3**.) Clearly, a female fetus does not need to produce its own ovarian sex hormones to become physically and behaviorally female.

ACTIVATIONAL EFFECTS OF SEX HORMONES ON BEHAVIOR

Effects of Androgens

As we saw earlier, testosterone activates sexual behavior of male rodents. The same is true for all male mammals that have been studied, including humans. The ability to have an erection and engage in sexual intercourse depends on the presence of testosterone, either from functioning testes or from injections of the hormone.

Davidson, Camargo, and Smith (1979) performed a carefully controlled double-blind study of the effects of testosterone on the sexual behavior of men whose testes failed to secrete normal amounts of androgens. The men were given monthly injections of a placebo or one of two different doses of a longlasting form of testosterone. Compared with control injections, the testosterone had a large and statistically significant effect on the total number of erections and attempts at intercourse during the month following the injection, and the larger dose produced more of an effect than did the smaller dose. Thus, we may conclude that testosterone definitely affects male sexual performance.

If a man is castrated (the testes removed), his sex drive will inevitably decline. Usually he first loses the ability to ejaculate, then the ability to achieve an erection (Bermant and Davidson, 1974). But studies have shown that some men lose these abilities soon after castration, whereas others retain at least some level of sexual potency for many months. Injections or pills of testosterone quickly restores potency. It is possible that the amount of sexual experience prior to castration affects performance afterward. Rosenblatt and Aronson (1958) found that male cats who had copulated frequently before castration were able to perform sexually for much longer periods of time after the surgery. Perhaps the same is true for men.

Environment can affect testosterone levels: sexual activity raises the level, and stress lowers it. Even the *anticipation* of sexual activity can affect testosterone secretion. One careful observer (Anonymous, 1970) worked on a remote island, far from any women, and measured his beard growth every day by shaving with an electric razor and weighing the clippings. Just before his periodic trip to London his beard grew faster. Since the rate of beard growth depends upon testosterone levels, the anticipation of sexual activity in London appears to have increased his testosterone production.

Testosterone affects sex drive, but it does not determine the object of sexual desire. A homosexual man who receives injections of testosterone will not suddenly become interested in women. If the testosterone has any effect, it will be to increase his interest in sexual contact with other men.

Although the evidence shows clearly that testosterone affects men's sexual performance, we humans are uniquely emancipated from the biological effects of hormones in a special way. Not all human sexual activity requires an erect penis. A man does not need testosterone to be able to kiss and caress his partner or to engage in other noncoital activi-

ties. Men who have had to be castrated and who cannot receive injections of testosterone for medical reasons report continued sexual activity with their partners. We must remember that for humans sexual activity is not limited to coitus. (See **Figure 7.15**.)

It appears that androgens also activate sex drive in women. Waxenberg, Drellich, and Sutherland (1959) observed that women whose adrenal glands had been surgically removed because of cancer showed a decline in sexual activity and desire. The adrenal glands secrete a variety of hormones, including the androgens, androstenedione (AD) and testosterone. Of course, factors unrelated to the loss of the adrenal glands may have caused this decline. However, Schon and Sutherland (1960) have confirmed the importance of adrenal hormones. They observed that removal of the anterior pituitary gland, which causes a decrease in the hormonal output of the adrenal glands, also diminishes women's sex drive. (See **Figure 7.16**.)

There is other evidence that women's androgen

FIGURE 7.15   Human sexuality includes more than intercourse.

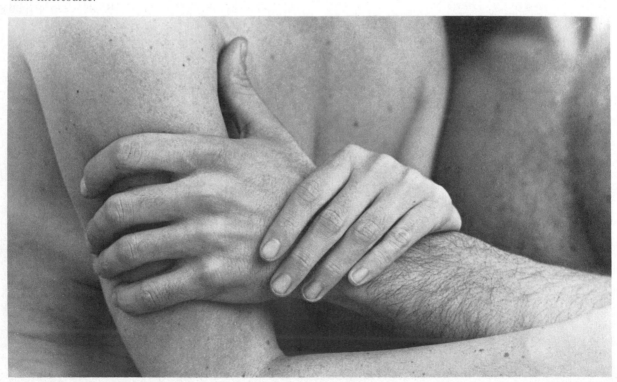

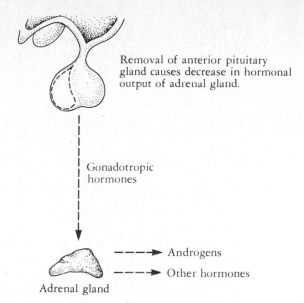

Removal of anterior pituitary gland causes decrease in hormonal output of adrenal gland.

Gonadotropic hormones

- - - -> Androgens

- - - -> Other hormones

Adrenal gland

FIGURE 7.16   Removal of the anterior pituitary gland decreases the secretion of androgens from the adrenal glands.

levels are correlated with their sexual desire. Salmon and Geist (1943) reported that testosterone has a stimulating effect on sexual desire and on the sensitivity of the clitoris to touch. Money and Ehrhardt (1972) reported that many women athletes who took steroids to increase their muscular strength reported an increase in sexual desire. (These steroids mimic some of the effects of androgens.) Persky, Lief, Strauss, Miller, and O'Brien (1978) studied the sexual activity of eleven married couples ranging in age from twenty-one to thirty-one. The subjects kept daily records of their sexual feelings and behavior and the experimenters measured their blood levels of testosterone twice a week. Couples were more likely to engage in intercourse when the woman's testosterone level was at a peak. In addition, the women reported finding intercourse more gratifying during these times.

In addition to these observational studies, carefully controlled experiments with female monkeys have demonstrated the role of androgens in female sexual activity. Everitt and Herbert (1969) administered a synthetic hormone that suppressed the secretion of all hormones by the adrenal glands. The synthetic hormone itself had no androgenic activity. The sexual behavior of these monkeys declined; they stopped presenting their hindquarters

to male monkeys and began to refuse their sexual advances. Injection of testosterone reversed these effects; the monkey's sexual interest and behavior returned. Together with the previously cited data, these results support the conclusion that androgens have an activational effect on a women's sex drive.

Effects of Progesterone and Estrogen

Although there is no evidence that female sex hormones have organizational effects on behavior, they do have activational effects. Both a normal female rat and a male rat that is castrated before the critical period of androgenization will exhibit female sexual behavior in adulthood, but only if progesterone and estrogen are present (for the castrated male this is accomplished through injections). The levels of these two sex hormones fluctuate during the *estrous cycle* of a female rat. An estrous cycle is roughly equivalent to a menstrual cycle, although it is much shorter—four to five days, compared with approximately twenty-eight. The female will receive the advances of a male only when her estrogen level is high. She will stand still while the male approches her. If he attempts to mount her, she will arch her back and move her tail to the side, giving him access to her genitals. In fact an estrous female often does not wait for the male to take the initiative—she engages in seductive behaviors such as hopping and wiggling her ears.

FIGURE 7.17   Changes in an ovarian follicle during a menstrual cycle. The follicle matures, discharges the ovum, and develops into a corpus luteum.

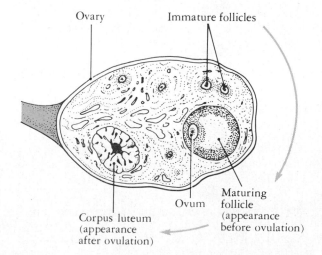

Ovary   Immature follicles

Maturing follicle (appearance before ovulation)

Ovum

Corpus luteum (appearance after ovulation)

These behaviors usually induce sexual activity by the male (McClintock and Adler, 1978).

A castrated female rat (one whose ovaries have been removed) is normally nonreceptive, even hostile, to the advances of an eager male. However, if she is given injections of estrogen and progesterone to duplicate the hormonal condition of the receptive part of her estrous cycle, she will receive the male or go after him. This is true whether her ovaries were removed immediately after birth or later in life, so ovarian hormones are not needed for organizational effects. If castrated before the critical period of androgenization, a male rat injected with estrogen and progesterone will show

FIGURE 7.18   A schematic diagram of the menstrual cycle. *A*: Secretion of follicle-stimulating hormone. *B*: Secretion of estrogen. *C*: Secretion of luteinizing hormone. *D*: Secretion of some estrogen and a large amount of progesterone. *F*: With menstruation, production of ovarian hormones stops.

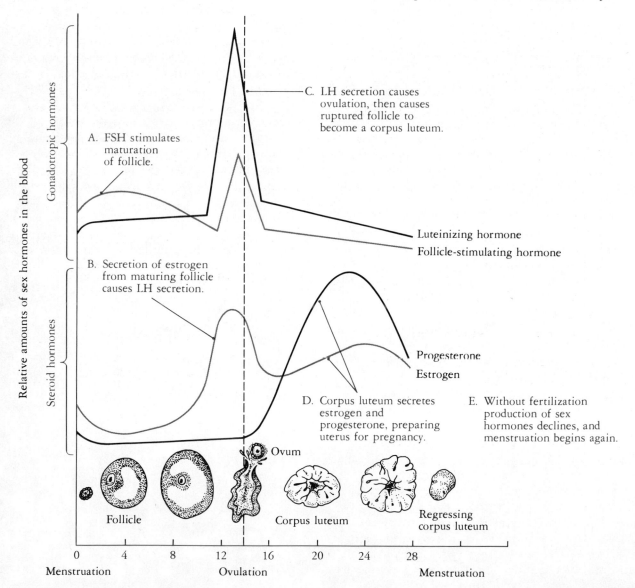

similar behavior—complete with hopping, ear-wiggling, and presentation of the hindquarters to a male that shows sexual advances.

Women and other female primates are unique among mammals in their sexual activity: they are potentially willing to engage in sexual behavior at any time during their reproductive cycle. It has been suggested that this phenomenon has made monogamous relationships possible; because the male can look forward to his mate's receptivity at any time during her menstrual cycle, he is less likely to look for other partners. However, some species form monogamous-pair bonds even though they mate during only one season of the year, and most primate species are promiscuous.

Although there is no nonreceptive time during a woman's menstrual cycle, the hormonal fluctuations do tend to affect a woman's sexual desire, though not to the same degree in all women. To understand these effects, we must first understand the menstrual cycle itself.

At the beginning of a cycle (just after the previous menstrual flow has ceased) the pituitary gland secretes gonadotropic hormones (especially one called *FSH,* or *follicle-stimulating hormone*), which stimulate the development of an *ovarian follicle,* a little bubble of cells in the ovary. Inside this bubble is a ripening ovum, the egg cell. (See **Figures 7.17 and 7.18,A.**) As the follicle matures, it secretes estrogen and a little progesterone.

The estrogen level continues to increase and stimulates the hypothalamus to release a surge of a gonadotropic hormone called *LH* (*luteinizing hormone*). The surge of LH causes the follicle to burst, releasing the ovum into the woman's abdominal cavity. This release is called ovulation. (See **Figure 7.18,B,C.**) The ovum then enters one of the *fimbria,* funnel-shaped structures at the end of the fallopian tubes. (See **Figure 7.19.**) It continues down the fallopian tube, where it may or may not become fertilized by a sperm.

After ovulation, luteinizing hormone causes the ruptured follicle to form a mass of tissue called a *corpus luteum* ("yellow body"). The corpus luteum produces some estrogen and a considerable amount of progesterone. As you recall, progesterone prepares the lining of the uterus for the possible implantation of a fertilized ovum. (See **Figure 7.18,D.**) If the ovum is not fertilized, and therefore is not implanted in the wall of the uterus, the

FIGURE 7.19   After ovulation, the ovum is swept into the fallopian tubes by the fimbria and travels toward the uterus.

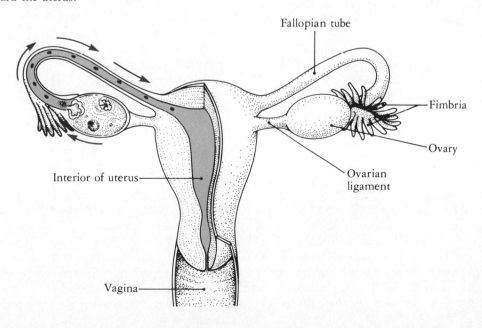

Fallopian tube

Fimbria

Ovary

Ovarian ligament

Interior of uterus

Vagina

corpus luteum stops producing estrogen and progesterone, and the lining of the uterus sloughs off, causing menstruation to begin. (See **Figure 7.18,E.**)

In summary, the estrogen level rises to a peak at midcycle, when ovulation occurs. After ovulation, progesterone begins to dominate, but some estrogen is still present. Toward the end of the cycle, the levels of both estrogen and progesterone fall, and menstruation begins.

Many women report having two periods of peak sexuality: at midcycle, around the time of ovulation, and just before and during menstruation. They also report two different kinds of sexual desire at these times; at midcycle they feel a need to be occupied sexually—to be possessed. Around the time of menstruation they feel more sexually aggressive; they want to envelop and "capture" the penis (Money and Ehrhardt, 1972).

Adams, Gold, and Burt (1978) provided clear evidence for the midcycle peak in a woman's sexuality. Women who were not taking birth control pills were more likely to masturbate or to initiate sexual activity with the partners around the time of ovulation. In contrast, women who took birth control pills, which prevent ovulation, did not show a midcycle peak.

Cycles in sexuality are also seen in other female primates. Loy (1970) observed the behavior of rhesus monkeys in a special free-ranging colony on Cayo Santiago, Puerto Rico. Nonpregnant females showed two peaks of sexuality—one at midcycle and another around the time of menstruation.

An interesting study by Van de Castle and Smith (1971) found that women's dreams tend to vary during the menstrual cycle in ways related to changes in sexual desire. During the menstrual phase (the time when women tend to feel more aggressive sexually) the women had more dreams of aggression directed toward males, but not toward females, and of friendly advances toward both males and females. During the nonmenstrual phase, they had more dreams of experiencing aggression from men, but not from other women, and of many more encounters with men, aggressive or not. These results support the conclusion that hormonal changes during the menstrual cycle have an effect on a woman's sexuality.

◆ Progesterone appears to have a suppressive effect on the sexual behavior of a variety of female mammals, especially those with long estrous cycles or menstrual cycles, such as guinea pigs and monkeys (Bermant and Davidson, 1974). Low doses of progesterone stimulate sexual receptivity in these animals, but high doses suppress it.

The suppressive effect of high doses of progesterone is not as clear-cut in women as in other female mammals. Progesterone levels are highest between ovulation and menstruation, and for many women this is the low point of sexual desire. Furthermore, some women experience a decrease in sex drive if they take birth control pills containing progesteronelike hormones (James, 1971). Others experience either no effect or an effect so slight that the removal of their fear of pregnancy counteracts it (Gambrell, Bernard, Sanders, Vanderburg, and Buxton, 1976).

Unlike most other female mammals, women's sex drive does not depend on the presence of ovarian hormones. During menopause, when the ovaries suddenly cease to secrete hormones, women experience various uncomfortable symptoms, such as hot flashes, headaches, and depression, which can temporarily interfere with sex drive. The loss of estradiol tends to make the walls of the vagina thinner, and the decrease in vaginal secretions can make intercourse somewhat painful. However, with the use of a lubricant jelly, intercourse can be just as satisfying as it was before the ovaries ceased to function. Masters and Johnson (1966) report that frequent intercourse itself tends to retard the effects of menopause on the vagina. In fact, with pregnancy no longer a possibility, many women report an *increase* in desire for sexual activity. Occasionally a woman's ovaries must be removed during her reproductive years, but the "surgical menopause" that results is no different from the natural one; her sex drive is not directly affected.

Interim summary: No fetal gonadal hormones are necessary for the development of normal female sexual behavior in any mammal that has been studied, including humans. Androgens have organizational effects on sexual behavior, just as they do on physical development. At least in rodents, these hormones cause masculinization and defeminization by altering the brain's development. The activational effects of hormones refer to their effects in adulthood: androgens produce male sexual behavior in masculinized animals and estrogen and progesterone produce female sexual behavior in animals that have not been defeminized.

The strong organizational effect of prenatal androgenization in laboratory animals contrasts with data from humans. There is evidence that prenatal androgenization is responsible for some of the differences in social behavior of human males and females, but the effect is undoubtedly much smaller than that produced by the environment. Prenatally androgenized women report heterosexual preference and normal sex drive. In humans, androgens activate male sexual behavior, and apparently female sexual behavior as well. Estrogen and progesterone have an influence on the sex drive of some women, but women's sexual behavior does not depend on these hormones.

EFFECTS OF PHEROMONES

Another class of compounds beside sex hormones has a profound effect on the behavior and reproductive physiology of many species of animals. Recently investigators have studied the possibility that these substances, called *pheromones,* might have effects on humans, as well.

◆   The word *pheromone* was coined by Karlson and Luscher (1959) from the Greek *pherein,* "to transfer," and *hormon,* "to excite." Pheromones are chemicals released by one animal that affect the physiology or behavior of another. Usually, a pheromone is detected by the olfactory system (sense of smell), but in some cases it can be eaten or absorbed through the skin. Pheromones serve as sexual attractants in a number of species. For example, many female insects release a pheromone that is carried on the wind and attracts males from a great distance away.

Several phenomena related to sex pheromones in mammals influence preferences for sex partners, pregnancy, and estrous or menstrual cycles. For example, Mainardi (cited by Bruce, 1960a) reported that female mice show a preference for males of other genetic strains as sex partners. This preference appears to be controlled by the male's odor. Its selective value is probably to increase the likelihood of outbreeding (which is genetically healthier).

The *Lee-Boot effect* (van der Lee and Boot, 1955)

and the *Whitten effect* (Whitten, 1959) demonstrated that females can influence each other's estrous cycles. Female mice housed together in groups of four tend to become *pseudopregnant;* that is, although they are virgins, their endocrine systems respond as if the mice were pregnant (Lee-Boot effect). If mice are housed in larger groups their estrous cycles become longer and longer, and eventually stop (Whitten effect). These effects are controlled by pheromones in the urine of the mice; the presence of female urine alone can cause the phenomena.

The Lee-Boot and Whitten effects occur only when females are housed apart from males. If a normal male mouse is present, an odor in his urine causes their cycles to resume and to become synchronized (Bronson and Whitten, 1968). The urine of a castrated male mouse has no effect.

The *Bruce effect* (Bruce, 1960a, 1960b) is a particularly interesting phenomenon: when a recently impregnated female mouse encounters a normal male mouse other than the one that impregnated her, the pregnancy is very likely to fail. This effect is also caused by a substance secreted in the urine of intact males, but not males that have been castrated. Thus a male mouse is able to kill the genetic material of another male and impregnate the female himself.

It appears that at least some of these phenomena occur in humans. For example, Collet, Wertenberger, and Fiske (1954) observed a rather high percentage of unusually long menstrual cycles in female college students. The investigators hypothesized that these long cycles reflected normal developmental changes in young women. However, McClintock (1971) noted that most of the women in this study had attended all-female colleges. To determine whether this phenomenon resembled the Whitten effect in female mice, she studied the menstrual cycles of women attending an all-female college. McClintock found that women who spent a significant amount of time together tended to have synchronized cycles—their menstrual periods began within a day or two of each other. In addition, females who regularly spent some time in the presence of males tended to have shorter cycles than those who rarely met males.

Russell, Switz, and Thompson (1977) obtained evidence that women's menstrual cycles synchronize in response to olfactory stimuli, thus suggesting the presence of pheromones. They collected daily samples of underarm sweat from a woman whose presence appeared to influence the synchronization of several women's cycles. The samples were dissolved in alcohol and were swabbed three times each week, in the order in which they were originally taken, on the upper lips of other women. The upper lips of control subjects were swabbed with pure alcohol. The cycles of the women who received the extract began to synchronize. The cycles of those who received the control substance were not affected.

Many investigators have studied the possibility that olfactory stimuli affect sexual attraction in primates. For example, Keverne and Michael (1971) reported that fatty acids secreted by a female monkey's vagina around the time of ovulation made the females more sexually attractive to males, suggesting that the chemicals served as sex-attractant pheromones. This phenomenon would make sense, because it would encourage sexual intercourse during the time the female is most likely to become pregnant. However, Goldfoot, Krevetz, Goy, and Freeman (1976) presented data suggesting that the monkeys in Michael's laboratory *learned* to respond the way they did. If olfactory stimuli had an effect, it was probably because the males were detecting the odor of previously deposited semen. Goldfoot and his colleagues attempted to replicate the results of Keverne and Michael under conditions that would not permit learning to take place, and they failed to obtain evidence for the effects of pheromones. In addition, their analyses indicate that the substances isolated by Keverne and Michael were secreted during the latter part of the menstrual cycle, and not around the time of ovulation. Thus, the evidence that pheromones influence sexual attraction in primates is not at all conclusive.

Some investigators have studied the possibility that odors produced by vaginal secretions may affect a woman's attractiveness. Doty, Ford, Preti, and Huggins (1975) found that both males and females rated these odors as unpleasant, although secretions that were obtained around the time of ovulation were rated as less unpleasant. Thus, a woman's menstrual cycle appears to affect the odor of her vaginal secretions, but there is no direct evidence that these changes increase her attractiveness.

Even though there is currently no evidence that pheromones play a role in sexual attraction in primates, the familiar odor of a sexual partner may have a positive effect on sexual arousal. Although we are not generally conscious of the fact, we can identify other people on the basis of olfactory cues. For example, a study by Russell (1976) found that people were able to distinguish by odor between T-shirts that they had worn and those previously worn by other people. They could also tell whether the unknown owner of a T-shirt was male or female. Thus, it is likely that men and women can learn to be attracted by their partners' characteristic odors. However, this is a different phenomenon from the responses produced by pheromones, which apparently need not be learned.

HUMAN SEXUAL BEHAVIOR

EFFECTS OF EROTIC IMAGERY IN MEN AND WOMEN

◈ Men and women respond in basically the same way to visual and tactual sexual stimuli, but they ap-

FIGURE 7.20   Many women are sexually aroused by photographs of romantic situations such as those found on greeting cards.

pear to differ in the kinds of stimuli, imagery, and fantasy they consider erotic. Sigusch, Schmidt, Reinfeld, and Wiedemann-Sutor (1970) and Schmidt and Sigusch (1970) studied the attitudes and sexual responses of fifty men and women toward sexual stimuli. They measured sexual arousal by monitoring penile erections and vaginal lubrication with electronic sensing equipment.

The subjects looked at pictures of couples in romantic situations, showing affection and kissing, and in explicitly sexual situations, engaging in intercourse. The women reported finding the pictures of romantic situations sexually arousing, and physiological measures confirmed their statements. (See **Figure** 7.20.) However, most of them reported finding the sexually explicit pictures distasteful, even though the monitoring apparatus showed that these pictures also aroused them. Presumably, this distaste is enculturated; many women are taught that it is not proper to show an interest in erotic materials. Thus, some women are likely to avoid erotica even though they can become as stimulated by them as men. The men reported the pictures of sexual behavior to be arousing (and the physiological measurements agreed), but unlike the women, they were not aroused by the romantic pictures.

Money and Ehrhardt (1972) describe the kinds of stimuli to which men and women respond. If a male responds sexually to a picture of an attractive woman, he tends to imagine her as a sex object; figuratively, he takes her out of the picture and uses her. A woman might also respond to an erotic picture of another woman, but in this case she imagines herself in the woman's situation. On the other hand, a picture of a naked man is generally not arousing to heterosexual males *or* females. Evidence from the editor of *Playgirl,* a magazine that features pictures of nude men, confirmed this finding. The editor stated in a television interview that the pictures that elicit the most fan mail from their female readers tend to be those featuring the man in a scene that appears to have some "story" to it. A simple picture of a naked man, however good-looking, does not elicit many letters of admiration.

For many women, the romantic story appears to be at least as important as actual sexual behavior in providing sexual arousal. In fact, Stoller (1970) has characterized romantic stories of the "true confession" type as women's pornography. These stories are very different from pornographic stories preferred by men, and because men tend to write the laws, antipornographic statutes are aimed against the kinds of narratives that appeal to males.

TABLE 7.4   The most prevalent types of sexual fantasies, by sex and sexual preference

Males	Females
Heterosexual	
1. Replacement of established partner	1. Replacement of established partner
2. Forced sexual encounter with female	2. Forced sexual encounter with male
3. Observation of sexual activity	3. Observation of sexual activity
4. Homosexual encounters	4. Idyllic encounters with unknown men
5. Group sex experiences	5. Lesbian encounters
Homosexual	
1. Imagery of male sexual anatomy	1. Forced sexual encounters
2. Forced sexual encounters with males	2. Idyllic encounter with established partner
3. Heterosexual encounters with females	3. Heterosexual encounters
4. Idyllic encounters with unknown men	4. Recall of past sexual experience
5. Group sex experiences	5. Sadistic imagery

Adapted from Masters, W.H., and Johnson, V.E. *Homosexuality in Perspective.* Boston: Little, Brown, 1979.

Masters and Johnson (1979) interviewed heterosexual and homosexual males and females and found
that the subject matter of their sexual fantasies bore
striking similarities, although the gender of the
sex partner in the fantasies differed according to
the person's orientation. (See **Table 7.4.**)

THE HUMAN SEXUAL RESPONSE

William Masters and Virginia Johnson have revolutionized sex research by obtaining real evidence
about a myth-laden topic, the physiology of sex.
(See **Figure 7.21.**) Their direct observations of sexual activity in the laboratory have provided insight
into the human sexual response. (See Masters and
Johnson, 1966; Masters, Johnson, and Kolodny,
1982.)

FIGURE 7.21   William Masters and Virginia
Johnson, a husband-and-wife team of a physician and
a psychologist, are the modern pioneers in research on
human sexuality.

The Male Sexual Response

◆ EXCITEMENT PHASE   The critical sign of sexual
arousal in a man is erection of the penis, because
it most reliably indicates interest in sexual activity
and because it is a prerequisite for sexual intercourse. The penis contains several spongy chambers
that are filled with blood. These chambers are very
elastic, and if blood is pumped into them under
high pressure, they will expand and become rigid.
Normally, the flow of blood into the penis and the
flow out of it are equal. However, sexual arousal
causes the arteries leading into the penis to increase
in diameter, thus increasing the flow of blood
through them. The spongy chambers become distended with blood and the penis becomes large and
rigid.

Probably the most effective stimulus of sexual
arousal is the anticipation of exciting and enjoyable
sexual activity. This anticipation makes sexual contact itself more arousing; the sight of his sex partner and the feel of his partner's skin against his
become intensely pleasurable. Thus sexual arousal
feeds upon itself. Anticipation produces an erection, which makes the penis more sensitive to touch.
If the man's partner caresses his genitals, the erection becomes even more intense, and contact becomes even more exciting and pleasurable.

The *excitement phase* is extremely variable in
its nature and duration. What people do to arouse
each other and how long they do it depend on their
prior experience, their situation, and their mood.

PLATEAU PHASE   The insertion of a man's penis in
his partner's vagina causes another increase in arousal.
The stimulation resulting from the friction between the penis and vagina and the contact of their
bodies bring excitement to a peak level. Masters
and Johnson describe this level as the *plateau phase*
because it can remain at a sustained high level for
a considerable time. Like the excitement phase, the
plateau phase lasts as long as the partners want—
or are able—to continue it.

Physiologically, the plateau phase is characterized by somewhat elevated blood pressure, heart
rate, and rate of respiration. The penis is quite
erect. The scrotum becomes wrinkled by the contraction of small muscles that occupy a layer of the
skin; this wrinkling draws the testes up against the

man's body. For some unknown reason this elevation of the testes is important for the next phase of the male sexual response—orgasm.

ORGASMIC PHASE   Normally, the plateau phase leads to the *orgasmic phase.* During the plateau phase a man normally modulates his activity in order to control his degree of arousal, keeping himself short of orgasm. When this inhibition either fails or is deliberately relaxed, the orgasmic phase begins.

During orgasm, the man's penis ejaculates semen, a thick, viscous liquid containing the sperm. Semen is produced mainly by the seminal vesicles and the *prostate.* (See **Figure 7.22.**) Ejaculation occurs in two phases, *emission* and *expulsion.* During the emission phase, the prostate and seminal vesicles contract, emptying their semen into the urethra, the tube that carries urine or semen through the penis. During the expulsion phase, strong contraction of muscles in the base of the penis propel the semen through the urethra. The ejaculatory muscles contract forcefully several times, at a rate of approximately four contractions every three seconds.

A man can feel both phases of ejaculation. The emission phase provides a feeling of ejaculatory inevitability, a gathering of forces for the expulsion. The first few muscular contractions that force the semen out of the penis provide the peak experience of the sexual response. During this time the man usually stops making pelvic movements, holding himself rigid, with his penis deep in his partner. This response may have direct biological utility in assuring the deposition of semen where it is most likely to cause fertilization. Excitement rapidly falls off, and subsequent contractions of the ejaculatory muscles become less forceful and provide less sensation.

Masters and Johnson found that physiological measures indicate that masturbation often produces

FIGURE 7.22   The male genitourinary system. The seminal vesicles and prostate glands produce most of the fluid portion of semen.

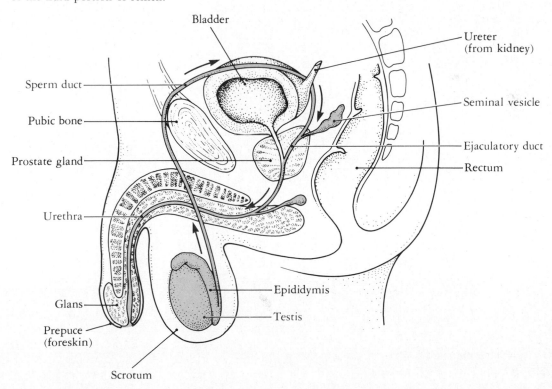

a more intense orgasm than intercourse does, but few men prefer a lonely orgasm to a shared one.

RESOLUTION PHASE   The changes that occurred during the excitement phase and plateau phase reverse themselves during the *resolution phase*. The arteries leading to the penis constrict so that less blood flows in and the penis becomes less rigid. The man relaxes and his heart rate and breathing rate subside. For some time, he is physiologically incapable of arousal and ejaculation. This *refractory period* is variable; the younger the man, the shorter it tends to be.

The Female Sexual Response

◆ EXCITEMENT PHASE   For a woman as for a man, the most effective stimulus for sexual arousal is the

FIGURE 7.23   The response of a woman's sex organs during intercourse. (From Masters, W.H.,

Johnson, V.E., and Kolodny, R.C. *Human Sexuality*. Boston: Little, Brown, 1982.)

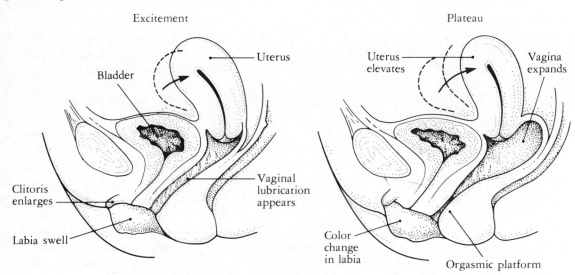

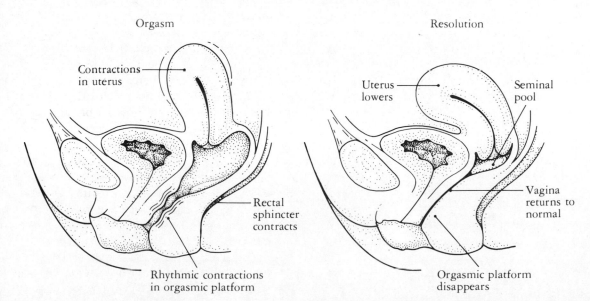

anticipation of a pleasurable sexual encounter. (It has been noted that a person's most important erogenous zone is his or her own brain.) Touch—especially when it involves her breasts, genitals, and thighs—also induces sexual arousal.

The first signs of sexual arousal in a woman are an increase in blood flow to the genitals and the secretion of fluid in the vagina, which serves as a lubricant to facilitate the entry of a penis. Researchers used to believe that a set of glands whose ducts end in the vagina provided the vaginal lubrication, but Masters and Johnson found that these glands provide only a few drops of fluid. By attaching a movie camera to an artificial penis with a built-in camera lens and observing the results as volunteers masturbated with this device, Masters and Johnson found that the lubricating fluid oozes from the walls of the vagina much as sweat oozes from the skin. In fact, in genetic males who have undergone a sex-change operation, even surgically constructed vaginas produce adequate lubrication.

The outer and inner labia also respond during the excitement phase. The outer labia normally meet each other at the midline, covering the opening of the vagina. During the excitement phase they grow thinner and pull apart. The inner labia become swollen with blood; this swelling adds almost a half inch to the length of the vagina. The clitoris, located at the upper junction of the inner labia, also responds to sexual excitement. It becomes engorged with blood, usually increasing in size enough so that the end of it (the *glans clitoris*) protrudes from beneath its hood. (See **Figure 7.23, top left.**)

The breasts also respond to sexual excitement. The nipples become erect, standing out from the surrounding pink or brown areola ("little area") surrounding them, especially if the woman's partner stimulates them. Some women's breasts also grow somewhat larger, although this response is diminished in women who have previously given birth.

PLATEAU PHASE   After intercourse begins, excitement continues to mount, and the woman enters the plateau phase. The inner labia remain swollen with blood and turn dark pink or red. The clitoris retracts behind its hood. The outer third of the vagina becomes much swollen and distended with

blood, causing the formation of what Masters and Johnson call the *orgasmic platform*. (See **Figure 7.23, top right.**) This swollen platform serves to hold onto the penis and forms a kind of dam that will hold a pool of semen where it can come in contact with the opening of the uterus.

During the latter part of the plateau phase, the areolae often swell so much that the nipples appear to retract into them. This apparent loss of nipple erection sometimes puzzles a man who has been caressing the woman's breasts, for it gives the false appearance of a loss of sexual interest.

ORGASMIC PHASE   During orgasm, a woman's orgasmic platform begins a series of contractions, at the rate of four contractions every three seconds (the same rate as the man's expulsion of semen), which soon become slower and weaker. (See **Figure 7.23, bottom left.**) As in males, almost all the muscles of the body become involved. However, whereas males tend to stop thrusting, a woman is likely to increase the rate of pelvic movements during orgasm.

Prior arousal is very important in determining whether a woman achieves orgasm. If she is not sufficiently aroused, and if the male reaches the plateau phase too quickly, he may have his orgasm before she is able to. Gebhard (1966) found that a woman is more likely to achieve orgasm if there has been considerable foreplay before intercourse.

Earlier researchers, including Sigmund Freud, suggested that there were two types of female orgasm: clitoral orgasm and vaginal orgasm. The vaginal orgasm was held to be more "mature"; clitoral orgasm, because it could be achieved by masturbation, was considered less fulfilling. However, Masters and Johnson found that there are no physiological distinctions between orgasms caused by clitoral stimulation during masturbation and those caused by vaginal penetration during intercourse. The fact is, the clitoris is stimulated when the penis moves within the vagina, even when the organs do not come in contact with each other; the stretching of the skin in the genital region causes the clitoris to rub against the hood of skin that covers it.

Nevertheless, like men, most women prefer an orgasm resulting from sexual intercourse, complete with insertion of a penis in the vagina, to an orgasm resulting from masturbation. (Few women masturbate by inserting anything in the vagina; most massage the area around the clitoris, causing this organ to rub against its hood. Even if a woman uses a penis-shaped vibrator, she is unlikely to place it in her vagina.) Although the physiological nature of the orgasm may be the same no matter how it is achieved, it is clear that the total emotional experience cannot be reduced to a mere throbbing of the orgasmic platform.

RESOLUTION PHASE Many women are able to achieve more than one orgasm during intercourse, so the resolution phase does not necessarily follow the first orgasmic phase. If the woman wants another orgasm, and if the man is willing and able to continue, she may re-enter the plateau phase and then proceed to orgasm several times more.

The resolution phase, the period of sexual relaxation, may be somewhat delayed if the man has not yet ejaculated and continues with intercourse. When both partners are finished, the changes that occurred during the excitement and plateau phases reverse themselves. The areolae resume their normal shape, the nipples lose their rigidity, and the breasts return to their normal size. The orgasmic platform disappears, and blood drains from the inner labia. The uterus, which was pulled up during intercourse, drops down. If the woman is lying on her back when intercourse is over, the uterus now opens directly on the pool of semen deposited by the man, increasing the likelihood that a large number of sperm will be able to swim up to the fallopian tubes. (See **Figure 7.23, bottom right.**)

If a woman becomes aroused but does not achieve orgasm, the resolution phase will be very prolonged, and the excess blood in the pelvic region will be drained very slowly. Occasionally this process will result in painful cramps. Sometimes a man who reaches orgasm too soon and cannot continue intercourse helps his partner achieve orgasm by means of clitoral stimulation.

NEURAL MECHANISMS OF SEXUAL BEHAVIOR

Both the sympathetic and parasympathetic divisions of the autonomic nervous system (described in Chapter 3) control the reproductive organs. The nerves that exert this control, and also receive sensory information from them, are attached to the lower part of the spinal cord. Tactual stimulation of the penis or clitoris is the most important sensory event that causes excitement and orgasm. It is interesting to note that the glans penis and clitoris are insensitive to light touch and warmth but do respond to heavy touch, pain, and cold. It is somewhat ironic that the pleasurable sensation that men and women receive from stimulation of these regions is provided mostly by pain fibers.

Most of the research on the neural circuits that control sexual responses in humans has involved people whose spinal cords have been severed, and most of these people have been men. More males suffer damage to their spinal cord because of their greater participation in warfare and other activities that expose them to serious injury. Furthermore, most researchers are probably reluctant to ask to examine the genital responses of paralyzed women.

Studies have shown that the neural reflex mechanisms necessary for erection and ejaculation, the essential parts of the male sexual response, are located in the lower part of the spinal cord. For example, the penis of a man whose spinal cord is severed is likely to become erect when it is stimulated, and continued stimulation can lead to ejaculation (Comarr, 1970). In fact, men with spinal cord damage have become fathers through artificial insemination of their wives with semen obtained through mechanical stimulation. If these reflex mechanisms were located in the brain or upper part of the spinal cord, the injury would disconnect them from the genitals, and the men would no longer be capable of erection and ejaculation. (See Figure 7.24.)

The neural reflex mechanisms for vaginal lubrication and female orgasm are probably also located in the spinal cord. One reason we lack solid information on these responses is that male erection and ejaculation are more easily detected than signs of arousal in women. Studies of other female animals have shown results analogous to those in males. If an experimenter stimulates the genitals of a female rat or cat whose spinal cord has been severed, the animal will exhibit normal sexual reflexes, arching her back and moving her tail to the side as if to receive the male (Beach, 1967; Hart, 1969). Female orgasm is primarily a human phenomenon;

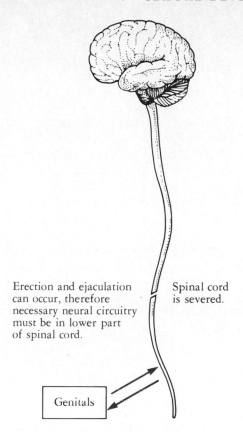

Erection and ejaculation can occur, therefore necessary neural circuitry must be in lower part of spinal cord.

Spinal cord is severed.

Genitals

FIGURE 7.24   Because some men with spinal-cord damage can have an erection and ejaculate, the neural reflex mechanisms for these functions must be within the spinal cord.

therefore, studies of women will be necessary to determine whether the vaginal contractions that occur during orgasm are organized in the spinal cord.

Neural control mechanisms in the brain turn the spinal reflex mechanisms on or off in response to thoughts and environmental stimuli and also give rise to sexual sensations. A man with a damaged spinal cord may achieve an erection and ejaculate, but he cannot feel what is happening. He will never get an erection in response to thoughts or sights that previously aroused him. Feelings, thoughts, and visual perception occur in the brain, and a cut through the spinal cord prevents the brain from communicating with the neural sexual mechanisms in the spinal cord. Men with spinal-cord damage report that they become sexually

aroused by kissing, engage in sexual fantasies, and experience orgasm mentally (though not physically) during erotic dreams (Blumer and Walker, 1975). The feelings of sexual arousal, erection, and orgasm occur despite the fact that nothing is happening to the genitals.

There is also good evidence that the brain normally inhibits the activity of the spinal-cord reflex mechanisms so that they do not respond to actual stimuli at times when sexual activity is not contemplated. For example, if a man strokes the inner surface of his thigh, it is unlikely that he will get an erection unless he has decided to masturbate. However, if he is in a private and secluded place, and a close female friend strokes his thigh, he is likely to get an erection. The spinal cord received the same sensory information in both cases. But when a man strokes his own thigh, the brain normally sends an inhibitory message that prevents the reflex mechanisms in the spinal cord from responding. When a woman does the stroking, the brain sends no inhibitory message, so the stimulation can activate the neural mechanisms of the spinal cord. In fact the brain can send an excitatory message. Suppose the woman says, "I'm going to stroke your thigh—let's see what happens." Even before her hand touches him, the man's penis is likely to start responding.

Research with animals has substantiated that the brain controls (through inhibition) the sexual reflex mechanisms of the spinal cord. For example, Hart (1967) has found that a normal male dog will not exhibit an ejaculatory response to mechanical stimulation of its penis unless it can see and smell a sexually receptive female dog. However, if the dog's spinal cord has been severed this inhibitory control is removed. Now, mechanical stimulation is effective by itself; a receptive bitch need not be present. (See **Figure 7.25.**) Hart also obtained evidence suggesting that the brain controls the refractory period. Normal dogs have a refractory period of more than thirty minutes after an ejaculation, whereas dogs with severed spinal cords can respond again in as little as five minutes. The spinal cord appears to be ready for more before the brain is.

Other evidence indicates that the brain directly stimulates, as well as inhibits, the male sexual response. A series of experiments in MacLean's laboratory (MacLean, Dua, and Denniston, 1963; Dua

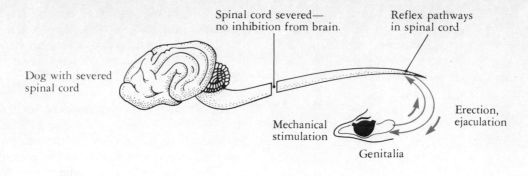

Spinal cord severed—
no inhibition from brain.

Reflex pathways
in spinal cord

Dog with severed
spinal cord

Mechanical
stimulation

Erection,
ejaculation

Genitalia

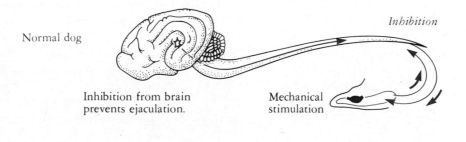

Normal dog

Inhibition

Inhibition from brain
prevents ejaculation.

Mechanical
stimulation

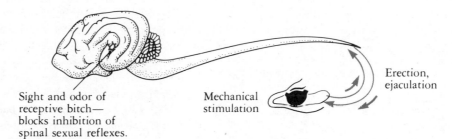

Sight and odor of
receptive bitch—
blocks inhibition of
spinal sexual reflexes.

Mechanical
stimulation

Erection,
ejaculation

FIGURE 7.25   The rationale of the experiment by Hart (1967). (Adapted from Carlson, N.R. *Physiology of Behavior*, 2nd ed. Boston: Allyn and Bacon, 1981.)

and MacLean, 1964) showed that electrical stimulation of a variety of interconnected brain structures causes erection or ejaculation or both in male squirrel monkeys. The fact that a nonerect penis can emit semen indicates that the neural mechanisms for erection and ejaculation are separate.

Some studies with laboratory animals seem to show that male and female sexual responses are organized differently in the brain; one region appears to stimulate mounting behavior (typical of males) and another to stimulate assumption of the female sexual posture.

Destruction of the ***medial preoptic area*** (just in front of the hypothalamus) abolishes mounting be-

havior in both male and female rats. In addition, when testosterone is implanted directly into the medial preoptic area of a castrated male rat (which is normally sexually inactive), the animal will exhibit mating behavior (Johnston and Davidson, 1972). This evidence suggests that testosterone facilitates male sexual behavior by stimulating neurons located in the medial preoptic area.

Destruction of the medial preoptic area in female rats also abolishes malelike mounting behavior that is occasionally seen in female rats (Heimer and Larsson, 1966/1967; Singer, 1968). And, in addition, it disrupts maternal behavior; female rats no longer construct nests and care for their babies

(Numan, 1974). It is not known whether there is some relation between male sexual behavior and maternal behavior or whether the medial preoptic area is coincidentally important for both kinds of activity. However, lesions of the medial preoptic area do not decrease the female response of receptive posturing; in fact, they appear to increase it (Heimer and Larsson, 1966/1967).

Mathews and Edwards (1977) found that female sexual behavior is disrupted by destruction of another area: the ventromedial hypothalamus, which is located just behind the medial preoptic area. (We encountered this part of the brain in Chapter 5 in its role in the control of food intake.) Male sexual behavior is not affected by these operations. Implantation of estradiol into this region facilitates female sexual responses in castrated female rats (Pfaff, 1980). Presumably, estrogen from a normal female rat's ovaries acts by stimulating neurons there.

Damage to the temporal lobes, which appears to affect an animal's choice of an appropriate sex object, is discussed in the next section.

Interim summary: Although males and females are sometimes referred to as members of "opposite" sexes, there are many similarities in their sexual responses. As we saw in the previous section, the sex drives of both men and women respond to androgens. As we saw in this section, men and women respond in similar fashion to erotic stimuli and engage in similar kinds of erotic fantasies, although social factors can have strong influences. The human sexual response for both male and female consists of the excitement, plateau, orgasmic, and resolution phases. Although men and women have different kinds of genitals, the kinds of physiological effects that occur during intercourse are similar. Even orgasm is accompanied by rhythmic contractions that occur at approximately the same rate, four every three seconds.

Evidence obtained from men with damaged spinal cords, supplemented by additional information provided by experiments with dogs, suggests that the male sexual reflexes of erection and ejaculation are produced by activation of reflex mechanisms in the lower part of the spinal cord. When the spinal cord is severed, inhibitory control from the brain no longer restricts the ejaculatory response (in dogs) to times when a receptive female is present. Be-

cause electrical stimulation of various parts of the brain can cause erection and ejaculation, it is apparent that the connections between the brain and reflex mechanisms in the spinal cord can convey excitatory, as well as inhibitory, influences.

Other research suggests that different areas of the brain affect certain kinds of sexual responses. Destruction of the medial preoptic area of rats abolishes mounting behavior, and destruction of the ventromedial hypothalamus abolishes receptive posturing. In addition, if estradiol or testosterone is implanted into the medial preoptic area or ventromedial hypothalamus of castrated male or female rats, their sexual behavior will be restored; thus, these regions appear to play a role in the control of sexual behavior in males and females, respectively.

VARIATIONS IN SEXUAL BEHAVIOR

Variations refer to differences from a perceived norm, or "standard," and few issues are as value-laden as the issue of what constitutes "normal" sexual behavior. What one person regards as pleasurable and acceptable sexual activity another may regard as "perverse" or "indecent," even in matters of the sexual relations between husband and wife. Yet human sexual activity is limited only by a person's physical capacity and his or her imagination. The behaviors discussed in this section are variations from our society's prevailing norm of heterosexuality. They have no inherent values, only the ones we attach to them.

HOMOSEXUALITY

◈ Homosexual behavior (engaging in sexual activity with members of the same sex; from Greek *homos*, "the same") is seen in male and female animals of many different species. This widespread occurrence of homosexual behavior makes it difficult to refer to it objectively as "unnatural." However, humans are apparently the only species that regularly exhibit exclusive homosexuality. Other animals, if they are not exclusively heterosexual, are likely to be bisexual (engaging in sexual activity with members of both sexes), not homosexual. In contrast,

FIGURE 7.26   Many homosexuals are happy and emotionally healthy.

the number of men and women who describe themselves as exclusively homosexual exeeds the number who describe themselves as bisexual.

There is no evidence that homosexuality is a disorder. The fact that homosexuals appear to have more problems in adjustment reflects the fact that our society at large treats them differently. Therefore, even if we observe more neuroses in homosexuals, we cannot conclude that their maladjustment is directly related to their sexual preference. In a society that was absolutely indifferent to a person's sexual orientation, homosexuals might be as well adjusted as heterosexuals. The fact that a large number of homosexuals are well adjusted and happy with themselves (Bell and Weinberg, 1978) suggests that homosexuality is not always associated with emotional difficulties. See **Figure 7.26.**)

Some researchers have suggested that homosexuality is an emotional disturbance caused by faulty child rearing. For example, one study suggested that male homosexuals tend to be the only child, or the youngest child, or the youngest male in their family (Westwood, 1960). Others have reported that fathers of homosexuals tend to be cold and unaffectionate or even hostile (Evans, 1969; Siegelman, 1974) and that their mothers tend to be domineering and physically intimate (Bieber et al., 1962). Many clinicians have concluded that the boys lack an adequate male figure on which to model their behavior and continue to need male affection that they never received from their father.

Much of the data in these studies were gathered from people who went to a psychiatrist or clinical psychologist for help with emotional problems. Therefore, they were not necessarily typical of all homosexuals, and we cannot know whether their homosexuality was a direct result of an unhappy childhood, or whether their emotional instability and homosexual preference were purely coincidental.

A very ambitious project reported by Bell, Weinberg, and Hammersmith (1981) studied a large number of male and female homosexuals, most of whom had not sought professional psychological assistance. The researchers obtained their subjects by placing advertisements in newspapers, approaching people in gay bars and bookstores, and asking known homosexuals to recommend friends. The study took place in San Francisco, where homosexuals form a large part of the population.

The subjects were asked about their relations with their parents, siblings, and peers, and about their feelings, gender identification, and sexual activity. The results provided little or no support for traditional theories of homosexuality.

The major conclusions of the study were as follows:

1. Sexual preference appears to be determined prior to adolescence and prior to homosexual or heterosexual activity. The most important single predictor of adult homosexuality was a self-report of homosexual feelings, which usually occurred three years before genital homosexual activity. This finding suggests that homosexuality is a deep-seated tendency. It also tends to rule out the suggestion that seduction by an older person of the same sex plays an important role in the development of homosexuality.

2. Most homosexual men and women have engaged in some heterosexual experiences during childhood and adolescence, but, in contrast to their heterosexual counterparts, found these experiences unrewarding. This finding is also consistent with the existence of a deep-seated predisposition prior to adulthood.

3. There is a strong relation between gender nonconformity in childhood and the development of homosexuality. Gender nonconformity is characterized by an aversion in boys to "masculine" behaviors and one in girls to "feminine" behaviors. For example, among the male subjects, 11 percent of the homosexuals, compared with 70 percent of the heterosexuals, reported having enjoyed boys' activities very much. In contrast, 46 percent of the homosexuals reported having enjoyed girls' activities, compared with 11 percent of the heterosexuals. The same pattern held true among the women; 62 percent of the homosexuals described themselves as having been masculine during childhood, compared with 10 percent of the heterosexuals.

However, childhood interests are not invariable predictors of later sexual preference. Approximately half of the homosexual men were "masculine" during childhood, while nearly a quarter of

the heterosexual men were "feminine." Similarly one-third of the homosexual women were "feminine" during childhood while approximately one-fifth of the heterosexual women were "masculine."

4. Poor relationship with a father is a modest but significant predictor of homosexuality *in both males and females*. However, a person's relationship with his or her mother does not seem to predict later sexual preference. This finding contradicts earlier theories of homosexuality suggesting that a boy's relations with his mother are of paramount importance in the development of homosexuality. Moreover, the fact that a poor relationship with the father was associated with homosexuality gives no indication of cause and effect; that is, a distant or hostile father might drive a child to homosexuality, or a child whose behavior did not conform to his or her gender might antagonize or distress a father and thus lead to a bad relationship.

As the researchers admit, the results of the study are consistent with the hypothesis that homosexuality is at least partly determined by biological factors. That is, biological variables may predispose a child to behavior that is more typical of the other sex and eventually to sexual arousal by members of his or her own sex. Such behavior often results in poor relations with peers and parents.

◆ Is there evidence for biological causes of homosexuality? We can immediately rule out the suggestion that male homosexuals are deficient in testosterone or have excessive levels of estrogen or progesterone in their blood. Although some studies have found evidence of androgen deficiencies in male homosexuals, it is well known that stress can affect production of these hormones (Rose, Bourne, Poe, Mougey, Collins, and Mason, 1969). Tests of homosexuals who have difficulty accepting their own sexual orientation or who feel harassed by society are likely to show that homosexuals have lower testosterone levels than those of most heterosexuals. However, it appears that well-adjusted male homosexuals have normal levels of testosterone (Tourney, 1980).

Another possible biological cause of male homosexuality is inadequate prenatal androgenization of the brain, which might result in a preference for the sexual partner that a woman would normally prefer—namely, a man. Or perhaps some genes are associated with sexual preference; a certain percentage of homosexuals might be said to "inherit" their orientation. Some slight evidence from research with rats suggests that disturbances in prenatal androgenization can cause male homosexuality. Ward (1972) created a stressful situation by exposing pregnant rats to bright lights. Their male offspring, when they grew up, were deficient in male sexual behavior and responded to estrogen and progesterone by showing female sexual behavior. Presumably, the stress caused the mothers' adrenal glands to secrete hormones that suppressed the production of testosterone in the testes of their male fetuses. (See **Figure 7.27**.) Whether prenatal

FIGURE 7.27   Maternal stress suppresses the secretion of testosterone in the experiment by Ward (1972).

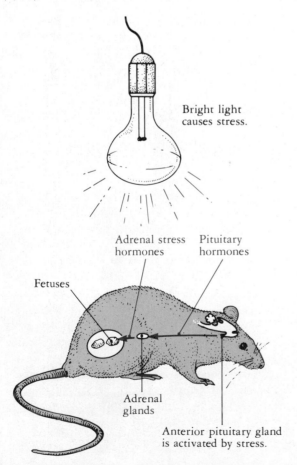

Bright light causes stress.

Adrenal stress hormones

Pituitary hormones

Fetuses

Adrenal glands

Anterior pituitary gland is activated by stress.

stress plays a role in some cases of human homosexuality is an unanswered question.

You will recall that androgens have two organizational effects on the sexual behavior of male rodents: masculinization and defeminization. Masculinization refers to the organization of mounting behavior, and defeminization to suppression of the tendency to accept the advances of a male and to adopt the female posture. Although human sexual behavior is not sexually dimorphic, it is conceivable that androgenization accomplishes two different effects in human males: masculinization (establishment of a tendency to perceive females as sex partners), and defeminization (suppression of the tendency to perceive males as sex partners). If this hypothesis is correct, and if these two phenomena occur at different times during prenatal development, we would predict that some males would be exclusively heterosexual (their brains would be masculinized and defeminized), some bisexual (their brains would be masculinized but *not* defeminized), and some exclusively homosexual (their brains would be neither masculinized nor defeminized).

Attempts to identify a genetic role in homosexuality have provided strong but not conclusive evidence. For example, Kallman (1952) studied a large number of genetically identical twins and found that all had the same sexual preference; if one was homosexual, so was the other. Heston and Shields (1968) studied a remarkable family of fourteen children that contained three pairs of male identical twins. Two of the pairs were homosexual and one pair was heterosexual. No environmental factor could be found to explain why two of the pairs, but not the third, became homosexual. Identical male twins of different sexual orientation (one homosexual, the other heterosexual) are apparently rare; Zuger (1976) found only nine cases in the scientific literature.

The biological causes of female homosexuality have been studied far less than those of male homosexuality. One study with rats suggests that the prenatal environment may play a role. Clemens (1971) found that the probability of malelike mounting behavior in female rats was related to the number of their brothers. Presumably, when a female fetus shares the uterus with several brothers, her brain is affected by their androgens, and hence her behavior is slightly masculinized.

Our knowledge of the factors that influence sexual preference remains indefinite. The study by Bell, Weinberg, and Hammersmith suggests that future research should focus on the sex-related behavior of children and try to determine the factors, biological and environmental, that influence its development.

PARAPHILIAS

Paraphilias, or "unusual loves," are directed at an astonishing variety of sexual objects. People have been sexually attracted to animals, young children, dead people, specific parts of the body (especially feet or hair), or objects such as shoes or underwear. Many people who exhibit paraphilias are unable to function sexually in a more normal manner unless the object of their fetish is present. (See **Figure 7.28.**)

Most people who develop paraphilias are men. As Money and Ehrhardt put it, "Nature makes more errors in the male" (1972, p. 148). It appears that male sexuality is more easily disrupted than female sexuality, perhaps because something must be *added* to make a male, since a female develops if androgenization does not take place. If the ad-

FIGURE 7.28   Manufacturers and merchants are happy to supply articles for a variety of sexual practices.

ditions are not accomplished properly, then abnormalities are likely to result. It is also possible that differences in socialization account for the higher incidence of paraphilias in men.

A special interest in some part of another person's anatomy does not necessarily indicate the presence of a paraphilia. It would not be considered unusual for a man to become aroused by the sight of a woman combing her beautiful, flowing hair or to become even further aroused by touching and stroking her hair. However, if he showed no interest in having intercourse with her and received all his gratification through contact with her hair, we would conclude that his preference was abnormal. (Remember, abnormal does not mean evil; it simply means "not usual.")

Like every other psychological abnormality, paraphilias have been blamed on improper child-rearing practices, but little or no progress has been made with this hypothesis. Another suggestion is that classical conditioning indelibly attaches a person's sexual response to unusual objects. As we saw in Chapter 4, this suggestion has some experimental support. However, the conditioning model does not explain why some people seem more susceptible than others to developing paraphilias, nor does it account for the higher incidence in males. Finally, there is the suggestion that abnormalities in brain functioning account for at least some paraphilias.

Sexual Dysfunctions and Brain Abnormalities

◆ The temporal lobes appear to play a role in the recognition of sex objects. Partial destruction of this region in male monkeys (Schreiner and Kling, 1956) or cats (Green, Clemente, and DeGroot, 1957) causes *hypersexuality*. Perhaps *pansexuality* would be a better term (*pan* means "all"). The cats in the second study attempt to copulate with everything in sight—other males, stuffed toys, furniture, or the experimenter's leg. They appear unable to distinguish appropriate sex objects from inappropriate ones.

Many humans with temporal lobe abnormalities also display sexual dysfunctions. One common disorder of the temporal lobe is *focal epilepsy*. Epilepsy is a brain disorder that is characterized by an uncontrolled storm of neural firing. *Focal* epilepsy refers to the abnormal firing of neurons in a restricted portion of the brain, most commonly in one or both temporal lobes. Depending on its severity and location, this abnormal activity results in various behaviors, including stereotyped and repetitive movements, convulsions, or simply episodes of blank staring.

Many males and females with temporal lobe epilepsy are *hyposexual*—uninterested in sex (Blumer, 1975; Blumer and Walker, 1975). If this disorder begins before puberty, the person will undergo normal changes in primary and secondary sex characteristics but may never experience sexual arousal. Usually, successful treatment of the seizures with medication will increase sexual interest. Sometimes medication does not alleviate the epilepsy, and part of the abnormal temporal lobe is removed. If the surgery stops the seizures, the patient usually experiences normal sexual desire, and sometimes *hypersexuality*.

Blumer and Walker (1975) report the following case of hyposexuality associated with temporal lobe epilepsy.

> A boy developed normally until the age of 12 years, when he had an attack in which he became rigid with head retracted and eyes staring. In subsequent years, the episodes continued—sometimes occurring daily and again not for a week or so. . . . Although his secondary sexual characteristics developed normally, he developed no sexual arousal and throughout his 20s he had little interest or curiosity about women, with whom he had many associations in church work. The spells continued despite anticonvulsant medication and at age 30 his [abnormal] right temporal lobe was removed. The attacks ceased completely. A few months after the operation, he began to notice how attractive women were. He took up dancing but he almost gave it up when, for the first time in his life, he experienced an erection when he held a woman in his arms. This embarrassment heightened one evening 6 months after his operation, when at the age of 31 he had his first emission [of semen]. He later married and at age 40 continued to consummate his marriage with great regularity. (pp. 207–208)

This and other studies suggest that the temporal lobes play an inhibitory role in the control of sexual activity. When an epileptic focus (region of neural irritation) is active, it stimulates neurons in the rest of the temporal lobe. This stimulation produces hyposexuality. Surgical destruction of part of the temporal lobe removes this source of inhibition and produces normal or even unusually high levels of sexual interest.

A few patients with temporal lobe epilepsy exhibit paraphilias immediately after having a seizure. One man with temporal lobe epilepsy would be gripped by a compulsion to stare at a safety pin, would then have an epileptic seizure, and afterward dress in his wife's clothing. Removal of part of the left temporal lobe cured his disorder (Mitchell, Falconer, and Hill, 1954).

Thus, there is good evidence that at least some cases of paraphilia are a result of abnormalities in the temporal lobe. However, without further evidence it would be unwise to conclude that *all* paraphilias have a neurological basis.

Transvestism

◆ *Transvestism,* or cross-dressing (from *trans,* "across," and *vestire,* "to dress"), involves wearing clothes appropriate to the other sex. Like other paraphilias, transvestism is observed almost exclusively in males. Of course, society does not treat cross-dressing by males and females in the same way. A man who dresses in women's clothing is called abnormal. A woman who dresses in men's clothing is called fashionable. Often one member of a lesbian couple will dress in masculine clothing, but the clothes themselves probably do not provide sexual stimulation as they do for the transvestite. Similarly, some male homosexuals dress as women, but the clothes are usually a means to an end; they are worn to attract other men. (See **Figure 7.29.**)

The true transvestite is almost always heterosexual and is often married. Many men are stimulated to some extent by the sight of women's underclothes. Superficially, at least, it is easy to explain this phenomenon. Underclothes are seen in pictures of attractive, scantily clad women, and they are the last garments to come off when a woman undresses for intercourse. Thus it is not surprising to find that underclothes themselves elicit a certain amount of sexual interest. It is only when a man receives all or most of his sexual gratification by

FIGURE 7.29   Homosexual transvestites are more likely to show themselves in public, but most transvestites are heterosexual and practice their cross-dressing in private.

wearing these garments himself that we would consider his behavior to be abnormal.

TRANSSEXUALISM

The wish to be a member of the opposite sex is called *transsexualism.* Again, many more men than women are transsexuals, despite the obvious social and economic advantages males have in our society. Like transvestites, transsexuals want to dress in the clothes of the other sex, but for very different reasons. A transvestite male enjoys having a penis and derives sexual gratification from it. A transsexual male wants to become—indeed, feels that he really is—a female. He despises his penis and wants to get rid of it. Money and Tucker (1975) describe the incredible case of a transsexual man who tried the "loose-tooth" solution to his problem. He tied one end of a string around his penis, fastened the other end to a doorknob, and slammed the door.

From what we know of the organizational effects of hormones, we might speculate that inadequate prenatal androgenization causes transsexualism. However, there is no evidence for or against this hypothesis at present. Experts on transsexualism like John Money (see Money and Ehrhardt, 1972) believe that most instances of this disorder are results of child-rearing practices that do not encourage the person to be content and confident with his or her own sexuality. For example, if a child's parents really wanted a girl but got a boy, they might treat the child ambiguously and inconsistently—sometimes pretending he is a girl, then feeling guilty for doing so and consequently punishing the "feminine" behaviors in their child that they had previously enjoyed seeing. Such treatment might well have adverse effects on the child's gender identification. This hypothesis sounds reasonable, but we still do not have enough evidence to consider it proved.

CONCLUDING REMARKS

Sexual development begins early in embryonic life with the differentiation of the primordial gonads into testes or ovaries. If testes are present, they secrete androgens, which cause male sexual organs to develop; otherwise, a female develops. Androgenization is called an *organizational* effect. It probably affects human brain tissue as well as the reproductive organs.

At puberty, the gonadotropic hormones cause the gonads to secrete their hormones. These hormones (estradiol and AD in females, testosterone in males) cause further sexual development—the emergence of the primary and secondary sex characteristics. Although the sexual behavior of female mammals with estrous cycles depends on estrogen and progesterone, these hormones have only a minor effect on women's sexual behavior. Their sexual desire, like that of men, is much more dependent on androgens.

Although neural mechanisms in the spinal cord control the activity of the genitals, sexual arousal and gratification are ultimately properties of the brain and are affected by experience and learning.

Human sexual behavior includes many variations on the norm of heterosexual intercourse. We do not know what causes homosexuality, although recent research suggests that the tendency toward homosexuality is influenced by biological factors more than by social ones. No good evidence has linked homosexuality with particular types of child-rearing practices. Abnormal sexual behaviors (paraphilias) are often associated with brain dysfunctions, especially of the temporal lobes. Transvestism, practiced mostly by heterosexual males, is distinct from transsexualism, a desire to be a member of the opposite sex. Like the other paraphilias, transsexualism is most common in males.

Although an individual's sex life is a personal, private matter, scientific investigation of its nature in no way diminishes its quality. A thorough understanding of the social and biological determinants of sexual behavior will enable us to help those who are afflicted by sexual dysfunctions, and thus enhance at least some people's sex lives.

GUIDE TO TERMS INTRODUCED IN THIS CHAPTER

activational effect   p. 262

adrenal gland   p. 264   Figure 7.16

adrenogenital syndrome   p. 269   Table 7.2

androgen insensitivity syndrome   p. 272   Figure 7.14

androgenization   p. 262   Figures 7.4, 7.5, 7.9

androgen   p. 263   Table 7.1

androstenedione (AD)   p. 263   Table 7.1

anterior pituitary gland   p. 263   Figures 7.6, 7.16

autosome   p. 256

bipotential   p. 257   Figures 7.3, 7.5

Bruce effect   p. 279

clitoris   p. 259   Figures 7.5, 7.23

corpus luteum   p. 277   Figures 7.17, 7.18

defeminization   p. 266

epididymis   p. 258   Figures 7.4, 7.22

estradiol   p. 263   Table 7.1

SUGGESTIONS FOR FURTHER READING

Several excellent books about sex are available today. I can recommend *Human Sexuality* by W.H. Masters, V.E. Johnson, and R.C. Kolodny (Boston: Little, Brown, 1982). The discussion is scholarly but the style is clear and easy, and there are excellent illustrations, including several clever cartoons. *Sexual Signatures: On Being a Man or a Woman* by J. Money and P. Singer (Boston: Little, Brown, 1975) describes the formation of gender identity. This interesting and well-written book is designed for the general public, so its style is light and easy. *Sexual Preference: Its Development in Men and Women* by A.P. Bell, M.S. Weinberg, and S.K. Hammersmith (Bloomington: Indiana University Press, 1981) is the official publication of a recent survey conducted by the Kinsey Institute for Sex Research; it discusses the variables that appear to affect the development of homosexual or heterosexual preference. *Exploring Human Sexuality,* by D. Byrne and L. Byrne (New York: Harper & Row, 1977) includes a variety of interesting and informative articles.

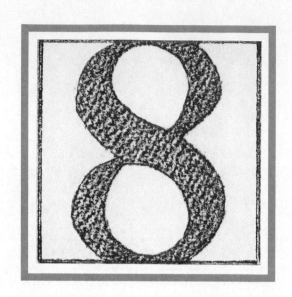

8

VISION AND

VISUAL

PERCEPTION

L E A R N I N G ◆ O B J E C T I V E S

Our senses are the means by which we experience the world; everything we learn is transmitted to our brains by sensory nerves. Without sensory input a human brain would be useless and functionless. This chapter and the next discuss our sense organs and how sensory information is organized into experience. This chapter discusses only vision because of all the senses, it has been the subject of the most research. The eye is a very complicated sense organ, and most people value sight above all the other sense modalities; if forced to choose, they would rather lose any other sense than vision. (See **Figure 8.1**.)

SENSORY PROCESSING

Experience is traditionally divided into two classes, sensation and perception. Most psychologists define *sensation* as the awareness of simple properties of stimuli, such as brightness, color, warmth, or sweetness, and *perception* as the awareness of more complex characteristics of stimuli. According to these definitions, seeing the color red is a *sensation,* but seeing an apple is a *perception.* Psychologists used to believe that perceptions depended heavily

FIGURE 8.1   Vision is very important to humans and human activities. We are able to extract information quickly and efficiently from a complex environment.

on learning, whereas pure sensations involved innate, "prewired" physiological mechanisms. However, neither behavioral nor physiological research has provided a clear boundary between "simple" sensations and "complex" perceptions. Indeed, research has shown that experience is essential to the development of some of the most elementary features of sensory systems. Therefore, in this chapter and the next I will use the term perception to refer to all sensory experience.

Perception depends on learning the relations between various sensory experiences. For example, a child apparently sees the full moon as almost close enough to touch, but an adult perceives it as far away. Furthermore, perceptions are based both on what the perceiver does and on what the object being perceived does. If you move your eyes so that your gaze follows a spot of light that is slowly moving around in the dark, the image of the object on your retina remains fairly constant. However, you will correctly perceive that the object is moving, because of the movement of your eye muscles.

Sense organs can respond directly to the environmental stimuli of light, sound, odor, taste, or touch, but the brain cannot. Sensory information must be introduced to the brain through neural impulses—action potentials of axons in sensory nerves. To serve as an effective stimulus, an environmental event must cause a unique pattern of neural activity that the brain can distinguish from all other patterns. Two processes—*transduction* and *sensory coding*—transform sensory events into neural activity, and hence are basic to the ways in which we perceive the world.

TRANSDUCTION

◈ *Transduction* (literally, "leading across") is the process by which the sense organs convert energy from environmental events into neural activity. In this age of computers, such a function is referred to as an interface. To a computer technologist, an interface is a device that translates environmental events (such as closures of switch contacts or the scanning of perforations on computer cards) into the electrical "language" that a computer can understand. Similarly, our sense organs serve as interfaces between brain and environment. Each sense organ responds to a particular form of energy given off by an environmental stimulus and translates that energy into neural firing to which the brain can respond. The means of transduction are as diverse as the kinds of stimuli we can perceive. In most senses, specialized *receptor cells* release chemical neurotransmitters that stimulate neurons, and thus alter the rate of firing of their axons. In the body senses, neurons respond directly to physical stimuli, without the intervention of specialized receptor cells. **Figure 8.2** illustrates these two processes schematically.

FIGURE 8.2   Two general types of receptors.

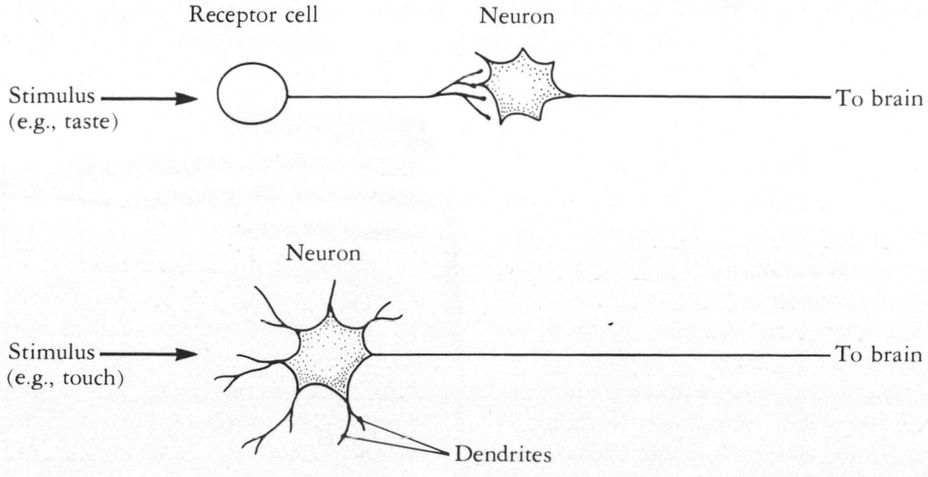

SENSORY CODING

As we saw in Chapter 3, nerves are bundles of axons, each of which can do no more than transmit action potentials. These action potentials are fixed in size and duration; they cannot be altered. Yet our sense organs must respond differently to a multitude of stimuli, and therefore the nerves conveying the information to the brain must carry distinctive messages. For example, we are capable of discriminating among approximately 7.5 million different colors, if we were permitted to examine them side by side. We can recognize touches to different parts of the body, and further discriminate the degree of pressure involved and the sharpness or bluntness, softness or hardness, and even the temperature of the object touching us. Because differences in the action potentials themselves cannot be altered, differences in stimuli must be encoded by other means.

A code is a system of symbols or signals representing information. Spoken English, written French, semaphore signals, magnetic fields on a recording tape, and the electrical ones and zeroes in the memory of a computer are all codes. So long as we know the rules of a code, we can convert a message from one medium to another without losing any information. Although we do not know the precise rules used by the sensory systems to transmit information to the brain, we do know that they take two general forms: anatomical coding and temporal coding.

Anatomical Coding

Since the early 1800s, when Johannes Müller formulated his doctrine of specific nerve energies (discussed in Chapter 1), we have known that the brain learns what is happening through the activity of specific sets of neurons. Sensory organs are located in different places in the body and send their information to the brain through different nerves. Because the brain has no direct information about the physical energy impinging on a given sense organ, it uses *anatomical coding;* that is, it interprets the location and type of sensory stimulus according to which incoming nerve fibers are active. For example, if you rub your eyes and thus mechanically stimulate their light-sensitive receptors you will see stars and flashes. Because motor plan-

ning and execution systems of the frontal lobes of your brain were responsible for your rubbing your eyes, you know that the stars and flashes are not real lights. However, to the visual-processing regions of your brain the activity of the axons of the optic nerves represents light, however this activity is initiated.

Other sensory modalities are far less accessible to artificial stimulation of this kind, so they are less easily deceived. (People are not likely to poke a stick in their ear or nostril to see what happens when they touch the receptors that respond to sounds or odors.) But experiments performed during surgery have confirmed that we perceive different sensations through anatomical coding: electrical stimulation of the nerves that convey taste produces a sensation of taste, electrical stimulation of the auditory nerve produces a buzzing noise, and so forth.

We use forms of anatomical coding to distinguish not only among the sensory modalities themselves but also among stimuli of the same sensory modalities. Obviously, sensory coding for the body surface is anatomical: different nerve fibers innervate different parts of the skin. Thus, we can easily discriminate a touch on the arm from a touch on the knee. Central sensory mechanisms maintain a similar coding scheme; most individual neurons in the somatosensory systems of the brain, up to and including the somatosensory cortex, respond best to a touch applied to a particular portion of the body's surface. Neighboring neurons in the somatosensory cortex are most likely to respond to touch applied to nearby locations on the skin. Thus, the somatosensory system contains a neural "map" of the skin. The primary visual cortex also maintains a map of the visual field, and the inner ear codes one aspect of sound anatomically—pitch.

Temporal Coding

Temporal coding is the transmission of information in terms of time. The simplest form of temporal code is *rate*. By firing at a faster or slower rate according to the intensity of a stimulus, an axon can communicate quantitative information to the brain. Thus the firing of a particular set of neurons (anatomical code) tells *where* the body is being touched; the rate at which these neurons fire (temporal code) tells *how intense* that touch is. So far as we know, all sensory systems use rate of firing

on test (last sem)

to encode the intensity of stimulation. It is possible that the nervous system uses more complex forms of temporal codes, but this has yet to be scientifically established.

PSYCHOPHYSICS

Nineteenth-century Europe was the birthplace of *psychophysics,* the systematic study of the relation between the physical characteristics of a stimulus and the perceptions they produce. To study perceptual phenomena, scientists had to find reliable ways to measure people's perceptions.

The Principle of the Just-Noticeable Difference

◈ In nineteenth-century Germany, Ernst Weber, an anatomist and physiologist, investigated the ability of humans to discriminate between various stimuli, and discovered a principle that held true for all sensory systems: the *just-noticeable difference (jnd).* For example, when he presented subjects with two metal objects and asked them to say whether they differed in weight, he found that people reported that two weights felt the same unless they differed by a factor of 1 in 40; that is, a person could just barely distinguish a 40-gram weight from a 41-gram weight, an 80-gram weight from an 82-gram weight, or a 400-gram weight from a 410-gram weight. Psychologically, the difference between a 40-gram weight and a 41-gram weight is equivalent to the difference between an 80-gram weight and an 82-gram weight: one jnd. Different senses had different ratios; for example, the ratio for detecting differences in the brightness of white light is approximately 1 in 60. These ratios are called *Weber fractions.* (See **Figure 8.3**.)

Gustav Fechner, another German physiologist, used Weber's concept of the just-noticeable difference to measure people's perceptions. Assuming

FIGURE 8.3   Ernst Weber (1795–1878) discovered that the smallest noticeable difference in two stimuli was a constant fraction of their magnitude.

FIGURE 8.4   Gustav Fechner (1801–1887), using Weber's principle of the just-noticeable difference, developed psychophysical methods by which experienced sensation could be measured.

1. Experimenter sets the brightest of these lights to be equal.

2. Experimenter gradually changes the brightness of this light until the subject says they look different.

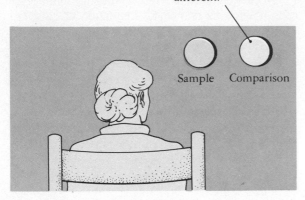

Sample   Comparison

FIGURE 8.5   The method for determining a just-noticeable difference (jnd).

that this was the basic unit of a perceptual experience, he measured the absolute magnitude of a perception in jnds. (See **Figure 8.4.**)

Suppose we wanted to measure the strength of a person's perception of a light with a particular intensity. We could seat the subject in a dark room, facing two disks of frosted glass with a lightbulb behind each whose brightness we could adjust. One of these would serve as the sample stimulus, the other as the comparison stimulus. (See **Figure 8.5.**) We would start with the sample stimulus turned

FIGURE 8.6   A hypothetical range of perceived brightness in jnds as a function of intensity.

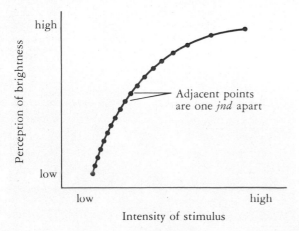

off completely and increase the brightness of the comparison stimulus just until our subject could detect a difference. That value would be one jnd. Then we would set the sample stimulus to that intensity (one jnd) and again increase the brightness of the comparison stimulus just until our subject could tell them apart again. The new value of the comparison stimulus would be two jnds. We would continue making these measurements until our stimuli became as bright as we could make them or until they became uncomfortably bright for our subject. Finally, we could construct a graph indicating the strength of a perception of brightness (in jnds) in relation to the intensity of a stimulus. The graph might look something like **Figure 8.6.**

Signal-Detection Theory

Psychophysical methods rely heavily on the concept of a ***threshold,*** in which an observer crosses from not perceiving to perceiving. The just-noticeable difference can also be called a ***difference threshold***—the minimum detectable difference between two stimuli. An ***absolute threshold*** is the minimum value of a stimulus that can be detected—that is, discriminated from no stimulus at all. Thus, the first comparison in the experiment that I just described, using a dark disk as the sample stimulus, measured an absolute threshold. The subsequent ones measured difference thresholds.

Even early psychophysicists realized that a threshold was not an absolutely fixed value. When an experimenter flashes a very dim light a subject may report seeing it on some trials but not on others. By convention, the threshold is the point at which a subject detects the stimulus 50 percent of the time. This definition is necessary because of the inherent variability of the activity in the nervous system. Even when they are not being stimulated, neurons are never absolutely still; they fire every now and then. If a very weak stimulus occurs when neurons in the visual system happen to be quiet, the brain is likely to detect it. But if the neurons happen to be firing, the effects of the stimulus are likely to be lost in the "noise."

One effective method uses ***signal-detection theory*** to measure a person's sensitivity to changes in physical stimuli (Green and Swets, 1974). According to this theory, every stimulus event requires discrimination between *signal* (stimulus) and *noise* (consisting of both background stimuli and random activity of the nervous system).

Suppose you are seated in a quiet room, facing a small warning light. The experimenter tells you that when the light flashes you *may* hear a faint tone one second later. Your task is to say "yes" or "no" after each flash of the warning light, according to whether you heard the tone. At first the task is easy: some flashes are followed by an easily heard tone; others are followed by silence. You are confident about your yes and no decisions. But as the experiment progresses the tone gets fainter and fainter, until it is so soft that you have doubts about how you should respond. The light flashes. What should you say? Did you really hear a tone or were you just imagining it?

At this point your *response bias* could have an effect. Suppose you want to be very sure that you are correct when you say "yes," because you would feel foolish saying you have heard something that is not there. Your response bias would be to err in favor of making hits and avoiding false alarms, even at the risk of making misses. On the other hand, your response bias could be to err in favor of detecting all stimuli, even at the risk of making false alarms. (According to the terminology of signal-detection theory, *hits* are saying "yes" when the stimulus is presented, *misses* are saying "no" when it is presented, *correct negatives* are saying "no" when the stimulus is not presented, and *false alarms* are saying "yes" when the stimulus is not presented. Hits and correct negatives are correct responses; misses and false alarms are incorrect responses. See **Figure 8.7**.)

A person's response bias can seriously affect an investigator's estimate of the threshold of detection. A cautious person will appear to have a higher threshold than someone who does not want to let a tone go by without saying "yes." Therefore, signal-detection theorists have developed a method of assessing subjects' sensitivity, regardless of their initial response bias. They deliberately manipulate the response biases and observe the results of these manipulations on the subjects' judgments.

Suppose you were a subject in the experiment just described, and the experimenter promised you a dollar every time you made a hit, with no penalty for false alarms. I suspect you would tend to say "yes" on every trial, even if you were not sure you had heard the tone. On the other hand, if the experimenter announced she would fine you a dollar every time you made a false alarm and give you nothing for making hits, you would undoubtedly say "no" every time, because you would have everything to lose and nothing to gain: you would be extremely cautious in your judgments.

Now consider your response bias under a number of intermediate conditions. If you receive a dollar for every hit but are also fined fifty cents for every miss, you will say "yes" whenever you are reasonably sure you heard the tone. If you receive fifty cents for every hit but are fined a dollar for each false alarm, you will be more cautious, but if you are sure you heard the tone you will say "yes" to earn fifty cents. Figure 8.8 graphs your performance over this range of payoff conditions. (See **Figure 8.8**.)

The result is a *receiver-operating characteristic (ROC) curve,* named for its original use in research at the Bell Laboratories to measure the intelligibility of speech transmitted through a telephone system. The curve in Figure 8.8 shows performance when the sound is difficult to detect. If the sound were louder, so that you rarely doubted whether you heard it or not, you would make almost every possible hit and very few false alarms. The few misses you made would be under the low-payoff condition, when you wanted to be absolutely certain that you heard the tone. The few false alarms would occur when guessing did not matter because the fine for being wrong was low

FIGURE 8.7 The four possibilities in judging the presence or absence of a stimulus.

JUDGEMENT

		"Yes"	"No"
EVENT	Light *did* flash	Hit	Miss
	Light *did not* flash	False alarm	Correct negative

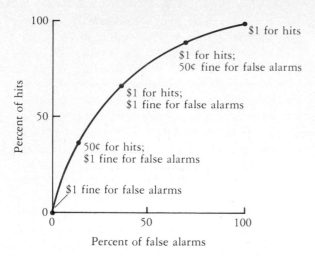

FIGURE 8.8   A receiver-operating characteristic (ROC) curve: percentage of hits and false alarms in judging the presence of a stimulus under several payoff conditions.

or nonexistent. The new ROC (color) is shown with the original one (black) in **Figure 8.9**. The difference between the two curves demonstrates that the louder tone is easier to detect. Detectability is measured by the relative heights of the peaks of curves measured perpendicular to a 45° line.

ROC curves can be obtained under a variety of conditions. They can measure one person's ability

FIGURE 8.9   Two ROC curves, obtained by presenting a more discriminable (colored curve) stimulus and a less discriminable (black curve) stimulus.

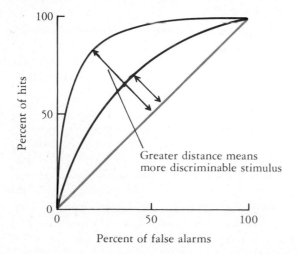

to detect two colors of light, to assess the sensitivity of his or her visual system to these stimuli; or they can measure the sensitivity of several people, to assess individual differences in their ability to detect stimuli. (I should note that there are other, less expensive ways to change people's response bias besides offering them payment. This is fortunate for researchers with limited budgets.)

The signal-detection method I just described is the best way to determine a person's sensitivity to the occurrence of a particular stimulus. Note that the concept of threshold is not used; instead, a stimulus is more or less detectable. The subject *decides* whether a stimulus occurred, and the consequences of making hits or false alarms can bias this decision. Signal-detection theory emphasizes that perception involves factors other than the activity of the sensory systems.

Interim summary: We experience the world through our senses. Your knowledge of the world stems from the accumulation of sensory experience and subsequent learning. But to study the nature of this experience scientifically, we must discover the physiological means by which we take in sensory experience.

All sensory experiences, not just visual ones, are the result of energy from events that are transduced into activity of receptors, which are either specialized cells or the dendritic endings of neurons. This transduction causes changes in the activity of axons of sensory nerves, which informs the sensory mechanisms of the brain about the environmental event. The information is coded both anatomically and temporally.

The ability to measure sensory experience is a prerequisite to dealing with it scientifically. In nineteenth-century Germany Weber and his successor Fechner began investigating the relation between the physical characteristics of stimuli and the perceptions they produced. Weber devised the concept of the just-noticeable difference, and Fechner used the jnd to measure the magnitude of sensations. In the twentieth century the signal-detection theory gave rise to methods that enabled psychologists to assess people's sensitivity to stimuli despite individual differences in response bias.

The principles of transduction and sensory coding, and the methods of psychophysics apply to all sensory modalities, including sight, smell, taste, hearing, and touch. The first—vision—is discussed in the rest of this chapter.

THE EYE

ANATOMY

◆ The eyes are important organs. Because they are delicate, they are well protected. Each eye is housed in a bony socket called the *orbit,* and can be covered by lids to keep dust and dirt out. The lids are edged by lashes that help keep foreign matter from falling into the open eye. The eyebrows help keep sweat on the forehead from dripping into the eyes. Reflex mechanisms provide additional protection: the sudden approach of an object toward the face or a touch on the surface of the eye causes automatic eyelid closure and withdrawal of the head.

Three opposing pairs of extraocular muscles move the eyes. (See **Figure 8.10.**) The term *extraocular,* "outside the eye," distinguishes them from the muscles in the eye itself. **Figure 8.11** shows a cross-section of a human eye. The outer white layer is the extremely tough *sclera* (from Greek *skleros,* "hard"). Eye surgeons need especially sharp needles to pierce this membrane. The transparent *cornea* forms a bulge at the front of the eye and admits light. The *conjunctiva,* a thin membrane, attaches to the eye near the edge of the cornea, lines the inside of the eyelids, and forms a sort of pouch around the eye. It is too clear and thin to be seen on the surface of the eye. (See **Figure 8.11.**).

FIGURE 8.10   The extraocular muscles, which move the human eye.

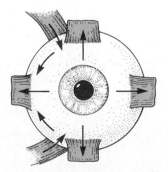

The *iris* consists of two bands of muscle that control the amount of light admitted into the eye. When the ringlike band of muscle contracts, the iris enlarges, constricting the size of the pupil. Contraction of the other muscle, whose fibers run radially, like spokes of a wheel, causes the iris to become more narrow, thus dilating the pupil.

The space immediately behind the cornea, called the anterior chamber, is filled with *aqueous humor,* which simply means "watery fluid." This fluid is constantly produced by tissue in the anterior chamber that filters it out of the blood. (A blockage of the passage that returns it to the blood can cause pressure to build up within the eye—a disorder known as glaucoma.) The aqueous humor nourishes the cornea and other portions of the front of the eye, which explains the circulation and renewal of this fluid. The need for a transparent cornea accounts for this unusual means of nourishment; our vision would not be very clear if we had a set of blood vessels across the front of our eyes.

The curvature of the cornea and of the *lens,* which lies immediately behind the iris, causes images to be focused on the back inner surface of the eye. The shape of the cornea is fixed, but the lens is flexible; a special set of muscles can alter its shape so that an observer's eyes can obtain images of either nearby or distant objects.

The posterior chamber, the great bulk of the eye, is filled with the *vitreous humor,* or "glassy fluid." This name, too, is apt, for the vitreous humor is not simply a liquid—it has strands and layers that give it shape. To remove vitreous humor during an operation, an eye surgeon cuts it with special scissors whose blades are snapped shut by compressed air. In this way the blades can cut the strands before they have time to move.

The *retina,* which lines most of the inner surface, performs the sensory functions of the eye. Embedded in the retina are over 130 million *photoreceptors*—receptor cells that transduce light into neural activity. The information from the photoreceptors is transmitted to neurons that send axons toward one point at the back of the eye—the *optic disk.* All axons leave the eye at this point and join the optic nerve, which travels to the brain. (See Figure 8.11 and **Color Plate 8.1.**) Because there are no photoreceptors in front of the optic disk, this portion of the retina is blind. If you have not

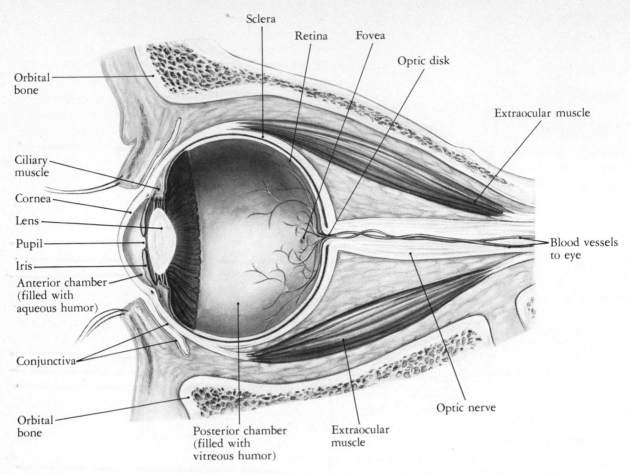

FIGURE 8.11   A cross-section of the human eye.
(Adapted from Carlson, N.R. *Physiology of Behavior*,
2nd ed. Boston: Allyn and Bacon, 1981.)

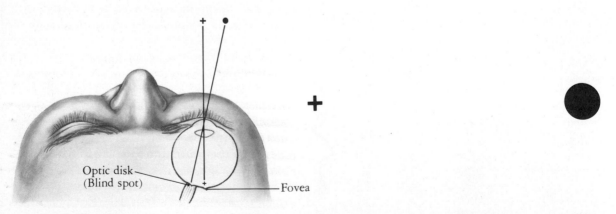

FIGURE 8.12   A test for the blind spot. With
the left eye closed, look at the + with your right eye
and move the page back and forth, toward and away
from yourself. At about 20 cm the black circle

disappears from your vision because its image falls on
your blind spot. (From Carlson, N.R. *Physiology of
Behavior*, 2nd ed. Boston: Allyn and Bacon, 1981.)

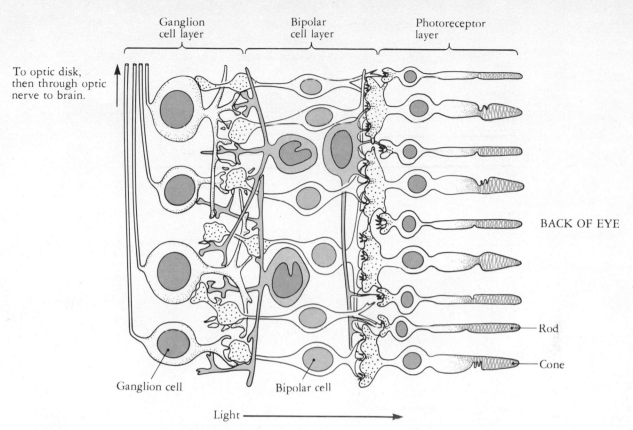

Ganglion cell layer Bipolar cell layer Photoreceptor layer

To optic disk, then through optic nerve to brain.

BACK OF EYE

Rod

Cone

Ganglion cell Bipolar cell

Light ⟶

FIGURE 8.13   The cells of the retina. (Redrawn by permission of the Royal Society and the authors from Dowling, J.E., and Boycott, B.B., *Proceedings of* *the Royal Society (London)*, 1966, Series B, *166*, 80–111.)

located your own *blind spot*, you might want to try the demonstration shown in **Figure 8.12.**

Before the seventeenth century it was thought that the lens sensed the presence of light. Johannes Kepler (1571–1630), the astronomer who discovered the true shape of the planets' orbits around the sun, is credited with the suggestion that the retina contains the receptive tissue of the eye. It remained for Christoph Scheiner (another German astronomer) to demonstrate in 1625 that the lens is simply a focusing device. After carefully peeling the sclera away from the back of an ox's eye, he was able to see an upside-down image of the world through the thin, translucent membrane that remained. As an astronomer, he was familiar with the fact that convex glass lenses could cast images, so he recognized the function of the lens of the eye.

Figure 8.13 shows a cross-section of the retina with its three principal layers. Light passes successively through the outermost **ganglion cell** layer,

the middle **bipolar cell** layer, and the innermost photoreceptor layer. Early anatomists were surprised to find the photoreceptors in the deepest layer. As you might expect, the cells that are located in front of the photoreceptors are transparent. (See **Figure 8.13.**)

Photoreceptors respond to light and pass the information on by means of a transmitter substance to the bipolar cells with which they synapse. Bipolar cells transmit this information to the ganglion cells, neurons whose axons travel across the retina and through the optic nerves. Thus, visual information passes through a three-cell chain to the brain: photoreceptor→bipolar cell→ganglion cell →brain.

A single photoreceptor responds only to the light that reaches its immediate vicinity, but a ganglion cell can receive information from many different photoreceptors. The retina also contains neurons that interconnect both adjacent photoreceptors and

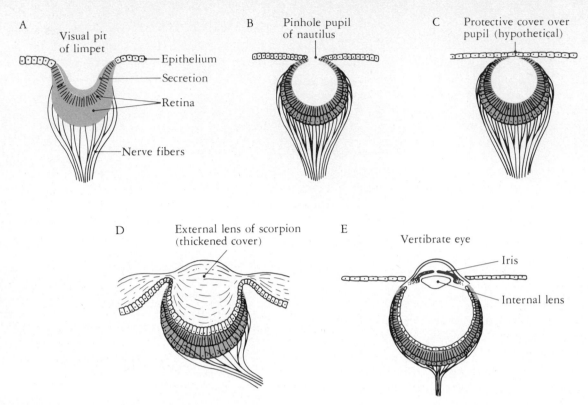

FIGURE 8.14   The probable evolution of the vertebrate eye. *A.* The visual pit of a limpet, a single-shelled mollusc. *B.* The eye of a nautilus, with its pinhole pupil. *C.* A hypothetical transitional stage showing a transparent protective cover over the pupil. *D.* The eye of a scorpion, with a lens that could have evolved from a protective cover. *E.* A vertebrate eye, with internal lens and adjustable pupil formed by the opening in the iris. (Adapted from Walls, G.L. The vertebrate eye and its adaptive radiation, *Cranbrook Institute of Science Bulletin,* 1942, *19.*)

adjacent ganglion cells. (See **Figure 8.13.**) The existence of this neural circuitry indicates that some kinds of information processing are performed in the retina.

The evolution of the vertebrate eye probably had a great deal to do with natural selection for increasingly efficient groupings of photoreceptors (Gregory, 1978). (See **Figure 8.14.**) Our most primitive ancestors probably had photoreceptors scattered over the surface of their bodies, as earthworms do. These evolved into patches collected at the back of a small depression, like the visual pit of the limpet (a small single-shelled mollusk), then probably into eyes with a small pinhole in the front, like the eyes of the nautilus (a large mollusk with a spiral shell). A pinhole serves as a primitive lens; in fact, a tin can with a small hole in one end and a piece of film in the other functions as a camera. Because a small hole can easily become plugged with debris, a transparent covering was probably the next step in evolution. Once a cover had evolved, there remained only the development of a cover with a bulge in it, to form a lens. Thereafter the opening could become larger, because the lens, and not the pinhole, could accomplish the focusing of the image on the photoreceptors at the back of the eye.

The human retina contains two general types of photoreceptors: *rods* and *cones.* The *fovea,* a small pit in the back of the retina, approximately 1 millimeter in diameter, contains only cones. (Look back at **Figure 8.11.**) Because most cones are connected only to one ganglion cell apiece, the fovea is responsible for our finest, most detailed vision.

When we look at a point in our visual field, we move our eyes so that the image of that point falls directly upon the cone-packed fovea. Thus the fovea provides us with our greatest visual acuity. (*Acuity* derives from Latin *acus,* "needle." We use the same concept when we say that someone has "sharp eyes"; we mean he or she can see extremely small details.) Cones are also responsible for our ability to see colors, a topic that is discussed later in this chapter.

Farther away from the fovea the number of cones decreases and the number of rods increases. Up to 100 rods may converge on a single ganglion cell. A ganglion cell receiving information from so many rods is sensitive to very low levels of light; a small quantity of light falling on many rods can effectively stimulate the ganglion cell on which their information converges. Thus rods provide our sensitivity to very dim light but provide little acuity.

The differences in the roles of rods and cones explains a sensory phenomenon that you may have discovered for yourself (and that may also account for some "sightings" of ghosts). If you are in the dark for a while you may notice a small, very dim light to the side of your gaze, but it will disappear as soon as you look directly at it. This is because the dim light is sufficient to stimulate ganglion cells that respond to rods but not cones. The rod-rich peripheral retina can detect the stimulus, but the rod-free fovea cannot.

TRANSDUCTION

Although light-sensitive sensory organs have evolved independently in a wide variety of animals—from insects to fish to mammals—the chemistry is essentially the same in all species; one molecule, derived from vitamin A, is the central ingredient in the transduction of the energy of light into neural activity. (Carrots are supposed to be good for vision because they contain a substance that the body easily converts to vitamin A.) In the absence of light, this molecule is attached to another molecule, a protein. The two molecules together form a *photopigment.* The photoreceptors of the human eye contain four kinds of photopigments, but their basic mechanism is the same. When a *photon* (a particle of light) strikes a photopigment, the photopigment splits apart into its two constituent mole-

cules. This event starts the process of transduction. The splitting of the photopigment causes a series of chemical changes that stimulate the photoreceptor and cause it to send a message to the bipolar cell with which it forms a synapse. The bipolar cell sends the message to the ganglion cells, which send it on to the brain. (See **Figure 8.15.**)

When they are intact, photopigments have a characteristic color. For example, *rhodopsin,* the photopigment of rods, is pink (*rhodos* means "rose" in Greek). However, once the photopigments are split apart by the action of light they lose their color—they become bleached. Franz Boll discovered this phenomenon in 1876 when he removed an eye from an animal and pointed it toward a

FIGURE 8.15   Transduction of light into neural activity and the transmission of information to the brain.

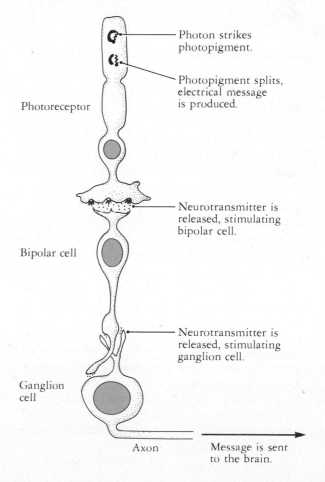

Photoreceptor

Photon strikes photopigment.

Photopigment splits, electrical message is produced.

Neurotransmitter is released, stimulating bipolar cell.

Bipolar cell

Neurotransmitter is released, stimulating ganglion cell.

Ganglion cell

Axon

Message is sent to the brain.

window opening upon a brightly lit scene. He then examined the retina under dim light and found that the image of the scene was still there. The retina was pink where little light had fallen and pale where the image had been bright. It was Boll's discovery that led investigators to suspect that a chemical reaction was responsible for the transduction of light into neural activity.

After light has caused a molecule of photopigment to become bleached (split), energy from the cell's metabolism causes the two molecules to recombine, and the photopigment is ready to be bleached by light again. Each photoreceptor contains many thousands of molecules of photopigment. The number of intact molecules of photopigment in a given cell depends upon the relative rates at which they are being split by light and being put back together by the cell's energy. The brighter the light, the more bleached photopigment there is. This leads us to the topic of the next section.

ADAPTATION TO LIGHT AND DARK

The easiest way to introduce the phenomenon of visual adaptation is to ask you to remember how difficult it is to find a seat in a darkened movie theater. If you have just come in from the bright sun, your eyes do not respond well to the low level of illumination. However, after a few minutes you can see rather well—your eyes have adapted.

To be detected, a photon must bleach (split) a molecule of rhodopsin. When high levels of illumination strike the retina, the regeneration of rhodopsin falls behind the bleaching process. With only a small percentage of the rhodopsin molecules intact, the rods are not very sensitive to light. If you enter a dark room after being in a brightly lit room or in sunlight, there are too few intact rhodopsin molecules for your eyes to respond immediately to dim light. The probability that a photon will strike an intact molecule of rhodopsin is very low. However, after a while the regeneration of rhodopsin overcomes the bleaching effects of the energy of light. The rods become full of unbleached rhodopsin, and a photon passing through a rod is likely to find a target. The eye has undergone *dark adaptation*.

Even before the development of electron microscopes permitted detailed examination of rods and cones, psychologists were able to demonstrate their functional differences by studying the process of dark adaptation. Hecht and Schlaer (1938) exposed a subject's eyes to bright illumination and then completely darkened the room. To determine the detection threshold, they gradually increased the intensity of a small spot of light until the subject reported seeing it. As dark adaptation proceeded, the subject's visual detection threshold got progressively lower; the eyes became progressively more sensitive to light. (A *low* threshold denotes greater sensitivity, because a lower stimulus intensity is able to produce a sensation.)

Figure 8.16 shows the results of the dark-adaptation experiment. Each point on the vertical axis indicates the intensity of light necessary to produce a sensation (the threshold). (Note that the scale on the vertical axis is logarithmic; a log value of 8 is 100,000 times greater than a log value of 3.) The figure shows clearly that the process of dark adaptation is not smooth and continuous; a break occurs after about seven minutes in the dark. (See **Figure 8.16**.)

The discontinuity in the dark-adaptation curve is called the *rod-cone break.* The function is really two curves, not one. Cones, which are less sensitive than rods, complete their regeneration of photopigments in five to seven minutes. The part of the curve before the break represents their activity. Rods

FIGURE 8.16   A dark adaptation curve showing a rod-cone break. (From Hecht, S., and Schlaer, S. *Journal of the Optical Society of America,* 1938, *28,* 269–275.)

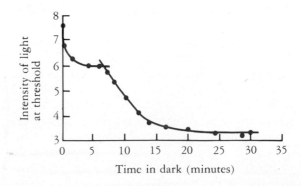

are slower to regenerate rhodopsin, but they are more sensitive to light, so we see the effect of their adaptation only after the cones are completely dark adapted.

How can we be sure that the break is due to differences in the rate of dark adaptation of rods and cones and that cones are responsible for the top curve and rods for the bottom one? A rather simple experiment provides the answer. Before I describe it, try to see whether you can think of it yourself. Here is a hint: remember that the fovea contains only cones.

* * *

Here is how the evidence can be obtained. If a subject looks directly at a small spot of light only the fovea (which contains just cones) will be stimulated. A dark adaptation curve obtained this way contains only the upper limb. However, if the spot of light appears off to the side so that it stimulates more peripheral portions of the retina (where both rods and cones are located) the dark-adaptation curve contains both limbs.

There is more evidence that rods and cones differ in their functions. Some people's retinas lack cones altogether. Dark-adaptation curves obtained from these people show only the lower limb. Because the rhodopsin in their photoreceptors quickly bleaches out, they must avoid bright light or they will become temporarily blind. Because their foveas are empty, their visual acuity is very poor. These people also lack color vision. These symptoms provide evidence for all the differences in the

functions of the rods and cones: cones are less sensitive to light but mediate our most detailed vision, and they are necessary for the perception of color.

SIMULTANEOUS CONTRAST

There are mechanisms in the retina that increase our sensitivity to features of our environment. The small gray squares in Figure 8.17 appear to differ in brightness, but in fact do not. (See **Figure 8.17.**) Through the phenomenon of *simultaneous contrast,* if two adjacent regions of the visual scene differ in brightness, the visual system exaggerates the difference; a gray square looks darker against a white background and lighter against a black background.

Simultaneous contrast appears to be caused by *lateral inhibition,* which is illustrated in Figure 8.18. This figure shows a mosaic of hypothetical receptors that are interconnected in such a way that each one, when stimulated by light, will inhibit its neighbors. If light falls on one receptor, its rate of firing will increase, and this activity will depress the firing rate of the receptors that surround it. (In the figure, relative shades of gray represent relative firing rates. See **Figure 8.18.**) By depressing the activity of the surrounding cells, lateral inhibition produces more of a contrast between the stimulated receptor and its neighbors.

Figure 8.19 illustrates the significance of lateral inhibition. This figure shows the six panels of a

FIGURE 8.17 Simultaneous contrast. The gray square on the right appears lighter than the one on the left, although they are the same shade.

Each receptor
inhibits its neighbors.

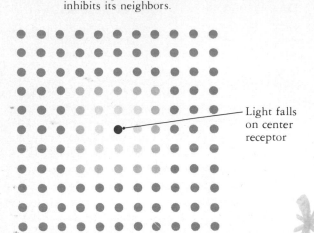

Light falls
on center
receptor

FIGURE 8.18 Lateral inhibition exaggerates the difference between the stimulated receptor (center) and its neighbors. (The shading indicates the receptors' level of activity.)

"gray scale" used by photographers to calibrate their equipment. Each panel appears to be not quite uniform in color; its left side looks lighter than its right, and consequently the gray scale appears to be subdivided by dark vertical lines. (See **Figure 8.19.**) Lateral inhibition adds these contrasting features, apparently so that we can more easily detect differences in brightness in the environment (in fact, the panels are uniform in brightness and

FIGURE 8.19 Although each shade of gray is uniform across its width, lateral inhibition produces the impression of dark or light lines between each panel.

there are no vertical lines between them). The visual system exaggerates information that might be important to us.

COLOR VISION

Among mammals, only primates have true color vision. A bull does not charge a red cape; he charges what he sees as an annoying gray object being waved at him. Among nonmammals, many birds and fishes have excellent color vision; the brightly colored lure may really appeal to the fish as much as to the angler who buys it.

Experiments have shown that there are three types of cones in the human eye, each containing a different type of photopigment. Each type of photopigment is most sensitive to a particular *wavelength* of light; that is, light of a particular wavelength most readily causes a particular photopigment to split. Thus, different types of cones are stimulated by different wavelengths of light. Information from the cones enables us to perceive colors.

To understand color vision we must know something about the physical nature of light. Wavelength is an important physical characteristic of light. Light from an incandescent source, such as the sun, consists of radiant energy similar to radio waves and contains a mixture of many frequencies. Because the speed of radiant energy is always constant—186,000 miles per second—the frequency of vibration determines the wavelength of the energy. The faster the vibration, the shorter the wavelength. (See **Figure 8.20.**)

The wavelength of visible light ranges from 380 through 760 *nanometers (nm,* billionths of a meter). Ultraviolet radiation, X rays, and cosmic rays are also forms of radiant energy, but have shorter wavelengths. Infrared radiation and radio waves have longer wavelengths. (See **Color Plate 8.2.**)

Wavelength is related to color, but the terms are not synonymous. First, color is a perceptual term, not a physical one. A particular wavelength does not have a color; it can only be said to produce a *sensation* of color in an animal with color vision. To say that humans *see* 435-nm light as blue is quite different from saying that 435-nm light *is* blue. Second, the *spectral colors* (the colors we see in a rainbow, which contains the entire spectrum

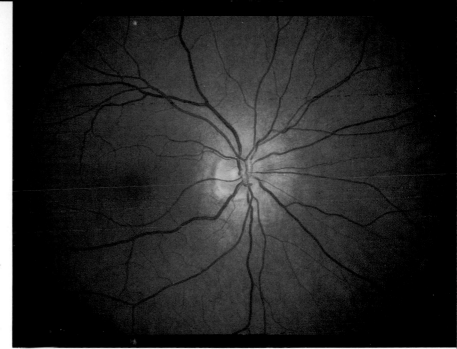

COLOR PLATE 8.1 A view of the back of the eye showing the retina, fovea, optic disk, and blood vessels. (Courtesy of Douglas G. Mollerstuen, New England Medical Center.)

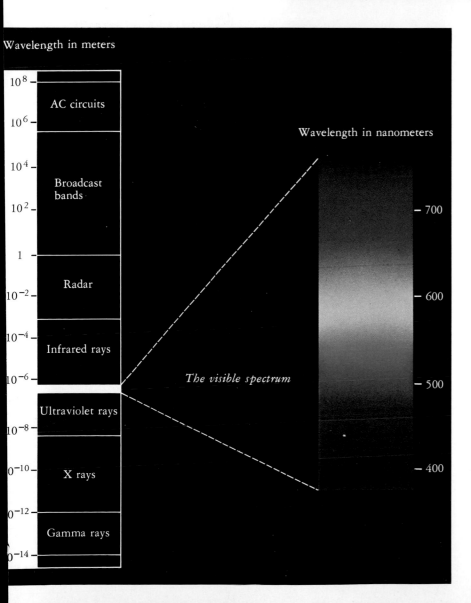

Wavelength in meters

AC circuits

Broadcast bands

Radar

Infrared rays

Ultraviolet rays

X rays

Gamma rays

10^8
10^6
10^4
10^2
1
10^{-2}
10^{-4}
10^{-6}
10^{-8}
0^{-10}
0^{-12}
0^{-14}

Wavelength in nanometers

The visible spectrum

— 700

— 600

— 500

— 400

COLOR PLATE 8.2
The electromagnetic spectrum.

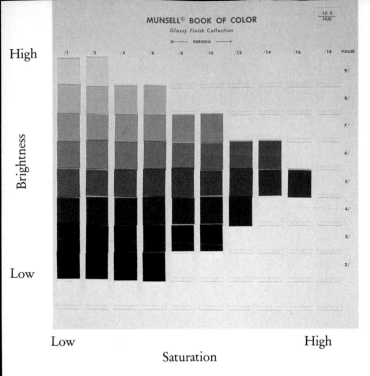

High

Brightness

Low

Low   High

Saturation

COLOR PLATE 8.3 These colors have the same dominant wavelength (hue), but different saturation and brightness. (Courtesy of Munsell Color Corporation.)

COLOR PLATE 8.4 A color circle showing fully saturated hues of different wavelengths. The reddish-purple hues between 380 and 700 nanometers are not part of the spectrum, but consist of mixtures of these two wavelengths. Pairs of hues on opposite sides of the circle are complementary; when added together they produce a colorless grey.

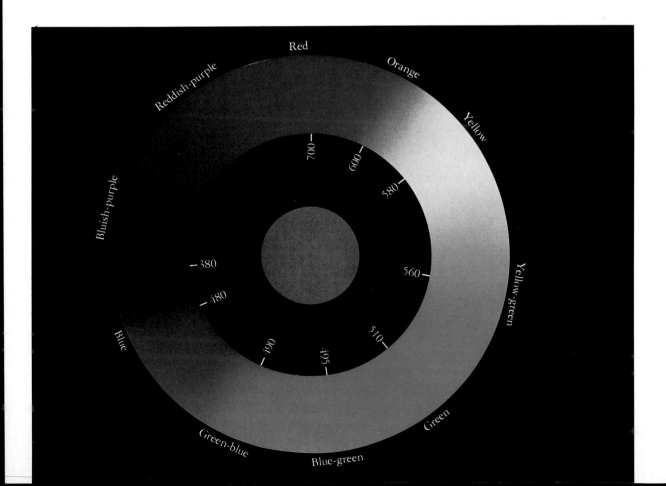

COLOR PLATE 8.5   White light can be split into a spectrum
of colors with a prism and recombined through another prism.

COLOR PLATE 8.6   Additive color mix-
ing. When blue, red, and green light of the proper
intensity are shone together the result is white
light. (Courtesy of GATF.)

COLOR PLATE 8.7   A possible arrangement
of blue, red, and green cones in the human retina,
based on the model proposed by Walraven (1974).

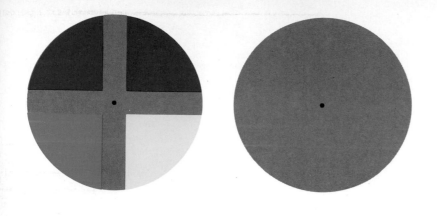

COLOR PLATE 8.8 A negative afterimage. Stare for several seconds at the dot in the center of the left figure; then quickly transfer your gaze to the dot in the center of the right figure. You will see colors that are complementary to the originals.

COLOR PLATE 8.9 A negative afterimage. Stare for several seconds at the center of the painting; then look at a sheet of white paper.

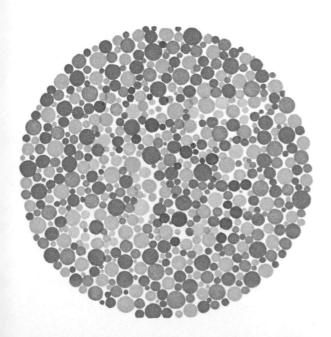

COLOR PLATE 8.10 A figure commonly used to test for defective color vision. People with red/green color blindness will fail to see the 5 or the 7. (Courtesy of American Optical Corporation.)

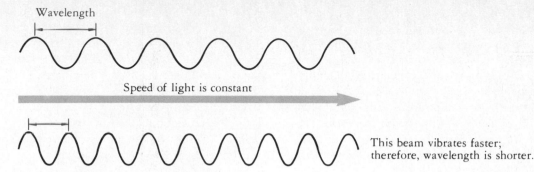

FIGURE 8.20   Because the speed of light is constant, faster vibrations produce shorter wavelengths.

of visible radiant energy) do not include all colors that we can see, such as brown, pink, and the metallic colors silver and gold. The fact that not all colors are found in the spectrum means that differences in wavelength alone cannot account for the differences in the colors we can perceive.

The Dimensions of Color

◆ Most colors can be described in terms of three physical dimensions: wavelength, intensity, and purity. Three perceptual dimensions corresponding to these physical dimensions describe what we see. (See **Table 8.1**.) The *hue* of most colors is determined by wavelength; for example, light with a wavelength of 540 nm is perceived as green. A color's *brightness* is determined by the intensity, or degree of energy, of the light that is being perceived, all other factors being equal. However, as we shall see in a later section on perception of light and dark, our perceptions of brightness of an object are greatly influenced by the surrounding scene.

The third perceptual dimension of color is *saturation.* Saturation is roughly equivalent to purity. A fully saturated color consists of light of only one wavelength; the spectral colors of the rainbow are all fully saturated. If white light (light containing a mixture of all wavelengths) is mixed with light of a particular wavelength, the result will be a desaturated color. For example, when red light (650 nm) is added to white light, the result is pink light. Pink is thus a less-saturated version of red. Color Plate 8.3 illustrates how a color with a particular dominant wavelength (hue) can vary in its brightness and saturation. Color Plate 8.4 illustrates a ring containing colors with different hues. (See **Color Plates 8.3 and 8.4**.)

Color Mixing

◆ The circle shown in Color Plate 8.4 demonstrates the fact that not all hues can be specified by wavelength; some hues are not found in the visual spectrum. There is a gap between red (700 nm) and

TABLE 8.1   Physical and perceptual dimensions of color

Perceptual dimension	Physical dimension	Physical characteristics
Hue	Wavelength	Frequency of oscillation of light radiation
Brightness	Intensity	Amplitude of light radiation
Saturation	Purity	Intensity of dominant wavelength, relative to total radiant energy

violet (420 nm), but psychologically no gap exists. The colors blend, and there do not appear to be any sudden shifts in hue. (See **Color Plate 8**.4.) Theoretically, if we start with the longest wavelength (red) and move through shorter and shorter wavelengths we eventually get to violet—we should be *as far away from red as we can be.* But even though we have moved through the entire spectrum, perceptually we have arrived back very near our starting point; violet does not look all that different from red.

Why do violet and red look so similar, when they are at opposite ends of the spectrum? To illustrate the paradoxical nature of this phenomenon consider the keyboard of a piano. Low-frequency notes are found at the left. If we play each key from left to right, we hear sounds of higher and higher frequency (that is, shorter and shorter wavelength). The top note sounds nothing like the lowest one. If the sound spectrum were analogous to the color spectrum, then the top notes of a piano would sound similar to the lowest ones. However, this is not the case. Why do violet and red look so similar, when they are at opposite ends of the spectrum? The physics of light provides no solution to this paradox. The perception of hues as a continuous sequence is a psychological phenomenon. The colors on the color circle between red and violet are not part of the spectrum; they are mixtures of various amounts of red and violet light. We perceive these mixtures as individual colors, intermediate in hue to the colors that produce them. We do not see the original two component colors.

Vision is a *synthetic* sensory modality; that is, it synthesizes (puts together) rather than analyzes (takes apart). We see an intermediate color rather than the two components. (In contrast, the auditory system is analytic. If a high note and a low note are played together on a piano we hear both notes instead of a single, intermediate tone.) The addition of two or more lights of different wavelengths is called *color mixing.* This procedure is very different from paint mixing, and so are its results. If we pass a beam of white light through a prism we break it into the spectrum of the different wavelengths it contains. If we recombine these colors by passing them through another prism, we obtain white light again. (See **Color Plate 8**.5.)

When we mix paints we are subtracting colors,

not adding them together. If we mix red, orange, yellow, and green paint and so on through violet, we will not produce white paint. Mixing two paints always yields a darker result: blue paint and yellow paint yield green paint. But mixing two beams of light of different wavelengths always yields a brighter color. For example, when red and green light are shone together on a piece of white paper, we see yellow. In fact, we cannot tell a pure yellow (575 nm) from a synthesized one made of the proper intensities of red and green light. To our eyes, both yellows appear identical.

To reconstitute white light, we do not even have to recombine all the wavelengths in the spectrum. If we shine a blue light, a green light, and a red light together on a sheet of white paper and properly adjust their intensities, the place where all three beams overlap will look perfectly white. (See **Color Plate 8**.6.)

Color Coding in the Retina

◈ In 1802 Thomas Young, a British physicist and physician, noted that the human visual system can synthesize any color from various amounts of almost any set of three different wavelengths. Young hypothesized that the eye contains three types of color receptors, each sensitive to a different hue, and that the brain synthesizes colors by combining the information received by each type of receptor. He suggested that these receptors were sensitive to the psychologically "pure" colors blue, green, and red.

Subsequent experiments have shown that the cones in the human eye do contain three types of photopigments, each of which preferentially absorbs light of a particular wavelength: 435, 540, and 565 nm. Although Color Plate 8.4 shows that in fact these wavelengths correspond to blue, green, and yellow, by convention the receptors are referred to as blue, green, and red cones. Red and green cones are present in about equal proportions, but there are far fewer blue cones. **Color Plate 8**.7 shows a hypothetical arrangement. A color television screen uses our ability to synthesize all the colors we see in the picture from only three hues. If you look at the screen with a magnifying glass you will see closely spaced red, green, and blue dots. All the colors we see are produced by different intensities of those dots.

Several scientists after Young devised theories that took account of the fact that yellow is also a psychologically "pure" hue. Late in the nineteenth century Ewald Hering, a German physiologist, noted that the four primary hues appeared to belong to pairs of complementary (in this case, opposing) colors: red/green and yellow/blue. We can imagine a bluish green or a yellowish green, a bluish red or a yellowish red; however, we cannot imagine a greenish red or a yellowish blue. Hering suggested that we cannot imagine these blends because there are two types of photoreceptors, one kind responding to green and red, and the other responding to yellow and blue. The responses are coded by an *opponent process.*

Recordings of the electrical activity of single neurons in the retina have shown that Hering's opponent-process theory is correct, but that it applies to ganglion cells and not to photoreceptors. Two types of ganglion cells encode color vision: red/green and yellow/blue. In the dark, a red/green ganglion cell fires at a steady rate. However, if red light shines on nearby cones the cell will begin to fire at a faster rate (E, an excitatory effect); green light will make the cell fire at a slower rate (I, an inhibitory effect). Thus, the cell encodes red and green in opposing fashion: an increase in rate encodes the presence of red light while a decrease

encodes green light. Similarly, yellow/blue ganglion cells respond faster to yellow light and more slowly to blue light. (See **Figure 8.21.**)

Figure 8.22 diagrams the effects from stimulation of each type of cone on the firing of these two classes of ganglion cells. The arrows do not imply direct neural connections, only *effects*. (See **Figure 8.22.**) This mechanism explains why we never see a reddish green or a yellowish blue. Because different sets of axons transmit information about red/green and yellow/blue to the brain, the two sets can fire independently. That is, red/green axons can fire rapidly, signaling red, while the yellow/blue axons fire slowly, signaling blue. As a result we perceive a combination of red and blue. By similar means we can perceive greenish blue, reddish yellow, or greenish yellow. But red and green or yellow and blue cannot be signaled simultaneously; an axon cannot fire quickly and slowly at the same time. A perfectly balanced mixture of red and green will cause no change in the firing rate of the red/green ganglion cells, because the excitatory and inhibitory effects will cancel each other.

A color has more than a particular hue; it also has a particular saturation and brightness. Red/green and yellow/blue ganglion cells cannot specify all three dimensions. Another type of ganglion cell, called a black/white cell, responds only to bright-

FIGURE 8.21   Opponent process: the effect of various hues of light on the activity of yellow/blue and red/green ganglion cells.

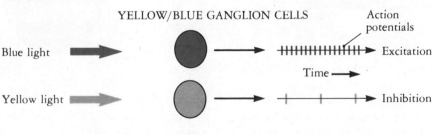

YELLOW/BLUE GANGLION CELLS

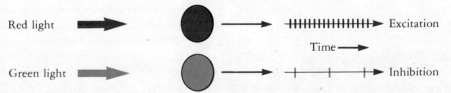

RED/GREEN GANGLION CELLS

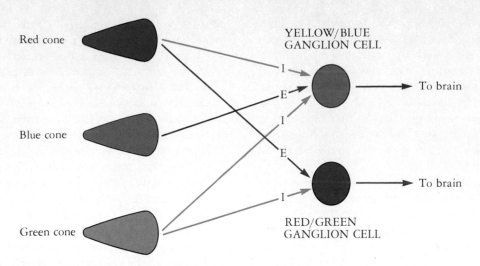

FIGURE 8.22   Opponent process: hypothetical connections between cones and yellow/blue and red/green ganglion cells.

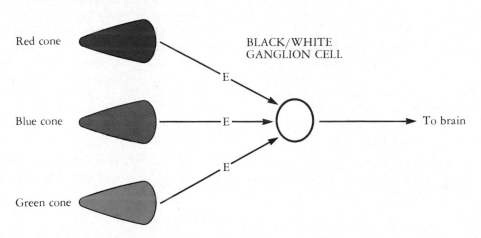

FIGURE 8.23   Hypothetical connections between cones and black/white ganglion cells.

ness. Black/white cells are stimulated by all three kinds of cones. (See **Figure 8.23.**) Visual mechanisms in the brain perceive brightness and saturation of colors by comparing the activity of these cells with those of the red/green and yellow/blue cells.

Negative Afterimages

◆ The figures in Color Plate 8.8 demonstrate an interesting property of the visual system—the formation of a *negative afterimage.* Stare at the dot in the center of the lefthand circle (the one with the patches of color) for approximately thirty seconds. Then quickly look at the dot in the center of the blank gray circle to the right. You will have a fleeting experience of seeing four colors that are *complementary,* or opposite, to the ones to the left. (See **Color Plate 8.8.**) Complementary items are those that go together to make up a whole. In this context, complementary colors are those that make white (or shades of gray) when added together. To me, the complements of the blue, red, green, and yellow of the left figure are orangish yellow, pale blue, magenta, and purple.

Two processes account for our perception of negative afterimages: bleaching of photopigments and adaptation of the ganglion cells. When cones in one region of the retina are stimulated with color of a particular hue, some are stimulated more than others, and their supply of photopigment becomes more bleached out. These cones are then less able than the others to respond to a balanced source of illumination like the gray square. The more vigorous response of the other cones produces an unbalanced input to the ganglion cells, resulting in the perception of the complementary color. Negative afterimages also occur because neurons that are excited or inhibited for a long period of time adapt to these influences, and hence show a "rebound" effect when the excitation or inhibition is removed. For example, a ganglion cell that is inhibited by a green cone for twenty seconds will adapt to this influence and fire more rapidly than normal when balanced illumination strikes the retina.

Negative color afterimages can be quite striking. Color Plate 8.9 shows a picture of a young woman painted by Johann von Goethe. If you stare at a single point (such as her nose) for a few seconds, then quickly look at a piece of plain white paper, you will see a fleeting image of her again, this time in more normal colors. (See **Color Plate 8.9.**)

The existence of complementary colors has nothing to do with the intrinsic properties of light. The only reason that they make white light when mixed together is that our visual systems are constructed the way they are. Complementary colors are pairs of colors that stimulate the photoreceptors in such a way that they produce a perfect balance between the excitatory and inhibitory influences on the red/green and yellow/blue ganglion cells, so that the firing rate of these cells does not change. However, the brightness detector (black/white ganglion cell) receives excitatory input from all three types of cones, and its firing rate goes up. Thus, the brain receives a message of having perceived bright, colorless light—white.

Defects in Color Vision

Approximately one in twenty males has some form of defective color vision. These defects are some-

times called color blindness but the latter term should probably be reserved for the very few people who cannot see any color at all. Males are affected more than females because many of the genes for producing photopigments appear to be located on the X chromosome. Because males have only one X chromosome, a defective gene there will always be expressed.

There are many different types of defective color vision. Two of the three described here involve the red/green system. People with these defects confuse red and green. Their primary color sensations are yellow and blue; red and green both look yellowish. Color Plate 8.10 shows one of the figures from a commonly used test of defective color vision. A person who confuses red and green will not be able to see the 5 or the 7. (See **Color Plate 8.10.**) The most common defect, called *protanopia,* appears to result from a lack of the photopigment for red cones. The fact that people with protanopia have relatively normal acuity suggests that they do have red cones, but that they are filled with green photopigment (Boynton, 1979). To a protanope, red looks much darker than green. In a mild form of protanopia called *protanomaly,* the red cones are sensitive to light of 545 nm rather than to the normal 575 nm. This wavelength is intermediate between normal red and normal green. The second form of red/green defect, called *deuteranopia,* appears to result from the opposite kind of substitution: green cones are filled with red photopigment.

The third form of color defect, called *tritanopia,* involves the yellow/blue system and is much rarer: it affects fewer than 1 in 10,000 people. Tritanopes see the world in greens and reds; to them a clear blue sky is a bright green, and yellow looks pink. Unlike protanopia and deuteranopia, the faulty allele that causes tritanopia is carried on an autosome, not an X chromosome. This defect appears to involve loss of blue cones, but because there are far fewer of these than of red and green cones to begin with, it is not possible to determine whether the cones are missing or filled with one of the other photopigments.

There is an extremely rare condition of true color blindness in which people have functioning cones but are completely unable to discriminate hues. These people see the world in black and white.

Unlike people whose retinas lack cones (and who consequently have poor vision), these people have normal acuity. This condition is probably a combination of protanopia or deuteranopia with tritanopia within the same individual: their red and green cones contain only one photopigment and they lack blue cones.

Interim summary: You now have a better idea of how your visual experiences are transduced and transmitted to the brain. This section has described the anatomy of the eye and how it responds to light and perceives color. The retina contains photoreceptors: rods and cones. The energy from light is transduced into neural activity when a photon strikes a molecule of photopigment, splitting it into its two constituents. This event causes the photoreceptor to send information to the ganglion cells, by means of the bipolar cells.

When an image of the visual scene is cast upon the retina, each part of the image has a specific hue, brightness, and saturation. The red, blue, and green cones respond in proportion to the amount of each of these wavelengths contained in the light striking them. The encoded information is transmitted through red/green, yellow/blue, and black/white ganglion cells, which send axons to the brain. The amount of activity in the red/green, yellow/blue, and black/white axons from each part of the retina gives rise to the perception of an image, complete with color.

VISUAL PERCEPTION

The visual system performs many remarkable tasks. The brain receives fragments of information from hundreds of thousands of axons of the optic nerves and combines and organizes them into the perception of a scene—objects with different forms, colors, and textures, residing at different locations in three-dimensional space. Even when our eyes move, exposing the photoreceptors to entirely new patterns of visual information, our perception of the scene before us does not change. We see a stable world, not a moving one, because the brain keeps track of the constantly changing patterns of neural firing.

If you can conveniently do so, take a break from your reading now and go for a short walk—even if it is only around the room. Think of what you are seeing—shapes, figures, background, shadows, areas of light and dark—as you move and as your eyes move. Your knowledge of the objects and their relative location is extensive, and you have a good idea of what they will feel like, even if you have not touched them. If the lighting suddenly changes (if lamps are turned on or off or a cloud passes in front of the sun) the amount of light reflected by the objects in the scene changes too, but your perception of the objects remains the same—you see them as having the same shape, color, and texture as before. Similarly, you do not perceive an object as increasing in size as you approach it, even though the image it casts upon your retina does get larger. These perceptions of form, movement, and space are the remaining topics of this chapter.

PERCEPTION OF LIGHT AND DARK

◆ Experiments have shown that people can judge the whiteness or grayness of an object very well, even if the level of illumination changes. If you look at a sheet of white paper in either bright sunlight or in shade, you will perceive it as being white, even though the intensities of its image on your retina differ. If you look at a sheet of gray paper in sunlight, it may in fact reflect more light to your eye than a white paper located in the shade, but you will still see the white paper as white and the gray paper as gray. (See **Figure 8.24**.)

This phenomenon is known as *brightness constancy*. Katz (1935) demonstrated brightness constancy by constructing a vertical barrier and positioning a light source so that a shadow was cast to the right of the barrier. In the shadow he placed a gray square card on a white background. In the lighted area on the left of the barrier he placed a number of shades of gray and asked subjects to choose one that would match the gray square in the shadow. (See **Figure 8.25**.) His subjects matched the grays not in terms of the light that the cards actually reflected, but in terms of the light they *would have* reflected if both had been viewed under the same level of illumination. In other words, the subjects compensated for the dimness of the shadow. The match was not perfect, but it was much closer than it would have been if perception of brightness were made solely from the

FIGURE 8.24   A demonstration of brightness constancy. The paper looks equally bright in the shade or sunlight, because we judge its brightness relative to its surroundings.

amount of light in the image of the cards on the retina.

The perception of white and gray, then, is not a matter of absolutes. In the first place, there is no such thing as gray light. If you place a red or blue filter in front of a source of light and shine it on a piece of white paper, the illumination will look red or blue, but if you use a gray filter the result will be a dimmer white light, not a gray light. Second, gray is a color that cannot exist in isolation; it is perceived only if white or brighter shades of gray are also present. If an illuminated gray card is the only object you can see in an otherwise dark room, it will look white, not gray. Also, if white is eliminated from a scene, the brightest gray becomes white. In other words, people perceive the brightest neutrally colored object in the environment as white and perceive the brightness of other colors relative to it. For example, you perceive a ceiling painted a rather dark off-white color as pure white unless a piece of white paper is placed next to it for comparison. Furthermore, you see the white of a ceiling or wall as white even where it is in shadow. In fact people often do not even see shadows unless they specifically look for them.

PERCEPTION OF FORM: FIGURE AND GROUND

◆ If you look at the scene in front of you, you will observe that most of what you see can be categorized as either object or background. Objects appear as things, and have a particular location in space; they have *form*. The background is essentially formless and serves mostly as a texture behind the objects. The distinction between an object and a background is not rigid; a picture hanging on a wall can appear as an object or as part of the background, depending on whether you pay specific attention to it. And some pictures can provide ambiguous clues; does **Figure 8.26** illustrate two faces or a wine goblet?

FIGURE 8.25   The experiment by Katz (1935), which demonstrated brightness constancy.

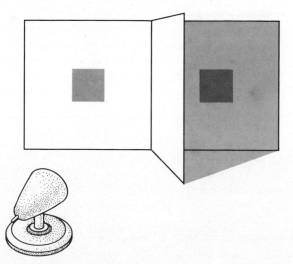

FIGURE 8.26   A drawing in which figure and ground can be reversed. You can see either two faces against a white background or a wineglass against a dark background.

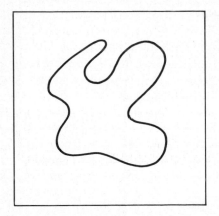

FIGURE 8.27   We immediately perceive even an unfamiliar figure when the outline is closed.

Psychologists use the terms *figure* and **ground** to label an object and its background, respectively. Even without three-dimensional cues, we tend to organize what we see in terms of figure and ground. In fact, it is difficult *not* to see figure and ground in a drawing such as the one shown in **Figure 8.27.**

What rules determine which parts of a scene we perceive as figure, and which parts as ground? If the pattern of stimulation is that of a well-known object, it will almost certainly be seen as a figure,

FIGURE 8.28   We tend to perceive a group of smaller elements as a larger figure.

but so will an unfamiliar, meaningless form such as the one you saw in Figure 8.27. Therefore, although familiarity is important for perception of form, it is not necessary. If it were, we would have difficulty perceiving objects we have never seen before.

One of the most important aspects of form perception is the existence of a *boundary*. If the visual field contains a sharp and distinct change in brightness, color, or texture, an edge is perceived. If this edge forms a continuous boundary, the space enclosed by the boundary will probably be perceived as a figure. The form you saw in Figure 8.27 is perceived as such because of its distinct border. But the presence of an actual line is not necessary for the perception of form. Figure 8.28 shows we tend to perceive small elements arranged in groups as larger figures (See **Figure 8.28.**)

The tendency to perceive elements as belonging together has been recognized for many years. Earlier this century, a group of psychologists organized a theory of perception called **Gestalt psychology.** *Gestalt* means "form," but Gestalt psychologists use the term to mean more than that. Their essential thesis is that the whole, in perception, is more than the sum of its parts. Visual perception cannot be understood simply by analyzing the scene into its elements because what we see depends on the *relations* of these elements with each other.

Organizational Laws of Gestalt Psychology

Elements of a visual scene can combine in various ways to produce different forms. Gestalt psychologists have observed that several principles can predict the combination of these elements.

The law of *proximity* states that elements that are closest together will be perceived as belonging together. **Figure 8.29** demonstrates this principle.

FIGURE 8.29   The Gestalt principle of proximity. Different spacing of the dots produces four vertical or horizontal lines.

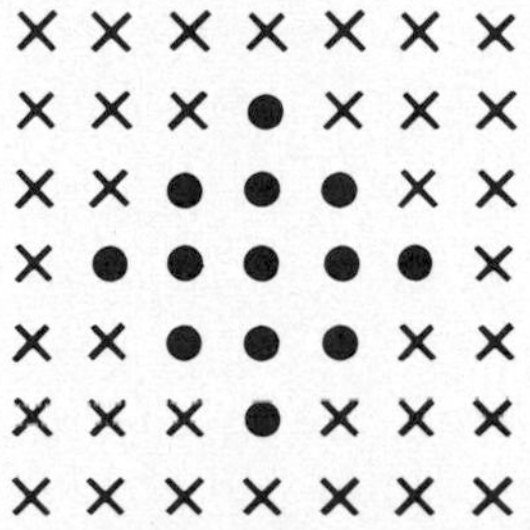

× × × × × × ×
× × × ● × × ×
× × ● ● ● × ×
× ● ● ● ● ● ×
× × ● ● ● × ×
× × × ● × × ×
× × × × × × ×

FIGURE 8.30   The Gestalt principle of similarity. Similar elements are perceived as belonging to the same form.

The pattern on the left looks like four vertical columns, whereas the one on the right looks like four horizontal rows.

The law of *similarity* states that elements that look similar will be perceived as part of the same form. It is easy to see the diamond inside the square in **Figure 8.30**.

Good continuation refers to predictability or simplicity. Which of the two sets of colored dots best describes the continuation of the line of black dots in **Figure 8.31**? If you see the figure the way

I do, you will choose the colored dots that continue the curve down and to the right. It is simpler to perceive the line following a smooth course than suddenly making a sharp bend. Figure 8.32 illustrates a similar principle. It is possible to see two complex lines that do not cross each other, but it is simpler to describe the figure as a straight line superimposed on a wavy line, and most people tend to perceive it this way. (See **Figure 8.32**.)

The law of *closure* states that we often supply missing information to close a figure and separate it from its background. For example, Figure 8.33 looks a bit like a triangle, but if you cover the gaps with a pencil the figure undeniably looks like a triangle. (See **Figure 8.33**.)

In **Figure 8.34**, the nonexistent—but still very apparent—triangle looks brighter than the background. Apparently our visual system, in perceiving a figure against a ground, emphasizes the figure and makes it more vivid. Certainly, lateral inhibition within the retina cannot account for this instance of simultaneous contrast.

The final Gestalt law of organization relies on movement. The law of *common fate* states that elements that move in the same direction will be perceived as belonging together and forming a figure. In the forest, an animal will be camouflaged if its surface is covered with the same elements that are found in the background—spots of brown, tan, and green—because its boundary will be obscured. There will be no basis for grouping the elements on the animal. As long as the animal remains stationary, it remains well hidden. However, once it moves, the elements on its surface will move to-

FIGURE 8.31   The Gestalt principle of good continuation. It is easier to perceive a smooth continuation than an abrupt shift.

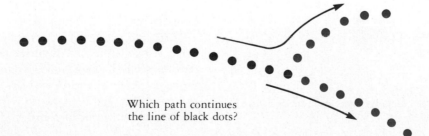

Which path continues the line of black dots?

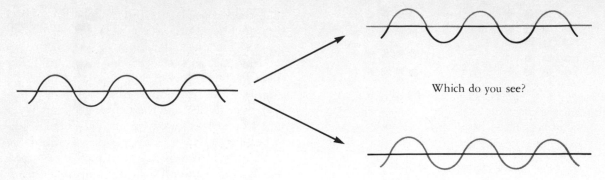

FIGURE 8.32   The Gestalt principle of good continuation. Which do you see?

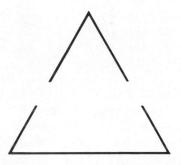

FIGURE 8.33   The Gestalt principle of closure. We tend to supply missing information to close a figure and separate it from its background. Lay a pencil across the gaps and see how strong the perception of a complete triangle becomes.

FIGURE 8.34   Even when boundaries are not present, we can be fooled into seeing them. The triangle with its point down looks brighter than the surrounding area.

gether, and the animal's form will quickly be perceived.

Other Characteristics of Figure-Ground Relations

All other factors being equal, we will see a black area as figure and a white area as ground. In **Figure 8.35**, people are slightly more likely to see a black fan against a white background than the reverse. Possibly our experience with black letters against white paper accounts for this tendency.

Another principle emerges in the next figure. Do you see a black fan or a white one? (See **Figure 8.36**.) Almost everyone sees a white fan, because the blades are arranged vertically, and there is a strong tendency to see verticals as figure rather than as ground.

Most people see one part of Figure 8.37 as white columns against a black background, and the other as black columns against a white background. Which way do you see them—and can you explain why? (See **Figure 8.37**.) If you are like me, you saw black columns on the left and white columns on the right. The *symmetry* of the patterns accounts for this perception: the edges of the black patterns on the left are mirror images of each other, and the same is true for the white patterns on the right.

With the exception of verticality, and perhaps black versus white, all the principles of form perception seem to make good common sense. We group together elements that are similar or close to each other, and we tend to reject patterns that are complex in favor of those that are simple and

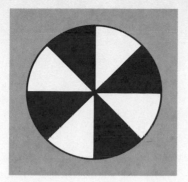

FIGURE 8.35 Do you see a fan with black blades against a white background or a fan with white blades against a black background?

FIGURE 8.36 Most people see a fan with white blades against a black background. Can you figure out why?

FIGURE 8.37 Which columns are white, and which are black? Why?

predictable. If you look about you, you will find that you can use these principles to explain why you perceive some parts of the visual scene as figure and others as ground.

PHYSIOLOGICAL MECHANISMS OF FORM PERCEPTION

◆ In recent years we have learned much about how the visual system encodes information, especially from two prominent researchers, David Hubel and Thorsten Wiesel of Harvard University. They have inserted *microelectrodes,* extremely small wires with microscopically sharp points, into various regions of the visual system of cats and monkeys to detect the electrical disturbances that accompany the ac-

tion potentials of individual neurons (Hubel and Wiesel, 1977, 1979).

The signals that are detected by the microelectrodes are electronically amplified, and are sent to a recording device so that they can be studied later. They are also sent to a loudspeaker, where the action potentials are converted into easily recognizable crackling noises.

After positioning a microelectrode close to a neuron, Hubel and Wiesel presented various stimuli on a large white screen in front of the anesthetized animal. The anesthesia makes the animal unconscious but does not prevent neurons in the visual system from responding. They moved a stimulus around on the screen until they located the point where it had the largest effect on the neuron. Almost always, the neurons responded to stimuli in a limited portion of the visual field. Next, they presented various shapes to learn which stimulus produced the greatest response from the neuron. (See **Figure 8.38.**)

They found that neurons in the thalamus, and those in the primary visual cortex that are stimulated directly by them, changed their firing rate

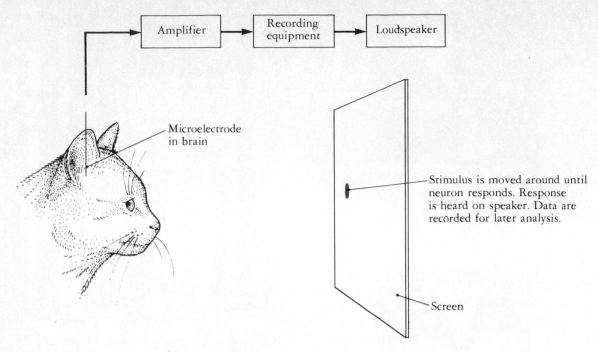

FIGURE 8.38   The procedure used by Hubel and Wiesel.

most when a spot of light was shone on a restricted region of the retina. That portion of the visual field corresponding to this region is called the neuron's *receptive field.* If they moved the spot of light just slightly, the neuron stopped responding and its neighbors began responding instead. (See **Figure 8.39.**)

From their experiments Hubel and Wiesel concluded that the geography of the visual field is retained in the visual cortex. That is, they observed a point-to-point relation between the real world and the surface of the visual cortex. However, the map on the brain is distorted, with the largest amount of area given to the center of the visual field, which projects on the fovea. They also concluded that cells in the primary visual cortex are arranged hierarchically; that is, one set of neurons analyzes a simple feature and passes this information on to another set of neurons; the second set analyzes more complex features and passes this information on to yet another set of neurons; and so on.

The primary visual cortex, like other areas of the cerebral cortex, is composed of several layers, like a sandwich. The neurons that receive infor-

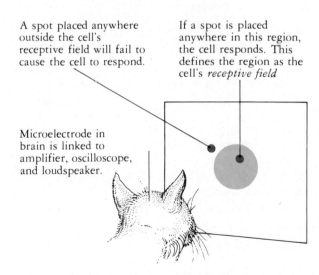

A spot placed anywhere outside the cell's receptive field will fail to cause the cell to respond.

If a spot is placed anywhere in this region, the cell responds. This defines the region as the cell's *receptive field*

Microelectrode in brain is linked to amplifier, oscilloscope, and loudspeaker.

FIGURE 8.39   Locating a neuron's receptive field.

mation directly from the thalamus are located in one of the middle layers. Neurons in the layer just above this one also have restricted receptive fields, but instead of responding to spots they respond to

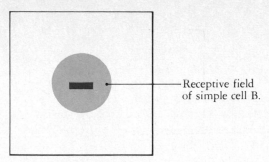

Receptive field
of simple cell B.

Simple cell B responds
best to a line with
this orientation.

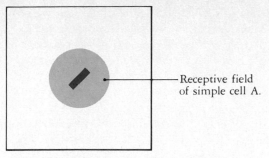

Receptive field
of simple cell A.

Simple cell A responds
best to a line with
this orientation.

FIGURE 8.40   The kind of stimulus that
produces the best responses in simple cells in the
visual cortex.

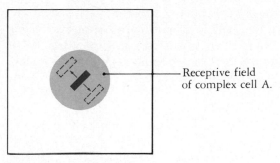

Receptive field
of complex cell A.

Complex cell A responds
best to a line with this
orientation, moving at right
angles to its long axis.

FIGURE 8.41   The kind of stimulus that
produces the best responses in complex cells in the
visual cortex.

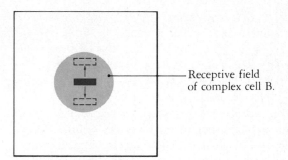

Receptive field
of complex cell B.

Complex cell B responds
best to a line with this
orientation, moving at right
angles to its long axis.

lines, and to lines of a particular orientation. For example, one might respond to a vertical line, another to a line rotated ten degrees from the horizontal. Hubel and Wiesel call neurons that respond this way *simple cells.* (See **Figure 8.40.**)

Other layers of visual cortex contain *complex cells.* Like simple cells, these respond to lines of a particular orientation. However, they have somewhat larger receptive fields, and unlike simple cells they respond best to lines that are moving at right angles to their angle of orientation. (See **Figure 8.41.**)

Hubel and Wiesel note that although neurons in the primary visual cortex appear to analyze suc-

cessively more complex forms of stimuli, each neuron has information about only a restricted area of the visual field. Therefore, the primary visual cortex cannot analyze shape and form; higher levels of perceptual analysis must take place elsewhere. To understand better why this is so, consider this analogy. Imagine a large group of people, each of whom is examining a small part of a visual scene with a telescope mounted on a tripod. Each telescope is aimed at a different part of the scene, and none can be moved. Obviously, none of the people can describe what is happening in the scene in front of them. They can report spots, lines, colors, and movements from a small part of the scene, but they cannot perceive the whole. If the people could talk with each other, they could share their information and possibly make some inferences about what was going on in front of them. Or they could report what they are seeing to someone else, who would put all the reports together and come up with a perception of the scene. We know that neurons in the primary visual cortex share their information only with their immediate neighbors, so the first possibility is ruled out. However, neurons in the primary visual cortex *do* send information to another place—the visual association cortex. Unlike neurons in the primary visual cortex, those in the visual association cortex respond best to complex stimuli, and they continue to respond even when the stimulus is moved around so that its image falls on different parts of the retina.

The effects of damage to the primary visual cortex and to the visual association cortex support these research findings. When the primary visual cortex is damaged, the person becomes blind in some portion of the visual field. (The exact location depends on where the brain damage is.) In contrast, damage to the visual association cortex produces varying amounts of difficulty comprehending the *meaning* of what is seen. A person with damage to the left visual association cortex usually has difficulty reading, whereas a person with damage to the right visual association cortex usually has difficulty recognizing familiar objects by sight.

FIGURE 8.42   A visual sine-wave grating. The graph of brightness below is in the form of a sine wave.

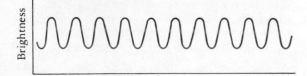

Although the work of Hubel and Wiesel is very well respected, other investigators have suggested slightly different interpretations of their data. For example, neurons in the visual cortex may not respond best to lines and sharp edges, but to gradual changes in brightness, different neurons responding to different rates of change in brightness. These stimuli are known as *sine-wave gratings,* because the changes in brightness follow a sine-wave function. (See **Figure 8.42**.)

EFFECTS OF EXPERIENCE

◈ It has been known for some time that the lack of a stimulating visual environment can prevent normal development of the visual system. In fact Hubel and Wiesel received a Nobel prize in 1981 for discovering that neurons in the visual cortex will never respond to stimulation of both eyes unless the animal has experience with binocular vision early in life. (The importance of this phenomenon to perceptual development was discussed in Chapter 6.)

Until recently, most investigators believed that innately determined neural connections produced the responses of the simpler elements of the visual system. But Hirsch and Spinelli (1971) showed that experience can alter the responses of even the simplest elements, which suggests that the neural connections can be affected by what an organism sees. They raised kittens in the dark from birth to the age of three weeks, then fitted them with a pair of goggles and allowed them to run about in the light for a time each day. The goggles presented very special stimuli to each eye; the right eye saw only vertical lines and the left eye saw only horizontal lines. (See **Figure 8.43**.)

After several weeks of training Hirsch and Spinelli recorded the responses of neurons in the cats' visual cortex and found cells that previous investigators had never seen. These cells responded best to vertical lines shown to the right eye and to horizontal lines shown to the left eye. Thus, the features detected by neurons in the visual cortex are at least partially affected by the animal's early visual environment.

A study by Ball and Sekuler (1982) suggests that feature detectors can be modified even in the visual system of adults. The experimenters trained

FIGURE 8.43 A kitten wearing the training goggles from one of Spinelli's experiments. The horizontal and vertical stripes on the outside of the goggles are for identification purposes only; the actual stimuli are contained inside the goggles and are illuminated by transparent openings at the sides (out of which the kitten cannot see). The cardboard cone prevents the kitten from dislodging the goggles. (From Carlson, N.R. *Physiology of Behavior,* 2nd ed. Boston: Allyn and Bacon, 1981.)

people to detect extremely small movements. Each subject sat in front of a display screen. A series of dots would appear, scattered across the face of the screen, and would either all move an extremely small distance or remain stationary. The dots always moved in the same direction, but the direction was different for each person in the experiment. After several sessions, the subjects' sensitivity was assessed by the techniques of signal-detection theory, described earlier. (The subjects received two cents for each hit or correct negative and were fined one cent for each miss or false alarm.) Each person was good at detecting movement only in the direction in which he or she had been trained; the training did not increase their detection of movements in other directions. The effect was still present when the subjects were tested again ten weeks later.

The fact that the subjects learned to detect a small movement in a particular direction, and not small movements in general, suggests that their visual systems were modified at a rather elementary level. Possibly they acquired new sets of feature

detectors that responded to movement in a particular direction. As yet we have no way of knowing where these hypothetical detectors are.

Interim summary: Although the physiological basis of visual perception is still poorly understood, there are rules that govern the way we see our world. Most phenomena of visual perception depend on relations among different elements of the scene before us. We perceive the brightness of an object relative to the brightness of objects around it; thus, objects retain a constant brightness under a variety of conditions of illumination. The Gestalt organizational laws of proximity, similarity, good continuation, closure, and common fate describe some of the ways we distinguish figure from ground.

There is little physiological evidence concerning complex aspects of visual perception, but investigators have learned much about the activity of neurons that participate in the early stages of perception. Studies of the electrical activity of single neurons in the brain have shown that cells in the thalamus respond to spots of light in their receptive field and thus there is a point-by-point correlation between the visual field and the surface of the visual cortex. In addition, both simple cells and complex cells in the visual cortex respond to lines of a particular orientation; the receptive field of complex cells is larger, and they respond best when the lines move. Cells in the visual association cortex respond to complex stimuli presented almost anywhere in the visual field. Experience, too, has an effect on visual perception. Although it was thought that simple features were analyzed by innate properties of the visual system, research has shown that visual deprivation prevents some mechanisms from developing properly, and special visual experience early in life will cause the development of novel-feature detectors.

PERCEPTION OF MOVEMENT

The law of common fate, mentioned earlier, states that elements that move together are perceived as being part of the same figure and therefore give rise to the perception of form. This phenomenon enables us to detect moving objects quickly and easily. The eyes also make their own movements, and the brain can compensate for eye, head, and body movements. This compensation enables us to determine whether parts of the visual field are stationary or in motion.

Eye Movements

◆ Our eyes are never completely at rest, even when our gaze is fixed upon a small point. Three types of movement can be observed. (1) Fast, aimless, jittering movements occur, probably similar to the fine tremors that are seen in the hand and fingers when we attempt to keep them still. (2) Superimposed on these random tremors are slow drifting movements that move the image on the retina a distance of approximately twenty cone widths. These slow drifts are terminated by (3) quick movements that bring the image of the fixation point back to the fovea.

◆   Besides these resting movements, there are three types of "purposive" eye movements: conjugate movements, saccadic movements, and pursuit movements.

Conjugate movements are cooperative movements that keep both eyes fixed upon the same target, or more precisely, keep the image of the target object on corresponding parts of the two retinas. If you hold up a finger in front of your face, look at it, and then bring your finger closer to your face, your eyes will make conjugate movements toward your nose. If you then look at an object on the other side of the room your eyes will rotate outward, and you will see two separate blurry images of your finger. Conjugate eye movements are very important in the perception of space.

When you scan the scene in front of you, your gaze does not roam slowly and steadily across its features. Instead, your eyes move in jerky *saccadic movements*—you shift your gaze abruptly from one point to another. When you read a line in this book, your eyes stop several times, moving very quickly between each stop. Although you can make smaller saccades, you cannot consciously control the rate of movements between each stop; during each saccade the eyes move as fast as they can. Only by performing a *pursuit movement*—say, by looking at your finger while you move it around—can you make your eyes move more slowly.

Experimental recordings of the axons that control the eye muscles show that they fire at their maximum rate during all but the smallest saccades. Thus, variations in the amplitude, or strength, of muscular contractions do not control differences in the degree of eye movements. Instead, the movements are *timed;* the brain controls a saccade from one point to another by turning on the appropriate eye muscles for just the right amount of time. The cerebellum appears to be most responsible for this timing, for damage to this part of the brain disrupts normal saccadic movements.

The mechanism that controls saccades does not appear to use feedback from what the eyes see. The eyes do not move until the image of the target falls on the appropriate part of the retina and then stop moving. Instead, each saccade is *ballistic*—the eye is "aimed and fired" at the target and hits it almost perfectly every time. Try making some aimed saccades yourself. Hold your hands straight out in front of you about a foot apart and raise your index fingers. Look back and forth from one finger to the other. Your eyes will snap to their targets with very little error.

Perception of Movement in the Absence of Motion

◆ If you sit in a darkened room and watch two small lights that are alternately turned on and off, you will see a single light moving back and forth between two different locations. You will not see the light turn off at one position and then turn on at the second position; if the distance and timing are just right, the light will appear to stay on at all times, quickly moving between positions. This response is known as the *phi phenomenon.* Theater marquees and "moving" neon signs make use of it.

This characteristic of the visual system accounts for the fact that we perceive the images in motion pictures and on television as continuous rather than separate. The images actually jump from place to place, but we see smooth movement.

Interpretation of a Moving Retinal Image

How can we tell the difference between an object that moves while our eyes are still and one that stays still while our eyes move? If you look at a single point of light in an otherwise dark room, your eye movements and movements of the light will produce exactly the same effect: the image of the light will change its location on your retina. The slow, *unintentional,* drifting movements of your eyes will cause you to perceive the light as wandering around. But it you *intentionally* move your eyes around, up and down, and side to side, you will perceive the point of light as remaining stationary. In other words, intent seems to play an important role. If you move your eyes on purpose, the spot of light seems to remain in the same place. If your eyes move unintentionally, you perceive the light as having moved.

You need not go to a dark room to demonstrate this phenomenon. Close your left eye and look slightly down and to the left. Press your finger against the upper eyelid of your right eye and make your right eye move a bit. The scene before you appears to be moving, even though you know better. The brain mechanism that controls your eye muscles did not "intend" to move them; therefore, your visual system interprets the movement of the image on the retina as movement of the scene. (See **Figure 8.44.**)

Try this experiment. Put the front of a small flashlight (or any other source of bright light) a few inches from your eye. Close the other eye, turn on the light, and stare at it for a few seconds to produce an afterimage. Push your finger against your eyelid as you did in the previous demonstration, thus creating movement manually. Although the world appears to move as it did before, the afterimage will appear to be stationary; it remains on the same place on your retina.

Now produce another afterimage with the bright light, close both eyes, and move them around (with your eye muscles, not your finger). This time the afterimage appears to move, following your eyes whichever way they turn. Because your brain commanded your eye muscles to move your eyes, the image of a stationary object would be expected to move around on your retina. However, the afterimage remains on the same part of the retina; thus, your visual system interprets the spot as moving around in response to the movements of your eyes.

FIGURE 8.44 A schematic explanation of why passive movement of the eye results in perception of movement of the visual scene.

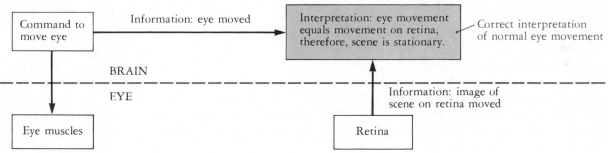

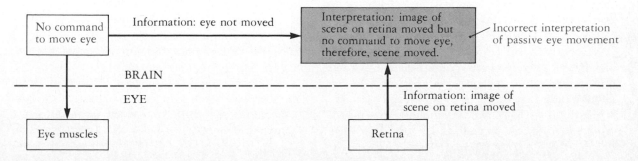

Besides perceiving absolute movements, we perceive the movements of objects relative to one another. Sometimes we can be fooled. You may have sat in an automobile at a stoplight when the vehicle next to you started to move forward. For a moment you were uncertain whether you were moving backward or the other vehicle was moving forward. Only by looking at nonmoving objects such as buildings or trees could you be sure.

In general, if two objects of different size are seen moving relative to each other, the smaller one is perceived as moving and the larger one as standing still. Generally, this is true in our environment: people we see at a distance move against a stable background, flies move against an unmoving wall. Thus, even when an experimenter moves both figure and background we nevertheless tend to perceive the background as stationary.

Stabilized Images

◆ Although the small, jerky movements that the eyes make when at rest are random and involuntary, they appear to have a definite purpose. Riggs, Ratliff, Cornsweet, and Cornsweet (1953) devised a way to project *stabilized images* on the retina. A stabilized image is one that remains in one location on the retina. They mounted a small mirror in a contact lens worn by the subject and bounced a beam of light off it. They then projected the image onto a white screen in front of the subject, bounced it off several more mirrors, and finally directed it toward the subject's eye. (See **Figure 8.45**.) The path of the light was arranged so that the image on the screen moved in perfect synchrony with the eye movements. If the eye moved, so did the image; thus, the image that the experimenters projected always fell on precisely the same part of the retina despite the subject's eye movements. Under these conditions, details of visual stimuli began to disappear. At first the image was clear but then a "fog" drifted over the subject's field of view, obscuring the image. After a while, some images could not be seen at all.

These results suggest that elements of the visual system are not responsive to an unchanging stimulus. The photoreceptors or the ganglion cells, or perhaps both, apparently cease to respond to a constant stimulus. The small, involuntary movements of our eyes keep the image moving, and thus keep

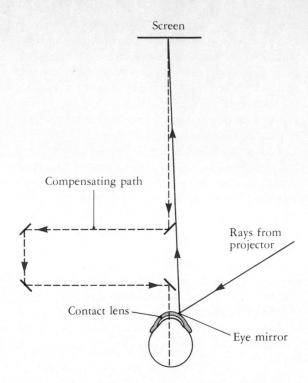

FIGURE 8.45   A procedure for stabilizing an image on the retina. (From Riggs, L.A., Ratliff, F., Cornsweet, J.C., and Cornsweet, T.N. *Journal of the Optical Society of America*, 1953, *43*, 495–501.)

the visual system responsive to the details of the scene before us.

Interim summary: Eyes make several kinds of movements. Vision, though popularly thought to be a passive experience (eyes being our windows on the world), requires the behavior of looking: movements of eyes and head. The eyes have a repertoire of movements that function for visual perception. Experiments with stabilized images show that the small, involuntary movements keep the image moving across the photoreceptors and prevent them from adapting to a constant stimulus. When we are engaged in looking, we use other eye movements, including saccades (which are quick timed movements from point to point) and pursuit movements.

Because our bodies might well be moving while we are visually following some activity in the outside world, the visual system has to make further compensations. The visual system keeps track of the commands to the eye muscles and compensates for the direction in which the eyes arc pointing. Movement is perceived when objects move relative to each other. In particular, the smaller object is likely to be perceived as moving across the larger one. Movement is also perceived when our eyes follow a moving object, even though its image remains on the same part of the retina. To show how important the brain's coordination of this activity is, you have only to "fool" the brain's visual mechanisms by a push against the eye that causes it to move passively.

PERCEPTION OF SPACE

Form Constancy

Besides being able to perceive the forms of objects in our environment, we are able to judge their relative location in space quite accurately. Furthermore, when we approach an object or when it approaches us, we do not perceive it as getting larger. Even though the image of the object on the retina gets larger, we perceive this change as being due to a decrease in the distance between ourselves and the object. Our perception of the object's size remains relatively constant. (See **Figure 8.46.**)

Close one eye and look closely at a bright light, then look at this book so that you see the afterimage superimposed on it. Move the book back and forth, closer and farther from your eye. You will see that the afterimage appears to change in size. When the book is near you it is small; when it is far it is larger. If you look across the room to the wall, the afterimage will look even larger. Thus, the true size of the afterimage (measured on your retina) is constant, but when you perceive it at different distances your perception of its size changes. The brain compensates for perceived distance in perception of size.

The relatively unchanging perception of an object's size and shape when it moves relative to us is called ***form constancy***. (People also refer to *size constancy*, but size is simply one aspect of form.) In the nineteenth century, Herman von Helmholtz suggested that form constancy was achieved by ***unconscious inference***. We know the size and shape of a familiar object; therefore, if the image it casts upon our retina is small, we perceive it as being far away. If the image is large, we perceive it as being close. In either case, we perceive the object itself as being of the same size. Form constancy also works for rotation; the central ring representing the horizon in **Figure 8.47** looks circular even

FIGURE 8.46   Size constancy. Although the retinal image of the apple is larger when the apple is

nearer, we tend to perceive it as being the same size whether it is near us or far away.

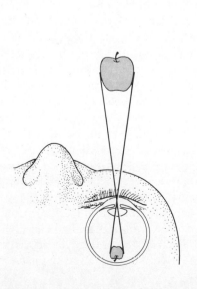
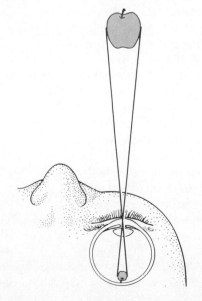

though the image it casts on our retina is that of an ellipse.

We are usually also fairly accurate at estimating the size and shape of unfamiliar objects. If we know an object's distance from us, we can compute its actual size from the size of its image on the retina; an object that produces a large retinal image is perceived as big if it is far away, but small if it is close. Apparently the visual system performs this computation. Therefore, perception of an object's true size and shape requires knowledge of its distance from us.

PERCEPTION OF DISTANCE

We perceive distance by means of two kinds of cues: binocular ("two-eye") and monocular ("one-eye"). Only animals with eyes on the front of the head (such as primates, cats, and some birds) can obtain binocular cues. Monocular cues are potentially available to any species with good form vision.

Binocular Cues

◆ CONVERGENCE   You will recall that the eyes make conjugate movements so that both look at (converge on) the same point of the visual scene. If an object is very close to your face, your eyes are turned inward. If it is farther away, they look more nearly straight ahead. Thus, the eyes can be used like rangefinders; the brain controls the extraocular muscles, so it knows the angle between them, which is related to the distance between the object and the eyes. (See **Figure 8.48.**)

RETINAL DISPARITY   An even more important factor in the perception of distance is the information provided by *retinal disparity*. If you hold your finger up in front of you and look past it into the distance you will see a double image of your finger. Because your eyes are directed toward objects in the distance, and not toward your finger, the image of your finger falls on different portions of the retina in each eye. The degree of retinal disparity provides an important clue about an object's distance.

The perception of depth from retinal disparity is called *stereopsis*. (I discussed its development in Chapter 6.) When you look at a stereoscope you

FIGURE 8.47   Form constancy. Because of the context, we perceive the metal rings of this armillary sphere as round, even though the image they cast on our retina is that of an ellipse.

see a three-dimensional image. An experiment by Julesz (1965) demonstrated that the disparity produces the effect of depth. Using a computer, he produced two displays of randomly positioned dots in which the location of some dots differed slightly. If the dots were placed properly, the two displays gave the impression of depth when viewed through a stereoscope.

Figure 8.49 shows a pair of these random-dot stereograms. If you look at them very carefully you will see that some of the dots near the center have been moved slightly to the left. (See **Figure 8.49.**) Some people can look at these figures without using a stereoscope and see depth. If you want to try, hold the book at arm's length and look at the space between the figures. Now pretend you are looking "through" the book, into the distance. Each image will become double, since your eyes are no longer converged properly. If you try hard, you might make two of these images fuse into one, located right in the middle. If you keep looking, eventually you might see a small square in the center of the image, raised above the background.

Electrical recordings of individual neurons in the visual system of the brain have found a class

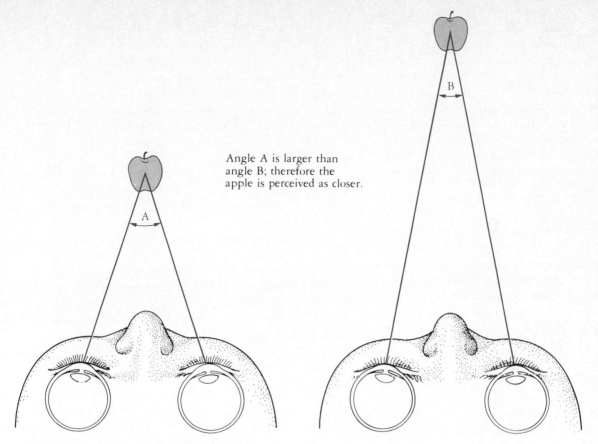

Angle A is larger than
angle B; therefore the
apple is perceived as closer.

FIGURE 8.48 When the eyes converge on a
nearby object the angle between them is greater than
when they converge on a distant object. The brain
uses this information in perceiving the distance of an
object.

FIGURE 8.49 A pair of random-dot stereograms.
(From Julesz, B. *Scientific American*, 1965, 38–48.)

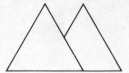
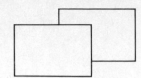

FIGURE 8.50   Use of the principle of good form in the perception of depth. The objects are perceived as identical pairs, but the ones on the left look closer to each other than those on the right.

of cells that respond only when there is a slight disparity between the image of an object on both retinas. (This is the effect that would occur if an object was not quite at the point of convergence of the gaze of the eyes.) Thus, it appears that some neurons compare the activity of neurons with corresponding receptive fields for both eyes and respond when there is a disparity.

Monocular Cues

◈ GOOD FORM   Just as the Gestalt law of good continuation plays a role in form perception, a prin-

ciple of *good form* affects our perception of the relative location of objects: we perceive the object with the simplest border as being closer. Figure 8.50 contains two drawings that can be seen either as complex two-dimensional figures or as two simple objects, one in front of the other. Because we tend to resolve an ambiguous drawing according to the principle of good form, we almost always see two objects. (See **Figure 8.50.**)

PERSPECTIVE AND TEXTURE   Figure 8.51 shows two columns located at different distances. The drawing shows *perspective;* parallel lines that recede from us tend to converge at a single point. Because of perspective we perceive the columns as having the same size even though they produce retinal images of different sizes. (See **Figure 8.51.**) In contrast, the next figure shows two mirrors that produce retinal images of the same size, but the one toward the right is perceived as larger. (See **Figure 8.52.**)

In a natural environment that has not been altered by humans we seldom see converging lines

FIGURE 8.51   Perspective gives the appearance of distance and makes the two columns look similar in size.

FIGURE 8.52   Although the two mirrors are drawn to the same size, perspective makes the one to the right look larger.

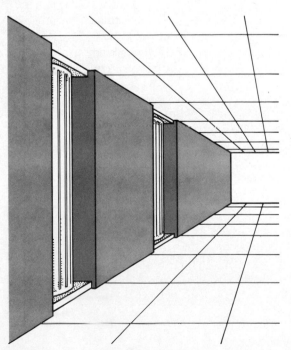

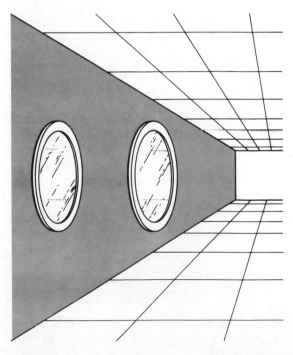

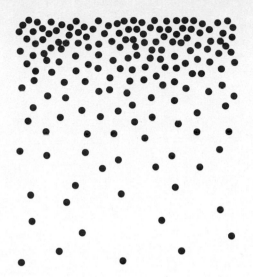

FIGURE 8.53   Texture can produce an appearance of distance.

FIGURE 8.54   Variation in detail, in the form of haze, produces an appearance of distance.

that denote perspective. Earlier in our evolutionary history we did not see streets, large buildings, and railroad tracks. Did we acquire the ability to use perspective cues only after producing these features of the landscape, or is there a counterpart of perspective to be found in nature?

Texture, another cue we use to perceive distance, is closely related to perspective. **Figure 8.53** shows how the texture of a background can give the impression of depth. Dots more closely spaced provide a finer texture, giving the impression of distance. Drawings that use perspective lines also achieve this effect: as the lines get closer together they produce a finer-grained texture. (Look back at **Figure 8.51**.)

The earth's atmosphere can also supply texture. Parts of the landscape that are farther away become less distinct because of haze in the air. The artist who made the engraving shown in the next figure used this phenomenon, among others, to impart the perception of distance. (See **Figure 8.54**.)

EFFECTS OF HEAD AND BODY MOVEMENTS   The information derived from our movements relative to other objects also helps us perceive distance. If you focus your eyes on an object close to you and move your head from side to side, your image of the scene moves back and forth behind the nearer object. If you focus your eyes on the background

while moving your head from side to side, the image of the nearer object passes back and forth across the background. Head and body movements cause the images from the scene before us to change; the closer the object, the more it changes, relative to the background. The information contained in this relative movement helps us perceive distance.

Figure 8.55 illustrates the kinds of cues that are supplied when we move with respect to features in the environment. The top part of the figure shows three objects at different distances from the observer: a man, a house, and a tree. The lower part shows the views that the observer will see from five different places (P_1–P_5). The changes in the relative locations of the objects provide cues to their distance from the observer. (See **Figure 8.55**.)

Interim summary: Because the size and shape of a retinal image varies with the location of an object relative to the eye, accurate form perception requires perception of an object's location in space. Binocular cues (from convergence and retinal disparity) and monocular cues (from the principle of good form, perspective, texture, and the effects of head and body movements) help us perceive distance.

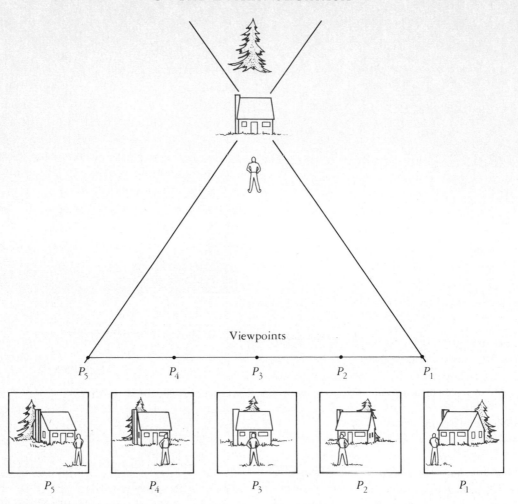

FIGURE 8.55   As we move, we make inferences about distance from the relative positions of objects in the environment. (From Haber, R.N., and Hershenson, M. *The Psychology of Visual Perception.* New York: Holt, Rinehart and Winston, 1973.)

CONCLUDING REMARKS

Vision, to most people, is the most important sensory modality. Through it we learn to recognize family and friends, see their facial expressions and gestures, learn to read, perceive objects we can never touch, and find our way around our environment. It provides us information about the size, shape, color, and movement of objects at a distance. Through vision we gain our most significant aesthetic experiences in the form of art and other beautiful images, experiences rivaled only by music.

The eye and the visual systems of the brain are remarkably complex, yet the perceptions they produce seem so simple. If you look around, you do not see complicated relationships, perspective, differential movement, saccades, and slow drifts. You see objects and places.

GUIDE TO TERMS INTRODUCED IN THIS CHAPTER

absolute threshold   p. 304
anatomical coding   p. 302
aqueous humor   p. 307   Figure 8.11
bipolar cell   p. 309   Figure 8.13, 8.15

SUGGESTIONS FOR FURTHER READING

Many books have been written about vision and visual perception. An excellent starting point is an inexpensive paperback by R. L. Gregory, *Eye and Brain,* 3rd ed. (New York: McGraw-Hill, World University Library, 1978). Gregory thoroughly knows his subject and writes with wit and style. The book contains excellent illustrations, many in color. Another fine book is *Vision* by D. Marr (San Francisco: W. H. Freeman, 1983). Marr finished the manuscript while battling serious illness—he never lived to see his book published.

HEARING, TASTE, SMELL, AND THE BODY SENSES

LEARNING ◆ OBJECTIVES

VISION INVOLVES the perception of objects in three dimensions, at a variety of distances, and with a multitude of colors and textures. These complex responses may involve either a single point in time or an unchanging scene. The other senses analyze much simpler stimuli (such as an odor or a taste) or depend upon time and stimulus change for the development of a complex perception. For example, the sense of touch quickly adapts: soon after we put on a wristwatch we do not even feel its presence. To perceive a solid object in three dimensions by means of touch we must manipulate it—turn it over in our hands or move our hands over its surface. The stimulus must change over time for a full-fledged perception of form to emerge. The same is true for audition. By its very nature, acoustic information must change over time. We hear nothing meaningful in an instant.

AUDITION

Most people consider the sense of hearing second in importance only to vision. In some ways, it is *more* important. A blind person can converse and communicate with other people almost as well as a sighted person. However, someone who cannot hear must depend on other people's knowledge of sign language or their willingness to communicate slowly by careful lip movements or by writing. A deaf person cannot easily join the conversation of a group of people. Although our eyes can transmit much more information to the brain, the ears convey some of our most important forms of social communication. (See **Figure 9.1.**)

THE STIMULUS

◆ Sound consists of rhythmic pressure changes in air. As it moves toward you, a vibrating object com-

FIGURE 9.1   In social interactions, what we hear is often as important as what we see.

FIGURE 9.2   Changes in air pressure from sound waves move the eardrum in and out.

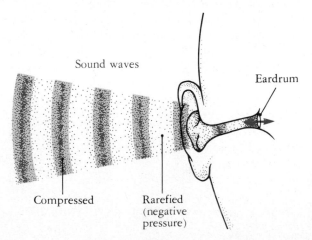

Sound waves

Eardrum

Compressed

Rarefied (negative pressure)

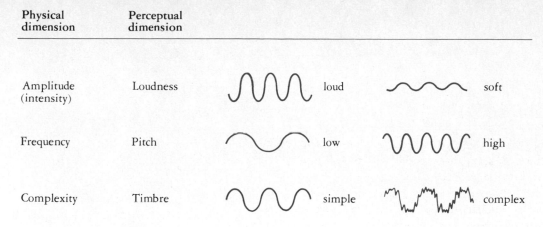

Physical dimension	Perceptual dimension				
Amplitude (intensity)	Loudness	∿∿∿	loud	∼∼∼	soft
Frequency	Pitch	∼∼∼	low	∿∿∿	high
Complexity	Timbre	∼∼∼	simple	⌇⌇⌇	complex

FIGURE 9.3   The physical and perceptual dimensions of sound waves.

presses molecules of air; as it moves away, it pulls the molecules farther apart. As a pressure wave arrives, it bends your eardrum in. The following wave of negative pressure (when the molecules are pulled farther apart) causes your eardrum to bulge out. (See **Figure 9.2.**)

Sound waves are measured in frequency units of cycles per second called **Hertz (Hz).** The human ear perceives vibrations between approximately 30 and 20,000 Hz. Sound waves can vary in **intensity** and **frequency.** These variations produce corresponding changes in perceptions of **loudness** and **pitch.** (See **Figure 9.3.**) However, the relation is not perfect; if a pure tone is increased in intensity the perceived pitch rises slightly. A third psychological dimension, *timbre,* corresponds to the complexity of the sound vibration.

ANATOMY OF THE EAR

◆ When people refer to the ear they usually mean what anatomists call the *pinna*—the flesh-covered cartilage attached to the side of the head. (*Pinna* means "wing" in Latin.) But the pinna performs only a small role in audition; it helps funnel sound toward the middle and inner ear, where the business of hearing gets done. (See **Figure 9.4.**)

The eardrum (the *tympanic membrane*) is the first of a set of structures of the middle ear that respond to sound waves and pass the vibration on to the receptive cells in the inner ear. The eardrum

is attached to the first of a set of three bones of the middle ear called the *ossicles.* These bones act together, in lever fashion, to transmit the vibrations of the tympanic membrane to the fluid-filled structure of the inner ear that contains the receptive organ. Movement of the tympanic membrane is transmitted first to the *malleus* ("hammer"), then to the *incus* ("anvil"), and finally to the *stapes* ("stirrup"). This elaborate arrangement is necessary because transmission of sound vibrations from the air into a liquid is extremely inefficient; more than 99 percent of the energy simply bounces off the surface of the liquid. However, the tympanic membrane absorbs much of the energy, and although the lever arrangement reduces the size of the movement, so that the footplate of the stapes moves less than the tympanic membrane, the force is correspondingly increased. Thus, the vibrations are efficiently transferred to the fluid filling the inner ear.

When the ear confronts a dangerously loud sound, the stapedius muscle contracts, moving the ossicles in such a way as to reduce the amount of energy transmitted to the inner ear, and thus reducing the amount of damage that might occur. This protective mechanism is called the *stapedius reflex.*

The *vestibule* ("entrance"), a bone surrounding part of the inner ear, contains two openings, the *oval window* and the *round window.* The stapes presses against a membrane behind the oval window and transmits sound waves through it into the

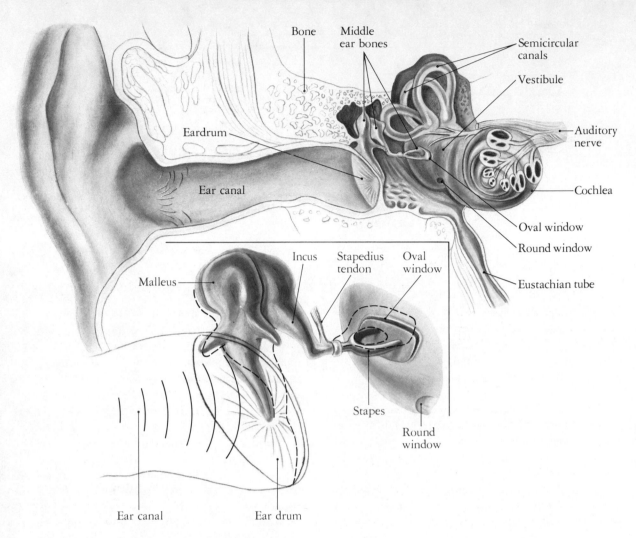

FIGURE 9.4   Anatomy of the auditory system.
(From Carlson, N.R. *Physiology of Behavior,* 2nd ed.
Boston: Allyn and Bacon, 1981.)

fluid of the inner ear. Attached to the vestibule is the *cochlea,* the bony structure that contains the receptive organ. (*Kokhlos* means "snail," which accurately describes its shape—see **Figure 9.4.**) The cochlea is divided into two parts by the *basilar membrane,* which varies in width and flexibility. As we shall see, this variation permits us to hear and analyze sounds of different frequencies. When the footplate of the stapes presses against the membrane behind the oval window, pressure builds up on the fluid above the basilar membrane, which causes the membrane to bend downward. (See **Fig-**

ure 9.5.) This action transmits the pressure to the portion of the cochlea on the lower side of the basilar membrane. The displaced fluid causes a membrane behind the round window to bulge out. Thus, we perceive sound when vibrations cause the membrane behind the oval window to move in and out, in turn causing the basilar membrane to flex back and forth.

Some people suffer from a middle ear disease that causes the bone to grow over the round window. These people have a severe hearing loss. However, a surgical procedure called *fenestration,*

Outer ear   Middle ear   Inner ear

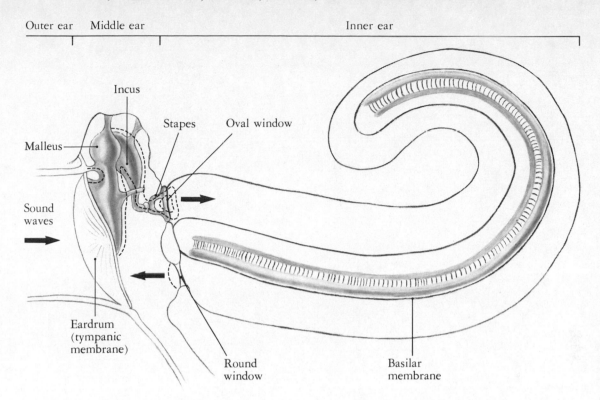

FIGURE 9.5   When the stapes pushes against the membrane behind the oval window, the membrane behind the round window bulges outward.

or "window-making," in which a tiny hole is drilled in the bone where the round window should be, can restore the patient's hearing.

TRANSDUCTION OF AUDITORY INFORMATION

◈ The cochlea contains the receptive organ for sound, the *organ of Corti,* which resides on the basilar membrane. This organ consists of a structure of supporting cells into which are embedded the *auditory hair cells,* which transduce mechanical energy caused by the flexing of the basilar membrane into neural activity. (See **Figure 9.6.**)

The auditory hair cells possess *cilia* ("eyelashes"), which are hairlike protrusions. The ends of the cilia are embedded in a fairly rigid shelf (the *tectorial membrane*) that hangs over the basilar membrane like a balcony. When sound vibrations cause the basilar membrane to flex back and forth,

they exert force upon the cilia, while the overhanging tectorial membrane remains stationary. The pull on the cilia is translated into neural activity. (See **Figure 9.6.**)

The auditory hair cells, like the photoreceptors in the retina, are incapable of producing action potentials. However, there is an electrical charge across their membrane, and this charge is somehow altered when a force is exerted on the cilia. The change in the electrical charge liberates a neurotransmitter at a synapse between the auditory hair cell and the dendrite of a neuron of the auditory nerve. The release of the transmitter substance excites the neuron, which sends action potentials through the auditory nerve to the brain. (See **Figure 9.6.**)

ENCODING OF PITCH

As we have seen, pitch is closely related to the frequency of vibration of sound waves. The audi-

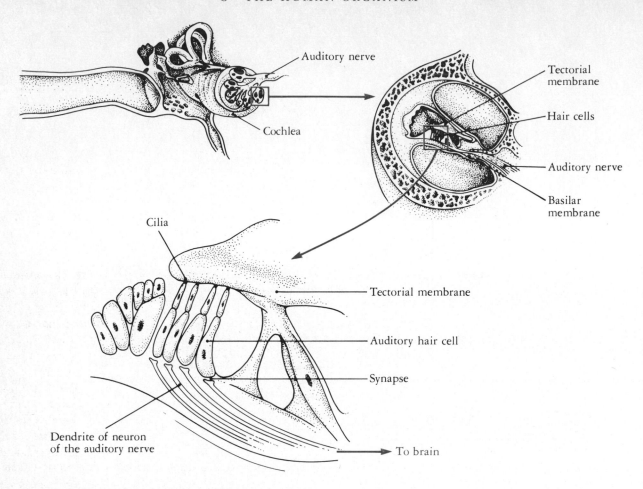

Auditory nerve

Cochlea

Tectorial membrane

Hair cells

Auditory nerve

Basilar membrane

Cilia

Tectorial membrane

Auditory hair cell

Synapse

Dendrite of neuron of the auditory nerve

To brain

FIGURE 9.6   The transduction of sound vibrations in the auditory system.

tory system encodes pitch by both an anatomical and a temporal code.

Anatomical Coding

◈ Because tones of different frequencies vary along a temporal (time) dimension scientists originally thought that the neurons of the auditory system represented pitch by means of a temporal code—namely, the firing in synchrony with the vibrations of the basilar membrane. However, they subsequently learned that axons cannot fire rapidly enough to represent the high frequencies that we can hear. A good, young ear can hear frequencies of more than 20,000 Hz, but axons cannot fire more than 1000 times per second. Therefore, high-frequency sounds, at least, must be encoded by some method other than frequency of neural firing.

The pitch of most frequencies of sound is encoded anatomically. The variations in the thickness and flexibility of the basilar membrane serve as the basis for the sensory coding of the frequency of a sound. Different frequencies of sound transmitted to the membrane behind the oval window cause different parts of the basilar membrane to flex back and forth. The higher the frequency of the stimulation, the closer to the oval window the flexing occurs. (See **Figure 9.7.**) However, the stimulated region is rather broad.

◈ Two basic types of evidence indicate that pitch is coded anatomically. First, direct observations of the basilar membrane, pioneered by the great auditory scientist Georg von Békésy (1899–1972), have shown that the region of maximum displacement depends on the frequency of the stimulating

High-frequency pure tone:
Basilar membrane flexes
near oval window.

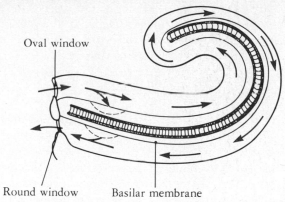

Oval window

Round window   Basilar membrane

Medium-frequency pure tone:
Basilar membrane flexes midway
between oval window and end.

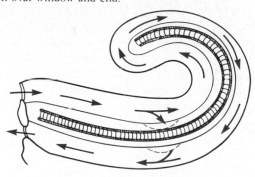

FIGURE 9.7   Different frequencies of sound
vibrations cause flexing of different portions of the
basilar membrane.

tone (von Békésy, 1960). Many people can discriminate two tones whose frequencies differ by as
little as 2 Hz. Given the broad area of displacement
in the basilar membrane, it is hard to understand
how such fine discriminations are possible. You
will recall that lateral inhibition in the visual system exaggerates the contrast between two areas that
differ only slightly in brightness. In the auditory
system, lateral inhibition probably exaggerates the
differences in the firing rates of the neurons that
are stimulated by flexing of the basilar membrane.
The most-stimulated neurons suppress their neighbors more than their neighbors suppress them.

A second piece of evidence comes from studies
that have found that damage to specific regions of
the basilar membrane causes loss of ability to perceive specific frequencies. The discovery that some
antibiotics damage hearing (for example, deafness
is one of the side effects of the antituberculosis
drug streptomycin) has helped auditory researchers
investigate the anatomical coding of pitch. Stebbins, Miller, Johnsson, and Hawkins (1969) administered antibiotics to different groups of animals
for varying times. Afterward they removed the animals' cochleas and examined them. The longer the
exposure, the more hair cells that were killed.
Damage started at the end of the basilar membrane
nearest the oval window, and progressed toward
the other end. Tests of the ability of the animals
to perceive tones of different frequencies indicated
a progressive decline beginning with the loss of the
ability to detect the highest frequencies. The animals' hearing loss exactly paralleled the death of
the hair cells.

Another type of experiment explains why loud
sounds are injurious to hearing. If an animal is
exposed to an extremely loud sound of a particular
frequency, it will sustain irreversible damage to the
hair cells on the portion of the basilar membrane
corresponding to that frequency. The cilia will be
torn right off of the hair cells (Smith, 1947). Likewise, people exposed to intense high-frequency sound
from jet engines or rock concerts may suffer permanent damage to the hair cells. The sound of the
jet engines can be attenuated by wearing special
protective ear muffs. I suppose that the same could
be done at a rock concert, but that would seem to
defeat the purpose of attending the concert in the
first place. Instead, some cotton or a piece of tissue
paper in the ear canals can reduce the intensity of
the damaging-frequency sounds without seriously
affecting other frequencies. As we age, our hearing
gets progressively worse, starting with high frequencies—it seems a shame to hasten this process
unnecessarily.

Temporal Coding

◈ Kiang (1965) recorded the electrical activity of single axons in the auditory nerve and found many
that responded to particular frequencies. Presumably, these axons are stimulated by hair cells located on different regions of the basilar membrane;
that is, they convey information about frequency
that is encoded anatomically. However, Kiang did

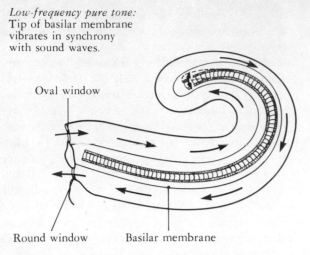

Low-frequency pure tone:
Tip of basilar membrane
vibrates in synchrony
with sound waves.

Oval window

Round window   Basilar membrane

FIGURE 9.8   Low-frequency sound vibrations
cause the end of the basilar membrane to flex in
synchrony with the vibrations.

not find any axons that responded uniquely to frequencies lower than 200 Hz—and yet tones lower than 200 Hz are easily perceived. How, then, are the lower frequencies encoded?

The answer is this: lower frequencies appear to be encoded temporally. The end of the basilar membrane farthest from the oval window vibrates as a whole to low-frequency stimulation. Neurons that are stimulated by hair cells located there are able to fire in synchrony with these vibrations, thus firing at the same frequency as the sound. (See **Figure 9.8.**)

The best evidence that low frequencies are encoded temporally and not anatomically comes from an experiment by Miller and Taylor (1948). These investigators used **white noise** as a stimulus. White noise consists of a random mixture of all of the perceptible frequencies of sound—it sounds like the *sssh* that is heard when a television or FM radio is tuned between stations. White noise stimulates *all* regions of the basilar membrane because it contains all frequencies of sound; therefore, no anatomical coding is possible.

Miller and Taylor presented subjects with white noise that passed through a hole in a rotating disk. By spinning the disk at various speeds, the noise could be chopped up into brief pulses, presented at various frequencies. When the frequency was less than 250 Hz the subjects could accurately

identify its pitch. Above 250 Hz the perception of pitch disappeared. These findings indicate that the brain must use temporal information received from the auditory nerve in the perception of pitch. At lower frequencies, bursts of neural firing occur in synchrony with the pulses of white noise.

ENCODING OF LOUDNESS

◆ As we saw, the loudness of a sound corresponds closely with the amplitude of the sound waves. (Look back at Figure 9.3.) For those frequencies that are high enough to be represented by anatomical coding on the basilar membrane, loudness is encoded by the rate of firing of the axons in the auditory nerve. Pitch is encoded by *which* neurons fire, loudness by *how fast* they fire.

Tones of frequencies below 250 Hz, which are encoded by frequency of firing, can vary in perceived loudness; some are loud, others are soft. We do not yet know exactly how the auditory system encodes the loudness of low-frequency tones. If frequency of firing represents pitch, perhaps loudness is encoded by the *number* of neurons that fire during each cycle of the stimulus; the more intense the stimulus, the more neurons fire in response.

ENCODING OF SPATIAL LOCATION

◆ When we hear an unexpected sound we usually turn our heads quickly to face its source. We make this response with rather high accuracy. And once our face is oriented toward the source of the sound, we can detect changes in its location by as little as one degree. To do this we use relative loudness and difference in arrival time (or phase difference).

Relative loudness is the most effective means of perceiving the location of high-frequency sounds. Acoustic energy, in the form of vibrations, does not in fact pass through solid objects. Low-frequency sounds can easily make a large object such as a wall vibrate, setting the air on the other side into motion and producing a *new* sound across the barrier. But large objects effectively damp out high frequencies by casting a "sound shadow."

So far as sound vibrations go, the head is a large object. Thus, if a source on your right produces a high-frequency sound, your right ear will receive more intense stimulation than your left ear. Your

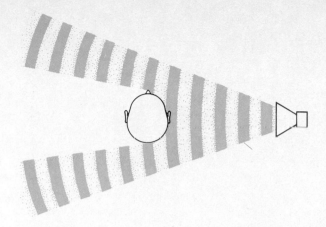

FIGURE 9.9   The head casts a shadow for high-frequency sound vibrations.

head does not transmit the sound very well, so your left ear will be in a "shadow." (See **Figure 9.9.**) You can easily confirm this mechanism by listening to a high-frequency sound delivered through earphones. If you deliver a different intensity of stim-

ulation to each ear, you will perceive the source of the sound as coming from the side with the greater stimulation.

The second method, which works best for frequencies below approximately 3000 Hz, involves detecting differences in the arrival time of waves of sound pressure at each eardrum. A 1000-Hz tone produces waves of pressure approximately one foot apart. Since the distance between a person's eardrums is somewhat less than half that, a source of 1000-Hz sound located to one side of the head will cause one eardrum to be pushed in while the other eardrum is being pulled out. In contrast, if the source of the sound is directly in front of the listener, both eardrums will move in synchrony. (See **Figure 9.10.**)

Recordings of the firing of the individual axons of the auditory nerve have shown that their responses tend to occur at a particular part of the cycle of the sound wave. Thus, a source of sound that is located to the side of the head, as in the lefthand drawing of Figure 9.10, will cause the neurons in the right and left auditory nerves to fire

FIGURE 9.10   *Left.* When the source of a 1000-Hz tone is to the right, the pressure waves on each eardrum are out of phase; one eardrum is pushed in while the other is pushed out. *Right.* When the source of a sound is directly in front of a person, the vibrations of the eardrums are synchronized.

Source of 1000-Hz
tone is to the right.

Source of tone
is in front.

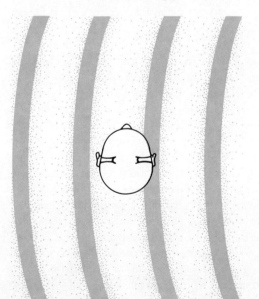

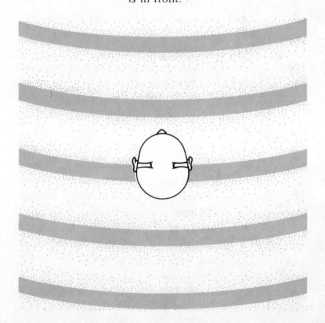

FIGURE 9.11   The high, shrill pitch of the siren, punctuated with sharp blasts on the horn, provides a stimulus that is easy to localize.

at different times. The brain is able to detect this disparity, which causes the sound to be perceived as being off to one side. In fact, the brain can detect differences in firing times of a fraction of a millisecond (a thousandth of a second). The easiest stimuli to locate are those that produce brief clicks, which produce brief bursts of neural activity. Apparently it is easiest for the brain to compare the arrival times of single bursts of incoming information. (See **Figure 9.11.**)

Other animals can also detect the location of a sharp, short burst of sound more easily than a smooth, steady one. Birds capitalize upon this capability. When a male bird stakes out his territory, he sings with a very sharp, staccato song that is easy to localize. In effect he is announcing, "Keep away, males, I am here and this place is mine!" In contrast, if a predator appears in the vicinity, many birds will emit alarm calls that warn the others of the danger without endangering themselves by revealing their own location. The alarm call usually consists of steady whistles that start and end slowly. Because the call has no sudden changes in loudness

it is more difficult to localize; it seems to be coming from everywhere. If you go for a walk in the woods sometime, try to listen for both types of calls.

ENCODING OF TIMBRE

◆ You can easily distinguish between the sounds of a violin and a clarinet, even if they are playing tones of the same pitch and loudness. This fact makes it clear that pitch and loudness are not the only perceptual characteristics of a sound. Sounds can vary greatly in complexity; they can start suddenly or gradually increase in loudness, be short or long, thin and reedy, or full and vibrant. Because sounds can vary in time, an infinite number of different ones can be produced. This enormous variety is in large part due to an important characteristic of sound called timbre.

The combining, or *synthesis,* of two or more simple tones, each consisting of a single frequency, can produce a complex tone. It does not matter how the tones are added together. Electrical signals

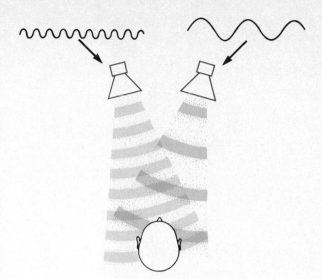

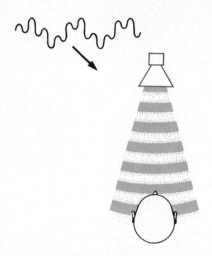

Both people hear identical sounds

FIGURE 9.12 Sound mixing. The ear hears the same result whether the sound comes from one speaker or from two speakers closely spaced.

Conversely, complex sounds that have a regular *periodicity*—that is, a repeating sequence of waves—can be reduced through analysis into several simple tones. Figure 9.13 shows a waveform produced by the sound of a clarinet (upper curve). The curves beneath it show the amplitude and frequency of the various simple waves that can be shown, math-

FIGURE 9.13 The shape of a sound wave from a clarinet (top) and the individual frequencies into which it can be analyzed. (From *Stereo Review*, June 1977.)

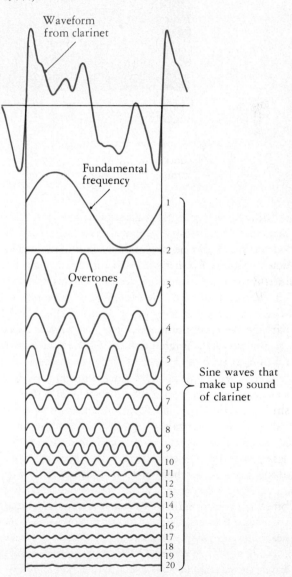

can be mixed, and the result sent to a loudspeaker, or two different loudspeakers can be used. The result is the same, so far as the ear is concerned. (See **Figure 9.12.**) For example, an electronic synthesizer produces a mixture of sounds of different frequencies, each of which can be varied in amplitude. Thus, it can synthesize the complex sounds of a clarinet or oboe or can assemble completely new sounds not produced by any other source.

FIGURE 9.14   The auditory system performs remarkable analyses. People can distinguish the characteristic timbres of different instruments in the complex waveform funneled toward the audience by the concert shell.

ematically, to produce the waveform. (See **Figure 9.13.**)

An analysis like the one shown in Figure 9.13 specifies the *timbre* of a sound. We can tell a clarinet from another instrument because each instrument produces sounds consisting of different sets of simple tones called *overtones.* Their frequencies are multiples of the *fundamental frequency,* or the basic pitch of the sound. Timbre, then, is the distinctive combination of overtones with the fundamental tone. The fundamental tone and each of the overtones cause several different parts of the basilar membrane to flex; thus the ear analyzes a complex sound, just as the author of Figure 9.13 did. Information about the fundamental tone and each of the overtones is sent to the brain by means of anatomical coding, and a complex tone with a particular timbre is perceived. (See **Figure 9.14.**)

Interim summary: Were you to sit at a synthesizer, you would have at your fingertips the means to produce a vast array of sounds. You would also have at your disposal an auditory system sophisticated enough to differentiate among these sounds. The physical dimensions of the synthesizer's sound—

amplitude, frequency, complexity—would be translated into the perceptual dimensions of loudness, pitch, and timbre for sounds ranging from 30 to 20,000 Hz. Sound-pressure waves put the process in motion by setting up vibrations in the tympanic membrane, which are passed on to the ossicles. Vibrations of the stapes create pressure changes that cause the basilar membrane to flex back and forth, which causes the hair cells of the organ of Corti to move relative to the tectorial membrane. The resulting pull on the cilia of the hair cells stimulates them to secrete a transmitter substance that excites neurons of the auditory nerve. This process informs the brain of the presence of a sound. Two different means of encoding enable the brain to differentiate the multitude of sounds that can be produced.

High-frequency sounds are coded anatomically; different parts of the basilar membrane flex in response to different frequencies. Low-frequency vibrations are coded temporally; the end of the basilar membrane vibrates in synchrony with the sound, which causes the axons in the auditory nerve to fire at the same frequency. To locate the source of a sound, should it come from different speakers, you have available two means: low-frequency sounds are located by differences in the arrival times in each ear, and high-frequency sounds are located by differences in intensity caused by the "sound shadow" cast by the head.

As you produce sounds of more and more complex timbre the auditory system will analyze them into their constituent frequencies, each of which causes a part of the basilar membrane to flex. The brain will then hear what you have played on the synthesizer.

GUSTATION

◆ Taste, or *gustation,* is the simplest of the sense modalities. We can perceive only four qualities of taste: *sourness, sweetness, saltiness,* and *bitterness.* Taste is not the same as flavor. Flavor depends on odor as well as taste. You have probably noticed that the flavors of food are diminished when you have a head cold. This occurs not because your taste buds are inoperative, but because odor-laden air has difficulty reaching your receptors for the sense of smell. Without their characteristic odors to serve as cues, onions taste much like apples, although apples do not make your eyes water. Even a steak tastes like salty cardboard if we cannot smell it. (See **Figure 9.15.**)

RECEPTORS

◆ The tongue has a somewhat corrugated appearance, being marked by creases and bumps. The bumps are called *papillae* (from Latin "pimple"). Each papilla contains a number of *taste buds* (in some cases as many as 200). A taste bud contains a number of receptor cells, each of which is shaped rather like a segment of an orange. The cells have hairlike projections called *microvilli* that protrude through the pore of the taste bud into the saliva that coats the tongue and fills the trenches of the papillae. (See **Figure 9.16.**) Chemicals that are dissolved in the saliva stimulate the receptor cells, probably by interacting with special receptor sites on the microvilli. These receptor sites might resemble the ones that play a role in synaptic transmission. The receptor cells synapse with dendrites of neurons that send axons to the brain through several different cranial nerves.

THE FOUR QUALITIES OF TASTE

The surface of the tongue is differentially sensitive to taste. The tip is most sensitive to sweet and salty substances; the sides to sour substances; and the back of the tongue, the back of the throat, and the soft palate overhanging the back of the tongue to bitter substances. (See **Figure 9.17.**) Researchers have examined and tested individual taste buds by placing a small, pointed glass tube over one and applying gentle suction, which makes the taste bud turn inside out. Experiments have shown that many taste buds respond to more than one quality; some respond to all four.

The physical properties of the molecules that we taste determine the nature of the taste sensations. For example, *salty* substances must ionize, or break

FIGURE 9.15 Flavor includes odor as well as taste; food is not simply sweet, sour, salty, or bitter.

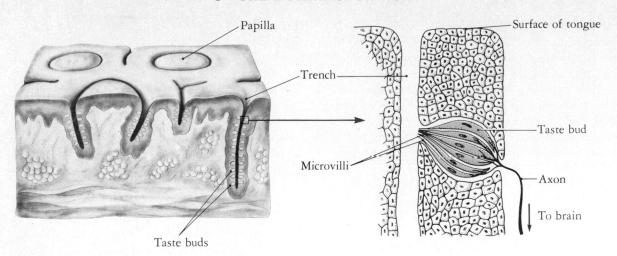

FIGURE 9.16   *Left*. Papillae on the surface of the tongue. *Right*. A taste bud.

into charged particles when they dissolve. The "model" salty substance is, of course, table salt—sodium chloride (NaCl). Other chlorides, such as lithium or potassium chloride, and some other salts, such as bromides or sulfates, are also salty in taste, but none tastes quite so salty as sodium chloride. This fact suggests that the specific function of salt-tasting receptors is the identification of sodium

FIGURE 9.17   Different regions of the tongue are especially sensitive to different tastes.

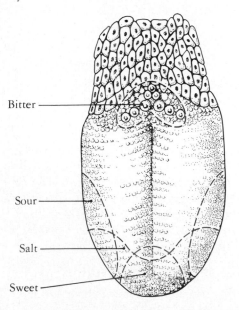

chloride. Sodium (which most commonly comes in the form of sodium chloride) plays a unique role in the regulation of our body fluid. If the body's store of sodium falls, we cannot retain water, and our blood volume will fall. The result can be heart failure. Deprivation of sodium stimulates thirst because of loss of water by the kidneys, and also produces a strong craving for the salty taste of sodium chloride.

The craving for sodium chloride appears to be innate. Experiments have shown that a rat whose body has been artificially depleted of sodium will immediately begin to drink a concentrated salt solution even if it never previously experienced a need for sodium (Krieckhaus and Wolf, 1968). One sad case demonstrating the need in humans involved a boy who began eating large quantities of salt each day, pouring it over his food and even eating it plain. He was put into a hospital, his pleas for salt were ignored, and he soon died. Afterward, it was realized that he had suffered from a glandular deficiency that prevented his kidneys from retaining sodium. His innate craving enabled him to survive by eating salt until he was prevented from doing so.

Both *bitter* and *sweet* substances seem to consist of large, nonionizing molecules. It is not yet possible to predict, merely on the basis of shape, whether a molecule will taste bitter or sweet (or neither). Some molecules (such as saccharine) stimulate both sweetness and bitterness receptors; they taste sweet at the front of the tongue and bitter at the back of the palate and throat. It is likely that the function of the bitterness receptor is avoidance of poison. Many plant alkaloids are poisonous, and most of them taste bitter. The sweetness receptor enables us to recognize the sugar content of fruits and other nutritive plant foods.

Most *sour* tastes are produced by acids, and in particular by the hydrogen ion (H^+) contained in acid solutions. The sourness receptor probably serves as a warning device against substances that have undergone bacterial decomposition, most of which become acidic. Most wholesome, natural foods that were present in an earlier environment tasted sweet or salty, not bitter or sour.

An interesting chemical contained in the African "miracle fruit" produces a shift in the normal sensory coding of taste. After a person eats this fruit (or puts some of its extract on the tongue), substances that previously tasted sour, such as a lemon, now taste sweet. African tribespeople who produced a rather disagreeable, sour-tasting beer discovered that after they ate miracle fruit, the beverage tasted sweet and delicious. The miracle fruit does not merely *mask* the sour taste—it *converts* it into sweetness.

OLFACTION

The sense of smell—*olfaction*—is one of the most interesting and puzzling of the sense modalities. For one thing, odors have a powerful ability to evoke old memories and feelings, even many years after an event. At some time in their lives, most people encounter an odor that they recognize as having some childhood association, even though they cannot identify it. This recognition has been called the "Proust effect" from a vivid description of such an event in Marcel Proust's book, *Remembrance of Things Past.*

Although other animals, such as dogs, have more sensitive olfactory systems, we should not underrate our own. We can smell some substances at lower concentrations than our most sensitive instruments can detect. Some of the reason for the apparent differences in sensitivity of our olfactory system and those of other mammals is that they

FIGURE 9.18   Being closer to the ground, dogs make more effective use of their sense of smell.

put their noses where the odors are the strongest— just above ground level. For example, watch a dog following an odor trail. The dog sniffs along the ground, where odors of the passing animal have clung. Even a bloodhound's nose would not be very useful if it were kept five feet above the ground. (See **Figure 9.18**.)

Odors play a very important role in the lives of most mammals. Although we do not make use of olfaction in identifying one another, we do use it to avoid some dangers, such as food that has spoiled. In fact, the odor of rotten meat will trigger vomiting—a useful response, if some of the rotten meat has been swallowed. Other animals recognize friend and foe by means of smell and use odors to attract mates and repel rivals. The reproductive system of some animals can be controlled by odors. As we saw in Chapter 7, the estrous cycle and reproductive behavior of laboratory mammals—and even the menstrual cycle of women—can be influenced by the odors emitted by other animals of the same species.

ANATOMY OF THE OLFACTORY SYSTEM

◆ **Figure** 9.19 shows the anatomy of the olfactory system. The receptor cells lie in the *olfactory mu-cosa.* These one-inch-square patches of mucous membrane are located on the roof of the nasal sinuses, just under the base of the brain. The receptor cells are true neurons, sending axons up through small holes in the bone above the olfactory mucosa. The axons synapse on neurons in the *olfactory bulbs,* which are enlargements at the ends of the stalk-like olfactory nerves. The process of transduction is unknown. The most widely accepted hypothesis is that the interaction between odor molecule and receptor is similar to that of transmitter substance

FIGURE 9.19   The olfactory system.

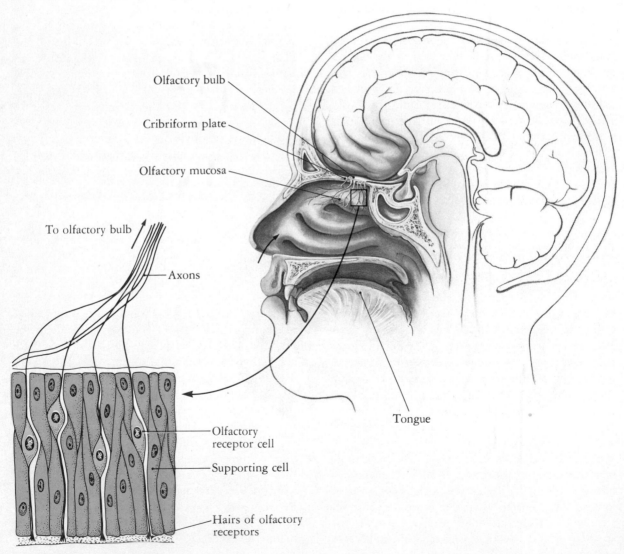

and receptor site on a neuron. Thus, similar mechanisms may transduce the stimuli for taste and olfaction.

THE DIMENSIONS OF ODOR

We know that there are four taste dimensions and that a color can be specified by hue, brightness, and saturation, but we still do not know what the dimensions of odor might be. It seems reasonable that there *are* dimensions, if only because the alternatives seem so implausible. We do not know how many odors we can identify, but the number is very large. It seems unlikely that we have separate receptors for each odor. Such a requirement would involve a phenomenal number of different receptors, and it undoubtedly takes more than a single receptor cell to produce a sensation. Moreover, it would not explain the fact that we can smell and learn to identify new, synthetic chemicals that were not in existence while our olfactory system was evolving. It does not seem likely that we possess unique olfactory receptors for every new odor that exists or is yet to be synthesized by chemists.

Most people agree that some odors resemble one another. The smell of rotten eggs is not at all like the smell of lemons, but pine oil and cedar oil smell rather similar. Thus, it seems plausible that there is a limited number of "odor primaries," and that our olfactory system identifies an odor by determining the degree to which it resembles each of the primaries. The hue of a color can be specified by measuring the excitation produced in red, green, and blue receptors; perhaps the olfactory system works in a similar way. (See **Figure 9.20**.)

The problem is to determine how many "odor primaries" there might be. Amoore (1970) consulted *Bielstein,* a compendium of chemical compounds that describes, among other things, their odors. He was able to reduce the descriptive adjectives there to a list of seven: camphoraceous, ethereal, floral, musky, pepperminty, pungent, and putrid. The fact that people find these seven adjectives necessary may mean that there are seven odor primaries, just as the perceptual priority of red, green, yellow, blue (and black and white) was found to have a physiological basis.

Amoore also hypothesized that there were receptors on the cilia of the olfactory cells with spe-

FIGURE 9.20 What words would you use to describe the smell these fish undoubtedly have? Is the smell a unique one or does it seem like a mixture of several primary odors?

Molecule

Hypothesized receptor

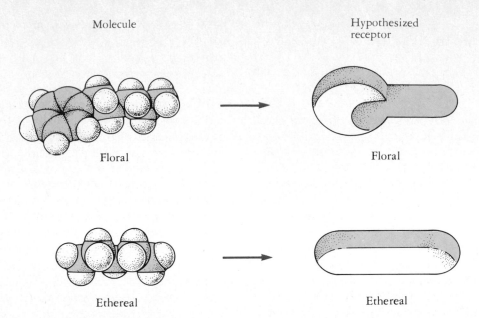

Floral

Floral

Ethereal

Ethereal

FIGURE 9.21   Two sample shapes of Amoore's primary odor molecules and their hypothetical receptors. (Adapted from Amoore, J.E., Johnston, J.W., and Rubin, M. The Stereochemical theory of odor. *Scientific American,* 1964, *210* (2), 42–49.)

cific shapes to accommodate odor molecules with particular three-dimensional configurations. (**Figure 9.21** shows two examples.) According to this hypothesis, a particular molecule might fit the pepperminty receptors fairly well, the floral receptors a little less well, the ethereal even less well, and the others not at all. Thus, the brain would receive signals of an odor that is strongly pepperminty, moderately floral, and slightly ethereal, combining these dimensions to produce the perception of a unique odor.

There is not enough supporting evidence to prove Amoore's theory and not enough contradictory evidence to disprove it. Some people appear to be unable to identify whole classes of odors, just as color-blind people cannot identify whole classes of colors. Perhaps these people lack one of the various types of odor receptors. However, the classes of odors that they cannot detect often do not correspond well with Amoore's hypothetical primaries. Furthermore, although there is some similarity between the three-dimensional shapes of molecules that are judged to be similar in odor, there are also some glaring discrepancies: some similarly shaped molecules smell very different, and some differently shaped molecules smell similar. Finally, although it is possible to synthesize sounds or colors, it is impossible to reproduce one odor by mixing several "simple" odors together.

Some scientists have rejected the notion that the shape of odor molecules is important and are investigating such characteristics as their vibration or emission of energy. Whatever the mechanism of odor recognition is, the answer appears to be a long way off.

Interim summary: Both gustation and olfaction are served by cells with receptors that respond selectively to various kinds of molecules. Taste buds have four kinds of receptors, responding to molecules that we perceive as sweet, salty, sour, or bitter. To most organisms, sweet and salty substances taste pleasant, whereas sour or bitter substances taste unpleasant. Sweetness and saltiness receptors permit us to detect food and sodium chloride. Sourness and bitterness receptors help us avoid substances that might be toxic.

Olfaction is a remarkable sensory modality. We can distinguish countless different odors, and can even recognize smells from childhood even though we cannot remember when or where we encountered them. Although we recognize similarities between different odors, most seem unique. Unlike visual and auditory stimuli, odors do not easily blend; when visiting a carnival we can smell the odors of popcorn, cotton candy, crushed grass, and diesel oil in a single sniff. However, most investigators believe that there are olfactory primaries of some kind even though they have not yet been discovered.

THE SOMATOSENSES

The body senses, or *somatosenses,* include our ability to respond to touch, vibration, pain, warmth, coolness, limb position, muscle length and stretch, tilt of the head, and changes in the speed of head rotation. The number of sensory modalities represented in this list depends on one's definition of sensory modality. However, it does not matter really whether we say that we respond to warmth and coolness by means of one or two sense modalities; in this case, the important thing is to understand how our bodies are able to detect changes in temperature.

Many experiences require simultaneous stimulation of several different sensory modalities. For example, taste and odor alone do not determine the flavor of spicy food; mild (or sometimes not-so-mild) stimulation of pain detectors in the mouth and throat gives Mexican food its special characteristic. Sensations such as tickle and itch are apparently mixtures of varying amounts of touch and pain. Similarly, our perceptions of the texture and three-dimensional shape of objects that we touch involve cooperation among our senses of pressure, muscle and joint sensitivity, and motor control (to manipulate the object). If we handle an object and find that it moves smoothly in our hand, we conclude that it is slippery. If, after handling this object, our fingers subsequently slide across each other without much resistance, we perceive a feeling of oiliness. If we sense vibrations when we move our fingers over an object, it is rough. And so on—if you close your eyes as you manipulate some soft and hard, warm and cold objects, you can make yourself aware of the separate sensations that interact and give rise to a complex perception.

The following discussion of the somatosenses groups them into three major categories: the *skin senses,* the *internal senses,* and the *vestibular senses.*

THE SKIN SENSES

◆ The entire surface of the human body is innervated (supplied with nerve fibers) by the dendrites of neurons that transmit somatosensory information to the brain. Cranial nerves convey information from the face and front portion of the head (including the teeth and the inside of the mouth and throat); spinal nerves convey information from the rest of the body's surface. **Figure 9.22** shows a sixteenth-century drawing of the spinal nerves. All

FIGURE 9.22 A sixteenth-century drawing by Vesalius of the peripheral nervous system.

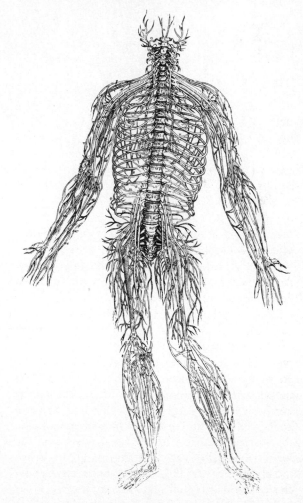

Hairy skin

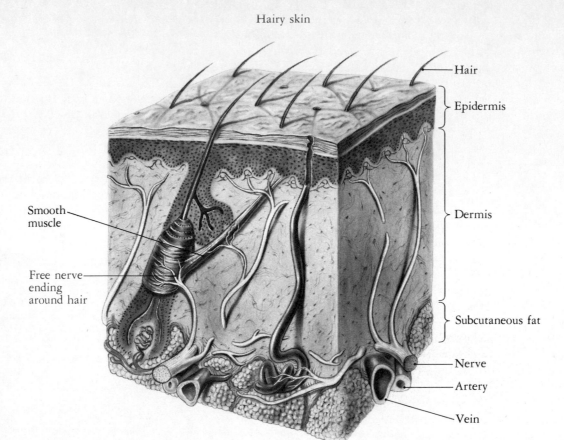

FIGURE 9.23   Sensory receptors in hairy skin. (From Carlson, N.R. *Physiology of Behavior.* 2nd ed. Boston: Allyn and Bacon, 1981.)

somatosensory information is detected by the dendrites of neurons; the system uses no separate receptor cells. However, some of these dendrites have specialized endings that modify the way in which they transduce energy into neural activity.

Figures 9.23 and 9.24 show the sensory receptors found in hairy skin and in smooth, hairless skin (such as that on the palms of the hands or the soles of the feet). The most common type is the *free nerve ending,* which resembles the fine roots of a plant. Free nerve endings infiltrate the middle layers of both smooth and hairy skin and surround the hair follicles in hairy skin. If you bend a single hair on your forearm you will see how sensitive the free nerve endings are. (See **Figure 9.23**.) Investigators have identified many other types of specialized dendritic endings than are shown in the two figures, but most authorities now believe that these are either artificially produced by the process of preparing and staining the skin for microscopic examination or are functionless "dead ends" produced during development, when the dendrites hit some obstruction in the underlayers of the skin.

Attempts to correlate a specific sensory ending with a specific stimulus have not been very successful. Only one of the special receptive endings is known definitely to have a special function: the *Pacinian corpuscle.* (See **Figure 9.24**.) Pacinian corpuscles are sensitive to movement; when they are moved, their axons fire a brief burst of impulses. These are thought to be the receptors that inform us about vibration.

Most investigators now believe that the quality of somatosensory stimuli is represented by some

Hairless skin

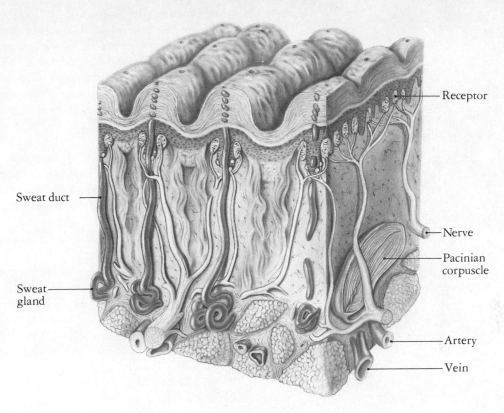

FIGURE 9.24 Sensory receptors in hairless skin.
(From Carlson, N.R. *Physiology of Behavior*, 2nd ed.
Boston: Allyn and Bacon, 1981.)

sort of complex pattern of activity from several different types of receptors. There is a good deal of evidence supporting this claim. For example, the cornea of the eye, which contains only free nerve endings, is very sensitive to pain, warmth, and cold. Furthermore, *psoriasis* (a congenital skin disease) produces gross changes in the innervation of the afflicted skin, including degeneration of many of the encapsulated dendritic endings. Yet despite these changes the afflicted skin responds to all the normal sensory stimuli.

Temperature

◆ There is general agreement that different sensory endings produce the sensations of warmth and coolness. Detectors for coolness appear to be lo-

cated closer to the surface of the skin. If you suddenly place your foot under a stream of rather hot water, you may feel a brief sensation of cold just before you perceive that the water is really hot; this sensation probably results from short-lived stimulation of the coolness detectors located in the upper layers of the skin.

Our temperature detectors respond best to *changes* in temperature. Within reasonable limits, the air temperature of our environment comes to feel "normal." Temporary changes in temperature are perceived as warmth or coolness. Thus, our temperature detectors adapt to the *ambient* (that is, surrounding, or environmental) temperature. If you place one hand in a pail of hot water and the other in a pail of cold water, the intensity of the sensations of heat and cold will decrease after a few

FIGURE 9.25   The air temperature here is probably not within "reasonable limits," and continues to feel cold.

minutes. If you then plunge both hands into a pailful of water that is at room temperature, it will feel hot to the cold-adapted hand and cold to the hot-adapted hand. It is mainly the change in temperature that is signaled to the brain. Of course, there are limits to the process of adaptation. Extreme heat or cold will continue to feel hot or cold, however long we experience it. (See **Figure 9.25**.)

Pressure

◈ Sensory psychologists speak of touch and pressure as two separate senses. They define touch as the sensation of very light contact of an object with the skin, and pressure as the sensation produced by more forceful contact. There is also good evidence that two different kinds of sensory endings mediate sensations of vibration, depending on the frequency (cycles per second) of stimulation.

Sensations of pressure occur only when the skin is actually moving, which means that the pressure detectors respond only while they are being bent. Just how the motion stimulates the neurons is not known. If you rest your forearm on a table and place a small weight on your skin, you will feel the pressure at first, but eventually you will feel nothing at all, if you keep your arm still. You fail to feel the pressure not because your brain "ig-

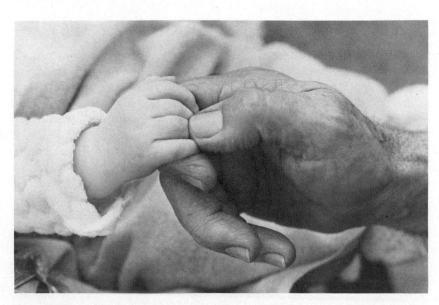

FIGURE 9.26   Our fingers are especially sensitive to touch.

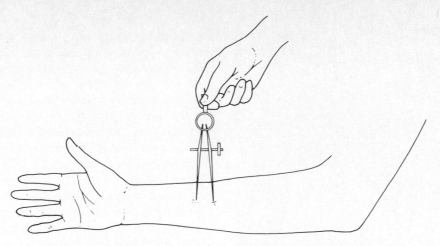

FIGURE 9.27   The method for determining the two-point discrimination threshold.

nores" incoming stimulation; your sensory endings actually cease sending impulses to your brain. This phenomenon is called **sensory adaptation.** Studies that have measured the very slow, very minute movements of a weight sinking down into the skin have shown that sensations of pressure cease when the movements stop. With the addition of another weight on top of the first one, movement and sensations of pressure begin again (Nafe and Wagoner, 1941). A person will feel a very heavy weight indefinitely, but the sensation is probably pain rather than pressure.

Sensitivity to subtle differences in touch and pressure varies widely across the surface of the body. The most sensitive regions are the lips and the fingertips. (See **Figure 9.26.**) The most common measure of the tactile discrimination of a region of skin is the **two-point discrimination threshold.** The experimenter touches the subject with one or both legs of a pair of dividers and asks the person to say whether the sensation is coming from one or two points. (See **Figure 9.27.**) The farther apart the legs of the dividers must be before the person reports feeling two separate sensations, the lower the sensitivity of that region of skin.

Pain

◆ Pain is a complex sensation involving not only intense sensory stimulation but also an emotional component; a given sensory input to the brain might be interpreted as pain in one situation and as pleas-

ure in another. For example, when people are sexually aroused, they become less sensitive to many forms of pain and often even find such intense stimulation pleasurable. Sometimes wounded soldiers who have survived a fierce battle refuse painkilling drugs; presumably, the sensation from their wound telling them that they are alive offsets the negative effects of their pain.

There is good physiological evidence for a distinction between the sensation of pain and its emotional component. Opiates such as morphine diminish the sensation of pain by stimulating opiate receptors on neurons in the brain; these neurons participate in mechanisms that block the transmission of pain information to the brain. In contrast, some tranquilizers (such as Valium) depress neural systems that are responsible for the emotional component of pain, but do not diminish the intensity of the sensation. Thus, people who have received a drug like Valium will report that they feel the pain just as much as they did before, but that it does not bother them much. (See **Figure 9.28.**)

Evidence from surgical procedures also supports the distinction between sensation and emotion. Prefrontal lobotomy, like the administration of tranquilizers such as Valium, blocks the emotional component of pain but does not affect primary sensation. Therefore, operations similar to prefrontal lobotomy (but much less drastic) are sometimes performed to treat people who suffer from chronic

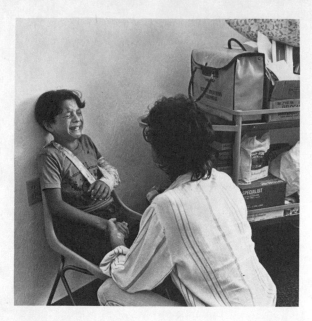

FIGURE 9.28   The emotional components of pain are related to the circumstances of its occurrence. In strange and fearful situations the experience of pain can be especially intense.

pain that cannot be alleviated by other means.

We do not yet know the nature of the immediate stimulus (or stimuli) for pain. One thing that painful stimuli have in common is the ability to produce tissue damage. Many investigators believe that pain detectors—which appear to consist of free nerve endings—are stimulated by chemicals released by damaged tissue. Keele (1966) devised a technique for studying the chemicals that produce pain. He placed some *cantharides* (Spanish fly) on the skin, which causes a blister to form. He then picked off the top of the blister and gently washed the sore with a sterile salt solution. He placed solutions of various substances on the raw skin (and hence, exposed free nerve endings) and asked subjects to rate the intensity of the pain that was produced.

Experiments like these supply useful information, but it is difficult to separate primary from secondary effects. For example, pain sensations are closely related to the concentration of the potassium ion in solutions that are placed on the blisters. Does this ion produce pain because it directly stimulates the pain detectors or because it produces tissue damage that causes another substance to be

released, which in turn stimulates the detectors? More research is needed to answer this question.

You may be acquainted with the term "Spanish fly" in another context. This extract of the cantharides beetle is reputed to be an *aphrodisiac*—a substance that increases a person's sex drive. It does nothing of the sort. When it is ingested it causes an irritation and itching of the mucous membrane of the urinary tract, which produces an urge to rub the affected area. That urge is quite distinct from sexual arousal.

Many noxious stimuli elicit two kinds of pain—an immediate sharp, or "bright," pain followed by a deep, dull, sometimes throbbing pain. Presumably, different types of nerve endings mediate these two types of pain. For example, a hard blow from a blunt object to a large muscle will produce only the deep, dull pain. Of the two sensations, deep pain is usually the most unpleasant. If your intellectual curiosity and gullibility are great enough, you can demonstrate these phenomena yourself. Take one shoe off and stand facing a wall, about six inches away. Standing on your shoe-clad food, draw your shoeless foot back and quickly swing it forward in an arc. You will feel a sudden flash of bright pain in your toes, followed shortly by a more enduring deep pain.

Bright and dull sensations of pain can be distinguished physiologically. Various regions of the thalamus relay somatosensory information to the cerebral cortex. Mark, Ervin, and Yakovlev (1962) found that surgical destruction of one part of the human thalamus diminished sensitivity to deep pain without affecting sharp pain or sensitivity to touch and pressure. Destruction of a different region diminished sensitivity to touch and sharp pain but did not affect deep pain. Therefore, these two types of pain appear to be distinct.

Pain or the fear of pain is one of the most effective motivators of human behavior. However, it also serves us well in the normal course of living. We escape from stimuli that damage our body, and we subsequently learn to avoid them. People who have a genetically caused lack of pain sensation suffer many injuries. They receive cuts and burns from objects that normal people would feel and withdraw from. In some cases, broken bones have gone unset, and inflamed appendixes have ruptured without any warning signals. Even our adjustments in posture are motivated by pain; one young woman who lacked sensitivity to pain died of spinal injuries caused by her failure to shift her posture periodically (Sternbach, 1968).

THE INTERNAL SENSES

◈ Sensory endings located in our internal organs, bones and joints, and muscles convey painful, neutral, and in some cases pleasurable sensory information. Although most tissue in the interior of the body is insensitive to cutting, burning, or crushings—manipulations that would assuredly produce pain if they were applied to the skin—the walls of most internal organs contain receptive endings that respond to stretch, producing sensations of pain. Their excellent sensitivity to stretch manifests itself in discomfort when, for example, our intestines are distended with gas, a gall bladder or appendix is swollen, or a kidney stone passes through a ureter.

Bones are covered by a membrane that is richly innervated with sensory endings. Foreign objects rarely touch this membrane, but when they do, excruciating pain can result. The membranes that line the joints between bones contain another type of sensory ending, whose output provides us with information regarding our limb position and movement. Membranes in joints also contain pain receptors; when they are inflamed with arthritis, even normal bone movements can stimulate these nerve endings and produce pain.

Finally, the muscles themselves are enclosed by a tough sheath of tissue that contains free nerve endings. When a strained muscle becomes swollen and inflamed, this sheath is stretched, causing the pain of an aching muscle.

◈ Within the body of the muscle itself are still more sensory endings. Muscles are attached to bones by incredibly tough bands of fibers called tendons. A set of stretch detectors that make up the *Golgi tendon organ* are located at the junction between muscle and tendon. (See **Figure 9.29.**) These sensory endings fire at a high rate when the stretch on a tendon becomes excessive. The result is an automatic, reflexive inhibition of the neurons in the spinal cord that activate contraction of the muscle. This inhibitory system helps prevent damage to the tendons or bones from an excessively strong contraction. Some weightlifters have received injections of a local anesthetic near the tendons of some muscles to prevent the Golgi tendon organs from signaling neurons in the spinal cord to inhibit muscular contraction. As a result they can lift even heavier weights. (Some have also been known to snap their tendons or break their arms.)

Muscle spindles, another set of stretch detectors, are distributed throughout the muscle and inform the brain about changes in muscle length. (See **Figure 9.30, top.**) You cannot "feel" the information from the muscle spindles, but the brain uses the information from these receptors and from joint receptors to keep track of the location of parts of the body and to control muscular contractions. If you are holding your forearm parallel to the ground and a weight is suddenly placed in your hand,

FIGURE 9.29   Activity from the Golgi tendon organ excites neurons in the spinal cord that inhibit the firing of the motor neuron, thus reducing the strength of muscular contraction. (From Carlson, N.R. *Physiology of Behavior,* 2nd ed. Boston: Allyn and Bacon, 1981.)

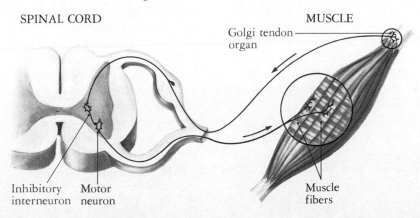

SPINAL CORD

MUSCLE

Golgi tendon organ

Inhibitory interneuron   Motor neuron

Muscle fibers

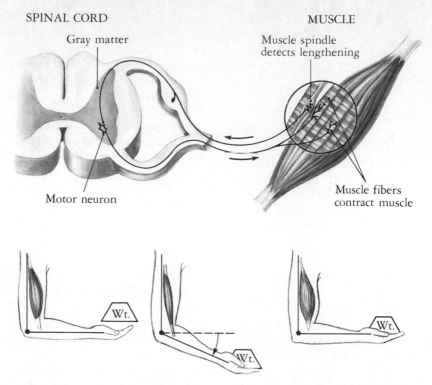

FIGURE 9.30   *Top.* Lengthening of the muscle activates the muscle spindles, which excite the motor neurons in the spinal cord and increase the strength of muscular contraction. *Bottom.* The action of muscle spindles compensates for the addition of a weight in the hand by bringing the arm back to its original position. (From Carlson, N.R. *Physiology of Behavior,* 2nd ed. Boston: Allyn and Bacon, 1981.)

stimulation from the muscle spindles causes an automatic increase in the strength of the muscular contraction, thereby compensating for the additional weight. (See **Figure 9.30, bottom.**)

THE VESTIBULAR SENSES

◆ What we call our "sense of balance" in fact involves several senses, not just one. If we stand on one foot and then close our eyes, we immediately realize how important a role vision plays. If we were deprived of sensory input from our joints and muscles, we would immediately fall down. The *vestibular apparatus* of the inner ear provides only part of the sensory input that helps us to remain upright.

The vestibular apparatus does provide information that is useful in maintaining posture. The three *semicircular canals,* oriented at right angles to one another, detect changes in rotation of the head in any direction. (See **Figure 9.31.**) These canals contain a liquid, and rotation of the head makes the liquid flow, stimulating the nerve fibers that innervate them.

You can perform an experiment with another person that demonstrates the operation of the semicircular canals. Spin someone seated in a swivel chair or have the person stand and turn around for thirty seconds or so. After the person stops rotating, his or her eyes will involuntarily move from side to side. If you watch the eyes carefully, you will see that they repeatedly move in one direction, and then snap back to the place where they started. These eye movements are called *nystagmus.* The rapid movement takes place in the same direction as the rotation.

Another set of inner ear organs is the pair of *vestibular sacs.* (See **Figure 9.31.**) These contain crystals of calcium carbonate that are embedded in a gelatinlike substance attached to receptive hair

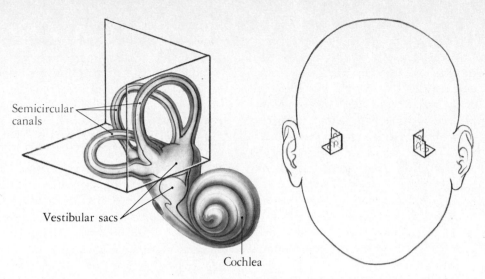

FIGURE 9.31 The three semicircular canals and two vestibular sacs located in the inner ear. Note the location of the cochlea. (From Carlson, N.R. *Physiology of Behavior,* 2nd ed. Boston: Allyn and Bacon, 1981.)

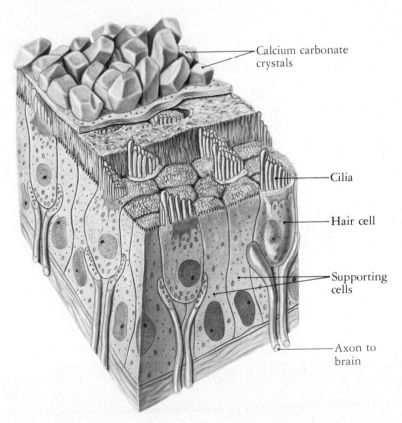

FIGURE 9.32 The sensory tissue located within the vestibular sacs. (From Carlson, N.R. *Physiology of Behavior,* 2nd ed. Boston: Allyn and Bacon, 1981.)

cells. In one sac the receptive tissue is on the wall; in the other it is on the floor. When the head tilts, the weight of the calcium carbonate crystals shifts, producing different forces on the cilia of the hair cells. (See **Figure 9.32.**)

The vestibular sacs are very useful in maintaining an upright head position. They also participate in a reflex that enables us to see clearly even when the head is being jarred. When we walk, our eyes are jostled back and forth. The jarring of the head stimulates the vestibular sacs to cause reflexive movements of the eyes that partially compensate for the head movements. People who lack this reflex because of localized brain damage must stop walking in order to see things clearly—for example, to read a street sign.

We know that the vestibular sacs provide the sensory input that can produce motion sickness, because slow, repetitive stimulation of the vestibular sacs can produce nausea and vomiting in a susceptible individual. It is difficult to imagine what useful function this mechanism performs. It undoubtedly served our ancestors in some way unrelated to modern means of transportation.

Interim summary: The somatosenses gather several different kinds of information from different parts of the body. The skin senses of temperature, touch and pressure, vibration, and pain inform us about the nature of objects that come in contact with our skin. Imagine a man attempting to climb a rock cliff. As he reaches for a firm handhold overhead, the Pacinian corpuscles in his fingers detect vibration as he runs his fingers over the rock, which helps him determine its texture and find cracks into which he can insert anchors for his rope. Perhaps temperature receptors in his fingers tell him whether the rock is exposed to the sun and has warmed up, or whether it is in the cool shade. If he cuts his skin against some sharp rock, free nerve endings give rise to sensations of pain, caused by tissue damage. Presumably he is too intent on his task to notice sensations from his internal organs, although he would certainly feel a painful stimulus like a kidney stone, and if he thinks that he is slipping he will most assuredly feel a queasy sensation caused by his internal reaction to a sudden release of adrenalin. (When he reaches the top and enjoys a hot cup of tea he can savor a comfortable, warm feeling from his stomach.) As he climbs, he relies heavily on sensory receptors in his muscles and joints, which inform his brain of movement and location of his arms and legs; the vestibular senses help him keep his balance.

CONCLUDING REMARKS

Although vision is in many ways the most important sensory modality, the others contribute to the richness of experience. Because of the role that speech plays in human culture, audition is extremely important for social behavior. Along with vision, it provides information about distant events. Except for olfaction, which can tell us about sources of aromatic molecules far upwind, the other sensory modalities deal with things near our body, including things important to us, such as the touch of a loved one. The somatosenses and the vestibular senses are closely tied to our own movement. When we feel an object we do not do so passively; we move our hands over it to determine its shape, texture, and temperature. In fact, the primary information from vestibular senses and from the muscle and joint receptors is produced by our own movement. Without this information we would stumble and fall.

Every profound thought, every experience, every brilliant deduction owes its existence to the sensory modalities. Without sensory input the brain would be an unconscious, useless mass of tissue. As philosophers realized long ago, all knowledge comes through the sense organs. The marvelous complexity of our sensory systems is revealed by the marvelous complexity of our thoughts and experiences.

GUIDE TO TERMS INTRODUCED IN THIS CHAPTER

auditory hair cell   p. 344   Figure 9.6
basilar membrane   p. 344   Figures 9.5–9.7
bitterness   p. 353   Figure 9.17
cilia   p. 345   Figure 9.6
cochlea   p. 344   Figures 9.4, 9.31
free nerve ending   p. 360   Figure 9.23

SUGGESTIONS FOR FURTHER READING

There are many excellent books on hearing. I can especially recommend *Fundamentals of Hearing* by W.A. Yost and D.W. Nielsen (New York: Holt, Rinehart and Winston, 1977). *Molecular Basis of Odor* by J. Amoore (Springfield, Ill.: C.C. Thomas, 1970) is rather old, but it is interesting and written in a readable style. R. Sternbach's book on *Pain: A Psychophysiological Analysis* (New York: Academic Press, 1968) is even older, but it contains many interesting examples.

A scholarly yet entertaining textbook by M. Matlin entitled *Perception* (Boston: Allyn & Bacon, 1983) has an excellent chapter on taste, with many applications about food and beverage tasting.

PART • D

COGNITIVE

BEHAVIOR

The next four chapters discuss psychological research into the major aspects of human cognition or "knowing": consciousness, memory, language, and intelligence.

We humans are aware of ourselves; we know this is true because we can say so to each other. Consciousness is one of the most fascinating of all psychological phenomena. Why are we aware of ourselves? What brain mechanisms give rise to consciousness? Chapter 10 discusses these questions and some possible answers, along with the related topics of sleep, attention, hypnosis, and ways consciousness can be altered and controlled.

Chapter 11 surveys research into human memory and the cognitive processes related to learning and remembering (and forgetting) information. Chapter 12 examines communication through language and children's acquisition of language. Finally, Chapter 13 discusses the nature of human intelligence. Is the IQ score a valid measure of ability? Can intelligence be inherited? The answers to these questions are important to society as well as to psychologists seeking to understand human cognition.

CONSCIOUSNESS

L E A R N I N G ◆ O B J E C T I V E S

THIS CHAPTER explores the nature of human self-awareness—knowledge of our own existence, behavior, perceptions, and thoughts. This is the most common, and probably the most important, meaning of consciousness. What factors affect consciousness? How do we direct our consciousness from one event to another, paying attention to some stimuli and ignoring others? What is the role of brain functions in consciousness? What is hypnosis—can another person really take control of our thoughts and behavior? How does a person control his or her consciousness through meditation? Why do we regularly undergo the profound alteration in consciousness called sleep? We do not yet have all the answers to these questions, but we have made much progress. Our own consciousness is a private experience. We infer that other people are conscious from their behavior—in particular, from their speech and writing. In fact the *sole* criterion for consciousness is verbal. We conclude that other people are conscious—that they know they exist—because they *tell* us so.

CONSCIOUSNESS AS A SOCIAL BEHAVIOR

◆ Why are we aware of ourselves? What purpose is served by our ability to "know" that we (and the rest of the world) exist? If we view consciousness as an adaptive trait of the human species, the most likely explanation lies in its relation to communication. Because of our ability to communicate we are aware of ourselves. Thus, consciousness is primarily a social phenomenon.

Certainly humans are not unique in their ability to communicate with other living creatures. Dogs can snarl at each other, birds can sing to proclaim their territories, monkeys can assert their dominance or submission by facial expressions. Animals can communicate with prospective mates to signal readiness. Most can communicate to a rival that a fight is unnecessary—the signaler is willing to submit. Thus, the ability to signal one's probable behavior (loosely referred to as "intentions") has important survival value. (See Figure 10.1.)

Human language can communicate much more than intentions; for example, it is also a means of enlisting help from other people. We can communicate many of our requests nonverbally, just as other animals can. However, through language we can make much more complex requests. To ask another person to perform a particular action, we must be able to express our needs verbally—we must have *verbal access* to them. If we cannot talk about them we cannot request assistance. Second, behaviors that we request from other people must be under *verbal control*—words must be capable of causing the person addressed to perform the behaviors. If a verbal request cannot elicit the behaviors (assuming the person is already willing to cooperate), the request is useless.

The concepts of verbal access and verbal control are important ones and require some elaboration. Many events occur in our bodies to which we have no verbal access. For example, we cannot tell another person whether our parathyroid gland is secreting its hormones. However, we do have verbal access to the physiological events that occur when we go for a prolonged time without food or water; we can tell someone else that we are hungry or thirsty. The selective advantage to having verbal access to the physiological conditions of hunger and thirst is that we can ask other people for help in obtaining food or water.

Verbal control refers to the effect of words on the behavior of other people. A person raised completely apart from other people would not be able to talk, because there would be no reason to do so;

FIGURE 10.1   The ability to communicate is not unique to humans. Here an adolescent female ape greets an adolescent male. Presumably, a degree of self-awareness accompanies the ability to communicate.

verbal access

verbal control

speech would have no effect on his or her environment. Speech is useful to us because it can elicit behaviors from other people. When we can elicit specific behaviors from other people by the sounds that we make or the marks that we put on a piece of paper, the behaviors are said to be under verbal control.

Consciousness, then, can be seen as a consequence of our ability to communicate—internally, with ourselves, or externally, with others. We are conscious of the needs that we can talk about and of the behaviors that are under verbal control.

Not all communication can be said to be conscious. For example, we saw in Chapter 6 that when they are cold, baby mice automatically emit an ultrasonic cry that elicits behavior from their mother. We do not have to assume that the baby mice are conscious of the cold or that the mother is conscious of being called. This kind of communication is automatic and apparently unlearned. Species-typical communications like these probably do not fall in the domain of consciousness.

Some human communications are also automatic, and therefore probably unconscious. An infant's smile is automatically elicited by stimuli such as a high-pitched voice or a human face (or even a picture of a circle with dots on it that look like eyes). It will automatically cry when it is cold or in pain. Even social interactions between adults are filled with nonverbal exchanges by means of subtle postural or facial expressions. (These are often referred to as "body language.") Have you ever met someone you found rather attractive but soon realized that he or she did not like you and wanted to discourage your attention? You couldn't say exactly what the person did, but something in his or her manner was discouraging. You received some signs that you were not conscious of, but their *effects* were plain. One of the abilities of a good novelist is to be able to recognize these nonverbal behaviors and express them in words.

Although we sometimes communicate with other people unconsciously, much of our nonverbal communication is conscious and deliberate. For example, when a traffic policeman signals us to stop, he is certainly aware of what he is doing, and so are we. When we wave hello or beckon to someone to come over we are certainly aware that we are communicating. Thus, we have a language of movements that serves the same function as words. The important feature seems to be that we are conscious of the gestures that we *could* put into words, if we chose. The policeman could say "Stop!" but instead he signals nonverbally because we might not hear him. We beckon to a friend because we do not want to shout across the room. The fact that we use a hand gesture rather than words does not make our behavior nonconscious. (See **Figure 10.2.**)

Although the principal benefit of communication is its capacity to affect the behavior of other people, it has other advantages. Through communication, one person's experience can be shared with others. We are not limited to learning about things that we have directly observed; we can profit from what other people have learned by listening to them speak or reading what they have written.

FIGURE 10.2 Not all conscious human communication is expressed through words.

This fact has made it possible for human culture to evolve. Just as members of a particular species profit from the "discoveries" made by genetic mutations of their ancestors, we can profit from the discoveries made by our ancestors and passed down to us through writing or oral traditions. Each generation can start where the previous one left off.

We can also communicate with ourselves. This capacity is another important consequence of having verbal access to our perceptions and feelings and verbal control over our behavior. We can make plans in words, think about the consequences of these plans in words, and use words to produce behaviors—all without actually *saying* the words, but by thinking them. Surely the brain mechanisms that permit us to understand words and produce speech are the same ones we use to think in words. Of course, thinking in words stops short of firing the neurons that move the muscles that we use to speak.

In support of this hypothesis, investigators have noted that deaf people who use sign language to communicate with each other often make small movements with their hands when they are thinking to themselves, just as those of us who can hear and speak sometimes talk to ourselves under our breath. Apparently we exercise our expressive language mechanisms, whatever they are, when we think.

The ability to think in words about what we are doing enables us to engage in *verbally mediated* behaviors. Activities involving verbal mediation include logical analysis, development of philosophic systems of thought, and formulation of the rules of the scientific method. Even some skills can be learned through verbal mediation. Consider a person who is learning to drive a car with a manual transmission. "Let's see, push in the clutch, move the shift lever to the left and then down—there, it's in gear—now let the clutch come up—oh! It died—I should have given it more gas. Let's see, clutch down, turn the key . . ." This behavior eventually becomes automatic, but at first it is verbally mediated.

To be sure, not all thinking is verbally mediated. If we have verbal access to our nonverbal thinking, we are conscious of it. If we do not have verbal access, we are not conscious of it. Suppose you are preparing to walk across a wide stream that is strewn with large rocks. Your problem is to get to the other side without falling, by jumping from rock to rock. You will not use words for this project. Instead, you will probably look at the rocks in front of you and mentally try out various possible paths. As you proceed across the stream you will continue to revise your plan, estimating distances, deciding which of several alternatives is safest and most direct. This process will undoubtedly call on many of the brain mechanisms that participate in walking and jumping; in other words, the planning will involve private locomotion just as thinking in words involved private talking. But although this planning does not require words, you are perfectly able to describe what you are doing. You can tell someone else that you are thinking about this rock—"No, it isn't wide enough—that one looks too slippery—there, that's the one." You have verbal access to the nonverbal mental processes that you use in crossing the stream.

In contrast, there are some nonverbal mental processes to which we do not have verbal access. For example, skilled activities such as riding a bicycle or performing gymnastic routines require very complex sequences of muscular contractions. These sequences cannot be learned verbally. Words help, of course, but the only way to learn is to watch skilled people perform the behaviors and then to practice them. (See **Figure 10.3.**) You can learn how to work the gearshift of a car by reading a book, but you cannot read a book on how to ride a bicycle and then expect to get on one and begin riding right away. You would have to learn the movements that are necessary to keep from falling. I know that I learned to ride a bicycle long before I could say that I had to turn the wheel to the right whenever I began falling in that direction. The fact that I gained verbal access to this rule only after years of riding proves that I did not need this verbal access to know how to ride.

Although consciousness may be synonymous with activity of the verbal mechanisms of the brain, we need not conclude that only humans are conscious. The evolutionary process is incremental: new traits and abilities build upon ones that already exist. Some forms of communication among animals are automatic and probably do not involve conscious-

FIGURE 10.3   Words may help describe some
nonverbally mediated behaviors, but they must be
learned through imitation and practice.

ness. Others can be learned, just as we learn our
own verbal language. Certainly your dog can learn
to communicate with you. The fact that it can
learn to tell you when it wants to eat, go for a
walk, or play probably means that it is conscious,
also. We humans have much more verbal access to
our needs and perceptions, which means that our
consciousness is better developed. But if the ability
to communicate evolved, then we must conclude
that consciousness developed along with it.

 There are some cases in which verbal activity is
not synonymous with consciousness. Some people
whose brains have been injured by degenerative
processes show no comprehension of speech but
repeat everything that is said to them, rather like
 a parrot. Because their speech does not express their
needs or describe things that are happening to them
it can be regarded as a nonconscious phenomenon.

Interim summary: Consciousness, as it is defined here, can be viewed as synonymous with verbal processes. Its physiological basis is the activity
of language mechanisms of the brain. The private
use of language ("thinking to oneself") is clearly
conscious. Private nonverbal processes are conscious if we can describe them—if their activities
are available to neural mechanisms of language.
Just as clearly, we are conscious of *external* events
only if we can think (and verbalize) about them.
Verbal access is the ability to describe, in words,
private events such as perceptions, feelings, and
plans. *Verbal control* is the capacity of verbal stimuli
to elicit behaviors from other people. *Verbal mediation* is the role played by verbal stimuli in controlling special kinds of complex behaviors (such
as logical thinking) that exist only because our brains
possess verbal mechanisms.

This view of human self-awareness is not the only one, but it seems to be the most useful one, for it helps present a unified picture of a variety of phenomena related to consciousness.

ATTENTION

◆ Not all events that can enter consciousness actually do so. Just as some automatic behaviors occur without our awareness, there are stimuli that we do not notice. As I concentrate on thinking and writing I am not conscious of other things that happen around me. If someone asks me about them later, I will not be able to recall them. If I had wanted to, I could have paid attention to these events, making information about them available to the verbal systems of my brain. As a result I would have been able to think (and talk) about them. Clearly, *selective attention* is an important component of human consciousness.

In this context, attention refers to what we do to gain verbal access to stimuli that are currently present. At any one moment, several stimuli are acting upon our sense receptors. If asked to do so, we can describe any of them in detail, directing our attention toward the relevant stimulus. That is, we transmit the activity in the appropriate part of our perceptual systems to our verbal system.

EFFECTS OF ATTENTION ON VERBAL MEMORY

◆ Attention is not only important in determining which stimuli will be accessible to verbal mechanisms; it also plays an important role in memory. When someone presents new information to us verbally, our attention determines whether we will be able to remember it.

Cherry (1953) obtained evidence of this phenomenon through experiments involving *dichotic listening.* (*Dichotic* means "divided into two parts"). He placed earphones on his subjects and presented recordings of different spoken messages to each ear. He asked them to *shadow,* or repeat, the message presented to one ear. Shadowing ensured that they would pay attention to the message, processing it verbally. (See **Figure 10.4.**)

The subjects were able to shadow the message, but they repeated it in a rather monotonous voice, probably because of the great demands this task places on the verbal system. Shadowing involves listening to the sounds in one ear, recognizing them as words, and remembering them while repeating

FIGURE 10.4 "Shadowing" a message that is presented by means of headphones.

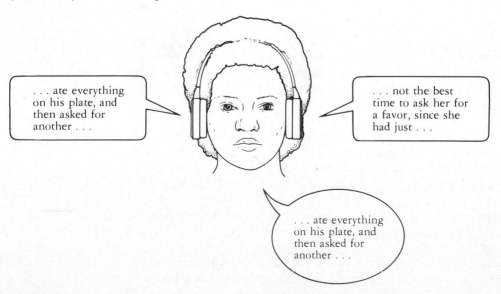

. . . ate everything on his plate, and then asked for another . . .

. . . not the best time to ask her for a favor, since she had just . . .

. . . ate everything on his plate, and then asked for another . . .

words that were heard a few seconds ago. These activities may occupy the verbal system so completely that it can no longer also exert control over inflections in tone. The subjects did not realize how listless and monotonous they sounded—apparently they paid little attention to the sounds of their own voices.

The information that entered the unattended ear appeared to be lost. When questioned about what that ear heard, subjects responded that they heard something, but they could not say what it was. Even if the voice presented to the unshadowed ear began to talk in a foreign language they did not notice. When an unshadowed voice was played backward, a few subjects said only that there was something funny about the voice in that ear. However, if the voice switched from male to female, they later recalled this change.

The results might suggest that a channel of sensory input (in this case, one ear) can simply be turned off. Perhaps neurons in the auditory system that detect sound from the unattended ear are inhibited so that they cannot respond to sounds presented to that ear. However, other data show that some information, by its very nature, can break through into consciousness. For example, if the subject's name is presented to the unattended ear, he or she will very likely hear it and remember it later. A study by Von Wright, Anderson, and Stenman (1975) showed that words that had previously been presented along with an unpleasant electric shock would produce an emotional reaction when the words were presented to the unattended ear. Even when the subject was not attending to the voice in a verbal sense, the information produced a nonverbal response—an emotional reaction that was previously classically conditioned to a particular word.

Besides being able to notice and remember some characteristics of information received by the unattended sensory channel, we are able to store information temporarily as it comes in. No doubt you have had the following sort of experience. You are intently reading or thinking about something, when you become aware that someone has asked you a question. You look up and say, "What?" but then answer the question before the other person has had a chance to repeat it. You first became aware that you had just been asked a question, but

you did not know what had been asked. However, when you thought for a moment, you remembered what the question was—you heard it again in your mind's ear, so to speak. The information, held in temporary storage, was made accessible to your verbal system.

Treisman (1964) showed that people can follow a message that is being shadowed even if it switches from one ear to another. Suppose a subject is shadowing a message presented to the left ear, and the message to the right ear is unshadowed. (See **Figure 10.5**.)

The subject will probably say, "crept out of the swamp," and not "crept out of flowers." Apparently, the switch occurs when the message begins to make no sense. However, by the time the subject realizes that "crept out of flowers" makes no sense, the rest of the message, "the swamp," has already been presented to the right ear. Given the fact that subjects could continue the message without missing any words, they must be able to retrieve some words from memory. Thus, even though the unshadowed message cannot be remembered later, it produces some trace that can be retrieved if attention is directed to it soon after the words are presented.

Sometimes we have to sort out one message from several others without the benefit of such a distinct cue; we seldom hear one voice in one ear and another in the other. For example, we might be trying to converse with one person while we are in a room with several other people who are carrying on their

FIGURE 10.5   Switching from one ear to the other while shadowing a dichotically presented message.

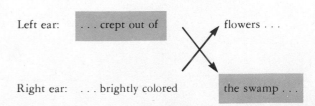

own conversations. Our task is easier if the person has a different voice from those of the other people in the room (for example, a female voice among male voices). We can also partially duplicate the dichotic listening task by turning the head so that one ear is nearer to the person who is speaking.

Even if you are in a situation like that shown in Figure 10.6, you can usually sort out one voice from another. (See **Figure 10.6.**) In this case you are trying to listen to the person opposite you and to ignore the cross-conversation of the people to your left and right. Your ears receive a jumble of sounds, but you are able to pick out the ones you want, stringing them together into a meaningful message and forgetting the rest. This task takes some effort; following one person's conversation in such circumstances is more difficult when what he or she is saying is not very interesting. If you overhear a few words of another conversation that seems more interesting, it is hard to strain out the cross-conversation.

It is also possible to decode one meaningful message from a recording of several messages spoken by the same person, played through the same loud-speaker. Although you may hear several words simultaneously, you select the one that best fits the message being followed, and reject (and forget) the others. The task is easiest if the messages differ in content, and difficult to impossible if they are very similar.

ATTENTION AND VERBAL CONTROL OF BEHAVIOR

The evidence presented in the previous section suggests that we cannot remember verbal information unless we pay attention to it when it is presented. Attention appears to be necessary to verbal memories. (A classically conditioned emotional response to a word is not a verbal memory.) However, some behaviors can be learned without attention or awareness.

An experiment by Carter (1973) demonstrated that people's behavior can be trained without their awareness. He seated each of his subjects (college students) in front of a panel containing a light and an electrically operated counter, with a telegraph key beside his or her hand. The subjects were told to figure out how to press the key in a pattern that would earn the most points. Points would be signaled by the flashing light and totaled by the counter. The subjects began pressing the key, varying their rate of responding as they tried to figure out what the pattern was. Clearly, they were paying attention to the key and to the light and counter on the panel, which indicated when they were correct. However, the subjects did not know that the key presses they made *had no effect* on how many points they would earn. Instead, the experimenter watched the subjects through a one-way mirror and operated the light and the counter whenever they blinked their right eye. Soon the subjects began to blink rapidly; the contingency between blinking and the flashing light was effective in reinforcing eyeblink. When the experimenter stopped awarding points, the blinking ceased (extinguished), but the subjects kept pressing away at the key.

When Carter questioned his subjects later, it was clear that they were unaware of the connection between their blinking and the awarding of the points. In fact, some appeared not to believe him. Some were so sure they had not been blinking at a high rate that Carter offered to prove to them that the experiment was valid by letting them serve as research assistants. They accepted his chal-

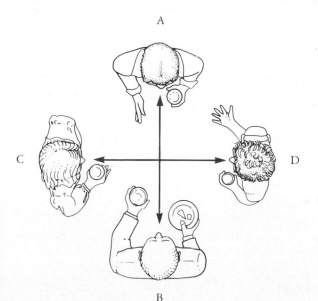

FIGURE 10.6   The cocktail party phenomenon. Two conversations can be carried on simultaneously.

lenge and, after helping him, were convinced. (And Carter, a graduate student at the time, obtained free help.)

Carter's experiment shows that although attention appears to be necessary for gaining verbal access to information, it is not necessary for learning and performing nonverbal tasks.

CONTROL OF ATTENTION: HABITUATION

Habituation, which was first discussed in Chapter 4, has direct relevance to consciousness. Novel stimuli have the ability to capture our attention. This effect is obviously useful, because a new stimulus might be important: it could either signal danger or an unexpected opportunity. For example, if you sit in a quiet room, a sudden stimulus such as a noise or a movement will cause you to become more alert, and you will look at the source of the stimulus. Your pupils will dilate slightly, your heart rate will briefly increase, and the level of electrical activity in your brain will indicate that you have become more alert and aroused. Your muscles may even jerk a bit, if the stimulus was particularly startling. We call this set of reactions the orienting response. If the noise occurs repeatedly, your response will become less and less pronounced, until you finally fail to react. Your response has habituated to the stimulus. The usefulness of habituation is obvious: if the stimulus occurs again and again and is plainly not important, it should be ignored. (Of course, if it *is* important you will not ignore it. For example, you will continue to respond to an aversive stimulus that elicits a defensive reaction.)

Habituation might appear to be a more passive process than selective attention. After all, selective attention involves noticing and thinking about a stimulus; habituation involves merely ignoring a stimulus. Yet we can become habituated to a stimulus of one intensity and exhibit an orienting response to the same stimulus presented at a lower intensity. For example, once we are habituated to a bright light flash, we are surprised by a dim one. It is as if any stimulus that is different from the one we have come to expect is capable of arousing us.

Expectation, then, seems to play a large role in habituation, which implies that unconscious analysis of incoming information must occur—just as it does for information presented to the unattended ear in a dichotic listening task. If a click is sounded every two seconds a subject's orienting response to it will soon habituate. But if the click suddenly stops, an orienting response will occur a little more than two seconds after the last click—just after the time the click should have been heard. I have observed a similar phenomenon while giving a lecture when the ventilating system went off. The sudden silence made me stop, and all of us in the room suddenly looked up at the place where the sound had been coming from. Clearly, our orienting response was not produced by energy striking our sense receptors. The eliciting stimulus was the *absence* of energy.

Sokolov (1963) has suggested a model that can account for this phenomenon. When a stimulus is presented repeatedly, a brain mechanism constructs a memory for the stimulus. Thereafter, as the brain receives information from the sense organ, it is compared with the memory. If sensation and memory match, we ignore the stimulus—it does not produce an orienting response. Unless we are paying special attention to the stimulus, we will not be aware of it. However, a stimulus that is different from the memory evokes an orienting response, and we pay attention to it. (See **Figure 10.7.**)

This model explains how the sudden absence of a click can arouse us after our response has become habituated through hearing one every two seconds. Presumably, some neural activity in the brain, representing the memory for the click, also occurs every two seconds. If the neural activity occurs at the same time as a click, no orienting response occurs; the click was expected. However, when the click stops, the neural activity occurs without a matching stimulus. The comparison mechanism detects a difference, and triggers the orienting response.

We humans are usually conscious of our own orienting responses. Our verbal system has access to the mechanisms that produce them, and the triggering of one directs our attention to the novel stimulus. However, because this response occurs

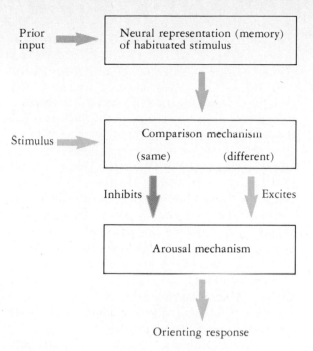

FIGURE 10.7   When a regularly presented stimulus is omitted, the omission elicits an orienting response.

also in other animals, the orienting response and its habituation are clearly not verbally mediated activities.

Interim summary: As we saw earlier in the chapter, consciousness can be analyzed as a social phenomenon, derived through evolution of brain mechanisms that are responsible for our ability to communicate with each other (and, in addition, with ourselves). However, because of the limited capacity of the brain, at any one time there is much going on in our environment that we cannot verbalize or think about. Through selective attention we are conscious of some stimuli and not others; later, we can remember and talk about only those stimuli to which we paid attention. For example, dichotic listening experiments show that what is received by the unattended ear is lost within a few seconds unless something causes us to take heed of it. The factors that control our attention include novelty, verbal stimuli like those of an experimen-

ter, and our own assessment of the significance of what we are perceiving.

CONSCIOUSNESS AND THE BRAIN

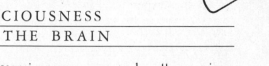

Human consciousness seems to be all one piece. When you see a flower, approach it, grasp and pick it, and lift it to your nose to smell it, the same person sees the flower, touches it, hears the stem snap, and smells it. In other words, the seeing, touching, hearing, and smelling parts of your brain all supply perceptions to the same consciousness—the consciousness that decides to approach, pick, and smell the flower. You have verbal control over the behaviors, and verbal access to the perceptions.

One function that is not connected to verbal mechanisms in the normal brain is smiling. Stand in front of a mirror and smile. Try to make the smile a big, happy one. This smile does not look like the kind you make when you are very happy or hear an amusing joke. You probably feel a bit awkward trying to make the smile look genuine. Apparently it is hard to produce a real smile because we cannot exert direct verbal control over the brain mechanisms that produce it. As we saw in Chapter 6, smiling is a species-typical response; it is seen in children who have been blinded since birth. Unlike various culturally determined gestures, it does not have to be learned. Under verbal control, we can move the muscles of our face to produce an expression that *resembles* a smile, but we cannot produce a real one unless we are amused or especially happy. With a lot of practice, people such as models or actors can generate good fake smiles, but the verbally controlled product is never quite the same as the real thing.

Researchers who have examined the effects of damage to the human brain have found that a unified consciousness depends on specific sets of axons that interconnect various regions of the cortex. In an intact brain, information is shared freely among the various systems, so that many different kinds of experience are accessible to verbal mechanisms, and many different behaviors can come under verbal control. Destruction of the fibers produces a fragmented consciousness—various parts of the brain receive information about various aspects of the environment, but there is no longer an exchange of information among them.

CROSS-MODAL TRANSFER OF INFORMATION

Information can be shared among our visual, somatosensory, motor, and verbal systems. If we are shown a simple object that we have never seen before, we can easily choose it from among several different objects in the dark. In other words, when we see an object we have a good idea of what it will feel like, and when we feel an object we have a good idea of what it will look like. We can also describe its shape after either touching it or seeing it. The ability to recognize new objects by using a sensory system different from the one that perceived it previously is known as *cross-modal transfer of information.* Most other animals are incapable of such a transfer. For example, monkeys, who have visual and somatosensory systems that are nearly

as good as ours, can easily be trained to reach toward an object that they can see, but not touch, in order to obtain a treat like a raisin. They can also be trained to select the correct object in the dark, by touch. But they cannot use visually learned information in a tactually guided test, or vice versa. Special tasks can be constructed to permit cross-modal transfer of information in monkeys, but the ability of most nonhuman animals to perform such a task is clearly limited. Unlike monkeys, higher primates such as gorillas and chimpanzees are capable of cross-modal transfers. According to Geschwind (1965), what we higher primates have in common is a profusion of bundles of long *cortical association fibers.* Far fewer of these fibers are found in the brains of other mammals.

As you will recall from Chapter 3, the cortex of the human brain contains sensory areas, motor areas, and association areas. The association cortex deals with perceptions, thoughts, and plans rather than elementary sensations and particular muscular contractions. Most areas of the association cortex are

FIGURE 10.8   A photograph of the left half of a human brain. The brain has been sliced in two and the right half has been removed. Some of the cerebral cortex has been dissected away, leaving bundles of cortical association fibers. (From Gluhbegovic, N., and Williams, T.H. *The Human Brain: A Photographic Atlas.* Hagerstown, Md.: Harper & Row, 1980.)

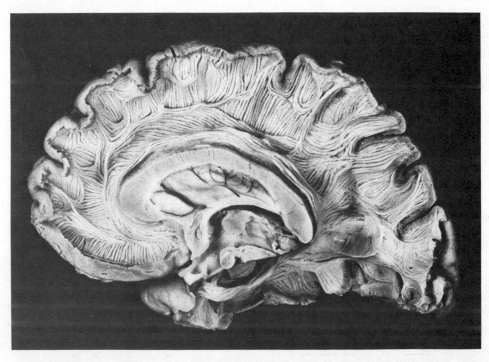

concerned with a specific sensory modality or with the control of movement. For example, the visual association cortex lies adjacent to the primary visual cortex, the frontal (motor) association cortex lies adjacent to the primary motor cortex, and so on. The cortical association fibers interconnect these areas and are, according to Geschwind, the means by which cross-modal transfers of information take place. (See **Figure 10.8.**)

It is a reasonable hypothesis that these connections among the various areas of the association cortex are prerequisites for being able to learn to talk, write, listen, and read. Words are themselves cross-modal symbols. For example, a concrete noun is a set of sounds representing a tangible object that can be seen, felt, smelled, or the like. The word itself can be heard, read or written. Thus, language cannot exist without the cortical association fibers. Suppose someone places a number of objects in front of you and asks you to point to the pencil. You hear the words, look at the objects, and point out the pencil. Your auditory, visual, and motor systems must all exchange information if you are to perform this task. (See **Figure 10.9.**)

Given the fact that the brains of the higher apes

also contain an abundance of cortical association fibers, perhaps, to a more limited extent, they too are capable of learning language. As we shall see in Chapter 12, people have trained chimpanzees and gorillas to communicate surprisingly well through sign language. The ability to learn these behaviors suggests that the consciousness of these animals is closer than that of other animals to our own.

LACK OF VERBAL ACCESS TO VISUAL PERCEPTIONS: A CASE OF VISUAL AGNOSIA

◆ The usual method of investigating someone's perceptions is to ask the person to describe them. If the descriptions are different from those that most people would provide, we conclude that the perceptions are abnormal. But there is evidence that verbal descriptions (and consciousness) of perceptions can be abnormal even when perceptual systems are working properly.

Recently a colleague (David Margolin) and I studied a young man whose brain had been damaged by an inflammation of the blood vessels and

FIGURE 10.9   You are asked to choose a pencil from a group of objects.

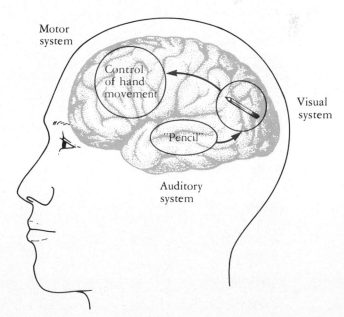

who consequently suffered from visual agnosia. He had great difficulty identifying common objects by sight. For example, he could not say what a hammer was by looking at it, but he quickly identified it when he was permitted to pick it up and feel it. He was not blind; he could walk around without bumping into things, and he had no trouble making visually guided movements to pick up an object that he wanted to identify. The simplest explanation is that his disease had damaged the neural circuits responsible for visual perception.

Although the patient had great difficulty in visually identifying objects or pictures of objects, he often made hand movements that appeared to be related to the object he could not identify. For example, when he was shown a picture of a pistol he stared at it with a puzzled look, then shook his head and said that he couldn't tell what it was. While continuing to study the picture, he clenched his right hand into a fist and began making movements with his index finger. When we asked him what he was doing, he looked at his hand, made a few tentative movements with his finger, then raised his hand in the air and moved it forward each time he moved his finger. He was unmistak-

ably miming the way a person holds and fires a pistol. "Oh!" he said. "It's a gun . . . a pistol." Clearly, he was not aware what the picture was until he paid attention to what his hand was doing. On another occasion, once he looked at a picture of a belt and said it was a pair of pants. We asked him to show us where the legs and other parts of the pants were. When he tried to do so, he became quite puzzled. His hands went to the place where his belt buckle would be (he was wearing hospital pajamas) and moved as if he were feeling one. "No," he said. "It's not a pair of pants—it's a belt!"

Although the patient's visual system was not normal, it functioned better than we could infer from only his verbal behavior. That is, his perceptions were clearer than his words indicated. The fact that he could mime the use of a pistol or feel an imaginary belt buckle with his hands indicated that his visual system worked well enough to initiate appropriate nonverbal behaviors, though not the appropriate words. Once he felt what he was doing he could name the object. The process might involve steps such as those shown in **Figure 10.10**.

Although the patient lost his ability to read, speech therapists were able to teach him to use

FIGURE 10.10   Hypothetical exchanges of information within the brain of the patient with visual agnosia.

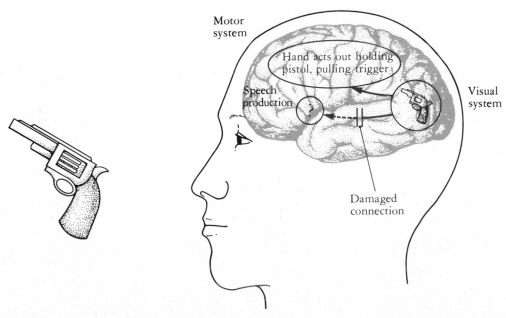

finger spelling to read. He could not say what a particular letter was, but he could learn to make a particular hand movement when he saw it. After he learned the finger-spelling alphabet used by deaf people, he could read slowly and laboriously by making hand movements for each letter and feeling the words that his hand was spelling out.

The fact that this patient could make hand movements indicating that he had perceived an object does not mean that he was conscious of his visual perception all along. Nonverbal behavior does not always indicate consciousness. Certainly, Carter's subjects were not aware that their rate of blinking increased in response to the flashing light. Our patient's gestures were not intended as signals to us that he understood what he was looking at. They were automatic, and at first they surprised him as much as they surprised us.

This case supports the conclusion that consciousness is synonymous with activity of the brain's verbal system. Disruption of the normal interchange between the visual perceptual system and verbal system precludes identification of a visually presented object. Chapters 11 and 12 describe some other relevant effects of brain damage on memory and language.

THE SPLIT-BRAIN SYNDROME

◆ One surgical procedure demonstrates dramatically how various brain functions can be disconnected from each other and from verbal mechanisms. It is used for people who have very severe epilepsy that cannot be controlled by drugs. Violent storms of neural activity begin in one hemisphere and are transmitted to the other by the *corpus callosum,* the largest bundle of association fibers in the brain, connecting corresponding parts of cortex on one side of the brain with those of the other. Both sides of the brain now engage in wild neural firing, and stimulate each other, causing a generalized epileptic seizure. These seizures can occur many times each day and prevent the patient from leading a normal life. Neurosurgeons discovered that cutting the corpus callosum (the *split-brain operation*) greatly reduced the frequency of epileptic seizures. (See **Figure 10.11.**)

Gazzaniga and his associates (Gazzaniga, 1970; Gazzaniga and LeDoux, 1978) have studied these

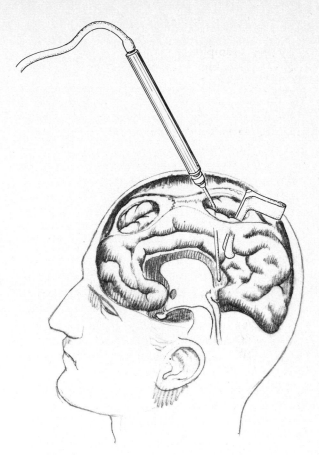

FIGURE 10.11   The split-brain operation. (From Gazzaniga, M.S. *Fundamentals of Psychology.* New York: Academic Press, 1973.)

patients extensively. After the two hemispheres are disconnected, they operate independently; their sensory mechanisms, memories, and motor systems can no longer exchange information. The effects of these disconnections are not obvious to the casual observer, for the simple reason that only one hemisphere—in most people, the left—controls speech. The right hemisphere of a person with a split brain can understand speech reasonably well, but it is poor at reading and spelling, and because Broca's speech area is located in the left hemisphere, it is totally incapable of producing speech.

Because only one side of the brain can talk, most observers do not detect the independent operations of the right side of a split brain. Even the patient's left brain has to learn about the independent existence of the right brain. One of the first things that the patients say they notice is that the left hand seems to have a "mind of its own." Patients find themselves putting down a book held in the left hand, even if they are reading it with great interest. At other times, they surprise themselves by making obscene gestures (with the left hand) at inappropriate times. Each side of the brain is connected to the opposite side of the body, controlling its movements and receiving sensations from it. Thus, the right hemisphere controls the movements of the left hand, and these unexpected movements puzzle the left hemisphere, the side of the brain that controls speech.

One exception to the crossed representation of sensory information is the olfactory system. When a person sniffs a flower through the left nostril, only the left brain receives a sensation of the odor. Thus, if the right nostril of a patient with a split brain is plugged up, leaving the left nostril open, the patient will accurately identify odors verbally.

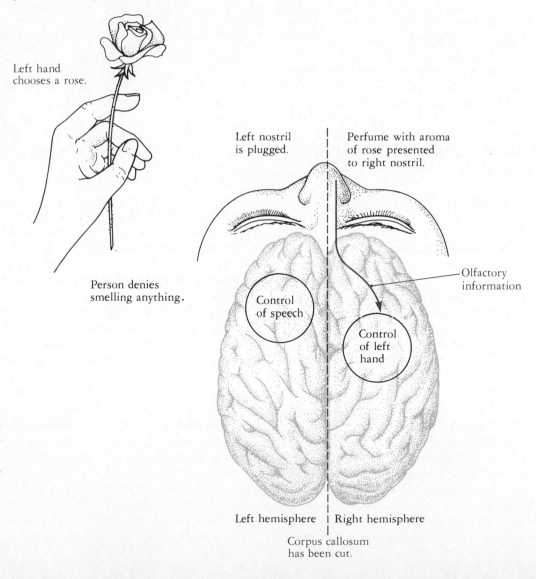

FIGURE 10.12   Identification of an object in response to an olfactory stimulus by a blindfolded person with a split brain.

Left hand chooses a rose.

Person denies smelling anything.

Left nostril is plugged.

Perfume with aroma of rose presented to right nostril.

Olfactory information

Control of speech

Control of left hand

Left hemisphere | Right hemisphere

Corpus callosum has been cut.

If the odor enters the right nostril, the patient will say that he or she smells nothing. But in fact the right brain has perceived the odor, and can identify it. This is demonstrated when the patient is told to reach for some objects that are hidden from view by a partition. If asked to use the left hand, he or she will select the object that corresponds to the odor—a plastic flower for a floral odor, a toy fish for a fishy odor, a model tree for the odor of pine, and so forth. The right hand fails this test, since it is connected to the left hemisphere, which did not smell the odor. (See **Figure 10.12.**)

Sometimes the hands conflict in everyday activities, one trying to put a book down, and the other trying to pick it up to read it. (Can you guess which hand is which?) It was even reported that a man with a split brain attempted to beat his wife with one hand and protect her with the other. Did he *really* want to hurt her? Yes and no, I guess.

As we saw in Chapter 3, the left hemisphere, besides being able to read, write, and speak, is good at other tasks that require verbal abilities, such as mathematics and logic, whereas the right hemisphere excels at tasks of perception and has a much greater artistic ability. If a patient with a split brain tries to use his or her right hand to arrange blocks to duplicate a geometric design provided by the experimeter, the hand will hopelessly fumble around with the blocks. Often, the left hand (controlled by the right hemisphere) will brush the right hand aside and easily complete the task. It is as if the right hemisphere gets impatient with the clumsy ineptitude of the hand controlled by the left hemisphere.

The effects of cutting the corpus callosum reinforce the conclusion that the unity of consciousness depends on the integrity of the neural connections that permit various brain structures to communicate with each other. Consciousness is not an intangible property that pervades all the parts of the brain.

Interim summary: Although our consciousness is normally unified, its components can be separated and made to operate independently, usually by damage to cortical association fibers. Our ability to combine information from several different sensory modalities into a single unified perception appears to depend on connections among the various association areas of the cerebral cortex. Because language is a symbolic code that requires such cross-modal transfer of information, it depends on these connections.

The fact that the unity of consciousness requires communication among various parts of the brain is demonstrated vividly by the effects of the split-brain operation. Although a person whose corpus callosum has been severed can make perceptual judgments with the right hemisphere, he or she cannot talk about them and appears to be unaware of them. And as the examination of the patient with visual agnosia shows, brain damage within the cerebral hemispheres can disrupt a person's verbal access to (awareness of) perceptual mechanisms without destroying these mechanisms.

HYPNOSIS

Hypnosis is a specific and unusual form of verbal control that apparently enables one person to control another person's behavior, thoughts, and perceptions. A person can be induced to bark like a dog, act like a baby, or tolerate being pierced with needles.

◆ Hypnosis, or *mesmerism* was discovered by Franz Anton Mesmer, an Austrian physician in the eighteenth century. He found that when he passed magnets back and forth over people's bodies (in an attempt to restore their "magnetic fluxes" and cure them of disease), they would often have convulsions and enter a trancelike state, during which almost miraculous cures could be achieved. (See **Figure 10.13.**) As Mesmer discovered later, the patients were not affected directly by the magnetism of the iron rods; they were responding to his undoubtedly persuasive and compelling personality. We now know that convulsions and trancelike states do not necessarily accompany hypnosis, and we also know that hypnosis does not cure physical illnesses. Mesmer's patients obviously had psychologically produced symptoms that were alleviated by suggestions made while they were hypnotized.

THE INDUCTION OF HYPNOSIS

◆ A hypnotized person can be alert, relaxed, tense, lying quietly, exercising vigorously, or in any other condition that is normal while he or she is not

FIGURE 10.13 Franz Anton Mesmer (1734–1815) discovered hypnosis. His practice flourished in France until a commission (whose membership included Benjamin Franklin) wrote a report criticizing his methods.

hypnotized. There is no need to move an object in front of someone's face or to say "You are getting sleepy"; an enormous variety of techniques can be used to induce hypnosis in a susceptible person. The only essential feature seems to be the subject's understanding that he or she is to be hypnotized. Moss (1965) reports having sometimes simply said to a well-practiced subject, in a normal tone of voice, "Please sit in that chair and go into hypnosis," and the subject complied in a few seconds. Sometimes this approach worked even on volunteers who had never been hypnotized before.

Obviously, soothing, friendly words are more persuasive than hostile ones, but most investigators agree that no special tricks are necessary to induce hypnosis. This is not to say that the words the hypnotist uses have no effect; if he or she emphasizes the word *sleep,* the subjects are more likely to enter a drowsy trance than a relatively alert one.

PHENOMENA OF HYPNOSIS

◆ All of the things that a hypnotized person can do have also been done, at one time or another, by unhypnotized people. In other words, the degree of control exerted over a hypnotized subject is not very different from the control the hypnotist would have over the subject in a nonhypnotized state. Moreover, it is easy to simulate a hypnotic state.

FIGURE 10.14 An engraving from *Antimagnetism, or the Origin, Progress, Decline, and Refutation of Animal Magnetism* written in 1784. The illustration satirizes Mesmer's claim to be able to gather "animal magnetism" and direct it toward the cure of illness.

This fact does not mean that hypnosis is fakery; rather, it indicates that hypnosis is not a magical state in which a person acquires special powers or becomes someone else. (See **Figure 10.14**.) Perhaps we need not think of hypnosis as a radically different state of the organism, but rather as a condition in which some normal capabilities and tendencies (such as suggestibility) are permitted full rein, while others (such as social inhibition) are held somewhat in abeyance.

Suggestibility

Hypnotized people are very suggestible; they will do things in conformity with what the hypnotist says, even to the extent of appearing to misperceive reality. Under hypnosis, people can be instructed to do things that they would not be expected to do under normal conditions, such as acting out imaginary scenes or pretending to be an animal. Hypnotized people can be convinced that an arm cannot move or is insensitive to pain, and then act as if that is the case; hypnosis can be used to induce paralysis or anesthesia. They can also be made to see things that are not there (*positive hallucination*) or can be persuaded that objects that are actually present are gone from view (*negative hallucination*).

One of the most dramatic phenomena of hypnosis is that of *posthypnotic suggestibility,* in which a person is given instructions under hypnosis and follows those instructions after returning to a nonhypnotized state. For example, the hypnotist might tell a subject that he will become unbearably thirsty when the hypnotist winds her watch. Usually the hypnotist also admonishes the subject not to remember anything upon leaving the hypnotic state, so that *posthypnotic amnesia* is also achieved. After leaving the hypnotic state, the subject acts normally and professes ignorance of what he perceived and did during hypnosis, sometimes apologizing for not having succumbed to hypnosis. The hypnotist later winds her watch, and the subject suddenly leaves the room to get a drink of water.

Antisocial Behavior

◆ It has been suggested that people can be induced to commit antisocial acts—even crimes—while under hypnosis, but most professionals assert that people cannot simply be told to perform an act that violates their moral code, such as picking up a gun and killing someone on command. Some people have also suggested that hypnotized subjects can be made to misperceive a situation and thus inadvertently do violence to their code of conduct. For example, a subject might be given a gun and told to "shoot at that paper target," the target actually being another person. However, after reviewing attempts to trick or directly induce people into committing antisocial acts under hypnosis, Barber (1961) concluded that hypnosis does not lower people's inhibitions against committing criminal acts, nor does it appear that people can be tricked into committing them.

People's expectations about hypnosis appear to play an important role in their behavior while under hypnosis. If we believe that hypnotized subjects will act silly if asked to do so, we feel no reluctance to do likewise under hypnosis, because we know that *we are not responsible* for our behavior. In lectures to two sections of an introductory psychology class, Orne (1959) told one section (falsely) that one of the most prominent features of hypnosis was a rigidity of the preferred (that is, dominant) hand. Later, he arranged a demonstration of hypnosis during a meeting of students from both sections. Several of the students who had heard that the dominant hand became rigid showed this phenomenon when hypnotized.

Subjects' knowledge of the hypnotist also affects their expectations about whether they will be asked to do something genuinely harmful. Suppose a subject is asked to throw the contents of a bottle labeled "SULFURIC ACID—DANGER" into the face of the hypnotist with the admonition, "Go ahead, throw it at me." If the subject does so, we need not conclude that he or she has been tricked into committing a violent act. Perhaps the subject realized that the hypnotist was unlikely to ask for a faceful of sulfuric acid, and thus that the contents of the bottle must in fact be harmless.

Another factor is the willingness of an unhypnotized person to perform an antisocial act. Most studies have failed to use control groups to determine the limits of an unhypnotized person's behavior. Instead, they simply show that hypnotized people will do remarkable things. Milgram (1963, 1974) instructed unhypnotized subjects to press a button that supposedly delivered a shock whenever a "trainee" (hidden behind a wall) made a wrong answer in a learning task. The strength of the shock was gradually increased during the experiment. As noises, pleas, and finally screams came through the wall, many of the subjects continued to press the button, under the instructions of the experimenter. Even after silence suggested that the "trainee" had died, subjects continued to push the button while the experimenter turned up the voltage, demanding through the intercom that the "trainee" respond.

When Milgram's studies were first published, psychologists and lay people alike were amazed at what the subjects would do. If Milgram's subjects had been hypnotized, the experiment would have been taken as a demonstration of the frightful power of hypnosis. Such results make it imperative that appropriate control groups be used in any experiment that attempts to determine whether hypnosis can induce people to commit antisocial acts.

Abnormal Perception and Paralysis

◆ Paralysis, anesthesia, hallucinations, and related phenomena can all be induced while a subject is hypnotized. However, all of these states are also seen in people who are not hypnotized. For example, hysterical paralysis (a neurotic paralysis that exists in the absence of any physiological cause) appears to be identical to hypnotic paralysis, although they have different causes. Likewise, an experiment by Pattie (1937) indicates that local anesthesia induced by hypnotic suggestion is not the same as anesthesia produced by drugs. Pattie suggested to hypnotized subjects that they could feel nothing in one hand. He then had them cross their wrists so that their forearms formed an X, turn their palms together, interlace their fingers, and twist their hands toward their bodies until their thumbs pointed upward. (See **Figure 10.15**.) In such a position, it is very difficult for someone to tell which hand is being touched by another person. (Try it yourself. Fold your hands as shown in Figure 10.15, have someone touch three or four fingers in rapid succession, and try to say to which hand the touched fingers belong.) Pattie touched several fingers on both of the subjects' hands and asked them to count the number of times they were touched. If in fact they could not feel sensations from the "anesthetized" hand, they should not have counted the touches made to this hand, but they included many of these in the total count. It therefore appears that hypnotized subjects were not anesthetized; they simply acted as if they were.

Many studies have also shown that hypnotically induced blindness or deafness does not take the same form that it would if the sensory systems of the brain were no longer being stimulated. For example, Miller, Hennessy, and Leibowitz (1973) used the Ponzo illusion, shown in Figure 10.16 to test the effects of hypnotically induced blindness. Although the two parallel horizontal lines in the left portion are the same length, the top one looks longer than the bottom one. (See **Figure 10.16, left.**) This effect is produced by the presence of the slanted lines to the left and right of the horizontal ones; if these are not present, the horizontal lines appear to be the same length. (See **Figure 10.16, right.**) Through hypnotic suggestion, the experimenters made the slanted lines "disappear," but even though the subjects reported that they could

FIGURE 10.15   The procedure used by Pattie (1937).

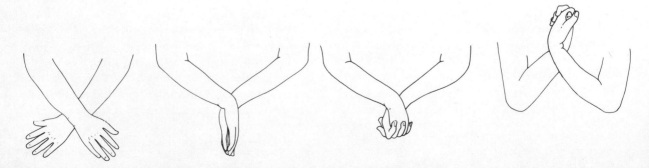

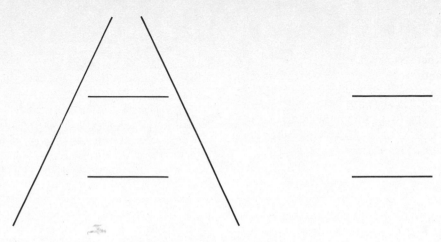

FIGURE 10.16 The Ponzo illusion. The short horizontal lines are actually the same length.

not see the slanted lines (a negative hallucination), they still perceived the upper line as being longer than the lower one. This result indicates that the visual system continues to process sensory information during hypnotic blindness; otherwise, the subjects would have perceived the lines as equal in length. The reported blindness does not appear to occur because of altered activity of the visual system, but because of altered activity of the verbal system (and of consciousness).

EXPLANATIONS OF HYPNOSIS

Hypnosis has been called a special case of learning, a transference of the superego, a goal-directed behavior shaped by the hypnotist, a role-playing situation, and a restructuring of perceptual-cognitive functioning. In other words, no one yet knows what it is. Hypnosis has been described as a state of enhanced suggestibility, but that is a description, not an explanation. The following hypotheses remain only possibilities.

An Analogy: Disconnected Brain Mechanisms

The case of visual agnosia, which I described earlier, illustrates that complex brain mechanisms can function without the subject's consciousness. Perhaps hypnosis is a form of disconnection. For example, a hypnotized person may be unable to "see" an object because the hypnosis has produced a functional blockage of the exchange of information between some components of the visual system and

verbal mechanisms. That is, the visual processing occurs normally, but neural inhibition prevents transmission of some of the messages to the verbal system, and thus prevents verbal access to (and consciousness of) some or all aspects of visual perception. This hypothesis suggests that the subject's perceptions are not brought under the verbal control of the hypnotist; rather, the perceptions can be prevented from affecting the person's verbal behavior (and consciousness).

As for the fact that hypnotized subjects perform behaviors that are unlikely at other times, perhaps hypnosis simply removes the social inhibitions that normally prevent people from doing things in public that would make them feel foolish. As mentioned earlier, in such cases the subjects' expectations also undoubtedly play a role. Hypnosis provides a good excuse for behaving strangely because people do not have to feel responsible for their behavior.

Finally, when inducing positive hallucinations—perceptions of stimuli that are not actually present—the hypnotist may merely control the subject's behavior (including verbal behavior) instead of bringing his or her perceptions under control. That is, the hypnotist suggests that the subject sees something, and the subject, convinced that the object is there, acts as if he or she sees it.

Hypnosis as Participation in a Story

All the behavioral and perceptual phenomena discussed so far in this book have obvious survival value for the organism; that is, a functional analysis of behavioral phenomena usually suggests a plausible reason for the occurrence of the behavior. If hypnotic phenomena occurred only when a person was hypnotized, it would be difficult to understand how the brain happened to evolve in such a way that people could be hypnotized. A suggestion by Theodore Barber (1975) indicates that at least some aspects of hypnosis are related to events that can happen every day.

Barber argues that hypnosis should not be viewed as a special state, in the way that sleep is a state; rather, the suspension of self-control that occurs during hypnosis is very similar to "participation" in the story of a movie or novel. When we go to a movie or read a book we generally do so with the intent of becoming "swept up" in the story. We willingly let the author or filmmaker lead us through a fantasy. When we read a book or hear a story we even imagine the scenes and the events that occur in them. We feel happy when good things happen to characters that we identify with and like, and feel sad when bad things happen to them. Certainly, we express a full range of emotions while watching a good movie or reading a good book. (If the movie or book is a poor one, we do not enter the fantasy world.) Perhaps these imagined events are similar to the positive hallucinations experienced during hypnosis.

If hypnosis is related to our ability to participate vicariously in a story, then we have at least a starting point for a functional explanation of hypnosis. One of the ways people can affect other people's behavior verbally is to get them to imagine themselves in the speaker's place. We call this phenomenon empathy; it is easier to obtain assistance from others if they can imagine themselves in our place and thus see how important their help is to our well-being. Surely, the ability to think about another person's situation empathetically facilitates cooperation and assistance. Perhaps our moral codes owe their existence at least partly to this phenomenon.

Barber's description of his own thoughts while being hypnotized by a colleague demonstrates a striking similarity to participating vicariously in a story.

The experimenter begins by asking me to clasp my hands together tightly with fingers interlaced. He then states, "Your hands are hard, solid, rigid. They are very rigid and solid. They are two pieces of steel that are welded together. They are rigid, solid, stuck together." He continues with these kinds of suggestions for about 30 seconds and finally states, "Try to take your hands apart. Notice that the harder you try, the more difficult it becomes. Try to take them apart; you can't."

. . . At the present time, I see this type of test situation as a valuable and useful experience . . . I want to experience those things that are suggested . . ., and I believe or expect that I, and other investigators, can experience the suggested effects . . . if we temporarily put aside critical or analytical thoughts such as "It's impossible for my hands to become stuck together." . . . I cooperate and "think with" or "imagine" those things that are suggested. . . . I continue to focus my thoughts on the rigidity in the hands and to imagine that they are made of welded steel. I pull on the hands but they feel very tight, like a solid piece of metal. . . . Finally, the experimenter states, "Now relax your hands. You can now easily unclasp them." After I relax the hands, I have a feeling of pleasant surprise to see how easily they now come apart. (Barber, 1975, p. 7)

SUSCEPTIBILITY TO HYPNOSIS

◆ Not everyone can be hypnotized, and attempts to relate personality to hypnotic susceptibility have yielded few definitive results. Susceptibility does not appear to be related strongly to any particular personality type. An early study by Eysenck (1947) seemed to indicate that neurotics are more susceptible than well-adjusted people, but later studies have failed to confirm this, and in fact suggest that well-adjusted people are *more* susceptible to hypnosis (Moss, 1965). In a review of the literature, Hilgard (1975) notes that many personality characteristics that one would expect to be related to hypnotic susceptibility are not, and that different experiments often produce conflicting results. The one personality trait that does appear to be related to susceptibility to hypnosis is a rich, vivid imagination. Such people would also tend to be especially likely to participate vicariously in a story.

USES OF HYPNOSIS

Hypnosis can play a useful role in dentistry and medicine. It can be used to suppress the pain of childbirth or of having one's teeth drilled, to prevent gagging when a dentist is working in a patient's mouth, and to help people break a bad habit such as smoking or overeating. Hypnosis is a useful tool for research into human consciousness. Finally, hypnosis is often used in psychotherapy to help the patient discuss painful memories whose inaccessibility is impeding progress.

Interim summary: Hypnosis is a form of verbal control over a person's consciousness in which the hypnotist's suggestions affect some of the subject's perceptions and behaviors. Although some people have viewed hypnosis as a mysterious, trancelike state, investigations have shown its phenomena to be similar to many phenomena of normal consciousness. Because control groups are seldom used, we cannot conclude that hypnosis causes people to perform behaviors that they would not otherwise perform. It is possible that many people, if earnestly asked to do so, would be willing, say, to bark like a dog in public. We must also consider the fact that being hypnotized provides a face-saving excuse for doing things that might be considered foolish. There is no single way to induce hypnosis, and responses depend very much on what the hypnotist said. If he or she stresses sleepiness, subjects will become sleepy; if he or she tells the subjects to remain alert, they will do so.

Barber suggests that being hypnotized is similar to participating vicariously in a narrative, which is something we do whenever we become engrossed in a novel, movie, or drama, or even in the recounting of a friend's experience to us. When we are engrossed this way we experience genuine feelings of emotion even though the situation is not "real."

CONTROL OF CONSCIOUSNESS

Given that every culture has its means for altering consciousness, it appears that humans want at least occasional changes in awareness. Even children enjoy spinning around to make themselves dizzy. Some means of altering consciousness have become commonplace, such as the ingestion of coffee, tea, alcohol, or tobacco. Many people use other, illegal drugs, such as marijuana.

The expectations and customs of a society significantly influence the effects that drugs have on a person's consciousness. For example, when coffee drinking was associated with religious ritual long ago, it undoubtedly caused a much more striking change in consciousness than it does now when it is dispensed into a styrofoam cup from the local vending machine. Similarly, when the smoking of tobacco was a part of American Indian rites, it almost certainly induced a greater change in consciousness than it does in the average cigarette smoker today.

Yet the urge to alter, expand, or even escape from one's consciousness does not require the use of drugs. Since the beginning of history, people have developed ways to change their consciousness by means of self-control. For example, the ancient Hebrews and early Christians often fasted for many days, undoubtedly because of the effects that their altered metabolism had upon their consciousness. In earlier times there was also much more emphasis on ritualized chants and movements, such as those of the Jewish Hasidim and Cabalists. However, the Christian Pentecostal sect today practices dances

FIGURE 10.17 Meditation through Yoga.

and chanting that would not seem strange to thirteenth-century mystics, and these encourage the "taking over" of one's consciousness.

The one function that all methods of changing consciousness have in common is an alteration in *attention*. The various exercises can be divided into those that remove attention from the stimuli around us and those that increase attention to events that we no longer notice, including our own behaviors that have become automatic and relatively nonconscious. We refer to exercises in both categories as meditation. (See **Figure 10.17**.) Forms of meditation have developed in almost every culture. Zen Buddhism, Yoga, Sufism, and Taoism are best known and most influential in Eastern societies, where they first developed, but there is also a tradition of meditation in the Western world. Christian monasteries continue the tradition of meditation and contemplation, and even the ritualized recitation of the rosary and the clicking of the beads undoubtedly derives from an earlier ritual designed to change one's consciousness.

TECHNIQUES FOR
WITHDRAWING ATTENTION

◆ The goal of most meditation exercises is to remove attention from all sensory stimuli—to think of absolutely nothing. The various techniques require that the meditator direct his or her attention to a single object, such as a specially prepared symbol; to a spoken or imagined word or phrase; to a monotonous sound, such as the rushing of a waterfall; or to a repetitive movement, such as breathing or touching the tips of each of the four fingers with the thumb. A Tibetan monk might say, "Om mani padme hum"; a Christian monk might say, "Lord Jesus Christ, have mercy on me"; and a Sufi might say, "La illaha illa'llah." The basic effect of all the chants is the same.

By concentrating on an object, a sound, or a repetitive movement, we can learn to ignore other stimuli. We achieve this kind of focus to some degree when we read a book intently or attempt to solve a problem. The difference is that the book or problem supplies a changing form of stimulation. Thoughts, words, images, and ideas flow through our minds. In contrast, a person attempting to achieve a meditative trance selects an inherently static object of attention that leads to habituation. By concentrating on this unchanging source of information, constantly bringing his or her attention back to it, the person achieves a state of utter concentration on *nothing*.

The important effects of such a state are not the ones that can be measured by laboratory instruments. One of these is increased EEG synchrony, which is consistent with a condition in which the brain is processing very little information. Sometimes, apparently, the meditator simply falls asleep, although he or she is usually not aware of these lapses and afterward denies having done so. Physiological measurement, then, demonstrates that something different is going on during a meditative state. However, although the effects that the meditator experiences must have a physiological basis, they are not to be measured by so crude an instrument as the electroencephalograph.

Withdrawal of attention appears to have two primary goals: to reduce verbal control over nonverbal functions of the brain and to produce afterward a "rebound" phenomenon—a heightening of awareness and an increase in attention. The second goal is identical to that of consciousness-awakening exercises, discussed in the next section.

The effects of damage to or disruption of cortical association fibers, like those produced by the split-brain operation, demonstrate that the brain has many nonverbal functions, especially the perceptual, spatial, and artistic abilities that appear to be located primarily in the right atmosphere. Meditation exercises seem to depress verbal processing so such functions can operate without inhibition. However, we cannot be sure that this is what is happening, because people must use the verbal system to describe afterward what they experienced during meditation. Perhaps we should just accept their claims that it is a desirable experience, without demanding a description.

TECHNIQUES FOR INCREASING AND
DISHABITUATING CONSCIOUSNESS

◆ Habituation to most stimuli in our environment enables us to concentrate on those important to our survival. For instance, I can remember very little about showering, shaving, and dressing this morning or about driving back and forth between my home and office. When driving along a highway we do not concentrate on the position of our hands on the steering wheel, its texture under our fingers, or the road vibrations through our body. Neither do we notice the shape of the windshield opening, the color of the hood, the outline of the guardrails as we go past them, or any of the myriad other stimuli to which we could attend. Sometimes we drive over a very familiar route and suddenly arrive at our destination without being able to remember anything about the journey, or at least large parts of it. Obviously, we did the right things, because we got there, but for all we can remember about the trip, we may as well have been unconscious. Our attention is left free for noticing dangers to which we must either respond or be killed. The relative infrequency of automobile accidents attests to the efficiency of our attentional mechanisms in monitoring the information that we must process to survive.

However, given our awareness that we must grow older and finally die, habituation to everything around us would prevent us from making the most of life. The beautiful things and moments may not contain stimuli that are important to our survival, but they are certainly important to the enjoyment of life. Techniques for increasing awareness are designed to reduce habituation, at least partially.

The easiest way to defeat habituation and automatic functioning is to encounter novel stimuli. If we go to new places and have new experiences we are more likely to be aware of what is going on around us. Moreover, there is a worthwhile side effect: when we return home many of the old stimuli seem fresh and new again, at least for a while. We recover from some of our habituation.

Another way to notice things is to do them differently. Many ancient traditions suggest doing routine tasks in different orders or with the unaccustomed hand and making oneself concentrate on just what happens. By analyzing the details of the habituated stimuli, we force them into consciousness.

Doing something dangerous, or at least something that places great demands on skill and coordination, can also heighten awareness by presenting unexpected stimuli to which we must react. Activities such as driving a car too fast, rock climbing, skiing, and hang gliding require us to be

aware of what is going on around us and to remain vigilant at all times. Many people report that they never feel so "alive" as when they are in danger. (See **Figure 10.18**.)

Finally, as I mentioned earlier, a very effective means of increasing our attention to the world around us is to remove ourselves from it temporarily. Almost all the meditative traditions, new and old, stress that the world appears to be more real after a period of withdrawal of attention from it. This

FIGURE 10.18   A roller-coaster ride is fun because it provides an exciting, somewhat frightening experience without real danger. The effect is to heighten self-awareness.

heightened awareness undoubtedly occurs because attentional mechanisms, which have been suppressed by concentration on an unchanging stimulus, now "rebound," and we notice much more than we previously did.

Interim summary: Techniques of meditation have been used since the beginning of history, and include methods for increasing or decreasing attention to the external world. Even the withdrawal of attention causes a rebound that leads the practitioner to look at his or her surroundings with revitalized awareness. We still do not understand meditation physiologically, but a reasonable analysis can be made in terms of habituation and selective attention: the person pays strict attention to a simple stimulus such as a visual pattern, a word, or a monotonous, repetitive movement, and as the response to the repeated stimulus habituates, he or she is left with a relatively empty consciousness.

SLEEP

Sleep is certainly a state of altered consciousness; during sleep we have dreams that can be just as vivid as waking experiences, and yet we forget most of them as soon as they are over. In fact there are two distinct kinds of sleep, thus two states of altered consciousness. We spend approximately one-third of our lives sleeping—or trying to. Many people are preoccupied with sleep or with the lack of it. They consume tons of drugs each year in an attempt to get to sleep. Advertisements for non-prescription sleeping drugs imply that a night without a full eight hours of sleep is a physiological and psychological disaster. Does missing a few hours—or even a full night—of sleep actually harm us? What does sleep do for us?

THE STAGES OF SLEEP

Sleep is not a uniform state. We can sleep lightly or deeply; we can be restless or still; we can have vivid dreams or our consciousness can be relatively blank. Researchers who have studied sleep have found that its stages usually follow an orderly, predictable sequence.

Most sleep research takes place in a sleep laboratory. Because a person's sleep is affected by his or her surroundings, a sleep laboratory contains one or more small bedrooms, furnished and decorated to be as homelike and comfortable as possible. Sleep during the first night or two is likely to be somewhat different from usual, because of the new environment. However, by the third night sleep is essentially normal, and from this point on, observations can be considered useful.

The most important apparatus of the sleep laboratory is the *polygraph,* which is located in a separate room. This machine records on paper the output of various devices that can be attached to the subject. For example, the polygraph can record the electrical activity of the brain (an *EEG,* or *electroencephalogram*) through small metal disks pasted to the scalp; electrical signals from muscles (an *EMG,* or *electromyogram*) or from the heart (an *EKG,* or *electrocardiogram*); or eye move-

TABLE 10.1   Devices used in sleep research

Device	Function
Electrodes attached to scalp: electroencephalogram (EEG)	Measurement of brain activity
Electrodes attached to chin: electromyogram (EMG)	Measurement of muscular activity
Electrodes attached around eye: electroculogram (EOG)	Measurement of eye movements
Electrodes attached to fingers	Measurement of galvanic skin response (GSR), skin resistance
Electrodes attached to arms and legs: electrocardiogram (EKG)	Measurement of electrical activity of heart
Strain gauge around chest or temperature probe in front of nose	Measurement of respiration
Penile plethysmograph	Measurement of penile erections
Vaginal blood flow monitor	Measurement of blood flow in walls of vagina

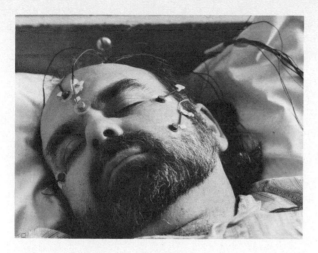

FIGURE 10.19   A subject prepared for a night's sleep in a sleep laboratory.

ments (an *EOG,* or *electroculogram*) through small metal disks attached to the skin around the eyes. Other special transducers can detect respiration, sweating, skin or body temperature, and a variety of other physiological states. (See **Table 10.1.**)

Let us look at a typical night's sleep of a male college student on his third night. EEG electrodes are attached to his scalp, EMG electrodes to his chin, EKG electrodes to his chest, and EOG electrodes to the skin around his eyes. (See **Figure 10.19.**) Wires connected to these electrodes are plugged into the amplifiers of the polygraph. The output of each amplifier causes a pen on the polygraph to move up and down while a long, continuous sheet of paper moves by.

The EEG record distinguishes between alert and relaxed wakefulness. When a person is alert, the tracing looks rather irregular, and the pens do not move very far up or down; the EEG shows high-frequency, low-amplitude electrical activity called

beta activity. When a person is relaxed and perhaps somewhat drowsy, the record shows *alpha activity,* a medium-amplitude, medium-frequency (8–12 Hz) rhythm. (See **Figure 10.20.**)

The technician leaves the room, the lights are turned off, and the subject closes his eyes. As he relaxes and grows drowsy his EEG changes from beta activity to alpha activity. The first stage of sleep, called stage 1, still contains some alpha activity, marked by the colored bracket in Figure 10.21, A. The EMG shows that his muscles are still active and his EOG indicates slow, gentle, rolling eye movements. (See **Figure 10.21, A.**) As sleep progresses, it gets deeper and deeper, moving through stages 2, 3, and 4. The EEG gets progressively slower in frequency and higher in amplitude. (See **Figure 10.21, B, C, D.**) Stage 4 consists mainly of *delta activity,* characterized by relatively high-voltage waves occurring at 3–5 Hz. Our subject becomes less responsive to the environment and it becomes more difficult to awaken him. Environmental stimuli that caused him to stir during stage 1 produce no reaction during stage 4. The sleep of stages 3 and 4 is called *slow-wave sleep.*

Stage 4 sleep is reached in less than an hour and continues for about a half hour. Then, suddenly, the EEG begins to indicate lighter levels of sleep, back through stages 3 and 2 to the activity characteristic of stage 1. The subject's heart begins to beat more rapidly and his respiration alternates between shallow breaths and sudden gasps. The EOG shows that the subject's eyes are darting rapidly back and forth, up and down. The EEG record looks like that of a person who is awake and active. Yet the subject is fast asleep. His hands and feet twitch occasionally, and his breathing is irregular. (See **Figure 10.21, E.**)

At this point the subject is dreaming. He has

FIGURE 10.20   *Top.* Beta activity, characteristic of alert wakefulness. *Bottom.* Alpha activity, characteristic of relaxed, drowsy wakefulness or light sleep.

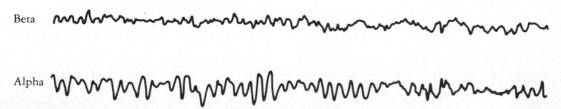

Beta

Alpha

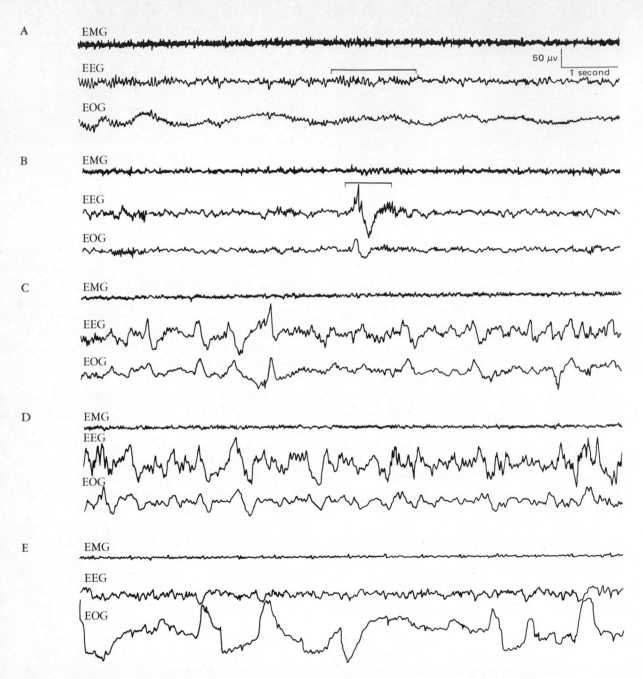

FIGURE 10.21   An EEG recording of the various stages of sleep. *A.* Stage 1. The bracket indicates alpha activity. *B.* Stage 2. The bracket indicates a waveform often seen during this stage. *C.* Stage 3. *D.* Stage 4. Note the predominance of delta activity, the high-amplitude, low-frequency waves. *E.* Stage REM. Note the low-amplitude, high-frequency waves, the relative lack of activity in the EMG, and the prominent eye movements (EOG). (From Cohen, D.B. *Sleep & Dreaming: Origins, Nature and Functions.* New York: Pergamon Press, 1979.)

Eye movements:

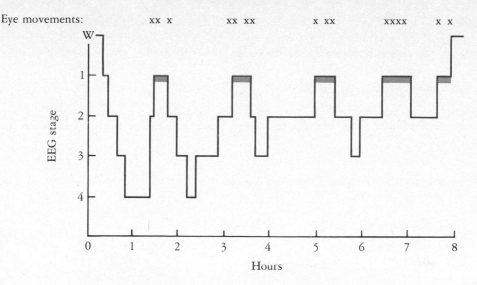

FIGURE 10.22 Typical progression of stages during a night's sleep. (From Hartmann, E. *The Biology of Dreaming*. Springfield, Ill.: C.C. Thomas, 1967.)

entered another stage of sleep that has several names, including paradoxical sleep, active sleep, rapid eye movement (REM) sleep, and desynchronized sleep. The most popular name is ***REM sleep.*** REM sleep lasts about twenty to thirty minutes, followed by approximately one hour of slow-wave sleep. A typical night's sleep consists of four or five of these ninety-minute cycles. Figure 10.22 shows a record of a person's stages of sleep; the colored shading indicates REM sleep. (See **Figure 10.22**.)

A person in REM sleep exhibits a desynchronized EEG, rapid eye movements, brief twitches of the hands and feet, and rapid, irregular heart rate and breathing. The EMG shows that the facial muscles are still. In fact, physiological studies have shown that, aside from occasional twitching, a person actually becomes paralyzed during REM sleep. Males are observed to have partial or full erections, which are usually not associated with sexual arousal, although both males and females sometimes have dreams of a sexual nature, occasionally ending with orgasm. Studies have found that women's vaginal secretions increase during REM sleep.

DREAMING

States of Consciousness During Sleep

A person who is awakened during REM sleep and asked whether anything was happening will almost always report a dream. The typical REM-sleep dream resembles a play or movie—it has a narrative form. Conversely, reports of narrative, storylike dreams are rare among people awakened from slow-wave sleep. In general, mental activity during slow-wave sleep is more nearly static; it involves situations rather than stories and generally unpleasant ones. For example, a person awakened from slow-wave sleep might report a sensation of being crushed or suffocated. The painting shown in **Figure 10.23** was inspired by a dream typical of slow-wave sleep.

Unless their sleep is heavily drugged, almost everyone has four or five bouts of REM sleep each night, with accompanying dreams. Yet unless the dreamer awakens while they are in progress, they are lost forever. Some people who claimed not to have had a dream for many years slept in a sleep laboratory and found that in fact they did dream. They were able to remember their dreams because the investigator awakened them during REM sleep.

The fact that we recall dreams only if we awaken during their progress explains why light sleepers tend to remember more dreams than heavy sleepers—and why we are most likely to recall dreams that occur toward morning, around the time we are likely to awaken. Many people in psychotherapy learn to remember their dreams so that they can discuss them with their therapists. Ap-

FIGURE 10.23   *The Nightmare* (1781), by Johann
Heinrich Füssli, Swiss, 1741–1825. (Gift of Mr. and
Mrs. Bert L. Smokler and Mr. and Mrs. Lawrence A.
Fleischman, Detroit Institute of Arts.)

parently, they somehow learn to awaken during
REM sleep.

The reports of people awakened from REM and
slow-wave sleep make it clear that people are conscious during sleep, even though they may not
remember any of their experiences then. Lack of
memory for an event does not mean that it never
happened, only that there is no permanent record
accessible to conscious thought during wakefulness. Thus we can say that slow-wave sleep and
REM sleep reflect two different states of consciousness.

There is more continuity between dreaming and
waking consciousness than we would ordinarily
suppose. A number of studies have shown that people can tell an experimenter whenever a dream begins by pushing a hand-held switch. Brown and
Cartwright (1977) used this technique and found
that subjects who were awakened after pressing the
button almost always reported that they were
dreaming. This study shows that instructions given
during wakefulness can control a person's behavior
during sleep. In what is probably a similar phenomenon, many people can set an "internal alarm
clock" and awaken at a particular time the next
morning.

Eye Movements During REM Sleep

Early investigators suggested that eye movements
during REM sleep indicated that sleepers were

watching their dreams—the eye movements represented those that people would make to look at their imaginary environment. Later research has indicated that this explanation is indeed correct. Roffwarg, Dement, Muzio, and Fisher (1962) recorded eye movements during REM sleep and then awakened the subjects to obtain a narrative of the dream. One of the experimenters who did not know what eye movements had actually occurred studied the dream and made a list of the eye movements that would have been expected to occur. The correspondence between actual and predicted eye movements was very good. In fact a later study (Dement, 1974) showed that the correspondence was as good for dreams as it was during waking, when an experimenter tried to predict a subject's eye movements while looking at a real scene.

Symbolism in Dreams

For as long as humans have used language to communicate, dreams have played a special role in society. Some people have acted as interpreters of dreams. Battles have been averted or begun because of a general's dream. People have decided on their careers, marriage partners, and place of residence on the basis of what their dreams told them. Today, many books are available to tell us what our dreams really mean. Do dreams in fact have some special, hidden meaning that we can extract from them? (See **Figure 10.24**.)

Investigators who have studied REM sleep dreams carefully report that most dreams are extremely prosaic (Hall, 1966). The overwhelming majority of them occur in ordinary places, and not much happens. Even if the situation seems to demand strong emotion, the dreamer often reports that he or she did not feel very excited or upset; almost everything is taken for granted in a dream. In contrast, people often do appear to be upset when they are awakened from the kinds of dreams that occur in slow-wave sleep.

If most dreams are so prosaic, why do we remember such bizarre ones? The explanation appears to lie in the sheer number of dreams. Each of us has an estimated 150,000 dreams during a lifetime, and even if we remember only a small

FIGURE 10.24   We have all had unusual dreams. Do these dreams have a hidden meaning?

percentage of them, that is still a large number of dreams. We are most likely to dwell upon, and tell others about, only the most interesting and unusual dreams. The dull, commonplace ones are quickly forgotten.

◆   Nowadays not many people believe that dreams can predict the future, but many do believe that the proper interpretation of a dream could give them some insight into their own psyches. Sigmund Freud attributed much to dreams and started a tradition of a particular form of dream analysis. He believed that dreams had a *latent* ("hidden") *content,* consisting of wishes that came out of unfulfilled sexual desires, especially those resulting from sexual conflicts during infancy that had never been resolved. Although the latent content was what the dream was really about, Freud argued that social taboos prevented the dreamer from confronting the topic of the dream directly. Instead, the latent content was disguised in a way that could safely be tolerated. The latent content was transformed into the dream's *manifest content*—the actual, simple description of the dream's plot. Dreams were assumed to be full of symbols and hidden meanings. For example, any elongated object—a pencil, a tree, a stick, or a chimney, to name but a few—represented a penis. Vaginas were symbolized by any sort of container, even an automobile or a boat. Riding a horse, shooting a gun, or even climbing a flight of stairs was taken to represent sexual intercourse.

◆   Most of Freud's followers today would expand the scope of a dream's latent content to include more than sexual matters; they agree that people are motivated by other kinds of urges, as well. But is the basic notion of hidden symbols correct? There is no doubt that some objects or occurrences are symbolized, but is the meaning of all these symbols hidden from the dreamer? And is it not possible that sometimes the symbol is not a symbol at all, but is really what it seems to be? Does a dream about paddling a canoe through some rapids invariably symbolize unexpressed sexual desires? Does the canoe necessarily represent a woman's sexual organs? Or is it possible that it is just a canoe, and the dream represents a not-so-subtle desire to go canoeing?

Hall, who admits to the validity of symbolism in dreams, does not believe that the symbols are usually hidden. For example, a person may plainly engage in sexual intercourse in one dream and have another dream that involves shooting a gun. Surely the "real" meaning of shooting the gun need not be hidden from a dreamer who has undisguised dreams of sexual intercourse at other times or who has an uninhibited sex life during waking. Why should this person disguise sexual desires while dreaming? As Hall says, people use their own symbols, and not those of anyone else. They represent what the dreamers think, and therefore their meaning is usually not hidden from them.

Dreams do assuredly tell us something about the dreamer. Consider the following dream, reported by a woman who appears to be unhappy with life and does not seem to have a very good marriage:

> I dreamed that my unit head at camp had been doing little mean things to me. She seemed to exclude me from her conversation, to comment only when my work was unsatisfactory and to reprimand me in front of others. I was extremely unhappy. I felt that I could not tell of my unhappiness to anyone, not even to my husband. Somehow I had the feeling that no one would understand me. (Hall, 1966, p. 105.)

Given the woman's situation, we need not make any assumptions about hidden meaning. Perhaps the leader at the camp represents the dreamer's mother, but, as Hall says, this assumption does not really add to our understanding.

Consider this dream:

> My girl and I were skiing down a long brushy slope. We were holding hands, then I fell and she fell over me into a big powdery drift. We sat up laughing, snow up to our necks. I kissed her and when I opened my eyes we were in a log cabin sitting before a fire. We smiled at each other. "You said this would be nice. It's wonderful," she said. "Mmmmmmmmmmmuuuuuuuummm," I replied. (Hall, 1966, pp. 105–106.)

The desires expressed in this dream seem very clear, not hidden.

The following dream is symbolic, but the dreamer is fully aware of its meaning.

> I was at a gas station where I work and my friend Bob was there also working. It seemed to me that he was new and inexperienced at the job, because I was watching him check the oil on a car. He pulled out the oil dipstick and looked at it. At this point

I went up to him rather angrily and said, "Bob, in order to check the oil you have to wipe off the oil on the dipstick first and then put the dipstick back in, pull it out and then get a reading." He thanked me for my help and the dream ended. (Hall, 1966, pp. 101–102.)

The dreamer said later that the checking of the oil represented sexual intercourse, and that his friend Bob was not doing it right—he was visiting prostitutes, and the dreamer wished he would stop doing so. The symbolism is rather primitive and direct, but the important thing is that it is the *dreamer's* symbolism. Suppose a race-car driver has a dream about checking the oil of his car on the night before a big race. Unless the dreamer says otherwise, would it not be most reasonable to assume that he or she was worrying about the engine, rather than expressing a hidden sexual desire?

The view that symbols in dreams are the private property of the dreamer is supported by the results of experiments that have attempted to insert material into dreams by presenting subjects with stimuli or situations before or during sleep. According to a summary of studies on dreaming, "Subjects most often select something other than [what the experimenter intends]. . . . If they do dream of [what the experimenter intends]. . . , it is most often represented in some personal associative way rather than directly, making identification difficult. . . ." (Webb and Cartwright, 1978, p. 243.) In other words, the symbols that the subject uses may disguise the material from the experimenter, but not necessarily from the dreamer.

Sometimes people dream about things that they avoid thinking about while awake, and these dreams may be filled with symbols whose significance they cannot recognize. In such cases a good psychotherapist may be able to use information from the dreams to understand what problems are bothering his or her client and to help the client with his or her difficulties. However, we cannot infer from these relatively rare situations that all dreams of all people are filled with symbols whose meanings can be understood only by a person with special training.

FUNCTIONS OF SLEEP

We do not yet know definitely what functions sleep performs. One hypothesis is that sleep provides our bodies (including our brains) with a chance to repair themselves. Another views sleep simply as a behavioral response.

Sleep as Repair

Perhaps our bodies just get worn out by waking activities for sixteen hours or so. There is a definite relation between the number of hours we stay awake and how sleepy we feel. Perhaps waking activity uses up some vital substances that can be regenerated only when we sleep. Or perhaps wakefulness produces some toxic chemicals that are broken down during sleep. However, there is no compelling evidence to support either of these possibilities. The amount of physical activity people engage in has a rather small effect on the amount of sleep they need.

Shapiro, Bortz, Mitchell, Bartel, and Jooste (1982) found that people who had participated in a long (ninety-two kilometer) running race slept longer than normal the following two nights. Slow-wave sleep increased about 45 percent, while REM sleep decreased. The data suggest that slow-wave sleep plays a role in helping people recuperate from the effects of muscular exertion. However, *lack* of exercise does not significantly reduce sleep; Ryback and Lewis (1971) had healthy subjects spend six weeks resting in bed, and observed no changes in either REM or slow-wave sleep. Thus, it is unlikely that the sole function of sleep is recuperation from the effects of exercise the previous day.

Researchers have found that some other physiological events appear to be tied to sleep. For example, the rate of protein synthesis in the brains of cats greatly increases during REM sleep, and human growth hormone is secreted during the first bout or two of slow-wave sleep (Drucker-Colin and Spanis, 1976; Takahashi, 1979). However, we cannot conclude that we sleep *in order to* produce brain proteins; the increased neural activity that accompanies REM sleep may cause the increase in protein synthesis. In addition, the secretion of growth hormone in some people is not related to slow-wave sleep. Researchers have not yet found any toxic chemicals that are produced during wakefulness that must be disposed of during sleep, nor have they found any vital substances that are used up during wakefulness that must be manufactured during sleep. For now we must conclude that the evidence for sleep as repair is not very strong.

◆ THE EFFECTS OF TOTAL SLEEP DEPRIVATION　The effects of starvation are easy to detect: the person loses weight, becomes fatigued, and will eventually die if he or she does not eat again. By analogy, it should be easy to discover why we sleep by seeing what happens to a person who goes without sleep. The intense discomfort that we experience when we are deprived of sleep makes us feel that sleep is more than an adaptive response; we consider it necessary for our well-being. Yet research shows that sleep deprivation does little more than make the person feel extremely sleepy.

Several dozen people have been kept awake for upward of 200 hours, without any remarkable effects (Dement, 1974; Webb, 1975). People who are kept awake for so long get very sleepy, of course. Their eyelids itch and droop, and they have trouble doing dull, routine tasks. However, when they are properly motivated, they can perform almost as well as they did before the sleep deprivation began.

A famous case was reported in which a disk jockey stayed awake for several days to gain publicity for a charity and became "psychotic" as a result of his sleep deprivation. But his case appears to be unique; other people who have stayed up just as long remained perfectly stable. Therefore, his psychosis cannot be blamed directly upon the lack of sleep. His abnormal behaviors appear to have been the result of stress (which sleep deprivation certainly causes) in a susceptible individual. Most people get a bit grouchy if they are kept awake for ten days, but they do not become crazy. (See **Figure 10.25**.)

Feelings of sleepiness do not continue to increase indefinitely as the period of sleep deprivation goes on. Sleepiness follows the day-night cycle, reaching its maximum around 4:00 A.M. During the day, subjects find it fairly easy to ward off sleep. And when they finally go to sleep again, they do not make up all the sleep that they missed. Most of them sleep approximately fifteen hours, and feel fine after that.

These results certainly do not support the hypothesis that sleep serves a vital physiological func-

FIGURE 10.25　During the Depression, dance marathons awarded cash prizes to couples who could stay awake and dance the longest. Sleep deprivation causes exhaustion, not psychosis.

tion. When we miss sleep we get very sleepy but there is no evidence that our bodies suffer any measurable harm.

◆ THE EFFECTS OF REM-SLEEP DEPRIVATION There is considerable evidence that although total sleep deprivation does little more than make a person very sleepy, *selective* deprivation of REM sleep has demonstrable effects. People who are sleeping in a laboratory can be selectively deprived of REM sleep; an investigator awakens them whenever the polygraph record indicates that they have entered REM sleep. The investigator must also awaken control subjects just as often at random intervals to eliminate any effects produced by being wakened several times.

Experimenters can selectively deprive laboratory animals of REM sleep by housing them in cages that contain a small island surrounded by water. The island often consists of an upturned flower pot; hence the term *flower-pot technique.* (See **Figure 10.26.**) When the subject (usually a mouse) enters REM sleep, its muscles become paralyzed, its head slumps, and its face splashes into the water, causing the animal to awaken. Soon the animal learns not to enter REM sleep while it is on the platform.

If an animal or person is deprived of REM sleep for several nights and is then allowed to sleep without interruption, the onset of REM sleep becomes more frequent. It is as if a need for REM sleep builds up, forcing the organism into this state more often. In addition, when the subject is no longer awakened during REM sleep, a rebound phenomenon is seen—the subject engages in much more REM sleep than normal during the next night or two, as if the organism were "catching up" on something important that is missed.

The saying "Things will look better in the morning" appears to be true. Sleep (particularly REM sleep) appears to play a role in the assimilation of emotionally related material. For example, Greenberg, Pillard, and Pearlman (1972) had subjects view a film of a very gruesome circumcision rite performed by a primitive tribe. This film produces anxiety when it is watched the first time, but if it is watched again on a later date, the effect is much smaller. Greenberg and his colleagues showed the film twice, on two separate days, to two groups of subjects. One group was permitted

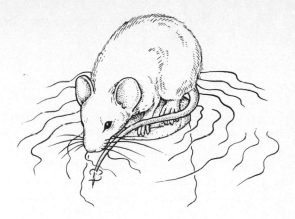

FIGURE 10.26 The flower-pot technique. (From Carlson, N.R. *Physiology of Behavior,* 2nd ed. Boston: Allyn and Bacon, 1981.)

to sleep normally; the other was deprived of REM sleep. The sleep-deprived subjects showed much less reduction of anxiety at the second viewing than the subjects who were permitted to obtain REM sleep. The results suggest that REM sleep may perform a role in reducing anxiety produced by events that occurred during the day; perhaps we really do "work things out" during REM sleep.

A large number of studies with laboratory animals have shown that deprivation of REM sleep affects retention of new tasks learned during the previous day. For example, Rideout (1979) gave hungry mice one opportunity to run through a maze each day and find food at the end. After each day's trial he deprived them of REM sleep by putting them on a small platform in a cage filled with water. The mice who were deprived of REM sleep learned their way around the maze more slowly than the mice who were not deprived of REM sleep.

◆ It also appears that the amount of REM sleep that takes place is related to the amount of new information learned the previous day. Block, Hennevin, and Leconte (1978) trained rats to run through a maze and measured the amount of REM sleep that they subsequently engaged in. They found that REM sleep increased as soon as training began but declined again to normal levels as soon as the subjects learned how to get through the maze quickly. Figure 10.27 shows that running speed (colored curve) increased suddenly after the sixth day, whereas REM sleep (black curve) increased

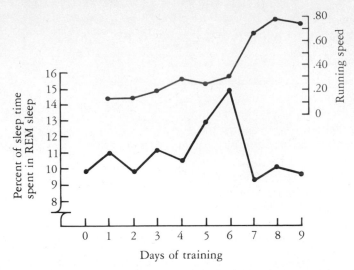

FIGURE 10.27   Percentage of sleep time spent in REM sleep (black curve) and maze-learning performance (colored curve) during training. (From Block, V., Hennevin, E., and Leconte, P. In *Neurobiology of Sleep and Memory*, edited by R.R. Drucker-Colin and J.L. McGaugh. New York: Academic Press, 1978.)

during training, reached a peak on the sixth day, and then declined. (See **Figure 10.27.**)

We cannot be sure what REM sleep accomplishes, but there appears to be a definite relation between this state and the learning and assimilation of emotional experiences. The sleep of a newborn infant is mostly REM sleep. Does this fact have any relation to the tremendous amount of learning that occurs early in life, or is it somehow related to the growth and development of the brain? Perhaps both factors are important.

Sleep as a Response

Another view, championed by Webb (1975), is that sleep is an instinctive behavioral response, like sexual intercourse. That is, there is no physiological need for sleep or sexual intercourse as there is for food and water. Rather, sleep serves a useful purpose for the survival of the individual and the species—or at least it did when the brain mechanisms of sleep were evolving.

There is no doubt that sleep is an active function of the brain. Sleep is definitely a response, not simply a state that we enter by default when we are not awake. The brain does not just "run down" at the end of the day. An ingenious experiment by

Magni, Moruzzi, Rossi, and Zanchetti (1959) proved that an animal sleeps because parts of the brain (we could call them "sleep circuits") become active and put the rest of the brain to sleep.

The investigators tied off some branches of the blood vessels leading to a cat's brain, isolating the blood supply of the brain stem from the front part (including the cerebral hemispheres). They permitted the cat to fall asleep and then injected an anesthetic into the brain stem. This treatment caused the animal to awaken. Thus, anesthesia of the brain stem brings a period of sleep to an end. Magni and his colleagues concluded that some portion of the brain stem contains circuits that produce sleep. If these circuits are suppressed by an anesthetic, the cat cannot sleep. (See **Figure 10.28.**)

Further confirmation that sleep is an active process comes from experiments that have permanently isolated the front part of the brain from the hind part by cutting entirely through the middle of the pons. This procedure causes insomnia; cats with this brain transection remain awake 80 to 90 percent of the time, compared with approximately 40 percent for normal animals (Batini, Moruzzi, Palestini, Rossi, and Zanchetti, 1959; 1959). (See **Figure 10.29.**) These experiments suggest that sleep

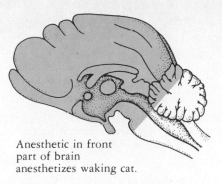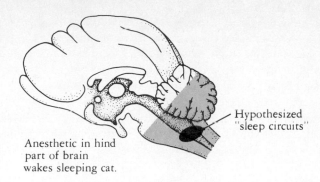

Anesthetic in front
part of brain
anesthetizes waking cat.

Anesthetic in hind
part of brain
wakes sleeping cat.

Hypothesized
"sleep circuits"

FIGURE 10.28   The experiment by Magni,
Moruzzi, Rossi, and Zanchetti (1959).

is a state that occurs when some neural system becomes active. The precise location of this circuit is not yet known.

Now let us consider Webb's suggestion that sleep is a response that is useful for the survival of a species. Different animals sleep for very different amounts of time, and the time seems to be related both to the animal's way of obtaining food and to its exposure to predators. In general, animals that have a safe place to stay will sleep for relatively long periods, unless they have high metabolic rates that require a lot of food gathering. The short-tailed shrew has a safe burrow but sleeps very little; it must eat around the clock or die. The ground

FIGURE 10.29   The results of transection of the pons.

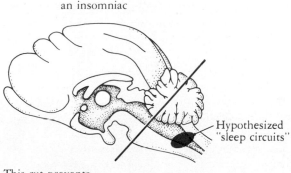

Animal becomes
an insomniac

Hypothesized
"sleep circuits"

This cut prevents
hypothesized sleep circuit
from affecting rest of brain.

squirrel also has a safe burrow, but because this animal is larger and consequently has a lower metabolic rate, it does not need to eat so often. It sleeps fourteen hours a day. So does a gorilla, who obviously does not need to sleep in a burrow. Cattle, sheep, deer, zebras, and other animals that can be preyed upon sleep very little—about two hours per day—and only in brief naps.

These sleeping patterns make sense in terms of the ecological niche of each species. For example, most primates are well adapted to daytime activity. They are agile and have good vision. Most are adept at climbing trees. Their sense of smell is not very useful in detecting animals that are dangerous to them; they rely principally on vision, although audition is also important. Some primates are principally vegetarians and obtain their foods from bushes and trees. These nutrients are readily available during the day, so there is no advantage to gathering them at night. Primate species ancestral to our own were omnivorous, eating plants and other animals. Their principal method of killing other animals was to use a weapon. This activity is visually guided, and thus requires daylight.

Most primates, then, are best adapted to the daylight world. Food is harder to obtain at night, and exposure to predators is greater because it is harder to see other animals; it makes good sense to find a safe place to stay during the night and to remain inactive there rather than moving around and wasting energy. Thus, it is plausible to view sleep as an adaptive instinctual behavior—one that keeps the animal quiet and out of harm's way.

The logic of this hypothesis is persuasive, and this account may well be correct. However, it does not necessarily follow that the *only* functions accomplished by sleep are safety and energy conservation. It is possible that the neural mechanisms for sleep originally evolved for these purposes but subsequently took on additional functions, such as synthesis of protein in the brain, facilitation of memory storage, and emotional assimilation.

SLEEP DISORDERS

Some of the things that sleep researchers have learned can help people with sleep-associated disorders.

Insomnia

Almost everyone has probably suffered from insomnia at least once. A few people have difficulty sleeping most nights; some of them take sleep medications for their ailment. Yet, according to most sleep researchers, sleep medications are the major *cause* of insomnia. Thus, insomnia is today's most prevalent *iatrogenic* ("physician-produced") *disorder,* because physicians succumb to pressure from their patients to give them sleeping pills.

So far as anyone knows, insomnia is not a disease. It is a symptom of a variety of conditions, including depression, anxiety, or chronic pain, and can even be produced by the anticipation of a happy event; a child may well lose sleep the night before a birthday party. There is no evidence that some people's brains contain a faulty sleep mechanism that can be fixed with a drug.

Sleep medications provide only symptomatic relief; the sleep produced by them is not normal, and relief is temporary. People need ever-increasing doses, and soon become dependent on the drug. Sleep medications suppress REM sleep, but even with escalating doses of the drug, a more normal amount of REM sleep begins to occur, as if a compensatory mechanism made it break through the effects of medication. Discontinuation of the drug produces a rebound effect: the brain's REM sleep mechanism recovers, and restlessness, unpleasant dreams, and frequent awakenings predominate throughout the night. One or two such experiences are usually enough to convince most people that they "need" the sleeping pills to which they have

become addicted. As people increase the number of sleeping pills taken each night, they reach a point where they are still drugged when they awaken. When it becomes difficult to function normally in the morning, they resort to stimulants to counteract the effects of the depressant drugs. Finally, they become addicted to alternating doses of depressants and stimulants in order to sleep and wake.

Not everyone becomes caught in such a cycle. Many people use sleep medications only rarely, or in low doses. But it is worth considering whether sleeping pills are *ever* necessary. A sedative or tranquilizer may be appropriate for some situations, such as counteracting shock when a loved one has died. But in the absence of such circumstances, it is important to realize that a sleepless night—or even two or three in a row—does not appear to cause any physiological harm. People who tend toward neuroticism and hypochondria generally feel that they *need* sleep, that they will somehow be harmed if they do not get enough of it. Since worrying about insomnia is a common cause of insomnia, just knowing that a sleepless night is harmless will often solve the problem. Other people use real or imagined insomnia as an excuse for their lack of success in life, telling themselves that they would do much better if only they could get enough sleep. For these people, insomnia may serve as a defense against the painful reality of their lives.

Many people who believe themselves to be insomniacs actually are not. We are often very poor at estimating how much sleep we get. Many people have reported lying awake all night, yet the record obtained in a sleep laboratory shows that they actually fell asleep in approximately thirty minutes and got seven or eight hours of sleep. Many of these people feel better as soon as they find out just how much sleep they are getting.

In addition to people who do not sleep a so-called normal amount and those who imagine that they do not, there are a few people who have recurring dreams of lying in bed, trying to fall asleep. The next day, they often feel as bad as if they had really stayed awake.

A common cause of insomnia in old people or infants is *sleep apnea.* (*Apnea* means "without breathing".) People with sleep apnea cannot sleep and breathe at the same time. When they fall asleep, they stop breathing, the content of carbon dioxide in their blood builds up, and they awaken, gasping for air. After breathing deeply for a while, they go back to sleep and resume the cycle. Some people who suffer from sleep apnea are blessed with a lack of memory for this periodic sleeping and awakening; others are aware of it and dread each night's sleep. It has been suggested that sleep apnea accounts for the **sudden infant death syndrome** ("crib death") that mysteriously kills babies in their sleep. It is believed that a mild infection, combined with an underdeveloped respiratory center (located in the medulla), is responsible for the children's failure to awaken when they stop breathing.

◆ Insomnia can neither kill nor disable you. If a more basic problem, such as depression, seems to be causing your insomnia, get professional help. If there are no obvious causes and the insomnia is not severe, try doing your worrying, or whatever else it is that might interfere with sleep, *before* going to bed. Make bed a place where you sleep, not where you worry. Establish and follow a regular routine when you get ready for bed. If you do not fall asleep in a reasonable amount of time, do not lie there fretting. Get up and do something else, and do not go back to bed until you feel drowsy. Even if you are up most of the night, stay up until you feel sleepy enough to doze off as soon as you get into bed. Remember that you will survive even if you miss a night's sleep. Make yourself get up at a regular time; if you make yourself get up in the morning you will probably find it easier to fall asleep the next night.

Disorders Associated with REM Sleep

◆ Two important characteristics of REM sleep are dreaming and paralysis. It is likely that the paralysis results from a mechanism that prevents us from acting out our dreams. In fact, damage to certain areas of a cat's brain will produce just that result: the cat, obviously asleep, acts as if it were participating in a dream (Jouvet, 1972). It walks around stalking imaginary prey and responding defensively to imaginary predators.

Dreams and muscular paralysis are fine when a person is lying in bed. But sometimes a person is struck down by paralysis while actively going about his or her business. He or she falls to the ground and lies there, paralyzed but fully conscious. These attacks of **cataplexy** (*kata,* "down"; plēxis, "stroke") usually last less than a minute. Attacks of cataplexy are usually triggered by strong emotional states, such as anger, laughter, or even lovemaking. People who have cataleptic attacks tend also to enter REM sleep as soon as they fall asleep, in contrast to the normal ninety-minute interval.

People who suffer from cataplectic attacks also tend to have vivid **hypnagogic hallucinations** just before they fall asleep, which are almost certainly premature dreams. These are often continuations of events that have actually occurred. For example, a patient in a sleep lab experienced a hypnagogic hallucination in which the experimenter, who had just attached the electrodes, was attempting to cut off his ear with a scalpel (Dement, 1974). Thus, the disorder appears to involve overactive REM-sleep mechanisms; cataplexy is probably caused by inappropriate activity of the brain mechanism that keeps a person paralyzed during dreaming.

Cataplexy can be treated by drugs that increase the activity of neurons that use a particular transmitter substance (serotonin) to communicate with other neurons. In contrast, LSD and mescaline, drugs that produce visual hallucinations, *inhibit* the activity of serotonin-secreting neurons. These facts suggest that there may be a relation between dreams and hallucinations caused by LSD; serotonin-stimulating drugs reduce them, whereas serotonin-inhibiting drugs make them more likely to occur.

Cataplexy and hypnagogic hallucinations are symptoms of a more general disorder called **narcolepsy** (literally, "numbness seizure"). Another common symptom of narcolepsy is a **sleep attack,** a sudden wave of irresistible sleepiness. Unlike attacks of cataplexy, sleep attacks can be warded off temporarily, until the person can get to a safe place. After a brief period of normal sleep, the person wakes up feeling refreshed. Sleep attacks can usually be controlled with amphetamine.

Disorders Associated with Slow-Wave Sleep

◆ Several phenomena occur during the deepest phase (stage 4) of slow-wave sleep. These include sleepwalking, night terrors, and enuresis. Sleeptalking also occurs during non-REM sleep, but usually during its lighter stages.

Sleepwalking can be as simple as getting out of bed and right back in again, or as complicated as walking out of a house and climbing into a car. (Fortunately, sleepwalkers apparently do not try to drive.) We know that sleepwalking is not the acting out of a dream, because it occurs during stage 4 of slow-wave sleep, when the EEG shows synchronous slow waves and the person's mental state generally involves a static situation not a narrative. Sleepwalkers are difficult to awaken, and once awakened they are often confused and disoriented. However, contrary to popular belief, it is perfectly safe to wake them up.

Sleepwalking is *not* a manifestation of some deep-seated emotional problem. Most sleepwalkers are children, who almost invariably outgrow it. The worst thing to do, according to sleep researchers, is to try to get them treated for it. Of course, a house inhabited by a sleepwalker should be made as safe as possible and the doors should be kept locked at night. For some reason, sleepwalking runs in families; Dement (1974) tells of a family whose grown members were reunited for a holiday celebration. In the middle of the night they woke to find that they had all gathered in the living room—during their sleep.

Sleeptalking sometimes occurs as part of a REM sleep dream, but more often, it occurs during slow-wave sleep. Often it is possible to carry on a conversation with the sleeptalker; this fact indicates that the person is very near the edge of sleep and waking. During this state sleeptalkers are very suggestible. So-called truth drugs are used in an attempt to duplicate this condition, so that it is possible to question a person who is not on guard against giving away secrets and is not functioning well enough to tell elaborate lies. Unfortunately for the interrogators (and fortunately for the rest of the population), there are no foolproof, reliable truth drugs.

Night terrors, like sleepwalking, occur most often in children, who wake, screaming with terror. When questioned, they do not report a dream, and they often seem confused. Usually they fall asleep quickly without showing any aftereffects, and seldom remember the events the next day. Night terrors are not the same as nightmares, which are simply frightening dreams from which one happens to awaken. It appears that night terrors are caused by sudden awakenings from the depths of stage 4 sleep.

The sudden, dramatic change in consciousness is a frightening experience for the child.

The final disorder of slow-wave sleep, *enuresis,* or "bedwetting," is fairly common in young children. Most children outgrow it, just as they outgrow sleepwalking or night terrors. Emotional problems can trigger enuresis, but bedwetting does not itself indicate that a child is psychologically unwell. The problem with enuresis is that, unlike the other stage 4 phenomena, there are aftereffects that must be cleaned up. Parents dislike having their sleep disturbed and get tired of frequently changing and laundering sheets. The resulting tension in family relations can make the child feel anxious and guilty and thus unnecessarily prolong the disorder.

◆ Fortunately, a simple training method often cures enuresis. A moisture-sensitive device is placed under the bedsheet; when it gets wet it causes a bell to ring. Because a child releases a few drops of urine before the bladder begins to empty in earnest, the bell wakes the child in time to run to the bathroom. In about a week, most children learn to prevent their bladders from emptying and manage to wait until morning. Perhaps what they really learn is not to enter such a deep level of stage 4 sleep, where the mechanism that keeps the bladder from emptying seems to break down.

CONCLUDING REMARKS

This chapter has explained consciousness in terms of verbal control, verbal mediation, and verbal access. It has also described the basic phenomena related to consciousness, including its role in attention, habituation, effects of destruction of cortical association fibers, hypnosis, meditation, and sleep. Although consciousness is a private phenomenon, we can study it through public phenomena; namely, the behaviors of other people—words, gestures, facial expressions of emotion, and the like. Those aspects of consciousness that do not manifest themselves in behavior can never reveal themselves to us. This chapter suggests that study of social behaviors will reveal all that is essential to consciousness, because this phenomenon is a byproduct of our ability to communicate with others:

thinking to ourselves and being aware of our own existence derives from our ability to talk about our existence and experiences to others.

GUIDE TO TERMS
INTRODUCED IN
THIS CHAPTER

SUGGESTIONS FOR
FURTHER READING

A book by B. Wallace and L.E. Fisher, *Consciousness and Behavior* (Boston: Allyn and Bacon, 1983), provides more information about a variety of topics related to consciousness, including some that I did not discuss in this chapter, such as extrasensory perception (ESP). *The Origin of Consciousness in the Breakdown of the Bicameral Mind* by J. Jaynes (Boston: Houghton Mifflin, 1976) presents the provocative hypothesis that human consciousness is a recent phenomenon that emerged long after the evolution of the human brain, as we know it now. It is not necessary to agree with Jaynes's thesis to enjoy reading this scholarly book. Another provocative thesis is advanced by A. Weil in *The Natural Mind* (Boston: Houghton Mifflin, 1972), who argues that altering one's consciousness is an innate human need. His research on the Indian tribes of South America shows how cultures other than our own attach religious significance to states of altered consciousness.

If you would like to learn more about hypnosis you would enjoy *Hypnotism, Imagination, and Human Potentialities* by T.X. Barber, N.P. Spanos, and J.F. Chaves (New York: Pergamon Press, 1974) or *Hypnosis for the Seriously Curious* by K.S. Bowers (Monterey Calif.: Brooks/Cole, 1976). Applications are described in *Applied Hypnosis: An Overview* by B. Wallace (Chicago: Nelson-Hall, 1979).

Three interesting and informative books on sleep are *Some Must Watch While Some Must Sleep* by W.C. Dement (San Francisco: W.C. Freeman, 1974), *Sleep: The Gentle Tyrant* by W.B. Webb (Englewood Cliffs, N.J.: Prentice-Hall, 1975), and *Sleep and Dreaming: Origins, Nature and Functions* by D.B. Cohen (New York: Pergamon Press, 1979).

MEMORY

LEARNING ◆ OBJECTIVES

YOU HAVE already seen how animals and humans use memory in purely behavioral terms; Chapter 4 described how reinforcement and punishment can alter behavior. However, most of our learning does not require overt, obvious reinforcement; more subtle reasons motivate us than the bits of food given to a rat that is learning to press a lever or run through a maze. For humans, opportunities to solve problems and learn new material serve as conditioned reinforcers; these activities have become ends in themselves. This fact, along with people's desire to gain approval from others, makes it unnecessary for experimenters investigating human memory to reinforce the behavior of their subjects explicitly. This chapter describes how people learn and remember information, and how learned information is organized in their brain.

AN OVERVIEW

As we all know, the mere ability to perceive new information is no guarantee that we will be able to remember it later. We have all experienced reading or hearing and understanding something, but being unable to remember it later. Thus, it is clear that not everything we perceive becomes part of our permanent store of memories.

There appear to be at least three forms of memory, each with a distinct physiological basis. The first form, called *sensory memory,* lasts for a very brief time—perhaps a second or less—and is difficult to distinguish from perception.

The information contained in sensory memory represents the original stimulus fairly accurately—such as a brief image of a sight we have just seen or a fleeting echo of a sound we have just heard. Generally, we are not aware of sensory memory; no analysis appears to be performed on the information while it remains in this form. Its function appears to be to hold onto information long enough for its transfer to the next form, *short-term memory.*

Short-term memory is an immediate memory for stimuli that have just been perceived. We can remember a new item of information (such as a telephone number) as long as we want to simply by rehearsing it. However, once we stop rehearsing the information there is no guarantee that we will be able to remember it later. That is, it may or may not get stored in *long-term memory.*

There is a definite limit to the amount of information that short-term memory can hold. For example, read the following numbers to yourself just once, and then close your eyes and recite them back.

1 4 9 2 3 0 7

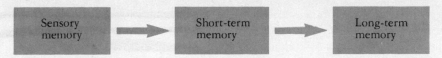

FIGURE 11.1 This model of human memory is too simple.

You probably had no trouble remembering them. Now try the following set of numbers, but go through them only once before you close your eyes.

7 2 5 2 3 9 1 6 5 8 4

Very few people can repeat eleven numbers; in fact you may not have even bothered to try, seeing how many numbers there were. Short-term memory has definite limits. No matter how much you practice, you will probably not be able to recite more than seven to nine independent pieces of information. (As we shall see later, there are ways to organize new information so that you can remember more than seven to nine items, but in such cases they can no longer be considered independent.)

If you wanted to, you could recite the numbers again and again until you had memorized them; that is, you could rehearse the information in short-term memory until it was eventually stored in long-term memory. The fact that there are eleven numbers would present no obstacle; long-term memory can accommodate an unlimited number of items of information. The difference in the capacities of short-term and long-term memory indicate that these forms of memory are separate entities.

Most people find it difficult to conceive of short-term memory as a form of memory at all. Generally, they think of the ability to recite back a set of numbers immediately as something different from actually *remembering* the numbers; when most people refer to memory they mean *long-term* memory.

Some psychologists argue that there is no real distinction between short-term and long-term memory, that they are different phases of a continuous process. They object to conceiving of memory as a series of separate units with information flowing from one to the next, as in **Figure 11.1**. And indeed such a "compartment" model is too simple. Short-term memory is closely related to recall of information from long-term memory. Thinking about old information (from long-term memory) is very similar to thinking about new information that has just been perceived. However, several arguments support a distinction between short-term and long-term memory. As we shall see, a lot happens to the way in which new information is retained during the first few seconds after it is received. Even if memory is a continuous process, and short-term and long-term memory refer merely to rapidly changing or relatively stable phases, the distinction is useful. Items in short-term memory are "in our thoughts." A newly perceived stimulus that is in short-term memory is one that we are currently attending to; it is in our consciousness. In contrast, we actively think about very little of the information in long-term memory at any given time. For example, there is probably no item of information that we know better than our own names, but the name is not something we must "think about" all the time. Whenever we need to remember it, it is there.

This distinction does not mean that information in short-term memory *must* be conscious. As we saw in Chapter 10, behaviors can be learned and performed without verbal awareness. For example, Carter trained his subjects to blink their eyes without their being aware of what was happening. However, most investigators who study human memory deal with information that the subject is clearly aware of. As a result, we know little about the details of nonconscious memory processes. For the time being it will be most convenient to think of short-term memory as the immediate storage of newly perceived information to which we have verbal access—that is, of which we are "aware."

SENSORY MEMORY

We are not generally aware of sensory memory. Information that we have just perceived remains in

sensory memory for a very brief time—just long enough to be transferred to short-term memory. A thunderstorm at night provides us with an opportunity to become aware of sensory memory. When a bright flash of lightning reveals a scene, we *see* things before we *recognize* them. That is, we see something first, then study the image that is left behind. We probably have a sensory memory for each sense modality. So far, research efforts have focused on the two most important, iconic and echoic memory.

ICONIC MEMORY

Visual sensory memory is referred to as *iconic memory* (*icon* means "image"). To study this form of memory, Sperling (1960) presented visual stimuli to subjects by means of a *tachistoscope* (from *tachistos,* "most swift"; *skopein,* "to see"). (See **Figure 11.2.**) Sperling flashed a set of nine letters, such as those shown below, on the screen for 0.05 second.

P Q B

C Z L

R K F

On the average, subjects were able to identify only four or five letters but reported that they could *see* more; the image faded too fast to permit identification of them all.

To determine whether the capacity of iconic memory accounted for this limitation, Sperling asked the subjects to recall the letters in only one of the three horizontal lines. If a high, middle, or low tone was sounded, they were to identify the letters in the top, middle, or bottom line. If people are warned beforehand which line they should pay attention to, they have no difficulty getting all three letters right. But Sperling sounded the tone *after* flashing the letters on the screen. The subjects had to select the line from the *image* that they still had; that is, they had to retrieve the information from iconic memory. With brief delays, they recalled a line of letters with perfect accuracy. For example, after seeing all nine letters flashed on the screen they would hear the high tone, direct their attention to the top line of letters in their iconic memory, and "read them off." These results indicate that all nine letters were stored in iconic memory.

Sperling also varied the delay between the presentation of the nine letters and the tone. If the delay was longer than one second, performance fell to slightly above 50 percent. This result indicates that the image of the visual stimulus fades quickly

FIGURE 11.2   The woman on the right looks at stimuli presented in the tachistoscope while the experimenter records her responses.

from iconic memory. This factor explains why subjects who were asked to report *all* the letters failed to report more than four or five. They had to scan their visual sensory memories and identify each letter. Once they were identified, they could be retained in short-term memory. This process takes time, and the image was fading while the scanning occurred. Although all nine letters were originally present in iconic memory, there was time to recognize and report only four or five before they faded.

ECHOIC MEMORY

◆ Auditory sensory memory, aptly called *echoic memory*, is of prime importance in the comprehension of speech. Spoken words consist of a series of sounds that encode information. When we hear a word pronounced, we hear individual sounds one at a time. We cannot identify the word until we have heard all the sounds, so we must store them in memory until all have been received. For example, if someone says *mallet*, we may think of a kind of hammer; but if someone says *malice*, we will think of something entirely different. The sound *mal* has no meaning by itself in English, so we do not identify it as a word. However, once the last syllable is uttered, we can put the two syllables together and recognize the word. At this point, the word enters short-term memory. Echoic memory holds a representation of the initial sounds until the word is complete.

We encountered an example of the operation of echoic memory in Chapter 10, in the discussion of dichotic listening. In this procedure, subjects listen to a message from one earphone while ignoring the message that is being presented simultaneously through the other earphone. If a signal is given, the listener can pay attention to the message that was just received in the unattended ear and can catch the words that were just heard before they slip away. Even when we are not paying attention, information remains in sensory memory long enough to be "caught" and transferred to short-term memory. Our attention determines which information is caught and which is lost. (See **Figure 11.3**.)

Massaro (1970, 1972) first presented subjects with a series of very brief (0.02-second) low and high tones and asked subjects to identify each tone

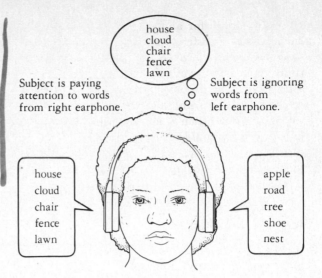

Subject is paying attention to words from right earphone.

Subject is ignoring words from left earphone.

house
cloud
chair
fence
lawn

house
cloud
chair
fence
lawn

apple
road
tree
shoe
nest

Words stop; subject is asked to say the last word from the left earphone.

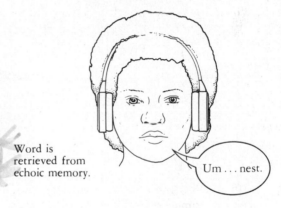

Word is retrieved from echoic memory.

Um . . . nest.

FIGURE 11.3 The dichotic listening task.

after it was presented. Next, he presented a masking tone of medium pitch after each high or low tone at intervals, ranging from no delay to a delay of 5 seconds. (See **Figure 11.4**.) Figure 11.5 shows the results. If the masking tone came right after the test tone, the subjects correctly identified the test tone only about 60 percent of the time. (This is very poor performance. Given that there were only two tones to identify, we would expect a score of 50 percent from guessing alone.) The greater the delay between test tone and masking tone, the more likely the subjects were to identify the first tone correctly. (See **Figure 11.5**.)

The results of Massaro's study show that raw auditory information appears to be stored in echoic

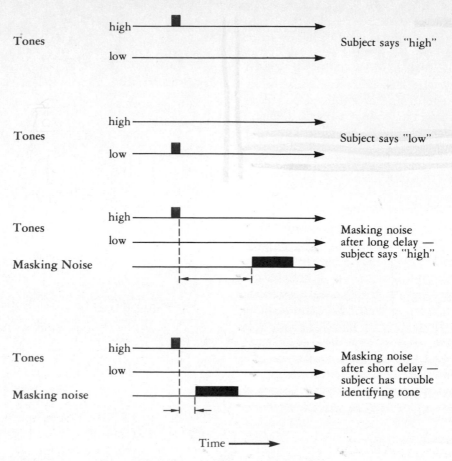

FIGURE 11.4   The procedure used by Massaro (1970).

memory, and that even a decision to classify a tone as high or low takes some time. If another tone displaces the "echo" of the first tone before the decision is made, the subject cannot correctly identify it.

Moray, Bates, and Barnett (1965) performed an experiment similar to Sperling's study of iconic memory. They placed four loudspeakers around the subjects and played a recording of up to eight different letters through each speaker. In their laps the subjects held a display panel with lights mounted on it. Immediately after the broadcast of the letters, one of the lights came on, indicating which speaker the subject should respond to. (See **Figure 11.6**.) As in the Sperling experiment, the subjects' partial reports were better than their full reports; more was stored in echoic memory than could be

"dumped" into short-term memory. Like iconic memory, echoic memory can hold more information than we can consciously attend to.

◆   Interim summary: Memory exists in three forms: sensory, short-term, and long-term. The characteristics of each differ, which suggests that they differ physiologically as well. Sensory memory is very brief, and provides temporary storage until the newly perceived information can be stored in short-term memory. Short-term memory is memory that we are usually aware of. Although its capacity is limited to something under ten items of independent information, we can rehearse information as long as we choose, thus making it more likely that we will remember it indefinitely—that it will enter long-term memory.

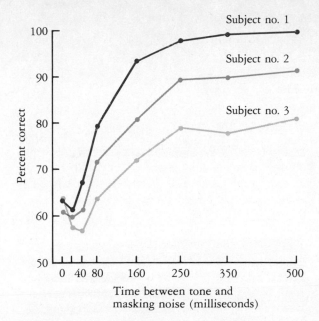

FIGURE 11.5   The results of Massaro's experiment. (From Massaro, D.W. *Journal of Experimental Psychology*, 1970, 85, 411–417.)

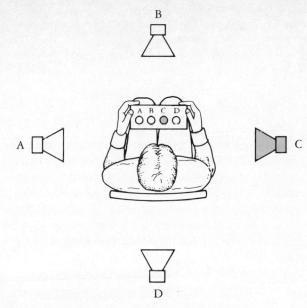

FIGURE 11.6   The procedure used by Moray, Bates, and Barnett (1965).

SHORT-TERM MEMORY

◆ ENCODING OF INFORMATION

Sensory memory represents information quite faithfully. For example, the image in iconic memory seems to contain most of the features of the scene that was just perceived. Indeed, some investigators believe that the basis of iconic memory is, in large part, activity of the cells in the retina that persists for a short while after an image is gone. But short-term memory is much more than a simple representation of an image, a sound, or a touch; it is an interpretation of events, so that they have meaning. For example, say the group of words below, look away from the page, and recite the words from memory.

along got the was door crept locked slowly
he until passage the he to which

No doubt you found the task hopeless; there was just too much information to store in short-term memory. Now try the following group of words:

He slowly crept along the passage until

he got to the door, which was locked.

This time you were probably much more successful. Once they are arranged in a sequence that makes sense, the same fifteen words are not difficult to store in short-term memory. Clearly, it is not simply the number of syllables that determines how much information can be put into short-term memory; rather, the limit depends on how much *meaning* the information has. The first set is merely fifteen different words, as unconnected as a list of fifteen different numbers. Given that few people can immediately recite back more than seven to nine independent items, it is not surprising that we find it impossible to store fifteen assorted words in short-term memory. However, when the items are related we can store many more of them. This means that we do not store them as a list of words; instead, they are encoded in terms of meaning. When we recite back the sentence, we convert the encoded meaning back into words. The ease with which we convert the stored meaning (plus other information) into words gives us the false impression that short-term memory contains a faithful representation of the sounds of the words themselves.

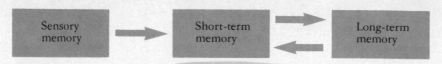

FIGURE 11.7   Revised (but still too simple) model of human memory.

In the past some psychologists asserted that we encode *all* verbal material stored in short-term memory acoustically, and that we encode information by meaning only in long-term memory. However, the fact that it is easier to remember a meaningful sentence than a random set of words indicates that meaning is encoded in short-term memory.

But our ability to organize information in short-term memory in terms of meaning must require the use of long-term memory. After all, if words have meaning to us, we must have learned this meaning previously; that is, it has been stored in long-term memory. Figure 11.7 is a modification of the diagram that was presented in Figure 11.1 to take account of the role that long-term memory plays in organizing information in short-term memory. (The diagram is still incomplete.) (See **Figure 11.7.**)

The preceding example (the man creeping along the passage) makes it obvious that information is encoded in short-term memory according to *previously learned rules*. In this example, the previously learned rules concerned the meaning of words and the ways in which they may be combined to produce sentences. The *retention* of information in short-term memory involves *retrieval* of information from long-term memory, because that is where the previously learned rules are stored. We know the meanings of words because we have learned them; they are stored in long-term memory. Thus if we hear the word *tree,* we do not merely store those three sounds ($t + r + ee$) in short-term memory; we also retrieve the meaning of the sounds from long-term memory and store that meaning. We might even summon an image of a tree.

George Miller (1956) was the first to consider explicitly how information might be encoded in short-term memory. In a series of experiments he showed that only about seven *independent* items (such as numbers, letters, words, or tones with particular pitches) could be stored in short-term memory. However, we would probably have no difficulty retaining the numbers written below in short-term memory, even though there are ten of them.

1 3 5 7 9 2 4 6 8 0

These numbers are easy to retain in short-term memory because we can remember a rule instead of ten independent numbers. **Chunking** is Miller's term for the use of rules that were previously stored in long-term memory to organize information just received in short-term memory. Short-term memory can organize incoming information into about seven chunks according to these previously learned rules. Thus, the amount of information we can store in short-term memory depends on the particular rules we use to organize the information.

Anyone familiar with the number system used by computers will have no difficulty chunking any sequence of eighteen ones and zeroes. To demonstrate the role of chunking in short-term memory, I occasionally ask eighteen students in a class to say either "one" or "zero," then write the sequence, which I obviously could not have memorized in advance, on the board. For example, I might get the following series:

0 1 0 1 1 0 1 0 0 0 1 0 1 1 1 0 0 0

I study the list for a few seconds, look away, and go on with my lecture. Then I stop and say, "Here are the numbers," and write them on the board. Because I have had experience with computers, which use only ones and zeroes for internal storage, I can look at any sequence of three ones and zeroes and immediately recognize it as representing a number from 0 to 7, in accordance with the following rules:

000 = 0	100 = 4
001 = 1	101 = 5
010 = 2	110 = 6
011 = 3	111 = 7

I study the eighteen numbers by groups of three and convert them into their numerical equivalents, as follows:

$$\underline{010} \quad \underline{110} \quad \underline{100} \quad \underline{010} \quad \underline{111} \quad \underline{000}$$
$$2 \qquad 6 \qquad 4 \qquad 2 \qquad 7 \qquad 0$$

As a result, I have to remember only six items, not eighteen. I recite "264270" to myself several times, and continue to rehearse the numbers while I say a few more sentences to the class (this is the hardest part). Then I decode 264270 into the zeroes and ones.

We perform precisely the same kinds of conversions every day, although we are usually unaware of doing so. We perceive an endless stream of sensory information and process it into chunks according to rules stored in long-term memory. For example, we use rhythm and rhyme patterns to help ourselves remember poetry. We use our knowledge of the rules of grammar to organize verbal material, even when it appears to consist of nonsense words. Consider the following:

a vap koob desak the citar
molent um glox nerf

An experiment by Epstein (1961) demonstrated that subjects found it easier to remember nonsense words like these if the words were put into a sentence form, even though the sentence had no meaning. The "sentence" below contains the same words, in the same order, but word endings like -y, -s, -ed, and -ly give the impression of grammatical structure.

A vapy koobs desaked the citar
molently um glox nerfs.

Lewis Carroll's poem "Jabberwocky," in *Through the Looking-Glass,* demonstrates this phenomenon:

'Twas brillig, and the slithy toves
Did gyre and gimble in the wabe:
All mimsy were the borogroves,
And the mome raths outgrabe.

It is clear that short-term memory is more than a way station between perception and long-term memory. For example, as I write this paragraph I think not only about the words that I have just written (represented in short-term memory) but also about what I want to say next. To make these plans, I must use information that is already stored in long-term memory. Because short-term memory contains information that we are currently thinking about, including information that has been retrieved from long-term memory, some investigators prefer not to distinguish between short-term and long-term memory, and use the term *activated memory* or *working memory* to refer to the part of long-term memory that we are currently thinking about. Its contents include new and old information.

The fact that activated or working memory contains both old and new information does not mean that we must discard the distinction between short-term and long-term memory; most psychologists continue to use these terms because, as we shall see later, there is evidence for a physiological distinction between them. We can even consider the *remembering* of a memory to be a short-term memory itself. For example, think about the last time you mailed a letter. This information, and your awareness of thinking about it, are presently in your working memory, just as newly presented information would be. If I ask you later, "Do you remember thinking about the last time you mailed a letter?" you will undoubtedly be able to say "Yes." Thus, information can reach short-term memory from the act of remembering as well as from the sensory systems.

SENSORY REPRESENTATION

Evidence indicates that we have separate short-term memories for each sensory modality: vision, audition, the somatosenses, taste, and olfaction. We probably also have a motor short-term memory, where we store information about movements that we have just made, and possibly where we rehearse movements that we are thinking about making.

Effects of Intramodal Interference

Many experiments have shown that *intramodal* interference is much more severe than *intermodal* interference (*intra* means "within," *inter* means "between"). That is, when we attempt to retain information in short-term memory we are more likely to be confused by additional information if it is presented through the same sense modality (intramodal interference) rather than through a dif-

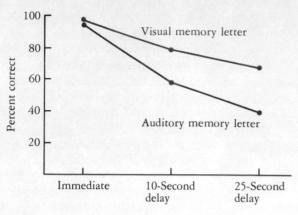

FIGURE 11.8   Memory for a visually or acoustically presented letter immediately after presentation and after ten or twenty-five seconds of shadowing an acoustically presented message. (Based on data from Kroll, N.E.A., Parks, T., Parkinson, S.R., Bieber, S.L., and Johnson, A.L. *Journal of Experimental Psychology,* 1970, *85,* 220–224.).

ferent one (intermodal interference). In one such experiment, Kroll, Parks, Parkinson, Bieber, and Johnson (1970) presented subjects either visually or acoustically with a single letter (the "memory letter") to be retained in short-term memory. Immediately afterward they had the subjects shadow a spoken list of unrelated letters—that is, the subjects were to repeat back the letters while listening to them. Ten or twenty-five seconds after hearing or seeing the memory letter, the subjects were asked to recall it. Figure 11.8 shows the results. When the subjects were asked to repeat the letter with no delay (that is, without having to shadow a list of letters), retention was virtually perfect (around 96 percent). In contrast, ten or twenty-five seconds of shadowing interfered with retention of a spoken memory letter; retention of a visually presented letter was much better. (See **Figure 11.8.**)

The results of this experiment suggest that auditory and visual short-term memory are distinct; a verbal task displaces information in auditory short-term memory more easily than information in visual short-term memory. Presumably, the subjects could maintain an image of the visually presented memory letter while showing the list of unrelated letters, whereas they found it much more difficult to retain the sound of a letter while attending to the list.

Through the series of experiments below, you can demonstrate to yourself the existence of several relatively independent activated or working memories, each devoted to a sense modality.

1. Get a pencil and paper. Write the word *antidisestablishmentarianism.* Do not copy it from the book; spell the word out by yourself. Pay close attention to what you do as you write the word.

* * *

You probably sounded the word out to yourself as you wrote it, converting the mental sounds into letters. You needed to "hear" a long, unfamiliar word in order to produce the hand movements that are necessary for writing it down.

2. Now turn the paper over and write *antidisestablishmentarianism* again while performing another verbally mediated behavior: sing "Happy Birthday" while you try to write the word. (If you are not alone and do not want to attract attention to yourself, at least whisper the words to the song).

* * *

This time you probably found it very difficult to write *antidisestablishmentarianism.* If you managed to write it you probably did so during pauses between words of the song. This task demonstrates that working memory has a limited capacity; it cannot mediate two complicated behaviors at the same time.

3. Now perform another complex task—one that does not require verbal mediation. Draw a picture of a house while singing (or whispering) "Happy Birthday."

* * *

You probably had no trouble performing this task. Whereas both singing and writing require auditory working memory, drawing a picture from memory is probably mediated by your visual system; your visual memory of a house guides the movements of your hand. It is easy to draw a picture and sing a song at the same time. This task demonstrates that some tasks do not compete with each other; a verbally mediated task (singing) and a nonverbally mediated task (drawing a picture) appear to use different brain resources.

4. Now turn the paper over to the word *antidisestablishmentarianism* that you wrote for experiment 1. Write the word again while singing "Happy

Birthday," but this time *copy* the word, writing it beneath the first version.

*   *   *

This time you probably had no trouble, because you did not have to sound out the word when you wrote it. Your motor system could control movements of your fingers when using the previously written word as a model. Thus, even though your verbal system was busy finding the words to "Happy Birthday" and controlling your singing them, you had no trouble copying *antidisestablishmentarianism*.

The four experiments demonstrate that two tasks that use the same kind of sensory material (in this case singing and writing a long unfamiliar word) are very difficult to perform. Two tasks that use different kinds of information (singing and drawing a picture or copying a long word) can be performed together rather well. Therefore, we can conclude that short-term (working) memory has several components, organized in terms of a specific sense modality.

Here is another problem for you. Try singing "Happy Birthday" while you sign your name. Do it with your eyes closed so that you have no visual feedback. You will probably be able to do this easily. Why? What kind of long-term memories are guiding your hand and finger movements? It does not appear to be acoustic, for there is no interference with the singing.

Effects of Brain Damage

◆ The evidence presented in the previous section does not in itself prove that different neural systems mediate the various sensory components of short-term (working) memory. To determine whether these memories are anatomically separate, we need physiological evidence.

Geschwind, Quadfasel, and Segarra (1968) reported the case of a woman who suffered severe brain damage from inhaling gas from an unlit water heater. As Figure 11.9 shows, the damage completely spared the auditory cortex, the auditory association cortex (Wernicke's area), Broca's speech area, and the fibers that connect these regions. (See **Figure 11.9.**) The result of the damage was *isolation aphasia.* The woman remained in a hospital for nine years, until she died. During this time she made few voluntary movements except with her eyes, which were able to follow moving ob-

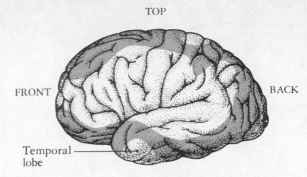

FIGURE 11.9   The brain damage sustained by a woman with isolation aphasia, reported by Geschwind, Quadfasel, and Segarra (1968).

jects. She did not initiate speech, answer questions, or give any signs that she understood the speech of others. However, she could repeat words that were spoken to her. Furthermore, if the words were spoken to her with a foreign accent, she would repeat them without the accent, so she obviously had a long-term memory for the pronunciation of English words. And if someone said, "Roses are red, violets are blue," she would respond with "Sugar is sweet, and so are you." She even learned new poems and songs. Clearly, then, the undamaged areas of her brain were necessary and sufficient for short-term and long-term auditory memory—enabling her to speak and to learn new sequences of words—but the damaged areas were essential to her ability to understand the meaning of these words.

FIGURE 11.10   Visual memories appear not to be stored in the undamaged part of the brain of the woman with isolation aphasia.

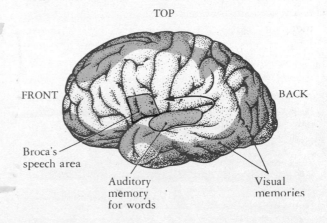

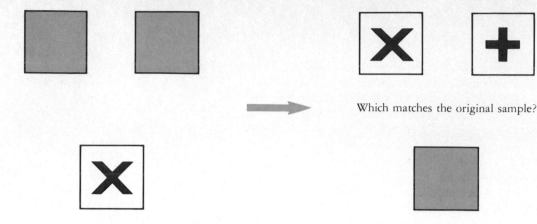

FIGURE 11.11   The delayed matching-to-sample task.

The evidence from this case localizes auditory short-term to the undamaged regions of the patient's cortex. Damage to these regions in other patients disrupts auditory memory, leaving visual and somatosensory memories intact. Thus, we can conclude that different regions of the cerebral cortex mediate memories obtained from stimuli perceived by the various sensory modalities. (See **Figure 11.10.**)

Kovner and Stamm (1972) obtained evidence from monkeys that support this conclusion. First, they operated on the monkeys, placing wires on various regions of the cerebral cortex. They attached these wires to a connector fastened to the top of each animal's head, so that they could transmit electrical current through the wires while the animals were performing their task. The electrical current disrupted the normal functioning of the region of cortex where the wire was located. Then they trained the monkeys in a ***delayed matching-to-sample task.*** They briefly showed the animals a visual pattern—the sample. After a delay of several seconds with no pattern present, they showed two patterns, one of which was the same as the sample. If the monkey touched the pattern that matched the sample, it was given a piece of food. If it touched the other pattern, no food was delivered. (See **Figure 11.11.**)

The delayed matching-to-sample task required the monkeys to compare their memory of a visual stimulus with an actual stimulus. Thus, the animals had to use their visual short-term memory to decide which pattern to select.

The current was turned on during the delay interval, while the image of the sample pattern was stored in visual short-term memory. Stimulation in the visual association cortex on the temporal lobe disrupted performance; stimulation in other regions had no effect. The current appeared to "erase" the image. Thus, visual short-term memories appear to be located in this region of the visual association cortex.

As a control procedure the experimenters also trained the monkeys in a ***simultaneous matching-to-sample task,*** which required the animals to indicate which of two patterns at the bottom of the screen matched the one above. (See **Figure 11.12.**) Because the sample was always present, no image of it had to be stored in visual short-term memory. In this case, electrical brain stimulation had no effect at all; the animals performed normally.

All the findings above suggest that visual and auditory short-term memories are distinct. Additional evidence supports the same conclusion for other sense modalities, though not so clearly as the studies cited here. However, all these short-term memories interact with each other.

READING: CROSS-MODAL ENCODING IN SHORT-TERM MEMORY

We have seen that the encoding of information in short-term memory proceeds according to previously learned rules; for example, the sounds of words

Which matches the sample above?

FIGURE 11.12   The simultaneous matching-to-sample task.

are encoded according to meaning, and patterns of zeroes and ones can be translated into numbers from zero to seven. Thus, retrieval from long-term memory (where the rules are stored) affects the nature of the information stored in short-term memory. The information retrieved from long-term memory does not have to be of the same sensory modality as the incoming information. For example, visual

short-term memory can draw from long-term memories that were originally learned acoustically. Look at the following words. *Without saying them aloud,* can you determine whether or not they rhyme?

tie fly

Of course you can. You can see the words, store them in visual short-term memory, and almost immediately withdraw the meaning *and information about the sounds* of these words from long-term memory. You compare the mental sounds and note that the words rhyme. Your knowledge of the sounds that the words make comes from previously learned acoustical information. Once you retrieve the acoustic information from long-term memory, it too is stored in short-term memory. Thus, you have a dual representation of the words *tie* and *fly*—visual short-term memory of their appearance on the page, and auditory short-term memory of their sounds. In addition, you retrieve information about the meaning of the words. You might even summon an image of a person preparing (tying) some artificial flies that are used as fishing lures. (See **Figure 11.13.**)

The fact that visually presented material (especially verbal material) causes a rapid retrieval of

FIGURE 11.13   When we see the words *tie* and *fly* we quickly recognize that they rhyme. The words may also evoke related images.

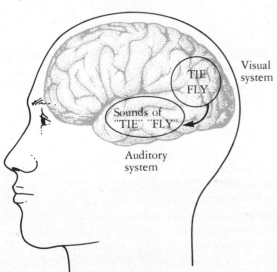
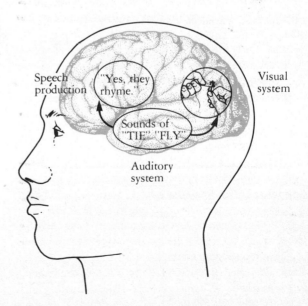

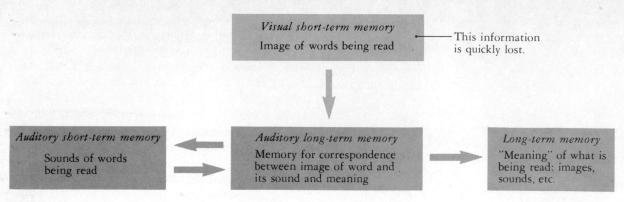

FIGURE 11.14   Some details of the retrieval of information from long-term memory.

acoustically coded information from long-term memory is of obvious importance in the use of language. We often see a word, encode it acoustically and by meaning, and forget about it in a visual sense; that is, we do not continue to picture what the letters look like on the page. This is probably the process involved when we read; new information is constantly entering visual short-term memory, driving out the old. As we recognize words, we encode the corresponding sounds and meaning, and some representation of meaning enters long-term memory. (See **Figure** 11.14.)

Conrad (1964) showed how important acoustic coding of visual information can be. He briefly showed lists of six letters to his subjects and then asked them to write the letters down. The errors the subjects made were almost always acoustic rather than visual. That is, people were more likely to write D for T (these letters sound similar) than they were to write O for Q (these letters look similar). The results imply that the subjects read the letters, encoded them acoustically ("said them in their minds"), and remembered them by rehearsing the letters as sounds. During this process they might easily recall a D as a T.

Although we usually encode verbal material acoustically when we read it, it is possible to interfere with this coding, leaving only visual coding in short-term memory. Peterson and Johnson (1971) had subjects read a series of letters and then count aloud. The counting task made it difficult for them to encode the letters acoustically. Control subjects were silent, so they were able to rehearse the letters to themselves.

Try the experiment yourself. Look at the letters below, then look away and count from 85 to 100. See if you can "say the letters to yourself" as you count.

B   L   R   F   Q   D

The control subjects in Peterson and Johnson's study showed acoustic confusions upon recall. For example, they might say the letter T instead of D. However, the subjects who counted aloud did not make acoustic errors, although they remembered fewer letters, because they were not able to practice them acoustically. The results suggest that visual presentation of verbal material normally causes storage of the information in both visual and auditory short-term memory. However, when auditory mechanisms are kept busy processing verbal information (in this case, counting) the information is coded only visually.

Deep dyslexia, a syndrome produced by brain damage, provides further evidence for dual encoding of visually perceived information in both auditory and visual short-term memory. (*Dyslexia* means "reading disorder.") It is produced by severe damage to the left hemisphere, somewhere near the boundary of the occipital, temporal, and parietal lobes. This form of dyslexia is called "deep" because the words the patients speak are usually similar in meaning to the words that they attempt to read; a word's meaning is, metaphorically speaking, deeper than its acoustic representation. Patterson and Marcel (1977) described two cases of this disorder. Their patients could understand spoken speech and could repeat words that they heard.

However, they made many errors in reading. For example, *dream* might be read as "sleep." They could most easily read concrete nouns that are easy to picture, such as *lecture* or *marriage.* They had much more difficulty with less tangible words, such as *event* or *scene.*

Perhaps the patients with deep dyslexia cannot acoustically encode visually presented verbal material in short-term memory. When Patterson and Marcel read aloud nonsense words like *dube, plosh,* or *widge,* the patients had no trouble repeating them. However, they were unable to read such words themselves; they could not "sound the words out." Usually they did not even try to pronounce a nonsense word. When they did, their errors were in-teresting. For example, one patient read the non-sense word *glem* as *jewel.* In this case, the word's resemblance to *gem* may have conjured up an image of a gem, and information about this image was transmitted to Broca's area, where it was translated into the spoken word *jewel.* (See **Figure 11.15.**)

It is clear that we encode information several ways, regardless of the sensory modality through which we have received it. Conrad showed that subjects make acoustic errors when they attempt to recall printed letters, Peterson and Johnson showed that acoustic errors for printed letters are eliminated when verbal rehearsal is prevented, and the phenomenon of deep dyslexia demonstrates that we normally read two ways: acoustically and vis-

FIGURE 11.15   A hypothetical explanation for a patient's reading of *glem* as "jewel." (Adapted from

Carlson, N.R. *Physiology of Behavior,* 2nd ed. Boston: Allyn and Bacon, 1981.)

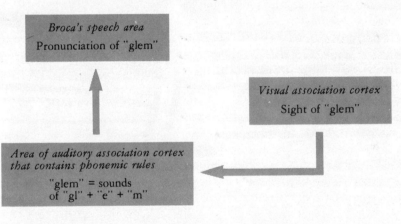

Normal person

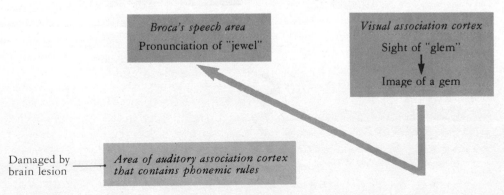

Patient with deep dyslexia

ually. Thus, we cannot say that any one sense modality accounts for short-term memory.

FAILURE OF SHORT-TERM MEMORY: DECAY OR INTERFERENCE?

The essence of short-term memory is its transience; hence its name. At present, there is good evidence that new information displaces older information from short-term memory and that previously stored information causes confusion. There is also less compelling evidence that information naturally decays from short-term memory if it is not rehearsed.

Decay

◆ In an attempt to assess the decay of information in short-term memory, Peterson and Peterson (1959) presented subjects with a set of three consonants, such as HRF, then immediately gave them a number and told them to count backward by threes from that number. For example, the number might be 417; the subjects would say, "414, 411, 408, 405," etc. The task made it difficult for the subjects to rehearse the letters acoustically at the same time. At various intervals after presenting the three letters, the experimenters stopped subjects and asked them to recall the letters. Figure 11.16 shows the results: the proportion of letters that were retained fell steadily over the eighteen-second interval. (See **Figure 11.16**.) The researchers concluded that short-term memory for the letters simply decayed over time if the material was not rehearsed. However, as we shall see, others have disputed this interpretation.

Proactive Interference

◆ There is good evidence that previously learned information can affect short-term memory. For example, suppose you are asked to read lists containing the words *muskrat, beaver, weasel, ermine, rabbit,* and *opossum* and were later given a list with the words: *mink, otter,* and *badger,* then asked to count backwards by threes from 578. After thirty seconds you are asked to recall the most recent words. Probably you will confuse the words that were presented on both occasions, even though the earlier words were in long-term and not short-term memory.

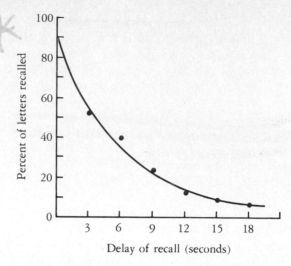

FIGURE 11.16   Percentage of letters recalled after various delays. (From Peterson, L.R., and Peterson, M.J., *Journal of Experimental Psychology,* 1959, *58,* 193–198.)

This effect is called ***proactive interference;*** previously learned information acts *forward in time,* or *proacts,* causing confusion when we attempt to learn more information later. Proactive interference probably affects the encoding of information in short-term memory, especially when the new information is similar to what we just learned. When we store new information in short-term memory we encode it in terms of previously learned information, retrieved from long-term memory. In this case when we read the words we might imagine a muskrat, a beaver, a weasel, and so on. If we later try to use similar cues to encode other information (such as mink, otter, and badger), confusion is likely to result—it is difficult to maintain clear, separate images of all these furry little animals.

Keppel and Underwood (1962) suggested that proactive interference was an important factor in the study by Peterson and Peterson, which purported to demonstrate that information in short-term memory decayed. Having noted that the Petersons administered two practice trials before their test, Keppel and Underwood used the same procedure but kept track of what happened in the first two trials. As Figure 11.17 shows, the first two trials did have an effect on those that followed: there was no evidence of decay on the first trial,

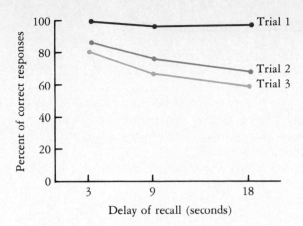

FIGURE 11.17   Percentage of items correctly recalled after the first presentation of the list. (From Keppel, G., and Underwood, B.J., *Journal of Verbal Learning and Verbal Behavior*, 1962, *1*, 153–161.)

some on the second, and even more on the third. (See **Figure 11.17**.) We cannot conclude that decay *never* occurs, but given that performance did not decline until the second trial, we must also allow for the role of proactive interference in the progressive decline thereafter.

Displacement

There is no doubt that displacement of information occurs in short-term memory. Suppose someone asks you to remember the sequence 34156, then to repeat the sequences 14635, 63154, 41356, and 53416, and finally to recall the original sequence. You will find the task hopeless; the intervening information will have made you forget the order of the original set. Numerous studies have shown that new information can displace existing information in short-term memory, and that the more similar the new information is to the existing information, the more likely interference is.

CONSOLIDATION

The transfer of information from short-term to long-term memory is usually called *consolidation*. As you will learn later, the better organized the information is, the easier it is to understand and remember it. A classic procedure illustrates the essential features of consolidation.

The Serial-Position Curve

The best way to learn about the principles established by an experiment is to be a participant yourself. First, find someone to serve as the experimenter. Give this book to the experimenter and ask him or her to recite the list of words on page 432 one at a time, pausing about two seconds between each word. (Don't look at the words yourself beforehand.) The experimenter must not hurry through the list. As soon as he or she has spoken the last word, the experimenter is to say, "OK." At this cue, write down as many of the words as you can, in any order. If you cannot find anyone to help you, use two pieces of paper, exposing only one word at a time as you move down the list. (See **Figure 11.18**.) When you get to the end of the list, write down all the words that you remember. There is no time limit for recalling the words.

* * *

As your experimenter read the list, you probably started repeating the first few words in order, mentally rehearsing them: *shirt,* then *shirt, flower,* then *shirt, flower, telephone,* and so on, until you realized that you could not get through all the items. You may have felt a twinge of anxiety: all those words, and you would forget them unless you did something! Perhaps you then started picturing the objects that the words represented, visualizing a chimney when you heard that word, or your own shoes when you heard *shoe.* When you heard the

FIGURE 11.18   Follow this procedure if you do not have someone to read the words to you.

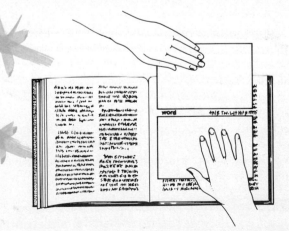

shirt

flower

telephone

carpet

sky

typewriter

basket

chimney

necktie

tree

picture

shoe

lamp

napkin

carrot

experimenter say, "napkin . . . carrot . . . OK," you probably wrote *carrot* down first, because you knew that was the last word in the list and the word was still fresh in your mind. Next you may have written down *napkin,* because it was the next-to-last word presented to you.

Once you "got rid of" the last word or two you probably tried to recall some of the images that you had formed, such as the chimney or the shoe. You probably also went back to the beginning of the list and recited the first few words—the ones you were able to rehearse until the list became too long. There is a good chance that you remembered the beginning of the list. Then you tried to picture more of your images and perhaps recalled some pairs of words that are normally associated, such as *shirt* and *necktie.*

If people are given a list of words to memorize, they tend to remember the first few words and the last few words the best, as Figure 11.19 illustrates. This *serial-position curve* represents the mean percent of items remembered in each of the locations on a list of fifteen words. (The words were presented to each person in a different order, in case some words were easier to remember than others; that is, the order of presentation was counterbalanced.) (See **Figure 11.19.**)

DELAY OF REPORTING AND THE RECENCY EFFECT
Facility in recalling the last few words in a list is

known as the *recency effect.* The following rationale explains this phenomenon: (1) Because short-term memory has a limited capacity, it can store only a few independent items at any one time; (2) if short-term memory is as full of information as it can be, the entry of new information displaces information that is already there; thus (3) short-term memory will contain the most recently perceived information.

Suppose you were unable to write down the last word or two right away because a delay was imposed after the last word was presented to you. If you kept rehearsing them, you could retain them, and eventually they would enter long-term memory. But if you were prevented from rehearsing them, the recency effect would be eliminated. Glanzer and Cunitz (1966) presented a list of fifteen words to two groups of subjects. They asked one group to recall the words right away; the other group was required to wait for thirty seconds before attempting to recall them. To make it difficult for the subjects to rehearse any information that they had in short-term memory, the researchers required the second group to count aloud during the thirty-second interval.

Figure 11.20 shows the results. The black curve represents the recall of subjects who started without delay. (This is the same curve shown in Figure 11.19.) The colored curve represents the performance of subjects who were required to count aloud for thirty seconds before beginning their recall. This group did not remember the last few words better than the earlier ones. (See **Figure 11.20.**)

These data are consistent with the conclusion that short-term memory can store only a few items, that the most recent items are the easiest to retrieve, and that new information displaces older information. Furthermore, the effect of the delay interval suggests that without some sort of rehearsal, we will eventually lose information that is stored in short-term memory.

OPPORTUNITY FOR REHEARSAL AND THE PRIMACY EFFECT   The fact that the first few items of a list are easier to remember than those in the middle is known as the *primacy effect* (*primacy* means "the state of being first"). The explanation is simple, if we assume that we need rehearsal (or some sort of

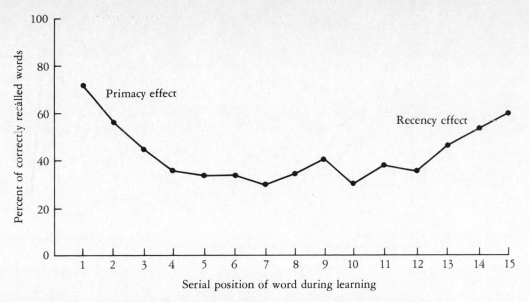

FIGURE 11.19   A serial-position curve. (From
Glanzer, M., and Cunitz, A.R., *Journal of Verbal
Learning and Verbal Behavior,* 1966, *5,* 351–360.)

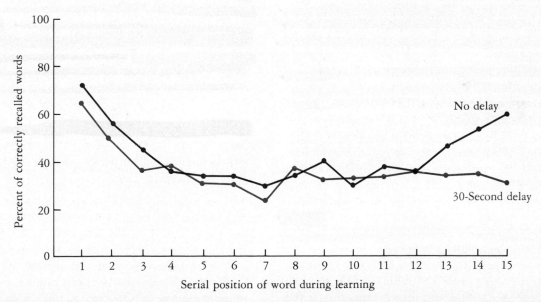

FIGURE 11.20   Serial-position curves obtained
after no delay (black curve) and after a delay of thirty
seconds (colored curve). Note the lack of the recency
effect in the colored curve. (From Glanzer, M., and
Cunitz, A.R., *Journal of Verbal Learning and Verbal
Behavior,* 1966, *5,* 351–360.)

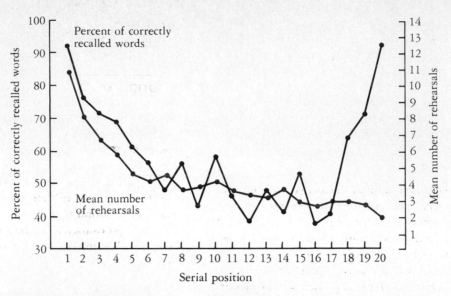

FIGURE 11.21   Probability of recall (black curve) and number of rehearsals (colored curve) as a function of serial position. (From Rundus, D., and Atkinson, R.C., *Journal of Verbal Learning and Verbal Behavior*, 1970, *9*, 99–105.)

elaboration of the material in short-term memory) in order to store information in long-term memory. The more time we spend in this rehearsal or elaboration, the more likely it is that the information will enter long-term memory and be available for recall later.

It is easy to rehearse the first few words, but as we hear more and more words, we reach a point where it becomes impossible to review them all. Rundus and Atkinson (1970) asked subjects to rehearse out loud and made tape recordings of their practice. They found that subjects rehearsed the words at the beginning of the list more often than the later ones. Figure 11.21 shows the number of rehearsals of each item. (This curve is similar to the first part of the serial-position curve.) The fact that the first few items received more rehearsal may account for the primacy effect. The relation between rehearsal and recall broke down at the end of the list because of the recency effect, but the last few items were withdrawn from short-term, not long-term, memory. (See **Figure 11.21**.)

In another experiment, Waugh and Norman (1965) asked their subjects to rehearse only the *current* item—that is, the one that was just presented—and not to go back and rehearse earlier items. Thus, if the subjects followed instructions, each item received approximately the same amount of rehearsal, and subjects could not link stimuli like "shirt" and "necktie" because doing so would involve thinking about more than one item. Waugh and Norman found that this procedure eliminated the primacy effect. Because all items received the same amount of rehearsal, the first few were not recalled any better than the ones in the middle.

Effects of Head Injury on Consolidation

From the earliest times, people have observed that a blow to the head can affect memory. Let us consider an imaginary case.

Fred, a baseball player, is standing on first base. The pitcher begins his windup, and Fred takes a few steps toward second base. The pitch is wild, and the catcher loses his balance while reaching for it. Taking advantage of the momentary confusion, Fred runs for second base. The catcher sees him running, jumps to his feet, and throws the ball to second base just as Fred arrives there. Fred's foot touches the base in time, but his head comes between the ball, which has been thrown a bit high, and the second baseman's glove. The ball hits Fred just above the ear, and he crumples to the ground. He regains consciousness in the dugout, sees his teammates gathered around him, and sits up slowly. "What happened to me?" he asks. He sits for a while, dazed, then shakes his head tentatively and decides that he will be all right. "I'm OK. I'll go back on base." He leaves the dugout and heads for first base. "Hey!" one of his teammates yells. "You were on second—you stole second base." Fred looks at him incredulously but notes that other teammates are nodding. It must be true. He walks to second base, feeling puzzled.

In innumerable similar incidents, people have been bumped on the head and have forgotten what happened immediately before the injury. A blow to the head makes the brain bump against the inside of the skull, and this movement apparently disrupts its normal functioning. Short-term memory is affected, but not long-term memory. A lack of memory for events that occurred just before an injury is called *retrograde amnesia*. In the case of our baseball player, Fred stood on first base long enough to form a long-term memory for having been there. He saw the wild pitch, ran to second base, and got hit on the head. His memory of the run to second base was in short-term storage and was destroyed when the normal functioning of his brain was temporarily disrupted.

From such events we can draw two tentative conclusions. Because only recently perceived information is disrupted by a minor head injury (1) short-term and long-term memory must be physiologically different, and (2) the transfer of information from short-term to long-term memory must take time. Information stored in fragile short-term memory is consolidated into the more stable long-term memory.

Effects of Electroshock Treatment on Consolidation

In 1937, Ugo Cerletti, an Italian psychiatrist, developed a treatment for mental illness that later became important for the study of the consolidation of memory. Previously, von Meduna had noted that schizophrenic patients who were also subject to epileptic seizures showed improvement immediately after each attack. Von Meduna reasoned that the violent storm of neural activity in the brain that constitutes an epileptic seizure somehow improved the patients' mental condition. He de-

veloped a way to produce seizures by administering a drug, but the procedure was dangerous. Cerletti discovered that the local slaughterhouse applied a jolt of electricity to animals' heads to stun them before killing them. The electricity appeared to produce a seizure that resembled an epileptic attack. He decided to try to use electricity to induce a seizure more safely.

Cerletti tried the procedure on dogs and found that an electric shock to the skull did produce a seizure and that the animals recovered with no apparent ill effects. He then used the procedure on humans and found it to be safer than the chemical treatment previously used. As a result, *electroshock treatment* became one of the most used—and most abused—treatments for mental illness. Although it is useful for treatment of severe psychotic depression, as we shall see in Chapter 18, we now know that electroshock treatment is not useful for the treatment of schizophrenia.

As soon as electroshock treatment came into therapeutic use, it was seen to produce amnesia for recent events. Zubin and Barrera (1941) confirmed that people who received electroshock treatments could not remember afterward what had happened just before the electric current was applied. These investigators asked patients to learn a list of words before receiving an electroshock treatment. The subjects could not recall the words they had learned immediately before electroshock, but they could remember words they had learned earlier.

Soon investigators recognized electroshock treatment as a means of producing amnesia in experimental animals, thus preventing the consolidation of memory. For example, Chorover and Schiller (1965) placed rats on a small wooden platform surrounded by a floor consisting of metal rods. When the animals stepped off the platform onto

FIGURE 11.22   An apparatus for training a passive avoidance response.

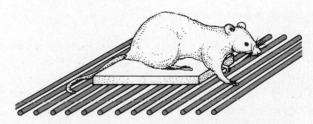

the rods, an electric current was passed through the metal gridwork, giving the animals a brief, painful footshock. Normally, animals that receive such a shock remain on the platform when they are placed there the next day. (See **Figure 11.22.**) Chorover and Schiller administered an electroshock after the footshock, through earringlike clips attached to the animals' ears. Some animals received the electroshock immediately after the footshock; others received it after a delay period. Figure 11.23 shows that the rats that received the electroshock right away appeared to have forgotten the footshock: when tested the next day, they stepped right off the platform. The rats that received the electroshock after a delay of thirty seconds remained on the platform the next day; they acted as if they remembered the footshock. (See **Figure 11.23.**)

These results indicate that electroshock treatment, like head injury, prevents consolidation. Probably the storm of neural activity disrupts short-term memory and thus prevents the transfer of information to long-term memory. A single electroshock treatment does not damage long-term memory, but repeated treatment can cause permanent harm. Patients who have received hundreds of electroshock treatments have suffered long-term memory loss and become unable to learn anything new.

Because a single electroshock treatment disrupts

short-term memory but not long-term memory, we can conclude that the brain stores old and new memories in different ways. The most likely explanation is that short-term memories are held by means of neural activity; that is, the information is encoded as a particular pattern of neural firing. Rehearsal amounts to an intentional prolonging of this activity. If something disrupts the pattern before consolidation takes place, the information is lost. An electroshock treatment can produce the disruption by causing neurons to fire wildly, and a mild head injury can temporarily depress the ability of neurons to respond normally.

The physiological evidence suggests that long-term memory involves some physical change in the neural structure of the brain that is not disrupted by electroshock treatment or by mild head injury. That is, there seems to be some sort of "wiring change" that encodes the information. For example, certain synapses between neurons may change in size, or new synaptic connections may develop.

Interim summary: Information in short-term memory is encoded (chunked) according to previously learned rules; thus, information in long-term memory determines the nature of the coding. Although short-term memory holds only about seven items of independent information, efficient coding means that this limit is not very restrictive.

Because short-term memory contains information retrieved from long-term memory as well as newly perceived information, many investigators conceive of it as a "working" memory. Research data and a set of informal experiments have shown that each sensory modality has its own short-term (working) memory, although their contents are shared by means of interconnections. Physiological evidence (the effects of isolation of the speech areas and the stimulation study with monkeys) supports this conclusion. Complex behaviors like reading involve cross-modal encoding of information. Brain damage can disrupt the ability to decode letters into sounds (deep dyslexia) without destroying the ability to recognize the meaning of words that represent concrete objects.

Not all information that enters short-term memory subsequently enters long-term memory (is consolidated). Some is lost by proactive interference from previously learned material. Other information is displayed by new material before it

FIGURE 11.23 Avoidance as a function of delay between receiving a footshock and receiving electroshock treatment. (From Chorover, S.L., and Schiller, P.H. *Journal of Comparative and Physiological Psychology*, 1965, 59, 73–78.)

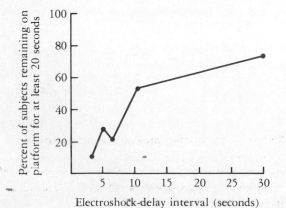

can be consolidated. Although it is possible that some short-term memories may be lost by decay, the evidence is not compelling.

The experiments relating to the nature of the serial-position curve confirm what we have already concluded from everyday experience: short-term memory has a limited capacity, and information there is subject to displacement by new information; and long-term memory has unlimited capacity and receives information by means of rehearsal or elaboration of items contained in short-term memory. Data from head injuries and electroshock treatment provide evidence that long-term and short-term memory are physiologically different: short-term memory probably involves neural activity (which can be prolonged by rehearsal) and long-term memory probably involves permanent structural changes in neurons.

LONG-TERM MEMORY

SENSORY CODING IN LONG-TERM MEMORY

Like short-term memory, long-term memory retains information that is encoded in terms of sense modality and in terms of links with information that was learned earlier (that is, *meaning*). Although some investigators have suggested that long-term memory retains only meaning, independent of the sensory modality through which the information was learned, everyday experience suggests otherwise. Sensory coding occurs in long-term memory: we can recognize previously learned information by sight, sound, touch, smell, and taste. *Recognition* involves remembering that the stimulus is similar to one we previously perceived; this process requires us to withdraw information from long-term memory. If long-term memories did not contain sensory information, we could not recognize information received through our sense modalities. For example, if acoustic information were not stored in long-term memory, we could never recognize a series of sounds as words.

As we saw from the case of the woman with brain damage caused by poison gas, the auditory cortex (including Wernicke's area) is both necessary and sufficient for short-term and long-term auditory memory. Another syndrome illustrates the localization of auditory long-term memory and provides evidence concerning storage of the meaning and spelling of words.

People with minor damage to Wernicke's area, a region of the auditory association cortex, have difficulty perceiving closely related speech sounds, such as *tip, dip,* and *pip* (Luria, 1970). They also make acoustical errors in *writing.* For example, a patient who is asked to write *dart* may write *tart.* The error does not involve a misunderstanding of the word itself; even when asked to write the word for "that thing with feathers and a sharp point that you throw at a target in an English pub," the patient will write *tart,* not *dart.* The problem involves confusion of letters that have similar sounds but not of letters that take similar movements to produce (handwritten *a* and *o*).

A plausible explanation stems from the fact that we first learn words acoustically; we hear the speech of other people and learn which sounds are associated with which objects and actions. Subsequent recognition of the words is based on acoustic information. Because Wernicke's area is necessary for these processes, it appears that our memory for the sounds of words is stored at least partly there. The same holds true for spelling; when we learn to spell, we learn the association between the letters and the sounds they make. Thus, minor damage to Wernicke's area impairs both the ability to distinguish between similar sounds and the ability to spell words correctly.

People who have been deaf since birth provide a natural control groups for this phenomenon. They never learn the association between the sound of a word and its meaning. They learn that the sight of a printed word (or the hand movements that represent a word by sign language) is associated with the sight and touch of a particular object or action. (See **Figure 11.24.**) There is no opportunity to sound the word out and spell it phonetically, as people with hearing do. (A young child trying to write will make lip movements accompanying the writing movements. In fact, Luria also found that young children had great difficulty writing if they were required to keep their mouth open or hold their tongue between their teeth to prevent speech.) Damage to Wernicke's area does *not* affect the spelling ability of deaf people (Luria, 1970), because no auditory learning takes place. Thus, deaf people and those who can hear store memories for spelling in different places in the brain.

FIGURE 11.24   A word expressed in sign language is based on visual and somatosensory features, not acoustic ones.

People who can write and speak Chinese constitute another control group. Written Chinese is not phonetic; the symbols represent pictures or ideas, not sounds. Because each word has its own character, Chinese people learn the relation between the meanings of words and the appearance of the corresponding characters (and the movements one makes to draw them). Therefore, spoken and written Chinese are two separate languages. Chinese speakers who suffer damage to Wernicke's area have difficulty in auditory recognition, but their writing is unaffected (Luria, 1970). Similarly, Japanese words can be represented phonetically, by *kana* symbols, or pictorially (like Chinese), by *kanji* symbols. (See **Figure 11.25.**) Damage to Wernicke's area disrupts the writing of *kana* (acoustically coded) symbols but not *kanji* (visually coded) symbols (Sasanuma, 1975). Thus, *the place in the brain where the memory for a symbol is stored depends on the sense modality through which it was learned*.

People whose Wernicke's area is totally destroyed lose not only the ability to spell words, but also the memory of their *meaning*. Their talk is a babble of meaningless syllables and phrases. However, if the damage is limited to Wernicke's area they can respond appropriately—though nonverbally—to visual stimuli. For example, they can demonstrate how to use a toothbrush or a knife and fork, and they generally respond appropriately in social situations.

A patient that I studied provided yet another example of the storage of different memories in different parts of the brain. The woman had suffered a stroke that damaged the parietal region of her brain. Her speech was excellent and she appeared to be intelligent and alert, but she had difficulty with spatial relations. For example, she could not tell time any longer by looking at a clock with hands and was unable to draw a simple three-dimensional representation of a house. She also had difficulty talking about the things she had difficulty perceiving. For example, when I asked her, "Is the floor up or down?" she would say "up" as often as "down," even though she could point to the floor when asked to do so. When I asked her to choose the appropriate word for a sentence like

FIGURE 11.25   Japanese *kanji* symbols, derived from Chinese characters, provide no guide to pronunciation and must be learned individually.

"After a preliminary discussion, they got _____ to business," she immediately said "down." Thus, she was unable to use words like *up* or *down* in sentences signifying spatial relations, but for other sentences using the same words she performed normally. Her case provides evidence that different meanings of the same word are stored in different parts of the brain. The spatial meaning of down requires the parietal cortex; other meanings do not. We may conclude that long-term memories are organized in the brain according to categories that are closely related to specialized functions of different parts of the brain.

As we saw in Chapter 10, cognitive processing in the brain can occur cross-modally. The same is true for interactions among different long-term memories. That is, when we retrieve a memory of an object we can simultaneously recall what it looks like, sounds like, and feels like. Even though the memories of these properties appear to be stored in different locations, they are somehow tied together, undoubtedly by cortical association fibers. Thus, any form of sensory input can cause the retrieval of all modes of storage. The sight of a kitten

FIGURE 11.26   Does the image of the kitten evoke for you a somatosensory memory?

recalls its furry softness; the sound of a whistle in the distance evokes an image of a train. (See **Figure 11.26.**)

STORAGE OF MEMORY

◆ One way to store information from short-term memory in long-term memory is to rehearse it. But there are more and less efficient ways to rehearse.

Rehearsal

Suppose someone gives you the following words to remember:

tree   house   man   car

You could simply repeat this sequence until you learned it, but remembering would be much easier if you pictured a scene involving the words: a *tree* falls on a *house* and makes it collapse. A *man* emerges from the wreckage, gets into his *car,* and drives off for help. Picturing that scene once or twice is probably far more effective than saying the four words to yourself a dozen times. (Try it.)

Craik and Watkins (1973) have designated two kinds of rehearsal: *maintenance* and *elaborative rehearsal.* Maintenance is a repetition of words in short-term memory without any attempt to make sense of them; the repetition simply *maintains* the information in short-term memory. In contrast, elaborative rehearsal consists in organizing the information so that it forms a coherent whole, and especially so that it becomes integrated with prior information in long-term memory.

Craik and Watkins presented their subjects with several lists of words and asked them to remember the last four words on each list, rehearsing them aloud, because they would be tested after a delay. After each list was presented, the subjects rehearsed the four words and easily repeated them, then they moved on to the next list. After some lists there was a long delay interval, so that the four words were rehearsed many times. At the end of the experiment, the subjects were asked to recall as many of the rehearsed words as they could. This came as a surprise; the subjects had thought they were through with a list of words as soon as they moved on to the next one.

The results showed that the likelihood of recalling a particular word was not related to the amount of rehearsal. The words that had been rehearsed many times were *not* more likely to be remembered than words that had been rehearsed only a few times. Craik and Watkins concluded that the rehearsals were merely a form of maintenance; the subjects kept the information in short-term memory, but because they made no attempt to elaborate on the information, to process it and fit it in with other information already in long-term memory, rehearsal had little effect on the subjects' ability to retrieve it later.

The evidence suggests that the process of consolidation entails far more than making short-term memories solid—it entails the cataloging of new information, the integration of new information with old, and the construction of retrieval cues. There might indeed be such a thing as passive, rote learning, but the role of cataloging is so important that it overshadows less active forms of memory storage.

Cataloging and the Formation of Retrieval Cues

When a book is purchased by a library, it is cataloged before being put into the stacks. The cataloging is organized by author, title, and subject to enable readers to find the book. Suppose the book is about hypnosis. A person interested in this subject will look up "hypnosis" in the card catalog, find the entry, and make a note of the code number identifying the location of the book. Without the cataloging system, the reader would probably be unable to find the book. And if the book is not cataloged and placed in the proper location in the stacks, it may as well not be there at all. The same is true for memories. It is one thing to store information in long-term memory; it is quite another to retrieve it. The information must be "cataloged" when it is stored so that it will be accessible later.

◆ USE OF CONTEXT   An ingenious experiment by Craik and Tulving (1975) demonstrates the importance of the construction of retrieval cues. Subjects were handed cards, each containing a printed sentence with a missing word, denoted by a blank line, such as "The _____ is torn." After reading the sentence, the subjects looked at a word flashed on a screen, then pressed a button as quickly as possible to signify whether or not the word fit the sentence. In this example, *dress* would fit, but *table* would not.

The sentences varied in complexity. Some were very simple, such as:

She cooked the _____.

The _____ is torn.

Others were complex, such as:

The great bird swooped down and carried off the struggling _____.

The old man hobbled across the room and picked up the valuable _____.

The same word could be used for either a simple or complex sentence: "She cooked the *chicken*," or "The great bird swooped down and carried off the struggling *chicken*." All subjects who participated saw a given word once, in either a simple or a complex sentence.

No mention was made of a memory test, so there was no reason for the subjects to try to remember the words. However, after responding to the sentences, they were presented with them again and asked to recall the words they used. Figure 11.27 shows that subjects were more likely to remember a word if it previously fit into a complex

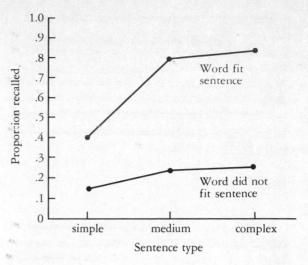

FIGURE 11.27   Proportion of words recalled as a function of the complexity of the sentence in which they were embedded. (From Craik, F.I.M., and Tulving, E. *Journal of Experimental Psychology: General,* 1975, *104,* 268–294.)

sentence than if it fit into a simple one. If a word did not fit the sentence at all, it was unlikely to be remembered, and complexity had no effect. (See **Figure 11.27.**)

These results suggest that the likelihood of recalling a word depends on the number of cues that are associated with it. Consider the different images conjured up by the two sentences:

He dropped the *watch.*

The old man hobbled across the room and picked up the valuable *watch.*

The second sentence is rich with cues for retrieval of the target word. The more elaborate the context, the more links that can be formed among different individual memories. There is no need to retrieve the word *watch* in isolation; the word, or rather an image of the object it represents, is associated with a visual image of a scene in which the object fits.

CATEGORIZATION   One way to form retrieval cues is to organize information into categories. If you try to recite as many concrete nouns as you can think of, you will probably find yourself going through different categories, saying as many related words as you can before trying a new category. Or you might picture a scene, such as a familiar room, and describe the items contained in that scene. You will not retrieve nouns randomly from memory; there will be some order and organization to your recall. In fact, lack of organization when trying to recite words spontaneously is a characteristic of damage to the frontal cortex.

◆ An experiment by Tulving and Psotka (1971) showed how important categorization is for storage and retrieval of information. They presented subjects with six lists of twenty-four words like the following: *zinc, copper, aluminium, bronze; orange, apple, pear, melon; hut, cottage, tent, hotel; cliff, river, hill, volcano; captain, corporal, sergeant, colonel; ant, wasp, beetle, mosquito.* They presented each list three times, then asked the subjects to recall the words. **Figure 11.28** presents the results. The colored curve shows that the recall of words from the most recently presented lists was best. The gray curve shows a strong effect of ***retroactive interference;*** that is, the most recent lists appeared to interfere with retrieval of earlier words from long-term memory. The black curve shows performance when subjects were given the names of the categories of the words they had read, such as metals, fruits, and build-

ings. With these category names as retrieval cues, the subjects did very well at recalling the words. In fact their performance was about as good as when memory was tested immediately after learning each list. Retroactive interference did not occur; items from early lists were recalled nearly as well as items from later ones.

The results show that people classify and categorize information even if they are not asked to do so, and that information about categories serves as an effective retrieval cue for the items in them. The results also suggest that retroactive interference, at least as it applies to long-term memory, does *not* involve displacement of old items by new ones. There is an anecdote about an ichthyology professor who refused to learn his students' names because every time he learned a student's name he forgot the name of a fish. However, the experiment by Tulving and Psotka suggests that old memories remain despite the introduction of newer ones. With appropriate retrieval cues, we can recall older items as well as new ones.

MEANING: EPISODIC AND SEMANTIC LONG-TERM MEMORY

◆ Long-term memory not only stores sensory information about original perceptions of certain particular stimuli; it also transforms information, organizing it in terms of meaning. A study by Sachs (1967) shows that as a memory gets older, sensory information becomes somewhat less important than meaning. Subjects read a passage of prose containing a *test sentence* but were not told which one it was. One test sentence was:

> He sent a letter about it to Galileo,
> the great Italian scientist.

At varying intervals (from 0 to 160 syllables later) Sachs presented another sentence (the *comparison sentence*) and asked the subjects whether it was the same as or different from the earlier one. The comparison sentence was sometimes the same and sometimes different. Differences might involve meaning or only word order, as in the following:

> Galileo, the great Italian scientist,
> sent him a letter about it.
> (different meaning)

FIGURE 11.28   Mean number of words recalled as a function of number of lists that were learned between original learning and testing. (From Tulving, E., and Psotka, J. *Journal of Experimental Psychology.* 1971, 87, 1–8.)

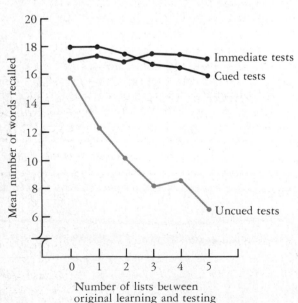

He sent Galileo, the great Italian scientist,
a letter about it.
(same meaning, different word order)

The results, shown in Figure 11.29, reveal that
the subjects found it easy to tell any of the sentences apart when there was no delay between the
original sentence and the comparison sentence.
When a delay was introduced they had difficulty
remembering the specific word order of the original
sentence, but they made very few errors in meaning, even with a 160-syllable delay. (See **Figure
11.29**.) Thus, information about the *form* of a sentence disappears faster than information about its
meaning as the sentence enters long-term memory.

The distinction between information about specific items and more general information about
meaning has led to the suggestion that there are
two kinds of long-term memory: ***episodic memory***
and ***semantic memory*** (Tulving, 1972). Episodic
memory consists of memory about specific things
we have done, seen, heard, felt, tasted, and so on.
Semantic memory consists of more abstract and
conceptual rules, such as our knowledge that the
sun is a star and that humans are mammals. We
can remember when we formed episodic memories.
That is their very nature; they are memories of
episodes, with information about specific perceptions along with information that places it in a
context of time. In contrast, we probably forget

FIGURE 11.29   Results of the experiment by
Sachs (1967).

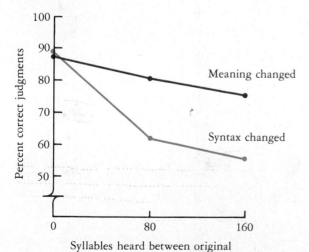

when we learned that the sun is a star. Although
we have developed semantic memories on specific
occasions—someone told us that the sun is a star,
or we read this fact in a book—we have come across
this information so many times that we have forgotten when we first learned it. In this sense, then,
a particular item in semantic memory contains *less*
information than a similar item in episodic memory.

When I come to work I always park my car in
the lot adjacent to the building. When I leave the
building each evening I have to remember where
I parked my car that day. This information is episodic. I know that I parked my car somewhere in
the lot, but sometimes I cannot remember just
where. The reason I sometimes forget is that I have
parked my car in that lot so many times that one
episode becomes confused with the others. Similarly, episodic memories blur together to yield semantic memory. For this reason, neuropsychological investigations are unlikely to prove that episodic
and semantic memories are anatomically distinct.

Semantic memory can be more than degraded
episodic memory. It is also a product of thinking
about what we have already learned. Sometimes we
think about things that we already know (we retrieve information from long-term memory and put
it in working memory). We think things over,
realize that some facts are related, and come to
some conclusions. These conclusions are stored in
long-term memory; they are something new that
we know. If we remember the occasions when we
came to these conclusions, the memory will be
episodic. More likely, we will forget these details
and develop a new semantic memory. For example,
in writing this book I have read articles and books
by many other people, and have taken notes to help
me remember what I read. Later I have looked at
the notes and thought about what I have learned.
Sometimes I realize that several different experiments are related; I can infer a common principle
from them. Forming a conclusion causes it to be
stored in my long-term semantic memory.

RECONSTRUCTION:
MEMORY AS A CREATIVE PROCESS

People can remember more information later when
the items presented fit together and form a coherent story. Consider the following set of sentences:

A store contained a row of wooden cages.
A man bought a dog. A child wanted an
animal. A father drove to his house. . . .
A boy was delighted with a gift.

deVilliers (1974) presented one group of subjects with these sentences and another group with the following set:

The store contained a row of wooden cages.
The man bought a dog. The child wanted
the animal. The father drove to his house. . . .
The boy was delighted with the gift.

When tested later, the subjects who had read the first set remembered less information. The second set of sentences is identical to the first, except that the definite article (*the*) replaces indefinite articles (*a, an*). Both sets of sentences contain the same amount of information, yet the use of the definite article suggests that the statements are connected. The use of the word *the* implies that the noun to which it refers is familiar; it is something that the reader or listener already knows something about. Therefore, people encountering the second set of sentences tended to perceive them as connected parts of a story. Presumably, items of information are encoded and stored more effectively when they are part of a whole, and their coherence facilitates later retrieval.

◆ Much of what we retrieve from long-term memory is not an accurate representation of what actually happened previously; it is a plausible account of what might have happened, or even of what we think *should* have happened. An experiment by Bartlett (1932) called attention to this fact. He had his subjects read a story or essay or look at a picture, then asked them later on several occasions to retell the prose passage or draw the picture. Each time, the subjects "remembered" the original a little differently. If a story contained peculiar and unexpected sequences of events, the subjects tended to retell the story in a more coherent and sensible fashion, as if they had revised their memories to make the information accord more closely with their own conceptions of reality. Bartlett concluded that people remember only a few striking details of an experience, and that during recall they *reconstruct* the missing portions in accordance with their own expectations.

Many studies have confirmed Bartlett's conclusions and have extended his findings to related phe-

nomena. An experiment by Spiro (1976) illustrates that people will remember even a rather simple story in different ways, according to their conceptions of reality. Two groups of subjects read a story about an engaged couple, in which the man was opposed to having children. In one version, the woman was upset to learn this, because she wanted to have children. In the other version, the woman also did not want to have children.

After reading the story, the subjects were asked to fill out some forms. While collecting the forms the experimenter either said nothing more about the story or "casually mentioned" one of two different endings: the couple got married and have been happy ever since, or the couple broke up and never saw each other again.

Two days, three weeks, or six weeks later, the subjects were asked to recall the story they had read. If at least three weeks had elapsed the subjects who heard an ending that contradicted the story tended to "remember" information that resolved the conflict. For example, if they had read that the woman was upset to learn that the man did not want children, but were later told that the couple was happily married, the subjects were likely to "recall" something that would have resolved the conflict, such as that the couple had decided to adopt a child rather than have one of their own. If subjects had read that the woman also did not want children but were later told that the couple broke up, then they were likely to "remember" that there was a difficulty with one set of parents. In contrast, the subjects who heard an ending that was consistent with the story they had read did not remember any extra facts; they did not need them to make sense of the story. For example, if they heard that the couple disagreed about having a child and later broke up, no new "facts" had to be added.

Experiments like this indicate that learning new information and recalling it later are not the passive processes that are implied by the terms *storage* and *retrieval;* we do not simply place an item of information in a filing cabinet and pick it up later. We organize and integrate information in terms of what we already know about life and have come to expect about particular experiences. Thus, when we recall the memory later, it is likely to contain information that was not part of the original experience.

AIDS TO MEMORY: MNEMONIC SYSTEMS

◆ Some things are exceedingly easy to remember. Suppose you are walking down the street and see someone fall from the roof of a building. You will not have to rehearse this information verbally to remember it; you see it so vividly that the scene remains with you always. Similarly, you can probably remember the missing word in the sentence: "The old man hobbled across the room and picked up the valuable _____." And can you remember the sequence of four words listed earlier? (Hint: the first one is *tree*.)

When we can imagine information vividly and concretely, and when it fits into the context of what we already know, it is easy to remember later. People have known this fact for millenia and have devised systems for remembering things in order to take advantage of it. All *mnemonic systems* (from Greek *mneme,* or "memory") make use of information that is already stored in long-term memory to incorporate new information.

Mnemonic systems do not simplify information; in fact, they make it more elaborate. *More* information is stored, not less. However, the additional information makes the material easier to recall. Furthermore, mnemonic systems organize new information into a cohesive whole, so that retrieval of part of the information ensures retrieval of the rest of it. (If you remember the tree falling on the house, you can probably remember all the other words on the list.) These facts suggest that the ease or difficulty with which we learn new information depends not on *how much* we must learn, but on *how well it fits with what we already know.* The better it fits, the easier it is to retrieve.

Method of Loci

In Greece before the sixth century B.C., few people knew how to write, and those who did had to use cumbersome clay tablets. Consequently, oratory skills and memory for long epic poems (running for several hours) were highly prized, and some people earned a living by using them. Because people could not carry around several hundred pounds of clay tablets, they had to keep important information in their heads. To do this, the Greeks devised the *method of loci* (*loci* means "places").

To use the method of loci, would-be mnemon-ists (memory artists) had to memorize the inside of a building. In Greece, they would wander through public buildings, stopping to study and memorize various locations and arranging them in order, usually starting with the door of the building. After memorizing the locations, they made the tour mentally. To learn a list of words, they would visualize each word in a particular location in the memorized building and picture the association as vividly as possible. For example, for the word *love* they might imagine an embracing couple leaning against a particular column in a hall of the building. To recall the list, they would imagine each of the locations in sequence, "see" the word, and say it. To store a speech, they would group the words into concepts and place a "note" for each concept at each location.

Mnemonists could use a single building as a "memory temple" to store many different sequences. Modern psychologists still cannot explain why sequences from different speeches or poems did not become confused with each other.

Narrative Stories

Another useful aid to memory is to organize information into a narrative, as in the example of a tree falling on a house. Bower and Clark (1969) showed that even inexperienced subjects can use this method. The investigators asked subjects to try to learn twelve lists of 10 concrete nouns. They gave some of the subjects the following advice:

> A good way to learn the list of items is to make up a story relating the items to one another. Specifically, start with the first item and put it in a setting which will allow other items to be added to it. Then, add the other items to the story in the same order as the items appear. Make each story meaningful to yourself. Then, when you are asked to recall the items, you can simply go through your story and pull out the proper items in their correct order.

A typical narrative, described by one of the subjects, was as follows (list words are italicized): "A *lumberjack darted* out of the forest, *skated* around a *hedge* past a *colony* of *ducks.* He tripped on some *furniture,* tearing his *stocking* while hastening to the *pillow* where his *mistress* lay."

Control subjects were merely asked to learn the lists and were given the same amount of time as the "narrative" subjects to study them. Immediate

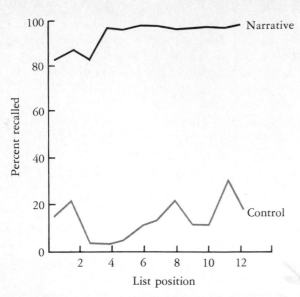

FIGURE 11.30 Percentage of words recalled by control subjects and by subjects who used a narrative strategy. (From Bower, G.H., and Clark, M.C. *Psychonomic Science,* 1969, *13,* 181–182.)

recall after each list had been rehearsed was equivalent. However, when all the lists had been learned, recall of all 120 words was far superior in the group that had constructed narrative stories. **Figure 11.30** shows the results.

Interim summary: Some memories survive the transitory nature of sensory memory and short-term memory and become part of long-term memory. Once there, they need no longer be rehearsed or "thought about," but will remain for later use. Neuropsychological evidence indicates that long-term memory, like short-term memory, is located in separate modality-specific regions of the brain. For example, memory for the spelling of words may be located in different regions, depending on whether a person learns symbols in association with specific sounds (as with the letters used in the English language) or in association with visual stimuli (as with Chinese ideograms or Japanese *kanji* symbols). The case of the woman with parietal-lobe damage shows that the memory of different meanings of a single word can be located in different regions of the cerebral cortex. Because these memories are linked for people without brain damage, we experience a unified memory.

Memories are cataloged and cross-referenced in long-term storage. The establishment of contextual retrieval cues and names of categories seem to be the most important factors in the later retrieval of information. In support of this assertion, you can probably remember the end of the sentence, "The great bird swooped down and carried off the struggling _____," and some of the names of metals,

FIGURE 11.31 A model of human memory that includes some of the features discussed in this chapter. Only auditory and visual memory are

considered; a more complete model would include the other sense modalities and motor memory.

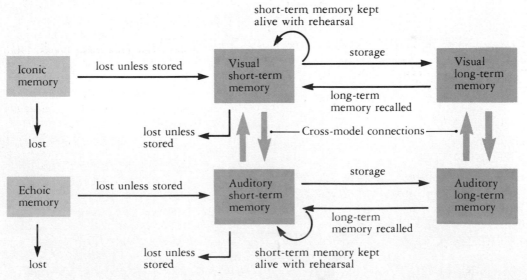

fruits, and buildings that I mentioned earlier. Mere rehearsal is not a good method for learning new material.

Episodic memory and semantic memory refer to different degrees of specificity in long-term memories: we can remember the time and place we learned an episodic memory, but not a semantic memory. However, semantic memories are not simply degraded episodic memories; in some cases they are logical deductions from other memories.

Recall is not simply the replaying of a tape that has been recorded in our brain; it entails a process of reconstruction that sometimes introduces new "facts" that we perceive as memories of what we previously experienced. As the effectiveness of mnemonic systems attests, memory is not limited by complexity; in fact, complex information is often easier to learn than simple information, so long as it is internally consistent and can be integrated with what we already know.

CONCLUDING REMARKS

The rules by which information is encoded in sensory memory, short-term memory, and long-term memory appear to be different; so do the physical means by which the information is represented in the brain. Memories appear to be specific to the sense modalities but are linked with each other cross-modally.

Figure 11.31 summarizes some of the more important features of the memory process.

GUIDE TO TERMS INTRODUCED IN THIS CHAPTER

SUGGESTIONS FOR FURTHER READING

Given the importance of learning and forgetting in almost everyone's life, it is not surprising that many popular books have been written about human memory. *The Mind of a Mnemonist* by A.R. Luria is the great Russian neurologist's account of a man with an extraordinary memory (New York: Basic Books, 1968). *Memory Observed: Remembering in Natural Contexts* by U. Neisser (San Francisco: W.H. Freeman, 1982) consists of studies about remembering in natural contexts, rather than arbitrary ones contrived in the laboratory. *Memory* by E.F. Loftus (Reading, Mass.: Addison Wesley, 1980), written for the general reader, discusses the tricks our memories can play on us when we try to remember what we have seen.

If you are interested in improving your own memory, there are dozens of books to choose from, including L.S. Cermak's *Improving Your Memory* (New York: Norton, 1975) and *The Memory Book* by R. Lorayne and J. Lucas (New York: Stein & Day, 1974).

LANGUAGE

LEARNING ◆ OBJECTIVES

WITH THE exception of sexual behavior (without which our species would not survive), communication is probably the most important of all human social behaviors. This chapter discusses verbal communication (nonverbal communication is examined in Chapter 14). As we saw in Chapter 10, our use of language can be private—we can think to ourselves in words or write diaries that are meant to be seen by no one but ourselves—but language evolved through social contacts among our early ancestors. Speaking and writing are clearly social behaviors: we learn these skills from other people and use them to communicate with them. (See **Figure 12.1.**)

◆   Many psychologists use the term ***verbal behav-***

ior to refer to the use of language—the acts of speaking, listening, writing, or reading—because it emphasizes the fact that speaking, listening, writing, and reading *are* behaviors and, like other behaviors, can be studied. Linguists have studied the "rules" of language and have described precisely what we do when we speak or write. On the other hand, researchers in ***psycholinguistics*** (a branch of psychology) are more concerned with human cognition than with the particular rules that describe language. Psycholinguists are interested in how children acquire language—how verbal behavior develops and how children learn to speak from their interactions with adults. They also investigate the role of cognitive development in the

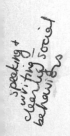

450

FIGURE 12.1 Communication is an important social behavior.

acquisition of language. These issues, rather than the concerns of linguists, are the focus of this chapter. The major topics discussed here are the functions of language, the perception of speech, understanding meaning, the brain mechanisms involved in verbal behaviors, and children's acquisition of speech. It also considers whether other primates can acquire verbal behaviors.

◆ Our verbal behavior, both written and oral, is orderly. Linguists would say that our speech follows grammatical rules. For example, English sentences contain noun phrases and verb phrases, and most questions in English are formed by placing the modal auxiliary in front of the verb. But both linguists and psycholinguists acknowledge that people who use language correctly do not consciously learn these rules. (Most people do not know what a modal auxiliary is even though they can use it properly.) Linguists did not invent the rules of language any more than physicists invented the laws of thermodynamics; they discovered them by studying people's speech and writing. The rules

are *descriptions of what people do* when they engage in verbal behavior; they are not *prescriptions for* verbal behavior.

This distinction becomes clearer if we consider another skilled behavior: riding a bicycle. Physicists know how we can balance on a vehicle with two narrow wheels: it involves inertia, gyroscopic effects of rotating wheels, locating our center of gravity, and other factors, all of which can be incorporated into complicated mathematical equations. Still, knowing these rules does not really help a person to ride a bicycle. A physicist who wants to learn to ride a bicycle must learn the same way that a child does—by getting on and trying.

Similarly, our behavior must conform to the rules of our language or we will not be understood by others. However, we do not have to be able to *state* these rules, any more than a bird has to "know" the laws of aerodynamics in order to be able to fly.

THE FUNCTIONS OF LANGUAGE

The ability to engage in verbal behavior confers decided advantages on our species. As we saw in Chapter 10, we can profit from the experiences of others, even from those of people who died long ago, and share the results of our own experiences. (see **Figure 12.2.**) We can request from other people specific behaviors and information that are helpful to us. We can provide information to other people so that their behavior will change in a way that benefits them (or us). Consider the effects of the following statements:

Don't step on that rock; it will tip
and you'll fall into the river.

Please hold that knot for me while I tie
another one.

Which way am I supposed to turn this?

Whenever you do that I get very angry.

Give me some milk, Mommy.

The sink is full of dirty dishes.

◆ The three major functions of oral and written language are: providing information, requesting information, and requesting a behavior. (For convenience, in the rest of this chapter "speaker" will

FIGURE 12.2 A papyrus containing portions of the Bible, written during the early fourth century. The words existed for years in oral form before being preserved in writing.

also designate "writer," and "listener" will also designate "reader.") Technically the second and third functions belong to the same category: a request for information is a request for a particular kind of behavior from the listener; but for our purposes it is worthwhile to maintain a distinction between them, especially since the forms taken by the two kinds of requests are different.

PROVIDING INFORMATION

Much of our verbal behavior provides other people with information. If all goes well, the listener learns something and adds new information to memory.

(See **Figure 12.3**.) But as we saw in Chapter 11, the contents of memory are organized and classified by category; people's classification schemes directly affect the storage and retrieval of information. Therefore, the listener will be able to absorb new information and retrieve it later only if it is stored appropriately. The verbal behavior of the speaker takes account of this fact. For example, a listener will be able to store even complex and detailed new information in short-term memory if the items are organized into a meaningful unit—a sentence. Compare the difficulty involved in storing the following two sets of fifteen words:

> along got the was door crept locked slowly
> he until passage the he to which

> He slowly crept along the passage until
> he got to the door, which was locked.

By retrieving information that is already contained in long-term memory, the listener can easily organize the second set of words in short-term memory and subsequently store it in long-term memory.

A speaker who imparts new information helps the listener by placing it in the context of what he or she expects the listener to know already. Suppose Sue says to John:

> The man I was telling you about finally died.

From this sentence we can conclude that Sue has previously told John about a particular man (*The man I was telling you about*) and that the man's death has been expected (*finally*). The only new information is that the man died. But a simple sentence containing only the new information—*He died*—would not permit John to categorize this information; he would not know where to put it in his memory. *The man I was telling you about* identifies the appropriate category—in this case, a man whom Sue has already mentioned to John.

Sometimes a listener fails to identify the category of old information to which the speaker is referring. For example, John may say, "What man?" Sue will then provide more information. She may say, "You know, the one I was telling you about at the party at Will's house last Saturday."

Because new information must be organized into categories that have already been established in long-term memory, it is essential that the speaker make explicit which is old information and which is new.

FIGURE 12.3 Most instances of speech provide information to listeners.

The communication must be a cooperative endeavor: the speaker uses special behaviors (rules) to specify which information is old and which is new; the listener must indicate whether he or she recognizes the old information. Clark and Haviland (1977) call the cooperation between speaker and listener the *given-new contract*.

When we say something to another person, unless we are socially inept, we watch for signs that we are being understood—that the listener is identifying old (given) information. Consider the following two exchanges:

You remember that car I sideswiped? (Listener nods.) Well, it turns out that it belongs to Julie's boss.

I was telling Charlie that . . . (puzzled look on listener's face) . . . you know, my roommate's brother . . .

Clearly, a speaker must be sensitive to both verbal and nonverbal signs of comprehension and puzzlement. Because writers do not have the benefit of such feedback, they must be particularly careful to identify old information for their readers. If they do not provide adequate cues so that their readers can organize new information in terms of what they already know, the information will not go into long-term memory.

A speaker uses several methods to identify old (given) and new information for a listener. Two of these are stress and choice of article.

Stress

Stress, in spoken language, refers to the emphasis placed on a syllable or word. Stress is one of the most important cues that we use to distinguish old from new information. Say the following sentences to yourself, placing stress on the italicized words:

> *Frank* helped the old man.
>
> Frank helped the *old* man.
>
> Frank helped the old *man*.

The stress highlights the new information. In terms of the given-new contract, in the first sentence the given (what the listener already knows) is *Someone helped the old man;* the new item is *Frank.* In the second sentence, the given is *Frank helped a man* (there were probably several men that the sentence could refer to); the new information is that the man he helped was *old.* In the third sentence, the given is *Frank helped an old person* (perhaps an old man and an old woman were present); the new item is *man.*

Choice of Article

Speakers also identify given and old information through the choice of articles—*a, an,* and *the.* Old or given information is usually identified by the definite article (*the*), new information by indefinite articles (*a* or *an*). For example, *I bought the car* implies that the listener has already heard about the car to which the speaker is referring; on the other hand, *I bought a car* implies that this is a newly mentioned car, not one that the listener already knows something about; thus the listener need not look for a particular car in his or her memory.

Consider the use of indefinite and definite articles in the following passage, as new items of information (a car, an old woman) become old information:

"I just bought *a* new car. I am very pleased with it. The salesman told me that *the* car was previously owned by *an* old woman who just drove it to church on Sundays. One thing that puzzles me is that the paint on the steering wheel of *the* car is all worn off even though the odometer says that *the* car was driven only 2000 miles, but the salesman said that *the* old woman had a lot of acid in the sweat from her hands."

REQUESTING INFORMATION

The second major function of speech is to request information; if the verbal behavior is successful, the listener becomes a speaker who provides information.

Wh- Questions

Most requests for information are signaled by a question that begins with a *wh-* word, such as *who, what, when, where, why,* and *which. How* is also considered a *wh-* word, even though it is not spelled that way. A *wh-* question contains an incomplete assertion (a statement of fact), phrased so as to elicit information from the listener. In other words, a *wh-* question is a fill-in-the-blank request to the listener; the *wh-* word represents the blank to be filled. The question *Where is the bathroom?* can be rephrased as *The bathroom is where?* The listener provides the information that fits the blank.

With a *wh-* question, the speaker tells the listener that he or she knows some old (given) information but needs some new information. The listener must identify the old information, retrieve it from memory, identify what new information is being requested, and supply the missing information. Consider the following questions:

> Who carried the box away?
>
> When did the lamp get broken?
>
> How did Ruth manage to convince her?

In the first question, the old information is *Someone carried the box away;* the requested new information is *Who is that someone?* and so on.

Yes/No Questions

Often the speaker wants to determine whether a hypothesis is true or false. Suppose you think that Charlotte's birthday is next week, but you are not sure. You ask a friend, "Is Charlotte's birthday next week?" You expect a yes or no answer, or perhaps "I don't know."

Most yes/no questions begin with an auxiliary verb: "Does she . . .," "Will they . . .," "Has it . . .," "Are you . . .," "Should I . . ." A rise in voice pitch at the end of the sentence provides an additional cue that the sentence is a question. Accordingly, your friend can identify *Is Charlotte's birthday next week?* as a yes/no question because the auxiliary verb *is* is at the beginning of the sentence and because you have raised the pitch of your voice at the end of the sentence. He or she responds as if the question were: *True or false: Charlotte's birth-day is next week.* Having determined the assertion that is to be evaluated, your friend must locate the appropriate information, decide whether the assertion matches the information in memory, and say "yes" or "no."

Some yes/no questions involve both old information (what we already know to be true) and new information (what we are uncertain about). When we ask questions like this, we must construct the sentence so that the listener will recognize which is which. If you ask, "Was it Judy who had to drive Jim home?" you are asserting that *Someone had to drive Jim home* and are asking whether the someone was Judy. If you ask, "Was Jim the one whom Judy had to drive home?" you are asserting that *Judy had to drive someone home* and are asking whether that someone was Jim.

To find out whether listeners check language representing given information or language representing new information, Hornby (1974) uttered assertions and after each one showed subjects a set of two pictures to determine whether the assertion was correct. Each sentence contained two nouns, one representing given information, the other new information. Making use of Sperling's finding that iconic memory fades rapidly, Hornby flashed each set of pictures on a screen very briefly (0.05 second), so that the subjects had time to check on the accuracy of only one noun.

For example, the subjects were asked to evaluate the truth of the assertion *It is the BOY who is petting the cat,* which is equivalent to asking them *Is it the BOY who is petting the cat?* The given is *Someone is petting the cat;* the new information is *The boy is that someone.* If the subjects were shown the lefthand picture in Figure 12.4, they would look at the child, note that it was a girl, and say that the assertion was false. If they were shown the right-hand picture they would look at the child, note that it was a boy, and say that the assertion was true. (See **Figure 12.4.**) The image disappeared before the subjects had a chance to see what kind of animal the boy was petting. If the assertion was *It is the CAT which the boy is petting,* the subjects would identify *cat* as new information and say "true" for the lefthand figure and "false" for the righthand figure. (See **Figure 12.4.**) The subjects noticed a discrepancy in new information 72 percent of the

FIGURE 12.4   The sort of stimuli used by Hornby.

time but detected only 39 percent of discrepancies in old information. The results indicate that a listener who is asked a yes/no question (1) determines which parts of the question represent given information and which represent new information, (2) assumes that the given information is true, and (3) tries to determine whether the new information is correct. Clearly, they checked out the new information first; the new information is the targeted material.

REQUESTING A BEHAVIOR

Requests for specific behaviors are called ***directives.*** *Shut the door! Carry out the garbage,* and *Please stop at the store on your way home and buy some milk* all request an action from the listener. So do indirect statements such as *Don't you think it's cold in here?* (meaning "Close the window"), *Would you mind doing that somewhere else?* (meaning "Go away and do that somewhere else!") or *Boy, that looks delicious!* (meaning "Please give me some").

Directives may take a variety of forms, depending largely on who is speaking, who is being spoken to, and the nature of the message. (See **Figure 12.5.**) Clearly, requesting a behavior is an important social skill, and knowledge of the appropriate form for the request is essential. If you want to find out what time it is from a well-dressed older stranger, you might say "Excuse me, could you tell me what time it is?" If you feel timid about

FIGURE 12.5   Many instances of speech are requests of the listener to perform a behavior.

approaching the stranger, you might be even more indirect: "I wonder if you'd mind telling me the time." The listener understands these polite forms of address as requests to tell the speaker what time it is, and not as questions about whether he is wearing a watch and is capable of telling time, or whether he would mind consulting his watch. You might approach a casually dressed teenager with a slightly less polite, but also somewhat friendlier and more familiar request, such as "Hi! Do you have the time?"

All users of a language understand the protocol for the use of directives. Everyone recognizes that *You have to do this* is an impolite form of address unless the speaker is citing a rule or giving instructions. For example, it is quite acceptable to say *You have to put the thread through this hole before you can hook it onto the lever.* In fact, *Would you mind putting the thread through this hole first?* would sound silly. In other situations, the most emphatic form of direction is actually the most polite. *You've got*

to try this cake!* is more polite than *Will you please try a piece of this cake.* In the latter case the listener will find it hard to refuse such a serious request, even if he or she wants no cake.

Interim summary: Language, the second most important human social behavior, is an orderly system of communication. Although all its users follow the rules, few are able to articulate them. In discussion of the three major functions of verbal communication we have seen that the distinction between old and new information is important, because communication requires that both parties talk about the same things and events. Most utterances contain both old and new information; the old information identifies the common topic of communication (what speaker and listener already know) and the new part identifies what the listener is to learn (or tell the speaker about).

PERCEPTION OF SPEECH

When we speak to someone we produce a series of sounds in a continuous stream, punctuated by pauses and modulated by stress and changes in pitch, such as the following sentence (the italics indicate stress; the arrow indicates a rise in pitch):

I*told*hershecould*bor*rowyour*book*
Was that o*kay* ↑

We write sentences as sets of words, with spaces between them. But we *say* sentences as a string of sounds, emphasizing some, quickly sliding over others, raising the pitch of our voice on some, lowering it on others. We maintain a regular rhythmic pattern of stress. We pause at appropriate times, but not after each word.

RECOGNITION OF SPEECH SOUNDS

The human auditory system performs a formidably complex task in enabling us to recognize speech sounds. These sounds vary according to the sounds that precede and follow them, the speaker's accent (and other peculiarities of speech), and the stress placed on the syllables in which they occur. *Phonemes* are the elements of speech—the smallest units of sound that contribute to the meaning of a word. For example, the word *pin* consists of three phonemes: /p/ + /i/ + /n/. Thus, the first step in recognizing speech sounds is to identify phonemes.

1. *Effects of neighboring sounds.* The phoneme /b/ sounds different in the words *borrow, bush,* and *crab,* but we recognize the same sound in all three. We can distinguish among the three *b* sounds, only if we listen carefully. Say *borrow* and *bush* aloud; you will note that your lips are puckered a bit more when you say the *b* in *bush.* Also, you let out a little puff of air after pronouncing the *b* sound in *borrow* and *bush,* but not after pronouncing the *b* in *crab.*

In other cases two sounds may be exactly the same, but we recognize them as different phonemes because different sounds precede or follow them. If we pronounce *writer* and *rider* casually, as in normal speech, we say the *t* and *d* exactly the same way, using the "flap *d*"; the end of the tongue takes a backward-moving slap at the ridge just behind the upper front teeth. But we can distinguish *I hired a writer* from *I hired a rider.* Say these sentences aloud and try to figure out how you distinguish them. Say them quickly and casually, without forcing the *t* and *d* sounds.

* * *

The only difference in pronunciation is that the *i* in *rider* is held a little longer than the *i* in *writer.* This fact is an example of a ***phonological rule.*** (*Phonology* is the study of the ways that various languages combine phonemes.) When we say a word quickly, we sometimes pronounce voiced consonants (in this case the phoneme /d/) and unvoiced consonants (the phoneme /t/) the same way. However, when we do this we also lengthen the vowel that precedes the voiced consonant.

2. *Effects of a speaker's accent or speech peculiarities.* A speaker from rural Tennessee might say *right* in the way a Californian would say *rot.* A Bostonian's *Mary* and *merry* sound the same. A Japanese person speaking English often pronounces *l*s as *r*s. Despite these differences in pronunciation, we quickly adjust to a speaker's accent and perceive his or her speech without much trouble. We recognize that the Tennesseean's *ah* sound in *right* is the same phoneme as the Californian's *aye* sound in *right.*

3. *Effects of stress.* A speech sound is shaped by the stress it receives. For example, compare the *o* sound in *potion* and *polite.* The *o* in *potion* is pronounced with the lips pursed, because the syllable *po* is stressed. The *o* in *polite* is pronounced with the lips in a relaxed position.

Perception of Consonants: Five Channels of Analysis

An important study by Miller and Nicely (1955) investigated how English-speaking people identify consonants. The researchers presented their subjects with sixteen consonants followed by the vowel *a* of *father* (*ma, ta, ka,* and so on) at a variety of intensities, from very soft to very loud. They also presented a background of white noise (a sound similar to the *sssh* made by an FM radio that is tuned between stations), which made it difficult to identify the consonants when they were presented softly. The errors that the subjects made were not random. For example, when they misperceived the sound *n* it was seldom identified as *f,* but they often identified it as *m.*

Miller and Nicely found that five distinguishing features could account for their subjects' ability to discriminate among the sounds. Table 12.1 shows their classification scheme. (Study this table and pronounce the consonants to yourself so that you will understand the kinds of sounds these features describe. See **Table 12.1.**) According to these results, the auditory system analyzes the sound of consonants by monitoring the (1) voicing, (2) nasality, (3) stridency, (4) duration, and (5) some characteristic of timbre provided by the lips, front of the tongue, or back of the tongue. To test one aspect of this hypothesis, Miller and Nicely eliminated the use of ***voicing*** as a cue. Voicing, which is produced by vibration of the vocal cords, provides a sound that is much lower in pitch than the clicks, buzzes, and hisses that form the other consonant sounds. The experimenters found that when they filtered out these low-frequency sounds from speech, consonants that differed only in voicing

TABLE 12.1   Miller and Nicely's five channels for perceiving English consonants

Channel and distinctions	Consonants
Voicing	
Voiced	b d g v ð z ʒ m n
Unvoiced	p t k f θ s ʃ
Nasality	
Nasal	m n
Not nasal	all others
Stridency	
Strident	f θ s ʃ v ð z ʒ
Not strident	p t k b d g m n
Duration	
Long	s ʃ z ʒ
Short	all others
Place of articulation	
Lips	p f b v m
Front of tongue	t θ s d ð z n
Middle or back of mouth	k ʃ g ʒ

Note: θ = *th,* as in *throw;* ʃ = *sh;* ʒ = *zh,* as in *azure;* ð = *th,* as in *this.*

(such as *p* versus *b, s* versus *z, d* versus *t,* and *k* versus *g*) sounded the same to the subjects.

Let us analyze why *n* and *m* are often confused, whereas *n* and *f* are not. Both *n* and *m* are (1) voiced, (2) nasal, (3) not strident, and (4) of short duration. They differ only in that (5) *n* is made with the front of the tongue, whereas *m* is made with the lips. On the other hand, *f* is (1) not voiced, (2) not nasal, (3) strident, (4) of short duration, and (5) pronounced with the lips: *n* and *f* have only one feature in common—their short duration. With so many differences, the sounds are unlikely to be confused.

◆ **Details of One Channel of Analysis**

There has been much research into how we discriminate among phonemes. Here we shall consider in detail the channel of analysis that permits us to discriminate between the sounds *b* and *p.* Try to figure out the difference yourself by saying *pa* and *ba.* Pay attention to what the sounds are like, not to how you move your lips to make them.

* * *

The difference is very subtle. When you say *pa* you first build up a little pressure in your mouth. When you open your lips a puff of air comes out. The *ah* sound does not occur immediately, because the air pressure in your mouth and throat keeps air from leaving your lungs for a brief time. When you say *ba* you do not first build up pressure. Your vocal cords start vibrating as soon as your lips open. As we saw, the vibration of your vocal cords is called voicing. The delay in voicing that occurs when you say *pa* is very slight—only 0.06 second. Try saying *ba* and *pa* aloud several times and note the difference. Your vocal cords will start vibrating just a little later when you say *pa.*

Lisker and Abramson (1970) presented subjects with a series of computer-generated sounds consisting of a puff followed by an *ah.* The sounds varied only in one way—the amount of time between the puff and the *ah.* When we speak, we make a puff for *pa* but not for *ba.* However, even though the computer always produced a puff, subjects reported that they heard *ba* when the delay was short and *pa* when it was long. If the delay in voicing was between 0.02 and 0.03 second, they reported hearing *ba* on some trials and *pa* on others, but never some blend of the two; their perceptions were *categorical*—that is, the subjects perceived only two categories of phonemes: /p/ and /b/. As Figure 12.6 shows, subjects discriminated between the phonemes /p/ and /b/ strictly according to the delay in voicing. (Negative delays mean that the *ah* sound started *before* the puff.) Note how sharp the criterion is. (See **Figure 12.6.**)

The delay in voicing that permits us to distinguish between *p* and *b* is known as *voice-onset time.* The sounds of *g* versus *k* and *d* versus *t* are also distinguished by voice-onset time; if you say the sounds *ga-ka* and *da-ta,* you will note delays in voicing after *ka* and *ta.*

Phonological Constraints

◆ Some combinations of sounds just cannot be made by the human speech apparatus and thus cannot occur in any language. For example, many conso-

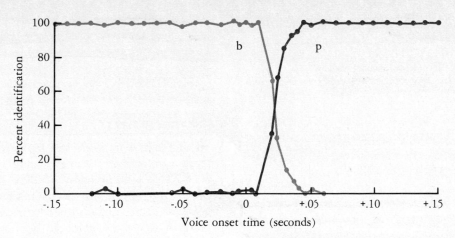

FIGURE 12.6 Identification of a sound as *ba* or *pa* as a function of voice-onset time. (From Lisker, L., and Abramson, A. Proceedings of the Sixth International Congress of Phonetic Sciences, Prague, 1967. Prague: Academia, 1970.)

nants cannot follow one another immediately; they must have a vowel or a pause between them: we can say *bim* but not *bmi*. Furthermore, any language uses only a portion of the combinations of sounds that humans can make. For example, English-speakers can easily pronounce the pattern *zyik* (say *zhee ick,* with the *zh* sound of azure) but the word sounds very un-English. Greenberg and Jenkins (1964) found that people could readily rate how "English" a particular sequence sounded to them, and that their judgments agreed closely with the actual occurrence of these sequences in the English language. Clearly, we have a bias toward hearing the sequences of speech sounds that are used in our native language; if a sequence is ambiguous, we tend to hear it in a way that most closely resembles the preferred order in English. In other words, our perception of speech shows *phonological constraints*—restrictions on the kinds of sound combinations that we are likely to perceive.

Day (1968, 1970) confirmed that our auditory system performs a rapid analysis of the sounds we hear, and that our experience with our native language biases how we perceive sequences of speech sounds. He presented two sound sequences to his English-speaking subjects through earphones. The subjects heard the same voice simultaneously saying *banket* in one ear and *lanket* in the other. Thus,

| Left ear: | **blanket** | |
| Right ear: | **lanket** | say "blanket" |

| Left ear: | **sin** | |
| Right ear: | **pin** | say "spin" |

| Left ear: | **tak** | sometimes say "task" |
| Right ear: | **tass** | sometimes say "tax" |

FIGURE 12.7 The procedure and results of the experiment by Day (1968, 1970).

the phonemes /b/ and /l/ occurred together, one in each ear. Sometime people heard two separate sequences of sounds, but when the sequences merged, the subjects always heard *blanket,* never *lbanket.* Similarly, *sin* and *pin* merged to *spin,* never to *psin.* However, when *tak* and *tass* were presented together, the subjects sometimes heard *task* and sometimes *tax.* Either combination is acceptable in English. (See **Figure 12.7.**) Information stored in short-term memory makes use of rules contained in long-term memory. Apparently, these rules permit English-speakers to encode the sequence of phonemes /b/ + /l/ in long-term memory, but not the sequence /l/ + /b/.

RECOGNITION OF WORDS IN CONTINUOUS SPEECH

Context

The perception of continuous speech involves different mechanisms from those used in the perception of isolated speech sounds. Because speech is full of hesitations, muffled sounds, and sloppy pronunciations, many individual words are hard to recognize out of context. For example, when Pollack and Pickett (1964) isolated individual words from a recording of normal conversations and played them back to another person, the person correctly identified the words only 47 percent of the time; when they presented the same words in the context of the original conversation, the subjects identified and understood almost 100 percent of them. These findings confirm that the context of speech provides significant cues to our recognition of words. (See **Figure 12.8.**)

Warren (1967) has also studied the role of contextual cues in our ability to perceive speech and has found that we can "fill in" missing information. He presented a recording of a sentence that had a cough spliced into it, in place of a speech sound (* marks the cough):

The state governors met with their respective legi*latures convening in the capital city.

Nineteen of the twenty people who listened to the

FIGURE 12.8   Isolated words are more difficult to identify than words presented in context.

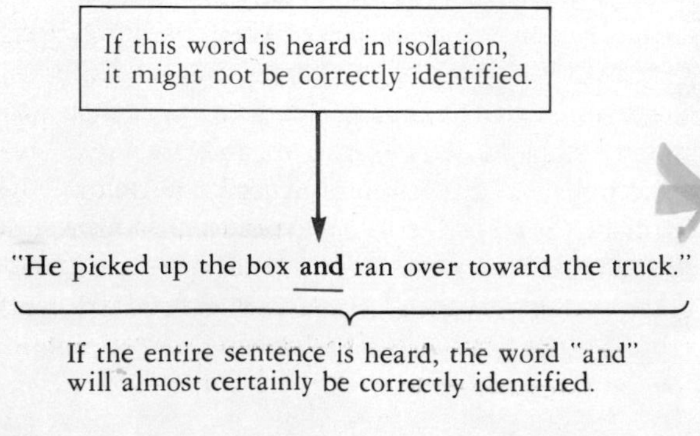

If this word is heard in isolation, it might not be correctly identified.

"He picked up the box **and** ran over toward the truck."

If the entire sentence is heard, the word "and" will almost certainly be correctly identified.

sentence failed to notice that anything was missing; when the information was encoded into short-term memory, the missing phoneme was filled in. In contrast, when a missing phoneme was replaced by silence rather than by a noise (*legi latures*), the subjects readily noticed the gap. Warren's results indicate that the human auditory system is prepared to fill in speech sounds that are obscured by noise, but that it does not cope with a "hole" in the stream of speech.

A study by Warren and Warren (1970) confirms that people fill in a missing phoneme according to context. The subjects heard the following four sentences with a sound replaced by a cough.

It was found that the *eel was on the axle.

It was found that the *eel was on the shoe.

It was found that the *eel was on the orange.

It was found that the *eel was on the table.

They heard the words as *wheel, heel, peel,* and *meal.*

Rhythm and Stress

One of the cues provided in continuous speech is rhythm. The speaker cooperates with the listener by talking with a regular cadence—a repetitive beat—that helps the listener locate individual words. For example, say *hippity-hop, downtown.* Note how long it takes you to pronounce each word. If you are like most speakers of English, you rate of speech was faster on *hippity-hop,* slower on *downtown.* The former contains four syllables; the latter contains two, yet it takes most people the same time to pronounce each word. We tend to space our stressed syllables evenly, like this:

HIP pit y HOP

DOWN   TOWN

Try another pair: *abracadabra, think snow.*

AB ra ca DAB ra

THINK SNOW

Higgins (1972) showed that listeners are very sensitive to the cadence of a sentence. If he electronically shortened some portion of a recorded sentence, subjects would judge the speech as unnatural. If he lengthened adjacent portions of speech, thus restoring the original time between "beats," the subjects reported that the speech sounded normal again.

Besides talking with a regular cadence, speakers stress words that they want the listener to be sure to hear—words that are crucial to understanding, or that are rare, or that might not be expected from the context of the sentence. Consider the following examples:

Make sure you open the *exhaust* valve first.

(Important word: stress is added to distinguish the word from possible alternatives, such as the intake valve.)

It was truly an *eleemosynary* act.

(Rare word: stress is added in the hope—probably vain—that the listener will hear and understand the unusual word.)

He said that we'd have to *think* or swim.

(Unexpected word: stress is added to make sure that the listener hears *think,* not *sink.*)

Shields, McHugh, and Martin (1974) have shown that stress definitely alerts the listener to the significance of a speech sound. They asked subjects to listen to a sentence and try to identify the first word containing *b.* The *b* occurred in a nonsense word, *benkik,* that was pronounced with stress on either the first or second syllable. For example:

You will have to curtail any morning sightseeing plans, as the plane to BENkik leaves at noon.

You will have to curtail any morning sightseeing plans, as the plane to benKIK leaves at noon.

The subjects were more likely to notice the *b* in a stressed syllable (*BENkik*) than in an unstressed one (*benKIK*). Given that they more readily perceived information contained in stressed syllables, it appears that our auditory system gives priority to processing sounds that receive stress. Thus, the speaker's tendency to stress important information is matched by the listener's tendency to analyze this information first.

UNDERSTANDING MEANING

To get a listener to act upon speech, the speaker must follow the "rules" of language, using words with which the listener is familiar and combining them in specific ways. For example, *Mary hit John* means something very different from *John hit Mary;* an English-speaker combines the words in one way if Mary does the hitting and in another if John does the hitting. In many languages, word order is an important cue to meaning.

Some people use different rules, in accordance with geographic location or social class. If a person says "I done did it!" we cannot conclude that the speaker is not following the "rules of English grammar," only that he or she is following different rules from the ones that other people may follow. This speaker will never say "I did done it!" or "I do did it!" The rules that he or she follows do not permit these alternatives. One disadvantage in a society in which different groups of people use different linguistic rules is that when communication between groups becomes difficult, misunderstandings become more frequent. Another is that members of higher socioeconomic groups tend to perceive the speech of people from lower socioeconomic groups as "wrong" and to label the speakers "inferior."

Syntactic Analysis

Syntactic Rules

We use cues not only from word order but also from added particles such as *-ing, -ed, -s,* or *pre-;* modifiers such as *not;* and auxiliaries such as *did* or *has.* That is, we respond to the *syntax* of the sentence (*syntax,* like *synthesis,* comes from Greek *syntassein,* "to put together"). Syntax is the science of grammatical construction. The rules that describe how we put words together to form sentences are called **syntactic rules.**

Some commonly used sentences do not require syntactic analysis. For example, we respond to sentences like *Put it down! Be quiet! What time is it?* or *Wait a minute!* as automatically as to single-word commands like *Stop!* or *Duck!* We have heard these groups of words so often that we pay no attention to the structure of the sentences or the meaning of the individual words. However, most sentences we encounter each day we have never heard before. For example, most of the sentences in this book are new to you; you have never heard or read them before. But you can understand them. (I hope.) How do we understand the meaning of sentences that we have never encountered before?

FIGURE 12.9   Although most sentences we hear are unique, we are able to understand their meaning.

Apparently, one of the things we do is analyze the syntactic structure of the sentence—that is, we undo it or take it apart and determine what syntactic rules were used to put it together. Once we understand the rules, we can understand the meaning that is intended by the speaker. We are no more conscious of this process than a child is conscious of the laws of physics when he or she learns to ride a bicycle. (See **Figure 12.9**.)

◆ ANALYSIS INTO CONSTITUENT PARTS   Consider the following sentence:

> Peter and Ralph carefully moved
> the part into position.

The sentence seems to break naturally into two parts:

> (Peter and Ralph)
> (carefully moved the part into position).

A pause between these parts seems quite natural. In contrast, consider the following division:

> (Peter and Ralph carefully moved the)
> (part into position).

This division does not seem right; a pause after *the* does not sound natural. Let us break the sentence down, step by step, until we get down to the smallest groups of words that seem to go together:

> Peter and Ralph carefully moved
> the part into position.

> (Peter and Ralph)
> (carefully moved the part into position).

> ((Peter) (and) (Ralph))
> ((carefully) (moved the part into position))

> ((Peter) (and) (Ralph))
> ((carefully) ((moved) (the part) (into position))).

This kind of analysis indicates the relatedness or relative closeness of the words of a sentence. In the final division, *Peter* and *and* are separated by only two parentheses, whereas *Ralph* and *carefully* are separated by four. Similarly, *carefully* appears to be further from *moved* (three parentheses) than *moved* is from *the part* (two parentheses). In fact, people reading a sentence aloud are most likely to pause at the places that receive the most parentheses when the sentence is divided like the one above. Fodor and Bever (1965) tested the validity of such an analysis by presenting the following sentence to their subjects *one line at a time.*

> *Divided into constituent parts*
> During World War II,
> even fantastic schemes
> received consideration
> if they gave promise
> of shortening the conflict.

> *Arbitrarily divided*
> During World War
> II, even fantastic
> schemes received
> consideration if they gave
> promise of shortening the
> conflict.

The subjects found it easier to read and understand the text that was divided into its constituent parts; an interruption in the middle of a constituent was confusing. (Remember, they saw only one line at a time.) This result suggests that readers (and presumably listeners) analyze sentences piece by piece. Once a constituent begins, perhaps they accumulate the words in short-term memory and hold them there until the constituent ends. Then they analyze the structure of that constituent and encode its meaning more efficiently (perhaps by chunking).

Ammon (1968) presented subjects with recordings of sentences like the following:

The polite actor thanked the old woman who carried the black umbrella.

Here is the same sentence, broken down into its smallest constituents:

((The (polite actor)) (thanked ((the (old woman)) (who (carried (the (black umbrella)))))).

At the end of each sentence, Ammon presented one of its words and asked the subjects to say the word that followed it. For example, the correct response to *polite* would be *actor*. The speed of the subjects' responses reflected the "relatedness" of the two words. The sequence *polite actor* was fastest (no parenthesis), *who carried* was slower (one parenthesis), and *actor thanked* was slowest (three parentheses). The results suggest that short-term memory for a sentence may be stored as a group of constituent parts.

FUNCTION WORDS Words can be classified according to whether they are *function words* or *content words*. Function words include determiners, quantifiers, prepositions, and words in similar categories: *a, the, to, in, some, many, and, but, when, since,* and so on. Content words include nouns, verbs, and most adjectives and adverbs: *apple, rug, went, caught, heavy, mysterious, thoroughly,* and *disparagingly*. Content words express meaning; function words express the relations between content words. (See **Figure 12.10.**)

Because a function word almost always marks the beginning of a new constituent in a sentence, when we hear a function word we tend to listen for a group of words that will go with it. Consider the following sentence:

She walked *through* the field *that* had been harvested *several* days ago.

The function words *through, that,* and *several* mark the beginnings of constituent phrases.

A study by Fodor and Garrett (1967) provides evidence that we use function words as cues to mark the beginning of a constituent part, indicat-

FIGURE 12.10 Content words express meaning.

ing that the previous one is over. For example, the following sentences convey the same meaning.

The pen that the author used was new.

The pen the author used was new.

The first sentence uses a function word (*that*) to mark the beginning of a constituent (*that the author used*). A listener can hear the word *that* and assume that a new constituent is beginning. In the second sentence the listener cannot make a decision to mark the beginning of a new constituent until he or she hears the word *used;* it is difficult to predict what the next word will be. And in fact Fodor and Garrett's subjects more easily understood the sentence containing the word *that*. Thus, besides indicating the relations between words, function words are important cues to the dividing points between the constituent parts of a sentence.

Semantic Analysis

Understanding the meaning of a sentence involves more than analysis; the listener or reader must also decode the meaning of the words in the sentence. *Semantics* (from Greek *sēma,* or "sign") is the study of the meanings represented by words.

Sometimes we can understand what a speaker or writer means even though the syntax of a sentence is ambiguous. Consider the following sentence.

Frank discovered a louse combing his beard.

The *syntax* of this sentence does not tell us whether Frank was combing Frank's beard, the louse was combing the louse's beard, or the louse was combing Frank's beard. But our knowledge of the world and of the usual meaning of words tells us that Frank was doing the combing—people, not lice, have beards and combs. We perform a semantic analysis.

Just as function words help us determine the syntax of a sentence, content words help us determine its meaning. For example, even with its function words removed, the following sentence still makes pretty good sense.

man placed ladder tree climbed picked apples

You can probably fill in the function words yourself and get: *The man placed the ladder against the tree, climbed it, and picked some apples.* We can often guess at function words, which is fortunate, because they are normally unstressed in speech and are the most likely to be poorly pronounced.

We use content words to understand the meaning of ambiguous sentences (for example, we know that a louse does not have a beard) and sentences with complicated syntactic structures. Consider the following sentence (from Stolz, 1967):

The vase that the maid that the agency hired dropped broke on the floor.

The sentence is convoluted, but its content words enable us to make some sense of it: the vase broke, the maid dropped, and the agency hired. The sentence below has precisely the same syntactic structure, but its content words are less specific in what they refer to.

The dog that the cat that the girl fought scolded approached the colt.

It is almost impossible to understand this sentence. We cannot assign the nouns (dog, cat, girl) to the verbs (fought, scolded, approached) on the basis of meaning, so we must depend entirely on syntax, which is extremely complex. A speaker saying a sentence like the one above deserves to be misunderstood.

Fillenbaum (1974a,b) showed that we sometimes ignore syntax when we hear a sentence. Instead, we pay attention to the meaning of the words as they relate to our experience. Thus, semantics can override syntax. Consider the following sentences:

John dressed and had a bath.

Don't print that or I won't sue you.

Over 60 percent of Fillenbaum's subjects failed to notice that these sentences have rather peculiar meanings. The subjects would paraphrase the second sentence as *If you print that, I'll sue you.* But that is not what it says. (Read the sentences again— very carefully.) When asked to re-examine the original sentence, only about half the subjects noticed the peculiarity, and many who did notice the discrepancy said that they knew what the sentence was really *supposed* to mean, so they rephrased it. Thus the syntax of a sentence partly determines what information enters short-term memory, but our previous nonverbal experiences (such as bathing and dressing) also play an important role.

Interim summary: The recognition of words in continuous speech is a complex process. Phonemes are recognized even though their pronunciation is affected by neighboring sounds, by accents and speech peculiarities, and by stress. Miller and Nicely discovered that our ability to distinguish among the sixteen consonants that they tested depended on five channels of analysis: voicing, nasality, stridency, duration, and place of articulation. Other studies show that we distinguish between voiced and unvoiced consonant phonemes such as /b/ and /p/ by means of voice-onset time, a 0.06-second delay in vibration of the vocal cords after opening the lips. When voice-onset time is varied in computer-generated speech, our speech is categorical: we always hear a voiced or unvoiced consonant, never an intermediate one. In addition, our perception of speech sounds is constrained by phonological rules; we tend to hear ambiguous sounds as those that are used in our language.

Our recognition of words in continuous speech is far superior to our ability to recognize them when they have been isolated. Related to this phenomenon is the fact that we tend not to hear noises that obscure speech sounds; if we understand what we hear, our short-term memory encodes the entire words, with the missing phonemes restored. The speaker helps the listener to understand what is being said by adding rhythm and stress; for example, stress marks important, rare, or unexpected words.

Meaning is a joint function of syntax and semantics. All users of a particular language observe syntactic rules (although these may vary according to geographic location and social class) that establish the relations of the words to each other. Sentences longer than a few words consist of several constituents: closely related units of a few words. We use pauses and function words to mark the beginnings of new constituents. Content words refer to object, actions, and the characteristics of objects and actions, and thus can express meaning even in some syntactically ambiguous sentences.

BRAIN MECHANISMS

Studies of the verbal behavior of people with brain damage suggest that mechanisms involved in perceiving and producing speech are located in different areas of the cortex.

PERCEPTION AND PRODUCTION: EVIDENCE FROM WERNICKE'S APHASIA AND BROCA'S APHASIA

Wernicke's aphasia results from damage to Wernicke's area, in the auditory association cortex of the temporal lobe. (See **Figure 12.11.**) People with this disorder show a severe deficit in understanding speech, and they produce fluent but meaningless speech; their speech is full of function words, which are especially important for syntax, but has very few content words. Broca's aphasia results from damage to Broca's area, in the frontal cortex. (See **Figure 12.11.**) People with this disorder speak slowly and laboriously and use very few function words. However, their speech is usually meaningful to other people, because it contains content words, which are essential to semantics.

The most likely explanation for Wernicke's aphasia is that the temporal lobe contains the perceptual mechanisms for decoding speech and the memory for the sequences of sounds that constitute words (especially content words). Damage to this region impairs speech perception and makes it difficult for people with Wernicke's aphasia to think of words with which to express thoughts; thus their speech lacks meaning. The symptoms of Broca's aphasia suggest that memories for the sequences of muscular movements necessary for speech are located in the back part of the frontal lobe. These people, with an intact Wernicke's area, can think of content words but cannot easily articulate them, since their expressive mechanism is damaged. But why does their speech lack function words, and why is the speech of a person with Wernicke's aphasia so full of them?

Some people with Broca's aphasia show an extremely severe deficit in both the comprehension and production of syntax: they have difficulty understanding a sentence in which syntax is crucial to express meaning, and they cannot themselves use syntactic rules in speech. This condition is known as *agrammatism.*

To test agrammatic subjects for speech comprehension, Schwartz, Saffran, and Marin (1980) showed them a pair of drawings, read a sentence aloud,

TOP

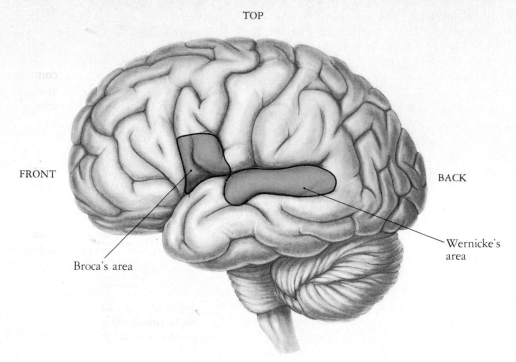

FRONT   BACK

Wernicke's area

Broca's area

FIGURE 12.11   The location of Broca's area and Wernicke's area.

and then asked them to point to the appropriate picture. The subjects heard forty-eight sentences such as *The clown applauds the dancer* and *The robber is shot by the cop.* For the first sample sentence one picture would show a clown applauding a dancer, and the other would show a dancer applauding a clown. On average, the brain-damaged subjects responded correctly to only 62 percent of the pictures (chance would be 50 percent). In contrast, the performance of normal people would be around 100 percent on such a simple task. In another study, Saffran, Schwartz, and Marin (1980) obtained evidence of the subjects' deficits in the use of syntactic rules by showing them simple pictures and asking them to say what was happening. Here are some of the responses:

Picture of a girl giving flowers to her teacher: Girl . . . wants to . . . flowers . . . flowers and wants to . . . The woman . . . wants to . . . The girl wants to . . . the flowers and the woman.

Picture of a boy being hit in the head by a baseball: Boy is hurting to it.

Picture of a woman kissing a man: The kiss . . . the lady kissed . . . the lady is . . . the lady and the man and the lady . . . kissing.

Picture of a boy giving a valentine to a girl: The boy and a valentine and a girl . . . boy . . . the boy put the valentine into this girl.

Patients with agrammatism usually have large lesions in the left frontal cortex, damaging more than Broca's area. Given that the frontal lobes govern motor control and, more generally, planning, it is not surprising that damage there impairs the production of proper syntax. Syntactic rules involve motor operations in the sense that they entail putting a word into its proper position, adding the correct ending to a verb, and so on. It is somewhat more surprising that these lesions also impair comprehension. Thus, we cannot say that speech perception is strictly a function of Wernicke's area. It appears that the mechanisms that permit us to translate meaning into syntax are also necessary for us to extract meaning from syntax; encoding and decoding use the same brain mechanisms.

If this explanation is true, we can understand why the speech of people with Wernicke's aphasia is full of function words: they have lost the mechanisms that mediate the memories of the sounds and meanings of content words, but retain the mechanisms that control utterances of function words (which are encoded in memory by the movements that produce them). Their speech is controlled by speech mechanisms in the frontal lobe with little meaningful input to guide them, and therefore it consists mostly of function words.

SEMANTICS: EVIDENCE FROM ISOLATION APHASIA

Evidence from another type of aphasia indicates that perception of speech (that is, recognition of words) and comprehension of the meaning of speech require different brain mechanisms. (Of course, speech perception, which involves Wernicke's area, is necessary for comprehension of its meaning; if a person cannot perceive the words, he or she cannot understand their meaning.) Isolation aphasia is caused by brain damage that spares Wernicke's area, Broca's area, and their interconnections but severely damages the rest of the cerebral cortex. In Chapter 11 we examined the case of a woman with such damage. Her speech consisted of memorized poems and phrases or repetitions of what had just been said, and she showed no signs of understanding either what she said or what other people said to her. However, if someone said an ungrammatical phrase she often repeated it with correct grammar. She had no difficulty saying function words or content words.

This case indicates that although mechanisms in Wernicke's area and Broca'a area put thoughts into words, brain mechanisms outside the primary speech areas initiate these thoughts. In addition, Wernicke's area decodes sounds into words (and Broca's area decodes their syntax), but mechanisms in other parts of the brain understand the meaning of these words.

PROSODY

◈ When we speak, we stress some words, raise or lower the pitch of our voice, and impart a regular rhythm to what we say. These features of oral speech are called *prosody.* Their importance is indicated by the fact that we use symbols to indicate them when we write. Punctuation marks are representations of prosodic elements: commas signify short pauses, periods longer ones, question marks a rise in voice pitch, exclamation marks emphatic speech, and italics special stress. It would be difficult to understand text that lacked these symbols.

Not much is known about which brain functions are involved in the production and comprehension of the prosodic elements of speech, but it appears that the right hemisphere is more important than the left. The right hemisphere is also important in the perception and production of rhythms, musical sequences, and the facial gestures related to emotion. Given that all these functions play a role in prosody, it is not surprising that damage to the right hemisphere can disrupt prosody without affecting syntactic and verbal content. The resulting disorder is called *aprosodia.*

Weintraub, Mesulam, and Kramer (1981) tested the prosodic skills of people with damage to their right hemisphere. In one experiment they asked their subjects to point to a picture that corresponded to a word that they heard. For example, they presented a picture of a greenhouse and a picture of a house that was painted green and asked which one the subjects would choose if they heard *GREEN house* and which one they would choose if they heard *GREEN HOUSE* (both words equally stressed). The patients did significantly worse than control subjects.

Weintraub and her colleagues also asked their subjects to listen to two sentences and say whether they were the same or different. If the sentences differed in stress or intonation the brain-damaged subjects were likely to say that they were the same. For example, they tended not to notice the difference between *Margo plays the piano?* and *Margo plays the piano.* They also had difficulty *repeating* prosodic features; they did not raise the pitch of their voices at the end of sentences, and if they stressed a word, it tended to be the wrong one.

Finally, the investigators observed the patients' use of stress in their own speech. They presented two contrasting sentences and then asked a question about them. For example, a subject might see the following two sentences:

The man walked to the grocery store.

The woman rode to the shoe store.

The subjects were then asked to answer a question by reading one of the sentences. If a normal person is shown these questions and is asked, "Who walked to the grocery store, the man or the woman?" he or she will probably say, "The *man* walked to the grocery store," with stress on *man* because it represents new information requested by the speaker. The patients with right-hemisphere brain damage chose the correct sentence but either failed to stress a word or stressed the wrong one.

Ross (1981) claims to have found that some aprosodias caused by damage to the right hemisphere correspond to the language problems that are produced by left-hemisphere damage; that is, damage to the right temporal lobe causes comprehension deficits but not expressive deficits, and damage to the right frontal lobe causes expressive deficits but not comphrehension deficits. Because his conclusions are based on a small number of cases, we cannot consider his assertions to be proved, but other investigators will undoubtedly study them further.

READING

Apparently, when we read aloud, we use at least two different methods: *phonetic reading* involves seeing individual letters (or small groups of letters) and decoding them into sounds, which we then pronounce; *whole-word reading* involves seeing a word as a whole and then pronouncing it. Studies of people who have sustained brain damage show that damage to one process does not always seriously affect the other.

Phonological Dyslexia

Brain-damaged people with *phonological dyslexia* have great difficulty reading phonetically. They can read words that they learned before their stroke or head injury, but they cannot read unfamiliar ones. In particular, they cannot read nonwords such as *flape, buflig,* or *strudge,* whereas most normal people can pronounce these sequences of letters by using phonetic rules. The fact that the patients can con-

tinue to read words they already know suggests that they are using a method other than phonetic reading. Presumably, this method involves whole-word recognition.

The exact location of the damage that causes phonological dyslexia is not known, but it usually involves the region near the junction of the parietal, temporal, and occipital lobes.

Surface Dyslexia

In contrast, people with *surface dyslexia* have no trouble reading phonetically, but they appear to have difficulty with whole-word reading. People with this disorder find it easier to read regularly spelled words than irregularly spelled ones. Regularly spelled words are those that conform to the common rules of spelling, such as *church, happy, late,* or *establishment.* Most people can easily "sound out" these words by using phonetic rules (such as the facts that each letter has a specific sound, that *ch* and *th* make special sounds, and that an *e* at the end of a word makes an internal vowel long rather than short). Irregularly spelled words do not follow these rules; therefore, we read words such as *listen* (the *t* is silent), *pint* (the *i* is long rather than short), and *yacht* (the *ch* is silent) by the whole-word method. A person with surface dyslexia sometimes pronounces *pint* as "pinnt" and *yacht* as "yatchet" but can read nonwords that conform to the common rules of spelling.

The Two Phases of Whole-Word Reading: Recognition and Pronunciation

Whole-word reading entails two phases: *recognition* and *pronunciation.* For most of us, these two phases occur in such rapid sequence that we are unaware that they are separate. However, evidence indicates that recognition of a word is not synonymous with the ability to say it. A colleague and I (Margolin and Carlson, 1982) studied a woman who had received a head injury in an automobile accident, resulting in severe damage to the left temporal lobe. Her speech was fluent, but she had severe *anomia;* that is, when speaking she had trouble finding words, especially concrete nouns. For example, when talking about her horse she might forget the word and say, "You know, an animal

. . . I keep it out in the back . . . it's big . . . I take it for rides . . . oh, I know what it is, I just can't say it to you." She had no difficulty pronouncing words once she thought of them or was reminded of them. If we said, "Do you mean *horse?*" she would reply, "Yes, horse!" The patient also had difficulty naming objects shown in pictures, such as a lamp, a boat, a pair of scissors, or a nest. Moreover, when we tested her ability to read simple words or pronounceable nonwords such as *jess* or *blit,* she failed utterly.

At first we concluded that the subject had lost the ability to read either phonetically or by the whole-word method. But further testing showed that although the woman could not *pronounce* the words she was shown, she could *recognize* them. When we showed her a printed word along with four pictures, one of which contained the object represented by the word, she chose the correct picture 66 percent of the time (chance would be 25 percent). Similarly, when we showed her one picture along with four printed words, she chose the correct word 85 percent of the time. Thus, in both cases she was able to match words that she could not read with pictures that she could not name. (See **Figure 12.12.**) Because our subject could not have performed so well unless she could recognize words, we concluded that her wholeword recog-

nition was relatively intact. Chance and additional testing confirmed this view when one day, when she was trying (without success) to read some words that I had typed, she suddenly said, "Hey! You spelled this one wrong." Indeed, I had. But even though she saw that the word was misspelled she could not read it. The next day I gave her a list of eighty pairs of words, one spelled correctly and the other incorrectly. She went through the list quickly and easily, identifying 95 percent of the misspelled words, although she was able to read only five words.

Figure 12.13 shows a hypothetical model of some of the reading processes discussed in this section. (See **Figure 12.13.**)

Interim summary: The effects of brain damage suggest that the memory of the sounds of words is located in Wernicke's area and the memory of the muscular movements needed to produce them is located in Broca's area. Thus, Wernicke's area is necessary for speech perception and Broca's area for its production. Wernicke's aphasia is characterized by fluent but meaningless speech, scarce in content words but rich in function words. Presumably, function words and other syntactic features of speech related to motor operations involve mechanisms in the frontal lobes. Semantics, or meaning, requires other areas of cortex, which contain memories of the relations among words and the concepts they denote.

A person has two means of recognizing and pronouncing written words: phonetic reading and whole-word reading. These two abilities seem to be functions of different areas of the brain. A person with phonological dyslexia can only read by the whole-word method, whereas a person with surface dyslexia can only read phonologically. Presumably, a normal person uses both methods, recognizing familiar words by their shape and decoding unfamiliar ones by phonological rules. Recognizing a word is not synonymous with pronouncing it; a patient who could not read a word aloud could match words with pictures and recognize misspelled words. Thus verbal communication is very complex, using many different mechanisms located in different areas of the brain.

FIGURE 12.12   One of the stimuli presented to the anomic, dyslexic patient in the study by Margolin and Carlson (1982).

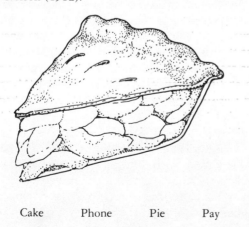

Cake   Phone   Pie   Pay

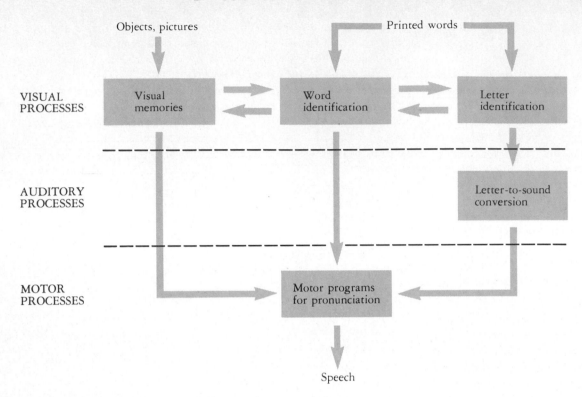

FIGURE 12.13   A hypothetical model of some of
the processes involved in reading a word aloud.

DEVELOPMENT OF VERBAL BEHAVIOR IN CHILDREN

How do children learn to communicate verbally
with other people? How do they master the many
rules needed to transform a thought into a coherent
sentence? How do they learn the meanings of thousands of words? And *why* do they do all these things?
Do other people shape their babble into words by
appropriately reinforcing their behavior, or do innate
mechanisms ensure the acquisition of language
without reinforcement? This section addresses these
and other questions related to children's verbal development.

THE PRESPEECH PERIOD AND THE FIRST WORDS

Perception of Speech Sounds

An infant's auditory system is remarkably well developed. Wertheimer (1961) found that a newborn
infant in a delivery room can turn its head toward
the source of a sound. An infant two or three weeks
of age can discriminate the sound of a voice from
nonspeech sounds. By the age of two months, a
baby can tell an angry voice from a pleasant one;
an angry voice produces crying, whereas a pleasant
one causes smiling and cooing.

Psychologists have developed a clever technique
to determine what sounds a very young infant can
perceive. A special pacifier nipple is placed in the
baby's mouth. The nipple is connected by a plastic
tube to a pressure-sensitive switch that converts the
infant's sucking movements into electrical signals.
These signals can be used to turn on auditory stimuli; each time the baby sucks, a particular sound
is presented. (See **Figure 12.14**.)

If the auditory stimulus is novel, the baby usually begins to suck at a high rate. If the stimulus
remains the same, its novelty wears off (habituation
occurs) and the rate of sucking goes down. With
another new stimulus, the rate of sucking again
suddenly increases, unless the baby cannot discrim-

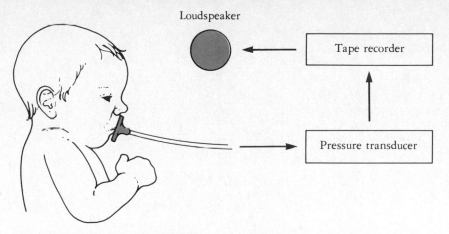

FIGURE 12.14 A procedure used to investigate auditory perception by infants. The baby's sucking action on the nipple turns on the tape recorder.

inate the difference; if the stimuli sound the same to the infant, its rate of sucking remains low after the change. Figure 12.15 shows some data collected by this procedure (Trehub, 1976). The rate of sucking per minute increased in response to the sound *zah,* then declined during habituation over a five-minute period. When the auditory stimulus was changed to *rah,* the rate of sucking suddenly increased again, indicating that the infant could discriminate between the two sounds. (See **Figure 12.15.**)

Using this technique, Eimas, Siqueland, Jus-

FIGURE 12.15 Data from the auditory perception procedure shown in Figure 12.14. (From Trehub, S.E. *Child Development,* 1976, 47, 466–472.)

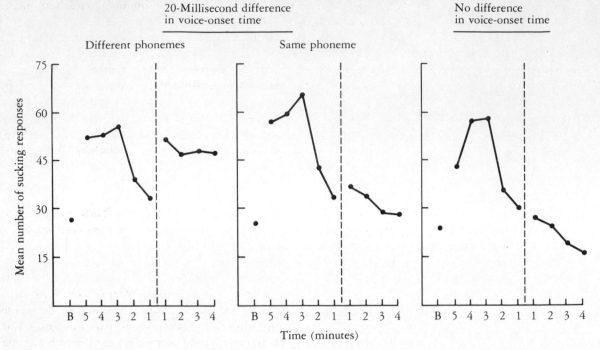

FIGURE 12.16   Evidence of categorical perception in a one-month-old infant. (From Eimas, P.D., Siqueland, E.R., Jusczyk, P., and Vigorito, J. *Science,* 1971, *171,* 303–306.)

czyk, and Vigorito (1971) found that one-month-old infants could tell the difference between the sounds of the consonants *b* and *p*. Like Lisker and Abramson (1970), in the study presented earlier, they presented the sounds *ba* and *pa,* synthesized by a computer. The infants, like the adult subjects in the earlier study, discriminated between these sounds at a voice-onset time of 0.02 second. Furthermore, they appeared to sort the sounds into two categories, corresponding to what adults would hear as *ba* and *pa.* (See **Figure 12.16.**)

Some psycholinguists have concluded from data like these that the human auditory system contains innate, "pre-wired" mechanisms that sort speech sounds into discrete categories. However, a number of experiments suggest that animals with no observed speech-analyzing abilities respond categorically to sounds like *pa* and *ba.* For example, Kuhl and Miller (1975, 1978) trained chinchillas to respond differently to the sounds of *pa* and *ba* and found that in these animals, too, the criterion for discrimination is very close to that of humans.

Stages of Infant Speech Sounds

◆ Kaplan and Kaplan (1971) have outlined the following four stages of early vocalizations in infants.

STAGE 1: CRYING   Everyone knows that crying is the first sound that a baby makes. As we saw in Chapter 6, this aversive stimulus is important in obtaining behaviors from the baby's caretakers.

STAGE 2: OTHER VOCALIZATIONS AND COOING   At about one month of age, infants start making other sounds, including one that is called *cooing* because of the prevalence of the *oo* sound. Often during this period babies also make a series of sounds that resemble a halfhearted attempt to mimic the sound of crying.

STAGE 3: BABBLING   At around six months, a baby's sounds begin to resemble those that occur in speech. Some researchers (including Mowrer, 1960) have suggested that speech emerges from babbling. They claim that an infant's babbling contains all the sounds that occur in all languages of the world, and that learning to speak involves a selection process—a narrowing of the range of sounds to those that are actually used in the child's native language. However, although a baby produces some sounds that are not heard in English (such as the sound of the French *u* or the German *ü*), it does not by any means produce all the sounds that *are* heard in English (Oller, Wieman, Doyle, and Ross, 1976). These come during later stages of language development.

STAGE 4: PATTERNED SPEECH At about one year of age, a child begins to produce words. The transition between stages 3 and 4 can occur gradually or abruptly. Sometimes there is a period of silence for several days or weeks during which the child stops babbling altogether, followed by the beginning of patterned speech.

The first sounds that children use to produce speech appear to be the same across all languages and cultures: the first vowel is usually the soft *a* sound of *father,* and the first consonant is a *stop consonant* produced with the lips—*p* or *b*. Thus the first word is often *papa* or *baba*. The next feature to be added is *nasality,* which converts the consonant *p* or *b* into *m*. Thus, the next word is *mama*. Naturally, mothers and fathers all over the world recognize these sounds as their children's attempts to address them.

The development of speech sounds continues for many years. Some sequences are added very late. For example, the *str* of *string* and the *bl* of *blink* are difficult for young children to produce; they usually say *tring* and *link,* omitting the first consonant. Most children recognize sounds in adult speech before they can produce them. Consider this conversation (Dale, 1976):

ADULT: Johnny, I'm going to say a word two times and you tell me which time I say it right and which time I say it wrong: *rabbit, wabbit*.

CHILD: *Wabbit* is wight and *wabbit* is wong.

Although the child could not pronounce the *r* sound it is clear that he could recognize it.

THE TWO-WORD STAGE

◈ When children start putting two words together their linguistic development takes a leap forward.

It is at this stage that linguistic creativity really begins. Consider the creativity in *allgone outside,* said by a child when the door was closed.

Like first sounds, children's two-word utterances are remarkably consistent across all cultures that have been observed. Children use words in the same way, no matter what language their parents speak. Even deaf children who learn sign language from their parents and children who can hear put two words together in the same way (Bellugi and Klima, 1972); deaf children whose parents do not know sign language invent their own signs and use them in orderly, "rule-governed" ways (Goldin-Meadow and Feldman, 1977). Thus, the grammar of children's language at the two-word stage appears to be universal.

For many years, investigators described the speech of young children in terms of adult grammar, but it is now recognized that their speech simply follows different rules. Young children are incapable of forming complex sentences, partly because their vocabulary is small, partly because their short-term "working" memory is limited (they cannot yet encode a long string of words), and partly because their cognitive development has not yet reached a stage where they can learn complex rules of syntax.

Researchers have used a variety of strategies to uncover young children's regularities of speech and to deduce from these the "rules" that children use. For example, Miller and Ervin-Tripp (1964) recorded two statements by a child: *Christy room* (meaning "This is Christy's room") and *Christy room* (meaning "Christy is in the room"). What grammatical rules enable two different meanings to result in use of the same two words? Yet it appears that this two-word speech is orderly and that "rules" do govern much of what young children say. Wieman (1974) noted that children often stress one of the words in their two-word sentences; for example, a child may say *CHRISTY room* in one situation and *Christy ROOM* in another. Say these two-word sentences to yourself, stressing the capitalized word. Can you guess which means "Christy is in the room" and which means "This is Christy's room"?

* * *

Most people guess correctly (which means that they are really not guessing, I suppose). Wieman recorded many instances of two-word speech and classified the words according to form and function. Seven categories emerged: (1) new or contrasting information (as opposed to given or old information), (2) location, (3) possession, (4) noun object, (5) action, (6) pronoun object, and (7) agent that performs some action. These classes occurred in a hierarchy: if a child's statement contained words from two different classes, the stress fell on the word from the higher-order class. (See **Table 12.2.**) For example, suppose that a child whose speech is at the two-word stage wants to say, "This is Christy's room." *Christy* is possessive, since she is the owner of the room, whereas *room* is a noun object. Because possession is higher in the hierarchy than noun object, it receives the stress. The child says *CHRISTY room.* On the other hand, suppose that the child wants to say, "Christy is in her room." Now *Christy* is a noun object, and *room* is a location where that object (person) is to be found. Location is higher in the hierarchy than noun object, so *room* receives the stress: *Christy ROOM.*

Wieman's analysis is only one of the many approaches developed to reveal the regularities of children's speech at the two-word stage, and undoubtedly, more regularities will become apparent. The importance of Wieman's conclusions is their support for the idea that children's speech is orderly and that the rules that govern stress are complex; they are determined by the relation between the meanings of the two words.

One of the difficulties in determining the rules of children's grammar is that the words by themselves often do not provide enough information for us to infer the meaning of an utterance. Wieman's analysis can be tested only when an observer is present to determine what the child intends to say; the words themselves are ambiguous. If we know nothing about the context of the two sentences, we cannot classify the words. Thus, an adequate description of the regularities of children's speech must take account of the functions that the words perform, and not simply their form. The rules are semantic as well as syntactic.

ACQUISITION OF ADULT RULES OF GRAMMAR

◆ We tend to assume that the simplest rules of grammar are the first to be learned. The trouble with this assumption is that so far there is no accurate way of assessing the complexity of a particular linguistic rule. If we follow children around and record their speech, we can determine the chronological order in which they use grammatical rules. Yet it is possible that children have to master some rules that are relatively complex but very important for communication before they learn simpler rules that are not needed very often. This possibility must govern the following considerations about how children learn adult linguistic "rules."

As children develop past the two-word stage, they begin to learn and use more and more of the grammatical rules that adults use: verbs are used more often, articles are added, prepositional phrases are mastered, and sentences become more complex. These results involve the use of *inflections* and function words. Function words, you recall, are the little words that help shape the syntax of a sentence. Inflections are special particles that we add to words to change their syntactic or semantic function. For example, the inflection *-ed* changes most verbs into the past tense (*change* becomes *changed*), *-ing* makes a verb into a noun (*make* becomes *making*), and *-'s* indicates possession (*Paul's truck*). Table 12.3 shows the approximate order in which children acquire some of these inflections and function words. (See **Table 12.3.**)

It is more difficult for children to add an inflection or function word to their vocabulary than to add to a new content word, because the rules that govern the use of inflections or function words are more complex than those that govern the use of most content words. In addition, content words usually refer to concrete objects or activities. The

---

T A B L E 12.2 A stress hiererchy for the sentences of children at the two-word stage

Most stress	New or contrasting information
↑	Location
	Possession
	Noun object
	Action (usually a verb)
	Pronoun object
Least stress	Agent

TABLE 12.3   The order in which children acquire some English suffixes and function words

Item	Example
1. Present progressive: *ing*	He is sit*ting* down.
2. Preposition: *in*	The mouse is *in* the box.
3. Preposition: *on*	The book is *on* the table.
4. Plural: *-s*	The dog*s* ran away.
5. Past irregular: e.g., *went*	The boy *went* home.
6. Possessive: *-'s*	The girl*'s* dog is big.
7. Uncontractible copula *be*: e.g., *are, was*	*Are* they boys or girls? *Was* that a dog?
8. Articles: *the, a, an*	He has *a* book.
9. Past regular: *-ed*	He jump*ed* the stream.
10. Third person regular: *-s*	She run*s* fast.
11. Third person irregular: e.g., *has, does*	*Does* the dog bark?
12. Uncontractible auxiliary *be*: e.g., *is, were*	*Is* he running? *Were* they at home?
13. Contractible copula *be*: e.g., *'s, -re*	That*'s* a spaniel. They*'re* pretty.
14. Contractible auxiliary *be*: e.g., *-'s, -'re*	He*'s* doing it. They*'re* running slowly.

Adapted from Clark, H.H., and Clark, E.V. *Psychology and Language.* New York: Harcourt Brace Jovanovich, 1977, after Brown (1973).

rules that govern the use of function words are rarely made explicit; a parent seldom says, "When you want to use the past tense, add *-ed* to the verb"—nor would a young child understand such a pronouncement. Instead, children must listen to speech and figure out how to express such concepts as the past tense. Studies of children's speech have told us something about the process by which this occurs.

The most frequently used verbs in most languages are *irregular;* among other peculiarities, forming the past tense of such verbs in English does *not* involve adding *-ed.* (Examples are *go/went, catch/caught, throw/threw, buy/bought, be/was, see/saw,*

can/could.) The past tense of such verbs must be learned individually. Because irregular verbs are more common than regular ones, children learn them first, producing the past tense easily in sentences such as *I came, I fell down,* and *She hit me.* Soon afterward, they discover the regular past-tense inflection and expand their vocabulary, producing sentences like *He dropped the ball.* But they also say *I comed, I falled down,* and *She hitted me.* Having learned a rule, they apply it to all verbs, including the irregular ones that they were previously using correctly. In fact it takes children several years to learn to use the regular past tense correctly.

Some English verbs have two acceptable past-tense forms, regular and irregular, such as *light/lit* or *light/lighted, thrive/throve* or *thrive/thrived.* It has been suggested that many of our verbs that are now regular were previously irregular, and that the tendency of children to overregularize the past tense rule caused them to become regular.

ACQUISITION OF MEANING

How do children learn to use and understand words? The simplest explanation is that they hear a word spoken at the same time that they see (or hear, or touch) the object to which the word refers. After several such pairings, they add a word to their vocabulary. Suppose we give a boy a small red plastic ball and say *ball.* After a while, the child says *ball* when he sees it.

Yet we cannot conclude from this behavior that the child knows the meaning of *ball.* So far, he has encountered only one referent for the word—a small one made of red plastic. If he says *ball* when he sees an apple or an orange, or even the moon, we must conclude that he does not know the meaning of *ball;* he has **overextended** the word. On the other hand, if he uses the word to refer only to the small red plastic ball, his error would be called an **underextension.** Table 12.4 lists some examples of children's overextensions in learning the meanings of new words.

Both overextensions and underextensions are normal; a single pairing of a word with the object does not provide enough information for accurate generalization. Suppose someone is teaching you a foreign language. She points to a penny and says *pengar.* Does the word mean "penny," "money,"

TABLE 12.4   Some overextensions made by children while learning new words

Word	Original referent	Application
mooi	moon	Cakes, round marks on windows, writing on windows and in books, round shapes in books, round postmarks, letter *o*
buti	ball	Toy, radish, stone sphere at park entrance
ticktock	watch	All clocks and watches, gas meter, firehose wound on spool, bath scale with round dial
baw	ball	Apples, grapes, eggs, squash, bell clapper, anything round
mem	horse	Cow, calf, pig, moose, all four-legged animals
fly	fly	Specks of dirt, dust, all small insects, child's own toes, crumbs of bread, a toad
wau-wau	dog	All animals, toy dog, soft house slippers, picture of an old man dressed in furs

Adapted from Clark, H.H., and Clark, E.V. *Psychology and Language.* New York: Harcourt Brace Jovanovich, 1977, after Clark (1973).

"coin," or "round"? You cannot decide from this one example. Without further information you may overextend or underextend the meaning of the word if you try to use it. If your teacher then points to a dollar bill and again says *pengar,* you will deduce (correctly) that the word means "money." (See **Figure 12.17.**)

Many words, including function words, do not have physical referents. For example, prepositions such as *on, in,* and *toward* express relationships or directions, and a child needs many examples to learn how to use them appropriately. Pronouns are also difficult; for example, it takes a child some time to grasp the notion that *I* means the speaker— *I* means "me" when I say it, *I* means "you" when you say it. In fact parents usually avoid personal pronouns in speaking with their children; instead they use sentences such as *Does baby want another one?* (meaning "Do you want another one?") and *Daddy will help you* (meaning "I will help you").

Abstract words such as *apparently, necessity, thorough,* and *method* have no direct referents and must be defined in terms of other words. Therefore, children cannot learn their meanings until after they have learned many other words. Explaining the meaning of *apparently* to a child with a limited vocabulary would be as hopeless a task as my using

FIGURE 12.17   This could be "tummy," "soft," or "round."

a Russian dictionary (not a *Russian-English* dictionary) to determine the meaning of a Russian word. Given that I do not understand Russian, the definition would be just as meaningless to me as the word being defined.

WHY CHILDREN LEARN LANGUAGE

◆ The linguistic accomplishments of young children are remarkable. Even a child who later does poorly in school learns the rules of grammar and the meanings of thousands of words. Some children fail to work hard at school, but no normal child fails to learn to talk. What shapes this learning process, and what motivates it? (See **Figure 12.18.**)

There is vigorous controversy about why children learn to speak, and especially to speak grammatically. Noam Chomsky, a noted linguist, observed that the recorded speech of adults is not as correct as the dialogue we read in a novel or hear in a play; often it is ungrammatical, hesitating, and full of unfinished sentences. In fact Chomsky (1965) characterized everyday adult speech as "defective" and "degenerate." If this is really what children hear when they learn to speak, it is amaz-

ing that they manage to acquire the rules of grammar.

Language Acquisition as an Innate Ability

◆ The view that children learn regular rules from apparently haphazard samples of speech has led many linguists to conclude that the ability to learn language is innate; all a child has to do is to be in the company of speakers of a language. McNeill (1970) has proposed that a child's brain contains a "language acquisition device," which contains rules of "universal grammar"; because each language expresses these rules in slightly different ways, the child must learn the details, but the basics are already there in the brain.

There are several problems with the assumption that children do not have to learn the "rules" of grammar. First, assuming that a behavior or capability is innate effectively stops investigation into its origins. It is better to investigate first and to eliminate all other possibilities. Second, people often support this assumption with the claim that children learn language easily, whereas adults learn a new language only with great difficulty. Allegedly the ability to learn a language is at a peak during

FIGURE 12.18   Why do children exert the effort that is needed to learn verbal behaviors?

childhood and declines as people get older. However, this assertion is based on unfair comparisons. Most of a child's waking hours are spent in language practice—both in speaking and in listening to the speech of other people. Most adults who try to learn a new language spend no more than an hour or two each day practicing it. Finally, although adults often speak to one another carelessly and ungrammatically, they are less likely to do so when addressing young children.

How Adults Talk to Children

◆ It has been known for some time that parents use short, simple, well-formed, repetitive sentences and phrases when speaking to their children (Brown and Bellugi, 1964). Their speech does not contain the kinds of faults that supposedly characterize adult speech. In a comprehensive review of the literature, deVilliers and deVilliers (1978) found that adults' speech to children is characterized by clear pronunciation, exaggerated intonations, and careful distinctions between similar-sounding phonemes, relatively few abstract words and function words, and a tendency to isolate constituents that undoubtedly enables young children to recognize them as units of speech. In addition, most speech is in the present tense and refers to tangible objects that the child can see. (See **Figure 12.19**.)

Whether they are parents or not, adults tend to act as tutors when talking with children, prompting their answers:

ADULT: What do you want?

CHILD: (no response)

ADULT: You want what?

Adults also often expand children's speech by imitating it but putting it into more complex forms (Brown and Bellugi, 1964):

CHILD: Baby highchair.

ADULT: Baby is in the highchair.

CHILD: Eve lunch.

ADULT: Eve is having lunch.

CHILD: Throw daddy.

ADULT: Throw it to daddy.

Finally, adults tend to provide a running commentary about what is happening:

ADULT: Now I'm going to pick up the red ball. See the red ball? Here it is. Oh! Baby dropped it! Baby dropped the red ball. It bumped baby's toe. It's rolled far away.

People also make allowances for the age of the child. Mothers talk differently to two-year-olds than

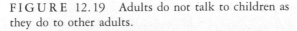

FIGURE 12.19   Adults do not talk to children as they do to other adults.

to ten-year-olds (Snow, 1972a); even four-year-old children talk differently to two-year-olds than they do to adults or other four-year-olds (Shatz and Gelman, 1973).

It seems unlikely that these differentiated speech patterns are innately determined. Snow (1972a) compared the speech patterns of a mother talking to a child with her speech patterns when she only pretended to be talking to a child. The woman's speech when the child was absent was simpler than it would have been if addressed to an adult, but when the child was present it was simpler still. Clearly, then, feedback from children is important.

The Role of Feedback from Children

The most important factor controlling adults' speech to children is the child's attentiveness. An experiment by Snow (1972b) showed that children pay more attention to a tape recording of speech directed to a child than to a recording of speech directed to an adult. Other researchers have found that children respond best to speech that is slightly more complex than their own (Shipley, Smith, and Gleitman, 1969). Interacting with someone who has achieved slightly greater competence appears to be an optimum strategy for most learning; for example, if you want to improve your tennis game, you should play with someone a bit better than

FIGURE 12.20 A child reinforces an adult's verbal behavior and regulates its level of complexity by displaying signs of attention.

you. A poorer player is no challenge, and if you play with someone of professional quality you will hardly get a chance to return the ball.

Both adults and children are very sensitive to whether or not another person is paying attention to them. When a child looks interested we continue with what we are doing. When we notice signs of inattention, we advance or simplify our level of speech until we regain the child's attention. Thus, children modify adults' speech, keeping it at the optimal level of complexity. (See **Figure 12.20**.)

The Role of Reinforcement

As we saw in Chapter 4, reinforcement plays an important role in learning: favorable consequences of a particular behavior can make that behavior occur more often. Critics of the notion that reinforcement plays an important role in the acquisition of language stress the fact that parents seldom praise their children for speaking or correct their ungrammatical utterances, yet children manage to learn very complex behaviors. Therefore, they claim, reinforcement cannot be important. The following examples from Brown, Cazden, and Bellugi (1969) illustrate this tendency. When Eve said to her mother *He a girl* (meaning "You are a girl"), her mother ignored the inappropriate choice of a pronoun and the lack of a verb and said "That's right." Similarly, Eve's mother accepted *Her curl my hair,* because that is what she was doing. However, when Sarah said *There's the animal farmhouse* (which was grammatically acceptable but factually incorrect) she was corrected; the picture that she was looking at was one of a lighthouse.

Skinner (1957) suggested that the use of language is shaped by contingencies in the child's environment, much as complex behaviors can be shaped in other animals through the reinforcement of behaviors that are successively closer and closer to the final form. Most linguists and many psychologists have vigorously objected to Skinner's model, on the grounds discussed above. However, a careful analysis shows that much of this criticism misses an essential feature of reinforcement.

Reinforcement is a process by which the *effects* of a behavior increase the likelihood that the behavior will occur again. Reinforcement is not synonymous with *reward;* it can occur without the deliberate intervention of another person. If I look for wild edible mushrooms in the woods and consistently find them in damp places but not in dry ones, then my searching for them in damp places is reinforced, but my searching for them in dry places is not. No one needs to watch me and drop mushrooms at my feet when I perform the appropriate behavior. I am reinforced for looking in damp places by effects of the laws of nature: mushrooms grow in damp places; therefore, I will find them only if I look there.

Similarly, the fact that parents do not often reward their children's speech behaviors with praise or tangible reinforcers (such as candy) does not contradict the idea that reinforcement plays an important role in the acquisition of verbal behavior. It is the *effects* of speech that are reinforcing: a child who says "Milk!" is likely to receive a glass of milk. The adult does not give the child the milk as a reward for saying *milk*, but as a response to a request. However, the adult's intention is irrelevant. The glass of milk serves as a reinforcer for the verbal behavior that was instrumental in getting it delivered.

Speech provides more subtle (and probably more important) reinforcers. We humans are social animals; our behavior is strongly affected by the behavior of others. It is readily apparent to anyone who has observed the behavior of children that the attention of other people is extremely important to them. Children will perform a variety of behaviors that get other people to pay attention to them. They will make faces, play games, even misbehave in order to attract attention. And, above all, they will talk. Consider yourself in the child's place. Adults or other children are likely to pay attention to you if you start talking to them. If they cannot understand your speech, they are unlikely to maintain their attention.

Thus, reinforcement plays at least two roles in the acquisition of speech. Speech can cause people to provide useful things such as glasses of milk or toys or other amusements, or it can elicit attention and social interaction. Reinforcement can even play a role in the acquisition of the rules of grammar. Simple speech suffices for simple requests. However, more complex requests require more complex speech. If this speech is to be understood, it must be in a form that adults can recognize; that is, it

must be grammatical (although the "rules" do not have to be the full-fledged rules of adult speech—these come slowly and gradually). The acquisition of grammatical speech, then, is reinforced *by the effects of speech that is understood.* For example, a child does not receive explicit reinforcers for learning to use the future tense properly. Instead, reinforcement comes from the effects of using the future tense; the child can get an adult to promise that he or she *will do* something.

It is impossible to prove conclusively that reinforcement is crucial in the acquisition of language. To prove this claim, an experimenter would have to respond to the speech of some children and ignore others or deliberately "misunderstand" them, giving them a toy when they ask for a glass of milk and paying attention to them when they are silent instead of when they speak. Obviously, such an experiment is unconscionable: how satisfactory would the experiment be if the child really failed to learn to speak?

Interim summary: Studies using the habituation of a baby's sucking response have shown that the human auditory system is capable of discriminating among speech sounds soon after birth. This fact has been cited as evidence for innate mechanisms for speech acquisition, but the capabilities of human auditory analysis are not unique; birds such as parrots and mynahs can perceive and mimic human speech sounds. Human vocalization begins with crying, then develops into babbling and finally patterned speech. During the two-word stage children begin to combine words creatively, saying things that they have never heard. Their speech is governed by "rules"; they stress one of the words according to a hierarchy of categories of form and function. Children unconsciously adopt the rules, and adults unconsciously understand them.

As young children gain more experience with the world and with the speech of adults and older children, their vocabulary grows and they learn to use adult rules of grammar. Although the first verbs they learn tend to have irregular past tenses, once they learn the regular past tense rule (add *-ed*) they apply this rule even to irregular verbs they previously used properly.

Psychologists disagree about what motivates a child to learn language; some believe that innate brain mechanisms contain universal grammatical rules whose details are shaped by the child's native language and others believe that verbal behavior is like any other behavior, shaped by the contingencies of reinforcement. As we saw in an earlier section, the human brain contains mechanisms that must function properly for a person to understand speech and use it meaningfully. But at present there is no proof that language develops without reinforcement; a careful analysis of the role that language plays in a child's social interactions suggests that the consequences of learning and using language are reinforcing.

LANGUAGE IN OTHER PRIMATES

The members of most species can communicate with one another. Even insects communicate; a female moth that is ready to mate can release a pheromone that will bring male moths from miles away. And a dog can tell its owner, by bringing its leash in its mouth and whining at the door, that it wants to go for a walk. But until recently, humans were the only species with *language,* that flexible system that uses symbols to express so many meanings.

In the 1960s Beatrice and Roger Gardner, of the University of Nevada, began Project Washoe (Gardner and Gardner, 1969, 1978), a remarkably successful attempt to teach sign language to a female chimpanzee named Washoe. Previous attempts to teach chimps to learn and use human language focused on speech (Hayes, 1952). These failed because chimps lack the control of tongue, lips, palate, and vocal cords that humans have, and thus they cannot produce the variety of complex sounds that characterize human speech.

Gardner and Gardner realized this limitation and decided to attempt to teach Washoe a *manual language*—one that makes use of hand movements. Chimps' hand and finger dexterity is almost as good as ours, so the only limitations in their ability would be cognitive ones. The manual language the Gardners chose was *Ameslan, the American sign language* used by the deaf. Ameslan is a true language; it contains function words and content words and has regular grammatical rules. People can communicate in Ameslan as fast as in spoken languages; they can even make puns based on similarities among signs, just as we make puns based on similarities among the sounds of words.

Washoe was one year old when she began learning Ameslan; by the time she was four, she had a vocabulary of over 130 signs. Like children, she used single signs at first, then began to produce two-word sentences such as *Washoe sorry, gimme flower, more fruit,* and *Roger tickle.* Sometimes she strung three or more words together, using the concept of agent and object: *You tickle me.* She asked and answered questions, apologized, made assertions—in short, did everything that a child would do at the same stage of development (although children of the same calendar age would have reached a higher stage of language development). She showed overextensions and underextensions, just as human children do. Occasionally she even made correct generalizations by herself. After learning the signs for the verb *open* (as in *open box, open cupboard*), she used it to say *open faucet,* in requesting a drink.

Inspired by Project Washoe's success, a number of other investigators have taught other chimpanzees and a gorilla to use sign language. Washoe's training started relatively late in her life, and her trainers were not, at the beginning of the project, fluent in Ameslan. Other chimpanzees, raised from birth by humans who are native speakers of Ameslan, have begun to use signs when they are three months old (Gardner and Gardner, 1975).

Many psychologists and linguists have questions whether the behavior of these animals can really be classified as verbal behavior. For example, Terrace, Petitto, Sanders, and Bever (1979) argue that the apes simply learned to imitate the gestures made by their trainers, and that sequences of signs such as *please milk please me like drink apple bottle* (produced by a young gorilla) are nothing like the sequences that human children produce. Others have challenged these criticisms (Bindra, 1980; Patterson, 1980), and the issue remains controversial. (See **Figure 12.21.**)

Certainly, the verbal behavior of apes cannot be the same as that of humans. If apes could learn to communicate verbally as well as children can, then humans would not be the only species to have developed language. The usefulness of these studies rests in what they can teach us about our own

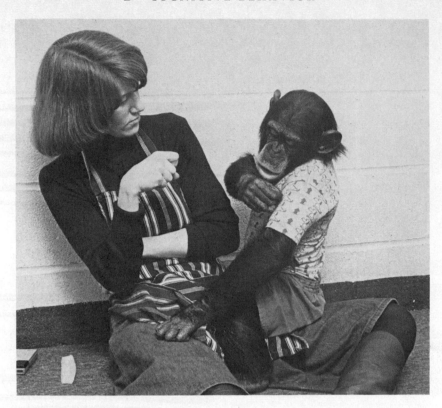

FIGURE 12.21   Psychologists dispute the
significance of the ability of nonhuman primates to
learn to use Ameslan signs.

language and cognitive abilities. Through them we
may discover what abilities animals need in order
to communicate the way we do. They may also
help us understand the evolution of these capacities.

These studies have already provided some useful
information. For example, Premack (1976) has
taught chimpanzees to "read" and "write" by arranging plastic tokens into "sentences." Each token represents an object, action, or attribute such
as color or shape, much the way words do. His
first trainee, Sarah, whom he acquired when she
was one year old, learned to understand complex
sentences such as *Sarah insert banana in pail, apple
in dish.* When she saw the disks arranged in this
order, she obeyed the instructions.

Sarah also learned to use word order to denote
agent-action-object, and she applied this syntactic
rule to construct new sentences such as *Debby cut
banana.* She even constructed a syntactic rule of her
own; she spontaneously combined *Mary give Sarah
apple* with *Mary give Sarah orange,* producing *Mary
give Sarah apple orange.* These linguistic accomplishments are modest in comparison with those of humans. For example, Premack notes that chimpanzees have never been observed to combine *Mary
gives me apple* with *I like Mary* to produce *Mary's
giving me apple is why I like her.* However, it is
possible that the linguistic accomplishments of humans and chimpanzees involve similar kinds of
cognitive abilities, differing only in degree.

Chimpanzees apparently can use symbols to represent real objects and can manipulate these symbols logically. These abilities are two of the most
powerful features of language. For Premack's chimpanzees a blue plastic triangle means "apple." If
the chimpanzees are given a blue plastic triangle
and asked to choose the appropriate symbols de-
noting its color and shape, they choose the ones
that signify "red" and "round," not "blue" and

"triangular." Thus, the blue triangle is not simply a disk that the animals can use to obtain apples; it *represents* an apple for them, just as the word *apple* represents it for us.

Savage-Rumbaugh, Rumbaugh, Smith, and Lawson (1980) obtained more evidence that chimpanzees can use symbols in the representational way that humans do. They tested two chimpanzees that had previously learned a language similar to the one used by Premack and his colleagues; that is, specific visual patterns represented objects, actions,

and other concepts. First, the experimenters taught the chimps to sort real objects according to the categories "food" and "tool"; the animals quickly learned to place a piece of beancake, a slice of orange, and a slice of bread in one bin and a key, a stick, and some money into another. (See **Figure 12.22, A.**).

Next, the trainers taught the chimps symbols representing the two categories they had learned, pairing the three foods with one symbol and the three tools with another. Once the animals learned

FIGURE 12.22 The procedure of the study by Savage-Rumbaugh et al. (From Savage-Rumbaugh, E.S., Rumbaugh, D.M., Smith S.T., and Lawson, J. *Science,* 1980, *210,* 922–925.)

Items learned   Items tested

A. Sorting objects

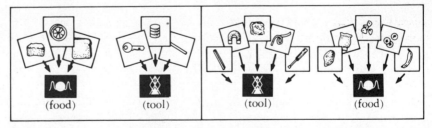

B. Labeling objects

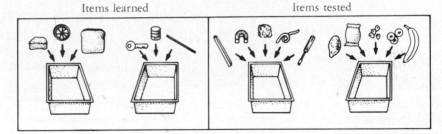

C. Labeling photographs

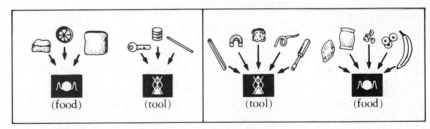

D. Labeling lexigrams

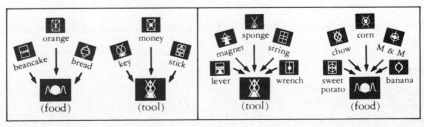

these, they were tested with a variety of other foods and tools (such as peanut, celery, jelly, and raisins versus scrub brush, shovel, screwdriver, and scissors). The chimps responded appropriately; they had learned that the symbols referred to the categories, not simply to the three items in the categories. (See **Figure 12.22, B.**)

The third phase involved the same tasks as the second, but with photographs instead of real objects. The results were about the same. (See **Figure 12.22, C.**).

Finally, the experimenters paired the previously learned symbols for the beancake, orange, bread, key, stick, and money with the symbols representing the categories "food" and "tool." When the chimpanzees were tested with these symbols, they responded appropriately. In other words, they had learned to classify symbols, as well as objects. (See **Figure 12.22, D.**) These results indicate that chimpanzees can learn to use symbolic logic; if real objects are grouped in categories, then the symbols that denote these objects also belong to the same categories.

Other studies have used "chimpanzee language" to study other cognitive skills of these animals. For example, Woodruff, Premack, and Kennel (1978) found that their fourteen-year-old chimpanzee,

Sarah, was able to conserve volume. (You may recall from Chapter 6 that Jean Piaget studied the cognitive skill of conservation extensively.) Woodruff and his colleagues showed Sarah two tall cylinders containing equal volumes of water (dyed blue), then poured the contents of one cylinder into a wider container. Naturally, the level of water was lower in this one. Next the trainer gave Sarah a dish containing two plastic tokens, representing "same" and "different" and immediately left the room, so as not to tell Sarah inadvertently which symbol to choose by making unconscious gestures. Sarah had previously learned how to use these tokens: if two objects were the same she had put "same" between them; if they were different she had put "different" between them. Sara responded by putting the "same" token between the two containers of water. (See **Figure 12.23.**)

Sarah also conserved the volume of solids when their shape was transformed; that is, she placed a "same" token between a ball of modeling clay and the same amount of clay rolled into a different shape. However, she was unable to compare the same or different numbers of objects. Having demonstrated no understanding of the concept of number, she could not be tested for conservation of this concept.

FIGURE 12.23   A chimpanzee demonstrates conservation of liquid. (From Woodruff, G.,

Premack, D., and Kennel, K. *Science,* 1978, *202,* 991–994.)

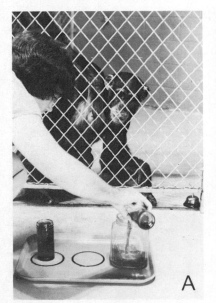

A   B   C

These studies of the ability of other primates to learn language enable us to analyze some of the types of experiences that are necessary for acquiring the skills involved in producing and understanding speech. To the extent that apes can be taught at least some of the rudiments of language, their behaviors provide some hints about the ways in which humans acquire these skills.

CONCLUDING REMARKS

In discussing how we perceive, acquire, and use language, this chapter has built on topics of previous chapters. For example, verbal ability depends on cognitive abilities that engage memory, described in Chapter 11; Chapter 10 examined language in terms of its contributions to human consciousness and the advantages it confers on our species. Learning how to speak, an important part of a child's cognitive development, was discussed in Chapter 6. Chapter 3 described some of the brain mechanisms necessary for speaking and comprehending speech; and the basic principles of learning, discussed in Chapters 4 and 5, have direct bearing on the possible role of reinforcement in language development.

Language is a beautiful medium for thought and expression. We can appreciate fine prose and poetry, enjoy the sound of an actor's voice, converse with a loved one, listen to our children's first words, and think thoughts that could never occur without language. What we know about language so far is a pitifully small part of the entire picture; the quest for an understanding of verbal behavior, the most complex of all our activities, has just begun.

GUIDE TO TERMS
INTRODUCED IN
THIS CHAPTER

SUGGESTIONS FOR
FURTHER READING

An excellent introduction to psycholinguistics is *Psychology and Language* by H.H. Clark and E.V. Clark (New York: Harcourt Brace Jovanovich, 1977). If you are interested in knowing more about how children learn language you should read *Language Acquisition* by J.G. deVilliers and P.A. deVilliers (Cambridge Mass.: Harvard University Press, 1978). "Comparative Psychology and Language Acquisition" by R.A. Gardner and B.T. Gardner (*Annals of the New York Academy of Science*, 1978, *309*, 37–76) and *Language in Primates: Perspectives and Implications* edited by J. de Luce and H.T. Wilder (New York: Springer-Verlag, 1983) describe attempts to teach language to apes.

INTELLIGENCE

LEARNING ◆ OBJECTIVES

JUST AS people differ in temperament, so they differ in skills and abilities, including the ability to perform various intellectual tasks. What is the nature of these individual differences? Is intelligence a single general trait or a composite of many independent, specific abilities? How much of the observed differences is due to heredity, and how much to the effects of environment? How can we measure abilities? Because research into the last question has increased our understanding of all these issues, we shall consider intelligence testing first.

INTELLIGENCE TESTING

Assessment of intellectual ability, or intelligence testing, is a controversial topic because of its importance in modern society. Unless people have special skills that suit them for a career in sports or entertainment, their economic success depends heavily on formal education, and admission to colleges and eligibility for scholarships are largely determined by the results of tests. Because the scores achieved on these tests have important implications for the quality of people's adult lives, testing has become one of the most important areas of applied psychology. Today there are hundreds of tests of specific abilities, such as manual dexterity, spatial reasoning, vocabulary, mathematical aptitude, musical ability, creativity, and memory. There are also general tests of scholastic aptitude, some of

which you have probably taken yourself. These tests vary widely in reliability, validity, and ease of administration.

FROM MANDARINS TO GALTON

Undoubtedly humans have been aware of individual differences in abilities since our species first evolved. Some people were more efficient hunters, some were more skillful at constructing tools and weapons, some were more daring and clever warriors. As early as 2200 B.C., Chinese administrators tested civil servants (mandarins) periodically to be sure that their abilities qualified them for their jobs. But in Western cultures differences in social class were far more important than individual differences in ability until the Renaissance, when the modern concept of individualism came into being.

◆   Although the term *intelligence* is an old one, deriving from Latin *intellectus* ("perception" or "comprehension"), its use in the English language dates only from the late nineteenth century, when it was revived by the philosopher Herbert Spencer and by the biologist-statistician Sir Francis Galton (1822–1911), the most important early investigator of individual differences in ability. Galton was strongly influenced by his cousin, Charles Darwin, who stressed the importance of inherited differences in the physical and behavioral traits related to species survival. Galton observed that there were family differences in ability and concluded that intellectual abilities were heritable. Having noted that people with low ability were poor at making sensory discriminations, he decided that tests involving such discriminations would provide valid measures of intelligence.

In 1884 Galton established the Anthropometric ("human-measuring") Laboratory at the International Health Exhibition in London. His exhibit was so popular that afterward his laboratory became part of the South Kensington Museum. He tested over 9000 people on seventeen variables, including height and weight, muscular strength, and the ability to perform sensory discriminations.

FIGURE 13.1 *Top:* A mathematically derived normal curve. *Bottom:* A curve showing the distribution of IQ scores of 850 children of 2½ years of age. (From Terman, L.M., and Merrill, M.A. *Stanford-Binet Intelligence Scale.* Boston: Houghton Mifflin, 1960; material cited pertains to the 1960 edition and not to the 4th edition, 1985. Reproduced by permission of The Riverside Publishing Co.)

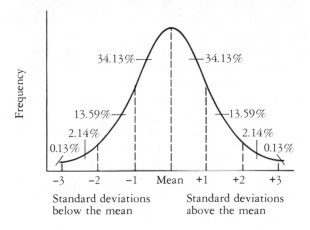

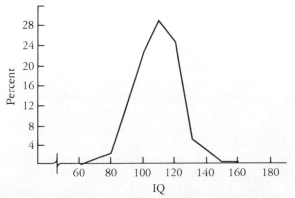

One task involved detecting small differences in the weights of objects of the same size and shape. Later research proved that tests of sensory discrimination were poor predictors of academic or vocational success, so Galton's research program was not continued after his death.

Nevertheless, Galton made some important contributions to the study of individual differences. His systematic evaluation of large numbers of people and the methods of population statistics he developed served as models for the statistical tests that are now used in all branches of science. His observation that the distribution of most human traits closely resembles the normal curve developed by the Belgian statistician Quetelet is the foundation for many modern tests of statistical significance. (See **Figure 13.1.**)

Galton also outlined the logic of a measure he called *correlation*—the degree to which variability in one measure is related to variability in another. From this analysis Karl Pearson derived the correlation coefficient (r) that is used today to assess the degree of statistical relation between variables. In addition, Galton developed the logic of *twin studies* and *foster parent studies* to assess the heritability of a human trait. These methods are discussed later in the chapter.

THE BINET-SIMON TEST

Alfred Binet, a French psychologist, disagreed with Galton's conception of human intelligence. He and a colleague (Binet and Henri, 1896) suggested that a group of simple sensory tests could not adequately determine a person's intelligence. They recommended measuring a variety of psychological abilities—such as imagery, attention, comprehension, imagination, judgments of visual space, and memory for various stimuli—that appeared to be more representative of the traits that distinguished people of high and low intelligence. (See **Figure 13.2.**)

To identify children who were unable to profit from normal classroom instruction and needed special attention, Binet and another colleague, Theodore Simon, assembled a collection of tests, many of which had been developed by other investigators, and published the **Binet-Simon Scale** in 1905. The tests were arranged in order of difficulty, and

FIGURE 13.2   Alfred Binet (1857–1911) developed a test of intellectual ability that is still used today, in revised form.

the researchers obtained *norms*—distributions of scores obtained by children of different ages. Binet and Simon also provided a detailed description of the testing procedure, which was essential for obtaining reliable scores. Without a standardized procedure for administering a test, different testers can obtain different scores from the same child.

Binet revised the 1905 test in order to assess the intellectual abilities of both normal children and those with learning problems. The revised versions provided a procedure for estimating a child's *mental age*—the level of intellectual development that could be expected for an average child of a particular age. For example, if a child of eight scored as well as average ten-year-old children, his or her mental age would be ten years. Binet did not develop the concept of the IQ, or intelligence quotient. Nor did he believe that the mental age derived from the test scores expressed a simple trait

called intelligence; rather, he conceived of the score as the average of several different abilities.

THE STANFORD-BINET TEST

◆ Lewis Terman, of Stanford University, translated and revised the Binet-Simon test in the United States. The test, published in 1916, became known as the *Stanford-Binet Scale.* Revisions by Terman and Maud Merrill were published in 1937 and 1960. The scale consists of various tasks grouped according to mental age. Simple tests include identification of parts of the body and remembering which of three small cardboard boxes contains a marble. Intermediate tests include tracing a simple maze with a pencil and repeating five digits orally. Advanced tests include explaining the difference between two abstract words that are close in meaning (such as *fame* and *notoriety*) and completing complex sentences.

The 1916 Stanford-Binet scale contained a formula for computing the *intelligence quotient,* or *IQ,* a measure devised by Stern (1914). Its rationale is quite simple: If the test scores indicate that a child's mental age is equal to his or her chronological age (that is, calendar age), then the child's intelligence is average; if the child's mental age is above or below his or her chronological age, then the child is more or less intelligent than average. This relation is expressed as the quotient of mental age (MA) and chronological age (CA). The result is called the *ratio IQ:*

$$IQ = \frac{MA}{CA} \times 100$$

The quotient is multiplied by 100 to eliminate fractions. For example, if a child's mental age is ten and chronological age is eight, then his or her IQ is (10 ÷ 8) × 100, or 125.

The 1960 version of the Stanford-Binet replaced the ratio IQ with the *deviation IQ.* Instead of using the ratio of chronological age to mental age, the new measure compared a child's score with those received by other children of the same chronological age. Suppose a child's score is one standard deviation above the mean for his or her age. (See Chapter 2 for a discussion of standard deviation.) The standard deviation of the older ratio IQ scores is 16 points, and the score assigned to the average

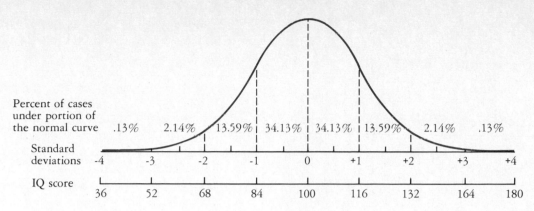

Percent of cases
under portion of
the normal curve   .13%   2.14%   13.59% 34.13% 34.13% 13.59%   2.14%   .13%

Standard
deviations   -4   -3   -2   -1   0   +1   +2   +3   +4

IQ score
                36   52   68   84   100   116   132   164   180

FIGURE 13.3   The rationale for calculating the
deviation IQ score.

IQ is 100 points; thus, the child's score is 100 plus 16 (the standard deviation), or 116. A child who scores one standard deviation below the mean receives a deviation IQ of 84 (100 − 16). (See **Figure 13.3.**)

◆   As you recall from Chapter 2, the adequacy of a measure is represented by its reliability and validity. Reliability is the likelihood a person will receive the same score if the measurement is made more than once. High reliability is achieved by means of standardized test administration and objective scoring: all people are exposed to the same situation during testing and all testers score responses in the same way. A reliability score can be thought of as the correlation between two test scores for the same person on two occasions; a perfect score is 1.0. The reliability of the revised 1937 IQ score was found to be very high, ranging from .98 for people with low IQs to .90 for people with high IQs.

Validity is the correlation between test scores and an actual measurement of the variable that is being assessed—the *criterion.* For example, suppose you plan to estimate a person's wealth by observing how many money-related words he or she uses when describing a picture that illustrates a story. (This example is fictitious; no one has developed such a test—I think.) You can determine the validity of the test by seeing how accurately it estimates people's actual wealth (the criterion).

But it is impossible to assess the validity of any test of intelligence, because the variable that is being measured (intelligence) is an abstraction; there

is no criterion measure. The IQ correlates rather well with success in school (between .40 and .75). This fact, together with the fact that intellectual ability plays at least some role in academic success, makes it likely that the IQ has some validity.

WECHSLER'S TESTS

◆ When David Wechsler was chief psychologist at New York City's Bellevue Psychiatric Hospital, he developed several popular and well-respected tests of intelligence. The Wechsler-Bellevue, published in 1939, was revised in 1942 for use in the armed forces and was superseded in 1955 by the *Wechsler Adult Intelligence Scale (WAIS).* This test was revised again (WAIS-R) in 1981. The *Wechsler Intelligence Scale for Children (WISC),* first published in 1949 and revised in 1974, closely resembles the WAIS. Wechsler also devised an intelligence test for preschool children, a memory scale, and other measures of ability.

The WAIS consists of eleven subtests, divided into two categories, verbal and performance. **Table 13.1** lists the subtests and a typical question or problem for each. **Figure 13.4** shows a person taking one of them—block design. The norms obtained for the WAIS permit the tester to calculate a deviation IQ score.

The WAIS has become the most popular individually administered adult intelligence test. Like the Stanford-Binet, it is very reliable. An important advantage is that it tests verbal and performance abilities separately. Neuropsychologists

FIGURE 13.4   A subject working on one of the problems of the block design subtest of The Wechsler Adult Intelligence Scale, Revised (WAIS-R).

often use it because people with brain damage tend to score very differently on the performance and verbal tests; thus, comparisons of performance and verbal test scores suggest the presence of undiagnosed brain damage. Because people who have had few educational and cultural opportunities often do worse on the verbal tests than on the performance tests, the WAIS is useful in estimating what their score might have been in a more favorable environment.

THE USE AND ABUSE OF INTELLIGENCE TESTS

Many kinds of institutions use intelligence tests and tests of specific abilities. Schools that group students according to ability usually do so on the

TABLE 13.1   WAIS-R subtests and typical questions or problems

Subtests	Typical questions or problems
Verbal	
Information	"What is the capital of France?"
Digit span	"Repeat these numbers back to me: 46239."
Vocabulary	"What does 'conventional' mean?"
Arithmetic	"Suppose you bought six postcards for thirteen cents each and gave the clerk a dollar. How much change would you receive?" (Paper and pencil cannot be used.)
Comprehension	"Why are we tried by a jury of our peers?
Similarities	"How are goldfish and canaries similar to each other?"
Performance	
Picture completion	Tester shows the subject a picture with a missing part (such as a mouse without its whiskers) and says, "Tell me what's missing."
Picture arrangement	The tester shows a series of cartoon pictures (without words) and instructs the subject to arrange them in the proper sequence.
Block design	The tester shows a picture and four or nine blocks divided diagonally into red and white sections, then instructs the subject to arrange the blocks so that they match the design in the picture.
Object assembly	The tester gives the subject pieces of cardboard cut like a jigsaw puzzle and instructs him or her to assemble it. (When properly assembled the pieces form the shape of a common object.)
Digit symbol	The tester presents a set of ten designs paired with the ten numerals and instructs the subject to write the corresponding symbols beneath each of a large series of numerals.

FIGURE 13.5   Each year thousands of high-school students in North America take achievement tests, the scores of which are used by college and university admission committees.

basis of test scores. Schools also administer tests to students who appear to be slow learners, to assess educational needs that may require participation in a special program. At selective academic institutions, test scores usually serve as an important criterion for admission. Similarly, many business organizations use ability tests to screen job candidates. Because test scores have such important consequences for people's opportunities, it is essential to know whether intelligence tests are valid and whether they are used appropriately. (See **Figure 13.5**.)

◆   Critics of intelligence testing have argued that intelligence tests do not measure people's abilities at all; rather, they measure what people have learned. Therefore, people's educational opportunities in the home, neighborhood, and school directly influence their performance on intelligence tests. Consider the effects of a person's family background and culture on his or her ability to answer questions such as "Who wrote *Romeo and Juliet?*" What is a hieroglyphic?" "What is the meaning of cata-

comb?" and "What is the thing to do if another boy (or girl) hits you without meaning to?" (Vernon, 1979, p. 22). Obviously, a child from a middle-class family is much more likely to be able to answer the first three questions than an equally intelligent child from a deprived environment. The answer given to the fourth question is also likely to be culturally determined. Test constructors have responded to this criticism, and modern tests are much less likely to contain questions that are obviously biased culturally.

Predicting and Measuring Performance

◆ Critics' objections to the more general issue that intelligence tests measure what people have learned, and not what they *can* learn, are also valid. It is clear that two people with identical innate abilities can have very different IQ scores. But this fact does not necessarily mean that intelligence tests are useless. Perhaps what a person has learned is useful in predicting how well he or she will continue to learn in the future.

Intelligence tests have been found to be rather good predictors of a child's scholastic performance. As mentioned before, the correlation between scores on the 1960 Stanford-Binet and school grades ranges from .40 to .75 (Aiken, 1982). However, critics of these tests question the need for teachers to *predict* children's academic performance. After all, teachers are in a position to observe performance. What information do intelligence tests provide that teachers cannot observe in their classrooms?

Another potential abuse of intelligence tests is to deprive children who have scored poorly of opportunities to receive an education that will make them competitive later in life. According to Kenneth Clark:

> The I.Q. cannot be considered sacred or even relevant in decisions about the future of the child. It should not be used to shackle children. An I.Q. so misused contributes to the wastage of human potential. The I.Q. can be a valuable educational tool within the limits of its utility, namely, as an index of what needs to be done for a particular child. The I.Q. used . . . to determine where one must start, to determine what a particular child needs to bring him up to maximum effectiveness, is a valuable educational aid. But [to use] the I.Q. as an end product or an end decision for children is criminally neglectful. The I.Q. should not be used as a basis for segregating children and for predicting—and, therefore, determining—the child's educational future. (1965, p. 129)

Intelligence tests, then, should not be used to label children; they should be used to assess what children need to learn. Ebel (1966) points out additional dangers. First, children who discover that they have scored poorly on an intelligence test are likely to suffer feelings of inferiority and may become disinclined to try to learn, believing that they cannot. Second, undue emphasis on testing may affect a school's curriculum and methods of teaching; teachers and administrators may try to teach information and skills that are measured by the tests instead of basing their curriculum on the children's needs. On the other hand, intelligence testing can be used to assess the value of experimental teaching methods and curricula. Using results from objective testing, educators can decide whether to retain, modify, or abandon new classroom procedures. Clearly, schools should use in-

telligence tests with great caution. If the results are not themselves used intelligently, such tests are actually harmful.

Identifying Specific Learning Needs

Intelligence testing has other potential benefits when used in accordance with Binet's original purpose—to identify students who require special instruction. Children with severe learning problems are likely to develop a strong sense of inferiority if they are placed in classes with children whose academic progress is much faster than theirs, and will probably benefit most from special teaching methods. The tests can also identify exceptionally bright students who are performing poorly because they are bored with the pace of instruction or who have been labeled as "troublemakers" by their teachers.

Many otherwise bright children suffer from various specific learning disabilities. Some have trouble learning to read or write, or perform poorly at arithmetic or motor skills. For example, some children have difficulty learning to recognize letters of the alphabet; a deficit in visual perception makes it difficult for them to learn to read. Others can recognize the letters but have trouble blending the individual sounds that each letter represents. These difficulties (and others) are collectively called *dyslexia,* literally, "bad reading."

Dyslexic children are often frustrated by the contrast between their inability to read and their other abilities. They may act out this frustration through disruptive behavior at school and at home, or they may simply stop trying to excel at anything. As a result, they are sometimes stigmatized as mentally retarded and denied the opportunity for a good education. In this situation, tests of intellectual abilities are extremely useful. By identifying a specific learning disability in an otherwise bright child, testing helps ensure remedial action and prevents mislabeling.

Identifying Degrees of Mental Retardation

Binet's original use of intelligence tests—to identify children who learn more slowly than most others and who therefore need special training—is still important. Some children are so deficient in intellectual abilities that they require institutional care. Intelligence tests are accepted means of evaluating

FIGURE 13.6   A mentally retarded adult.

the extent of a child's disabilities, and thus of the most appropriate remedial program.

The term *mental retardation* was applied to children with severe learning problems because they appeared to achieve intellectual skills and competencies at a significantly later age than most children. Their achievements came more slowly; thus, their developmental stages appeared to be retarded. Although most mentally retarded people were formerly relegated to a bleak and hopeless existence in institutions, many successful training programs have been instituted in recent years. The causes of mental retardation are discussed later in this chapter.

Mental retardation is often accompanied by deficits in physical and social skills. (See **Figure 13.6.**) The most severe classification, *profound mental retardation,* designates people with a mental age of under three years, with IQ scores under 25. These people usually have severe brain damage, and they almost always also have physical defects. Few of them learn to read and write unless they are trained by special methods. They need custodial care. Approximately 0.1 percent of the population can be classified as profoundly mentally retarded.

Trainable mental retardation designates people with mental ages ranging from three to seven-and-a-half years, with IQ scores of 25 to 50. Many of these people also require custodial care. People in this category constitute approximately 0.3 percent of the population.

Educable mental retardation designates people with mental ages of seven-and-a-half to eleven years, with IQ scores of 50 to 75. These people constitute approximately 2.6 percent of the population. With adequate training, most educable mentally retarded people can lead independent lives and perform well at jobs that do not require a great deal of intellectual ability.

Interim summary: Although the earliest known instance of ability testing was carried out by the ancient Chinese, modern intelligence testing dates from the efforts of Galton to measure individual differences. Although he made a significant contribution to the field of measurement, his use of tests of simple perceptual abilities has been abandoned in favor of tests that attempt to assess more complex abilities, such as memory, logical reasoning, and vocabulary.

Binet developed a test that was designed to assess students' intellectual abilities in order to identify children with special educational needs. Although the test that superseded his, the Stanford-Binet scale, provided for calculation of the IQ, Binet believed that "intelligence" was actually a composite of several specific abilities. For him, the concept of mental age was a convenience, not a biological reality. Wechsler's two intelligence tests, the WAIS for adults and the WISC for children, are widely used today. The information provided by the verbal and performance scores helps neuropsychologists diagnose brain damage and can provide at least a rough estimate of the innate ability of poorly educated people.

Reliability of modern intelligence tests is excellent, but it is still difficult to assess their validity. Since no criterion measure of intelligence exists, intelligence tests are validated by comparing the scores with measures of achievement, such as scholastic success.

Intelligence tests can have both good and bad effects on people who take them. The principal benefit is derived by identifying children with special needs (or special talents) who will profit from special programs. The principal danger is stigmatizing those who score poorly and depriving them of the opportunity for good jobs or further education.

THE NATURE
OF INTELLIGENCE

◆ There is no doubt that people vary widely in intellectual abilities such as problem solving, acquisition and use of vocabulary, and efficiency in learning new information. The question remains whether intelligence is a global trait or a composite of separate, independent abilities. The fact that we take a test that yields a single IQ score does not in itself mean that intelligence is a single general characteristic. It is possible that the abilities to learn the meanings of words, to understand mathematical reasoning, and so on are completely independent; for example, a person can be excellent at spatial reasoning but poor at solving verbal analogies. Even investigators who believe that intelligence is a global trait acknowledge that people also have specific intellectual abilities and that these abilities are at least somewhat independent. But there is still disagreement between those who believe that specific abilities are totally independent and those who believe that one general factor influences them all.

SPEARMAN'S TWO-FACTOR THEORY

◆ Charles Spearman (1927) proposed that a person's performance on a test of intellectual ability is determined by two factors: *g,* a general factor, and *s,* a factor that is specific to a particular test. Spear-

man did not call his *g* factor intelligence; he considered the term too vague. However, his definition of *g* seems similar to what we call intelligence: *g* represents a person's ability to perform "eduction of relations and correlates." *Eduction* (not "*education*") is the process of drawing or bringing out, figuring out from given facts. Roughly speaking, Spearman equated eduction with logical analysis and deduction.

Empirical evidence for Spearman's two-factor theory comes from correlations between various tests of intellectual ability. The governing logic is as follows. Suppose we administer ten different tests to a group of people. If each test measures a separate, independent ability, the score of any individual on any one test will be unrelated to his or her score on any other; the correlations between them will be approximately zero. However, if each test measures abilities that are simply manifestations of a single trait, the scores will be perfectly related; the intercorrelations will be close to 1.0. In fact the intercorrelations among a group of tests are neither zero nor one; most tests that are designed to measure specific intellectual abilities are at least moderately correlated: a person who scores well on a vocabulary test also tends to score well on other tests, such as arithmetic or spatial reasoning. The correlations between various tests of mental ability usually range from .30 to .70; that is, the tests have from 10 percent to 50 percent of their variance in common. (You will recall that the common variance between two variables is equal to the square of the correlation coefficient, or r^2.)

Spearman concluded that a general factor (*g*) accounted for the common variance shared among different tests of ability. Thus, a person's score on a particular test depended upon two things: the person's specific ability (*s*) on the factor being measured (such as spatial reasoning) and his or her level of *g,* or general reasoning ability. However, even though Spearman's data were consistent with his theory, they do not prove that his theory is correct. The fact that two tests are correlated does not prove that they share a common *g* factor; they could be sharing a common *s* factor instead. For example, if we construct and administer two tests, one consisting of fifty multiplication problems and the other of fifty division problems, we will undoubtedly find that people who do well on one also tend to do well on the other. But this correlation is not necessarily evidence for a common *g* factor; more likely, the tests share a common *s* factor, because multiplication and division are similar tasks. Only special methods such as factor analysis can suggest how much of the correlation between two tests can be attributed to an *s* factor and how much to a *g* factor.

EVIDENCE FROM FACTOR ANALYSIS

◈ Table 13.2 presents an *intercorrelation matrix* of the WAIS subtests, constructed from data obtained by Birren and Morrison (1961) in a study of 933 people. To find a correlation between any two tests, locate the row that contains one of the tests, the column that contains the other, and read the number where row and column intersect. For example, the correlation between comprehension (subtest 2) and vocabulary (subtest 6) is .60. (See **Table 13.2.**)

The high correlation between these two tests indicates that they measure similar abilities. Vocabulary measures the ability to supply definitions of words, and people learn the meaning of words by listening to others and by reading. Thus, when they learn the meanings of new words, they probably also learn new facts; and the comprehension subtest presents factual questions such as "Why are

we tried by a jury of our peers?" In contrast, we might expect that the abilities required to repeat a list of numbers are rather different from those needed to assemble a set of blocks into a geometric pattern; and in fact the correlation between the WAIS digit-span and block-design subtests is only .24. Look at the matrix in Table 13.2 to see which types of tests appear to measure similar abilities. (See **Table 13.2.**)

Factor analysis, a statistical method developed by Spearman and Pearson, permits investigators to discover common factors in an intercorrelation matrix. Table 13.3 lists the results of a factor analysis on the data of Table 13.2. A, B, and C represent the three factors that have been isolated. (See **Table 13.3.**)

The numbers in the three columns are called *factor loadings.* They are somewhat like correlation coefficients in that they express the degree to which a particular test is related to a particular factor. For the various subtests on factor A, the largest loading is for vocabulary, followed by information, comprehension, and similarities. In the middle range are picture completion, arithmetic, picture arrangement, and digit symbol. Digit span, object assembly, and block design are the smallest. (See **Table 13.3.**) Although verbal subtests make the most important contribution, almost all make

---

TABLE 13.2   Matrix of correlations among WAIS subtests

Subtests	1	2	3	4	5	6	7	8	9	10	11
1. Information	—	.50	.45	.49	.30	.67	.24	.48	.34	.35	.25
2. Comprehension	.50	—	.38	.43	.22	.60	.20	.41	.32	.36	.24
3. Arithmetic	.45	.38	—	.32	.39	.39	.23	.32	.36	.28	.24
4. Similarities	.49	.43	.32	—	.22	.54	.25	.40	.35	.31	.25
5. Digit span	.30	.22	.39	.22	—	.29	.26	.26	.24	.26	.16
6. Vocabulary	.67	.60	.39	.54	.29	—	.33	.44	.32	.40	.26
7. Digit symbol	.24	.20	.23	.25	.26	.33	—	.27	.28	.27	.26
8. Picture completion	.48	.41	.32	.40	.26	.40	.27	—	.48	.44	.38
9. Block design	.34	.32	.36	.35	.24	.32	.28	.48	—	.37	.49
10. Picture arrangement	.35	.36	.28	.31	.26	.40	.27	.44	.37	—	.29
11. Object assembly	.25	.24	.24	.25	.16	.26	.26	.38	.49	.29	—

From Aiken, L.R. *Psychological Testing and Assessment,* 4th ed. Boston: Allyn and Bacon, 1982, after Birren and Morrison (1961).

TABLE 13.3   Three factors derived by factor analysis of scores on WAIS subtests

SUBTESTS	FACTORS		
	A	B	C
Information	.70	.18	.25
Comprehension	.63	.12	.24
Arithmetic	.38	.35	.28
Similarities	.57	.12	.27
Digit span	.16	.84	.13
Vocabulary	.84	.16	.18
Digit symbol	.24	.22	.29
Picture completion	.41	.15	.53
Block design	.20	.14	.73
Picture arrangement	.35	.18	.41
Object assembly	.16	.06	.59

Adapted from Morrison, D.F. *Multivariate Statistical Methods.* New York: McGraw-Hill, 1967.

at least a moderate contribution. We might be tempted to call this factor "general intelligence," although the name is arbitrary. How does the distribution of weights correspond to your own concept of intelligence? On factor B, digit span loads vary heavily (.84), but other tests register much lower. Arithmetic and digit symbol have moderate loadings. This factor appears to be related to maintaining information in short-term memory and manipulating numbers. Factor C appears to be determined mainly by block design, object assembly, picture completion, and picture arrangement. A good name for this factor might be "spatial ability."

This factor analysis suggests that a person's performance on the WAIS is largely determined by three factors. However, the analysis does not provide names for the factors. We could easily argue that factor A should be called "verbal skill" rather than "general intelligence" and assert that this factor is not a general one at all; perhaps it *appears* to be general only because verbal ability is a part of much of our learning. Although factor analysis can give hints about the nature of intelligence, it cannot provide definitive answers.

Furthermore, factor analysis can never be more meaningful than the individual tests on which it is performed. For example, experience has shown that the WAIS is a useful predictor of scholastic performance and (to a lesser extent) of vocational success. Thus, it appears to measure some important abilities. But a factor analysis of the subtests will never reveal other important skills that may *not* be measured by the WAIS. To identify the relevant factors in human intelligence, one must include an extensive variety of tests in the factor analysis.

The factor analysis shown in Table 13.3 consists

TABLE 13.4   A hypothetical matrix of correlations among several physical measurements

Measurements	1	2	3	4	5	6	7	8	9
1. Arm length	—	.69	.72	.66	.24	.17	.30	.28	.22
2. Finger length	.69	—	.81	.78	.34	.25	.29	.19	.33
3. Torso length	.72	.81	—	.82	.22	.31	.19	.24	.30
4. Foot size	.66	.78	.82	—	.21	.26	.32	.29	.16
5. Flesh thickness	.24	.34	.22	.21	—	.58	.62	.71	.63
6. Waist circumference	.17	.25	.31	.26	.58	—	.78	.73	.80
7. Hip circumference	.30	.29	.19	.32	.62	.78	—	.69	.66
8. Arm circumference	.28	.19	.24	.29	.71	.73	.69	—	.89
9. Thigh circumference	.22	.33	.30	.16	.63	.80	.66	.89	—

of factors that have been chosen to be independent of each other; that is, the intercorrelations of the factors are zero. Other types of factor analysis, using different assumptions and procedures, permit the extraction of factors that are related to each other.

There is a sound rationale for extracting correlated factors. Consider a hypothetical example. Suppose that we obtain a number of physical measures of people's bodies—arm length, finger length, torso length, foot size, thickness of a pinch of flesh, and circumference of waist, hips, arms, and thighs—and prepare a table of intercorrelations such as the hypothetical ones presented in **Table 13.4.** If we perform a factor analysis we will surely obtain two factors: height and weight. Although a person's weight can certainly vary without affecting his or her height (getting fatter does not make a person become taller), differences in height are nevertheless related to differences in

FIGURE 13.7   Five tests that correlate well with Cattell's g_f factor. (From Form B, Scales II and III, IPAT Culture-Fair Test. By permission of the Institute of Personality and Ability Testing, 1602 Coronado Drive, Champaign, Illinois, and the Cattell Scale II, Harrap & Co.)

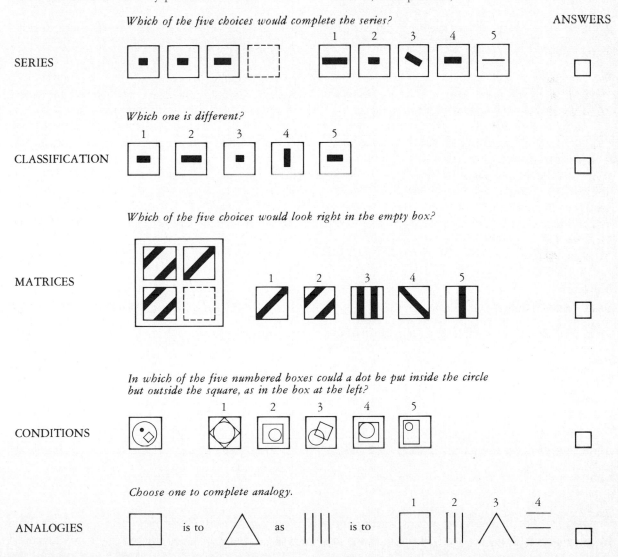

weight. In general, taller people are heavier than shorter people. Therefore, it would be inappropriate in this case to perform a factor analysis that extracts uncorrelated factors.

◆ Many investigators have performed factor analyses on tests of intellectual abilities that yield correlated factors. For example, Louis Thurstone (1938) administered a battery of fifty-six tests to 218 college students, then performed a factor analysis and extracted seven factors, which he labeled verbal meaning, number, space, perceptual speed, word fluency, memory, and inductive reasoning. At first, Thurstone thought that his results contradicted Spearman's hypothesized g factor. However, Raymond Cattell suggested that because Thurstone's factors were not independent, a second factor analysis could be performed on them. If the analysis successfully extracted a common factor, Spearman's g factor would receive support. In other words, if Thurstone's seven factors themselves had a second-order factor in common, this factor might be conceived of as general intelligence.

Cattell performed a second-order factor analysis and found not one but several factors. He and Horn (1966) later confirmed these results in Cattell's own laboratory, using his own tests. The first two factors appear to account for most of the variability. Cattell called these *fluid intelligence* (g_f) and *crystallized intelligence* (g_c). (You may recall these terms from Chapter 6 in the discussion of the effects of aging on intelligence.) Fluid intelligence is defined as essentially nonverbal, relatively culture-free mental efficiency. Presumably, it is most closely related to a person's innate capacity for intellectual performance—a potential ability to learn and solve problems. In contrast, crystallized intelligence represents what a person has accomplished through the use of his or her fluid intelligence—what he or she has learned.

Figure 13.7 illustrates items from five subtests that load heavily on the g_f (fluid intelligence) factor. Although verbalization can help solve these problems, they are essentially nonverbal in form. In addition, the items differ from the types of problems encountered in school, and they do not appear to be closely tied to cultural experience. (See **Figure 13.7**.)

Tests that load heavily on g_c (crystallized intelligence) include word analogies and tests of vocabulary, general information, and use of language.

Theoretically, g_c depends on g_f. Fluid intelligence supplies the native ability, whereas experience with language and exposure to books, school, and other learning opportunities develop crystallized intelligence. If two people have the same experiences, the one with the greater fluid intelligence will develop the greater crystallized intelligence. How-

TABLE 13.5   Summary of tests with large factor loadings on g_f or g_c

TESTS	APPROXIMATE FACTOR LOADINGS	
	g_f	g_c
Figural relations: Deduction of a relation when this is shown among common figures	.57	.01
Memory span: Reproduction of several numbers or letters presented briefly	.50	.00
Induction: Deduction of a correlate from relations shown in a series of letters, numbers, or figures, as in a letter series test	.41	.06
General reasoning: Solving problems of area, rate, finance, and the like, as in an arithmetic reasoning test	.31	.34
Semantic relations: Deduction of a relation when this is shown among words, as in an analogies test	.37	.43
Formal reasoning: Arriving at a conclusion in accordance with a formal reasoning process, as in a syllogistic reasoning test	.31	.41
Number facility: Quick and accurate use of arithmetical operations such as addition, subtraction, and multiplication	.21	.29
Experiential evaluation: Solving problems involving protocol and requiring diplomacy, as in a social relations test	.08	.43
Verbal comprehension: Advanced understanding of language, as measured in a vocabulary or reading test	.08	.68

Adapted from Horn, J.L. "Organization of Abilities and the Development of Intelligence." *Psychological Review*, 1968, 75, 249.

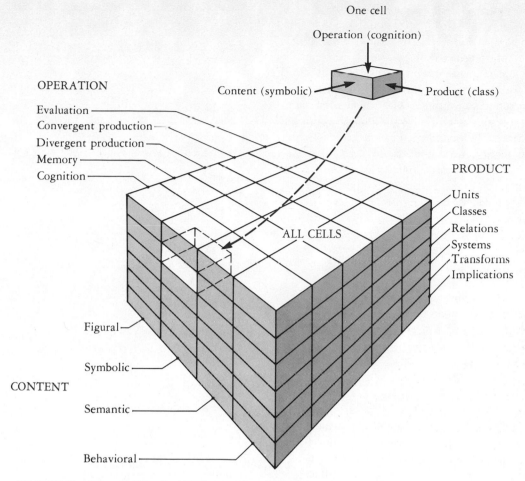

One cell

Operation (cognition)

Content (symbolic) → ← Product (class)

OPERATION

Evaluation
Convergent production
Divergent production
Memory
Cognition

PRODUCT

Units
Classes
Relations
Systems
Transforms
Implications

ALL CELLS

Figural

Symbolic

CONTENT

Semantic

Behavioral

FIGURE 13.8   Guilford's 120 factors of intelligence. (From Guilford, J.P. *The Nature of Human Intelligence.* New York: McGraw-Hill, 1967.)

ever, a person with a high fluid intelligence exposed to an intellectually impoverished environment will develop a poor or mediocre crystallized intelligence. **Table 13.5** presents a summary by Horn (1968) of tests that load on g_f and g_c.

◈   Some investigators question the existence of a general intelligence factor. For example, J.P. Guilford (1967) has conceptualized intelligence as a structure with three dimensions: the *mental operations* that are performed on a given task, the *content* on which the mental operation is performed, and the resulting *product*. He has identified five types of operations, four types of content, and six types of products, for a total of 5 × 4 × 6, or 120

factors. (See **Figure 13.8**.) Guilford claims to have identified 98 of these factors in his research.

No two investigators agree about the nature of intelligence. However, most believe that a small number of common factors (such as Cattell's g_f and g_c) account for at least part of a person's performance on intellectual tasks. Most of them reject Guilford's suggestion that intelligence consists of a large number of completely independent factors.

STABILITY OF IQ SCORES

◈ It is a common belief that the IQ score measures a permanent and rather stable attribute. However, the best evidence on this issue indicates otherwise. In a longitudinal study of sixty-one children born in Berkeley, California, Jones and Bayley (1941) measured the children's IQs repeatedly from the ages of one month to eighteen years. Table 13.6 presents the correlations between the measurements taken at various ages with the final measurement at age eighteen. The values for the children under six years of age represent the mean of three measurements, taken one to six months apart. (See **Table 13.6.**) The table indicates that the scores of IQ tests administered early in life have no relation to IQ scores received later. However, the correlation improves substantially, reaching approxi-

TABLE 13.6   Correlations between IQ scores measured at various ages and scores measured at age eighteen

Age at measurement	r at 18 years
1–3 months	.05[a]
4–6 months	− .01[a]
7–9 months	.20[a]
10–12 months	.41[a]
13–15 months	.23[a]
18–24 months	.55[a]
27–36 months	.54[a]
42–54 months	.62[a]
6 years	.77
7 years	.80
8 years	.85
9 years	.87
10 years	.86
11 years	.93
12 years	.89
13 years	.93
14 years	.89
15 years	.88
16 years	.94
17 years	.90

[a]Mean of three measurements taken one to three months apart.

Adapted from Brody, E.B., and Brody, N. *Intelligence: Nature, Determinants, and Consequences.* New York: Academic Press, 1976.

TABLE 13.7   Changes between IQ scores measured at various ages and score measured at age seventeen

Age at testing	Range of changes (IQ points)	Mean change (IQ points)
6 months	2–60	15.7
1 year	1–75	16.6
2 years	0–40	14.5
3 years	0–39	14.1
4 years	2–34	12.6
5 years	1–27	10.8
6 years	0–34	11.1
7 years	1–27	9.2
8 years	0–25	8.7
9 years	0–22	9.6
10 years	1–26	9.5
11 years	1–21	7.8
12 years	0–18	7.1
14 years	0–18	5.8

Adapted from Brody, E.B., and Brody, N. *Intelligence: Nature, Determinants, and Consequences.* New York: Academic Press, 1976.

mately .90 around age ten or eleven. Table 13.7 presents the range of observed changes between a person's score at various ages and his or her score at age seventeen. (See **Table 13.7.**) A child's IQ score does not remain fixed; even after age ten the IQ can change by 20 points. Moreover, because the sample in this study included only white, English-speaking, middle-class children, the variability seen here is likely to underestimate the variability that would be obtained from a more heterogeneous population.

Interim summary: Intelligence is still a controversial concept. Although it is often represented by a single score, the IQ, modern investigators do not deny the existence of specific abilities. What is controversial is whether a general factor also exists. Spearman believed so; he named the factor *g* and demonstrated that people's scores on a variety of specific tests of ability were correlated. He believed that specific factors (*s*) also existed. Thurstone performed a factor analysis on 57 individual tests that revealed the existence of seven factors, and not a single *g* factor. However, Cattell reasoned that since these factors were themselves correlated, a factor analysis on *them* was justified. He obtained two factors, and confirmed this with analyses of tests of his own. The nature of the tests that weighted heavily on these two factors suggested the names *fluid* and *crystallized* intelligence, the former representing a person's native ability and the latter representing what a person learns.

THE ROLES OF HEREDITY AND ENVIRONMENT

Ideally, investigation of the role of hereditary and environmental factors in intellectual ability should resemble any other scientific enterprise: evidence should be obtained; hypotheses should be formulated and tested; and subsequent discussion, analysis, and constructive debate should lead to additional hypotheses and data gathering. However, discussion of this issue has been characterized by animosity, personal attacks, emotional outbursts, defensive posturing, and even a scandal involving one of the most respected figures in the field.

Apparently some scientists reason that if heredity has a role in intellectual ability, then some people may conclude that some racial groups are intrinsically "inferior" to others. Such a conclusion would give legitimacy to differential treatment of people on the basis of race. To avoid such an outcome, some people have attempted to discredit the work of others whose evidence suggests that hereditary factors play a role in intelligence.

Among other things, this section attempts to

FIGURE 13.9 Sir Francis Galton (left) and his cousin Charles Darwin (right). The fact that family resemblances are often seen in artistic talents and intellectual skills as well as physical appearance suggests to some that abilities are heritable.

analyze and dispose of many misconceptions that cloud the issue. If we understand how genetic and environmental influences manifest themselves and interact with each other, we will be less likely to draw unjustified conclusions. (See **Figure 13.9**.)

THE MEANING OF HERITABILITY

◆ *Heritability* expresses the proportion of observed variability in a trait that is a direct result of genetic variability. The value of this measure can vary from zero to 1.0. The heritability of most physical traits in most cultures is very high; for example, eye color is affected almost entirely by hereditary factors and little, if at all, by the environment. Thus, the heritability of eye color is close to 1.0.

Heritability merely describes what occurs in a given population; it does not express a primary biological truth. An example may make this distinction clear. Consider the heritability of hair color in adult residents of North America. If you guess that it is 1.0 (or close to it) you will be wrong. Hair color can be altered by environmental factors such as sunlight, bleach, and dye. The fact that an individual has hair of a particular color does not mean that his or her chromosomes necessarily account for this hue. The answer might be found in a bottle. The surface appearance is all we can observe. And because both genetic factors and environmental factors (the use or nonuse of bleach and dyes) can affect the color of a person's hair, the heritability of hair color in North American culture is less than 1.0.

In contrast, almost all young Eskimos have black hair, whereas older Eskimos have gray or white hair. The variability in the alleles that determine hair color is essentially zero; therefore, the heritability of hair color in the Eskimo culture is also zero. Because all the members of this population possess the same alleles for hair color, all variability is explained by an environmental factor: age.

These examples make it clear that measures of heritability do not tell us how much a trait depends on biology. As with hair color, we are forced to infer the heritability of a person's intelligence from his or her observed performance. Thus, looking at a person's IQ score is equivalent to looking at the color of a person's hair. Clearly, even if hereditary factors do influence intelligence, the heritability of this trait must be considerably less than 1.0 be-

cause, as we have seen, so many environmental factors can influence it.

INTERACTION BETWEEN HEREDITY AND ENVIRONMENT

Interaction refers to events whose effects influence each other. Suppose that all mechanical devices in the world were designed so that only righthanded people could operate them, including paper-and-pencil tests of intelligence and tests of manual dexterity. People who were congenitally lefthanded would, in general, perform more poorly. Their measured IQ would be lower than that of righthanded people, and they would have trouble obtaining skilled jobs because mechanical devices would be harder for them to operate. Their lower test scores (and probably lower grades) would make it harder for them to get into college. Therefore, they would be considered less "intelligent" than righthanded people.

This hypothetical example illustrates how hereditary and environmental factors can interact. Suppose that the heritability of handedness is very high (although in fact there is evidence that it is not). Suppose too that the biological potential for intelligence is highly heritable and that environmental factors such as disease, injury, early experiences, and education also strongly affect intelligence. In these circumstances lefthanded people are destined to have a low measured intelligence because the extreme righthanded bias in the environment makes it difficult for them to profit from educational experiences that help righthanded people develop their intelligence. Environmental factors (educational experiences) interact with hereditary factors (handedness). A poor education results in a low IQ in everyone. A good education results in a high IQ in most people. However, lefthanded people will tend to score poorly because their environment interacts unfavorably with their handedness.

The effects of genetic variation and environmental variation on the observed variation of a trait can be expressed in a simple formula.

observed variance =
　　genetic variance + environmental variance

or:

505

$$OV = GV + EV$$

This formula cannot apply in an environment that discriminates against lefthanded people. There, genetic and environmental variance cannot account for phenotypic variance (the variance in the observed trait, namely IQ score). Another term must be added to express the interaction of genetic and environmental factors ($GV \times EV$). Thus:

$$OV = GV + EV + (GV \times EV)$$

◈ As you will see in a later section, evidence for an interaction effect in human intelligence is circumstantial, not direct. However, Cooper and Zubek (1958) gathered evidence in the laboratory that illustrates the interaction between heredity and environment. They raised "maze-bright" and "maze-dull" rats in three different environments and then tested their ability to learn a maze. You will recall from Chapter 6 that Tryon (1940) successfully bred two strains of rats for their ability to learn a maze. After several generations, maze-bright rats learned a maze *much* faster than maze-dull rats. Cooper and Zubek raised three groups of both strains of rats in a standard environment, an impoverished environment, and an enriched environment containing many objects with which the rats could interact.

FIGURE 13.10 Mean number of errors of maze-dull and maze-bright rats raised in various environments. (Based on data from Cooper, R.M., and Zubek, J.P. *Canadian Journal of Psychology*, 1958, *12*, 159–164.)

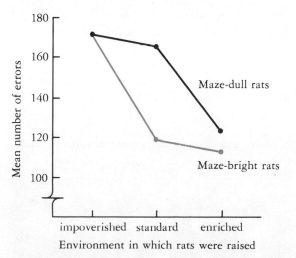

The results, shown in Figure 13.10, reveal a strong interaction between heredity and environment. All rats raised in the impoverished environment performed poorly; they made many errors while learning the maze. Rats that were raised in the enriched environment all performed well; when they had been raised in a more favorable environment, even the maze-dull rats did rather well. Only under the standard conditions did the two strains of rats perform differently. (See **Figure 13.10**.)

From these results we can conclude that (1) heredity has a strong effect on a rat's ability to learn a maze, (2) a rat's early environment has a strong effect on its ability to learn a maze, and (3) the effect of a rat's heredity depends on the environment in which it is raised; the two factors interact. Although we have no comparable experimental data from humans, the graph suggests that it is important to provide people with an optimal environment, whatever their heredity may be.

PRENATAL AND POSTNATAL FACTORS

◈ Both biological and environmental prenatal and postnatal factors can affect intellectual abilities. Although the discussion here considers these factors in terms of Cattell's notions of a general fluid and crystallized intelligence, its conclusions apply equally to specific abilities.

A newborn infant cannot be said to possess any significant intellectual abilities; rather, it is more or less capable of developing them during its life. Therefore, prenatal influences can be said to affect a fetus's *potential* fluid intelligence. Fluid intelligence is an important variable in the acquisition of knowledge and various intellectual skills. Factors that impair it will necessarily also impair crystallized intelligence.

Prenatal influences may be either genetic or nongenetic; genetic factors may be hereditary or nonhereditary. For example, the most obvious known causes of mental retardation are disorders such as Down's syndrome and phenylketonuria, discussed in Chapter 3. Down's syndrome is caused by abnormal genetic material—the presence of an extra twenty-first chromosome; it is not a heritable disorder. (See **Figure 13.11**.) Hereditary genetic influences include (among other factors) inherited metabolic disorders such as phenylketonuria that interfere with normal brain development. Phenylketonuria

FIGURE 13.11   A child with Down's syndrome
learning the concept "round."

results in brain damage and mental retardation unless it is recognized early in life so that a special diet can be administered. It is conceivable that hereditary differences in brain chemistry and structure affect potential fluid intelligence.

Prenatal environmental factors include physical trauma (perhaps through injury to the mother in an automobile accident); and toxic effects from diseases contracted by the mother during pregnancy, such as German measles, or from smoking or the ingestion of alcohol or poisons such as mercury or lead. Some of these can result in mental retardation. Positive factors include an excellent diet and good medical care for the mother.

From birth onward, a child's brain continues to develop. Environmental factors can either promote or impede that development. Postnatal factors such as birth trauma, diseases that affect the brain, or toxic chemicals can prevent optimal development and thereby affect fluid intelligence. For example, encephalitis, when contracted during childhood, can result in mental retardation. So can the ingestion of poisons such as mercury or lead.

Educational influences in the environment, including (but not limited to) schooling, enable a child to acquire crystallized intelligence. A less-than-optimal environment prevents the fullest possible realization of potential crystallized intelligence. Experience with mentally retarded people demonstrates this point. Known causes account for only approximately 25 percent of observed cases of mental retardation. This fact, together with the fact that people whose mental retardation has no obvious physical cause are likely to have close relatives who are also mentally retarded, strongly suggests that many of the remaining 75 percent of cases are hereditary. On the other hand, undocumented environmental causes can produce brain damage in members of the same family; thus, not all cases of *familial* mental retardation are *hereditary*.

Clearly, the interaction effects of environmental factors and hereditary and nonhereditary genetic factors are complex. The effects of hereditary factors on adult intellectual ability are necessarily indirect; many environmental factors exert their effects throughout a person's life. Given that an adult's intellectual abilities are the product of a long chain of events, it is impossible to isolate the effects of the earliest factors:

Conception: A person's genetic endowment sets limits on his or her brain anatomy, and thus on his or her g_f.

Prenatal development: Good nutrition and a normal pregnancy result in optimal brain development, and optimal g_f.

Drugs, toxic substances, poor nutrition, and physical accident can impair brain development, thus lowering g_f.

Genetic disorders such as PKU and Down's syndrome can impair brain development, thus lowering g_f.

Birth: Anoxia or head trauma can cause brain damage, thus lowering g_f.

Infancy: The brain continues to develop and grow. Good nutrition continues to be important.

Sensory stimulation and interaction with a responsive environment is important for cognitive development. An infant's environment and g_f jointly determine its g_c.

Later life: A person's g_c continues to be jointly determined by his or her environment and g_f.

Brain damage is more likely to affect specific abilities than general factors, although metabolic disturbances or infections of the brain can reduce g_f and g_c.

Late in life, dementing diseases such as Alzheimer's disease can severely reduce g_f and g_c. Normal aging usually causes a decline in g_f but leaves g_c relatively intact.

FAMILY STUDIES OF INTELLIGENCE

By now it is clear that intelligence is an arbitrarily defined trait. Intelligence tests give some indication of a person's ability to perform well academically and in some occupations, and research indicates that there is some meaning to the concept of a general factor in intellectual ability. Although a single number cannot express the complexity of a person's pattern of performance on a variety of tasks, the heritability of IQ continues to be a topic of interest to researchers. Their reasoning usually takes into account the crucial factors of genetic and environmental variability, discussed earlier in this chapter, and generally follows three major considerations:

1. Heritability depends on the observed variability of genetic factors in a given population. Because the ancestors of people living in many developed Western nations came from all over the world, genetic variability is likely to be much higher there than it would be in an isolated tribe of people in a remote part of the world. Therefore, if variability in IQ scores is at all affected by heredity, it will be more so in, say, North American culture than in the isolated tribe.

2. The relative importance of environmental factors in intelligence depends on the amount of environmental variance (EV) that occurs in the population. In a society with no relevant environmental variability—one in which all children were raised in the same way by equally skilled and conscientious caretakers, all schools were equally good, all teachers had equally effective personalities and teaching skills, and no one was discriminated against—the effects of EV would be small and those of GV (genetic variance) would be large.

3. Heritability is affected by the degree to which genotype and environment interact. Suppose that because of genetic differences some people are calm and others are excitable. Suppose that excitable people will profit most from a classroom in which distractions are kept to a minimum and teachers are themselves calm and soothing. Further suppose

that the calm students will profit most from an exciting classroom that motivates them to work their hardest. If this were true, there would be an interaction between heredity and environment. If all students were taught in a calm classroom, the excitable children would perform best, and hence learn more and obtain better IQ scores. If all students were taught in an exciting classroom, the calm children would benefit more. The ($GV \times EV$) factor would be large.

Researchers studying the heritability of IQ have tried to measure these interactive effects by gathering data from families with twins.

Twin Studies

◈ Because monozygotic (identical) twins share the same set of chromosomes, they are genetically identical. They have also shared virtually the same environment in the uterus. For all practical purposes, they are two examples of the same person. (See **Figure** 13.12.) Some researchers have tried to estimate the heritability of IQ by studying many sets of monozygotic twins who were separated at birth and raised in different families.

There are several problems inherent in such studies. One is the necessary limits on the size of the sample population. Studies that have found a high correlation in IQ between isolated pairs of monozygotic twins—say, .90—do show that the heritability of IQ is also high—81 percent ($.90^2$)—but only for their own sample of twins. Some of these studies have also failed to take sufficient account of the similarity of the environments in which isolated twins were raised. If the home and school environments of isolated twins are similar, environmental variability will be low, so estimates of heritability will necessarily be high. If some individuals were fostered in wealthy homes, some in poor ones, some in loving homes, some in homes in which they were regularly abused, some in so-

FIGURE 13.12   Monozygotic (identical) twins.

cieties with compulsory education, some in cultures where schools are unknown, the correlation would undoubtedly be lower.

Munsinger (1975a, 1975b) has revealed several related problems. First, adopted children are often not typical of the population as a whole. During the 1920s and 1930s, when many of these studies were performed, adopted children tended to be very carefully selected from a large population of illegitimate babies. Sometimes adoptive parents were given "return privileges"; they could bring back children who did not meet their expectations. The less desirable children were left in the orphanages. (Because fewer children are available for adoption today, there is less selection. The data presented later are based on recent studies that are less likely to be biased by this effect.) (See **Figure 13.13**.)

Second, adoption agencies often attempt to place brighter and healthier children in families with better education and higher socioeconomic status. This tendency introduces a spurious correlation between adoptive child and foster parent that increases the estimate of environmental effects and lowers the estimate of hereditary effects.

Finally, most biological parents are in their early twenties when they have their first child, whereas foster parents usually adopt a child only after discovering that they cannot have one of their own. In addition, they often have to wait to adopt a child. Therefore, they tend to be older, usually in their early thirties. Parental age may have effects on a child's intellectual development.

Other estimates of heritability have compared monozygotic twins with dizygotic twins, both reared

FIGURE 13.13   An infant girl from India, adopted by a North American couple. Nowadays adopted children are often from different ethnic groups or cultures than their adoptive parents.

together. Where monozygotic twins have identical genetic material, dizygotic twins are no more closely related than any two siblings who were born at different times. On the average, 50 percent of the chromosomes of a dizygotic twin are the same as those of the other twin (compared with 100 percent for monozygotic twins). Because twins who are reared together share approximately the same environment, researchers have estimated heritability by observing the difference in the correlation between the two types of twins.

These studies have found a higher correlation between monozygotic twins than between dizygotic twins. The problem with these results is that the formulas using the difference in correlation between monozygotic twins and dizygotic twins to estimate heritability of the observed trait are based on the assumption that the environments of monozygotic twins are as similar as the environments of dizygotic twins. However, the concept of environment embraces more than the superficial aspects of a person's surroundings. Although dizygotic twins are born at the same time and live in the same household, perhaps even sharing the same bedroom, their environments are not identical in all details.

Because dizygotic twins look much less similar than monozygotic twins, they are more likely to be treated differently by other people, including family members. They are much less likely to be dressed alike. Their personalities, and thus their interactions with other people, are also likely to be different. (As we shall see in Chapter 16, personality traits are at least somewhat heritable.) If dizygotic twins have less similar environments than monozygotic twins, their measured intelligence will be somewhat less similar than it would be in identical environments. This difference in environmental similarity will artificially inflate the estimate of heritability.

Many studies have used these two methods to estimate the heritability of IQ scores. Data from the earlier studies suggested that hereditary factors accounted for approximately 80 percent of the observed variance, environmental factors for approximately 20 percent. Most of these data were obtained before World War II from white North American and northern European populations. Even if they were accurate, these estimates would not mean that changes in a person's environment can produce only a 20-percent change in his or her IQ score. A heritability estimate never indicates how much effect environmental factors *can* have on a trait; it indicates only how much of the variability of that trait in that population appears to be related to the environmental variation that is naturally present. Suppose we raised some babies in stimulating responsive environments, others in mediocre environments, and others in environments so impoverished that words were never spoken. The babies in the impoverished environment would never even learn to talk, and their IQs would be very low. We would find that environmental factors accounted for nearly 100 percent of the observed variance in this population, with genetic factors being almost negligible.

Family-of-Twins Studies

◆ More recent studies, using methods that yield more accurate estimates, indicate that the heritability of intelligence, as measured by IQ tests, is lower than previously supposed. The most sophisticated method, the *family-of-twins design,* involves the study of adult monozygotic twins, their spouses, and their offspring (Henderson, 1982). Thus, such studies embrace several relationships: the monozygotic twins themselves, siblings (the twins' children), half-siblings (the children of one twin are, genetically speaking, the half-siblings of the children of the other twin), and the parents and their offspring. Geneticists have devised formulas to calculate the heritability of a trait from the values of the correlations between various family members.

Using these formulas, Rose, Harris, Christian, and Nance (1979) obtained estimates of heritability of IQ ranging from .40 based on the half-sib relationship to .56 based on the offspring-parent relationship. They also found that mothers had more effect than fathers on some measures of intellectual ability: the children in the two families of female monozygotic twins were more similar than children in the families of male monozygotic twins (Rose, Boughman, Cory, Nance, Christian, and Kang, 1980). Because monozygotic twin males and females are genetically identical and because they tend also to be behaviorally similar, the effect appears to be an environmental one; that is, the behavior of mothers affects the test scores of children more than does the behavior of fathers. The maternal effect found by Rose and his colleagues undoubtedly reflects the fact that mothers tend to spend more time with their young children than fathers do. If most children were raised by fathers, a paternal effect would probably be observed instead.

The 1980 study also found no evidence for sex differences in mate selection based on intelligence. Because people choose their own mates on a nonrandom basis, parents will obviously be similar on several variables. A common stereotype asserts that men choose their wives on the basis of beauty, whereas women choose their husbands on the basis of intelligence and other factors related to their ability to provide for them. However, Rose and his colleagues found no evidence for this stereotype; the intelligence test scores of the wives of male monozygotic twins were as similar as the scores of the husbands of female monozygotic twins.

Table 13.8 presents correlations in intelligence of people with varying kinships and estimates of the relative contributions of genetic and environmental factors based on these data, obtained from a summary of several recent studies by Henderson (1982). The top portion of the table shows that the correlation between two people is indeed related to their genetic similarity. (See **Table 13.8, top.**) The bottom portion shows that the estimates of the importance of common genetics and common environment vary considerably, depending on the type of comparison made. Estimates of genetic influence range from 25 to 58 percent, and estimates of common environmental influence range from 4 to 28 percent. (See **Table 13.8, bottom.**)

Estimates of heritability are much lower for specific intellectual traits than for general factors. For example, Foch and Plomin (1980) tested monozygotic and dizygotic twins on a number of tests of intellectual ability and found a significant difference in monozygotic-dizygotic correlations on only one, but strong environmental effects on nine.

TABLE 13.8   Correlations in intelligence of pairs of people with varying kinships and estimates of relative contributions of genetics and environment

Relationship	Rearing	Percentage of genetic similarity	Correlation	Number of pairs
Same individual	—	100%	.87	456
Monozygotic twins	together	100	.86	1417
Dizygotic twins	together	50	.62	1329
Siblings	together	50	.41	5350
Parent-child	together	50	.35	3973
Parent-child	apart	50	.31	345
Foster parent–adopted child	together	?	.16	1594
Unrelated persons	together	?	.25	601
Spouses	together	?	.29	5318

Comparison	Estimates of contributions of genetics and environment to variability in intelligence	
	Genetics	Environment
Monozygotic twins together versus dizygotic twins together	.58	.28
Parent-offspring together versus parent-offspring apart	.50	.04
Siblings together versus siblings apart	.25	.25

Adapted from Henderson, N.D. *Annual Review of Psychology,* 1982, *33,* 403–440.

Plomin and DeFries (1979) performed a factor analysis on the scores of 5587 pairs of twins who took five subtests of the National Merit Scholarship Qualifying Test. (The data were originally collected in a study by Loehlin and Nichols, 1976.) They found a single factor that accounted for more than 70 percent of the variance that could be attributed to heredity. They also found a single factor that accounted for almost 70 percent of the variance that could be attributed to differences in environment. Thus, both genetics and environment appeared to have general rather than specific effects on test performance.

These and other results suggest that a general intellectual capacity is inherited but that specific abilities are not. In contrast, twin studies on specific personality traits have found monozygotic twins to be much more similar than dizygotic twins. Thus, specific personality traits appear to be more heritable than specific intellectual abilities.

Interim summary: There is excellent evidence that heredity affects intellectual ability. There is also excellent evidence that environmental factors have an effect, too. Neither of these conclusions should be surprising. Heredity appears to affect a general factor much more than specific abilities, which are more strongly influenced by environment.

Sir Cyril Burt

The scandal I mentioned earlier involved a large number of studies performed by Sir Cyril Burt and his colleagues on twins raised together and apart, whose conclusions supported the heritability of IQ. This British psychologist had a long and distinguished career, and his research results and writings affected millions of British schoolchildren, who were assigned to different school systems on the basis of scores that they received on tests of intelligence. After Burt's death it became apparent that he had falsified some of his data. He even invented a fictitious colleague, with whom he coauthored a number of papers (Kamin, 1974; Hernshaw, 1979). As a result of this scandal, many people claimed that the entire field of investigation of the effects of heredity on intelligence had been discredited. However, the fact that one person falsified data

does not impugn the integrity of other researchers. None of the data presented in this chapter are based on Burt's publications.

Kamin (1974) has also pointed out that many prominent early researchers into intelligence testing expressed prejudice toward other ethnic and racial groups. However, we evaluate scientific hypotheses by collecting and analyzing data, not by examining the personal defects of the people who proposed them.

INTELLIGENCE FROM AN EVOLUTIONARY PERSPECTIVE

To evaluate the heritability of intellectual ability, some investigators have considered what this trait might mean to the survival of the species. Stenhouse (1974) discussed the biological characteristics that might have been selected for what we refer to collectively as intelligence. He suggested that there are four important factors:

1. *Sensory and motor abilities.* To respond intelligently to the environment, an organism must be able to perceive a large variety of environmental events and perform a large variety of behaviors. The more sensory modalities an organism possesses and the more environmental features it is able to detect with each of its sensory systems, the better it can exploit its environment. Similarly, a greater motor capacity guarantees a larger repertoire of responses. For example, without their excellent visual system and dextrous hands and fingers, humans would never have developed written forms of language.

2. *Memory.* The ability of an organism to remember what it has perceived and what behaviors it has performed is obviously related to its ability to learn to behave flexibly and intelligently.

3. *Generalization.* Organisms that can extract the essential features of a particular experience and appropriately generalize them to other situations will be able to profit most from experience.

4. *Inhibition of instinctual responses.* A species develops instinctual responses to particular classes of stimuli early in its evolutionary history. These "wired-in" responses serve a species well in a restricted range of environments. However, to ex-

ploit a wide range of environments, individuals must often suppress these responses in favor of learned ones. They must also suppress previously learned responses in new environments, when the "rules of the game" change. (In mammals, this ability appears to be especially dependent upon the frontal lobes of the brain. As we saw in Chapter 3, humans with frontal-lobe damage exhibit primitive responses and reflexes, and have great difficulty changing their strategy in a task when the experimenter changes the way that a problem must be solved.)

THE ISSUE OF RACE AND INTELLIGENCE

Efforts to relate intelligence to race are of little scientific interest. First, people who pursue the issue usually define race in a meaningless and illogical way. Second, because the environments of people of different racial groups differ, it is impossible to assess the relative effects of heredity and environment.

Defining Racial Groups

◆ A biologist uses term *race* to identify a population of plants or animals that has some degree of reproductive isolation from other members of the species, with which it is perfectly capable of interbreeding. For example, collies, cocker spaniels, and beagles constitute different races. In these cases, reproductive isolation is imposed by humans; however, within obvious size limits, different breeds of dogs readily mate with each other.

Any isolated group of organisms will, as a result of chance factors and of differences in local environment, become genetically different over time. Groups of humans whose ancestors mated only with other people in a restricted geographic region tend to differ from other groups on a variety of hereditary traits, including stature, hair color, skin pigmentation, and blood type. The migrations of humanoid ancestors to different parts of the world many thousands of years ago led to genetic differences among people whose recent ancestors lived in different parts of the world. However, many other migrations and conquests since ancient times have caused the interbreeding of many different groups of people. As a result, human racial groups are much more similar than, say, races of dogs, and classifying people on the basis of race is a difficult and somewhat arbitrary matter. Baker (1974) developed a typical classification scheme: (1) *Australasid,* the original non-European inhabitants of Australia, Melanesia, and Tasmania; (2) *Europoid,* the original inhabitants of Europe, Arabia, northern Russia, and Ethiopia; (3) *Negroid,* the original black inhabitants of parts of central and southern Africa, such as Zaire, Senegal, southern Sudan, and Zimbabwe; (4) *Khoisanid,* the so-called Hottentots and Bushmen, who originally inhabited southwest Africa and the Kalahari Desert; (5) *Mongoloid,* the original inhabitants of Mongolia, central China, and southeast Asia; and (6) *Indianid,* the original (pre-Columbian) inhabitants of Mexico and Central and South America. Other groups are blends of these six.

Baker's classification scheme is only one of many, and not all biologists accept it. Furthermore, as Theodosius Dobzhansky, an eminent evolutionary geneticist, put it,

> If the classification of human races is in an unsatisfactory state, the understanding of their origins and biological significance is still more so. . . . solid and conclusive evidence concerning the adaptive significance of racial traits in man is scant in the extreme, and the best that can be offered are plausible speculations and surmises. (1962, pp. 269, 271)

◆ People who ask: "Are there racial differences in intelligence?" almost always mean: "Are blacks inherently less intelligent than whites?" The comparison groups tend to be white and black people in the United States or in other racially mixed Western countries.

Many researchers have used the trait of skin pigmentation to classify people by race. Two chemicals, melanin and keratin, cause skin to be black and yellow, respectively; a combination produces brown skin; and the skin of pale people contains little of either substance. As we saw in Chapter 6, there is good evidence that skin pigmentation serves as a protection against the effects of sunlight (Loomis, 1967). Such protection is important near the equator, where the sun is intense all year, but is less important in temperate zones. Because vitamin D is synthesized primarily through the action of sun-light on deep layers of the skin, lack of pigmentation was advantageous to residents of northern latitudes, except to those living in arctic regions, where vitamin D was readily available from fish and seal meat.

The selective advantage of differences in skin pigmentation is obvious, but there is no plausible reason to expect them to be correlated either with other physical measures or with measures of intellectual ability. Both the tallest (the Masai) and the shortest (Pigmy) people in the world have black skin. Nor are shape of nose or forehead, hair texture, blood groups, and many other physical features well correlated with skin pigmentation. We would never classify varieties of dogs by color, assigning golden retrievers and chihuahuas to one group and black Labradors and scotties to another. Why, then, should we do so with humans?

Although the issue of race and intelligence as presently conceived does not appear to be meaningful, it would be scientifically interesting to study the effects of different environments on inherited intellectual capacity. One such investigation might involve human populations whose ancestors came from desert regions, cold regions, humid regions, regions with widely fluctuating temperatures, regions with a high level of endemic disease, regions where food is difficult to obtain, regions where food is easily available, regions where the last ice age affected the indigenous population, regions where trade has been important, and regions that have been isolated and self-sufficient. Direct comparisons of the intellectual ability of these people could tell us which environmental factors have been important in natural selection for intellectual ability. However, these factors would not be synonymous with racial differences.

The crucial obstacle to performing such a study is the fact that it is not possible to measure inherited intellectual ability. If two people have had approximately the same environment, we can assume that they have had the same opportunity to use their biological capacity to develop intellectual skills. Their test scores are at least roughly proportional to their innate intellectual capacity. But this condition, equal environments, will never be met when we try to compare different populations of people.

Other Environmental Differences

◆ A large number of studies have established that Americans who are identified as black score an average of 85 on IQ tests, whereas Americans who are identified as white score an average of 100. Thus, although some blacks score better than some whites, on the average, whites do better on these tests.

We still do not know why these difference exist, but it is likely that environmental factors play an important role. In the United States, as in many other countries, racial membership is a cultural phenomenon, not a biological one. A man with three grandparents of European origin and one grandparent of African origin is defined as black, unless he keeps this fact secret and "passes" (defines himself) as white. Black people and white people are treated differently; the average black family is poorer than the average white one; blacks usually attend schools of lesser academic quality than whites; pregnant black women usually receive poorer medical care than their white counterparts and their diet tends to be not as well balanced; and so on. In these circumstances, it would not be surprising if people's IQ scores differed in accordance with whether they had been raised as blacks or as whites.

Some investigators have attempted to use statistical means to "remove" the effects of environmental variables, such as socioeconomic status, that account for differences in performance between blacks and whites. These efforts are subject to criticism on several grounds. However, a study by Scarr and Weinberg (1976) provides unambiguous evidence that environmental factors can substantially increase the measured IQ of a black child. Scarr and Weinberg studied ninety-nine black children who were adopted while they were young into white families of higher-than-average educational and socioeconomic status. The expected average IQ of black children in the same area who were raised in black families was approximately 90. The average IQ of the adopted group was observed to be 105.

Some authors have flatly stated that there are no racial differences in biologically determined intellectual capacity. However, this claim, like the one asserting that blacks are inherently less intelligent than whites, lacks scientific support. Although we know that blacks and whites have different environments, and that a black child raised in an environment similar to that of a white child will receive a higher IQ score, the question of racial, hereditary differences cannot be answered. Given that there is at least as much variability in intelligence between two people selected at random as there is between the average black and the average white, knowing a person's race tells us very little about how intelligent he or she may be.

The interesting and more valid racial questions are those that will be addressed by social psychologists and anthropologists. These include issues like the prevalence of prejudice, ethnic identification and cohesiveness, fear of strangers, and the tendency to judge something that is different as inferior.

CONCLUDING REMARKS

Although there is still disagreement about the nature of intellectual abilities, the evidence suggests that a general factor accounts for a large part of the variability in people's scores on a variety of tests. Because verbalization plays such a large part in understanding and answering test questions and in learning facts in general, it is possible that this general factor is verbal ability. Regardless of the nature of a general factor, it is clear that there are also specific intellectual abilities. The fact that brain damage can produce specific deficits (such as the loss of perceptual abilities or of the ability to orient oneself in space) indicates that specific skills appear to require different brain mechanisms. Therefore, it is not surprising that specific abilities can vary from person to person.

Although Cattell's model of intelligence has not yet been proven correct, his concepts of fluid and crystallized intelligence are useful for describing the important distinction between potential and actual abilities. Finally, an understanding of heritability and the interacting roles of heredity and environment clear up misunderstandings that are prevalent in the general population. Heritability is a measure of the degree to which observed variability in a particular trait in a particular population is controlled by genetic variability. If there is no genetic variability, then it cannot be responsible for observed individual differences in that trait.

The degree to which environmental factors influence an observed trait depends on how much environmental and genetic variability exist in a population.

GUIDE TO TERMS INTRODUCED IN THIS CHAPTER

Binet-Simon Scale   p. 489

criterion   p. 491

deviation IQ   p. 490   Figure 13.3

dyslexia   p. 494

educable mental retardation   p. 495

factor analysis   p. 497   Table 13.3

factor loading   p. 497   Table 13.3

family-of-twins design   p. 510   Table 13.8

g (general factor)   p. 496

heritability   p. 504

intelligence quotient (IQ)   p. 490

intercorrelation matrix   p. 497   Tables 13.2, 13.4

mental age   p. 490

mental retardation   p. 495

norm   p. 490

profound mental retardation   p. 495

ratio IQ   p. 490

s (specific factor)   p. 496

Stanford-Binet Scale   p. 490   Table 13.1

trainable mental retardation   p. 495

Wechsler Adult Intelligence Scale (WAIS)
p. 491   Table 13.1, Figure 13.4

Wechsler Intelligence Scale for Children (WISC)
p. 491

SUGGESTIONS FOR FURTHER READING

The controversy surrounding the topic of intelligence (especially the use and abuse of IQ testing and the heredity of intelligence) accounts for the many books available. Leon Kamin and Hans Eysenck engage in a spirited (and sometimes rather personal) exchange in *Intelligence Controversy: H.J. Eysenck vs Leon Kamin* (New York: John Wiley & Sons, 1981). S. Scarr's *Race, Social Class, and Individual Differences in IQ*

(Hillsdale, N.J.: Lawrence Erlbaum Associates, 1981) is an excellent discussion of the interrelations among these topics. *Flowers for Algernon* by D. Keyes (New York: Harcourt, Brace & World, 1966) is a fictional account that explores the relations among intelligence, social status, and individual happiness. J.R. Vale's *Genes, Environment, and Behavior* (New York: Harper & Row, 1980) discusses the interactions between heredity and environment and the role of these interactions in behavior and abilities.

The authoritative volume on intelligence tests, their administration, and their interpretation is J. Sattler's *Assessment of Intelligence and Special Abilities* (Boston: Allyn and Bacon, 1981).

PART • E
SOCIAL
BEHAVIOR

Social behaviors, broadly defined as those that influence, or are influenced by, the behavior of other people, form a part of almost all human existence. We have already seen that the behavior of other people toward us provides potent reinforcers and punishers, and that sexual behavior and language are significant social behaviors. We have also seen that consciousness undoubtedly evolved along with human society; it is unlikely that a solitary organism could evolve self-awareness. Finally, intelligence, as we typically define it, develops through learning from other people.

Emotions, discussed in Chapter 14, are an essential part of human life, not only because we feel them but also because we express them to others. The expression of our feelings through nonverbal communication is a coun-

terpart to our use of language. Chapter 14 also discusses aggression, an emotional social behavior that has important implications for our species.

Chapter 15 examines how social psychologists make inferences about the causes of people's behavior, the formation of attitudes and how they can be changed, the influences of other people on an individual's behavior, attraction between individuals, and the behavior of people working in groups.

Chapter 16 considers the study of human personality—which is largely based on observation of individuals' social behavior—including how psychologists attempt to define and measure personality traits and to describe the basic principles that determine human personality.

EMOTION

LEARNING ◆ OBJECTIVES

THE NATURE OF EMOTION

◆ In a real sense, emotions are what life is all about. Life without emotion would be bland and mean- ingless. The situations that produce strong feelings are the ones that matter to us. In contrast to moods and temperament, emotions are relatively brief subjective feelings. *Moods* are longer-lived and

FIGURE 14.1   Nanook's joy upon first hearing a phonograph is evident from his facial expression.

522

generally weaker than emotions. Much less is known about mood states than about emotions, because the conditions that elicit them are less distinct. Chapter 17 discusses moods and their pathological expressions. *Temperament,* which is even longer-lived than mood, refers to a person's general disposition, or typical pattern of affective reaction to various situations. Some people are especially sensitive to criticism and easily become angry or depressed. Others are generally cheerful and tend to see the bright side of things. Temperament is an aspect of personality, the topic of Chapter 16.

Just as motivation is intimately related to reinforcement and punishment, emotions are intimately related to motivation. Emotions such as joy, fear, disgust, and anger are evoked by stimuli that have the power to reinforce or punish our behavior. Perhaps, then, emotions are the subjective aspect of motivation and reinforcement. Reinforcement makes us happy, punishment makes us sad, and the anticipation of one or the other makes us feel hope or fear.

Although emotions themselves are private, most behaviors that occur in association with them are social. Emotional behaviors include overt approach or avoidance behaviors, defensive or aggressive behaviors, positive social behaviors like sexual activities or parental behavior, and the expressions of emotion (such as smiles and frowns) that convey our feelings to other people. (See **Figure 14.1**.)

Many people who have studied emotions have focused on certain aspects—the kinds of situations that produce them, the kinds of feelings that people report, the behaviors they engage in, or the physiological changes they undergo. All these approaches increase our understanding of emotion. But emotions are more than feelings, behaviors, or patterns of physiological response. Emotions are the products of judgments. For example, after a performance a pianist may perceive the applause as praise for an outstanding performance, judging it to be a positive evaluation of her own worth. She feels pride and satisfaction. In this case, her emotional state is produced by social reinforcement—the expression of approval and admiration by other people. However, if the pianist believes that she has performed poorly, she may judge the applause as the mindless enthusiasm of people who have no taste or appreciation for music, and feel only con-

tempt. Furthermore, the person who turned the pages of the music is also present on the stage, but does not evaluate the applause as praise for anything he did. The applause may even make him feel jealous. Clearly, a given set of stimuli does not always elicit the same emotions; rather, the judgments made about the significance of the stimuli determine the emotion felt. Thus, the study of emotion requires more than the investigation of any single aspect. (See **Figure 14.2**.)

THE MYTHOLOGY OF EMOTION

There are many misconceptions about the nature and functions of our emotions. Four of these are examined below.

We Are Not Responsible for Our Emotional Behavior

Despite the fact that *emotion* comes from Latin *emovere,* meaning "to move out, to shake," we almost

FIGURE 14.2   The facial expressions of these football players tell us something about their judgment of the significance of the game they have just played.

always describe an emotion as something that *happens to us*. Until recently, the word *passion* (which comes from the same root as *passive*) was commonly used to describe feelings of emotion. As Solomon (1976) puts it:

> Our language and our thinking about the passions is riddled with this myth of passivity; we "fall in" love, much as one might fall into a tiger trap or a swamp. We find ourselves "paralyzed" with fear, as if we had been inoculated with a powerful drug. We are "plagued" with remorse, as if by flies or mosquitos. We are "struck" by jealousy, as if by a Buick; "felled" by shame, [like] a tree by an ax; "distracted" by grief, as if by a trombone in the kitchen; "haunted" by guilt, as if by a ghost; and "driven" into anger, as if pushed by a prod. Our richest poetic metaphors, grown trite with overuse, are images of passivity. We are "heartbroken," "crushed," "smitten," "overwhelmed," "carried away," and "undone" by passion. (p. xv)

Through constant use, these metaphors seem perfectly natural. When we experience an emotion, we tend to perceive ourselves as passive and helpless. From this perception it follows that perhaps we are not to be held responsible for our behavior when we are emotionally aroused. How many of us have heard (or said), "I couldn't help it; I was so angry that I just couldn't think straight"? Laws in many countries provide milder penalties for crimes committed "in the heat of passion." In most jurisdictions of the United States if a person gets angry at someone and kills him or her right away, the most serious charge possible is second-degree murder; if there is enough "provocation," the charge might be manslaughter. However, if the person waits until the next day to kill the victim, the charge will be one of first-degree murder, because the murder is "premeditated"; the murderer's passion has had time to cool, and the crime must therefore have been the result of reasoning. People are not held entirely responsible for an act that they are "forced to commit" by a strong emotion, but they *can* be blamed for all acts that are considered to be "reasoned."

The notion that we are not responsible for our emotions or for our behavior when we are gripped by them permits us to indulge in unbecoming behavior and later to absolve ourselves of blame, at least partially. We can get away with hurting others or acting foolishly so long as we can point to an overpowering emotion that "made us do it." It appears that society as a whole suffers as a result. If people have an excuse for bad behavior they are more likely to engage in it.

In contrast, we do not attempt to absolve ourselves of responsibility for *good* acts. Imagine someone saying, "I just couldn't help myself. I saw her drowning and before I knew it I was struck by an altruistic frenzy. When I regained control of myself, I found that I had dragged her onto the shore." We attribute such acts to our intellect, so that we can take credit for them, while blaming bad behaviors on our uncontrollable emotions.

Intense Emotions Disorganize Rational Behavior

A corollary of the doctrine of helplessness is that emotions tend to disorganize rational behavior. In many cases this claim is simply a justification for the notion that we are not responsible for our emotional behaviors. If intense emotions always disorganize rational behavior, how do we explain the fact that, in the heat of extreme anger, we so often find exactly the right thing to say to deeply wound our adversaries? Afterward we may say, "I didn't really mean to hurt you that way—I didn't know what I was saying." Yet our intellect was organized enough that we could dip into memory and come up with something calculated to do the most damage. Apparently the heat of passion does not necessarily make people stupid.

Sometimes strong emotional states arising from species-typical responses interfere with performance of behavior that is appropriate in our technological society. For example, when we encounter dangerous situations we must hide, fight, or flee. If we must flee for our lives, our energy resources are best expended in vigorous muscular movement. The autonomic nervous system directs our blood flow to our muscles. The release of hormones increases our heart rate, blood pressure, and rate and depth of breathing, and converts glycogen into glucose. All these responses facilitate gross motor activities such as running. However, they make it more difficult for us to exercise the control and inhibition necessary to perform fine motor tasks.

Suppose you stop your car in a remote area, get out, lock the doors, and start out on a hike. Suddenly a bear appears from behind some brush and runs toward you. You turn toward your car, the only place to hide. You must find the appropriate key on your key ring, orient it properly, place it in the slot, and turn the key in the right direction. Meanwhile the bear is rapidly running toward you. How efficient would your performance be?

Emotions Are Unreasonable and Irrational

It is often said that emotions are unreasonable and irrational—they come to us unbidden. Nothing could be further from the truth; emotions are often the results of intellectual activity. For example, applause may evoke quite different emotions in a pianist, depending on her appraisal of her performance. Or a physician may notice some symptoms in himself that suggest the presence of a fatal disease. His subsequent fear and anxiety arise from his intelligence and education; he knows enough to be frightened by symptoms that would not bother other people.

Sometimes emotions appear to occur too quickly to be products of intellectual judgment. For example, a person may hear a particular sound and experience an unpleasant sinking sensation in his or her stomach. It may take the person a moment to realize what is causing distress. Through classical conditioning, emotional responses can be evoked by stimuli that were previously paired with stimuli that elicit appetitive or defensive responses.

Emotions Are Primitive

Finally, emotions are held to be primitive. There is some truth to this claim. Emotional behaviors (especially defensive and aggressive behaviors) and emotional expressions (such as smiles and frowns) are in large part biological, in the sense that many components of our emotional responses are stereotyped and species-typical. However, even though many emotional behaviors are primitive in this sense, the control of these behaviors is often learned.

Just as the range of intellectual abilities increases as we ascend the phylogenetic scale from protozoan to human, so the range of emotions also increases. A wide variety of species can express fear and rage, but humans are capable of being afraid of or angry at more things than any other species. We can also feel proud, sullen, embarrassed, loving, or ashamed.

PRACTICAL PROBLEMS OF RESEARCH

◆ No single, comprehensive theory of emotion has good empirical support. Theories based on experimental data are restricted in scope, and those that take into account the range and subtlety of human emotion also involve a great deal of unsupported speculation. These problems necessarily limit progress in scientific investigations of emotion.

One of the major difficulties in objectively studying human emotions is *producing* them in subjects. Researchers can ask a subject to make a facial expression that corresponds to a particular emotion, but they cannot expect the subject actually to experience fear, ecstasy, or grief. Only motivationally significant situations can reliably produce strong emotions, and such situations are difficult to produce in the laboratory. Furthermore, the methods that would produce strong emotions are unethical.

Fear is probably the easiest emotion to evoke, and earlier investigators used clever strategems to frighten their subjects. One investigator attached difficult-to-remove electrodes to a subject's fingers. The electrodes soon began to produce "accidental" shocks, the "old, unreliable" equipment began to smoke, and the experimenter showed fright himself, trying to fix the apparatus before the subject was electrocuted. The deceit succeeded in making the subject frightened, but concern with the ethical treatment of subjects rules out such procedures today. Studies that proposed to treat subjects this way would be turned down by research review committees, and scientific journals would refuse to publish them.

Another problem with the study of emotion is that emotions depend on cognitive appraisal of a situation and on the individual's temperament. Thus, we cannot fully understand emotion until we understand more about our cognitive abilities and the nature of personality differences. Furthermore, a complete understanding of emotion will require a better understanding of the nature of the processes of reinforcement and punishment.

CLASSIFICATION OF EMOTIONS

◆ There is no general agreement about how many emotions there are. The English language is full of words that denote concepts of emotion; Averill (1975) has identified over 500. The two general systems for classifying emotions divide them into *categories* or *dimensions.* Psychologists who assign emotions to categories conceive of them as distinct, independent entities. Other psychologists believe that a small number of factors, or dimensions, underlie all emotions; a particular emotion consists of a certain amount of dimension A, of dimension B, and so on, just as a particular color consists of a specific brightness, saturation, and hue.

CATEGORIES

According to Tomkins (1962, 1963; Izard and Tomkins, 1966), emotions are innate biological response systems, and the most important aspect of these systems is facial expression. Thus, Tomkins based his classification on types of facial expressions, on the assumption that distinct patterns of facial expressions indicate the presence of distinct emotional states. He assigned emotions to eight categories: *interest/excitement,* expressed by a fixed stare with the eyebrows down; *enjoyment/joy,* expressed by a smile; *surprise/startle,* expressed by raised eyebrows and an eyeblink; *distress/anguish,* expressed by crying; *fear/terror,* expressed by wide open eyes, withdrawal, sweating, trembling; *shame/humiliation,* expressed by a lowering of the head and eyes; *contempt/disgust,* expressed by a sneer; and *anger/rage,* expressed by a frown, clenched jaw, and reddening of the face.

Other investigators have asked subjects to sort cards, each containing a word that denotes an emotional concept, into separate piles, each containing words with similar meanings. This procedure can provide reliable results, uncontaminated by subjective evaluations of the experimenters, but even if there is a limited number of emotional states, not all the words necessarily have the same meaning for all subjects. For example, are hatred and contempt different emotions? Nor is there agree-

ment as to whether the experimenters should assign an arbitrary number of categories or allow each subject to use as many as he or she likes. If freedom is allowed, how can the researcher compare a classification system based on eight categories with one based on twenty-six? So far no solutions to these problems have been found.

DIMENSIONS

Whereas categories are independent "pigeonholes" into which items can be sorted, dimensions are variable quantities. For example, the location of an object in space can be specified in terms of three dimensions. With a change in any of these dimensions, the object assumes a new, unique location. Similarly, several investigators conceive of an emotion as a unique blend of a few simple dimensions.

Millenson (1967) suggested three dimensions are basic to all emotions: fear, anger, and pleasure. These dimensions are all related to reinforcement: fear is produced by anticipation of an aversive stimulus, anger by the removal of a reinforcer, and pleasure by anticipation of reinforcement or the elimination of an aversive stimulus. A "pure" emotion—such as pleasure, elation, or ecstasy—consists of only one of these dimensions but can vary in intensity. Emotions that are not "pure" contain certain amounts of two or three of the factors. (See **Figure 14.3.**) For example, Millenson suggests that a child who steals a cookie experiences both the pleasure of eating it and the fear caused by anticipation of punishment. The resulting compound emotion is usually labeled as *guilt.* (See **Figure 14.4.**)

Other investigators have derived dimensions of emotion by having subjects rate the emotional expressions of other people, either by observing them directly or through photographs. Instead of trying to divide the responses into categories, they use factor analysis to identify a set of dimensions that might characterize the subject's ratings. For example, Frijda (1968) found six dimensions around which the ratings of his subjects were found to cluster: pleasantness versus unpleasantness, intensity of arousal, attention versus rejection, social evaluation, surprise, and simple versus complicated.

The validity of the results of such studies depends on three conditions: the ability of the actor

validity

FIGURE 14.3   The facial expressions of these children taunting British troops in Northern Ireland suggest that they are experiencing a mixture of anger and pleasure, and probably some fear, as well.

to portray the entire range of human emotions, the range of labels given to the subjects to choose from, and the appropriateness of the mathematical model used to derive the dimensions. The last element is the most complicated, because different models can produce very different results. The fact that a particular method yields reliable results when applied to the data does not prove that emotions are in fact composites of various dimensions. Verifying this assertion requires independent means of measurement, and so far such a method has not been found.

Interim summary: Emotions are the feelings produced by motivationally relevant situations. Psychologists have concerned themselves with the situations that produce them, the behaviors associated with them, and the physiological changes that accompany them. Because we often use emotions to excuse our own bad behavior, almost all societies have myths about emotions: we are not responsible for our emotional behaviors, emotions disorganize our behavior, they are unreasonable and irrational, and they are primitive.

Studies of emotions confront practical problems, including the ethical problems associated with contriving situations that will produce them in experimental subjects. Even defining emotions is still

FIGURE 14.4   According to Millenson's model of emotion, when a child steals a cookie, the composite fear and pleasure causes the emotion of guilt.

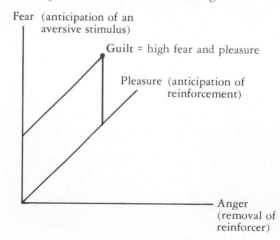

a problem. The two principal forms of classification are categories and dimensions. Tomkins's eight categories of facial expressions and Millenson's three dimensions (fear, anger, and pleasure) are good representatives of the two types of approaches. However, we do not know how many emotions there are, whether they fall into separate and independent categories, or whether they consist of mixtures of a few primary dimensions. As a result, psychologists have restricted their investigations to particular, limited aspects of emotion.

EXPRESSION AND RECOGNITION OF EMOTION

Expressions of emotion are important in social situations. Studies have shown that when people try to judge the true feelings of others they trust facial expressions the most, tone of voice next, and words last (Mehrabian and Ferris, 1967; Mehrabian and Wiener, 1967). In recognition of this fact, we sometimes try to hide our true feelings, attempting to appear impassive or even to display an emotion different from what we feel. (See **Figure 14.5.**) At other times, we may exaggerate our emotional response to make sure that others see how we feel. For example, if a friend tells us about a devastating

experience, we make sure that our facial expression conveys sadness and sympathy.

EXPRESSION OF EMOTION: AN INNATE OR LEARNED BEHAVIOR?

Darwin's Contributions

Charles Darwin (1872/1965) pointed out the evolutionary significance of the ability of animals to send and receive messages concerning their emotional state. For example, a young chimpanzee finds it useful to detect annoyance in a full-grown male while there is still time to get away from him. Darwin suggested that emotional expressions are innate, unlearned responses consisting of a complex set of movements, principally of the facial muscles.

Darwin obtained evidence for his assertion by observation of his own children (like Piaget later), and through correspondence with people living in various isolated cultures around the world. His rationale was that if people all over the world, no matter how isolated, show the same facial expressions of emotion, then these expressions must be inherited instead of learned. The logic of this reasoning goes like this. When groups of people are isolated for many years, they develop different languages. Thus, we can say that the words people use are arbitrary; there is no biological basis for

FIGURE 14.5   Former U.S. President Richard Nixon and his family as he announces his resignation.

Their facial expressions undoubtedly hide their real feelings.

using the word "hand" to represent the thing that all people have at the end of their arm, because languages other than English use different sets of sounds and symbols to represent the same thing. However, if facial expressions are inherited, then they should take the same form in people from all cultures, despite their isolation from one another.

Darwin claimed that people in different cultures used the same patterns of movement of facial muscles to express a particular emotional state. Here is one of Darwin's descriptions:

Mr. J. Scott, of the Botanic Gardens, Calcutta has obligingly sent me a full description. . . . He observed during some time, himself unseen, a very young Dhangar woman from Nagpore, the wife of one of the gardeners, nursing her baby who was at the point of death; and he distinctly saw the eyebrows raised at the inner corners, the eyelids drooping, the forehead wrinkled in the middle, the mouth slightly open, with the corners much depressed. He then came from behind a screen of plants and spoke to the poor woman, who started, burst into a bitter flood of tears, and besought him to cure her baby. (1872/1965, pp. 185–186)

Such an expression of sadness is identical to one that would be seen in Western society. (See **Figure 14.6**.) Thus, Darwin concluded, patterns of facial expression are universal, and this fact strongly implies that they are inherited.

Criticisms of Darwin

◆ A number of subsequent investigators challenged Darwin's conclusions on the grounds that his data were biased. For example, here are two of the questions he put to his correspondents:

(1) Is astonishment expressed by the eyes and mouth being opened wide, and by the eyebrows being raised?

FIGURE 14.6   Compare this facial expression with Darwin's description.

(2) When in low spirits are the corners of the mouth depressed, and inner corner of the eyebrows raised by that muscle which the French call the "grief muscle"? The eyebrows in this state become slightly oblique, with a little swelling at the inner end; and the forehead is transversely wrinkled in the middle part, but not across the whole breadth, as when the eyebrows are raised in surprise. (1872/1965, p. 15)

The form of these questions told the correspondent what Darwin hoped to hear, exerting some degree of pressure to comply. Darwin was unaware of this issue of bias in human research, whereas modern psychologists have learned to be sensitive to it.

Many investigators concluded not only that Darwin's methods were flawed, but also his conclusions were incorrect. For example, Williams (1930) described a festive ceremony held in Melanesia, in the southwest Pacific:

The guests, arriving in their several parties, come riding single file into the village, each party headed by its man of first importance, befeathered club on shoulder. No smile adorns his face, but rather an expression of fierceness, which however unsuited it may seem to the hospitable occasion, is nevertheless [considered to be] good form. (p. 29)

Another investigator (Klineberg, 1938) noted that expressions of emotion are not consistent even in Western society:

Not only may joy be expressed without a smile, but in addition the smile may be used in a variety of situations in a manner quite different from what appears to be its original significance. Even in our own society, we know that a smile may mean contempt, incredulity, affection, and serve also as part of a purely social greeting devoid of emotional significance. . . . (p. 194)

A Possible Reconciliation: Cultural Regulation of Emotional Expression

Ekman and Friesen (1971) noted that even though Darwin's data were not gathered under carefully controlled conditions, and even though the observations of Williams and Klineberg were accurate, Darwin's conclusions, and not those of his critics, were correct. Ekman and Friesen noted that the facial muscles can be used for tasks other than the expression of emotion. They can also be used to produce three special types of nonverbal behavior: illustrators, regulators, and emblems.

Illustrators are movements that, along with changes in pitch and stress of the voice, emphasize words or phrases—they complement prosodic elements of speech. For example, a person may raise his or her brow to mark an important word. *Regulators* are used to control the give-and-take in a conversation. They are facial expressions that say such things as "Hurry up, get to the point," or "Hold it, I don't understand what you are saying," or "That's very interesting, tell me more." (Imagine yourself holding a conversation and making faces that express these requests.) Chapter 12 discussed people's use of these expressions in fulfilling the "given-new contract" that people obey when they talk with each other. Finally, *emblems* are expressions that convey a specific meaning within a given culture. For example, if you wink at someone you are saying that you and the recipient are sharing something private—a joke, perhaps. A smile might mean simply "hello" and not necessarily denote happiness. None of these uses of the facial muscles can really be said to be expressions of emotions, even though emotions may be present.

Ekman (1973, 1980) notes that we must not confuse true expressions of emotion with the use of facial movements for the display of illustrators, regulators, or emblems. These three phenomena are part of a person's culture, just as language is. An investigator who mistakes one of them for expressions of emotion is likely to make erroneous conclusions. For example, the fierce grimace of a Melanesian tribesman is an emblem that probably means "Here I am, an important man, and we're all going to have a great time!" His facial expression should not be interpreted as an actual expression of anger.

If Ekman and Friesen are correct about the effects of cultural control on facial expressions in social situations, then it should be possible to detect differences in these expressions when people of different cultures are among other people or alone. Presumably, the facial expressions that occur when people are alone reflect their emotional states more accurately than the expressions that occur in the presence of other people.

Ekman and his colleagues (Ekman, Friesen, and

Ellsworth, 1972; Friesen, 1972) showed a distressing film to Japanese and American college students, both in groups and singly. Because the Japanese culture discourages public display of emotion, the researchers expected that the Japanese students would show fewer facial expressions of emotion when in public than when alone, and far fewer than the American students under both conditions.

The researchers recorded the facial expressions of their subjects with hidden cameras while the subjects viewed a film showing a gruesome and bloody coming-of-age rite in a primitive tribe. The results were as predicted. When the subjects were alone, American and Japanese subjects showed the same facial expressions. When they were with other people from their culture, the Japanese students were less likely to express negative emotions and more likely to mask these expressions with polite smiles. Thus, people from both societies used the same facial expressions of emotion but were subject to different social controls.

This evidence indicates the role of cultural influences on people's use of facial expressions for more than showing emotions. However, the question remains whether facial expressions of emotion are biologically determined or learned from other members of one's culture. The fact that Japanese and American people who were tested alone reacted in the same way to the film suggests that at least some facial expressions are not culture specific. However, because these two cultures are not isolated, we could have learned from each other. Thus, the results are not conclusive.

CROSS-CULTURAL STUDIES

◆ In 1967 and 1968 Ekman and Friesen visited an isolated tribe in a remote area of New Guinea—the South Fore tribe. This group of 319 adults and children had never been exposed to Western culture. They had never seen a movie, or lived in a Western town, or worked for a Caucasian. Therefore, if they were able to identify accurately the emotional expressions of Westerners as well as those of members of their own tribe, and if their own facial expressions were the same as those of Westerners, it would seem that these expressions were not culturally determined.

Because translations of single words from one language to another are not always accurate, Ekman and Friesen told little stories to describe an emotion instead of presenting a single word. They

FIGURE 14.7 In a study by Ekman and his colleagues, subjects were asked to match the story with the appropriate photograph. (From Ekman, P.

The Face of Man: Expressions of Universal Emotions in a New Guinea Village. New York: Garland STPM Press, 1980.)

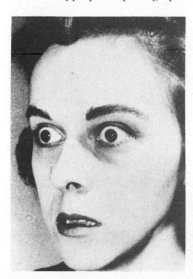  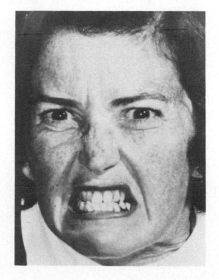

told the story to a subject, presented three photographs of Westerners depicting three different emotions, and asked the subject to choose the appropriate one. Here are three examples of the stories:

> *Fear*—She is sitting in her house all alone and there is no one else in the village; and there is no knife, ax, or bow and arrow in the house. A wild pig is standing in the door of the house and the woman is looking at the pig and is very afraid of it. The pig has been standing in the doorway for a few minutes and the person is looking at it very afraid and the pig won't move away from the door and she is afraid the pig will bite her.
>
> *Happy*—Her friends have come and she is happy.
>
> *Anger*—She is angry and is about to fight. (Ekman, 1980, p. 130)

Now look at Figure 14.7 to see whether you would have trouble matching the story with the photograph. (See **Figure 14.7**.)

(From Ekman, P. *The Face of Man: Expressions of Universal Emotions in a New Guinea Village.* New York: Garland STPM Press, 1980.)

FIGURE 14.8   In a study by Ekman and his colleagues, subjects were asked to make faces (shown in the photographs) when they were told the stories.

"Your friend has come and you are happy."

"Your child has died."

"You are angry and about to fight."

"You see a dead pig that has been lying there a long time."

TABLE 14.1 Judgments of emotion by people in the Fore tribe of New Guinea

Emotion described	Percent whose judgments agree with those made by members of literate cultures
Happiness	92
Sadness	79
Anger	84
Disgust	81
Surprise	68
Fear resulting from anger, disgust, or sadness	80
Fear resulting from surprise	43

Adapted from Ekman, P., and Friesen, W.V. Constants across cultures in the face and emotion. *Journal of Personality and Social Psychology*, 1971, *17*, 124–129.

Table 14.1 shows that the Fore tribespeople accurately identified all the expressions except for surprise and fear, which they tended to confuse, perhaps because for the people of this tribe surprising events are often also dangerous ones. (See **Table 14.1.**)

In a second study, Ekman and Friesen asked their subjects to make the kind of face that they thought people would make if they were experiencing the events recounted in the little stories. The researchers videotaped these efforts, made photographs of the appropriate frame, and showed the photographs to American college students, who accurately identified all emotions portrayed except surprise and fear (which is consistent with the judgments of Western expressions by the Fore people). Four photographs of the expressions of the Fore people are shown in Figure 14.8. The caption beneath each photograph describes the stories that were used to elicit the expressions. (See **Figure 14.8.**)

The results of this careful cross-cultural study (and of others that have produced similar data) suggest strongly that situations that would be expected to have motivational significance produce consisent patterns of contraction in the facial mus-

cles, whatever the person's culture. This conclusion suggests that the patterns of movement are inherited—wired into the brain, so to speak. The consistency of facial movements suggests an underlying consistency of emotional feeling throughout our species.

FACIAL EXPRESSIONS IN BLIND PEOPLE

◆ Other researchers have compared the facial expressions of blind and normally sighted children. The rationale is that if the facial expressions of both groups are similar, then the expressions are natural for our species and do not require learning by imitation. (Studies in blind adults would not be conclusive, because adults would have heard enough descriptions of facial expressions to be able to pose them.)

Summaries of studies of blind children (Woodworth and Schlosberg, 1954; Izard, 1971) found that in fact the facial expressions of young blind and sighted children are very similar, but that as blind children grow older, their facial gestures tend to become somewhat less expressive. This fact suggests that social reinforcement is important in maintaining our displays of emotion. However, the evidence clearly shows that we do not have to learn to smile, frown, or show other feelings with our facial gestures. Both the cross-cultural studies and the investigations with blind children confirm the naturalness of these expressions.

COMMUNICATION OF EMOTION IN NONHUMAN PRIMATES

Although the cross-cultural studies and observations of blind children suggest strongly that emotional *expression* by means of facial movements is innate, we cannot conclude from them that *recognition* of these expressions is also innate. It is quite possible that children learn what these expressions mean by observing others. The only way to determine whether the recognition is innate would be to isolate children from birth and later introduce them to society and see whether they responded appropriately to facial expressions of emotion. Obviously, this kind of study is impossible. However, studies with another species of primates have provided some interesting data.

R.E. Miller and his colleagues (Miller, Murphy, and Mirsky, 1959; Miller, Banks, and Ogawa, 1962, 1963; Miller, Banks, and Kawahara, 1966) have performed a number of experiments that demonstrate the ability of monkeys to communicate emotional states by means of facial gestures. Monkeys were taught to press a lever whenever a signal light was turned on. If they did not press the lever within a few seconds after the light came on, they received an electric shock. The animals readily learned the task. Next, two monkeys were tested in a divided task at the same time, in separate rooms. One monkey had the lever, the other had the signal light. The task worked as before: one animal had to press the lever a few seconds after the signal light came on, or else *both* animals received a shock. A closed-circuit television system recorded the facial expressions of the monkey who had only the signal light (the sender), and a television monitor was placed in the room of the monkey who had the lever (the receiver). The pair performed very well; the receiver was able to detect something (fear?) in the facial expression of the sender whenever the signal light came on, and pressed the lever to avoid the impending shock. (See **Figure 14.9.**)

The results show that monkeys can communicate at least one kind of emotion by means of facial gestures. Observations made in laboratory colonies and in the wild leave no doubt that many other emotions, such as anger, fear, sexual arousal, or pleasure can also be communicated.

Miller, Caul, and Mirsky (1967) used the same technique to determine whether learning and socialization are necessary for a monkey's production and recognition of facial expressions of emotion. They used animals that had been reared in isolation in Harlow's laboratory. (These monkeys were described in Chapter 6.) The monkeys had no trouble perceiving the light and learning to press the lever in response. Next, the researchers paired the isolated monkeys with normal monkeys and with other isolated monkeys as senders or receivers. A pair of isolated monkeys was a disaster; they managed to avoid only 10 percent of the shocks. A normal-isolate pair (the isolate serving as the receiver) did just as poorly. However, the isolate-normal pair did nearly as well as the normal-normal pair. (See **Figure 14.10.**)

These results suggest that the isolated monkeys made the appropriate facial gestures when the signal light came on and that the normal monkeys correctly read their expressions. However, the isolated monkeys failed to respond appropriately to the facial expressions of another monkey. Perhaps the organization of facial expression is part of a biological response system that does not require socialization, but *recognition* of facial expressions must be learned.

FIGURE 14.9   The procedure used by Miller and his colleagues.

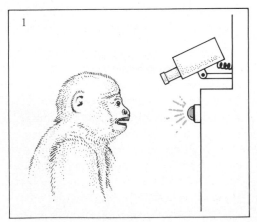

Sender

Receiver

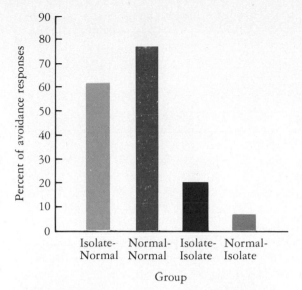

FIGURE 14.10   Data from the monkey communication study. (Miller, R.E., Caul, W.F., and Mirsky, I.A. *Journal of Personality and Social Psychology*, 1967, 7, 231–239.)

The experiment demonstrated that the isolates managed to communicate an expression (perhaps of fear) on most of the trials. But they also appeared to communicate this emotion at inappropriate times. When a normal monkey served as the sender, a normal receiver made few responses when the sig-

nal lamp was off; that is, few false alarms were sent. However, when an isolated monkey served as the sender, the receiver made many responses at inappropriate times. It was as if the isolated sender lacked good control over its emotional expressions and sent many false alarms. Perhaps socialization is not necessary for learning how to express fear, but the proper *control* of this response does require interaction with other monkeys.

The results of this study suggest that a monkey requires socialization early in life in order to respond correctly to another monkey's facial expression of fear. However, it also appears that some emotional expressions are innately recognized. For example, Sackett (1970) found that isolated infant monkeys made no response to colored slides of older monkeys exhibiting facial expressions that indicate threat. But by the age of three months, these monkeys showed great fear of the expressions, even though they had never seen or been harmed by another live monkey. Obviously, the infant monkeys' fear could not have been learned; presumably, all that was necessary for this response was for their brain to become sufficiently developed. (See **Figure 14.11.**)

Interim summary: The effect of emotions on social behavior is seen in the facial gestures that we make to express our feelings to others. In fact, we

FIGURE 14.11   Reactions of isolated infant monkeys at various ages to color slides of various objects. (From Sackett, G.P. In *Miami Symposium on the Prediction of Behavior, 1968,* edited by M.R. Jones. Coral Gables, Fla.: University of Miami Press, 1970.)

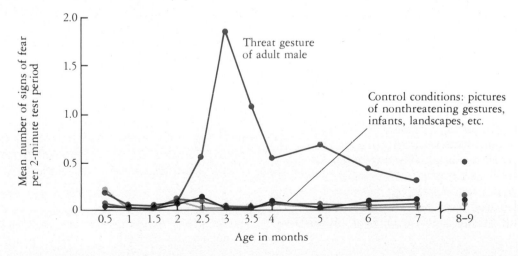

tend to trust people's facial expressions and tone of voice more than the meaning of their words. Darwin believed that the expression of emotion by facial gestures was innate; the muscular movements were inherited behavioral patterns. Although subsequent researchers criticized his data as biased and challenged his conclusions, more recent evidence suggests that Darwin was correct. Contradictory evidence came from deliberate, learned use of facial gestures as emblems: nonverbal substitutes for words.

In their study with Japanese and American subjects tested alone and in groups, Ekman and his colleagues found that cultural controls can affect people's facial expression of emotions, but that the basic form of expression among both cultures is the same. This conclusion was supported by more elaborate studies with people of the Fore tribe, who recognized facial expressions of Westerners, and made facial gestures that were clear to Westerners.

Studies with blind children and with monkeys raised in isolation also indicate that facial expressions of emotion are innate, although they can be affected by learning: the facial gestures of blind children tend to disappear unless they are explicitly reinforced, and isolated monkeys exhibit poorer control over facial gestures than their normally raised counterparts. The studies by Miller and his colleagues further suggest that monkeys must learn to recognize expressions of emotion, although Sackett's study indicates that at least one gesture (threat) produces fear in monkeys with no social experience.

PHYSIOLOGICAL EXPLANATIONS OF EMOTIONS

It is easy to understand why, from very early times, people have associated emotions with physiological responses. Strong emotions can cause increased heart rate, irregular breathing, queasy feelings in the internal organs, trembling, sweating, reddening of the face, or even fainting. The question is, do these physiological changes *constitute* emotion, or are they merely symptoms of some other underlying process? Do we feel frightened because we tremble, or do we tremble because we are frightened? (See **Figure 14.12**.)

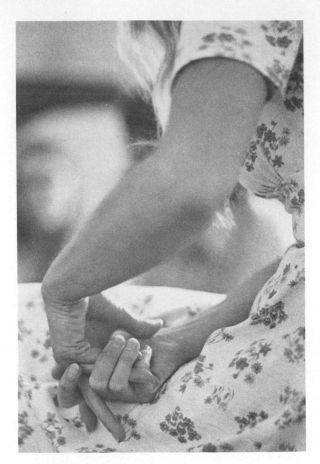

FIGURE 14.12   Is this woman's agitation *caused* by her anxiety or is it one of the responses that *constitutes* her anxiety?

THE JAMES-LANGE THEORY

William James (1842–1910), an American psychologist, and Carl Lange (1834–1900), a Danish physiologist, independently suggested similar explanations for emotion, which most people refer to collectively as the **James-Lange theory.** Basically, the theory states that emotion-producing situations elicit an appropriate set of physiological responses, such as trembling, sweating, and clenching of the fists. The brain receives sensory feedback from the organs that produce these responses, and the feedback constitutes emotion. As James put it:

. . . the bodily changes follow directly the perception of the exciting fact, and . . . our feelings of the same changes as they occur is the emotion. Common sense says we lose our fortune, are sorry, and weep; we meet a bear,

are frightened, and run; we are insulted by a rival, are angry, and strike. The hypothesis here to be defended says that this order of sequence is incorrect, that the one mental state is not immediately induced by the other and that the bodily manifestations must first be interposed between. The more rational statement is that we feel sorry because we cry, angry because we strike, afraid because we tremble, and not that we cry, strike, or tremble, because we are sorry, angry or fearful, as the case may be.

. . . If we fancy some strong emotion, and then try to abstract from our consciousness of it all the feelings of its bodily symptoms, we find we have nothing left behind, no "mind stuff" out of which the emotion can be constituted and that a cold and neutral state of intellectual perception is all that remains. (James, 1890, pp. 449–451)

To James, the fact that emotions are no more than a perception of our physiological responses suggested some practical consequences. We can "conquer undesirable emotional tendencies . . . by assiduously, and in the first instance cold-bloodedly, go[ing] through . . . the *outward movements* of those contrary dispositions which we prefer to cultivate" (p. 462). In other words, if we practice smiling at someone who makes us angry, our anger will eventually disappear.

James's description of the process of emotion might strike you as being at odds with your own experience. Most of us feel that we experience emotions directly, internally. The outward manifestations of our emotions seem to us to be secondary events. But have you ever found yourself in an unpleasant confrontation with someone else and discovered that you were trembling, even though you did not think that you were so bothered by the encounter? Or did you ever find yourself blushing in response to some public remark that was made about you? Or did you ever find tears coming to your eyes while watching a film that you did not think was affecting you? What would you conclude about your emotional states in situations like these? Would you ignore the evidence from your own physiological reactions?

Chapter 15 describes a topic of research called attribution, the process by which we make conclusions about the causes of other people's behavior. James's conclusions are closely related to the process of attribution; he suggests that our own emotional feelings are based on what we find ourselves doing and on the sensory feedback we receive from the activity of our internal organs. Where feelings of emotions are concerned, we are self-observers.

There is not much direct experimental support for the James-Lange theory, any more than there is for any other theory of emotion. James was a brilliant thinker and a persuasive writer, and the influence of his appeals to introspection and common sense is still strong. Furthermore, his theory has no been *disproved,* although many arguments have been directed against it.

Walter Cannon (1871–1945), a prominent physiologist, offered five major criticisms of the James-Lange theory (Cannon, 1927).

1. "The viscera {internal organs] are relatively insensitive structures." Thus, feedback would be poor, and we could not possibly discriminate the many emotions we can experience merely from our internal organs.
2. "The same visceral changes occur in very different emotional states."
3. "Artificial induction of the visceral changes typical of strong emotions does not produce them." Thus, injection of a hormone that increases heart rate does not cause the subject to experience an emotional change.
4. "Visceral changes are too slow to be a source of feeling." After all, emotional changes can be abrupt.
5. "Total separation of the viscera from the central nervous system does not alter emotional behavior."

However, more recent evidence suggests that Cannon's criticisms are not relevant. For example, although the viscera are not sensitive to cutting and burning, they provide much better feedback than Cannon suspected. Moreover, people are sensitive to a wide variety of patterns of activity in the viscera, and many changes in the viscera can occur rapidly enough so that they *could* be the causes of feelings of emotion.

Cannon cited the fact that cutting the sensory nerves between the internal organs and the central nervous system does not abolish emotional behavior in animals. However, this does not prove that *feelings* of emotion survive this surgical disruption. We do not know how the animal feels; we know only that it will snarl and attempt to bite if it is threatened. In any case, James did not attribute all emotion to the internal organs; he also said that feedback from muscles was important. The threat might make the animal snarl and bite, and the feedback from the facial and neck muscles might constitute a "feeling" of anger, even if feedback from the internal organs was cut off.

Hohman (1966) collected data from humans that established the importance of feedback from physiological responses in feelings of emotion. He questioned people who had suffered damage to the spinal cord about how intense their emotional feelings were. If feedback is important, one would expect that emotional feelings would be less intense if the injury were high (that is, close to the brain) than if it were low, because a high spinal-cord injury would cut off more of the body from the brain. In fact, this is precisely what Hohman found: the higher the injury, the less intense the feeling. (See **Figure 14.13.**)

The comments of patients with high spinal in-

jury suggest that the severely diminished feedback does change their feelings but not necessarily their behavior.

> I sit around and build things up in my mind, and I worry a lot, but it's not much but the power of thought. I was at home alone in bed one day and dropped a cigarette where I couldn't reach it. I finally managed to scrounge around and put it out. I could have burned up right there, but the funny thing is, I didn't get all shook up about it. I just didn't feel afraid at all, like you would suppose.
>
> Now, I don't get a feeling of physical animation, it's sort of cold anger. Sometimes I act angry when I see some injustice. I yell and cuss and raise hell, because if you don't do it sometimes, I've learned people will take advantage of you, but it doesn't have the heat to it that it used to. It's a mental kind of anger. (Hohman, 1966, pp. 150–151)

These comments suggest that we do not necessarily engage in emotional behavior *because of* our feelings; lacking these feelings, people still engage

FIGURE 14.13 The rationale for Hohman's investigation of the intensity of feelings of emotion in men with spinal cord damage. (Redrawn from Carlson, N.R. *Physiology of Behavior,* 2nd ed. Boston: Allyn and Bacon, 1981.)

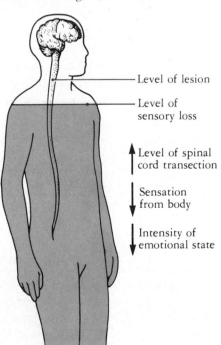

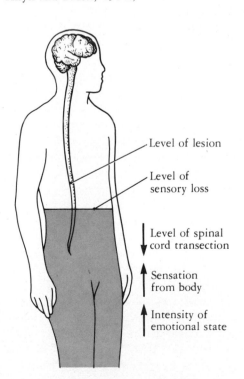

in the same behaviors for "rational" reasons. Perhaps these are also the real causes of the emotional behavior of people with the spinal cord intact.

OTHER PHYSIOLOGICAL THEORIES

Besides criticizing the James-Lange theory, Cannon proposed one of his own. He suggested that emotions are produced by activity of the thalamus, which sends information to and receives information from all regions of the cerebral cortex and participates in the control of autonomic and skeletal muscular responses. When emotion-producing stimuli are perceived, Cannon said, the messages sent by the thalamus to the cortex cause us to perceive the emotion, and those sent to the viscera and skeletal muscles cause the physiological emotional response. (See **Figure 14.14**.)

As a result of continuing research on brain functions, more recent investigators have located the source of emotions in the hypothalamus or in the *limbic system* (a series of brain structures that includes the hypothalamus and parts of the thalamus). However, these suggestions have not increased our understanding of emotion. They simply indicate that a given structure is necessary for an animal to produce an integrated display of emotional behavior.

THE INADEQUACY OF PHYSIOLOGICAL THEORIES OF EMOTION

Physiological investigation is essential to our understanding of emotional responses; as a physiological psychologist I would be the last person to deny the importance of these studies. But theories that focus only on physiological mechanisms can never provide an adequate explanation of emotion. For one thing, emotions are more than a set of physiological responses, even if these responses are essential to feeling emotion. As we saw earlier, in most cases emotions are more than automatic reactions to stimuli—they are often products of *judgments*. Our assessment of a particular situation determines how we will feel, and this assessment

FIGURE 14.14   Cannon's physiological theory of emotion.

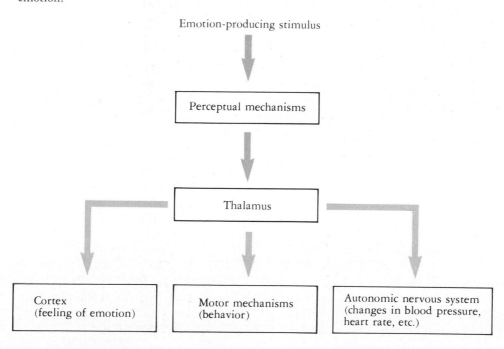

Emotion-producing stimulus

Perceptual mechanisms

Thalamus

Cortex
(feeling of emotion)

Motor mechanisms
(behavior)

Autonomic nervous system
(changes in blood pressure,
heart rate, etc.)

FIGURE 14.15   This woman's emotion is best
understood in terms of her past experiences, not by an
analysis of her physiological responses.

necessarily precedes any physiological response. To
achieve a complete explanation of emotion, we must
also know how a person's perception and experience
cause a particular emotion to occur in a particular
situation. (See **Figure 14.15.**)

The exceptions are our almost immediate responses to certain threatening stimuli. For example, classically conditioned responses appear to be
automatic and independent of cognition. If we are
walking across a street, the sound of screeching
tires will probably produce a surge of adrenalin and
a rapidly beating heart before we have time to assess what is happening. There is nothing innately
threatening about the sound of screeching tires,
but we have learned of their association with fast-
moving cars.

THE NEUROPSYCHOLOGY OF EMOTION

◆ Although we cannot explain emotions simply as
physiological responses, the emotional behavior of
people who have suffered brain damage has provided some insights. In general, the right hemisphere appears to play a more important role in
both feelings and expressions of emotion and in the
perception of emotions in other people. Within the

cerebral hemispheres, the temporal and frontal lobes
appear to play an important role in governing emotion and emotional behavior.

Effects of Brain Damage on Emotional Expression and Recognition

For a long time clinicians have noted differences
in the emotional behavior of patients with damage
to the right or left hemispheres. People who have
sustained damage to the left hemisphere often suffer a *catastrophic reaction,* an episode of severe
anxiety and depression, presumably in response to
their awareness of their neurological deficits. In
contrast, people with right-hemisphere damage are
often indifferent to their disorder. People with
damage to either hemisphere often have a paralyzed
arm and leg, but those with damage to the right
hemisphere, even when they acknowledge that they
cannot walk, often continue to make plans that do
not take account of their impairments, and show
no concern about their deficits. One man I met
had suffered a stroke that produced severe damage
to his right hemisphere. His left arm and leg were
totally paralyzed. He was confined to a wheelchair
because he could not walk. However, on several
occasions he cheerfully wheeled to the door of the
rehabilitation center so that he could "go for a walk

outside." This man was very intelligent, receiving superior scores on verbal subtests of the WAIS even after his stroke. However, some aspects of his judgment were impaired.

Presumably, the right hemisphere is specialized to some extent for recognizing emotionally relevant situations and for organizing the pattern of emotional responses. Thus, people with a damaged left hemisphere become anxious and depressed because their intact right hemisphere recognizes the devastating nature of the neurological impairments and assigns emotional significance to this assessment. But when the right hemisphere is damaged, although the left hemisphere can perform an objective inventory of these impairments, no emotional significance is attached to the results of the inventory. The patient acts cheerful and indifferent; the left hemisphere just does not seem to care.

Just as the left posterior regions of the cerebral cortex are important for the perception of speech and the left frontal regions for the production of speech, it appears that similar regional specialization exists in the right hemisphere for the recognition and production of emotional expressions. Ross (1981) reported case studies of patients who received damage to the right posterior frontal cortex, to the right parieto-temporal cortex, and to both regions. Frontal damage impaired the patients' use of facial gestures and tone of voice to express emotion, but not their comprehension of other people's emotional expressions. In contrast, patients with posterior damage could produce emotional expres-

FIGURE 14.16   The study by Ross (1981).

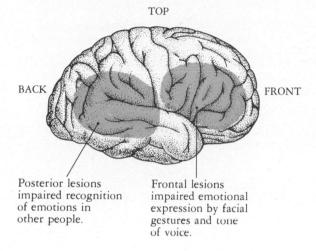

TOP

BACK   FRONT

Posterior lesions impaired recognition of emotions in other people.

Frontal lesions impaired emotional expression by facial gestures and tone of voice.

FIGURE 14.17   Presumably, cortical mechanisms are responsible for the recognition of stimuli that arouse emotions, but the activity of subcortical structures evokes the feelings themselves.

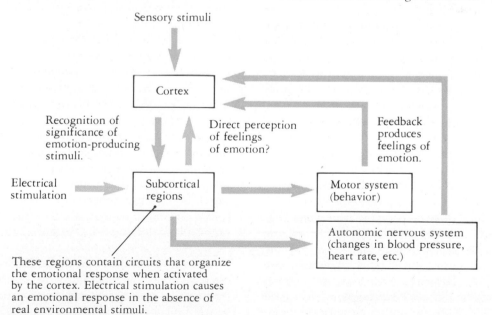

Sensory stimuli

Cortex

Recognition of significance of emotion-producing stimuli.

Direct perception of feelings of emotion?

Feedback produces feelings of emotion.

Electrical stimulation

Subcortical regions

Motor system (behavior)

Autonomic nervous system (changes in blood pressure, heart rate, etc.)

These regions contain circuits that organize the emotional response when activated by the cortex. Electrical stimulation causes an emotional response in the absence of real environmental stimuli.

sions but could not recognize those of other people. Large lesions damaged both production and recognition. (See **Figure 14.16.**)

The results of Ross's study are particularly interesting because they seem to be analogous to disturbances in language production and comprehension that follow damage to the corresponding areas of the left hemisphere. However, the conclusions are based on the data from only a few patients, and the results must be confirmed by other investigators before we can confidently accept them as fact.

Although the cerebral cortex is important in the evocation of emotional states in situations that normally produce them, the feelings themselves probably arise from the activity of subcortical regions, especially the limbic system and hypothalamus. (The fact that these regions control the autonomic nervous system probably accounts for the importance of feedback, as Hohman showed.) The best evidence for this assertion comes from the effects of electrical stimulation of the human brain. Stimulation of many subcortical regions can elicit feelings of pleasure, anger, fear, or rage (Sem-Jacobsen, 1968). These subcortical regions are presumably activated by circuits in the cerebral cortex that recognize the motivational significance of stimuli that normally evoke emotion. (See **Figure 14.17.**)

Hemispheric Differences in Emotional Behavior in Normal People

◈ Studies involving people with intact brains support the conclusions from neuropsychological data that the right hemisphere plays a special role in emotion. Ley and Bryden (1979) presented pictures of faces expressing various emotional states. The pictures were briefly presented either to the right or the left of the subject's point of gaze, so that the visual information was sent to the left or right hemispheres. (Although the hemispheres are united by the corpus callosum, it is assumed that the information received directly from the sensory system is richer in detail than the information relayed from the other side.) When the right hemisphere was the direct recipient of the visual information, the subjects made more accurate judgments of the emotional significance of the facial expressions. (See **Figure 14.18.**) Dimond, Farrington, and Johnson (1976) and Dimond and Farrington (1977) used special contact lenses to project an image of a motion picture on either the left or right half of sub-

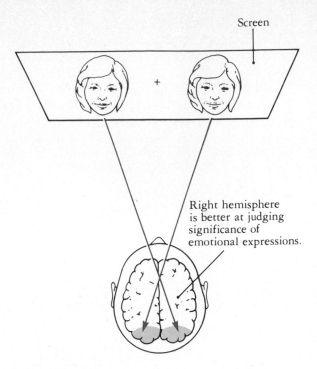

FIGURE 14.18   The study by Ley and Bryden (1979).

jects' retinas, no matter where they directed their eyes. When the right hemisphere was the primary viewer of the movie, the subjects were more likely to react emotionally, showing signs of autonomic activation.

The right-hemisphere advantage does not appear to be restricted to visually presented material. Safer and Leventhal (1977) presented passages read in a happy, angry, or neutral tone of voice. The subjects listened to the passage with either their right or left ear. (Although each ear sends auditory information to both hemispheres, the projections from each ear to the opposite hemisphere appear to be more important for auditory perception than their projections to the hemisphere on the same side.) In this experiment, too, the right hemisphere seemed to be more accurate than the left in rating the significance of the tone of the voice.

Interim summary: From the earliest times, people recognized that emotions were accompanied by feelings that seemed to come from inside the body, which probably provided the impetus for developing physiological theories of emotion. James and

Lange suggested that the physiological and behavioral reactions to emotion-producing situations were *interpreted* by people as states of emotion, and that emotional states were not the causes of these reactions. Cannon criticized this theory but many of the physiological data on which his criticisms were based were later shown to be incorrect. Hohman's study of people with spinal cord damage supported the James-Lange theory—people who could no longer feel the reactions from most of their body reported that they no longer experienced intense emotional states. However, the loss of feelings did not necessarily affect their behavior; thus, emotional feelings and behaviors may be at least somewhat independent.

In any case, theories of emotion based on physiological reactions cannot explain *why* emotions occur. Such explanations will require understanding of the situations that produce emotions and our ability to recognize them.

Neuropsychological studies have shown that the right hemisphere plays a more important role in perceiving the emotional significance of situations, expressing emotion, and perceiving the emotional expressions of other people. In particular, the frontal lobes may contain expressive mechanisms, and the posterior lobes may contain perceptual mechanisms. Because studies have shown that electrical stimulation of subcortical regions evokes emotional feelings or elicits emotional behaviors, it is likely that the cortical mechanisms of emotion control the activity of subcortical circuits.

SELF-ASSESSMENT: THE ROLE OF COGNITION IN EMOTION

Considerable research has suggested that although our feelings of emotion do depend on perception of our physiological reactions, the assessments we make depend very much on cognitive processes. Many people have noticed a difference between physiological response and emotion. For example, Bertrand Russell (1960) wrote:

> Some people say that the physiological changes correlated with . . . secretions *are* the emotions. . . . As everyone knows, the adrenal glands secrete adrenalin, which produces the bodily symptoms of fear or rage. On one occasion my dentist injected a considerable amount of the substance into my blood in the course of administering a local anesthetic. I turned pale and trembled, and my heart beat violently; the bodily symptoms of fear were present, as the books said they should be, but it was quite obvious to me that I was not actually feeling fear. I should have had the same bodily symptoms in the presence of a tyrant about to condemn me to death, but there would have been something extra which was absent when I was in the dentist's chair. What was different was the cognitive part: I did not feel fear because I knew there was nothing to be afraid of. In normal life, the adrenal glands are stimulated by the perception of an object which is frightful or enraging; thus there is already a cognitive element present. . . . But when adrenalin is artificially administered, this cognitive element is absent and the emotion in its entirety fails to arise. . . ." (pp. 226–227)

SUBJECTIVE INTERPRETATION OF DRUG-INDUCED AROUSAL

Schachter (1964) proposed that emotions are determined *jointly* by perception of physiological responses and by cognitive assessment of a specific situation. He described three conditions that elicit emotion:

> . . . given a state of physiological arousal for which an individual has no immediate explanation, he will "label" this state and describe his feelings in terms of the cognitions available to him. To the extent that cognitive factors are potent determiners of emotional states, . . . precisely the same state of physiological arousal could be labelled "joy" or "fury" or any of a great diversity of emotional labels. . . .
>
> . . . given a state of physiological arousal for which an individual has a completely appropriate explanation (e.g., "I feel this way because I have just received an injection of adrenalin"), no evaluative needs will arise, and the individual is unlikely to label his feelings in terms of the alternative cognitions available. . . .
>
> . . . given the same cognitive circumstances, the individual will react emotionally or describe his feelings as emotions only to the extent that he experiences a state of physiological arousal. (p. 53)

Thus, to Schachter, emotion is cognition plus emotional reaction in the form of physiological arousal. Both are necessary.

To test this hypothesis, Schachter and Singer (1962) arranged to induce physiological arousal in groups of subjects placed in various situations. All subjects were told that they were part of an investigation of the effects of a vitamin called "suproxin" on visual perception. No such vitamin exists. They gave some subjects injections of adrenalin, a hormone that stimulates a variety of autonomic effects associated with arousal, such as increased heart rate and blood pressure, irregular breathing, warming of the face, and mild trembling. Other subjects received a control injection of a salt solution, which has no physiological effects.

Next the researchers placed some subjects in an anger-provoking situation, in which they were treated rudely and subjected to obnoxious test questions such as following: "How many men, besides your father, has your mother slept with? (a) one, (b) two, (c) three, (d) four or more." Others were treated politely and saw the antics of another "subject" (a confederate who was hired by the experimenters) who acted silly and euphoric. The experimenters hoped that these two situations, together with the physiological reactions produced by the injections of adrenalin, would promote either negative or positive emotional states.

Finally, some subjects were correctly informed that the injections they received would produce side effects such as trembling and a pounding heart. Others were told to expect irrelevant side effects or none at all. Schachter and Singer predicted that the subjects who knew what side effects to expect would correctly attribute their physiological reactions to the drug and would not experience a change in emotion. Those who were misinformed would note their physiological arousal and conclude that they were feeling especially angry or happy, as the circumstance dictated. The subjects reported their emotional states in a questionnaire.

The results were not as clear-cut as the experimenters had hoped. The adrenalin did not increase the intensity of the subjects' emotional state; however, subjects who expected to experience physiological arousal as a result of the injection reported much less of a change in their emotional state, *whether they received the adrenalin or the placebo;* they felt less angry or happy after having been exposed to one of the emotional situations. These results suggest that we *interpret* the significance of our physiological reactions, rather than simply experiencing them as emotions.

Nisbett and Schachter (1966) provided further evidence that subjects can be fooled into attributing their own naturally occurring physiological responses to a drug, and thus into feeling less "emotional." First, they gave all subjects a placebo pill (one with no physiological effects). Half the subjects were told that the pill would make their hearts pound, their breathing increase, and their hands tremble; the other half (the control subjects) were told nothing about possible side effects. Then the researchers strapped on electrodes and gave the subjects electric shocks. All subjects presumably experienced pain and fear, and consequently their heart rate and breathing increased, they trembled and so on. The subjects who perceived their reactions as drug-induced were able to tolerate stronger shocks than the control subjects and they reported less fear and pain. Thus, cognition can affect people's judgments about their own emotional states, and even their tolerance of pain.

EFFECTS OF FALSE FEEDBACK ON EMOTIONAL FEELINGS

Just as we can apparently "explain away" our physiological arousal, our beliefs about our physiological responses can affect our judgments, even if the beliefs are untrue. Valins (1966) showed ten colored slides of nude women in varying sequences to male subjects. They were told that their heart rates were to be recorded during the slide show; the "old fashioned" electronic equipment used was so crude that it allowed the subjects to hear what they assumed to be their own heartbeats. In fact, the subjects actually heard a prerecorded heartbeat, not their own. During presentation of five of the ten slides, the subjects heard an increase in heart rate, which led them to conclude that these five pictures caused autonomic arousal. When asked to rate the pictures of the women after having seen all ten, they showed a preference for the ones associated with the phony increase in heart rate.

The preference was a lasting one; in a follow-up study, Valins (1968) found that even after the deception was explained, the subjects insisted that they still liked slides of the "increased heart rate" women better. (The selection of the five slides was counterbalanced, so that the set was different for each subject.) According to Valins, when the subjects thought they heard their heart rate increase, they looked at the slide more carefully, to find out what there was about the woman that aroused them. The careful scrutiny revealed interesting features that they found pleasing.

Interim summary: Although emotional states are sometimes produced by automatic, classically-conditioned responses, some psychologists have suggested that the perception of our own emotional state is not determined solely by physiological feedback, but also by cognitive assessment of the situation in which we find ourselves. Schachter and his colleagues found that information about the physiological reactions of drugs (or placebos) affected subjects' reports about their emotional state. In one study they even tolerated more intense electric shocks because they had been told that their physiological reactions were effects of a drug; hence they apparently discounted their own fear. Valins showed that false feedback about subjects' physiological reactions affected their judgments about the attractiveness of nude women, and that these judgments were not altered by informing them about the deception. While these results do not support any single comprehensive theory of emotion, they do underscore the importance of cognitive factors in emotion and the complexity of the phenomenon.

EMOTIONAL BEHAVIOR: AGGRESSION

Of the various kinds of emotionally related social behavior, two are especially important: sexual activity (already discussed in Chapter 7) and aggression. (See **Figure 14.19**.)

Aggression is a serious problem in human society; every day we hear or read about incidents involving violence and cruelty, and undoubtedly thousands more go unreported. If we are to provide a safe environment for everyone, we must learn more about the causes of aggressive behavior. Probably many factors influence a person's tendency to commit acts of aggression, including childhood experiences, exposure to violence on television and in movies, peer-group pressures, hormones and drugs, and malfunctions of the brain. Various aspects of aggressive behavior have been studied by zoologists, physiological psychologists, sociologists, social psychologists, political scientists, and psychologists who specialize in the learning process.

FIGURE 14.19 Aggression is an all-too-common aspect of human life.

ETHOLOGICAL STUDIES OF AGGRESSION

The Social Relevance of Intraspecific Aggression

◆ The utility of species-typical behaviors such as sexual activity, parental behavior, food gathering, and nest construction is obvious; it is easy to understand their value to survival. But violence and aggression are also seen in many species, including humans. If aggression is harmful, one would not expect it to be so prevalent in nature. Ethologists—zoologists who study the behavior of animals in their natural environments—have analyzed the causes of aggression and have shown that it, too, often has value for the survival of a species.

There are two basic forms of aggression. *Predation,* an attack by an animal of one species upon an animal of another as a source of food, should probably not be classified as an emotional behavior. A lion killing a zebra, a bird catching a fish, or a fisherman pulling in his net is simply obtaining food. The other form, *intraspecific aggression,* involves an attack by one animal upon another member of its species.

Ethologists have shown that intraspecific aggression has several biological advantages. First, it tends to disperse a population of animals, forcing some into new territories, where necessary environmental adaptations may increase the flexibility of the species. Second, when accompanied with rivalry among males for mating opportunities, intraspecific aggression tends to perpetuate the genes of healthier, more vigorous animals.

Human cultures, however, are very different, even from those of other species of primates. Perhaps intraspecific aggression has outlived its usefulness for humans and we would benefit from its elimination. In any case, we must understand the causes of human aggression to eliminate it or to direct it to useful purposes.

Threat and Appeasement

◆ Ethologists have discovered a related set of behaviors in many species: ritualized threat gestures and appeasement gestures. *Threat gestures* enable an animal to communicate aggressive intent to an-

other before engaging in actual violence. For example, if one dog intrudes into another's territory the defender will growl and bare its teeth, raise the fur on its back (presumably making it look larger to its opponent), and stare at the intruder. Almost always, the dog defending its territory will drive the intruder away. Threat gestures are particularly important in species whose members are able to kill each other (Lorenz, 1966; Eibl-Eibesfeld, 1980). For example, wolves often threaten each other with growls and bared teeth but rarely bite each other. Similarly, rattlesnakes "Indian wrestle" until one opponent is pinned down, but they almost never bite each other. (A rattlesnake is not immune to its own poison.) Because an all-out battle between these pairs of animals would probably end in the death of one and the serious wounding of the other, the tendency to perform ritualized displays rather than engage in overt aggression has an obvious advantage to the survival of the species. (See **Figure 14.20.**)

To forestall an impending attack, one of the animals must show that it does not want to fight—

FIGURE 14.20   Poisonous Australian black snakes, like rattlesnakes, wrestle to establish dominance; they do not bite each other..

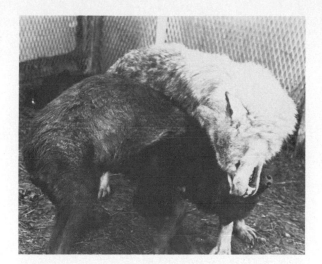

FIGURE 14.21   The submissive wolf shows appeasement behavior by exposing its throat to the dominant wolf.

FIGURE 14.22   Staring at an opponent constitutes a threat gesture in humans as well as in chimpanzees.

that it admits defeat. The submissive animal makes an *appeasement gesture.* If a pair of wolves get into a fight, one usually submits to the other by lying down and exposing its throat. The sight of a helpless and vulnerable opponent presumably terminates the victor's hostility, and the fight ceases. The aggression of the dominant animal is *appeased.* (See **Figure 14.21.**)

Probably the most easily recognized examples of these behaviors for humans are those from Jane Goodall's studies of chimpanzees living in the wild (Goodall, 1968). Threat gestures include:

Glaring or staring opponent into submission
Raising arm above head or hunching shoulders
Swaggering back and forth from foot to foot
Stamping the ground with the feet
Hooting and screaming at the opponent

Appeasement gestures include:

Whimpering while showing teeth and gums
Bowing or crouching down
Reaching out the hand to be touched
Sexually presenting (whether male or female)

Sometimes the submissive animal elicits *reassurance gestures* from the dominant chimpanzee; through these the winner seems to communicate

that it will not hurt the loser. The gestures include:

Patting on the head
Touching the outstretched hand
Mounting the opponent and making a few perfunctory sexual gestures

If you saw these behaviors yourself, you probably would have no trouble identifying them. In fact you may already have seen some of them, slightly modified, in humans. (See **Figure 14.22.**) Suppose you are a male of average size standing at a bar next to a muscular, 280-pound male wearing a jacket with a skull-and-crossbones stenciled on the back. Would you stare directly at his face? And if he happened to stare at you, would you stand up tall and meet his gaze or slouch down a bit, displaying a diffident look on your face?

Although we can recognize the threat and appeasement behaviors of chimpanzees as similar to those of humans, our societies are very different. Thus, even though similar neural mechanisms may underlie these displays in both species, the conditions under which they are elicited are very different. Furthermore, the complexity of our culture suggests that many other factors affect our learning when to act aggressively and when to appease.

VARIABLES THAT AFFECT HUMAN AGGRESSION

Imitation of Aggression

Consider the significance of a conversation like this one:

> PARENT: I don't know what to do with Johnny. His teacher says he is simply impossible. He just can't keep from hitting and kicking other children.
>
> FRIEND: Perhaps he needs more discipline.
>
> PARENT: But I spank him all the time!

Why does Johnny persist in being aggressive, even though this behavior is regularly punished? Some psychologists would suggest that instead of suppressing his violent behavior, frequent spankings have *taught* him to be aggressive. When his parents become upset with his behavior, they resort to physical violence. And Johnny learns to imitate them.

A large percentage of nonviolent people may have been spanked at least once when they were children, with no obvious harm. But it is clear that when parents habitually resort to aggression, their children are likely to do the same. In the extreme case of child abuse, parents who beat their children usually turn out to have been victims of child abuse themselves; this unfortunate trait seems

FIGURE 14.23   Too often, television characters choose a violent solution to their problems.

to be passed along like an unwanted family heirloom (Parke and Collmer, 1975).

Most parents do not beat their children or even spank them frequently, but there is another opportunity for imitation that is of concern to society—examples of violence on television or in movies. All too often, the heroes disdain peaceful solutions to their problems and instead seek them through fighting. (See **Figure 14.23.**) Most people would agree that it would be unfortunate if real people were as violent as the ones we see on television. Does the continued observation of violence in the mass media lead children to choose aggressive means to solve their problems, or are the spokespersons for the television networks correct when they argue that children have no trouble separating fact from fancy, and that they only give us what we want anyway?

◆ LABORATORY STUDIES   Some of the most interesting research on children's imitation of violence comes from the laboratory of Albert Bandura (see Bandura, 1973). In one particularly significant set of experiments an adult attacked a large, inflated clown doll (affectionately referred to in the literature as a "Bobo doll"). One group of children watched the attack; some witnessed in person, others on television. Another group watched the adult engage in innocuous behaviors. Later, the children were allowed to play in the room where the doll was kept.

All the children who had seen the adult beat Bobo, either in person or on television, imitated the adult's behavior, giving the doll a savage beating. The children who watched innocuous behaviors did not display aggression toward the doll. It was also clear that the children's aggressive behavior was modeled on that of the adult. Those who had seen the adult kick the doll, use a hammer to hit it, or sit on top of it and pound its face did the same. Figure 14.24 shows the model behavior of the adult (top) and the imitative behavior of the children. (See **Figure 14.24.**)

Other research by Bandura and his colleagues has shown that viewing another person's aggressive behavior has complex effects. For example, some children saw a film of a person being aggressive. The person was either rewarded or punished for the aggression. Children who saw the person being re-

FIGURE 14.24   *Top:* Aggressive behavior of the model. *Middle and bottom:* Imitative behavior by children. (From Bandura, A., Ross, D., and Ross, S.A. *Journal of Abnormal and Social Psychology,* 1961, 66, 3–11.)

warded were more aggressive, whereas those who watched the person being punished subsequently made fewer attacks on the Bobo doll. We cannot conclude that one group of children, but not the other, *learned* to attack the doll. When the experimenter later offered the children a reward for imitating the model, *both groups* started beating Bobo. Thus, it is clear that all the children had learned the aggressive response. The sight of the model being punished had inhibited the children's expression of the learned behaviors, so that they did not act out what they had learned until direct reinforcement of these behaviors removed this inhibition.

Seldom do laboratory experiments dealing with complex issues provide such unambiguous results, and in this case such clear application to the issue of violence in the mass media.

FIELD STUDIES   Field studies have yielded less clearcut results than laboratory studies. One reason is that experiments that attempt to manipulate real-life situations are difficult to carry out. Field studies have furnished no direct evidence that longterm viewing of violence on television causes children to be more violent. This fact does not mean that violence on television has no effect on youngsters, only that definitive studies remain to be performed.

Lefkowitz, Eron, Walder, and Huesmann (1977) observed a correlation between boys' viewing of violence and their later behavior. They reported that the greater boys' preference was for violent television at age eight, the greater their aggressiveness was both at that age and ten years later, at age eighteen. (Girls were found to be much less aggressive, and no relation was observed between television viewing and violence.) The correlation between program preference and later aggressiveness was .31; that is, slightly less than 10 percent ($.31^2$) of the variability in the boys' violence at age eighteen was related to their earlier preference. Thus, even if the television viewing influenced the violence, the effect was small.

The authors concluded that there is a cause-and-effect relation between early viewing of television violence and later aggression, and several statistical analyses of the data lend some support to this conclusion. However, a correlation between two variables does not prove that one causes the other. It is possible that children who are violent at age eight (for whatever reason) prefer to watch violent programs on television. Their preference may therefore be a *symptom,* rather than a *cause,* of their aggressiveness.

Feshbach and Singer (1971) carried out a bold and interesting field study in an attempt to manipulate directly the amount of violence seen by boys, and thus to determine whether the viewing would affect their later aggressiveness. With the cooperation of directors of various private boarding schools and homes for neglected children, half of the teenage boys were permitted to watch only violent television programs, the other half only nonviolent ones. Six months later, no effect was seen on the behavior of the boys in the private schools. The boys in the homes for neglected children who had watched violent programs tended to be slightly *less* aggressive than those who had watched the nonviolent ones.

Two factors prevent us from concluding that violent television programs promote pacifism or at least have no effect. First, by the time people reach their teens, they may be too old to be affected by six months of television viewing; the critical period may come earlier. If this assumption is true, it suggests that it does not matter what an adult watches. Second, some of the boys resented not

FIGURE 14.25 We should try to promote more constructive models than the kind that produce behaviors like this.

being allowed to watch their favorite (in this case violent) television programs, and most of these boys already displayed violent behaviors. Therefore, the displeasure of the violent boys who watched the nonviolent programs probably may have made them more aggressive.

As with many other complex social issues, we lack definitive evidence that television violence makes members of our society more aggressive. However, the stakes in this issue are high enough that we should tolerate some uncertainty and choose what is clearly the lesser of two evils. Given both the possibility that violence on television has a harmful effect and the fact that no harm can come from reducing the amount of aggression on the airwaves, we should make every effort to provide a more peaceful and constructive model of human behavior to our children. (See **Figure 14.25.**)

Frustration and Aggression

◈ An influential hypothesis proposed by Dollard, Doob, Miller, Mowrer, and Sears (1939) stated that frustration causes aggression. In general usage, the term *frustration* refers to an unpleasant feeling produced by an unfulfilled desire. However, Dollard and his colleagues defined ***frustration*** specifically as "an interference with the occurrence of an in-stigated goal-response at its proper time in the behavior sequence"—that is, as a condition that prevents the occurrence of an expected reinforcer. Expectation (implied by the term "goal-response") plays a crucial role in the definition of frustration. For example, I cannot be said to be frustrated by not winning the Irish sweepstakes. However, if I am very thirsty and put my last piece of change in a vending machine to get something to drink, my response of drinking—which I expect to be able to do—is frustrated if the machine keeps my money but fails to deliver a beverage.

According to Dollard and his colleagues, frustration invariably increases an organism's tendency to engage in aggressive behavior and accounts for *all* instances of aggression. Their rationale was that frustration produces a drive that motivates the aggressive behavior; if this drive finds an outlet in the form of aggressive behavior, it will be reduced and the organism will no longer behave aggressively. This hypothetical phenomenon was originally suggested by Freud's psychodynamic theory

of personality and is called *catharsis*. A later section discusses the role of catharsis in aggression.

An analysis by Berkowitz (1978) disposes of the hypothesis that all aggressive acts are caused by frustration. Aggressive behaviors, like any other, can be reinforced. A dog can be trained to attack. An assassin can be hired to kill another person. Frustration does not play a causal role in either of these cases. Pain is also an effective agent in producing aggressive behavior. If two animals are placed in a small cage and receive electric shocks to their feet, they are likely to fight.

On the other hand, although some forms of aggression do not involve frustration, perhaps frustration invariably increases an organism's tendency to behave aggressively. However, even in this case some psychologists have concluded that frustration will not produce aggression if the interference is reasonable. Pastore (1952) asked subjects how they would feel if they were in various situations—for example, if they were waiting for a bus and saw one pass them by without stopping. They responded that if the bus simply drove by, they would feel angry; however, if the bus had a sign on it showing that it was not in service but was on its way to the garage, they would not feel angry. Perhaps we are likely to engage in aggressive behavior (become angry) only when there seems to be no good reason for the frustration.

The possibility remains that the subjects in this experiment were simply giving socially acceptable responses, and that they would actually have felt angry in both cases. To investigate this possibility, Burnstein and Worchel (1962) had their subjects work in groups on a common task. In each group, a confederate hired by the experimenters frustrated their progress. In one group the confederate appeared to have a hearing defect, which accounted for his interruptions; in the other, the confederate appeared to be interrupting for no good reason.

When the subjects were asked whether they wanted to eliminate any members of their group, they rejected the confederate who had frustrated their progress without apparent cause, but not the man with the hearing defect. However, the subjects admitted privately that they would have liked to reject him as well. Apparently they refused to do so in the group setting because they thought they would have looked bad to the other people.

Thus, it is possible that frustration does increase aggressive tendencies, but that other conditions (such as social controls) can suppress these tendencies.

Berkowitz (1978) had subjects sit on a bicycle and attempt to adjust their rate of pedaling to match that of a person in another room. Signal lights indicated whether they should pedal faster or slower. In fact, there was no partner in the other room. The subjects were told that they would receive five dollars if they matched their partner's speed for the entire trial. Control subjects were not told that they would win a prize, and consequently had no expectations that could be frustrated.

Near the end of the run, frustration was introduced: the subjects suddenly failed to match their partner's speed. Some subjects were told that a malfunction of the equipment had caused the failure; others were told that their partners were at fault. Subjects in both experimental groups reported that they were angry; subjects in control groups did not. Thus, frustration caused anger even when it was caused by factors apparently outside of anyone's control.

The next phase of the experiment tested actual aggression, when the subjects had an opportunity to punish the fictitious partner's behavior by pressing a button that allegedly delivered a loud, noxious noise. The perceived source of frustration did have an effect on aggressive behavior: subjects who believed that the partner was to blame pressed the button more often and longer than did those who blamed the apparatus or had not expected to receive a reward.

Given the results of these and other experiments, Berkowitz has suggested modifying the frustration-aggression hypothesis to account for the effects of other aversive stimuli, including pain. In our evolution, pain became a potent elicitor for aggressive behavior; if an animal was in pain and another animal was present, the latter was likely to be the source of the pain. Thus, animals who attacked despite being in pain were more likely to survive than those who failed to respond.

Berkowitz and Frodi (1977) found that pain does elicit aggressive behavior in humans. They induced pain in volunteer subjects by having them place a hand in a tank of very cold water. The effect is painful but does not cause physical harm. Control subjects placed a hand in cool water. After seven minutes, the subjects were permitted to reward or punish the behavior of a (fictitious) person in the next room. Subjects who were experiencing pain administered more shocks than did control subjects. They also reported feeling annoyance, irritation, and anger, as well as pain and discomfort.

In conclusion, at least some forms of aggression appear to be produced by aversive stimuli, frustration being just one example. In addition, aggression, like any other species-typical behavior, can be inhibited.

Aggression and Catharsis

◈ Dollard and his colleagues have accepted Freud's suggestion that aggression consists of response tendencies that are energized by a drive, and this hypothesis has been incorporated into many ethological theories. Various physiological and environmental influences increase the level of this drive. Once aroused, the aggressive drive must eventually find some sort of outlet in actual aggressive behavior or in some symbolic substitute. The Freudian and ethological models of aggression emphasize the importance of *catharsis* (*katharsis* is Greek for "purge"). According to Freud, if a person does not satisfy energized aggressive drives by acting out the hostile feelings or by some means of symbolic aggression, the person will direct the aggression inward, and mental disorders will ensue. Presumably the spilling out of hostility through catharsis leaves the person in a healthy, relaxed state. (See **Figure** 14.26.)

EXPERIMENTAL RESEARCH ON CATHARSIS Experimental evidence suggests that acting out aggression tends to lead to even *more* aggression.

Geen, Stonner, and Shope (1975) made some subjects angry by having a confederate unfairly give them an excessive number of electric shocks while they were attempting to solve a problem. Afterward some subjects were given the opportunity to punish their tormentor by supposedly delivering a shock whenever he made an error in a learning task. During a second learning task, all subjects were given the same opportunity. However, this time they could turn a dial to determine how intense the shock would be. The subjects' blood pressure was taken several times during the experiment. According to the catharsis model, the sub-

FIGURE 14.26 This prison inmate expresses his hostility symbolically through his artistic efforts. Do activities like these reduce the tendency toward violent behaviors?

jects who were able to punish the confederate twice should have shown less anger during the second learning task—their anger should have been released during the first task—whereas those who did not punish their tormenter during the first learning task should still have been angry and have set the shock intensity higher.

The blood-pressure readings were in accord with the catharsis hypothesis: after each opportunity to punish the confederate, the subjects' blood pressure fell, presumably reflecting a decrease in anger. However, the *behavioral* effects were just the opposite: subjects who had shocked the confederate during the first learning task shocked him even more during the second, and their responses on a questionnaire indicated that they felt more hostile toward him. Although aggression appeared to purge anger, it seemed also to increase aggressive tendencies.

Perhaps the opportunity to be aggressive has a beneficial effect on a person's feelings, and thus lowers his or her blood pressure. However, the reduction of unpleasant feelings creates the conditions for *negative reinforcement,* achieved through the termination of an aversive stimulus. Thus, when a person gives vent to feelings of hostility and feels better afterward, the experience tends to increase the likelihood that aggressive behavior will recur.

◆ SYMBOLIC CATHARSIS The noted ethologist Konrad Lorenz and others have suggested that people can achieve catharsis merely by watching or participating in some form of ritualized violence rather than by actual aggression. According to Lorenz, "The most important function of sport lies in furnishing a healthy safety valve for that most indispensable and, at the same time, most dangerous form of aggression that I have described as collective militant enthusiasms . . ." (1966, p. 272).

However, the evidence indicates otherwise. Patterson (1974) administered a paper-and-pencil test of hostility to high school football players at two different times and found that they appeared to become more aggressive after the football season than before it. In a laboratory study, Ryan (1970) made subjects angry and gave some of them the opportunity to hit a "cathartic pounding appara-tus" with a rubber mallet. The exercise failed to relieve their hostility. When they were tested in a "learning experiment" like the one described ear-lier, they delivered as many fictitious shocks to their antagonist as the control subjects did.

Exercise does appear to relieve aggressive feel-ings, but for other reasons. For example, if you are angry with someone and go out and run for a cou-ple of miles, you will probably come back feeling much less hostile. There are two reasons for this phenomenon: first, physical exhaustion is likely to make anyone feel less inclined to pick a fight; sec-ond, any intervening activity that distracts a person for a sufficient amount of time—such as counting to ten if someone makes you angry—is likely to allow aggressive tendencies to dissipate. Thus, the role of catharsis in aggression remains unsolved.

Distraction by Means of Competing Responses

◆ There do appear to be other ways to decrease vio-lence. One is to divert anger by engaging in be-haviors that are incompatible with aggression. For example, if an angry confrontation appears to be brewing in a group of people, a "peacemaker" may try to forestall an outbreak of hostility by making jokes. Often the people turn to laughter rather than aggression, and the situation is defused.

This method also works in the laboratory. Baron (1974) first had a confederate anger his subjects and then showed them some funny cartoons. Con-trol subjects looked at neutral pictures of scenery or works of art. The subjects who looked at the cartoons gave briefer shocks to the confederate dur-ing the final part of the study, when they had a chance to retaliate. Further research may prove that other kinds of distractions are useful in decreasing aggression.

BIOLOGY OF AGGRESSION

There is good evidence from a variety of animals that many forms of aggressive behavior are species-typical responses. Two kinds of violent behavior that closely resemble predation and intraspecific aggression appear to be organized in the brains of several species of mammals. It is likely that some simple elements of attack are innately organized in

the human brain; as almost every parent learns, young children will bite in response to frustration. However, most aggressive behaviors in humans are more complex, and these patterns are undoubtedly learned.

Brain Mechanisms of Attack

◆ Aggressive behaviors in most animals follow a fairly rigid, stereotyped form. Because the same response patterns are observed even in animals raised in iso-lation, it seems likely that these behaviors are or-ganized or programmed in the brain. Somehow, neural circuits must contain the information needed to identify an opponent and to control the threat displays and sequence of movements that consti-tute an attack. Flynn and his colleagues (Flynn, Vanegas, Foote, and Edwards, 1970) have studied the neural mechanisms that arouse, inhibit, and organize aggressive behaviors in cats' brains. Other investigators have extended their findings to spe-cies such as rats, opossums, and rhesus monkeys.

It appears that the processes of organization, excitation, and inhibition are located in different parts of the brain. Flynn and his colleagues placed wires directly in the hypothalamus and periaque-ductal gray matter of cats' brains. They found that electrical stimulation elicited two kinds of attack on another animal, depending on where the stim-ulation occurred. Stimulation of the medial hypo-thalamus produced **affective attack,** which looks like real rage and is probably similar to aggressive violence in humans. The cats arched their backs, spat and hissed, and lashed out with their claws at anything that moved. Stimulation more toward the side of the hypothalamus produced **quiet-biting attack,** which resembles simple predation. The cats acted excited but not angry. If they saw a rat or other appropriate prey they sank down into a hunt-ing posture, twitched their tails, carefully crept up to the other animal, and suddenly pounced on it.

It appears that attack sequences are organized in the periaqueductal gray matter, and that the hypo-thalamus plays a role in arousing or inhibiting these behaviors. When Flynn and his colleagues de-stroyed portions of the periaqueductal gray matter, the cats stopped attacking rats and mice, even if their hypothalamus was electrically stimulated. The "on buttons" in the hypothalamus were useless when the machinery of the midbrain was gone. (See **Fig-ure 14.27, top.**) After the hypothalamus was sur-

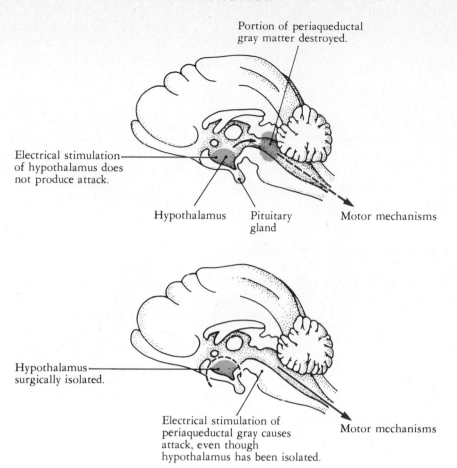

Portion of periaqueductal
gray matter destroyed.

Electrical stimulation
of hypothalamus does
not produce attack.

Hypothalamus   Pituitary   Motor mechanisms
                gland

Hypothalamus
surgically isolated.

Electrical stimulation of
periaqueductal gray causes   Motor mechanisms
attack, even though
hypothalamus has been isolated.

FIGURE 14.27   *Top:* Attack behaviors appear to be organized in the periaqueductal gray matter; when portions of it are destroyed, the cat does not attack another animal even if its hypothalamus is stimulated. *Bottom:* The arousal and inhibition of attack appear to be influenced by activity of the hypothalamus.

gically disconnected, electrical stimulation of the periaqueductal gray matter still caused attack behavior; even with the "on buttons" gone, the machinery could still be directly stimulated. (See **Figure 14.27, bottom.**)

One other brain structure influences aggressive behavior, but its precise role is uncertain. The *amygdala* (a Greek word meaning "almond-shaped") lies deep in the temporal lobes. Damage to various parts of the amygdala can make an animal either more or less aggressive than normal, and electrical stimulation can either arouse or inhibit attack. Some investigators (for example, Mark and Ervin, 1970) believe that malfunctions of the amygdala account for some cases of irrational violence in humans. (See **Figure 14.28.**)

In a variety of species, then, patterns of aggres-sive attack appear to be organized in the periaq-ueductal gray matter of the midbrain. The hypo-thalamus excites or inhibits these circuits and is itself excited or inhibited by the amygdala. Un-doubtedly, these structures are controlled by still other brain mechanisms. For example, the cerebral cortex enables the animal to recognize that a par-ticular environmental situation calls for aggression.

Psychosurgery: A Cure for Human Violence?

◈ A number of neurosurgeons, aware of the results of these experiments with animals, have attempted to control instances of human violence by means of brain surgery. Some people exhibit periods of extreme rage in which they attempt to kill anyone in their presence. Often they "black out" during these episodes, remembering nothing that hap-

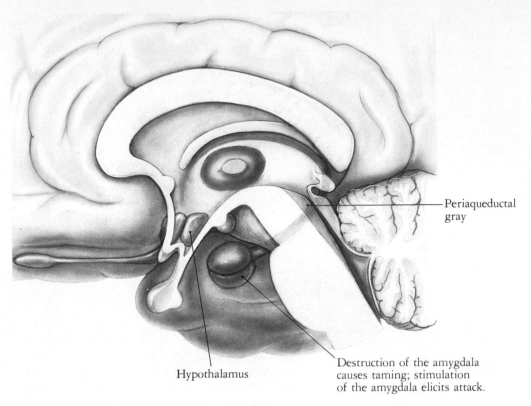

Periaqueductal
gray

Destruction of the amygdala
causes taming; stimulation
of the amygdala elicits attack.

Hypothalamus

FIGURE 14.28   Destruction of the amygdala
causes taming. Stimulation of the amygdala elicits
attack behavior.

pened or only dimly recalling a fit of violence that
they deeply regret.

In a few rare cases, these fits of rage have occurred after a head injury, and surgical removal of
damaged brain tissue has successfully eliminated
them. One woman was thrown from a horse and
received a skull fracture. Afterward she suffered
from epileptic seizures that triggered bouts of violence. It was found that a piece of bone was pressing on her temporal lobe. The bone was lifted away
from the brain, and some damaged tissue, including part of the amygdala, was removed. The
operation eliminated the seizures and the fits of
aggression (Mark, Sweet, and Ervin, 1972). This
case is not an example of psychosurgery.

More controversial is the removal of brain tissue
to alter a person's behavior, without direct evidence that the tissue is abnormal. Such procedures
constitute *psychosurgery.* For example, several
surgeons have removed parts of the amygdala,

hypothalamus, or periaqueductal gray matter in
attempts to cure irrationally violent people of aggressive tendencies. The rationale was that there
must be something wrong with the brain mechanisms that control aggressive attack.

Elliot Valenstein (1973) has challenged this line
of reasoning, and pointed out three major problems
of psychosurgery. First, many neurosurgeons have
demonstrated "tunnel vision" when interpreting the
results of animal experiments. For example, a rhesus monkey whose amygdala has been destroyed
may be less likely to attack the experimenter, but
is "taming" the primary effect of the surgery? These
monkeys also exhibit inappropriate social behavior
with other monkeys and are consequently attacked
for infractions of the rules. Kling, Lancaster, and
Benitone (1970) captured some wild rhesus monkeys, removed a portion of their amygdalas, and
released them after the animals recovered. Within
a few weeks the monkeys were dead; some were

killed by their fellows, and some starved. Such results indicate that surgical destruction of the amygdala does more than produce "taming."

Second, preoperative and postoperative evaluations are often carelessly done. The main criterion for success is often whether the procedure makes it easier for the supervisory personnel in an institution to handle the patient. As a result of the generally low quality of observations, it is impossible to evaluate the usefulness of psychosurgery in the alleviation of violence.

Finally, alternative means of therapy are often neglected, and surgery is sometimes attempted first rather than as a last resort. Consider a case reported by Gross (1971):

A good example is Jimmy, whom we saw at age 9 because of serious rage reactions and aggressiveness leading to threatened expulsion from school. He was one of nine children, and the only one who had any behavior problem. In fact, the other children were considered outstanding in the community and at school. Jimmy had an identical twin, Johnny, who was considered a "model child." Jimmy's EEG showed left temporal spikes; Johnny's was negative. On [an

anticonvulsant drug] Jimmy became an entirely different boy, a "model child" like his twin. When medication was omitted for a short time, he reverted to his old self by the third day. . . . p. 89)

This was a clear-cut case, and one with a happy ending. The source of the disorder was in fact in the brain, and was eliminated without brain surgery.

In general, Valenstein is pessimistic about the usefulness of psychosurgery to cure violence, and most neuropsychologists and physiological psychologists agree. We do not yet know enough about neural mechanisms of aggressive behavior to justify removing parts of the human brain unless these parts are definitely shown to be diseased. Some forms of psychosurgery, designed to alleviate suicidal depression or compulsive behaviors, *do* show promise. These are discussed in Chapter 18.

Hormones and Aggression

◆ In birds and most mammals, androgens appear to exert a strong effect on aggressiveness. You will recall from Chapter 7 that androgens have both an organizational effect and an activational effect on

FIGURE 14.29   Organizational and activational effects of androgens on intermale aggression in male rats.

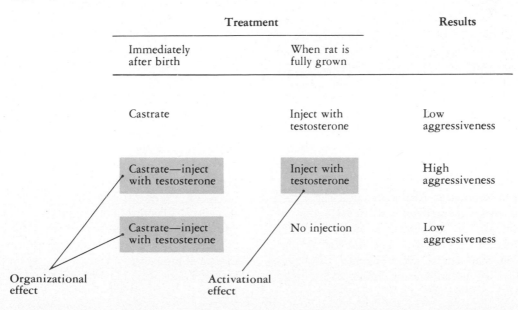

Treatment		Results
Immediately after birth	When rat is fully grown	
Castrate	Inject with testosterone	Low aggressiveness
Castrate—inject with testosterone	Inject with testosterone	High aggressiveness
Castrate—inject with testosterone	No injection	Low aggressiveness

Organizational effect

Activational effect

male sexual behavior; the presence of androgens during prenatal life *organizes* the development of the growing brain, which causes the development of circuits that can be *activated* by androgens in adulthood. The activation produces male sexual behavior.

Androgens appear to exert the same effects on some forms of aggressive behavior. If a male mouse is raised in isolation, it will demonstrate *intermale aggression,* fiercely attacking other male mice. But if male mice are castrated early in life, before their brains have matured, they will not attack another male when they grow up, even if they are given injections of testosterone (Conner and Levine, 1969). (See **Figure** 14.29.)

Given that men are generally more aggressive than women (Maccoby and Jacklin, 1974) and that male sexual behavior in humans depends on the presence of testosterone, perhaps this hormone also influences men's aggressive behavior. However, there is no good evidence that this is the case. Bremer (1959) reported the effects of castration on 224 Norwegian men who were convicted of physical assault or various sex offenses. The operations reduced or eliminated the men's sex drives and the aggression associated with their sex offenses, but not non-sex-related aggression.

Nevertheless, it is possible that hormones play an activational role in human aggression. Androstenedione (AD), a hormone closely related to testosterone, is produced by the adrenal glands. Even after castration, then, some male hormones are present. Perhaps a level of male hormone that is insufficient to stimulate male sex drive is still high enough to stimulate aggressiveness. There are a few reports that drugs that counteract the effects of male hormones (both testosterone and AD) seem to suppress aggressive behavior in men with records of criminal violence (Moyer, 1976). However, there is not yet enough evidence to permit any definite conclusions.

Interim summary: Although aggression serves useful purposes in many species, most human societies attempt to suppress it in order to protect its victims. Studies of other species reveal the presence of mechanisms to avert violence: threat gestures warn of an impending attack and appease-ment gestures propitiate the potential aggressor, who sometimes then emits reassurance gestures.

Although some simple human aggressive behaviors may be innate, most are learned. (See **Figure** 14.30.) In the laboratory, Bandura's studies demonstrate dramatically the effect of a model on children's subsequent aggression, but show that inhibitions can be learned, as well. Field studies are not so conclusive; observational studies have revealed a modest relation between preference for violent television shows and boys' aggressiveness, but we cannot be sure that the relation is causal. An attempt to manipulate aggression by forcing children to watch violent or nonviolent shows was inconclusive because many children resented their loss of choice.

The frustration-aggression hypothesis suggests that thwarting an organism's opportunity to obtain a reinforcer is the sole cause of aggression. However, some forms of aggression are not caused by frustration; for example, violence can be explicitly reinforced. Berkowitz suggested that unpleasant stimuli such as pain and the effects of frustration increase an organism's tendency to behave aggressively, but that social influences can control the expression of these tendencies.

The catharsis hypothesis has received mixed support. Although the opportunity to engage in aggression may indeed relieve a person's *feelings* of anger they are likely to increase further violence. And there is no evidence that symbolic aggression such as involvement in contact sports reduces the tendency toward violent behavior.

Biological studies have revealed the presence of neural circuits that control at least two forms of violent behavior: predation (not actually a form of aggression) and affective attack. General excitatory and inhibitory effects by the amygdala (probably in response to social stimuli) and immediate control by the hypothalamus are exerted on the mechanisms in the periaqueductal gray matter that program the sequence of behaviors that constitute an attack. These studies suggested to neurosurgeons that uncontrollable violent behavior may be eliminated by surgical destruction of the amygdala or parts of the hypothalamus or periaqueductal gray matter. However, as Valenstein observes, the rationale is not sound, being based on studies with

FIGURE 14.30 This woman with her child, fathered by a German soldier during World War II, is being driven from a French village after having had her head shaved.

animals that looked only at limited aspects of behavior. In addition, preoperative and postoperative evaluations of the patients' behavior have not been thorough and unbiased, and in some cases reversible treatments such as drug therapy have not been attempted.

The fact that most male animals are more aggressive than females led to investigations of the role of androgens in intraspecific aggression. Indeed, testosterone has both organizational and activational effects on intermale aggression, just as it has on male sexual behavior. Although the data from humans are limited, testosterone appears to affect forms of aggression related to sexual behavior but not others.

CONCLUDING REMARKS

Although no comprehensive theory of emotion has yet been developed, we can form some tentative conclusions. First, emotions are not simply inborn, stereotyped physiological reactions to particular stimuli. Some reactions *are* innate, such as a baby's fear and withdrawal responses to loud noises, but the number of such reactions is small compared with the number of emotions that humans can experience. Furthermore, emotions are not merely things that "happen to us"; our judgments play a crucial role in determining our emotional states. The fact that people can be fooled into various interpretations of their own emotional states suggests that recognizing our own emotions is not a simple process. We appear to examine our physiological responses and to use this information, together with information about what is going on in the environment, to decide how we feel. If the recognition of our own emotional states were automatic—that is, if we made no judgments but just "felt" them—it would be impossible to alter people's feelings by misinforming them about their physiological responses.

Cross-cultural studies and studies of blind children indicate that the facial expression of many emotions appears to be inborn. In contrast, studies with isolated monkeys suggest that the recognition of the facial expression of fear must be learned, although the ability to recognize a threat gesture appears to be innate.

A study of patients with damage to the upper regions of the spinal cord has shown that physiological reactions are very important to the intensity of our emotions. However, these reactions are not essential to emotional *behavior;* the same patients acted much as they did before, even though they did not feel the emotions so intensely.

Studies of the neuropsychology of emotion indicate that the right hemisphere is more important than the left. In addition, the frontal cortex appears to be more important for emotional expression, whereas the parieto-temporal cortex is more important for recognition of emotional states in other people.

Aggression, one of the most important emotional behaviors, occurs in a variety of situations and undoubtedly has many causes. The occurrence of aversive stimuli is probably the most important one. Threat and appeasement displays are seen in many species of animals and probably have counterparts in humans. At least some instances of violent behavior appear to be produced by the activity of innate brain mechanisms, but the expression of aggressive behaviors is subject to learned controls.

GUIDE TO TERMS INTRODUCED IN THIS CHAPTER

affective attack   p. 554

amygdala   p. 555   Figure 14.28

appeasement gesture   p. 547   Figure 14.21

catastrophic reaction   p. 540

category   p. 526

catharsis   p. 552

dimension   p. 526   Figure 14.4

emblem   p. 530

frustration   p. 551

illustrator   p. 530

intermale aggression   p. 538   Figure 14.29

intraspecific aggression   p. 546

James-Lange theory   p. 536

limbic system   p. 539

mood   p. 522

predation   p. 546

psychosurgery   p. 556

quiet-biting attack   p. 554

reassurance gesture   p. 547

regulator   p. 530

temperament   p. 523

threat gesture   p. 546   Figure 14.21

SUGGESTIONS FOR FURTHER READING

The Passions by R.C. Solomon (Garden City, N.Y.: Doubleday, Anchor Press, 1976) is an interesting discussion of the nature of emotion by a philosopher. In particular, he explores the mythology of emotions. William James's *Principles of Psychology* (New York: Henry Holt, 1890) provides insights into the history of our thinking about emotion. *The Face of Man: Expressions of Universal Emotions in a New Guinea Village* by P. Ekman (New York: Garland STPM Press, 1980) discusses cross-cultural studies on the expression and recognition of emotion. C.E. Izard provides a general account in *Human Emotions* (New York: Plenum Press, 1977).

A number of books are devoted to specific emotions, especially unpleasant ones. In *The Psychobiology of Aggression* (New York: Harper & Row, 1976), K.E. Moyer discusses the evolution and neural and hormonal control of aggressive behavior. *Fear and Courage* by S.H. Rachman (San Francisco: W.H. Freeman, 1978) examines two related emotions and the conditions that elicit them. K. Lorenz's *On Aggression* (New York: Harcourt Brace Jovanovich, 1966) is a classic description of the famous ethologist's views about the causes of violence.

15

SOCIAL

PSYCHOLOGY

L E A R N I N G ◆ O B J E C T I V E S

◆ THIS CHAPTER examines the effects that people have on each other's behavior. Social psychologists often study the behavior of people in groups, but unlike sociologists, they study the behavior of the *individual* within the group, not the group itself.

Interactions with other people affect all aspects of human behavior. Human development depends on the influence of other people, from infancy to old age. We learn from other people, through instruction or by example. The important people in our lives shape our emotions, thoughts, and personalities. Our perceptions, which we think of as private, solitary events, are affected by our interactions with others. Social psychologists have found that even the most personal and supposedly subjective aspects of human life, such as interpersonal attraction, can be studied objectively. We should not be disappointed that phenomena such as reinforcement play a role in determining with whom we fall in love. Instead, we should appreciate the intricate interplay of biological and social factors that control behaviors that are important both to the survival of our species and to the individual happiness of its members.

Earlier chapters have already discussed some of the topics of social psychology: sexual behavior, aggression and the expression of emotion, the role of social reinforcement in learning and conditioning, and language. This chapter surveys several additional topics studied by social psychologists: attribution, or how we try to explain the causes of our own and other people's behavior; attitudes and persuasion; social influences, including conformity, compliance, and obedience; interpersonal attraction; and group processes, including social facilitation and decision making by groups.

ATTRIBUTION

Our behavior is affected by stimuli in our environment, and aside from the necessities of life, such as food, water, and air, the behavior of other people provides our most significant reinforcing and punishing stimuli. We gain a sense of our worth from the presence or absence of signs of others' approval and respect.

◆   But it is clear that not everyone we meet influences our behavior. Some people affect us a great deal, others very little. One of the factors determining whether a person's behavior affects our own is our perception of the reasons for the other person's behavior. For example, smiles and friendly gestures from another person are generally reinforcing, but these behaviors will have less of an effect on you if the smiling, friendly person is trying to entice you to make an expensive purchase. You will realize that the person's friendly behaviors may be stimulated by a desire to make a commission

on the sale rather than by your own attractive personality and charm. Therefore, you will probably not take these behaviors too seriously. On the other hand, if someone has no plausible reason for ingratiating himself or herself with you, you are more likely to perceive his or her friendly behavior as a reflection of a genuine interest in you. (See **Figure 15.1**.)

This example illustrates a phenomenon that is currently one of the most important topics in social psychology, ***attribution.*** We seek to *attribute* people's behavior to the most likely causes, and our ability to do so is an exceedingly important social skill. Knowing why people act as they do may help us predict what they will do in a particular situation, and thus help us promote pleasant interactions and avoid unpleasant ones. We will probably be less susceptible to their attempts to manipulate

FIGURE 15.1   Is this man interested in you or does he simply act that way out of his own self-interest?

us. We may even be able to use our attribution skills to understand our own behavior.

The study of attribution has had a profound impact on social psychology. It has affected our understanding of persuasion, interpersonal attraction, group behavior, self-evaluation, and attitudes and opinions. It has even affected the study of human personality.

THE IMPLICIT PSYCHOLOGIST

As we saw in Chapter 12, everyone who is able to use a language knows a large set of complex rules of grammar, but few people know how to describe those rules. Similarly, although we all attribute causes to events every day, often without giving the matter much thought, the reasons for the choices we make are not always obvious to us. Our knowledge of human behavior is based on attributions. From them we construct theories of social behavior. These theories allow us to organize our observations and to predict the probable outcomes of our own behavior. If our theories are good ones we can affect the behavior of other people in ways that benefit us.

Implicit psychology involves both attribution and the formation of private theories of reality. Unlike the theories of psychologists, in which the methods, assumptions, and data are explicitly stated, implicit psychological theories are private and often cannot be explained by their owner. Indeed, people do not regard their implicit theories as theories at all, but as facts. Consequently, they tend not to revise the theories when provided with contradictory data. Many prejudices and superstitions can best be understood as products of faulty implicit theories of human nature.

THE COVARIANCE METHOD

◆ Harold Kelley (1967, 1971) has suggested that we reach most of our conclusions about the causes of events by the *covariance method*. *Covariance* refers to a phenomenon in which two events are observed to vary together or simply to occur together, like thunder and lightning. According to Kelley's definition of the covariance method, "The effect is attributed to that condition which is present when the effect is present and which is absent when the effect is absent" (1967, p. 194). For example, if John blushes, stammers, and becomes inarticulate whenever Susan is in the room but acts and speaks normally when she is not, we will decide that her presence flusters him.

Scientists also use the covariance method to determine the causes of natural phenomena. You may recall from Chapter 2 that psychologists try to discover the causes of behaviors by observing which events and behaviors tend to occur together, and then using the covariance method to form hypotheses about cause-and-effect relations. However, scientists take the process one step further than most of us do in our daily lives: they perform an experiment, manipulating one variable (the independent variable) to see whether this manipulation affects the other one (the dependent variable).

Most of the attribution that occurs in normal social situations involves only the gathering of data and the formation of hypotheses. Occasionally, however, we also perform "experiments" to test our hypotheses: *I wonder if she's interested in me. I'll look directly at her and see whether she smiles back or turns away.* More often, we observe other people's behavior and form conclusions based on our past experience.

DISPOSITION VERSUS SITUATION

◆ The primary classification that we make concerning the causes of a person's behavior is the relative importance of *situational factors* versus *dispositional factors* (Heider, 1958). One of the tasks of socialization is to learn what behaviors are expected in various kinds of situations. In this way we learn both what to expect from others and to behave so as not to elicit disapproval. Once we learn that in certain situations most people act in a specific way, we expect others to act similarly in those situations. For example, when people are introduced they are expected to look at each other, smile, say something like "How do you do?" or "It's nice to meet you," and perhaps offer to shake the other person's hand. If people act in conventional ways in given situations, we are not surprised. Their behavior appears to be dictated by social custom—

FIGURE 15.2   We cannot make any inferences about the personalities of these people from their behavior, because their actions conform to social custom.

by the characteristics of the *situation*—and we therefore learn very little about them as individuals. (See **Figure 15.2**.)

As we get to know other people, we also learn what to expect from them as individuals. We learn about their *dispositions*—the kinds of behaviors that they tend to engage in. We learn to characterize people as friendly, generous, suspicious, pessimistic, or greedy by observing their behavior in a variety of situations. Sometimes we even make inferences from a single observation. If someone's behavior is seriously at variance with *situational demands,* we attribute his or her behavior to internal, or dispositional, causes (Jones and Davis, 1965). For example, if we see a person refuse to hold a door open for someone in a wheelchair, we assign some negative personality characteristics to him or her. Similarly, if a young boy receives some candy and shares it with his little sister we attribute a generous nature to the child, because we assume that young children are typically selfish.

In contrast, if we observe that a person conforms to situational demands we tend to give his or her behavior very little significance and do not use it to make dispositional attributions. This phenomenon is called *discounting.* For example, if someone asks an acquaintance for the loan of a coin to make a telephone call, we do not conclude that the person is especially kind and generous if he or she complies. The request is reasonable and costs little; the situational demand is to lend the money. However, if the person has some change but refuses to lend it, we readily attribute dispositional factors such as stinginess or meanness to that person.

SOURCES OF INFORMATION

Kelley (1967, 1971, 1973) has also suggested that we attribute the behavior of other people to external (situational) or internal (dispositional) causes on the basis of *consensus, consistency,* and *distinctiveness.*

If a behavior is *consensual*—that is, if it is shared by a large number of people—we tend to attribute

FIGURE 15.3   In Scotland, this man's behavior is consensual, and says little about his personality. However, in North America, where kilts are seldom worn, his behavior would not be consensual, and we would conclude that he is somewhat eccentric.

the behavior to external causes. The behavior is assumed to be demanded by the situation. For example, if the weather is hot and you see a group of people splashing in the water of a fountain, you will probably conclude that they are trying to get some relief from the oppressive heat. You attribute their behavior to external causes. However, if you see only one person cavorting in the water while others watch, you will probably conclude that he or she is showing off. If only one person does something, he or she must be doing it for personal, or internal, reasons. (See **Figure 15.3**.)

We also base our attributions on *consistency*—that is, on whether a person's behavior occurs reliably over time. For example, if you meet someone for the first time and notice that she speaks slowly and without much expression, stands in a slouching posture, and sighs occasionally, you will probably conclude that she has a sad and listless disposition. Now suppose that after she has left, you mention to a friend that the young woman seems very passive and depressed. Your friend says, "No, I know her pretty well, and she's usually very cheerful and friendly." With this new evidence about her behavior you will reassess your conclusion and perhaps wonder what happened to make her act so sad. If a person's pattern of behavior is consistent, we attribute the behavior to internal causes; inconsistent behaviors lead us to seek external causes.

Distinctiveness is closely related to consistency. If a person behaves in the same way under different circumstances, we attribute the behavior to personality characteristics—to his or her disposition. However, if the person acts one way in one kind of situation and another way in different circumstances, we tend to attribute the behavior to external causes—the situation. For example, suppose a mother observes that her little boy is generally polite and well behaved, but that whenever he plays with the child across the street, he comes home with his clothes dirty and acts sassy toward her until she has rebuked him a few times. She does not conclude that her boy is rude or messy; she will probably conclude that the child across the street has a bad influence on him. Because her child's rude and messy behavior occurs only under distinctive circumstances, she attributes it to external causes.

ISOLATING CAUSES

◆ Often we encounter complex situations in which a particular event may have many possible causes. How do we weigh the possible causes and decide which is the most important?

The most obvious way is to try to obtain more information. Suppose we learn that someone has decided to marry a handsome, rich, rude man. Why has she chosen to do so? The fact that he is rude suggests that he has other qualities that offset this characteristic—perhaps either his good looks or his wealth. If we learn that the woman has just inherited a large fortune, we will discount greed as a motive and probably conclude that she is attracted to his looks. However, if we learn that she is poor and has an ailing parent to support, we will probably conclude that his wealth is his primary attraction for her.

A considerable amount of research indicates that if we are unable to obtain much information about the causes of an event, we attribute the cause to the most salient stimuli. For example, Taylor, Fiske, Close, Anderson, and Ruderman (1978) prepared a set of color slides of a group of six men supposedly engaged in conversation. A tape recording presented their conversation. The projector showed a picture of each participant when he was speaking, so that the subjects could determine who said what. Although all subjects heard the same soundtrack (a brainstorming session for a publicity campaign), the composition of the group shown in the slides

varied: some subjects saw three whites and three blacks while others saw five whites and one black. The subjects were asked to rate the amount of influence that one of the black men had on the other people during the discussion. When there was only one black person in the group, subjects rated his influence as greater than when there were three blacks, because of his distinctiveness.

Distinctiveness appears to be an important variable in determining the causes of an ambiguous situation. Other studies have shown that a single woman in a group of men, a single man in a group of women, or even a person wearing a different style of clothing is given more credit for the outcome of the discussion.

ATTRIBUTIONAL BIASES

When we make attributions we do not act like impartial, dispassionate observers; our biases affect our conclusions about the actor (the person performing the behavior). This section describes the more important biases and some research into their causes.

The Fundamental Attributional Error

◆ When attributing the behavior of an actor to possible causes, an observer tends to overestimate the significance of dispositional factors and underestimate the significance of situational factors. If we see a driver turn in front of an oncoming car, we are more likely to say "She is a terrible driver" than "She was distracted by her children yelling in the back seat." Ross (1977) calls this bias the *fundamental attributional error.* Most of the other attributional biases can be explained as consequences of this one.

The fundamental attributional error is remarkably potent. Even when evidence indicates otherwise, people seem to prefer dispositional explanations to situational ones. A study by Ross, Amabile, and Steinmetz (1977) demonstrates this tendency. Pairs of students played a contrived "quiz game" in which the questioner was permitted to ask any question he or she wanted to, no matter how obscure or esoteric. In this situation a person can easily stump someone else by choosing some topic that he or she knows more about than the average person. After the game the subjects were asked to rate both

TABLE 15.1   Ratings of general knowledge of self and opponent in a mock quiz game

CONDITION	MEASURE	
	Rating of self	Rating of opponent
Subjects devised questions		
Subject as questioner	53.5[a]	50.6[b]
Subject as contestant	41.3[a,c]	66.8[b,c]
Experimenter prepared questions		
Subject as questioner	54.1	52.5
Subject as contestant	47.0	50.3

Note: scores with the same superscripts differed significantly from each other.

Adapted from Ross, L.D., Amabile, T.M., and Steinmetz, J.L. *Journal of Personality and Social Psychology*, 1977, *35*, 485–494.

their own level of general knowledge and that of their opponent. Table 15.1 lists the ratings. Subjects who played the role of contestant tended to rate the questioner as much more knowledgeable than themselves. (See **Table 15.1.**) Apparently they attributed the difficult questions to factors internal to their opponents rather than to the situation. When the subjects served as questioners, they did not make an internal attribution; they rated themselves as only slightly more knowledgeable than the person they questioned. (See **Table 15.1.**) Thus, a person is less likely to make the fundamental attributional error when he or she is the actor (the person who is performing the behavior—in this case, the questioner).

An experiment by Storms (1973) showed that the fundamental attributional error also plays a role when a person witnesses his or her own behavior as an observer would. Storms had pairs of subjects carry on a discussion and videotaped one of them during the conversation. One group of subjects later watched a tape of the other subject (the same perspective that they had during the discussion). Another group saw themselves as their partners had. After viewing the videotape, the subjects were asked to rate the degree to which their own behavior was due to dispositional versus situational causes. (See **Figure 15.4.**) The results were as predicted. Subjects who did not see a tape of themselves attributed their own behavior to situational factors. Those who saw themselves as others would see them showed the fundamental attributional error: they judged

FIGURE 15.4   The procedure used by Storms (1973).

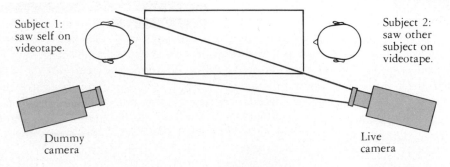

Subject 1: saw self on videotape.

Subject 2: saw other subject on videotape.

Dummy camera

Live camera

their own behavior as being a consequence of dispositional factors. (See **Figure 15.5.**)

Another study showed that it is possible to perform the reverse manipulation. Regan and Totten (1975) asked their subjects to empathize with the actors—to try to see the situation in the way the other person might. In contrast with observers who were not told to empathize, these subjects tended to make situational rather than dispositional attributions of the actor's behavior. For example, an empathetic observer might say that the actor's nervous laughter was a response to a strange experimental setting, whereas a nonempathetic observer might say that the actor was an anxious sort of person. These results indicate that altering the observer's perspective on the situation can reduce or eliminate the fundamental attributional error.

Why do we make the fundamental attributional error when we observe the behavior of others but not when we explain the causes of our own behavior? Jones and Nisbett (1971) suggest two possible reasons. First, we have a *different focus of attention* when we view ourselves. When we ourselves are doing something we see the world around us more clearly than we see our own behavior. However, when we observe someone else, we focus our attention on what is most salient and significant: that person's behavior, and not the situation in which he or she is placed.

A second possible reason for these differences in attribution is that *different types of information* are available to us about our own behavior and that of other people. We have more information about our own consistency (we are more likely to remember how we acted under the same circumstances at different times) and we also have a better notion of which stimuli we are attending to.

False Consensus

The second attributional error is the tendency of an observer to perceive his or her own response as representative of a general consensus. Thus, if someone disagrees with the observer or behaves in a way that the observer would not, the actor is seen as deviant. This error has been called *false consensus.*

Ross, Greene, and House (1977) asked college students to walk around campus for thirty minutes while wearing a large sandwich-board sign that

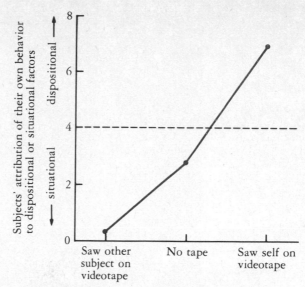

FIGURE 15.5.   Attribution of an actor's behavior to dispositional or situational factors, depending on the observer's point of view. (Based on data from Storms, M.D. *Journal of Personality and Social Psychology,* 1973, 27, 165–175.)

read "EAT AT JOE'S"; they were told it was part of a study on communication techniques. After deciding whether they would wear the sign, the students were asked to estimate how many of their peers would volunteer. Those who agreed to wear the sign thought that approximately two-thirds of their peers would also agree to do so; those who refused thought that most of their peers would also refuse. The results indicate that people's estimates of what other people will do are influenced by their own inclinations.

One explanation accounts for false consensus in terms of defense of ego or self-esteem. Presumably, people do not like to think of themselves as being too different from other people, so they prefer to think that most other people will act the way they do.

Another possible explanation is that people tend to place themselves in the company of others who are similar to themselves (Ross, 1977). (See **Figure 15.6.**) As we shall see later in this chapter, an important variable in interpersonal attraction is similarity in behavior and attitudes. Thus, when people conclude that other people are more similar

FIGURE 15.6   The people at this convention
share a common interest in science fiction.

to themselves than they actually are, the error may
be a result of a sampling bias rather than of a need
to minimize damage to their egos.

Overreliance on the Particular, Underreliance on the General

◆ The fundamental attributional error represents a
tendency to overgeneralize; that is, people are willing to impute a personality characteristic to an
individual on the basis of a single observation. If
we see someone get angry we tend to judge her as
hot-tempered. If we see someone stumble on a crack
in the sidewalk we tend to label him as clumsy.
In contrast, we seldom pay much attention to general tendencies as explanations for specific instances
of behavior.

Ross (1977) provided a good example of the
tendency to ignore general predictor variables,
similar to the following problem: I (a professor of
psychology) have a friend who is a professor. He
likes to swim laps in the pool every lunch hour.
He also likes to play tennis and if he can find an

opponent he will even play in the dead of winter,
if the court can be swept clear of snow. Which of
the following is his field: (a) sports medicine or (b)
psychology?

If you said "psychology" you were most likely
to be right, because I am a professor of psychology
and am therefore likely to have friends who are also
professors of psychology. In addition, there are many
more professors of psychology than professors of
sports medicine. Yet you may have chosen alternative (a) or at least seriously considered it. The
image of an athletic, tennis-playing person seems
to be such a distinctive cue that it is difficult to
"play the odds."

An anecdote by Kahneman and Tversky (1973)
also illustrates the tendency to overgeneralize from
one observation. When Israeli flight instructors were
urged to praise their students whenever they exhibited a good performance they resisted doing so
because of their previous experience. They had observed that whenever they praised an especially good
performance the student did worse, rather than

better, the next time he tried; reinforcement seemed to make the student try less hard. In contrast, whenever a student performed terribly, criticism led to improvement the next time. Can you detect the error in the instructors' reasoning?

* * *

Consider what a student's performance would be if he received neither praise nor criticism. After exceptional performance on one trial, you would predict that his performance on the next trial would be less than exceptional. (Otherwise you must change your definition of "exceptional.") If the instructor praises a fine performance and observes a less able performance the next time, he is likely to attribute the decline to his praise. On the other hand, if a student performs worse than usual on one trial he is likely—by chance—to do better on the next. If the instructor criticizes him after the terrible performance and sees improvement he concludes that the criticism had an effect.

A study by Borgida and Nisbett (1977) confirms that information about the "odds" is less powerful than specific instances of behavior. They provided college students with information about courses based on ratings of students who had previously enrolled in them. The information came from summaries of the ratings of many students and from face-to-face contact with a few students who had taken the courses. The students were then asked to choose the courses that they would like to take. Although the summaries provided the best information because they came from a large number of students, the face-to-face contacts had a stronger effect on the students' choices.

Motivational Biases

Most of the attributional biases discussed so far are logical, or intellectual. Other biases appear to be related to motivation—to processes that have personal significance for the observer.

CREDIT FOR SUCCESS, BLAME FOR FAILURE People tend to attribute successful outcomes of their own behavior to internal causes but their failures to external causes. For example, a person is likely to perceive a high score on a test as a reflection of his or her intelligence and motivation, but low scores to an unfair examination, boring and trivial subject matter, or lack of opportunity to study properly.

Johnson, Feigenbaum, and Weiby (1964) enlisted students in an educational psychology course in a trial program of teaching mathematics to fourth-grade boys. The experimenters prearranged the boys' test performance so that the performance of some boys improved during the teaching sessions, while the performance of others stayed the same or got worse. The "teachers" who had worked with boys whose test performance improved later cited their own teaching skills as the cause. Those who had worked with boys who did not improve blamed the poor performance on the low motivation or intelligence of the learner.

The perception of outside observers is quite different from the perception of a person who has personal involvement with the success or failure of an enterprise. Beckman (1970) performed an experiment similar to the one I just described but obtained attributional judgments both from the teachers and from observers. Unlike the teachers, the observers blamed the teachers for the students' poor performance but attributed good performance to the students' intelligence and motivation.

A review of the literature has shown that people are not inevitably self-serving in their attributions (Arkin, Cooper, and Kolditz, 1980). For example, Ross, Bierbrauer, and Polly (1974) devised an extremely realistic teacher-student situation in which the teachers were able to make detailed observations of their students' performance. With more information available, they were less likely to blame the students for their failure while taking credit for success. Thus, although we give ourselves the benefit of the doubt when the causes of success or failure are not clear, we will make attributions that are not favorable to ourselves when our observations demand them.

MOTIVATIONAL RELEVANCE Another element that influences our attributions of behavior to either dispositional or situational factors is the motivational relevance of the consequences of this behavior for the actor. Thibaut and Riecken (1955) arranged for undergraduates at Harvard University to make a request of both a person of higher status (a well-dressed, confident-acting man who had just received his Ph.D. and joined the faculty) and a person of lower status (a poorly dressed, self-deprecating undergraduate from a college that a Harvard student was likely to hold in low esteem). Both people (confederates of the experimenters) complied with the subjects' requests. When asked to explain why the people complied with their requests, the students attributed the compliance of the higher-status person to dispositional factors, and that of the lower-status person to situational factors. Apparently, the subjects assumed that because the higher-status person had nothing to gain from agreeing to assist them, he must have done so because he was helpful and considerate; in contrast, because the lower-status person was perceived as being less free to choose, he complied because the subjects' request was persuasive.

THE ILLUSION OF PERSONAL CAUSATION Independent of the tendency to take credit for our successes and to avoid blame for our failures, we appear to have a tendency to assume that when we do something, our action will have an effect on subsequent events, even when logically these events cannot be related to our behavior. We have a fallacious belief in *personal causation.* In an experiment illustrating this phenomenon, Langer (1975) allowed some subjects to select a fifty-cent lottery ticket and simply handed one to others. When asked later how much money they would accept to sell their ticket, the subjects who had been given a ticket were willing to sell it for approximately two dollars, whereas those who had selected their ticket wanted almost nine dollars. The element of choice led to an illusion of personal causation; the chosen ticket was perceived as more likely to be a winner.

FIGURE 15.7 Self-image versus reality, according to a cartoonist satirizing Hitler.

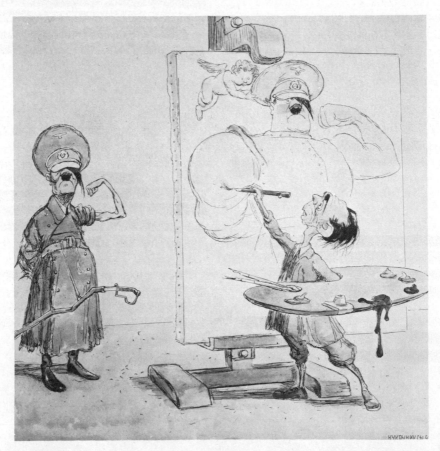

The illusion of personal causation may be an innate tendency. More likely, however, it is simply a generalization from our previous experience with reality. When we intend our behavior to have an effect on the environment it often does. We push something and it moves. We say something and other people react. Thus, we come to regard our own efforts as causal. Because some people are more successful than others at making things happen, different people will have different degrees of belief in the potency of their efforts. (See **Figure** 15.7.) This important personality variable is discussed in Chapter 16.

Interim summary: The conclusions that people make about the causes of the behavior of people around them have important effects on their own attitudes and behavior. We are all students of social behavior, since we are all members of society, and the ability to understand the causes of other people's behavior and predict what they are likely to do is an important skill. Only recently have psychologists begun to study the factors that govern this process of attribution.

Like scientists, people use the covariance method to determine cause-and-effect: events that occur together are assumed to be causally related. We attribute particular instances of behavior to two types of causes: situational and dispositional. If a behavior is consensual (many people are acting the same way) we attribute it to situational factors. If a behavior is consistent (a person acts the same way in a variety of situations) we attribute it to dispositional factors. If a behavior is distinctive, occurring only under certain circumstances, we attribute it to situational factors.

Ross identified the fundamental attributional error: overreliance on dispositional factors, underreliance on situational factors. We are most likely to make the fundamental attributional error when trying to understand the causes of other people's behavior, because we are more aware of the environmental factors that effect our own behavior. As experiments showed, changing a person's point of view or asking him or her to empathize with other people can change the tendency to commit the fundamental attributional error.

False consensus refers to the tendency to believe that others act and believe much as we do. Another

error, overreliance on the particular and underreliance on the general, leads us to ignore good solid data in favor of a personal anecdote. For example, a person may rely more on the experience a friend has had with a particular car than on a published consumer survey of 2000 owners. We also tend to take credit for success and shun blame for failure, and many of us have an exaggerated belief in the efficacy of our own behaviors.

ATTITUDES AND PERSUASION

The investigation of attitudes and factors that influence their change formerly constituted the bulk of research in social psychology (Eagly and Himmelfarb, 1978). During the 1960s, interest in the topic sharply declined, principally because many studies found a low correlation between people's expressed attitudes and actual observed behavior. However, in the past few years experiments have shown that under certain conditions people's attitudes and behavior are rather closely associated. Once psychologists were able to demonstrate that attitudes really could predict behavior, interest in the field revived.

FORMATION OF ATTITUDES

The ways in which we form our attitudes are somewhat similar to the ways in which we are persuaded to change them. However, the process of attitude formation is usually more subtle than that of attitude change. Attitudes have both an *affective* and a *cognitive* component. The affective component consists of the kinds of feelings that a particular topic arouses. The cognitive component consists of a set of beliefs about that topic.

Affective Components of Attitudes

Affective components of attitudes can be very strong and pervasive. The bigot feels uneasy in the presence of certain religious, racial, or ethnic groups; the nature lover feels exhilaration from a pleasant walk through the woods. These feelings are probably established principally through direct or vicarious classical conditioning.

Direct classical conditioning is straightforward.

Suppose you meet someone who seems to take a delight in embarrassing you. She makes clever, sarcastic remarks that disparage your intelligence, looks, and personality. Unfortunately, her remarks are so clever that your attempts to defend yourself make you appear even more foolish. After a few encounters with this person, it is likely that the sight of her or the sound of her voice will immediately evoke feelings of dislike and fear in you. Your attitude toward her will be negative.

Vicarious classical conditioning undoubtedly plays a significant role in transmitting parents' attitudes to their children. People are skilled at detecting even subtle signs of fear, hatred, and other negative emotional states in other people, especially when they know them well. Thus, children perceive their parents' prejudices and fears even if these feelings are unspoken. A child who sees its parents recoil in disgust at the sight of members of some ethnic group is likely to learn to react in the same way. Humans have a strong tendency to acquire classically conditioned responses themselves by observing them to be elicited in other people by the conditional stimulus.

Berger (1962) demonstrated the effectiveness of observation. Subjects watched another person jerk his arm violently just after a buzzer was sounded. Some subjects were told that the person they were watching was receiving painful electric shocks; others were told that they should expect him to jerk his arm voluntarily from time to time.

After watching the person for several minutes, the subjects were tested for signs of classical conditioning. Berger presented the sound of the buzzer and measured the observers' skin conductance, which is related to the amount of sweating, and thus to emotional arousal. Those who believed that the person they were observing had been receiving painful electric shocks were more then three times as likely to show signs of autonomic arousal than those who thought he was not.

The affective component of attitudes tends to be rather resistant to change; it persists for some time even after a person has altered his or her opinion on a particular subject. For example, a person may successfully overcome a childhood racial prejudice and be completely fair and impartial in dealing with people of other races but experience unpleasant emotional arousal at the sight of a ra-

cially mixed couple. This discrepancy between belief and feelings often makes people feel guilty.

Cognitive Components of Attitudes

We acquire most beliefs about a particular topic quite directly: we hear or read a fact or opinion, or other people reinforce our statements expressing a particular attitude. Someone may say to a child: "Blacks are lazy" or "You can't trust whites" or "We Czechs are better than those Slovaks." A group of racially prejudiced people will probably ostracize a person who makes positive statements about minority groups. Or conscientious parents may applaud their child's positive statements about other ethnic groups or about social issues such as environmental conservation.

Children in particular form attitudes through imitating, or *modeling,* the behavior of people who play an important role in their lives. Children usu-

FIGURE 15.8   The tendency to identify with a group is strong in humans.

ally repeat opinions expressed by their parents. In the United States, many children label themselves as Democrats or Republicans long before they know what these political parties stand for. Often they ask their parents, "What are we, Republicans or Democrats?" without considering whether they might have any choice in the matter. The tendency to identify with the family unit (and, later, with peer groups) provides a strong incentive to adopt the group's attitudes. (See **Figure 15.8**.)

PERSUASION

Persuasion is the process by which people induce others to change their attitudes. Many variables affect this process—who the persuader is, what he or she has to say, how it is said, and how receptive the person is to the argument.

Characteristics of the Communicator

◆ Attitude change often depends a great deal on who presents the message. Some people are more persuasive than others. The three most important factors in the communicator's ability to change other people's opinions appear to be expertise, motives, and attractiveness.

EXPERTISE   Expertise refers to the amount of knowledge that the communicator appears to have about the topic of the message. For example, people are likely to accept a surgeon's assertion that a particular operation is dangerous, because he or she is considered an expert on the topic of surgery. Producers of television commercials also try to make their actors look like experts. The man who recommends cough medicine to you sits at a large desk, in front of a bookcase full of weighty-looking books. He dresses in dignified, "doctorlike" clothes and tries to convey the impression that he really knows what he is talking about.

Aronson, Turner, and Carlsmith (1963) demonstrated the importance of the communicator's expertise in persuasion. They asked college students to evaluate two passages of poetry, then showed them evaluations that were supposedly written either by a famous poet (T.S. Eliot) or by a student at a small college. (In fact the experimenters wrote the evaluations.) The students read evaluations that were very similar to their own, somewhat different from

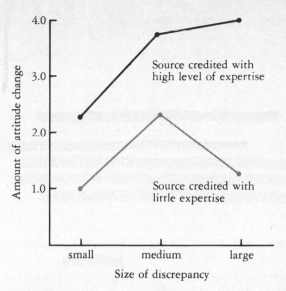

FIGURE 15.9   Amount of attitude change caused by high- and low-credibility sources as a function of discrepancy between the subject's and the persuader's expressed attitude. (From Baron, R.A., and Byrne, D. *Social Psychology: Understanding Human Interaction,* 2nd ed. Boston: Allyn and Bacon, 1977; after Aronson, Turner, and Carlsmith (1963).)

them, or very different from them. Later the subjects were asked to evaluate the poems again, and the experimenters measured the amount of shift in their opinions. Figure 15.9 shows the results. The messages supposedly written by the communicator with a high level of expertise (T.S. Eliot) were much more effective in altering the subjects' opinions than were those supposedly written by another student. In fact if the students believed the message to have been written by a source with little expertise, they appeared to be better able to resist the persuasive effects of the message. (See **Figure 15.9**.) Apparently, to change someone's mind, the communicator must do so in small steps, unless he or she is an expert on the subject (or knows how to act like one).

MOTIVES   Suppose a woman who sells Tornado vacuum cleaners tells you that they are better than Cyclone vacuum cleaners. Probably you will not find this message persuasive. You will attribute her assertion to the fact that she stands to make money from the sale, rather than to a genuine belief. In contrast, if an automobile salesman tells you not to buy the more expensive model because the only difference between it and the cheaper one is some fancy trim, you will probably believe him, because he stands to make less money from the sale of the cheaper model.

Attribution theory explains these reactions. We attribute causal relations to events that occur together. We know that a sale results in a commission for the salesperson, which is a reinforcing event, so when the person tries to make a sale we attribute his or her efforts to a desire to make money. But if a salesperson urges a potential customer to buy a product that results in a smaller commission—an event that would produce less reinforcement—we perceive this behavior as *distinctive:* it is not what we would expect most people to do in this situation. Distinctive behaviors are interpreted as being internally caused. Because we have ruled out greed, we conclude that the person is honest and trustworthy.

Another important motivational factor is our perception of whether or not the communicator *wants* to persuade us. If we think that the communicator does not really care about convincing us, the message is more persuasive. Advertisers capitalize on this fact by producing commercials in which an actor portraying an average man or woman, supposedly filmed by a hidden camera, compares two brands of toilet paper, scouring powder, or some other product and concludes that the sponsor's brand is better. We are meant to believe that the person has no stake in the outcome, and thus is not trying to persuade the television viewer. Attribution theory can also explain this phenomenon. If we cannot attribute the "average person's" behavior to motivational variables like greed, we conclude that he or she believes that the product is actually better.

Walster and Festinger (1962) arranged for married female college students to "overhear" a conversation in which two people discussed whether husbands who were college students should spend more time at home with their wives. The speakers concluded that they should. Walster and Festinger told some of the women that the speakers knew

FIGURE 15.10 We tend to believe people who are attractive, but still not too different from us.

that they were being listened to; the other subjects thought that the speakers were unaware of them. The latter subjects were more likely to have their opinions changed by the experience. Presumably, because they believed that the message could not have been directed at them, they assumed it was unbiased.

◆ ATTRACTIVENESS   People find a message from an attractive person more persuasive than one from an unattractive person. The two most important characteristics of attractiveness are physical good looks and similarity to the viewer. (See **Figure 15.10**.) Mills and Harvey (1972) have suggested that these characteristics affect persuasiveness because they present a good model for the recipient, who sees the communicator's attractiveness and wants to be more like him or her. In an attempt to become more similar to the model, the recipient adopts his or her attitudes. If the persuader is too different from the recipient, the gap will be too large to bridge, and the recipient will not try to change.

◆ WHEN DOES IT MATTER?   The effectiveness of a persuasive message is related to characteristics of the communicator only when the recipient does not consider the topic to be important (Petty and Cacioppo, 1981). For example, Chaiken (1980) exposed subjects to persuasive messages from likeable or dislikable communicators. Some messages contained several arguments; others contained a few. Some subjects expected to be interviewed later about the topic; others did not. Subjects who did not expect to be interviewed later were affected by the likability of the persuader and not by the number of arguments. Those who expected to be interviewed later were not affected by the likability of the persuader; instead, their attitude change was affected by the number of arguments.

Apparently, when an issue is made to be important to the recipient, people pay more attention to the nature of a persuasive message, and less attention to its source. (Perhaps this finding suggests why so many political candidates seem to prefer to avoid real issues during their campaigns for office.)

Characteristics of the Message

◆ Although persuasion depends on the characteristics of the communicator, most people are persuaded by the content of a message and not merely by who presents it.

ARGUMENTATION   People who hope to persuade others to their own point of view often wonder whether it is more effective to present specific arguments that support a particular opinion or merely express an opinion; to present arguments only in favor of their own position or arguments for both sides of the issue. The answer is: it depends.

If the communicator is attractive, then argumentation is less important, perhaps because the recipients model the persuader's behavior instead of concentrating on the logic of the message. However, if the communicator is an authority on the subject, arguments do count; the appeal to the recipients is apparently more logical (Norman, 1976).

If people initially favor the communicator's viewpoint to some degree, it is more effective to present only one-sided arguments; the recipient may find arguments for the other side to be persuasive. However, if the recipients initially favor the opposing point of view, it is easier to persuade them by first presenting arguments for their side, then subsequently discrediting them with arguments for the opposite position (Baron and Byrne, 1981). Apparently, the two-sided presentation seems less biased, and thus more persuasive.

REPETITION   The more often we encounter something, the more we tend to like it, or at least not object to it. For example, in the late 1960s, many people were outraged by seeing males wearing their hair long. However, few people today object to the style, and many older men who formerly objected to long hair now wear it long themselves. You may also have heard (or said) something like: "I know it's ugly, but I've grown so used to it that I've come to like it."

A clever experiment by Mita, Dermer, and Knight (1977) showed that subjects preferred pictures of themselves that looked like their images in a mirror: reversed from left to right. (People's faces are not symmetrical; the right and left sides differ in shape, and people often part their hair on one side.) However, they preferred pictures of friends that were *not* reversed. Because we most often see our own face in a mirror, we become accustomed

FIGURE 15.11   Mita, Dermer, and Knight
(1977) found that people prefer a reversed picture of
themselves and an unreversed picture of their friends.

to a reversed image of ourselves, whereas we see our friends' faces unreversed. Repeated exposure to a particular stimulus seems to make us prefer it to others. (See **Figure 15.11**.)

The effect of exposure also applies to people's preferences for words. Zajonc (1968) found that when subjects chose the word they preferred from pairs of antonyms (fast-slow, hot-cold, and so on), 82 percent of the time they chose the word that was in more frequent everyday use. When he presented nonwords such as *afworbu, civadra,* and *zabulon,* he found that the more times these novel stimuli were presented, the better the subjects liked them.

Many other studies have demonstrated the positive effect of exposure on preference, with stimuli ranging from geometric figures to musical compositions. But two other factors interact with frequency of exposure. First, only relatively complex stimuli profit from repeated observation; apparently people get tired of simple stimuli (Smith and Dorfman, 1975). Second, repetition of even complex stimuli loses its effect when carried on indef-

initely (Zajonc, Shaver, Travis, and Kreveld, 1972). (Sponsors of television commercials should learn about this finding.)

FEAR   Fear can be used not only to compel obedience ("Do this or I'll shoot you!") but also to change people's attitudes. Most messages that attempt to persuade you to stop smoking, to fasten your seatbelt, or to lose excess weight are based on fear: if you don't do this, the results will be lung cancer, a mangled body, or a heart attack. (See **Figure 15.12**.)

Experiments have attested the effectiveness of fear-producing methods of persuasion. Pictures of rotten teeth and diseased gums persuade people of the importance of oral hygiene more effectively than pictures of plastic teeth (Evans, Rozelle, Lasater, Dembroski, and Allen, 1970). If the fear-inducing message also contains a specific recommendation of action, it is even more persuasive (Rogers, 1975). Rogers cites three factors that make fear-inducing messages effective in changing attitudes: (1) the noxiousness of the event being depicted, (2) the perceived likelihood that the event may occur, and (3) the perceived effectiveness of the recommended response in avoiding the event.

Harris and Jellison (1971) have suggested that specific recommendations are especially effective in fear-inducing messages because they give the recipient a way to reduce his or her fear vicariously. Thus, the message arouses fear, which is an unpleasant state, but when the subject imagines himself or herself performing the recommended behavior, the fear decreases. In yet another instance of negative reinforcement, the decrease in fear vicariously reinforces the recipient for covertly performing the behavior and presumably increases the probability that he or she will actually perform the behavior.

Characteristics of the Recipient

Not everyone is equally susceptible to persuasion. For example, a biochemist can be persuaded about some topic in his or her field by another biochemist but not by the uninformed opinions of a television actor, even if the actor is attractive and is a good public speaker. If the recipient knows a topic well, it is difficult to change his or her opinions unless the argument is supported by fact.

When the topic of a persuasive message is unrelated to the recipient's field of expertise, the recipient's personality characteristics play an important role. The most important of these appears to be *self-esteem*. A person whose self-esteem is low tends to be receptive to a persuasive message. People with high self-esteem are much more resistant; they have confidence in their own opinions and less need to conform and be accepted by the communicator.

Self-esteem is also related to intelligence; intelligent people are likely to have confidence in their own abilities, whereas less intelligent people are likely to be aware of their shortcomings. Eagly and Warren (1976) found that intelligent people tended to be more persuaded by complex messages, because they could understand the arguments more easily than less intelligent subjects could. However, when presented with a simple message unsupported by arguments, intelligent people were

FIGURE 15.12   This bumper sticker attempts to persuade by arousing our fear of exposure to radioactivity.

considerably *less* likely than others to be persuaded. Presumably they had enough confidence in themselves to resist a message that contained no supporting facts.

Less enduring characteristics of the recipient are also important. Salespeople have known for a long time that a recipient's mood plays a role in his or her persuadability. The "three-martini lunch" is designed to put a prospective client into a good mood so that he or she will be more likely to buy. In fact Janis, Kaye, and Kirschner (1965) found that subjects who received a snack were more likely to be persuaded than those who did not.

Development of Resistance to Persuasion

◆ Social psychologists have studied the ways of helping people resist persuasion. Just as the best way to inoculate people against many diseases is to expose them to a mild form of the illness in order to organize their defenses against it, the best defense against persuasion is previous exposure to the arguments. McGuire and Papageorgis (1961) presented two kinds of arguments to subjects on various issues with which they were likely to agree. Some subjects heard a *supportive defense,* consisting of arguments in favor of the issue; others heard a *refutational defense*—a presentation of several arguments on the other side of the issue, followed by counterarguments refuting them. A few days later, the experimenters presented the subjects with persuasive messages opposing their previous point of view. Subjects who had heard the refutational defense were much more likely to maintain their original opinion; a taste of the opposition's arguments strengthened them against the effects of persuasion.

Some studies have confirmed the effectiveness of refutational defense, whereas others have found that it is no more effective than supportive defense (Cialdini, Petty, and Cacioppo, 1981). The distinguishing variable appears to be the nature of the topic. If the topic is an assertion that our culture takes for granted as being true, then refutational defense is especially effective. Presumably, most people are unfamiliar with arguments against cultural truisms; thus, inoculation against them is especially effective.

ATTITUDES AND BEHAVIOR

◆ People do not always behave as their expressed attitudes and beliefs would lead us to expect. In a classic example, LaPiere (1934) drove through the United States with a Chinese couple. They stopped at over 250 restaurants and lodging places and were refused service only once. Several months after their trip, LaPiere wrote to the owners of the places they had visited and asked whether they would serve Chinese people. The response was overwhelmingly negative; 92 percent of those who responded said that they would not. Clearly, their behavior gave less evidence of racial bias than their expressed attitudes did.

As I mentioned earlier, many studies in the 1960s (such as Wicker, 1969) observed a poor relation between attitudes and behavior, and Abelson (1972) even suggested that the concept of attitudes be dispensed with altogether. However, subsequent studies have shown that attitudes and behavior are related, although several factors can affect the relation.

Degree of Specificity

One important variable that affects the correspondence between a person's attitude and behavior is the degree of specificity. If you measure a person's general attitude toward a topic, you will be less likely to be able to predict his or her behavior; behaviors, unlike attitudes, are specific events. As the attitude being measured becomes more specific, the person's behavior becomes more predictable. For example, Weigel, Vernon, and Tognacci

TABLE 15.2 Correlation between willingness to join the Sierra Club and various measures of related attitudes

Attitude scale	Correlation
Importance of a pure environment	.06
Pollution	.32
Conservation	.24
Attitude toward the Sierra Club	.68

Based on Wiegel, R.H., Vernon, D.T.A., and Tognacci, L.N. *Journal of Personality and Social Psychology,* 1974, *30,* 724–728.

(1974) measured people's attitudes toward a series of topics that increased in specificity from "a pure environment" to "the Sierra Club" (an American organization that supports environmental causes). They used the subjects' attitudes to predict whether they would volunteer for various activities to benefit the Sierra Club.

Table 15.2 shows the results. A person's attitude toward environmentalism was a poor predictor of whether he or she would volunteer, but his or her attitude toward the Sierra Club itself was a much better predictor. (See **Table 15.2.**) For example, a person might favor a pure environment, but also dislike organized clubs or have little time to spare for meetings. This person would express a positive attitude toward a pure environment but would not volunteer for any activities to support the club.

Self-Attribution

Another variable that affects the relation between attitude and subsequent behavior is the way in which the person has formed his or her attitude. If a person has developed an attitude that is based on the opinions or persuasive arguments of other people the attitude will usually be a poor predictor of behavior. In contrast, an attitude formed through *self-attribution* is likely to be an excellent predictor of behavior.

Self-attribution occurs as a result of the fact that we are all self-observers. We see how we behave in various situations and make attributions about our own dispositions just as we make them about other people's. If we observe that someone else habitually avoids talking with fat people we can conclude that the person has a negative attitude toward them. If we find ourselves avoiding fat people we can make a similar self-attribution.

A number of studies have found that when a person has had the opportunity to perform relevant behaviors he or she is more likely to express attitudes that are consistent with subsequent behaviors. For example, Regan and Fazio (1977) had some subjects spend time playing with five puzzles; others merely heard descriptions of the puzzles. All subjects were asked to rate their interest in each puzzle.

Later, the subjects were given some "free time" during which they could play with the puzzles if they chose. The correlation between ratings and later activity with the puzzles was .54 for subjects who had actually played with the puzzles, but only .20 for those who had merely heard them described. Therefore, it appears that attitudes that are based on people's previous behavior are better predictors of their future behavior.

Constraints on Behavior

Other more obvious factors, such as existing circumstances, also produce discrepancies between attitudes and behaviors. For example, a young man might have a very positive attitude toward a young woman. If he were asked, he might rate kissing her very highly. However, he is never observed to engage in this behavior, because the young woman has plainly shown that she is not interested in him. No matter how carefully we measure the young man's attitudes, we cannot predict his behavior without additional information (in this case, from the young woman).

COGNITIVE DISSONANCE

◆ Although we usually regard our attitudes as causes of our behavior, our behavior also affects our attitudes. Two major theories attempt to explain the effects of behavior on attitude formation. The oldest theory, developed by Leon Festinger (1957), is that of *cognitive dissonance.* According to Festinger, when we perceive a discrepancy between our attitudes and behavior, between our behavior and self-image, or between one attitude and another, an unpleasant state of dissonance results. In the earlier example, a person feels guilty if she believes herself to be racially unprejudiced but finds that she avoids the company of racially mixed couples. The woman experiences a conflict between her belief in her own lack of prejudice and the evidence of prejudice from her behavior. This conflict produces dissonance, which is aversive. (See **Figure 15.13.**)

In Festinger's view, an important source of human motivation is *dissonance reduction;* the aversive state of dissonance motivates a person to reduce it. (Because dissonance reduction is removal of an aversive stimulus it constitutes a negative reinforcer.) A person can achieve dissonance reduction by (1) reducing the importance of one of the

FIGURE 15.13   What conflicts do you think are engendered in this police officer, who must ignore the personal insult? How do you think he resolves the cognitive dissonance that the conflict produces?

dissonant elements, (2) adding consonant elements, or (3) changing one of the dissonant elements.

Suppose a student believes that he is intelligent, but he invariably receives bad grades in his courses. Because the obvious prediction is that intelligent people get good grades, the discrepancy causes the student to experience dissonance. To reduce this dissonance, he may decide that grades are not important—that intelligence is not very closely related to grades. He is (1) reducing the importance of one of the dissonant elements—the fact that he received bad grades in his courses. Or the student can dwell on the fact that his professors were unfair or that his job leaves him little time to study. He is reducing dissonance by (2) adding consonant elements—other factors account for his poor grades and hence explain the discrepancy between his perceived intelligence and grades. Finally, the student can (3) change one of the dissonant elements: he can either start getting good grades or revise his opinion of his own intelligence. Other factors (how

hard he is willing to work, how important it is for him to feel that he is intelligent) will determine which of these strategies he chooses.

Conflict Resolution

The theory of cognitive dissonance predicts that our decision-making behavior should have an effect on our attitudes. The effect should be strongest when we make a difficult decision based on conflicting tendencies. For example, suppose a young lawyer is offered two jobs. One is at a prestigious firm that pays well and offers good chances for advancement but expects only top-notch work from its employees; the firm has a reputation for firing even veteran employees if their performance lags. The other offer is from a less prestigious firm; if she takes this job, she will never fulfill her ambitions for recognition. However, the working conditions are pleasant and the firm is very loyal to its employees; few employees are ever fired. Thus, the lawyer would be assured of lifelong employment.

Suppose the young lawyer is initially torn between these two choices but finally decides to accept one of the job offers. Once the choice is made, her attitudes will probably undergo change. If she chooses the high-powered firm, she is likely to perceive the practice of rewarding an employee's loyalty, as opposed to his or her ability, as a weak and contemptible practice, because this belief will reduce any residual doubts about the wisdom of her choice. Conversely, if she chooses the other firm, she will probably tell herself that loyalty is an important virtue and that she is glad she did not commit herself to work in such an inhumane place. Besides, the fact that she will not have to worry about losing her job means that she can concentrate on the task at hand and will actually become a better lawyer.

Even in trivial matters, people tend to shift their attitudes once they have made a decision. Knox and Inkster (1968) asked people at the betting windows of a racetrack how confident they were that their horse would win. They questioned half of the people just before they had made their bets, the other half just afterward. The people who had already made their bets were more confident than those who had not yet paid; presumably, once they had paid, they started dwelling on the virtues of their horse and the defects of the others.

Attitudes and Expenditures

◆ Festinger's theory of cognitive dissonance accounts for yet another relation between behavior and attitudes—our tendency to value an item more if it costs us something. For example, some people buy extremely expensive brands of cosmetics even though the same ingredients are used in much cheaper brands. Presumably they believe that if an item costs more it must work better. Following the same rationale, most animal shelters sell their stray animals to prospective pet owners, not only to help defray their operating costs but also because they assume that a pet that has been purchased will probably be treated better than one that was obtained free. (See **Figure 15.14**.)

Aronson and Mills (1959) verified this phenomenon. The experimenters subjected female college students to varying degrees of embarrassment as a prerequisite for joining what was promised to be an interesting discussion about sexual behavior. To produce slight embarrassment, they had the subjects read five sex-related words (such as *prostitute, virgin,* and *petting*) to the experimenter, who was male. To produce more severe embarrassment, they had the women read aloud twelve obscene four-letter words and two sexually explicit passages of prose. The control group read nothing at all. The "interesting group discussion" turned out to be a tape recording of a very dull conversation. (When psychologists put their mind to it, they can produce excruciatingly dull material. Sometimes this even happens inadvertently.)

Festinger's theory predicts that the women who had to go through an embarrassing ordeal in order to join the group would experience some cognitive dissonance. They gave up something—some pride or self-esteem—to obtain a goal that they initially perceived to be worthwhile: the privilege of par-

FIGURE 15.14 We usually value things that cost us more than things we obtain free.

ticipating in an interesting discussion. This investment should make them perceive the "discussion" more favorably, so that their effort would not be perceived as having been completely without value. The results were as predicted: the subjects who had been embarrassed the most rated the discussion higher than did the control subjects or the subjects who experienced very slight embarrassment. Clearly, we value things at least partly by how much they cost us. (See **Figure 15.15**.)

Induced Compliance

It is commonly believed that although it is possible to induce people to do something, it is much harder to get them to change their opinions. However, Festinger's theory of cognitive dissonance and supporting experimental evidence indicate otherwise. Under the right conditions, when people are coerced into doing something or paid to do so, the act of compliance causes a change in their attitudes.

Dissonance theory predicts that dissonance occurs when a person's behavior has outcomes that are harmful to self-esteem; there is a conflict between the person's belief in his or her own worth and the fact that he or she has done something that damages this belief. The person will then seek to justify his or her behavior. In some cases, the ends clearly justify the means, and the person's self-esteem does not suffer, as when Lady Godiva rode naked down the street in order to save the townspeople from having to pay a heavy and unfair tax to her odious husband. Since the goal was worthwhile, she did not lose face in doing so.

On the other hand, suppose you are having a picnic at a park. While idly throwing stones, you happen to break a beer bottle that someone carelessly discarded. You think vaguely about retrieving the broken pieces of glass, but somehow you do not get around to doing it. Later you hear the cries of a little girl who has been playing nearby and has cut her feet badly on the broken glass. You will feel ashamed of yourself for not having picked up the pieces of broken glass, but you will probably try to lighten your share of the blame by saying to yourself, "The slob who left the bottle there is really responsible" and "Why weren't that girl's parents watching her more closely?"

Similarly, a poorly paid vacuum-cleaner salesperson is likely to convince himself that the shoddy merchandise he sells is actually good. Otherwise, he must live with the realization that he is always lying to prospective customers and doing them a disservice by persuading them to buy one. On the other hand, an executive of one of the commercial television networks might know that the programs she produces are sleazy, mindless drivel, but she is so well paid that she does not feel bad about producing them. Her high salary justifies her job and probably also provides her with enough self-esteem that she has decided that the public "gets what it deserves," anyway.

Festinger and Carlsmith (1959) verified this observation by having subjects perform boring tasks such as putting a number of spools on a tray, dumping them out, putting them on the tray again, dumping them out again, and so on. After this exercise, the experimenter asked the subjects whether they would help out in the study by trying to convince the subject who followed them that the task was interesting. Some subjects received one dollar for doing so, others twenty dollars. Control subjects were paid nothing; their assistance was presumably an expression of willingness to help the experimenter. It was predicted that the subjects who were paid only one dollar would perceive the task as being relatively interesting. They had been

FIGURE 15.15   Ratings of a discussion by people who sustained varying amounts of embarrassment. (Data based on Aronson, E., and Mills, J. *Journal of Abnormal and Social Psychology*, 1959, 67, 31–36.)

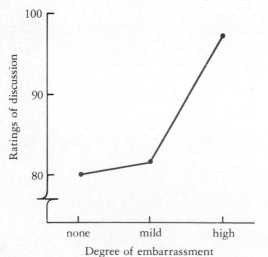

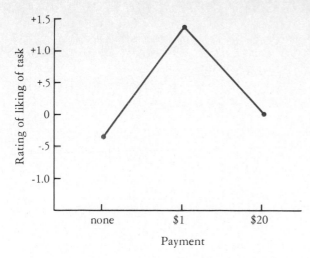

FIGURE 15.16   Ratings of liking of task by people who received no payment or payment of one dollar or twenty dollars. (Based on data from Festinger, L., and Carlsmith, J.M. *Journal of Abnormal and Social Psychology,* 1959, *58,* 203–210.)

induced to lie to a "fellow student" (a confederate of the experimenters) for a paltry sum. Like the vacuum-cleaner salesman, they should convince themselves of the worth of the experiment so as to maintain their self-esteem. **Figure 15.16** shows that the poorly paid subject did in fact rate the task better than control subjects or those who were well paid. Clearly, our actions *do* have an effect on our attitudes; when faced with inconsistency between our behavior and our attitudes, we often change our attitudes to suit our behavior.

SELF-PERCEPTION

Daryl Bem (1972) has proposed an alternative to the theory of cognitive dissonance. He defines *self-perception theory* in the following way:

> Individuals come to "know" their own attitudes, emotions, and other internal states partially by inferring them from observations of their own overt behavior and/or the circumstances in which this behavior occurs. Thus, to the extent that internal cues are weak, ambiguous, or uninterpretable, the individual is functionally in the same position as an outside observer, an observer who must necessarily rely upon those same external cues to infer the individual's inner states. (p. 2)

Bem notes that an observer who attempts to make judgments about someone's attitudes, emotions, or other internal states must examine the person's behavior for clues. He suggests that people analyze their own internal states in a similar way, making causal attributions about their own behavior.

Bem's theory derives from an analysis of behavior in terms of reinforcement, punishment, and discriminative stimuli that signal the particular contingencies in a particular situation. In other words, the theory uses the principles of operant conditioning to explain a person's behavior and attitudes.

Bem provided the following example to illustrate his claim. Suppose you see a friend running into the room, holding a broom over his head. Many psychologists assert that you would have to know what his intentions were—what his goal was in performing this behavior. If a mouse has run into the room just beforehand, you will probably assume that your friend is chasing the mouse with the intent of killing it or driving it outside again. If the mouse has run into the room just afterward, you will probably assume that the mouse is chasing your friend; his intent is to escape from it. Finally, if there is no mouse at all, you may wonder whether your friend was angry at you and is planning to attack you with the upraised broom. Your attributions are based on your observations of environmental stimuli, namely, the presence or absence of a mouse and its relation to your friend's entering the room. You have no way of looking inside your friend's head to see whether he is determined to kill the mouse or is afraid of it. (We will assume that you cannot see the expression on his face.) Therefore, you cannot understand his behavior by discovering his intent. Instead, you *analyze the situation.* You perceive that the mouse is the stimulus controlling your friend's behavior, and thus attribute his behavior to it. You may conclude that your friend is determined or afraid, but only *after* you have decided what accounts for his behavior. (See **Figure 15.17.**)

When we make conclusions about our own internal states, such as attitudes or intents, our reasons are often very clear; the situation provides such obvious clues that there is no doubt about why we have behaved in a given way. If we see a

FIGURE 15.17   We use environmental cues to attribute the same behavior to different causes.

mouse and start chasing it with a broom we know exactly why we are running with a broom in our hands. In more complex situations, an analysis of the situation does not provide clear-cut reasons. If we cannot determine the causes from the situation, we must turn to our own behavior for clues.

You will recall the experiment by Festinger and Carlsmith (1959) in which students who were paid only one dollar later rated a boring task as more interesting than did those who were paid twenty dollars. How does self-perception theory explain these results?

Suppose an observer watches a subject who has been paid one dollar to deliver a convincing speech to another student about how interesting a task was. Because being paid such a small sum is not a sufficient reason for calling a dull task interesting, the observer will probably conclude that the student actually enjoyed the task. Lacking good evidence for external causes, the observer will attribute the behavior to a dispositional factor—interest in the task. Bem argues that the subject makes the same inferences. Because the subject was not paid enough to tell a lie, he or she must have enjoyed the task. The principal advantage of self-perception theory is that it makes fewer assumptions than dissonance theory; it does not postulate a motivating, aversive drive state. Thus it has the advantage of parsimony. If two theories are equally good at predicting behavior, the *parsimonious* one (the one that is stingy in the number of assumptions it requires) is preferable. Furthermore, as we shall see later, self-perception theory also explains

phenomena that dissonance theory cannot account for.

REPORTS OF ATTITUDE CHANGE

◆ So far we have assumed that reports of attitudes are trustworthy—that subjects rate their attitudes truthfully. But research indicates that this is not always the case. In some situations a person's expressed attitude appears to be affected by his or her desire to look good to others. This phenomenon has been called *impression management;* we manage people's impression of ourselves so that we appear in a favorable light.

When a person appears to change his or her attitude, an observer does not simply note this fact in a neutral manner. Instead, the observer often forms positive or negative opinions about the actor. Consider this story, reported in a newspaper:

> The Very Republican Lady from Columbus, Ohio, looked sternly at former Texas Gov. John Connally and asked: "What are your views on the ERA?" "I'm for it," Connally shot back. "I've been for it since 1962." The Very Republican Lady, obviously no fan of the Equal Rights Amendment, glared. After a short, pained silence, Connally began to revise and extend his remarks. "Actually, I have mixed feelings," he said, "If the amendment would weaken or destroy family life, I'd have to take another look. . . . I wouldn't have voted to extend the time for ratification. That was wrong. . . . So for all practical purposes I guess you could say I'm against it today." (Copyright 1983, Des Moines Register and Tribune Company.)

Governor Connally seemed to change his attitude in a rather short time. The apparent reason for his change is disapproval of a potential voter and, by implication, of other voters who shared her point of view. Does this change of attitude affect your opinion of governor Connally?

In general, when a person is persuaded to change his or her opinion, an observer will rate the person as being somewhat less attractive and intelligent, whereas the persuader will rate the person positively (Cialdini, Braver, and Lewis, 1974; Cialdini and Mirels, 1976). If people are aware of this phenomenon, then perhaps they will admit to different amounts of attitude change, depending on whether or not there are witnesses present.

Braver, Linder, Corwin, and Cialdini (1977) asked subjects the following question: "How favorable would you be toward shortening the number of years of medical training for doctors, thus permitting the training of more doctors and the lengthening of each doctor's active practice?" After giving their answers they joined two other people who were supposedly other subjects. One of them (the persuader) gave a persuasive speech in favor of shortening the duration of medical training.

The subjects were then exposed to one of four experimental conditions: (1) the observer left, leaving the subject in the presence of only the persuader; (2) the persuader left, leaving the subject in the presence of only the observer; (3) neither of them left; and (4) both of them left. The subjects were then asked again to give their opinion about the length of medical training. Figure 15.18 shows the results. If only the persuader was present, subjects expressed a relatively favorable response to the suggested decrease in length of training. If both persuader and observer were present, subjects expressed a slightly less favorable opinion. If subjects were alone or if only an observer was present, they expressed somewhat unfavorable opinions. (Numbers higher than 3.5 indicate agreement; those below 3.5 indicate disagreement.) (See **Figure 15.18**.)

All subjects heard exactly the same persuasive arguments; the only difference was in the situation in which their attitudes were measured the second time. It seems reasonable to attribute their expressed opinions to something other than genuine attitude change; they appeared (consciously or not) to express an opinion that would make the best impression on their audience.

FIGURE 15.18   Subjects' agreement with a persuasive argument in the presence or absence of an observer and/or persuader. (Based on data from

Braver, S.L., Linder, D.E., Corwin, T.T., and Cialdini, R.B. *Journal of Experimental Social Psychology,* 1977, *13,* 565–576.)

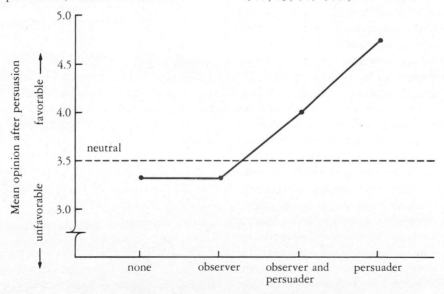

People present with subject during attitude testing

Interim summary: Although the topic of attitudes and persuasion fell into disrepute for several years, we now understand the principal reasons for poor correspondence between attitudes and behavior: differences in degree of specificity of the attitude and behavior, the opportunity a person has had to observe his or own attitude-related behavior, and external constraints that prevent a person's acting on his or her attitudes.

Attitudes have affective components, primarily formed through direct or vicarious classical conditioning, and cognitive components, formed through direct instruction or through instrumental conditioning or modeling.

Effectiveness of attempts to persuade a person to change his or her attitudes depends on several factors. Relevant characteristics of the communicator include expertise, apparent motives, and attractiveness. Thus, a good-looking expert who appears to have no stake in persuading someone else will be the best persuader. However, when the issue is an important one, factors other than the characteristics of the communicator will play the most important role. Relevant characteristics of the message include argumentation, repetition, and fear. If a person initially does not favor the communicator's side of the issue or if the communicator is perceived as an expert, then the most effective message is one that contains arguments on both sides of the issue. If the person initially agrees with the communicator or if the communicator is attractive, then the most effective message is one that presents one-sided arguments. The use of fear is most effective if the message describes how a change in attitude and behavior will avoid the unpleasant events it describes; presumably, the arousal and elimination of fear produces vicarious negative reinforcement. Finally, the relevant characteristics of the recipient include his or her own expertise, self-esteem, intelligence, and mood. Intelligent experts with high self-esteem are difficult to persuade, unless the message contains well-reasoned arguments.

Festinger's theory of cognitive dissonance suggests reasons for interactions between attitudes and behavior. It proposes that discrepancies between attitudes and behavior, behavior and self-image, or one attitude and another leads to the unpleasant state of cognitive dissonance. Reduction of this dissonance by changing the importance of dissonant elements, adding consonant ones, or changing one of them, provides negative reinforcement. The theory explains why we more highly value things that cost us something, and predicts that behaviors—even induced compliance—can lead to attitude changes.

Bem's alternative to cognitive dissonance—self-perception theory—suggests that many of our attitudes are based on self-observation. When our motives are unclear, we look to the situation for the stimuli and probable reinforcers and punishers that cause us to act as we do. For example, subjects who are paid one dollar to persuade fellow students to perform a boring task have a more favorable attitude toward it because genuine interest is a more likely explanation for their own behavior than the receipt of such a small sum.

Another important variable is impression management—we sometimes profess attitudes in order to please a persuader or to appear to others that we have enough self-confidence not to be easily manipulated.

It is clear from the data presented in this section that no single theory can account for the formation and alteration of attitudes. Human behavior is complex and entails evaluation of a wide range of possible causal factors.

SOCIAL INFLUENCES

The previous section discussed the ways in which a person's attitudes can be changed. This section discusses three ways in which social influences can control or alter a person's *behavior*. *Conformity* entails behaving as the group does—modeling one's responses on the example set by the people with whom one interacts. *Compliance* is more straightforward; it consists in doing something that another person requests. If someone who is burdened with packages asks you to open a door, your doing so is an act of compliance. *Obedience* differs from compliance only in degree; a behavior is ordered rather than requested.

CONFORMITY

◆ Most of us cherish our independence and like to think that we do what we do because *we* want to

FIGURE 15.19   Most of us feel more comfortable
when we look and act like the other people around
us.

do it, not because others decree that we should.
But none of us is immune to social influences, and
most instances of conformity benefit us all. If we
see someone whose face has been disfigured by an
accident or disease, we do not stare at the person
or comment about his or her appearance. If someone drops a valuable item, we do not try to pick
it up and keep it for ourselves. If we lose a tennis
match, we do not cry and pout; instead, we smile
and congratulate the victor. If we have a cold, we
try not to sneeze in someone else's face. Each society has developed norms that define the ways in
which we should behave in various situations, and
following these norms generally makes us feel more
comfortable and also helps the group function
smoothly. (See **Figure 15.19.**)

The Asch Effect

◈ Solomon Asch (1951) demonstrated just how powerful social influences can be, even on simple perceptual judgments. He asked several groups of seven
to nine students to estimate lengths of lines that
were presented on a screen. A sample line was shown
at the left, and the subjects were to choose which
of the three lines to the right matched it. (See
Figure 15.20.) The subjects gave their answers
orally.

In fact there was only one subject in each group;
all the others were confederates of the experimenter. The seating was arranged so that the subject
answered last. Under some conditions, the confederates made incorrect responses. When they made
incorrect responses on six of the twelve trials in an
experiment, 76 percent of the subjects went along
with the group on at least one trial. Under control
conditions, when the confederates responded accurately, only 5 percent of the subjects made an
error.

FIGURE 15.20   An example of the stimuli used
by Asch (1951).

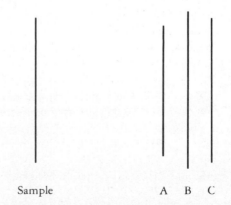

Sample   A   B   C

Group pressure did not affect the subjects' perceptions; it affected their behavior. That is, the subjects went along with the group decision even though the choice still looked wrong to them. When they were questioned later, they said that they started doubting their own eyesight or thought that perhaps they had misunderstood the instructions. The subjects who did not conform also felt uncomfortable about disagreeing with the other members of the group.

The Asch effect shows how strong the tendency to conform can be. Faced with a simple, unambiguous task in a group of strangers who showed no signs of disapproval when the subject disagreed with them, a large majority of subjects nevertheless ignored their own judgments and agreed with the obviously incorrect choice made by the others.

Factors That Affect Conformity

The same variables that affect persuasiveness also affect conformity. For example, we are more likely to conform if the other members of the group are attractive and have higher status than we do. We are also more likely to conform if we cannot attribute their judgments to external factors. For example, if several of your friends wear T-shirts with a particular slogan because they have been paid to do so by an advertiser, you are unlikely to purchase one of these shirts yourself unless you also get paid. But if your friends start wearing these shirts without explanation, you are much more likely to see them as the "in" thing and to start looking for one to buy.

People have often suggested that women are more susceptible than men to pressures to conform, because women are traditionally viewed as "socially oriented," in contrast to the more independent "career orientation" of men. Although some studies have supported this assertion, Sistrunk and McDavid (1971) have shown that an unintentional bias contaminated the results of these studies. They noted that the topics chosen for the studies were generally conceived of as "male" topics, and that perhaps the women simply perceived men as being better experts on them. (Whether they actually were better experts is irrelevant; what matters is the perceptions.)

Sistrunk and McDavid prepared a list of topics,

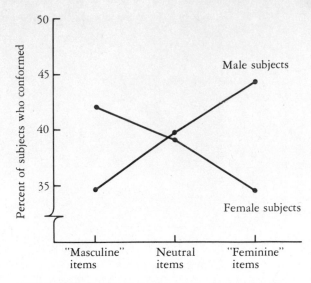

FIGURE 15.21   Percentage of male and female subjects who conformed as a function of the perceived masculinity and femininity of the items. (Based on data from Sistrunk, F., and McDavid, J.W. *Journal of Personality and Social Psychology*, 1971, *17*, 200–207.)

some "male-related," some "female-related," and some neutral. (Perhaps I should say "neuter.") Both males and females were given fictitious ratings of "200 college students" and were asked to give their own. Figure 15.21 shows that males conformed most when the item was "female-related," females when the item was "male-related." On neutral items, males and females showed the same amount of conformity. (See **Figure 15.21**.) What looked like a sex-related characteristic was found to be an example of the variable of expertise, discussed earlier. A person who doubts his or her own expertise on a topic is more likely to conform to group judgments about that topic.

COMPLIANCE

Many of the factors that affect conformity also affect compliance. For example, if people believe that most other people have complied with a particular request, they tend to do so themselves. When Schofield (1975) merely asked twenty females college students to read and review some pamphlets, only seven agreed to do so. When she also said, to another group of twenty, that "she was pleased that

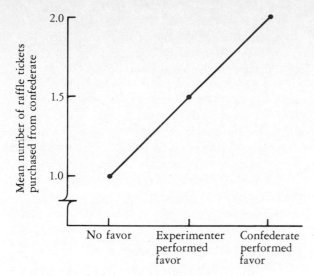

FIGURE 15.22   Mean number of raffle tickets purchased from a confederate when subjects received a favor or no favor from the experimenter or confederate. (Based on data from Regan, D.T. *Journal of Experimental Social Psychology,* 1971, 7, 627–639.)

most women in the previous groups" had complied with her requests, seventeen subjects agreed to help.

Compliance and Equity Theory

Homans (1961) suggested that an important component of compliance is *equity*. Most social relations are governed by fairness and equity; we do something for someone else, and someone does something for us. Often, the person for whom we do something is not the same person who does something for us; we assume that "If I were she, I'd expect someone else to do what I'm doing." The classic example is the fact that we do not repay to our parents the money they spent in raising us; instead, we do the same for our own children.

Regan (1971) showed that people do appear to take equity into account when they decide whether or not to comply with a request. A group of college students participated in an experiment that was supposedly involved with art appreciation. During a break, some subjects were treated to a soft drink by the experimenter or by another "subject" (a confederate); others received nothing. After the experiment, the confederate asked the subject to purchase some raffle tickets that he was selling.

Compliance was measured by the number of tickets that each subject bought. Figure 15.22 shows the results. The subjects whom the confederate treated to a soft drink purchased the most raffle tickets. Getting a free drink from the experimenter also had an effect. Perhaps the subjects responded to the example of doing a favor for someone else; they probably thought well of the experimenter and, with this example fresh in mind, complied with the confederate's request so that they would be thought well of too. (See **Figure 15.22.**)

Compliance and Transgression

If an accident or other circumstances cause us to harm someone else, we are likely to comply with requests made by that person. For example, Carlsmith and Gross (1969) had subjects participate in a "learning task." The subject served as teacher, and another "student" (a confederate) served as learner. The subject informed the learner when he was wrong by operating a switch that (1) purportedly delivered an electric shock to the learner or (2) sounded a buzzer.

Afterward the learners asked the teachers whether they would be willing to circulate a petition to help stop the construction of a freeway through a redwood forest in California. Twenty-five percent of the subjects who had simply buzzed the learner complied, compared with 75 percent of the subjects who believed they had administered a shock. Equity theory suggests that the subjects were doing a favor for the victim in compensation for the pain they had caused.

Compliance and Self-Esteem

A person who transgresses—that is, hurts someone or violates a social rule—becomes more likely to comply with a request. McMillen (1971) has suggested that another factor besides equity theory can account for this compliance: when we transgress, we not only feel guilty; we also suffer a loss in self-esteem. In support of this suggestion, McMillen and Austin (1971) found that transgressors who were subsequently told that they had done very well on a personality test were less likely than control subjects to comply with a request; the increased self-esteem apparently reduced their tendency to atone for their misdeed.

OBEDIENCE

Milgram's Studies

Suppose someone told you to torture an innocent man who was strapped in a chair. Of course you believe you would refuse to do so. But a series of experiments by Stanley Milgram found that many people were willing to do just that.

Milgram (1963) advertised for subjects in local newspapers to obtain as representative a sample as possible. The subjects served as the teacher in what they were told was a learning experiment. A confederate (a middle-aged accountant) serving as the learner was strapped into a chair "to prevent excessive movements when he was shocked," and electrodes were attached to his wrist. (See **Figure 15.23.**) The subjects were told that "although the shocks can be extremely painful, they cause no permanent tissue damage."

The subject was brought to a separate room, where there was an apparatus containing dials, buttons, and a series of switches that supposedly delivered 15 to 450 volts. The subject was to use this apparatus to deliver shocks to the learner in the other room. Beneath the switches were descriptive labels ranging from "SLIGHT SHOCK" to "DANGER: SEVERE SHOCK." (See **Figure 15.24.**)

The learner gave his answers by pressing the appropriate lever on the table in front of him. Each time he made an incorrect response, the experimenter told the subject to throw another switch and give a larger shock. At the 300-volt level, the learner pounded on the wall and then stopped responding to the questions. The experimenter told the subject to consider no answer as an incorrect answer. At the 315-volt level, the learner pounded the wall again. If the subject hesitated in delivering a shock, the experimenter said, "Please go on." If this admonition was not enough, he said, "The experiment requires that you continue," "It is absolutely essential that you continue," and, finally, "You have no other choice; you *must* go on." The factor of interest was how long the subjects would continue to administer shock to the hapless victim.

A majority of subjects gave the learner what they believed to be the 450-volt shock, despite the fact that he pounded the wall twice and then stopped responding altogether. (See **Figure 15.25.**)

In a later experiment, when the confederate was placed in the same room as the subject and his struggling and apparent pain could be observed, 37.5 percent of the participants—over one-third—obeyed the order to administer further shocks (Milgram, 1974). Thirty percent were even willing to hold his hand against a metal plate to force him to receive the shock.

Milgram's experiments indicate that a significant percentage of people will blindly follow orders, no matter what the effects are on other people. Clearly, the tendency to obey an authority figure is amazingly strong. Perhaps, we should emphasize to our children the importance of doing no harm to others as least as much as we emphasize obedience.

Obedience and Group Pressure

Peer pressure has a strong effect on whether a person obeys orders. In separate studies, Milgram (1964, 1965) had subjects work only with the experimenter or with the experimenter and two "assistants" who would help them decide what the shock level should be. In the first study, the confederates suggested that the shock level be increased after each incorrect answer. **Figure 15.26** shows that subjects who acted in the presence of confederates (colored curve) administered more intense shocks than those who worked only with the experimenter (black curve). In the second study, the experimenter himself kept increasing the shock level, but the confederates left the experiment, refusing to go on; one left after the 150-volt level, and the other after the 210-volt level. **Figure 15.27** shows that subjects who were tested with peers who eventually refused to continue (colored curve) stopped sooner than those who worked only with the experimenter (black curve).

Together, the studies confirm that in the company of ruthless people, we are more willing to be cruel ourselves. In the company of people who refuse to obey orders to hurt someone else, we ourselves are more likely to refuse to continue causing harm.

Obedience and the Fundamental Attributional Error

Most people find the results of Milgram's studies surprising; it seems impossible that for such a large

FIGURE 15.23   A "learner" (confederate) being strapped in a chair in one of Milgram's studies. (From Milgram, S. *Obedience to Authority.* New York: Harper & Row, 1974.)

FIGURE 15.24   Milgram's "shocking" device. (From Milgram, S. *Obedience to Authority.* New York: Harper & Row, 1974.)

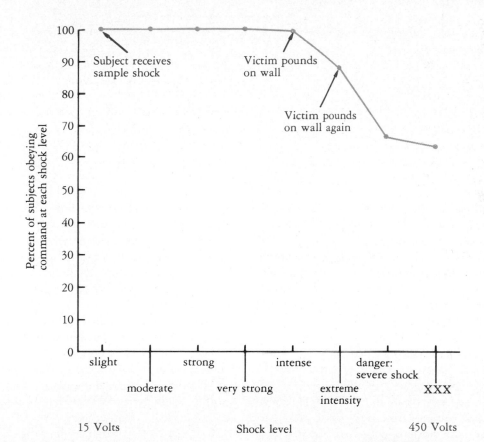

FIGURE 15.25   Data from one of Milgram's studies of obedience. (From Baron, R.A., and Bryne, D. *Social Psychology: Understanding Human Interaction,* 2nd ed. Boston: Allyn and Bacon, 1977; after Milgram, 1963.)

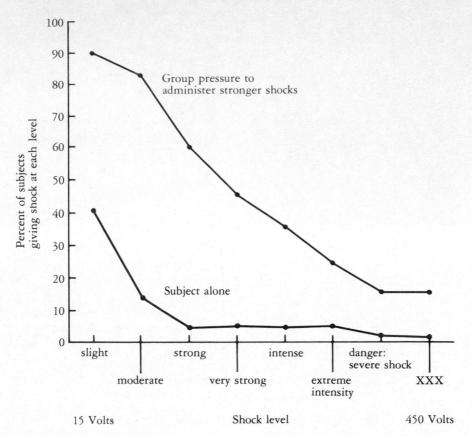

FIGURE 15.26   Results of Milgram's obedience study with "peers" present who were willing to continue shocking the "learner." (From Baron, R.A., and Byrne, D. *Social Psychology: Understanding Human Interaction,* 2nd ed. Boston: Allyn and Bacon, 1977; after Milgram, 1964.)

proportion of people the social pressure to conform to the experimenter's orders is stronger than the subject's own desire not to hurt someone else. As Ross (1977) points out, this misperception is an example of the fundamental attributional error. People tend to underestimate the effectiveness of situational factors and to overestimate the effectiveness of dispositional ones.

Interim summary: Social influences include a tendency to conform to the prevailing behaviors of the group, to comply with other people's requests, and to obey their orders. Although many people regard conformity as an undesirable trait, most examples of conformity are beneficial to society. Conformity is affected by variables like those that affect attitudes—namely, the attractiveness and status of the other group members and the apparent presence or absence of external reasons for their behavior. Asch found that the pressure to conform is strong even when other group members showed no signs of disapproval for perceptual judgments that differed from theirs. Females are no more likely than males to conform.

The variables that affect compliance are similar to those that affect conformity. In addition, compliance is affected by equity—if people have been done a favor by someone else they are more likely to comply with another person's request. They are also more likely to do so if they believe that they have harmed the other person or have suffered a loss of self-esteem that may be rectified by an act of compliance.

Milgram's studies surprised many people with

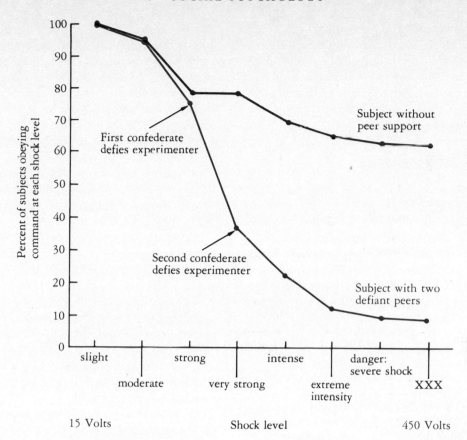

FIGURE 15.27   Results of Milgram's obedience study with "peers" present who were unwilling to continue shocking the "learner." (From Baron, R.A., and Byrne, D. *Social Psychology: Understanding Human Interaction,* 2nd ed. Boston: Allyn and Bacon, 1977; after Milgram, 1965.)

their demonstration of people's willingness to obey an authority figure even when the results of their obedience apparently hurt someone else. They also showed that peer pressure can modify this tendency either positively or negatively.

INTERPERSONAL ATTRACTION

Humans are social animals. We make friends, eat and drink together in groups, join clubs, and form close associations with our mates and children. For most of us, the behavior of other people serves as our most significant source of reinforcing and aversive stimuli. Why do we enjoy the company of some people and not others?

A number of factors determine *interpersonal attraction*—people's tendency to approach each other and evaluate each other positively. Some of these factors are characteristics of the individuals themselves; others are determined by the environment.

The simplest and most parsimonious explanation for interpersonal attraction is that people who serve as sources of reinforcing stimuli for each other tend to remain in each other's company. As you will recall from Chapter 4, stimuli that are regularly associated with reinforcing stimuli will themselves become reinforcing stimuli, through the process of classical conditioning. Thus, we learn to prefer the company of people who regularly provide us with social reinforcement.

The nature of social reinforcement is quite varied. Acknowledgment of our abilities and accomplishments and appreciation of our intelligence and wit are certainly desirable characteristics in a close friend. Other characteristics, such as talent and physical attractiveness, also endear others to us; having an attractive and accomplished friend suggests both to ourselves and to other people that we too are worthy of respect.

POSITIVE EVALUATION

Humans have a real need to be evaluated positively—to be held in high regard by other people. This need is expressed in interpersonal attraction. Byrne and Rhamey (1965) studied the effects of positive personal evaluations on attraction. First, they asked subjects to express their attitudes toward twelve issues. Then they described a fictitious stranger, explaining what his attitudes were on the

FIGURE 15.28   Ratings of the description of a stranger who was said to have evaluated the subject positively or negatively as a function of similarity between stranger and rater. (From Baron, R.A., and Byrne, D. *Social Psychology: Understanding Human Interaction,* 2nd ed. Boston: Allyn and Bacon, 1977; after Byrne and Rhamey, 1965.)

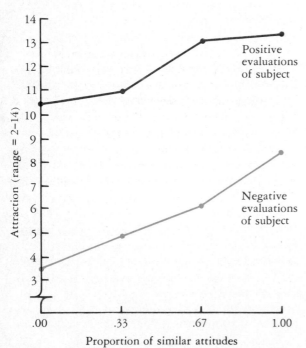

twelve issues. The subjects were told that the stranger had read their attitude survey and had accordingly evaluated the subjects positively or negatively. Finally, the experimenters asked the subjects to rate the amount of attraction they felt toward the stranger. As Figure 15.28 shows, subjects reported being more attracted if the stranger's attitudes were similar to their own. However, the most important factor was whether the stranger approved of the subject; subjects who were evaluated positively reported being much more attracted to the stranger than did those who were rated negatively. (See **Figure 15.28.**)

In situations involving real people, the effects of evaluation are even more pronounced. Geller, Goodstein, Silver, and Sternberg (1974) had female college students individually join group discussions with two other women, confederates of the experimenter. During the discussion, the confederates either treated the subject normally or ignored her, showing a lack of interest in what she said and changing the subject whenever she spoke. The subjects who were ignored found the conversations distressing; they felt very unhappy and even gave *themselves* poor ratings. Being ignored is a form of negative evaluation by other people, and it exerts a powerful effect.

SHARED OPINIONS

A second factor that influences interpersonal attraction is the degree to which people hold similar opinions. This factor, too, can be explained in terms of social reinforcement. Presumably, a person who shares our opinions is likely to approve of us when we express them. Also, having friends who have similar opinions guarantees that our opinions are likely to find a consensus; we will not often find ourselves in the unpleasant position of saying something that brings disapproval from other people.

Byrne and Nelson (1965) measured various attitudes of their subjects and then had them read descriptions of the attitudes of a stranger. After learning about this person's attitudes, the subjects rated how much they liked or disliked the stranger. The scatterplot shown in Figure 15.29 presents the results. The points, which represent individuals, cluster along an imaginary diagonal line; there was

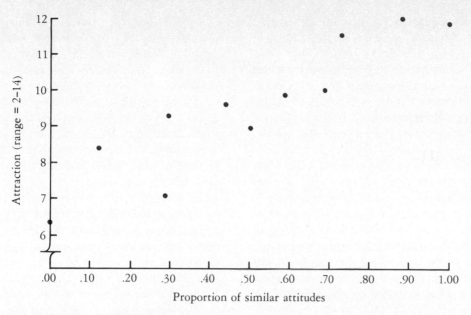

FIGURE 15.29   Ratings of attraction toward a stranger as a function of similarity in attitudes between stranger and rater. (From Byrne, D., and Nelson, D. *Journal of Personality and Social Psychology,* 1971, *1,* 659–663.)

an excellent relation between shared attitudes and attraction. The more similar the stranger's attitudes were to those of the subjects, the better the stranger was liked. (See **Figure 15.29**.)

In the real world, similarity of attitudes is not the only factor determining the strength of interpersonal attraction. Other kinds of similarity are also important, such as age, occupational status, and ethnic background. Friends tend to have similar backgrounds as well as similar attitudes.

PHYSICAL APPEARANCE

We do judge by the characteristic that is supposed to be only skin deep; men prefer beautiful women, and women prefer handsome men. Again, social reinforcement provides a likely explanation for this phenomenon. Although aesthetics (such as our attraction to a beautiful painting) may account in part for our attraction to goodlooking people, self-esteem probably plays a more important role. Someone who is seen in the company of a well-regarded person and is obviously favored by this person is likely to be well regarded by other people ("If she likes him, then he must really have something going for him").

Walster, Aronson, Abrahams, and Rottman (1966) studied the effects of physical appearance at a dance at which college students were paired by a computer. Midway through the evening, the experimenters asked the subjects to rate the attraction they felt toward their partners and to say whether they thought they would like to see them in the future. For both sexes, the only characteristic that correlated with attraction was physical appearance. Intelligence, grade-point average, and personality variables seemed to have no significant effect. However, Berscheid, Dion, Walster, and Walster (1971) found that although physical appearance may be the most important variable in determining attraction between people who are randomly paired by a computer, when people choose their own partner they tend to pick someone who is about as physically attractive as they are.

When people first meet someone with a good physical appearance, they rate the person as probably holding attitudes similar to their own (Schoedel, Frederickson, and Knight, 1975) and tend to assume that they have good personalities, successful marriages, and high occupational status (Dion, Berscheid, and Walster, 1972; Adams and Huston, 1975). In fact physically attractive people usually *do* possess many of these characteristics, probably because they receive favorable treatment from society.

Beauty is also a matter of personal preference; a person whom we perceive as goodlooking is someone who conforms to our concept of good looks. For example, Peterson and Curran (1976) had undergraduate women look at photographs and rate the physical attractiveness of undergraduate men who were wearing either long or short wigs. Some women rated the short-haired men higher; others preferred the long-haired men. The women who preferred the short-haired men tended to be more conservative and more religious than the other subjects. They probably used hair length to identify the men whom they perceived as holding similar attitudes, and thus perceived these men as more attractive. Thus, a person's attitudes can affect his or her concept of physical beauty.

FAMILIARITY

Fortunately for the majority of us who are not especially beautiful or handsome, the variable of exposure influences people's attitudes toward others; the more frequent the exposure, the more positive the attitude.

Bukoff and Elman (1979) had female college students look at photographs of male college students and rate their physical attractiveness. Then the subjects looked at the photographs again a variable number of times and later rated the men's physical attractiveness again. Familiarity had a significant, positive effect; the more times a man's face had been seen, the more positively it was rated.

PROPINQUITY

Propinquity, or nearness, is not a psychologically interesting variable, but it is undoubtedly an important one in determining interpersonal attraction.

Festinger, Schachter, and Back (1950) found that the likelihood of friendships between people who lived in an apartment house was related to the distance between the apartments in which they lived; the closer the apartments, the more likely the friendship. People were also unlikely to have friends who lived on a different floor, unless their apart-

ment was next to a stairway, where they would meet people going up or down the stairs. In suburban housing development, neighbors are more likely to be friends if their driveways are adjacent to each other (Whyte, 1956). Even in a classroom, people who sit together are more likely to become friends. Segal (1974) asked trainees in the Maryland State Police School to list classmates whom they would like to have for friends. Almost half the people they listed had last names that began with letters near theirs in the alphabet. (Can you guess why?)

Even in the brief time it takes to participate in an experiment, propinquity affects interpersonal attraction. Saegert, Swap, and Zajonc (1973) had college women participate in an experiment supposedly involving taste. Groups of two students (all were subjects—no confederates this time) had entered booths, where they tasted and rated various liquids. The movements of the subjects from booth to booth were choreographed so that pairs of women were together from zero to ten times. Afterward, the subjects rated their attraction to each of the other people in the experiment. The amount of attraction the subjects felt toward a given person was related to the number of interactions they had had. (See **Figure 15.30.**)

It is not hard to see why propinquity has a strong effect on interpersonal attraction. Given that we are attracted to people who reinforce us, we must have the opportunity to experience some occasions of reinforcement. While we are discovering each other's attitudes, frequent encounters will increase each other's apparent physical attractiveness.

LIKING AND LOVING: DIFFERENCES IN NATURE OR DEGREE?

The simplest explanation for the intense interpersonal relation we call love is that it is simply a strong form of liking; the feeling we have for the person who is our lover is qualitatively no different from the attraction that we feel for other people, except for the added feelings derived from sexual intimacy, if that occurs. However, some studies have suggested that love is qualitatively different from liking—that the phenomena of reinforcement cannot explain some of the factors that affect the special kind of interpersonal attraction that people

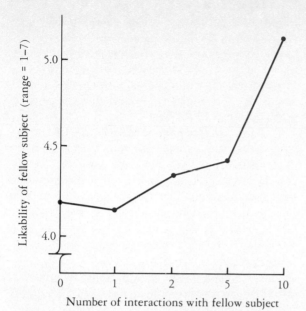

FIGURE 15.30   The rated likability of a fellow
subject as a function of number of interactions. (Based
on data from Saegert, S.C., Swap, W., and Zajonc,
R.B. *Journal of Personality and Social Psychology*, 1973,
25, 234–242.)

can feel. As Walster and Berscheid have put it,
"Passion sometimes develops in conditions that
would seem more likely to provoke aggression and
hatred" (1971, p. 47).

Dutton and Aron (1974) had an attractive young
woman interview male college students as they
walked across a suspension bridge spanning a gorge
280 feet deep. The bridge was 5 feet wide, 450
feet long, and had "a tendency to tilt, sway, and
wobble, creating the impression that one is about
to fall over the side" (p. 511). The same woman
interviewed control subjects on a more conventional, sturdy bridge spanning a 10-foot drop.

The men who were interviewed on the suspension bridge appeared to find the woman more attractive than did those who were interviewed on
the ordinary one. They were more likely to make
sexually related responses to a brief personality test.
Perhaps more significantly, they were much more
likely to telephone the woman later. The inter-
viewer gave her telephone number to all subjects
with the suggestion that they call her if they wanted
to discuss the experiment further.

The results suggest that the anxiety evoked by
standing on a precarious suspension bridge increased the men's sexual attraction toward the
woman. At first, this finding appears to be incompatible with the suggestion that interpersonal attraction stems from reinforcement. The subjects
met the woman in the context of aversive stimuli,
not reinforcing ones; therefore, she should subsequently have become an aversive stimulus herself
and elicited avoidance behaviors, not telephone calls.

Dutton and Aron explained their results in terms
of attribution theory: a man experiences increased
arousal in the presence of a woman; he attributes
it to the most significant stimulus—the woman—
and concludes that he is attracted to her. Later he
acts on this conclusion by telephoning her.

Several researchers acknowledge that adversity
and unpleasant arousal seem to increase interpersonal attraction between men and women. Rubin
(1973) notes couples of mixed religious background report stronger degrees of romantic love.
Presumably, the conflict that followed their choice
of each other (especially among other family members) provided arousal that strengthened their mu-
tual attraction. Similarly, an ancient Roman expert
advised men to take their women to the Colosseum
to see the gladiators fight, because the experience
would increase their amorousness. (See **Figure
15.31**.)

But Kenrick and Cialdini (1977) suggest that
misattributed arousal is not the best explanation
for this phenomenon. First, it is unlikely that a
person who is standing on a swaying suspension
bridge cannot identify the source of his or her arousal;
most people have more insight than that into the
source of their emotions. If the subjects correctly
attribute their arousal to the bridge, they will not
need to attribute it to the woman standing on it.
Furthermore, a person who is present in an aversive
situation does not necessarily become an aversive
stimulus by association; instead, he or she can become a conditioned reinforcer. Consider what happened to the subjects. They started walking across
a narrow, swaying bridge suspended above a deep
gorge and met a calm, attractive young woman
who stopped them and asked them to participate
in an experiment. They spent several minutes talking with her, then continued on their way. Probably this encounter reduced rather than increased

FIGURE 15.31   Humphrey Bogart and Lauren Bacall in "The Big Sleep." Adversity often increases romantic attraction, as many filmmakers have realized.

fear. The woman seemed calm and reassuring and accustomed to standing on the bridge; therefore, she served as an example to the students. Her presence may also have distracted them from the view of the rocks far below. Because the reduction of an aversive stimulus is a negative reinforcer, the men's increased attraction toward the woman can be accounted for in terms of reinforcement, not misattribution. The woman's presence became a conditioned reinforcer because it was associated with reduction of fear.

This conclusion is consistent with the results of many studies performed with other animals. For example, you will remember from Chapter 6 that infant monkeys cling to their mothers when they are frightened by novel stimuli. In addition, ethologists have noted that the presence of predators causes animals to congregate. Undoubtedly this tendency exists in humans too—when we are faced with danger or adversity we seek the company of other people.

A study by Dutton and Aron (1974) demonstrated that the presence of another person can reduce aversive arousal. They led a group of male subjects to expect to receive either a weak or a strong and painful electric shock, or no shock. During a delay period some subjects waited alone; others waited with a young woman. Presumably, the subjects who anticipated receiving a strong shock were unpleasantly aroused. As in the bridge experiment, subjects who were expecting a shock reported more attraction than did those who were not expecting shock. Dutton and Aron also asked the subjects to rate their level of anxiety. Those who waited with the young woman reported less anxiety than did control subjects who waited alone. Although the investigators explained the increased attraction in terms of attribution theory, the fact that the woman's presence decreased the subjects' arousal provides important support for the negative-reinforcement hypothesis.

The negative-reinforcement hypothesis can also explain Rubin's (1973) findings on couples of mixed religious background. The aversive feelings produced by family conflicts are decreased when the couples are together. Thus, the presence of the partner is reinforcing. (How many couples have reported that a crisis brought them closer together?)

Interim summary: Although the factors that influence interpersonal attraction are complex and are not yet fully understood, they all appear to involve social reinforcement (and, in the case of lovers, physical reinforcement). In turn, people learn to act in ways that reinforce the behavior of friends and lovers, to maintain and strengthen their ties with them. Attraction is increased by positive evaluation of oneself by the other person, by shared opinions, by physical good looks, and by familiarity. Furthermore, propinquity provides the opportunity to get to know, and like, other people.

Although attribution undoubtedly plays an important role in interpersonal attraction—for example, our beliefs about why other people act as they do certainly affects how much we like them—a careful analysis suggests that the reason that people's romantic bonds can be strengthened by adversity lies in the phenomenon of negative reinforcement. The presence of another person makes an unpleasant situation more tolerable, and this reduction of the strength of an aversive stimulus confers to the other person the status of a conditioned reinforcer.

GROUP PROCESSES

This section considers the interactions of people within groups, including the ways in which an audience affects a person's performance and how groups of people reach decisions. These activities qualify as *group processes.*

SOCIAL FACILITATION

◆ Triplett (1897) published the first experimental study on *social facilitation.* He had people perform a number of simple tasks, such as turning the handle of a fishing reel. He found that his subjects turned the crank faster and for a longer time if other people were present. Although many other studies found the same effect, some investigators reported just the opposite phenomenon—if the task was difficult and complex, the presence of an audience *impaired* the subjects' performance. You yourself have probably noticed that you have difficulty performing some tasks if someone is watching you.

Robert Zajonc (1965) has suggested an explanation both for the phenomenon of social facilitation and for the opposite effect. He claims that the presence of people who are watching a performer (or whom the performer *perceives* as watching) raises that person's arousal level. Presumably, the increase in arousal has the effect of increasing the probability of performing dominant responses. When the task is simple, the dominant response is generally the correct one, so an audience improves performance. When the task is complex, a person can

perform a number of different responses and must decide which one is appropriate. The presence of the audience makes the selection of the appropriate behavior more difficult, because the increased arousal tends to cause the person to perform the dominant response, which may not be the correct one. Suppose you are trying to assemble an intricate piece of machinery. A part is sticking. You want to bang on it, but you know that doing so will not help. You must be patient and gently manipulate it into place. Just then, a curious bystander approaches you and stands close to you, asking if he or she can watch. You say yes and turn back to the task. The part seems to be giving you even more trouble than before, and you suddenly start banging on it.

Subsequent experiments have supported Zajonc's explanation. Martens (1969) tested the prediction that the presence of a group increases a person's level of arousal. While subjects performed a complex motor task alone or in the presence of ten people, the experimenter determined physiological arousal by measuring the amount of sweat that was present on the subjects' palms. The presence of an audience produced a clear-cut effect: the subjects who performed in front of other people had sweatier palms.

An experiment by Zajonc and Sales (1966) showed that the presence of an audience can raise the probability of dominant responses. The experimenters read aloud a list of fictitious Turkish words and had subjects pronounce each of them from one to sixteen times. Then they asked the subjects to watch a screen, on which the words would be flashed too rapidly to be seen clearly, and to guess which word had been presented. In fact the experimenters flashed a meaningless jumble of shapes on the screen. Subjects who performed this part of the task alone guessed that they saw many of the words that they had heard. They were more likely to say the words that they had rehearsed more often, but they also chose a good number of the least-practiced ones. Other subjects performed in the presence of two people who had supposedly asked the experimenter whether they could watch the procedure. With this audience present, the subjects tended to stick with the words that they had practiced the most; it was as if their increased arousal caused them to make only the dominant responses. Perhaps they found

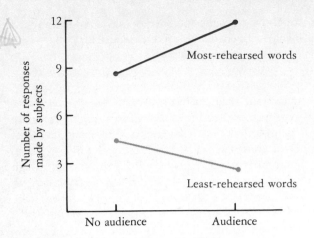

FIGURE 15.32   Number of responses of most-rehearsed and least-rehearsed words made by subject in the presence or absence of an audience. (Based on data from Zajonc, R.B., and Sales, S.M. *Journal of Experimental Social Psychology,* 1966, 2, 160–168.)

it harder to think of the words that they had not rehearsed often. (See **Figure 15.32.**)

Why does the presence of a group increase a person's arousal? One important factor seems to be whether subjects perceive the group as observing (and thus evaluating) their performance. Cottrell, Wack, Sekerak, and Rittle (1968) had their subjects perform a task like the one used by Zajonc and Sales. During the word-guessing phase, some subjects were tested alone; others were tested in the presence of two blindfolded or unblindfolded people. Only the subjects who were actually watched by other people showed the expected increase in dominant responses. The phenomenon of group facilitation thus appears to be closely related to a person's self-esteem.

SOCIAL LOAFING

Usually people try harder when a group of other people is watching, but under some conditions the presence of a group results in a decrease in effort, or *social loafing.* Thus, sometimes the whole is less than the sum of its individual parts. Many years ago Ringelmann (cited by Dashiell, 1935) measured the effort that people made when pulling a rope in a mock tug-of-war contest against a device that measured the exerted force. Presumably,

the force exerted by eight people pulling together in a simple task would be at least the sum of their individual efforts, or even somewhat greater than the sum, because of the phenomenon of social facilitation. However, Ringelmann found that the total force exerted was only about half what would be predicted by the simple combination of individual efforts. The subjects exerted less force when they worked in a group.

More recent studies have confirmed these results and extended them to other behaviors. For example, Latané, Williams, and Harkins (1979) asked subjects alone, in pairs, or in groups of six to shout as loudly as they could. The subjects wore earphones that played a loud noise so that they could not hear the shouting of the other subjects, and blindfolds, so that they could neither observe nor be observed by the other people in their group. When subjects shouted alone they made more noise than when they shouted in groups; their group effort was only 82 percent of their individual effort.

The variable of identifiability seems to determine whether the presence of a group will produce social facilitation or social loafing. In a follow-up study, Williams, Harkins, and Latané (1981) asked subjects to shout as loud as they could individually or in groups. Subjects who were told that the equipment could measure only the total group effort shouted less loudly than those who were told that the equipment could measure individual efforts. The latter shouted just as loudly in groups as they did alone. These results suggest that a person's efforts in a group activity depend largely on whether or not other people can observe his or her individual efforts. If they can, social facilitation is likely to occur; if they cannot, then social loafing is likely.

As Latané and his colleagues point out, social loafing has implications for group efforts outside the laboratory. First, social loafing is observed in tasks that require intellectual effort. For example, Petty, Harkins, and Williams (1980) found that subjects who participated in a group effort to evaluate a persuasive message worked less hard at the task than did subjects who had to perform their own evaluations. Consequently, the subjects who worked in a group were more susceptible to persuasion by a message with poor arguments than subjects who had prepared their own arguments.

Latané and his colleagues also point out the relevance of their studies to an observation made by Turner (1978). Apparently, it is difficult to achieve good quality control on the production line at pickle factories. Dill pickle halves must be stuffed into jars by hand, and only pickles of certain sizes will do; long ones will not fit and short ones will float around in the jar, looking "cheap and crummy." Because the conveyor belt moves inexorably, workers tend to fill the jars with whatever pickles are at hand; if they stop to look for pickles of the proper size, the jars pile up. Jars that are filled with the pickles of the wrong size must be culled by inspectors, adding considerably to production costs. But, because there is no way to tell which worker has filled which jar, there is little incentive for a worker to choose the pickles carefully.

The phenomenon of social loafing lends itself very nicely to a behavioral analysis in terms of reinforcement. When someone's own efforts can be measured by other people, that person is the potential recipient of social reinforcers such as approval or acknowledgment of a job well done. In other words, *contingencies of reinforcement* are present. When a person's efforts are submerged in that of a group, these contingencies cannot apply, and the quality of individual effort declines.

DECISION MAKING BY GROUPS

Common sense suggests that a group decision is likely to be cautious and conservative. If a group of people is able to reach agreement on an issue, that consensus must lie within the range of opinions held by all its members. Therefore, although some individuals may hold extreme opinions, a group decision is likely to be middle-of-the-road. (See **Figure 15.33**.)

Stoner (cited by Baron and Byrne, 1981) performed the first experimental study to cast doubt on this common belief. Stoner asked individuals and groups of people to decide on the appropriate course of action in a variety of situations. Each situation had a conservative and a risky alternative. For example, the subjects were asked to decide whether a fictitious individual should accept a secure but poorly paying job or a high-paying one with a newly formed company that might fold. The conservative decision would be to take the secure job.

FIGURE 15.33   This council of Bakhtiari tribesmen are deciding the fate of a man who stole an animal. Research indicates that group decisions like this are usually not the average of the individual opinions.

The group decisions tended to be *less* conservative than individual ones. When subjects met in a group and discussed the alternatives they were more likely to select the risky choices than when they made the decisions by themselves. This finding became the subject of controversy among social psychologists. A number of studies confirmed Stoner's results, such as Myers and Lamm (1976). But it also became apparent that group decisions were sometimes *more* conservative than decisions made by individuals. If the average opinion of the members of the group was slightly on the side of risk-taking, then discussion would result in a group decision that was even more risky. If the average opinion was slightly conservative, the discussion would produce an even more conservative decision. In other words, group discussion tended to polarize the average opinion—to produce a more extreme version of the views of individual members. (See **Figure 15.34**.)

A variety of experiments and field studies indicate that group polarization is a widespread phenomenon. If subjects pretend that they are serving on a jury, their original decisions tend to become more extreme after group discussion (Myers and Kaplan, 1976). Similarly, Lamm and Sauer (1974) found that group discussion leads to higher demands during collective bargaining. There appear to be two principal causes of group polarization: social comparison and the exchange of persuasive arguments.

Social Comparison

Few people like to regard themselves as average. We tend to compare our performance with that of others in the hope that we will come out better on at least some measures. For example, when subjects participate in psychological experiments the question they most often ask the experimenter when the study is over is "How well did I do, compared with the others?" Most business executives rate themselves as more ethical than average (Baumhart, 1968). Most people believe that they are less prejudiced than the norms for their community (Levitan, 1965). In addition, people generally have a high regard for those who hold a somewhat more

FIGURE 15.34 A schematic explanation of the principle of shift away from a neutral position.

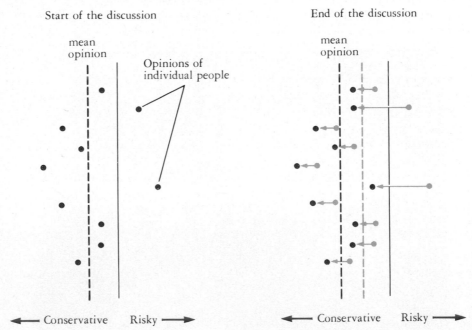

extreme position than they do. Eisinger and Mills (1968) found that people rated extremists on their own side of an issue as being more sincere and competent than moderates. The social desirability of being "better than average" appears to be well established.

Perhaps, as Brown (1974) suggests, this general tendency at least partly accounts for group polarization. Once a person learns what the average opinion of the group is, he or she adopts an even more extreme attitude, which is therefore "better" than the one held by the group as a whole. If a large number of the members of the group shift their attitude in this way, the result will be the observed group polarization effect.

There is some evidence to support this hypothesis. Baron and Roper (1976) used a perceptual phenomenon, the **autokinetic phenomenon,** to assess the effects of social comparison. When a person looks at a point of light in a dark room, the light appears to move slightly even though it remains still; hence the term *autokinetic* ("self-moving"). Some subjects were told that people who see especially large movements tend to be especially intelligent. The subjects viewed the light in groups, discussed the amount of apparent movement, and then came to a decision.

If the subjects believed that the size of the autokinetic phenomenon was related to intelligence, their group discussion resulted in polarization. That is, once an initial discussion showed what the average estimate of movement was for the group, members then started making estimates that were more extreme than the average. Presumably, they wanted to demonstrate to themselves (or to the others) that they were more intelligent than the group average. In contrast, if the subjects were not told that the size of the autokinetic phenomenon was related to intelligence, group polarization did not occur; the group decision was simply the average of the subjects' initial ratings.

Exchange of Persuasive Arguments

When a group of people discuss a situation, they explain the reasons for their positions—in other words, they present arguments in favor of their views. Because it is unlikely that any one member of the group has previously considered all the ar-

guments in favor of a given position, it is likely that the discussion provides the participants with even more arguments in support of the opinion that they hold. Therefore, the shift in opinion (which leads to group polarization) may be a result of this new information.

Experimental support for this suggestion comes from Ebbesen and Bowers (1974). Their subjects listened to tape recordings of contrived discussions in favor of risky and conservative decisions. The persuasive arguments expressed in these discussions ranged from 90 percent favoring the risky choice to 90 percent favoring the conservative choice. After listening to the recordings, the subjects were asked to give their own opinions. Figure 15.35 shows the results: the proportion of arguments in favor of the risky or conservative choice strongly influenced the subjects' decision. (See **Figure 15.35.**)

In general, the arguments expressed in a group discussion tend to be in favor of the average group bias (Vinokur and Burnstein, 1974). Perhaps peo-

FIGURE 15.35   Mean shift in subjects' recommendations as a function of the proportion of group arguments that favored taking a risk. (From Baron, R.A., and Byrne, D. *Social Psychology: Understanding Human Interaction,* 2nd ed. Boston: Allyn and Bacon, 1977; after Ebbesen and Bowers, 1974.)

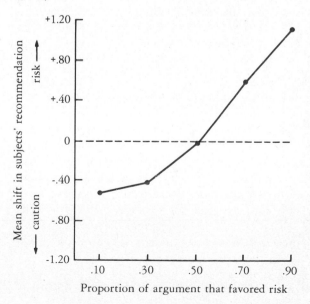

Proportion of argument that favored risk

ple are simply reluctant to present arguments that the group as a whole might regard unfavorably. Group polarization may result at least partly from this one-sided exposure.

Interim summary: When they are part of a group, or observed by others, people act differently than when alone. In general, the presence of observers increases the likelihood that the performer will make the dominant response; depending on the complexity of the task, this effect can either facilitate or inhibit performance. When performing as part of a group, a person's efforts will usually be less vigorous if his or her individual contribution cannot be measured. This phenomenon is called social loafing.

Contrary to popular belief, decisions made by groups are often less conservative than the average opinion of the individual members before the discussion begins. Two phenomena appear to account for this polarization of opinion: social comparison and exchange of persuasive arguments. Most people prefer to regard themselves as above average, so many adopt a somewhat more extreme opinion after they learn what the general opinion of the group is. In addition, in group discussions people tend not to express arguments contrary to what the group as a whole favors, which means that most of the arguments will be on one side of the issue. In all of these group-related phenomena we see the importance of self-esteem, which is obviously related to social reinforcement.

CONCLUDING REMARKS

The discussion of some of the aspects of social behavior in this chapter may simply have confirmed conclusions that you had already made on the basis of your own experience. You are already an expert on social behavior. Because each of us uses attribution to construct his or her own theory of social behavior, we must understand the working of this process before we can understand how people affect each other.

The investigation of the ways in which people try to understand the causes of each other's behav-

ior is rather recent, but it has had considerable influence on a variety of research topics in social psychology. For example, we now know that our attitudes are influenced by the inferences we make about the persuader's motives. We observe our own behavior in ways that resemble our obsevations of others and make similar causal attributions about ourselves. Causal attribution also affects interpersonal relations; we come to know about others through observing their behavior.

In many experiments investigating the causes of social behavior, social psychologists have used techniques to deceive their subjects. For example, many studies have used confederates who acted as if they were fellow subjects. The reason for this deception is obvious: to reveal the variables that affect people's behavior in real life, the situations created by the experimenters must appear to be realistic. At the same time, to assess the effects of social interactions, investigators must control those interactions. Therefore, someone must act out a part in a little drama so that the subject's responses can be measured. Whenever a psychological experiment involves deception of subjects, an independent committee carefully scrutinizes the procedure to be sure that the subjects will not undergo unnecessary embarrassment or stress. All subjects are told about the deception after participating in the experiment.

GUIDE TO TERMS INTRODUCED IN THIS CHAPTER

attribution　p. 565　Figures 15.1–15.3, 15.5
autokinetic phenomenon　p. 607
cognitive dissonance　p. 583　Figures 15.15, 15.16
compliance　p. 590
conformity　p. 590
consensus　p. 567　Figure 15.3
consistency　p. 568
covariance method　p. 566
discounting　p. 567
dispositional factor　p. 566
dissonance reduction　p. 583

SUGGESTIONS FOR FURTHER READING

Perspectives on Attributional Processes by J.H. Harvey and G. Weary (Dubuque, Iowa: W.C. Brown, 1981) discusses modern research on attribution. D.J. Schneider, A.H. Hastorf, and P.C. Ellsworth describe how we form impressions about other people in *Person Perception* (2nd ed.; Reading, Mass.: Addison-Wesley, 1979). R.E. Petty and J.T. Cacioppo's *Attitudes and Persuasion: Classic and Contemporary Approaches* (Dubuque, Iowa: W.C. Brown, 1981) discusses these topics in depth.

Other books about specific topics in social psychology include *Residential Crowding and Design,* edited by J.R. Aiello and A. Braum (New York: Plenum, 1979), and *Victims of Groupthink: A Psychological Study of Foreign-Policy Decisions and Fiascoes* by I.L. Janis (Boston, Mass.: Houghton Mifflin, 1973).

PERSONALITY

W E ALL realize that people are unique individuals. No two people are precisely the same in appearance and style of behavior. However, we learn to recognize particular patterns of behavior and to describe them as, say, serious, frivolous, lazy, diligent, honest, sly, mean, or friendly. Soon after we meet someone we begin to form opinions about his or her patterns of behavior. For example, if we see someone abuse his subordinates we will probably label him as autocratic. We will probably also use this label to make predictions about his behavior in other contexts; we will expect that he is also domineering with his wife and children.

Our tendency to assume that people's personality traits are stable—that the same kinds of behavior will occur in a wide variety of situations—is simply another form of the fundamental attributional error, discussed in the previous chapter. That is, we tend to perceive other people's behavior as being caused by internal, dispositional factors but to perceive our own behavior as determined by our particular situation. Thus, we are more willing to attribute personality traits to other people than to ourselves. Identifying stable personality traits in other people provides us with information that we use to function effectively in society. If we see an acquaintance steal an item from a store we will probably label him as dishonest and will not trust him in a business dealing. Similarly, if we see a teenage girl walk out of a tavern drunk, we will probably label her as irresponsible and will not hire her as a babysitter.

Like everyone else, psychologists are interested in predicting behavior. They attempt to determine what behavioral traits people possess and to assess the value of these traits in predicting people's behavior in various situations. But psychologists are also interested in understanding *why* people differ from each other. Describing a personality trait and explaining it are two different matters. Many of us tend to "explain" behavior simply by naming it. You may recall this phenomenon, called the *nominal fallacy,* from Chapter 2. Suppose you go to a party with a friend and notice a man who is acting nasty and belligerent. You ask your friend, who seems to know him, what is wrong with him. She says, "That's George. He always gets mean when he gets drunk." "Oh," you say, "that explains it." But psychologists are not satisfied with "explanations" like these. Giving the phenomenon a label (George is a "mean drunk") may have some value in predicting George's behavior, but this description does not explain it: you do not know why he drinks or what alcohol does to change his behavior.

However, identification is the first step to explanation. We must classify phenomena before we can explain them. Thus, research on human personality requires two kinds of efforts: identifying personality traits and determining the variables that produce and control them.

Psychologists disagree about many aspects of human personality, including which factors (biological and environmental) are responsible for various personality traits, which is the best way to classify individual differences, and even whether stable differences in personality exist. However, almost all attempts to identify personality traits are based in some way on theories about the causes of human behavior. This chapter discusses research on identifying and classifying human personality traits, the validity and implications of various classification schemes, and the methods of personality assessment used to determine whether a classification scheme is valid. It also discusses three major theories that attempt to explain the factors that shape human personality: the psychodynamic approach, the behavioristic approach, and the humanistic approach.

PERSONALITY TRAITS

TYPES AND TRAITS

◆ It has long been apparent that people differ in temperament, or personality characteristics. The earliest known explanation for these individual differences is the humoral theory, proposed by Galen in the second century and based on then common medical beliefs. The body was thought to contain four humors, or fluids: yellow bile (*kholē*), black bile (*melankholē*), phlegm (*phlegma*), and blood (*sanguis*). People were classified according to the disposition supposedly produced by the predominance of one of these humors in their system. *Choleric* people, who had an excess of yellow bile, were bad-tempered and irritable. (An intestinal upset, which at the time was attributed to biliousness, would make anyone irritable.) *Melancholic* people, with an excess of black bile, had a gloomy and pessimistic temperament. *Phlegmatic* people, whose bodies contained an excessive amount of phlegm, were sluggish, calm, and unexcitable, presumably because phlegm is viscous and slow moving. *Sanguine* people had a preponderance of blood, which made them cheerful and passionate. Their ruddy appearance indicated that they were energetic and "hot-blooded." (See **Figure 16.1**.)

Although later biological investigations discredited this theory, the notion that people could be divided into different *personality types* persisted long afterward. Theories of personality type attempt to assign people to different categories, which vary in accordance with the theory. For example, Freud's theory, which maintains that people go through different stages of psychosexual development, predicts the existence of different types of people who have problems associated with these stages. Another theory, devised by Hans Eysenck, an English psychologist, involves the personality types of *extraversion* and *introversion* (literally,

FIGURE 16.1 The effects of the four humors, according to a medieval artist. From left to right: choleric, melancholic, phlegmatic, and sanguine.

"turning outward" and "turning inward"). Here are his definitions:

> The typical introvert is a quiet, retiring sort of person, introspective, fond of books rather than people; he is reserved and distant except to intimate friends. He tends to plan ahead, "looks before he leaps," and mistrusts the impulse of the moment. He does not like excitement, takes matters of everyday life with proper seriousness, and likes a well-ordered mode of life. He keeps his feelings under close control, seldom behaves in an aggressive manner, and does not lose his temper easily. He is reliable, somewhat pessimistic, and places great value on ethical standards.
>
> The typical extravert is sociable, likes parties, has many friends, needs to have people to talk to, and does not like reading or studying by himself. He craves excitement, takes chances, often sticks his neck out, acts on the spur of the moment, and is generally an impulsive individual. He is fond of practical jokes, always has a ready answer, and generally likes change; he is carefree, easygoing, optimistic, and "likes to laugh and be merry." He prefers to keep moving and doing things, tends to be aggressive and loses his temper quickly; altogether his feelings are not kept under tight control, and he is not always a reliable person. (Eysenck and Rachman, 1965, p. 19)

Personality types are very useful in formulating hypotheses, because when a theorist is thinking about personality variables it is easiest to think of extreme cases—prototypes, so to speak. Of course, the personality types outlined in some theories have no validity. After identifying and defining personality types, it is essential to determine whether these types actually exist, and whether knowing a person's personality type leads to valid predictions about his or her behavior in a variety of situations. More important, however, most modern investigators reject the notion that individuals can be assigned to discrete categories; instead, they generally conceive of individual differences as quantitative rather than qualitative. That is, if Eysenck's definitions of introversion and extraversion are valid, people differ from each other in degree on this dimension: one person is more introverted than another, but less introverted than a third. Instead of classifying people by categories, or types, most investigators prefer to measure the degree to which an individual expresses a particular *personality trait*. (See **Figure 16.2**.)

A simple example illustrates the difference between types and traits. We could classify people

FIGURE 16.2   These girls appear to differ in their degree of extraversion.

into two different types, tall people and short people. Indeed, we use these terms in everyday speech. But we all recognize that height is best conceived of as a *trait*, as a dimension on which people can differ. We can easily observe that people differ in height in a *continuous* rather than a *dichotomous* manner. If we measure the height of a large sample of people we will find instances all along the distribution, from very short to very tall. (See **Figure 16.3**.)

Other individual differences are dichotomous. If we classify people according to gender we will find that two categories are sufficient (excluding a very small proportion of people with genetic or developmental anomalies). (See **Figure 16.4**.)

So far, all behavioral traits that can be measured with any degree of accuracy seem to be distributed along a curve, as shown in Figure 16.3. Thus, to most investigators, the term *personality type* simply refers to the extremes of a continuous distribution. An "extravert," like a "tall" person, does not belong to a discrete category; rather, he or she scores high on the dimension of introversion–extraversion. (See **Figure 16.5**.) Similarly, although gender is distributed in a dichotomous fashion, measurements of "masculinity" or "femininity" (tendencies to behave according to male or female stereotypes) are distributed continuously in the population. Masculinity–femininity can be conceived of as a bipolar scale, with individuals differing from one another in degree. We might expect the distribution to look something like the curve shown in Figure 16.6; males and females tend to be clustered toward opposite ends of the scale, but there is considerable overlap. (See **Figure 16.6**.) Any scale of masculinity–femininity will be culturally dependent; just as different theories predict different personality traits, different societies regard different behaviors as "masculine" and "feminine."

FIGURE 16.3 The distribution of height is continuous, not dichotomous.

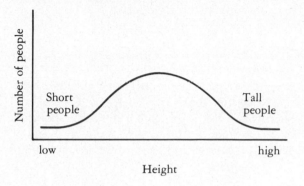

FIGURE 16.4 The distribution of gender is dichotomous.

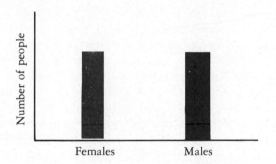

FIGURE 16.5 "Introverts" and "extraverts" represent two ends of a continuous distribution.

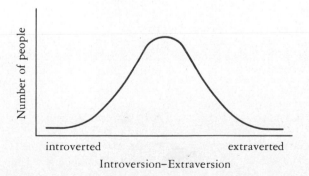

FIGURE 16.6 The distribution of gender-related behavior is continuous and bimodal.

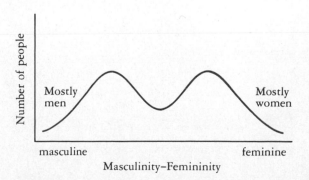

IDENTIFICATION OF PERSONALITY TRAITS

For centuries, people have assessed personality traits on a rather casual, informal basis. However, psychological research on personality requires more careful measurement. The first task is to identify and define personality traits. In most cases, the prediction comes from a theory of personality. The second step is to develop a measurement device. The third and final step is to assess the validity of the measurement device. This last task is complex and time consuming.

The general approaches to the identification of personality traits begin with theories of personality that predict specific differences among people's behavior. For example, Freud's psychodynamic theory of personality (discussed in detail later) predicts that people may become fixated in various stages of psychosexual development. Another theory, by William Sheldon (Sheldon and Stevens, 1942), predicts that people with different physiques will exhibit different temperaments. Once the predictions have been made, tests are developed to measure these traits. A large sample of people take the tests, and experiments are performed to determine whether the tests make it possible to predict their behavior in various situations. If the tests prove valid as a means of predicting behavior, the theory gains support.

Factor analysis, described in more detail in Chapter 13, is another means of identifying personality traits. This method entails making a large variety of observations of the behavior of a large number of people. Usually the observations are limited to responses to a number of questions on a paper-and-pencil test. Mathematical procedures permit the investigator to determine which items tend to be answered in the same way by a given person, and hence to infer the existence of common factors. Suppose we have a four-item test with the following questions:

1. I attend parties as frequently as I can.
2. I often get bored when I am alone.
3. I worry about my health a lot.
4. I often get an upset stomach.

If we give this test to a group of people and calculate the correlations between individual items, we might obtain the results shown in Table 16.1.

The results show that questions 1 and 2 and questions 3 and 4 correlate well with each other, but that 1 and 2 correlate poorly with 3 and 4. Thus, if a person said "yes" to question 1, he or she also tended to say "yes" to question 2; similarly, a "yes" to question 3 was associated with a "yes" to question 4. However, a person's answer to questions 1 and 2 did not predict how he or she would answer 3 and 4. Clearly, the test measures two factors. One factor is related to a person's interest in socializing with other people, and the other is related to excessive concern with health.

In practice, psychologists ask people hundreds of questions and identify the factors mathematically, not by inspection. Also, the factors are not so obvious as the ones derived from this simple test. It would be easy to think of names for the two factors involved above, but it is often difficult to name the factors obtained through a factor anal-

TABLE 16.1   Hypothetical intercorrelations on a four-item personality test

ITEM	CORRELATION			
	1	2	3	4
1. I attend parties as frequently as I can.	—	.88	.32	.21
2. I often get bored when I am alone.	.88	—	.19	.24
3. I worry about my health a lot.	.32	.19	—	.69
4. I often get an upset stomach.	.21	.24	.69	—

TABLE 16.2   Cattell's sixteen personality factors, obtained by factor analysis

Factor	Description of high score	Description of low score
A	Outgoing, participating	Reserved, detached
B	Intelligent, abstract thinking	Less intelligent, concrete thinking
C	Emotionally stable, calm	Emotionally less stable, easily upset
E	Assertive, stubborn	Humble, conforming
F	Sober, serious	Happy-go-lucky, enthusiastic
G	Conscientious, rule-bound	Evades rules, feels few obligations
H	Venturesome, uninhibited	Shy, restrained, timid
I	Tender-minded, sensitive	Tough-minded, realistic
L	Suspicious, hard to fool	Trusting, free of jealousy
M	Imaginative, careless of practical matters	Practical, regulated by external realities
N	Shrewd, calculating	Forthright, natural
O	Apprehensive, troubled	Self-assured, confident
Q_1	Experimenting, liberal, free-thinking	Conservative, respecting established ideas
Q_2	Self-sufficient, resourceful	Group-dependent, "joiner"
Q_3	Controlled, follows self-image	Undisciplined self-conflict, follows own urges
Q_4	Tense, frustrated, driven	Relaxed, tranquil, unfrustrated

Based on Cattell, R B , and Stice, G.F. *Handbook for the Sixteen Personality Factor Questionnaire.* Champaign, Ill.: Institute for Personality and Ability Testing, 1962.

ysis. Cattell (1946) has used the factor-analytic method to identify sixteen personality factors. **Table 16.2** lists them in order of importance.

You will recall from Chapter 13 that the factor-analytic method has a very important drawback: the conclusions can never be better than the questions that are asked of the subjects. For example, the simple four-item test presented above misses much that is important in distinguishing the temperament of one person from another; there are no questions about a person's tendency to conform, religiousness, tolerance of other people's mistakes, or any of a wide variety of possible characteristics. Thus, it would make a very poor test of personality. If a test does not contain questions related to some important traits, those traits will never emerge as factors in the analysis. Therefore, the construction of test items must be guided by at least a vague theoretical notion of what is important in human personality, so that significant traits

will not be missed. Even the factor-analytic method requires theorizing by the investigator.

MEASUREMENT OF PERSONALITY TRAITS

After identifying personality traits, an investigator must devise a way to measure them. The two general approaches to this task are the rational strategy and the empirical strategy.

The Rational Strategy

The *rational strategy* of measurement requires a theoretical definition of a trait. From this definition the investigator makes predictions about the behavior of people who differ with respect to the trait. For example, to develop a test of extraversion–introversion, an investigator would list a number of ways in which the behavior of people at the extremes of the dimension would be expected to differ, and then write items that were relevant to these differences. Extraverts would be expected to answer "yes" to "I attend parties as frequently as I can" but "no" to "I like to take long walks by myself." The test would consist of a number of items like these. A person's score would be the total number of "extraverted" responses.

The success of this strategy depends on two important factors. First, the theory must be correct, at least with respect to the trait that is being assessed. Second, there must be a good correspondence between a person's response and his or her behavior in the situations depicted in a particular question. If a person affirms that he or she likes to take long walks alone but in fact never does so, then the question is not measuring what the test constructor thinks it is.

The Empirical Strategy

The second way to devise a test that measures a personality trait is the **empirical strategy**. An investigator who uses this method does not care whether a person's answer bears any relation to reality. For example, it would not matter whether a person takes long walks alone; it would matter only that a person tends to *answer the question* in a particular way, and that the answer correlates with other measures of the trait in question. To devise a test of extraversion–introversion by empirical means, a psychologist would write a test with a large number of questions, much as the investigator using the factor-analytic method would. After administering the test to a group of people containing a large number of introverts and extraverts (the **criterion group**), the investigator would perform a statistical analysis of their answers, retaining those questions that were answered differently by the extraverts and introverts and discarding all the others. The investigator would then devise a new test, using only the good questions, and administer it to a new group of introverts and extraverts. The decision to retain a particular item would be completely empirical. For example, if extraverts, but not introverts, answered "yes" to the item "I prefer oak trees to maples," the question would be used again. It would not matter that there was no logical relation between the item and the trait being assessed.

The empirical method can be used only when

the investigator already knows how to identify the traits to be measured. There must be some way to measure the *criterion*—in this case, extraversion–introversion. Investigators generally use the empirical strategy of test construction when the usual way to measure a personality trait is difficult and expensive—for example, if the measurement requires hours of individual testing by a specially trained person. If a simple paper-and-pencil test can be devised that classifies people in the same way as the rational method, an obvious savings can be accomplished.

Construct Validation

In practice, the rational and empirical strategies must be used together. The products of empirical strategies must be consistent with theories based on experimental data. The convergence of these two methods—the process by which tests validate theories and theories validate tests—is known as **construct validity**. For example, suppose a psychologist develops a theory that predicts that extraverts and introverts should act in particular ways in a particular situation. She administers a test of extraversion–introversion to a number of people and selects a sample of high scorers and low scorers. She enlists these people as subjects for an experiment in which they are placed in the relevant situation. She observes that extraverts and introverts act as she predicted in that situation. This finding supplies some evidence that her theory is correct and that the test actually measures what it is supposed to. (However, it does not *prove* that the theory and test are accurate.)

Suppose the psychologist did not obtain the results that she expected. She found that extraverts and introverts did not differ in their behavior in the experimental situation. There are three possible reasons for this outcome: (1) extraversion–introversion is not a stable personality trait, (2) the test does not actually measure extraversion–introversion, or (3) the psychologist's theory about the behavior of extraverts and introverts is incorrect. Only analysis of the data and subsequent research can determine which of the alternatives is correct.

As you can see, the process of construct validity is not so much a specific method as a description of what happens in the scientific community. Psychologists who are engaged in personality research use personality tests to validate their theories, and in so doing, validate the tests they use. The process is a slow one that operates step by step; no single experiment proves the validity of test or theory.

OBJECTIVE TESTS OF PERSONALITY

Many kinds of tests have been devised to measure personality traits. The two major types are objective tests and projective tests. The responses that subjects can make on *objective tests* are severely constrained by the test designer; the questions asked are unambiguous, and explicit rules for scoring the subjects' responses can be specified in advance. Responses are usually restricted to agreement or disagreement with a statement (yes/no or true/false) or to selection from a set of alternatives (multiple choice).

One of the oldest, most widely used objective tests of personality is the ***Minnesota Multiphasic Personality Inventory (MMPI),*** devised by Hathaway and McKinley in 1939. (See **Figure 16.7.**) Their original purpose in developing the test was to produce an objective, reliable method for diagnosing various personality traits that were related to a person's mental health. This test would be valuable in assessing people for a variety of purposes. It would provide a specific means of determining how effective psychotherapy was; improvement in people's scores over the course of treatment would indicate that the treatment was successful.

Hathaway and McKinley used the empirical strategy to devise their test. They wrote 504 true/false items and administered the test to several groups of people in mental institutions in Minnesota who had received diagnoses of specific disorders. These diagnoses had been obtained by psychiatric interviews with the patients. Such interviews are ex-

FIGURE 16.7   The MMPI.

pensive, so a simple paper-and-pencil test that accomplished the same result would be quite valuable. The control group consisted of relatives and friends of the patients, who were tested when they came to visit them. (It is questionable whether these people constituted the best possible group of normal subjects.) The responses were analyzed empirically, and the questions that correlated with various diagnostic labels were included in various scales. For example, if people who had been diagnosed as paranoid tended to say "true" to "I believe I am being plotted against" this question would become part of the paranoia scale.

The current revised version of the MMPI includes over 500 questions, grouped into ten clinical scales and four validity scales. (See **Table 16.3.**) A particular item can be used on more than one scale. For example, both people who are depressed and those who are excessively concerned with the state of their health tend to agree that they have gastrointestinal problems. The clinical scales include a number of diagnostic terms traditionally used to label psychiatric patients, such as hypochondriasis, depression, or paranoia.

The validity scales were devised to provide the tester with some assurance that the subjects are answering questions reliably and accurately, and that they can read the questions and pay attention to them. The *? scale* (cannot say) is simply the number of questions not answered. A high score on this scale indicates either that the person finds some questions irrelevant or that the person is evading issues that he or she finds painful.

The **L scale** (lie) contains questions such as "I do not read every editorial in the newspaper every day" and "My table manners are not quite as good at home as when I am out in company." A person who disagrees with questions like these is almost

---

TABLE 16.3   Scales of the MMPI

Scales	Criteria
Validity scales	
? (Cannot say)	Number of items left unanswered
L (Lie)	15 items of overly good self-report, such as "I smile at everyone I meet" (answered true)
F (Frequency)	64 items answered in the scored direction by 10 percent or less of normals, such as "There is an international plot against me" (answered true)
K (Correction)	30 items reflecting defensiveness in admitting to problems, such as "I feel bad when others criticize me" (answered false)
Clinical scales	
Hs (Hypochondriasis)	33 items derived from patients showing abnormal concern with bodily functions, such as "I have chest pains several times a week" (answered true)
D (Depression)	60 items derived from patients showing extreme pessimism, feelings of hopelessness, and slowing of thought and action, such as "I usually feel that life is interesting and worthwhile" (answered false)
Hy (Conversion hysteria)	60 items from neurotic patients using physical or mental symptoms as a way of unconsciously avoiding difficult conflicts and responsibilities, such as "My heart frequently pounds so hard I can feel it" (answered true)
Pd (Psychopathic deviate)	50 items from patients showing a repeated and flagrant disregard for social customs, emotional shallowness, and inability to learn from punishing experiences, such as "My activities and interests are often criticized by others" (answered true)

certainly not telling the truth. A high score on the L scale suggests the need for caution in interpreting other scales and also reveals something about the subject's personality. In particular, people who score high on this scale tend to be rather naive; more sophisticated people realize that no one is perfect and do not try to make themselves appear to be so.

The **F scale** (frequency) consists of items that are answered one way by at least 90 percent of the normal population. A high score on this scale indicates carelessness, poor reading ability, or very unusual personality traits. The usual responses are "false" to items such as "I can easily make other people afraid of me, and sometimes do for the fun of it" and "true" to items such as "I am liked by most people who know me."

The **K scale** (defensiveness) was devised to identify people who are trying to cover up their feelings to guard against internal conflicts that might cause them emotional distress. A person receives a high value on the K scale by answering "false" to questions such as "Criticism or scolding hurts me terribly" and "At periods my mind seems to work more slowly than usual." People who score very *low* on this scale tend to be in need of help or to be unusually immune to criticism and social influences.

Because the MMPI was devised by empirical means, the scales that are based on diagnostic categories can be only as valid as the original classification of the patients. Despite this potential drawback, the MMPI has proved to be very useful in clinical diagnosis. Research has shown that various patterns of responding on more than one scale are correlated with a variety of psychological problems. For example, it is said that a person who suffers great emotional discomfort, against which

TABLE 16.3 Scales of MMPI (*continued*)

Scales	Criteria
Clinical scales (cont.)	
Mf (Masculinity–femininity)	60 items from patients showing homoeroticism and items differentiating between men and women, such as "I like to arrange flowers" (answered true, scored for femininity)
Pa (Paranoia)	40 items from patients showing abnormal suspiciousness and delusions of grandeur or persecution, such as "There are evil people trying to influence my mind" (answered true)
Pt (Psychasthenia)	48 items from neurotic patients showing obsessions, compulsions, abnormal fears, and guilt and indecisiveness, such as "I save nearly everything I buy, even after I have no use for it" (answered true)
Sc (Schizophrenia)	78 items from patients showing bizarre or unusual thoughts or behavior, frequent withdrawals and delusions and hallucinations, such as "Things around me do not seem real" (answered true) and "It makes me uncomfortable to have people close to me" (answered true)
Ma (Hypomania)	46 items from patients showing emotional excitement, overactivity, and flight of ideas, such as "At times I feel very 'high' or very 'low' for no apparent reason" (answered true)
Si (Social introversion)	70 items from persons showing shyness, little interest in people, and insecurity, such as "I have the time of my life at parties" (answered false)

Adapted from Aiken, L.R. *Psychological Testing and Assessment,* 4th ed. Boston: Allyn and Bacon, 1982. Copyright 1943, renewed 1970 by the University of Minnesota. Published by the Psychological Corporation, New York, N.Y. All rights reserved.

he or she has few defenses, will probably score high on the Pt scale (psychasthenia) and low on the K scale (defensiveness). In contrast, a person who engages in antisocial behavior and harms other people tends to score high on both the Pt scale and the Ma scale (hypomania). Thus, the uses of the MMPI have been extended beyond its authors' original intentions.

As well as being used in clinical assessment, the MMPI has also been used extensively in personality research, and a number of other tests, including the *California Psychological Inventory* and the *Taylor Manifest Anxiety Scale,* have been based on it.

PROJECTIVE TESTS OF PERSONALITY

◈ **Projective tests** of personality are quite different in form from objective ones. They are designed to be ambiguous, so that the person's answer will reveal more about him or her than will agreement or disagreement with a statement provided by the test constructor. The assumption is that the subject will "project" his or her personality into the ambiguous situation and thus make responses that give clues to this personality. In addition, the ambiguity of the test makes it unlikely that subjects will have preconceived notions about which answers are socially desirable. Thus it will be difficult for a subject to give biased answers in an attempt to look better (or worse) than he or she actually is.

The Rorschach Inkblot Test

One of the oldest projective tests of personality is the **Rorschach Inkblot Test,** published in 1921 by Hermann Rorschach, a Swiss psychiatrist. The test consists of ten pictures of inkblots, originally made by spilling ink on a piece of paper that was subsequently folded in half, producing an image symmetrical around the line of the fold. Five of the inkblots are black-and-white and five are in color. (See **Figure 16.8.**) The subject is shown each card and asked to describe what it looks like. Then the cards are shown again, and the subject is asked to point out the features that he or she used to determine what was seen. The responses, and the nature of the features that the subject uses to make them, are scored on a number of dimensions.

In the following example described by Pervin

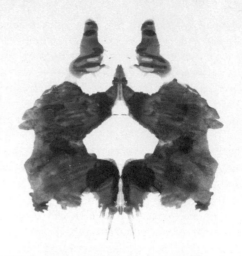

FIGURE 16.8   An item from the Rorschach test. The card is printed in black with patches of red. (From Rorschach, H. *Psychodiagnostics*. Bern, Switzerland: Hans Huber, 1921, 1948.)

(1975), a person's response to the inkblot shown in Figure 16.8 might be: "Two bears with their paws touching one another playing pattycake or could be they are fighting and the red is the blood from the fighting."

The scoring of this response, also described by Pervin, would be as follows: *large detail* of the blot was used, *good form* was used, *movement* was noted, *color* was used in the response about blood, an *animal* was seen, and a *popular response* (two bears) was made. A possible interpretation of the response might be:

> Subject starts off with popular response and animals expressing playful, "childish" behavior. Response is then given in terms of hostile act with accompanying inquiry. Pure color response and blood content suggest he may have difficulty controlling his response to the environment. Is a playful, childlike exterior used by him to disguise hostile, destructive feelings that threaten to break out in his dealings with the environment? (Pervin, 1975, p. 37)

Although traditionally the interpretation of people's responses to the Rorschach test was based on psychoanalytic theory, many investigators have used it in an empirical fashion. That is, a variety of different scoring methods have been devised, and the scores obtained by these methods have been correlated with clinical diagnoses, just as investigators have done with people's scores on the MMPI. The style and content of the responses are not interpreted in terms of a theory (as Rorschach did) but are simply correlated with other measures of personality.

The Thematic Apperception Test

Another popular projective technique, the *Thematic Apperception Test (TAT),* was developed by the American psychologists Henry Murray and C.D. Morgan to measure various psychological *needs.* People are shown a picture of a very ambiguous situation, such as the one in **Figure 16.9,** and are asked to tell a complete story about what is happening in the picture, explaining the situation, what led up to it, what the characters are thinking and saying, and what the final outcome will be. Presumably, the subjects will "project" themselves into the scene, and their story will reflect their own needs. As you might imagine, scoring is difficult and requires a great deal of practice and skill. The tester attempts to infer the psychological needs expressed in the stories.

Phares (1979) has presented six responses of one woman to TAT cards and a clinician's interpretation of these responses. The questions asked by the examiner are in parentheses.

FIGURE 16.9 An item from the Thematic Apperception Test. (From Murray, H.A. *Thematic Apperception Test.* Cambridge, Mass.: Harvard University Press. Copyright 1943 by the President and Fellows of Harvard College, copyright 1971 by H.A. Murray.)

Card 3BM. Looks like a little boy crying for something he can't have. (Why is he crying?) Probably because he can't go somewhere. (How will it turn out?) Probably sit there and sob hisself to sleep.

Card 3GF. Looks like her boyfriend might have let her down. She hurt his feelings. He's closed the door on her. (What did he say?) I don't know.

Card 9GF. Girl looks like somebody's run off and left her. She's ready for a dance. Maid's watching to see where she goes. (Why run off?) Probably because she wasn't ready in time.

Card 10. Looks like there's sorrow here. Grieving about something. (About what?) Looks like maybe one of the children's passed away.

Card 13MF. Looks like his wife might have passed away; he feels there's nothing more to do.

Card 20. Looks like a man that's ready to rob something. Hiding behind a high fence of some kind. Has his hand in his pocket with a gun ready to shoot if anybody comes out.

(Interpretation)   The TAT produced responses that were uniformly indicative of unhappiness, threat, misfortune, a lack of control over environmental forces. None of the test responses were indicative of satisfaction, happy endings, etc. . . . In summary, the test results point to an individual who is anxious and, at the same time, depressed. Feelings of insecurity, inadequacy, and lack of control over environmental forces are apparent, as are unhappiness and apprehension. These factors result in a constriction of performance that is largely oriented toward avoiding threat and that hampers sufficient mobilization of energy to perform at an optimal level. (Phares, 1979, p. 273)

The pattern of responses in this case is quite consistent; few people would disagree with the conclusion that the woman is sad and depressed. However, not all people provide such clear-cut responses. As you might expect, it is much more difficult to interpret differences in the stories of people who are relatively well adjusted. As a result, it is difficult to distinguish between people with different, but normal, personality traits.

◆   Just as the Rorschach test has provided raw material for empirically determined scales, the TAT has been used to provide responses for a variety of personality tests. For example, David McClelland and John Atkinson devised a scoring system to measure a person's **need to achieve,** or to perform successfully at a variety of tasks. Subjects' stories are examined for a number of characteristics that are related to the need to achieve, such as a stated need for achievement, the anticipation that some goal will be fulfilled, working to surmount an obstacle, or the existence of a character who encourages the protagonist to try hard to succeed.

Various studies by McClelland and his colleagues validated the measurement of the need to achieve. Atkinson and McClelland (1948) used the test to determine whether an easily manipulated biological need would be expressed in the stories constructed by subjects. Groups of subjects were requested not to eat for one, four, or sixteen hours, so that their need for food (hunger) would vary. The subjects were given the Thematic Apperception Test and their stories examined for food-related content. The hungrier the subjects were, the more their stories dealt with obtaining food. Thus the test gives evidence of a biological need.

To see whether the TAT also indicates the presence of a psychological need, McClelland, Atkinson, Clark, and Lowell (1953) attempted to manipulate the need to achieve in various groups of subjects and to determine whether these manipulations resulted in different achievement scores on the Thematic Apperception Test. All subjects were first given a paper-and-pencil test, but different groups received different instructions about the test. The *achievement-oriented group* was told that the task was a test of ability used by the U.S. government to select people for positions of leadership. The test was conducted formally, and subjects were required to put their names on the paper. No information was given to the subjects about their scores on the test. The *success group* and the *failure group* were treated the same way, except that the subjects were told that they had done very well or very poorly on the test. Subjects in the *relaxed group* took the test in informal conditions under the supervision of a graduate student who said he was trying to standardize a test he was developing. The subjects were told not to put their names on the papers.

After taking the test (and, in the case of the success and failure groups, receiving information about how well they supposedly did), subjects were given the Thematic Apperception Test, which was scored for the need to achieve. The results are shown in **Figure 16.10**. The subjects in the relaxed group, who had not been told they were taking an aptitude test, had the lowest scores. The experience of

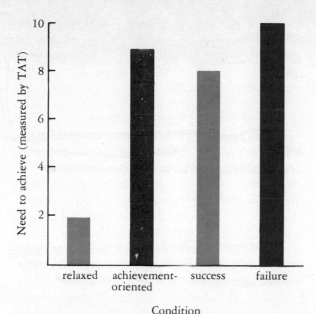

FIGURE 16.10 TAT measurement of four groups' need to achieve after performance on a test during various conditions. (Based on data from McClelland, Atkinson, Clark, and Lowell, 1953.)

the other subjects, particularly those who thought they had failed, appears to have stimulated their need to achieve. The results of this study support the use of the Thematic Apperception Test as a measure of the need to achieve. The experiment also provides an example of test assessment by means of construct validity.

Interim summary: Personality characteristics can be conceived of as types or traits. The earliest theory of personality classified people into types according to their predominant humor, or body fluid. Today most psychologists conceive of personality differences as being represented by quantitative traits. The search for meaningful personality traits goes through three steps. First, a theory must identify possible traits and make some predictions about how they will affect people's behavior. Next, the investigator must devise tests to measure the traits. Finally, the test must be validated by comparing people's behavior with their test scores. Traits can also be derived through factor analysis, but even this method entails some theoretical speculation.

Tests can be constructed by rational or empirical means. The rational strategy requires a detailed

theory that can predict the behavior of people with various personality traits; the test is constructed in accordance with these predictions. The empirical strategy requires that the investigator first identify (perhaps by an expensive and time-consuming method) people who do or do not possess a particular personality trait. The investigator assembles a criterion group consisting of a mixture of such people and gives them a large number of test items. Only those items that are answered differently by people with and without the trait are retained in the final form of the test.

Objective tests contain items that can be answered and scored objectively, such as true/false or multiple-choice tests. One of the most important objective personality tests is the Minnesota Multiphasic Personality Inventory, which was empirically devised to discriminate among people who had been assigned various psychiatric diagnoses, but which has since been used widely in research on personality. Projective tests, such as the Rorschach Inkblot Test and the Thematic Apperception Test, contain ambiguous items that presumably elicit answers that reveal aspects of the subjects' personalities. Because answers can vary widely, test administrators must receive special training to interpret them.

This section has considered the measurement of personality traits; in the next we shall examine what psychologists believe to be the role of personality traits in determining behavior.

TRAITS VERSUS SITUATIONS AS PREDICTORS OF BEHAVIOR

◆ The introduction to this chapter noted that the concept of personality is useful to the extent to which it permits us to predict the behavior of different individuals. Personality traits are assumed to be relatively stable; if they were not, then useful predictions would be impossible. (See **Figure 16.11.**) Walter Mischel (1968, 1976) has severely criticized the concept of personality traits. He has suggested that situations, and not traits, best predict behavior. Consider two situations: a party to celebrate someone's winning a large sum of money in a lottery and a funeral. Certainly people will be much more talkative, cheerful, and outgoing at the party than at the funeral. In contrast, suppose you know a person's score on a test of extraver-

FIGURE 16.11   Psychologists disagree about whether personality traits are stable.

sion–introversion. How much will this knowledge enable you to predict whether he or she will be talkative and outgoing? It would seem that knowing the situation has much more predictive value than knowing the test score.

Cross-Situational Reliability

A number of studies have shown that people tend to behave inconsistently (Mischel, 1968; Bem, 1972). For example, various personal characteristics, such as attitude toward authority, moral behavior, and sexual identification, have typically showed a *cross-situational reliability* of less than .30. That is, the correlation between a person's attitude or behavior in two different situations was less than .30. As you recall from Chapter 2, predictability can be expressed as the percentage of variability of one measure that can be accounted for by another measure, which is equal to the square

of the correlation. This means that knowledge of a person's identity can explain less than 10 percent ($.30^2 = .09$) of the variability in his or her behavior. If personality traits account for only 10 percent of the variability of human behavior, then perhaps the assessment of personality traits is not very useful.

Other psychologists responded to these criticisms. For example, Epstein (1977) noted that traits are more stable than some measures suggested. He made two general points. First, assessments of cross-situational reliability usually involve testing a group of people on two occasions and correlating their behavior in one situation with their behavior in the other. Epstein showed that repeated measurements across several days yielded much higher correlations; reliability measures approached .80.

Second, the question, "Which is more important in determining a person's behavior, the situation or his or her personality traits?" is almost identical to the question, "Which is more important in determining a person's intelligence, heredity or environment?" and the answer to both questions is "It depends." As we saw in Chapter 13, heritability depends on the particular population that is being considered. For example, heritability of hair color is zero in a population that is homogeneous for this trait, such as Eskimos, but high in heterogeneous populations. Similarly, the degree to which personality traits can be used to predict behavior depends on the variability of that trait within the population and on the variability of the situations.

Epstein suggests a useful analogy. Suppose we want to predict how long it takes a person to finish a race. We test a very heterogeneous group of people—young, old, fat, thin, athletic, and sedentary—in a 100-meter and a 200-meter race. Obviously, we would predict that people will take longer to finish the 200-meter race. However, the range of finishing times will be very great. In fact it will undoubtedly take less time for the faster runners to finish the 200-meter race than it will take the slower runners to finish the 100-meter race. Knowing which race a person runs, then, does not tell us much. In contrast, knowing a person's running ability tells us much more. In this case, the trait of running ability is more informative than the length of the race.

Now suppose all the contestants are male Olympic-class runners. It is likely that all of them will finish the race within a few seconds of each other. In this case, if we want to predict how long it will take for each runner to finish, the more useful information will be the race in which the contestant is running, not his running ability. The situation is much more predictive than the personal characteristics of the runners.

More recently, Mischel (1977, 1979) has acknowledged that personality traits are also often important. The importance depends on a number of factors, including the variability of situations and the homogeneity of the population that is being observed. Mischel (1977) also points out that some situations, by their very nature, severely constrain a person's behavior whereas others permit a wide variety of responses.

> Psychological "situations" . . . are powerful to the degree that they lead everyone to construe the particular events the same way, induce *uniform* expectancies regarding the most appropriate response pattern, provide adequate incentives for the performance of that response pattern and require skills that everyone has to the same extent. A good example of a powerful stimulus is a red light; it exerts powerful effects on the behavior of most motorists because they all know what it means, are motivated to obey it, and are capable of stopping when they see it. Therefore it would be easier to predict drivers' behavior at stop lights from knowing the color of the light than from making inferences about the "conformity," "cautiousness," or other traits of the drivers.
>
> Situations are weak to the degree that they are not uniformly encoded, do not generate uniform expectancies concerning the desired behavior, do not offer sufficient incentives for its performance, or fail to provide the learning conditions required for successful genesis of the behavior. An example of such a weak stimulus is the blank card on the TAT projective test with the instructions to create a story about what might be happening; clearly the answers depend more on the storytellers than on the card. (Mischel, 1977, p. 347)

Thus, in *powerful situations,* the situation is important, and not the personality traits of the actor. In contrast, *weak situations* do not predict a person's behavior; his or her behavior depends on personal variables.

Just as situations can be classified as strong or weak, we can probably classify personality variables as strong or weak in their predictive value. Consider a person who is so terribly depressed that she

FIGURE 16.12   To what do you attribute this woman's behavior—her personality, the situation, or an interaction between the two?

will not talk to anyone, but hangs her head, weeping quietly. She does so whether she is alone in her room or among a group of people at a party. Or consider a violent psychopath who attacks anyone who comes near him. He has to be restrained to be prevented from hurting others. The behavior of these people is much less dependent on situations than the behavior of most people. Although these are extreme cases, it seems likely that some personality variables predict behavior better than others in a variety of situations.

Personality and situations are usually conceived of as independent variables, but this is not always true. In laboratory settings, experimenters are assigned to various situations; here, situation and personality are truly independent. However, as Bem and Allen (1974) point out, people in real life are more able to choose the situations they enter. Thus, even though a party is a moderately strong situation and would tend to produce extraverted behaviors, introverted people may stay away from parties to avoid situations that encourage behaviors with which they are not comfortable. Similarly, extraverts may avoid situations in which they are alone. Under these circumstances, traits *interact* with situations.

In acknowledgment of this interaction, psychologists appear to have reached a consensus in the situation–trait controversy. The original question, "Which is more important in determining a person's behavior, the situation or his or her personality traits?" has proved too simplistic. Some types of personality traits will prevail in most situations, some situations will dictate the behavior of most of the participants, and there are interactions between situation and personality that require the analysis of both variables. (See **Figure 16.12.**)

Self-Monitoring: Stability as a Personality Trait

The controversy over whether traits or situations are more useful predictors of behavior has led to the discovery that some people are more influenced than others by situational demands. Thus, the stability of a person's behavior in a variety of situations appears to be a personality trait. People who change their behavior to suit the situation (that is,

show less stability in their behavior) are said to score highly on the trait of *self-monitoring.* (See **Figure 16.13.**)

Snyder (1974) proposed that people who are strong self-monitors should be expected to make more social comparisons between individuals and should be good at both assessing other people's emotions and expressing their own. Using the rational strategy, he constructed a self-monitoring test of twenty-five true/false questions that appeared to be related to his conception of self-monitoring, such as "I am not always the person I appear to be" and "In different situations and with different people, I often act like very different persons." The test appears to correlate well with other measures, such as peer ratings. In addition, professional and amateur actors score higher than nonactors (Snyder, 1979) and self-monitoring people are better than others at remembering information about a person whom they expect to meet; presumably, they pay attention to the person's character-

FIGURE 16.13   People who score high on the trait of self-monitoring tend to fit their behavior to the situation.

istics so that they can act accordingly (Berscheid, Graziano, Monson, and Dermer, 1976).

The self-monitoring trait is more than a measure of the inconsistency of a person's behavior. Indeed, in some situations self-monitoring people are *more* consistent than others. Snyder and Monson (1975) videotaped discussions held by groups of subjects, all of whom had signed forms giving their consent for the tapes to be shown to other members of their psychology class. Thus, the subjects undoubtedly perceived their own behavior as being highly visible to a large number of people. The experimenters predicted that in this situation self-monitoring people would attempt to convey an image of consistency. The results supported experimenters' expectations: people who scored high on the self-monitoring scale tended to be consistent in the public situation and inconsistent in a private discussion that was not videotaped. In contrast, the behavior of people who scored low on the self-monitoring scale remained the same in the two situations.

The concept of self-monitoring as a personality trait is relatively new, and its value remains to be proved through further experimental research.

HERITABILITY OF PERSONALITY TRAITS

◆ The discussion of the heritability of behavioral traits in Chapter 14 presented considerable evidence that at least some aspects of a person's temperament are genetically influenced. However, until 1980 there was no clear evidence that family environment also has an effect on personality.

In a large study of 800 sets of adolescent twins, Loehlin and Nichols (1976) used tests to measure a variety of personality characteristics and estimated their heritability by comparing dizygotic and monozygotic twins. They found a substantial contribution of heredity; monozygotic twins were generally more similar in temperament than dizygotic twins. (Of course, the study is subject to the criticisms of the twin method discussed in Chapter 14.) Table 16.4 summarizes some of the data from this study and others carried out in the United States, England, and Scandanavia on two measures of personality, extraversion and neuroticism. All report substantial contributions from heredity. Environmental family influences were not statistically significant. (See **Table 16.4**.)

What relation does a family's environmental influence have to a child's personality traits? So far, correlations between biologically unrelated children who are raised in the same household are in general not significantly different from zero. Similarly, correlations between foster parent and adopted child are around zero (Henderson, 1982). These results do not mean that a parent's behavior has no effect on a child's personality. Most of the studies have looked for correlations—that is, a resemblance between a child and his or her parents or sibs. However, a parent's particular behavior pattern may produce a reliable but *different* behavior

TABLE 16.4   Estimates of heritability of neuroticism and extraversion

SAMPLE	NUMBER OF PAIRS	HERITABILITY	
		Neuroticism	Extraversion
U.S. adolescents	793	.53	.59
English children	287	.44	.56
English adults	542	.41	.50
Finnish women	5632	.59	.74
Swedish men	6793	.56	.61

Adapted from Henderson, N.D. *Annual Review of Psychology*, 1982, *33*, 403–440.

pattern in the child. For example, children may model themselves on parents who are moderately domineering, but the children of extremely domineering parents may find them intimidating, and react by becoming submissive. If these effects occur, a simple correlation between parent and child would be close to zero, even though there is a cause-and-effect relation.

Another problem with assessing the heritability of personality traits is the fact that a particular temperament may be associated with different behaviors at different stages of development; that is, a particular set of behaviors at one age may imply very different personality traits at different ages. For example, Buss and Plomin (1975) criticized a study that attempted to assess personality traits at a variety of ages. They noted that both of the following behaviors were characterized as "low distractibility": "will not stop crying when diaper is changed and fusses after eating even when rocked" (two months) and "can read a book while television set is at high volume and does chores on schedule" (ten years) (p. 227). Although in a general sense both behaviors show a lack of distractibility, it does appear that very different personality characteristics are involved.

A recent study of monozygotic and dizygotic twins with an average age of 7.6 years observed significant effects of family environment on personality (Plomin and Foch, 1980). Instead of using tests of personality, the investigators observed actual behavior: activity (measured by a device attached to each child's waist), fidgeting while sitting for nine minutes in a beanbag chair, vigilance while participating in a boring task, selective attention in a distracting environment, and aggression (directed toward an inflatable Bobo doll). In contrast to previous studies, Plomin and Foch found little evidence for a genetic effect on these behaviors; the correlations between fraternal twins and identical twins were approximately equal. Instead, the evidence showed that family environment had a significant effect, especially on activity, selective attention, and aggression.

This study is particularly interesting because its results contrast so sharply with studies that use personality tests. Obviously, more research is needed to confirm these results and explain the reasons for the differences. Only when personality and its development through different stages of life are well defined will the relative roles of heredity and environmental factors be understood.

CAUSAL ATTRIBUTION: IMPLICATIONS FOR PERSONALITY

In Chapter 15 I discussed the process of causal attribution and the variables that affect the way in which we make inferences about cause-and-effect relations in our environment. Psychologists have discovered that the process of attribution also has important implications for personality. Attribution affects both how we perceive the personality traits of other people and how we ourselves behave.

Attribution of Personality Traits

As we saw in Chapter 15, we base our conclusions about other people's behavior on the sequence in which events occur and on the degree of *consensuality, consistency,* and *distinctiveness* of their behavior. If someone's behavior is consensual, we attribute it to the situation, and not to the personality characteristics of the performer. (If everyone stands when the national anthem is played, we do not conclude that they are all especially patriotic.) If the behavior is consistent, we attribute it to personality traits. (If a person always acts cheerful, we conclude that he or she has a cheerful disposition, not that he or she just happened to receive good news.) Likewise, if the behavior is distinctive, we attribute it to personality traits. (If one person remains seated when the national anthem is played, even though everyone else is standing, we conclude that he or she does so for reasons related to personality.)

We also develop informal personality theories of our own to understand and predict the behavior of other people. (As you will recall from Chapter 15, this phenomenon is known as implicit psychology.) We have expectations about what behavior should occur in a particular situation, and if people's behaviors violate these situational demands, we conclude that they do so because of their personality characteristics. In contrast, we discount a behavior that is expected; if a person's behavior conforms to the situational demands we make no conclusion about his or her personality characteristics.

Consider the following hypothetical situation. A man enters a store, takes a gun from his pocket, robs the clerk, and kills him. He runs to a car waiting outside and is driven away by an accomplice. The two are later apprehended by the police and indicted for murder. Below are six possible endings for the story. Consider each one and decide whether you would attribute the person's behavior to situational or to dispositional factors. If you attribute the behavior to personality traits, decide which traits they would be.

1. There are no eyewitnesses to the murder. The driver of the car is given immunity from prosecution if he will testify against the gunman. The driver agrees and testifies.
2. There are no eyewitnesses. The driver is given immunity but refuses to testify and is indicted for murder with his comrade.
3. There are no eyewitnesses. The driver is not given immunity but nevertheless testifies against the gunman.
4. There are no eyewitnesses. The driver is not given immunity and does not testify against the gunman.
5. There is an eyewitness who was in the store at the time of the killing. The witness testifies against the gunman.
6. There is an eyewitness, but she refuses to testify at the trial.

* * *

Here are my conclusions; see how they compare with yours. I attribute ending 1 to situational factors (the driver has a powerful motive for testifying: he avoids the possibility of being convicted for murder); ending 2 to dispositional factors (the driver's refusal to testify against the gunman indicates that he is very loyal); ending 3 to dispositional factors (perhaps the driver did not expect the clerk to be killed and is so opposed to the taking of life that he does not want the murder to go free); ending 4 to situational factors (the driver does not want to give testimony that will hurt himself unless there is a good reason to do so); and ending 5 to situational factors (the eyewitness's behavior is consensual: witnesses to crimes are expected to testify). We cannot be sure about the reasons for the sixth outcome. Perhaps the witness fears retaliation from friends of the gunman (which would be a

situational factor), or perhaps she hates authority and sympathizes with criminals (which would be a dispositional factor).

It should be apparent that the process of causal attribution plays an essential role in our perception of the personality traits of other people. In fact, psychologists who are engaged in personality research use the same process, although more formally.

Locus of Control

Research has revealed that the nature of people's beliefs about the causes of their own behavior constitutes an important personality trait. As we saw in Chapter 15, if all other factors are equal, we tend to attribute our own behavior to situational factors but the behavior of others to their personality. When we perform a behavior, our attention tends to be focused on the environment. This focus emphasizes the importance of the situation. However, when we watch the behavior of other people our attention is focused on them, so we tend to see their personality characteristics as the reasons for their behavior.

Although we tend to focus on the situational factors that are responsible for our behavior, most of us believe that our personality traits and intentions are at least partly responsible for what we do. But this belief is not uniform; people differ in the degree of control they attribute to themselves. Some people believe that fate, or a deity, or people in authority determine what happens to them; they attribute their behavior to *external control*. Others believe that their destiny is up to them; they accept credit for their successes, and responsibility for their failures. These people attribute their behavior to *internal control*. The two groups are called *externals* and *internals*, respectively.

At first glance it might appear that attribution to internal control would always be better, but this is not true for all situations. A slave who believes that he is responsible for his own situation is obviously going to be unhappier than one who realizes that external forces have shaped his fate. In some environments, belief in external control is both logical and desirable. (See **Figure 16.14**.) For example, Lao (1970) has shown that black people in the southern United States are most likely to be mentally and emotionally healthy if they attribute

FIGURE 16.14   The fate of U.S. citizens of Japanese descent, placed in internment camps during World War II, was certainly a result of external events.

their social status to external forces and their personal accomplishments to internal forces—their own efforts. These attributions are obviously realistic: a black person's social status receives its definition from a predominantly white society, but beyond this inescapable fact, the person will not accomplish much unless he or she exerts considerable effort.

A variety of personality tests have been devised to measure a person's belief in internal versus external control. The original test was the *Rotter I–E Scale* (Rotter, 1966). Here are a few sample questions:

4. _____a. In the long run people get the respect they deserve in this world.
   _____b. Unfortunately, an individual's worth often passes unrecognized no matter how hard he tries.

10. _____a. In the case of the well prepared student there is rarely if ever such a thing as an unfair test.

   _____b. Many times exam questions tend to be so unrelated to course work that studying is really useless.

13. _____a. When I make plans, I am almost certain that I can make them work.
   _____b. It is not always wise to plan too far ahead because many things turn out to be a matter of good or bad fortune anyhow.

26. _____a. People are lonely because they don't try to be friendly.
   _____b. There's not much use in trying too hard to please people, if they like you, they like you.

It is obvious that Rotter used a rational strategy to devise the scale. It is also fairly obvious which alternatives would be scored as internal and which as external. Indeed, Jackson and Paunonen (1980) note that many investigators have criticized the scale for the fact that the significance of the alternatives is obvious to the subject, because subjects may tend to answer in a way that they believe will make them look good to the experimenter. Another criticism has been that people may differ in their beliefs about the causes of good and bad outcomes, making internal attributions for one and external attributions for the other (Gregory, 1978). The Rotter I–E scale does not distinguish between these two types of attributions.

Many studies have shown that the internal–external trait is an important personality variable. It seems probable that this trait is a function of learning, or experience. Whatever the cause may be, internals and externals act very differently in most situations. (See **Figure 16.15**.)

In many psychological experiments, internals appear to go their own way. If they think they have figured out what the experimenter wants them to do, they behave contrary to the external control. Strickland (1970) tried to reinforce subjects' choice of the verb from among four words written on

cards. She would nod and say "um-hm" each time a verb was chosen. Internals who perceived the strategy apparently did not like being manipulated; they tended to avoid choosing verbs until the experimenter stopped nodding and saying "um-hm." These subjects appeared willing to demonstrate that they knew the correct answer, so long as doing so did not make them look as if they were being manipulated.

Internals are not simply more stubborn than externals. Ritchie and Phares (1969) found that internals and externals were equally susceptible to changes in their opinions if they were given well-reasoned arguments. However, externals were more swayed by statements attributed to authority figures (such as the Secretary of the United States Treasury) than by those attributed to their own peers (such as a college sophomore). Internals were not affected by the source of the statement.

Internals and externals also differ in their reactions to tasks that appear to be controlled by chance or skill. Rotter and Mulry (1965) ascertained whether subjects were internals or externals on the basis of the Rotter I–E Scale. They then had the subjects perform a difficult perceptual matching task. Half the subjects were told that their performance would depend on their skill; the other half that their success would depend on chance. The task was constructed so that all subjects made the same number of correct choices. The experimenters measured the length of time the subjects took to decide which response to make.

Internals, who had confidence in the effects of their own efforts, took longer to decide which choice to make when they believed the task depended on skill than when they believed it depended on chance. Externals took approximately the same amount of time to choose in both conditions. Figure 16.16 shows the results. Although the mean decision time was higher under the chance condition, the difference was not statistically significant. (See **Figure 16.16**.)

A study by Karabenick and Srull (1978) found another interesting difference between internally and externally controlled people. Subjects performed tasks whose outcome appeared to be a result of either luck or skill. As in the study by Rotter and Mulry, the experimenters controlled the subjects' success on these tasks. After performing the

FIGURE 16.15 Would you expect chess playing to appeal more to internals or externals?

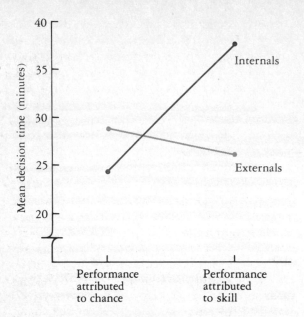

FIGURE 16.16   Mean decision time of internals
and externals on tasks whose outcomes were perceived
to depend on skill or on chance. (Based on data from
Rotter and Mulry, 1965.)

task, the subjects were asked to report their scores
to the experimenter. Internals tended to exaggerate
their score in the skill-determined task, and externals tended to exaggerate their score in the luck-
determined task. The subjects appeared to exaggerate the scores on the kinds of tasks that were
most important to their own self concept ("I'm a
skillful person" versus "I'm a lucky person").

There have been numerous other studies on locus of control. One more deserves mention here
because it shows, again, that laboratory research
can suggest useful strategies for real-life situations.

It has long been assumed that academic achievement is determined almost solely by intelligence.
However, McClelland and Atkinson's research on
achievement motivation caused investigators to focus on this variable, and studies showed that the
need to achieve can be at least as important as
intelligence. This finding alerted psychologists to
the importance of personality variables in academic
success. The Coleman report (Coleman et al., 1966)
pointed out that the most important variable in
predicting the success of poor, slumdwelling children was their degree of belief that their scholastic
achievements were a result of their own effort.

An important study by Richard deCharms (1972)
confirmed this conclusion. In an ambitious attempt
to teach children to become internals—to develop
a belief in their power to determine their own fate—
he established a training program that taught black
teachers from black inner-city schools how to in-
still self-concepts of internal control. The emphasis
was on developing achievement motivation, the
ability to set realistic goals, and acceptance of the
concept of self as the origin of one's fate.

The training sessions changed the teachers' behavior. Children in the classrooms of trained teachers rated their teachers as more encouraging of behaviors and attitudes of internal origin than did
children in the classrooms of nontrained teachers.
Furthermore, the children's scores on a modified
I–E scale (with questions that were appropriate to
their age) showed a shift toward internal control.
Figure 16.17 dramatically illustrates the change.
The four graphs show the scores for four groups of
children whose progress was followed through the
fifth, sixth, and seventh grades. One group received special training in the sixth and seventh
grades, the second group received only seventh-
grade training, the third group only sixth-grade
training, and a fourth group received no special
training at all. Increases in the I–E scores coincided
with the training. (See Figure 16.17.)

Besides scoring differently on the I–E scale, the
children who had received training appeared to enjoy school more; they had fewer absences than untrained children. Furthermore, those who received
the special training scored better on achievement
tests than their untrained peers. Normally, the gap
between the performance of inner-city black children and the national norms widens as the children
get older. This did not happen in the case of the
trained children; although they continued to score
below the national average, the gap did not widen.
These important results indicate the need for further research in this area.

Interim summary: Psychologists dispute the
significance of personality traits; some have asserted that situations are much more important
than traits in determining a person's behavior, while
others insist that traits have good predictive validity. In fact, it appears that some situations impose
severe constraints on behavior. In these situations

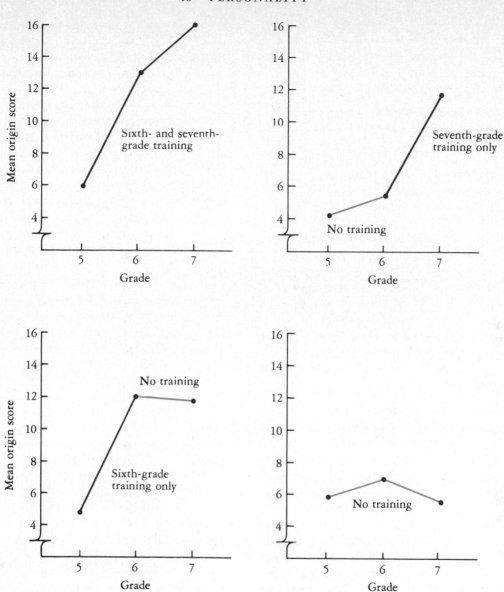

FIGURE 16.17 Academic performance of inner-city children with standard training and special internality training. (From deCharms, R. *Journal of Applied Social Psychology*, 1972, 2, 95–113.)

almost everyone acts the same way. Other situations are less constraining, so that people with different personality traits will act in different ways. In addition, situations and traits may interact; some people may avoid certain situations and seek others, thus placing themselves in situations that call for the kinds of behaviors that they are most comfortable with. Research has shown that a person's consistency in a variety of situations is itself a personality trait; people who score high on the trait of self-monitoring tend to adjust their behavior to what is expected of them by the circumstances.

Many studies have shown that personality traits are affected by heredity, but only recently have psychologists obtained good evidence for environmental family influences. The relation between a child's behavior and that of his or her parents may be complex, and hence simple correlational methods may fail to reveal them. The best evidence for environmental family influences has come from studies that observed actual behaviors rather than answers on personality tests.

We saw in Chapter 15 that causal attribution is an important aspect of social behavior. Because predicting other people's behavior is an important social skill, personality research has included investigation of the kinds of deductions people make about the personality traits of themselves and of other people. An important personality trait concerns a person's perceived locus of control; externals believe that their fate is governed by outside forces whereas internals believe that their fate is determined by their own efforts.

This section has discussed the strategies that psychologists use to develop concepts and tests of pesonality traits and how they attempt to determine whether these traits are stable. Instead of summarizing the many theories of personality that have been developed, the rest of the chapter describes in detail three theories that take very different approaches.

THE PSYCHODYNAMIC
APPROACH TO PERSONALITY

◈ The work of Sigmund Freud has had a profound and lasting effect on twentieth-century society. Terms such as *ego, id, libido, repression, rationalization, Oedipus complex,* and *fixation* became as familiar to most Western laypeople as to clinicians. Before Freud formulated his theory, people believed that most behavior was determined by rational, conscious processes, although strong emotions might drive some to do irrational things. Freud was the first to claim that what we do is *often* irrational, and that the reasons for our behavior are seldom available to conscious mental processes. The mind, to Freud, was a battleground for the warring factions of instinct, reason, and conscience. The term *psychodynamic* refers to this struggle among various aspects of personality.

Sigmund Freud (1856–1939) was a Viennese physician who acquired his early training in neurology, in the laboratory of Ernst Wilhelm von Brücke, an eminent physiologist and neuroanatomist. Freud's work in the laboratory consisted mostly of careful anatomical observation rather than experimentation. This approach also characterized his later work with human behavior; he made detailed observations of individual patients and attempted to draw inferences about the structure of the human psyche from these cases. He did not try to carry out any psychological experiments. Freud's disciples have continued in his tradition of observing and analyzing the verbal reports of patients.

Freud hoped to obtain a position at a university and continue his research, but the fact that he was Jewish made it impossible for him to obtain such a post. He therefore decided to set up a private medical practice of his own. Before doing so, he studied in Paris with Jean Martin Charcot, who was investigating the usefulness of hypnosis as a treatment for hysteria. Patients with hysteria suffer paralysis of some part of the body, or loss of one of the senses, without any detectable physiological cause. The fact that hypnosis could be used either to produce or to alleviate these symptoms sug-

FIGURE 16.18   A photograph of Freud taken around the time he studied in Paris with Charcot.

gested that they were of psychological origin. Charcot suggested that hysterical symptoms were caused by some kind of psychological trauma. Freud was greatly impressed by Charcot's work and became even more interested in problems of the mind. (See **Figure 16.18.**)

Freud returned to Vienna and opened his medical practice. He began an association with Josef Breuer, a prominent physician who helped him get his practice established. Freud and Breuer together published a book called *Studies on Hysteria,* and one of the cases cited in it, that of Anna O., provided the evidence that led to some of the most important tenets of Freud's theory.

Anna O. was treated by Breuer twelve years before he and Freud published their book. She suffered from an incredible number of hysterical symptoms, including loss of speech, disturbances in vision, headaches, and paralysis and loss of feeling in her right arm. Under hypnosis, Anna was asked to go back to the times when her symptoms

FIGURE 16.19 Bertha Pappenheim, the real Anna O.

had started. Each of her symptoms appeared to have begun just when she was unable to express a strongly felt emotion. While under hypnosis, she experienced these emotions again, and the experience gave her relief from her hysterical symptoms. It was as if the emotions had been bottled up, and reliving the original experiences uncorked them. This release of energy (which Breuer and Freud called *catharsis*) presumably eliminated the hysterical symptoms.

The case of Anna O. is one of the most-reported cases in the annals of psychotherapy. However, Breuer's original description appears to be inaccurate in some of its most important respects (Ellenberger, 1972). Apparently the woman was not at all cured by Breuer's hypnosis and psychotherapy. Ellenberger discovered the existence of hospital records indicating that Anna O. (actually, Bertha Pappenheim) continued to take morphine for the distress caused by the disorders that Breuer had allegedly cured. Freud appears to have learned later that the cure was a fabrication, but this fact did not become generally known until recently. However, Breuer's failure to help Anna O. with her problems through hypnosis and psychotherapy does not mean that we must reject psychoanalysis. Although Breuer's apparent success inspired Freud to examine the unconscious, Freud's theory of personality must stand or fall on its own merits, evaluated by more modern evidence. (See **Figure 16.19.**)

The case of Anna O., along with evidence obtained from his own clinical practice, led Freud to reason that human behavior is motivated by instinctual drives, which, when activated, supply psychic energy. This energy is aversive, because the nervous system seeks a state of quiet equilibrium. According to Freud, if something prevents the psychic energy caused by activation of a drive from being discharged, psychological disturbances will result. (As we saw in Chapter 5, not all psychologists agree that organisms invariably seek a state of reduced drive.)

STRUCTURES OF THE MIND: THE ID, EGO, AND SUPEREGO

◆ Freud was struck by the apparent fact that psychological disturbances could stem from events that a person could no longer consciously recall, although they could be revealed during hypnosis. This phenomenon led him to conclude that the mind consists of both unconscious and conscious elements.

Freud divided the mind into three structures: the *id*, the *ego*, and the *superego*. The id contains the *libido*, which is the primary source of motivation; this force is insistent and is unresponsive to the demands of reality. The operations of the id are completely unconscious. Its forces provide the energy for all psychic processes.

The ego is the self. It controls and integrates behavior. It acts as a mediator, negotiating a compromise between the pressures of the id, the counterpressures of the superego, and the demands of reality. The ego's functions of perception, cognition, and memory perform this mediation. The ego is driven by the *reality principle*, or the ability to delay gratification of a drive until an appropriate goal is located. To ward off the demands of the id, the ego uses *defense mechanisms* (described later). Some of the functions of the ego are unconscious.

The superego is subdivided into the *conscience* and the *ego-ideal*. The conscience is the internalization of the rules and restrictions of society. It determines which behaviors are permissible and punishes wrongdoing with feelings of guilt. The ego-ideal is an internalization of what the person would like to be—of his or her goals. The superego, like the id, is unconscious and is subject to irrational thought. For example, guilt feelings are not always rational.

◆   Freud found the mind to be full of conflicts. A conflict might begin when one of the two primary drives, the *sexual instinctual drive* or the *aggressive instinctual drive,* was aroused. These drives demand gratification but are often held in check by *internalized prohibitions* against the behaviors the drives tend to produce. Internalized prohibitions are characteristics of the superego. They are rules of behavior learned in childhood that defend the person from the guilt that he or she would feel if the instinctual drives were able to express themselves. The result of the conflict is a *compromise formation*—a compromise between the demands of the drive and the suppressive effects of internalized prohibitions. Freud believed that phenomena such as dreams, artistic creations, and slips of the tongue (we now call them *Freudian slips*) were examples of compromise formation.

Freud believed that the *manifest content* of a dream—its actual story line—is only a disguised version of its *latent* (hidden) *content,* which is produced by the unconscious. The latent content might be an unexpressed wish related to the sexual or aggressive instinctual drives. For example, a small boy might want to kill his father and sleep with his mother (thus satisfying both instinctive drives). However, if he did this in a dream he would experience very painful guilt and anxiety. Therefore, the *preconscious* (an intermediate system between the conscious and unconscious) transforms the nasty wishes of the unconscious into a more palatable form; the manifest content of the dream might be that his father became ill, and that the boy helped his mother around the house, assuming some of his father's chores. These chores would substitute for the sexual activity that his unconscious was really interested in. The manifest content of this dream manages to express, at least partly, the latent content supplied by the unconscious.

DEFENSE MECHANISMS

According to Freud, the ego contains defense mechanisms that become active whenever unconscious instinctual drives of the id come into conflict with prohibitions of the superego. The signal for the ego to utilize one of its defenses is the state of *anxiety* produced by an intrapsychic conflict. This unpleasant condition motivates the ego to apply a defense mechanism, and thus reduce the anxiety. Ten of the most important defense mechanisms are described below.

◆   *Repression* is a means of preventing an idea, feeling, or memory from reaching consciousness. For example, Freud theorized that Anna O. had repressed the memories that caused the conflicts underlying her hysterical symptoms. Repression is the one phenomenon described by Freud that has received experimental attention.

Isolation is a form of partial repression involving the *affective* part of an idea (that is, the feelings that accompany an emotion-laden memory or thought), leaving only the *intellectual* part in consciousness. For example, a person might talk unemotionally about a traumatic love affair, without feeling any of the painful emotions that were present at the time.

FIGURE 16.20 Many crusaders are actually fighting their own impulses.

Reaction formation involves replacing a threatening idea with its opposite. An often-cited example of a reaction formation is that of a person who is aroused and fascinated by pornographic material but whose superego will not permit this enjoyment. In consequence, he or she becomes a militant crusader against pornography. (See **Figure 16.20**.)

Reaction formation can be a very useful defense mechanism, permitting sexually acceptable interaction with the forbidden object. The crusader against pornography often studies the salacious material to see just how vile it is, so that he or she can better educate others about its harmful nature. Thus, enjoyment becomes possible without feelings of guilt.

Projection involves denial of one's own unacceptable desires and the discovery of evidence of these desires in the behavior of other people. For example, a man who is full of repressed hostility may perceive the world as being full of people who are hostile to him. In this way he can blame someone else for any conflicts in which he engages.

Undoing is a form of repentance for a wish or action that causes guilt. For example, a mother who, in a fit of anger, wishes her child dead, may later shower affection on the child to undo her previous wish and prove to herself that she really is a good mother.

Sublimation is the diversion of psychic energy from an unacceptable drive to an acceptable one. For example, a person may feel strong sexual desire but find its outlet unacceptable because of internalized prohibitions. Despite repression of the drive, its energy remains and finds an outlet in another drive, such as artistic or other creative activities. (See **Figure 16.21**.)

Freud considered sublimation to be a significant factor in artistic and intellectual creativity. Because people have a fixed amount of drive available for motivating all activities, surplus sexual drive that is not expended in its normal way can be used to increase a person's potential for creative achievements.

Displacement is the substitution of a "safe" target of an instinctual drive for a "dangerous" one. Whereas sublimation consists in diverting energy from an impermissible desire into a different drive, displacement consists in diverting the impermissible desire to a different goal. The target of the drive, not the drive itself, is altered. For example, a boy who feels hostility toward his father may direct his hostility toward other children, becoming a bully.

Turning against the self is a special form of displacement of the aggressive instinctual drive. In this case the substitute goal is one's self. Hostile thoughts toward another person are transformed into self-hatred.

Rationalization is the process of inventing an acceptable reason for a behavior that is really being performed for another, less acceptable, reason. For example, a man who feels guilty about his real reasons for purchasing a magazine containing pictures of naked men or women may say, "I don't buy the magazine for the pictures. I buy it to read the interesting and enlightening articles it contains."

Conversion is the provision of an outlet for in-

FIGURE 16.21   Freud suggests that artistic expression is often a result of sublimation of unacceptable psychic energy. He might have even found the strong vertical lines to be symbols of sexuality and power.

trapsychic conflict in the form of a physical symptom. The conflict is transformed into blindness, deafness, paralysis, or numbness. (This phenomenon has also been called *hysteria,* which should not be confused with the common use of the term, meaning "running around and shouting and generally acting out of control.") Anna O.'s problem would be described as a conversion reaction. For example, a person might develop blindness so that he or she will no longer be able to see a situation that arouses a strong, painful intrapsychic conflict. In Chapter 17 we will examine the case of a man who became hysterically blind, apparently because he became jealous watching his wife nurse their child.

FREUD'S PSYCHOSEXUAL THEORY OF PERSONALITY DEVELOPMENT

◆ Freud believed that the prime mover in personality development was the sexual instinctive drive, which is present in everyone from earliest childhood. In the healthy person, its outlet depends on the person's level of physical development.

Because a newborn baby can do little more than suck and drink, its sexual drive finds an outlet in these activities. Even as the baby becomes able to engage in more complex behaviors, it continues to receive most of its sexual gratification orally. The early period of the *oral stage* of personality development is characterized by sucking and is passive in character. Later, the baby becomes more aggressive and derives its pleasure from biting and chewing.

The *anal stage* of personality development begins during the second year of life. Now the baby begins to enjoy emptying its bowels (*anal* is derived from *anus,* the opening of the large intestine). Early in this stage, called the *expressive period,* the baby enjoys expelling its feces. Later, in the *retentive period,* it derives pleasure from storing them up.

At around age three, children discover that it is fun to play with their penis or clitoris and they enter the *phallic stage.* (*Phallus* means "penis," but Freud used the term bisexually in this context.) Children also begin to discover the sex roles of their parents and attach themselves to the parent of the opposite sex. A boy's attachment to his mother is called the *Oedipus complex,* after the Greek king of mythology who unknowingly married his mother after killing his father. A girl's attachment to her father is called the *Electra complex.* In Greek mythology, Electra (along with her brother) killed her mother and her mother's lover to avenge her father's death.

In boys, the Oedipus complex normally becomes repressed by age five, although the conflicts that occur during the phallic stage continue to affect his personality throughout life. A boy's wish to take his father's place is suppressed by his fear that his father will castrate him as punishment. (In fact Freud believed that young boys regarded females as castrated males.) The conflict is finally resolved when the boy begins to model his behavior on that of his father—he achieves *identification* with him.

Girls supposedly experience fewer conflicts than boys do during the phallic stage. The chief reason for their transfer of love from their mother (who provided primary gratification during early life) to their father is *penis envy.* A girl discovers that she and her mother lack this organ, so she become attached to her father, who has one. This attachment persists longer than the Oedipus complex, because the girl does not have to fear castration as revenge for usurping her mother's role. However, according to Freud, penis envy eventually becomes transformed into a need to bear children. The missing penis is replaced by a baby.

Between the end of the phallic stage and the beginning of the *genital stage,* there is a *latency period* of several years, during which the child's sexual drive is mostly submerged. At the onset of puberty, the person begins to form adult sexual attachments to age-mates of the opposite sex. The sexual drive finds its outlet in heterosexual genital contact—hence the term *genital* stage.

Freud's psychosexual theory of personality development has been extremely influential because of its ability to explain personality disorders in terms of whole or partial *fixation,* or "holding in place," at an early stage of development. For ex-

ample, fixation at the oral stage might result from early (or delayed) weaning from breast to bottle to cup. Someone whose personality is fixated at the early oral stage might be excessively passive. "Biting" sarcasm or compulsive talking represent fixation at the later, aggressive phase of the oral stage. Other oral-stage activities include habits like smoking and excessive eating.

Improper toilet training can result in fixation at the anal stage. People fixated at the anal-expressive period are characterized as destructive and cruel, anal-retentives as stingy and miserly. Finally, people who do not successfully pass through the phallic stage may experience a variety of emotional problems. Freud believed that homosexuality stemmed from unresolved problems that occurred during this stage.

ASSESSMENT OF FREUD'S PSYCHODYNAMIC THEORY

Although Freud's psychodynamic theory has had a profound effect on psychological theory, psychotherapy, and literature, his theory has received little experimental support, mainly because he referred to concepts that are poorly defined and that cannot be observed directly. How is one to study the ego, the superego, or the id? How can one prove (or disprove) that an artist's creativity is the result of displaced aggressiveness or sexual drive?

The one Freudian phenomenon that has undergone experimental testing is repression. This phenomenon is very important to Freud's theory because it is one of the primary ego defenses and because it operates by pushing memories (or newly perceived stimuli) into the unconscious. Thus, experimental verification of repression would lend some support to Freud's notions of intrapsychic conflict and the existence of the unconscious.

However, the results have not been conclusive. Typically, repression experiments ask subjects to learn some material associated with an unpleasant, ego-threatening situation, then compare their memory for the information with that of subjects who learned the material under nonthreatening conditions. If repression occurs, the threatened subjects should remember less of the material than the nonthreatened subjects. Some studies have reported positive results, but later experiments have shown that other, non-Freudian phenomena could explain them more easily. Perhaps the most important fact is that none of the experiments can really be said to have threatened the subjects' ego, producing the level of anxiety that would lead to the activation of a defense mechanism. Any experimental procedure that did so would probably be unethical.

One representative experiment on repression used a threat to the ego that has a certain amount of plausibility. D'Zurilla (1965) showed subjects ten pictures of inkblots, with two words beneath each inkblot, and asked the subjects to select the word that best described each inkblot. After making their ten choices, subjects in the experimental group were told that the task they had just performed was a test of latent homosexuality (homosexual tendencies that have not yet been fully expressed) and that they had chosen nine out of ten responses indicating this tendency. Control subjects were merely told that they were helping the experimenter develop a new psychological test. Five minutes later, both groups were tested to see how many of the twenty words they could remember. The experimental subjects remembered fewer of the words than the control subjects did, perhaps because they were repressing painful memories. The experimenter then told the experimental subjects that they had been deceived, and that the test had nothing at all to do with homosexuality. In a subsequent memory test the experimental subjects did as well as controls. Perhaps the repression has been lifted; because the memories were no longer painful and ego threatening, the conscious was given free access to them.

But there is a simpler explanation. The subjects were questioned about what they thought about during the five-minute period right after the first test. Most of the experimental subjects reported that they had been thinking about the test and brooding about the inkblots, their alleged homosexual tendencies, and related subjects. This fact is quite the opposite of what Freud would predict; the subjects should have *avoided* these thoughts if they were painful. Perhaps the poor performance in the first recall test of the twenty words simply stemmed from interference; the subjects were preoccupied with thinking about what they had just been told about themselves. They were prob-

ably more interested in worrying about their scores on the test than in trying to remember the twenty words for the experimenter.

This experiment suggests the difficulty involved in testing even the most specific prediction of Freud's theory. It is very difficult (and perhaps impossible) to prove that a person's behavior is a result of unconscious conflicts.

Interim summary: Freud believed that the mind was full of conflicts between the primitive urges of the libido and the prohibitions of the superego. These conflicts tended to be resolved through compromise formation, and through ego defenses such as repression, sublimation, and reaction formation. His theory of psychosexual development, a progression through the oral, anal, phallic, and genital stages, provided the basis for a theory of personality and personality disorders. Although Freud was a brilliant and insightful thinker his theory has not been experimentally verified, primarily because most of his concepts are unobservable, and therefore untestable. Even though many modern psychologists do not believe his psychodynamic theory to be correct, Freud made an important contribution to psychology with his realization that not all the causes of our behavior are available to our consciousness; many are unknown to us. In Chapter 18 we shall examine psychoanalysis, the therapeutic technique based on his theory of personality.

THE BEHAVIORISTIC
APPROACH TO PERSONALITY

◆ Freud's influence on twentieth-century thought is rivaled only by that of B.F. Skinner. Like Freud, Skinner has been a prolific writer, with a style that is either beautifully insightful and persuasive or infuriatingly wrong, according to the reader's point of view. Perhaps it is unfair to Skinner to call his view of human personality a theory, because he dislikes the term, at least as most psychologists use it. Skinner does not believe that most concepts dear to the hearts of personality theorists, such as ego, unconscious, anger, fear, or anxiety, are of any use in understanding human behavior. Instead, we must simply study an individual's behavior in response to his or her environment. What we need to determine are the relations between stimuli and responses; nothing is gained by assuming the existence of personality structures within the individual. Here is how Skinner puts it:

> It is often said that a science of behavior studies the human organism but neglects the person or self. What it neglects is a vestige of animism, a doctrine which in its crudest form held that the body was moved by one or more indwelling spirits. When the resulting behavior was disruptive, the spirit was probably a devil; when it was creative, it was a guiding genius or muse. Traces of the doctrine survive when we speak of a *personality,* of an ego in ego psychology, or an *I* who says he knows what he is going to do and uses his body to do it, or of the role a person plays as a persona in a drama, wearing his body as a costume. (1974, p. 184)

OPERANT CONDITIONING AND PERSONALITY

Skinner believes that human behavior is ultimately explainable in terms of the principles of operant conditioning. This approach is called **radical behaviorism.** *Radical* derives from the Latin word *radix,* meaning "root." Hence, radical behaviorism is behaviorism that is pure to the root.

Chapter 4 outlined the principles behind Skinner's views on human personality. We do what we do because in past situations some behaviors have been reinforced and others punished. We *discriminate* among various stimuli and respond appropriately. If we are reinforced for performing a particular behavior in the presence of a particular stimulus we *generalize* our responding to similar stimuli. Sometimes we behave *superstitiously* because a particular response is fortuitously followed by a reinforcing stimulus that would have occurred regardless of what we did. And, of course, our behavior is reinforced by a much wider range of stimuli than food or water; it is controlled by smiles and frowns, by our own self-appraisal, and by a variety of conditioned reinforcers. (Conditioned reinforcers can be remote from primary rewards; a miser derives pleasure from a set of digits written in his or her bankbook.)

In Skinner's view, personality traits are best conceived of as behavioral tendencies produced by a person's history of reinforcement. For example, if a child's performance is reinforced on a variable-interval or variable-ratio schedule, he or she is likely to become industrious; intermittent reinforcement leads to steady work and good resistance to extinction. Conversely, if a child is given frequent, noncontingent reinforcers independent of his or her

FIGURE 16.22 Social reinforcement—sometimes obvious, sometimes subtle—shapes our behavior and our personality.

performance, the child will probably learn to be lazy. A child who is frequently punished will probably become timid and fearful or especially aggressive, depending on the schedule of punishment. Although Skinner does not rule out hereditary factors in temperament, he views a person's conditioning history as more important and more interesting. (See **Figure 16.22.**)

REJECTION OF INTERVENING VARIABLES

Ego, id, instinctual drive, and the like are not directly observable phenomena; they are presumed to be internal functions of the individual. These *intervening variables* are located within the individual, between environmental stimuli and the person's behavioral responses. Skinner regards intervening variables as useless clutter obscuring the stimulus-response relations that we should seek to identify.

◆   Some psychologists object to Skinner's dismissal of intervening variables. But there can be no argument about the danger of the nominal fallacy. That is, we can use the term *lazy* to describe a pattern of behavior: sleeping more than usual, allowing one's living quarters to become messy, quitting most tasks before they are finished, and the like. The word *lazy* serves as a shorthand description of a complex set of responses. It is perfectly logical and acceptable to use it in this way. But suppose someone says "Henry sleeps all day, lives like a pig, and never finishes anything he starts *because he is lazy.*" This statement makes no sense. We cannot use a descriptive term like *lazy* as an *explanation* for behavior.

If we discard all the intervening variables that are part of every personality theory, how do we account for human behavior? Skinner is chiefly interested in a *functional analysis* of behavior, that is, a study of cause-and-effect relations. For example, an investigator performing a functional analysis would not report that people drink because they are thirsty; he or she would try to discover the events that predict that a person will drink. Suppose we observe that people tend to drink when the air temperature is very high, when they have just eaten salty food, or when they have lost blood. We would then propose these events as causes of drinking.

To make sure that our conclusions were correct, we would manipulate the variables to see whether we could control people's drinking behavior. If we find that putting people in hot rooms or having them eat salty food or removing some of their blood (there may be some practical difficulties here) results in drinking, then we can conclude that these events *cause* drinking. In one of these procedures, we may offer someone a slice of very salty pizza. She eats it, enjoys it, and accepts another slice. And another. After a while she asks for a drink of water. Suppose someone who did not see the subject eat the pizza asks us to explain why she drank the water. The correct explanation is not "Because she is thirsty," but "Because she just ate several slices of salty pizza." In this simple example, we know that certain environmental events (such as a hot climate or the ingestion of salt) produce drinking, along with the feeling we call thirst. But most human behavior cannot be so easily explained. Therefore, we tend to be less critical when someone "explains" a complex behavior in terms of unobservable internal processes.

THE MYTH OF FREE WILL

◆ Because Skinner's emphasis on a functional analysis of behavior leaves no room for intervening variables, it also rejects the notion of *free will*. We all feel that we have at least some control over our own behavior. (In fact, as we saw earlier, this belief has proved to be an important personality variable, influencing internality versus externality.) However, if there is a physical cause for every event, free will must be a myth. Either behavior is a part of an orderly physical universe or it is not. Our inability to predict someone's behavior with any certainty does not mean that his or her behavior does not have real, physical causes.

Even people who do not believe in free will *feel* as if they have it. Skinner would say that the feeling that we have free will has been useful for the survival of our species. Perhaps a feeling of responsibility for our own actions is part of what makes us the social animals we are. For example, if we perceive that we have hurt someone else, the perception is accompanied by feelings of guilt, which are aversive. Thus, our hurtful behavior is punished; we become less likely to do again what we did to that person. Also, if we believe that other people are responsible for their own behavior, we feel justified in rewarding their behavior when it is good and punishing it when it is bad. Therefore, a belief in free will probably led humans to use the principles of operant conditioning long before they were formally articulated. Such a belief was probably essential to the development of an orderly society, even if the belief is scientifically incorrect. According to Skinner, the concept of free will is a myth that we no longer need. Rational humans can apply the principles of reinforcement now that these are becoming understood.

REJECTION OF INNATE PERSONALITY TRAITS

Skinner considers it fruitless to describe human behavior in terms of innate personality traits. He objects even more to innate mental structures such as those described by Freud. He prefers to describe the ego, superego, and id as three kinds of contingencies of reinforcement that a person encounters when he or she interacts with other people. Elements like the ego, superego, and id appear to be universal because the contingencies are universal in the environment, not because they are inherent in our biology. According to Skinner, the ego is "the product of the practical contingencies in daily life, necessarily involving susceptibilities to reinforcement and the punitive contingencies arranged by other people." In other words, the ego describes the everyday existence of the person. The superego is "mainly the product of the punitive practices of a society which attempts to suppress the selfish behavior generated by biological reinforcers, and it may take the form of imitating society . . . as the injunctions of parents, teachers, and others become part of its repertoire." The id describes "man's . . . innate susceptibilities to reinforcement, most of them almost necessarily in conflict with the interests of others" (Skinner, 1974, p. 166). (See **Figure 16.23**.)

Skinner's conception of the id, ego, and superego as contingencies of reinforcement rather than as innate personality structures provides a useful approach to understanding the causes of human behavior. Contingencies of reinforcement can be observed; mental structures cannot. As Skinner suggests, we should stick with that which is observable.

FIGURE 16.23   This man's innate susceptibilities to reinforcement seem to have placed him in conflict with others.

Skinner's analysis of Freud's ego defense mechanisms illustrates the contrast between the two approaches. *Webster's Third International Dictionary* defines, in primarily Freudian terms, *repression* as "a process or mechanism of ego defense whereby wishes or impulses that are incapable of fulfillment are kept from or made inaccessible to consciousness." In contrast, Skinner defines repression as the phenomenon whereby "behavior which is punished becomes aversive, and by not engaging in it or not 'seeing it,' a person avoids conditioned aversive stimulation. There are feelings associated with this [process], but the facts are accounted for by the contingencies" (1974, p. 171).

Likewise, whereas Freud defined sublimation as the redirection of the energy behind an unacceptable instinctual drive into another, permissible drive, Skinner describes the concept in much simpler terms, completely avoiding mention of internal processes such as drives and conflicts: "If two forms of behavior are both reinforced and if only one of them is punished, the other is more likely to occur" (p. 173).

Skinner does not make a serious attempt to study enduring personality traits that might be a result of a person's heredity. He is interested in predicting and controlling behavior, and nonmodifiable behaviors do not hold much interest for him. Although he recognizes the importance of an organism's genetic inheritance, he places more stress on the role of genetics in the evolution of species than on the role of heredity in individual differences. In his view, the role of natural selection is similar to that of reinforcement: the contingencies of the environment shape the behavioral repertoire of an individual organism through reinforcement and determines the behavioral capacities and tendencies of the species through natural selection.

CRITICISM OF SKINNER'S EXPLANATION OF HUMAN PERSONALITY

◆ Skinner has attacked beliefs that are cherished by many people, and in turn his analysis of the causes of human behavior has been vigorously criticized. Perhaps the most important issue raised by his critics is the generality of the principles of reinforce-

ment. The behavior of rats and pigeons in operant chambers, like other natural phenomena, follows certain general principles. It is also well known that schedules of reinforcement can alter human behavior; many studies have shown that if an effective reinforcer is identified and is made contingent on a person's behavior, the frequency of that behavior will change.

But critics also question whether all, or even a large part, of human behavior occurs as a result of contingencies of reinforcement. It is one thing, they say, to explain the behavior of a hungry rat in a cage with a lever and a food dispenser, and another thing altogether to explain the behavior of a human in a social situation. Humans are much more complex, and they engage in cognitive operations that cannot be explained by reinforcement and punishment. Moreover, critics argue that Skinner's attempts to identify the stimuli that explain a person's behavior in a particular situation are mere guesses; he cannot be sure that a particular stimulus is a reinforcer, a punisher, or a neutral

FIGURE 16.24   The causes of behavior are often obscure.

stimulus. Perhaps the reasons for the behavior are entirely private, known only to the person who is being observed. (See **Figure 16.24**.)

Another criticism of radical behaviorism is that it largely ignores individual differences that are caused by heredity. Although this criticism is true, we do not yet know how important it is, because we do not know whether people with different genetic endowments respond in different ways to the contingencies of reinforcement and punishment. If a great deal of variability in human behavior is a result of genetic mechanisms then a purely environmental approach such as Skinner's will never account for that variability.

The controversy persists. Whichever approach is most successful in predicting and explaining human behavior will endure; the others will be consigned to the history books.

Interim summary: Skinner's approach to the understanding of the causes of behavior is based on the principles of reinforcement and punishment that were described in Chapter 4. His analysis consists of examining the reinforcement and punishment contingencies present in a person's environment along with the discriminative stimuli that signal the fact that these contingencies are operating. He attributes different patterns of behavior of different individuals (their personality traits) to their previous experience with different kinds of contingencies.

The behavioral approach has found many applications. Programmed instructional techniques, which are becoming more and more important with the advent of inexpensive computers, are based on behavioral principles. Behavior changes are sought by therapists who attempt to manage reinforcement contingencies to eliminate their client's maladaptive behaviors and substitute more adaptive ones. (We shall examine these techniques in Chapter 18.) Behaviorism is also the parent of other approaches to the study of personality. For example, social learning theory (Bandura, 1977) applies the principles of reinforcement to human motivation and social interactions. This approach embraces concepts such as expectancy and emphasizes phenomena such as observational learning, which Skinner acknowledges but does not devote much attention to. Many investigators agree with Skin-

ner about the importance of reinforcement but disagree with his insistence that intervening variables be abandoned; they hypothesize emotional and cognitive structures to which they assign explanatory value.

THE HUMANISTIC APPROACH TO PERSONALITY

◆ The third approach to understanding and explaining human personality is at the other extreme from Skinner's scientific rigor. The term *humanistic psychology* applies to a variety of approaches to the study of human behavior, all of which share a belief in the importance of *holism*. The holistic view of behavior stresses the importance of studying the entire person, without attempting to isolate particular variables that are common to everyone. Proponents of this view argue that it is invalid to consider average scores in the behavior of a group of subjects. No one is average; each person is unique and must be studied as an individual. (Skinner would agree that the individual is the proper subject for investigation, but he would disagree with the assertion that each person follows his or her own unique set of laws; in his view, we are all subject to the same principles of behavior.)

The rejection of general laws of behavior is inconsistent with the methods of science. Indeed, humanistic psychologists argue that scientific experiments will never provide an adequate explanation of human behavior. Humanistic psychologists characterize experiments as artificial and unnatural and claim that they yield trivial results; the use of the scientific method rules out the investigation of human characteristics that cannot be precisely measured. The problem, according to humanistic psychologists, is that these characteristics are the very ones that make humans what they are.

Humanistic psychologists' method of investigation consists in close observation of a relatively small number of people. Whereas Freud obtained most of his information from people who came to him for assistance with a psychological problem, humanistic psychologists emphasize the importance of studying people who are normal; generalizations about human behavior should not be based solely on cases of abnormality.

MASLOW'S THEORY OF SELF-ACTUALIZATION

◆ The humanistic psychologist who had the most influence on personality theory was Abraham Maslow (1908–1970). Maslow devised a theory of human personality based on a *hierarchy of needs.* These needs are innate, although most of the ways in which they may be gratified must be learned. Failure to gratify a need will result in a psychological or physiological dysfunction. The need will remain important to the person until it is satisfied. On the other hand, a need that is consistently gratified will cease to be important, and growth of the individual can occur, with other, less primitive needs becoming important. Healthy growth, then, is a shifting of the relative importance of needs from the most primitive to the most advanced— the most "human."

According to Maslow, the hierarchy contains five classes of basic needs. He discussed two additional ones, *cognitive needs* (needs to know, understand, and explore) and *aesthetic needs* (needs for symmetry, order, and beauty) but did not place them in his hierarchy. (See **Figure 16.25.**)

Physiological needs include the needs for food, water, warmth, and sexual contact. Deprivation of physiological needs causes illness. Preoccupation with these needs (because of difficulty in gratifying them) blocks growth. For example, impoverished people living under conditions of nearstarvation will not be motivated by psychological needs that are found farther up the hierarchy. They will be unable to engage in higher forms of human activity, such as philosophy or art.

Safety needs include the needs for security, dependency, freedom from fear, and a stable and structured environment. Insufficient gratification of safety needs will lead to a preoccupation with them, and possibly to various forms of neurosis.

Needs for belongingness and love include a striving for strong interpersonal relations with a lover and with a family group or clan. Prolonged deprivation of the needs for belongingness and love lead to feelings of rejection and loneliness, which can result in severe psychological disturbances.

Need for esteem includes the need to feel competent and in control of one's own life (self-esteem) and a desire to be well regarded by other people. (See **Figure 16.26.**) A person who fails to gratify the need for esteem will develop feelings of inferiority and helplessness, which may manifest themselves in depression.

Need for self-actualization is the final need, which can be fulfilled only if the others have been satisfied. This last need is the most difficult to define. In Maslow's own words, "What a man *can* be, he *must* be. He must be true to his own nature. [Self-actualization is a] desire to become more and more what one idiosyncratically is, to become everything that one is capable of becoming" (1970, p. 46). According to Maslow, a self-actualizing person has a more efficient perception of reality; demonstrates greater acceptance of self, others, and nature; is more spontaneous; pays more attention to problems outside himself or herself; is more comfortable with solitude and privacy; shows greater independence from culture and environment; appreciates a variety of experiences; identifies fully with humanity; engages in more profound interpersonal relationships; is more creative; and has a more philosophical sense of humor.

Maslow would say that for most people in our society physiological needs cease to be of significant importance (except during periods of deprivation) rather early in life. People are much more likely

FIGURE 16.25   Maslow's hierarchy of needs.

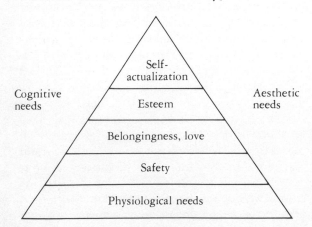

FIGURE 16.26 Examples of fulfillment of cognitive needs and needs for esteem.

and thus reduce the tension. (At least in this regard, Maslow was a drive theorist like Freud.)

On the other hand, the need for self-actualization provides what Maslow called **growth motivation.** In contrast to deficiency motivation, which is a response to a lack, growth motivation stimulates development of a person's potential. At this stage they are beyond the gratification of needs and are striving for self-actualization. Even their perceptions and cognitions change from those of deficiency to those of "being." People no longer strive to obtain things they need; because their needs are met they strive to become better, more effective, more self-actualized.

CRITIQUE OF MASLOW'S THEORY OF PERSONALITY

◆ As a prescription for living one's life, Maslow's description of the self-actualizing person has much to recommend it. All of us would like to have a more efficient perception of reality, a greater adaptation to the environment, greater spontaneity and creativity, and so on. Readers of Maslow's works are likely to come away feeling that they should try to make better persons of themselves. But as a theoretical description of the basis of human personality, Maslow's work suffers badly.

The theory is inherently untestable; its concepts are not well defined and are not susceptible to experimental verification. It is difficult to predict from Maslow's theory how a particular person would behave in a particular situation. For example, Maslow asserts that a person must be true to his or her own nature. But exactly what is a person's true nature, and how can we ever know when it is achieved? Maslow and his followers would not be troubled by this uncertainty, because in their view experimentation is not an appropriate way to study human behavior. But if we cannot perform controlled observations, we cannot determine whether the theory is correct. Lacking specific definitions and criteria, we can never evaluate it.

Many of the criticisms that advocates of humanistic psychology direct against psychological theories of personality are valid; current attempts to explain human behavior *do* miss much of the complexity of the human organism. To produce testable hypotheses, psychologists must often sim-

to suffer some deprivation of the needs for belongingness and love and for esteem. Many (perhaps most) people never completely outgrow a preoccupation with these needs; their behavior is said to be driven by **deficiency motivation.** Deficiency motivation is an aversive state of tension that makes the person seek the goals that will fulfill the need,

plify. But this fact does not mean that scientific study *cannot* explain human behavior, in all of its complexity. It means only that after approximately eighty years of scientific research in psychology most of the task still lies ahead. It should come as no surprise that we have a long way to go before we can construct an adequate theory of human behavior.

CONCLUDING REMARKS

Personality traits are patterns of behavior that show at least some degree of stability from situation to situation. Indeed the stability of a person's behavior in a variety of situations is itself a personality trait. Although factor analysis has been used to derive some traits, most have been drawn from theories of human behavior. Theories of personality are of more than academic interest; practical applications, in the form of psychotherapeutic methods, have been based on them.

Once a personality trait is hypothesized it must be tested by some means of measurement, either by a specialized test or (more rarely) by direct observation of a person's behavior. Tests may be devised rationally or empirically. Rational tests contain items evolved by logical deduction that appear to measure the behaviors or attitudes that would be expressed by a person with a particular trait. Empirical tests contain items that are answered in a particular way by people with the trait (the criterion group), culled from a large preliminary sample of test items.

All of us attempt to infer the personality characteristics of other people and even of ourselves. Some people believe that their own behavior determines their fate while others blame fate. Psychologists call these people *internals* or *externals,* depending on their perceived locus of control.

Of the three major theories of personality reviewed, demonstrating the psychodynamic, behavioristic, and humanistic approaches, Freud's and Skinner's have been the most influential in psychology. Freud pointed out the importance of unconscious motivation and concluded that a person's behavior is a product of conflicting mental structures. Personality was determined by the ways that these conflicts were resolved, and by factors that influenced the way people passed through the stages of psychosexual development. In contrast, Skinner deals only with observable relations between environmental stimuli and behavior, discarding intervening variables. Although his explanation of human behavior is based on principles derived from experimental data, many psychologists dispute his application of these principles to human behavior and argue for the importance of cognitive and emotional influences.

GUIDE TO TERMS INTRODUCED IN THIS CHAPTER

SUGGESTIONS FOR FURTHER READING

Personality testing and research on personality traits receive thorough coverage in general texts such as *Personality: Theory, Assessment, and Research* by R.J. Gatchel and F.G. Mears (New York: St. Martin's Press, 1982). *Locus of Control in Personality* by E.J. Phares (Morristown, N.J.: General Learning Press, 1976) discusses the role of attributions of internality and externality in personality characteristics.

The best resources on the general theories of personality discussed in this chapter are the works of the people who formulated these theories. One of these is Sigmund Freud's *General Introduction to Psychoanalysis* (trans. J. Riviere, rev. ed; New York: Permabooks, 1957). An interesting discussion of Freud's life as well as his writings is *The Life and Work of Sigmund Freud* by E. Jones (New York: Basic Books, 1953). In *About Behaviorism* (New York: Vintage Books, 1976) B.F. Skinner presents his views about the causes of human behavior. A. Bandura's *Social Learning Theory* (Englewood Cliffs, N.J.: Prentice-Hall, 1977) presents an account of human behavior derived from the behavioristic tradition. A.H. Maslow discusses his views about human behavior and human potential in *The Farther Reaches of Human Nature* (New York: Viking Press, 1971).

PART · F

ABNORMAL

BEHAVIOR

Because the human organism is extremely complex, it is not surprising that sometimes things go wrong. Whether because of environmental factors or biological defects or both, some people's behavior is maladaptive. Psychologists and other mental health professionals have discovered that the maladaptive behavior of many people falls into one of several recognizable patterns. Thus, one of the first steps in understanding and eliminating maladaptive behaviors is classifying them. Once patterns are recognized, common causes can be sought.

Chapter 17 describes the more serious mental disorders and what is known about their causes. Chapter 18 discusses the various treatments devised by psychologists and physicians. Mental disorders remain a puzzling problem, and many of them are difficult to treat. As in any other field where there are overwhelmingly more good intentions than known facts, people disagree about the efficacy of various treatments. As we shall see, self-selection, problems with defining the goals of treatment, and differences in the skills of practitioners make it particularly difficult to apply the scientific method to the evaluation of various treatments.

THE NATURE

AND CAUSES

OF MENTAL

DISORDERS

LEARNING ◆ OBJECTIVES

LIFE IS complex, and things do not always go smoothly. We are all beset by major and minor tragedies, but we usually manage to cope with them. Occasionally we find ourselves behaving irrationally, having trouble concentrating on a single topic, or experiencing feelings that do not seem appropriate for the circumstances. Sometimes we brood about imaginary disasters or harbor hurtful thoughts

FIGURE 17.1 People develop a variety of defenses against threats.

about people we love. For most of us, however, these problems remain occasional and do not cause much concern.

But the lives of some people are dominated by disordered thoughts, or disturbed feelings, or inappropriate behaviors. Their problems become so severe that they cannot cope with life. Consequently they either withdraw from it, or seek the help of others, or are judged unfit by society and are placed in an institution. What goes wrong?

We all develop defenses against real or imagined threats to our self-concept—strategies that help us overcome our own defects, or help us cope with demands placed on us by others. (See **Figure 17.1**) For example, a boy who is constantly criticized by an overbearing, demanding parent may learn to be passive and nonresponding, so that the attacks will cease as soon as possible. This strategy may be very adaptive in interactions with his parent, but it would clearly be maladaptive if he were to use it too readily when he was stressed by other social situations.

◆ Some kinds of mental disorders are relatively easy to explain; although the person's behavior is clearly inappropriate and maladaptive, it can be seen as an exaggeration of a reaction that a "normal" person could have. These disorders have traditionally been called **neuroses.** In contrast, **psychoses** reflect severe disruptions in thought processes. Psychotic behavior is illogical and qualitatively different from the behavior of either normal people or people with neuroses. Psychotic people appear to be crazy; they are not simply overreacting to stress. Although investigators and therapists often try to explain specific psychotic behaviors as strategies for coping with life problems, in most cases the explanations are not nearly so satisfactory as they are for other kinds of mental disorders. As we shall see, some people believe that whereas neu-

roses are learned disorders of behavior, psychoses result from biological defects (although they may be triggered by stress).

This chapter concentrates on anxiety disorders, somatoform disorders, dissociative disorders, dysthymic disorders, and psychoses. The descriptions of these disorders necessarily make distinctions that are not always easy to make in real life; the essential features of the more important mental disorders are simplified for the sake of clarity. Moreover, clinicians rarely encounter cases that are clear-cut and thus as easily classified as the ones included here. Space does not permit coverage of the features in our society—such as crime and delinquency, problems of marriage and family life, social inequities, war, and problems of personal adjustment—that cause mental stress in many people but do not lead

FIGURE 17.2　The room of this young patient in a mental hospital looks much like that of any other teenager.

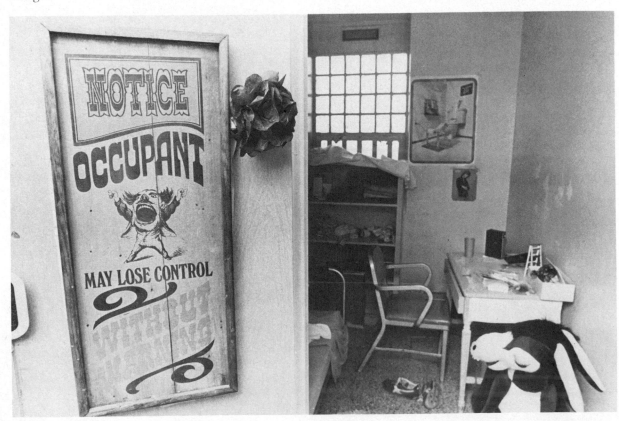

to the diagnosis of a specific mental disorder. Fortunately, more and more people are coming to realize that there is no sharp line dividing normal and abnormal behavior, and that they need not be "sick" to profit from professional advice and help concerning their feelings and behavior. (See **Figure 17.2.**)

CLASSIFICATION AND DIAGNOSIS

THE VALUE OF CLASSIFICATION

There are dangers in classifying a person's mental disorder. No classification scheme is perfect and no two people with the same diagnosis will behave exactly the same way. However, once people are labeled, they are likely to be perceived as having all the characteristics that are assumed to accompany that label; their behavior will probably be perceived selectively and interpreted in terms of the diagnosis. Mental health professionals, like other humans, tend to simplify things by pigeonholing people.

◆ A study by Rosenhan (1973) demonstrated the strength of this tendency through methods that created a stir among clinical psychologists and psychiatrists. After testing volunteers to be sure that they were in no way psychotic, he arranged for them to seek admission as patients in various psychiatric hospitals. To gain admission, they complained of only one symptom—that they heard voices saying "empty," "hollow," and "thud." (Hallucinations are significant symptoms of schizophrenia.) All other statements were as true and accurate as they could make them, and they did not behave abnormally. Furtheremore, once they were admitted, they did not complain of the voices any more.

Most of the volunteers were diagnosed as psychotic. Once they were in the hospitals, Rosenhan says, the staff explained their behavior as symptomatic of their mental illness. None of the mental health professionals realized that the pseudopatients were normal, although some of their fellow patients did, apparently from the fact that they openly took notes. One patient said, "You're not crazy. You're a journalist or a professor. You're

checking up on the hospital" (Rosenhan, 1973, p. 252). When the pseudopatients were released, the diagnosis in almost every case was "schizophrenia, in remission." (*Remission* means "a lessening in extent or degree.")

When these results were published, a number of people concluded that psychiatric diagnosis was a useless endeavor, if it could not distinguish between normal people and schizophrenics. However, a closer examination of the facts shows that the data do not warrant this conclusion. The clinicians were not required to distinguish between *normal* people and people with a mental disorder; they were required to detect that some people were *pretending* to have symptoms of schizophrenia. In fact Spitzer (1975) has shown that on the basis of the data the clinicians had, no other diagnosis would have been justified. He notes that the pseudopatients insisted on admission to the hospitals, which itself is an important symptom of mental or emotional disturbance. Moreover, their behavior after admission was not in fact normal; a normal person would go to the nursing station and say, "I'm really not crazy—I just pretended to be. Now I want to be released." The pseudopatients remained passive.

Rosenhan's study and Spitzer's criticism have stimulated much public discussion about an important issue. They also reinforce the value of the logic used in scientific investigations, discussed in Chapter 2. We should certainly criticize any tendency of mental health professionals to view patients' behavior only in terms of an initial psychiatric diagnosis. However, we should not blame them for making a reasonable diagnosis when a patient lies about symptoms that are almost never found in people who are not psychotic.

Because labeling can have bad effects, perhaps we should abandon all attempts to classify and diagnose mental disorders. However, proper classification does have advantages for a patient.

◆ With few exceptions, the recognition of a specific diagnostic category precedes the development of a successful treatment for that disorder. Treatments for diseases such as diabetes, syphilis, tetanus, and malaria were found only after the disorders could be reliably diagnosed. Any patient has a multitude of symptoms, and before the cause of a disease (and hence its treatment) can be discovered, the primary symptoms must be identified. For example, a mental disorder called **Graves' disease** is characterized by irritability, restlessness, confused and rapid thought processes, and, occasionally, delusions and hallucinations. Little was known about the endocrine system during the nineteenth century, when Robert Graves identified the disease, but we now know that this syndrome results from oversecretion of thyroxin, a hormone produced by the thyroid glands. Treatment involves prescription of antithyroid drugs or surgical removal of the thyroid glands, followed by administering appropriate doses of thyroxin. Graves's classification scheme was devised many years before the disease could be understood, but once enough was known

about the effects of thyroxin, physicians were able to eliminate an entire class of mental disorder.

On a less spectacular scale, different kinds of neuroses respond to different kinds of behavioral treatments, and different psychoses respond to different drugs. If future research is to discover causes and treatments, we must be able to classify specific mental disorders reliably and accurately.

Another important reason for properly classifying mental disorders is the fact that some disorders have a good prognosis—the patient is likely to improve soon and unlikely to have a recurrence. Other disorders have progressive courses, from which the patient is less likely to recover. In the first case, the patient can obtain reassurance about his or her future; in the second, the patient's family

---

TABLE 17.1   The DSM-III classification of disorders

Axis I. Clinical syndromes	Schizophrenic disorders (*cont.*)
Disorders usually first evident in infancy, childhood, or adolescence	Paranoid
Mental retardation	Undifferentiated
Attention deficit disorder	Residual
Conduct disorder	Paranoid disorders
Anxiety disorders of childhood or adolescence	Psychotic disorders not elsewhere classified
Other disorders of infancy, childhood, or adolescence	Affective disorders
Eating disorders	Major affective disorders
Stereotyped movement disorders	Bipolar disorder
Other disorders with physical manifestations	Mixed
Pervasive developmental disorders	Manic
Organic mental disorders	Depressed
Organic brain syndromes	Major depression
Organic mental disorders whose etiology is listed	Other specific affective disorders
Dementias arising in the senium and presenium	Cyclothymic disorder
Substance-induced organic mental disorders	Dysthymic disorder (depressive neurosis)
Organic brain syndromes whose etiology or pathophysiology is . . . [outside the classification system] or is unknown	Atypical affective disorders
Substance use disorders	Atypical bipolar depression
Schizophrenic disorders	Atypical depression
Disorganized	Anxiety disorders
Catatonic	Phobic disorders
	Agoraphobia with panic attacks
	Agoraphobia without panic attacks
	Social phobia
	Simple phobia

can obtain assistance in making realistic plans about his or her future.

THE DSM-III CLASSIFICATION SCHEME

Mental disorders can be classified in a number of ways, but the system most commonly used in North America today is the one proposed in the American Psychiatric Association's *Diagnostic and Statistical Manual III (DSM-III).* Table 17.1 lists these classifications, with several subclassifications omitted for the sake of simplicity. (See **Table 17.1**.)

The DSM-III classification scheme was devised in an attempt to provide a reliable, universal set of diagnostic categories, with diagnostic criteria specified as explicitly as possible. However, this classification scheme is based on no single, underlying principle. Some categories seem to have been chosen with an eye to third-party reimbursement. Critics have suggested that problems such as "tobacco withdrawal" or "developmental arithmetic disorder" have been officially labeled as mental disorders so that clinicians can receive compensation for their services from insurance companies and public welfare organizations.

Beck, Ward, Mendelson, Mock, and Erbaugh (1962) performed an interesting investigation to determine how well psychiatrists could agree on the diagnosis of mental patients according to the then current DSM-I classification scheme (an earlier version of DSM-III). In one week, two members of a team of four highly experienced psychiatrists

---

TABLE 17.1   The DSM-III classification of disorders (*cont.*)

Anxiety disorders (*cont.*)	Factitious disorders
Anxiety states	Disorders of impulse control not elsewhere classified
Panic disorder	Adjustment disorder
Generalized anxiety disorder	Psychological factors affecting physical condition
Obsessive-compulsive disorder	Conditions not attributable to a mental disorder that are a focus of attention or treatment
Post-traumatic stress disorder	
Acute	*Axis II, Specific developmental disorders and personality disorders*
Chronic or delayed	
Somatoform disorders	Specific developmental disorders
Somatization disorder	Developmental reading disorder
Conversion disorder	Developmental arithmetic disorder
Psychogenic pain disorder	Developmental language disorder
Hypochondriasis	Developmental articulation disorder
Atypical somatoform disorder	Personality disorder
Dissociative disorders	Paranoid personality disorder
Psychogenic amnesia	Schizoid personality disorder
Psychogenic fugue	Schizotypical personality disorder
Multiple personality	Histrionic personality disorder
Depersonalization disorder	Narcissistic personality disorder
Atypical dissociative disorder	Antisocial personality disorder
Psychosexual disorders	Borderline personality disorder
Gender identity disorders	Avoidant personality disorder
Paraphilias	Dependent personality disorder
Psychosexual dysfunctions	Compulsive personality disorder
Other psychosexual disorders	Passive-aggressive personality disorder

TABLE 17.2   Percentage of diagnostic agreement within various diagnostic categories

Category	Number of diagnoses	Percentage of agreement
Neurotic depression	92	63
Anxiety reaction	58	55
Sociopath	11	54
Schizophrenic reaction	60	53
Involutional melancholia	10	40
Personality trait disturbance	26	38

Note: These diagnostic categories are now obsolete.

From Beck, A.T., Ward, C.H., Mendelson, M., Mock, J.E., and Erbaugh, J.K. *American Journal of Psychiatry,* 1962, *119,* 351–357.

interviewed 153 patients upon their admission to a mental health facility. **Table 17.2** presents the six most frequently used categories and the percentages of agreement. Of all patients diagnosed, only 54 percent were assigned to the same category by both examining psychiatrists. These results sound poor, but a closer look at the data provides a more hopeful picture. Some people are obviously mentally disturbed, but the pattern of their symptoms does not fall clearly into any one classification. On those judgments that the psychiatrists felt confident about, agreement was 81 percent, which is very high. Furthermore, when the psychiatrists made a second choice of a diagnostic label, agreement on at least one choice was 84 percent.

◆   In a later study, Ward, Beck, Mendelson, Mock, and Erbaugh (1962) reexamined the data to determine the reasons for the psychiatrists' disagreements. They found three. Inconsistency in the patient's behavior accounted for 5 percent of the disagreements. Sometimes a patient said different things to different clinicians; in this case neither the clinicians nor the system of classification is to blame for differences in diagnosis. Inconsistency in interpretation and diagnosis accounted for 32.5 percent of disagreements. The sources of inconsistency were the different training, experience, and temperament of the clinicians. Finally, inadequacies of the diagnostic system accounted for the largest proportion of inconsistencies—62.5 percent. This result emphasizes the importance of the classifica-

tion system. Continued research will tell whether the current DSM-III system is an improvement over its predecessors.

Interim summary: Rosenhan's study indicates that once a diagnosis is made, people tend thereafter to view a patient's behavior selectively; this tendency should be carefully guarded against. However, the fact that the pseudopatients were lying about important symptoms prevents us from concluding that diagnoses are inherently unreliable. The value of classification and diagnosis lies in the potential identification of diseases with common causes. Once diseases are classified, research can be carried out with the goal of finding useful therapies. The principal classification scheme in North America is the DSM-III, which provides explicit criteria for diagnosing mental disorders.

NONPSYCHOTIC MENTAL DISORDERS

◆ Nonpsychotic mental disorders used to be called neuroses. The term *neurosis,* which simply means "neural disorder," is poor because it provides no explanation of the phenomenon. However, I use this term in this introductory discussion because it is so established in our society.

Neuroses are strategies of perception and behavior that have gotten out of hand; they are characterized by pathological increases in anxiety and/or by defense mechanisms that are applied too rigidly, so that they have become maladaptive. Neurotic people are anxious, fearful, depressed, and generally unhappy. However, they do not suffer from delusions or severely disordered thought processes, like people who are afflicted with psychoses. Furthermore, they almost universally realize that they have a problem; most neurotics are only too aware that their strategies for coping with the world are not working.

Neurotic behavior is characterized by avoidance rather than confrontation of problems. People with neuroses turn to imaginary illnesses, oversleeping, or convenient forgetfulness to avoid having to confront stressful situations. Even normal people sometimes use these strategies. Any teacher can attest that a disproportionate number of students seem to be struck by illness and other emergencies just before examination time. But a neurotic adopts avoidance as a way of life. (See **Figure 17.3**.)

Neurotic people tend to limit their functioning severely through overdependence on their maladaptive strategies, and the increasing hopelessness

FIGURE 17.3   Avoidance as a way of life is one of the distinguishing features of neuroses.

of their situation makes them cling even more tenaciously to self-defeating patterns of behavior. These defenses are all they know. Their imagined problems inevitably produce real ones, and eventually they may turn to someone for help in their despair.

The DSM-III has dropped the term *neurosis*. In its place are the anxiety, somatoform, and dissociative disorders, some of which were not previously labeled as neuroses, and dysthymic disorder (previously called depressive neurosis), now classified as an affective disorder. The seven most important—generalized anxiety disorder, obsessive-compulsive disorder, phobic disorder, conversion disorder, hypochondriasis, the dissociative disorders, and dysthymic disorder—are discussed below.

ANXIETY DISORDERS

Several important types of mental disorders are classified as anxiety disorders, with fear and anxiety as the salient symptoms. One category, *anxiety states,* includes chronic generalized anxiety disorders, episodic panic disorders, and obsessive-compulsive disorders. Patients have no adequate defense against the first two states; those suffering from obsessive-compulsive disorders use stereotyped rituals to reduce anxiety. *Phobic disorders,* another category of anxiety disorders, are characterized by excessive fears of specific objects or situations.

Generalized Anxiety Disorder

DESCRIPTION   Most people with a ***generalized anxiety disorder*** suffer from at least some anxiety all the time. Furthermore, the fear is usually not specific to any particular object or situation; people with these disorders are afraid of almost everything. They are often struck with episodic attacks of acute anxiety, periods of acute and unremitting terror that grip them for variable lengths of time, from a few seconds to a few hours. (These attacks have the specific name ***panic disorder*** in the DSM-III.) The physical symptoms of an anxiety attack include such things as shortness of breath, clammy sweat, perceived irregularities in heart beat, dizziness, a perceived need to urinate and defecate, and intestinal upset. The victim of an anxiety attack often feels that he or she is going to die. Leon

no defense against anxiety

(1977) describes a thirty-eight-year-old man who suffered from frequent attacks of anxiety.

> During the times when he was experiencing intense anxiety, it often seemed as if he were having a heart seizure. He experienced chest pains and heart palpitations, numbness, shortness of breath, and he felt a strong need to breathe in air. He reported that in the midst of the anxiety attack, he developed a feeling of tightness over his eyes and he could only see objects directly in front of him (tunnel vision). He further stated that he feared that he would not be able to swallow.
>
> . . . The intensity of the anxiety symptoms was very frightening to him and on two occasions his wife had rushed him to a local hospital because he was in a state of panic, sure that his heart was going to stop beating and he would die. His symptoms were relieved after he was given an injection of tranquilizer medication. . . . He began to note the lo-

cation of doctors' offices and hospitals in whatever vicinity he happened to be . . . and he became extremely anxious if medical help were not close by. (Leon, 1977, pp. 112, 117)

Between anxiety attacks (which some never experience, but which others can experience up to several times each day), people with a generalized anxiety disorder have difficulty concentrating or making decisions, tend to suffer from disturbances of sleep (insomnia, nightmares, general restlessness), overreact to sudden noises, and are usually in a state of general muscular tension. They are frequently abusers of alcohol, tranquilizers, and sleeping pills.

Anxiety is a normal reaction to many stresses of modern life, and none of us are completely free from it. In fact, anxiety is undoubtedly useful in causing us to be more alert and to take important things seriously. (See **Figure** 17.4.) It is when even the simplest and least threatening of events causes anxiety, or when people unrealistically become afraid of failing tasks that should provide no problems to them that anxiety is characterized as a mental disorder.

POSSIBLE CAUSES   Parental influence appears to be an important factor in the development of a generalized anxiety disorder. Jenkins (1969) observed that people with this disorder tend to come from families with neurotic mothers and in which the parents hold up a high standard of accomplishment while simultaneously failing to recognize the actual achievements of their children.

Of all the nonpsychotic disorders discussed in this chapter, generalized anxiety disorder is the least adaptive, and this fact makes it difficult to explain. Panic attacks themselves may provide a certain amount of relief—for example, by enabling a person to avoid a difficult decision—but the disorder is very painful. Unlike people with other nonpsychotic disorders, those with a generalized anxiety disorder do not make excessive use of defense mechanisms; instead, they are exposed to battering by what they perceive as a hostile and pain-provoking world.

It has been suggested that generalized anxiety disorder is a form of learned helplessness, a syndrome that is presumably caused by a perception (valid or otherwise) of powerlessness in affecting

FIGURE 17.4   Anxiety is normal (and appropriate) in some situations.

one's own fate (see Chapter 5). A feeling of helplessness would certainly make a person feel anxious, because it implies vulnerability to misfortune at any time. However, we have no evidence that a person develops this disorder in the same way that an animal learns not to acquire an avoidance response.

Obsessive-Compulsive Disorder

◆ DESCRIPTION   As the name implies, people with an *obsessive-compulsive disorder* suffer from *obsessions*—thoughts that will not leave them—and *compulsions*—behaviors that they cannot keep from performing. Unlike people with generalized anxiety disorders, obsessive-compulsives have a defense against anxiety, namely, their compulsive behavior. Unfortunately, the need to perform this behavior often becomes more and more demanding on their time, until it interferes with their careers and daily lives.

There are two principal kinds of obsessions: doubt or uncertainty, and fear of doing something that is prohibited. We all experience doubts about future activities (such as whether to look for a new job, eat at one restaurant or another, or wear a raincoat or take an umbrella) and about past activities (such as whether we have turned off the coffeepot and whether we should have worn dressier clothes), but these uncertainties, trivial and important, preoccupy some obsessive-compulsives almost completely. Others are plagued with fear that they will do something terrible—swear aloud in church, urinate in someone's living room, kill a loved one, or jump off a bridge—although they seldom actually do something unsocial. Kraines (1948) described the case of a young woman who

. . . complained of having "terrible thoughts." When she thought of her boy-friend she wished he were dead; when her mother went down the stairs, she "wished she'd fall and break her neck"; when her sister spoke of going to the beach with her infant daughter, the patient "hoped that they would both drown." These thoughts "make me hysterical. I love them; why should I wish such terrible things to happen? It drives me wild, makes me feel I'm crazy and don't belong to society; maybe it's best for me to end it all than to go on thinking such terrible things about those I love." (p. 183)

Unlike obsessive fears, compulsions are usually acted upon. Shakespeare's Lady Macbeth is the classic case of a person beset with a compulsion to wash imaginary blood off her hands, after she and her husband, upon her urging, killed the king. "Out, damned spot! out, I say! . . . What, will these hands ne'er be clean? . . . Here's the smell of blood still; all the perfumes of Arabia will not sweeten this little hand" (*Macbeth,* act 5, scene 1; see **Figure 17.5**). The cause of Lady Macbeth's compulsive behavior is clear—she felt guilty about having committed murder. In real life it is rare that the reason for a compulsion is so evident. Klein and Howard (1972) describe an actual case:

. . . he felt a compulsive, irrational need to look into a mirror and stare into his eyes, feeling that they were "stiff." . . . Striving to cease staring at his eyes, he painted over all the mirrors in his house. But then he began to look for dirt in the indentations of his hands. When he no longer could tolerate this, he wore gloves, but became obsessed with the thought of the dirt that might be in the glove stitching. Then he had to stare at his trousers and shoes, check his socks and shoelaces, count the holes in his belt,

FIGURE 17.5   Shakespeare's Lady Macbeth.

straighten his underwear, and determine if his eyebrows were straight. The time spent performing these rituals increased from minutes to hours a day. He constantly thought about committing suicide. (p. 209)

Davison and Neale (1974) report the case of a woman who washed her hands more than 500 times a day because she feared being contaminated by germs. The hand washing persisted even when her hands became covered with painful sores. Why she developed a fear of bacterial contamination was not explained, but the reason was probably not so clearcut as Lady Macbeth's.

Most of us have been obsessed by persistent thoughts and have been afflicted by compulsions from time to time. For example, sometimes a tune (often an irritating commercial jingle) just will not go away. And if we are under stress, we often find ourselves repeating some habitual task. Almost everyone will become annoyed if he or she is prevented from performing some pet habit. An obsessive-compulsive disorder can be viewed as normal thought and behavior patterns carried to the extreme.

◆ POSSIBLE CAUSES   There are several possible causes for an obsessive-compulsive disorder. Unlike simple anxiety states, this disorder can be understood in terms of defense mechanisms. First, obsessions can be viewed as devices to occupy the mind and displace painful thoughts. This strategy is seen in normal behavior; a person who "psychs himself up" before a competitive event by telling himself about his skill and stamina is also keeping out self-defeating doubts and fears. Like Scarlett O'Hara in *Gone with the Wind*, with her "I'll think about it tomorrow," we all say, at one time or another, "Oh, I'll think about something else" when our thoughts become painful.

If painful, anxiety-producing thoughts become frequent, and if turning to alternate patterns of thought reduces anxiety, then the principle of reinforcement predicts that the person will turn to these patterns more frequently. Just as an animal learns to jump a hurdle to escape a painful foot shock, a person can learn to think about a "safe" topic in order to avoid painful thoughts. If the habit becomes firmly established, the obsessive thoughts may persist even after the original reason for turning to them—the situation that produced the anxiety-arousing thoughts—no longer exists. A habit can outlast its original causes.

Compulsive behavior sometimes stems from feelings of guilt, as Lady Macbeth's did; the person commits the act in an attempt to atone for past misdeeds. Compulsions can also be attempts to provide order and stability in an otherwise unpredictable environment. Almost everyone is comforted by a regular routine, and in times of stress the need for order becomes greater.

It is also possible that compulsions are related to the peculiar superstitious behaviors that can be produced in animals. You may recall the hungry pigeons, described in Chapter 4, who were regularly given a bit of food every fifteen seconds. They eventually adopted strange behaviors and performed them as if these were what brought about the reinforcement, even though the food was delivered no matter what they did. Perhaps some human compulsions are learned similarly. (Consider the gambler who blows on the dice or makes some other gesture to "bring luck.")

Phobic Disorders

◆ DESCRIPTION   *Phobic disorders* include some of the most interesting mental disorders with an array of inventive names. (See **Table 17.3.**)

Almost all of us have one or more irrational fears of specific objects or situations, and it is difficult to draw a line between these fears and a phobic disorder. If someone is afraid of spiders but manages to lead a normal life by avoiding getting close to them, it would seem inappropriate to say that the person has a mental disorder. Similarly, many otherwise normal people are afraid of speaking in public. The term *phobic disorder* should be reserved for people whose fear makes their lives difficult. One of the diagnostic criteria of the DSM-III is "significant distress because of the disturbance." Agras, Sylvester, and Oliveau (1969) have estimated that up to 7.7 percent of the population (based upon a sample of New Englanders) have a "phobia," but that only .22 percent of the population are severely disabled by their fears.

The DSM-III recognizes three subtypes of phobic disorders: agoraphobia, social phobia, and simple phobia. *Agoraphobia* (*agora* means "open spaces") is a fear of "being alone or in public places from which escape might be difficult or help not avail-

TABLE 17.3   Names and descriptions of some phobias

Name	Object or situation feared
Acrophobia	Heights
Agoraphobia	Open places
Algophobia	Pain
Astraphobia	Storms, thunder, lightning
Claustrophobia	Enclosed places
Hematophobia	Blood
Mysophobia	Contamination or germs
Monophobia	Being alone
Nyctophobia	Darkness
Ochlophobia	Crowds
Pathophobia	Disease
Pyrophobia	Fire
Syphilophobia	Syphilis
Zoophobia	Animals, or a specific animal

From Coleman, J.C. *Abnormal Psychology and Modern Life*, 5th ed., Glenview, Ill.: Scott, Foresman, 1976.

able in cases of sudden incapacitation, e.g., crowds, tunnels, bridges, public transportation." ***Social phobia*** is an exaggerated "fear of, and compelling desire to avoid, a situation in which the individual is exposed to possible scrutiny by others and fears that he or she may act in a way that will be humiliating or embarrassing." ***Simple phobia*** includes all other phobias, such as fear of snakes, darkness, or heights. (See **Figure 17.6**.)

◆ POSSIBLE CAUSES   Psychoanalytic theory attributes phobias to distress caused by intolerable unconscious impulses, such as an unresolved Oedipus or Electra complex. Whether or not this is true, almost all psychoanalysts and behaviorists believe that phobias are learned by means of classical conditioning (Chapter 4 discussed this explanation at some length). The following example, reported by Hofling (1963), illustrates this process.

> Miss E.M., a woman . . . 22 years of age, was referred to a psychiatrist . . . for treatment of a set of severe phobias. . . . after a number of interviews the precipitating conflict could be elucidated.
>
> At the time of onset, Miss M. had been doing

FIGURE 17.6   This painting expresses a phobic reaction to dogs. (*Animals*, 1941, by Rufino Tamayo. Oil on canvas; H 30 1/8″, W 40″. Collection, The Museum of Modern Art, New York.)

secretarial work. . . . Although intellectually competent and physically very attractive, the patient had always been extremely shy in any personal situation involving a man. She led a restricted social life and very seldom went out on dates. . . . While working for the firm, Miss M. secretly developed a romantic interest in one of the young executives, an interest that she scarcely acknowledged even to herself. She . . . learned, in casual office conversation, that he was married.

. . . One morning, arriving at work an unaccustomed few minutes late, Miss M. found herself alone in an elevator with the young executive. The man made a complimentary but slightly suggestive remark about the patient's dress. Miss M. blushed and became highly embarrassed, tense, and anxious. By dint of considerable effort, she managed to get through the day's work. The next morning, as she was about to enter the elevator, she experienced an attack of anxiety so severe as to verge upon panic. She left the building, walked about for nearly an hour, and then was able to return. This time she climbed six flights of stairs to the office.

During succeeding days the patient made several efforts to use the elevator, but she invariably found herself becoming too anxious to do so. . . . Eventually, the use of the stairs became as disturbing as that of the elevator. At this point, the patient was compelled to ask for a leave of absence. . . . At no point did the patient consciously associate her attacks of anxiety with the young executive. . . . she considered the nature of her illness to be inexplicable. (pp. 325–326)

The patient suffered a severe anxiety attack after her encounter with the man in the elevator. Although clinicians would disagree about the reasons for her shyness and avoidance of sexual desires, all would agree that the aversive experience created the conditions for the phobia. The woman learned to avoid the elevator, where the experience occurred. Unfortunately, the learning generalized to other stimuli, including the stairway, and as a result it became impossible for her to continue working in the building.

Some people can also learn fears by observing others. Bandura and Rosenthal (1966) had subjects watch a confederate sitting in a chair, wired to some electrical apparatus. Each time a buzzer was sounded, the confederate withdrew his hand and acted as if he were in pain. After witnessing this sequence several times, the subjects, who never received a shock, gave physiological evidence of an emotional reaction to the sound of the buzzer when it was presented alone.

To say that phobias are learned through classical conditioning does not explain this disorder completely. Many people have traumatic experiences, but few of them go on to develop phobic disorders. Perhaps some people are more susceptible to developing phobias than others. Lacey and Lacey (1962) have observed that some people are especially reactive to unpleasant stimuli. Apparently, some people have a very *labile,* or changeable (from Latin *labes,* "a falling or sinking in") autonomic nervous system, which predisposes them to acquire conditioned fears.

SOMATOFORM DISORDERS

The primary symptoms of *somatoform disorder* are physical (*soma* means "body"). Two of the more important somatoform disorders are the conversion disorder and hypochondriasis.

Conversion Disorder

◆ DESCRIPTION *Conversion disorders,* formerly called *hysterical neurosis, conversion type,* are characterized by physical complaints that have no underlying organic pathology. The former term derives from *hystera,* or "uterus," because of the ancient belief that various emotional and physical ailments in women could be caused by the uterus, which wandered around inside the body, searching for a baby. (As a remedy, Hippocrates recommended marriage.) The modern use of the word hysteria does not imply any gynecological problems; conversion disorders can afflict men and women alike.

The term *conversion,* when applied to a mental disorder, refers to the development of sensory or motor impairments: psychological blindness, deafness, loss of feeling, or paralysis. These syndromes are called conversion reactions because of the psychoanalytic theory that the energy of an unresolved psychic conflict is diverted into a physical symptom. Hofling (1963) describes one such case:

The patient had taken the day off from work to be at home with his wife and [newborn] baby. During the afternoon, he had felt somewhat nervous and tense, but had passed off these feelings as normal for a new father. . . .

. . . the baby awoke and cried. Mrs. L. said that she would nurse him. . . . As she put the baby to her breast, the patient became aware of a smarting sensation in his eyes. He had been smoking heavily and attributed the irritation to the room's being filled with smoke. He got up and opened a window. When the smarting sensation became worse he went to the washstand and applied a cold cloth to his eyes. On removing the cloth, he found that he was completely blind.

. . . psychotherapy was instituted. . . . The visual symptoms disappeared rather promptly, with only very mild and fleeting exacerbations during the next several months. . . .

. . . He had been jealous of the baby—this was a difficult admission to make—and jealous on two distinct counts. One feeling was, in essence, a sexual jealousy, accentuated by his own sexual deprivation during the last weeks of the pregnancy. The other was . . . a jealousy of the maternal solicitude shown the infant by its mother. (pp. 315–316)

The sensory disorders of paralyses of people with conversion disorders do not result from damage to the nervous system, but this fact does not mean that these people are faking their illness. People who deliberately pretend that they are sick in order to gain some advantage, such as avoiding work, are said to be *malingering.* Although it is not always easy to distinguish malingering from a conversion reaction, two criteria are useful. First, people with a conversion reaction are usually delighted to talk about their symptoms in great detail, whereas malingerers are reluctant to do so, for fear of having their deception discovered. Second, people with a conversion reaction usually describe the symptoms with great drama and flair but do *not* appear to be upset about them. This blasé attitude is so striking that it has been called *la belle indifference,* "fine unconcern."

Conversion disorders must also be distinguished from two other syndromes, psychosomatic disorders and hypochondriasis. Hypochondriasis is described in the next section. *Psychosomatic disorders* are real, organic illnesses that are caused or made worse by psychological factors. For example, extreme stress can (in a susceptible individual) cause gastric ulcers, asthma, or other physical symptoms. An ulcer caused by stress is a real ulcer, not

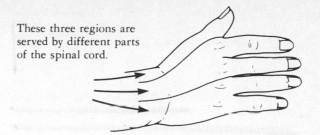

These three regions are served by different parts of the spinal cord.

Anesthesia of only the hand is not anatomically possible.

FIGURE 17.7 Glove anesthesia is physiologically impossible because the three major regions of the hand are served by different parts of the spinal cord.

an imaginary one. Successful treatment requires reduction of the person's level of stress as well as surgical or medical treatment of the lesion in the stomach.

The particular physical symptoms of people with conversion reactions change with the times and with people's general sophistication. For example, around the turn of the century, patients commonly developed "glove" or "stocking" anesthesias; the skin over their hands or feet would become perfectly numb. It is physiologically impossible for these anesthesias to occur as a result of nerve damage; the patterns of anesthesia produced by organic means would be very different. Today people seldom suffer such a naive disorder. (See **Figure 17.7**.)

Because conversion reactions can affect any part of the body, it is very important that clinicians distinguish between organic illness and conversion disorders. There is nothing to prevent a person with a conversion reaction from also having an organic illness. Whitlock (1967) examined the subsequent medical history of patients with various kinds of nonpsychotic mental disorders and found that more than 60 percent of those diagnosed as having conversion disorders later developed organic diseases, in contrast to 5 percent of people with other types of mental disorders. The ailments of the people with "conversion disorders" included head injury (received before diagnosis), stroke, encephalitis, and brain tumors.

◆ POSSIBLE CAUSES   Psychoanalytic theory suggests that the psychic energy of unresolved conflicts (especially those involving sexual desires that the patient is unwilling or unable to admit to having) becomes displaced into physical symptoms. In other words, psychoanalysts regard conversion reactions as primarily sexual in origin.

Behaviorists have suggested that conversion reactions can be learned for a variety of reasons. This assertion gains support from the fact that people with this disorder usually suffer from physical symptoms of diseases with which they are already familiar (Ullman and Krasner, 1969). A patient often mimics the symptoms of a friend. Furthermore, the patient must receive some kind of reinforcement for having the disability; he or she must derive some benefit from it.

Ullman and Krasner have cited a case that was originally reported by Brady and Lind (1961). A soldier developed an eye problem that led to his discharge, along with a small disability pension. He worked at a series of menial jobs, returning periodically to the hospital for treatment of his eye condition. He applied for a larger disability pension several times but was turned down because his vision had not become worse. After twelve years, the man, who was currently being forced by his wife and mother-in-law to spend his spare evenings and weekends doing chores around the house, suddenly became "blind." Because of his total disability, he was given special training for the blind and received a larger pension. He also received a family allowance from the community and no longer had to work around the house. In this case, both criteria described by Ullman and Krasner were fulfilled—the patient was familiar with the disorder (indeed, he had a real eye disorder) and his symptoms were reinforced.

Hypochondriasis

◆ DESCRIPTION   There is probably a bit of the hypochondriac in all of us. It is said that almost every first-year medical student suffers from mild hypochondria when he or she learns the symptoms of so many diseases. (And perhaps you have been searching you own behavior patterns while reading the descriptions of the mental disorders in this chapter.) However, *hypochondriasis* is a condition in which a person adopts illness as a way of life. (*Hypochondria* means "under the cartilage." Greek physicians thought that the disorder occurred when black bile collected under the breastbone, which is made of cartilage.) Hypochondriasis is different from conversion disorders and psychosomatic illness, both of which have physical symptoms. Hypochondriacs usually do not have precise symptoms, and they tend to indulge in a great deal of self-diagnosis. They usually read about diseases and watch television programs with medical themes, coming down with each new disorder they learn about. Often their self-descriptions are a hodgepodge of medical terminology. Coleman (1976) quotes a patient as saying that he had "ptosis of the transvex colon." (*Ptosis* refers to drooping, especially of an upper eyelid, and *transvex* is a meaningless word that probably refers to the *transverse* colon.)

Menninger (1945) published the following letter from a woman with severe hypochondriasis. The letter shows the vagueness of her symptoms and the wide scope of her complaints.

Dear Mother and Husband:

I have suffered terrible today with drawing in throat. My nerves are terrible. My head feels queer. But my stomach hasn't cramped quite so hard. I've been on the verge of a nervous chill all day, but I have been fighting it hard. It's night and bedtime, but, Oh, how I hate to go to bed. Nobody knows or realizes how badly I feel because I fight to stay up and outdoors if possible.

I haven't had my cot up for two days, they don't want me to use it.

These long afternoons and nights are awful. There are plenty of patients well enough to visit with but I'm in too much pain.

The nurses ignore any complaining. They just laugh or scold.

Eating has been awful hard. They expect me to eat like a harvest hand. Every bite of solid food is agony to get down, for my throat aches so and feels so closed up. . . .

With supper so early, and evening so long, I am so nervous I can't sleep until so late. I haven't slept well since I've been here. My heart pains as much as when I was at home. More so at night. I put hot water bottle on it. I don't know if I should or not. I've been wanting to ask some Dr.

I had headache so badly in the back of my head last night and put hot water bottle there. My nurse said not to.

They don't give much medicine here. Mostly Christian Science it seems! Well I must close or I never will get to sleep. My nurse gets off at 8:15 so she makes me go to bed by then.

My eyes are bothering me more.

Come up as soon as you can. My nose runs terrible every time I eat.

The trains and ducks and water pipes are noisy at night.

                                                    Annie

◆ POSSIBLE CAUSES Coleman (1976) lists three important factors in the development of hypochondriasis. (1) *Overemphasis on body functions in early life.* A child who hears a lot of medical complaints from parents and other relations is likely to adopt a similar pattern of behavior. Furthermore, if overprotective parents become alarmed about every cough and sneeze, the child may become oversensitive to his or her own physical condition. Finally, if a genuine illness or injury early in life brings attention and special favors, symptoms of illness are likely to be reinforced.

(2) *A disappointing life situation as a precipitating factor.* Hypochondriasis is often triggered by life crises such as those that often occur when people are in their forties or fifties, when they tend to realize that their lives are not now, and probably never will be, all that they had hoped for. Of course, not all people develop hypochondriasis if they suffer a midlife crisis; other disorders can occur instead, or the person can simply weather the crisis. However, if their early training has predisposed them to a preoccupation with health, they are more likely to develop hypochondriasis.

(3) *Maintenance of the hypochondriacal pattern by reinforcement.* Normally, hypochondriacs receive benefit from their condition. They get sympathy and support (at least at first), and they can manipulate people by making them feel guilty about their (the patient's) misfortune. Also, like people with a conversion disorder, they can get out of unpleasant chores and other responsibilities. Finally—and

perhaps most important—they can use the imaginary illness to absolve themselves of personal responsibility for the general lack of achievement in their lives.

DISSOCIATIVE DISORDERS

Description

◆ Like *conversion disorder,* the term **dissociative disorder** comes from Freud. According to psychoanalytic theory, a person develops a dissociative disorder when a massive repression fails to keep a strong sexual desire from consciousness. As a result, the person resorts to dissociating one part of his or her mind from the rest. Dissociative disorders can be either serial—occurring in sequence— or simultaneous. The most common serial dissociative reaction is **amnesia,** in which a person "forgets" all his or her past life, along with the conflicts that were present, and begins a new one. Because amnesia can also be produced by physical means—such as epilepsy, drug or alcohol intoxication, or brain injury resulting from a stroke, encephalitis, malnutrition coupled with chronic alcoholism, or a blow to the head—clinicians must be careful to distinguish between amnesia of organic and psychogenic origin. Any person with amnesia must undergo a complete neurological examination and appropriate laboratory tests.

Hofling (1963) reports a case of psychogenic amnesia.

> An attractive young girl . . . was brought to the receiving ward by a taxicab driver, who stated that after entering his cab at the airport the girl had seemed utterly confused, being unable to give a destination or even to give her own identity.
>
> . . . She was cooperative in the examination, but completely unable to relate events in her personal life prior to her having stepped into the cab. . . . the patient retained memory of the events of the ride to the hospital and events occurring in the receiving ward. In fact, aside from the loss of memory and a mood of mild anxiety and depression, the mental status findings were normal. . . . She even could express opinions on certain subjects (preferring one form of music, literature, athletics, to another) although she could not recall the experiences upon which the opinions were based.
>
> In the patient's purse were an airplane ticket,

showing that she had arrived on the morning plane from an eastern city, and a driver's license giving her name, Miss K.B., her age, 19. . . . In response to questions, the patient could only say that the name and address sounded vaguely familiar; she had no sense of their belonging to herself. As the questions continued, she became increasingly anxious without knowing why.

. . . with the patient's somewhat hesitant agreement, she was given sodium pentothal intravenously and interviewed. . . . Within half an hour, the amnesia had cleared completely. The purpose of the airplane trip had been a rendezvous with a twice-divorced man of 30, of whom the girl's parents violently disapproved. With the recovery of this memory, Miss B. became, for the first time, very upset, and she began to weep. (pp. 322–323)

A *fugue* (pronounced "fyoog") is a special form of amnesia in which the person leaves and starts a new life elsewhere. (*Fugue* means "flight.") Henderson and Gillespie (1950) reported the following case of psychogenic amnesia compounded by fugue.

A clergyman, the Rev. Ansell Bourne, disappeared from a town in Rhode Island. Eight weeks later a man calling himself A.J. Brown, who had rented a small shop six weeks previously in a town in Pennsylvania and had stocked it with confectionery, etc., woke up in a fright and asked who he was. He said he was a clergyman, that his name was Bourne, and that he knew nothing of the shop or of Brown. He was subsequently identified as the Rev. Ansell Bourne by his relatives, and remained terrified by the incident and unable to explain it. (p. 192)

Multiple personality is a very rare, but very striking, dissociative disorder. The DSM-III defines this condition as "the existence within the individual of two or more distinct personalities, each of which is dominant at a particular time." In addition, "each individual personality is complex and integrated with its own unique behavior patterns and social relationships." Only about a hundred cases of multiple personality have been documented, but this disorder has received much attention; most people find it fascinating to contemplate several different personalities, most of

FIGURE 17.8   Actress Joanne Woodward portraying two of Eve's personalities from the film *The Three Faces of Eve.*

whom are unaware of each other, existing within the same individual. (See **Figure 17.8.**) Lipton (1943) gave an account of the case of Sara and Maud K.

> . . . in general demeanor, Maud was quite different from Sara. She walked with a swinging, bouncing gait contrasted to Sara's sedate one. While Sara was depressed, Maud was ebullient and happy.
>
> . . . in so far as she could Maud dressed differently from Sara. Sara had two pairs of slippers. One was a worn pair of plain gray mules; the other, gaudy, striped, high-heeled, open-toed sandals. Sara always wore the mules. Maud would throw them aside in disgust and don the sandals. Sara used no make-up. Maud used a lot of rouge and lipstick, painted her fingernails and toenails deep red, and put a red ribbon in her hair. She liked red and was quickly attracted by anything of that color. Sara's favorite color was blue.
>
> Sara was a mature, intelligent individual. Her . . . I.Q. [was] 128. [Maud's I.Q. was 43.] Sara's vocabulary was larger than Maud's, and she took an intelligent interest in words new to her. When Maud heard a new word, she would laugh and mispronounce it or say, "That was a twenty-five cent one." In sharp contrast to Sara, Maud's grammar was atrocious. A typical statement was, "I didn't do nuttin'." Sara's handwriting was more mature than Maud's.
>
> Sara did not smoke and was very awkward when she attempted it. Maud had a compulsion to smoke. At times she insisted she "had to" and would become agitated and even violent if cigarettes were denied her. She would smoke chain fashion as many cigarettes as were permitted. . . .
>
> Maud had no conscience, no sense of right and wrong. She saw no reason for not always doing as she pleased. She felt no guilt over her incestuous and promiscuous sexual relationships. Sara on the other hand had marked guilt feelings over her previous immoral sexual behavior.
>
> It seemed that Sara changed to Maud at the point when Sara's feeling of guilt was greatest. (pp. 41–44)

Possible Causes

Dissociative disorders are usually explained as responses to a severe conflict resulting from intolerable impulses or guilt stemming from an actual misdeed. Leahy and Martin (1967) describe a man who became subject to amnesia after World War II. While he was amnestic, he did not recognize his wife, and spoke to her as if she were French;

he also acted as if he thought he was in France, where he had been stationed during the war. The episodes were disturbing to the man's family, and he sought psychotherapy.

Under hypnosis, he described an important experience he had had during the war. He and an officer who outranked him were in charge of four German prisoners and became separated from the rest of the unit. When the officer ordered him to shoot the prisoners, the patient said that he refused to do so, threw his rifle to him, and ran out of the hut to rejoin his unit. The patient relived the experience several times under hypnosis and showed some improvement. The relief was short-lived, however, and when the patient came back to the hospital and was hypnotized again, he admitted that he had not rejoined his unit after leaving the hut. Instead, he had come back and had stabbed the officer to death in order to protect the German prisoners. This experience was relived with intense emotion, and this time the catharsis seemed to work; the patient's amnesia disappeared.

Partly because they are so rare, dissociative disorders are among the least understood of the mental disorders. In general, the dissociation is advantageous to the person. Amnesia includes forgetting about a painful or unpleasant life. A person with fugue not only forgets but also leaves the area to start a new existence. Finally, multiple personalities allow a person to do things that he or she would really like to do but cannot, because of the strong guilt feelings that would ensue. The alternate personality can be one with a very weak conscience.

DYSTHYMIC DISORDER

◆ The term *dysthymic disorder,* formerly called *depressive neurosis,* is derived from Greek *thymos,* meaning "spirit" or "temper." Thus, dysthymia (pronounced "dis-THIGH-me-a") is a disorder of spirit.

Dysthymia is a condition of extreme sadness caused by a personal tragedy such as the death of a loved one, loss of a job, or arrest and conviction for a crime. Obviously, sadness and depression are natural consequences of such events; the difference between normal depression and a dysthymic disorder is one of degree.

It is sometimes difficult to distinguish a dysthymic disorder from the major affective disorders, which are psychoses. The best distinguishing feature is that although people with dysthymic disorder feel hopeless and dejected, their thought processes are not severely disordered, and they do not suffer from delusions. Davison and Neale (1974) describe the following case:

> The patient, a thirty-six-year-old woman, had just been readmitted to a psychiatric hospital. Her husband reported that during the past few weeks she had virtually stopped behaving, seeming to lose interest in all activities, both household chores and hobbies. During the intake interview, the woman's sadness was very apparent; her speech was slow, her posture stooped, and her facial expression was almost frozen in a look of extreme grief. When asked when she had begun to feel depressed and why, she reported that "About a month ago, everything just seemed to start to go wrong. My husband lost his job and two of my children became very ill. There just wasn't anything I could do about it." (p. 176)

These symptoms indicate a diagnosis of dysthymic disorder. However, the woman then went on to say: "When I first noticed myself getting depressed I knew that I couldn't do anything about it. No one would help because of my wickedness. I'm being punished for my past sins and have been given over to the devil" (p. 176). This delusion rules out a diagnosis of dysthymic disorder. Delusions are characteristic of a more severe disorder, a psychosis.

Interim summary: People with nonpsychotic mental disorders, previously called neuroses, have adopted strategies that have a certain amount of immediate payoff but in the long run are maladaptive. We can understand most of their problems as exaggerations of our own. Although their fears and doubts may be unrealistic, they do not seem bizarre and illogical. In contast, psychoses involve obviously maladaptive features—delusions, hallucinations, disordered thought processes, and inappropriate emotional states.

Anxiety disorders include anxiety states and phobic disorders; anxiety states include generalized anxiety disorder, panic disorder, and obsessive-compulsive disorders. The first two are the least adaptive of all neurotic disorders; the person has no defense against his or her discomfort. In con-

trast, obsessive-compulsive disorders provide thoughts or behaviors that prevent the person's thinking about painful subjects, or ward off feelings of guilt and anxiety.

Phobic disorders can be explained by classical conditioning; some experience (usually early in life) causes a particular object or situation to become a conditioned aversive stimulus. The fear associated with this stimulus leads to escape behaviors, which are negatively reinforced by reduction of fear.

Somatoform disorders include conversion disorders and hypochondriasis. The conversion disorders include specific physical symptoms such as paralysis or sensory disturbance that are not produced by a physiological disorder. In most cases the patient derives some gain from his or her disability. Hypochondriacs exhibit less specific symptoms, and usually have a "complaining" personality, presumably as a result of overemphasis on body functions early in life, and a disappointing life situation. Their symptoms, like those seen in conversion disorders, are reinforced by sympathy and/or avoidance of unpleasantness.

Dissociative disorders are rare but interesting. Amnesia (with or without fugue) appears to be a withdrawal from a painful situation or from intolerable guilt. Because amnesia is a common symptom of brain injury or neurological disease, physical factors must be ruled out before accepting a diagnosis of psychogenic amnesia. Multiple personalities are even more rare, and presumably occur because they permit a person to engage in behaviors that are contrary to his or her code of conduct.

Dysthymic disorders are characterized by sadness and depression that follow a personal tragedy. Unlike psychotic depression (discussed later), dysthymic disorders do not include delusions or severe thought disorders.

SCHIZOPHRENIA

◈ *Schizophrenia,* the most common psychosis, includes several types, each with a distinctive set of symptoms. For many years there has been a controversy about whether schizophrenia is one disorder with various subtypes, or whether each type constitutes a distinct disease. A particular individual may, at different times, meet the criteria for different subtypes. However, because the prognosis differs for the various types of schizophrenia, they appear to differ at least in severity. As we shall see later, recent biological evidence suggests that there are two basic types of schizophrenia; these do not correspond to the DSM-III classifications.

The term *schizophrenia* comes from the Greek words *schizein,* "to split," and *phrēn,* "heart" or "mind." But the term does *not* imply a split or multiple personality. *Schizophrenia* is probably the most misused psychological term in existence. People often say that they "feel schizophrenic" about an issue when they really mean that they have mixed feelings about it. A person who sometimes wants to build a cabin in Alaska and live off the land and at other times wants to take over the family insurance business may be undecided, but he or she is not schizophrenic.

Eugen Bleuler, who coined the term *schizophrenia* in 1911, believed that this disorder resulted from splitting, or disorganization, of the various functions of the mind, so that thoughts and feelings no longer worked together normally. This concept is quite different from the notion of multiple personality; as S.H. Snyder (1974) puts it, the schizophrenic "cannot integrate a single personality, much less pull off . . . an effective presentation of three of them" (p. 80).

CHARACTERISTIC SYMPTOMS

This section describes the symptoms that are seen in all types of schizophrenia, although they may not all be present in any one person diagnosed as schizophrenic. Later sections will describe symptoms that are usually associated with a particular type of schizophrenia.

Thought Disorders

Disordered thought is probably the most important symptom of schizophrenia. Schizophrenics have great difficulty arranging their thoughts logically. In conversation, they jump from one topic to another, as new associations come up. Often they utter *neologisms* (new and meaningless words) or choose words for their rhyme rather than for their meaning. As a schizophrenic patient noted (in a period of relative lucidity):

My thoughts get all jumbled up. I start thinking or talking about something but I never get there. Instead, I wander off in the wrong direction and get caught up with all sorts of different things that may be connected with things I want to say but in a way I can't explain. People listening to me get more lost than I do. . . .

My trouble is that I've got too many thoughts. You might think about something, let's say that ashtray and just think, ah, yes, that's for putting my cigarette in, but I would think of it and then would think of a dozen different things connected with it at the same time. (McGhie and Chapman, 1961, p. 108)

Delusions

A delusion is a belief that is obviously contrary to fact, and many schizophrenics hold such beliefs. People with ***delusions of persecution*** believe that others are plotting against them. ***Delusions of grandeur*** entail false beliefs of one's power and importance, such as a conviction that one is really a messiah, or a famous scientist, or the possessor of powers that could destroy the world. ***Delusions of control*** are related to delusions of persecution; the person believes that he or she is being controlled by others by such means as radar or tiny radio receivers implanted in his or her brain. Cavanaugh and McGoldrick (1966) described the following case of a delusion of persecution:

. . . she . . . entertained many ideas of persecution, directed in particular against a man named "Casey." . . . He had "secret doors to her apartment." The people under her floors bothered her day and night. . . . She said people stuck their noses under the seats in movie theaters, telling her to get out. . . . She claimed she was from a very highborn family and that it was absurd, under these circumstances, for them to think her insane. (pp. 296–297)

An anonymous self-report (1955) described a delusion of grandeur.

. . . I was suddenly confronted with an overwhelming conviction that I had discovered the secrets of the universe, which were being rapidly made plain with incredible lucidity. The truths discovered seemed to be known immediately and directly, with absolute certainty. I had no sense of doubt or awareness of the possibility of doubt. . . . I was suddenly convinced that it was possible to prove rationally the existence of God. (p. 94)

Finally, here is a self-report of a delusion of control.

> . . . I discovered that the Persecutor was none other than the electric machine, that is, it was the "System" that was punishing me. I thought of it as some vast world-like entity encompassing all men. At the top were those who gave orders, who imposed punishment, who pronounced others guilty. But they were themselves guilty. Since every man was responsible for all other men, each of his acts had a repercussion on other beings. A formidable interdependence bound all men under the scourge of culpability. Everyone was part of the System. But only some were aware of being part. (Sechehaye, 1951, p. 165)

Of course, not all strange stories people tell are delusions, and the task of sorting fact from fancy is often difficult. Davison and Neale (1974) cite a case of a woman who thought she was being followed. Indeed, she was. Her husband had hired a private detective to keep track of her whereabouts. Countless movies have had themes involving a person's discovery of a bizarre plot, only to have other people dismiss the plot as a psychotic delusion.

Hallucinations

Hallucinations are perceptions of stimuli that are not actually present. The most common schizophrenic hallucinations are auditory, but they can also involve any of the other senses. The typical schizophrenic hallucination consists of voices talking to the person. Sometimes they order the person to do something; sometimes they scold the person for his or her unworthiness; sometimes they just utter meaningless phrases. Olfactory hallucinations are also fairly common; often these contribute to the delusion that others are trying to kill the person with poison gas. Boisen (1960) reported the following experience of hallucinations:

> There was music everywhere and rhythm and beauty. . . . I heard what seemed to be a choir of angels. I though it the most beautiful music I had ever heard. Two of the airs I kept repeating over and over until the delirium ended. . . . This choir of angels kept hovering around the hospital and shortly afterward I heard something about a little lamb being born up-stairs in the room just above mine. This excited me greatly and next morning I made some inquiries about that little lamb. . . .
>
> The next night I was visited, not by angels, but

> by a lot of witches. . . . I could hear a constant tap-tapping along the walls, all done according to some system. This was due, it seemed, to the detectives in the employ of the evil powers who were out to locate the exact place where I was. Then the room was filled with the odor of [sulfur]. I was told that witches were around and from the ventilator shaft I picked up paper black cats and broom-sticks and poke bonnets. I was greatly exercised, and I stuffed my blanket into the ventilator shaft. I finally not only worked out a way of checking the invasion of the black cats, but I found some sort of process of regeneration which could be used to save other people. I had, it seemed, broken an opening in the wall which separated medicine and religion. I was told to feel on the back of my neck and I would find there a sign of my new mission. I thereupon examined and found a shuttle-like affair about three-fourth of an inch long. (pp. 119–120)

This potpourri of symptoms included auditory, then olfactory, then visual hallucinations, followed by a delusion of grandeur, and, finally, a somatosensory hallucination.

Anxiety

Patients with schizophrenia often become frightened by their lack of control over their own thoughts and feelings, especially in the early part of a schizophrenic episode. Their world seems to be crumbling as they feel themselves descend into madness. As one patient put it:

> Everything seemed different and strange. It was like I had entered an alien world where nothing was the same as I had known it. I no longer knew who I was, or even where the environment left off and I began. I didn't even seem to exist anymore as a distinct person—just parts of me "floating around" here and there in space. (Coleman, 1976, p. 294)

Emotional Withdrawal

Schizophrenics often lose interest in the real world and withdraw into themselves. They may show indifference to events that would be expected to affect them deeply, such as the death of a close relative. Often they resist efforts to bring them back to reality and become hostile when a therapist attempts to do so. It is possible that the withdrawal is a defense against the panic and anxiety that occur early in episodes of schizophrenia.

TYPES OF SCHIZOPHRENIA

Most cases of schizophrenia do not fit neatly into one of the categories described below. Many are diagnosed as *undifferentiated schizophrenia;* that is, the patients have delusions, hallucinations, and disorganized behavior but do not meet the criteria for catatonic, paranoid, or disorganized schizophrenia. In addition, some patients' symptoms change after an initial diagnosis, and their classification changes accordingly.

Catatonic Schizophrenia

◈ *Catatonic schizophrenia* (from Greek *katateinein,* "to stretch or draw tight") is characterized by various motor disturbances, including *catatonic postures*—bizarre, stationary poses maintained for many hours—and *waxy flexibility,* in which the person's limbs can be molded into new positions, which are then maintained. Contrary to popular assumptions, catatonic schizophrenics are often aware of all that goes on about them and will talk about what happened after the episode of catatonia subsides. (See **Figure 17.9.**)

Immobility is not the only motor symptom of catatonic schizophrenia. People with the disorder often engage in bouts of wild, excited movement, becoming dangerous and unpredictable. Before modern medication eliminated almost all need to use straitjackets, it was catatonic schizophrenics who were most likely to wear these devices. (The word is *strait,* by the way, and not *straight.* To *straiten* means to "limit," or "restrict.") Davison and Neale (1982) describe the following case:

> Bob, a twenty-two-year-old, was admitted to the hospital after a brief period of bizarre behavior at home. His parents reported that for several days he had stayed in his room, coming out only for meals. Then, at dinner one evening, he suddenly "became rigid." Alarmed, the parents called the family physician, but by the time he arrived Bob had entered a period of intense activity. He ran through the house, rolled on the floor, and strenuously resisted efforts to restrain him. Finally, he was sedated and taken to the hospital.
>
> In the hospital Bob continued to alternate between periods of catatonic immobility and wild excitement. He refused to speak or eat and often did the exact opposite of what was requested of him,

FIGURE 17.9　A catatonic posture.

remaining in bed when asked to get up and remaining up when asked to go to bed. (p. 404)

Paranoid Schizophrenia

◈ The preeminent symptoms of *paranoid schizophrenia* are delusions of persecution, grandeur, or control, although delusions can also occur in other forms of schizophrenia. A case reported by Davison and Neale (1982) illustrates how bizarre the delusions of a paranoid schizophrenic can be. Roger felt that he was a "born soldier," and in fact wore an army jacket and kept his hair cut short, even though the army had rejected him for psychiatric reasons. After being treated on an outpatient basis for several weeks, he had to be committed to a hospital.

> He had threatened to blow up an army recruiting post, claiming that aliens from another planet had

taken over. He now believed that he was one of the last "true" earthmen. The aliens had already infiltrated the bodies of most human beings, beginning first with those of army men and then moving into the bodies of the rest of the human race as well. (p. 406)

The word "paranoid" has become so widely used in ordinary language that it has come to mean "suspicious." However, not all paranoid schizophrenics believe that they are being persecuted. Some believe that they hold special powers that can save the world, or that they are Christ, or Napoleon, or the president of the United States.

Given the fact that paranoid schizophrenics are among the most intelligent of psychotic patients, it is not surprising that they often build up delusional structures incorporating an immense wealth of detail. Even the most trivial event is interpreted in terms of a grand scheme, whether it is a delusion of persecution or one of grandeur. The way a person walks, a particular facial expression or movement, or even the shapes of clouds can acquire special significance.

DSM-III recognizes a psychosis called *paranoia*, which is assumed to be distinct from paranoid schizophrenia. Not all clinicians agree; some argue that in most cases, a person with paranoia inevitably also begins to display the symptoms of schizophrenia. Paranoia consists of delusions *without* the thought disorders that characterize schizophrenia. That is, a pure paranoid will be perfectly rational about everything but his or her delusion, and even that will be logically consistent. Starting with an incorrect premise, paranoid patients piece together grand schemes, especially those of persecution. Paranoids are extremely resistant to therapy; if a person tries to convince them that they are really not being persecuted, they tend to view the attempts as a part of the plot to get them off their guard. To a paranoid, almost everyone is a part of the plot and plays a role in his or her delusion.

Disorganized Schizophrenia

◆ *Disorganized schizophrenia* once had a relatively innocuous-sounding name, *hebephrenic schizophrenia*. (Hebe, the Greek goddess of youth and spring, was usually portrayed as being rather silly.

Thus, *hebephrenia* denotes a "silly mind.") However, disorganized schizophrenia is a serious disorder. Usually it is progressive and irreversible. People with disorganized schizophrenia often display signs of emotion, especially silly laughter, that are inappropriate to the circumstances. Also, their speech tends to be a jumble of words: "I came to the hospital to play, gay, way, lay, day, bray, donkey, monkey" (S.H. Snyder, 1974, p. 132). The speech of a seriously deteriorated hebephrenic is often called a *word salad*. Cavanaugh and McGoldrick (1966) have reported a typical case of disorganized schizophrenia:

. . . she grew gradually worse, lost interest in everything, could not concentrate, became extremely impulsive, talked in a rambling, incoherent manner, became extremely silly with apparently unmotivated laughter, and would frequently cry and scream. . . . The following monologue illustrates her disordered stream of speech. . . . "When was I born? April 1, 1915. I have a pair of roller skates. We take exercise. I went in the front door and out the back. I took a bath, lady. I studied physiology. They taught me to eat lots of milk." To the accompaniment of silly giggling, she continues: "Lady with the white dress" (meaning the physician) "my grandfather was drowned in a well. So was my grandmother. I was vaccinated for smallpox. I had a blood test taken, lady!"

. . . The marked changes in personality and disposition, mental confusion, poverty of thought, rambling and incoherent speech, memory defects, emotional deterioration, fleeting and changeable illusions, silliness, lack of insight and judgment, in addition to the other symptoms indicated above, warranted the diagnosis of schizophrenia, hebephrenic [disorganized] type. (p. 258)

Schizophreniform Disorder

◆ Although the DSM-III assigns *schizophreniform disorder* (formerly called an *acute schizophrenic episode*) to the category of "psychotic disorders not elsewhere classified," this disorder differs from schizophrenia only in its shorter duration. Because episodes tend to begin and end rapidly, patients are likely to be overwhelmed by the sudden changes in their thought processes and are therefore also likely to feel panic and anxiety. Acute schizophrenic episodes also tend to be *undifferentiated;*

that is, they involve a wide variety of symptoms. Schizophreniform disorder has the best prognosis of all types of schizophrenia.

CAUSES

Early Predictors

◆ Eugen Bleuler (1911/1950), one of the pioneers in the diagnosis and study of schizophrenia (see **Figure 17.10**), divided the disorder into *process* and *reactive* forms. A patient with a general history of good mental health was designated as reactive, on the assumption that the disorder was a *reaction* to stressful life situations. Typically, these patients soon recovered, and few experienced another episode. Today these people would receive a diagnosis of either schizophreniform disorder or a brief reac-

FIGURE 17.10   Swiss psychiatrist Eugen Bleuler (1857–1939).

tive psychosis, depending on whether a plausible source of stress could be identified. Patients with indications of mental pathology early in life were designated as process schizophrenics and were considered to have a chronic disorder. Process schizophrenia would include all the other types of schizophrenia described above.

Evidence from modern research supports the distinction between process and reactive schizophrenia. Clinicians have observed that the symptoms displayed by the patients at the time of diagnosis can be used to predict the likelihood of eventual recovery. Astrup and Noreik (1966) followed patients over a thirty-year period and compared their clinical symptoms with the outcome of their disorder. Predictors of eventual recovery were delusions, thought disturbances, hallucinations, and change of personality at the onset of the schizophrenic episode. Presumably, these symptoms are characteristic of the fast onset of a reactive form of schizophrenia. Unfavorable signs were long duration of illness, emotional blunting, and inadequate motor reflexes. As we shall see, these results are consistent with the distinctions between *positive* and *negative* symptoms that have recently been made as a result of biological studies.

If process schizophrenia does have its roots in early life, then it is important to determine what the early signs are. If people with a high risk of schizophrenia can be identified early enough, it might be possible to institute some forms of therapy before the disorder becomes advanced. The early symptoms might also indicate whether the causes of schizophrenia are biological, environmental, or both.

◆ Watt and Lubansky (1976) attempted to relate childhood behavior patterns to schizophrenia in adulthood. First, they obtained a list of all patients from ages fifteen to thirty-four in mental institutions in Massachusetts. They also obtained a list of students who had attended the public high school in a large Boston suburb and identified among them fifty-four who later became schizophrenic patients. They selected a group of control subjects who had not developed schizophrenia, matching them with the patients on the basis of age, sex, race, and social class of the parents. Then the researchers examined the comments of the subjects' teachers in their school records and attempted to relate the kinds of comments that were made with the probability of a later onset of schizophrenia.

There were sharp sex differences in the results. Boys who had become schizophrenic were rated as less conscientious and as more abrasive and antisocial than the control subjects. Teachers found them disagreeable and described them as emotionally unstable. In contrast, the girls who had become schizophrenic were generally described as withdrawn or introverted, insecure, and passive. The control girls tended to be rated as more nervous, restless, and emotional. No strong differences were seen in intelligence or academic achievement. Preschizophrenics had somewhat lower IQ scores and scholastic performance, but the difference was not great, and childhood intelligence was not related to the amount of time spent in a mental hospital later.

The results support the hypothesis that schizophrenia is a disorder that strikes people who are different from others even in childhood. The study reveals nothing about whether these differences result from physiological disorders or from the behavior of other family members during the schizophrenics' infancy and early childhood.

Identifying the Essential Feature of Schizophrenia

As we have seen, schizophrenia is characterized by thought disorders, delusions, hallucinations, and emotional changes, and, in some cases, by motor disturbances. Many investigators have attempted to identify a single, essential feature that can account for all these symptoms. S.H. Synder (1974) reviews these efforts and casts doubt on most of the hypotheses. One of these claims that **anhedonia**, or lack of pleasure, characterizes all schizophrenics; that is, schizophrenia prevents the operation of reinforcement on a person's behavior. But Snyder notes that this feature is even more characteristic of the psychotic affective disorders than of schizophrenia.

A second hypothesis claims that overanxiety is the essential feature—that all schizophrenics find their symptoms threatening. However, people with anxiety disorders display anxiety and fear, but without the thought disturbances that affect schizophrenics. Furthermore, many schizophrenics do not exhibit much anxiety.

A third hypothesis, based on psychoanalytic theory, maintains that all schizophrenia results from the assertion of control by the primitive unconscious. According to this view, the id, with its impulsiveness and lack of logic, assumes direct control over the mind of the schizophrenic. This hypothesis is impossible either to prove or to disprove, because the unconscious is not observable. Furthermore, it does not explain *why* the unconscious takes over.

A fourth view maintains that schizophrenics' thought disorders are essential, and that the anhedonia, anxiety, and other symptoms follow from them. This claim seems plausible but does not precisely define a thought disorder or explain what might cause it.

Snyder also cites the work of David Shakow (1962), who has attributed all the thought disorders of schizophrenics to disruption of attention. Shakow maintains that all schizophrenics have trouble focusing their thoughts on the relevant topic. Instead of ignoring the many possible associations that a given topic can evoke, schizophrenic patients attempt to pursue them all.

> If there is any creature who can be accused of not seeing the forest for the trees, it is the schizophrenic. If he is of the paranoid persuasion, he sticks even more closely than the normal person to the path through the forest, examining each tree along the path, sometimes even each tree's leaves, with meticulous detail. If at the other extreme he follows the hebephrenic pattern, then he acts as if there were no paths, for he strays off the obvious path entirely; he is attracted not only visually but even by smell and taste, by any and all trees and even the undergrowth and flora of the forest, in a superficial flirting, apparently forgetting in the meantime about the place he wants to get to. (Shakow, 1962, p. 14)

Schizophrenics seem to have trouble keeping "on track"; they keep branching off, following associations that are not related to the main theme and, in the case of paranoia, magnifying the significance of these associations. Perceptions, as well as thoughts, appear to be affected. In the excerpt below, an intelligent and articulate woman reports her thoughts and perceptions during an earlier schizophrenic episode. She appears to characterize her experience as difficulty in controlling the focus of her attention.

Each of us is capable of coping with a large number of stimuli, invading our being through any one of the senses. We could hear every sound within earshot and see every object, line, and color within the field of vision and so on. It is obvious that we would be incapable of carrying on any of our daily activities if even one-hundredth of all these available stimuli invaded us at once. So the mind must have a filter which functions without our conscious thought, sorting stimuli, and allowing only those which are relevant to the situation at hand to disturb consciousness. And this filter must be working at maximum efficiency at all times, particularly when we require a high degree of concentration. What happened to me . . . was a breakdown in the filter, and a hodgepodge of unrelated stimuli were distracting me from things which should have had my undivided attention. (McDonald, 1960, p. 218)

A number of laboratory experiments support the hypothesis that the essential feature of schizophrenia is a disordered attentional mechanism. For example, Rappaport (1967) presented schizophrenic and normal subjects with up to seven auditory messages, played simultaneously. The subjects were asked to pay attention to one of the messages and to repeat it back. The schizophrenic subjects had more trouble than the normal subjects in discriminating between the relevant and irrelevant information.

Heritability

So many studies have demonstrated the heritability of schizophrenia that most investigators do not dispute the issue. In one of the best studies, Kety, Rosenthal, Wender, and Schulsinger (1968) examined Denmark's *folkeregister*, which contains a lifelong record of Danish citizens. From it, they compiled two lists: one of children who had been adopted and who later became schizophrenic, and one of adopted children who did not. They found that the incidence of schizophrenia in the adoptive families of people who were schizophrenic was as low as in the adoptive families of control subjects who were not schizophrenic, but that the incidence of schizophrenia in the children's *biological* families was much higher than normal. Because the children were raised by their adoptive families, and not by their biological families, there are no grounds for concluding that learning played a role in the transmission of the disorder; rather, the transmis-

sion would appear to have been hereditary. (See **Figure 17.11**.) The same study found that only chronic (process) schizophrenia was related to schizophrenia in the biological family. Acute (reactive) schizophrenia was *not* related to a family history of mental disturbances. This finding further supports the conclusion that the process and reactive forms of schizophrenia are indeed different, with different causes.

In another study, Heston (1966) compared the children of schizophrenic and nonschizophrenic mothers, all of whom were adopted by other families within two weeks of birth. Seventeen percent of the children of schizophrenic mothers later became schizophrenic, whereas none of the children of the nonschizophrenic mothers did. Moreover,

FIGURE 17.11   The results and conclusions of the adoption study by Kety, Rosenthal, Wender, and Schulsinger (1968).

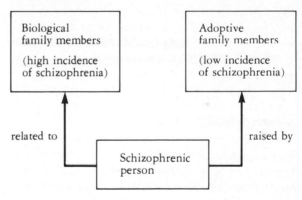

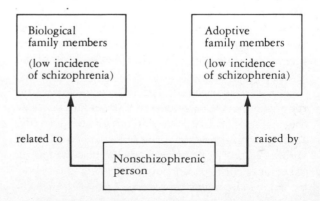

approximately half of the children of the schizophrenic mothers had serious emotional problems. Many were arrested for antisocial crimes, and others became drug addicts or alcoholics. It appears that the children received some form of deleterious genetic information from their schizophrenic mothers.

Although the heredity studies have shown that the likelihood of developing schizophrenia increases significantly if a person has schizophrenic relatives, this disorder is not a simple trait that is inherited like eye color. Most people with schizophrenic relatives do not develop schizophrenia. Studies estimate that even if both parents are schizophrenic, the probability that their child will develop schizophrenia is 30 percent or less.

Most investigators believe that a person inherits a *predisposition* to become schizophrenic; in their view, most enviornments will foster normal development, whereas others will trigger various disorders, including schizophrenia. Until recently, the important factors were thought to be social ones, and schizophrenia to be a reaction to stress in susceptible individuals. Although social factors cannot be ruled out, evidence now suggests that at least some cases of schizophrenia may result from disease. This evidence will be reviewed later.

Biochemical Factors

◆ One way to determine the cause or causes of schizophrenia would be to induce its characteristic symptoms under controlled conditions. And indeed, certain chemicals do cause schizophrenic behavior. Earlier in this century, when cocaine was cheap and freely available, there was an epidemic of cocaine psychoses, caused by chronic, large injections of the substance. (Today the drug is usually sniffed in relatively small amounts, so psychotic reactions are less common. The high price of the drug is probably the limiting factor.) Heavy users of cocaine developed a syndrome that closely resembled paranoid schizophrenia, and in fact many were diagnosed as having this disorder. The addicts became suspicious and believed that others were plotting against them, heard voices talking to them, and often had tactile hallucinations, such as the feeling that small insects had burrowed under their skin.

Clinicians have also observed that abuse of amphetamine (whose pharmacological effects are similar to those of cocaine) causes a temporary psychosis that resembles schizophrenia. Griffith, Cavanaugh, Held, and Oates (1972) used seven subjects who were users of amphetamine but who had no previous history of psychotic behavior. (Experimentally, it would have been better to use subjects who had never taken amphetamine, but ethical considerations rule out this approach.) The experimenters administered a very heavy dose—10 milligrams of dextroamphetamine every hour. All seven of the subjects became psychotic within two to five days. At first the subjects lost their appetite and could not sleep. About eight hours before overt signs of psychosis occurred, they became withdrawn and would not discuss their thoughts and feelings. Later, the subjects admitted that during this time they began to have paranoid thoughts, but they felt that these were drug induced and fought to keep control over them. When the psychosis finally emerged, the subjects began to talk about it. They all developed paranoid delusions, including one of being controlled by a "giant oscillator." Their symptoms disappeared a few hours after discontinuing the drug.

Amphetamine and related substances also make all kinds of naturally occurring schizophrenia worse: paranoids become more suspicious, disorganized schizophrenics sillier, and catatonics more rigid or hyperactive. Davis (1974) injected an amphetaminelike drug into schizophrenic patients whose symptoms had abated. Within one minute, each patient's condition changed "from a mild schizophrenia into a wild and very florid schizophrenia." One of them began to make a clacking noise, then pounded a pad of paper with a pencil until he shredded it. He had been "sending and receiving messages from the ancient Egyptians."

There are other drugs that make people behave abnormally, but only those with the biochemical effects of amphetamine and cocaine produce psychoses that would be diagnosed as schizophrenia. For example, LSD or mescaline psychoses are very different from schizophrenia. Although some investigators have tried to relate schizophrenia to the symptoms of these drugs, the hallucinations they produce are primarily visual, whereas schizophrenic hallucinations are typically auditory. Hollister (1962) tape-recorded interviews with schizophrenics and subjects who had taken psychedelic drugs, then played the recordings to var-

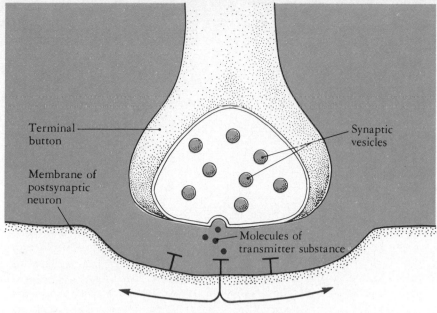

Terminal button

Membrane of postsynaptic neuron

Synaptic vesicles

Molecules of transmitter substance

Activation of receptor site excites or inhibits postsynaptic neuron.

FIGURE 17.12   Synaptic transmission.

ious mental health professionals. The raters had no trouble distinguishing a schizophrenic from a person under the influence of the drugs.

The fact that large doses of amphetamine can induce schizophrenia, or something very like it, suggests that some built-in biochemical defect acts in a similar way to affect the brains of people in whom schizophrenia occurs naturally. Support for this hypothesis comes not only from evidence that the tendency to develop schizophrenia is hereditary, as discussed earlier, but also from the fact that *antipsychotic drugs,* with biochemical effects *opposite* to those of amphetamine, reduce or eliminate the symptoms of both amphetamine-induced psychosis and naturally occurring schizophrenia.

Both amphetamine and the antipsychotic drugs act on synapses, the junctions between nerve cells in the brain. As you may recall from Chapter 3, one neuron passes on excitatory or inhibitory messages to another by liberating a small amount of transmitter substance from its terminal button into the synaptic cleft. The chemical activates receptors on the surface of the receiving neuron, and the activated receptors either excite or inhibit the receiving neuron. (See **Figure 17.12.**)

THE BIOCHEMISTRY OF AMPHETAMINE PSYCHOSIS The neurons of the brain employ a variety of different chemicals as transmitter substances. Two in particular are affected by cocaine and amphetamine: dopamine and norepinephrine. Cocaine and amphetamine enhance the activity of synapses that utilize dopamine and norepinephrine by (1) causing the release of these transmitter substances, (2) directly stimulating the receptors on the receiving neurons, and (3) retarding the rate at which the transmitter substances are returned to the terminal button of the sending neuron. This last effect is the most important; it keeps the transmitter substances in contact with the receptors on the receiving neurons for a longer-than-normal time. (See **Figure 17.13.**) Because cocaine and amphetamine stimulate synapses that use dopamine and norepinephrine as transmitter substances, it is possible that schizophrenia results from a biochemical defect that causes one or both of these types of synapses to be abnormally active.

THE BIOCHEMISTRY OF ANTIPSYCHOTIC DRUGS People with a diagnosis of schizophrenia constitute the largest proportion of patients in mental hos-

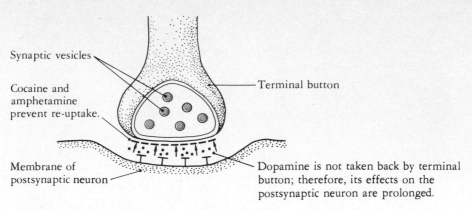

Synaptic vesicles

Cocaine and
amphetamine
prevent re-uptake.

Terminal button

Membrane of
postsynaptic neuron

Dopamine is not taken back by terminal
button; therefore, its effects on the
postsynaptic neuron are prolonged.

FIGURE 17.13   The effects of cocaine and
amphetamine on terminal buttons that secrete
dopamine.

pitals. Until around 1955, the number of patients in mental hospitals grew steadily every year; then the number of patients began to decline. (See **Figure 17.14.**) Several factors led to this decrease, including a growing tendency to treat patients in community-based facilities. But one of the most important factors was the introduction of ***chlorpromazine*** (trade name Thorazine).

◆   Chlorpromazine and other antipsychotic drugs are remarkably effective in alleviating the symptoms of schizophrenia. Hallucinations diminish or disappear, delusions become less striking or cease

FIGURE 17.14   Number of patients in public mental hospitals from 1900 to 1975. (Redrawn from Bassuk, E.L., and Gerson, S. *Scientific American,* 1978, *238,* 46–53.)

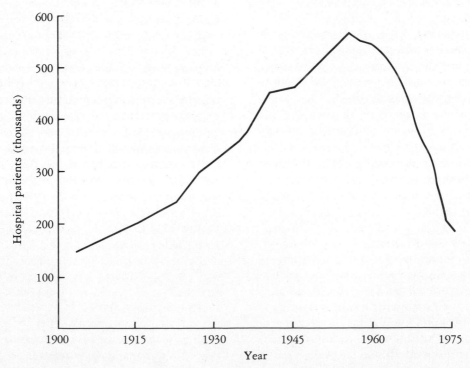

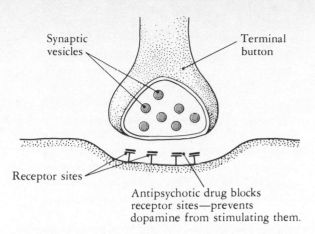

Synaptic vesicles

Terminal button

Receptor sites

Antipsychotic drug blocks receptor sites—prevents dopamine from stimulating them.

FIGURE 17.15   By blocking dopamine receptors on the postsynaptic membrane, antipsychotic drugs interfere with the neuron's response to this transmitter substance.

altogether, and the patients' thought processes become more coherent. These drugs are not merely tranquilizers; for example, they cause a patient with catatonic immobility to begin moving again, as well as cause an excited patient to quiet down. In contrast, true tranquilizers such as Librium or Valium only make a schizophrenic slow-moving and groggy.

The principal effect of the antipsychotic drugs appears to be the inhibition of dopamine synapses through blocking the receptors on the receiving neurons. When dopamine is released from the terminal buttons of the sending neurons, it causes very little response in the receiving neurons. (See **Figure 17.15**.) The fact that chlorpromazine and the other antipsychotic drugs are effective in alleviating the symptoms of both naturally occurring schizophrenia and amphetamine psychosis suggests that both of these disorders stem from overactivity of dopamine synapses.

THE ROLE OF DOPAMINE   Research with laboratory animals suggests that a system of dopamine-secreting neurons controls an important component of the brain's attentional mechanism. For example, after destroying this system on one side of rats' brains, Ungerstedt and Ljungberg (1974) observed that the animals ignored sensory stimuli that were presented to one side of the body. If damage to

this system of dopamine-secreting neurons causes an animal to ignore sensory stimuli, then overactivity of this system may produce the opposite effect: the organism will pay too much attention to all sensory stimuli and thus will be unable to distinguish important stimuli from trivial ones. As we have seen this is one of the primary features of schizophrenia.

SCHIZOPHRENIA AS A NEUROLOGICAL DISORDER

◆ Although the dopamine hypothesis has for several years been the dominant biological explanation for schizophrenia, recent evidence suggests that it can offer only a partial explanation. From the early days of treatment with antipsychotic drugs clinicians recognized that some patients' symptoms were not improved by medication. Crow and his colleagues (Crow, 1980; Crow, Cross, Johnstone, and Owen, 1982) suggest that the reason for this failure to improve is that there are two types of schizophrenic symptoms, positive and negative. Positive symptoms include the hallmarks of schizophrenia: delusions, hallucinations, and thought disorders. Negative symptoms include loss of emotional response, decreased speech, lack of drive, and diminished social interaction. Because antipsychotic drugs alleviate positive, but not negative, symptoms of schizophrenia (Angrist, Rotrosen, and Gershon, 1980), perhaps those patients who do not get better with medication have primarily negative symptoms.

Once investigators began paying more attention to negative symptoms they discovered evidence for brain damage. For example, Stevens (1982b) notes that many patients with chronic schizophrenia demonstrate symptoms that clearly indicate neurological disease, especially with regard to eye movements: decreased rate of eye blink, staring, lack of blink reflex in response to a tap on the forehead, turning of the eyes to the side accompanied by an arrest in speech, poor visual pursuit movements, poor pupillary reactions to light, and elevation of the eyebrows. In addition, catatonia is seen in nonpsychotic patients with a variety of neurological disorders. When she examined slices of brains of deceased schizophrenic patients, Stevens

(1982a) found clear evidence for brain damage that suggested either a disease process that had occurred earlier in life and had partly healed or one that was slowly progressing at the time of the patient's death. Other investigators examined CAT scans of patients with schizophrenia. For example, Weinberger and Wyatt (1982) compared CAT scans of the brains of fifty-eight schizophrenics and fifty-six controls matched by age. They found that the ventricles of the schizophrenic patients were, on average, twice as large as those of the normal subjects. Enlargement of the hollow ventricles of the brain indicates the loss of brain tissue elsewhere; thus, the evidence implied some kind of neurological disease.

Loss of brain tissue, as assessed by CAT scans, appears to be related to negative symptoms of schizophrenia, not positive ones (Johnstone, Crow, Frith, Stevens, Kreel, and Husband, 1978). In addition, patients with loss of brain tissue respond poorly to antipsychotic drugs (Weinberger, Bigelow, Kleinman, Klein, Rosenblatt, and Wyatt, 1980). These studies suggest that positive and negative symptoms have different causes: positive symptoms are a result of overactivity of dopamine synapses whereas negative symptoms are produced by actual loss of brain tissue.

Several studies have suggested that the cause of brain damage may be a viral infection. Torrey, Torrey, and Peterson (1977) noted that people who were born in late winter are significantly more likely to develop schizophrenia than those born during other times of the year. Similar seasonal variation is seen in diseases that are known to be caused by viruses, such as chickenpox and measles. Torrey, Yolken, and Winfrey (1982) analyzed cerebrospinal fluid from schizophrenic and control subjects and found antibodies for *cytomegalovirus (CMV),* a herpeslike virus, in 11 percent of the schizophrenics but none of the controls. Herpeslike viruses are known to be able to produce brain damage.

Stevens (1982b) suggests that schizophrenia is produced by a combination of hereditary and environmental factors in the following way: infection with CMV early in life will, in a genetically susceptible individual, cause brain damage, probably by triggering the person's immune system to begin attacking his or her own brain. She notes several similarities between schizophrenia and multiple sclerosis, a neurological disorder that most investigators believe to be caused by these means. Both schizophrenia and multiple sclerosis show seasonal variation, both are more prevalent in people who spent their childhood in northern latitudes and living in crowded conditions. In addition, both diseases are characterized by three patterns: (1) episodic attacks followed by more or less complete remissions; (2) recurrent attacks followed by only partial remissions, thus leading to increasing deficits; and (3) insidious onset followed by slow, steady, relentless progression of symptoms. Perhaps the positive symptoms are caused by attacks that somehow increase the activity of dopamine synapses. Each attack also produces some brain damage that gives rise to negative symptoms.

Interim summary: The principal positive symptoms of schizophrenia include thought disorders; delusions of persecution, grandeur, and control; and hallucinations. The principal negative symptoms include withdrawal, apathy, and poverty of speech. The DSM-III classifies schizophrenia into several subtypes, including undifferentiated, catatonic, paranoid, and disorganized, but it appears that the distinctions between process and reactive schizophrenia, and between positive and negative symptoms, are more important. Studies have suggested that the essential feature is a problem with control of attention, and that the other symptoms (at least the positive ones) follow from it.

People who develop chronic, process schizophrenia appear to be different from other people even as children, which suggests that the disorder has its roots very early in life. Indeed, heritability studies have shown a strong genetic component in schizophrenia, although they do not rule out the possibility of interaction with adverse environmental situations as a causal factor.

Positive symptoms of schizophrenia can be produced in normal people, or made worse in schizophrenics, by drugs that stimulate dopamine synapses (cocaine and amphetamine) and can be reduced or eliminated by those that block dopamine receptors (the antipsychotic drugs). These facts have led to the dopamine hypothesis: schizophrenia is caused by an inherited biochemical deficit that causes dopamine neurons to be overactive, producing disorders in attentional mechanisms.

More recent studies indicate that schizophrenia can best be conceived of as two different disorders. The positive symptoms are produced by overactivity of dopamine neurons and can be treated with the antipsychotic drugs, but the negative ones, which do not respond to these drugs, are caused by brain damage. Investigators have found direct evidence of brain damage by inspecting slices of deceased patients' brains and CAT scans of living patients. The fact that most schizophrenic patients were born during late winter and early spring, the fact that the disorder shows a particular geographical distribution, and the fact that antibodies for cytomegalovirus have been found in their cerebrospinal fluid strengthen the conclusion that a neurological disease may be present. Perhaps the virus causes no brain damage in people with non-schizophrenic heredity but damages the brains of people with an inherited susceptibility to the disease. This pattern appears to be the case with multiple sclerosis.

Much more research will be necessary before investigators can determine whether overactivity of dopamine synapses does indeed produce positive symptoms of schizophrenia and a viral infection does indeed produce the brain damage that results in negative symptoms. But biological explanations for schizophrenia will not lessen the usefulness of behaviorally oriented therapies (discussed in the next chapter) in the treatment of this disorder. Experience has shown that it is not enough merely to dose a schizophrenic patient with Thorazine. It is also important to teach the person how to structure a new life and how to cope with the many problems that he or she will encounter in reentering society. Behaviorally oriented therapies are the only hope for those patients with predominantly negative symptoms, who are not helped by antipsychotic drugs.

THE AFFECTIVE DISORDERS

DESCRIPTION

◆ In contrast to schizophrenia, whose principal symptom is thought disorders, the *affective disorders* are primarily disorders of emotion. There appears to be no environmental cause for the major affective disorders; the illness seems to be a result of something in the patient. The most severe affective disorders are *bipolar disorder* and *major depression*. Bipolar disorder is characterized by alternating periods of mania (wild excitement) and depression; major depression is unrelieved by bouts of mania. Dysthymic disorder was described earlier with other nonpsychotic mental disorders because it differs from the major affective disorders in its lack of delusions and hallucinations, its relatively

FIGURE 17.16   Depression sometimes has no obvious environmental cause.

low severity and short duration, and the presence of environmental causes.

Because one of the differences between dysthymic disorder and the major affective disorders is the presence or absence of environmental causes, it is important to determine whether an episode of depression is related to a stressful event. (See **Figure 17.16.**) However, this determination is not always easy, as Mendels (1970) points out. He outlines the following four possible relations between environmental stress and depression.

1. *The stress is a temporal coincidence.* We all experience difficulties and strains in the course of everyday living, and only a minority of us develop symptoms sufficiently severe after such experiences to bring them to a psychologist or a psychiatrist. It is therefore possible that the stress events that the patient associates with the onset of his illness are unrelated to the illness.

2. *The so-called stress event may arise as a consequence of the illness.* This is exemplified in a man who explains his depression as a result of having recently lost an important position. Careful [investigation] might reveal that he had lost his position because of increasing inefficiency associated with the earlier onset of the depression.

3. *The stress experience may interact with an underlying predisposing factor* or in some way activate a latent problem in a vulnerable personality.

4. *The stress event may, in fact, have been the major cause of the depression,* either because of the nature or the intensity of the stress. An example would be a woman who is depressed because her husband and children were all killed in [an automobile] accident. (p.28)

Mania

◈ *Mania* (the Greek word for "madness") is characterized by wild, exuberant, unrealistic activity. During manic episodes, people are usually elated and self-confident; however, contradiction or interference tends to make them very angry. Their speech and, presumably, their thought processes, become very rapid. They tend to flit from topic to topic and are full of grandiose plans, but their thoughts are less disorganized than those of a schizophrenic. Manic patients also tend to be restless and hyperactive, often pacing around ceaselessly. Davison and Neale (1982) record a typical interaction.

THERAPIST: Well, you seem pretty happy today.

CLIENT: Happy! Happy! You certainly are a master of understatement, you rogue! (Shouting, literally jumping out of seat.) Why I'm ecstatic. I'm leaving for the West coast today, on my daughter's bicycle. Only 3100 miles. That's nothing, you know. I could probably walk, but I want to get there by next week. And along the way I plan to contact a lot of people about investing in my fishing equipment. I'll get to know more people that way—you know, doc, "know" in the biblical sense (leering at therapist seductively). Oh, God, how good it feels. It's almost like a nonstop orgasm. (p. 232)

Because very few patients exhibit only mania, the DSM-III classifies all cases in which mania occurs as bipolar disorder. Patients with bipolar disorder usually experience alternate periods of mania and depression. Each of these lasts from a few days to a few weeks, usually with several days of relatively normal behavior in between. Many therapists have observed that there is something brittle and unnatural about the happiness during the manic phase; that the patient is making himself or herself be happy to ward off an attack of depression. A report by Masserman (1961) implies just such a defense.

He neglected his meals and rest hours, and was highly irregular, impulsive, and distractive in his adaptations to ward routine. Without apparent intent to be annoying or disturbing he sang, whistled, told pointless off-color stories, visited indiscriminately, and flirted crudely with the nurses and female patients. Superficially he appeared to be in high spirits, and yet one day when he was being gently chided over some particularly irresponsible act he suddenly slumped in a chair, covered his face with his hands, began sobbing, and cried, "For Pete's sake, doc, let me be. Can't you see that I've just got to act happy?" (pp. 66–67)

One type of antidepressant drug, *lithium carbonate,* is effective in treating bipolar disorder, though as yet no one knows why. Lithium carbonate is a simple inorganic compound. Its active ingredient is the element lithium, a metal that is closely related to sodium, which is found in ordinary table salt. (In fact lithium chloride was used as a sodium-free salt substitute until it was found to be toxic in large doses.)

Depression

Depressed psychotics are extremely sad, slow-moving, and full of self-directed guilt. Beck (1967) identified five cardinal symptoms of depression: (a) a sad and apathetic mood, (2) a negative self-concept, (3) a desire to withdraw from other people, (4) sleeplessness and loss of appetite and sexual desire, and (5) change in activity level, to either lethargy or agitation. Most people who are labeled "depressed" have a dysthymic disorder. Very few have a major affective disorder. However, the fact that many people who do suffer from major depression or the depressed phase of bipolar disorder commit suicide makes them potentially fatal disorders.

Depressed psychotics often have delusions, especially that their brains or internal organs are rotting away. Often they believe that they are being punished for unspeakable and unforgivable sins, as in the following dialogue, reported by Coleman (1976).

TH.: Good morning, Mr. H., how are you today?

PT.: (Long pause—looks up and then head drops back down and stares at floor.)

TH.: I said good morning, Mr. H. Wouldn't you like to tell me how you feel today?

PT.: (Pause—looks up again) . . . I feel . . . terrible . . . simply terrible.

TH.: What seems to be your trouble?

PT.: . . . There's just no way out of it . . . nothing but blind alleys . . . I have no appetite . . . nothing matters anymore . . . it's hopeless . . . everything is hopeless.

TH.: Can you tell me how your trouble started?

PT.: I don't know . . . it seems like I have a lead weight in my stomach . . . I feel different . . . I am not like other people . . . my health is ruined . . . I wish I were dead.

TH.: Your health is ruined?

PT.: . . . Yes, my brain is being eaten away. I shouldn't have done it . . . If I had any willpower I would kill myself . . . I don't deserve to live . . . I have ruined everything . . . and it's all my fault.

TH.: It's all your fault?

PT.: Yes . . . I have been unfaithful to my wife and now I am being punished . . . my health is ruined . . . there's no use going on . . . (sigh) . . . I have ruined everything . . . my family . . . and now

myself . . . I bring misfortune to everyone . . . I am a moral leper . . . a serpent in the Garden of Eden . . . why don't I die . . . why don't you give me a pill and end it all before I bring catastrophe on everyone. . . . No one can help me. . . . It's hopeless . . . I know that . . . it's hopeless. (p. 346)

Victims of major depression usually report that time seems to pass very slowly, but laboratory studies have shown that their estimates of elapsed time are as good as those of normal people (Mézey and Cohen, 1961). Such patients also believe that their intelligence is impaired, but studies have shown that depressed psychotics score as high as normal people on tests of intelligence (Granick, 1963). In general, depressed patients magnify and exaggerate evaluations of themselves. If they succeed at a task, they feel much better than normal people, and if they fail, they feel much worse (Loeb, Beck, Diggory, and Tuthill, 1966).

POSSIBLE CAUSES

Psychoanalytic Theory

◆ Freud believed that the roots of depression are established when a child becomes fixated at the oral stage of psychosexual development. This particular fixation produces an excessively dependent personality. Later in life, if a loved one dies, the person *introjects,* or "incorporates," the dead person. Unconscious hostility toward the dead person, along with anger at being deprived of his or her company, becomes directed inward. The self-directed hostility eventually creates the feelings of guilt and unworthiness that characterize depression. For people whose depression occurs without any apparent environmental stress, Freud hypothesized a *symbolic* loss of a loved one. For example, a person might interpret cross words as a sign that a loved one no longer returns his or her affection.

There are serious problems with the psychoanalytic explanation of depression. First, many investigators dispute the reality of Freud's stages of psychosexual development and deny that people can become fixated in the oral stage. Certainly there is no solid evidence that such a fixation occurs. Second, Freud's theory does not explain why people direct hatred at themselves instead of turning inward the *love* they feel toward the dead person.

Finally, the concept of symbolic loss is a useless intervening variable: it cannot be observed—and therefore can never be proved or disproved.

A Cognitive Theory

Beck (1967) has suggested that the changes in affect seen in depressive psychoses are not primary, but instead are secondary to changes in cognition. That is, the primary disturbance is a distortion in the person's view of reality. For example, a person may see a blemish on the surface of his or her car and conclude that the car is ruined. Or a person whose recipe fails may see the unappetizing dish as proof of his or her unworthiness. Or a nasty, dunning letter from a creditor is seen as a serious and personal condemnation.

In contrast with psychoanalytic theory, which emphasizes the role of the unconscious in the emergence of mental disorder, Beck's theory emphasizes the role of a person's judgment in ascertaining his or her own emotional state. Though not yet proved correct, this theory has served a useful function in alerting therapists to the importance of considering the thought processes, as well as the feelings, of a patient with an affective psychosis.

Heritability

Like schizophrenia, the affective disorders appear to have a genetic component. People who have close relatives with a major affective disorder are ten times more likely to develop these disorders than are people without afflicted relatives (Rosenthal, 1970). Furthermore, if one monozygotic (identical) twin suffers from an affective psychosis, the likelihood that the other twin will also be afflicted is 68 percent, compared with a likelihood of 27 percent for dizygotic (fraternal) twins. The apparent existence of a genetic component suggests that people may inherit certain physiological traits that increase their vulnerability to affective psychoses. However, the heritability of affective disorders is not yet as well established as that of schizophrenia.

Biochemical Factors

Two forms of medical treatment that have proved successful in alleviating the symptoms of affective disorders are *electroconvulsive therapy (ECT)* and *antidepressant drugs.* Their success indicates that physiological disorders may underlie these conditions. Because no one knows how electroconvulsive therapy works, discussion of this treatment is deferred until Chapter 18. More is known about the pharmacological effects of the antidepressant drugs, and this knowledge has led investigators to speculate that the affective disorders may have physiological causes.

Currently, two types of antidepressant drugs are in widespread use. The effects of lithium carbonate in relieving bipolar disorder were discussed earlier. The other class includes the *tricyclic antidepressant drugs,* such as imipramine. (*Tricyclic* refers to their molecular structure.) Experiments with laboratory animals have shown that these drugs exert their effects principally on synapses that utilize norepinephrine or another transmitter substance, *serotonin.* They retard the return of these transmitter substances into the terminal button that released them, and hence prolong their effects on the receiving neuron. Like amphetamine in its effects on dopamine synapses, imipramine and other tricyclic antidepressants facilitate the activity of norepinephrine and serotonin synapses.

Other drugs, including *reserpine,* which is used to treat high blood pressure, can *cause* episodes of depression. Norepinephrine synapses control the size of the blood vessels, and thus play a role in regulating blood pressure. When the blood vessels are constricted, blood has more difficulty in flowing through them, so blood pressure rises. Reserpine lowers blood pressure by impairing the activity of norepinephrine synapses, thus causing the muscles in the blood vessels to relax. However, apparently because the drug also lowers the effectiveness of norepinephrine and serotonin synapses in the brain, a common side effect is depression. This side effect strengthens the argument that brain biochemistry plays an important role in depression.

Several studies have found evidence for biochemical differences in the brains of people with affective disorders. It is not possible to take samples of transmitter substances directly from living brains. But when transmitter substances are released, a small amount gets broken down by enzymes in the brain, and some of the breakdown products accumulate in the cerebrospinal fluid or pass into the bloodstream and collect in the urine. Investigators have analyzed cerebrospinal fluid and urine for these substances.

For example, Träskman, Asberg, Bertilsson, and Sjöstrand (1981) measured the level of *5-HIAA,* a compound that is produced when serotonin is broken down, in the cerebrospinal fluid of depressed people who had attempted suicide. The levels of 5-HIAA were significantly lower than that of control subjects, which implies that there was less activity of serotonin-secreting neurons in the brains of the depressed subjects. In fact, 20 percent of the subjects with levels below the median subsequently killed themselves, whereas none of the patients with levels above the median committed suicide. Taube, Kirstein, Sweeney, Heninger, and Maas (1978) obtained evidence for decreased activity of neurons that secrete norepinephrine; they found low levels of *MHPG* (produced when this transmitter substance is broken down) in the urine of patients with affective disorders. Thus, decreased activity of serotonin- and norepinephrine-secreting neurons appears to be related to depression. Presumably, the tricyclic antidepressant drugs alleviate the symptoms of depression by increasing the activity of these neurons.

Although the brain biochemistry of patients with affective disorders appears to be abnormal, we cannot be certain that a biochemical imbalance is the first event in a sequence that leads to depression. It is possible that environmental stimuli cause the depression, which then leads to biochemical changes in the brain. For example, the brain levels of norepinephrine are lower in dogs who have been presented with an inescapable electric shock and have developed learned helplessness (Miller, Rosellini, and Seligman, 1977). The dogs certainly did not inherit the low norepinephrine levels; they acquired them as a result of their experience. The facts imply that a tendency to develop affective psychoses is heritable, and that low levels of norepinephrine are associated with these disorders. However, the cause-and-effect relations have yet to be worked out.

Relation to Sleep Cycles

◆ A characteristic symptom of the affective disorders is sleep disturbances. Usually, people with the major affective disorders have little difficulty falling asleep, but awaken early and are unable to get to sleep again. (In contrast, people with dysthymic disorder are more likely to have trouble falling asleep and have trouble getting out of bed the next day.) Kupfer (1976) reported that depressed patients tend to enter REM sleep sooner than normals, and spend an increased time in this state during the last half of sleep, which probably accounts for their early awakening. Noting this fact, Vogel, Vogel, McAbee, and Thurmond (1980) deprived depressed patients of REM sleep by awakening them whenever the EEG showed signs that they were entering this stage. Remarkably, the deprivation decreased their depression. These findings are supported by the fact that in cats, treatments that alleviate depression, such as electroconvulsive therapy and the tricyclic antidepressant drugs, profoundly reduce REM sleep (Scherschlicht, Polc, Schneeberger, Steiner, and Haefely, 1982).

Goodwin, Wirz-Justice, and Wehr (1982) suggest that the affective disorders are caused by disturbance in the brain mechanisms that control sleep–waking cycles. They reviewed a large number of studies that they and other investigators had performed, and found that many physiological and biochemical rhythms were disrupted in depressed people. In fact, they could sometimes predict when a person with bipolar disorder would switch from mania to depression by observing changes in their daily rhythm of fluctuations in body temperature. These interesting findings and speculations will have to be confirmed by future research.

Interim summary: The affective psychoses are primarily disorders of emotion, although delusions are characteristically present also. Bipolar disorder consists of alternating periods of mania and depression, whereas major depression consists of depression alone. Although an important distinguishing feature of the affective psychoses is lack of an environmental precipitating factor, it is often difficult to determine cause-and-effect relations between a person's life situation and psychological disturbance.

Freud suggested that fixation in the oral phase of psychosexual development was the cause of depression, but this explanation has not received empirical support. Beck has called people's attention to the fact that although the affective psychoses involve emotional reactions, these may at least in part be based on faulty cognition.

Heritability studies strongly suggest a biological component to the affective disorders, which receives support from the fact that biological treatments (lithium in the case of bipolar disorder and ECT, tricyclic antidepressant drugs, and REM sleep deprivation in the case of depression) effectively reduce their symptoms, whereas reserpine can cause depression. These facts, and additional evidence from biochemical analysis of the breakdown products of norepinephrine and serotonin in depressed patients, suggest that depression results for underactivity of neurons that secrete norepinephrine and/or serotonin. However, the finding that stress can reduce the amount of norepinephrine produced in an animal's brain warns us to be careful about making inferences about cause-and-effect.

Recent evidence suggests that the primary physiological disorder in the affective psychoses may manifest itself in abnormalities in sleep–waking rhythms. REM sleep deprivation alleviates symptoms of depression, and all known biological treatments themselves reduce REM sleep.

CONCLUDING REMARKS

Besides having to simplify disorders that are typically complex, I have had to exaggerate the distinction between normalcy and mental disorder. I must emphasize again the fact that there is no sharp line that divides normal behavior from abnormal. At the extremes there is no mistaking a person with, say, a phobic disorder, schizophrenia, or a major affective disorder for a normal person. But most people do not fall at the extremes, and all of us recognize aspects of our own behavior in many of the descriptions of people with mental disorders.

I am sure that a good number of you have at least one relative who has received a diagnosis of a serious mental disorder, and were distressed by my reports of data that show that schizophrenia and the major affective disorders appear to have a heritable component. I would offer the following reassurances: mental disorders are not strongly heritable. At best, a tendency toward developing them

is inherited, and even in the worst case (two schizophrenic parents) the probability of being diagnosed as having a schizophrenic episode is less than 30 percent. The probability of developing severe, chronic schizophrenia is much less than that. In addition, schizophrenia usually shows its first manifestations early in life. If a person has enjoyed good mental health through his or her teens, it is very unlikely that he or she will become schizophrenic later. Finally, drug treatment and psychotherapy for schizophrenia and the affective disorders has released many people from institutional care and given them the hope of leading normal lives.

In this chapter we have seen some of the more important forms of mental disorders. In the next chapter I shall describe some of the attempts that have been made to help people who suffer from them.

GUIDE TO TERMS INTRODUCED IN THIS CHAPTER

SUGGESTIONS FOR FURTHER READING

Severe and Mild Depression by S. Arieti and J. Bemborad (New York: Basic Books, 1978) and *Schizophrenia* by K. Bernheim and R. Lewine (New York: Norton, 1979) discuss two of the most common psychological disturbances. *Case Studies in Abnormal Behavior* by R. Meyer and Y. Osborne (Boston: Allyn and Bacon, 1982) presents several accounts of specific cases of mental disorders and describes their diagnosis and treatment. *Obsessions and Compulsions* (Englewood Cliffs, N.J.: Prentice Hall, 1975) by S. Rachman covers the range of obsessive-compulsive behaviors, from the tunes that won't leave our minds to crippling disorders. S. Snyder's *Madness and the Brain* (New York: McGraw-Hill, 1974) describes the physiology of schizophrenia and the affective psychoses. Finally, *Labeling Madness,* edited by T. Scheff (Englewood Cliffs, N.J.: Prentice-Hall, 1975), discusses the problems involved in classifying mental disorders.

THE TREATMENT

OF MENTAL

DISORDERS

LEARNING ◆ OBJECTIVES

HISTORICAL BACKGROUND

EARLY TREATMENT OF MENTAL ILLNESS

◆ Mental disorders have been with us since human existence began. For most of that time, people afflicted with these disorders have been regarded, at various times, with awe or with fear. Sometimes the delusions of people whom we would now probably classify as paranoid schizophrenics were regarded as prophetic; the people were seen as instruments through whom gods or spirits were speaking. More often, the people were considered to be occupied by devils or evil spirits and were made to suffer accordingly. The earliest known attempts to treat mental disorders involved *trephining,* or drilling holes in a person's skull. Presum-

ably, the opening was made to permit evil spirits to leave the victim's head. In prehistoric times, this procedure was performed with a sharp-edged stone; later civilizations, such as the Egyptians, refined the practice. Signs of healing at the edges of the holes in prehistoric skulls indicate that some people survived these operations. (See **Figure 18.1.**)

Many painful and degrading practices were directed at people's presumed possession by evil spirits. Those who were thought to be unwilling hosts for evil spirits were subjected to curses or insults designed to persuade the demons to leave; if these had no effect, exorcism was tried, to make the person's body an unpleasant place for devils to reside, through beatings, starving, near-drowning, and the drinking of foul-tasting concoctions. Many people who were perceived as having accepted their

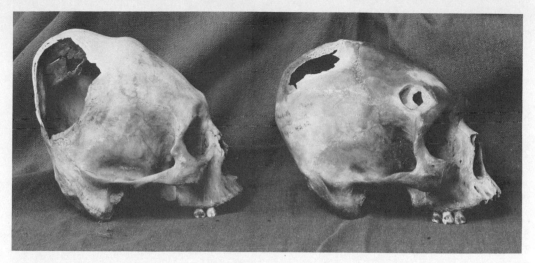

FIGURE 18.1   Prehistoric skulls showing trephining.

condition voluntarily—as being in league with the devil—actively participated in their own prosecution and conviction. The delusional schemes of psychotics often include beliefs of personal guilt and unworthiness, and in a society that accepted the notion that there were witches and devils, these people were ready to imagine themselves as being evil and degraded. They "confessed" to unspeakable acts of sorcery and welcomed their own persecution and punishment. Consider the following case, which occurred during the Middle Ages.

> A certain woman was taken and finally burned, who for six years had an incubus devil {an evil spirit that has sexual intercourse with a sleeping woman} even when she was lying in bed at the side of her husband. . . . the homage she has given to the devil was of such a sort that she was bound to dedicate herself body and soul to him forever, after seven years. But God provided mercifully for she was taken in the sixth year and condemned to the fire, and having truly and completely confessed is believed to have obtained pardon from God. For she went most willingly to her death, saying that she would gladly suffer an even more terrible death if only she would be set free and escape the power of the devil. (Stone, 1937, p. 146)

Until the eighteenth century, Europeans accepted the idea that devils and spirits were responsible for peculiar behaviors in some people. A few believed that these disorders reflected diseases, and that they should be treated medically, with compassion for the victim. Johann Wier, a sixteenth-century physician, was among the first to challenge the entire concept of witchcraft. He argued that most people who were being tortured and burned for practicing witchcraft in fact suffered from mental illness. The church condemned his writings as heretical, and banned them until the twentieth century. However, even within the church some people began to realize that the prevailing beliefs and practices were wrong. Saint Vincent de Paul, a seventeenth-century priest, wrote: "Mental disease is no different to bodily disease and Christianity demands of the humane and powerful to protect, and the skillful to relieve the one as well as the other" (cited in Coleman, 1976, p. 37).

As belief in witchcraft and demonology waned, clergymen, medical authorities, and the general public began to regard people with mental disorders as ill, and torture and persecution eventually ceased. However, the lives of these people were not necessarily better as a result. Undoubtedly, many people with mental disorders were regarded as strange but harmless and managed to maintain a marginal existence in society. Others were sheltered by their families. The unfortunate ones were those who were consigned to the various "asylums" that were established for the care of the mentally

FIGURE 18.2   A crib used to restrain violent
patients.

FIGURE 18.4   A rotating chair, used in the early
nineteenth century to treat people with mental
disorders.

FIGURE 18.3   The "tranquilizing chair" devised
by Benjamin Rush.

ill. Most of these mental institutions were hide-
ously inhumane. Patients were often kept in chains
and sometimes wallowed in their own excreta. Those
who displayed bizarre catatonic postures or who
had fanciful delusions were exhibited to the public,
for a fee. Many of the treatments designed to cure
mental patients were little better than the tortures
that had previously been used to drive out evil
spirits. Patients were tied up, doused in cold water,
bled, made to vomit, spun violently in a "tranquilizing chair," and otherwise assaulted by the

fruits of "modern science." (See **Figures 18.2–18.4.**)

The mistreatment of the mentally ill did not go
unnoticed by humanitarians. A famous and effective early reformer was Philippe Pinel (1745–1826),
a French physician. In 1792, Pinel was appointed
as director of La Bicetre, a mental hospital in Paris.
Pinel believed that most mental patients would
respond well to kind treatment. As an experiment,
he removed the chains from some of the inmates,
took them out of dungeons, and allowed them to
walk about the hospital grounds. The experiment
was a remarkable success; an atmosphere of peace
and quiet replaced the previous noise, stench, and
general aura of despair. Many patients were eventually discharged. His success at La Bicetre was
repeated when he was given charge of Salpêtrière
Hospital. (See **Figure 18.5.**) From what we now
know about psychoses, many patients eventually
recover—or at least get much better—without any
treatment at all. But if a person was put in one of
the mental institutions that existed at the time, he
or she never had a chance to show improvement;
the conditions would seem to have been designed
to *prevent* recovery.

Pinel's success encouraged similar reforms elsewhere. In the United States, the campaign for humane treatment of mental patients was led by Do-
rothea Dix (1802–1887), who raised millions of

FIGURE 18.5   Philippe Pinel releasing the shackles from patients at Salpêtrière Hospital.

dollars for the construction of mental hospitals and spurred the reform of many mental health facilities. The process took a long time; until very recently, some large mental hospitals were little more than warehouses for severely affected patients, who received little or no treatment, but were merely provided with the necessities of life. Today there is much greater emphasis on treatment in community-based facilities, and the discovery of the antipsychotic drugs has freed many patients who would otherwise have spent their lives in institutions.

THE DEVELOPMENT OF PSYCHOTHERAPY

◆ The modern history of specific treatments for mental disorders probably began with Anton Mesmer (1734–1815), an Austrian physician who practiced in Paris in the late eighteenth and early nineteenth centuries. He devised a theory of "animal magnetism," in which he attempted to effect cures by means of iron rods and bottles of chemicals. What he actually did was to hypnotize his patients, and thereby alleviate some of their symptoms, especially those of neurotic hysteria. Accordingly, hyp-

nosis was first known as *mesmerism*. (See **Figure 18.6**.)

A French neurologist, Jean Charcot (1825–1893), began his investigations of the therapeutic uses of hypnosis when one of his students hypnotized a woman and induced her to display the symptoms of a conversion reaction (formerly called hysteria). Charcot examined her and concluded that she was, in fact, a hysterical patient. The student then woke the woman, and her symptoms vanished. Charcot had previously believed that hysteria had an organic basis, but this experience changed his opinion, and he began investigating its psychological causes.

Just before Sigmund Freud began private practice, he studied with Charcot in Paris and observed the effects of hypnosis on hysteria. Freud's association with Charcot, and later with Breuer, started him on his life's study of the determinants of personality and the origins of mental illness. As we saw in Chapter 16, Freud formulated a psychodynamic theory of personality, which has proved to be one of the most influential attempts to explain human behavior. He also founded the practice of psychoanalysis, which many psychiatrists use today to treat patients with psychological problems.

FIGURE 18.6   Mesmer's apparatus for treating
hysterical anesthesias and paralyses.

The rest of this chapter describes the three general approaches to the treatment of mental disorders: psychotherapies, behavior therapies, and biological treatments. The psychotherapies include a variety of treatments that emphasize talk between the therapist and the client as a means of discovering the reasons for the client's problems. Insight into these reasons helps the client solve the problems. In contrast, behavior therapies downplay the importance of insight and concentrate on eliminating maladaptive behaviors and replacing them with adaptive ones. Biological treatments attempt to change a person's behavior medically, by altering the state of the nervous sytem. In practice, most clinical psychologists are not unalterably wedded to a particular system of therapy. Although each therapist discovers that he or she deals best with particular kinds of problems, most prac-

titioners adopt a variety of techniques to achieve therapeutic results with their clients.

PSYCHOTHERAPIES

The case of Anna O., who was supposedly cured of her hysteria by talking about various conflicts while under hypnosis, probably marks the beginning of *insight therapy*. Insight therapy is based on the assumption that people are essentially normal, but that they learn maladaptive thought patterns and behaviors. Once a patient understands the causes of his or her problems, they will cease; insight will lead to a cure.

Most forms of psychotherapy (those that are not based on physiological treatment or on classical or instrumental conditioning procedures) rely upon insight for behavior change. Some therapies, such as psychoanalysis, emphasize causes in the patient's past. Others, such as client-centered therapy, emphasize the present; they attempt to get the patient to see the bad effects of his or her patterns of behavior and to find more adaptive ways of living. Similarly, group therapies attempt to bring people together so that the therapist and other members of the group can help each person see himself or herself as others do. Therapists who use transactional analysis help their patients discover the roles that they are playing so that they can abandon these maladaptive strategies.

PSYCHOANALYSIS

Description

◆ Freud's psychodynamic theory of personality serves as the basis for *psychoanalysis,* the first formal psychotherapeutic procedure devised. Psychoanalysis means just what its name implies: a person's psyche, or mind, is analyzed. By bringing unconscious conflicts to consciousness, the client comes to understand the reasons for his or her behavior and realizes that the childhood conditions under which the causes developed no longer exist. As a result the conflicts are resolved.

The first step, bringing the unconscious to light, involves relaxing or tricking the ego's defense mechanisms, which suppress unconscious thoughts. One technique used to accomplish this goal is *free association,* in which the client is encouraged to talk about anything and everything that he or she thinks of. Before beginning free association, the psychotherapist says something like this:

> In ordinary conversation, you usually try to keep a connecting thread running through your remarks excluding any intrusive ideas or side issues so as not to wander too far from the point, and rightly so. But in this case you must talk differently. As you talk various thoughts will occur to you which you like to ignore because of certain criticisms and objections. You will be tempted to think, "that is irrelevant or unimportant, or nonsensical," and to avoid saying it. Do not give in to such criticism. Report such thoughts in spite of your wish not to do so. Later, the reason for this injunction, the only one you have to follow, will become clear. Report whatever goes through your mind. Pretend that you are a traveler,

describing to someone beside you the changing views which you see outside the train window. (Ford and Urban, 1963, p. 168)

The alert psychotherapist notes the dominant themes in the client's narrative and attempts to interpret any symbolism that represents disguised unconscious thoughts. The therapist also notes any awkwardness, hesitations, or abrupt changes of subject, which may indicate that the client is approaching painful topics. These examples of *resistance* are considered to be significant indications of the source of the person's problems.

Another source of data concerning the unconscious is dreams. Because the ego defenses are more relaxed during sleep, the content of dreams often suggests the nature of the client's conflicts. The latent, or hidden, content of a dream is inferred from its manifest, or apparent, content. Similarly, hypnosis may be used to uncover the client's unconscious thoughts.

As psychotherapy progresses, the therapist begins interpreting free associations and dreams for

FIGURE 18.7   A psychoanalytic session.

the client, in order to increase the person's insight. The interpretations must come at the proper stage of analysis; if they are presented prematurely, the client may rebel and his or her resistance increase.

During psychoanalysis the client generally forms a *transference neurosis*, transferring his or her feelings toward a dominant childhood figure—usually a parent—to the psychoanalyst. Transference is seen as beneficial, and the psychoanalyst encourages its development by remaining a rather vague, shadowy figure seated behind the client's head. Using the relation that develops between client and therapist, the therapist can infer the childhood relations that caused the conflicts to develop. (See **Figure 18.7.**)

Evaluation

The scientific basis of psychoanalysis has not been established. As we saw in Chapter 16, the foundations of Freud's theory of personality remain unproved. But even though the theory cannot be confirmed, we should be able to assess the effectiveness of the psychoanalytic method—after all, it is results that count most. However, it is difficult to evaluate the effectiveness of psychoanalysis, because only a small proportion of people with mental disorders qualify for this method of treatment: intelligent, articulate individuals who are motivated enough to spend three or more hours a week for several years working very hard to uncover unconscious conflicts. In addition, they must be able to afford the psychoanalyst's fees, which are very high. (Psychoanalysts maintain that it is in the interests of clients to make a financial sacrifice, because doing so encourages them to take the procedure seriously.) These qualifications rule out most psychotics, as well as people who lack the time or money to devote to such a long-term project. Furthermore, many who enter psychoanalysis become dissatisfied with their progress and leave; in other cases the therapist encourages a client to leave, if he or she decides that the latter is not cooperating fully. Thus, those who actually complete a course of psychoanalysis do not constitute a random sample, and we cannot conclude that psychoanalysis works because a high percentage of the group is happy with the results. Those who have dropped out are not counted.

Another problem in evaluating psychoanalysis is the difficulty of explicitly defining the changes that are being sought in the client. For example, one of the goals is to lift unconscious repressions, but how can the therapist determine when this goal is achieved? Perhaps a client's insight into his or her behavior demonstrates success. But some critics have argued that insight is no more than a client's acceptance of the therapist's belief system (Bandura, 1969). In fact one critic (Levy, 1963) has asserted that the unconscious does not exist—that it is merely a disagreement between therapist and client about the causes of the client's behavior.

Another problem in evaluating psychoanalysis is that psychoanalysts have a way to "explain" their failures: they can blame them on the client. If the client appears to accept an insight into his or her behavior but that behavior does not change, the insight is said to be merely "intellectual." This escape clause makes the argument for the importance of insight completely circular, and therefore illogical: if the client gets better, the improvement is due to insight; however, if the client's behavior remains unchanged, real (as opposed to "intellectual") insight did not occur. An equivalent in logic would be to argue that wearing a charm (and sincerely believing in it) will cure cancer. If some people who wear the charm get better, then the charm obviously works; if some people die, then they obviously were not believers.

Many psychiatrists today practice a form of therapy based on psychoanalytic principles but do not require clients to embark on a full-fledged, years-long program of intensive psychoanalysis. These practitioners have in fact adapted an eclectic approach to treatment, discussed later in the chapter.

CLIENT-CENTERED THERAPY

Description

Client-centered therapy was developed by Carl Rogers, an American psychologist. (See **Figure 18.8.**) It is based on a loosely formulated theory of human behavior similar to that of Abraham Maslow (described in Chapter 16). Rogers believes that people are basically good and that they all possess an innate drive toward self-actualization. A person who exists in an environment of *unconditional positive regard* will follow his or her own instincts

FIGURE 18.8 Carl Rogers, founder of client-centered therapy.

for goodness and will become a self-actualizing person without any psychological disturbances. Problems occur when a person's concept of the *ideal self* begins to differ significantly from his or her concept of the *real self*. This discrepancy occurs when people fail to pay attention to their own internal evaluations of their self-concept, accepting the evaluations of others instead. The faulty self-concept inevitably conflicts with experience, and the person becomes unhappy and dissatisfied.

The primary objective of Rogers's therapeutic approach is to help the client pay attention to his or her own feelings, so that these innate tendencies toward goodness can emerge. Only by using these feelings as guides can the person move toward a life-style that will be most gratifying for that individual.

The first requirement is that the therapist provide an atmosphere of unconditional positive regard so that the client can come to believe that his or her feelings are worthwhile and important. Once the client begins to pay attention to these feelings, a self-healing process begins. The therapist must be not only warm and friendly but also empathetic; he or she must use this empathy to try to help the client articulate these feelings. For example, a client usually has difficulty at first in expressing feelings

verbally. The therapist tries to understand the feelings underlying the client's confused state and helps the client put them into words. Through this process the client learns to understand and heed his or her own drive toward self-actualization and goodness. Adaptive behaviors will automatically replace maladaptive ones. The following interaction illustrates this process.

ALICE: I was thinking about this business of standards. I somehow developed a sort of knack, I guess, of—well—habit—of trying to make people feel at ease around me, or to make things go along smoothly . . . .

COUNSELOR: In other words, what you did was always in the direction of trying to keep things smooth and to make other people feel better and to smooth the situation.

ALICE: Yes. I think that's what it was. Now the reason why I did it probably was—I mean, not that I was a good little Samaritan going around making other people happy, but that was probably the role that felt easiest for me to play. I'd been doing it around the home so much. I just didn't stand up for my own convictions, until I don't know whether I have any convictions to stand up for.

COUNSELOR: You feel that for a long time you've been playing the role of kind of smoothing out the frictions or differences or what not . . . .

ALICE: M-hum.

COUNSELOR: Rather than having any opinion or reaction of your own in the situation. Is that it?

ALICE: That's it. Or that I haven't been really honestly being myself, or actually knowing what my real self is, and that I've been just playing a sort of false role. Whatever role no one else was playing, and that needed to be played at the time, I'd try to fill it in. (Rogers, 1951, pp. 152–153)

Evaluation

Unlike many other clinicians, who prefer to rely on their own judgments, Rogers himself has stimulated a considerable amount of research on the efficacy of client-centered therapy. He has recorded therapeutic sessions so that various techniques can be evaluated. As you may recall from Chapter 4, Rogers used to refer to his therapy as *nondirective*, on the assumption that the therapist did no more than provide the proper atmosphere for facilitating a client's self-change. However, Truax (1966) examined recordings of Rogers's therapeutic sessions and discovered that Rogers selectively reinforced (with warmth and approval) "healthy" statements by his clients. Nonhealthy statements were *not* reinforced. This finding does not discredit client-centered therapy. Rather, it shows the basic importance of the principle of reinforcement. Rogers's simply adopted the most effective strategy for altering a person's behavior. As a consequence of Truax's findings, Rogers ceased referring to his therapy as nondirective.

Butler and Haigh (1954) attempted to determine whether client-centered therapy does narrow the gap between a person's real and ideal selves. They tested three groups of college students: those with psychological problems who embarked on a course of client-centered therapy, those who had psychological problems but did not undergo therapy, and those who were normal and did not receive therapy. At the beginning of the study, the experimenters asked all students to rate themselves both as they were right then and as they would like to be. The rating technique used was a *Q-sort.* The subjects received a set of cards, each containing a statement such as: "Is highly tense and anxious most of the time" or "Is likable," and sorted them into piles according to the aptness of the descriptions. The subjects performed ratings for both the real self and the ideal self. After the members of the first group had gone through a course of therapy, all the subjects rated themselves again using the same technique.

The results were favorable to client-centered therapy. The first ratings showed a greater difference between real and ideal self-concepts in students with psychological problems than in normal students, and in the second rating the gap narrowed for the treated but not the untreated group. As measured by the Q-sort technique, Rogers's client-centered therapy appears to bring a person's real and ideal selves into closer correspondence.

However, this experiment did not prove that this change was caused specifically by client-centered therapy, for there was no control for a possible placebo effect. You may recall from Chapter 2 that the effects of therapeutic drugs must be determined through comparison with the effects of innocuous sugar pills, to be sure that the improve-

ment has not occurred merely because the patient *thinks* that the pill has done some good. Placebo effects can also occur in psychotherapy; the person knows that he or she is being treated and gets better because he or she believes that the treatment should lead to improvement. Most studies that evaluate psychotherapeutic techniques do not include control groups for placebo effects. For one thing, it is difficult to design "mock therapy" sessions during which the therapist does nothing therapeutic, but convinces the patient that therapy is taking place. Practically speaking, however, if patients get better after a course of client-centered therapy, it does not matter why.

Davison and Neale (1974) point out what is probably a more important criticism of client-centered therapy. Rogers assumes that once a person begins to heed his or her own feelings, maladaptive behaviors will automatically cease. But this assumption has by no means been proved. For example, a person with a severe feeling of inferiority may withdraw from the company of other people and hence never learn the social skills that we all develop through interactions with others. Even if therapy did improve the person's self-concept, he or she would still have problems in society. As Davison and Neale point out, it is also necessary

FIGURE 18.9   A session of client-centered therapy.

to help people develop social skills; changes must occur in both behavior and self-concept to produce significant improvement.

One other limitation requires mention. Like psychoanalysis, client-centered therapy is not appropriate for serious problems such as psychoses; it is most effective for people who are motivated enough to want to change and who are intelligent enough to be able to gain some insight concerning their problems. (However, client-centered therapy is much more affordable and less time-consuming than traditional psychoanalysis.) (See **Figure 18.9.**)

Most ordinary, decent, neurotic people would probably enjoy and profit from talking about their problems with a person as sympathetic as Carl Rogers. Although his theoretical formulation of human behavior is unlikely to have a lasting influence on the science of psychology, his insights into the dynamics of the client-therapist relationship have had a major impact on the field of psychotherapy.

RATIONAL-EMOTIVE THERAPY

Description

◆ In contrast to client-centered therapy, *rational-emotive therapy,* developed in the 1950s by a clinical psychologist named Albert Ellis, is highly directive and confrontational. Rational-emotive theory asserts that psychological problems are the result of faulty cognitions; therapy is therefore aimed at changing people's beliefs.

According to Ellis and his followers, emotions are the product of cognition. A *significant activating event* (A) is followed by a highly charged *emotional consequence* (C), but it is not correct to say that A has caused C. Rather C is a result of the person's *belief system* (B). There, inappropriate emotions (such as depression, guilt, and anxiety) can be abolished only if change occurs in a person's beliefs and perceptions. It is the task of the rational-emotive therapist to dispute the person's beliefs and to convince him or her that they are inappropriate.

The prevailing principle in rational-emotive theory is that the universe is logical and rational; the appropriate means of understanding it is the scientific method of controlled observation. Magic and superstition have no place in the belief system of a healthy, rational person. Therefore, the therapist attempts to get the client to describe his or her irrational beliefs, so that these beliefs can be challenged and defeated. As Ellis puts it, the rational-emotive therapist is "an exposing and nonsense-annihilating scientist" (Ellis, 1979, p. 187).

Rational-emotive theory asserts that people have the capacity for rational understanding and thus possess the resources for personal growth. Unfortunately, they also have the capacity for self-delusion and acceptance of irrational beliefs. Ellis (1979) has compiled the following list of irrational cognitive practices.

◆ Among their biological tendencies to be self-defeating are powerful proclivities (1) to be overwhelmed, frequently, by the great difficulty of changing thinking and acting . . . even when [some thoughts and behaviors produce] much more unpleasant results than [others]; (2) to desire greatly many patently harmful goals and things and to convince themselves that they *need,* or *must have,* what they merely *want* or *prefer;* (3) to find it most difficult to unlearn even the most inefficient habits; (4) to remain attached to many prejudices and myths learned during childhood; (5) to be overvigilant and overcautious on innumerable occasions when they could just be sanely watchful; (6) to be sorely afflicted with the "need" to prove they are superior to other humans, and that they are in some significant ways omnipotent; (7) to easily jump, when one of their views proves to be ill-founded, to an extremely opposite view that is equally foolish; (8) to resort frequently to automaticity and silly routines, when their better interests would clearly be served by conscious thinking and rethinking; (9) to keep forgetting that something is noxious, even when they have considerable evidence of its harmfulness; (10) to engage in enormous amounts of wishful thinking; (11) to find it "too hard" to sustain valuable efforts and self-disciplines and, instead, to be continually "lazy" and procrastinating; (12) to *demand* rather than to *want* others to treat them justly, and to dwell interminably on the fact that people often don't; (13) to condemn themselves instead of only assessing their poor behavior; (14) to overgeneralize about events that have occurred in the past or may occur in the future; (15) to easily become physically or psychosomatically affected when they make themselves emotionally upset. (p. 195)

Rational-emotive therapy seeks to rid people of all these illogical and counterproductive tendencies. Several of these tendencies receive special emphasis: the tendency to perceive a desirable event as an absolute necessity, the need to be better than everyone else, and the perception of failure as a disaster. If a man avoids social gatherings because he is afraid that someone else will not like or approve of him, a therapist would say something like this: "Suppose that the worst happens. He hates you. He finds that you are a real jerk. You would say to yourself, 'I *can't stand* that! It is absolutely *awful* that he doesn't like me! Because I can't make him like me I am a *worthless person!*' But that is not true. Actually, it is undesirable that he does not like you. It would be much nicer if he did. Being liked is definitely better than not being liked. But it is illogical and unproductive to perceive the rejection as a disaster."

Although rational-emotive therapy is much more directive than client-centered therapy, there are some similarities. Just as Rogers emphasizes unconditional positive regard, Ellis and his followers attempt to engender a feeling of *full acceptance* in their clients. They teach that self-blame is the core of emotional disturbance, and that it is possible for people to learn to stop continuously rating their own personal worth and measuring themselves against an impossible standard. They emphasize that people will be happier if they can learn to see failures as unfortunate events, not as disastrous ones that confirm the lack of their own worth. Unlike a Rogerian therapist, a rational-emotive therapist will vigorously argue with his or her client, attacking beliefs that the therapist regards as foolish and illogical.

Unlike psychoanalysis, which seeks the source of a person's psychological problems in traumatic childhood experiences, rational-emotive therapy does not require a client to reconstruct and relive the original traumatic experiences. The emphasis is on the here and now. It may be useful to discuss some early experiences in order to uncover and correct the client's beliefs, but focusing on past misfortunes will only harm the client, so long as faulty cognitive systems are interpreting these events. The only way to improvement is through a restructuring of these systems.

Rational-emotive psychology also differs from psychoanalytic theory in denying the existence of an entity called "the unconscious." It relies on brief, incisive questioning by the therapist to make peo-

ple aware of the reasons for some of their behaviors. In fact, the therapist often ridicules the client's irrational beliefs in an attempt to get him or her to reject them. Transference is neither necessary nor desirable. Therapy differs from the client-centered approach in that although the therapist needs to be an effective teacher and guide, he or she does not need to be especially empathetic.

Evaluation

Rational-emotive therapy has appeal and potential usefulness for those who can enjoy and profit from intellectual teaching and argumentation. The people who are likely to benefit most from this form of therapy are those who are self-demanding and who feel guilt for not living up to their own standards of perfection. People with severe thought disorders, such as schizophrenia and the affective psychoses, are less likely to respond to an intellectual analysis of their problems.

Rational-emotive therapy has received considerable attention, and many therapists who adopt an eclectic approach use some of its techniques with some of their clients. In some ways the theory can be seen as a systematized form of a common-sense approach to living. However, most other psychotherapists disagree with Ellis's denial of the importance of empathy in the relation between therapist and client.

GROUP PSYCHOTHERAPY

Description

Group psychotherapy became common during World War II, when the stresses of combat produced psychological problems in many of the members of the armed forces and the demand for psychotherapists greatly exceeded the supply. What began as an economic necessity became an institution, once the effectiveness of group treatment was recognized.

Because most psychological problems involve interactions with other people, it is often worthwhile to treat these problems in a group setting. Such a setting permits the therapist to observe and interpret actual interactions without having to rely on clients' descriptions, which may be selective or faulty. Furthermore, a group can bring social pres-

FIGURE 18.10 A session of group therapy. The
video recorder and television in the background are
used to help people see themselves as others do.

sures to bear on the problems of its members; if a
person receives comments about his or her behavior
from all the members of a group, the message is
often more convincing than if a psychotherapist
delivers it in a private session. Finally, the process
of seeking causes of maladaptive behavior in other
people often helps a person gain insight into his
or her own problems. (See **Figure 18.10.**)

The structure of the group session varies widely.
Some sessions are little more than lectures, in which
the therapist presents information about a problem
that is common to all members of the group, followed by discussion. For example, in a case involving a person with severe mental or physical
illness the therapist explains to family members the
nature, treatment, and possible outcomes of the
disorder, then answers questions and allows people
to share their feelings about what the illness has
done to their family.

◆ PSYCHODRAMA J.L. Moreno (1959) developed a
form of structured group therapy called *psychodrama,* in which clients are asked to act out some
of their problems by pretending that they are
members of the cast of a play. Some clients assume
the role of actor while others serve as the audience.
The therapist serves as director, commenting on

the actors' performances and keeping the "plot"
moving in a useful direction.

One of the techniques developed as a part of
psychodrama is *mirroring,* in which one member
of the group is asked to act out a particular
maladaptive pattern of behavior that is displayed
by another member. The object of this exercise is
to help the person whose behavior is being mir-
rored to see himself or herself as others do, and
therefore to gain insight that will facilitate change.
In group therapy sessions today, videotape recordings are often made of clients' interactions with
others, in order to "mirror" precisely what other
people see.

◆ TRANSACTIONAL ANALYSIS Another form of interpersonal therapy emphasizes the nature of a person's interactions with other people. This approach, called *transactional analysis,* was developed
by Eric Berne (1964, 1972). Berne believed that
we all play essentially three roles in our interactions
with others: those of *child, adult,* and *parent.* He
called these roles *ego states.* We learn our parent
role from our own parents and sometimes (inap-
propriately) use it on a spouse or friend, giving
unneeded advice "for their own good." Our child
role consists of demands for immediate gratifica-

tion of our wants, or a desire to have others make our decisions for us—to assume the parent role. The adult ego state is the healthy, independent one that we should strive for.

People (especially married couples) often enter into transactions in which they play roles that serve either childish or parental needs but that lead ultimately to conflict and unhappiness. Berne has characterized these interactions as *games,* because they appear to have a set of rules and to lead to predictable outcomes. Here are some examples from Berne (1964).

Why Don't You—Yes But [YDYB]

"Why Don't You—Yes But" occupies a special place in game analysis, because it was the original stimulus for the concept of games. It was the first game to be dissected out of its social context, and . . . it is one of the best understood. It is also the game most commonly played at parties and groups of all kinds. . . .

WHITE: My husband always insists on doing our own repairs, and he never builds anything right."

BLACK: "Why doesn't he take a course in carpentry?"

WHITE: "Yes, but he doesn't have time."

BLUE: "Why don't you buy him some good tools?"

WHITE: "Yes, but he doesn't know how to use them."

RED: "Why don't you have your building done by a carpenter?"

WHITE: "Yes, but that would cost too much."

BROWN: "Why don't you just accept what he does the way he does it?"

WHITE: "Yes, but the whole thing might fall down."

Such an exchange is typically followed by a silence. . . . YDYB can be played by any number. The agent presents a problem. The others start to present solutions, each beginning with "Why don't you . . .?" To each of these White objects with a "Yes, but. . . ." A good player can stand off the others indefinitely until they all give up, whereupon White wins. (p. 116)

Now I've Got You, You Son of a Bitch [NIGYSOB]

White needed some plumbing fixtures installed, and he reviewed the costs very carefully with the plumber before giving him a go-ahead. The price was set, and it was agreed that there would be no extras. When the plumber submitted his bill, he included a few

dollars extra for an unexpected valve that had to be installed—about four dollars on a four-hundred-dollar job. White became infuriated, called the plumber on the phone and demanded an explanation. The plumber would not back down. White wrote him a long letter criticizing his integrity and ethics and refused to pay the bill until the extra charge was withdrawn. The plumber finally gave in.

It soon became obvious that both White and the plumber were playing games. . . . White took the opportunity to make extensive criticisms of the plumber's whole way of living . . . exploiting his trivial but socially defensible objection . . . to vent the pent-up furies of many years on his cozening opponent, just as his mother might have done in a similar situation. (pp. 85–86)

Berne's therapeutic technique is a form of group insight therapy in which people come to recognize the games they play and to realize that the roles are maladaptive and self-defeating. The goal of therapy is to replace these games with healthy, adult relationships.

◆ FAMILY THERAPY   Family therapy has recently become an important technique for clinical psychologists. Very often, it is not enough to deal with the problems of an individual. People are the products of their environment; the structure of a person's family is a significant part of that environment. Often, it is impossible to help an unhappy person without also restructuring relations with his or her family members. (See **Figure 18.11.**)

In many cases a family therapist meets with all members of a client's family and analyzes the ways in which individuals interact with each other. He or she attempts to get family members to talk to each other instead of addressing all comments and questions to the therapist. The therapist observes as much as possible the data about the interactions—how individuals sit in relation to each other, who interrupts whom, who looks at whom before speaking—to try to infer the nature of family interrelations. For example, there may be barriers between family members; perhaps a father is unable to communicate with one of his children. Or two or more family members may be so "enmeshed" that they cannot function independently; they constantly seek each other's approval and, through overdependence, make each other miserable.

FIGURE 18.11 A session of family therapy.

Salvador Minuchin (1974), a psychiatrist, has devised an approach called **structural family therapy.** He observes a family's interactions and draws simple diagrams of the relationships that he infers from the behavior of the family members. He identifies the counterproductive relationships and attempts to restructure the family in more adaptive ways. For example, he might diagram a family structure with father (F) on one side and mother (M) on the other side, allied with son (S) but estranged from daugher (D):

$$\frac{F}{MS|D}$$

He would then attempt to restructure the family as follows:

$$\frac{HW}{SD}$$

Husband (H) and wife (W) would replace mother and father, emphasizing that their primary relation should be the one between spouses. The healthiest family interactions stem from an effectively functioning *marital subsystem,* consisting of husband and wife. A marriage that is completely child oriented is always dysfunctional (Foley, 1979). And alli-

ances between one parent and one or more children are almost always detrimental to the family.

After inferring the family structure, the therapist attempts to restructure it by replacing pathological interactions with more effective, functional ones. He or she suggests that perhaps all members of the family must change if the client is to make real improvement and then gets family members to "actualize" their transactional patterns—that is, to act out their everyday relationships. Restructuring techniques include forming temporary alliances between the therapist and one or more of the family members, increasing tension in order to trigger changes in unstable structures, assigning explicit tasks and homework to family members (for example, making them interact with other members), and providing general support, education, and guidance. Sometimes the therapist visits the family at home. For example, if a child in a family refuses to eat, the therapist will visit during mealtime, in order to see the problem acted out as explicitly as possible.

The basic premise of family therapy seems sound: effective treatment of a person's problems often involves making changes in a significant part of that person's environment; namely, his or her family. However, there is no clearly defined theory or set of procedures to help family therapists effect these changes; nor are there clear guidelines for assessing them. Until a more explicit and formal method has been developed, the efficacy of family therapy is likely to depend on the skill and personality of the individual practitioner.

Evaluation

A bewildering variety of group therapies have been developed. (See **Figure 18.12**.) Members are asked to lead blindfolded partners around, to develop trust; people meet in the nude, to establish openness and eliminate hypocrisy and the trappings of status that we convey by our modes of dress; people vent their anger and hostility in emotional confrontations; groups meet in long marathon sessions with the assumption that fatigue will weaken defenses and permit people to encounter their real selves—the list could go on indefinitely. Each method has its adherents, but there is little objective evidence about the efficacy of these techniques. Some have proved to be fads and are fading in popularity, and others will undoubtedly do likewise. However, it is clear that much can be accomplished in groups that cannot be accomplished in private sessions, and future research will undoubtedly lead to more effective ways of treating people's psychological problems in groups.

Interim summary: Psychotherapies are based primarily on conversation between therapist and client. The oldest form, psychoanalysis, was devised by Freud. Psychoanalysis attempts to discover the forces that are warring in the client's psyche and resolve the inner conflicts by bringing to consciousness his or her unconscious drives and the defenses that have been established against them. *Insight* is the primary form of therapy.

Whereas psychoanalysis regards humans as products of primitive biologically determined urges, client-centered therapy is based on the premise that people are basically healthy and good, and that their problems result from their failure to evaluate themselves in terms of their own self-concept, instead judging themselves by other people's standards. This tendency is rectified by providing an environment of unconditional positive regard, in which clients can find their own way to mental health.

Rational-emotive therapy is also based on the assumption that people's psychological problems stem from faulty cognitions, but its practitioners use many forms of persuasion, including ridicule,

FIGURE 18.12   A group psychotherapy session using conventional means to get people to relax and interact with each other unguardedly.

to get people to abandon these cognitions in favor of logical and healthy ones. Although they believe that significant activating events give rise to emotional consequences, the particular consequences that occur depend upon people's belief systems. Relief from distress is achieved by changing these belief systems, not reliving the past.

A variety of group therapies have been developed to take advantage of the fact that many people's problems can be helped more efficiently, and more effectively, in group settings. Practitioners of psychodrama, transactional analysis, and family therapy all attempt to understand people's interactions with others, and help them learn how to establish more effective ones.

BEHAVIOR THERAPY

◆ Traditional psychotherapies (especially psychoanalysis) are based on the assumption that understanding leads to behavioral change: once a person gains insight into the causes of his or her maladaptive behavior, that behavior will cease and will be replaced by adaptive behavior. However, insight is often *not* followed by behavioral change. Some therapists have decided that it is better to focus on a person's maladaptive behavior than to speculate on its causes. The *behavior itself* is the problem, and not the historical reasons for its development. Consequently, the goal is to change the behavior by whatever means are found to be most effective.

Practitioners of behavior therapy employ a variety of techniques based on the principles of classical and instrumental conditioning (defined and described in Chapter 4). The emphasis in classical conditioning is on the stimuli that elicit new responses that are contrary to the old, maladaptive, ones. In instrumental conditioning (also called operant conditioning), the emphasis is on the responses made; adaptive responses are selectively reinforced, and maladaptive ones ignored or punished.

The fact that behavior therapy is based on the results of experimental research makes it no less difficult to use and requires no less sensitivity or clinical experience on the part of the therapist. A successful behavior therapist must be able to determine what behaviors and emotional reactions need

to be changed, find out what stimuli can serve as effective reinforcers, and successfully alter the client's environment in a way that produces desirable changes. Many would-be therapists have tried behavioral methods and found that "reward didn't work." Perhaps they never found effective reinforcers, or the procedures they followed were inadequate. Perhaps their clients derived more reinforcement from making the therapist look foolish than from experiencing the "reinforcing" stimuli that they were being offered. In any event, empirical research has proved the efficacy of the techniques described in this section.

SYSTEMATIC DESENSITIZATION

◆ One technique of behavior therapy has been especially successful in eliminating some kinds of neurotic fears and phobias. This technique, called *systematic desensitization,* was developed by Joseph Wolpe, of the Temple University School of Medicine. Its goal is to remove the unpleasant emotional response that is produced by the feared object or situation and replace it with an incompatible one—relaxation.

First the client is trained is achieve complete relaxation. There is an emphasis on deep-muscle relaxation, but the essential task is to learn to respond quickly to suggestions to feel relaxed and peaceful, so that these suggestions can elicit a relaxation response. Second, the client and therapist construct a hierarchy of anxiety-related stimuli. Table 18.1 presents a hierarchy constructed with a subject who had an intense fear of taking examinations. The situations provoking least fear are at the top. (See **Table 18.1**.)

Finally, the conditional stimuli (fear-eliciting situations) are paired with the stimuli that elicit the learned relaxation response. For example, a person with a fear of taking exams is instructed to relax, and then to imagine entering a classroom to begin a new course. If the client reports no anxiety, he or she is instructed to move to the next item and imagine hearing the professor announce a small quiz two weeks hence; and so on. Whenever the client begins feeling anxious, he or she signals to the therapist with some predetermined gesture— say, by raising his or her finger. The therapist instructs the client to relax and, if necessary, de-

TABLE 18.1   Desensitization hierarchy for test anxiety

Fear ratings	Hierarchy items
0	Beginning a new course
10	Hearing an instructor announce a small quiz two weeks hence
25	Having a professor urge you personally to do well on an exam
40	Trying to decide how to study for an exam
45	Reviewing the material I know should be studied—listing study to do
50	Hearing an instructor remind the class of a quiz one week hence
65	Hearing an instructor announce a major exam in three weeks and its importance
70	Standing alone in the hall before an exam
75	Hearing an instructor announce a major exam in one week
80	Getting an exam back in class
80	Anticipating getting back a graded exam later that day
80	Thinking about being scared and anxious regarding a specific exam
85	Talking to several students about an exam right before taking it
85	Studying with fellow students several days before an exam
90	Hearing some "pearls" from another student which you doubt you'll remember, while studying in a group
90	Cramming while alone in the library right before an exam
90	Thinking about being anxious over schoolwork in general
95	Thinking about not keeping up in other subjects while preparing for an exam
95	Talking with several students about an exam immediately after
100	Thinking about being generally inadequately prepared
100	Thinking about not being adequately prepared for a particular exam
100	Studying the night before a big exam

Note: 0 = total relaxation; 100 = maximum tension.
From Kanfer, F.H., and Phillips, J.S. *Learning Foundations of Behavior Therapy*. New York: Wiley, 1970.

scribes a less threatening scene. The client is not permitted to feel severe anxiety at any time. Gradually, over a series of sessions (the average is around eleven), the client is able to get through the entire list.

Systematic desensitization is a very successful technique for people who have a specific phobia (as opposed to generalized fear and anxiety). The fact that this technique always has a specific goal makes it possible to assess its success or failure objectively.

A number of experiments have found that all the elements of systematic desensitization are necessary for its success. For example, a person will not get rid of a phobia merely by participating in relaxation training or by constructing hierarchies of fear-producing situations; only *pairings* of the anxiety-producing stimuli with instructions to relax will reduce the fear. One testimonial to this fact comes from a study by Johnson and Sechrest (1968), which attempted to reduce the fear of taking examinations in a group of college students. Students who underwent systematic desensitization received significantly higher grades on their final examination in a psychology course than did the groups of control subjects who were also taking the course but who received either no treatment, or relaxation training alone.

AVERSIVE CLASSICAL CONDITIONING

Sometimes people are attracted by stimuli that most of us would ignore, and they engage in maladaptive behavior as a result of this attraction. Fetishes (such as a sexual attraction to women's shoes) are the most striking examples. The technique of *aversive classical conditioning* attempts to establish an unpleasant response (such as a feeling of fear or disgust) to the object that produces the undesired behavior. For example, a person with a fetish for women's shoes might be given painful electric shocks while viewing color slides of women's shoes. This technique has been shown to be moderately effective (Kanfer and Phillips, 1970).

Very often, *covert sensitization* is used to establish the unpleasant response to the object. The person to be treated does not actually experience the aversive stimulus but imagines it. Wisocki (1970) describes the use of covert sensitization in the treatment of a clothes-folding compulsion of a twenty-seven-year-old woman. Her ritual involved the following behaviors:

> . . . (a) ends of clothes brought together; (b) wrinkles smoothed out; (c) item folded carefully once; (d) item unfolded and smoothed over again; (e) folded neatly a second time (this process might be carried out several times until she was satisfied as to the lack of wrinkles); (f) carried to a dresser drawer across the room (each item carried individually); (g) drawer opened and item carefully placed on appropriate pile of clothing. If it became wrinkled at this point, it was refolded. (It was also sometimes necessary to refold the entire pile of clothes.) (h) drawer closed; (i) drawer opened to check neatness; (j) drawer closed; (k) patient turns attention to next item. (p. 235)

Wisocki had the woman imagine various disgusting scenes, in an attempt to make the ritual

become aversive to her. Here is a typical description:

> You're in the laundry room. There is a pile of clothing in front of you. You take one thing . . . it's a towel . . . and you fold it once and put it aside. You look over at it and think that it's not quite wrinkle-free and you decide to refold it. As soon as you have that thought, you get a queasy feeling in the pit of your stomach. Vomit comes up into your mouth. It tastes bitter and you swallow it back down. Your throat burns. But you take the towel and start to refold it anyway. Just as you do that, your stomach churns and vomit comes out of your mouth—all over the clean clothes, your hands, the table, over everything. You keep vomiting and vomiting. Your eyes are watering; your nose has mucus coming out of it. You see vomit all over everything. You think that you should never have tried to fold that towel a second time—a few slight wrinkles make no difference—and you run from the room. Immediately you feel better. You go and clean yourself up and smell fresh and feel wonderful. (p. 235)

According to Wisocki's report, covert sensitization seems to have succeeded in ending the client's compulsion for clothes folding. However, because the woman wanted to do her own housework, therapy also had to establish a new set of behaviors through a technique discussed in the next section.

INSTRUMENTAL CONDITIONING

Behavioral techniques are often used to alter the behavior of mentally retarded or emotionally disturbed people who are difficult to communicate with. Isaacs, Thomas, and Goldiamond (1960) have reported the case of a forty-year-old man with schizophrenia who had been admitted to a hospital nineteen years before and had not spoken one word to anyone during those years. A therapist decided to use instrumental conditioning to try to get him to speak once again. After observing the patient for a while, the therapist discovered that he enjoyed chewing gum. The therapist would hold up a stick of gum and, when the patient looked at it, would give it to him. Soon he began paying attention to the therapist and would look at the piece of gum as soon as it was brought out.

Next, the therapist held up a piece of gum, waited until the patient moved his lips, and immediately reinforced the movement. Next, a reinforcer was delivered only after the patient made a sound. Once the patient was reliably making a sound whenever the stick of gum was held up, the therapist held one up and said "Say 'gum.' "After a few minutes the patient finally said "gum"—his first word in nineteen years. Six weeks after the training had begun, the patient said, "Gum, please," adding the extra word on his own, and soon thereafter began talking with the therapist. Behavioral methods worked where others had failed. (You may recall from Chapter 4 that the technique used to train an improbable response is called shaping.)

Sometimes the appropriate response need not actually be performed in the presence of the therapist. *Covert reinforcement* uses a strategy similar to that of covert sensitization. Instead of receiving an actual reward for an actual behavior, the client imagines that he or she is performing a desired behavior and then imagines receiving a reward; behavior and reinforcement are experienced vicariously.

After helping her client establish an aversion to compulsive clothes folding, Wisocki (1970) had the woman imagine herself doing the job without being perfectionistic, allowing a few wrinkles to develop in the folded clothes. Next, it was established that the client very much enjoyed practicing ballet, sipping sweet tea, eating Italian food, golfing, walking in a forest, completing a difficult job, being praised, having people seek her out for company, and being with happy people. The client was to imagine herself enjoying one of these reinforcers whenever the therapist said "Reinforcement." A typical training session went as follows:

> Relax and imagine that you are in the laundry room, standing in front of the day's laundry. You think to yourself that you'll really have to hurry folding these clothes so that you can go shopping with a friend ("Reinforcement"). You impatiently shove the clothes to one side ("Reinforcement"). You take the next item, fold it quickly and it's a little wrinkled, but you put it on top of the other things ("Reinforcement"). (p. 236)

After a total of eight two-hour sessions, the client became much more efficient in her housework. Not only clothes folding, but also other activities such as bedmaking and washing dishes took much less time. As long as one year later the client remained satisfied with her improved performance.

Punishment of Maladaptive Behaviors

In general, punishment is not nearly so good a training method as positive reinforcement. For one thing, the person who is being punished may form negative associations with the person who administers the punishment. Second, there is a tendency to *overgeneralize*—to avoid performing a whole class of responses related to the one that is specifically being punished. For example, a child might not tell her father any more lies after being punished for doing so, but she might also stop sharing her fantasies with him. Unfortunately, it is usually easier to punish a response than it is to figure out how to reinforce other responses that will replace the undesirable one. And when we are angry, we often find that it is satisfying (rewarding) to punish someone.

However, in some therapeutic situations, especially those in which the undesirable response is clearly harmful to the client, punishment is the most effective technique for eliminating an undesirable behavior. Cowart and Whaley (1971) reported the case of an emotionally disturbed child who persisted in self-mutilation. He banged his head against the floor until it was a swollen mass of cuts and bruises. As a result, he had to be restrained in his crib in a hospital for the mentally retarded. Obviously, the consequences of such confinement are serious for a child's development. After conventional techniques had failed, the therapist attached a pair of wires to the child's leg and placed him in a room with a padded floor. The child immediately began battering his head against the floor, and the therapist administered an electric shock through the wires. The shock, which was certainly less damaging than the blows to the head, stopped the child short. He seemed more startled than anything else. He started banging his head against the floor again and received another shock. After very few repetitions of this sequence the boy stopped his self-mutilation and could safely be let out of his crib.

Modeling

To change the behavior of a laboratory animal, an experimenter must either reinforce certain behaviors that are already present or shape a new one.

In some cases, this appears to be the only way to effect change in humans, as with the schizophrenic patient who was induced to talk by rewards of chewing gum. However, even in this case the therapist did not simply wait until the patient spontaneously uttered a *g* sound. Instead, the therapist said, "Say 'gum.'" He provided a model for the patient to follow.

Humans (and many other animals) have the ability to learn from the experience of others. As we have already seen, people can experience reinforcement and punishment vicariously. They can also imitate the behavior of other people, watching what they do and, if the conditions are appropriate, performing the same behavior. This capability provides the basis for the technique of modeling. Behavior therapists have found that clients can make much better progress when they have access to a model providing samples of successful behaviors to imitate. Bandura (1971) describes a modeling session with people who had a phobic fear of snakes.

> The therapist himself performed the fearless behavior at each step and gradually led subjects into touching, stroking, and then holding the snake's body with gloved and bare hands while the experimenter held the snake securely by head and tail. If a subject was unable to touch the snake following ample demonstration, she was asked to place her hand on the experimenter's and to move her hand down gradually until it touched the snake's body. After subjects no longer felt any apprehension about touching the snake under these secure conditions, anxieties about contact with the snake's head area and entwining tail were extinguished. The therapist again performed the tasks fearlessly, and then he and the subject performed the responses jointly; as subjects became less fearful, the experimenter gradually reduced his participation and control over the snake, until eventually subjects were able to hold the snake in their laps without assistance, to let the snake loose in the room and retrieve it, and to let it crawl freely over their bodies. Progress through the graded approach tasks was paced according to the subjects' apprehensiveness. When they reported being able to perform one activity with little or no fear, they were eased into a more difficult interaction. (p. 680)

This treatment eliminated fear of snakes in 92 percent of the subjects who participated.

There are probably several reasons for the success of the modeling technique. Subjects learn to make new responses by imitating those of the therapist

and are reinforced for doing so. When they observe a confident person approaching and touching a feared object without showing any signs of emotional distress, they probably experience a vicarious extinction of their own emotional responses. In fact, Bandura reports that, "having successfully overcome a phobia that had plagued them for most of their lives, subjects reported increased confidence that they could cope effectively with other fear-provoking events" (1971, p. 684), including their reaction to encounters with other people.

Token Economies

The principle of instrumental conditioning has been used on a large scale in various institutions (such as mental hospitals and homes for the retarded), with generally good success. In such institutions residents are often asked to do chores, both to keep operating costs low and to engage them in active participation in their environment. In some instances, other specific behaviors are also targeted as desirable and therapeutic, such as helping other residents who have more severe problems. To promote these behaviors, therapists have designed *token economies.*

The principle is extremely simple. A list of tasks is compiled and residents receive tokens as rewards for performing the tasks. Later they can exchange these tokens for snacks, other desired articles, or various privileges. Thus, the tokens become conditioned reinforcers for desirable and appropriate behaviors. The system includes both a "pay scale" for the various tasks and "prices" for the privileges. **Table 18.2** presents a typical "pay scale." **Figure 18.13** shows the strong effects of the contingencies of the pay scale: the amount of time spent performing the desirable behaviors was high when the reinforcement contingencies were imposed, but low when they were not (Ayllon and Azrin, 1968).

Although token economies are based on a simple principle, they are very difficult to implement. A mental institution includes patients, caretakers, housekeeping staff, and professional staff. If a token economy is to be effective, all the staff who deal with residents must learn how the system is to work; ideally, they should also understand and agree with its underlying principles. A token economy can easily be sabotaged by a few people who believe that the system is foolish, wrong, or in some way threatening to themselves. If these ob-

TABLE 18.2   Examples of a pay scale in a token economy

Types of jobs	Number of jobs per day	Duration	Tokens paid
Special services			
Errands Leaves the ward on official errands throughout the hospital grounds, delivering messages and picking up supplies and records pertaining to the ward	1	20 min.	6
Tour guide Gives visitors a 15-minute tour of the ward, explaining the activities and token system; answers visitors' questions about the ward	1	15 min.	10
Nursing assistant Assists staff with the preparation of patients to be seen by the medical doctor; assists staff with the control of undesired interaction between patients	1	10 min.	10
Self-care activities			
Grooming Combs hair, wears: dress, slip, panties, bra, stockings and shoes	3		1
Bathing Takes a bath at time designated for bath (once a week)			1
Tooth brushing Brushes teeth or gargles at the time designated for tooth brushing	1		1
Exercises Participates in exercises conducted by the exercise assistant	2		1
Bed making Makes own bed and cleans area around and under bed	2		1

Adopted from Ayllon, T., and Azrin, N.H. *The Token Economy: A Motivational System for Therapy and Rehabilitation.* New York: Appleton-Century-Crofts, 1968.

stacles can be overcome, token economies work very well (Ayllon and Azrin, 1968).

EVALUATION OF BEHAVIOR THERAPY

◆ Psychotherapists with traditional orientations have criticized behavior therapy for its focus on the symptoms of a psychological problem, to the exclusion of its roots. Some psychoanalysts even argue that the treatment of symptoms is dangerous; in their view, the removal of one symptom of an intrapsychic conflict will simply produce another,

perhaps more serious, symptom. This hypothetical process is called **symptom substitution**.

However, there is little evidence that symptom substitution occurs. It is true that many people's behavior problems are caused by conditions that existed in the past and often these problems become self-perpetuating. For example, a child may (for one reason or another) begin wetting its bed. The nightly awakening irritates the parents, who must change the bedclothes and the child's pajamas. The disturbance often disrupts family relationships. The child develops feelings of guilt and

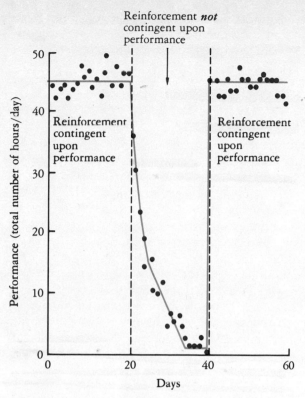

Reinforcement *not* contingent upon performance

Reinforcement contingent upon performance

Reinforcement contingent upon performance

FIGURE 18.13   The effects of a token economy system of reinforcement on patients' performance of specified chores. (From Ayllon, T., and Azrin, N. *The Token Economy: A Motivational System for Therapy and Rehabilitation.* New York: Appleton-Century-Crofts, 1968. By permission Prentice-Hall, Englewood Cliffs, N.J.)

insecurity and as a result wets the bed more often. Instead of analyzing the sources of family conflicts, a therapist who uses behavior therapy would install a device in the child's bed that rings a bell when he or she begins to urinate. The child awakens and goes to the bathroom to urinate and soon ceases to wet the bed. The elimination of bed wetting causes rapid improvement in the child's self-esteem and in the entire family relationship. Symptom substitution does not appear to occur (Baker, 1969).

A criticism with real substance is that behaviors learned under one set of conditions may fail to occur in different environments; that is, the behavior change may not generalize to other situations. This problem is especially acute in the treatment of alcohol addiction; addicts may abstain from drinking under laboratory conditions but go on a binge as soon as they are released.

Specific techniques have been designed to increase the generalization of the results of behavior therapy. For example, Drabman, Spitalnik, and O'Leary (1973) rewarded a group of disruptive boys for performing desirable behaviors such as participating in classroom activities like reading. The reinforcement was effective; the frequency of disruptive behaviors declined and academic activity increased. To make the change as permanent as possible, the experimenters also rewarded the boys when the ratings of their own behavior agreed with those of their teacher. In other words, they were trained to evaluate their behaviors in terms of both those that should be reinforced and those that should not be. The assumption was that the self-evaluations would become conditioned reinforcers because they would initially be paired with actual reinforcement. Thus, the process of self-evaluation would continue to reinforce the boys' behavior even after the period of training. Judging from the excellent results, the procedure succeeded.

There are some situations in which behavior therapy should not be used. For example, a person who is involuntarily confined to an institution should not be subjected to aversive techniques unless he or she clearly wants to participate or unless the benefits far outweigh the discomfort, as in the case of the child who stopped battering his head against the floor after he received a few mild electric shocks for doing so. The decision to use aversive techniques must not rest only with people who are directly in charge of the residents, lest the procedures eventually be used merely for the sake of convenience. The decision must involve a committee containing people who serve as advocates for the patient.

In other situations, behavior therapy may not be appropriate either because it is unfeasible or because it raises unanswerable ethical issues. For example, a person may come to a therapist because his homosexuality causes him great anguish. The client asks for help and is willing to undergo whatever treatment is necessary; no coercion is involved. The therapist faces the dilemma of whether to embark on a course of treatment in which aversive stimuli are associated with other males or to try to help the client accept his sexual orientation and develop a better self-image. If the homosexuality is deep-seated, behavior therapy may make the client shun *all* sexual stimuli. It is not enough to learn the techniques of behavior therapy; one must also learn to recognize the circumstances in which these techniques are appropriate.

Interim summary: Behavior therapists attempt to use the principles of classical and instrumental (operant) conditioning to modify behavior: to eliminate fears or replace maladaptive behaviors with adaptive ones. Systematic desensitization uses classical procedures to condition the response of relaxation to stimuli that were previously fear-producing. In contrast, aversive classical conditioning attempts to condition an unpleasant response to a stimulus with which the client is preoccupied, such as a fetish.

Whereas classical conditioning involves automatic approach and avoidance responses to particular stimuli, instrumental conditioning involves reinforcement or punishment for particular behaviors in particular situations. The most formal system is that of token economies, which arrange contingencies in the environment of people who reside in institutions; the system of payment and reward is obvious to the participants. But not all instances of reinforcement and punishment are overt; they can also be vicarious. With the guidance of therapists, people can imagine their own behavior with its consequent reinforcement or punishment. Modeling has been used as an important adjunct to instrumental conditioning; therapists who use this effective technique provide specific examples of the desirable behaviors.

Although some people view behavior therapy as simple and rigid application of principles of conditioning, therapists must be well-trained, sensitive people if the techniques are to be effective. The major problem with behavior therapy is people's tendency to discriminate the therapeutic situation from similar ones in the outside world, thus failing to generalize their behavior to situations outside the clinic.

BIOLOGICAL TREATMENTS

As we saw in Chapter 17, the most effective single treatment for schizophrenia and the affective psychoses is medication. Besides drug therapy, there are two other forms of biological treatment: electroconvulsive therapy and psychosurgery.

DRUG THERAPY

Antipsychotic Drugs

Antipsychotic drugs have had a profound effect on the treatment of schizophrenia. Although they do not "cure" schizophrenia, they reduce the severity of its most prominent symptoms, delusions and hallucinations, apparently by blocking dopamine receptors in the brain. (Pharmacological stimulation of these neurons with drugs such as amphetamine produces symptoms of schizophrenia, and inhibition with the antipsychotic drugs reduces them.) Presumably the overactivity of these synapses in a system that controls the functioning of attentional processes is an important factor in the development of schizophrenia. This system connects neurons in the brain stem—in the *ventral tegmental area*—with those in the hypothalamus, cortex, and parts of the limbic system near the front of the brain. (See **Figure 18.14.**)

Another system of dopamine-secreting neurons in the brain is involved in control of movement. This system connects the *substantia nigra* ("black substance") in the brain stem with basal ganglia. Occasionally, this system of neurons degenerates spontaneously in older people, producing Parkinson's disease. Symptoms of this disorder include tremors, muscular rigidity, loss of balance, difficulty in initiating a movement, and impaired breathing that makes speech indistinct. In extreme cases the person is bedridden.

The major problem with the antipsychotic drugs is that they do not discriminate between these two pathways of dopamine-secreting neurons; the drugs interfere with the activity of both the attentional circuit and the motor circuit. Consequently, a patient being treated for schizophrenia often shows disturbance in control of movement and other symptoms of Parkinson's disease. One of these, loss of facial expression, can have serious consequences, because it is sometimes misdiagnosed as a recurrence of one of the symptoms of schizophrenia, lack of affect (Snyder, 1974). A resulting increase in dosage to counteract the presumed recurrence makes the problem worse. In fact all the parkinsonian side

This system is involved in control of movements.

This system is involved in attention. Overactivity may cause schizophrenia.

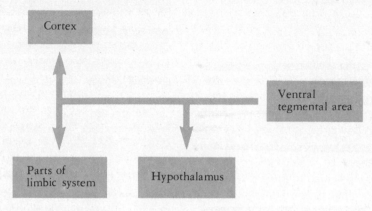

FIGURE 18.14   The two major dopamine systems. *Top:* The motor system; *bottom:* The system involved in reinforcement and attention.

effects are usually temporary and can be controlled by adjusting the dosage of the medication.

A related problem is that symptoms of motor impairment sometimes do not appear until after several years of medication. Symptoms of **tardive dyskinesia** (*tardive* means "late-developing"; *dyskinesia* refers to a disturbance of movement) include facial grimacing and involuntary movements of the tongue, mouth, and neck. Severely affected patients have difficulty talking, and occasionally the movements interfere with breathing. The symptoms can temporarily be alleviated by an *increase* in dosage, which only increases and perpetuates the patient's dependence on the medication (Baldessarini and Tarsy, 1980). This side effect argues forcefully for the necessity of careful monitoring of patients' symptoms and for restriction of antipsychotic medication to the minimum effective dosage.

Clinicians and researchers continue to hope for the development of antipsychotic drugs that will affect only the dopamine neurons that are part of the attentional mechanism of the brain and that

will not interfere with the neurons that are involved in the control of movement. Because the biochemistry of these two types of neurons differs slightly, there is some basis for this hope.

Antidepressant Drugs

◆ Like the uses of antipsychotic drugs, those of the antidepressant drugs, the tricyclic antidepressants and lithium carbonate, were discussed in Chapter 17. The tricyclic drugs are most effective in the treatment of major depression, lithium in the treatment of bipolar affective disorders or simple mania. Patients' manic symptoms usually decrease as soon as their blood levels of lithium reach a therapeutic level (Gerbino, Oleshansky, and Gershon, 1978). In patients with bipolar disorder, once the manic phase is eliminated, the depressed phase does not return. Lithium appears to be remarkably free of side effects, but an overdose of the drug is toxic. Therefore, the patient's blood should be monitored periodically.

As we saw in Chapter 17, a common side effect of the hypotensive drugs such as reserpine is depression. Thus it should not be surprising that the principal side effect of the tricyclic antidepressant drugs is elevated blood pressure (hypertension). This effect makes treatment of a depressed person with high blood pressure a difficult problem. On the one hand, a patient with high blood pressure stands a good chance of suffering heart attacks or strokes. On the other hand, for many people major depression makes life not worth living.

Antianxiety Drugs

◆ *Antianxiety drugs,* better known as tranquilizers, are the most abused of all drugs. Many people take drugs such as Librium and Valium to combat the most common symptom of neurosis: anxiety. People with neuroses (or tendencies toward them) are especially prone to drug dependency in their search for a crutch to help them. Because some busy physicians find it easier to give a patient a prescription than to try to find out what is causing the anxiety, people rarely have trouble obtaining these drugs. If necessary, people hooked on tranquilizers will shop around until they find a physician who will oblige them.

Antianxiety drugs undoubtedly serve a useful purpose in helping people cope with transient crises.

They are also effective in reducing the withdrawal symptoms of alcohol and opiate addictions. Sometimes they are used as antidotes for overdoses of stimulant drugs. But there is no "disease state" that is alleviated by the antianxiety medications. Chronic, long-term use of tranquilizers is probably not in anyone's best interest (Baldessarini, 1977).

ELECTROCONVULSIVE THERAPY

◆ *Electroconvulsive therapy (ECT)* involves applying a pair of metal electrodes to a person's head and then passing a brief surge of electric current through them. The jolt produces a storm of electrical activity in the brain (a seizure) that renders the person unconscious. The wild firing of the neurons that control movement produces convulsions—violent thrashing movements of head, trunk, and limbs, followed by muscular rigidity and trembling. After a few minutes, the person falls into a stuporous sleep. Today patients are anesthetized and paralyzed before the current is turned on. This procedure eliminates the convulsion but not the seizure, which is what delivers the therapeutic effect. (See **Figure 18.15**.)

ECT has a bad reputation among many clinicians because it has been used to treat disorders

FIGURE 18.15   A patient being prepared for ECT.

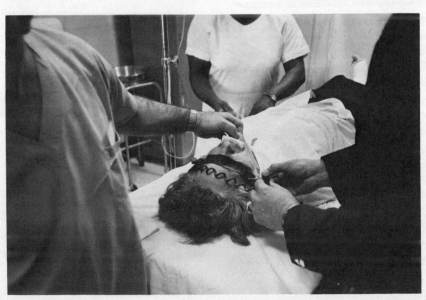

such as schizophrenia for which it has no useful effects, and because patients have received excessive numbers of ECT treatments—as many as hundreds. Originally, ECT was thought to alleviate the symptoms of schizophrenia, because schizophrenic people who also had epilepsy often appeared to improve just after a seizure. Subsequent research has shown that ECT has little or no effect on the symptoms of schizophrenia. However, it been shown to be singularly effective in treating severe depression (Baldessarini, 1977). Although no one knows for certain why ECT alleviates depression, it is possible that it does so by reducing REM sleep. As we saw in Chapter 17, people with major depression engage in abnormally large amounts of REM sleep, and REM-sleep depression is an effective antidepressant therapy.

A case report by Fink (1976) illustrates the response of a depressed patient to a course of electroconvulsive therapy. A forty-four-year-old widow had been hospitalized for three months for severe depression. A course of three ECT treatments per week was prescribed for her by her therapist's supervisor. Unknown to her therapist (a trainee), the first twelve treatments were subthreshold; that is, the intensity of the electrical current was too low to produce seizures. (The treatments could be regarded as placebo treatments.) Although both the patient and therapist expected the woman to show some improvement, none was seen. In the next fourteen treatments, the current was raised to a sufficient level to produce seizures. After five actual seizures, both the patient and therapist noticed an improvement. The woman began to complain less about various physical symptoms, to participate in hospital activities, and to make more positive statements about her mood. She became easier to talk with, and the therapist's notes of their conversations immediately proliferated. The fact that these responses occurred only after several actual seizures suggests that improvement stemmed from the biological treatment and not simply from the therapist's or patient's expectations.

Some patients with affective psychoses do not respond to the antidepressant drugs, but a substantial percentage improve after a few electroconvulsive treatments. Because antidepressant medications are generally slow-acting, taking ten days to two weeks for their therapeutic effects to begin,

severe cases of depression are often treated with a brief course of ECT to reduce the symptoms right away. The patients are then maintained on the antidepressant drug.

The second criticism of ECT is well justified. Too many ECT treatments will produce permanent loss of memory (Squire, 1974) and probably also cognitive deficits. Thus, although a prolonged series of treatments is not necessary to achieve therapeutic results, it is likely that even a small number of treatments causes at least some permanent brain damage. Therefore, the potential benefits of ECT must be weighed against its potential damage. Electroconvulsive therapy must be used only when the patient's symptoms justify it. Because ECT undoubtedly achieves it effects through the biochemical consequences of the seizure, pharmacologists may discover new drugs that can produce its rapid therapeutic effects without its deleterious ones. Once this breakthrough occurs, electroconvulsive therapy can be discarded.

PSYCHOSURGERY

One form of treatment for mental disorders is even more controversial than ECT. *Psychosurgery* is the treatment of a mental disorder, in the absence of obvious organic damage, by means of brain surgery. As you may recall from Chapter 14, brain surgery to remove a tumor or diseased neural tissue or to repair a damaged blood vessel is *not* psychosurgery, and there is no controversy about these procedures.

Psychosurgical treatment has no scientific basis, and it produces permanent, irreversible brain damage. Together, these facts form a convincing argument for banning the procedures, and in fact some jurisdictions in the United States have done so. However, although it has not proved effective in reducing or eliminating violent behavior, as was originally hoped, there is some evidence that psychosurgery has greatly improved the lives of mentally disturbed people who were formerly desperate for relief. This evidence has apparently been strong enough to convince even former critics. For example, Elliot Valenstein, in an excellent and influential book (1973), concluded that psychosurgical procedures were generally very poorly evaluated; few surgeons made careful measurements of their patients' symptoms before and after an operation, and the emphasis was often on manageability, not on actual remission of symptoms. However, a more recent report by a commission composed of experts, including Valenstein and other skeptics (U.S. National Commission for the Protection of Human Subjects of Biomedical and Behavioral Research, 1977), has drawn much more favorable conclusions about psychosurgery.

Psychosurgery was first performed in 1935, as an experimental procedure to investigate brain functions. Carlyle Jacobsen and two colleagues had been attempting to train a chimpanzee to perform a task that required the animal to note the presence of food, wait for a predetermined period, and then locate the food. One chimpanzee, Becky, did not take well to this ask; she appeared to be "neurotic." The experimenters reversed her behavior by performing a *prefrontal lobotomy*. This procedure disconnects the frontmost portion of the brain, effectively eliminating its functions. (See **Figure 18.16.**) The more commonly used medical term is *leucotomy* ("cutting of white matter"). The following extract from the experimenters' report describes the chimp's behavior before and after the procedure.

> In the normal phase, this animal was extremely eager to work and apparently well motivated; but this subject was highly emotional and profoundly upset whenever she made an error. Violent temper tantrums after a mistake were not infrequent occurrences. She observed closely loading of the cup with food, and often whimpered softly as the cup was placed over the food. If the experimenter lowered or started to lower the opaque door to exclude the animal's view of the cups, she immediately flew into a temper tantrum, rolled on the floor, defecated and urinated . . . .
>
> When this animal was [given a prefrontal lobotomy], a profound change occurred. The chimpanzee offered its usual friendly greeting, and eagerly ran from its living quarters to the transfer cage, and in turn went properly to the experimental cage. The usual procedure of baiting the cup and lowering the opaque screen was followed. But the chimpanzee did not show any excitement and sat quietly before the door or walked around the cage. Given an opportunity to choose between the cups it did so with its customary eagerness and alacrity. However, if the animal made a mistake, it showed no evidence of emotional disturbance but quietly awaited the loading of the cups for the next trial . . . . (Jacobsen, Wolf, and Jackson, 1935, pp. 9–10)

Egas Moniz, a Portuguese psychiatrist, noted the similarity between Becky's behavior and that of people with mental disorders. He persuaded Almeida Lina, a neurosurgeon, to try the procedure on a human patient, and the first operation was performed in November 1935. Moniz himself supervised only about 100 prefrontal lobotomies and

FIGURE 18.16   The technique of prefrontal lobotomy. (Adapted from Freeman, W., and Watts, J.W. *Psychosurgery in the Treatment of Mental Disorders and Intractable Pain*, 2nd ed. Springfield, Ill.: C.C. Thomas, 1950.)

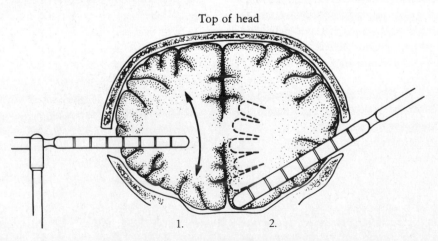

Top of head

1.   2.

wanted to wait for an evaluation of long-term results before recommending the procedure for more patients. (Ironically, a patient who had received a lobotomy shot Moniz, and the bullet lodged in his spine, causing paralysis of the lower part of his body.) In 1949 Moniz received a Nobel Prize "for his discovery of the therapeutic value of prefrontal leucotomy in certain psychoses."

The award by the Nobel Committee was definitely premature; the procedure was found to have serious side effects, such as apathy and severe blunting of emotions, intellectual impairments, and deficits in judgment. Nevertheless, the procedure was soon in common use for a variety of conditions, most of which were not improved by the surgery. It is estimated that approximately 40,000 prefrontal lobotomies were performed in the United States alone. A simple procedure, called "ice pick" prefrontal lobotomy by its critics, was even performed on an outpatient basis. (See **Figure 18.17.**) The development of antipsychotic drugs and increasing attention to the serious side effects of prefrontal lobotomy led to a sharp decline in the use of this procedure during the 1950s. Today they are no longer performed.

A few surgeons have continued to refine the technique and now perform a procedure called a **cingulectomy,** which involves cutting the **cingulum bundle,** a band of nerve fibers that connects the prefrontal cortex with parts of the limbic system. (See **Figure 18.18.**) The purpose of a cingulectomy is to disconnect "thoughts and emotions," to relieve mental tension, and to "take the sting out of experience." According to the Commission on Psychosurgery (1977), these more restricted operations do not appear to produce the intellectual impairments or changes in personality that often occurred after prefrontal lobotomies. In fact, people's IQ test scores often improve after surgery, because their other problems are alleviated and they can devote more attention to the task at hand. The only reliable negative finding is an impairment of patients' ability to change their strategy in a problem-solving task. Another possible result is a mild, temporary blunting of affect.

Cingulectomies have been shown to be effective

FIGURE 18.17   "Ice pick" prefrontal lobotomy. (Adapted from Freeman, W. *Proceedings of the Royal Society of Medicine,* 1949, *42 (suppl.),* 8–12.)

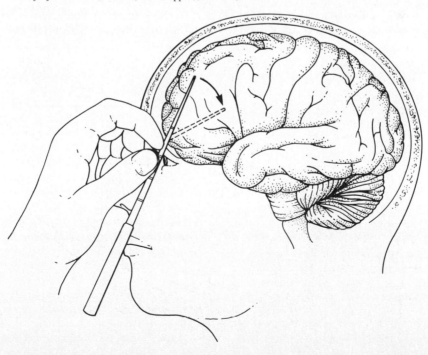

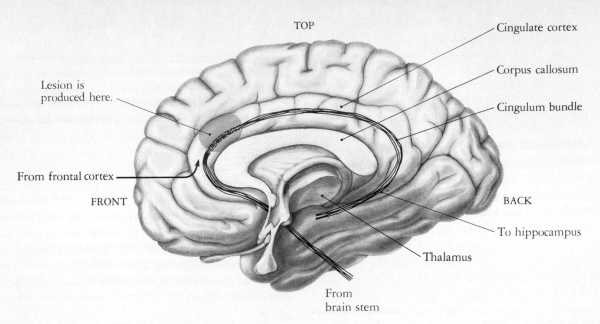

FIGURE 18.18   The cingulectomy procedure.

in helping people who suffer from severe compulsions, such as the following case.

> Her day was totally occupied with checking and rechecking actions such as washing, dressing and household tasks. She had, for example, to wash her face in a special order—starting with the left side, nose, right side, forehead—up to thirteen times. A similar elaborate system was involved in her bathing, which took her over an hour each day. After washing clothes she had to squeeze them a certain way, repeating the proceedings twenty-two times, the bottom of the bowl was then examined, checking the maker's mark numerous times to make sure the bowl was empty. Cleaning her teeth was a major task, taking over a half an hour . . . .
>
> Household chores such as washing-up or polishing a table were completely impossible for her, as they took so long and caused her such distress. Her husband and mother were, therefore, forced into running her home and, on medical advice, her two children were at boarding school. The patient felt extreme guilt at her disruption of the family's existence and, at times, felt very depressed and that life was not worth living . . . . (National Commission, 1977, app. 1, pp. 39–40)

The same report presents a case history of an obsessive-compulsive patient who was given a cin-

gulectomy after other therapeutic techniques failed to help:

> *Case History 1230.* This is a 37 year old white female who is presently married for the second time and who has one child.
>
> Her illness had been present for ten years, precipitated by sadistic beatings in her first unhappy marriage. She was first seen in 1962 for confusion, fear of being alone, and treated with psychotherapy and given adjunctive medications with only minimal improvement. Following this, she was given treatment including more than 20 ECTs.
>
> In May 1965 she married for the second time. In August of that year her symptoms recurred when she became pregnant. The obsessive-compulsive symptoms continued during pregnancy and psychotherapy combined with anxiety medication and major tranquilizers did not relieve her emotional state. In 1966 she became depressed. She was maintained on antidepressants and monthly supportive visits until it became necessary to hospitalize her for a course of 6 ECTs. The ECT relieved the depression but did not alter her obsessive-compulsive symptoms. Her obsessions were related chiefly to cleaning . . . the house, setting the table and dressing, all of which were done over and over again. Added to these symptoms was a passive-dependent personality with some schizoid loose thinking. It became necessary for her mother

to move into the house. The patient also developed a type of nervous dermatitis in her hands which required cortisone injections. This patient underwent a psychosurgical procedure in 1971. Improvement was noticed about 6 weeks after the operation. She made the decision along with her mother. She stated that she has no regrets and that it helped her.

Her postoperative condition has been good. She has been able to raise her family and run her home effectively. Her performance on the psychological tests {was} varied. Some subtests of the IQ test were below normal but her overall level was within normal limits. She failed to grasp any of the concepts of the Wisconsin Card Sorting Test. (National Commission, 1977, app. 2, pp. 68,69)

According to the commission, psychosurgery appears to be of most value in the treatment of affective disorders; it does not significantly curtail thought disturbances. The report stresses the importance of carefully evaluating each case. In one flagrantly inadequate evaluation, a surgeon noted that the surgery produced "no or little changes in intellect and discriminative ability," using as the only criterion the patient's ability to knit after the operation (Winter, 1972). Surgeons should not be expected to perform a psychological evaluation.

In its report, the commission managed to debunk a few popular myths about psychosurgery. One is that blacks and other minority groups have been disproportionately subjected to psychosurgery as a result of racial and ethnic prejudice. In fact the commission found that very few members of minority groups have received psychosurgery. Because most people who undergo psychosurgery are recommended to neurosurgeons by a private psychiatrist, most of the patients are white and middle class.

If psychosurgery is ever used, it should be used only as a last resort, and never on a patient who cannot assent to treatment. The effects of psychosurgery are permanent; there is no way to reverse a brain lesion. Perhaps more effective behavioral techniques and new drug treatments will eventually make psychosurgical procedures obsolete.

Interim summary: Biological treatments for mental disorders include drugs, ECT, and psychosurgery. Research has shown that treatment of the positive symptoms of schizophrenia with antipsychotic drugs, of major depression with the tricyclic antidepressant drugs, and of bipolar disorder with lithium carbonate are the most effective ways to alleviate the symptoms of these disorders. Although ECT is an effective therapy for depression, its use should be reserved for cases where rapid relief is critical, because the seizures may produce brain damage. Probably, antianxiety drugs (tranquilizers) should not be used to treat people with neurotic anxiety, because these people are especially susceptible to becoming addicted. The most controversial treatment, psychosurgery, is rarely performed today. Its only presently accepted use, in the form of cingulectomy, is for treatment of crippling compulsions that cannot be reduced by more conventional means.

ECLECTIC TREATMENT

In its description of the various kinds of psychotherapies, this chapter may have given the impression that practitioners usually employ only one approach. They may be psychoanalysts, client-centered therapists, rational-emotive therapists, group psychotherapists, family therapists, behavior therapists, or physicians who prescribe drugs. In fact some psychotherapists do describe themselves in these terms. But the majority of clinical psychologists probably describe their own therapeutic preference as eclectic.

Eclectic (from Greek *eklegein*, "to single out") means "choosing what appears to be the best from diverse sources, systems, or styles." The eclectic clinical psychologist attempts to learn what is good about each of many different approaches. If a client seems to be avoiding discussion of some painful childhood events that may still be affecting his or her behavior, the therapist may use hypnosis or free association to uncover these memories and try to work them out. For a client with a simple, isolated phobia, the therapist may use systematic desensitization to alleviate the problem. If the problem seems to involve interactions with other family members, the therapist may meet with the entire family. If the client seems to be too self-critical, the therapist may attempt to change his or her beliefs about what is necessary and what is desirable. For a client who appears to be suicidal the therapist may consult a psychiatrist for elec-troconvulsive therapy and/or a course of antide-pressant drugs.

The average person who visits a clinical psy-chologist for help with a problem will probably not be able to identify the therapist's theoretical orientation, because the therapist will most likely adopt the technique that he or she believes is best suited to the client's problem.

EVALUATION OF THERAPIES AND THERAPISTS

◆ Several factors make it extremely difficult to eval-uate the efficacy of a particular form of therapy or the effectiveness of an individual therapist. One is the problem of *measurement*. It is very difficult to measure a person's dysfunction. There are no easily applied, commonly agreed-upon criteria for mental health. Therefore, it is difficult to make valid be-fore-and-after measurements.

Ethics also sometimes prevents clinicians from using a purely scientific method of evaluation, which requires that experimental and control groups be constituted in equivalent ways. Leaving a person who appears to be suicidal untreated, so that com-parisons can be made with similar people who receive therapy, presents risks that almost all ther-apists would consider unacceptable.

Self-selection, or clients' initial choices of a certain therapeutic approach, and the resulting impossi-bility of establishing either a stable sample popu-lation or a control group, also makes it difficult to compare the efficacy of various kinds of therapies. Many patients change therapists or leave therapy altogether. What conclusions can we make about the effectiveness of the therapy by looking only at the progress made by the clients who remain? With what control group can we compare them?

◆ In a pioneering paper on psychotherapeutic eval-uation, Eysenck (1952) examined nineteen studies assessing the efficacy of psychotherapy. He re-ported that of the people who remained in psycho-analysis as long as their therapists thought they should, 66 percent showed improvement. Simi-larly, 64 percent of people treated eclectically showed

an improvement. However, 72 percent of people who were treated only custodially in institutions (receiving no psychotherapy) showed improve-ment. In other words, people got better just as fast by themselves as they did in therapy. This was obviously not a favorable finding for psycho-therapy.

Subsequent studies have not been much more favorable. Some investigators (including Eysenck) have concluded that it is unethical to charge a per-son for psychotherapy, because there is little sci-entific evidence that it is effective. Others say that the problems involved in performing scientific re-search are so great that we must abandon the attempt to evaluate therapies; validation of the ef-ficacy of therapy must rely on the therapist's clin-ical judgment. Many forms of therapy have never been evaluated objectively, because their practi-tioners are convinced that the method works and reject objective confirmation as unnecessary.

A number of more recent studies have compared the efficacy of insight psychotherapies, behavior therapies, and drug treatments. In a review of these studies, Luborsky, Singer, and Luborsky (1976) found that individual therapies worked about as well as group therapies, client-centered therapy was just about as effective as other types of individual therapy, and that behavior therapy was somewhat more effective than insight therapy. (To be fair, it is easier to evaluate the achievements of behavior therapy because its goals tend to be more limited and specific than those of other therapies.) They found that drug therapy was superior to psycho-therapy, but that a combination of drugs and psy-chotherapy achieved better results than did either element alone. For the treatment of psychosomatic disease, the combination of medical therapy and psychotherapy was far superior to medical therapy alone. Of thirty-three studies comparing psycho-therapy with control groups (no therapy), twenty found a statistically significant advantage to psy-chotherapy and thirteen found no difference. *No* study found that the control group did signifi-cantly better.

Considering the enormous expense and effort in-volved in psychotherapy, an impartial observer must admit that there is rather scanty evidence for its usefulness. Yet few people would recommend that psychotherapy be abandoned. We need to find ways to make psychotherapy more effective or to evaluate its effects more precisely, or both.

◆   An interesting study by Luborsky, Chandler, Auerbach, Cohen, and Bachrach (1971) investigated the factors that influence the outcome of a course of psychotherapy. They examined patient variables, treatment variables, and therapist variables. The important *patient variables* were psychological health at the beginning of the therapy, adequacy of personality, the patient's motivation for change, level of intelligence, level of anxiety (more anxious patients tended to do better), and education and socioeconomic status. Some of the variables seem to be self-confirming; if you are in fairly good psychological shape to begin with you have a better chance of improving. In addition, if you are well educated and have adequate social and financial resources, your condition will probably improve. The finding that anxiety is a good sign probably indicates a motivation to improve.

The only significant *treatment variable* was the number of sessions of therapy. No one type of therapy appeared to be better than another. However, because a larger number of treatments took more time, we cannot assume that the treatments themselves were responsible for the improvement; perhaps the mere passage of time was all that was necessary.

Several *therapist variables* were significant. These were the number of years that he or she had been practicing, similarity in the personality of therapist and client, and the ability of the therapist to communicate empathy to the client. The finding that the more experienced therapists had more success with their clients is very encouraging; it suggests that therapists learn something from their years of experience, which in turn implies that *there is something to learn.* Thus, we have some reason to believe that the process of psychotherapy is not futile.

◆   The fact that the ability of the therapist to express empathy is a significant variable has suggested to several investigators (such as Fix and Haffke, 1976) that a therapist's most important function is to change the client's thoughts and behaviors by social reinforcement. You will recall that Truax (1966) found that Carl Rogers was inadvertently reinforcing statements from his clients

that indicated improvement. Therapists who demonstrate warmth and understanding are most successful in reinforcing desirable statements and behaviors from their patients. Cold, uninvolved therapists simply have less impact. Truax and Carkhuff (1964) have distinguished between effective and ineffective therapists in the following way:

> Patients whose therapists offered a high level of unconditional positive warmth, self-congruence or genuineness, and accurate empathetic understanding showed significant positive personality and behavioral change on a wide variety of indices, and . . . patients whose therapists offered relatively low levels of these conditions during therapy exhibited significant deterioration in personality and behavioral functioning. (pp. 130–131)

To illustrate what is meant by effective empathy, Fix and Haffke (1976) describe three hypothetical encounters between an adolescent client and a therapist. The first communicates a high level of empathy.

PATIENT: That's when Dad said, "Come here, Stupid."

THERAPIST: Ouch!

PATIENT: I didn't mind. I just shrugged my shoulders and walked away.

THERAPIST: "If that's all my help means to you, you can do the job yourself!"

PATIENT: Yeah; getting angry is one thing, but calling a guy a name is somethin' else.

THERAPIST: Especially from a guy's own Dad.

PATIENT: Yeah [voice quivering]. I don't want nothin' to do with him no more.

THERAPIST: "I don't want to be hurt like that again."

PATIENT: [long pause] And then I get angry and skip school and get in trouble. (p. 49)

The second dialogue involves a therapist who takes a rather mechanical view of empathy: repeat back to the client what he or she has just told you. This strategy is less likely to be successful.

PATIENT: That's when Dad said "Come here, Stupid."

THERAPIST: Your father called you stupid.

PATIENT: Uh . . . yes, but I just shrugged my shoulders and walked away.

THERAPIST: You just shrugged and walked off, as if you didn't care at all.

PATIENT: Yeah, and I don't. I don't want nothin' to do with him any more.

THERAPIST: You don't want to have anything more to do with your father because he called you stupid.

PATIENT: No. (p. 50)

This therapist seems to have reached a dead end with the client. Certainly, the client is not opening himself up so that a useful discussion can proceed.

In the third dialogue, the therapist pounces on any expression of emotion.

PATIENT: That's when Dad said "Come here, Stupid."

THERAPIST: Bet it made you angry.

PATIENT: No, I just shrugged my shoulders and walked away.

THERAPIST: But you were mad at him for calling you a name.

PATIENT: No, I just don't want nothin' to do with him no more.

THERAPIST: Oh, I see! You were hurt by what he said. It made you feel bad and you got angry. I'll bet that's why you skip school too. Huh?

PATIENT: [Silence].

THERAPIST: Now you're angry at me. (pp. 49–50)

These dialogues effectively illustrate what is meant by effective empathy. Clearly, the therapist in the first dialogue has elicited the most useful comments from his or her client and therefore has the best chance of influencing the client's behavior.

Several studies have suggested that the ability to express empathy is one of the traits that distin-

FIGURE 18.19   A therapist's effectiveness is closely related to his or her ability to express empathy. A high degree of empathy probably enhances the therapist's ability to provide social reinforcers and change clients' behaviors.

guish an experienced therapist from an inexperienced one. For example, Mullen and Abeles (1971) found that an experienced therapist was able to express empathy for a client whether the therapist liked the client or not, but that inexperienced therapists had difficulty expressing empathy for clients they did not like. And the characteristic that best predicted a favorable outcome was not whether the therapist liked the client, but whether he or she was able to express empathy (See **Figure 18.19**.)

CONCLUDING REMARKS

This chapter has tried to convey the ingenuity shown by clinicians in their efforts to help people with psychological problems. The magnitude of the task is formidable, and often the rewards are scanty, especially when objective research into the effects of their efforts shows so little.

One encouraging outcome of evaluative research is its implication that what the therapist does can indeed have an effect on the outcome; experienced and empathetic therapists are more likely to help their clients get better. Another is the general success achieved in behavior therapy, even though its goals are often circumscribed. Finally, even though clinical psychologists are not responsible for the development of the biological therapies, they can take heart from several studies showing that psychotherapy significantly improves the mental health of clients who receive drugs or electroshock treatment.

The research and writing of thousands of men and women have contributed to the information contained in this book. If this text has achieved all its purposes, you will now not only know more about human behavior than you did before, you will also have learned to be skeptical about unsupported statements about human behavior, and you will be convinced that the only way to find out how we work is to investigate ourselves scientifically. Even human thought and emotion are fair topics for science.

While writing this book I have enjoyed feeling that I have been talking with someone. If any of you would like to discuss with me what I have written (or not written), do let me hear from you. Write to me at the Department of Psychology,

Tobin Hall, University of Massachusetts, Amherst, Massachusetts 01003.

GUIDE TO TERMS INTRODUCED IN THIS CHAPTER

SUGGESTIONS FOR FURTHER READING

The full range of present-day treatments for mental disorders are well described in *Current Psychotherapies*, edited by R.J. Corsini (2nd ed.; Itasca, Ill.: R.E. Peacock, 1979). S. Minuchin describes his method of family therapy in *Families and Family Therapy* (Cambridge, Mass.: Harvard University Press, 1974). *Learning Foundations of Behavior Therapy* by F.H. Kanfer and J.S. Phillips (New York: Wiley, 1970) surveys the various techniques that have been used in behavior therapy. A very readable overview of the nature and treatment of mental disorders is provided in R. Kaplan and D. Sacuzzo's *Clinical Psychology* (Boston: Allyn and Bacon, 1984). Handy tools for aspiring clinicians are *The Psychotherapy Handbook*, edited by R. Herink (New York: NAL, 1980), which describes over 250 psychotherapies, and R. Meyer's *The Clinician's Handbook* (Boston: Allyn and Bacon, 1983), which is organized according to the classification system of DSM-III.

GLOSSARY

ABSOLUTE THRESHOLD The smallest value of a *stimulus* that can reliably be detected.

ACCOMMODATION 1. According to Jean Piaget, the process by which a child's behavioral *schemas* are altered by interaction with the environment. 2. Changes in the thickness of the lens of the eye, accomplished by the ciliary muscles, that focus images of near or distant objects on the *retina*.

ACETYLCHOLINE A *transmitter substance* that is released by the *terminal buttons* of some neurons in the brain and *peripheral nervous system*. Acetylcholine is the transmitter substance that causes muscles to contract.

ACTION POTENTIAL A brief electrochemical event that is carried by an *axon* from the cell body of the neuron to its *terminal buttons*, which in turn release *transmitter substance*, stimulating or inhibiting the neurons with which the terminal buttons form *synapses*.

ACTIVATED MEMORY Information that is currently being processed, consisting of new information and information that has recently been retrieved from *long-term memory*.

ACTIVATIONAL EFFECT Current effect of a *hormone*, which depends on the continued presence of the hormone. Examples are beard growth in men and milk production in women. See *organizational effect*.

ADJUNCTIVE BEHAVIOR Behavior that occurs when a highly motivated organism receives reinforcers intermittently; the behavior tends to be species typical, such as drinking, gnawing, or pecking at objects. Also called *interim behavior*.

ADRENAL GLAND An *endocrine gland* located just above the kidney that secretes several kinds of *hormones*. Some hormones help provide the muscles with nutrients and an increased blood supply for vigorous exercise; others control the body's mineral balance. The adrenal gland also produces sex hormones, such as *androstenedione* and *testosterone*.

ADRENOGENITAL SYNDROME Masculinization of a female caused by excessive secretion of *androgens* by the adrenal gland.

AFFECTIVE DISORDER Any of a variety of psychological disorders that alter emotion or mood; can be a state of excessive, unrealistic sadness (*depression*) or elation (*mania*).

AGRAPHIA Complete loss of the ability to write, caused by brain damage.

ALEXIA Complete loss of the ability to read, caused by brain damage. Usually the loss is not complete and is referred to as *dyslexia*.

ALLELE A particular form of a *gene* at a particular location on a *chromosome*. For example, blue and brown irises are produced by different alleles of the gene that causes the production of iris pigment.

ALPHA ACTIVITY Rhythmic activity of the *electroencephalogram,* a recording of the brain's activity, with a frequency between 8 and 12 cycles per second, usually indicating a state of quiet relaxation.

ALZHEIMER'S DISEASE A degenerative illness in which neurons of the *cerebral cortex* die. The result is loss of memory and other cognitive processes and ultimately death.

AMNESIA Loss of memory for events that should normally be subject to recall.

AMUSIA Loss of the ability to produce or comprehend the harmony and rhythm of music.

AMYGDALA A portion of the brain, located deep in the *temporal lobe*. Damage causes changes in emotional and aggressive behavior.

ANALGESIA Literally, complete loss of the sensation of pain, but the term usually refers to partial loss.

ANAL STAGE According to Freud, the second stage of psychosexual development, during which the infant obtains gratification by passing or retaining feces.

ANDROGEN The primary class of sex *hormones* in males. The most important androgen is *testosterone*.

ANDROGEN INSENSITIVITY SYNDROME A disorder in which a person's cells are incapable of responding to *androgens*. A genetic male with this condition will develop as an infertile female.

ANDROGENIZATION An *organizational effect* of *androgens* that causes a fetus to *differentiate* as a male.

ANDROSTENEDIONE (AD) An *androgen* that is secreted primarily by the adrenal glands. Androstenedione causes the growth of pubic and underarm hair in females at puberty.

ANHEDONIA Loss of the ability to experience pleasure.

ANIMISM A primitive belief that all animals, or even all moving objects, possess spirits providing their motive force.

ANTIDEPRESSANT DRUGS Drugs that are used to treat psychotic depression, one of the *affective disorders*. *Tricyclic antidepressant drugs,* such as imipramine, are used to treat *major depression; lithium carbonate* is used to treat *bipolar affective disorder*.

APPEASEMENT GESTURE A stereotyped gesture made by a submissive animal in response to a *threat gesture* by a dominant animal; tends to inhibit an attack.

APPETITIVE STIMULUS A stimulus that an organism will attempt to approach; appetitive stimuli can be used to reinforce a response.

APRAXIA   Difficulty in planning sequences of movements by a body part that is not paralyzed; generally caused by damage to the *parietal lobe* or *frontal lobe* of the brain.

ASSIMILATION   According to Jean Piaget, the process by which a new concept comes to elicit a child's behavioral *schema.*

ATTACHMENT   The process by which parent (or caretaker) and child form a mutually reinforcing system.

ATTRIBUTION   Assigning cause to an event, including a person's behavior, or assigning a personality characteristic to a person. Attributions can apply to others or to oneself.

AUTONOMIC NERVOUS SYSTEM   The part of the nervous system that controls the internal organs, blood vessels, sweat glands, and *endocrine glands.*

AUTOSHAPING   A procedure that causes certain species-typical behaviors to occur; for example, a pigeon begins pecking at a plastic disk that is briefly illuminated shortly before food is presented, even though feeding is not contingent on pecking.

AVERSIVE STIMULUS   A *stimulus* that an organism will attempt to *avoid* or *escape;* aversive stimuli can be used either to *punish* or *negatively reinforce* a response.

AVOIDANCE   The performance of a response that prevents an *aversive stimulus* from occurring. See *escape.*

AXON   A long, thin process of a neuron that divides into a few or many branches, ending in *terminal buttons.* See *action potential.*

BASAL GANGLIA   Structures near the center of the front part of the brain, which are involved in the control of movement and posture. *Parkinson's disease* and *Huntington's chorea* are two disorders caused by degeneration of parts of the basal ganglia.

BASILAR MEMBRANE   A membrane that divides the *cochlea* of the inner ear into two compartments. The receptive organ for audition, the *organ of Corti,* resides here.

BEHAVIORAL GENETICS   The study of the genetic basis of behavioral characteristics of organisms.

BEHAVIORISM   A movement in psychology that asserts that the only proper subject matter for scientific study in psychology is behavior.

BETA ACTIVITY   Irregular high-frequency activity of the *electroencephalogram,* a record of the brain's activity, usually indicating a state of alertness or arousal.

BIPOLAR DISORDER   A serious *affective disorder* characterized by alternating periods of *mania* and *depression;* a form of *psychosis.*

BRIGHTNESS   A perceptual dimension of color, most closely related to the radiant energy emitted by a visual stimulus.

BROCA'S APHASIA   Severe difficulty in articulating words, especially *function words,* caused by damage to Broca's area, a region of the *frontal cortex* on the left (speech-dominant) side of the brain.

BROCA'S SPEECH AREA   See *Broca's aphasia.*

BRUCE EFFECT   The termination of a pregnancy caused by the odor of a *pheromone* present in the urine of a male other than the male that impregnated the female; first identified in mice.

CATAPLEXY   A form of *narcolepsy* in which the person collapses, becoming temporarily paralyzed but not unconscious; usually triggered by anger or excitement; apparently related to the paralysis that normally accompanies *REM sleep.*

CATASTROPHIC REACTION   Severe and overwhelming depression in a person who has sustained brain damage, usually in the left hemisphere.

CATATONIC SCHIZOPHRENIA   A form of *schizophrenia* in which a person remains immobile, often in bizarre postures, or exhibits wild hyperactivity.

CATHARSIS   According to Freud, the release, through relatively harmless means such as symbolic aggression or vigorous sports, of a drive that might otherwise result in undesirable behavior.

CAT SCANNER   (CAT is an abbreviation of computerized axial tomography.) A device that uses a special X-ray machine and a computer to produce images of the brain that appear as slices taken parallel to the top of the skull.

CENTRAL NERVOUS SYSTEM   The brain and spinal cord.

CEREBELLUM   A pair of hemispheres resembling the cerebral hemispheres but much smaller and lying beneath and in back of them; controls posture and movements, especially rapid ones.

CEREBRAL CORTEX   The outer layer of the cerebral hemispheres of the brain. Specialized areas include the primary sensory and motor cortex, the association cortex, and regions that are necessary for speech comprehension and production.

CEREBROSPINAL FLUID (CSF)   A fluid similar to blood plasma that fills the hollow *ventricles* of the brain and in which the brain and spinal cord float.

CHROMOSOME   One of the structures composed of DNA that constitute the genetic material of the cell. Humans have twenty-three pairs of chromosomes, including one pair of sex chromosomes.

CHUNKING   The process by which information is simplified by rules, and hence can be remembered easily once the rules are learned. For example, the sequence 1 3 5 7 9 11 13 15 is easy to remember if a person knows the rule that describes odd numbers.

CLASSICAL CONDITIONING   The process by which a *defensive reflex* or *consummatory reflex,* normally produced automatically by an eliciting stimulus, comes to be produced by a previously neutral stimulus. The previously neutral stimulus is followed shortly by an eliciting stimulus (*unconditional stimulus*) that normally produces the response (*unconditional response*), and becomes, after several pairings, a *conditional stimulus* producing the *conditional response.*

CLINICAL PSYCHOLOGY   The branch of psychology devoted to the investigation and treatment of abnormal behavior and mental disorders.

CLOSURE   The tendency to see incomplete or partially obscured forms as complete and whole.

COCHLEA   A snail-shaped chamber set in bone in the inner ear, where audition takes place. See *basilar membrane*.

COGNITIVE DISSONANCE   An unpleasant state of tension caused when a disparity exists between concepts, especially those that are related to one's self-esteem.

COGNITIVE PSYCHOLOGY   The branch of psychology devoted to the investigation of perception, memory, concept formation, and other mental processes.

COMMON FATE   The tendency to perceive elements that move together in the same direction as belonging to the same figure in the foreground.

COMPARATIVE PSYCHOLOGY   The branch of psychology that studies the behavior of a variety of organisms in an attempt to understand the adaptive and functional significance of the behaviors and their relation to evolution.

COMPLEMENTARY COLORS   Colors that, when mixed, will produce a neutral *hue* (white or shades of gray). A *negative afterimage* is complementary to the color to which the eye was exposed.

COMPLIANCE   The performance of a behavior that was requested by another person.

COMPULSION   The feeling that one is obliged to perform a behavior, even if one prefers not to do so.

CONDITIONAL RESPONSE (CR)   After *classical conditioning* the response that is elicited by the *conditional stimulus*.

CONDITIONAL STIMULUS (CS)   After *classical conditioning* the stimulus that elicits the *conditional response*, which resembles the *unconditional response*.

CONDITIONED AVERSION   The process by which a novel stimulus, such as the taste of a food, followed by an unpleasant reaction, such as illness, results in an organism's avoiding the stimulus.

CONDITIONED PUNISHMENT   A process by which a previously neutral stimulus followed by an *aversive stimulus* itself becomes capable, through *classical conditioning*, of punishing a response.

CONDITIONED REINFORCEMENT   A process by which a previously neutral stimulus followed by an appetitive stimulus itself becomes capable, through *classical conditioning*, of reinforcing a response.

CONE   One of the *photoreceptors* in the retina, along with *rods*. Cones are responsible for acute daytime vision and for color perception.

CONFORMITY   The tendency to act in a way that is consistent with the norms of one's peer group.

CONFOUNDING OF VARIABLES   Inadvertent alteration of more than one *independent variable* during an experiment. The results of an experiment with confounded independent variables permit no valid conclusions about cause and effect.

CONJUGATE EYE MOVEMENT   The cooperative movement of the eyes that ensures that the image of an object falls on identical portions of both retinas.

CONSENSUS   General agreement within a group. In attribution theory, consensus refers to a behavior that is being performed by several people.

CONSERVATION   The tendency to perceive quantities, mass, and volume as remaining constant even if elements are moved or the shape of the substance is changed. According to Piaget, this is an important cognitive concept.

CONSOLIDATION   The process by which information in short-term memory is stored in long-term memory, presumably in the form of physical changes in neurons in the brain.

CONSUMMATORY REFLEX   Reflexes associated with species-typical behaviors that consummate a sequence; for example, salivation that accompanies eating, or increased blood pressure that accompanies fighting.

CONTENT WORD   A noun, verb, adjective, or adverb that conveys meaning. See *function word*.

CONTINGENT   Occurring only when certain conditions are fulfilled. If an appetitive stimulus is contingent on a particular behavior, the frequency of that behavior will usually increase.

CONTINUOUS REINFORCEMENT SCHEDULE (CRF)   A schedule whereby every occurrence of a particular response is followed by presentation of the reinforcer.

CONTROL GROUP   A comparison group used in an experiment, the members of which are exposed to the naturally occurring or zero value of the independent variable.

CONVERSION DISORDER   A psychological disorder in which a person experiences *amnesia* or physical symptoms such as anesthesia, paralysis, or illness without organic cause.

CORPUS LUTEUM   See *menstrual cycle*.

CORRELATION COEFFICIENT   A measurement of the degree to which two variables are related. A correlation of zero indicates no relation; perfect relation is ± 1.0. (A negative correlation indicates that large values of one variable are associated with small values of the other one.)

COVARIANCE METHOD   According to *attribution* theory, the strategy by which people infer causation; if events occur together we infer that one of them caused the other to happen.

COVERT REINFORCEMENT   A method used in the treatment of maladaptive behaviors in which the person imagines himself or herself performing adaptive behaviors and then being rewarded for doing so with pleasant situations.

CRANIAL NERVE   One of the twelve pairs of nerves that are directly attached to the brain.

CRITERION GROUP   A group of subjects whose behavior is used to validate a psychological test. For example, if people diagnosed as extraverted by other means tend to receive higher scores than randomly selected people on a test of extraversion, the test receives support as being valid.

CROSS-SECTIONAL OBSERVATION   Observation of the behavior of people of different ages at approximately the same time. See *longitudinal observation*.

CRYSTALLIZED INTELLIGENCE   According to Raymond Cattell, that part of a person's intellectual abilities that accumulates through experience. See *fluid intelligence*.

DARK ADAPTATION   The process by which the eye becomes capable of distinguishing dimly illuminated objects after going from a brightly lit region to a dark one. This process involves chemical changes in the *photoreceptors* of the *retina*.

DEFEMINIZATION An *organizational effect* of an *androgen:* suppression of the potential for an organism to engage in sexual behavior typical of the female of the species.

DEFENSE MECHANISM According to Freud, one of several methods by which the *ego* protects itself from conflicts between internalized prohibitions and drives.

DEFENSIVE REFLEX An innate, automatic response that tends to protect an organism from a potentially dangerous stimulus, usually by moving the threatened part away.

DELTA ACTIVITY Rhythmic activity of the *electroencephalogram,* a recording of the brain's activity, with a frequency between 3 and 5 cycles per second, indicating deep (slow-wave) sleep.

DELUSION A belief that is held even though evidence or logic shows it to be false. Delusions are important symptoms of psychoses. A delusion of control is a false belief that a person's thoughts and behaviors are being controlled by other people or other forces; a delusion of grandeur, that a person is famous, powerful, or important; and a delusion of persecution, that other people conspire to harm or thwart oneself.

DENDRITE A treelike part of a neuron on which the *terminal buttons* of other neurons form synapses.

DEPENDENT VARIABLE The event that is observed in an experiment. Manipulation of *independent variables* demonstrates whether or not they affect the value of dependent variables.

DEPRESSION A state of extreme sadness, usually characterized by slow thoughts and movements but sometimes by restless agitation. Psychotic depression includes *major depression* and the depressed phase of *bipolar affective disorder;* less serious neurotic depression includes *dysthymic disorder.*

DEUTERANOPIA A form of hereditary anomalous color vision, resulting from defective "green" *photoreceptors.*

DEVELOPMENTAL PSYCHOLOGY The branch of psychology that studies the changes in behavioral, perceptual, and cognitive capacities of organisms as a function of age and experience.

DICHOTIC LISTENING A task that requires a person to listen to one of two different messages being presented simultaneously to each ear through earphones.

DIFFERENCE THRESHOLD The smallest change in the value of a *stimulus* that can reliably be detected.

DIFFERENTIATION The process by which the cells of a developing organism become different from other cells and give rise to various organs of the body.

DISCOUNTING The tendency to reject *dispositional factors* as causes of a behavior when the behavior is apparently one that most people would perform under existing circumstances.

DISCRIMINATION The detection of differences between two stimuli or of a change in a *stimulus,* as shown by changes in an organism's behavior.

DISPLACEMENT According to Freud, one of the hypothetical ego *defense mechanisms,* in which energy from a prohibited drive is diverted into an irrelevant behavior.

DISPOSITIONAL FACTOR A cause of behavior that is related to one's personality characteristics and preferences. See *situational factor.*

DISSONANCE REDUCTION Resolution of a state of *cognitive dissonance,* accomplished through adding consonant elements that explain away the conflict, reducing the importance of the elements, or changing the dissonant elements.

DOCTRINE OF SPECIFIC NERVE ENERGIES Johannes Müller's observation that different nerve fibers convey specific information from one part of the body to the brain, or from the brain to one part of the body.

DOPAMINE A *transmitter substance* that is released by the *terminal buttons* of some neurons in the brain. Dopamine is apparently important in reinforcement, attention, and control of movement. Dopamine-secreting neurons may be involved in producing *schizophrenia.*

DOUBLE-BLIND METHOD An experimental procedure in which the subjects and experimenter do not know the value of the *independent variable* for a particular subject.

DOWN'S SYNDROME A disorder caused by the presence of an extra twenty-first chromosome, characterized by moderate to severe mental retardation and often by physical abnormalities; previously called mongolism.

DRIVE-REDUCTION HYPOTHESIS The hypothesis that a drive (resulting from physiological need or deprivation) produces an unpleasant state that causes an organism to engage in motivated behaviors. Reduction of drive is assumed to be reinforcing.

DUALISM The philosophic belief that humans consist of physical bodies and nonmaterial minds or souls.

DYSLEXIA Unusual difficulty in reading, caused by developmental factors or by brain injury.

DYSTHYMIC DISORDER Depression that is not severe or prolonged enough to be classified as psychotic.

ECHOIC MEMORY A form of *sensory memory* for sounds that have just been perceived.

EGO According to Freud, the structure of the mind that possesses memory and mediates the drives of the *id* and the internalized prohibitions of the *superego.*

EGOCENTRISM The tendency of young children to perceive the world solely in terms relative to themselves.

ELECTRA COMPLEX According to Freud, the desire of a girl to replace her mother as the object of her father's affections.

ELECTROCARDIOGRAM (EKG) The measurement and graphic presentation of the electrical activity of the heart, recorded by means of electrodes attached to the skin.

ELECTROCONVULSIVE THERAPY (ECT) Induction of a seizure by passing a brief shock of electricity through a person's head; used to treat severe psychotic depression. Also called electroshock treatment.

ELECTROCULOGRAM (EOG) The measurement and graphic presentation of the electrical activity caused by movements of the eye, recorded by means of electrodes attached to the skin adjacent to the eye.

ELECTROENCEPHALOGRAM (EEG) The measurement and graphic presentation of the electrical activity of the brain, recorded by means of electrodes attached to the scalp.

ELECTROMYOGRAM (EMG) The measurement and graphical presentation of the electrical activity of muscles, recorded by means of electrodes attached to the skin above them.

EMBLEM A facial gesture (such as a wink) that has a specific meaning in a given culture.

EMPIRICAL STRATEGY The development of psychological tests by presenting a variety of more or less randomly assembled items to a *criterion group*. Items that are regularly answered in one way by members of the criterion group are retained; the others are discarded.

EMPIRICISM The philosophic view that all knowledge is obtained through the senses.

ENDOCRINE GLAND A gland that secretes a *hormone* into the blood supply; for example, the *adrenal gland* and the *pituitary gland*.

ENDORPHIN A chemical secreted by neurons in the brain that produces analgesia and has reinforcing effects. The action of these chemicals is simulated by opiates such as morphine and heroin.

ENZYME A protein that serves as a biological catalyst, breaking certain molecules apart or causing certain molecules to be joined together.

EPILEPSY A neurological disorder characterized by uncontrolled activity of neurons in the brain called a seizure. Seizures are often accompanied by convulsions, behavioral arrests, or repetitive, stereotyped behaviors. The patient usually has *amnesia* for a seizure.

EPISODIC MEMORY Memory for specific information, including the time and place in which it was first learned. See *semantic memory*.

ESCAPE The performance of a response that terminates an *aversive stimulus*. See *avoidance*.

ESTRADIOL The primary *estrogen* in mammals.

ESTROGEN The principal class of sex *hormones* in females.

ESTROUS CYCLE The ovulatory cycle in mammals other than primates; the sequence of physical and hormonal changes that accompany the ripening and disintegration of ova. See *menstrual cycle*.

EXPERIMENTAL ABLATION The removal or destruction of a portion of the brain of an experimental animal for the purpose of studying the functions of that region; presumably, the functions that can no longer be performed are the ones that the region previously controlled.

EXTINCTION The reduction or elimination of a behavior caused by ceasing the presentation of the *reinforcing stimulus*.

EXTRAVERSION A *personality trait;* the tendency to seek the company of other people and to engage in conversation and other social behaviors with them.

FACTOR ANALYSIS A statistical technique involving study of the correlations among a large number of items in order to determine whether some common factors are responsible for patterns of correlation.

FETISHISM A disorder in which a person receives primary sexual stimulation and gratification from a class of inanimate objects.

FIXED-INTERVAL (FI) SCHEDULE A *schedule of reinforcement* in which the first response that is emitted after a fixed interval of time since the previous reinforcement (or the start of the session) is reinforced.

FIXED-RATIO (FR) SCHEDULE A *schedule of reinforcement* in which reinforcement occurs only after a fixed number of responses have been emitted since the previous reinforcement (or the start of the session).

FLUID INTELLIGENCE According to Raymond Cattell, the component of general intellectual ability that determines how likely a person is to profit from experience (that is, to develop *crystallized intelligence*).

FOCAL EPILEPSY A form of *epilepsy* that involves abnormal activity of neurons in a relatively localized region of the brain. Depending on the location of the focus, various behavioral effects are produced during a seizure.

FOLLICLE-STIMULATING HORMONE (FSH) A *gonadotropic hormone* secreted by the anterior pituitary gland. See *menstrual cycle*.

FORM CONSTANCY The tendency to perceive objects as having a constant form even when they are rotated or moved farther from or closer to the observer.

FOVEA A small pit near the center of the *retina*, containing densely packed *cones;* responsible for the most acute and detailed vision.

FREQUENCY The repetition rate of a periodic event, especially of sound vibrations. Frequency is closely related to *pitch*, a perceptual dimension of sound.

FRONTAL LOBE The portion of the *cerebral cortex* in front of the central fissure, including *Broca's speech area* and the motor cortex. Damage impairs movement, planning, and flexibility in behavioral strategies.

FRUSTRATION The prevention of an expected *appetitive stimulus;* said to result in aggression.

FUGUE A pathological behavior in which a person becomes amnestic and leaves his or her habitual environs.

FUNCTION WORD A preposition, article, and other word that conveys little of the meaning of a sentence but is important in specifying its grammatical structure. See *content word*.

FUNCTIONAL ANALYSIS An analysis of an organism's behavior in terms of the importance of the behavior to the organism's life; that is, in terms of its adaptive significance.

GANGLION CELL LAYER The layer of neurons in the *retina* that receive information from *photoreceptors* by means of bipolar cells, and from which axons proceed through the optic nerves to the brain.

GENE A functional unit of *chromosomes*, which contain the information that cells need to produce proteins, which serve structural purposes or serve as *enzymes*. Genes contain the instructions for development of an organism and for control of its maintenance and functions.

GENE POOL All of the genes contained in the chromosomes of a particular species or population of organisms.

GENERALIZATION An organism's tendency, once it has learned to emit a specific behavior when one *stimulus* is present, to emit that behavior when a similar stimulus is present.

GENERALIZED ANXIETY DISORDER A psychological disorder characterized by tension, overactivity of the *autonomic nervous system*, expectation of an impending disaster, and continuous vigilance for danger.

GENITAL STAGE According to Freud, the final stage of psychosexual development, in which a person receives gratification through genital sexual contact with a person of the opposite sex.

GENOTYPE The particular collection of *alleles* in an organism's *chromosomes*.

GLUCOSTATIC HYPOTHESIS The hypothesis that hunger is caused by a low level or availability of glucose, a condition that is monitored by specialized sensory neurons.

GLYCOGEN An insoluble carbohydrate that can be synthesized from glucose or converted to it; used to store nutrients.

GONADOTROPIC HORMONE A *hormone* secreted by the anterior pituitary gland that has *activational effects* on the ovaries or testes.

HABITUATION The gradual elimination of an *unconditional response* (especially an *orienting response*) by the repeated presentation of the *unconditional stimulus*. Habituation will not occur to especially noxious stimuli.

HERITABILITY The degree to which the variability of a particular trait in a particular population of organisms is a result of genetic differences between those organisms.

HOMEOSTASIS The process by which important physiological characteristics (such as body temperature and blood pressure) are regulated so that they remain at their optimal level.

HORMONE A chemical secreted by an *endocrine gland* that circulates through the blood and affects the growth or activity of cells located elsewhere in the body.

HUE A perceptual dimension of color, most closely related to the wavelength of a pure light. The effect of a particular hue is caused by the mixture of lights of various wavelengths.

HUNTINGTON'S CHOREA A neurological disorder characterized by uncontrollable jerky movements, especially of the limbs; caused by degeneration of neurons in the *basal ganglia*.

HYPNAGOGIC HALLUCINATION The perception of nonexistent objects and events just before sleep; a symptom of *narcolepsy*, presumably a premature dream.

HYPNOTIC SUGGESTIBILITY The tendency of a person to follow the suggestions of a hypnotist.

HYPOCHONDRIASIS A psychological disorder characterized by excessive concern and preoccupation with one's health, along with frequent fears of suffering from serious illness.

HYPOTHALAMUS A region of the brain located just above the *pituitary gland;* controls the *autonomic nervous system* and many behaviors related to regulation and survival, such as eating, drinking, fighting, shivering, and sweating.

HYPOTHESIS A statement, usually designed to be tested by an experiment, that expresses a tentative causal relation between variables.

ICONIC MEMORY A form of *sensory memory* that holds a brief visual image of a scene that has just been perceived.

ID One of Freud's three divisions of the mind (along with the *ego* and *superego*); contains the instinctual drives.

ILLUSTRATOR A facial gesture that adds emphasis to speech. An example is opening one's eyes wide while saying an important (stressed) word.

IMAGERY Visualization of a nonexistent object that one has previously seen; *activated memory* of a visual stimulus.

IMPLICIT PSYCHOLOGY A set of inferences (*attributions*) that people make in everyday life about the causes of people's behavior, including predictions of what they are likely to do.

IMPRESSION MANAGEMENT Performance of behavior that is calculated to give other people a particular impression of one's personal characteristics.

IMPRINTING The tendency of an infant to follow any significant moving object (usually the mother) that is encountered during the first day or two of life; seen especially in precocial birds, which can walk soon after hatching.

INCUS The "anvil"; the middle of the *ossicles,* or middle ear bones.

INDEPENDENT VARIABLE The variable that is manipulated in an experiment as a means of determining causal relations; manipulation of an independent variable demonstrates whether or not it affects the value of the *dependent variable.*

INSTRUMENTAL CONDITIONING *Operant conditioning;* increasing or decreasing the frequency of a response through contingent *reinforcement* or *punishment*.

INTELLIGENCE QUOTIENT (IQ) A simplified single measure of general intelligence; by definition, the ratio of a person's mental age to his or her chronological age, multiplied by 100; often derived by other formulas.

INTENSITY Amplitude of a physical stimulus; in audition, the intensity of a sound is closely associated with its *loudness* (a perceptual dimension); in vision, the intensity of a light is closely associated with its *brightness* (a perceptual dimension).

INTERIM BEHAVIOR See *adjunctive behavior.*

INTERMITTENT REINFORCEMENT A contingency whereby some, but not all, responses are reinforced. Behaviors that are reinforced intermittently are more resistant to extinction than behaviors that are reinforced on a *continuous reinforcement schedule.*

INTERRATER RELIABILITY The degree to which

two or more independent observers agree in their ratings of another organism's behavior, expressed in terms of a *correlation coefficient.*

INTRASPECIFIC AGGRESSION An attack by one organism on another member of the same species.

INTROSPECTION Literally, "looking within," in an attempt to describe one's own memories, perceptions, cognitive processes, or motivations.

INTROVERSION A *personality trait;* the tendency to avoid the company of other people, especially large groups of people; shyness.

JAMES-LANGE THEORY A theory of emotion that suggests that behaviors and physiological responses are directly elicited by situations, and that feelings of emotions are produced by feedback from these behaviors and responses.

JUST-NOTICEABLE DIFFERENCE (jnd) The smallest change in a stimulus that is reliably perceived; *difference threshold.*

KORSAKOFF'S SYNDROME An organic brain syndrome that is caused by chronic alcohol abuse or malnutrition and characterized by *amnesia* for events since the brain damage and inability to learn new information.

LATENCY PERIOD According to Freud, one of the stages of psychosexual development during which the child experiences little sexual drive; follows the *anal stage* and precedes the *phallic stage.*

LATENT CONTENT According to Freud, the hidden meaning of a dream—usually an unfulfilled desire—as opposed to the obvious plot, or *manifest content.*

LATENT INHIBITION The presentation of a neutral stimulus repeatedly so that the *orienting response* is *habituated,* making it difficult to use that stimulus as a *conditional stimulus* for *classical conditioning.*

LATERAL HYPOTHALAMUS The lateral portion of the *hypothalamus,* involved in control of a variety of species-typical behaviors, including eating, drinking, feeding, and sexual activity.

LATERAL INHIBITION A neurophysiological phenomenon in which a cell that is stimulated inhibits its neighbors; causes sharpening of a boundary between points of high and low stimulation.

LAW OF EFFECT Thorndike's observation that stimuli that are *contingent* on a response can increase (through *reinforcement*) or decrease (through *punishment*) response frequency.

LEARNED HELPLESSNESS A response to exposure to an inescapable *aversive stimulus,* characterized by reduced ability to learn a soluble avoidance task; thought to play a role in development of some psychological disturbances.

LEE-BOOT EFFECT The increased incidence of false pregnancies seen in female animals that are housed together; caused by a *pheromone* in the animals' urine; first observed in mice.

LIBIDO According to Freud, the psychic energy associated with instinctual drives.

LIMBIC SYSTEM A set of interconnected structures of the brain, important in emotional and species-typical behavior. Includes the *amygdala,* hippocampus, cingulate cortex, septum, and (usually) *hypothalamus.*

LITHIUM CARBONATE A simple salt that is used to treat *bipolar disorder.*

LONGITUDINAL OBSERVATION Observation of the behavior of one group of people at several different stages of development.

LONG-TERM MEMORY Relatively permanent memory. See *short-term memory.*

LOUDNESS A perceptual dimension of sound that is closely associated with *intensity* (amplitude).

LUTEINIZING HORMONE (LH) A *gonadotropic hormone.* See *menstrual cycle.*

MAJOR DEPRESSION Psychotic *depression* characterized by extreme sadness, feelings of guilt and unworthiness, and *delusions.*

MALINGERING Deliberate simulation of the symptoms of a real disease, generally to avoid work or unpleasant situations or to receive compensation.

MALLEUS The first of the three *ossicles,* or middle-ear bones, attached to the eardrum, or tympanic membrane; also called the "hammer."

MANIA Extreme exuberance, characterized by rapid thoughts, restlessness, sleeplessness, and grandiose plans; seen in *bipolar disorder.*

MANIFEST CONTENT According to Freud, the plot or description of the content of a dream. See *latent content.*

MASCULINIZATION An *organizational effect* of an *androgen* that causes the development of masculine body organs or body features and/or behaviors that are typical of males of the species.

MEDULLA The part of the brain stem that attaches to the spinal cord; contains part of the *reticular formation* and neural circuits that control respiration, heart rate, blood pressure, and other vital functions.

MENINGES A set of three membranes that encase the nervous system. (Singular is "meninx.")

MENSTRUAL CYCLE The monthly cycle of *ovulation* in primates. At the beginning of the menstrual cycle in primates (or *estrous cycle* in other mammals) the *gonadotropic hormones, follicle-stimulating hormone* and *luteinizing hormone,* cause the development of an *ovarian follicle,* a bubble of cells around an *ovum.* The ovum secretes an *estrogen,* which causes the anterior pituitary gland to secrete a surge of luteinizing hormone, which initiates ovulation. The cells of the ruptured follicle, under the influence of luteinizing hormone, develop into a corpus luteum, which secretes *progesterone,* the pregnancy hormone. If fertilization does not occur, the corpus luteum soon stops secreting hormones, and menstruation begins.

METHOD OF SUCCESSIVE APPROXIMATIONS See *shaping.*

MNEMONIC DEVICE A method by which information can easily be remembered, such as the method of loci.

MODEL A physical analogy for a physiological process; for example, computers have been used as models for various functions of the brain.

MODELING Changing a person's behavior by providing an example of desirable behavior and (usually) overtly or covertly reinforcing that behavior.

MOTOR NEURON A neuron whose *terminal buttons* form *synapses* with muscle fibers. When an *action potential* travels down its *axon* its associated muscle fibers will twitch.

MULTIPLE PERSONALITY A psychological disorder in which a person displays very different behaviors at different times, giving the impression of having distinct and different personalities.

MUTATION An alteration in the structure of a *gene* (the sequence of bases on the strand of DNA), caused by radiation, toxic chemicals, or breaks during cell division. Most mutations are disadvantageous, but a few confer a *reproductive advantage*. Mutations, along with *natural selection*, provide the basis for evolution.

NARCOLEPSY A neurological disorder in which a person suffers from irresistible sleep attacks and often *cataplexy* and *hypnagogic hallucinations*.

NATURAL SELECTION The process by which a particular *genotype* provides a *reproductive advantage* and thus becomes more prevalent; along with *mutations*, a component of evolution.

NEGATIVE AFTERIMAGE The image that is seen after a portion of the *retina* is exposed to an intense visual *stimulus;* a negative afterimage consists of color *complementary* to the physical stimulus.

NEGATIVE HALLUCINATION The perception that a *stimulus* that is present is actually absent; can be induced by hypnotic suggestion.

NEGATIVE REINFORCEMENT The removal or reduction of an *aversive stimulus* that is *contingent* on a particular response, with an attendant increase in the frequency of that response; *escape*.

NEOPHOBIA Fear of contact with a novel *stimulus*, especially a novel food.

NEUROLOGIST A physician who treats disorders of the nervous system.

NEURON The most important cell of the nervous system; consists of a cell body with *dendrites*, and an *axon* whose branches end in *terminal buttons* that synapse with muscle fibers, gland cells, or other neurons.

NEUROSIS A mental disorder of less severity than a *psychosis*. The term is not used in the new *Diagnostic and Statistical Manual III* of the American Psychiatric Association.

NOMINAL FALLACY The false belief that one has explained the causes of a phenomenon by identifying and naming it; for example, one does not explain lazy behavior by attributing it to "laziness."

NOREPINEPHRINE A *transmitter substance* that is liberated by the *terminal buttons* of some neurons. In the brain it appears to play a role in sleep and arousal and is also involved in the *autonomic nervous system*.

OBJECTIVE TEST A psychological test that can be scored objectively, such as a multiple-choice or true/false test.

OBSERVATIONAL STUDY Observation of two or more variables in the behavior or other characteristics of a group of people. Observational studies can reveal correlations but not causal relations among variables; the latter can be revealed only by experiments.

OBSESSIVE-COMPULSIVE DISORDER A neurotic disorder characterized by obsessions (recurrent, persistent thoughts and ideas) and *compulsions*.

OCCIPITAL LOBE The rearmost portion of the *cerebral cortex;* contains the primary visual cortex.

OEDIPUS COMPLEX According to Freud, the desire of a boy to replace his father and have sexual relations with his mother.

OPERANT CHAMBER An experimental chamber in which animals can be placed for *instrumental* (or operant) *conditioning;* contains a device to measure responses and provide *reinforcing* or *punishing* stimuli.

OPERANT CONDITIONING See *instrumental conditioning*.

OPERATIONAL DEFINITION The specification of a measurement or manipulation of a variable in terms of the operations that the experimenter performs to measure or manipulate it.

OPIATE ANTAGONIST A drug that blocks *opiate receptors*, making them insensitive to opiates.

OPIATE RECEPTOR *Receptor sites* on neurons that are activated by opiates, including the natural *endorphins* and opiates such as morphine or heroin.

ORAL STAGE According to Freud, the first stage of psychosexual development, in which an infant receives primary gratification by sucking.

ORGANIZATIONAL EFFECT An effect of a *hormone* that usually occurs early in development, producing permanent changes that alter the subsequent development of the organism. An example is *androgenization*. See *activational effect*.

ORGAN OF CORTI The receptive organ for audition, located on the *basilar membrane*.

ORIENTING RESPONSE The response by which an organism orients appropriate sensory receptors (such as eyes or ears) toward the source of a novel stimulus.

OSSICLES The three bones of the middle ear (*malleus*, "hammer"; *incus*, "anvil"; and *stapes*, "stirrup") that transmit acoustic vibrations from the tympanic membrane (eardrum) to the membrane behind the *oval window* of the *cochlea*.

OVAL WINDOW An opening in the bone surrounding the *cochlea* that permits the baseplate of the *stapes* to transmit acoustic vibrations to the receptive organ inside.

OVARIAN FOLLICLE A small bubble of cells that surround an *ovum* prior to *ovulation*. After ovulation the follicle becomes a *corpus luteum*.

OVULATION The release of a ripe *ovum*, which can subsequently be fertilized.

OVUM The female gamete; egg.

PANIC DISORDER A psychological disorder characterized by frequent panic attacks during which a person experiences great fear and symptoms such as loss of breath, heart palpitations, sensations of choking, dizziness, sweating, faintness, and fear of dying.

PARANOIA   A psychological disorder characterized by *delusions* of grandeur, persecution, or control. More commonly these symptoms are associated with paranoid *schizophrenia*.

PARIETAL LOBE   The region of the *cerebral cortex* behind the *frontal lobe* and above the *temporal lobe;* contains the somatosensory cortex; is involved in spatial perception, and memory for and planning of the execution of motor sequences.

PARKINSON'S DISEASE   A neurological disorder characterized by weakness, loss of balance, difficulty in initiating movements, and trembling of the limbs while resting; caused by degeneration of *dopamine*-secreting neurons that connect the brain stem with parts of the *basal ganglia*.

PERIAQUEDUCTAL GRAY MATTER   Neural tissue of the brain surrounding the cerebral aqueduct, a passage that connects two of the brain's *ventricles*. Many neurons with *opiate receptors* are located here, and destruction reduces or abolishes a number of species-typical behaviors.

PERIPHERAL NERVOUS SYSTEM   The *cranial* and *spinal nerves* and their associated structures; that part of the nervous system peripheral to the brain and spinal cord.

PERMANENCE   The concept that objects and people continue to exist even when they are hidden from view; develops during infancy.

PERSONALITY TRAIT   Relatively stable patterns of behavior that are at least somewhat predictable in a variety of situations.

PHALLIC STAGE   According to Freud, the third of the stages of psychosexual development, during which a person receives primary gratification from touching his or her genitals; precedes the *genital stage* and follows the *latency period*.

PHENOTYPE   The physical and behavioral characteristics of an individual organism that result from the joint influences of genetic and environmental factors.

PHENYLKETONURIA (PKU)   A hereditary disorder caused by the absence of an enzyme that converts the amino acid phenylalanine to tyrosine. The accumulation of phenylalanine causes brain damage unless a special diet is implemented soon after birth.

PHEROMONE   A chemical that is released by one organism and that affects the physiology or behavior of another. The usual means of communication is olfactory.

PHI PHENOMENON   The perceived movement that is caused by the turning on of two or more lights one at a time, in sequence; often used on theater marquees; responsible for the apparent movement of images in movies and television.

PHOBIA   Excessive, unreasonable fear of a particular class of objects or situations.

PHONEME   The minimum unit of sound that conveys meaning in a particular language, such as /p/.

PHONETIC READING   Reading by decoding the phonetic significance of letter strings, or "sound reading," as opposed to whole-word, or "sight" reading. Brain injury

can abolish one method without seriously affecting the other.

PHOTOPIGMENT   A protein dye (opsin) that is bonded to retinal, a substance derived from vitamin A; when struck by light it bleaches and stimulates the membrane of the *photoreceptor* in which it resides.

PHOTORECEPTOR   A receptive cell in the retina; *rods* and *cones* are photoreceptors.

PHYSIOLOGICAL PSYCHOLOGY   The branch of psychology that studies the physiological basis of behavior.

PITCH   A perceptual dimension of sound, most closely associated with *frequency*.

PITUITARY GLAND   An *endocrine gland* attached to the *hypothalamus* at the base of the brain.

PLACEBO   An inert substance that cannot be distinguished from a real medication by the patient or subject; used to please anxious patients or as the control substance in a *single-blind* or *double-blind* experiment.

POLYGENIC TRAIT   A trait that is influenced by the joint activity of many *genes*.

POSITIVE HALLUCINATION   The perception of an object that is not actually present; can be induced by hypnotic suggestion; a frequent symptom of *psychosis*.

POSITIVISM   A philosophic doctrine that asserts that humans can know nothing except phenomena that can be observed through the sense organs.

POSTHYPNOTIC SUGGESTIBILITY   The tendency of a person to perform a behavior suggested by the hypnotist some time after he or she has left the hypnotic state.

POSTSYNAPTIC NEURON   A neuron with which the *terminal buttons* of another neuron forms *synapses* and which is excited or inhibited by that neuron.

PREMACK PRINCIPLE   The assertion that the opportunity to engage in a preferred behavior can be used to reinforce the performance of a nonpreferred behavior.

PRESYNAPTIC NEURON   A neuron whose *terminal buttons* form *synapses* with and excite or inhibit another neuron.

PRIMARY PUNISHER   A naturally *aversive stimulus*, such as one that produces pain or nausea, which can be used to punish a response.

PRIMARY REINFORCER   A naturally *appetitive stimulus*, such as food, water, or warmth, which can be used to reinforce a response.

PRIMARY SEX CHARACTERISTICS   Sex organs such as genitals, gonads, and related organs.

PROACTIVE INTERFERENCE   The deleterious effect of learned information on the subsequent learning of similar information.

PROGESTERONE   A sex *hormone* that is secreted by the corpus luteum; maintains the lining of the uterus and supports pregnancy. See *menstrual cycle*.

PROJECTION   According to Freud, an ego *defense mechanism* in which a prohibited drive is attributed to another person.

PROJECTIVE TEST   A psychological test that attempts to determine a person's attitudes, personality, or motivation through his or her responses to ambiguous stimuli. The assumption is that because the stimuli provide few clues, the responses will characterize the subject.

PROTANOPIA Anomalous color vision, caused by defective "red" cones in the *retina*.

PSYCHOPHYSICS The branch of psychology that studies the relation of physical characteristics of stimuli to perceptual dimensions.

PSYCHOPHYSIOLOGY The measurement of peripheral physiological processes such as blood pressure and heart rate to infer changes in internal states such as emotions.

PSYCHOSIS A serious mental disorder, such as *schizophrenia* and the *affective disorders*.

PSYCHOSOMATIC DISORDER A real physical illness that is caused by psychological factors, especially emotional stress.

PSYCHOSURGERY The destruction of brain tissue in an attempt to eliminate maladaptive behavior or otherwise treat a mental disorder.

PUNISHMENT The suppression of a response by the *contingent* presentation of an *aversive stimulus* or the contingent removal of an *appetitive stimulus (response cost)*.

PURSUIT MOVEMENT The movements that the eyes make to maintain an image upon the *fovea*.

RATIONALIZATION According to Freud, one of the ego *defense mechanisms*, in which a person gives an acceptable reason for a behavior that is actually motivated by a prohibited drive.

RATIONAL STRATEGY The development of a psychological test by means of including items that appear to be related to the trait in question; contrasts with the *empirical strategy*.

REACTION FORMATION According to Freud, an ego *defense mechanism* in which a person experiences feelings opposite to a prohibited drive, such as disgust toward sexual material that the person actually finds interesting.

RECEPTOR SITE A location on the membrane of the *postsynaptic neuron* that responds to molecules of the *transmitter substance*. Receptor sites such as those that respond to opiates are sometimes found elsewhere on the surface of neurons.

RECOGNITION The identification of a *stimulus* as one that has been experienced before; a form of memory retrieval.

REFLEX An automatic response to a stimulus, such as the blink reflex to the sudden approach of an object toward the eyes.

REGULATOR A facial gesture by the listener that regulates the speech of the speaker, such as signs that the listener does or does not understand what the speaker is saying.

REINFORCEMENT The presentation of an *appetitive stimulus* (positive reinforcement) or the reduction or removal of an *aversive stimulus (negative reinforcement)* that is *contingent* on a response; reinforcement increases the frequency of the response.

REINFORCING STIMULUS (REINFORCER) A stimulus that, when *contingent* on a behavior, increases the occurrence of the behavior. See *reinforcement*.

RELIABILITY The repeatability of a measurement; the likelihood that if the measurement were made again it would yield the same value. See *validity*.

REM SLEEP A stage of sleep that is characterized by rapid eye movements, muscular paralysis, and dreaming.

REPRESSION According to Freud, an ego *defense mechanism* that prevents threatening material from reaching consciousness.

REPRODUCTIVE ADVANTAGE The effects of a particular *genotype* that enable an animal to have more offspring because of characteristics such as increased health and vigor or attractiveness to a potential mate.

RESPONSE COST A form of *punishment* in which a response is followed by the removal of an appetitive stimulus.

RETICULAR FORMATION A structure in the core of the brain stem that contains neurons important in the control of sleep, attention, arousal, and vital functions such as heart rate, respiration, and blood pressure.

RETINA The tissue at the back inside surface of the eye that contains the *photoreceptors* and associated neurons.

RETROSPECTIVE A research technique that requires subjects to report what happened in the past.

REUPTAKE The process by which a *terminal button* retrieves the molecules of *transmitter substance* that it has just released; terminates the effect of the transmitter substance on the *receptor sites* of the *postsynaptic neuron*.

RHODOPSIN The *photopigment* contained by *rods*.

ROD A *photoreceptor* that is very sensitive to light but cannot detect changes in *hue*. See *cone*.

ROUND WINDOW An opening in the bone surrounding the *cochlea* of the inner ear. A membrane behind the round window bulges in and out in response to pressure changes exerted by the baseplate of the *stapes* on the membrane behind the *oval window*.

SACCADIC MOVEMENT The rapid, ballistic movement of the eyes that is used in scanning a visual scene, as opposed to the smooth *pursuit movements* used to follow a moving object.

SATIATION The process of achieving satiety, having performed a sufficient amount of a *consummatory behavior*. As a result, the organism no longer seeks (for example) more food, water, or sex.

SATURATION A perceptual dimension of color; most closely associated with purity of a color; for example, red is saturated, pink is desaturated.

SCHEDULE OF REINFORCEMENT The scheme that determines the nature of *intermittent reinforcement*. See *fixed-ratio* and *fixed-interval schedules*.

SCHEMA In the theory of Jean Piaget, a behavior or behavioral sequence. See *accommodation*.

SCHIZOPHRENIA A serious mental disorder (*psychosis*) characterized by *delusions, hallucinations*, and often bizarre behaviors.

SECONDARY SEX CHARACTERISTIC External

distinguishing features of a mature person, such as facial hair or breasts.

SEMANTIC MEMORY   *Long-term memory* for information, but not for the time or circumstances of learning it. See *episodic memory*.

SEMICIRCULAR CANALS   A set of organs in the inner ear that respond to rotational movements of the head.

SENSORY ADAPTATION   Elimination of responding of sensory neurons to a moderate *stimulus* that is continuously applied, such as the failure to feel a wristwatch after it has been worn for a while.

SENSORY MEMORY   Very brief memory of a stimulus that has just occurred. See *iconic memory* and *echoic memory*.

SEROTONIN   A *transmitter substance* that is secreted by the *terminal buttons* of some neurons; appears to play a role in the control of sleep and has been implicated in the *affective disorders*.

SET POINT   The optimal value of a *system variable;* in the case of organisms, the optimal body temperature, level of blood oxygen, and so on.

SEX CHROMOSOME   The X and Y chromosomes, which determine an organism's gender. Normally, XX individuals are female, XY individuals are male.

SHAPING   The training of a very low-frequency response by successively reinforcing responses that are increasingly similar to the desired one; also called the *method of successive approximations*.

SHORT-TERM MEMORY   Memory for information that has just been presented; conceptually similar to *activated memory*, which also includes information that has just been retrieved from *long-term memory*.

SIGNAL-DETECTION THEORY   A method used to determine the sensitivity of a sensory system to a particular *stimulus*. Plotting the frequency of hits and false alarms in response to a stimulus under different payoff conditions produces a family of receiver-operating characteristic curves.

SIMULTANEOUS MATCHING-TO-SAMPLE TASK   A task that requires an organism to choose one of several stimuli that is identical to the sample *stimulus;* all stimuli are presented simultaneously.

SINGLE-BLIND METHOD   An experimental method in which the experimenter but not the subject knows the value of the *independent variable*. See *double-blind method*.

SITUATIONAL DEMAND   The effects of a particular situation on the behavior of people exposed to it; if most people act in a particular conventional way the situational demands are said to be strong.

SITUATIONAL FACTOR   A cause of behavior that is related to the situation rather than to the actor's *personality traits*. See *dispositional factors*.

SKINNER BOX   An informal name for an *operant chamber*.

SLEEP APNEA   A disorder characterized by inability to breathe while asleep.

SLOW-WAVE SLEEP   Sleep other than *REM sleep*, characterized by regular, slow waves on the electroencephalograph.

SOCIAL FACILITATION   The facilitating effect of a group of people on the behavior of one or more of its members.

SOCIAL PUNISHER   A punishing *stimulus* in the form of the behavior of another person, such as a frown or hostile words.

SOCIAL REINFORCER   A reinforcing *stimulus* in the form of the behavior of another person, such as a smile or kind words.

SPECIES-TYPICAL BEHAVIOR   A behavior that is seen in all or most members of a species, such as nest building, special food-getting behaviors, or reproductive behaviors.

SPINAL NERVE   Nerves that are attached to the spinal cord.

SPONTANEOUS RECOVERY   The recurrence of a behavior that was previously *extinguished*.

STANDARD DEVIATION   A statistic that expresses the variability of a measurement.

STANFORD-BINET SCALE   A test of intelligence for children; provides the standard measure of the *IQ*.

STAPES   One of the *ossicles* of the middle ear; the "stirrup," which transmits sound vibrations to the *cochlea*.

STATISTICAL SIGNIFICANCE   The likelihood that an observed relation or difference between two variables is not due to chance factors.

STEREOTAXIC APPARATUS   A device used to insert an object such as a wire or hypodermic needle into a particular part of the brain for the purpose of injecting or removing a substance, recording electrical activity, stimulating the brain electrically, or producing localized damage.

STIMULUS   A change in the environment that can be detected by the sense organs and is subsequently perceived by an organism.

SUBLIMATION   According to Freud, an ego *defense mechanism* in which a person finds an outlet for a prohibited drive in other behaviors, especially creative or artistic activity.

SUPEREGO   According to Freud, the part of the mind that incorporates prohibitions that a person has learned from society; the conscience.

SUPERSTITIOUS BEHAVIOR   A behavior that occurs in response to regular, noncontingent administration of an *appetitive stimulus* to a motivated organism.

SYMPTOM SUBSTITUTION   The hypothesis that if a maladaptive behavior is eliminated (for example, by *contingent punishment* or *reinforcement* of competing behaviors), then the causes of the behavior will remain and cause another maladaptive behavior to occur.

SYNAPSE   The junction between the *terminal button* of one neuron and the membrane of the *postsynaptic neuron*, which contains *receptor sites* that respond to the *transmitter substance* released by the terminal button.

SYNAPTIC CLEFT   The space between a *terminal button* and the membrane of the *postsynaptic neuron*.

SYNAPTIC VESICLE   A submicroscopic sac located in a *terminal button* and containing the *transmitter substance*.

SYSTEM VARIABLE   A variable in a system that is regulated; in living organisms, system variables include body temperature and blood pressure.

TARDIVE DYSKINESIA   A serious movement disorder that can occur when a person has been treated with antischizophrenic drugs for an extended period.

TEMPORAL LOBE   The portion of the *cerebral cortex* below the *parietal lobe* and containing the auditory cortex. Damage produces deficits in audition, speech perception and production, sexual behavior, visual perception, and/or social behaviors.

TERMINAL BUTTON   See *action potential.*

TESTOSTERONE   The principal *androgen*, or male sex hormone, secreted by the testes.

THALAMUS   A region of the brain near the center of the cerebral hemispheres. All sensory information except smell is sent to the thalamus and then relayed to the *cerebral cortex.*

THREAT GESTURE   A stereotyped gesture that signifies that one animal is likely to attack another member of the species. See *appeasement gesture.*

THRESHOLD   The minimum value of a *stimulus* that can be reliably detected (*absolute threshold*), or the minimum change that can be detected (*difference threshold*).

TIMBRE   A perceptual dimension of sound, determined by the complexity of the sound.

TOKEN ECONOMY   A scheme within an institution whereby residents' adaptive behaviors are regularly reinforced and maladaptive behaviors are not reinforced; the typical medium of reinforcement consists of tokens that can be exchanged for desirable commodities or special privileges.

TRANSDUCTION   The conversion of physical stimuli into electrical events in cells of sensory organs.

TRANSMITTER SUBSTANCE   See *action potential.*

TRANSSEXUALISM   The adoption of the identity of the opposite gender, sometimes including surgical changes and administration of sex hormones.

TRANSVESTISM   Wearing the clothes of the opposite gender; almost exclusively, the wearing of a woman's clothes by a man.

TRICYCLIC ANTIDEPRESSANT DRUG   A drug (for example, imipramine) used to treat *major depression;* named for the shape of the molecule.

TRITANOPIA   Anomalous color vision caused by defective "blue" cones.

TURNER'S SYNDROME   A condition caused by the presence of only one sex chromosome, an X chromosome. The person has no ovaries or testes and is morphologically female, but puberty must be induced by the administration of sex hormones.

TURNING AGAINST THE SELF   According to Freud, an ego *defense mechanism* in which a person punishes himself or herself for prohibited drives by means of self-directed aggression.

UNCONDITIONAL RESPONSE (UR)   See *classical conditioning.*

UNCONDITIONAL STIMULUS (US)   See *classical conditioning.*

VALIDITY   The degree to which a test or measurement is related to the variable it is designed to measure; a valid test is a perfect reflection of the psychological trait that it purports to measure.

VARIABLE-INTERVAL SCHEDULE   A *schedule of reinforcement* similar to a *fixed-interval* but characterized by a variable time requirement with a particular mean.

VARIABLE-RATIO SCHEDULE   A *schedule of reinforcement* similar to a *fixed-ratio* but characterized by a variable response requirement with a particular mean.

VENTRICLE   One of the hollow chambers in the brain that are filled with *cerebrospinal fluid.*

VENTROMEDIAL HYPOTHALAMUS   The medial part of the bottom of the *hypothalamus;* a part of the brain that is important for the expression of female sexual behavior. It also plays a role in the control of food intake; destruction leads to overeating and obesity.

VERBAL ACCESS   The ability to describe verbally a perception, thought, emotion, behavior, or memory.

VERBAL BEHAVIOR   Speaking, listening (with comprehension), writing, or reading.

VERBAL CONTROL   The ability to initiate, stop, or modify a behavior by means of *verbal behavior.*

VESTIBULAR APPARATUS   The receptive organs of the inner ear that contribute to balance and perception of head movement.

VISUAL AGNOSIA   The inability of a person who is not blind to recognize the identity or use of an object by means of vision; usually caused by damage to the brain.

VOICE-ONSET TIME   The delay between the initial sound of a voiced consonant (such as the puffing sound of the *phoneme* /p/) and the onset of vibration of the vocal cords.

VOICING   Vibration of the vocal cords, which accompanies some consonants and all vowels.

WAVELENGTH   The distance between adjacent waves of radiant energy; in vision, most closely associated with perceptual dimension of *hue.*

WERNICKE'S APHASIA   A disorder caused by damage to *Wernicke's area*, located in the *temporal lobe* (usually, the left), characterized by deficits in the perception of speech and by the production of fluent but rather meaningless speech.

WERNICKE'S AREA   See *Wernicke's aphasia.*

WHITTEN EFFECT   The synchronization of the menstrual or estrous cycles of a group of females, which occurs only when a male (or his *pheromone*) is present.

WHOLE-WORD READING   Identification of written words by perception of the word as a whole; contrasts with *phonetic reading.*

REFERENCES

ABELSON, R.P. Are attitudes necessary? In *Attitudes, Conflict, and Social Change,* edited by B.T. King and E. McGinnies. New York: Academic Press, 1972.

ADAMS, D.B., GOLD, A.R., & BURT, A.D. Rise in female-initiated sexual activity at ovulation and its suppression by oral contraceptives. *New England Journal of Medicine,* 1978, *299,* 1145–1150.

ADAMS, G.R., & HUSTON, T.L. Social perception of middle-aged persons varying in physical attractiveness. *Developmental Psychology,* 1975, *11,* 657–658.

AGRAS, S., SYLVESTER, D., & OLIVEAU, D. The epidemiology of common fears and phobias. Unpublished manuscript, 1969.

AIKEN, L.R. *Psychological Testing and Assessment* (4th ed.). Boston: Allyn and Bacon, 1982.

AINSWORTH, M.D.S. *Infancy in Uganda: Infant Care and the Growth of Love.* Baltimore: Johns Hopkins University Press, 1967.

AINSWORTH, M.D.S. The development of infant-mother attachment. In *Review of Child Development Research* (vol. 3), edited by B.M. Caldwell and H.R. Ricciuti. Chicago: University of Chicago Press, 1973.

AMBROSE, J.A. The development of the smiling response in early infancy. In *Determinants of Infant Behaviour I,* edited by B.M. Foss. London: Methuen, 1961.

AMMON, P.R. The perception of grammatical relations in sentences: A methodological exploration. *Journal of Verbal Learning and Verbal Behavior,* 1968, *7,* 869–875.

AMOORE, J.E. *Molecular Basis of Odor.* Springfield, Ill.: C.C. Thomas, 1970.

ANAND, B.K., & BROBECK, J.R. Hypothalamic control of food intake in rats and cats. *Yale Journal of Biology and Medicine,* 1951, *24,* 123–140.

ANDERSON, D.C., CROWELL, C.R., CUNNINGHAM, C.L., & LUPO, J.V. Behavior during shock exposure as a determinant of subsequent interference with shuttle box escape-avoidance learning in the rat. *Journal of Experimental Psychology: Animal Behavior Processes,* 1979, *5,* 243–257.

ANDERSON, J.R. *Language, Memory, and Thought.* Hillsdale, N.J.: Lawrence Erlbaum, 1976.

ANGRIST, B.J., ROTROSEN, J., & GERSHON, S. Positive and negative symptoms in schizophrenia—differential response to amphetamine and neuroleptics. *Psychopharmacology,* 1980, *72,* 17–19.

ANONYMOUS. An autobiography of a schizophrenic experience. *Journal of Abnormal and Social Psychology,* 1955, *51,* 677–689.

ANONYMOUS. Effects of sexual activity on beard growth in man. *Nature,* 1970, *226,* 869–870.

ANTELMAN, S.M., ROWLAND, N.E., & FISHER, A.E. Stress related recovery from lateral hypothalamic aphagia. *Brain Research,* 1976, *102,* 346–350.

ANTELMAN, S.M., & SZECHTMAN, H. Tail pinch induces eating in sated rats which appears to depend on nigrostriatal dopamine. *Science,* 1975, *189,* 731–733.

ANTELMAN, S.M., SZECHTMAN, H., CHIN, P., & FISHER, A.E. Tail pinch-induced eating, gnawing and licking behavior in rats: Dependence on the nigrostriatal dopamine system. *Brain Research,* 1975, *99,* 219–237.

APPLETON, T., CLIFTON, R., & GOLDBERG, S. The Development of behavioral competence in infancy. In *Review of Child Development* (vol. 4), edited by F.D. Horowitz. Chicago: University of Chicago Press, 1975.

ARENBERG, D. Cognition and aging: verbal learning, memory, and problem solving. In *The Psychology of Adult Development and Aging,* edited by C. Eisdorfer and M.P. Lawton. Washington, D.C.: American Psychological Association, 1973.

ARKIN, R., COOPER, H., & KOLDITZ, T. A statistical review of the literature concerning the self-serving attribution bias in interpersonal influence situations. *Journal of Personality,* 1980, *48,* 435–448.

ARONSON, E., & MILLS, J. The effects of severity of initiation on liking for a group. *Journal of Abnormal and Social Psychology,* 1959, *59,* 177–181.

ARONSON, E., TURNER, J.A., & CARLSMITH, J.M. Communicator credibility and communication discrepancy as determinants of opinion change. *Journal of Abnormal and Social Psychology,* 1963, *67,* 31–36.

ASCH, S.E. Effects of group pressure upon the modification and distortion of judgment. In *Groups, Leadership, and Men,* edited by H. Guetzkow. Pittsburgh: Carnegie, 1951.

ASTRUP, C., & NOREIK, K. *Functional Psychoses: Diagnostic and Prognostic Models.* Springfield, Ill.: C.C. Thomas, 1966.

ATKINSON, J.W., & McCLELLAND, D.C. The projective expression of needs: II The effect of different intensities of the hunger drive on thematic apperception. *Journal of Experimental Psychology,* 1948, *38,* 643–658.

AUSSEL, C., URIEL, J., & MERCIER-BODARD, C. Rat alphafetoprotein: Isolation, characterization, and estrogen-binding properties. *Biochimie*, 1973, *55*, 1431–1437.

AVERILL, J.R. A semantic atlas of emotional concepts. *Catalog of Selected Documents in Psychology*, 1975, 5, 330.

AYLLON, T., & AZRIN, N.H. *The Token Economy: A Motivational System for Therapy and Rehabilitation.* New York: Appleton-Century-Crofts, 1968.

AZRIN, N.H. *Agressive responses of paired animals.* Paper presented at Symposium of the Walter Reed Institute of Research, Washington, D.C., April, 1964.

BAER, D.M., PETERSON, R.F., & SHERMAN, J.A. Development of imitation by reinforcing behavioral similarity to a model. *Journal of the Experimental Analysis of Behavior*, 1967, *10*, 405–416.

BAKER, B.L. Symptom treatment and symptom substitution in enuresis. *Journal of Abnormal Psychology*, 1969, *74*, 42–49.

BAKER, J.R. *Race.* New York and London: Oxford University Press, 1974.

BALDESSARINI, R.J. *Chemotherapy in Psychiatry.* Cambridge, Mass.: Harvard University Press, 1977.

BALDESSARINI, R.J., & TARSY, D. Dopamine and the pathophysiology of dyskinesias induced by antipsychotic drugs. *Annual Review of Neuroscience*, 1980, *3*, 23–41.

BALL, K., & SEKULER, R. A specific and enduring improvement in visual motion discrimination. *Science*, 1982, *218*, 697–698.

BALTES, P., & SCHAIE, K. Aging and IQ: The myth of the twilight years. *Psychology Today*, October 1974, pp. 35–38.

BANDURA, A. *Principles of Behavior Modification.* New York: Holt, Rinehart and Winston, 1969.

BANDURA, A. Psychotherapy based upon modeling principles. In *Handbook of Psychotherapy and Behavior Change*, edited by A.E. Bergin and S.L. Garfield. New York: Wiley, 1971.

BANDURA, A. *Aggression: A Social Learning Analysis.* Englewood Cliffs, N.J.: Prentice-Hall, 1973.

BANDURA, A. *Social Learning Theory.* Englewood Cliffs, N.J.: Prentice-Hall, 1977.

BANDURA, A., & ROSENTHAL, T.L. Vicarious classical conditioning as a function of arousal level. *Journal of Personality and Social Psychology*, 1966, *3*, 54–62.

BANKS, M.S., ASLIN, R.N., & LETSON, R.D. Sensitive period for the development of human binocular vision. *Science*, 1975, *190*, 675–677.

BARBER, T.X. *Hypnosis: A Scientific Approach.* New York: Van Nostrand Reinhold, 1969.

BARBER, T.X. Responding to 'Hypnotic' Suggestions: An Introspective Report. *American Journal of Clinical Hypnosis*, 1975, *18*, 6–22.

BARON, R.A. The aggression-inhibiting influence of heightened sexual arousal. *Journal of Personality and Social Psychology*, 1974, *30*, 318–322.

BARON, R.A., & BYRNE, D. *Social Psychology: Understanding Human Interaction.* Boston: Allyn and Bacon, 1977, 1981.

BARON, R.S., & ROPER, G. Reaffirmation of social comparison views of choice shifts: Averaging and extremity effects in an autokinetic situation. *Journal of Personality and Social Psychology*, 1976, *33*, 521–530.

BARTLETT, F.C. *Remembering: An Experimental and Social Study.* Cambridge: Cambridge University Press, 1932.

BATINI, C., MORUZZI, G., PALESTINI, M., ROSSI, G.F., & ZANCHETTI, A. Persistent patterns of wakefulness in the pretrigeminal midpontile preparation. *Science*, 1958, *128*, 30–32.

BATINI, C., MORUZZI, G., PALESTINI, M., ROSSI, G.F., & ZANCHETTI, A. Effect of complete pontine transections on the sleep-wakefulness rhythm: the midpontine pretrigeminal preparation. *Archives Italiennes de Biologie*, 1959, 97, 1–12.

BAUMHART, R. *An Honest Profit.* New York: Holt, 1968.

BEACH, F.A. Cerebral and hormonal control of reflexive mechanisms involved in copulatory behavior. *Psychological Review*, 1967, 74, 289–316.

BEACH, F.A. Coital behavior in dogs. VI. Long-term effects of castration upon mating in the male. *Journal of Comparative and Physiological Psychology*, 1970, 70, 1–32.

BECK, A.T. *Depression: Clinical, Experimental, and Theoretical Aspects.* New York: Harper & Row, 1967.

BECK, A.T., WARD, C.H., MENDELSON, M., MOCK, J.E., & ERBAUGH, J.K. Reliability of psychiatric diagnosis 2: A study of consistency of clinical judgments and ratings. *American Journal of Psychiatry*, 1962, *119*, 351–357.

BECKMAN, L. Effects of students' performance on teachers' and observers' attributions of causality. *Journal of Educational Psychology*, 1970, *61*, 75–82.

BELL, A.P., & WEINBERG, M.S. *Homosexualities: A Study of Diversity Among Men and Women.* New York: Simon & Schuster, 1978.

BELL, A.P., WEINBERG, M.S., & HAMMERSMITH, S.K. *Sexual Preference: Its Development in Men and Women.* Bloomington: Indiana University Press, 1981.

BELL, S.M., & AINSWORTH, M.D. Infant crying and maternal responsiveness. *Child Development*, 1972, *43*, 1171–1190.

BELLUGI, U., & KLIMA, E.S. The roots of language in the sign talk of the deaf. *Psychology Today*, June 1972, pp. 61–76.

BELSKY, J. Child maltreatment: An ecological integration. *American Psychologist*, 1980, *35*, 320–335.

BEM, D.J. Self-perception theory. In *Advances in Experimental Social Psychology* (vol. 6), edited by L. Berkowitz. New York: Academic Press, 1972.

BEM, D., & ALLEN, A. On predicting some of the people some of the time: The search for cross-situational consistencies in behavior. *Psychological Review*, 1974, *81*, 506–520.

BERGER, S.M. Conditioning through vicarious instigation. *Psychological Review*, 1962, 69, 450–466.

BERKOWITZ, L. Whatever happened to the frustration-aggression hypothesis? *American Behavioral Scientist*, 1978, *21*, 691–708.

BERKOWITZ, L., & FRODI, A. Stimulus characteristics that can enhance or decrease aggression. *Aggressive Behavior*, 1977, *3*, 1–15.

BERKOWITZ, L., & WALSTER, E. (eds.) *Equity Theory: Toward a General Theory of Social Interaction.* New York: Academic Press, 1976.

BERMANT, G., & DAVIDSON, J.M. *Biological Bases of Sexual Behavior.* New York: Harper & Row, 1974.

BERNE, E. *Games People Play.* New York: Grove Press, 1964.

BERNE, E. *What Do You Say After You Say Hello?* New York: Grove Press, 1972.

BERSCHEID, E., DION, K., WALSTER, E., & WALSTER, G.W. Physical attractiveness and dating choice: A test of the matching hypothesis. *Journal of Experimental Social Psychology*, 1971, *7*, 173–189.

BERSCHEID, E., GRAZIANO, W., MONSON, T., & DERMER, M. Outcome dependency: Attention, attraction, and attribution. *Journal of Personality and Social Psychology*, 1976, *34*, 978–989.

BIEBER, I., DAIN, H.J., DINCE, P.R., DRELLICH, M.G., GRAND, H.G., GUNDLACH, R.H., KREMER, M.W., RIFKIN, A.H., WILBUR, C.B., & BIEBER, T.B. *Homosexuality: A Psychoanalytic Study.* New York: Basic Books, 1962.

BINDRA, D. Ape language. *Science*, 1980, *211*, 86.

BINET, A., & HENRI, V. La psychologie individuelle. *Année Psychologie*, 1896, *2*, 411–465.

BIRREN, J.E., & MORRISON, D.F. Analysis of the WISC subtests in relation to age and education. *Journal of Gerontology*, 1961, *16*, 363–369.

BLAZA, S. Brown adipose tissue in man: a review. *Journal of the Royal Society of Medicine*, 1983, *76*, 213–217.

BLEULER, E. *Dementia Praecox or the Group of Schizophrenias.* New York: International Universities Press, 1950. (Originally published, 1911.)

BLOCK, V., HENNEVIN, E. & LECONTE, P. Interaction between post-trial reticular stimulation and subsequent paradoxical sleep in memory consolidation processes. In *Neurobiology of Sleep and Memory*, edited by R.R. Drucker-Colín and J.L. McGlaugh. New York: Academic Press, 1977.

BLUMER, D. Temporal lobe epilepsy and its psychiatric significance. In *Psychiatric Aspects of Neurologic Disease*, edited by D.F. Benson and D. Blumer. New York: Grune & Stratton, 1975.

BLUMER, D., & WALKER, A.E. The neural basis of sexual behavior. In *Psychiatric Aspects of Neurologic Disease*, edited by D.F. Benson and D. Blumer. New York: Grune & Stratton, 1975.

BOISEN, A.T. *Out of the Depths.* New York: Harper & Row, 1960.

BOLLES, R.C. Species-specific defense reactions and avoidance learning. *Psychological Review*, 1970, *77*, 32–48.

BOLSTAD, O.D., & JOHNSON, S.M. Self-regulation in the modification of disruptive classroom behavior. *Journal of Applied Behavior Analysis*, 1972, *5*, 443–454.

BOOKMILLER, M.N., & BOWEN, G.L. *Textbook of Obstetrics and Obstetric Nursing* (5th ed.). Philadelphia: W.B. Saunders, 1967.

BORGIDA, E., & NISBETT, R.E. The differential viewpoint of abstract vs. concrete information on decisions. *Journal of Applied Social Psychology*, 1977, *7*, 258–271.

BOTWINICK, J., & STORANDT, M. *Memory, Related Functions and Age.* Springfield, Ill.: C.C. Thomas, 1974.

BOWER, G.H., & CLARK, M.C. Narrative stories as mediators for serial learning. *Psychonomic Science*, 1969, *14*, 181–182.

BOWLBY, J. Separation anxiety. *International Journal of Psychoanalysis*, 1960, *41*, 69–113.

BOYNTON, R.M. *Human Color Vision.* New York: Holt, Rinehart and Winston, 1979.

BRACKBILL, Y., ADAMS, G., CROWELL, D.H., & GRAY, M.L. Arousal level in neonates and preschool children under continuous auditory stimulation. *Journal of Experimental Child Psychology*, 1966, *4*, 178–188.

BRADY, J.P., & LIND, D.L. Experimental analysis of hysterical blindness. *Archives of General Psychiatry*, 1961, *4*, 331–359.

BRAVER, S.L., LINDER, D.E., CORWIN, T.T., & CIALDINI, R.B. Some conditions that affect admissions of attitude change. *Journal of Experimental Social Psychology*, 1977, *13*, 565–576.

BRELAND, K., & BRELAND, M. The misbehavior of organisms. *American Psychologist*, 1961, *16*, 661–664.

BREMER, J. *Asexualization.* New York: Macmillan, 1959.

BRODY, E.B., & BRODY, N. *Intelligence: Nature, Determinants, and Consequences.* New York: Academic Press, 1976.

BRONSON, F.H., & WHITTEN, W. Estrus accelerating pheromone of mice: assay, androgen-dependency, and presence in bladder urine. *Journal of Reproduction and Fertility*, 1968, *15*, 131–134.

BROWN, J., & CARTWRIGHT, R.D. Subject versus experimenter elicited dream reports: Who knows best? Unpublished manuscript cited by Cartwright, R.D., and Webb, W.B., Sleep and dreams. *Annual Review of Psychology*, 1978, *29*, 223–252.

BROWN, P.L., & JENKINS, H.M. Autoshaping of the pigeon's keypeck. *Journal of the Experimental Analysis of Behavior*, 1968, *11*, 1–8.

BROWN, R. Further comment on the risky shift. *American Psychologist*, 1974, *29*, 468–470.

BROWN, R., & BELLUGI, U. Three processes in the child's acquisition of syntax. *Harvard Education Review*, 1964, *34*, 133–151.

BROWN, R., CAZDEN, C.B., & BELLUGI, U. The child's grammar from I to III. In *Minnesota Symposium on Child Psychology* (vol. 2), edited by J. Hill. Minneapolis: University of Minnesota Press, 1969.

BRUCE, H.M. A block to pregnancy in the mouse caused

by proximity of strange males. *Journal of Reproduction and Fertility*, 1960a, *1*, 96–103.

BRUCE, H.M. Further observations on pregnancy block in mice caused by proximity of strange males. *Journal of Reproduction and Fertility*, 1960b, *1*, 311–312.

BUKOFF, A., & ELMAN, D. Repeated exposure to liked and disliked social stimuli. *Journal of Social Psychology*, 1979, *37*, 811–821.

BURNSTEIN, E., & WORCHEL, P. Arbitrariness of frustration and its consequences for aggression in a social situation. *Journal of Personality*, 1962, *30*, 528–541.

BURT, C. The concept of consciousness. *British Journal of Psychology*, 1962, *53*, 229–242.

BUSS, A.H., & PLOMIN, R. *A Temperament Theory of Personality Development*. New York: Wiley, 1975.

BUTLER, J.M., & HAIGH, G.V. Changes in the relation between self-concepts and ideal concepts consequent upon client-centered counseling. In *Psychotherapy and Personality Change*, edited by C.R. Rogers and R.F. Dymond. Chicago: University of Chicago Press, 1954.

BYRNE, D., & NELSON, D. Attraction as a linear function of proportion of positive reinforcements. *Journal of Personality and Social Psychology*, 1965, *1*, 659–663.

BYRNE, D., & RHAMEY, R. Magnitude of positive and negative reinforcements as a determinant of attraction. *Journal of Personality and Social Psychology*, 1965, *2*, 884–889.

CAMPBELL, D., SANDERSON, R.E., & LAVERTY, S.G. Characteristics of a conditioned response in human subjects during extinction trials following a single traumatic conditioning trial. *Journal of Abnormal and Social Psychology*, 1964, *68*, 627–639.

CAMPOS, J.J., LANGER, A., & KROWITZ, A. Cardiac responses on the visual cliff in prelocomotor human infants. *Science*, 1970, *170*, 196–197.

CANESTRARI, R.B. The effects of commonality on paired associate learning in two age groups. *Journal of Genetic Psychology*, 1966, *108*, 3–7.

CANNON, W.B. The James-Lange theory of emotions: A critical examination and an alternative. *American Journal of Psychology*, 1927, *39*, 106–124.

CANNON, W.B., & WASHBURN, A.L. An explanation of hunger. *American Journal of Physiology*, 1912, *29*, 444–454.

CARLSMITH, J.M., & GROSS, A.E. Some effects of guilt on compliance. *Journal of Personality and Social Psychology*, 1969, *11*, 240–244.

CARTER, E.N. The stimulus control of a response system in the absence of awareness. Unpublished doctoral dissertation, University of Massachusetts, 1973.

CATTELL, R.B. *Description and Measurement of Personality*. New York: World Books, 1946.

CATTELL, R.B. *Abilities: Their Structure, Growth, and Action*. Boston: Houghton Mifflin, 1971.

CAVANAUGH, J.R., & McGOLDRICK, J.B. *Fundamental Psychiatry*. Milwaukee, Wis.: Brice, 1966.

CERLETTI, U., & BINI, L. Electric shock treatment. *Bolletino ed Atti dell' Accademia Medica di Roma*, 1938, *64*, 36.

CHAIKEN, S. Heuristic versus systematic information processing and the use of source versus message cues in persuasion. *Journal of Personality and Social Psychology*, 1980, *39*, 752–766.

CHAPIN, F.S. *Experimental Designs in Sociological Research*. New York: Harper, 1947.

CHERRY, E.C. Some experiments on the recognition of speech, with one and with two ears. *Journal of the Acoustical Society of America*, 1953, *25*, 975–979.

CHOMSKY, N. *Aspects of the Theory of Syntax*. Cambridge, Mass.: MIT Press, 1965.

CHOROVER, S.L., & SCHILLER, P.H. Short-term retrograde amnesia in rats. *Journal of Comparative and Physiological Psychology*, 1965, *59*, 73–78.

CIALDINI, R.B., BRAVER, S.L., & LEWIS, S.K. Attributional bias and the easily persuaded others. *Journal of Personality and Social Psychology*, 1974, *30*, 613–637.

CIALDINI, R.B., & MIRELS, H. Sense of personal control and attributions about yielding and resisting persuasion targets. *Journal of Personality and Social Psychology*, 1976, *33*, 395–402.

CIALDINI, R.B., PETTY, R.E., & CACIOPPO, J.T. Attitude and attitude change. *Annual Review of Psychology*, 1981, *32*, 357–404.

CLARK, H.H., & HAVILAND, S.E. Comprehension and the given-new contract. In *Discourse Production and Comprehension*, edited by R.O. Freedle. Norwood, N.J.: Ablex Publishing, 1977.

CLARK, K.B. *Dark Ghetto. Dilemmas of Social Power*. New York: Harper & Row, 1965.

CLAVIER, R.M., & ROUTTENBERG, A. In search of reinforcement pathways: a neuroanatomical odyssey. In *Biology of Reinforcement: A Tribute to James Olds*. New York: Academic Press, 1980.

CLEMENS, L.G. Influence of prenatal litter composition on mounting behavior of female rats. *American Zoologist*, 1971, *11*, 617–618.

COLEMAN, J.C. *Abnormal Psychology and Modern Life* (5th ed.). Glenview, Ill.: Scott, Foresman, 1976.

COLEMAN, J.S., CAMPBELL, E.Q., HOBSON, C.J., McPARTLAND, J., MOOD, A.M., WEINFELD, F.D., & YORK, R.L. *Equality of Educational Opportunity*. Washington, D.C.: United States Government Printing Office, 1966.

COLLET, M.E., WERTENBERGER, G.E., & FISKE, V.M. The effect of age upon the pattern of the menstrual cycle. *Fertility and Sterility*, 1954, *5*, 437–448.

COMARR, A.E. Sexual function among patients with spinal cord injury. *Urologia Internationalis*, 1970, *25*, 134–168.

CONNER, R.L., & LEVINE, S. Hormonal influences on aggressive behaviour. In *Aggressive Behaviour*, edited by S. Garattine and E.B. Sigg. New York: Wiley, 1969.

CONRAD, R. Acoustic confusions in immediate memory. *British Journal of Psychology*, 1964, *55*, 75–83.

CONWAY, E., & BRACKBILL, Y. Delivery medication and infant outcome: An empirical study. *Monographs of the Society for Research in Child Development*, 1970, *35* (Serial No. 4), 24–34.

COOPER, R.M., & ZUBEK, J.P. Effects of enriched

and restricted early environments on the learning ability of bright and dull rats. *Canadian Journal of Psychology,* 1958, *12,* 159–164.

CORAH, N.L., ANTHONY, E.J., PAINTER, P., STERN, J.A., & THURSTON, D.L. Effects of perinatal anoxia after seven years. *Psychological Monographs: General & Applied,* 1965, 79, 1–34.

COTTRELL, N.B., WACK, D.L., SEKERAK, G.J., & RITTLE, R.H. Social facilitation of dominant responses by the presence of an audience and the mere presence of others. *Journal of Personality and Social Psychology,* 1968, 9, 245–250.

COWART, J., & WHALEY, D. Punishment of self-mutilation behavior. Unpublished manuscript cited by Whaley, D.L., and Malott, R.W. *Elementary Principles of Behavior.* New York: Appleton-Century-Crofts, 1971.

CRAIK, F.I.M., & TULVING, E. Depth of processing and the retention of words in episodic memory. *Journal of Experimental Psychology: General,* 1975, *104,* 268–294.

CRAIK, F.I.M., & WATKINS, M.J. The role of rehearsal in short-term memory. *Journal of Verbal Learning and Verbal Behavior,* 1973, *12,* 599–607.

CROW, T.J. Molecular pathology of schizophrenia: More than one disease process? *British Medical Journal,* 1980, *280,* 66–68.

CROW, T.J., CROSS, A.G., JOHNSTONE, E.C., & OWEN, F. Two syndromes in schizophrenia and their pathogenesis. In *Schizophrenia as a Brain Disease,* edited by F.A. Henn and G.A. Nasrallah. New York: Oxford University Press, 1982.

DALE, P.S. *Language Development: Structure and Function* (2nd ed.). New York: Holt, Rinehart and Winston, 1976.

DARWIN, C. *The Expression of the Emotions in Man and Animals.* Chicago: University of Chicago Press, 1872/1965.

DASHIELL, J.F. Experimental studies of the influence of social situations on the behavior of individual human adults. In *A Handbook of Social Psychology,* edited by C. Murcheson. Worcester, Mass.: Clark University Press, 1935.

DAVIDSON, J.M., CAMARGO, C.A., & SMITH, E.R. Effects of androgen on sexual behavior in hypogonadal men. *Journal of Clinical Endocrinology and Metabolism,* 1979, *48,* 955–958.

DAVIS, J.D., & CAMPBELL, C.S. Peripheral control of meal size in the rat: Effect of sham feeding on meal size and drinking rate. *Journal of Comparative and Physiological Psychology,* 1973, *83,* 379–387.

DAVIS, J.M. A two-factor theory of schizophrenia. *Journal of Psychiatric Research,* 1974, *11,* 25–30.

DAVISON, G.C., & NEALE, J.M. *Abnormal Psychology: An Experimental Clinical Approach.* New York: Wiley, 1974.

DAVISON, G.C., & NEALE, J.M. *Abnormal Psychology: An Experimental Clinical Approach* (3rd ed.). New York: Wiley, 1982.

DAY, R.S. Fusion in dichotic listening. Unpublished doctoral dissertation, Stanford University, 1968.

DAY, R.S. Temporal order judgments in speech: Are individuals language-bound or stimulus-bound? *Haskins Laboratories Status Report,* 1970, *SR-21/22,* 71–87.

DeCHARMS, R. Personal causation training in the schools. *Journal of Applied Social Psychology,* 1972, *2,* 95–113.

DEKABAN, A. *Neurology of Early Childhood.* Baltimore, Md.: Williams & Wilkins, 1970.

DE LACOSTE-UTAMSING, C., & HOLLOWAY, R.L. Sexual dimorphism in the human corpus callosum. *Science,* 1982, *216,* 1431–1432.

DEMENT, W.C. *Some Must Watch While Some Must Sleep.* San Francisco: Freeman, 1974.

DENNIS, W. Causes of retardation among institutional children: Iran. *Journal of Genetic Psychology,* 1960, *96,* 47–59.

DESCARTES, R. *Discourse on Method and Other Writings,* translated by F.E. Sutcliffe. Baltimore: Penguin Books, 1968, 41.

DESJARDINS, A. Personal communication, 1980.

DEUTSCH, J.A., YOUNG, W.G., & KALO-GERIS, T.J. The stomach signals satiety. *Science,* 1978, *201,* 165–167.

DeVILLIERS, J.G., & DE VILLIERS, P.A. *Language Acquisition.* Cambridge, Mass.: Harvard University Press, 1978.

DeVILLIERS, P.A. Imagery and theme in recall of connected discourse. *Journal of Experimental Psychology,* 1974, *103,* 263–268.

DIAMOND, M. Sexual identity, monozygotic twins reared in discordant sex roles and a BBC follow-up. *Archives of Sexual Behavior,* 1982, *11,* 181–186.

DIMOND, S.J., & FARRINGTON, L. Emotional response to films shown to the right or left hemisphere of the brain measured by heart rate. *Acta Psychologica,* 1977, *41,* 255–260.

DIMOND, S.J., FARRINGTON, L., & JOHNSON, P. Differing emotional response from right and left hemispheres. *Nature,* 1976, *201,* 690–692.

DION, K., BERSCHEID, E., & WALSTER, E. What is beautiful is good. *Journal of Personality and Social Psychology,* 1972, *24,* 285–290.

DOBZHANSKY, T. *Mankind Evolving.* New Haven: Yale University Press, 1962.

DOLLARD, J., DOOB, L., MILLER, N., MOWRER, O., & SEARS, R. *Frustration and Aggression.* New Haven: Yale University Press, 1939.

DONAHOE, J.W., CROWLEY, M.A., MILLARD, W.J., & STICKNEY, K.A. A unified principle of reinforcement: Some implications for matching. In *Quantitative Analysis of Behavior: 2. Matching and Maximizing Accounts,* edited by M.L. Commons, R.J. Herrnstein, and H. Rachlin. New York: Ballinger, 1982.

DOTY, R.L., FORD, M., PRETI, G., & HUGGINS, G.R. Changes in the intensity and pleasantness of human vaginal odors during the menstrual cycle. *Science,* 1975, *190,* 1316.

DRABMAN, R.S., SPITALNIK, R., & O'LEARY, K.D. Teaching self-control to disruptive children. *Journal of Abnormal Psychology,* 1973, *82,* 10–16.

DRUCKER-COLIN, R.R., SPANIS, C.W. Is there a sleep transmitter? *Progress in Neurobiology,* 1976, 6, 1–22.

DUA, S., & MAC LEAN, P.D. Location for penile erection in medial frontal lobe. *American Journal of Physiology*, 1964, *207*, 1425–1434.

DUTTON, D.G., & ARON, A.P. Some evidence for heightened sexual attraction under conditions of high anxiety. *Journal of Personality and Social Psychology*, 1974, *30*, 510–517.

D'ZURILLA, T. Recall efficiency and mediating cognitive events in "experimental repression." *Journal of Personality and Social Psychology*, 1965, *1*, 253–257.

EAGLY, A.H., & HIMMELFARB, S. Attitudes and opinions. *Annual Review of Psychology*, 1978, *29*, 517–554.

EAGLY, A.H., & WARREN, R. Intelligence, comprehension, and opinion change. *Journal of Personality*, 1976, *44*, 226–242.

EBBESEN, E.B., & BOWERS, R.J. Proportion of risky to conservative arguments in a group discussion and choice shift. *Journal of Personality and Social Psychology*, 1974, *29*, 316–327.

EBEL, R.L. The social consequences of educational testing. In *Testing Problems in Perspective*, edited by A. Anastasi. Washington, D.C.: American Council on Education, 1966.

EHRHARDT, A.A., GREENBERG, N., & MONEY, J. Female gender identity and absence of fetal hormones: Turner's syndrome. *Johns Hopkins Medical Journal*, 1970, *126*, 237–248.

EIBL-EIBESFELD, I. *The Biology of Peace and War*. New York: Viking Press, 1980.

EIMAS, P.D., SIQUELAND, E.R., JUSCZYK, P., & VIGORITO, J. Speech perception in infants. *Science*, 1971, *171*, 303–306.

EISINGER, R., & MILLS, J.P. Perception of the sincerity and competence of a communicator as a function of his position. *Journal of Experimental Social Psychology*, 1968, *4*, 224–232.

EKMAN, P. *Darwin and Facial Expression: A Century of Research in Review*. New York: Academic Press, 1973.

EKMAN, P. *The Face of Man: Expressions of Universal Emotions in a New Guinea Village*. New York: Garland STPM Press, 1980.

EKMAN, P., & FRIESEN, W.V. Constants across cultures in the face and emotion. *Journal of Personality and Social Psychology*, 1971, *17*, 124–129.

EKMAN, P., FRIESEN, W.V., & ELLSWORTH, P. *Emotion in the Human Face: Guidelines for Research and a Review of Findings*. New York: Pergamon Press, 1972.

ELLENBERGER, H.F. The story of "Anna O": A critical review with new data. *Journal of the History of Behavior Sciences*, 1972, *8*, 267–279.

ELLIS, A. Rational-Emotive Therapy. In *Current Psychotherapies* (2nd ed.), edited by R.J. Corsini. Itasca, Ill.: Peacock, 1979.

EPSTEIN, S. Traits are alive and well. In *Personality at the Crossroads: Current Issues in Interactional Psychology*, edited by D. Magnusson and N.S. Endler. Hillsdale, N.J.: Lawrence Erlbaum, 1977.

EPSTEIN, W. The influence of syntactical structure on learning. *American Journal of Psychology*, 1961, *74*, 80–85.

EVANS, R.B. Childhood parental relationships of homosexual men. *Journal of Consulting and Clinical Psychology*, 1969, *33*, 129–135.

EVANS, R.I., ROZELLE, R.M., LASATER, T.M., DEMBROSKI, T.M., & ALLEN, B.P. Fear arousal, persuasion, and actual versus implied behavioral change: New perspective utilizing a real-life dental hygiene program. *Journal of Personality and Social Psychology*, 1970, *16*, 220–227.

EVERITT, B.J., & HERBERT, J. Adrenal glands and sexual receptivity in female rhesus monkeys. *Nature*, 1969, *222*, 1065–1066.

EYSENCK, H.J. Primary social attitudes: I. The organization and measurement of social attitudes. *International Journal of Opinion Research*, 1947, *1*, 49–84.

EYSENCK, H.J. The effects of psychotherapy: An evaluation. *Journal of Consulting Psychology*, 1952, *16*, 319–324.

EYSENCK, H.J. *Dynamics of Anxiety and Hysteria*. London: Routledge and Kegan Paul, 1957.

EYSENCK, H.J., & RACHMAN, S. *The Causes and Cures of Neurosis: An Introduction to Modern Behavior Therapy Based on Learning Theory and the Principles of Conditioning*. San Diego: Knapp, 1965.

FALK, J.L. The nature and determinants of adjunctive behavior. In *Schedule Effects: Drugs, Drinking, and Aggression*, edited by R.M. Gilbert and J.D. Keehn. Toronto: University of Toronto Press, 1972.

FANTZ, R.L. The origin of form-perception. *Scientific American*, 1961, *204*, 66–72.

FANTZ, R.L., & NEVIS, S. Pattern preferences and perceptual-cognitive development in early infancy. *Merrill-Palmer Quarterly*, 1967, *13*, 77–108.

FESHBACH, S., & SINGER, R.D. *Television and Aggression*. San Francisco: Jossey-Bass, 1971.

FESTINGER, L. *A Theory of Cognitive Dissonance*. Stanford: Stanford University Press, 1957.

FESTINGER, L., & CARLSMITH, J.M. Cognitive consequences of forced compliance. *Journal of Abnormal and Social Psychology*, 1959, *58*, 203–210.

FESTINGER, L., SCHACHTER, S., & BACK, K. *Social Pressures in Informal Groups: A Study of a Housing Community*. New York: Harper, 1950.

FILLENBAUM, S. Pragmatic normalization: Further results for some conjunctive and disjunctive sentences. *Journal of Experimental Psychology*, 1974a, *102*, 574–578.

FILLENBAUM, S. Or: Some uses. *Journal of Experimental Psychology*, 1974b, *103*, 913–921.

FINK, M. Presidential address: Brain function, verbal behavior, and psychotherapy. In *Evaluation of Psychological Therapies: Psychotherapies, Behavior Therapies, Drug Therapies, and their Interactions*, edited by R.L. Spitzer and D.F. Klein. Baltimore: The Johns Hopkins University Press, 1976.

FIX, A.J., & HAFFKE, E.A. *Basic Psychological Therapies: Comparative Effectiveness*. New York: Human Sciences Press, 1976.

FLORY, R. Attack behavior as a function of minimum inter-food interval. *Journal of the Experimental Analysis of Behavior*, 1969, *12*, 825–828.

FLYNN, J., VANEGAS, H., FOOTE, W., & EDWARDS, S.B. Neural mechanisms involved in a cat's attack on a rat. In *The Neural Control of Behavior,* edited by R. Whalen, R.F. Thompson, M. Verzeano, and N. Weinberger. New York: Academic Press, 1970.

FOCH, T.T., & PLOMIN, R. Specific cognitive abilities in 5–12 year-old twins. *Behavior Genetics,* 1980, *10,* 507–520.

FODOR, J.A., & BEVER, T.G. The psychological reality of linguistic segments. *Journal of Verbal Learning and Verbal Behavior,* 1965, *4,* 414–420.

FODOR, J.A., & GARRETT, M.F. Some syntactic determinants of sentential complexity. *Perception and Psychophysics,* 1967, *2,* 289–296.

FOLEY, V.D. Family therapy. In *Current Psychotherapies* (2nd ed.), edited by R.J. Corsini. Itasca, Ill.: Peacock, 1979.

FORD, D.H., & URBAN, H.B. *Systems of Psychotherapy: A Comparative Study.* New York: Wiley, 1963.

FOX, R., ASLIN, R.N., SHEA, S.L., & DUMAIS, S.T. Stereopsis in human infants. *Science,* 1979, *207,* 323–324.

FREUD, A., & DANN, S. An experiment in group upbringing. In *The Psychoanalytic Study of the Child* (vol. 6). New York: International Universities Press, 1951.

FRIEDMAN, M.I., & STRICKER, E.M. The physiological psychology of hunger: A physiological perspective. *Psychological Review,* 1976, *83,* 409–431.

FRIESEN, W.V. Cultural differences in facial expression in a social situation: An experimental test of the concept of display rules. Unpublished doctoral dissertation, University of California, San Francisco, 1972.

FRIJDA, N.H. [Intelligence of man and intelligence of the machine: Remarks on simulation] *Cahiers de Psychologie,* 1968, *11,* 1–9.

FUHRMAN, W., RAHE, D.F., & HARTUP, W.W. Rehabilitation of socially withdrawn preschool children through mixed-age and same-age socialization. *Child Development,* 1979, *50,* 915–922.

GAMBRELL, R.D., BERNARD, D.M., SANDERS, B.I., VANDERBURG, N., & BUXTON, S.J. Changes in sexual drives of patients on oral contraceptives. *Journal of Reproductive Medicine,* 1976, *17,* 165–171.

GARCIA, J., & KOELLING, R.A. Relation of cue to consequence in avoidance learning. *Psychonomic Science,* 1966, *4,* 123–124.

GARDNER, D.B., HAWKES, G.R., & BURCHINAL, L.B. Noncontinuous mothering in infancy and development in later childhood. *Child Development,* 1961, *32,* 225–234.

GARDNER, R.A., & GARDNER, B.T. Teaching sign language to a chimpanzee. *Science,* 1969, *165,* 664–672.

GARDNER, R.A., & GARDNER, B.T. Early signs of language in child and chimpanzee. *Science,* 1975, *187,* 752–753.

GARDNER, R.A., & GARDNER, B.T. Comparative psychology and language acquisition. *Annals of the New York Academy of Science,* 1978, *309,* 37–76.

GAZZANIGA, M.S., & LeDOUX, J.E. *The Integrated Mind.* New York: Plenum Press, 1978.

GEBHARD, P.H. Factors in marital orgasm. *Journal of Social Issues,* 1966, *22,* 88–95.

GEEN, R.G., STONNER, D., & SHOPE, G.L. The facilitation of aggression by aggression: A study in response inhibition and disinhibition. *Journal of Personality and Social Psychology,* 1975, *31,* 721–726.

GEER, J.H., MOROKOFF, P., & GREENWOOD, P. Sexual arousal in women: The development of a measurement device for vaginal blood flow. *Archives of Sexual Behavior,* 1974, *3,* 359–364.

GELLER, D.M., GOODSTEIN, L., SILVER, M., & STERNBERG, W.C. On being ignored: The effects of the violation of implicit rules of social interaction. *Sociometry,* 1974, *37,* 541–556.

GELMAN, R. Logical capacity of very young children: Number invariance rules. *Child Development,* 1972, *43,* 75–90.

GERBINO, L., OLESHANSKY, M., & GERSHON, S. Clinical use and mode of action of lithium. In *Psychopharmacology: A Generation of Progress,* edited by M.A. Lipton, A. DiMascio, and K.F. Killam. New York: Raven Press, 1978.

GESCHWIND, N. Disconnexion syndromes in animals and man. *Brain,* 1965, *88,* 237–294, 585–644.

GESCHWIND, N., QUADFASEL, F.A., & SEGARRA, J.M. Isolation of the speech area. *Neuropsychologia,* 1968, *6,* 327–340.

GIBSON, E.J., & WALK, R.R. The "visual cliff." *Scientific American,* 1960, *202,* 2–9.

GLANZER, M., & CUNITZ, A.R. Two storage mechanisms in free recall. *Journal of Verbal Learning and Verbal Behavior,* 1966, *5,* 351–360.

GOLD, R.M., JONES, A.P., SAWCHENKO, P.E., & KAPATOS, G. Paraventricular area: Critical focus of a longitudinal neurocircuitry mediating food intake. *Physiology & Behavior,* 1977, *18,* 1111–1119.

GOLDBLATT, P.B., MOORE, M.E., & STUNKARD, A.J. Social factors in obesity. *Journal of the American Medical Association,* 1965, *21,* 1455–1470.

GOLDFARB, W. Emotional and intellectual consequences of psychological deprivation in infancy: A reevaluation. In *Psychopathology of Childhood,* edited by P.H. Hoch and J. Zubin. New York: Grune & Stratton, 1955.

GOLDFOOT, D.A., KREVETZ, M.A., GOY, R.W., & FREEMAN, S.K. Lack of effect of vaginal lavages and aliphatic acids on ejaculatory responses in rhesus monkeys: Behavioral and chemical analyses. *Hormones and Behavior,* 1976, *7,* 1–28.

GOLDIN-MEADOW, S., & FELDMAN, H. The development of language-like communication without a language model. *Science,* 1977, *197,* 401–403.

GOODALL, J. The behaviour of free-living chimpanzees in the Gombe Stream Reserve. *Animal Behaviour Monographs,* 1968, *1,* 165–301.

GOODGLASS, H. Agrammatism. In *Studies in Neurolinguistics,* edited by H. Whitaker and H.A. Whitaker. New York: Academic Press, 1976.

GOODWIN, F.K., WIRZ-JUSTICE, A., & WEHR, T.A. Evidence that the pathophysiology of depression and the mechanisms of action of antidepressant drugs both involve alterations in circadian rhythms. In *Typical and Atypical Antidepressants: Clinical Practice*, edited by E. Costa and G. Racagni. New York: Raven Press, 1982.

GOY, R.W., & GOLDFOOT, D.A. Hormonal influences on sexually dimorphic behavior. In *Handbook of Physiology* (Section 7, vol. 2, Part I), edited by R.O. Green. Washington, D.C.: American Physiological Society, 1973.

GOY, R.W., & MCEWEN, B.S. *Sexual Differentiation of the Brain.* Cambridge, Mass.: MIT Press, 1980.

GRAHAM, F.K., ERNHART, C.B., THURSTON, D., & CRAFT, M. Development three years after perinatal anoxia and other potentially damaging newborn experiences. *Psychological Monographs,* 1962 (76, Whole No. 522).

GRANICK, S. Comparative analysis of psychotic depressives with matched normals on some untimed verbal intelligence tests. *Journal of Consulting Psychology,* 1963, *27,* 439–443.

GRAVES, A.J. Attainment of conservation of mass, weight and volume in minimally educated adults. *Developmental Psychology,* 1972, *7,* 223.

GREEN, D.M., & SWETS, J.A. *Signal Detection Theory and Psychophysics.* New York: Krieger, 1974.

GREEN, J., CLEMENTE, C., & DeGROOT, J. Rhinencephalic lesions and behavior in cats. *Journal of Comparative Neurology,* 1957, *108,* 505–545.

GREENBERG, J.H., & JENKINS, J.J. Studies in the psychological correlates of the sound system of American English. *Word,* 1964, *20,* 157–177.

GREENBERG, R., PILLARD, R., & PEARLMAN, C. The effect of dream (stage REM) deprivation on adaptation to stress. *Psychosomatic Medicine,* 1972, *34,* 257–262.

GREGORY, R.L. *Eye and Brain* (3rd ed.). New York: World University Library, 1978.

GREGORY, W.L. Locus of control for positive and negative outcomes. *Journal of Personality and Social Psychology,* 1978, *36,* 840–849.

GRIFFITH, J.D., CAVANAUGH, J., HELD, N.N., & OATES, J.A. Dextroamphetamine: Evaluation of psychotomimetic properties in man. *Archives of General Psychiatry,* 1972, *26,* 97–100.

GRIFFITHS, M., & PAYNE, P.R. Energy expenditure in small children of obese and non-obese mothers. *Nature,* 1976, *260,* 698–700.

GROSS, M.D. Violence associated with organic brain disease. In *Dynamics of Violence,* edited by J. Fawcett. Chicago: American Medical Association, 1971.

GUILFORD, J.P. *The Nature of Human Intelligence.* New York: McGraw-Hill, 1967.

HAITH, M. Infrared television recording and measurement of ocular behavior in the human infant. *American Psychologist,* 1969, *24,* 279–283.

HAITH, M.M. Visual competence in early infancy. In *Handbook of Sensory Physiology* (vol. 8), edited by R. Held,

H. Leibowitz, and H.-L. Teuber. New York: Springer-Verlag, 1976.

HALL, E.T. *The Hidden Dimension.* New York: Doubleday, 1966.

HARLOW, H. *Learning to Love.* New York: J. Aronson, 1974.

HARRIS, L.J. Sex differences in spatial ability: possible environmental, genetic, and neurological factors. In *Asymmetrical Function of the Brain,* edited by M. Kinsbourne. Cambridge: Cambridge University Press, 1978.

HARRIS, V.A., & JELLISON, J.M. Fear-arousing communications, false physiological feedback and the acceptance of recommendations. *Journal of Experimental Social Psychology,* 1971, *7,* 269–279.

HART, B. Sexual reflexes and mating behavior in the male dog. *Journal of Comparative and Physiological Psychology,* 1967, *66,* 388–399.

HART, B. Gonadal hormones and sexual reflexes in the female rat. *Hormones and Behavior,* 1969, *1,* 65–71.

HAYES, C. *The Ape in Our House.* London: Gollancz, 1952.

HECHT, S., & SCHLAER, S. An adaptometer for measuring human dark adaptation. *Journal of the Optical Society of America,* 1938, *28,* 269–275.

HEIDER, F. *The Psychology of Interpersonal Relations.* New York: Wiley, 1958.

HEIMER, L., & LARSSON, K. Impairment of mating behavior in male rats following lesions in the preoptic-anterior hypothalamic continuum. *Brain Research,* 1966/1967, *3,* 248–263.

HENDERSON, D., & GILLESPIE, R.D. *A Textbook of Psychiatry for Students and Practitioners.* London: Oxford University Press, 1950.

HENDERSON, N.D. Human behavior genetics. *Annual Review of Psychology,* 1982, *33,* 403–440.

HERNSHAW, L.S. *Cyril Burt, Psychologist.* Ithaca, N.Y.: Cornell University Press, 1979.

HERRNSTEIN, R.J., & LOVELAND, D.H. Complex visual concept in the pigeon. *Science,* 1964, *146,* 549–551.

HESTON, L.L. Psychiatric disorders in foster home reared children of schiozphrenic mothers. *British Journal of Psychiatry,* 1966, *112,* 819–825.

HESTON, L.L., & SHIELDS, J.S. Homosexuality in twins: A family study and a registry study. *Archives of General Psychiatry,* 1968, *18,* 149–160.

HETHERINGTON, A.W., & RANSON, S.W. Experimental hypothalamohypophyseal obesity in the rat. *Proceedings of the Society for Experimental Biology and Medicine,* 1939, *41,* 465–466.

HIGGINS, J.M. The effect of speaker and pressure variation on the vibrotactile reception of selected spoken English phonemes. *Dissertation Abstracts International,* 1972, *32,* 5511.

HILGARD, E.R. Hypnosis. *Annual Review of Psychology,* 1975, *26,* 19–44.

HIMMS-HAGEN, J. Current status of nonshivering thermogenesis. In *Assessment of Energy Metabolism in Health and Disease,* edited by J.W. Kinney. Columbus, Ohio: Ross Laboratories, 1980.

HIRSCH, J., & KNITTLE, J.L. Cellularity of obese and nonobese human adipose tissue. *Federation Proceedings,* 1970, *29,* 1516–1521.

HIRSCH, H.V.B., & SPINELLI, D.N. Modification of the distribution of receptive field orientation in cats by selective visual exposure during development. *Experimental Brain Research,* 1971, *13,* 509–527.

HOFFMAN, F.G. *A Handbook on Drug and Alcohol Abuse.* New York: Oxford University Press, 1975.

HOFLING, C.K. *Textbook of Psychiatry for Medical Practice,* Philadelphia: Lippincott, 1963.

HOHMAN, G.W. Some effects of spinal cord lesions on experienced emotional feelings. *Psychophysiology,* 1966, *3,* 143–156.

HOLLISTER, L.E. Drug-induced psychoses and schizophrenic reactions: A critical comparison. *Annals of the New York Academy of Science,* 1962, 96, 80–88.

HOMANS, G.C. *Social Behavior: Its Elementary Forms.* New York: Harcourt, Brace, 1961.

HONIG, W.K., BONEAU, C.A., BURSTEIN, K.R., & PENNYPACKER, H.C. Positive and negative generalization gradients obtained after equivalent training conditions. *Journal of Comparative and Physiological Psychology,* 1963, *56,* 111–116.

HORN, J.L. Organization of abilities and the development of intelligence. *Psychological Review,* 1968, *75,* 242–259.

HORN, J.L. Human abilities: A review of research and theory in the early 1970s. *Annual Review of Psychology,* 1976, *27,* 437–485.

HORN, J.L., & CATTELL, R.B. Refinement and test of the theory of fluid and crystallized ability intelligences. *Journal of Educational Psychology,* 1966, 57, 253–270.

HORNBY, P.A. Surface structure and presupposition. *Journal of Verbal Learning and Verbal Behavior,* 1974, *13,* 530–538.

HUBEL, D.H., & WIESEL, T.N. The period of susceptibility to the physiological effects of unilateral eye closure in kittens. *Journal of Physiology* (London), 1970, *206,* 419–436.

HUBEL, D.H., & WIESEL, T.N. Functional architecture of macaque monkey visual cortex. *Proceedings of the Royal Society of London,* 1977, *198,* 1–59.

HUBEL, D.H., & WIESEL, T.N. Brain mechanisms of vision. *Scientific American,* 1979, *241,* 150–162.

HUGHES, J.G., EHEMANN, B., & BROWN, U.A. Electroencephalography of the newborn. *American Journal of Diseases of Children,* 1948, 76, 626–633.

INGLEFINGER, F.J. The late effects of total and subtotal gastrectomy, *New England Journal of Medicine,* 1944, *231,* 321–327.

ISAACS, W., THOMAS, J., & GOLDIAMOND, I. Application of operant conditioning to reinstate verbal behavior in psychotics. *Journal of Speech and Hearing Disorders,* 1960, *25,* 8–12.

IZARD, C.E. *The Face of Emotion.* New York: Appleton-Century-Crofts, 1971.

IZARD, C.E., & TOMKINS, S.S. Affect and behavior: Anxiety as a negative affect. In *Anxiety and Behavior,* edited by L.D. Spielberger. New York: Academic Press, 1966.

JACKSON, D.N., & PAUNONEN, S.V. Personality structure and assessment. *Annual Review of Psychology,* 1980, *31,* 503–551.

JACOBSEN, C.F., WOLF, J.B., & JACKSON, T.A. An experimental analysis of the functions of the frontal association areas in primates. *Journal of Nervous and Mental Diseases,* 1935, *82,* 1–14.

JAMES, W. *Principles of Psychology.* New York: Henry Holt, 1890.

JAMES, W.H. Coital rates and the pill. *Nature,* 1971, *234,* 555–556.

JAMES, W.P.T., & TRAYHURN, P. Thermogenesis and obesity. *British Medical Bulletin,* 1981, 37, 43–48.

JANIS, I.L., KAYE, D., & KIRSCHNER, P. Facilitating effects of "eating while reading" on responsiveness to persuasive communications. *Journal of Personality and Social Psychology,* 1965, *1,* 181–186.

JARVIK, L.F., & BLUM, J.E. Cognitive declines as predictors of mortality in discordant twin pairs—a twenty-year longitudinal study. In *Prediction of Life Span,* edited by E. Palmore and F.C. Jeffers. Lexington, Mass.: D.C. Heath, Lexington Books, 1971.

JENKINS, R.L. Classification of behavior problems of children. *American Journal of Psychiatry,* 1969, *125,* 1032–1039.

JOHNSON, S.B., & SECHREST, L. Comparison of desensitization and progressive relaxation in treating test anxiety. *Journal of Consulting and Clinical Psychology,* 1968, *32,* 280–286.

JOHNSON, T.J., FEIGENBAUM, R., & WEIBY, M. Some determinants and consequences of the teacher's perception of causation. *Journal of Experimental Psychology,* 1964, *55,* 237–246.

JOHNSTON, D., & DAVIDSON, J.M. Intracerebral androgen and sexual behavior in the male rat. *Hormones and Behavior,* 1972, *3,* 345–357.

JOHNSTONE, E.C., CROW, T.J., FRITH, C.D., STEVENS, M., KREEL, L., & HUSBAND, J. The dementia of dementia praecox. *Acta Psychiatrica Scandinavica,* 1978, *57,* 305–324.

JONES, A.P., & FRIEDMAN, M.I. Obesity and adipocyte abnormalities in offspring of rats undernourished during pregnancy. *Science,* 1982, *215,* 1515–1519.

JONES, E.E., & DAVIS, K.E. From acts to dispositions: The attribution process in person perceptions. In *Advances in Experimental Social Psychology* (vol. 2), edited by L. Berkowitz. New York: Academic Press, 1965.

JONES, E.E., & NISBETT, R.E. The actor and observer: Divergent perceptions of the causes of behavior. In *Attribution: Perceiving the Causes of Behavior,* edited by E.E. Jones, D.E. Kamouse, H.H. Kelley, R.E. Nisbett, S.

Valins, and B. Weiner. Morristown, N.J.: General Learning Press, 1971.

JONES, H.E., & BAYLEY, N. The Berkeley growth study. *Child Development,* 1941, *12,* 167–173.

JOUVET, M. The role of monoamines and acetylcholine-containing neurons in the regulation of the sleep-waking cycle. *Ergebnisse der Physiologie,* 1972, *64,* 166–307.

JULESZ, B. Texture and visual perception. *Scientific American,* 1965, *212,* 38–48.

KAGAN, J. The distribution of attention in infancy. In *Perception and Its Disorders,* edited by D.H. Hamburg. Baltimore: Williams & Wilkins, 1970.

KAGAN, J., & LEWIS, M. Studies of attention in the human infant. *Behavior Development,* 1965, *11,* 95–127.

KAHNEMAN, D., & TVERSKY, A. On the psychology of prediction. *Psychological Review,* 1973, *80,* 237–246.

KALLMAN, F.J. Comparative twin study on the genetic aspects of male homosexuality. *Journal of Nervous and Mental Disease,* 1952, *115,* 283–298.

KAMIN, L.J. *The Science and Politics of IQ.* Potomac, Md.: Lawrence Erlbaum, 1974.

KANFER, F.H., & PHILLIPS, J.S. *Learning Foundations of Behavior Therapy.* New York: Wiley, 1970.

KAPLAN, E.L., & KAPLAN, G.A. The prelinguistic child. In *Human Development and Cognitive Processes,* edited by J. Eliot. New York: Holt, Rinehart, and Winston, 1970.

KARABENICK, S.A., & SRULL, T.K. Effects of personality and situational variation in locus of control on cheating: Determinants of the congruence effect. *Journal of Personality,* 1978, *46,* 72–95.

KARLSON, P., & LUSCHER, M. "Pheromones": A new term for a class of biologically active substances. *Nature,* 1959, *183,* 55–56.

KATZ, D. *The World of Colour.* London: Kegan Paul, Trench, Trubner, 1935.

KEELE, C.A. Measurement of responses to chemically induced pain. In *Touch, Heat, and Pain,* edited by A.V.S. deRenuck and J. Knight. Boston: Little, Brown, 1966.

KELLEY, H.H. Attribution theory in social psychology. In *Nebraska Symposium on Motivation* (vol. 15), edited by D. Levine. Lincoln: University of Nebraska Press, 1967.

KELLEY, H.H. Attribution theory in social interaction. In *Attribution: Perceiving the Causes of Behavior,* edited by E.E. Jones, D.E. Kamouse, H.H. Kelley, R.E. Nisbett, S. Valins, and B. Weiner. Morristown, N.J.: General Learning Press, 1971.

KELLEY, H.H. The process of causal attribution. *American Psychologist,* 1973, *28,* 107–128.

KENRICK, D.T., & CIALDINI, R.B. Romantic attraction: Misattribution versus reinforcement explanations. *Journal of Personality and Social Psychology,* 1977, *35,* 381–391.

KEPPEL, G., & UNDERWOOD, B.J. Proactive inhibition in short-term retention of single items. *Journal of Verbal Learning and Verbal Behavior,* 1962, *1,* 153–161.

KERTESZ, A. Anatomy of jargon. In *Jargonaphasia,* edited by J. Brown. New York: Academic Press, 1981.

KETY, S.S., ROSENTHAL, D., WENDER, P.H., & SCHULSINGER, F. The types and prevalence of mental illness in the biological and adoptive families of adopted schizophrenics. In *The Transmission of Schizophrenia,* edited by D. Rosenthal and S.S. Kety. Elmsford, N.Y.: Pergamon Press, 1968.

KEVERNE, E.B., & MICHAEL, R.P. Sex-attractant properties of ether extracts of vaginal secretions from rhesus monkeys. *Journal of Endocrinology,* 1971, *51,* 313–322.

KIANG, N.Y.-S. *Discharge Patterns of Single Nerve Fibers in the Cat's Auditory Nerve.* Cambridge, Mass.: MIT Press, 1965.

KLAUS, M.H., JERAULD, R., KRIEGER, N.C., McALPINE, W. STEFFA, M., & KENNELL, J.H. Maternal attachment: Importance of the first postpartum days. *New England Journal of Medicine,* 1972, *286,* 460–463.

KLEIN, D.F., & HOWARD, A. *Psychiatric Case Studies: Treatment, Drugs, and Outcome.* Baltimore: Williams & Wilkins, 1972.

KLINEBERG, O. Emotional expression in Chinese literature. *Journal of Abnormal and Social Psychology,* 1938, *33,* 517–520.

KLING, A., LANCASTER, J., & BENITONE, J. Amygdalectomy in the free-ranging vervet (Cercopithecusalthiops). *Journal of Psychiatric Research,* 1970, *7,* 191–199.

KLOPFER, P.H., ADAMS, D.J., & KLOPFER, M.S. Maternal "imprinting" in goats. *Proceedings of the National Academy of Sciences,* 1964, *52,* 911–914.

KNITTLE, J.L., & HIRSCH, J. Effect of early nutrition on the development of rat epididymal fat pads: Cellularity and metabolism. *Journal of Clinical Investigation,* 1968, *47,* 2001–2098.

KNOX, R.E., & INKSTER, J.A. Postdecision dissonance at post time. *Journal of Personality and Social Psychology,* 1968, *8,* 310–323.

KNOX, V.J., CRUTCHFIELD, L., & HILGARD, E.R. *The nature of task interference in hypnotic dissociation.* Paper presented at the meeting of the Society of Clinical and Experimental Hypnosis, Newport Beach, Calif. 1973.

KOGAN, N. Categorizing and conceptualizing styles in younger and older adults, RB-73. Princeton, N.J.: Educational Testing Service, 1973.

KOOPMAN, P.R., & AMES, E.W. Infants' preferences for facial arrangements: A failure to replicate. *Child Development,* 1968, *39,* 481–487.

KOSSLYN, S.M. Scanning visual images: Some structural implications. *Perception and Psychophysics,* 1973, *14,* 90–94.

KOSSLYN, S.M. *Evidence for analogue representation.* Paper presented at the conference on Theoretical Issues in Natural Language Processing, Massachusetts Institute of Technology, Cambridge, Mass., July 1975.

KOVNER, R., & STAMM, J.S. Disruption of short-term visual memory by electrical stimulation of inferotemporal cortex in the monkey. *Journal of Comparative and Physiological Psychology,* 1972, *81,* 163–172.

KRAINES, S.H. *The Therapy of the Neuroses and Psychoses* (3rd ed.). Philadelphia: Lea & Fibiger, 1948.

KRIECKHAUS, E.E., & WOLF, G. Acquisition of sodium by rats. Interaction of innate mechanisms and latent learning. *Journal of Comparative and Physiological Psychology,* 1968, *65,* 197–201.

KROLL, N.E.A, PARKS, T., PARKINSON, S.R., BIEBER, S.L., & JOHNSON, A.L. Short-term memory while shadowing: Recall of visually and of aurally presented letters. *Journal of Experimental Psychology,* 1970, *85,* 220–224.

KUHL, P.K., & MILLER, J.D. Speech perception by the chinchilla: Voiced-voiceless distinction in alveolar plosive consonants. *Science,* 1975, *190,* 69–72.

KUHL, P.K., & MILLER, J.D. Speech perception by the chinchilla: Identification functions for synthetic VOT stimuli. *Journal of the Acoustical Society of America,* 1978, *63,* 905–917.

KUPFER, D.J. REM latency: A psychobiologic marker for primary depressive disease. *Biological Psychiatry,* 1976, *11,* 159–174.

LACEY, J.I., & LACEY, B.C. The law of initial value in the longitudinal study of autonomic constitution: Reproducibility of autonomic response patterns over a four-year interval. *Annals of the New York Academy of Science,* 1962, *98,* 1257–1290.

LAIR, C.V., MOON, W.H., & KAUSLER, D.H. Associative interference in the paired-associate learning of middle-aged and old subjects. *Developmental Psychology,* 1969, *1,* 548–552.

LAMM, H., & SAUER, C. Discussion-induced shift toward higher demands in negotiation. *European Journal of Social Psychology,* 1974, *4,* 85–88.

LANGER, E.J. The illusion of control. *Journal of Personality and Social Psychology,* 1975, *32,* 311–328.

LAO, R.C. Internal-external control and competent and innovative behavior among Negro college students. *Journal of Personality and Social Psychology,* 1970, *14,* 263–270.

LaPIERE, R.T. Attitudes and actions. *Social Forces,* 1934, *13,* 230–237.

LATANÉ, B., WILLIAMS, K., & HARKINS, S. Many hands make light the work: The causes and consequences of social loafing. *Journal of Personality and Social Psychology,* 1979, *37,* 823–832.

LEAHY, M.R., & MARTIN, I.C.A. Successful hypnotic abreaction after twenty years. *British Journal of Psychiatry,* 1967, *113,* 383–385.

LEECH, S., & WITTE, K.L. Paired-associate learning in elderly adults as related to pacing and incentive conditions. *Developmental Psychology,* 1971, *5,* 180.

LEFCOURT, H.M. *Locus of Control.* Hillsdale, N.J.: Lawrence Erlbaum, 1976.

LEFKOWITZ, M.M., ERON, L.D., WALDER, L.O., & HUESMANN, L.R. *Growing Up to Be Violent: A Longitudinal Study of the Development of Aggression.* New York: Pergamon Press, 1977.

LEON, G.R. *Case Histories of Deviant Behavior* (2nd ed.). Boston: Allyn and Bacon, 1977.

LEVY, L.H. *Psychological Interpretation.* New York: Holt, Rinehart and Winston, 1963.

LEWIS, M., & GOLDBERG, S. Perceptual-cognitive development in infancy: A generalized expectancy model as a function of mother-infant interaction. *Merrill-Palmer Quarterly,* 1969, *15,* 81–100.

LEY, R.G., & BRYDEN, M.P. Hemispheric differences in processing emotions and faces. *Brain and Language,* 1979, *7,* 127–138.

LIEBELT, R.A., BORDELON, C.B., & LIEBELT, A.G. The adipose tissue system and food intake. In *Progress in Physiological Psychology,* edited by E. Stellar and J.M. Sprague. New York: Academic Press, 1973.

LIPTON, S. Dissociated personality: A case report. *Psychiatric Quarterly,* 1943, *17,* 35–36.

LISKER, L., & ABRAMSON, A. The voicing dimension: Some experiments in comparative phonetics. *Proceedings of Sixth International Congress of Phonetic Sciences, Prague, 1967.* Prague: Academia, 1970.

LLOYD, C.W. The influence of hormones on human sexual behavior. In *Clinical Endocrinology* (vol. 2). New York: Grune & Stratton, 1968.

LOEB, A., BECK, A.T., DIGGORY, J.C., & TUTHILL, R. The effects of success and failure on mood, motivation and performance as a function of predetermined level of depression. Unpublished manuscript, University of Pennsylvania, 1966.

LOEHLIN, J.C., & NICHOLS, R.C. *Heredity, Environment, and Personality: A Study of 850 Sets of Twins.* Austin and London: University of Texas Press, 1976.

LOGAN, F.A. Decision making by rats: Delay versus amount of reward. *Journal of Comparative and Physiological Psychology,* 1965, *59,* 1–12.

LOOMIS, W.F. Skin pigment regulation of vitamin-D biosynthesis in man. *Science,* 1967, *157,* 501–506.

LORENZ, K. Companionship in bird life. In *Instinctive Behavior,* edited by C.H. Schiller. New York: International Universities Press, 1957.

LORENZ, K. *On Aggression.* New York: Harcourt Brace Jovanovich, 1966.

LOY, J. Perimenstrual sexual behavior among rhesus monkeys. *Folia Primatologica,* 1970, *13,* 286–297.

LUBORSKY, L., CHANDLER, M., AUERBACH, A.H., COHEN, J., & BACHRACH, H.M. Factors influencing the outcome of psychotherapy: A review of quantitative research. *Psychological Bulletin,* 1971, *75,* 145–185.

LUBORSKY, L., SINGER, G., & LUBORSKY, L. Comparative studies of psychotherapies: Is it true that "everybody has won and all must have prizes"? In *Evaluation of Psychological Therapies: Psychotherapies, Behavior Therapies, Drug Therapies, and their Interactions,* edited by R.L.

Spitzer and D.F. Klein. Baltimore: Johns Hopkins University Press, 1976.

LUCERO, M.A.   Lengthening of REM sleep duration consecutive to learning in the rat. *Brain Research,* 1970, *20,* 319–322.

LURIA, A.R.   The functional organization of the brain. *Scientific American,* 1970, *222,* 66–79.

MACCOBY, E.E., & JACKLIN, C.N.   *The Psychology of Sex Differences.* Stanford: Stanford University Press, 1974.

MacLEAN, P.D., DUA, S., & DENNISTON, R.H. Cerebral localization for scratching and seminal discharge. *Archives of Neurology,* 1963, *9,* 485–497.

MAGNI, F., MORUZZI, G., ROSSI, G.F., & ZANCHETTI, A.   EEG arousal following inactivation of the lower brain stem by selective injection of barbiturate into the vertebral circulation. *Archives Italiennes de Biologie,* 1959, *97,* 33–46.

MAIER, S.F., & JACKSON, R.L.   Learned helplessness: All of us were right (and wrong): Inescapable shock has multiple effects. In *Psychology of Learning and Motivation,* edited by G.H. Bower. New York: Academic Press, 1979.

MAIER, S.F., & SELIGMAN, M.E.   Learned helplessness: Theory and evidence. *Journal of Experimental Psychology: General,* 1976, *105,* 3–46.

MARGOLIN, D.I., & CARLSON, N.R.   *Common mechanisms in anomia and alexia.* Paper presented at the twentieth Annual Meeting of the Academy of Aphasia, Lake Mohonk, N.Y., October 1982.

MARK, V.H., & ERVIN, F.R.   *Violence and the Brain.* New York: Harper & Row, 1970.

MARK, V.H., ERVIN, F.R., & YAKOVLEV, P.I. The treatment of pain by stereotaxic methods. *Confina Neurologica,* 1962, *22,* 238–245.

MARK, V.H., SWEET, W.H., & ERVIN, F.R. The effect of amygdalotomy on violent behavior in patients with temporal lobe epilepsy. In *Psychosurgery,* edited by E. Hitchcock, L. Laitinen, and K. Vaernet. Springfield, Ill.: C.C. Thomas, 1972.

MARTENS, R.   Palmar sweating and the presence of an audience. *Journal of Experimental Social Psychology,* 1969, *5,* 371–374.

MASLOW, A.H.   *Motivation and Personality* (2nd ed.). New York: Harper & Row, 1970.

MASSARO, D.W.   Preperceptual auditory images. *Journal of Experimental Psychology,* 1970, *85,* 411–417.

MASSARO, D.W.   Preperceptual images, processing time, and perceptual units in auditory perception. *Psychological Review,* 1972, *79,* 124–145.

MASSERMAN, J.H.   *Principles of Dynamic Psychiatry* (2nd ed.). Philadelphia: W.B. Saunders, 1961.

MASTERS, W.H., & JOHNSON, V.E.   *Human Sexual Response.* Boston: Little, Brown, 1966.

MASTERS, W.H., & JOHNSON, V.E.   *Homosexuality in Perspective.* Boston: Little, Brown, 1979.

MASTERS, W.H., JOHNSON, V.E., & KO-

LODNY, R.C.   *Human Sexuality.* Boston: Little, Brown, 1982.

MATHEWS, D., & EDWARDS, D.A.   Involvement of the ventromedial and anterior hypothalamic nuclei in the hormonal induction of receptivity in the female rat. *Physiology & Behavior,* 1977, *19,* 319–326.

MAURER, D., & SALAPATEK, P.   Developmental changes in the scanning of faces by young infants. *Child Development,* 1976, *47,* 523–527.

MAYER, J.   Regulation of energy intake and the body weight: The glucostatic theory and the lipostatic hypothesis. *Annals of the New York Academy of Science,* 1955a, *63,* 15–43.

MAYER, J.   The role of exercise and activity in weight control. In *Weight Control: A Collection of Papers Presented at the Weight Control Symposium,* edited by E.S. Eppright, P. Swanson, and C.A. Iverson. Ames, Ia.: Iowa State College Press, 1955b.

McCLELLAND, D.C., ATKINSON, J.W., CLARK, R.W., & LOWELL, E.L.   *The Achievement Motive.* New York: Appleton-Century-Crofts, 1953.

McCLINTOCK, M.K.   Menstrual synchrony and suppression. *Nature,* 1971, *229,* 244–245.

McCLINTOCK, M.K., & ADLER, N.T.   The role of the female during copulation in wild and domestic Norway rats (*Rattus norvegicus*). *Behaviour,* 1978, *67,* 67–96.

McDONALD, N.   Living with schizophrenia. *Journal of the Canadian Medical Association,* 1960, *82,* 218–221.

McGHIE, A., & CHAPMAN, J.S.   Disorders of attention and perception in early schizophrenia. *British Journal of Medical Psychology,* 1961, *34,* 103–116.

McGLONE, J.   Sex differences in the cerebral organization of verbal functions in patients with unilateral brain lesions. *Brain,* 1977, *100,* 775–793.

McGUIRE, W.J., & PAPAGEORGIS, D.   The relative efficacy of various types of prior belief-defense in producing immunity against persuasion. *Journal of Abnormal and Social Psychology,* 1961, *62,* 327–337.

McMILLEN, D.L.   Transgression, self-image, and compliant behavior. *Journal of Personality and Social Psychology,* 1971, *20,* 176–179.

McMILLEN, D.L., & AUSTIN, J.B.   Effect of positive feedback on compliance following transgression. *Psychonomic Science,* 1971, *24,* 59–61.

McNEILL, D.   *The Acquisition of Language: The Study of Developmental Psycholinguistics.* New York: Harper & Row, 1970.

MEHRABIAN, A., & FERRIS, S.R.   Inference of attitudes from nonverbal communication in two channels. *Journal of Consulting Psychology,* 1967, *31,* 248–252.

MEHRABIAN, A., & WIENER, M.   Decoding of inconsistent communication. *Journal of Personality and Social Psychology,* 1967, *6,* 108–114.

MENDELS, J.   *Concepts of Depression.* New York: Wiley, 1970.

MENDELSON, J.   Role of hunger in T-maze learning

for food by rats. *Journal of Comparative and Physiological Psychology*, 1966, *62*, 341–349.

MENNINGER, K.   *The Human Mind* (3rd ed.). New York: Knopf, 1945.

MÉZEY, A.G., & COHEN, S.I.   The effect of depressive illness on time judgment and time experience. *Journal of Neurological and Neurosurgical Psychiatry*, 1961, *24*, 269–270.

MILGRAM, S.   Behavioral study of obedience. *Journal of Abnormal and Social Psychology*, 1963, *67*, 371–378.

MILGRAM, S.   Group pressure and action against a person. *Journal of Abnormal and Social Psychology*, 1964, *69*, 137–143.

MILGRAM, S.   Liberating effects of group pressure. *Journal of Personality and Social Psychology*. 1965, *1*, 127–134.

MILGRAM, S.   *Obedience to Authority*. New York: Harper & Row, 1974.

MILLENSON, J.R.   *Principles of Behavioral Analysis*. New York: Macmillan, 1967.

MILLER, D.T.   Locus of control and the ability to tolerate gratification delay: When it is better to be an external. *Journal of Research in Personality*, 1978, *12*, 49–56.

MILLER, G.A.   The magical number seven plus or minus two: Some limits on our capacity for processing information. *Psychological Review*, 1956, *63*, 81–97.

MILLER, G.A., & NICELY, P.   An analysis of perceptual confusions among some English consonants. *Journal of the Acoustical Society of America*, 1955, *27*, 338–352.

MILLER, G.A., & TAYLOR, W.G.   The perception of repeated bursts of noise. *Journal of the Acoustical Society of America*, 1948, *20*, 171–182.

MILLER, J.S., & GOLLUB, L.R.   Adjunctive and operant bolt pecking in the pigeon. *Psychological Record*, 1974, *24*, 203–208.

MILLER, R.E., & BANKS, J.H.   The determination of social dominance in monkeys by a competitive avoidance method. *Journal of Comparative and Physiological Psychology*, 1962, *55*, 137–141.

MILLER, R.E., BANKS, J., & KUWAHARA, H.   The communication of affects in monkeys: Cooperative reward conditioning. *Journal of Genetic Psychology*, 1966, *108*, 121–134.

MILLER, R.E., BANKS, J., & OGAWA, N.   Communication of affect in "cooperative conditioning" of rhesus monkeys. *Journal of Abnormal and Social Psychology*, 1962, *64*, 343–348.

MILLER, R.E., BANKS, J., & OGAWA, N.   Role of facial expression in "cooperative-avoidance conditioning" in monkeys. *Journal of Abnormal and Social Psychology*, 1963, *67*, 24–30.

MILLER, R.E., CAUL, W.F., & MIRSKY, I.A.   Communication of affects between feral and socially isolated monkeys. *Journal of Personality and Social Psychology*, 1967, *7*, 231–239.

MILLER, R.E., MURPHY, J.V., & MIRSKY, I.A.   Nonverbal communication of affect. *Journal of Clinical Psychology*, 1959, *15*, 155–158.

MILLER, R.J., HENNESSY, R.T., & LEIBOWITZ, H.W.   The effect of hypnotic ablation of the background on the magnitude of the Ponzo perspective illusion. *International Journal of Clinical and Experimental Hypnosis*, 1973, *21*, 180–191.

MILLER, W., & ERVIN-TRIPP, S.M.   The development of grammar in child language. In *The Acquisition of Language. Monographs of the Society for Research in Child Development*, edited by U. Bellugi and R. Brown, 1964 (29, Serial No. 92), 9–34.

MILLER, W.R., ROSELLINI, R.A., & SELIGMAN, M.E.P.   Learned helplessness and depression. In *Psychopathology: Experimental Models*, edited by J.D. Maser and M.E.P. Seligman. San Francisco: W.H. Freeman, 1977.

MILLS, J., & HARVEY, J.   Opinion change as a function of when information about the communicator is received and whether he is attractive or expert. *Journal of Personality and Social Psychology*, 1972, *21*, 52–55.

MINUCHIN, S.   *Families & Family Therapy*. Cambridge, Mass.: Harvard University Press, 1974.

MISCHEL, W.   *Personality and Assessment*. New York: Wiley, 1968.

MISCHEL, W.   *Introduction to Personality* (2nd ed.). New York: Holt, Rinehart, and Winston, 1976.

MISCHEL, W.   The interaction of person and situation. In *Personality at the Crossroads: Current Issues in Interactional Psychology*, edited by D. Magnusson and N.S. Endler. Hillsdale, N.J.: Lawrence Erlbaum, 1977.

MISCHEL, W.   On the interface of cognition and personality: Beyond the person-situation debate. *American Psychologist*, 1979, *34*, 740–754.

MITA, T.H., DERMER, M., & KNIGHT, J.   Reversed facial images and the mere-exposure hypothesis. *Journal of Personality and Social Psychology*, 1977, *35*, 597–601.

MITCHELL, W., FALCONER, M.A., & HILL, D.   Epilepsy and fetishism relieved by temporal lobectomy. *Lancet*, 1954, *2*, 626–630.

MOLTZ, H., LUBIN, M., LEON, M., & NUMAN, M.   Hormonal induction of maternal behavior in the ovariectomized nulliparous rat. *Physiology & Behavior*, 1970, *5*, 1373–1377.

MONEY, J., & EHRHARDT, A.   *Man & Woman, Boy & Girl*. Baltimore: Johns Hopkins University Press, 1972.

MONEY, J., & MATHEWS, D.   Prenatal exposure to virilizing progestins: An adult follow-up study of twelve women. *Archives of Sexual Behavior*, 1982, *11*, 73–82.

MONEY, J., & TUCKER, P.   *Sexual Signatures: On Being a Man or a Woman*. Boston: Little, Brown, 1975.

MOORE, B.R.   The role of directed Pavlovian reactions in simple instrumental learning in the pigeon. In *Constraints on Learning*, edited by R.A. Hinde and J. Stevenson-Hinde. New York: Academic Press, 1973.

MORAY, N., BATES, A., & BARNETT, T.   Experiments on the four-eared man. *Journal of the Acoustical Society of America*, 1965, *38*, 196–201.

MORENO, J.L. Psychodrama. In *American Handbook of Psychiatry* (vol. 2), edited by S. Arieti. New York: Basic Books, 1959.

MOSS, C.S. *Hypnosis in Perspective.* New York: McMillan, 1965.

MOWRER, O.H. *Learning Theory and Symbolic Processes.* New York: Wiley, 1960.

MOYER, K.E. *The Psychobiology of Aggression.* New York: Harper & Row, 1976.

MULLEN, J., & ABELES, N. Relationship of liking, empathy, and therapist's experience to outcome of therapy. *Journal of Consulting Psychology,* 1971, *18,* 39–43.

MUNSINGER, H. The adopted child's IQ: A critical review. *Psychological Bulletin,* 1975a, *82,* 623–659.

MUNSINGER, H. Children's resemblance to their biological and adopting parents in two ethnic groups. *Behavior Genetics,* 1975b, *5,* 239–254.

MURRAY, F.B. Acquisition of conservation through social interaction. *Developmental Psychology,* 1972, *6,* 1–6.

MYERS, D.G., & KAPLAN, M.F. Group-induced polarization in simulated juries. *Personality and Social Psychology Bulletin,* 1976, *2,* 63–66.

MYERS, D.G., & LAMM, H. The group polarization phenomenon. *Psychological Bulletin,* 1976, *83,* 602–627.

NADLER, R.D. Social factors in child development. In *Readings in Social Psychology,* edited by T.M. Newcomb and E.R. Hartley. New York: Holt, Rinehart and Winston, 1968.

NAFE, J.P., & WAGONER, K.S. The nature of pressure adaptation. *Journal of General Psychology,* 1941, *25,* 323–351.

NATIONAL COMMISSION FOR THE PROTECTION OF HUMAN SUBJECTS OF BIOMEDICAL AND BEHAVIORAL RESEARCH. *Report and Recommendations: Psychosurgery.* U.S. Government Printing Office, 1977.

NISBETT, R.E., & SCHACHTER, S. Cognitive manipulation of pain. *Journal of Experimental Social Psychology,* 1966, *2,* 227–236.

NOIROT, E. Selective priming of maternal responses by auditory and olfactory cues from mouse pups. *Developmental Psychobiology,* 1972, *5,* 371–387.

NORMAN, R. When what is said is important: A comparison of expert and attractive sources. *Journal of Experimental Social Psychology,* 1976, *12,* 294–300.

NOVAK, M.A., & HARLOW, H.F. Social recovery of monkeys isolated for the first year of life: 1. Rehabilitation and therapy. *Developmental Psychology,* 1975, *11,* 453–465.

NUMAN, M. Medial preoptic area and maternal behavior in the female rat. *Journal of Comparative and Physiological Psychology,* 1974, *87,* 746–759.

OAKLEY, A. *Sex, Gender and Society.* New York: Harper & Row, 1972.

OLDS, J. Commentary. In *Brain Stimulation and Motivation,* edited by E.S. Valenstein. Glenview, Ill: Scott, Foresman, 1973.

OLLER, D.K., WIEMAN, L.A., DOYLE, W.J., & ROSS, C. Infant babbling and speech. *Journal of Child Language,* 1976, *3,* 1–11.

ORNE, M.T. The nature of hypnosis: Artifact and essence. *Journal of Abnormal and Social Psychology,* 1959, *58,* 277–299.

OVERMEIER, J.B., & SELIGMAN, M.E.P. Effects of inescapable shock upon subsequent escape and avoidance responding. *Journal of Comparative and Physiological Psychology,* 1967, *63,* 28–33.

PARKE, R.D., & COLLMER, C.W. Child abuse: An interdisciplinary analysis. In *Review of Child Development Research* (vol. 5), edited by E.M. Hetherington. Chicago: University of Chicago Press, 1975.

PASTORE, N. The role of arbitrariness in the frustration-aggression hypothesis. *Journal of Abnormal and Social Psychology,* 1952, *47,* 728–731.

PATTERSON, A.H. *Hostility catharsis: A naturalistic quasi-experiment.* Paper presented at the annual convention of the American Psychological Association, 1974.

PATTERSON, F.G. Ape language. *Science,* 1980, *211,* 86–87.

PATTERSON, K.E., & MARCEL, A.J. Aphasia, dyslexia, and the phonological coding of written words. *Quarterly Journal of Experimental Psychology,* 1977, *29,* 307–318.

PATTIE, F.A. The genuineness of hypnotically produced anesthesia of the skin. *American Journal of Psychology,* 1937, *49,* 435–443.

PERSKY, H., LIEF, H.I., STRAUSS, D., MILLER, W.R., & O'BRIEN, C.P. Plasma testosterone level and sexual behavior of couples. *Archives of Sexual Behavior,* 1978, *7,* 157–173.

PERVIN, L.A. *Personality: Theory, Assessment, and Research.* New York: Wiley, 1975.

PETERSON, K., & CURRAN, J.P. Trait attribution as a function of hair length and correlates of subjects' preferences for hair style. *Journal of Psychology,* 1976, *93,* 331–339.

PETERSON, L.R., & JOHNSON, S.T. Some effects of minimizing articulation on short-term retention. *Journal of Verbal Learning and Verbal Behavior,* 1971, *10,* 346–354.

PETERSON, L.R., & PETERSON, M.J. Short-term retention of individual verbal items. *Journal of Experimental Psychology,* 1959, *58,* 193–198.

PETTY, R.E., & CACIOPPO, J.T. Issue involvement as a moderator of the effects on attitude of advertising content and context. *Advances in Consumer Research,* 1981, *8,* 20–24.

PETTY, R.E., HARKINS, S.G., & WILLIAMS, K.D. The effects of group diffusion of cognitive effort on attitudes: An information processing view. *Journal of Personality and Social Psychology,* 1980, *38,* 81–92.

PFAFF, D.W. *Estrogens and Brain Function: Neural Analysis of a Hormone-controlled Mammalian Reproductive Behavior.* New York: Springer-Verlag, 1980.

PHARES, E.J. *Clinical Psychology: Concepts, Methods, and Profession.* Homewood, Ill.: Dorsey Press, 1979.

PIAGET, J. *The Moral Judgment of the Child* (M. Gabain, trans.). New York: Harcourt, 1932.

PIAGET, J. *The Origins of Intelligence in Children* (M. Cook, trans.). New York: International Universities Press, 1952.

PIAGET, J. *The Early Growth of Logic in the Child* (E.A. Lunzer, and D. Pappert, trans.). London: Routledge and Kegan Paul, 1964.

PIERREL, R., & SHERMAN, J.G. Barnabus, the rat with college training. *Brown Alumni Monthly*, February 1963, pp. 8–12.

PLAPINGER, L., & McEWEN, B.S. Gonadal steroid-brain interactions in sexual differentiation. In *Biological Determinants of Sexual Behaviour*, edited by J.B. Hutchinson. Chichester: Wiley, 1978.

PLOMIN, R., & DeFRIES, J.C. Multivariate behavioral genetic analysis of twin data on scholastic abilities. *Behavior Genetics*, 1979, *9*, 505–517.

PLOMIN, R., & FOCH, T.T. A twin study of objectively assessed personality in childhood. *Journal of Personality and Social Psychology*, 1980, *39*, 680–688.

POLLACK, I., & PICKETT, J.M. Intelligibility of excerpts from fluent speech: Auditory vs. structural context. *Journal of Verbal Learning and Verbal Behavior*, 1964, *3*, 79–84.

POSTMAN, L. Verbal learning and memory. *Annual Review of Psychology*, 1975, *26*, 291–335.

PRECHTL, H.F.R. The directed head turning response and allied movements of the human baby. *Behaviour*, 1958, *13*, 212–242.

PREMACK, D. Reinforcement theory. In *Nebraska Symposium on Motivation*, edited by D. Levine. Lincoln: University of Nebraska Press, 1965.

PREMACK, D. Language and intelligence in ape and man. *American Scientist*, 1976, *64*, 674–683.

PROVENCE, S., & LIPTON, R.C. *Infants in Institutions*. New York: International Universities Press, 1962.

RACHMAN, S., & HODGSON, R.J. Experimentally-induced "sexual fetishism": Replication and development. *Psychological Record*, 1968, *18*, 25–27.

RAPPAPORT, M. Competing voice messages: Effects of message load and drugs on the ability of acute schizophrenics to attend. *Archives of General Psychiatry*, 1967, *17*, 97–103.

RAVELLI, G.-P., STEIN, Z.A., & SUSSER, M.W. Obesity in young men after famine exposure in utero and early infancy. *New England Journal of Medicine*, 1976, *295*, 349–353.

REGAN, D.T. Effects of a favor and liking on compliance. *Journal of Experimental Social Psychology*, 1971, *7*, 627–639.

REGAN, D.T., & FAZIO, R.H. On the consistency between attitudes and behavior: Look to the method of attitude formation. *Journal of Experimental Social Psychology*, 1977, *13*, 28–45.

REGAN, D.T., & TOTTEN, J. Empathy and attribution: Turning observers into actors. *Journal of Personality and Social Psychology*, 1975, *32*, 850–856.

RHEINGOLD, H.L. The effect of a strange environment on the behavior of infants. In *Determinants of Infant Behaviour* (vol. 4), edited by B.M. Foss. London: Methuen, 1969.

RHEINGOLD, H.L., & ECKERMAN, C.O. The infant separates himself from his mother. *Science*, 1970, *168*, 78–83.

RIDEOUT, B. Non-REM sleep as a source of learning deficits induced by REM sleep deprivation. *Physiology & Behavior*, 1979, *22*, 1043–1047.

RIEGEL, K.P., & RIEGEL, R.M. Development, drop, and death. *Developmental Psychology*, 1972, *6*, 306–319.

RIEGEL, K.P., RIEGEL, R.M., & MEYER, G. A study of the drop-out rates in longitudinal research on aging and the prediction of death. *Journal of Personality and Social Psychology*, 1967, *4*, 342–348.

RIESEN, A.H. Sensory deprivation: Facts in search of a theory. *Journal of Nervous and Mental Disorders*, 1961, *132*, 21–25.

RIGGS, L.A., RATLIFF, F., CORNSWEET, J.C., & CORNSWEET, T.N. The disappearance of steadily fixated visual test objects. *Journal of the Optical Society of America*, 1953, *43*, 495–501.

RITCHIE, D.E., & PHARES, E.J. Attitude change as a function of internal-external control and communicator status. *Journal of Personality*, 1969, *37*, 429–443.

ROBSON, K.S., & MOSS, H.A. Patterns and determinants of maternal attachment. *Journal of Pediatrics*, 1970, *77*(6), 976–985.

RODIN, J. Current status of the internal-external hypothesis for obesity: What went wrong? *American Psychologist*, 1981, *36*, 361–372.

ROFFWARG, H.P., DEMENT, W.C., MUZIO, J.N., & FISHER, C. Dream imagery: Relationship to rapid eye movements of sleep. *Archives of General Psychiatry*, 1962, *7*, 235–258.

ROGERS, C.T. *Client-centered Therapy*. Boston: Houghton Mifflin, 1951, renewed 1979.

ROGERS, R.W.A. A protection motivation theory of fear appeals and attitude change. *Journal of Psychology*, 1975, *91*, 93–114.

ROLLS, E.T., ROLLS, B.J., KELLY, P.H., SHAW, S.G., WOOD, R.J., & DALE, R. The relative attenuation of self-stimulation, eating, and drinking produced by dopamine-receptor blockade. *Psychopharmacologia*, 1974, *38*, 219–230.

ROSE, G.A., & WILLIAMS, R.T. Metabolic studies of large and small eaters. *British Journal of Nutrition*, 1961, *15*, 1–9.

ROSE, R.J., BOUGHMAN, J.A., CORY, L.A., NANCE, W.E., CHRISTIAN, J.C., & KANG, K.W. Data from kinship of monozygotic twins indicate maternal effects on verbal intelligence. *Nature*, 1980, *283*, 375–377.

ROSE, R.J., HARRIS, E.L., CHRISTIAN, J.C., & NANCE, W.E. Genetic variance in non-verbal intelligence: Data from the kinships of identical twins. *Science*, 1979, *205*, 1153–1155.

ROSE, R.M., BOURNE, P.G., POE, R.O.,

MOUGEY, E.H., COLLINS, D.R., & MASON, J.W. Androgen responses to stress. II. Excretion of testosterone, epitestosterone, androsterone, and etiocholanolone during basic combat training and under threat of attack. *Psychosomatic Medicine,* 1969, *31,* 418–436.

ROSENBLATT, J.S., & ARONSON, L.R. The decline of sexual behavior in male cats after castration with special reference to the role of prior sexual experience. *Behaviour,* 1958, *12,* 285–338.

ROSENHAN, D.L. On being sane in insane places. *Science,* 1973, *179,* 250–258.

ROSENTHAL, D. *Genetic Theory and Abnormal Behavior.* New York: McGraw-Hill, 1970.

ROSS, E.D. The aprosodias: Functional-anatomic organization of the affective components of language in the right hemisphere. *Archives of Neurology,* 1981, *38,* 561–569.

ROSS, L. The intuitive psychologist and his shortcomings: Distortions in the attribution process. In *Advances in Experimental Social Psychology,* edited by L. Berkowitz. New York: Academic Press, 1977.

ROSS, L.D., AMABILE, T.M., & STEINMETZ, J.L. Social roles, social control, and biases in social-perception processes. *Journal of Personality and Social Psychology,* 1977, *35,* 485–494.

ROSS, L., BIERBRAUER, G., & POLLY, S. Attribution of educational outcomes by professional and nonprofessional instructors. *Journal of Personality and Social Psychology,* 1974, *29,* 609–618.

ROSS, L.D., GREENE, D., & HOUSE, P. The "false consensus effect": An egocentric bias in social perception and attribution processes. *Journal of Experimental Social Psychology,* 1977, *13,* 279–301.

ROTHWELL, N.A., & STOCK, M.J. A role for brown adipose tissue in diet-induced thermogenesis. *Nature,* 1979, *281,* 31–35.

ROTTER, J.B. Generalized expectancies for internal versus external control of reinforcement. *Psychological Monographs,* 1966 (*80,* Whole No. 609).

ROTTER, J.B., & MULRY, R.C. Internal versus external control of decision time. *Journal of Personality and Social Psychology,* 1965, *2,* 598–604.

ROWLAND, N.E., & ANTELMAN, S.M. Stress induced hyperphagia and obesity in rats: A possible model for understanding human obesity. *Science,* 1976, *191,* 310–312.

ROZIN, P., & KALAT, J.W. Specific hungers and poison avoidance as adaptive specializations of learning. *Psychological Review,* 1971, *78,* 459–486.

RUBIN, Z. *Liking and Loving: An Invitation to Social Psychology.* New York: Holt, Rinehart and Winston, 1973.

RUCH, F.L. The differential decline of learning ability in the aged as a possible explanation of their conservatism. *Journal of Social Psychology,* 1934, *5,* 329–337.

RUNDUS, D., & ATKINSON, R.C. Rehearsal procedures in free recall: A procedure for direct observation. *Journal of Verbal Learning and Verbal Behavior,* 1970, *9,* 99–105.

RUSSEK, M. Hepatic receptors and the neurophysiological mechanisms controlling feeding behavior. In *Neurosciences Research* (vol. 4), edited by S. Ehrenpreis. New York: Academic Press, 1971.

RUSSELL, M.J. Human olfactory communication. *Nature,* 1976, *260,* 520–522.

RUSSELL, M.J., SWITZ, G.M., & THOMPSON, K. *Olfactory influences on the human menstrual cycle.* Paper presented at the meeting of the American Association for the Advancement of Science, San Francisco, June, 1977.

RYAN, E.D. The cathartic effect of vigorous motor activity on aggressive behavior. *Research Quarterly,* 1970, *41,* 542–551.

RYBACK, R.S., & LEWIS, O.F. Effects of prolonged bed rest on EEG sleep patterns in young, healthy volunteers. *Electroencephalography and Clinical Neurophysiology,* 1971, *31,* 395–399.

SACHS, J.S. Recognition memory for syntactic and semantic aspects of connected discourse. *Perception and Psychophysics,* 1967, *2,* 437–442.

SACKETT, G.P. Innate mechanisms, rearing conditions, and a theory of early experience effects in primates. In *Miami Symposium on the Prediction of Behavior, 1968,* edited by M.R. Jones. Coral Gables, Fla.: University of Miami Press, 1970.

SAEGERT, S.C., SWAP, W., & ZAJONC, R.B. Exposure, context, and interpersonal attraction. *Journal of Personality and Social Psychology,* 1973, *25,* 234–242.

SAFER, M., & LEVENTHAL, H. Ear differences in evaluating emotional tones of voice and verbal content. *Journal of Experimental Psychology: Human Perception and Performance,* 1977, *3,* 75–82.

SAFFRAN, E.M., SCHWARTZ, M.F., & MARIN, O.S.M. Evidence from Aphasia: Isolating the components of a production model. In *Language Production,* edited by B. Butterworth. London: Academic Press, 1980.

SALAPATEK, P. Pattern perception in early infancy. In *Infant Perception; From Sensation to Cognition* (vol. 1), edited by L.B. Cohen and P. Salapatek. New York: Academic Press, 1975.

SALK, L. Mother's heartbeat as an imprinting stimulus. *Transactions of the New York Academy of Sciences,* 1962, *24,* 753–763.

SALMON, U.J., & GEIST, S.H. Effect of androgens upon libido in women. *Journal of Clinical Endocrinology and Metabolism,* 1943, *172,* 374–377.

SASANUMA, S. Kana and kanji processing in Japanese aphasics. *Brain and Language,* 1975, *2,* 369–383.

SAVAGE-RUMBAUGH, E.S., RUMBAUGH, D.M., SMITH, S.T., & LAWSON, J. Reference: The linguistic essential. *Science,* 1980, *210,* 922–925.

SCARR, S., & WEINBERG, R.A. IQ test performance of black children adopted by white families. *American Psychologist,* 1976, *31,* 726–739.

SCHACHTER, S. The interaction of cognitive and physiological determinants of emotional state. In *Psychobiological Approaches to Social Behavior,* edited by P.H. Leiderman and D. Shapiro. Stanford: Stanford University Press, 1964.

SCHACHTER, S. Some extraordinary facts about obese humans and rats. *American Psychologist,* 1971, *26,* 129–144.

SCHACHTER, S., & SINGER, J.E. Cognitive, social and physiological determinants of emotional state. *Psychological Review*, 1962, *69*, 379–399.

SCHERSCHLICHT, R., POLC, P., SCHNEE-BERGER, J., STEINER, M., & HAEFELY, W. Selective suppression of rapid eye movement sleep (REMS) in cats by typical and atypical antidepressants. In *Typical and Atypical Antidepressants: Molecular Mechanisms*, edited by E. Costa and G. Racagni. New York: Raven Press, 1982.

SCHMIDT, G., & SIGUSCH, V. Sex differences in responses to psychosexual stimulation by films and slides. *Journal of Sex Research*, 1970, *44*, 229–237.

SCHOEDEL, J., FREDERICKSON, W.A., & KNIGHT, J.M. An extrapolation of the physical attractiveness and sex variables within the Byrne attraction paradigm. *Memory and Cognition*, 1975, *3*, 527–530.

SCHOFIELD, J.W. Effects of norms, public disclosure, and need for approval on volunteering behavior consistent with attitudes. *Journal of Personality and Social Psychology*, 1975, *31*, 1126–1133.

SCHON, M., & SUTHERLAND, A.M. The role of hormones in human behavior. III. Changes in female sexuality after hypophysectomy. *Journal of Clinical Endocrinology and Metabolism*, 1960, *20*, 833–841.

SCHREINER, L., & KLING, A. Rhinencephalon and behavior. *American Journal of Physiology*, 1956, *184*, 486–490.

SCHWARTZ, M.F., SAFFRAN, E.M., & MARIN, O.S.M. The word order problem in agrammatism. I. Comprehension. *Brain and Language*, 1980, *10*, 249–262.

SEARLE, L.V. The organization of hereditary maze-brightness and maze-dullness. *Genetic Psychology Monographs*, 1949, *39*, 279–325.

SECHEHAYE, M. *Autobiography of a Schizophrenic Girl*. New York: Grune & Stratton, 1951.

SEGAL, M.W. Alphabet and attraction: An unobstrusive measure of the effect of propinquity in a field setting. *Journal of Personality and Social Psychology*, 1974, *30*, 654–657.

SELIGMAN, M.E.P. Depression and learned helplessness. In *The Psychology of Depression: Contemporary Theory and Research*, edited by R.J. Friedman & M.M. Katz. Washington, D.C.: Winston-Wiley, 1974.

SEM-JACOBSEN, C.W. *Depth-electrographic Stimulation of the Human Brain and Behavior*. Springfield, Ill.: C.C. Thomas, 1968.

SHAKOW, D. Segmental set: A theory of the formal psychological deficit in schizophrenia. *Archives of General Psychiatry*, 1962, *6*, 1–17.

SHAPIRO, C.M., BORTZ, R., MITCHELL, D., BARTEL, P., & JOOSTE, P. Slow-wave sleep: A recovery period after exercise. *Science*, 1982, *214*, 1253–1254.

SHATZ, M., & GELMAN, R. The development of communication skills: Modifications in the speech of young children as a function of listener. *Monographs of the Society for Research in Child Development*, 1973 (38, Serial No. 152).

SHEFFIELD, F.D., & CAMPBELL, B.A. The role of experience in the "spontaneous" activity of hungry rats. *Journal of Comparative and Physiological Psychology*, 1954, *43*, 471–481.

SHEFFIELD, F.D., WULFF, J.J., & BACKER, R. Reward value of copulation without sex drive reduction. *Journal of Comparative and Physiological Psychology*, 1951, *44*, 3–8.

SHELDON, W.H., & STEVENS, S.S. *The Varieties of Temperament*. New York: Harper & Row, 1942.

SHIELDS, J.L., McHUGH, A., & MARTIN, J.G. Reaction time to phoneme targets as a function of rhythmic cues in continuous speech. *Journal of Experimental Psychology*, 1974, *102*, 250–255.

SHIPLEY, E.F., SMITH, C.S., & GLEITMAN, L.R. A study in the acquisition of language: Free responses to commands. *Language*, 1969, *45*, 322–342.

SHIRLEY, M.M. The first two years: A study of 25 babies, vol. I. Postural and locomotor development. *Institute of Child Welfare Monographs* (Series No. 6). Minneapolis: University of Minnesota Press, 1933.

SIEGELMAN, M. Parental background of male homosexuals and heterosexuals. *Archives of Sexual Behavior*, 1974, *3*, 3–18.

SIGUSCH, V., SCHMIDT, G., REINFELD, A., & WIEDEMANN-SUTOR, I. Psychosexual stimulation: sex differences. *Journal of Sex Research*, 1970, *6*, 10–24.

SIMS, E.A.H., & HORTON, E.S. Endocrine and metabolic adaptation to obesity and starvation. *American Journal of Clinical Nutrition*, 1968, *21*, 1455–1470.

SINGER, S. Hypothalamic control of male and female sexual behavior in female rats. *Journal of Comparative and Physiological Psychology*, 1968, *66*, 738–742.

SISTRUNK, F., & MC DAVID, J.W. Sex variable in conforming behavior. *Journal of Personality and Social Psychology*, 1971, *17*, 200–207.

SKINNER, B.F. Superstition in the pigeon. *Journal of Experimental Psychology*, 1948, *38*, 168–172.

SKINNER, B.F. *Verbal Behavior*. Englewood Cliffs, N.J.: Prentice-Hall, 1957.

SKINNER, B.F. *About Behaviorism*. New York: Vintage Books, 1974.

SMITH, G.F., & DORFMAN, D.D. The effect of stimulus uncertainty on the relationship between frequency of exposure and liking. *Journal of Personality and Social Psychology*, 1975, *31*, 150–155.

SMITH, K.R. The problem of stimulation deafness. II. Histological changes in the cochlea as a function of tonal frequency. *Journal of Experimental Psychology*, 1947, *37*, 304–317.

SNOW, C.E. Mothers' speech to children learning language. *Child Development*, 1972a, *43*, 549–565.

SNOW, C.E. *Young children's responses to adult sentences of varying complexity*. Paper presented at the Third International Congress of Applied Linguistics, Copenhagen, August, 1972b.

SNYDER, M. The self-monitoring of expressive behavior.

Journal of Personality and Social Psychology, 1974, *30*, 526–537.

SNYDER, M. Self-monitoring processes. *Advances in Experimental Social Psychology*, 1979, *12*, 85–128.

SNYDER, M., & MONSON, T.C. Persons, situations, and the control of social behavior. *Journal of Personality and Social Psychology*, 1975, *32*, 637–644.

SNYDER, S.H. *Madness and the Brain*. New York: McGraw-Hill, 1974.

SOKOLOV, E.N. *Perception and the Conditioned Reflex*. New York: Pergamon Press, 1963.

SOLOMON, P., LEIDERMAN, P.H., MENDELSON, J., & WEXLER, D. Sensory deprivation. *American Journal of Psychiatry*, 1957, *114*, 357–363.

SOLOMON, R.C. *The Passions*. Garden City, N.Y.: Doubleday, Anchor Press, 1976.

SPEARMAN, C. *The Abilities of Man*. London: Macmillan, 1927.

SPERLING, G.A. The information available in brief visual presentation. *Psychological Monographs*, 1960 (74, Whole No. 498).

SPIRO, R.J. Remembering information from text: Theoretical and empirical issues concerning the state of schema reconstruction hypothesis. In *Schooling and the Acquisition of Knowledge*, edited by R.J. Spiro and W.E. Montague. Hillsdale, N.J.: Lawrence Erlbaum, 1976.

SPITZER, R.L. On pseudoscience in science, logic in remission, and psychiatric diagnosis: A critique of Rosenhan's "On being sane in insane places." *Journal of Abnormal Psychology*, 1975, *84*, 442–452.

SQUIRE, L.R. Stable impairment in remote memory following electroconvulsive therapy. *Neuropsychologia*, 1974, *13*, 51–58.

STADDON, J.E.R. Schedule-induced behavior. In *Handbook of Operant Behavior*, edited by W.K. Honig and J.E.R. Staddon. Englewood Cliffs, N.J.: Prentice-Hall, 1976.

STADDON, J.E.R., & SIMMELHAG, V.L. The "superstition" experiment: A reexamination of its implications for the principles of adaptive behavior. *Psychological Review*, 1971, *78*, 3–43.

STAPP, J., FULCHER, R., NELSON, S.D., PALLAK, M.S., & WICHERSKI, M. The employment of recent doctorate recipients in psychology: 1975 through 1978. *American Psychologist*, 1981, *36*, 1211–1254.

STEBBINS, W.C., MILLER, J.M., JOHNSSON, L.G., & HAWKINS, J.E. Ototoxic hearing loss and cochlear pathology in the monkey. *Annals of Otology, Rhinology, and Laryngology*, 1969, *78*, 1007–1026.

STEIN, L., & RAY, O.S. Brain stimulation reward "thresholds" self-determined in rat. *Psychopharmacologia*, 1960, *1*, 251–256.

STENHOUSE, D. *The Evolution of Intelligence*. London: Allen and Unwin, 1974.

STERN, W. *The Psychological Methods of Testing Intelligence*. Baltimore: Warwick and York, 1914.

STERNBACH, R.A. *Pain: A Psychophysiological Analysis*. New York: Academic Press, 1968.

STEVENS, J.R. Neuropathology of schizophrenia. *Archives of General Psychiatry*, 1982a, *39*, 1131–1139.

STEVENS, J.R. Neurology and neuropathology of schizophrenia. In *Schizophrenia as a Brain Disease*, edited by F.A. Henn and G.A. Nasrallah. New York: Oxford University Press, 1982b.

STIRNIMANN, F. Ueber das farbempfinden Neugeborener. *Annales Paediatrici*, 1944, *163*, 1–25.

STOLLER, R.J. Pornography and perversion. *Archives of General Psychiatry*, 1970, *22*, 490–499.

STOLZ, W. A study of the ability to decode grammatically novel sentences. *Journal of Verbal Learning and Verbal Behavior*, 1967, *6*, 867–873.

STONE, S. Psychiatry through the ages. *Journal of Abnormal and Social Psychology*, 1937, *32*, 131–160.

STONER, J.A.F. A comparison of individual and group decisions involving risk. Unpublished master's thesis, School of Industrial Management, MIT, 1961.

STORMS, M.D. Videotape and the attribution process: Reversing actors' and observers' point of view. *Journal of Personality and Social Psychology*, 1973, *27*, 165–175.

STRICKLAND, B.R. Individual differences in verbal conditioning, extinction, and awareness. *Journal of Personality*, 1970, *38*, 364–378.

STROHNER, H., & NELSON, K.E. The young child's development of sentence comprehension: Influence of event probability, nonverbal context, syntactic form, and strategies. *Child Development*, 1974, *45*, 567–576.

STUNKARD, A.J., & BURT, V. Obesity and the body image: II. Age at onset of disturbances in the body image. *American Journal of Psychiatry*, 1967, *123*, 1443–1447.

SUOMI, S.J., & HARLOW, H.F. Social rehabilitation of isolate-reared monkeys. *Developmental Psychology*, 1972, *6*, 487–496.

SVEJDA, M.J., CAMPOS, J.J., & EMDE, R.N. Mother-infant "bonding": Failure to generalize. *Child Development*, 1980, *51*, 775–779.

TAKAHASHI, Y. Growth hormone secretion related to the sleep waking rhythm. In *The Functions of Sleep*, edited by R. Drucker-Colín, M. Shkurovich, and M.B. Sterman. New York: Academic Press, 1979.

TAUBE, S.L., KIRSTEIN, L.S., SWEENEY, D.R., HENINGER, G.R., & MAAS, J.W. Urinary 3-methoxy-4-hydroxyphenyleneglycol and psychiatric diagnosis. *American Journal of Psychiatry*, 1978, *135*, 78–82.

TAYLOR, S.E., FISKE, S.T., CLOSE, M., ANDERSON, C., & RUDERMAN, A. *Solo status as a psychological variable: The power of being distinctive*. Unpublished manuscript cited by Taylor, S.E., and Fiske, S.T. Salience, attention, and attribution: Top of the head phenomena. In *Advances in Experimental Social Psychology* (vol. 11), edited by L. Berkowitz. New York: Academic Press, 1978.

TERRACE, H.S., PETITTO, L.A., SANDERS, R.J., & BEVER, T.G. Can an ape create a sentence? *Science*, 1979, *206*, 891–902.

THIBAUT, J.W., & RIECKEN, H.W. Some determinants and consequences of the perception of social causality. *Journal of Personality*, 1955, *24*, 113–133.

THORNDIKE, E.L. *The Elements of Psychology.* New York: Seiler, 1905.

THURSTONE, L.L. *Primary Mental Abilities.* Chicago: University of Chicago Press, 1938.

TIMBERLAKE, W., & ALLISON, J. Response deprivation: An empirical approach to instrumental performance. *Psychological Review*, 1974, *81*, 146–164.

TOMKINS, S.S. *Affect, Imagery, Consciousness* (vol. 1, *The Positive Affects*). New York: Springer-Verlag, 1962.

TOMKINS, S.S. *Affect, Imagery, Consciousness* (vol. 2, *The Negative Affects*). New York: Springer, 1963.

TORREY, E.F., TORREY, B.B., & PETERSON, M.R. Seasonality of schizophrenic births in the United States. *Archives of General Psychiatry*, 1977, *34*, 1065–1070.

TORREY, E.F., YOLKEN, R.H., & WINFREY, C.J. Cytomegalovirus antibody in cerebrospinal fluid of schizophrenic patients detected by enzyme immunoassay. *Science*, 1982, *216*, 892–894.

TOURNEY, G. Hormones & homosexuality. In *Homosexual Behavior*, edited by J. Marmor. New York: Basic Books, 1980.

TRÄSKMAN, L., ÅSBERG, M., BERTILSSON, L., SJÖSTRAND, L. Monoamine metabolites in CSF and suicidal behavior. *Archives of General Psychiatry*, 1981, *38*, 631–636.

TRAYHURN, P., THURLBY, P.L., WOODWARD, C.J.H., & JAMES, W.P.T. Thermogenic defect in pre-obese ob/ob mice. *Nature*, 1977, *266*, 60–62.

TREISMAN, A.M. Selective attention in man. *British Medical Bulletin*, 1964, *20*, 12–16.

TRIPLETT, N. The dynamogenic factors in pacemaking and competition. *American Journal of Psychology*, 1897, *9*, 507–533.

TRONICK, E., ALS, H., ADAMSON, L., WISE, S., & BRAZELTON, T.B. The infant's response to entrapment between contradictory messages in face-to-face interaction. *Journal of the American Academy of Child Psychiatry*, 1978, *17*, 1–13.

TRUAX, C.B. Reinforcement and nonreinforcement in Rogerian psychotherapy. *Journal of Abnormal Psychology*, 1966, *71*, 1–9.

TRUAX, C.B., & CARKHUFF, R.R. Significant developments in psychotherapy research. In *Progress in Clinical Psychology*, edited by L.E. Abt and B.F. Reiss. New York: Grune & Stratton, 1964.

TRYON, R.C. Genetic differences in maze learning in rats. *Yearbook of the National Society for Studies in Education*, 1940, *39*, 111–119.

TULVING, E. Episodic and semantic memory. In *Organization of Memory*, edited by E. Tulving and W. Donaldson. New York: Academic Press, 1972.

TULVING, E., & PSOTKA, J. Retroactive inhibition in free-recall: Inaccessibility of information available in the memory store. *Journal of Experimental Psychology*, 1971, *87*, 1–8.

TURNER, S. The life and times of a pickle packer. *Boston Sunday Globe*, January 8, 1978, pp. 10–22.

TYSON, W. Personal communication, 1980.

ULLMAN, L.P., & KRASNER, L. *Psychological Approach to Abnormal Behavior.* Englewood Cliffs, N.J.: Prentice-Hall, 1969.

UNGERSTEDT, U., & LJUNGBERG, T. Central dopamine neurons and sensory processing. *Journal of Psychiatric Research*, 1974, *11*, 149–150.

VALENSTEIN, E.S. *Brain Control.* New York: Wiley & Sons, 1973.

VALINS, S. Cognitive effects of false heart-rate feedback. *Journal of Personality and Social Psychology*, 1966, *4*, 400–408.

VAN DER LEE, S., & BOOT, L.M. Spontaneous pseudopregnancy in mice. *Acta Physiologica et Pharmacologica Néerlandica*, 1955, *4*, 442–444.

VAN DE CASTLE & SMITH, 1971. Personal communication cited by Money, J., and Ehrhardt, A.A., *Man & Woman, Boy & Girl.* Baltimore: Johns Hopkins University Press, 1972.

VERNON, P.E. *Intelligence: Heredity and Environment.* San Francisco: Freeman, 1979.

VIDMAR, N. Effects of group discussion on category width judgments. *Journal of Personality and Social Psychology*, 1974, *29*, 187–195.

VINOKUR, A., & BURNSTEIN, E. Effects of partially shared persuasive arguments on group-induced shifts: A group problem-solving approach. *Journal of Personality and Social Psychology*, 1974, *29*, 305–315.

VON BÉKÉSY, G. *Experiments in Hearing.* New York: McGraw-Hill, 1960.

VOGEL, G.W., VOGEL, F., McABEE, R.S., & THURMOND, A.G. Improvement of depression by REM sleep deprivation. *Archives of General Psychiatry*, 1980, *37*, 247–253.

VON WRIGHT, J.M., ANDERSON, K., & STENMAN, U. Generalization of conditioned GSRs in dichotic listening. In *Attention and Performance V*, edited by P.M.A. Rabbitt and S. Dornic. London: Academic Press, 1975.

WADA, J.A., CLARKE, R., & HAMM, A. Cerebral hemispheric asymmetry in humans: Cortical speech zones in 100 adults and 100 infant brains. *Archives of Neurology*, 1975, *32*, 239–246.

WALLACE, M., & SINGER, G. Adjunctive behavior and smoking induced by a maze solving schedule in humans. *Physiology and Behavior*, 1976, *17*, 849–852.

WALSTER, E., ARONSON, V., ABRAHAMS, D., & ROTTMAN, L. Importance of physical attractiveness in dating behavior. *Journal of Personality and Social Psychology*, 1966, *4*, 508–516.

WALSTER, E., & BERSCHEID, E. Adrenaline makes the heart grow fonder. *Psychology Today*, June 1971, pp. 47–62.

WALSTER, E., & FESTINGER, L. The effectiveness of "overheard" persuasive communications. *Journal of Abnormal and Social Psychology*, 1962, *65*, 395–402.

WARD, C.H., BECK, A.T., MENDELSON, M.,

MOCK, J.E., & ERBAUGH, J.K. The psychiatric nomenclature: Reasons for diagnostic disagreement. *Archives of General Psychiatry*, 1962, 7, 198–205.

WARD, I. Prenatal stress feminizes and demasculinizes the behavior of males. *Science*, 1972, 175, 82–84.

WARREN, R.M. Perceptual restoration of missing speech sounds. *Science*, 1967, 167, 392–393.

WARREN, R.M., & WARREN, R.P. Auditory illusions and confusions. *Scientific American*, 1970, 223, 30–36.

WATSON, J.B. *Behaviorism* (rev. ed.). New York: Norton, 1930.

WATSON, J.S. Smiling, cooing and the "game." *Merrill-Palmer Quarterly*, 1973, 18, 323–339.

WATSON, J.S., & RAMEY, C.T. Reactions to responsive contingent stimulation in early infancy. *Merrill-Palmer Quarterly*, 1972, 18, 219–227.

WATT, N.F., & LUBANSKY, A.W. Childhood roots of schizophrenia. *Journal of Consulting and Clinical Psychology*, 1976, 44, 363–375.

WAUGH, N.C., & NORMAN, D.A. Primary memory. *Psychological Review*, 1965, 72, 89–104.

WAXENBERG, S.E., DRELLICH, M.G., & SUTHERLAND, A.M. The role of hormones in human behavior: I. Changes in female sexuality after adrenalectomy. *Journal of Clinical Endocrinology and Metabolism*, 1959, 19, 193–202.

WAYNER, M.J., SINGER, G., CIMINO, K., STEIN, J., & DWORKIN, L. Adjunctive behavior induced by different conditions of wheel running. *Physiology & Behavior*, 1975, 9, 115–130.

WEBB, W.B. *Sleep: The Gentle Tyrant*. Englewood Cliffs, N.J.: Prentice-Hall, 1975.

WEBB, W.B., & CARTWRIGHT, R.D. Sleep and dreams. *Annual Review of Psychology*, 1978, 29, 223–252.

WEIGEL, R.H., VERNON, D.T.A., & TOGNACCI, L.N. Specificity of the attitude as a determinant of attitude-behavior congruence. *Journal of Personality and Social Psychology*, 1974, 30, 724–728.

WEINBERGER, D.R., BIGELOW, L.B., KLEINMAN, J.E., KLEIN, S.T., ROSENBLATT, J.E., & WYATT, R.J. Cerebral ventricular enlargement in chronic schizophrenia: An association with poor response to treatment. *Archives of General Psychiatry*, 1980, 37, 11–13.

WEINBERGER, D.R., & WYATT, J.R. Brain morphology in schizophrenia: *In vivo* studies. In *Schizophrenia as a Brain Disease*, edited by F.A. Henn and G.A. Nasrallah. New York: Oxford University Press, 1982.

WEINTRAUB, S., MESULAM, M.-M., & KRAMER, L. Disturbances in prosody: A right-hemisphere contribution to language. *Archives of Neurology*, 1981, 38, 742–744.

WERTHEIMER, M. Psychomotor co-ordination of auditory-visual space at birth. *Science*, 1961, 134, 1692.

WESTWOOD, G. *A Minority: Report on the Life of the Male Homosexual in Great Britain*. London: Longmans, Green, 1960.

WHITE, B.L. *Fundamental early environmental influences on the development of competence*. Paper presented at the Third Western Symposium on Learning: Cognitive Learning, Bellingham, Wash., October 21–22, 1971.

WHITE, R.W. Motivation reconsidered: The concept of competence. *Psychological Review*, 1959, 66, 297–333.

WHITEHEAD, R.G., ROWLAND, M.G.M., HUTTON, M., PRENTICE, A.M., MÜLLER, E., & PAUL, A. Factors influencing lactation performance in rural Gambian mothers. *Lancet*, 1978, 2, 178–181.

WHITLOCK, F.A. The aetiology of hysteria. *Acta Psychiatrica Scandinavica*, 1967, 43, 144–162.

WHITTEN, W.K. Occurrence of anestrus in mice caged in groups. *Journal of Endocrinology*, 1959, 18, 102–107.

WHYTE, W.W., JR. *The Organization Man*. New York: Simon and Schuster, 1956.

WICKER, A.W. Attitudes versus actions: The relationship of verbal and overt behavioral responses to attitude objects. *Journal of Social Issues*, 1969, 25, 41–78.

WIEMAN, L.A. The stress pattern of early child language. Unpublished doctoral dissertation, University of Washington, 1974.

WIESEL, T.N., & HUBEL, D.H. Comparison of the effects of unilateral and bilateral eye closure on cortical unit responses in kittens. *Journal of Neurophysiology*, 1965, 28, 1029–1040.

WIESNER, B.P., & SHEARD, N. *Maternal Behavior in the Rat*. London: Oliver and Brody, 1933.

WILCOXON, H.C., DRAGOIN, W.B., & KRAL, P.A. Illness-induced aversions in rat and quail: Relative salience of visual and gustatory cues. *Science*, 1971, 171, 826–828.

WILLIAMS, D.R., & WILLIAMS, H. Auto-maintenance in the pigeon: Sustained pecking despite contingent nonreinforcement. *Journal of the Experimental Analysis of Behavior*, 1969, 12, 511–520.

WILLIAMS, F.E. *Orokaiva Society*. Oxford: Clarendon Press, 1930.

WILLIAMS, K., HARKINS, S., & LATANÉ, B. Identifiability as a deterrent to social loafing: Two cheering experiments. *Journal of Personality and Social Psychology*, 1981, 40, 303–311.

WINTER, A. Depression and intractable pain treated by modified prefrontal lobotomy. *Journal of Medical Sociology*, 1972, 69, 757–759.

WISOCKI, P.A. Treatment of obsessive compulsive behavior by the application of covert sensitization and covert reinforcement: A case report. *Journal of Behavior Therapy and Experimental Psychiatry*, 1970, 1, 233–239.

WOLFF, P.H. Observations on the early development of smiling. In *Determinants of Infant Behaviour* (vol. 2), edited by B.M. Foss. London: Methuen, 1963.

WOLFF, P.H. *The Causes, Controls and Organization of Behavior in the Neonate*. New York: International Universities Press, 1966.

WOLFF, P.H. Crying and vocalization in early infancy.

In *Determinants of Infant Behaviour* (vol. 4), edited by B.M. Foss. London: Methuen, 1969.

WOODRUFF, G., PREMACK, D., & KENNEL, K. Conservation of liquid and solid quantity by the chimpanzee. *Science,* 1978, *202,* 991–994.

WOODWORTH, R.S., & SCHLOSBERG, H. *Experimental Psychology.* New York: Holt, 1954.

ZAJONC, R.B. Social facilitation. *Science,* 1965, *149,* 269–274.

ZAJONC, R.B. Attitudinal effects of mere exposure. *Journal of Personality and Social Psychology Monograph Supplement,* 1968, 9, 1–27.

ZAJONC, R.B., & SALES, S.M. Social facilitation of dominant and subordinate responses. *Journal of Experimental Social Psychology,* 1966, *2,* 160–168.

ZAJONC, R.B., SHAVER, P., TRAVIS, C., & KREVELD, D.V. Exposure, satiation, and stimulus discriminability. *Journal of Personality and Social Psychology,* 1972, *21,* 270–280.

ZUBIN, J., & BARRERA, S.E. Effect of electric convulsive therapy on memory. *Proceedings of the Society for Experimental Biology and Medicine,* 1941, *48,* 596–597.

ZUGER, B. Monozygotic twins discordant for homosexuality: Report of a pair and significance of the phenomenon. *Comprehensive Psychiatry,* 1976, *17,* 661–669.

NAME INDEX

SUBJECT INDEX

Chapter 6

FIGURE 6.2 p. 203—Dr. Landrum B. Shettles. Figure 6.3 p. 204—Dr. Landrum B. Shettles. FIGURE 6.6 p. 207—Leonard Lee Rule III/Animals Animals. FIGURE 6.9 p. 210—Dr. Landrum B. Shettles. FIGURE 6.10 p. 210—Gerald Schatten/Florida State University. FIGURE 6.12 p. 212—Dr. Landrum B. Shettles. FIGURE 6.13 p. 212—Dr. Landrum B. Shettles. FIGURE 6.15 p. 215—Susan Lapides. FIGURE 6.21 p. 222—David S. Strickler/The Picture Cube. FIGURE 6.23 p. 224—The Granger Collection. FIGURE 6.27 p. 229—Frank Siteman. FIGURE 6.31 p. 232—Frank Siteman. FIGURE 6.32 p. 234—Frank Siteman. FIGURE 6.36 p. 238—Frank Siteman. FIGURE 6.38 p. 239—Jerry Howard/Positive Images. FIGURE 6.39 p. 241—Nina Leen/*Life Magazine*, Time Inc. FIGURE 6.46 p. 248—Martha Holmes/*Time Magazine*.

Chapter 7

FIGURE 7.1 p. 257—Frank Siteman. FIGURE 7.7 p. 263—Julie O'Neil/Stock, Boston. FIGURE 7.11 p. 268—Lucian Perkins/*The Washington Post*. FIGURE 7.12 p. 268—Jean-Claude Lejeune/Stock, Boston. FIGURE 7.13 p. 271—J. Berndt/Stock, Boston (left) and James Holland/Stock, Boston (right). FIGURE 7.15 p. 274—Frank Siteman/Stock, Boston. FIGURE 7.20 p. 280—Frank Siteman/Stock, Boston. FIGURE 7.21 p. 282—The Granger Collection. FIGURE 7.26 p. 290—Ira Kirschenbaum/Stock, Boston. FIGURE 7.28 p. 293—Robert V. Eckert, Jr./Stock, Boston. FIGURE 7.29 p. 295—J. Berndt/Stock, Boston.

Chapter 8

FIGURE 8.1 p. 300—Frank Siteman. FIGURE 8.3 p. 303—The Bettmann Archive. FIGURE 8.4 p. 303—The Granger Collection. COLOR PLATE 8.9—*Bust of a young girl in the reversed colors of an afterimage.* An illustration from Johann Wolfgang von Goethe's *Color Theory* (1810) in the collection of the Nationale Forschungsund Gedenkstätten der klassischen deutschen Literatur in Weimar.

Chapter 9

FIGURE 9.1 p. 342—Ellis Herwig/Stock, Boston. FIGURE 9.11 p. 350—Jerry Schrader/Stock, Boston. FIGURE 9.14 p. 352—Ellis Herwig/Stock, Boston. FIGURE 9.15 p. 353—Owen Franken/Stock, Boston. FIGURE 9.18 p. 355—Jeff Albertson/Stock, Boston. FIGURE 9.20 p. 357—Peter Menzel/Stock, Boston. FIGURE 9.22 p. 359—The Bettmann Archive. FIGURE 9.25 p. 362—Owen Franken/Stock, Boston. FIGURE 9.26 p. 362—James R. Holland/Stock, Boston. FIGURE 9.28 p. 364—Barbara Alper/Stock, Boston.

Chapter 10

FIGURE 10.1 p. 375—Wrangham/Anthro-Photo. FIGURE 10.2 p. 376—Pamela Schuyler/Stock, Boston. FIGURE 10.3 p. 378—Paul Conklin. FIGURE 10.13 p. 390—The Granger Collection. FIGURE 10.14 p. 390—The Granger Collection. FIGURE 10.17 p. 395—Watriss-Baldwin/Woodfin Camp & Associates. FIGURE 10.18 p. 397—David S. Strickler/The Picture Cube. FIGURE 10.19 p. 399—Michal Heron/Woodfin Camp & Associates. FIGURE 10.24 p. 403—Arthur Tress. FIGURE 10.25 p. 406—The Bettmann Archive.

Chapter 11

FIGURE 11.2 p. 418—Courtesy of Gerbrands Corporation. FIGURE 11.24 p. 438—David Cupp/Woodfin Camp & Associates. FIGURE 11.25 p. 439—Bernard Wolf/Omni-Photo Communications. FIGURE 11.26 p. 440—Bill Strode/Woodfin Camp & Associates.

Chapter 12

FIGURE 12.1 p. 451—Jerry Howard/Positive Images. FIGURE 12.2 p. 452—The Granger Collection. FIGURE 12.3 p. 453—Marc & Evelyne Bernheim/Woodfin Camp & Associates. FIGURE 12.5 p. 456—Frances M. Cox/Omni-Photo Communications. FIGURE 12.9 p. 462—Frank Siteman. FIGURE 12.10 p. 463—Barbara Alper/Stock, Boston. FIGURE 12.17 p. 476—Jerry Howard/Positive Images. FIGURE 12.18 p. 477—Ulrike Welsch. FIGURE 12.19 p. 478—Andrew Brilliant/The Picture Cube. FIGURE 12.20 p. 479—Frank Siteman. FIGURE 12.21 p. 482—H.S. Terrace/Anthro-Photo.

Chapter 13

FIGURE 13.2 p. 490—The Bettmann Archive. FIGURE 13.4 p. 492—Sepp Seitz/Woodfin Camp & Associates. FIGURE 13.5 p. 493—Arthur Grace/Stock, Boston. FIGURE 13.6 p. 495—Alan Carey/The Image Works. FIGURE 13.9 p. 503—The Granger Collection (left) and Historical Pictures Service, Chicago (right). FIGURE 13.11 p. 506—Rick Winsor/Woodfin Camp & Associates. FIGURE 13.12 p. 508—Harvey Stein. FIGURE 13.13 p. 509—Ellen Pines Sheffield/Woodfin Camp & Associates.

Chapter 14

FIGURE 14.1 p. 522—The Robert and Frances Flaherty Study Center, School of Theology at Claremont. FIGURE 14.2 p. 523—Frank Siteman/Stock, Boston. FIGURE 14.3 p. 527—Jim Anderson/Woodfin Camp & Associates. FIGURE 14.5 p. 528—United Press International. FIGURE 14.6 p. 529—James H. Karales/Peter Arnold. FIGURE 14.7 p. 531—P. Ekman (left), E. Gallob (middle), and E. Gallob (right). FIGURE 14.12 p. 536—Baron Wolman/Woodfin Camp & Associates. FIGURE 14.15 p. 540—Julian Calder/Woodfin Camp & Associates. FIGURE 14.19 p. 545—United Press International. FIGURE 14.20 p. 546—Helmut Gritscher/Animals Animals. FIGURE 14.21 p. 547—M.W. Fox/The Institute for the Study of Animal Problems. FIGURE 14.22 p. 547—Anna Kaufman Moon/Stock, Boston. FIGURE 14.23 p. 548—Ira Berger/Woodfin Camp & Associates. FIGURE 14.25 p. 550—Jill Freedman/Archive Pictures. FIGURE

14.26 p. 553—Ulrike Welsch. FIGURE 14.30 p. 559—Robert Capa/Magnum Photos.

Chapter 15
FIGURE 15.1 p. 565—Eric A. Roth/The Picture Cube. FIGURE 15.2 p. 567—Ulrike Welsch. FIGURE 15.3 p. 568—Ulrike Welsch. FIGURE 15.6 p. 572—Jim Anderson/Stock, Boston. FIGURE 15.7 p. 574—SCALA/Art Resource. FIGURE 15.8 p. 576—Norman Hurst/Stock, Boston. FIGURE 15.10 p. 578—Jim Anderson/Woodfin Camp & Associates. FIGURE 15.12 p. 581—Ellen Shub/The Picture Cube. FIGURE 15.13 p. 584—Eugene Richards/The Picture Cube. FIGURE 15.14 p. 585—Eric A. Roth/The Picture Cube. FIGURE 15.19 p. 591—Watriss-Baldwin/Woodfin Camp & Associates. FIGURE 15.31 p. 602—The Museum of Modern Art/Film Stills Archive. FIGURE 15.33 p. 605—Tony Howarth/Woodfin Camp & Associates.

Chapter 16
FIGURE 16.1 p. 613—The Bettmann Archive. FIGURE 16.2 p. 614—Joel Greenstein/Omni-Photo Communications. FIGURE 16.7 p. 619—Sepp Seitz/Woodfin Camp & Associates. FIGURE 16.11 p. 626—Charles Gatewood/Stock, Boston. FIGURE 16.12 p. 627—Peter Southwick/Stock, Boston. FIGURE 16.13 p. 628—Tim Carlson/Stock, Boston. FIGURE 16.14 p. 632—The Bettmann Archive. FIGURE 16.15 p. 633—Bob Clay/Jeroboam. FIGURE 16.18 p. 636—The Granger Collection. FIGURE 16.19 p. 637—The Granger Collection. FIGURE 16.20 p. 639—Joel Gordon. FIGURE 16.21 p. 640—J. Berndt/Stock, Boston. FIGURE 16.22 p. 643—George Bellerose/Stock, Boston. FIGURE 16.23 p. 645—Owen Franken/Stock, Boston. FIGURE 16.24 p. 646—Marjorie Nichols/The Picture Cube. FIGURE 16.26 p. 649—Ulrike Welsch (top) and John Running/Stock, Boston (bottom).

Chapter 17
FIGURE 17.1 p. 657—Michael Weisbrot/Stock, Boston. FIGURE 17.2 p. 658—Peter Southwick/Stock, Boston. FIGURE 17.3 p. 663—Arthur Tress. FIGURE 17.4 p. 664—Hope Alexander/Woodfin Camp & Associates. FIGURE 17.5 p. 665—Culver Pictures. FIGURE 17.8 p. 672—The Museum of Modern Art/Film Stills Archive. FIGURE 17.9 p. 677—Elinor S. Beckwith/Taurus Photo. FIGURE 17.10 p. 679—The Bettmann Archive. FIGURE 17.16 p. 687—Charles Harbutt/Archive Pictures.

Chapter 18
FIGURE 18.1 p. 697—University Museum, University of Pennsylvania. FIGURE 18.2 p. 698—The Bettmann Archive. FIGURE 18.3 p. 698—The Bettmann Archive. FIGURE 18.4 p. 698—Culver Pictures. FIGURE 18.5 p. 699—The Bettmann Archive. FIGURE 18.6 p. 700—Culver Pictures. FIGURE 18.7 p. 701—Judith D. Sedwick/The Picture Cube. FIGURE 18.8 p. 703—The Bettmann Archive. FIGURE 18.9 p. 704—Frank Siteman/The Picture Cube. FIGURE 18.10 p. 707—Jim Anderson/Woodfin Camp & Associates. FIGURE 18.11 p. 709—Linda Ferrer/Woodfin Camp & Associates. FIGURE 18.12 p. 710—James H. Karales/Peter Arnold. FIGURE 18.15 p. 720—Paul Fusco/Magnum Photos. FIGURE 18.19 p. 728—Meri Houtchens-Kitchens/The Picture Cube.